Municipal Decentralization and Neighborhood Resources

George J. Washnis

Published in cooperation with the
Center for Governmental Studies

The Praeger Special Studies program—utilizing the most modern and efficient book production techniques and a selective worldwide distribution network—makes available to the academic, government, and business communities significant, timely research in U.S. and international economic, social, and political development.

Municipal Decentralization and
and
Neighborhood Resources
Case Studies of
Twelve Cities

PRAEGER SPECIAL STUDIES IN U.S. ECONOMIC AND SOCIAL DEVELOPMENT

Praeger Publishers   New York   Washington   London

PRAEGER PUBLISHERS
111 Fourth Avenue, New York, N.Y. 10003, U.S.A.
5, Cromwell Place, London S.W.7, England

Published in the United States of America in 1972
by Praeger Publishers, Inc.

Library of Congress Catalog Card Number: 72-80467

Printed in the United States of America

Mayors, city councilmen, and administrators are faced with the challenge of creating more meaningful communication with citizens and of providing more effective services, even with dwindling resources. Their cities are confronted with the ills of our urban areas—turmoil and violence, poverty, racism, proliferation and overlapping of programs, inadequate finances, and the alienation and despair of people from all income and ethnic groups. City officials recognize the urgent need to adopt new approaches to problems.

Residents have expressed dissatisfaction with services provided by municipal departments and other public agencies. For a while this was most vocal in the poverty areas, exemplified in the community action (war on poverty) and Model Cities programs. In the last half of the 1960's, as civil disorder swept through many of our cities, it was apparent that among minority groups there was deep discontent for reasons far beyond the ineffectiveness of municipal services and that there were enormous gaps in communication between different segments of society. Now the increasingly unsilent voices of blue-collar and white-collar residents have come forth.

In recent years, a large number of local officials have come to believe that one part of the total solution is to take municipal government to the people by decentralizing services, establishing neighborhood offices, employing residents from the neighborhoods to run programs, and creating various forms of neighborhood citizen councils.

Decentralization has also been advocated by several national commissions. In 1967 the Advisory Commission on Intergovernmental Relations proposed the enactment of state legislation authorizing large cities to establish neighborhood subunits of government. The 1968 report of the National Advisory Commission on Civil Disorders (Kerner Commission) recommended that local governments develop neighborhood action task forces and neighborhood city halls to achieve more effective communication and to improve the delivery of services. In 1968 the National Commission on Urban Problems (Douglas Commission) endorsed the idea of little city halls and recommended more adequate city services, particularly in poor neighborhoods. The Committee for Economic Development, in its policy statement "Reshaping Government in Metropolitan Areas," recommends that central cities be divided into smaller community governments.

68623

Decentralization, of course, is not an entirely new idea to city government. Numerous municipal facilities, such as firehouses, police precinct stations, playgrounds, and public schools have long been located in outlying areas of many cities; and in some communities, branch offices of public and private agencies are to be found away from downtown. But whereas this older approach stressed convenience and efficiency, the recent emphasis of decentralization of municipal services has been concerned with communication, citizen attitude, and authority.

To learn how extensive this trend is, the Center for Governmental Studies, in conjunction with the International City Management Association, conducted a survey of the 800 largest cities and urban counties in the United States. Of the 437 communities responding, twenty-one indicated that they have what can be called "little city halls" (or their equivalent) and six more are planning them for the near future. Another fifty communities have municipally run multiservice centers. (See Appendix A.)

The next step was for the Center to conduct field surveys in some of the cities to learn about their practical experience in the organization and operation of neighborhood facilities and programs. Twelve cities were selected to provide a representative sample of different types of decentralization, regions, city size, and forms of municipal government (mayor-council, council-manager, etc.). These cities are Atlanta, Baltimore, Boston, Chicago, Columbus (Ohio), Houston, Kansas City (Missouri), Los Angeles, New York, Norfolk (Virginia), San Antonio, and San Francisco.

In this book George Washnis describes some of the experiences of these twelve cities, based upon his firsthand observations. He compares and analyzes the cities and discusses important decentralization concepts of interest to all citizens, particularly public officials, educators, and students of government. He also presents case studies of individual cities and detailed recommendations and more precise descriptions of how neighborhood offices function.

Mr. Washnis was assisted in the field work by James H. Ammons II, and he drew upon reports of two consultants—Donald Bourgeois on Columbus and Morton Coleman on Baltimore. During the project Elizabeth Miller and Yvonne Holland served as secretaries and Judy Chavkin and Madeline Wickler as editorial assistants. The study was made possible by a grant from the Ford Foundation. The opinions expressed in the report are those of the author and do not necessarily reflect the views of the board of directors and other staff of the Center for Governmental Studies or the Ford Foundation.

Howard W. Hallman
President
Center for Governmental Studies
Washington, D.C.

CONTENTS

APPENDIXES

Appendix

LIST OF TABLES

LIST OF ILLUSTRATIONS

TOWARD
A GREATER SENSE
OF COMMUNITY

Few officials or citizens need be told that improved communication links between City Hall and residents and the involvement of citizens in government in a more meaningful way are essential to strengthening our democratic ideals and improving government. Better government does not imply only making services more efficient, the flow of command smoother, and technological improvements. It also means citizens assisting in the decision-making process and creating a sense of community where people have trust in their institutions and live harmoniously in a city endowed with opportunities. Indeed, under these conditions services and government more likely may be improved.

The International City Management Association's Managing the Modern City points out that it appears extremely difficult to realize a truly participative system of organization government.

> It is also fervently, though perhaps heroically, to be hoped that enlightened, informal, professional management might be able to innovate pluralism into contemporary urban government; that the urban managerial and technical elite might become more socially and humanistically conscious and concerned than at present they generally are; and that, conceivably, it might be possible to fashion urban government that will serve citizens effectively and efficiently without becoming their master; that will disaccommodate, frustrate, and alienate them least; and that will provide maximally for their satisfaction, contentment, and happiness.[1]

However, most administrators and elected officials have important reservations and sensitivities about citizen participation but

3

realize neighborhood involvement is increasingly more important in
the creation of viable and stable communities. This book explores
the concept of sense of community and its relationship to the decentralization of both decision-making authority and municipal services.

THE MEANING OF "SENSE
OF COMMUNITY"

One definition of "sense of community" is the joining together
of human beings in reaching a goal or in maintaining preservation of
a memory.[2] In our context, we are interested in sense of community
as it relates to the aspirations of cities or neighborhoods rather than
private groups. Ethnic, religious, leisure, and business sense of community are secondary in this review. A sense of community may also
exist in one's world of sports, music, or work. However, we are interested primarily in sense of community from the citizen's relationship to local government, the services he receives, and his neighborhood life—only a fragment of the subject. In this case community is
the city or county, and it is one that does not jeopardize other communities while promoting the growth of its individuals.

Almost all meaningful opportunity comes through institutions;
therefore, to achieve a rich, full existence and improve the quality of
life, citizens must find ways to control institutions and participate in
deciding the future of institutions and systems which can stabilize or
vitalize, enslave or liberate the individual. Indeed, to add firmness,
stature, and dignity to individual growth, a sense of duty must exist,
along with greater participation in the governmental process.[3]

"Power, freedom, and community are the three qualities that
enable us to regard the city as a moral being," says Lawrence Haworth.
In some way we must enhance these qualities for the individual. The
artist, student, housewife, union leader, businessman, and disadvantaged
must become meaningfully involved in the decisions of government and
institutions. Urban administrators and elected officials cannot alone
experience the adventure of government and betterment of community
life and expect citizens to assist them with interest and intelligence.

The electoral process is not enough to achieve these objectives,
for it is mostly an impersonal, infrequent, and sometimes contrived
system. Regardless of how well we describe our system in relation
to other democracies, it simply has not been enough to achieve effective participatory democracy. Where there are elections by wards,
greater local options exist; but as populations grow, voter influence

is less. In council-manager cities and governments with nonpartisan elections, there is less feeling of participation. For the most part, professionals have provided a buffer between government and citizens, and some have secretly denounced citizen participation as too time-consuming and inefficient. However, some administrators have found rewards even with delays and have recognized that effective community participation takes something more than the voting process and ordinary means of communication.

There are varied opinions about the value of citizen participation. In an address to a Model Cities advisory council meeting in Chicago on February 26, 1971, Edward C. Banfield stated: "The politician's function—that is, finding the terms on which people whose interests and grievances are in conflict will act in relation to one another—is the most important function in the whole society—more important than that of the doctor, the teacher, the scientist." The political party is an institution to be strengthened and preserved as a way to get things done despite many disagreements, even though it rarely if ever uses the method of democracy, he indicated.

He believes citizen participation is one reason for administrative delay because some people are unwilling to be reasonable to the point of endless argument and nothing being done—at times a free-for-all. "To say the same thing the other way around, the more citizen participation you want, the less you must expect to achieve in the way of concrete results," he stated. He concluded by saying the majority must rule and that "no single issue can ever be as important as the process of peaceful, orderly, reasonable decision-making . . . it is in the long-run interest of all contestants to play by the rules and obey the umpire." Banfield is overly impressed with strong, organized political leadership, which has done little for participatory democracy and viable neighborhoods. Neighborhoods are being destroyed, and politicians and administrators know that there are dissatisfied citizens in our society who do not agree with established rules—the very essence of alienation and despair. Community leadership is needed, as well; and in most neighborhoods, effective mechanisms for sustained participatory government must be developed.

Paul Davidoff, an urban planner, states:

The fact that citizens' organizations have not played a positive role in formulating plans is to some extent a result of the enlarged weakness of municipal party politics. There is something very shameful to our society in the necessity to have organized "citizen participation."

Such participation should be the norm in an enlightened democracy. The formalization of citizen participation as a required practice in localities is similar in many respects to totalitarian shows of loyalty to the state by citizen parades.[4]

Urban officials must acknowledge that among the services of police, fire, sanitation and streets, there is also the service of improving sense of community and citizen dignity. Assuredly, reduction of crime will bring more people together in the streets and recreation areas; community centers will provide service and develop group spirit; rapid transit and jobs will promote greater freedom; and a good educational system will teach how to live together—all elements of sense of community. But to achieve its full objectives, much more needs to be done. As important as any element, citizens must be involved in the decision-making processes of our institutions if we wish to reduce alienation and improve the image and services of government, even while administrators impose their expertise on city problem solving.

Local government should be strengthened by a flexible and responsive organizational form that accepts innovation, new leadership, and increased challenges. Without the ability to meet the needs of the poor, create stability and harmony, and promote lasting economic strength, federal and state governments will more and more impose themselves on local government. With strong neighborhood authority and leadership, cities will not only be more likely to free themselves of revolution but will also evolve grass-roots support for maintaining municipal independence. It is more difficult for the state to diminish the city's home rule powers if they are shared with residents who believe in local determination.

In this sense, federal intervention in local affairs through the community action and Model Cities programs actually has strengthened local government, for it has allowed citizens to run programs and share control locally. This experience has developed a national policy to engage mayors and administrators in a wider scope of programs than ever before. It has challenged local officials to develop and operate programs of employment, social services, nutrition, and other human resource services in a comprehensive and more rational attack on urban ills. And it has brought into focus the need to coordinate private and public agencies, perfect intergovernmental relations, retrain and build new staff capacity, try new programs, and involve residents in the process.

So many new programs have now fallen legally or morally into
the laps of mayors and administrators that they have plenty of room
to share operations and decisions with neighborhood people. Human
resource problems have brought issues closer to neighborhood residents
than patching streets or building sewage plants. Even fighting crime
and picking up garbage has not aroused the citizen as much as food
distribution, day care, and community centers. Everything seems
closer now. And even in the middle- and higher-income areas, issues
of resource distribution, crime, and community stability have aroused
residents so that they too want to be part of the decision-making process.
It is more and more up to the elective and administrative leadership
to devise workable local systems of community interchange and shared
power.

Some officials may not wish to do anything. Some may wish to
extend participation but may be unable because of incongruous political
and social climates which require better timing. Others may wish to
take limited steps or enact comprehensive programs. Let us review
some of these alternatives.

TECHNIQUES FOR IMPROVING THE
SENSE OF COMMUNITY

To achieve a sense of community, cities use a variety of techniques, including citizen advisory boards, contracts with neighborhood
groups, employment of minority residents, little city halls, multiservice
centers, and a variety of innovative programs. Most of these concepts
can be placed under five models suggested by Henry J. Schmandt in a
recent conference paper on community decentralization.[5] These are
explained below, along with an approach termed the partnership model.

Organization Models

Exchange Model

The exchange model is a means of improving the communication
link between government and citizens through increased use of field
officers, little city halls, local citizen advisory boards, ombudsmen,
multiservice centers, and other methods of communication.

Most cities use at least one of these techniques. San Francisco
and St. Louis employ the most limited of these methods, utilizing field

officers working from the mayor's office but no neighborhood physical
facilities operated by the city. San Francisco also relies on physical
facilities operated by other agencies but primarily on television, press
conferences, and the expressive style of the mayor. Where a mayor
lacks convincing communicative styles, other methods become more
important.

In a survey conducted jointly by the Center for Governmental
Studies and International City Management Association, twenty of 800
cities and counties polled indicate use of little city halls or neighborhood offices. It is estimated that there are about 2,500 public and
private multiservice centers in the nation, many operated with some
city funds and staff. Our survey identified fifty cities that utilize
service centers for a variety of functions including some city programs.

Bureaucratic Model

The bureaucratic model involves the delegation of authority to
subordinate civil servants in the neighborhood and may take two forms:
functional and territorial. In the first type, locally based officials
(responsible to department heads at the city level) have power along
functional lines, such as in police precincts, refuse collection areas,
health districts, etc. In the second instance, authority over varied
functions is placed on a local manager or superintendent who is
responsible to the citywide executive.

Los Angeles has the most comprehensive physical decentralization
of functions. In some cases all main city hall services operate from
branch city halls but, as in most cities, it is a functional pattern because the local supervisors report to city department heads. There
is no overall manager of a mix of functions. This is the case in San
Antonio also.

Boston has a form of territorial decentralization. The managers
in the little city halls have authority over all activities within their
centers and report to one citywide director. They derive their strength
from the mayor, direct a form of mini-cabinet meetings, and attempt
to coordinate agencies operating in the area. The key ingredient for
both these patterns of bureaucratic decentralization is that local personnel are appointed by the existing city structure.

Modified Bureaucratic Model

The modified bureaucratic model is similar to the above except
that the district manager is responsible to both the city and, to a lesser

extent, to a neighborhood council representative of the residents. The
little city hall managers in Boston are primarily responsible to a
citywide director and to the mayor. They are also responsible to local
citizen advisory councils in some cases, although this is a very limited
responsibility. In New York, neighborhood city hall managers are
responsible to the major and to urban action task forces, although the
latter, too, have limited responsibility.

Chicago has directors in urban progress centers who have some
responsibility to service center boards, but there is little doubt that
control emanates from City Hall.

Development Model

The development model is represented by community corporations
which place policy and administrative functions under resident control
in order to undertake its own programs or to contract with the city or
other agencies. The community corporation is a private, nonprofit
organization, governed by a neighborhood board, and hires and fires
its own staff. There are over 1,000 community corporations in the
nation.[6]

A good example is Dayton's five satellite corporations, funded
by Model Cities, which hire their own staffs and operate programs
independently, but within guidelines originally established between
residents and the city. Most community action programs in cities
are operated by the community corporation technique.

Governmental Model

The governmental model is the creation of new political subunits
with powers similar to those of suburban towns or some neighborhood
school districts which have been given substantial legal powers. (See
Appendix B.) It is the most radical of the five models and is being
approached very slowly by city governments. Some fear that there is
already too great a proliferation of local government units and that
more would merely cause greater inefficiency and poorer services.
Moreover, cities approach it cautiously, for if charter or legislative
changes were made to create a system which later proved ineffective,
it would be difficult to reverse and may be even more damaging than
the present system. However, the Advisory Committee on Intergovernmental Relations recommendations allow dissolution at will by
city or county government. It believes subunits need not fragment
local government structure but may be used to harness some of the
resources and objectives of the inner communities.

In 1970, the Los Angeles City Council rejected proposed charter changes to allow the creation of boroughs with very limited powers as just another layer of bureaucracy. It also rejected the idea of neighborhood councils. The Boston Home Rule Commission recommended neighborhood districts and elected citizen boards sanctioned by legislative mandate. Legislative bodies have yet to act on these recommendations. In New York City, Mayor Lindsay has proposed charter changes for community districts and elected community boards having substantial decision-making authority. If the latter two concepts develop, they will come closest to the government model. The decentralized New York school board system could very well be considered a government model, for the boards are elected and have substantial authority in personnel and program matters.

Partnership Model

Schmandt's typology does not fully explore what might be termed the partnership arrangement, which appears to be both effective and the one most likely to take hold with municipal governments and neighborhood residents. It is stronger than the modified bureaucratic idea because the neighborhood board has the power to appoint and dismiss the local manager and to establish local policies and priorities within legal limitations and guidelines set by the city. It is a partnership because city officials agree to pass down authority by ordinance, charter, or contract and generally retain authority to help select a portion of the governing board; however, the board may be fully elected or selected by various techniques of consensus.

The partnership board does not have the same independence as a community corporation or the full legal powers of a separate government entity, but it has some of each. Very important to elected officials, it keeps the door unlocked so that they can change their minds about the arrangement without great legal difficulties, just in case things do not work out during the experimental phase. This diminishes the anxiety of some officials about the permanence of such creatures if they should turn into bureaucratic and oppressive monsters, as some have. More than a few boards have demonstrated failure, such as some under the Department of Labor's manpower programs, some community action boards, a council for neighborhood rehabilitation in St. Louis, a resident community center board in Evanston, and others. Nashville Model Cities is probably a good example of how a resident board and city officials have not been able to work together.

Partnership may be created through a series of bargaining sessions and a period of community development (until the dust settles)

in which compromises are reached to determine levels of power and
jurisdiction, very much custom-tailored for the community in question.
Too often technicians believe that models can be developed to cover
every situation. It may take considerable experimentation to perfect
the best system. And if there is a lesson to be learned, it is that failures guide one to better systems. If activists or political machines
dominate boards to the disadvantage of the client majority, alternative
selection methods should be employed, which may mean more than one
or two trials to reach success. If one believes in the objectives of
community involvement, the important thing is not to declare defeat
but to find the arrangement that works for your community. There is
one. The skilled mayor and administrator, faced with varying degrees
of citizen confrontation, have found it when faced with the challenge.

The partnership prototype is exemplified by numerous Model
Cities programs where boards have been given the authority to select
key staff persons and develop priorities, yet the city retains the power
of final decision and the ability to change the rules if it wants, mostly
accomplished through the process of negotiation. Its acceptance has
caused officials in a number of cities to recommend expanding the
Model Cities participation structure citywide to include all neighborhoods. Citywide citizen participation structures are being developed
in Washington, D.C., Seattle, Dayton, Boston, and New York.

Partnership is coming close to fruition in New York, where five
community boards determine capital improvement priorities, review
budgets, and make other local decisions. Shortly they may be allowed
to choose their own staff and participate in the selection of district
superintendents. Eventually these boards may be elected. The staff
seems to favor allowing each community to decide how it wants to
choose membership, similar to Boston's and Dayton's selection
methods.

Dayton's Model Cities may be the clearest example of partnership
where both resident boards and the city may veto programs with which
they disagree.

The five Chicago Near North multiservice centers, under the
Department of Human Resources, are a good example of partnership.
Although residents had to force their ideas upon the city, the program
is highly successful and well accepted in the neighborhood. The board,
chosen by consensus, selects staff, establishes policies, and operates
programs. The city, of course, can always veto or cut off funds.

The partnership model may very well help urban officials reach
the goals of sense of community. Partnership creates effective citizen

participation, penetrates bureaucratic personnel and policy-making structures so residents become part of the process, develops close ties between professionals and citizens, and instills in a local officer or manager (appointed by a community board) the responsibility for effectively interpreting and implementing city goals while he remains a citizen advocate.

NOTES

1. James M. Banovetz, ed., for International City Management Association, Managing the Modern City (Kingsport, Tenn.: Kingsport Press, Inc., 1971), p. 187.

2. Lawrence Haworth, The Good City (Bloomington, Ind.: Indiana University Press, 1963), p. 20.

3. Ibid., p. 59.

4. Paul Davidoff, "The Planner as Advocate," Journal of the American Institute of Planners, XXXI, 4 (December, 1965), p. 333.

5. Henry J. Schmandt, "Decentralization: A Structural Imperative," a paper written for a conference on public administration and neighborhood control held in Boulder, Colorado, in May, 1970, by the Center for Governmental Studies. It and the other conference papers will be published by Chandler Publishing Co. under the title Politics, Public Administration and Neighborhood Control.

6. For a fuller discussion of community corporations, see Neighborhood Control of Public Programs: Case Studies of Community Corporations and Neighborhood Boards (New York: Praeger, 1970).

PROGRAM GOALS

In general, the goal of each city with decentralized neighborhood services has been either to increase efficiency of service delivery to outlying areas—prevalent in those cities whose decentralization took place over a decade ago—or to expand services to areas of special need—common to those cities whose decentralization took place in response to the urban crisis—where the overriding goal was reducing racial tensions. In some cities, eruptions in black communities have had a mushrooming effect, releasing latent tensions among other minority communities as well as among "middle America" communities, so that programs which may have started out to serve only one or two areas have become citywide in order to prevent backlash from other segments.

It is becoming increasingly clear, therefore, that the goals of decentralization have had a significant effect on determining not only the type, number, and location of function and facilities, but also size, type of staff, hours of operation, and, of course, budget.

In cities where facilities do not meet needs, the political atmosphere of the city—for a number of possible reasons—is generally not supportive of decentralization and program leaders have not been able to make sufficient impact or to change it. And it is becoming more often the case that the city's financial resources are simply inadequate to provide what is needed.

In both Boston and New York, there are particularly strong pressures to reduce expenditures because of the city's overall financial plight. In 1971 budgets, both Boston and New York were

13

struggling to hold down projected deficits of $50 million and $350 million, respectively. This hindered expansion of decentralized programs because increased expenditures are usually necessary. Except for Boston and New York, it appears that most cities included in this review will continue at about the same levels of expenditure.

Types of Facilities

In addition to organizational models of decentralization described in Chapter 1, four principal types of decentralized facilities have emerged in the twelve cities, as outlined in Table 1 and described below. They are called, for purposes of this report, traditional, multiservice, new breed, and outreach. A comprehensive case study and recommendations for improvements for each of the twelve cities are presented after this chapter.

Traditional

Branch municipal facilities which place regular city services in field offices for purposes of efficiency and convenience are found in Los Angeles, San Antonio, and Kansas City.

Officials in these cities localized operations almost out of necessity. It was done in Los Angeles and Kansas City primarily for the convenience of citizens who live far from City Hall, although in Los Angeles, employee convenience was also a factor. In Los Angeles, too, decentralization was offered as a mild concession to the alienated communities which had been forced into annexation with the central city in order to receive utilities which by themselves they could not economically provide.

Kansas City's few financial services were decentralized primarily in response to pressure from residents, local chambers of commerce, and other neighborhood organizations.

As outlined in the case study, fear that a major fire might destroy most of the city's public works equipment prompted San Antonio to develop its three centers. Employee convenience has also resulted, but more as a by-product. The program has not been developed as a convenience to citizens, for few enter the centers, but more as a means to deploy men and equipment to do a better job for citizens. The competitive spirit generated among the three service area engineers has had an unusually good affect upon the improvement of services. (Generating this type of rivalry might be a worthwhile development for Los Angeles.)

TABLE 1

Municipally Directed Decentralized Neighborhood Services in Twelve Cities, March, 1971

Type	City	Name	Number	Budgeted Staff	Loaned Staff	Operations Budget	Location	Service Emphasis
Traditional Branch Municipal Facility	Los Angeles	Branch City Hall	11	1,086	0	$18,500,158	Citywide	All city services
	San Antonio	Area Service Center	3	900	0	7,000,000	Citywide	Public works
	Kansas City	City Hall Annex	2	4	0	30,746	Middle-Income	Finances
Multiservice Center	Chicago	Urban Progress Center	9, plus 6 outposts	400	600	2,800,000	Poverty Areas	Social welfare
	Norfolk	Multiservice Center	5	60	10	350,000	Low-Income	Social welfare
		Multipurpose Neighborhood Center	1	19	213 (part-time)	168,000	Poverty Area	Social welfare and recreation
Neighborhood City Hall Minimal In-House Services	New York	Urban Action Task Force	50 (9 NCH's)	300	0	2,000,000	Citywide	Complaints and special projects
	Atlanta	City Service Center	4	4	0	60,000	Poverty Areas	Complaints and special projects
	Houston	Neighborhood City Hall	3	3	0	60,000	Poverty Areas	Complaints and special projects
Multiple In-House Services	Boston	Little City Hall	14	100	30	1,000,000	Citywide	Complaints and special projects
	Baltimore	Mayor's Station	3	3	50	66,000	Mixed Income	Social welfare
	Columbus	Mini-City Hall	1	0	30	Existing Dept. Budgets	Poverty Area	Social welfare
Outreach Office	San Francisco	Mayor's Office of Outreach	0	2	0	30,000	Mixed Income	Complaints and special projects

Notes: Atlanta, Houston, Baltimore, and Columbus each have two-three additional central staff persons who devote part of their time to this program. Chicago staff and budgets are estimates because they are subdivided from the total OEO program. All cities expend capital outlay and program funds in addition to staff and operating monies. The source of all funds is primarily the city's general fund except in Chicago (OEO funds), Norfolk (Model Cities funds), New York City ($1 million Urban Coalition funds), and Boston ($200,000 Model Cities funds). New York expends $3,000,000 additionally for capital outlay projects from debt service tax monies.

Source: Center for Governmental Studies, Washington, D.C.

The centers in Los Angeles and Kansas City are located in outlying communities to lessen distance; those in San Antonio serve three
equal sections that take in the entire city. Developments in these
cities took place without particular focus on poverty or ethnic areas.
In Los Angeles and Kansas City only part of the population is served;
in San Antonio the centers serve the entire city because they were
created for a different reason.

Multiservice Centers

Multiservice centers provide many social services and some
municipal services in one location in Chicago and Norfolk. These
naturally have located their centers in disadvantaged areas because
poor people are the ones who use these services. Since Norfolk's
program was inspired by Model Cities funds, it services Model Cities
target areas, predominantly a black population. Chicago's centers
were started by Office of Economic Opportunity (OEO) funds, and they
serve a population that is heavily black but also contains a mix of other
ethnic groups. Economic and social considerations were the primary
factors determining location in these cities, and it appears that substantial physical plants never would have been created without federal
funds.

The goals of these two programs as well as those in cities
influenced by the little city hall concept have been to lessen racial
tensions, to improve services, and to develop an improved sense of
community through more effective communications.

The New Breed

Neighborhood city halls which emphasize communication, coordination, and a more personal involvement with individual citizens
and neighborhood problems, but with a minimal level of in-house
services, are in New York, Atlanta, and Houston. Cities which emphasize the neighborhood city hall aspects and also provide multiservice
functions are Boston, Baltimore, and Columbus.

In order to achieve these goals, Atlanta, Houston, Baltimore,
and Columbus chose to locate their centers in poverty areas, and
New York and Boston selected a citywide approach.

Atlanta located its operation in Community Action Program
(CAP) centers and the Model Cities headquarters building, all in
poverty and predominantly black areas, although some white areas—
a "hippie" section, for example—are served. The four mayor's

representatives respond to complaints from anywhere within the city. Department heads say they receive fewer irrelevant complaints because coordinators screen them first. A Police Department spokesman says, "We have better community relations in these areas." Others say it has relieved them from a "front-line citizen attack."

But Atlanta city offices are too small and their visibility is poor. John Robinson, director of the Department of Human Resources, and Daniel Sweat, chief administrative officer, both feel more centers and staff are needed. And HUD interns and Urban Corps volunteers are not numerous or permanent enough to make a lasting contribution for staff requirements.

In Houston, the business community, civic organizations, and apparently most citizens of all income levels have expressed favor for the program because they feel it has not only improved services in depressed areas but also has helped to stabilize the city, keep things "cool," and generally added to the progress of the city. The three trailers and one house (converted to offices) serve poor white, Mexican-American, and black areas.

Columbus placed its one mini-city hall in the Model Cities area, although some citizen groups felt that there are other areas of the city which could derive greater benefit from it, since Model Cities and CAP operate several neighborhood centers in the area.

Baltimore placed three centers in mixed racial and ethnic low-income and moderate-income areas because Mayor Thomas J. D'Alesandro II felt the sociopolitical dynamics of the city called for an equal concentration of concern for many diversified groups. One area is predominantly white and the others have mixed black and white populations, and there are varied ethnic groups in each area. An agreement between the city and CAP further stressed the location of the city centers outside of areas served by CAP. Although service centers function like little city halls, they are primarily multiservice centers, best located in disadvantaged areas near the people who need their social-welfare services most.

In Boston, little city halls (LCH) are located in all areas of the city but offer only a limited variety of services, most of which are not in the usual categories provided by multiservice centers. They concentrate on complaints and special neighborhood projects, but perform some services applicable to almost any neighborhood, such as housing inspection, police-community relations, and senior citizen activities. Mayor Kevin White chose a citywide approach on what appears to be justifiable grounds: alienation in the city was widespread; stabilization of middle- and higher-income communities was necessary to arrest deterioration of neighborhoods and loss of population from the central city; issues of crime, airport location, housing rehabilitation, and delivery of services were urgent in all sectors of the city. In addition, some areas had already petitioned for LCHs; city priorities could be more accurately determined if information came from all neighborhoods; citywide citizen councils and neighborhood government could be facilitated; and there was apprehension that a mere pilot program might just fade away. Also, there is little doubt that Mayor White envisioned LCHs as a politically astute way to reach the mass of citizens and to create voter goodwill.

In New York, shortly after initiating a half dozen neighborhood city halls in New York, Mayor John Lindsay decided that a much broader approach was necessary because alienation was seething among "middle Americans," and because it was also a good way to reach all constituents. Multiservice centers functioning under the Human Resources Administration, for example, must necessarily operate where need is greatest, but little city halls and urban action task forces (UATFs), which do not provide multiple social-welfare services, can operate anywhere because they deal primarily in complaints and special neighborhood projects.

The UATFs operate in fifty of the city's sixty-two community districts, so it can be defined fairly as a citywide program; however, because of the necessity for budget reductions in many programs, only six UATFs are fully staffed and have formal neighborhood councils with substantive decision-making authority. Some additional UATFs have staff and rent paid by voluntary private contributions.

Lindsay and White felt a citywide approach was necessary. They believed that the majority of citizens were not in sympathy with wholesale transfer of tax monies (local or federal) to a few minority groups. Particularly in Boston, larger ethnic groups reminded officials of their own struggles for survival in America and their determination not to relinquish gains. In both cities there was concern that a disproportionate share of federal money was already being concentrated in poverty areas through community action and other federal programs, and that even more would go in this direction with implementation of the Model Cities program. Decentralization in both a geographic and demographic context was seen as the most logical way to effectively bring all elements of the community together.

Outreach

Outreach consists of assignment of citizen advocates working from the mayor's office and to special areas in the city. San Francisco uses this approach, but there is criticism that the staff is not familiar enough with or interested in the neighborhoods.

Summary

More cities are looking with interest at the citywide approach for human and physical development projects. Dayton, Ohio, has established citizen councils throughout the city. Washington, D.C., is developing a citywide citizen structure designed after their Model Cities board. Kansas City is attempting to improve its citywide citizen structure, and Los Angeles plans to build at least two additional branch city halls in the near future. San Antonio already operates citywide with its service centers. And HUD's Model Cities special-revenue sharing program experiments with select cities already under Model Cities stresses the citywide approach for Model Cities programs. These actions may cause officials in cities with little city halls to consider broadening their approach, the extent of which depends greatly on their financial capabilities and upon the success of existing programs.

SERVICES

Emphasis on Public Works

Because public works and other "bread-and-butter" services are required in all parts of a city, their decentralization should be citywide. San Antonio's public works-oriented centers are the proto-type of citywide decentralization for limited functions. Programs with similar functions in some other communities serve the entire city also, but not with the same degree of decentralized authority as in San Antonio. Smaller cities operate these functions from a central yard; larger cities operate from district yards, but most represent only physical decentralization, with little authority delegated to district superintendents. The San Antonio public works director, Sam Granata, says, "I used to be a high priced clerk. Now I have time to plan and help develop policies." (This is so because area engineers absorb much of the local responsibility.) He intervenes for the community as a whole when area engineers become too narrow in outlook.

The budgets and personnel in the San Antonio and Los Angeles programs look large in comparison with other cities in this review; however, if public works field personnel in the district operations of other large cities are counted, budget figures are comparable. A unique feature of San Antonio is that it has housing and fire inspectors in the same decentralized centers as public works personnel.

Kansas City's $30,746 expenditure and four employees in two city hall annexes constitute a small program. The 30,000 financial transactions can easily be absorbed by existing personnel in the central city hall, but annexes are maintained for citizen convenience. To improve the program the city might do well to consider expanding to less fortunate areas, and to include more services tailored to neighborhood needs.

Services provided in the centers of the above three cities are not geared to human rehabilitation or neighborhood revitalization. They are simply normal city functions, and this is perhaps why there is little clamor for such centers from other areas of the city. Instead, citizen outcry is for Model Cities programs, which will soon assume the multiservice center role in the most hard-pressed areas of these cities and for community action programs, which have already absorbed some social-welfare functions. When new services and increased funding are offered, citizens take greater interest.

Emphasis on Human Resources

Multiservice centers in Chicago, Norfolk, and Baltimore all perform similar functions which emphasize human resources: family counseling, food programs, employment assistance, health services, training and education classes, Social Security and senior citizen assistance, day care, housing inspection, complaint processing, referrals, etc.

But funding is different in each city. Chicago operates its eighteen centers and outposts by utilizing part of its $54,000,000 CAP funds for this purpose. The city, however, contributes $12,000,000 in cash to the program as its local share. Norfolk uses Model Cities funds for its $168,000 operation. Baltimore operates its three stations with $66,000 of city funds and borrowed agency headquarters personnel. It spends the smallest amount of new monies and has achieved a high level of operating efficiency.

The largest variety of services is found in Chicago's program.
In addition to services mentioned above, its centers provide day-labor
assistance (jobs for people on a one-day basis), economic development,
language courses, Model Cities offices, hot food programs, and projects designed specifically for each neighborhood. The centers have
served over 3,000,000 clients since they were opened in 1965—clients
who might have given up in frustration and discouragement. In short,
through the centers, Chicagoans have received education, training,
counseling, and employment, and have developed a new sense of security.
Even Alderman Leon Depres, an Independent Democrat opposition
voice to Mayor Richard Daley, states that the service center program
is beneficial to the city. He believes it requires improvement and
should be less dominated from the "top," but that it is needed along
with other programs to assist the disadvantaged. There is a general
criticism of bureaucracy, and there is also criticism by center employees that central staffs are too large and would serve the city better
if more were located in the neighborhoods. Some civic organizations
believe that the program has great potential but has not yet achieved
it.

The Norfolk neighborhood multipurpose center has been extremely
beneficial during its short period of operation. Over 3,000 persons
are served monthly, mostly in recreational programs in the large
gymnasium and playground next to the center. A swimming pool will
increase this number. Hundreds are served each week by a permanent
staff of nineteen in regular social-welfare services.

The three centers in Baltimore each serve about 1,500 clients
monthly. The two largest functions—employment and probationary
services—handle about 500 cases apiece. There is a staff of about
twelve in each center, although one station is now being remodeled to
accommodate a staff of thirty.

In this program families are met in a reception area and processed effectively, quickly, and in a well-coordinated manner from
one agency to another—all on the same floor of this modest-size
store front operation. The size of the physical facilities in Baltimore
and Norfolk appear to come close to ideal for most efficient and
effective service.

Adaptations and Problems

Columbus' mini-city hall could be more effective with more
services. Its emphasis on human relations, youth services, and housing
inspections does not give it a broad enough base to be considered a

full-scale multiservice center where families may receive most social services in one stop. There is no overall director of the mini-city hall, services are uncoordinated, and the impression of many—including Model Cities and CAP personnel—is that it is primarily administrative, rather than a service center. It probably inherited many of these difficulties because it was not originally meant to be a multiple-service center, and merely added space for a few ongoing city operations.

The Columbus mini-city hall can be improved simply by designating a center director and adding services. The operation is already economical. It has no separate budget but uses parts of existing city department budgets and existing personnel. As in Baltimore, the city of Columbus transferred people from central offices to the neighborhood office but in few functional areas.

Boston Advocacy of Ombudsmen

For the most part, Boston's centers do not operate programs; rather, they assist in a variety of services, including employment, Social Security, senior citizen activities, housing and fire inspection, police-community relations, tax collections, food programs, referrals, information dissemination, ombudsmen, and complaint processing. In some centers there are day care and recreational programs but not many social-welfare services. CAP handles the latter.

The program emphasizes traditional city services, and most complaints (9,000 weekly) deal with city problems. Many program officials believe they have enough city problems to worry about without getting involved in social-welfare entanglements, and that a general city-service approach provides rationale for a citywide operation in contrast with dealing with poverty areas alone. The $1,000,000 (including $200,000 Model Cities funds) expenditure and services of about 100 employees for the program appear to be better justified when spread throughout the city.

"Complaint processing and information distribution is the 'bread and butter' operation of the Little City Halls," says David Davis, former director of the Office of Public Service, "but this is not enough to justify an existence by playing a numbers game with complaint statistics, even though the numbers are impressive." He believes project implementation is perhaps their most significant accomplishment. The little city hall managers have become citizen advocates (neighborhood ombudsmen); and they have led citizens successfully against the city and other agencies, when necessary, in battles of urban renewal, airport expansion, road construction, and many other neighborhood problems. They have helped in the improvement of service, delivery of food parcels, development of a heating task force to give aid to households without heat, initiation of a school lunch program, construction of a park, and other activities. It is primarily this function, Davis feels, that justifies the program. Citizens have been given new hope and have been shown how to get through the system successfully.

New York Concentration on Information and Complaints

New York's centers are really information and complaint offices with neighborhood ombudsmen who follow up complaints and assist in neighborhood projects. A few in-house services are provided in some centers, such as assistance to senior citizens for half-rate transit fares, information dissemination, and referral assistance. As in Boston, working with residents in projects involving neighborhood rehabilitation, block improvement, park development, crime reduction, drug education, zoning, and other matters constitutes their most important contribution. Originally, about $2 million—half from city funds and half from contributions by the Urban Coalition—financed fifty offices. Now only six offices are financed by the city, but six citizen councils functioning with these offices have been given authority to establish priorities and programs for $4,000,000 of capital improvement projects.

Task forces were formed to provide both a communications link and a surveillance technique to determine community problems. The caliber of their chairmen is important. They consist of deputy mayors, administrators, department heads, and other key officials. The work of chairmen is probably the most notable accomplishment of the task force, but performance varies greatly: some accomplish very little and some use the store fronts for personal advantage.

Atlanta and Houston: Inexpensive Support for the Mayor

Approximately $60,000 finances each of the programs for Atlanta and Houston. Atlanta's four centers are most economical because they are based in CAP buildings and the Model Cities headquarters. Houston uses small, inexpensive trailers for its three neighborhood city halls. Each city uses one mayor's aide and some part-time

clerical help for each center. Auto expenses and some operating costs
make up the rest of the budget.

There are no in-house services provided by the city in these
centers. However, CAP in Atlanta operates services within the center
where the city's offices are located. Houston's trailers limit services
to information distribution, referral, and some employment assistance.
The main function of both programs is to act as a base for neighborhood rehabilitation and as a work site for the mayor's aides in their
role of neighborhood ombudsmen. Each aide handles about fifteen
complaints daily in addition to his work on neighborhood development
projects. Naturally, some complaints are more easily handled than
others. For example, in a four-month survey period in Atlanta, 80
percent of complaints involving the Sanitation Department were corrected, while this was true in only 30 percent of the cases involving Police
Department complaints.

The program in Houston has been dramatically successful in
rehabilitating some neighborhoods and in providing improved service
in others because Mayor Louie Welch and the City Council committed
enough funds to bring about true change in entire areas. The "scattered
approach" of resolving complaints (as they arise, without preplanning)
has always been less efficient. It is preferable to program priorities
in a systematic and comprehensive fashion. For many cities, however,
a lack of resources has prevented this. But in Houston, listing the
proposed improvements in each neighborhood and then faithfully following through to completion have been the key factors of success. Citizens knew that wherever a neighborhood city hall was located, things
got done. This confidence, plus the "mayor's desk" (established to
receive grievances), City Council meetings in neighborhoods, thousands
of interviews by staff in black and Mexican-American areas, successful
job programs, and the excellent rapport established by Dr. Blair Justice (recent director of the Division of Human Relations) between his
department and minority groups have helped to create an approving
attitude from the public and official organizations. Even though Houston
experienced some racial strife in 1970, it was held to a minimum
largely because of these positive steps.

Rehabilitation of neighborhoods has been less comprehensive in
Atlanta than Houston; but even so, neighborhoods have been enhanced,
street lights added, refuse collection improved, rodent control effected,
and many low-cost services implemented. Although Atlanta's commitment of large capital improvement funds has not been on the scale of
Houston's, it has nevertheless done much to correct neighborhood
problems and to improve communication between residents and City
Hall.

San Francisco's Outreach: Short Span

The two mayor's aides in San Francisco's outreach program
each handle about ten to fifteen resident requests daily. The lack of a
neighborhood office appears to have made it more difficult to establish
rapport with residents. And since residents did not participate in the
selection of the aides, there is less confidence in them than might
otherwise be the case. Citizens feel that the wrong persons have been
chosen to serve their communities.

Filling in the gaps in neighborhood facilities are community
action centers, health centers, and a state multiservice center which
make up the base of neighborhood offices. The Model Cities program
will add one or two centers. In these physically decentralized facilities
Mayor Joseph Alioto may station city ombudsmen who are more attuned
to the highly diversified communities of San Francisco.

HOURS OF OPERATION

Most centers in the cities under discussion are open the same
hours as the main city hall. However, more comprehensive and well-
staffed multiservice centers are open in the evenings and part of each
weekend. Chicago's and Norfolk's centers, for example, are open
until 10 p.m. daily and also on weekends. Little city halls usually close
at 5 or 6 p.m. except when they are engaged in special projects (such
as voter registration), which may keep them open evenings or weekends.
A criticism of little city hall programs is that the centers close too
early. It is a valid criticism; however, most centers really operate
beyond closing hours because their managers attend many evening and
weekend meetings in the neighborhoods and make themselves available
most of the time.

II

FOR EACH CITY,
AN
INDIVIDUAL APPROACH—
CASE STUDIES
OF TWELVE CITIES

3

LOS ANGELES
IS FORCED
TO
REACH OUT

Area: 461 square miles
Population: 2,782,400
Mexican-American: 862,544
Black: 700,000

THE CITY AND ITS GOVERNMENT

Branch city halls (BCHs), as they are called in Los Angeles, are not an innovation. They have been in operation some thirty to forty years—almost as long as the communities in which they are located have been municipalities.

Even though there has always been a downtown, the saying goes that "Los Angeles is no city; it's a bunch of suburbs in search of a center." And approximately forty communities that lie within the city limits still maintain separate post office addresses. Eleven of these "neighborhoods" or "suburbs" have branch city halls, many of which were established even before the communities were annexed by the city.

The City

The continued existence of the branches of the city has never been seriously questioned—Los Angeles is simply too large, geographically, for one city hall. Some twenty-five miles separate its northern and southern tips, and it is fifteen miles wide—an area of 461 square miles, as compared with Boston's forty-three square miles and Manhattan's 22.3 square miles.

It is also large in population, the third largest in the country. Originally founded as a Spanish colony by Felipe de Neve in 1781, "the City of Los Angeles" became part of the United States in 1848 after the Mexican War and was incorporated as a city in 1850. Forty years later its population was 11,200, but by 1920 this figure was up to 577,000 and by 1930 it was 1,238,000.

The great gulf separating suburb from central city and one suburb from another is more than geographical. Psychological over-tones are there, too, as in most American cities. But in contrast with other cities, feelings of alienation among Angelenos are not res-tricted to the ghettos or barrios, nor are they caused only by socio-economic factors. Los Angeles' pattern of development has been a great factor in alienating high- and middle-income residents who had never intended to become part of the city when they settled in what were then independent communities. The fact that these communities have been forced over the years to annex with Los Angeles to receive adequate water supplies has left their residents resentful of central city government and unwilling to identify themselves by other than the original community names, i.e., San Pedro, Van Nuys, the "Valley" (San Fernando), etc. (Only very recently has water come under the operation of a metropolitan district agency, but the city still retains sewerage service as an annexation lever.)

Dissent has been so strong that the political history of the city is rife with secession proposals, particularly in the San Fernando Valley and the harbor area, and movements to establish boroughs.

The lack of feeling for the city as a whole has been analyzed by many urbanologists and writers, among them Myron Roberts, associate editor of the Los Angeles Magazine. He feels that Los Angeles people are basically rural-oriented in what he calls the "nonurban sense." As he puts it, "They think they live somewhere else." The big city is frightening, and most Los Angeles residents tend to hibernate in their houses surrounded by little walls. Says Roberts, "They are here not to share urban life, but to make money. Talk to anyone, and in twenty minutes he'll say, 'I never go to Los Angeles.' The terminology 'Southern California' has more meaning to them than Los Angeles."

Roberts believes that the first problem of Los Angeles is failure of citizens to see each other as common citizens in a "human city."

"It is a city built around the automobile—planned as a kind of machine by the men who built it.

"Residents never wanted a strong central city. They wanted their towns to be independent, so they developed a weak-mayor system. Perhaps it is up to this next generation of youth to develop some sense of cohesion among human beings."

The Government

Los Angeles' weak-mayor system consists of fifteen councilmanic districts whose councilmen are elected on a full-time, nonpartisan basis. They receive salaries of $17,500 per year. Staggered terms of office for councilmen, which prevents the mayor from developing reliable voting blocs, is just one of several charter provisions which place most of the power in the council's hands. The history of legislative predominance is a relatively long one in Los Angeles, dating from 1889, when the first city charter was revised to favor the legislature.

Another feature contributing to executive weakness is the commission system of departmental control, giving the mayor only indirect influence over selection of department heads. The charter gives lay commissioners, appointed by the mayor, power to select general managers and to administer departments; however, commissioners will ordinarily do what the mayor tells them to do.

In 1965, in response to recommendations by several charter study commissions, this system was somewhat altered. General managers of six departments were given responsibility for running their departments, and their boards of commissioners were placed in an advisory capacity; but the other departments were unchanged.

The city administrative officer (CAO), whose office was established in 1951, has no direct responsibility for department heads and is concerned primarily with financial control and program review. It is a system full of "checks and balances," but Dave Wilkins, chief administrative analyst for the city administrative officer, calls it "a system of all checks and no balances."

Ironically, with all the checks, the incumbent mayor, Sam Yorty, has still managed to be accused of being "power mad" and a "dictator" by some members of his council over the years.

BRANCH CITY HALLS

It is in this decentralized political environment and fragmented social milieu that BCHs operate as a natural feature of the terrain, and receive support from all sources. Their future is secure, because to remove them would only cause more citizen resentment toward the city, unwanted as a home by so many of its residents. Also, and perhaps most important, they generally provide desirable and effective

services. They are little affected by politics of the mayor or council,
even though councilmanic offices are located in six BCH buildings and
the mayor has an office in one.

Objectives

City officials tend to look with favor on the BCHs, recognizing
that they provide more convenient service to neighborhood residents
at least as efficiently as (and sometimes more than) the main city
hall. Some of the increased efficiency, they feel, is attributable to the
fact that employees live closer to their work and show greater concern
for neighborhood problems.

BCHs tend to provide a base for neighborhood identity, and a
center for business and some civic activity. Because of them, citizens
do feel somewhat closer to government and appreciate the fact that
they are getting service, even if they have little to say about it. Their
acceptance is enhanced by the display of beautiful structures, the
visibility of employees and expenditures of tax dollars, and a deemphasis on central control.

Physical Facilities and Locations

There are eleven BCHs in the Los Angeles area, serving all
income levels and varying widely in size, from the new San Fernando
Valley-Van Nuys eight-story structure and complex of several buildings
which employs 435 persons with operating costs of $7,408,920, to the
old but remodeled Watts structure, which employs 3.2 persons and
operates at $54,502. The eleven centers together spend $18,500,158
annually and employ 1,086 full-time civil service employees. Most
structures are not new but reflect extensive remodeling and enlarging.
In general, they are centrally located within the districts they serve
and enjoy good visibility.

Watts

The Watts BCH serves an almost all-black population of about
65,000 and operates out of a well-maintained, old building once used
as a municipal hall. While most branches provide four or five major
services—usually building code enforcement and permit issuance,
engineering, street maintenance, sanitation, and some planning services, for example—Watts has only a city clerk's office, a human
relations department, and a councilmanic office.

Scene of the 1965 riots which took place in its "curfew area," Watts is a district greatly in need of additional treatment. However, since it is located within ten miles of the main city hall, officials feel that other services can be easily obtained a "short distance away" and that an elaborate building is not needed.

Van Nuys and West Los Angeles

The Van Nuys complex is the most elaborate of the eleven, providing every service to its residents that can be found downtown. It serves a population of over a million people and an area of 252 square miles in the San Fernando Valley, which is somewhat isolated from the rest of the city by mountains and distance. The valley has one-third of the city's population and more than half of its area. This is the only branch having an elaborate switchboard; it is staffed by eleven persons who handle some 7,000 calls per week and operate on a twenty-four-hour-per-day basis.

West Los Angeles, a community of 200,000 persons, similar in socioeconomic features to Van Nuys, also has a large and elaborate BCH complex offering some sixteen services housed in several structures. It, too, operates a twenty-four-hour switchboard but is smaller than the one in Van Nuys.

Other branches have only small switchboards which operate during normal daytime working hours (branches maintain the same hours as the main city hall), but all are capable of switching any call, toll-free, downtown. This is an important service in Los Angeles, where sometimes a call from one neighborhood to the next involves toll fees. No citizen need ever place more than one call to reach any city department, either downtown or at a branch. The operators, however, do not process complaints—they merely pass them on.

Building Plans

Dr. C. Erwin Piper, CAO, states that the five-year capital improvement program for the city (which he says is followed very closely) includes plans for one new building each in Van Nuys and the West Valley (twenty-five miles from downtown), and a possible third in the Devonshire area. He believes that all councilmen want branch city halls in their areas, despite the fact that no intense competition over capital improvement projects is reflected in the actual allocation of building construction funds.

Expenditures and Staff

Expenditures of the BCHs are combined in the overall budgets of each central department; therefore, no specific breakdown of these expenditures is available. The city has 30,000 employees and a budget of over $500 million. Including proprietary (revenue-maintaining) departments, the figures are 47,000 employees and $1,200 million. (See Table 2.)

Personnel are selected through the regular civil service system and are assigned wherever necessary. A few officials criticize the duplication of some staff at both branch and central levels. But most feel the duplication is justified by better service to neighborhood residents. Less efficient use of some manpower is overcome by employees being closer to their jobs.

Management

Interdepartmental coordination does not exist in the BCHs. Direction and policy making emanate from central departments. There are no managers or coordinators—there are only field supervisors who handle complaints and make day-to-day decisions, such as which streets to patch, or which houses to process for demolition or rahabilitation. But major decisions on street paving or location of traffic signals, for example, or decisions on large expenditures are made by each department's general manager or commission—in many cases already decided in the five-year capital improvements budget approved by the City Council.

William Millburn, manager of the West Los Angeles branch of the Department of Building and Safety, indicates, for example, that his primary role is to supervise his immediate staff and carry out policies set forth by the general manager (equivalent to a city department head) and commission members.

City attorneys in BCHs primarily prosecute local criminal cases but seldom render legal decisions for the city. It is apparent that most action requiring decision making outside of local matters takes place downtown. Feedback from local department heads, however, is used by general managers and commissioners to help make policy decisions.

TABLE 2

Los Angeles City Government Branch City Hall
Functions, Employees, and Expenditures

Branch City Hall	Cost
Eagle Rock Municipal Building	$ 102,192
Hollywood-Wilshire Municipal Building	1,890,552
San Pedro Administrative Center	1,866,707
Sunland-Tujunga Municipal Building	255,480
Van Nuys Administrative Center	7,408,920
Venice Municipal Building	1,038,952
Watts Municipal Building	54,502
Westchester Municipal Building	671,061
West Los Angeles Administrative Center	3,065,760
West Valley Municipal Building	2,043,840
Wilmington Municipal Building	102,192
Total Estimated Operating Costs	$18,500,158

Department Occupancy	Number of Employees
Eagle Rock Municipal Building	
Building and Safety	1
Street Maintenance	5
Hollywood-Wilshire Municipal Building	
City Clerk	12
Municipal Arts	23
Engineering	62
Sanitation	4
Traffic	10
San Pedro Administrative Center	
Building and Safety	19
City Attorney	7
City Clerk	0.6
Fire	9
Human Relations	1
Planning	2
Contract Administration	3
Engineering	53
Personnel	3
Sanitation	4
Street Maintenance	6
Councilmanic Office	2
Sunland-Tujunga Municipal Building	
Building and Safety	15
Van Nuys Administrative Center	
Building and Safety	149
City Attorney	26
Planning	5
Traffic	8
City Clerk	20
Fire	17
Human Relations	1

(continued)

(TABLE 2 continued)

Branch City Hall	Cost
Department Occupancy	Number of Employees
Contract Administration	12
Engineering	155
Right of Way and Land	24
Street Maintenance	7
Sanitation	5
Social Service	2
Mayor	2
Councilmanic Office	2
Venice Municipal Building	
Building and Safety	11
Human Relations	1
Engineering	49
Watts Municipal Building	
City Clerk	0.2
Human Relations	1
Councilmanic Office	2
Westchester Municipal Building	
City Clerk	0.4
Fire	7
Engineering	22
Sanitation	4
Street Maintenance	5
Councilmanic Office	1
West Los Angeles Administrative Center	
Building and Safety	63
City Attorney	11
City Clerk	14
Planning	2
Contract Administration	4
Engineering	69
Street Maintenance	5
Traffic	10
Councilmanic Office	2
West Valley Municipal Building	
Planning	1
Traffic	8
Contract Administration	8
Engineering	93
Street Maintenance	7
Councilmanic Office	3
Wilmington Municipal Building	
Traffic	6
Total	1,086

Note: The expenditures in this table are estimated for each branch on the average cost per employee and include all costs except building depreciation.

Source: City administrator's office, City Hall, Los Angeles (July, 1970).

Councilmen

Six councilmanic district offices are located directly in BCHs, and several others are in nearby buildings.

These offices are the complaint and inquiry link between City Hall and the neighborhood residents. If a citizen has a complaint which he cannot resolve through normal channels, he goes to his councilman and usually gets results. Councilmen feel they are the ombudsmen and the ones who can really get things done.

The councilmen are paid $17,500 per year and engage almost full-time in their duties, although most have additional occupations. It is generally felt, however, that daily attendance at council meetings (the city charter requires them to meet at least five days each week) and all their other vast duties do constitute a full workweek for most.

Each councilman is authorized as many as eleven persons, to be selected by him and to work for him on city matters. Most councilmen choose to use the full budget allocated to them for this purpose, nor- mally selecting three deputies, several assistants, and other clerical personnel to help run their affairs. Most councilmanic staffs are based in the main city hall but spend some time in the district offices and considerable time at meetings of organizations, clubs, and civic groups in each district. They do not normally engage in organizing residents or in creating special community projects. In general, they handle administrative and political details and play a role in the com- munication network between citizens and councilman. Staff members are selected with these qualifications in mind. They are not employed to perform as citizen advocates.

A citizen role in the selection of deputies is practically nonexis- tent. As an example, in one case where the deputy is accepted by the residents, citizens feel that he may be a "nice guy" but gets little done. "Just look around. Nothing has changed. What good is someone if he can't get results?"

Councilman Edmund D. Edelman, who is also chairman of the City Council's Charter and Administrative Code Committee, has his office in a central business area in the Fifth District, easily accessible to most people he serves but not readily visible to the less informed. The income and educational level of the majority of his constituency are high, however, and they have better-than-average ability to "reach through the system." Therefore, he sees little need for his deputies to "walk the streets" and to knock on doors.

He is faced with serving approximately 200,000 persons located in seventeen smaller communities (Bel Air, Beverly Glen Canyon, Beverly Wood, Carthay Circle, Cheviot Hills, Century City, Fairfax, Holmby Hills, Palms, Pico-Robertson, Rancho Park, Roscomare Canyon, Stone Canyon, UCLA, West Pico, Westwood) in an area ten miles long and fifteen miles wide. This is a fairly typical situation for most councilmen.

Edelman's district office, in which he works one afternoon a week, and which is manned by one of his deputies three full days each week, receives approximately fifteen to twenty complaints daily, about five presented in person and the rest by telephone. Most require only one phone call to a department for results. In addition, he receives twenty to thirty letters per day and maintains a full-time secretary in his district office.

While this volume of work is reportedly typical of all fifteen district offices, the type and pattern of complaints vary from office to office; and not all councilmen keep precise records or tabulations. Also, there is no consolidation of data from the fifteen offices to any central source for evaluation and central management purposes.

Some councilmen feel that it is unnecessary to have district offices. Councilman James Potter of the Van Nuys district feels that the expense of staffing this office is not justifiable because of the lack of constituent traffic. Some councilmen do keep their offices open during regular city working hours. However, much of the time many of the offices located in the BCHs are locked during regular office hours, indicating that citizen business is conducted at the main city hall.

Despite the findings of the Los Angeles City Charter Commission that only a small percentage of people ever contact a councilman, Edelman is not in favor of the proposed city charter revision calling for the establishment of a regular ombudsman. He feels he is an ombudsman and, like most other councilmen, is confident of his ability to handle any citizen complaint. He is proud to be able to demonstrate to his constituency that he can get action. If other districts have greater problems, Edelman feels, "they can readily get additional assistance from City Council." For example, Councilman John S. Gibson of the Watts area, where great poverty and neglect exist, "could get another office and additional help if he would request it. If any area is too large to reach all of the people satisfactorily, more assistance is available. We shouldn't have a situation where citizens aren't being reached."

four councilmen, two school representatives, and a citizen from each
of six neighborhoods from the Model Cities target areas, plus two
chosen at large.

Each of the six Model Cities neighborhoods also has a neighborhood council, composed of twenty-eight citizens, which feed into the
advisory council. Members of these councils are paid ten dollars
each for each meeting attended and are intended to represent a cross
section of all citizens in the area.

These neighborhood councils may be the only real citizen link
to the main city hall. Some feel they may demonstrate a similar need
for councils in BCHs and other areas of the city.

Community Action Program

In 1962, the Youth Opportunities Board was formed as a "joint
powers agency" by city, county, and board of education to help coordinate all welfare and employment programs serving youth. The Office
of Economic Opportunity (OEO) later funded this group, which then became the official Community Action Program (CAP) agency with strong
city representation and influence on the board. City councilmen, however, declined to serve on it, apparently because of its controversial
nature.

Los Angeles' CAP, called Economic and Youth Opportunity Agency
(EYOA), consists of eight area offices staffed by one person each, but
this is the extent of the direct program, since almost all funds are
contracted with fourteen delegate agencies. Ernest Sprinkles, executive director, oversees their administration and directs certain youth
programs.

The city government staff initially put the EYOA application
together for funding. The mayor and two of his representatives sit
on the EYOA board. Relationships between the city and EYOA have
been without conflict partially because of the strong role the city has
played in its formulation and control.

In 1966, OEO turned down a proposal for area economic councils
and outreach centers, the first significant attempt to involve the poor,
realistically, in EYOA affairs and programs. This decision may have
been influenced by the fact that the state has three service centers
in the area in which EYOA operates (east Los Angeles, south-central
Los Angeles, and Venice), and the county of Los Angeles has four
centers, not directly related to EYOA but which perform many social

service and welfare functions. Both of these programs tend to diminish the service role of EYOA.

Sprinkles indicates that rapport with the administration has been good but little has been accomplished. He feels that a new, more vigorous approach is needed and that stronger communication links must be established between the city government and the people. "There is a strong feeling that the city has neglected our program and that most people have a negative attitude about EYOA because of strong city control and little citizen participation. There have been too many strings attached and unlike other CAP programs around the county, it does not have neighborhood centers or neighborhood councils."

Residents, however, do elect a neighborhood worker who represents them on the overall board of directors. Sprinkles indicates that he is now planning and seeking funds for eight area councils which will involve the poor in neighborhood organization, priority program planning, goal setting, budgeting and financial management, personnel selection, types of nonprofessional jobs, resident training, and evaluation of programs which may affect their lives. This is a first step in welding a more favorable relationship between EYOA and neighborhood people.

Sprinkles had developed elaborate plans and alternatives for grass-roots elections. He feels this is unquestionably the way to reach the people. "For too long there has been only discussion and no actual involvement of significant numbers of the poor." Citizen involvement has been accomplished primarily through the delegate agencies. Some feel this has been an effective method.

Los Angeles Chamber of Commerce

The Los Angeles Chamber of Commerce feels its rapport with the city government is very good. Neighborhood chambers want BCHs in their areas because they feel they provide needed services and help to stabilize the economic base. These organizations would be highly disturbed if the operation were discontinued.

An active participant in civic and government affairs, the Los Angeles Chamber of Commerce is beginning to take positions on major city programs and has set up a state and local government committee to analyze problems.

The Chamber has established a Management Council to examine problems and increase employment in blighted areas. Don Newcombe, presently doing public relations for the Los Angeles Dodgers, has been hired by the Chamber to work part-time with youth in the Management Council. So far, some 1,800 jobs have been found for youth and disadvantaged adults, and the council has been effective in securing big business participation and in working with black groups in Watts. The chamber estimates unemployment in Los Angeles may be 6.8 percent in general and as high as 45 percent among black youth. Since the cutback of government aerospace contracts, 22,000 engineers are out of work, placing a hardship on skilled as well as unskilled workers.

Newcombe indicates that most organizations are willing to work for community betterment, but it is difficult to secure any kind of coordination among groups. Newcombe and Chad McClellan, Management Council head, work through the National Alliance of Businessmen (NAB) for job commitments and use NAB staff member Truman Janks as a communications link to citizens through his weekly hour and a half radio program and his fieldwork.

A key problem in coordinating and getting the services down to the people is the vastness of the city and its transportation problems. Public transportation is scarce, inconvenient, and expensive—impractical, in most cases, to use in reaching a job. Even with an automobile, an uneducated person is in difficulty. "The expressways look like impregnable walls to him. This vastness also makes it difficult to get people to meetings. To have to drive over a hot freeway for an hour and a half to a meeting where little may be accomplished gets little enthusiasm," say Chamber officials.

Janks, from NAB, feels that the main city hall is too administratively oriented rather than people oriented. Few changes have taken place in Watts in regard to housing, jobs, and better schools. A few black business leaders have taken the initiative to move in the right direction, such as construction of a black-owned medical center and bank.

The Management Council has worked with the Watts Labor Action Council, headed by Ted Watkins, who has successfully started a string of service stations, cleaners, and auto mechanic shops, all of which hire Watts residents. The Labor Council has also arranged a shared-ride project. In Janks's opinion, much needs to be done to build a bridge between the citizens of Watts and the city administration.

"The ombudsman is not necessarily the way to this bridge," he says,
"because the ombudsmen would be City Hall men anyway, and not persons whom the citizens helped to select."

County Human Relations Division

The County Human Relations Division has eight field offices in
Los Angeles; four are in the Watts area, one located in the BCH and
supervised on a half-time basis. They deal with discrimination and
general complaints, sponsor workshops, and hold community meetings
to hear gripes and to help develop community plans. Ray Dawson,
supervisor of the Watts offices, estimates they receive about twenty
complaints per week. There would be more, he feels, if some decisions
could be made there. "Most people don't come in because they feel
nothing will be done anyway." Citizens have not participated in this
process very meaningfully.

PERCEPTIONS OF BRANCH CITY HALLS

Citizens view BCHs as a convenience to them in those areas
where service is good. The branches reinforce community identity
and serve as a display of the one type of government spending to
which citizens rarely object—direct spending in local communities,
where they feel a "fair share of the taxes ought to be spent anyway."
On the other hand, some people voice awareness of their lack of
influence on decisions or policy and seem to feel that they are being
patronized. They perceive these beautiful structures as being without
heads or ability to think.

"Bread and butter" complaints in Los Angeles, such as potholes,
rodents, weeds, etc., are far fewer than in the average big city, and
the citizen has less need to maintain contact with City Hall. When
something does not happen quickly enough, most citizens use their
councilman and normally get results. Alienation seems to creep in
over more complex problems of housing, air pollution, rapid transit,
and taxes—items which the average citizen knows will not be solved
at the BCH level, if they are solved at all. Some citizens view the
branch operation merely as a convenience for government and employees, and an easier way to collect permit fees and to process fines.
This feeling may still belong only to a minority of people, but it is
growing in poverty areas.

Residents express dissatisfaction with the city as well as with
most agencies. Many view the public employment agency in the Watts

area as "just another building and a place for addicts and winos to gather for their noon get-together." Except for a few meaningful things described above, Watts remains the same. Burned-out buildings remain; cabs refuse to go there; people live from day to day, not really caring what happens tomorrow. Little leadership exists.

The mayor and councilmen see BCHs as performing a valuable service and helping to dispel feelings of remoteness. The city administrative officer, general managers, and department commissioners view them as efficient and delivering an improved service. Most employees like their close proximity to their residences and a less bureaucratic atmosphere.

ANALYSIS AND RECOMMENDATIONS

Branch City Halls and Equality of Service

The eleven BCHs in Los Angeles provide improved service to citizens, saving them many millions of miles of travel annually in this expansive, sprawling city of 461 square miles. Even with the world's finest freeway system, drivers prefer to travel only a few miles and avoid the congestion and pollution of a ten- or fifteen-mile jaunt downtown. "If a city government wishes to be this large, for whatever reason, then it must responsibly and reasonably serve its citizens," people say. "Services located in neighborhoods are a proper use of our tax monies."

Scattered locations of BCHs are good for efficiency of government, for bringing employees closer to their work, and for lessening alienation of residents at the fringes. Regardless of added costs in building construction and personnel, and regardless of possible retardation of central city development, brought about through decentralization, the City Council would never think of closing the branches, because they are what the outlying communities want. Besides, BCHs provide a base for strengthening the present district government system and for furthering the idea of the councilman in the role of "mayor of his district."

Some BCHs provide every service that can be obtained at the main city hall, thus being particularly beneficial to the elderly, the uninformed, and those without transportation. Such decentralization of services is not experienced to this extent in any other major city in the United States.

However, this package of comprehensive service is offered in only a few of the eleven complexes, an inequality which will be difficult to maintain, particularly in light of the great need of some areas. Most cities have concentrated additional services in poverty areas, whereas in Los Angeles, in spite of its broad area approach, extra services have been placed in more affluent neighborhoods.

In general, extra effort is reflected in those services which tend to lessen travel time downtown. Delivery of regular services, such as refuse collection, street maintenance, rodent control, etc., is equal in all sections of the city, including Watts. Although poverty and social service functions are concentrated in depressed areas, primarily by state and county multiservice centers and delegate agencies of the Community Action Program, the greatest disparities are in housing, employment, and the more substantive areas.

Part of the imbalance will be alleviated when the proposed Model Cities multiservice center becomes operational in Watts, where service could stand improvement. The Watts BCH, with only human relations, city clerk, and councilmanic offices, could hardly tackle the major problems of the area. Yet, even now, a structure is there which could be expanded with additional services even though the area is only a few miles from the main city hall.

BCHs could be made more meaningful if they provided Social Security offices, welfare assistance, and senior citizen activities as well as regular city services. These functions would also save the citizen the long haul to the central city and would make the BCHs more popular.

Coordination and Central Management

Even now, BCHs with numerous services need managers or coordinators with overall knowledge of the operation to add direction. Preferably, each branch coordinator would report to a central coordinator responsible for overseeing all the branches; he, in turn, would report directly to the city administrative officer.

A central complaint office in the branches, as well as the main city hall, should be established under jurisdiction of the coordinators, working in conjunction with councilmanic offices. Complaint records from all offices would flow through branch coordinators to the central head of this division. The CAO and his staff would tabulate, process, and evaluate complaints from all city offices and departments for the purpose of improving central management techniques. Presently the CAO does not have detailed access to work data and performance records of each department. A directive prepared by him and approved by the mayor and City Council supporting this information-gathering technique could very well be put into effect now without charter changes.

The above would not only provide the mayor and City Council with a valuable information base for making decisions, establishing goals, and evaluating departmental performance; it would also improve the mayor's ability to direct through a strengthened and more know-ledgeable CAO and central management staff. This would be a desirable accomplishment in Los Angeles.

Councilmen vs. Ombudsmen

Regardless of official impressions, the city's regular channels of communication have not reached sufficient numbers of citizens. Particularly among the poor, in Watts and in other sections of the city, there are still many uninformed and apathetic citizens. The Watts councilmanic office, with its deputies, has only mildly touched the people. The "ombudsman" role of the councilman has not noticeably turned the tide of hostility or lessened feelings of forgottenness.

Most councilmen, however, express disfavor with the idea of appointed ombudsmen for two reasons. First, they believe client traffic would not warrant full-time ombudsmen offices in most areas; and second, they feel strongly that they already fill this role and are fully capable of handling all complaints in their areas (of approximately 200,000 persons each). For most sections of Los Angeles, particularly the higher-income areas, it appears to be true that the volume of complaints can be handled by councilmen. This says nothing, however, of the need for additional human resource services in each area, as well as a director-ombudsman to coordinate services and follow up individual and family problems on a regular, full-time schedule. It may take hours or even days of follow-up to process, counsel, and evaluate one case. In the less populous cities of Baltimore and Boston, for example, as many as 1,500 cases are handled monthly from one center servicing a small area. It takes trained counselors and evaluators, not easily found among elected officials, to settle these cases.

One problem is that there are at least two definitions of an ombudsman. In the American sense, he is mostly a citizen advocate working in the neighborhood to solve individual problems. He befriends

his client and treats every case as special. When such advocates
publicize their whereabouts and make themselves available at all
hours, hundreds of residents seem to come forward. It takes a full
staff to adequately process even a small number of cases. Citizens
do get better service under this system and they develop better feeling
about government.

In the Scandinavian sense, an ombudsman is an official of high
authority (with tenure and considerable independence), appointed by
the legislative branch to evaluate and improve the executive branch.
Ken Wilson, former chief of the Charter Commission staff, believes
this is what Los Angeles needs. In Chicago, investigators of the
Better Government Association (funded by private business and civic
sources) fulfill the Scandinavian role on the local level more closely
than any other American version, even though they are not officially
attached to government.

Los Angeles councilmen have the capacity to be Scandinavian-
type ombudsmen. This is largely why they resist appointing other
ombudsmen. However, councilmen are not very likely to investigate
themselves, and they do not have time to evaluate other branches of
local government (a full-time job in itself). The Chicago Better Government Association approach would be a worthy adjunct, if the gov-
ernment-supported concept of ombudsman does not come into fruition.

Most important, the lower range of ombudsmen are vital to
Los Angeles' ability to revitalize citizen attitudes. Appointment of
BCH coordinator-ombudsmen and family-counselor ombudsmen
should not hurt the City Council's pride.

Councilman Edelman states that if additional staff and offices
are needed in high problem areas, the City Council would readily
approve additional expenditures for this purpose. Thought certainly
ought to be given at this time to concentrating treatment in high-povert
areas with neighborhood ombudsmen.

Another reason for the apparently small clamor for ombudsmen
is that regular departmental complaints are minimal, and those that
exist are efficiently handled by departments themselves. Effective
city services tend to diminish the need for ombudsmen, but the concept is desirable nevertheless for achieving better communication,
independent evaluation of programs, project development, and long-
range casework. The present system does not do much about these
or alleviating alienation.

It is a fallacy of thinking in local government circles that as long as those functions directly responsible to city government are being handled well, obligations of public service are fulfilled. The "responsible city" concept indicates that city officials must go much further. The mayor and City Council must see to it that all agencies operating in their city are providing the best possible service in the best possible way. This means using city personnel for coordination and motivation in governments and organizations outside of its jurisdiction as well. After all, why should local government officials allow others to cause greater problems for the city than they have caused for themselves? Neglecting other influences would be fighting a losing battle.

City Council vs. Citizen Advisory Councils

Each time the issue of neighborhood government or councils comes forth, the City Council turns it down, although four or five councilmen are in favor of some kind of neighborhood organization. It appears, however, that no councilman wants to "freeze" such a requirement into the city charter.

Council President John Gibson states that he formed citizen advisory committees when he was first elected nineteen years ago and has been working with them successfully ever since. The establishment, either voluntarily or by ordinance, of some form of neighborhood councils and central ombudsmen is strongly encouraged by Council members Pat Russell and Thomas Bradley.

The search for meaningful neighborhood involvement will continue in Los Angeles. Some councilmen will rationalize that working with Boy Scouts, Rotary Club, and other civic organizations is enough citizen involvement. Others will want formalized relationships with citizens. At this time, however, there seems little chance that any innovative structures will develop.

Citizen involvement might well be advanced by formation of a City Council study commission to review experiences of other cities, such as Dayton, Ohio, and Kansas City, Missouri, where city funds are used to support citizen councils and pilot projects. In Los Angeles, the Model Cities agency is one kind of pilot project. But also, in those several districts where councilmen are anxious to develop citizen councils, the City Council should strongly consider supporting such requests.

Additionally, wherever citizens are anxious to tackle problems, neighborhood councils should be encouraged to form either on a voluntary basis or with City Council sanction. The district councilman could support the neighborhood council with part of his staff in those areas where appropriate. Such a council could relate to the functioning of the BCH, as well as to emergency matters and long-range planning. The results of this experiment could be reviewed periodically by the City Council to determine what additional steps might be taken.

FURTHER RECOMMENDATIONS

In order to highlight issues emerging from the Los Angeles experience with BCHs, the following suggestions are made as ways of strengthening this approach.

1. Services should be added to a number of BCHs, particularly those in the high-poverty areas, regardless of their proximity to the main city hall. This could involve as little as a transfer of existing staff, and would encourage deeper understanding and concern for localized problems. It would also indicate to citizens in the area that increased services are being provided. In Watts BCH, for example, the following types of services could be added: collection of taxes and utility bills, issuance of licenses and permits, environmental and housing inspection, community workers or neighborhood ombudsmen, Social Security assistance, employment assistance, and other services decentralized from agency offices. Though some of these services are located in the vicinity, the city should take initiative in pulling them together.

2. Each BCH should have a director-coordinator. Working closely with councilmanic offices, he would establish a central complaint and informational mechanism to receive data and pass it on to a central management office located in the city administrator's office.

3. The BCH coordinator would be responsible for conducting local meetings of district heads to relate to neighborhood problems and to viable local organizations. He could also serve as key staff person for any city-sanctioned citizen councils.

4. Decision making at the branch city hall level is practically non-existent. In order to make neighborhoods as well as BCHs more viable greater latitude should be given to local supervisors in assigning work schedules and establishing project and budget priorities according to the needs of the neighborhood.

5. The mayor might choose to appoint citizen advocates in various neighborhoods or communities while the City Council and its staff continue their ombudsman function. The BCH coordinator (or, if none exists, an area coordinator) should be responsible for assembling local data and coordinating local personnel and city functions, as well as stimulating interchange and understanding of all other agencies' functions. Community action agencies, state, county, and other units have been unable to fill this coordinative gap. Cities are gradually being encouraged to take the lead. This would be a first step toward accepting that challenge under the "responsible city" concept.

6. If individual councilmen wish to establish citizen councils in their own districts, the City Council should support them. It could treat one or two of these as pilot projects by providing sufficient resources for staff and other expenses. Additionally, the City Council should appoint a study committee to review present and future operations of citizen councils in other cities.

7. Area chambers of commerce, unions, women's associations, minority organizations, news media, and other civic groups should consider funding and operating a unit similar to the Better Government Association in Chicago (which is privately funded) to investigate improprieties or inefficiencies in agencies and at all levels of government. This is more than a committee. It is an action force that works. Mayor Yorty, in concert with civic leaders, could very well take the lead in forming such an association as a strong beginning effort to look at inefficiencies, bureaucratic overlapping, and slow governmental and agency response.

THE CRISIS OF CITY GOVERNMENT

As is true in any U.S. city in 1972, not everybody in Los Angeles is unhappy. And because Los Angeles has grown to be the third largest city in the United States, it can attract major industry and can provide most of its residents with a high standard of living in addition to scenic beauty and a warm climate. Because it has a reputation for having "clean" government, it also has avid boosters among its citizens—those who live well, generally, and see no necessity to change the system of government. As the Los Angeles Chamber of Commerce states, "It is not important what system works elsewhere, or that Los Angeles may have a different system from other cities. What is important is that the Los Angeles system works for Los Angeles."

Many others in and out of the city, however, do not think the

system works at all—even for Los Angeles. They point to enormous
problems of finances, race, urban renewal, and poverty which are not
being solved by a government designed for nineteenth-century needs;
one in which power is so diffused and the mayor is so hamstrung under
the elaborate system of checks and balances, or checks and no balances,
that nothing seems to get done. This opinion is shared by political
scientists Banfield and Wilson, who use Los Angeles as the prototype
of the extremely decentralized big-city government in their book on
contemporary urban politics.*

They conclude that in the framework of extreme decentralization
without strong political party control, it is almost impossible to pass
any kind of measure unless it includes "something for everyone."

It is not that some changes have not been made in Los Angeles—
the 1925 city charter has been amended 261 times in the city's history—
but these have not been sweeping changes directed at refocusing the
system. Most charter amendments have dealt with special needs and
individual problems.

Regardless of poor organization and political leadership, Los
Angeles is the most efficient and best-run of all the large cities in
America. Also, its corruption-free environment and political freedom
put it well ahead of Chicago, for example, in quality of life. But it
must learn to solve its pressing problems, or it too will fall into
deterioration.

CHARTER STUDY COMMISSION

In 1966 Mayor Yorty appointed a Charter Study Commission,
headed by Dr. Henry Reining, dean of the Von Klein Smid Center for
Public and International Affairs, University of Southern California,
to make a comprehensive examination of the 1925 charter and its
amendments in light of the city's present needs. The commission
submitted its report in July, 1969. Some of the recommendations
relevant to this report are summarized below with comments from
charter revision hearings held between July, 1969, and March, 1970,
and from additional interviews and research. Two of the recommendations listed below, numbers 14 and 15, on neighborhood councils

----

*Edward C. Banfield and James Q. Wilson, City Government (New
York: Random House, 1963), pp. 110-11.

and ombudsmen, respectively, are discussed in detail because they
are particularly germane to this report. The others are summarized
and presented here to provide a more comprehensive picture of the
functioning of Los Angeles government.

Relevant charter recommendations include the following:

1. Continue to elect the mayor and city attorney at large, and
fifteen city councilmen by districts. Apportion council on the basis
of population. The at-large election gives the mayor a little more
influence under this weak-mayor form, and election of councilmen
by districts continues to give at least some neighborhood representation. The commission feels that increasing this number would not
assure a more representative or effective legislative body. Some
feel it would allow greater citizen representation, as would apportioning by population rather than registered voters.

At the hearings, speakers from the Mexican-American community—Miguel García, Chicago Law Students Association; Sal Vills,
president, East Los Angeles Health Task Force; Ed Aguerre, LUCHA;
Joe Aragón, Mexican-American Law Students Association; Abe Topia,
Mexican-American Political Association; Judge Leo Sánchez, Superior
Court; and Gonzalo Molina, California Democratic Council—presented
statements in favor of expanding the City Council to seventeen members, apportioning councilmanic districts on the basis of population,
and terminating the practice of gerrymandering districts so that a
Mexican-American cannot be elected.

Generally, strong support was voiced at the hearings for appor-
tionment by population. In addition, it was pointed out that the Supreme
Court continues to expand the application of the one-man, one-vote
rule.

2. Elect an eleven-member Board of Education by districts
apportioned on the basis of population, to serve full-time with appropriate compensation. The commission states, "public education in
Los Angeles is facing three crises—financial, racial, and the uncertain
quality of educational achievement. District rather than at-large
elections will increase representativeness and a full-time board
with substantial salaries will increase effectiveness."

3. Incorporate standards of conduct for officers and employees
in the charter. The commission states, "Provisions to guide the conduct and prohibit certain actions of officials will promote public trust
and official accountability."

4. Retain and simplify existing election machinery, including provisions for initiative, referendum, and recall. The commission states, "Procedures for city elections have proven adequate and do not need to be revised; however, there should be a requirement for occupations of candidates to appear on the ballot and for the counting of ballots and pamphlets in Spanish to facilitate greater citizen participation."

5. Organize the City Council into a truly legislative branch, prohibit it from interference in departmental administration, eliminate the daily meeting requirement, and give it the power to appoint the ombudsman. The commission feels that legislative and executive functions are confused and that the City Council devotes too much time to making essentially administrative decisions and, as a result, has less time for important legislative matters.

6. Designate the mayor chief executive of the city and head of the executive branch, and organize the executive branch into an integrated management structure. The commission feels that the office of mayor is too weak to provide needed citywide leadership, that "the mayor exercises supervision over the affairs of the city but not control. He should be able to appoint and remove boards and executive officials, with appointments subject to council confirmation." The mayor would also be responsible for coordination of intergovernmental relations, an area now somewhat void.

The Los Angeles Chamber of Commerce opposes any provision which might give the mayor absolute power to dismiss department heads as "extremely dangerous." It says, "It would mean that in mayoralty campaigns one of the issues would be whether or not certain commissioners and department heads were to be removed. There would be no council checks on this very broad authority. If the mayor could fire at will, large sums of money would be put into campaigns to elect a particular mayor because of this ability to control." Under the present charter, only the mayor has power to initiate removal (except in the case of the city administrative officer). The Chamber of Commerce agrees with the charter that managers should be exempt from civil service and should be appointed by the mayor, subject to civil service standards and council confirmation. Removals, however, should require hearings by the City Council and council approval or disapproval.

The Chamber of Commerce feels that the mayor was never intended to be "executive officer" of the city in the sense of a full-time manager. "Managers are chosen for managerial skills, mayors

basically for political reasons. Campaigns are issues of policy, not
personal issues relating to a candidate's qualifications as a professional
manager. The mayor is not expected to have these skills and already
is overburdened with ceremonial and political duties and, therefore,
cannot be available from day-to-day for management responsibilities."

7. Retain the city attorney as an elected official to assure his
independence and impartiality.

8. Make the city administrative officer responsible to the mayor
alone, rather than to both mayor and City Council. The present arrangement of serving two bosses confuses authority and results in
weak and uncoordinated administration. This, the commission states,
will establish an integrated management organization, with the city
administrative officer serving as chief of staff to the mayor, and continuing to assist him in preparation of the budget.

"For the past eighteen years," the Los Angeles Chamber of
Commerce states, "the city administrative officer has served two
masters, as do hundreds of city managers across the country, and
has done it extremely successfully. In this independent stature, he
does not have to worry about being dismissed if he cannot please all
the elected officials."

9. Retain boards of commissioners for appeals, regulatory,
and advisory functions but discontinue their use as heads of departments. Allow the mayor and council to set commissioners' salaries
to make them more equitable. The present system diffuses executive
and legislative authority.

In addition, the League of Women Voters recommends that
agendas for each regular meeting of a board of commissioners should
be made available to the public at least forty-eight hours in advance,
so citizens can be aware of matters of interest to them.

The Community Relations Conference of Southern California
recommends that provisions should be devised both for selecting
commission members to insure realistic representation of the total
community and for an "early warning" system to alert interested
citizens to commission business and policy affecting their well-being,
in enough time to allow them to participate in the decision-making
process.

The commission feels that creating new and, hopefully, more
representative boards which would include minority representation

is a significant way of improving citizen participation. There are
now 130 citizen commissioners.

10. Continue existing organization and independent powers for
proprietary departments—airports, harbor, and water and power—and
establish guidelines and limitations for payments to the general fund.

11. Allow flexible framework for city government without
enumeration of departments, so that the mayor and council can organize
and modify departmental duties to meet immediate priorities, and
direct the bureaucracy to meet changing needs of a dynamic city.
Require departments to be managed by general managers, not citizen
boards; the exception would be the police department, because of the
controversial issues facing it and its need to be sensitive to grievances
of a diverse citizenry while remaining free to act without political
interference. The commission points out that city government generally
follows long-established procedures and operates through highly com-
partmentalized departments that individually often deal with only part
of an activity.

12. Establish an integrated financial organization and provide
for an appointed finance director. Preserve existing merit principles
and employee rights, but provide for the general manager to serve
as head of the personnel department and give the Board of Civil Service
Commissioners independent rule-making and appeals powers. General
managers should be appointed subject to civil service standards but
without civil service protection. Consolidate salary-setting authority
primarily in the personnel department.

Expand the scope of city planning to include economic and social
development, and make the director of planning head of the department.

13. Establish government structure in general provisions. Under
California constitutional law, the city charter is a limitation of power
and the present charter is too detailed and restrictive. Now, if a
city activity is obsolete, is overlapped by another agency, or is in-
appropriately placed, the problem is reinforced by the charter. Provide for review of the charter by a citizen panel every ten years.

The following two provisions are included in greater detail
because of their special relevance to this report.

14. Enable formation of neighborhood organizations with elected
boards and appointed neighbormen. The commission feels that local
communities lack effective means for communicating with and

contributing to large-scale centralized government. It says: "A self-defining and self-organizing neighborhood organization will provide an institutional channel for development and communication of community goals. An elected neighborhood board would work in an advisory capacity. It would be served by an appointed neighborman who would aid citizens and the board in meeting their needs. As a mechanism for increased citizen participation and involvement, a neighborhood board would be established only where citizens decided it would be a useful means of influencing the well-being and future of their communities, and reducing feelings of remoteness from the 'downtown' city hall." (See Appendix C.)

The charter hearings resulted in the following statements:

a. City administrative officer. At the charter hearings, the city administrative officer cited potential costs of neighborhood organizations and suggested that, at best, the concept should be scaled down to reduce the number of neighborhoods involved and to require that they pay their own expenses. He said that the neighborhood proposal has "too great a potential for ward politics at taxpayers' expense." He recommended dropping the proposal from the charter and suggested that the council and its committee hold meetings in BCHs as an alternative.

b. Community organizations. Some community groups expressed opposition to the neighborhood concept because of fear of additional layers of government, the feeling that neighborhood councils would be powerless to effect significant change, and their general satisfaction with the present system. These groups are the Los Angeles Chamber of Commerce, Citizens Committee to Save Elysian Park, and Silverlake Residents Association. The chief engineer of the Fire Department and Mr. Moir of the Planning Commission agreed with the groups.

c. Los Angeles Chamber of Commerce. The Los Angeles Chamber of Commerce stated that this proposal could result in some 500 neighbormen at city hall lobbying for the interests of their various areas and could cost $10 million per year.

d. Watts Coordinating Council. Ben Perry, chairman of the Urban Affairs Committee of the Watts Coordinating Council, urged enabling the formation of boroughs rather than neighborhood councils.

The Community Religious Conference of Southern California gave qualified support for the intent of the office of neighborman as an innovation for citizen participation, but said that in its present

form "it is a powerless instrument and would need basic revision
to enable it to deliver what is intended."

    f. Southside Chamber of Commerce. Dean Soles, vice-president
of the Southside Chamber of Commerce and chairman of the Eighth
Area Community Advisory Council, suggested that the neighborhood
and ombudsman proposals be removed and, instead, the City Council
be expanded to twenty-one members to improve representation.

    g. Junior Chamber of Commerce. The Junior Chamber of
Commerce opposes neighborhood councils because they feel their
impact would be unpredictable and their boards could turn into irre-
sponsible forums which would be able only to publicize problems without
having the power to solve them. Says JCC, "They might have greater
potential if they had power to raise revenues to alleviate neighborhood
problems."

    JCC indicates that many councilmen view the boards as training
grounds for potential rivals. Also, "some councilmen may capture
boards for their own use."

    h. Charter Commission summary of neighborhood councils.
The commission states there would not be any overlapping of boundaries; that election procedures would be adjusted by City Council
ordinance and would provide for adjustments or dissolutions when a
neighborhood did not meet the prescribed population parameters.
The City Council would also determine terms of board members and
rules for filling vacancies. Neighborhood boards would be part of
city government and board members, neighbormen, and staffs would
be city officials. Laws applicable to conduct of city officials would
apply to them. The City Council would provide for standards of conduct, handling of funds, and bonding of a treasurer. Neighbormen
would be employees of the city in exempt positions, responsible to
their respective neighborhood boards.

    The City Council would review and approve all budgets and
thereby have control over costs. City budget procedures would be
used and integrated into the city's annual budget process. The City
Council could designate neighborhood special assessment districts
for raising revenue. It would also be possible for neighborhoods to
pay their own way.

    In regard to "ward politics," the commission points out that
"the present system of councilmanic districts is a ward system."
The commission also states that the concept should no longer be

described as experimental, since there are neighborhood organizations in different forms in several cities throughout the country. "There should no longer be any doubt that means must be found to increase citizen involvement and participation in urban government.

"Increasing the size of the council does not answer the question because it is a different type of representation than that involved in neighborhood organizations."

The commission cites the following organizations and cities as supporters of some form of neighborhood government: Advisory Commission on Intergovernmental Relations, Commission for Economic Development, Kerner Commission, Department of HEW, Joint Economic Committee of the U.S. Congress, Chicago Riot Report, National Commission on Urban Problems, East Palo Alto and Stockton, California. (See Appendix D.)

The commission recommends neighborhood councils in preference to a borough concept, the latter having been first proposed in 1906 and again in 1909. Borough government is permitted in the present city charter. Reportedly, such enabling legislation was passed to assure residents of the cities of San Pedro and Wilmington—who were to vote on the question of consolidation with Los Angeles—that they would retain a degree of local self-government. The consolidation elections were successful, but San Pedro and Wilmington did not acquire borough status. They developed into an area called the Harbor.

In 1913, the Los Angeles City Council refused to act on a petition from Wilmington residents for the establishment of a borough government. Four years later the California Supreme Court ruled the charter's borough provisions void because they limited their formation to territory "hereafter annexed." The charter's borough provisions have subsequently undergone changes, but in the opinion of both the state legislative counsel and Los Angeles city attorney, the present provisions are invalid despite the fact that the state constitution now allows boroughs to be established in "all or part of a city."

In postwar years, agricultural areas, particularly the San Fernando Valley, Westchester, and West Los Angeles, became dissatisfied with the level of city service. In response to secession moves in the San Fernando and Harbor areas, Mayor Fletcher Bowran in 1948 proposed creation of five boroughs—San Fernando, Hollywood, West Los Angeles, Central, and Harbor—which would have locally elected policy boards authorized to locate and improve secondary streets, determine routes and procedures for garbage collection, locate stops for buses and streetcars, handle local zoning, and set the borough tax rate. No charter amendments were ever placed on the ballot.

In 1952 a more detailed borough plan was prepared but it never moved forward, either. It called for borough officials to direct decentralized city departments, with department heads providing general supervision and coordination. In a review of this, the Charter Commission states:

> . . . Advocacy of secession developed once more in the 1960's. In the first half of this decade, support for it emerged in Westwood over zoning changes permitting highrise apartments and office buildings, in Pacific Palisades over unhappiness about the level of police protection, and in the San Fernando Valley over services and taxes in general. Also, following the Watts riots in 1965, a militant organization in the area proposed the separation of the Watts portion of Los Angeles from the city.

> In December, 1964, the Charter and Administrative Code Committee of the City Council recommended the submission of a charter amendment to permit the establishment of boroughs in part or all of Los Angeles. At a council meeting in the same month the proposed amendment was altered to allow boroughs to be established only on a citywide basis, and the proposal was referred to the city attorney for his opinion on its legality. The city attorney's judgment was that a charter provision requiring the establishment of boroughs in every section of the city, if they were to be established at all, would be upheld by the courts, but that a feasible procedure to achieve the purpose of the amendment did not exist in the charter and would require further amendments. The proposed amendment was shortly withdrawn from council consideration and became inactive.

> In 1967 a motion was introduced in the council to have the Charter and Administrative Code Committee again explore the advisability of placing a borough charter amendment on the ballot. The committee recommended the submission to the voters of such an amendment, which would enable the organization of boroughs in part or all of the city and the selection of borough board members through election. The council turned down the committee's recommendation.

The most recent development was a proposal in 1968 by Councilman John S. Gibson, Jr., who represents the San Pedro-Wilmington area, to amend the charter to make it possible for the various portions of the city, at their individual discretion, to organize boroughs, which would be governed by elective boards. As stated with his motion, Councilman Gibson's reasons for the proposal were:

(1) The City has an area of more than 460 square miles, with its southern boundary approximately 50 miles distant from its northern boundary.

(2) Its population of nearly three million is composed of many communities with different social, financial, and ethnic groups.

(3) There is increasing need to establish a form of local government exercising jurisdiction over purely local matters which may be important to only one district in the City and do not concern the City as a whole.

(4) There appears to be increasing interest of citizens to become part of a decision-making body concerning problems and needs relating to their communities.

(5) A borough system would enable various sections of the city to have more say as to how locally-collected taxes should be spent with respect to local improvements and level of services.

(6) Provision for a borough form of government was made in the city charter of 1925, but was invalidated by a later amendment to the State Constitution.

Councilman Gibson's motion was sent to the Charter and Administrative Code Committee and subsequently referred to the Charter Commission for consideration.

In regard to the question of formation of neighborhood councils, at the commission's direction, Dr. Bollens, its consultant, made an extensive study to determine whether definable communities exist within the city and, if so, whether they could be used as

subunits of city government. The following conclusions
were reached.

(1) A citywide pattern of well-defined communities with
    district boundaries does not currently exist. To the
    contrary, considerable controversy is present in a
    number of instances over the dividing line between
    communities; there is even disagreement over
    whether certain "communities" are separate or
    actually part of larger communities.

(2) The various uses made of area divisions of the city,
    such as field service areas, statistical areas, plan-
    ning study districts, branch administrative centers,
    councilmanic districts, county and school district
    areas, and privately defined areas, do not furnish
    much assistance in deciding upon the exact terri-
    torial limits of communities within the city. (There
    are currently 65 statistical areas; 30 in Central Los
    Angeles, 18 in the San Fernando Valley, 12 in Western
    Los Angeles, and five in Southern Los Angeles. They
    range in estimated population from Porter Ranch
    with 1,400 people to Hollywood with approximately
    150,000 inhabitants. More than one-half of them
    have fewer than 40,000 residents.)

(3) Despite the fact that identification of communities
    was seldom the stated objective of the projects using
    area divisions, one does derive from a study of them
    a highly impressionistic view that communities do
    exist, but often imprecisely and seemingly at times
    in only embryonic form.

The Commission concluded that the identification of definable communities within the city was not the answer to the
problem of improving citizen and community participation
in city government. . . .

15. Adopt a new "responsible city" concept of municipal government service and a new office of ombudsman to process citizen complaints, maintain a central grievance file, and provide a government
referral service. The commission states: "There is a disparity
between views of city officials and citizens concerning adequacy of
citizens access and grievance mechanisms. Citizens are increasingly
frustrated by the city's lack of responsiveness and its inability to

solve certain problems. The ombudsman would not replace existing channels for communication of requests and complaints, but would provide recourse where present mechanisms prove unsatisfactory. The office would monitor performance of the executive branch and be a valuable input for council policy making." Ken Wilson, staff director of the commission, feels it is important that the ombudsman be part of the legislative branch. "In Oregon, the ombudsman works from the governor's office, which is fallacious," he believes.

The ombudsman would not have formal powers to effect change but would use only persuasion, publicity, and criticism as his remedial weapons. Dr. Reining* defines the position as somewhat like the "Israeli comptroller idea," to audit the administration and submit an independent annual audit to the council.

The commission reports:

The ombudsman concept has been adopted by five other countries—Finland, Denmark, West Germany, New Zealand, and England—and one American state—Hawaii. It has been proposed at the state level in California, Wisconsin, Maine, New York, New Mexico, Washington, and others, and one such office has been instituted on a trial basis in Nassau County, New York.

In California, the concept has been urged by a leader in the California State Assembly, but the necessary legislation has been defeated twice—in 1965 and 1967. Advocates feel the ombudsman is needed to guide and protect citizens in the face of growing complexities of government. They feel that although procedures exist by which citizens may gain access to government at all levels, these are not sufficient to meet the needs of a large segment of the population. The proponents believe such offices should be established at national, state, and especially local levels to provide a medium through which citizen complaints may be more easily heard. . . .

---

*Dr. Henry Reining is the Dean of the Von Klein Smid Center for Public and International Affairs at the University of Southern California at Los Angeles and Chairman of the Charter Study Commission.

The office of ombudsman, under the proposed charter, will be in the legislative branch. The ombudsman will be appointed by the City Council for a term of eight years. He will be qualified in accordance with civil service standards established by the Board of Civil Service Commissioners, but the office will be exempt from civil service rules. . . . The Council will be able to remove the ombudsman by a two-thirds vote. . . .

The ombudsman is part of the legislative branch because his duties are related to the council's oversight of administrative performance. While the ombudsman will be subordinate to the council in the legislative branch, the commission believes that a certain degree of independence would be desirable, and this is provided through an eight-year term and a two-thirds vote requirement for removal.

The commission suggests that the City Council provide funds equal to the average amount for offices of councilmen, and that ombudsmen be responsible for processing complaints and giving assistance on any government matters, regardless of jursidiction.

In conjunction with the ombudsman program, "the mayor and Council should adopt the responsible city concept and be ready to improve services to city residents that are not administered by the city," the commission states. As an example, the city no longer provides health services. They are now provided by the county, and there "is reason to believe these services are not up to par for city residents. The mayor should appoint an officer to oversee this and other matters to assure residents that the services being provided (and paid for) by them are satisfactory."

Additionally, the commission recommends provisions for standards of conduct for city officers and employees to cover such items as conflict of interest, campaign contributions, hours of work, absenteeism, interference with administrative activities, etc.

Reactions to the ombudsman proposal ranged from strongly unfavorable to favorable.

a. City administrative officer. At the hearings Dr. Piper opposed the ombudsman proposal based on cost and also said, "An ombudsman is not necessary so long as the citizen has direct access to his elected officials, i.e., mayor and Council, city administrative officer, grand jury, courts, and departmental commissions." He estimated it would cost a minimum of $139,453 annually.

b. Member of City Planning Commission. The chief engineer of the Fire Department and Mr. Moir, member of the City Planning Commission, opposed the proposal, saying "it would be an experimental concept."

c. Board of Police Commissions. The Board of Police Commissions recommended against it, saying, "It is the opinion of the commission that complaints and investigations should be received and made by those persons in city government having responsibility for effective administration of city government. It is the opinion of the commission that elected officials, particularly the mayor and councilmen, are fully capable of receiving and acting upon complaints. The commission feels particularly that the police commissioner, who is the actual head of the Police Department, properly should and does receive complaints and is also in a position to take corrective policy action, whereas the ombudsman would be a listening post without the power to change the responsibility for the proper operation of a city department."

d. Los Angeles Forward. The chairman of Los Angeles Forward stated that the ombudsman proposal, because it is controversial, should be placed on the ballot as a separate proposition to be decided by the voters.

e. 31st District PTA. The 31st District PTA recommended that "instead of an ombudsman . . . there be one council field deputy in each of the 15 council districts designated an ombudsman, with an office in the district, and that a central grievance file be established by the council."

f. Crenshaw Neighbors, Inc. Some citizens supported the proposal in general; others, like Crenshaw Neighbors, Inc., said, "It does not have sufficient power to effectively address citizen grievances," but did endorse the idea of a central grievance file.

g. Community Relations Council of Southern California. The Community Relations Conference of Southern California endorsed the concept on condition that charter language be added to provide the ombudsman with subpoena powers, that the office function as an information center, that it make an annual appraisal of all city services, and that there be provision in the charter for adequate budget and staff. They also recommended that "the proposed charter be amended

to include language providing for an annual review of the offices of
ombudsman and neighborman by an impartial evaluation panel composed
of representatives of business, labor, government, church, education
and both public and private human relations agencies; and the evaluation
panel be given power to recommend to City Council continuation or
redesign of both programs."

h. Junior Chamber of Commerce. The Junior Chamber of
Commerce views the arguments in favor of ombudsman and neighborhood boards as "not convincing, although both proposals have merito-
rious aspects. The office of ombudsman should be unnecessary so
long as citizens have direct access to elected public officials." They
do state, however, that it would be an alternate grievance route if a
citizen had an unsympathetic or unconcerned councilman, but conclude:
"Most complaints will involve welfare rights, which are primarily
controlled by county agencies; zoning, which is the jurisdiction of
the planning department; and police attitudes, which will not be amenda-
ble to ombudsman mediating."

i. Other organizations. The ombudsman is opposed as a powerless office by the Citizens Committee to Save Elysian Park, and also
by the Silverlake Residents Association.

j. Los Angeles Chamber of Commerce. The Los Angeles
Chamber of Commerce, in a 125-page analysis of the proposed charter,
indicates opposition to the ombudsman proposal. The Chamber feels
men of necessary stature are not likely to be attracted to serve and
that the conflict between the mayor and City Council could be intensi-
fied. "Establishing the office for eight years is too long for what is
admittedly an experiment. A central referral office could be a start
in directing inquiries to proper officials and a method could be devised
of compiling inquiries and grievances into periodic reports."

Greg O'Brien, assistant to the director of the Chamber of Commerce's Division of Government Relations, indicates that "the Chamber is basically for charter revision because the charter is unwieldly
and voluminous. On the question of ombudsmen, the Chamber recommends against it because there would be confusion in the minds of
the residents as to whom one goes with complaints, councilmen or
ombudsmen."

k. City attorney. The city attorney questioned whether the
cost of the program could be met within the $1.25 per $100 tax rate
limit included in the charter. This limit is for all general-fund purposes.

The Charter Commission indicates that cost factors could be raised in connection with any city office, and that cost is not usually used to limit the achievement of adequate representation. The commission stresses that "the reason this proposal was made is because there are people in Los Angeles who feel they do not have access to the city government and officials.

"Many people feel they do have acce.,s to city government, and city officials for good reasons feel that they are responsive to citizen needs. For these reasons it is difficult for officials to believe that there are persons who do not feel they have this access."

l. General expressions. Some civic groups expressed the feeling that City Council reaction to the Charter Commission recommendation was "irrational, a threatened feeling—one viewing the proposals as an indictment of the present system, a system which provides a high level of services through a fairly competent but bureaucratic civil service and government system."

m. Myron Roberts. Myron Roberts, associate editor of Los Angeles Magazine, feels that anything designed to make the government less bureaucratic is fine but is "not sure that the ombudsman is the answer. Any citizen can call most of the time and get a councilman, who almost always will resolve the complaint. Government takes plenty of time and energy to solve one citizen's problem but not one percent of citizens will bother to come in and not one in 100 knows the name of his councilman." He also believes an ombudsman probably would not have much to do.

On neighborhood councils, Roberts says he is willing to see them tried but feels they will not really solve any problems. "Councils and organizations may just be additional layers of bureaucracy. Americans are great joiners and can't avoid getting tied up in reading minutes and getting little accomplished." Ken Wilson, Charter Commission staff director, amplifies Roberts' point with his own view that "if the neighborhood council concept is not adopted, it is very remote that organizations would get together."

Roberts feels "the need to adopt these concepts or create efficiency is a myth—it is style that is important." Ken Wilson says, "Even a Lindsay would have problems in this government form."

However, Roberts feels that "neighborhood councils could give people a more tangible and potent way to make themselves heard—like Westchester, where the commission is generally angry and frustrated

about noise pollution of the airport—or San Fernando Valley which
may wish to raise hell about somebody's decision to spot zone a gas
station into a residential area."

n. Legality. The city attorney raised questions of legality
about several sections of the Charter Commission recommendations
which the commission felt "could just as easily be raised about provisions in the existing charter." An independent legal counsel has
verified the legal correctness of the commission's suggested adjustments, but the commission stresses that "the objective of preparing
provisions that are understandable to the citizen should remain a
paramount consideration."

o. General opposition to change. The commission feels that
"comments by most city officials and departments focused on the
general theme of opposition to change. For the most part, they wanted
their functions and organization structures to remain in the charter
unchanged. These people cannot be expected to support changes,
even when they represent needed overall improvements. Viewing
things habitually from the perspective of one functional aspect of
city government inhibits a view of the total city government as it is
and as it might be improved."

The commission made changes in its report and also concluded
that the new charter should be reconstituted as nine separate proposi-
tions to be voted upon rather than one comprehensive plan. It did not
compromise on its basic principles, however.

CITY COUNCIL ACTION ON THE NEW CHARTER

The City Council's Charter and Administrative Code Committee,
headed by Councilman Edelman, began its study of charter provisions
in July, 1969. It conducted twenty-seven public hearings, received
over seventy oral and written presentations, and presented its findings
to the entire City Council.

In September, 1970, the City Council approved by a vote of
twelve to one a proposed new city charter for placement on the November 3, 1970, general election ballot. However, the electorate gave
it a resounding defeat. The mayor was against it because it did not
give him enough additional power; employees from the Department
of Water and Power raised funds to defeat it because they wanted to
maintain their independent status; and much of the public apparently
was generally apprehensive about any change. It was placed on the

ballot for the second time in April, 1971, and was defeated again.
Since it gave additional administrative authority to the mayor, he
supported it; the proprietary departments supported it because it left
them alone; but it appears the public was not sold.

The provisions below were approved by the City Council for
the first test before the voters. In the second try those items referring
to the proprietary departments will apparently all be eliminated. Provisions for neighborhood councils and ombudsmen were eliminated
by the City Council before its first test.

Provisions on the ballot in November, 1970, were the following:

1. The mayor, subject to two-thirds Council approval, may
reorganize the departments, and three-fourths of the Council may
reorganize departments without the mayor's approval. Also, excessive
detail of department duties is eliminated. Presently, such action
requires a charter change by the electorate.

2. The CAO may conduct management audits and other functions
over the proprietary departments of Water and Power, and Harbor and
Airports. These departments will be required to make contributions
to the general fund.

3. General managers will administer all departments except
the Police Department and proprietary departments. They are to be
appointed and renewed by the mayor following civil service standards
and with Council approval. Commissions will still exist but be advisory.

4. The City Council will be apportioned on the basis of population
rather than registered voters, and a separate proposition will increase
its size to seventeen.

5. The City Council may provide for its own meeting place and
time. Daily meeting requirements are eliminated and the Council is
allowed to meet throughout the city.

6. The mayor will make two major reports to the Council and
give a state-of-the-city address annually. The mayor will also be
clearly responsible for administration of the affairs of the city.

7. There are special provisions to protect the environment,
parks, libraries, and recreation operations.

8. There will be a single salary-setting agency for all nonelected officials. Salaries of elected officials will be made more equitable.

9. The CAO formally is required to assist the mayor in administering the city. This is supposed to strengthen the mayor's role.

10. Adoption of a code of ethics is required.

The City Council has rejected several attempts and different versions of proposed neighborhood districts and ombudsmen, despite findings of the Los Angeles City Charter Commission that only a small percentage of people ever contact their councilman.

Most councilmen feel they can adequately handle all complaints and that they are in the best position to be ombudsmen. They feel that others acting in this capacity would simply be a duplication. Also, a number feel that citizen councils would be duplicating layers of government.

Councilman James Potter says, "A neighborhood council would just be an additional step to the bureaucratic system already so confusing to the taxpayer."

Council President John Gibson states that he has been using citizen advisory committees successfully ever since he was first elected some nineteen years ago. "All residents of these communities are invited to meet with us to further assist in handling problems at the community level," he says. "These meetings have been most successful in involving local citizens in the operation of their city government."

Councilwoman Pat Russell is very much concerned with responsible government and feels neighborhood decentralization is a key approach. However, she states, "I have been startled to encounter very little support among constituents for neighborhood councils or for an ombudsman. The major reason for the antipathy is the feeling that the councilman should fulfill these roles."

Councilman Thomas Bradley, one of three black councilmen, indicates strong favor for some form of neighborhood councils created voluntarily or by ordinance. He also favors a central ombudsman and staff. He feels that citizen councils should not be frozen into the charter, however: "Some problems are localized in nature and the best way to solve them is to generate community or neighborhood concern. This way I believe we could change the impersonal nature

of government and give people the feeling that their ideas and their
concerns really count."

POLITICS AND PROGRESS IN LOS ANGELES

Francis Carney summarizes Los Angeles politics by saying,
"Los Angeles is at present unbossed, is in the grip of no political
machine, and behind its formal government there lurks no covert or
semicovert 'power elite.'"* He indicates that district elections under
a nonpartisan system have helped in preventing growth of any machine
or of a dominating elite behind the scenes (while at-large elections
under nonpartisanship offer a tempting opportunity to informal slate-
making groups). "Neither labor nor business has been a power group.
At most they have been competing influence groups."

In Los Angeles voters not only vote for the man rather than the
party but also vote for fifteen different men in staggered elections
and elect a council of fifteen sovereigns. This diminishes power
politics.

However, there is no so-called mandate from the voters, since
only 25 percent turn out for a typical municipal election. Here, politics
seem unnecessary. "People are too busy pursuing the pleasures of
the area."

The editors of Los Angeles Magazine in the January, 1970,
issue take exception to the general belief that Los Angeles is a scattered
collection of suburbs. They contend: "It is indeed a single living
entity, the nation's second largest urban center. Yet it remains a
huge urban conglomerate. It shares with other urban areas the problems of haphazard planning, disfiguring of the environment, rising
crime and violence, dislocation of human identity and motivation
created by the remoteness of government, social diversity, rapid
change, affluence, and rising expectations (which fall short of realization).

"It is no longer experiencing spectacular growth. In 1969,
19,000 more people left Los Angeles County than settled here, but it

---

*"The Decentralized Politics of Los Angeles," Annals of the
American Academy of Political and Social Science (May, 1964), pp.
107-21.

is presently as large as Sweden and a million more than Switzerland. California itself has a population as large as Canada."

"Los Angeles' greatest failing might well be its lack of positive, pragmatic, on-the-scene leadership—that is, leadership in structuring our own environment in such a way as to alleviate much of the alienation or sense of nonparticipation that has come to characterize multi-million population urban societies. It needs leadership in new programs and in reforming many established practices and institutions."

There is belief that Mayor Yorty is not the man to provide the necessary leadership. He has continually battled with the City Council so that his citywide projects have hardly moved in any direction. And when he initiated a weekly radio program entitled "Ask Your Mayor," the Council demanded—and got—equal time for its own program, called "Ask Your Councilman."

Yorty alienated many people by turning against his own Democratic Party to support Richard Nixon in 1960. Even though he has been severely criticized, to date no major scandals have befallen his administration. His commission appointments have been praised, and the Police Department has kept Los Angeles relatively free of organized gambling and vice.

In a U.S. Senate hearing in August, 1966, Yorty said he had no authority and, therefore, could not move the city. He favors charter reform and a strong-mayor form of government, but there has been reluctance by the City Council to give it to him.

William J. Bird, Kaiser Industry vice-president and chairman of the Central Planning Commission, wants to build a core area attractive to people, where they will choose to live as well as work. He says, "The city lacks cohesion and leadership. It is hard to get people together and they tend to do their own thing. We need new buildings, culture, theatre, good restaurants, apartments, and human life in downtown."

The city is building City Hall East and Plaza Technical Center, at a cost of about $10 million, which will consolidate many departments now located in obsolete and decaying quarters. New, privately financed structures are springing up downtown. The present civic center and parks are attractive. The heart is beginning to take shape, but major problems of air pollution, mass transit, housing, and citizen alienation continue to exist.

ANALYSIS AND RECOMMENDATIONS

The Mayor and Power

Proposed charter revisions which allow the mayor to reorganize departments and appoint and remove general managers; make city commissions advisory; call upon the mayor to make reports and a state-of-the-city presentation; and provide him with competent assistance from the CAO are all elements that will strengthen the mayor. However, he still feels they give him too little power to lead the city.

Power to appoint and remove general managers without council approval would strengthen the mayor's hand to some degree, but he would still be limited by civil service regulations. If the mayor develops a nonpolitical and pragmatic case for dismissal, backed up by his technical staff (mainly the CAO), he should have little difficulty in removing a general manager who is not performing or is not leading his department progressively or in line with basic mayoral policies.

To have the CAO continue to be responsible to both mayor and Council is no different than the position of most city managers and CAOs in other cities. Mark Keane, executive director of the International City Management Association, advocates this approach for large as well as smaller cities. He feels the CAO, in order to be most effective, must administer policies of mayor and Council, and work in close relationship with both. It is only with agreed-on positions from both that the city will progress. What the mayor must do is win the majority of the City Council.

Mayor John Lindsay of New York operates under a strong-mayor form, but the city does not move very far without City Council and Board of Estimate approvals. Mayor Richard Daley of Chicago is in a weak-mayor system and moves everything in his direction because he has control of the City Council. Mayor Joseph Alioto of San Francisco functions in a weak-mayor form but has provided leadership primarily through a personal approach. In Los Angeles, greater leadership will come about when politics becomes more harmonious.

The City Council and Its Duties

The City Council should refrain from administration of government. This responsibility should be placed upon the CAO and general

managers. The Council should spend a greater amount of time in
meeting with citizen groups, holding neighborhood City Council meetings,
making their district offices full-time and more effective, studying
and acting upon the larger problems of air pollution, mass transit,
housing, unemployment, poverty, city-county relations, regional government, and long-range planning. It is too much for anybody in a
city the size of Los Angeles both to establish policy and to administer
it. Greater reliance should be placed upon the executive branch and
its administrative machinery. After all, the Council still has the
authority to approve or disapprove budgets and to change policies.

The Mayor and the CAO

The CAO, if voters give him power to audit departments and
set up more effective management techniques, could keep the Council
better informed and the departments under more effective control.
The Council would not have to involve itself as deeply in administrative
affairs. In the proposed charter revision, the CAO would have greater
latitude in setting up centralized data collection and evaluation systems
and other management techniques. The City Council, even without
charter changes, could assist him by providing him with data and by
supporting his efforts to coordinate and direct city departments,
BCHs, and other operations of local government.

The mayor has an opportunity to take a decisive leadership
role in all the major problem areas by working closely with the CAO
and obtaining technical support for his budget from a strictly professional staff. High-caliber personnel placed under direction of the
CAO rather than directly under the mayor's office would tend to
gather greater Council support for the mayor's programs. And even
if the charter is not approved, the City Council should request the
mayor to present a state-of-the-city address, and the mayor should
be more than willing to give it. For Los Angeles, now is the time
for the mayor and Council to cooperate; without cooperation, revising
the charter will mean little.

The Mayor and Leadership

The mayor can appoint task forces in each of the major goal
areas. Through them he can begin to look at regional issues and all
services which do not fall under city government jursidiction. He can
lead in the development of a Better Government Association concept,
as described earlier, to achieve greater effectiveness in government.

Formation of a mayor's cabinet and use of some of his fifty-man staff to guide such a movement, to act as ombudsmen in BCHs and other areas not so serviced, and to funnel information into a competent central management staff are all techniques that should be adopted to improve effectiveness.

Additionally, an atmosphere must be created to get the city moving so that people feel change and want to continue the forward motion. As Myron Roberts says, "It is the style that is important, more so than structural changes. People must be convinced that things are happening and that there is reason for pride in one's city."

It does take innovation and change to develop this atmosphere. But the mayor must start with what is available and try to elicit support of his councilmen. Together, with a reasonable degree of harmony, they must capture the heart of the citizenry.

SUMMARY OF RECOMMENDATIONS

The following recommendations are made in the hope that they stimulate thought and assist officials in Los Angeles:

1. A relationship must be developed between the mayor and City Council that concentrates less on their own differences and more on moving the whole city forward. The mayor should present his goals in a state-of-the-city address and, upon City Council approval, allow the administrative staff to carry them out. There is no need to wait for charter revisions to do this.

2. The City Council should concentrate more on enactment of policy and less on departmental administrative detail. It should allow the CAO to "run the administrative ship" and the mayor to give it command. City commissioners will normally do what the mayor wants them to do. The mayor should insist on more central control under the CAO.

3. The mayor should work more closely with the CAO as his professional backup, relying less on nonprofessional personnel to carry out his goals. In this manner, full departmental resources can be used, and there is greater likelihood of Council cooperation.

4. The mayor should formally convene a cabinet of key city officials to analyze city objectives and to work with any task forces he may wish to appoint. He should particularly consider an overall

task force to review regional concepts, duplicating and overlapping programs, and lack of programs and goals.

5. The mayor should use some of his present staff as ombudsmen in hard-pressed areas to establish communication links and solve citizen problems involving any level of government. And he should allow citizens a voice in the selection of any future neighborhood ombudsmen, who would be located in branch mayors' offices. He should revitalize the mobile complaint and information trailers, and make them work.

4

**SAN ANTONIO
DIVIDES
INTO QUARTERS**

Area: 160 square miles
Population: 650,000
Mexican-American: 273,000
Black: 78,000

THE CITY AND ITS GOVERNMENT

The City

San Antonio, located in Bexar County in south-central Texas,
has existed as a city since 1718 under Spanish, Mexican, and American
flags. San Antonio and Bexar County are still growing areas, and
together they make up a migration collection point for a forty-county
area in southern Texas.

The federal government is a dominant force in the economy of
San Antonio. With three air force bases, Fort Sam Houston, and the
Brooks Army Medical Center, the federal government is clearly the
area's largest employer. Tourism is important to the city's economy, and the city also functions as a distribution center for southern
Texas. There is some light manufacturing, but San Antonio cannot
be described as an industrial city.

The Government

San Antonio has the council-manager form of government. There
is a nine-member City Council; members run at-large and are elected

for overlapping terms. The mayor and vice-mayor are elected by the
Council. Councilmen receive $1,040 annually, and Mayor W. W.
McAllister receives $3,000 in addition, to pay for attending council
meetings. Service on the Council is definitely part-time. Members
do not have staffs or city-supplied offices outside the city hall. On
the present council, two members are Mexican-American, one is
black, and the rest are Anglos.

The city manager is appointed by the City Council. The manager
appoints city department heads, and they are responsible to him.

San Antonio moved toward consolidating its human services
efforts on June 1, 1970, by creating a Department of Human Resources.
It is expected to become the "urban umbrella" that will eventually
incorporate such other agencies as Model Cities, education, community relations, equal employment, and the Office of Economic
Opportunity (OEO). Dr. C. J. "Posty" Roberts heads the new department.

AREA SERVICE CENTERS

Locations

At present, decentralization of city government in San Antonio
is limited to three area service centers established under the Department of Public Works. These functions were decentralized in 1960
to prevent a possible fire from destroying all the city's public works
equipment, then housed under one roof, as well as to better serve a
city spread over a large geographical area (160.5 square miles).
City officials also saw increased efficiency and other advantages in
keeping equipment close to work sites, and in having workers near
their jobs. A round trip from a service center to downtown could
take as long as an hour.

The area service centers—Zarzamora, North Loop, and Southeast—divide the city about equally and serve approximately 200,000
persons each. Victoria, which is an automobile and truck maintenance
shop in the center of the city, and City Hall itself serve the business
district and nearby industrial and high-density residential areas. A
fourth center has been approved by voters and will be under construction soon.

Existing facilities are well placed, well marked, and beautifully constructed. Adequate parking space and several acres of "yard" and garage area for refuse and street equipment are available at each.

The North Loop center, opened in July, 1960, was San Antonio's first area service center; it presently houses agencies dealing with public works, housing inspection, health, fire, and city water inspection. North Loop is in a mixed and growing area, and will probably be enlarged.

The Zarzamora center, only several months younger than North Loop, has been in operation since October, 1960. Construction and supervision of the two are quite similar. The area served is also mixed, composed primarily of Mexican-American and Anglo residents, with a sprinkling of blacks. This racial composition is exemplified by the fact that clerks and receptionists speak Spanish for the benefit of the neighborhood people. Much like North Loop, however, few residents rely on Zarzamora as a problem-solving center.

The Southeast center, opened in October, 1962, is similar in operation, although somewhat different in appearance from the other two. It is a larger facility, with a meeting room in the basement designed to fulfill a need found lacking in the two older centers. As a result there is greater involvement with the neighborhood people. At present a neighborhood dancing class is held in the meeting room once a week, as well as citizen meetings. Plans are under way for a police outreach center to work out of the building.

Objectives

Main objectives of the centers appear to be economy and efficiency for the city government, and convenience for both citizens and city employees. They offer a number of services within a single, centrally located structure. They were instituted to save overhead costs on such items as gas, labor, and depreciation of equipment by eliminating long and unnecessary trips in service delivery. In general, they were designed to offer the San Antonio citizen more efficient city service but, perhaps more important, they were also intended to bring government closer to the people. A citizen no longer has to drive ten or fifteen miles to obtain a building permit or apply for a license. If he wishes to pay taxes or utility bills, an area center is but a few miles away. In addition, equipment housed locally can be on a particular job in a matter of minutes when necessary.

Looking ahead to the day when San Antonio would have a population exceeding one million, decentralization of the service centers
seemed a valid objective for the future. If the city developed in an
unbalanced fashion, other centers would be built and enlarged as
needed.

Staff and Budget

At present, 880 employees work out of the three centers and
maintenance shops. The bulk of the employees are public-works
oriented; however, ninety-seven of them are inspectors or clerical
or other personnel. North Loop center has twenty-six inspectors,
for example (see Table 3). Employees are selected by civil service
examinations and placed in one of several areas by department heads.
One defect is that there is no overall coordination of departments
within the centers.

The budget for personnel alone exceeds $7 million annually.
In addition, there are capital outlay costs for equipment and projects
totaling many millions of dollars. Budgets are determined centrally
by the city manager and each department head, with final approval
by the mayor and City Council. There is some flexibility in expenditures by area engineers so they may concentrate resources in problem areas. However, projects requiring large outlays are determined
by the central budgetary process.

Functions

The public works functions of the centers are primarily traffic,
street maintenance, street cleaning, drainage maintenance, refuse
collection and disposal, and forestry operations. Housing, health,
fire, and water department inspections are the other major services.
Citizens can obtain permits and licenses and pay some tax and utility
bills, but most stores in town also offer these services, so it is
unlikely they will be expanded.

Complaint follow-up forms are used, and all requests seem to
be properly handled and completed. Overall, services are well
performed and citizens seem to be satisfied with results. Centers
receive only a half-dozen complaints per week. General complaints
related to other city departments, however, are not encouraged;
therefore, the bulk of city requests is received centrally by the
various departments. The staff seems to be competent and dedicated.

TABLE 3

Functions and Employees, Area
Service Centers, San Antonio

Functions	Number of Employees
North Loop Service Center	
Public Works	283
Housing and Inspections	18 inspectors
Health	2 inspectors
Fire	5 inspectors
City Water Board	1 inspector
	25 subordinates
Southeast Service Center	
Public Works	287
Housing and Inspections	5 inspectors
Fire	4 inspectors
City Water Board	1 inspector
	9 subordinates
Zarzamora Service Center	
Public Works	213
Housing and Inspections	10 inspectors
Health	
Animal and Rodent Control	2 inspectors
Health Education	13 field representatives
Fire	2 inspectors
Total	880

Source: City Manager's Office, San Antonio, Texas (July, 1970).

The supervisor of each center is a public works area engineer who is not required to coordinate all departments located within the building complex. He supervises and administers all public works functions in his area and has considerable discretion as to deployment of personnel and setting of priorities, as long as decisions are made within guidelines of established policy set down by the city adminis- tration. Other departmental employees report directly to their depart- ment heads, who are located at the main city hall.

The feeling among department heads seems to be that if additional services were to be added in the human or social fields, they should be housed in separate buildings, even if located within the existing complexes. Some persons feel, however, that the service centers are not located in the most accessible population centers and that it would be better to locate social services in entirely different areas. City Manager Gerald Henckel indicates that police-community relations substations and other community relations functions may be added to the centers.

CITIZEN PARTICIPATION

The function of ombudsman or neighborhood advocate is not part of the service center program. No citizen advisory councils are associated with it; however, Henckel indicates that four citizen councils will very likely be created by the city to operate in four equally divided areas of the city. Their representation would probably be 50 percent each of citizens and city administration appointments. The level of their involvement has not yet been determined.

Sam Granata, public works director, expresses some concern with organized citizen involvement as a process which creates delays and irrelevant arguments over issues. He feels that if departments act competently and in a dedicated manner, citizen advisory councils are not needed. "I have a 650,000 man board which never adjourns," he points out. He feels he responds to every complaint, and his dedication seems evident.

Mel Sueltenfuss, assistant public works director, has an oppor- tunity to get closer to the people by serving on a Model Cities com- mittee concerned with public works matters. In providing service, he favors a total city approach, rather than locating them only in poverty areas. He also favors an ombudsman system, to be started in the Model Cities area first.

It appears that the city is moving toward greater overall citizen involvement and possible creation of ombudsmen for some of its existing operations.

ANALYSIS

San Antonio service centers have been geared to efficiency and more effective delivery of public works functions and inspection services. They have accomplished this and have proved that city services can be delivered to a large geographic area even with low resources.

Functions are truly decentralized because area engineers have considerable latitude in local decision making. The program has created competitiveness between centers, which has both advantages and disadvantages—stimulating higher productivity but developing "little empires." However, the overall effect has been good.

Coordination is not a function of the centers, but it very much exists at the central level; there is little question that the city manager is the key administrative officer and that all department heads report to him. There is little, if any, interference by elected officials in the administrative functions of the city. And there is little uncertainty by officials of the desirability of decentralized facilities. The mayor and City Council recognize their value, as did the citizens when they passed a September, 1970, referendum for a fourth center.

The city manager says the centers save him considerable time and allow him to concentrate on overall issues and long-range planning, rather than the day-to-day complaints of citizens. This is why the area engineers are given considerable latitude in decision making.

Director Granata says, "I used to be a high-priced clerk. Now I have time to plan and help develop policies." He takes strong hold over the area engineers, however, and enters into the decision-making process whenever it is necessary to settle disputes between them. Occasionally questions arise over loaning equipment from one area to another, with some engineers reluctant to let equipment leave the premises. When priorities and problems change, Granata enters the picture and decides what is best for the community as a whole— and provincialism ends.

City Manager Henckel indicates that at least the police-community relations function will be added to the centers and, perhaps

later, other human service functions as well, which may include
ombudsmen and center coordinators. Careful analysis should be
made of the location of all centers, to determine whether placing
these kinds of services at these locations will attract the clientele
that needs them most. The centers now are not located conveniently
near transit lines and traffic centers. New locations for different
functions may be more desirable, effective, and economical.

The city may take control of the Community Action Program
(CAP). It may also create its own citizen participation element in
the form of four citizen advisory councils, and place other social
service functions under its newly created Department of Human
Resources, which would act as an "urban umbrella" of programs.
Hopefully, it will provide councils with a degree of independence
that will maintain citizen interest and significant levels of participation.
If the seven existing CAP corporations are kept in operation, and the
four planned city administration citizen councils are used as overall
coordinating bodies, citizen conflict may be avoided. Dismembering
effective citizen councils, however, may cause greater citizen despair.
Existing CAP corporations could be used as vehicles to operate
decentralized federal and local services; the overall citizen councils,
as groups which reflect on an entire area's problems and priorities,
delegating operating authority.

RECOMMENDATIONS

In order to highlight some of the issues emerging from the San
Antonio experience, the following recommendations are made:

1. Additional functions should be placed in the area service
centers as long as they improve the delivery of services. Careful
study, however, should be made as to whether clients will tend to
use these centers or would be more inclined to use other, more
convenient locations. Decentralizing services in the wrong location
can be an expensive mistake. A pilot project should be tested without
significant capital outlay before deciding on a permanent approach.

2. Consideration should be given to adding neighborhood
ombudsmen to some area service centers, Model City multiservice
centers, CAP centers, and other locations. After testing their effectiveness, they can be shifted to the most appropriate areas.

3. Area service center engineers should be designated coordinators of all functions within their centers. This would tend, even

now, to stimulate greater efficiency and effectiveness of existing personnel. If new services are added, particularly in the human resources area, qualifications and motivations of coordinators would necessarily have to be reevaluated in light of new responsibilities. However, public works personnel, as well as others, should be encouraged to delve into all aspects of neighborhood problems and human concerns.

4. Center coordinators should hold staff meetings of key personnel in each center and periodically hold "mini cabinet" sessions with all district supervisors to elicit a new sense of neighborhood concern. Occasionally, these meetings could be held in conjunction with neighborhood groups.

5. Area service center coordinators could initially, and perhaps permanently, act as key staff liaison with planned citizen councils. The councils should have City Council support, staff assistance, and, most important, a reasonable degree of authority. A method of selecting citizens for membership on the councils should be devised that will truly provide grass-roots citizen membership—not participation merely from the "spokesmen." The community must be made to feel that council membership really represents them, or it loses its effectiveness.

6. Citizen councils and area ombudsmen can be a very valuable source of information feedback to central management for development of a citywide network of intelligence. As discussed in other sections of this study, some cities are using computer techniques in this regard; however, the proper management technique depends very much on types and amounts of information collected. In San Antonio this new source of neighborhood input may lead the city into more appropriate decision making. Its plans to create citizen councils and ombudsmen may be the catalyst.

7. Development of uniform area statistics and services is well under way in San Antonio because of existing service areas. It would be advisable to use these defined areas for new federal and local program boundaries, and to align existing programs within these areas in order to prevent and reduce overlapping and to effect better coordination of services. Attention placed on establishment of coterminous districts for some functions now will help to avoid an almost impossible situation later.

8. Few mayors, if any, have the power to unite various levels of government and myriad agencies in a common cause with agreed-

upon priorities to work toward a concerted attack on the city's problems. However, there is no other local official with as much strength and legal authority to begin at least the thinking process of the "responsible city" concept, whereby municipal government assumes the responsibility of the totality of a community's problems. Local elected officials cannot afford to allow others operating in their city to function ineffectively, in uncoordinated fashion, and with little concern for or understanding of the city's true priorities. If they do, urban areas will continue to slide backward.

In San Antonio, CAP and other programs have never been able to coordinate and motivate all necessary agencies and levels of government. Local government is being given the task and more power to do it. It must meet the challenge by whatever means are workable: coordinating cabinets, task forces, communications media, citizen councils, special investigative units, uniform districts, consolidation of functions (Department of Human Resources, for example, in San Antonio), and the image and leadership of the mayor. Some of these steps have been taken; others are needed.

5

**KANSAS CITY
TRIES TO MODERNIZE
OLD-STYLE
COMMUNITY COUNCILS**

Area: 316 square miles
Population: 500,000
Mexican-American: 6,512
Black: 121,000

THE CITY AND ITS GOVERNMENT

The City

Kansas City, Missouri's second largest metropolis, is an important industrial, commercial, and banking center. It is separated from Kansas City, Kansas, by the state line; but both are served by the same railroad terminals and transit and telephone systems.

Today, Kansas City is a major market for winter wheat and cattle. Meat packing and flour milling are the two leading industries, and apparel and related businesses are also important. In addition, Kansas City leads the nation in the manufacture of vending machines, is the country's second-largest assembly center for cars and trucks, and is an important warehousing center.

New structures on the city's horizon include a federal office building for 20,000 workers and a state office building. In 1969 a private concern, Hallmark Cards, began construction of the $115 million Crown Center model urban community. Kansas City International Airport is scheduled to open in 1972.

The metropolitan area's work force exceeds 742,000 and is constantly replenished from the outpouring of graduates and trainees from the area's business and technical schools, colleges, and universities.

About 74 percent of all employment here is in eleven major job categories: retail trade, service, transportation, communications, public utilities, wholesale trade, finance, insurance, real estate, contract construction, and government. Primarily, manufacturing has been closing the unemployment gap in the years since World War II.

The Government

The city government is the council-manager form. Mayor Ilus Davis is salaried at $15,000 and, even though a private attorney, spends almost full time on city problems. Councilmen receive $4,800 annually; six are elected from districts and six at large. Even though they spend a great deal of time at their city positions, they cannot serve full time. They pass complaints and most problems directly to the city manager or department heads. The city manager has an excellent team of department heads, administers well, and has earned the respect of his employees.

CITY HALL ANNEXES

Facilities and Functions

Kansas City is a sprawling metropolis whose residents are reluctant to go downtown for services if they can avoid it. To counteract this feeling of alienation, the city several years ago established two city hall annexes (the south and north annexes were established in 1966 and 1969, respectively).

Each provides financial services of tax collection, city sticker and dog license sales, issuance of permits and birth certificates, and water and ambulance bill collections.

The south city hall annex, now almost four years old, was first proposed by Councilman Swyden, with strong backing from the local Chamber of Commerce It is located in a two-room office in the basement of a firehouse in the Hickman Mills area, some thirteen miles from downtown. The local business community was quite influential in its creation and location.

The north annex, not yet two years old, was proposed by two other city councilmen, Mrs. Sarah Snow and J. D. Robins. Another group of business interests, in this case the Antioch Merchants Association, was influential in its creation. It is six miles from the main city hall and is located in a former police building.

The annexes also serve as centers for collection of surveys, including a recent one on city priorities. Both have microfilm equipment, which records information about payments of taxes, etc. The centers are equipped for walk-in service, and each annex has room for expansion of personnel and services. Some thought has been given to enlisting the services of a housing inspector in each, perhaps one day a week, and a city social worker; but this has not been acted upon.

The two annexes are now equipped with computer listings of tax and auto sticker rolls, and can use them for cross-reference, as well as to determine intracity resident mobility. This system will eventually lead to computerizing work loads and planning services needed in any given area.

Locations and Objectives

Both annexes are located in white, middle-class areas. Clearly their creation was in no way intended to serve the city's poverty neighborhoods. Rather, they were formed to assuage residents' fears of a central "power structure" and to provide greater convenience for residents living in the far north and south sides.

Staff, Budget, and Work Load

The centers do not handle an overly impressive workload. They processed 30,000 transactions in 1970, only a small percentage of the city's total business (see Table 4). In addition, only about ten to fifteen general complaints are received each month, which are handled on standard "request for service" forms. Two civil service employees (an administrative assistant and a clerk typist) are assigned to each center. Each works a five-day week, similar to staff at the main city hall. Total operating costs budgeted for 1970 for both annexes were $30,746, with salaries accounting for over $26,000 of this figure.

It is questionable that the city would have built such annexes from scratch. City Treasurer Paul A. Metz concedes that the business

TABLE 4

Transactions and Operating Costs
of City Hall Annexes, Kansas City,
Missouri, 1969

Function	North Annex		South Annex	
	Number	Amount	Number	Amount
Water Bills	3,175	$ 34,301.70	2,551	$ 33,845.96
City Stickers	9,250	53,807.40	15,148	91,084.85
Taxes	1,327	31,667.04	1,343	25,375.45
Dog Licenses	233	452.00	1,303	2,367.00
Hauling Permits	11	31.00	43	90.50
Formal Requests for Service	31		33	
Informal Requests for Service	34			
Other	108	2,178.85	31	62.00
	14,169	$122,437.99	20,452	$152,825.76

Yearly Operating Costs	
Salaries	$26,204
Telephone	2,502
Janitorial Service	1,100
Alarm System	190
Auto Allowance	350
Office Supplies	400
Total	$30,746

Source: Finance Department, Kansas City, Missouri (July, 1970).

handled at the two could easily be absorbed by the central city hall, with no increase in staff. Other city officials share this opinion.

But Metz also points out that the annexes are popular with residents, and he feels they would be quite disturbed if the annexes were eliminated. Metz sees them as much like "branch banks": convenient and, to some extent, taken for granted by the residents served. Since the annexes operate at such a low funding level, the City Council apparently has no desire to eliminate them. However, it does not appear that other annexes will be added.

An administrative aide to Metz, John Meehan, serves as liaison between the Finance Department and the city hall annexes. He agrees that people are distrustful of or do not know how to approach the central city hall. "People around here don't want to go downtown for anything," comments Meehan.

Larry Larson and Tom Bradford manage the north and south annexes, respectively. Larson, whose center is thirteen miles from downtown, concedes that the south annex is particularly popular with people living within a two- or three-mile radius. Residents living further away find it more convenient to go downtown.

DEPARTMENTAL PERFORMANCE
AND COMPLAINTS

Performance is at a high level for almost all departments. Department heads are competent and well-managed under this city manager system. Traditional city complaints (mostly public works) are held to a minimum. Major concerns now seem to have developed in the human problem areas, as is true in most cities.

The Public Information Office (central office of complaint and inquiry) handles some 4,000 complaints and 8,000 walk-in requests for information annually (see Table 5). Most complaints concern weeds and environmental problems.

The office has a staff of two persons who answer all complaints devotedly and apparently very satisfactorily. It has turned out to be a convenience to the public at small additional cost to the city. It is of significant aid to community councils, Model Cities, and the community action program (CAP) in the processing of their complaints.

TABLE 5

Statistics and Complaint Descriptions,
Public Information Office, Kansas City,
Missouri, 1969

Complaints Sent to Departments for Handling	
Department	Number of Complaints
Community Services-Animal Control	53
Fire-Fire Prevention	13
Health	
Environmental Services	
General	16
Housing Division	26
Air Pollution	12
Weeds	2,905
Trash-Junk	313
Rats	41
Septic Tanks	15
Dogs	4
Abandoned Vehicles	29
Police	30
Pollution Control-Sewers	48
Parks-Forestry Division	180
Public Works	
Buildings and Inspections	93
Engineering	17
Streets	179
Traffic	36
Miscellaneous	6
Water	10
Total Complaints Processed	4,026
Walk-in Requests for Information	8,000
Total Transactions	12,026

Note: Sixty-three tours of the main city hall, with a total participation of 1,961, were conducted in 1969.

Source: Public Information Office, Kansas City, Missouri (July, 1970).

94

CITIZEN PARTICIPATION

Citizen Reaction to Centers

Located in primarily white neighborhoods, the annexes tend to hold down some alienation there but they do not reach the city's black, Mexican-American, or rural-migrant population. In this sense, they are probably located in the least needed areas. Citizen input is minimal.

Other forms of decentralized services also have not been fully effective in this regard. The Mexican-American community feels left out of the multiservice center planned by the Model Cities program in a black area first; and rural folk are suspicious of both CAP and Model Cities, preferring to go directly downtown with their problems. It appears that service centers must be established in distinct communities in order to reach and satisfy those populations. The city indicates that the multiservice center is only the first of several and stresses its desire to have all residents use it until others are available.

Community Development Division

Municipal government's most effective citizen participation element is Kansas City's Community Development Division, part of the Community Services Department. It was created in 1943 in response to concern expressed by the City Council about the rising wave of juvenile delinquency during World War II and developed a broad citizen participation program, involving community and neighborhood councils. It quickly became apparent, however, that the problem of juvenile delinquency was only part of much greater, citywide concerns, and the division's mandate rapidly expanded.

The city was divided into twelve communities, each representing areas within school district lines. A community worker was assigned to each, and community councils were formed. In smaller areas, neighborhood councils sprang up. In 1949, an Association of Community Councils, composed of the presidents and secretaries of forty-five neighborhood groups, was organized to coordinate and strengthen efforts of the local bodies. This group is now inactive.

Although some of these councils are now dormant, particularly in poverty and Model Cities areas, many others are still active. Their concerns have expanded to education planning, zoning, and a variety of community activities. The division itself underwent extensive re-organization, with a stated goal of strengthening "a community's capacity to solve its own problems." It has placed increasing emphasis on service to community groups other than the traditional community and neighborhood councils. The community worker role has been strengthened by the formation of teams of community developers, each with a leader, and flexible assignments. Continuing in-service training for staff has been established in cooperation with the School of Social and Community Service of the University of Missouri.

Neighborhood councils handle hundreds of complaints each year, which are ultimately processed through the city's Public Information Office, in the main city hall. Every complaint is answered. When the Model Cities program first began in Kansas City, these existing councils were used by the program for planning and citizen input, and in two instances became the Model Cities neighborhood planning councils.

Jim Reefer, director of the Community Services Department, sees the community councils as a useful and vital force. Although he admits that some councils are much more active than others, he feels that the groups formulate practical goals and are useful in passing along local views to the city administration. In addition, with an organizational structure available, they can give quick response when problems arise.

He cites the Westport Community Council as being very active because they have something concrete to deal with—major traffic problems, the location of a junior college, and concerns of the merchants association and the hippie population. East Bottoms Council is functioning well because it is vitally concerned with pollution from a local plant and because it has good leadership, a necessary ingredient. By "setting up a desk" for department representatives at council meetings, greater interest has been generated, and citizens can meet face-to-face with city staff.

Reefer does sense a lack of communication and coordination among the groups, however. He attributes defeat of the December, 1969, city bond issue to lack of citizen communication and understanding of the issues. City Manager John Taylor concurs in the feeling that the city has lost contact with citizens.

The city budgeted $128,000 for staff assigned to work with neighborhood groups. The City Council discussed trimming this amount but finally agreed to approve it in full The feeling of some councilmen was that the city "doesn't have to support its enemies"—a reaction to criticism by the councils.

Reefer has thought about decentralized government, patterned along the lines of existing school districts, to handle zoning regulations and the like; but it is only an idea.

Ombudsmen

Although ombudsmen, as such, do not exist in Kansas City, the dozen or so community workers assigned to community councils by the Community Development Division perform some citizen advocate functions, helping to increase the level of citizen participation by their catalytic roles.

City Manager Taylor has expressed the possibility of turning these staff people into area generalists, by merely redirecting the focus of their jobs. This would come a step closer to the neighborhood ombudsman approach and would strengthen the channel of communication between the city and the citizen. (Stronger neighborhood ombudsmen are found in Boston, Houston, and Atlanta, for example.)

The Business Community

The business community's role in regard to citizens has been in the formation of job fairs and in the participation in minority employment programs. This has helped, to some extent, to improve relationships with the poor.

Max Norman, Chamber of Commerce representative for government relations, sees close rapport between his group and the city administration, as well. The city manager serves ex officio on the chamber's board of directors, and rapport is "excellent." Norman indicates that the central Kansas City Chamber supported creation of the two city hall annexes and continues to see their value.

MODEL CITIES PROGRAM

Now in its second action year, the Kansas City Model Cities program is in a position to serve people, so its influence can be felt. To some extent, city leaders look to the program as the vehicle for providing better communication between residents and the main city hall, and perhaps the best method to decentralize services.

For example, the Model Cities proposal calls for a number of resident educational advisory boards, "to provide a recognized means by which the residents of the model neighborhoods may eventually achieve the goal of active participation in the policy and activity functions of the school system." Four such boards are planned, but Model Cities presently funds only one. With few exceptions, the boards will be composed of local residents and will receive staff assistance from the Model Cities agency.

Model Cities has established six not-for-profit corporations to operate various segments of its program. It also funds seven citizen participation organizations, serving each of the seven model neighborhood areas. The corporations are run by their boards of directors, all local residents, and receive assistance from the Model Cities staff.

The present Model Cities Board of Directors membership is fourteen and will be expanded to twenty-one. The board is appointed by the mayor and is composed of seven Model Cities representatives, five at-large members, and two City Council members.

Kansas City estimates that the cost of the first Model Cities action year will be $8.7 million, of which the local Model Cities agency share is $2.5 million. Of the total, $314,722, all from Model Cities, will go to citizen participation structures. The biggest chunks in the Model Cities budget are for health, recreation and culture, and education. Other components in the planning document are municipal services, housing, transportation, welfare, crime, and economic development. However, the emphasis in the second action year will be on housing, economic development, and crime.

The relationship between Model Cities groups and CAP neighborhood councils is clearly spelled out in the Model Cities proposal:

> The existence of funded neighborhood groups performing
> similar functions in both the CAP program and the model
> cities program cannot be justified. Yet the amalgamation
> of both programs, however desirable, will not occur
> quickly or easily. It is proposed, therefore, that the
> Model Cities agency will initiate, during year one, a series
> of meetings with the Human Resources Corporation (the
> local CAP) with three major items on the agenda: (1)
> making the target areas of both agencies coterminous, by
> expansion of the Model Cities neighborhood boundaries;
> (2) forming new neighborhood corporations equally

representative of both agencies; and (3) determining the
financial commitment of each agency.

Model Cities Director James Threatt enjoys a close and comfortable working relationship with the city administration. He is
appointed by and is under supervision of the city manager. Threatt
believes it would be difficult to merge Model Cities and CAP because
of "differing philosophical concepts of citizen participation and the
fact that CAP has historically been an agency separated from local
government control." On the other hand, he feels that the strength
of Model Cities lies in the mayor and City Council, and that Model
Cities, "far from limiting itself to one economic or social group,
addresses itself to all the people in the area."

Threatt cites a number of city deficiencies he hopes his program can overcome. Among these are inadequacy of existing services
in slum areas; lack of coordination between services; fragmentation
and duplication of programs; and citizen ignorance of what services
are available.

COMMUNITY ACTION PROGRAM

Kansas City's community action agency is the Human Resources
Corporation (HRC), incorporated in October, 1964, and expanded two
years later with the formation of the Clay County and Platte County
Human Development Corporations. It now functions with some
decentralized services.

After a reorganization of the board, and neighborhood elections
in February, 1966, nine neighborhood centers were organized. Another
reorganization was held in 1968, to comply with the 1967 amendments
to the Economic Opportunity Act (EOA), and HRC was redesignated
the community action agency for Kansas City, Independence, Jackson,
Clay, and Platte counties. A board was then set up on the formula
prescribed by the EOA: with the city, labor, business, education,
civil rights, Head Start parents, and neighborhood groups represented.
Elections are held each May for area representatives of the poor.
The mayor is president of the board, and two councilmen and a
department head sit on it. Presently, the city manager serves as
treasurer of the CAP corporation.

HRC services are performed in the nine neighborhood centers,
except for the food stamp program, which operates out of twenty-
seven district centers. During the Kansas City civil disturbances,

HRC was commended for its job in providing shelter and food for those affected.

HRCs basic purpose is to stimulate better focusing of all available resources toward assisting low-income residents to attain the skills, knowledge, motivation, and opportunities necessary to become fully self-sufficient.

HRC centers provide the following kinds of services: physical facilities for a wide range of social and welfare services; community organization, outreach, intake, and referral; development of local human resources; staff services to area council boards and citizen assemblies; supervision of neighborhood workers; focal points for citizen participation in meetings which affect neighborhood residents; supervision of VISTA volunteers assigned to HRC.

As far as combining CAP and Model Cities is concerned, HRC officials express a definite desire to remain outside of city government in order to maintain more effective rapport with neighborhood residents. HRC feels it is performing well in all of its service areas, and sees no advantage in combining with any other agency. It is apprehensive about too much city involvement.

ANALYSIS

Kansas City's two city hall annexes are essentially branch offices of the Finance Department located in middle-class neighborhoods. They provide financial services but do not act as a focal point for resolving city problems. Thus, they are not like the little city halls which some cities have established to serve the neediest population, provide a multitude of services, increase communication with residents, and elicit feedback of neighborhood problems and concerns.

Location of the annexes was very much pressured by local business interests to maintain traffic in their areas and to retain some sense of local identity. The City Council recognized them as a way to hold down feelings of alienation by people in areas recently annexed and to lessen their apprehension of central government.

They have improved services somewhat because residents in these areas do not have to travel six to thirteen miles downtown to pay taxes, obtain licenses and permits, and transact other financial business. They are a convenience to residents in the areas they serve, but it does not appear that additional annexes will be funded for other areas.

The city relies on CAP and Model Cities for its most viable citizen participation components. It also feels the Community Development Division's forty-five neighborhood citizen councils offer a reasonable source of resident contact. However, a number of these councils are inactive, as it appears that issues and reasons for their existence have not been strong enough to pull them together into a meaningful association of citizen involvement. The councils as a group are not now capable of influencing the city on matters of bond referendums and other vital concerns.

But they could be. Jim Reefer, overall director of the program, is using community workers to strengthen the councils. He has also decentralized his operation by placing two members of his social work staff (not a part of the Community Development Division) in a Model Cities office and in a United Fund community center (the latter located in a Mexican-American section). The rest of his social work staff will operate the newly planned and decentralized Model Cities multiservice center. He likes the idea of decentralized citizen involvement for the entire city, patterned along lines of existing school or councilmanic districts, to handle zoning and other neighborhood matters. But decentralization of citizen power does not seem to be near.

City Manager John Taylor envisions the possibility of community workers acting as area generalists to serve the city similarly to neighborhood ombudsmen. He, too, feels citizen frustration and a lack of "sense of community."

Despite Kansas City's efficient government, where complaints are handled well, department heads and employees perform well, and the mayor and City Council and organizations hope for further progress and a solution to larger problems, citizens appear to be uninspired, bond issues fail, and there is widespread apathy.

RECOMMENDATIONS

1. With city hall annexes in two areas of the city, equal service should be provided in other distant areas and in low-income areas where residents may have difficulty in securing convenient transportation downtown. Location of city services in proposed multiservice centers would be a reasonable approach.

2. Annexes should have increased purpose and scope of services, to include housing code enforcement, employment processing, Social Security assistance, senior citizen programs, advocate planning,

branch offices of complaint and information, among others. For most economical use of staff, larger multiservice centers are advisable, so that employees can be borrowed and transferred from other agencies to a single building. This would be in addition to Model Cities and CAP programs, so that all income groups are reached by the city. (Baltimore and Boston are good examples where employees have been transferred from headquarters offices to field offices.)

3. Visibility of annexes should be increased through better signs and publicity. New quarters should be located in prominent, heavily traveled areas. Store front locations rather than low-visibility fire stations should be considered to give the program a fresh image of city concern. The mayor and City Council should take a unified and positive stand in development of outreach service centers. This program can be one of the most effective image builders for government at the same time that it improves services.

4. The role of community workers should be increased from organizers to neighborhood ombudsmen, to make their function more meaningful and to lend greater support to solution of resident problems. Additional neighborhood ombudsmen should be considered, with their selection effected by a partnership arrangement between the city and residents. The manager of each annex or center should be a director-ombudsman who can not only direct and coordinate a variety of agencies but can also act as a citizen-advocate. His selection, too, should be with agreement by local residents.

5. Wherever an annex and its additional services are located, the city administration should commit sufficient resources to effect meaningful improvements in the area besides those services provided within the centers. Additional street lights or paving, for example, would initially create greater visibility and a positive image for the program. These kinds of priorities should be established in the capital improvement budget in advance of locating new centers.

6. The existing city-financed program of citizen councils is a worthy step in improving citizen communication. However, they should be strengthened with sufficient operating funds and staff to make the present expenditure meaningful and the total concept successful. Most important, they ought to have increased responsibilities. For example, councils could review the city budget, assist in development of capital improvement priorities for each area, and participate in decisions on land use formulation, multiservice center location, selection of center directors and neighborhood ombudsmen (the citizen council would provide a list of three to five names from

which the mayor or city manager would select one), hours of operation
for centers, evaluation of services, and other matters to make the
process of citizen involvement meaningful. The mayor and City
Council should expect criticism from the councils and welcome it.
Together they will improve government.

7. The mayor and city manager should consider forming a citywide cabinet of officials from city and other public and private agencies
to resolve overall city priorities and goals, diminish duplication and
overlapping, set up more uniform operating districts, concentrate
resources in critical areas, and agree on approaches to mutual problems. This leadership must necessarily come from the mayor in his
pursuit of a "responsible city" concept, whereby he assumes responsibility for all matters affecting the life of his city, whether he has that
legal responsibility or not.

6

Area: 224.2 square miles
Population: 3,325,263
Black: 1,163,842

THE CITY AND ITS GOVERNMENT

The City

Chicago, seat of Cook County, Illinois, is the nation's second-largest city, the most important Great Lakes port, and the world's largest railroad terminal. Its airport, O'Hare International, is considered the world's busiest. The city's impressive skyline is still expanding. Among the newest buildings are the thirty-story Civic Center (equivalent in height to fifty stories) in the Loop (the downtown business area), and the cylindrical Marina City Towers apartments. The 100-story John Hancock Center, which opened in 1969, now ranks as the country's second tallest building. Two buildings even taller are now under construction—Sears Tower and Standard Oil Headquarters.

Chicago is a leading producer of steel, telephone equipment, appliances, electrical machinery, plastic products, and diesel engines. It boasts a Federal Reserve district bank, the Midwest Stock Exchange, the Chicago Mercantile Exchange, and the Chicago Board of Trade—the world's largest commodity futures market. The Atomic Energy Commission recently began construction of a $250 million high-energy proton accelerator, the world's most powerful, in nearby Weston.

The Government

Mayor Richard Daley (salary $35,000) has been in office since
1955 and functions in a weak-mayor-council form of government with
fifty aldermen elected by wards. As head of the city's Democratic
organization, the mayor influences the vast majority of aldermen; and
he controls all departments without much opposition, thus making his
position very strong. Thousands of patronage employees help the
mayor stay in power. Aldermen jealously guard their involvement
in ward politics and in doing favors for constituents but are limited
in skills, staff, and the time they can spend on handling resident problems.

With such strong leadership, programs move expeditiously and
there are few organizational delays. Although an estimated 35,000
of the city-county employees are appointed on a political basis as
"temporary civil service," most departments provide good service
compared with many older, large American cities. Mayor Daley has
appointed mostly competent and professional department heads who,
in the main, do their jobs well. He has used much new city and state
revenues to satisfy employee demands, as well as his skills as a
negotiator, to avoid the disastrous strikes that have occurred in New
York, for example. Relatively high salaries, a full complement of employees, many competent department heads, and the mayor's personal
ability to unite opposing forces keep the quality of services high.

However, this strong city hall control has created citizen distrust
and feelings of paternalism. Many citizens believe they do not truly
have a voice in elections or in helping to run their government and
neighborhoods. There is a feeling of helplessness in the throes of a
powerful political apparatus. But, at the same time, there is a feeling
of progress and growth and of being ahead of other communities faced
with a similar urban crisis; therefore, there is little pressure to
change the system. The progress seems to have been physical and
mostly in the central business district. Correction of human conditions is taking place at a much slower pace, but so it is with most
American cities.

City government in Chicago has been a forerunner in experimentation with decentralizing city services. Although Chicago has
no little city halls as such, it has used a base of federal funds from
the Office of Economic Opportunity (OEO) to decentralize some city
services. In 1965 the city began to provide decentralized services
in urban progress centers (UPCs) operated by the Chicago Committee
on Urban Opportunity (CCUO)—the city's community action agency.

UPCs and their outposts are located in poverty areas designated in the city's antipoverty plan. Additional decentralization took place later, when a series of small store front multiservice centers (MSCs) were funded under the juvenile delinquency program of the Department of Health, Education and Welfare. When this federal program was cut back, the city's Department of Human Resources (DHR) in 1969 assumed operation of the MSCs and received funds for it from CCUO as a delegate agency.

Decentralization in Chicago is designed to bring citizens and government services closer to one another, and to facilitate the dispensing of services.

URBAN PROGRESS CENTERS

Objectives

Since 1965, CCUO has established eight major UPCs, six outpost units, and a neighborhood service center to fulfill three major objectives:

1. To identify community needs through UPC structures and use of community representatives and advisory council members.

2. To establish agencies or other responsible public or private entities capable of responding to these needs, and to identify those already existing. (CCUO also acts as a catalyst to fund such activities.)

3. To implement and administer needed programming where other resources are inadequate, and to coordinate existing efforts.

On coordination, CCUO emphasized: "No single agency can competently and completely respond to the manifold problems confronting urban areas today. Coordination and cooperation are necessary. The poor are no longer going to be put off with fragmented and disconnected attempts to solve problems."

The centers were geared to be focal points of community services, leadership, and hope, and were placed in the worst poverty areas of the city. (See Map 1.) Besides providing needed services, the city administration hoped the program would provide a more effective communication link with residents and would create a feeling that government cares. The centers were to aid in reducing racial

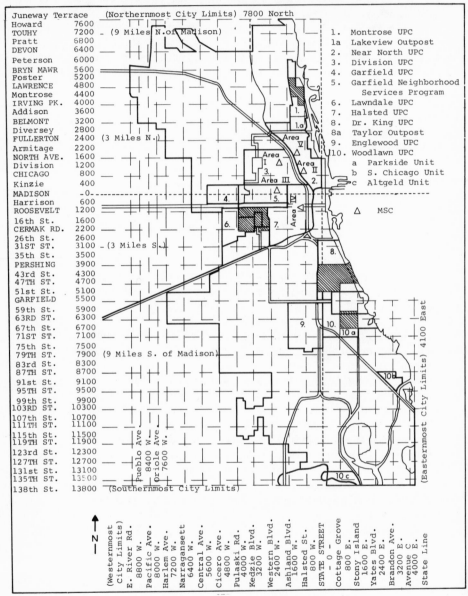

MAP 1

Urban Progress Center Districts and Outposts
and Model Cities Areas, Chicago

Juneway Terrace (Northernmost City Limits) 7800 North
Howard   7600
TOUHY   7200   (9 Miles N. of Madison)
Pratt   6800
DEVON   6400
Peterson   6000
BRYN MAWR   5600
Foster   5200
LAWRENCE   4800
Montrose   4400
IRVING PK.   4000
Addison   3600
BELMONT   3200
Diversey   2800
FULLERTON   2400 (3 Miles N.)
Armitage   2200
NORTH AVE.   1600
Division   1200
CHICAGO   800
Kinzie   400
MADISON   -0-
Harrison   600
ROOSEVELT   1200
16th St.   1600
CERMAK RD.   2200
26th St.   2600
31ST ST.   3100 (3 Miles S.)
35th St.   3500
PERSHING   3900
43rd St.   4300
47TH ST.   4700
51st St.   5100
GARFIELD   5500
59th St.   5900
63RD ST.   6300
67th St.   6700
71ST ST.   7100
75th St.   7500
79TH ST.   7900 (9 Miles S. of Madison)
83rd St.   8300
87TH ST.   8700
91st St.   9100
95TH ST.   9500
99th St.   9900
103RD ST.   10300
107th St.   10700
111TH ST.   11100
115th St.   11500
119TH ST.   11900
123rd St.   12300
127TH ST.   12700
131st St.   13100
135TH ST.   13500
138th St.   13800 (Southernmost City Limits)

1. Montrose UPC
1a Lakeview Outpost
2. Near North UPC
3. Division UPC
4. Garfield UPC
5. Garfield Neighborhood
       Services Program
6. Lawndale UPC
7. Halsted UPC
8. Dr. King UPC
8a Taylor Outpost
9. Englewood UPC
10. Woodlawn UPC
    a Parkside Unit
    b S. Chicago Unit
    c Altgeld Unit

△   MSC

Source: Planning Division, Chicago Committee on Urban Opportunity.

108

tension as well. The first executive director of CCUO was Dr. Denton
J. Brooks, Jr., now commissioner of the Department of Human Resources. The present director is Mrs. Murrell Siler.

Facilities and Budgets

UPC structures vary in size, depending upon program content
and the target area population; however, most are located in older,
unused warehouse, office, or store front buildings remodeled for this
program. The total CCUO budget in 1969 was $54,776,070, with the
city contributing $12,746,230 as its 20 percent local government share
to match OEO funds. The staff varies from a dozen or so in the outposts to over 400 in the Montrose Center, when all participating agency
personnel are included. CCUO staff budgets vary from $874,000 in
the Montrose Center to approximately $125,000 in the smaller outposts.

Montrose Center

A review of the Montrose program illustrates the major aspects
of the entire UPC program. The Montrose UPC, a four-story building
located in the northern part of the city, in a section called Uptown,
is the largest of the UPCs. It serves an area of four square miles
with a highly mixed population of 140,000. Though many are Appala-
chian whites, seven ethnic groups are represented. Two-thirds of
the population have incomes below the poverty line. The center has
17,000 participants per month, but this figure includes clients who
visit several times.

The center opened in 1965, with only ten employees. Now it
has 115 CCUO employees and nearly 300 from other agencies. Headed
by a director appointed by CCUO (the parent organization), it has an
advisory council of forty-one members appointed by CCUO's executive
director. Most members represent religious and social organizations
in the Montrose area.

A basic concept of the center is that residents should help their
neighbors, as well as upgrade themselves. The majority of personnel,
therefore, are nonprofessionals drawn from the neighborhoods. Both
professional and nonprofessional employees are on temporary civil
service status, recruited (interviewed and processed) by the center's
personnel department and referred to CCUO's central administrative
staff for final approval. There are political favorites as well as nonpolitical types. Government and private critics say this program, as

well as other new projects, is used to broaden the political base, in addition to fulfilling grant requirements—a good reason why the city seeks as much federal funds as it can get. This dual emphasis providing jobs as well as service is practiced by many cities, but political considerations are stronger here.

There is reportedly a significant "pecking order" (involving infighting and snobbism) among levels of employees who seek small status promotions. Much of this is created by the size of the operation, and it adversely affects performance. In spite of these deficiencies, the program provides better service than under the centralized bureaucratic arrangement, but at a marked increase in cost.

Montrose and most of the other centers are open from 6 a.m. to 10 p.m., Monday through Friday, and 8 a.m. to 10 p.m. on weekends. In emergencies the center may remain open on a twenty-four hour basis. These hours are longer than those in similar centers in other cities.

CCUO activities in the center include the following:

1. An Urban Life Department with thirty-five outreach workers, called community representatives (known as "reps"), who go door-to-door accepting any type of complaint, providing counseling and referral services, disseminating information, and assisting in recruitment for programs. They live in the area, know its people and resources, and act as citizen advocates. The system is criticized, however, for not selecting truly competent people who can effectively serve as neighborhood ombudsmen. Some officials feel it is more an employment program, benefiting those hired more than the thousands of other persons needing help. However, this has been a characteristic of neighborhood worker projects in OEO-funded programs in other cities as well. Intensive training of the "reps" would help, but has been minimal.

2. A mayor's information aide who receives and follows through on complaints about city government operations. Several forms are utilized in this operation—referral slips, family service logs, and action cards—which keep accurate account of action taken on requests and complaints. Officials say it is more quantitative than qualitative since the information aide has little ability to demand results and that precinct captains provide better service for most citizens. But the information aide does furnish a legitimate and organized method of handling numerous requests for information and complaints; and because it is tied to the Mayor's Office of Information and Inquiry (central office), a closer relationship to departments has developed.

3. The Community Services Department, which deals with problems of housing, health, consumer education, tenant-landlord relations, education, culture, recreation, and manpower.

4. Other CCUO programs with specialized staff are the work training unit, responsible for referring and supervising Neighborhood Youth Corps enrollees (ages sixteen to eighteen) recruited by the Human Resources Development Program (a cooperative project of CCUO and the Illinois State Employment Service); Head Start, which maintains an office to assist its North Side centers in providing social and education programs for disadvantaged preschoolers; Upward Bound Club, which encourages students to enter college programs; and the senior citizens program, which operates daily and provides hot meals according to ability to pay.

Non-CCUO center activities, which bring total personnel to about 400, are the following:

1. The Board of Education conducts day and evening classes in basic and adult education, general education development, and English.

2. The Board of Health, through its Division of Mental Health, operates the Lakeview-Uptown mental health center, one of its fourteen community mental health centers. Lakeview provides crisis intervention, group therapy, counseling and training of other agency personnel, and special counseling for delinquents. It has a mothers' counseling group and programs in selected public schools in the area, and conducts a lead poisoning detection campaign which periodically tests children from age one to six at various locations in the community.

3. The Chicago Association for Retarded Children-Head Start for Retarded Children treats children three and one-half to seven years of age to develop good speech and mental and physical control.

4. The Chicago Economic Development Corporation (formerly Small Business Opportunities Corporation) provides financial and management assistance to small, locally owned businesses; assists in developing new businesses; provides collateral for bank loans; helps businesses affected by urban renewal; develops plans for larger shopping centers; assists the Chicago Committee on Youth Welfare to encourage younger persons to enter business; and aids the Chicago Dwelling Association in providing housing improvement services.

5. The Department of Human Resources, Youth Services, assesses needs of youth and mobilizes local leadership to meet these needs.

6. The Cook County Department of Public Aid provides a full-time representative who explains services and refers applicants, but does not determine eligibility; provides a representative to determine food stamp eligibility two days per week; and houses a three-room model apartment in the center, which offers home economics training by trained home economists.

7. Hull House - Project Learn (Head Start) prepares 100 children age three and one-half to five for regular school experience.

8. The Illinois State Employment Service (ISES) operates a day labor office for men and women for temporary employment, but concentrates its major effort on providing permanent jobs for the unemployed and underemployed. ISES maintains a full staff at Montrose to screen and refer applicants; there were 41,867 placements in jobs and/or training by ISES in 1969 from all centers. This function is regarded as a highly successful operation because it has provided a considerable number of jobs for poverty residents, is an effective decentralized institutional change, and has lessened bureaucratic roadblocks.

9. The Robert R. McCormick Boys Club—The Graphic Arts Training School provides basic occupational skills to young men, ages eighteen to twenty-one, in photography, stripping, platemaking, pressing operations, and bindery.

10. United Charities-Legal Aid Bureau provides legal counsel for needy persons on matters of divorce, alimony, child support, custody and adoptions, financial and job problems, property and real estate cases, landlord-tenant disputes, claims before government agencies, school cases, and basic advice regarding signing of papers and contracts. However, legal aid services are being withdrawn from all centers for relocation elsewhere because of interference with the program by center directors and city officials. Legal aid personnel do not want to be centrally controlled.

11. The Model Cities office performs a limited function, mostly recruitment of Model Cities personnel with the assistance of ISES.

12. The Indigent Daily Food Program serves 1,500 hot meals per day at the center to any individual or family, with no declaration of indigency necessary. Because the program has attracted too many "wayward," alcoholic types, however, methods of distribution are being changed.

A permanent family record is maintained by a central records section on each person or family requesting service from the center. This 11" x 13" form holds information on dozens of questions pertaining to family size, income, housing conditions, health tests, employment status, education, welfare, pensions, program participation, etc. The intake center maintains these voluminous files and screens all applicants before they are referred to appropriate agencies. The procedures have been labeled by some as too bureaucratic and time-consuming. Chicago is a leader in decentralizing the bureaucracy, but it has assumed some of those cumbersome methods in its new system.

UPC Results

Published city reports, verified by program administrators, indicate that centers have provided significant services to neighborhood residents. In their five years of operation, they have had more than 3,000,000 visits, with many people using services repeatedly. There were 144,452 Head Start enrollments, more than 300,000 confirmed job and training placements, 112,400 youths enrolled in Neighborhood Youth Corps, 205,000 youths and adults placed in private employment, 90,000 blood samples taken for lead poisoning, 51,000 children inoculated, and 14,750 chest x-rays administered. In 1969, approximately 300,000 residents participated in programs of education, employment, training, recreation, cultural enrichment, and entertainment. (See Tables 6-8 and Chart 1.)

CCUO, through the UPCs, has also been given responsibility for administering the Parent and Child Center, Concentrated Employment Program, neighborhood service programs, day-care services, follow-through on Head Start, a Vietnam veterans' job program, and special projects with many other public and private agencies.

Executive Director Siler discusses the possibility of additional services for centers, including more traditional city government programs, such as housing inspections, weights and measures inspections, police-community relations, etc. The Dr. Martin Luther King, Jr. Center has weights and measures inspections. Montrose once had housing inspections, but they were abandoned because, reports former UPC Director Donald Smith, "Nothing could be done about the voluminous number of complaints. There is no sense in making inspections if you can't follow through. It merely increases despair." Court backlogs and lack of adequate relocation housing were partially responsible for lack of results. (Decentralized housing

TABLE 6

In-Center and Out-of-Center Services,
UPCs and Outpost Units, Chicago, March, 1965-70

Year	In-Center	In-Center and Out-of-Center
1965		a
1966	47,476	a
1967	84,547	a
1968	78,358	a
1969	82,724	131,881
1970	103,136	138,212

Source: Chicago Committee on Urban Opportunity (January, 1969).

TABLE 7

Services Requested By Persons Visiting UPCs
and Outpost Units, Chicago, January-March, 1970,
Compared with January-March, 1969

Services	Number 1970	Number 1969	Percent of Total 1970	Percent of Total 1969	Average per Month 1970	Average per Month 1969
Total	454,103	372,605	100.0	100.0	150,368	124,201
In-Center	344,741	242,043	76.4	65.0	114,914	80,681
Out-of-Center	34,176	35,114	7.6	9.4	11,392	11,704
Program Sites	72,186	95,448	16.0	25.6	24,062	31,816
Manpower	63,264	54,115	14.0	14.5	21,088	18,038
Education	72,685	96,365	16.1	25.9	24,229	32,122
Health	138,470	14,713	30.7	4.0	46,157	4,904
Social Welfare	30,256	26,571	6.7	7.1	10,085	8,857
Environmental	6,655	6,439	1.5	1.7	2,218	2,146
Community Development	11,325	8,638	2.5	2.3	3,775	2,879
Recreation, Culture	106,833	137,628	23.7	36.9	35,611	45,876
Other	21,615	28,136	4.8	7.6	7,205	9,379

Source: Chicago Committee on Urban Opportunity (January, 1971).

114

TABLE 8

Summary of In-Center Services, by UPC, Chicago, March, 1970

	Mar. 1970	Feb. 1970	Mar. 1969	Cumulative Total 1970 to Date	Year Ending Dec. 31, 1969	Total from Center Opening	Date Center Opened
All Centers	103,136	89,310	82,724	241,605	999,436	3,782,092	
North Side Centers	21,097	17,777	19,142	44,676	231,879	945,848	
Montrose	19,741	17,422	17,009	44,064	210,333	739,041	Feb. 1965
Near North Unit	1,356	355	2,133	612	21,546	206,807	Nov. 1965
West Side Centers	37,510	28,238	28,605	100,190	348,494	1,231,096	
Halsted	8,077	5,467	6,566	28,801	75,090	333,940	July 1965
Lawndale	8,928	7,578	6,003	12,576	75,337	343,539	Feb. 1965
Garfield NSP	7,741	6,708	4,123	13,289	51,255	192,712	Aug. 1965
West Garfield	4,875	3,590	7,719	6,757	83,084	162,435	June 1966
Division Street	7,889	4,895	4,194	38,767	63,728	198,470	June 1966
South Side Centers	44,529	43,295	34,977	96,739	419,063	1,605,148	
Englewood	8,473	5,189	6,672	28,796	89,035	371,074	June 1965
M. L. King, Jr.	9,311	14,696	9,459	25,613	114,251	525,885	Feb. 1965
Robert Taylor	4,038	1,821	1,950	9,099	25,277	112,784	Dec. 1965
Woodlawn	8,435	5,782	7,611	10,653	77,500	280,351	June 1965
Altgeld-Murray	4,042	3,305	4,785	6,389	59,234	156,801	May 1966
Parkside	1,615	1,492	2,316	2,687	31,241	64,805	Aug. 1966
South Chicago	8,615	11,010	2,184	13,502	22,525	93,448	Aug. 1966

Source: Chicago Committee on Urban Opportunity, Urban Progress Center Services Report (April, 1970).

115

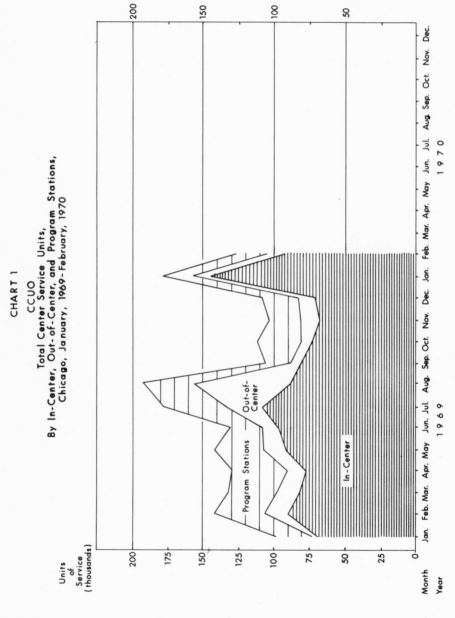

CHART 1

CCUO

Total Center Service Units,
By In-Center, Out-of-Center, and Program Stations,
Chicago, January, 1969-February, 1970

Units
of
Service
(thousands)

In-Center

Out-of-Center

Program Stations

Month   Jan. Feb. Mar. Apr. May Jun. Jul. Aug. Sep. Oct. Nov. Dec. Jan. Feb. Mar. Apr. May Jun. Jul. Aug. Sep. Oct. Nov. Dec.

Year   1 9 6 9   1 9 7 0

Source: Research Division, Chicago Committee on Urban Opportunity (April 7, 1970).

116

inspection in Boston and Baltimore are successful. In Boston, a special housing court is under consideration.)

DEPARTMENT OF HUMAN RESOURCES

The Department of Human Resources (DHR) was created January 1, 1969, as an official code department of Chicago to give the same attention to human problems as that shown other city problems. Dr. Denton J. Brooks moved from his position as executive director of CCUO to become the department's first commissioner.

The new department consolidated the Committees on Youth Welfare, Senior Citizens, and Joint Youth Development, along with new-resident and community service functions of the Committee on Human Relations, to eliminate duplication of services and strengthen support services of planning, research, public information, and department administration. This resulted in the following five divisions and a consolidated budget of $4,311,204 for 1970:

1. Community Services operates out of fifteen neighborhood units to stabilize the communities through liaison work with schools, students, and the community. It counsels on methods to prevent problems and to quiet rumors, and in this respect helps to identify leadership within the community; helps to organize tutoring and other educational programs; recruits for recreational and cultural activities and field trips; and helps to set up community organizations.

2. Family Services maintains programs of child care, consumer education, tutoring, and food and nutrition; processes consumer credit complaints; and assists in preparation of consumer protection legislation.

3. Correctional Services assists in rehabilitating youthful offenders and works in conjunction with the Illinois Youth Commission, Juvenile Court, and the Youth Division of the Chicago Police Department; in 1969, it provided assistance to 744 individuals and families under a new pilot program focusing on needs of victims of crimes committed by youths.

4. The Division of Senior Citizens conducts programs in adult education, consumer education, employment, health, housing, income maintenance, mental health, nutrition, retirement, planning, and transportation; cooperates with the Chicago Transit Authority in a reduced-fare plan; provides over 4,000 low-cost meals per week in thirty-two

locations for men and women over sixty years of age; and operates the foster grandparents program, which involves fifty-four elderly persons.

5. The Division of Manpower reviews and evaluates public and private man-power programs and provides staff for the Cooperative Area Manpower Planning System (CAMPS).

The DHR also is responsible for coordinating food and nutrition programs and day-care programs for the whole city. It sponsors summer recreational, cultural, and educational programs, involving some 500,000 persons in 1969. It operates two CAP programs and nine Model Cities projects delegated from the Model Cities agency.

There was disappointment by some that OEO-funded operations were not placed under DHR. However, ambiguity of future funding of OEO projects, staff and citizen conflicts, and the feeling that the CCUO operation was too big to be placed under one head responsible for several distinct divisions were reasons for their separation.

"This kind of thing must be done in steps," says Dr. Brooks. "It is much too difficult to try and merge all at once. When New York City tried it in their Human Resources Administration, Mitchell Ginsberg [former director of the administration] ended up with forty-four separate investigations because things got out of control."

Official relationships between CCUO and DHR are satisfactory. Food programs, day-care, senior citizen activities, and other projects are funded by CCUO to be operated by DHR in its five multiservice centers. Most of these services, however, are operated out of other neighborhood facilities because the multiservice centers are too small, with space for only a few offices. These centers were established to service the Near North area, which has higher-than-average citizen alienation.

"There is still exploration," states William Todhunter, a chief planner with DHR, "as to whether DHR is to be primarily a planning agency or an operator and deliverer of services." The recent reorganization is still too new to determine what Mayor Daley will eventually decide. However, there are no present plans to merge the two.

DHR MULTISERVICE CENTERS

Demography, Objectives, and Staff

The DHR operates five multiservice centers, which fall under the Division of Correctional Services. They engage in a wide variety of programs, such as direct service to hard-to-reach families by home visits, casework, group activities, counseling, and instruction in English for the Spanish-speaking. Center officials report that about 15,000 persons (many repeat clients) utilize their services every month. The centers are located in the Near North Lincoln Park community, an area of about 180,000 population, 20 percent black and 55 percent Spanish-American, each center serving neighborhoods of about six to ten square blocks and 30,000 residents.

Goals of the Near North multiservice center program are to build resident participation in community life; to enable families, neighborhood groups, organizations, agencies, and institutions to solve community problems; and to close the communication gap between them and local government. "We don't want to make them dependent on us," officials state.

The staff points out that people who participate in their programs are not meaningfully involved in other activities on the community level. "It would be an unserved group if not for this program," they say.

Each center has approximately six to twelve employees—a director, clerical workers, and community representatives (neighborhood ombudsmen). They coordinate and direct a variety of programs in nearby centers or store front operations, so that a fairly large complex of organizations and programs become involved through the multiservice center director's leadership. Multiservice centers themselves are located in two- or three-room store fronts or church basements. In most of the centers the feeling is that the central administration of DHR is too heavily staffed. "What do they do?" is a common remark. "The work is out here."

Many government and private observers agree that there is too much central staff in both CCUO and DHR agencies. Much of the blame is on federal reporting requirements, but also on reluctance to acknowledge that service emphasis should be placed in neighborhood operations—not the central office.

Functions

No large programs are conducted within the facilities, although some recreation and senior citizen activities, meetings, and classes are held in them. The centers primarily act as a catalyst, not only to receive complaints and requests but also to evaluate community needs and priorities toward developing a network of organizations to tackle local problems.

A typical month's services for the five centers consist of the following:

1. Employment: Making 300 telephone calls to forty-two companies, placing 225 persons. Periodically a jobmobile conducts job interviews and referrals from the field. ISES has placed staff in the central administration center and has served over 400 persons over a several-month period. The centers have set up baby-sitting pools.

2. Training: Aid in developing a summer training program for youth in health agencies and hospitals.

3. Library: Development of a program to bring mobile library units into each area.

4. Clean-up/Fix-up Program: Removal of 135 abandoned cars, streets and curbs repaired, lots cleared.

5. Program Catalyst: Staff was instrumental in starting new general adult education classes; welfare information club; community workshop on police relations; social awareness program for girls; lead poisoning testing; first aid classes; arts and crafts program; and recreational facilities in school buildings, housing authority property, churches, and store fronts. A health fair was held with fourteen major exhibits featuring Spanish translators at each booth. Health tests such as x-rays, diabetes test, and hearing and eye tests were administered.

6. Counseling and Assistance: Assistance in apartment hunting, aid to sick relatives, free lunches, Social Security and other benefits, emergency food and clothing, typing letters to secure copies of birth

certificates, obtaining affidavits, English and Spanish classes, help
from other agencies, legal aid, completion of forms and applications,
transportation for the elderly, home maintenance for the sick, accompanying children to library, school emergency cases, truancy
cases, urban renewal problems, and interim housing (see Table 9).

Residents have an excellent input into the program and are given
credit for having "really started it." Centers and staff are very well
accepted by the community, even by more militant or activist groups.

There is resident resentment against the city administration and,
even though the program is funded under a city agency, if it were to
become too closely identified with the administration, it would lose
much of its success in this area. City government is never mentioned
as being associated with the program.

"We are successful out here because the people think we are
independent and because they see real sincerity in the staff," say its
officials. "The less mention of City Hall, the better. So far, we are
not part of the power structure and don't have to check things out with
City Hall like the UPCs. As a result we have probably helped greatly
to maintain peace and harmony."

Many residents prefer the approach of the Near North multiservice centers because they offer a shopping center for social services without having to go through a newly established bureaucracy
with its inherent red tape, and having to see three or four people before you can get anything done. "No one wants to tell their story
four times," say residents.

"You come in a UPC at 8 a.m. and can't get interviewed until
11 a.m. It's just like any other agency," says a multiservice center
worker. "We make appointments for our clientele so they don't have
to wait for hours at the employment service. They know they're
coming and are received better. We also educate the citizen because
we don't want him to become dependent on us."

Warren Chapman, former director of the multiservice center
program, stated, "We try to deliver service right there after seeing
one person, and we don't get 'hung up' about economic qualifications
and other criteria." Much of the success is attributed to locating
programs in small store fronts on many different blocks, with the
result that less informed persons and those with language barriers
find it more convenient to use these facilities.

TABLE 9

Total Number of Participants and Participation in Multiservice Center Programs,
by Type of Service, Chicago, October, 1969

Type of Service	Carry-Overs	New Entrants	Reactivated	Total for Period	Dropouts	Inactive	Completions	Deletions	End of Period	Total Services This Period
Group Activities	2,776	922		3,698	50	171	210	431	3,267	32,557
Referrals	181	67		248			44	44	204	1,544
Counseling	143	2		145			1	1	144	483
Follow-up	219	79		298			60	60	238	1,734
Special Services	83	12		95			61	61	34	202
Family Services	136	20		156			19	19	137	731
Baby-Sitting Pool	72	1		73			37	37	36	300
Common Pantry	996	123		1,119					1,119	1,940
Staff Meeting		30		30			30	30		30
Community Meetings		92		92			92	92		92
Community Contacts		81		81			81	81		81
Teen Council		127		127			127	127		127
Adult Council		50		50			50	50		50
Canvassing		100		100			100	100		100
Adult Advisory Board		25		25			25	25		25
Community Adjustments	5			5					5	169
Employment Referrals	33	2		35					35	107
Employers Post	3			3					3	98
Job Placement	19			19					19	44
Housing	7			7					7	54
Girl Scouts		8		8					8	8
Lead Poisoning Tests		47		47			47	47		47
Contacts	358	20		378					378	1,536
Court Appearances*		4		4			4	4		16
Employment	32	25		57			57	57		99*
Housing Survey		40		40			15	15	25	73
Coordinating	183			183					183	547
Individual Interim	87			87					87	394
Neighborhood Advisory Bd.		11	1	12					12	19

*One-time event.

Notes: Total participants for end of October: 6,264.
Total times participants received service or participated in events: 41,485.

Source: Chicago Department of Human Resources (October, 1969).

Budget

The budget for the five centers and administrative office exceeds several hundred thousand dollars, paid from OEO funds delegated from CCUO. Originally HEW funded the centers through its juvenile delinquency program; but when that program was transferred to OEO, this left the DHR multiservice center program without funds. Eventually CCUO picked it up.

However, the city administration is dissatisfied with the Near North multiservice center program because it acts independently and encourages and accepts criticism of the administration. This year's budget was funded until June and then extended to the end of the year; however, there seems to be doubt whether funding will continue. Even this year's funding was in question. It was not until a representative group of angry citizens from these neighborhoods strongly protested to City Hall that funds were approved.

Director Siler of CCUO has supported the idea of making these centers satellites of her program, but multiservice center staff and resident insistence on maintaining their own identity has prevented this integration. These centers were originally formed because Near North residents felt they weren't getting their fair share of the city's services, and there is a fear that gains may disappear if they are "swallowed up" by CCUO.

Program Needs

Chapman stated that few employees leave the multiservice center program and that normally people prefer to work here than at UPCs because there is greater freedom of action. The director operates with one secretary and a part-time records clerk. He recommended three priority items to be accomplished: individual transportation for employees and group transportation for job seekers, a staff trainer, and petty cash and emergency funds for families.

On staff quality, Eli Baca, director of the Area Five multiservice center, believes that "a center director must first be acceptable to residents and then must be an administrator who can get things done, projects started, and develop the confidence of the people—not just be a complaint receiver. The operation is only as good as its director." Most directors in this project seemed to fill these qualifications.

Baca indicates need for more Spanish-speaking employees in the centers and elsewhere to serve the 300,000 Spanish-speaking

residents of the city. For example, he says, "Only one bilingual
Spanish-speaking person serves in the probationary office. We have
Spanish-speaking staff—that's why we can get closer to the people.
If we go, notários (notary publics) will spring up all over to serve
people. And it will be more costly to the citizen." Two UPCs—
Halsted and Division—have full staffs of bilinguals, but residents feel
this is not enough.

Many believe that City Hall doesn't pay much attention to this
area because 100,000 people refuse to become citizens and vote. Baca
feels citizenship should be made an immediate requirement.

Even though there are adverse feeling toward City Hall, Baca
relates, "I work with aldermen and precinct captains and our relationships are good. We should put them to work because they know
all the families and all are on the city payroll at $600-700 per month,
where they can get something done.

"The Young Lords and other youth groups come to me when they
need help because they figure the regular city employees are all
'Uncle Toms.' Settlement houses are threatened too because they
have never had to serve this kind of clientele."

Near North Urban Crisis Task Force

In conjunction with the multiservice center program, an Urban
Crisis Task Force composed of citizens representing the Near North
centers was created as a result of the Cabrini-Green conflict (a series
of violent incidents). The task force works toward solving many
special problems, particularly those of urban renewal, increasing
militancy and gang activities, wholesale interruptions of community
meetings by radicals, and disruption by "groups such as the SDS."
A report on the social climate states, "The total unrest over the rallies
in Lincoln Park and Gold Coast incidents speak for themselves and
left no section of the area untouched by social upheaval." The task
force has minimized this disruption and feels the need for the multiservice centers is even stronger to abate further problems.

MODEL CITIES PROGRAM

The $38 million Chicago Model Cities program is now in its
ninth month of the second action year. HUD has refused funds for
the second action year because Mayor Daley has not agreed to scatter

low-income housing sites in white neighborhoods. Agreement may
come about now that the mayoral election is over. The courts have
held that the projects must proceed, but appeals are pending. Meanwhile, city funds and some carry-over Model Cities funds from last
year keep the program going.

Model Cities plans to provide four comprehensive multiservice
centers which will have many social-welfare as well as a number of
local government services in them, stressing interagency cooperation.
New $2.8 million structures of 55,000 square feet each are proposed.
Land acquisition for these centers is now in process in the communities of Lawndale, Uptown, Woodlawn, and Near South, representing
an area of about 350,000 residents. Until the centers are constructed,
much of the service will be housed in temporary quarters. Among
the agencies planned in the centers are public aid, human resources,
police, fire, weights and measures, ISES, Commission on Senior
Citizens, Boards of Health and Education, Chicago Economic Development Corporation, legal aid, public library, CCUO, and a twenty-four-
hour Mayor's Office of Information and Inquiry. Additional links will
be made with City Hall through tours, a speakers' bureau, and information pamphlets to be distributed on all subjects and departments.

The Mayor's Office of Information and Inquiry will be either
within each center or in offices near heavy pedestrian traffic, operating
in conjunction with offices of the Commission on Human Relations
and the Registration of Citizen Complaints. They will be operated
primarily when heavy traffic prevails, such as on shopping nights
and when persons are returning from work. Five persons will staff
each office, with one overall project coordinator (director of information) and a total budget of $200,000 for all outposts. Plans call
for all types of complaints to be handled by the information representatives, so that citizens will not be passed from person to person
in order to get results.

Coordination with CCUO is good, since both programs are city-
directed and Model Cities funds nine projects for CCUO. Coordination
with most other agencies is also good. For example, ISES screens
applicants for Model Cities programs located at the UPCs. The
Model Cities staff, without statutory power, achieves some coordination
by relying on personal persuasion and the backing of the mayor to
encourage agencies to work together. But even with Mayor Daley's
power it has been difficult to get agencies to work together without
"buying into" them with HUD and OEO funds. However, decentralization, new hiring policies, simplified work procedures, and other
institutional changes have occurred in both Model Cities and the
community action programs.

CITIZEN PARTICIPATION
IN DECENTRALIZED PROGRAMS

Many national as well as local observers of antipoverty programs have been critical of the relative lack of citizen participation in the Chicago program. This study shows that there are differing approaches to citizen participation among the three Chicago programs.

Citizen Participation in CCUO

Although CCUO nominally meets OEO representation requirements for its governing board and neighborhood advisory councils, its interpretation of the "maximum feasible citizen participation" requirement has been to employ target area residents in UPCs and other programs rather than to involve them in decision making.

The governing board of CCUO consists of forty-eight members approved by the mayor, who serves as chairman. Clair Roddeweig, executive vice-chairman, a railroad executive, and close friend of Mayor Daley, functions as the active chairman. One member from each UPC advisory council serves on the governing board. The majority of members, however, are mayoral appointments and agency representatives. New appointments are made from applications acted on by the existing board.

UPC advisory councils are composed of neighborhood residents, some of whom are simply participants in neighborhood meetings or representatives of neighborhood organizations. The center director chooses almost all members, with the exception of those recommended by City Hall and local elected officials. These citizens form the nucleus of the councils, which in turn select and approve other members. There are no elections. Council sizes vary from twenty-nine to fifty-eight persons. In addition, each center has a youth council to listen and respond to the thinking of young people.

CCUO reports that residents of the inner city made it known that they wanted a voice in any program designed for them. "They were the first to know that they needed a different kind of help than had been forthcoming. They also wanted to plan an active role in any programming which was to affect their destiny," the committee stated in an initial report.

Director Claire Carr of the Montrose center believes that "the residents really feel it's their center." Tyrone Kenner, deputy director of CCUO, states that in almost every case citizens have chosen their own programs.

But opinions vary. "The UPC citizen councils are but a shadow of strong central control," says Alderman Leon Depres, an independent opposition voice to Mayor Daley. "There is no question that total control is from the top."

Many other CCUO programs have citizen advisory groups, such as Head Start's parents' council, which meets regularly. Each delegate agency "must have an advisory council as an integral part of its activity," CCUO reports. Counting all councils, citizen members number in the hundreds, but the main criticism is that they are almost always hand-picked and hardly ever independent. Their decision-making roles have always been designed to be weak. Key appointments are made and policy set almost entirely by the city administration through the CCUO board.

James V. Cunningham, of the University of Pittsburgh, in a study of citizen participation in ten cities during 1966-67, reported reluctance in Chicago to throw open selection of poverty boards to neighborhood elections out of fear of creating conflict and bitterness, and because the mayor did not consider it appropriate to give up any control of poverty programs. Cunningham concludes that this policy has caused repeated civil disorders.

A 1970 report of the University of Pittsburgh's Institute for Urban Policy and Administration states of Chicago's poverty area: "This is a territory of a million persons ruled politically by two dozen aldermen and ward committeemen in close alliance with the mayor. It was a political apparatus designed for control. It got to the mayor no real communication of the needs and aspirations of people who lived there."

Today, however, some lessons may have been learned. A new neighborhood programming project, using advisory councils to plan area programs, provides greater resident voice. Kenner states, "Regardless of whatever anyone says about control, I can't think of a single program the citizens didn't want that was forced on them. There may have been some programs they asked for that couldn't be funded because of lack of money, but I would say 98 percent of their desires have been heeded."

This may appear as a self-serving statement; but there is evidence that citizens have a lot more to say about programs, have turned back projects, initiate many projects of their own, and, at least, feel they are participating because they have entered into a dialogue with the power structure. In some areas it has been enough to satisfy residents because it is their first victory.

Citizen Participation in DHR

DHR has an advisory commission to review key programs and help formulate policy, composed primarily of twenty-seven leading business, civic, church, and agency persons. There are no neighborhood representatives. It is chaired by Patrick H. Hay, executive vice-president of the Penn-Dixie Cement Corporation. Members are appointed by the mayor in consultation with Commissioner Brooks. Dr. Brooks and the mayor make final policy decisions, as the commission's functions are advisory only.

Near North multiservice centers have an overall community advisory board of about eighty residents from all parts of the service area and all income levels. The board was formed by interested citizens coming together to work on mutual problems. Center directors make most of the membership recommendations, but the selection process is made at general assembly meetings and embodies a clear understanding as to which people are acceptable to the community as a whole. Local advisory councils for each center are in the process of being developed.

The council has built the program around what the people want. It selects center directors and staff, and formulates center programs. Over 250 people were screened by the council in the selection process, and every staff member was personally interviewed before employment. It is perhaps the strongest citizen participation element in Chicago.

Citizen Participation in Model Cities

The city's strong political structure has created a peculiar kind of citizen participation in the Model Cities program. Originally, all members were appointed. After HUD expressed dissatisfaction with the level of citizen participation, and the city's workable program citizen advisory groups recommended half of each of the four forty-member boards be elected, Mayor Daley concurred. While it appears that all Mayor Daley would need to do to gain control of each council is to get only one of his supporters elected in each area in addition to the twenty he appoints, he purposely chose to have Model Cities Director Erwin France select a representative cross-section of residents whose appointments would actually give greater voice to the grass-roots types, as opposed to local political figures. And election of some members would give decisiveness to the boards so their decisions would be less challengeable.

Even if all members were elected, the mayor would be assured of control because in only one area—Woodlawn—are antiadministration forces strong enough to win. But the city administration has been apprehensive that too strong political control in some areas is undesirable and may hurt the program. There is also a fear that some reputed crime figures may gain a more than desirable share of power. Semblance of and some actual participation of grass-roots residents is desired by the administration.

The April, 1970, election had 31,000 participants, or 30 percent of the eligible voters, one of the highest turnouts in the nation, but it was largely induced by the existing political structure. Except in the Woodlawn area, citizens had little chance of gaining control.

DEPARTMENTAL PERFORMANCE
AND COMPLAINTS

Appropriate methods of handling citizen complaints and inquiries have much to do with effectiveness of delivery of decentralized services. In addition to local complaint offices described previously, Chicago employs a central Mayor's Office of Information and Inquiry as well as one in the Department of Streets and Sanitation.

Mayor's Office of
Information and Inquiry

In 1969 over 50,000 complaints and 500,000 telephone inquiries were handled by the Mayor's Office of Information and Inquiry. In winter, when the temperature is below fifteen degrees, the office is open until 10:30 p.m., including weekends and holidays. It responded to some 3,600 complaints in 1969 from citizens whose homes lacked heat. Over 250,000 pieces of information were distributed, and tours of city facilities for 49,000 persons were conducted. Emergency housing and food are provided for needy families through a special fund.

"A personal reply is given to every one of the 50,000 complaints received," indicates Dennis Duffy, assistant director of the office. By using automatic electric typewriters, as many as 350 complaints per day can be answered by each unit, as compared with 125 per day when using typists. A seven-copy form is used by the ten-man staff to follow up replies from the various departments, with a two-week average reply time to citizens. Central staff and space allocations will be almost doubled in 1971 to provide intensive service for Model Cities residents and outposts in each of the four model cities areas.

There has been some criticism that the office does not properly follow up all inquiries but transfers too many to other departments. Duffy says every complaint received by telephone or personal contact is fully processed by his office and that only routine requests for information are transferred to other departments, such as inquiries on where an office or service is located.

"If that department does not properly respond, it may turn into a citizen complaint, whereby the citizen calls us and indicates that his problem hasn't been resolved. Then we follow up completely until a satisfactory answer has been obtained," he explains. "We never transfer complaints to other departments, only inquiries where there are no known problems. We are the problem solvers, and we will get an answer to the citizen in every case."

The office uses a variety of methods to obtain quick responses, including calling the office of an alderman when necessary. It provides effective service except where resources are short.

A mobile office that tours neighborhoods has direct radio communication to the Department of Streets and Sanitation and the Fire Alarm Office. Citizen inquiries are evaluated and answers provided on the spot. A camera is used to take pictures of serious conditions to instigate further action, and a sound system is available for public and community use.

When a citizen need arises to solve particular community problems, the office helps to organize local residents in cooperative efforts to find solutions jointly with city departments through Operation Pride, which carried out this function in four areas in 1969.

Department of Streets and Sanitation

The Department of Streets and Sanitation is the city's second largest department, with 7,500 employees and eight bureaus operating

in fifty political wards or work areas. It is the only department that
has its own division of information and inquiry, which handles some
300,000 calls annually pertaining to streets, sidewalks, lights, traffic
signals, signs, rodents, parking, refuse, dead animals, forestry, weeds,
and ice and snow complaints. Because this department receives more
complaints than any other, its separate complaint function considerably
relieves the central Office of Information and Inquiry. It does, however, work in cooperation with the mayor's office. While the latter
office is open only to 5 p.m., the Sanitation Department receives calls
on a twenty-four-hour basis by an automatic transfer to "night men."

ANALYSIS

Chicago has been a forerunner in developing the concept of one-
stop neighborhood service centers. Human Resources Commissioner
Brooks convinced the federal government in 1964 that it was sound
policy to mix Labor Department funds with OEO funds in a joint operation. Labor wanted to set up its own centers; but once this bottleneck
was broken, services from other departments were added.

Though some centers have grown too big or too bureaucratic,
they have effectively served tens of thousands of residents, institutionalized decentralization of traditional services, and made it possible
for agencies to cooperate with each other. Most critics say the services provided are desirable but could be more effective, and it has
been a high price to pay for the services received. However, it is
still too early to predict the long-range effects of the program.

Inevitably some elements of bureaucracy creep into a center
where 400 civil servants operate. This is a charge leveled not only
against large centers but also against some smaller ones, and not
only in Chicago. (Some of New York's Urban Action Task Force offices
of just one or two persons experience bureaucracy and disinterested
employees.) Neighborhood centers are hurt by such new developments of bureaucracy. To improve the centers, reception areas with
more interested workers, less initial paper work, and neighborhood
representatives (or ombudsmen) who show clients how to get through
the system might help.

However, some UPCs and their outposts have not fallen into
the bureaucratic trap. The multiservice centers under the DHR are
free of it. It is gratifying to see these small centers with their director-ombudsman pursue citizen complaints by every conceivable
method. Residents feel comfortable in approaching the offices,
greetings are cordial, and there is a sincere desire on the part of
staff to resolve problems.

The smallness and proximity to clients of the multiservice centers is very helpful, but most important is the trained, dedicated personnel. Most neighborhood representatives in the UPC program are not as well trained or interested. The latter appears largely as an employment program to benefit employees more than clientele. Immediate improvement of the program could be made by intensive training of "reps" and recruitment of those who really want to serve the community. The salary level of this position should also be improved if full and proper results are to be expected. A program of true neighborhood ombudsmen can be one of the most effective things the mayor can do.

Even with their problems, Chicago's neighborhood centers are serving people better than they were served without them. Several million client visits have been made since their inception, and many clients never would have received benefits from a central system. Many would not have bothered or known how to ask.

Alderman Leon Depres says, "The neighborhood centers are certainly doing some good. They are probably needed in other areas." But he too feels it is difficult to evaluate their total effect at this time.

Some observers feel that the centers are only temporary cures and not real solutions to long-range problems, designed to keep things cool but unable to bring about fundamental changes. But the jobs, education, and better health they provide do create lasting improvements, as does the development of at least some enlightened leadership and increased citizen involvement. Of these last two achievements, Depres says, "These may be all that are left when the program ends." And if so, it may have all been worthwhile.

New leadership is beginning to emerge, but citizen participation generally is weak in Chicago. There is little doubt that policy questions, personnel selection, and general control emanate from the top. The CCUO board is composed primarily of members of the mayor's liking and appointed by him. UPC citizen councils are appointed by the center directors, who are appointed by the administration. Local political leaders have strong influence on selection of favorites to the councils. But a reasonable number are "pure" resident types and, not surprisingly, many think and act independently, particularly as they begin to assume responsibilities for the neighborhood in which they live. CCUO's recently announced policy of giving councils greater voice in program development will help citizen participation.

Citizen involvement has probably been improved with the appointment of twenty of the forty members for each of the four Model

Cities councils. It is an unusual step by Mayor Daley to ensure a more respectable cross-sectional and representative council membership. The mayor allowed Model Cities Director Erwin France to make most of these choices. Full election of the councils, in all but the Woodlawn area, would have resulted in almost complete "machine" dominance. Whether Mayor Daley believed that too much political control would look bad, the wrong types would sit on the councils, different points of view were needed, the election of council members by only a bare majority would not lend weight to council elections, or whether the mayor was influenced in his decision by a citizen's council, his decision has turned out more favorably for citizens. And, most important, the citizens themselves believe they are participating more meaningfully than ever before. However, as pointed out in our recommendations, the 50 percent membership not elected should be chosen by some method of community consensus (door-to-door or other polling techniques) by an independent nonpartisan body. To obtain true resident involvement, selections should not be left up to one or even a few persons.

The Near North multiservice center citizens council is unquestionably the most independent participation unit. This is reflected in the positive attitude residents have about the program. However, although funded with CCUO funds, its independence is not sanctioned by the city; and it appears that greater controls will be placed on it, even if indirectly, by creating other, more financially secure centers nearby.

Citizen control is displeasing to the administration. It has no intention of creating neighborhood governments, as Daley's recent defeated mayoral opponent, Richard E. Friedman, suggested should be done. However, though all major policy decisions are made at the top, it is fair to say that citizens are being given a stronger voice and it will be difficult to take it away from them. Mayor Daley could make this voice stronger through a fairer technique of selecting membership.

In regard to the level of neighborhood service, the ability of local centers to function properly depends greatly on how well city departments and other agencies respond to complaints and requests for service. The Mayor's Office of Information and Inquiry does respond well to complaints and gives citizens answers in almost all cases. It is definitely an asset to Chicago and indicates that complaint offices in the Model Cities multiservice centers, as well as in other centers, ought to be encouraged.

Moreover, other outside agencies have performed better in their decentralized offices. However, most city departments respond at about the same level; and it still takes a call to an alderman, in many cases, to expedite matters. But city services appear to be fairly equal from ward to ward and are better than those found in most large American cities.

But it is unfair and difficult to compare Chicago with New York and Los Angeles and, certainly, smaller cities. New York does not run nearly as well but it is much bigger, constantly in growing pains, is not supported as well by its state government, has more intense density problems, and a poor political and administrative structure. Los Angeles runs well and its normal city services are as good as if not better than Chicago's; but it has a lower density, favorable climate, less physical obsolescence, a better-than-average civil service system, and a history of clean, efficient government. Chicago runs well because Mayor Daley has been able to unite most segments of the community; he demands and gets allegiance from the system; there is a full complement of employees; high union rates have been negotiated to keep the machinery running; and there are many competent department heads loyal to a structure that delivers.

It appears that Chicagoans are not all that dissatisfied with their government. Depres says, "If anything, the poorer neighborhoods get extra service because they need more, but it doesn't show up as well. It would be political suicide not to give service to certain wards because of their voting records. It's better politics to service all pretty much the same."

He and others sight faults, too. In 1970, the Chicago Better Government Association found loafing and falsification of records in the Forestry Department, and practically no service in an entire ward. This resulted in its transfer to the Department of Streets and Sanitation, where more effective supervision improved conditions. Of certain other departments there are charges of featherbedding, loafing, much less than a full day's work for a day's pay, small work loads, restrictive union regulations, and, of course, jobs based on one's ability to deliver votes. Some heavily Democratic wards get faster service and a few, more service. To achieve better results, neighborhood workers, too, deal with precinct captains, necessary in a tight political system. But it appears that services are spread fairly equally. Similar to the blend of City Hall control and little citizen participation, this is a blend of a deep-rooted political system and professionalism resulting in generally satisfactory service—but better service for some.

But Chicago is not alone in its problems of featherbedding, low productivity, and restrictive work rules. New York and Boston are

perhaps worse in this regard, with Los Angeles the most efficient.
In the problems of poor schools, high infant mortality rates, lack of
recreation space, pollution, congestion, and critical housing shortages
none of our urban areas fares well. The situations are so serious
that it is hardly fair to say that one is better off than another.

It remains to be seen who will concentrate on these issues and
solve them. Perhaps in its use of well-organized, service-oriented
neighborhood centers, Chicago will improve human resources and
widen citizen participation. I am sure the lessons of New York, which
is still organizing and behind in service, are being carefully watched.
On April 19, 1971, the Supreme Court refused to disturb a lower court
ruling that Chicago's patronage system denied non-Democratic candidates and voters an equal voice in government. Controls are tight,
but there are some signs that citizens are beginning to gain and take
hold. Hopefully, this involvement will be allowed to continue and
Mayor Daley will endorse human spirit as well as service.

RECOMMENDATIONS

In order to highlight some of the issues emerging from the
Chicago experience, the author makes the following suggestions for
improving the program.

1. CCUO should have at least as fair a system as Model Cities.
UPC advisory boards should be selected more like the Model Cities
advisory boards rather than being appointed by the center director.
A 50 percent election and 50 percent selection by directors would be
better; however, most acceptable would be a 50 percent election of
the board and the remainder selected by a technique of community
consensus, using a nonpartisan independent body to ensure equity.
The suggestion is perhaps too advanced for Chicago but worthy nevertheless.

2. The neighborhood programming project designed to use UPC
citizen advisory councils to plan programs is a good step in creating
greater citizen participation. However, it should also include citizen
involvement in the selection of some personnel and evaluation of programs. Citizens, for example, could present a list of acceptable
candidates from which the city makes its choices. Administrators
of UPCs should be made responsible to the advisory councils as well
as to the city administration. Without this involvement citizen participation will always remain weak.

3. The DHR multiservice center operation should continue to

be funded, and sufficient programming and operating funds should be
allocated. This is a system well-accepted by area residents and is
achieving its purpose. A reorganization at this time would not be
beneficial, and an attempt to put everything into a neat, well-disci-
plined package may do more harm than good. However, establishing
a larger, nonbureaucratic service center in the area as an adjunct,
and with the same level of resident participation, might improve the
program.

4. Many features of the DHR multiservice centers could benefit
the UPC outposts, such as appointment of dedicated administrator-
ombudsmen to operate the centers; development of well-trained neighborhood representatives (ombudsmen); coordinated program scheduling
of all projects in the neighborhood; and active citizen councils which
have some voice in selection of personnel, programs, and evaluation.

5. Sufficient bureaucracy agreed to even by many UPC officials
has crept into the UPCs to warrant some changes. Community "reps"
or other personnel, in addition to existing employees, could be assigned to receive clients so that waiting periods are held to a minimum.
These employees, acting in the capacity of neighborhood ombudsmen,
should be able to help in processing forms. In many cases neighborhood ombudsmen could provide a complete follow-through for clients
in order to dispel the feeling of excessive red tape.

6. The city administration should establish directives and the
means for center directors to conduct "mini-cabinet" meetings with
district superintendents and agency heads in order to effect better
coordination, agreement on priorities, and better understanding of
neighborhood problems. Internally, agencies also fail to coordinate
even though operating from the same building. Center directors'
authority should be strengthened.

7. The Mayor's Desk of Information and Inquiry should be more
prominently displayed in each UPC and the concept of City Hall assistance and concern emphasized. A mayor's aide, appointed by him,
should staff this service, display an attitude that City Hall truly wants
to assist citizens, and be given the authority to get things done. Whatever genuine concern the mayor harbors for service much of it is
hidden in a federal and state maze of funding and programming, even
though the city contributes $12 million as its share of CAP. In ad-
dition, the city should consider placing more local general-government
services into the centers, such as housing and health inspection, city
(neighborhood) planning, and utility and city bill collection, for example.

8. Neighborhood ombudsmen offices, which provide services particularly relevant to each community, should be considered for all income and ethnic areas of the city.

Area: 62 square miles
Population: 311,289
Black: 96,599

THE CITY AND ITS GOVERNMENT

The coastal city of Norfolk, Virginia, opened the first of four
planned multipurpose centers, the Berkley Neighborhood Center, in
1969. It is funded through its Model Cities effort. Although currently
geared to the myriad social, recreational, health, education, and
employment activities which constitute the Model Cities program, the
Berkley Center and scattered branch centers planned for other areas
of the city are expected to embody some of the functions traditionally
associated with City Hall.

The reality of this concept may not be far off. A recent HUD
grant of $1 million has been approved to build the city's second
multipurpose center, to serve the Huntersville neighborhood. Two
additional centers are planned in Brambleton and East Ghent.

Because Norfolk was one of the first cities chosen for Model
Cities planning funds (the very first in Virginia), the mayor's office
has been more than cooperative in the venture and is fully in accord
with plans to decentralize a number of city services.

The Government

Norfolk has operated successfully under the council-manager
form since 1918. The city manager is appointed by the City Council,

and as chief executive officer he has authority to hire and fire all department heads. The mayor and City Council are part-time officers receiving $600 and $400 monthly, respectively, and are elected at large for four-year overlapping terms. The mayor, who serves as president of the City Council, is elected from its members. The City Council does not get involved in the pursuit of complaints, "ombudsman fashion." Mayor Roy Martin is a dynamic figure who is leading the city primarily in cultural and business development, which appears to be highly successful in Norfolk.

Despite the fact that one-fourth of the city's population is Navy personnel (and therefore can be taxed only through utilities) and a good portion of the city area is tax-exempt, Norfolk enjoys a strong financial base and prosperous business and cultural activities.

The City and Its Environs

Norfolk is surrounded by the cities of Chesapeake, Virginia Beach, and Portsmouth, all of which see Norfolk as their central cultural and business district. Indeed, it has been dubbed the New York of the South. In the past, plans were under way to annex these areas within Norfolk city limits, but this never came about. Annexation evidently was resisted to avoid Norfolk's higher tax schedules and "black" problems.

Some persons would like to see such a merger in order to assure a good racial mix within the area, a stronger economic base, and more effective long-range planning. As it is, almost 30 percent of Virginia Beach and 40 percent of Chesapeake residents work in Norfolk.

Included in the now defunct annexation scheme might have been a truly decentralized city hall. Former City Manager Thomas Maxwell at first had given serious consideration to the idea but later, primarily due to the city's compact physical area, saw little reason for such a structure.

City Progress

John Talent, Chamber of Commerce official for planning and local government, calls the Norfolk city administration "as efficient and honest a government as you'll find anywhere." He gives credit to the mayor and various city officials for much of the new city pride, which he finds especially evident among the business community.

At one time the city never even met its United Fund goals, Talent admits, but now a new social conscience abounds. Businessmen are active on the Citizen's Advisory Committee and Model Cities council, as well as in the Tidewater Business League, a group dedicated to getting more blacks into business. The National Alliance of Businessmen program is also active in Norfolk; the business community, together with Southeastern Tidewater Opportunities Project (STOP, a community action program) and the local Concentrated Employment Program, has formed a consortium to create jobs and to train and place disadvantaged workers. The business community supports, without much hesitancy, the multiservice approach.

Talent believes the most important need for the area is a metropolitan approach to government in order to alleviate duplication, effect economies, and move the whole area toward greater development.

Official city figures reveal that approximately one-quarter of Norfolk's population is black, although Berkley Center Director Watt Newsome puts this figure somewhat higher, at about 35 percent. Although racial tensions do exist, much of the credit for so far avoiding out-and-out conflicts, according to city leaders, rests with an effective police-community relations effort; community action programs; and official city concern expressed through Model Cities, the multiservice approach, community development, and job programs. There have been some cases of arson at schools, but generally things have been quiet.

A new police chief, appointed from the ranks, has been commended for his ability to create a more efficient department as well as one much more responsive to minority needs. His appointment of a black officer to head the police community-relations division has been credited as one of his wisest decisions. The community relations officer has been praised highly and is extremely popular both with neighborhood groups and with the power structure.

A 1967 study of public administration and finance consultants urged Norfolk's Redevelopment and Housing Authority, Planning Commission, and other city agencies to work together to change the city's physical landscape.

A new civic center and the city's large cultural complex, SCOPE, were begun. A multimillion-dollar port authority and renovation of

the Norfolk International Terminals got under way. Citizens point
with pride to the city's Comprehensive Technical Vocational Center
on Military Highway. A number of new buildings and major renovations
have given a new look to the face of Norfolk.

When Congress passed Model Cities legislation, the Norfolk
Redevelopment and Housing Authority prepared the application for a
planning grant. But a new agency was established to develop the Model
Cities program.

THE MODEL CITIES PROGRAM

Norfolk was selected for Model Cities in November, 1967, and
subsequently received a $221,000 planning grant. The city manager
appointed Donald A. Slater director of the program in January, 1968;
and in August, 1969, Mayor Roy Martin was informed that the city plan
had been approved by HUD. Norfolk is now in its second action year.

Model Cities is closely supervised by the city administration and
works closely with STOP, bringing the city into closer contact with
the community action agency. The close ties between STOP and Model
Cities can be seen from the fact that Model Cities funds more than
70 percent of the STOP legal aid program, and during the summer
of 1970 STOP operated a Model Cities Neighborhood Youth Corps
program for 500 teenagers. There is a strong possibility that Model
Cities neighborhood assemblies and STOP neighborhood assemblies
might be merged, since they have so many interests and members in
common.

Councilman Robert Summers believes the two agencies should
merge, primarily to eliminate duplication and jealousies. Councilman
Joseph Jordon is not very optimistic about Model Cities potential
because, out of fear of controversy, it fails to provide programs the
city needs. Its main effect, he believes, has been to arouse citizen
interest; but he does not feel that the city administration will give
citizens any substantial controls.

The Model Cities program operates in the southeast section of
Norfolk, a residential district of some 2,500 acres and 38,000 people
(11 percent of the city's population).

This area forms a crescent around Norfolk's central business
district and is divided into five subareas.

1. Berkley. At one time the mile-square Berkley planning district
was a stable, thriving area with prosperous commercial and industrial
establishments. The physical condition of the area has gradually
deteriorated, and today its 10,800 residents suffer high tuberculosis
and low education and income rates. Nearly half of its families earn
under $3,000 a year. Berkley houses the city's large multipurpose
center.

2. Huntersville. An old residential community, Huntersville
has deteriorated to the point where its unemployment is one of the
highest in the Model Cities area (6.5 percent) and welfare recipients
reside at twice the city's average. About half the residents over age
twenty-five have less than an eighth-grade education. A branch office
of STOP, the local antipoverty agency, a fairly new public library, and
the Huntersville Model Cities office are located within its bounds.

3. Brambleton. One of the city's oldest areas, Brambleton faces
many of these same problems, in addition to an unemployment rate of
7.17 percent, well over twice the city's average. The area contains
a number of important public facilities, including Norfolk State College,
Wheatley Branch YWCA, Norfolk Community Hospital, and several
schools. There is a branch library which, under Model Cities, has
extended its hours and activities, including a neighborhood training
program for library aides. At present STOP has a neighborhood office
within the YWCA facilities.

4. East Ghent. With a population of about 6,000, East Ghent
harbors a considerable element of the city's hard-core unemployed,
with an unemployment rate of 8.84 percent. Traditional physical
features usually associated with slum conditions, however, such as
railroads and heavy industry alongside residential areas, do not exist
here. Nevertheless, nearly three-quarters of the area's housing is
substandard. The Municipal Arena and Center Theater, numerous
churches, and a branch library, as well as STOP and Model Cities
offices, are located within the area. Schools here are old, small, and
lacking in facilities.

5. Ghent. Ghent's problems are somewhat less acute than those
found in the other four Model Cities neighborhoods. Unemployment is
3.7 percent, compared with an overall city average of 3.3 percent.
The character of the area will be altered substantially by the city's
pending Ghent Conservation Project, under sponsorship of the Redevelopment and Housing Authority. Ghent boasts the Norfolk Museum of
Arts and Sciences, Leigh Memorial Hospital, Fire Station No. 3,
numerous churches, and two private schools. A medical center

providing a broad range of treatment facilities is located on the area's western edge.

From the beginning, serious attention was given to the community participation structure under the new effort. STOP, the local community action agency, had already established advisory councils in four of the target neighborhoods. The agency and the councils assisted in calling mass meetings to organize neighborhood assemblies for the Model Cities program. Nominating committees were formed and election procedures established.

The neighborhood advisory councils conducted a door-to-door campaign to bring residents into the preliminary meetings and to organize assemblies and vote for officers. Each neighborhood assembly elected a chairman, vice-chairman, program planning council representative, and secretary. Presently, each of the five neighborhoods elects three representatives to the board and the mayor appoints ten representatives from the city at large, for a total of twenty-five. Program committees were also formed.

The assembly meetings provided a public airing of resident views throughout the planning year. These views, in turn, were brought to the program planning council, Model Cities staff, and city administration. This program planning council, highest advisory body for the Model Cities effort, was made up of neighborhood assembly representatives and local agency officials, city department heads, and public agency administrators. State planning officials were represented on a separate program planning advisory board.

THE BERKLEY MULTIPURPOSE CENTER

Facility and Location

From the Model Cities planning process emerged the Berkley multipurpose center, located between the eastern and southern branches of the Elizabeth River, somewhat isolated from the rest of the city.

This large, two-story facility was donated to the city by the federal government (it is a former Naval Reserve training center) and completely renovated under a grant from HUD under the Neighborhood Facilities Program. Center Director is Watt D. Newsome, Jr.

Functions

The center offers a broad range of social services in conjunction
with the Model Cities program. These include day care, welfare,
recreation, mental health, general health, homemaking, adult education,
and employment activities. A probation office for Juvenile Domestic
Relations Court, a youth opportunity project funded by STOP, the Tidewater Legal Aid Society, Tidewater Area Business League, Senior
Citizen Volunteer Program, Lead Poisoning Control, and a branch of
the Virginia Employment Agency are all located here.

Newsome hopes to induce the city to provide additional city
service functions within the center. A city code enforcement project,
including tenant counseling and maintenance and financial advice,
operates out of the center and is aimed at advising residents about
health hazards and bringing homes up to acceptable health standards.
City complaints are received and information distributed.

Newsome would like to see the Social Security Administration
set up a satellite office at the center to involve not only the poor but
all residents of the community. So far, this has not materialized.

His ultimate goal is for the center to provide a central intake and
referral service so that residents might, by walking through one door,
receive information regarding all public and private services and
programs available to them. Its success, Newsome says, will depend
in large measure upon how effectively the follow-up system handles
resident needs.

In the center's first three months of operation, 7,915 people
took part in meetings and activities. However, most of the involvement
has been in recreational programs. In recent months, in cooperation
with citizens' groups, a black cultural class has been established.
Using private funds, a city pool was constructed on an adjacent site.

Staff and Hours

Of some 213 people hired (mostly part-time) to run the center's
programs since the fall of 1970, 163 were from surrounding neighborhoods. A basic staff of nineteen operates the center full-time.
Normally it is open six days a week, 8:30 a.m. to 9 p.m.; the hours
are kept flexible and are expandable should specific programs warrant.

A van provides transportation for those who need it. Volunteers help round out the core staff. (See Chart 2.)

COMMUNITY ACTION PROGRAM

Norfolk's antipoverty agency, STOP, has forty-three members—seventeen poor people elected from target areas, eleven agency representatives, and fifteen public officials. The general feeling among city officials is that there has been little coordination between STOP and the city, and that most city officials have shunned STOP for fear of getting involved in highly controversial issues. But City Councilman Robert E. Summers serves on STOP's executive committee and contributes regularly without fear of personal or political retribution.

Some STOP officials do not feel they are on the outside. One STOP employee indicated that relations were very good, pointing to such cooperative ventures as a recent job fair as evidence of teamwork. "After all," he says, "our job is to prod the administration and other agencies into actions we deem vital, so there has to be some conflict."

George C. Crawley, executive director of STOP, says there is no question of the city's support for STOP: "STOP was organized for the purpose of serving Norfolk and seven other communities. In this regard, we have not been and do not intend to become a Norfolk-only agency." Approximately 45 percent of STOP's services are directed to Norfolk, since the city constitutes that much of the service area.

"The Norfolk mayor and other city officials have been very cooperative in working with STOP. None has attempted to dictate our activities nor to keep us under a 'Norfolk Leash.' Hence, it is not hard to explain why the mayor of Norfolk or some department heads may not be in a position to speak in detail about what STOP is doing," Crawley states.

Generally, Norfolk endorses the regional approach to community action, and the city contributes funds based on a per capita formula. STOP operates a neighborhood center in the same area as the city's Berkley multipurpose center, and Crawley believes the two complement each other.

CHART 2

Referrals and Services of Berkley Multipurpose Neighborhood Center, Norfolk, Virginia

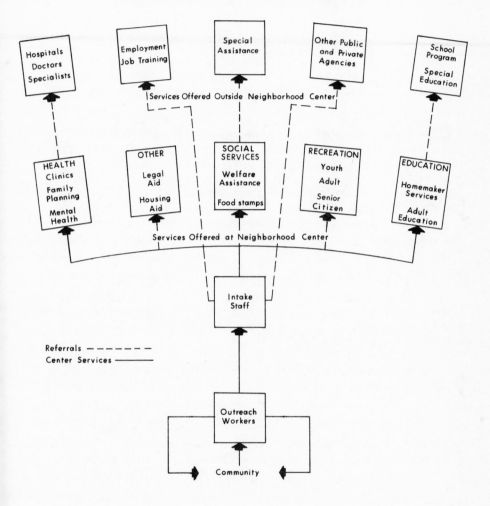

CITIZEN PARTICIPATION

Citizens' Advisory Committee

Norfolk's Citizens' Advisory Committee (CAC) is cited as the most "establishment" of its citizen participation structures but is effective, in the opinion of public officials. The mayor appoints, with City Council approval, its twenty-five members (fifteen citywide and ten by area). Its subcommittees involve an additional 200 citizens.

The committee, first formed some eight years ago to meet requirements of HUD's workable program for urban renewal, has had a sudden resurgence of vitality through competition with newer citizen groups under Model Cities and STOP umbrellas. However, Model Cities has taken away much of the action on major issues. Also, the Mayor's Committee on Youth Employment and Recreation has diminished the effect of CAC. It has been effective, however, in dealing with a number of city problems, assisted by city department heads and the City Council. City officials have gone into neighborhoods where meetings have been held.

CAC Vice-Chairman Ervin B. Hill, general manager of radio station WGMS, feels that the committee in recent years has directed itself mainly to racial problems and created the semblance of an urban coalition. He sees the body as "a catalyst between City Council and citizens, to make things happen."

Councilman Joe Jordon is less optimistic about CAC's involvement in significant community affairs. He visualizes it as being aimed more at "clean-up, fix-up" programs.

Hill feels strongly that the quality of leadership behind CAC determines its effectiveness. Clearly he takes his vice-chairmanship seriously. "You can make the committee what you want" is his feeling.

Mayor Martin expresses satisfaction with the CAC structure. He feels it reaches and represents the entire city, thus having a much broader appeal than either Model Cities or STOP citizen groups.

City Manager Thomas Maxwell says, "CAC is a very vital force and has done much good in the city." However, he is somewhat apprehensive about citizen councils in general. His experience with town hall meetings has been good and bad. He used them in University City, Missouri mostly to inform people. He says, "One or two people can dominate these meetings with trivia and nothing gets done."

But the city manager is in favor of citizens, rather than city officials, heading committees which confront citizens. Residents have greater empathy with citizens heading such committees than with city officials, he believes, because there is a feeling that a citizen performs this function to better the community and not to enhance his position. This emphasis on citizen leadership rather than government is an effective mechanism to involve citizens, but also one which may be used to protect city officials.

Councilman Jordan is more cynical about the power structure's motives. CAC was created to satisfy HUD urban renewal requirements, he feels, not by a government wishing to hear the voice of its constituents. Before 1960, Jordan says, the city resisted any efforts to create such a body, and it is still loath to listen to CAC's recommendations unless it is in basic agreement with them. The city is more interested in control than in service, Jordan believes. CAC, he feels, is not the catalyst many would have you believe. Any broadening of citizen participation will be done "begrudgingly and negatively" by the city, he says.

The Need for Ombudsmen

As would be expected, the desire for Norfolk to adopt the ombudsman system also varies among city officials. There are no plans for this type of proposal.

Mayor Martin, who feels fairly satisfied about the effectiveness and efficiency of the existing system, does not quite see the need for ombudsmen at this time. He has considered it, but sees no benefits from it that the city does not now enjoy.

City Manager Maxwell agrees. His opinion differs slightly, however, in that he sees CAC as presently handling the functions that would otherwise be given to an ombudsman.

In contrast, Councilman Jordan believes ombudsmen and multi-service centers are essential to the city. He would divide the city into seven areas, and have a rotating group of ombudsmen made up of current councilmen available in seven existing fire stations, the "perfect buildings" for this operation.

The city's seven councilmen are paid $400 per month and are not full-time officials. They all have other positions, mostly in salary ranges over $30,000, and apparently could not devote the time to a full ombudsman function. They are encouraged to pass on all complaints to the city manager in this strong council-manager form of government.

Although Public Works Director Chester Lewis has not considered the ombudsman question as such, he has thought of establishing a "trouble desk" to facilitate handling of complaints. But he is not sure whether such a system would not create more red tape than it would eliminate. City officials feel a central office of complaints for all city operations is not needed.

Chamber of Commerce official Talent sees no additional need for a coordinating group if it merely superimposes itself on existing bodies. Similarly, he expresses little enthusiasm for a cabinet structure within the mayor's office. He does, however, see the value of the ombudsman approach, particularly in Norfolk's Ocean View Beach area, one of the city's poorest (and, incidentally, white) neighborhoods.

Perceptions of Citizens

Interviews and questionnaires from residents reveal that Norfolk's populace feels it is "gaining on the system" in the sense of learning what services are available and how to get them. Most people noted economic gains as well.

Nevertheless, the general feeling is that more communication is necessary, both within and between neighborhoods. In addition, they would like to see more training for residents willing to participate in community activities. Educational opportunities should be well advertised so more people can take part.

As one resident put it, "We have come a long way, but then we were so far behind. This game of catching up is hard, but I can see the light just ahead."

While the people interviewed advocated widening communication channels, it is also true that a feeling of apathy pervades the city and

that citizen meetings, when held, generally are poorly attended.
Programs operating out of the Berkley center are hoping to overcome
this feeling, especially among the city's young people and its minority
groups.

ANALYSIS

Norfolk is a progressive city with a mayor, City Council, and
business community that take a strong lead in its economic development. Its new facade, stemming from intensive urban renewal efforts,
new civic and cultural centers, and better-than-normal availability of
resources make it the envy of many American cities. It has the capacity to solve its problems.

Yet there are undercurrents that all is not well, that some voices
are not being heard, that the poor are not being served. The Berkley
multipurpose center planned by the city and put into operation with
Model Cities and other HUD funds fills part of this gap. So will three
other Model Cities multiservice centers, soon to be established.
However, the city still needs to convince residents to come in, to participate, to contribute.

CAC is a viable force that has done much good in effecting better
communications and arousing some sense of community, even though
it is criticized for being too "establishment" and for concentrating on
minor issues and less significant projects. It could be improved by
increasing representation from those groups which feel they are not
being heard and by proper staffing. Since its key purpose is to search
out significant problem areas, this seems a most legitimate way of
doing it. Sufficient community action and Model Cities personnel, as
well as representation from other resident organizations, should help
make up the main body.

Holding neighborhood meetings with city and agency "desks" to
receive complaints is a commendable action of CAC. However, there
should be a closer tie-in with Model Cities and the various neighborhood community action councils. Initiative for this relationship would
most effectively come from Mayor Martin. The concept of uniting
federal, state, and local programs must necessarily receive its impetus
from the city administration. Local government is held responsible
by citizens for city progress or lack of it, and therefore it should
pursue, through whatever techniques possible, this "responsible city"
concept of stimulating and improving all agencies.

The city should not rely too heavily on the community action program for its citizen input or for the ombudsman function. In the Berkley center, as well as the newly planned Model Cities centers, a City Hall representative, funded by either Model Cities or the city, might very well be appointed by the city to operate a mayor's desk visible to all, and to function as a neighborhood ombudsman. Even though the center director is supposed to act in this capacity now, a much stronger advocate role is necessary. This would tend to make the centers more viable, and would more clearly establish lines of communication from the neighborhood to the city. It is the kind of visibility the mayor and City Council need — it would only help their image.

The use of fire stations or other unrelated city structures for this purpose would not be the best approach to achieving the above results. A new dimension in communication is needed to create a feeling of stronger city concern. Use of the same city structures will not attract now alienated clients.

SUMMARY OF RECOMMENDATIONS

To highlight issues emerging from the Norfolk experience the following suggestions are made to strengthen the approach.

1. CAC should be made more viable, with additional representation from the alienated, the young, and existing neighborhood councils, such as community action and Model Cities groups.

2. The city should consider permanent staff for CAC in addition to desirable and effective volunteer participation. The staff could come from new city funds or from the transfer of some departmental personnel to this function on a part-time basis. They would perform as liaison to city representatives in service centers, assemble data for city goals to be considered by the committee, and establish a formal mechanism for receipt of complaints and distribution of information. The staff would be responsible to CAC and the city administration, and would coordinate the various citizen participation structures in the city.

3. Mayor's representatives (or neighborhood ombudsmen), funded by Model Cities or city monies, should be placed in service centers as citizen advocates for neighborhoods, with the sanction of the city administration. Though the city does not now consider this vital, it should not rely solely on other agencies for citizen input.

4. The mayor should take strong initiative toward reinforcing communication links with neighborhoods. In addition to highly visible mayor's desks at each multipurpose center or Model Cities office, the mayor and City Council could benefit considerably by appearing more frequently in all neighborhoods as part of their formal meetings or subcommittee meetings.

5. Additional city services should be added to the centers. These may include collection of taxes, payment of utility bills (even though banks also assist in collection of utility bills), issuance of licenses and permits, additional housing inspection functions, city advocate planning functions, police-community relations office, ombudsman and complaint office, and other services appropriate to each area.

Area: 320 square miles

Population: 7,771,730   Puerto Rican: 777,173

Black: 1,125,600   Jewish: 1,942,913

THE CITY AND ITS GOVERNMENT

The City

New York, the nation's largest city and richest port, is a national leader in business, finance, manufacturing, communications, service industries, fashion, and the arts. It is also one of the world's leading ports, and headquarters of the United Nations.

The Government

Mayor John V. Lindsay (annual salary $50,000), whose term expires December 31, 1973, functions in a strong-mayor/council form of government with thirty-eight city councilmen (annual salaries $20,000, plus $5,000 contingency expenses), 27 elected from single-member districts, the council president elected at-large, and two elected at large from each borough by a method which almost assures two-party representation. The City Council's responsibilities are few. Its chief activities relate to the budget and "home rule" messages to the state legislature. There are five elected borough presidents (annual salaries $35,000), who, along with the mayor, comptroller, and president of the City Council, make up the Board of

Estimate. Borough presidents have two votes each, and the other
three members have four votes each, a total of twenty-two. The
mayor has control over all city departments, but his power is checked
by the City Council's and Board of Estimate's budget approval authority. The Board of Estimate must approve all substantial capital
projects, as well as decisions such as street closings, sale of city-
owned land, and leases of city property. It is a full-time participant
with the mayor in governing the city, a role City Council does not
have. Almost everything the mayor proposes needs board approval.
Some minor engineering and planning functions are operated from the
borough halls, which are similar to Los Angeles' branch city halls
but much more limited in scope.

Instead of over fifty separate line departments reporting to the
mayor, in 1966 the city was reorganized into the following nine administrations or superagencies to coordinate what were previously
separate agencies: health and environmental protection; housing and
development; human resources; municipal service; transportation;
finance; economic development; parks and recreation; and cultural
affairs. In 1970, Model Cities was also made into an administration.
Police, fire, corrections, and consumer affairs remain separate, as
do a number of commissions, boards, and agencies.

This reorganization came about as the result of a task force
study which indicated that the former government structure had the
following drawbacks:

1. Wasted time, money, and services, and distorted relationships of agencies to the central agencies of the city, to each other,
and to federal and state units.

2. Inhibited collection of information and intelligence necessary
for prudent policy choices.

3. Duplicated facilities for the same or similar functions.

4. Frustrated service delivery.

In addition to creating separate administrations, other offices
were created to perform specific management functions either within
the superagencies or as part of central management: Planning,
Programming and Budgeting; Office of Collective Bargaining; Policy
Planning Council (part of the Budget Bureau, it is the key coordinating
body, working in conjunction with the Rand Corporation, outside
management consultants); Management Service Unit; New York

Office for the Aging; Office of University Relations; Office of Contract
Compliance; Civic Assembly; Office of Administrative Management;
Management Advisory Council; Volunteer Coordinating Council; NYC
Urban Corps; and Central Publications Office. Many of these offices
are designed to centralize decision making over areas where there
had been little if any control, and to collect information about where
money can most effectively be used. But several dozen officials
report to the mayor, and the superagencies have made little progress
in coordinating functions, lessening burdens on the mayor, or attracting
administrators able to run effective departments. Central direction
takes place through one of two deputy mayors and several dozen
counselors and assistants.

By all admissions, next to the mayor the director of budget
is the most powerful office in the city. The mayor has gained control
of the Bureau of Budget as a central management tool in order to increase his power over departments. Second, the mayor's appointing
power of the chairman of the City Planning Commission (in effect
planning director) gives him additional leverage over departments.
But the strength that has been placed in the mayor's office is not
enough to cope with the City Council, Board of Estimate, unions,
banking interests, city comptroller, and the many other forces that
pressure the mayor from many directions.

There is discussion of new techniques to improve government,
such as decentralization. The Budget Bureau feels that centralization
does not make the case against decentralization and community
participation weaker, and it has suggested ways to give citizen councils
some budget authority, a few of which are being tried.

The mayor feels strongly that citizen involvement and improved
communication techniques are necessary for better government, and
has instituted the following:

1. A mayor's action center which responds to citizen complaints.

2. Neighborhood city halls.

3. Urban action task forces.

4. The service of "night mayor," which places responsible
executives of city agencies at City Hall after regular office hours
and throughout the night to handle complaints and emergencies.

5. The mayor's weekly TV program, with time set aside for questions from viewers.

Lindsay has now proposed a Plan for Neighborhood Government. This paper will discuss New York's most recent developments in neighborhood involvement (neighborhood city halls, urban action task forces, Plan for Neighborhood Government) and how they have been used to improve services and make government more responsive. To further understanding, it will also discuss citizen involvement and decentralization in relationship to two other active community participation agencies, community action and Model Cities. In view of Mayor Lindsay's closing all but a half-dozen neighborhood offices because of a severe city budget crisis, the proposed Plan for Neighborhood Government will be discussed, as well as the existing experimental program called Neighborhood Action Program.

NEIGHBORHOOD CITY HALLS AND URBAN ACTION TASK FORCES

History and Budget

Before the present neighborhood city hall (NCH) program was conceived in 1961, there were seven urban renewal site offices in Manhattan for social and physical rehabilitation under the Neighborhood Conservation Program. These were considered by many to be local "city halls" operated by the district director or "local mayor" and his staff, but were essentially established to conduct urban renewal projects. They did not have the same emphasis as the NCH program, and cannot be viewed as its genesis. Many cities in the early 1950's had such site offices to dispense project services, but they were not "tagged" as neighborhood city halls.

The idea of NCHs apparently sprang from Lindsay's 1965 political store fronts, but the first genuinely recognized NCH was opened in 1966 in East New York, in response to the spring riots of that year among Italians, blacks, and Puerto Ricans, and also out of a general need to communicate more effectively with neighborhood residents. In 1967 five more NCHs in store fronts and health centers, and three mobile units, were opened and funded with small operating budgets from private contributions ($320,000 annually the first two years and $620,000 the third year) and some funds indirectly borrowed from other accounts. The City Council and Board of Estimate had refused to fund them, overriding the mayor's veto in the belief they were mostly political institutions.

They served neighborhoods in four of the city's five boroughs
and operated with four to seven employees, some working from their
homes. Their primary role was to handle citizens' complaints at the
neighborhood level and improve communications between residents
and City Hall.

During the same period (1961-70) urban action task forces
(UATFs) were also established in forty-five (the number grew to
fifty) of the city's sixty-two planning districts, their boundaries
coinciding with "natural community" boundaries, as determined by
the Planning Commission.

By 1970, UATFs had absorbed the functions of NCHs, as well as
those of the city's Neighborhood Conservation and Better Block programs. Originally under the Division of Community Services, UATF,
in its expanded role, was moved to the Office of Neighborhood Government, created in early 1970 out of Mayor Lindsay's Plan for
Neighborhood Government.

The program was funded in 1970 at $5 million, of which $1
million came from the city's general fund, $1 million from the pri-
vately financed Urban Coalition, and $3 million from the city's
capital improvement fund.

In 1971, however, in an austerity move by the City Council, some
funds were cut from the program, and only six neighborhood offices
remain under a program called Neighborhood Action Program.

The staff for Neighborhood Action is being funded from the
capital budget, and although the program has been established only
by executive order, it is apparently receiving considerable support
from the City Council and Board of Estimate as a meaningful experiment in decentralization. They have increased the capital outlay
portion from $3 million to $4 million in 1971.

In the same economy move, UATF offices were eliminated
(formerly, twenty-five offices served the fifty UATFs), and the eighty-
eight-man staff drastically reduced. Those who remain will work
primarily from their homes, continuing citizen-advocate roles in the
community. Certain other UATF activities will also continue, un-
disrupted by loss of physical headquarters, such as UATF neighborhood meetings, and the Education Task Force, which, under mayoral
aide Barry Gottehrer, will continue to receive requests and act as
a base for information gathering. Reportedly, a few communities
are trying to raise money to keep their neighborhood UATF offices
and staff going.

Objectives of Decentralized Services

The goals of the various decentralized programs are stated by Mayor Lindsay in his Plan for Neighborhood Government, presented to elected officials and citizens in June, 1970:

1. To improve delivery of municipal services by making city agencies more responsive and accountable at the neighborhood level.

2. To reduce the alienation and distance which citizens feel toward a remote city government.

The city has approached these goals through neighborhood city halls, urban action task forces, strengthened community boards, community school boards, neighborhood conservation offices, Model Cities policy committees, community corporations, and a host of other citizen advisory councils. Together, these mechanisms have only partially fulfilled the need for communication and better service, and they are not widely regarded as successful. Mayor Lindsay feels that one decisive neighborhood body is needed in each district to coordinate agencies, plan economic development, review budgets, handle complaints, and act as a forum for local discussion. The new Office of Neighborhood Government is another stage in the evolutionary process of decentralizing government in New York. Located near the main city hall in Manhattan, it has forty-five employees who form the central management of the operation and concentrate on coordination. Executive Assistant to the Mayor Lewis Feldstein, administrator of the program, is responsible for maintaining effective channels of communication with all city departments, keeping the mayor fully informed about the operation and any serious community problems, and developing a responsible system of localized government. He and his staff attend numerous neighborhood meetings to discuss problems, sell the concept of neighborhood government, and achieve some coordination out of the multiple of organizations. The city's first attempt to accomplish some of these objectives was through the NCH and UATF programs. Their full description is necessary to understand the evolution of the Plan for Neighborhood Government.

Functions

Very few in-house services were conducted in NCH and UATF offices. Reduced-fare tickets for senior citizens were distributed, city information disseminated, complaints processed and answered,

space provided for activities of a nonpolitical nature for city councilmen and state assemblymen, staff assistance given to any community
organization desiring it, and planning and other special projects performed by the staff. Besides processing individual complaints, the
most important element seemed to be resolving special problems
affecting a large portion of a neighborhood, such as zoning cases,
drug abuse, park locations, neighborhood rehabilitation, etc.

Through the processing of complaints, the local staff was able
to more effectively pinpoint neighborhood problems and relay information to the mayor and central staff for development of priorities and
better management techniques. Citizen request forms were used to
process complaints and citizens were given a reply to their requests in
almost every case. In 1967, the first full year of operation, about
12,000 complaints were received by the NCHs; it increased to 80,000
annually. Combined with the UATFs, annual complaints and requests
totaled 500,000. Each neighborhood office received from ten to thirty
complaints and inquiries daily. Some received many more and a few
hardly any. Complaints from the field and the Mayor's Action Center
were not processed by computer or analyzed in any systematic
fashion, something which was felt necessary but never developed.

Directors of local offices still act as coordinators of area programs which involve more than one agency, assist community groups
in formulating plans for neighborhood rehabilitation, establish more
effective links with city departments, sponsor neighborhood meetings,
help to evaluate performance of departments and agencies working
in the area, inform local citizens about how agencies operate, and
assist in bringing key people together to help solve problems. Directors of the UATF offices dispersed recreation material, and
issued free sports tickets and other "hand-outs" to pacify neighborhoods. Since there never were enough to go around, antagonisms
were created. Under the Neighborhood Action Program this role will
probably be less meaningful.

Some UATF directors held bimonthly "mini-cabinet" meetings
of district superintendents and other key agency officials which included the police precinct captain, fire battalion chief, district welfare director, district health officer, district sanitation director,
etc. "Mini-cabinets" are a prime function for directors under the
Neighborhood Action Program. The aim is to make district superintendents more responsive to neighborhood problems, achieve
cooperation, and avoid duplication of services. Some success has
been achieved, but better response from district superintendents is
needed if real progress is to be made.

To improve the concept, the Office of Neighborhood Government has proposed the following steps:

1. Attendance at community cabinet meetings should be required of the key city officials who have operating responsibility for that area as a part of their job.

2. City officials attending these meetings should have the power and the discretion to make key local decisions without the need to clear everything with their supervisor downtown.

3. City agencies should identify the scope and level of services they provide by community planning district so that the community board and the community cabinet may address questions of priorities, allocation, and needs.

4. The redistricting of city agencies to conform to community districts should move ahead. Otherwise, local line officials will have to attend far too many community board meetings because their service district would overlap several community districts.

5. The community board should be representative and have legitimacy, so line agencies could work with the board as a representative of the entire community.

In Washington Heights, located between 155th and 229th Streets in Manhattan, with a population of 500,000, the NCH was managed by John Van Putton and housed in a store front with five rooms of office space and a meeting room capable of holding about twelve persons. The area has 120 organizations operating within it, none strongly militant or activist. Van Putton held monthly "mini-cabinet" meetings, met continually with citizen groups, and made himself available on many weeknights and weekends in the center. Numerous special projects were conducted, such as a fashion show which attracted over 7,000 neighborhood residents. The bulk of his time was spent following up citizen complaints and requests, and citizens felt he performed a vital service.

The Flushing-Hillcrest NCH opened in May, 1969, on the ground floor of an office building and was slightly more spacious than the one in Washington Heights. A meeting room for twenty-five to thirty persons was used by a variety of community groups. Located in a middle-class area of Queens, its problems differed markedly from those in poverty areas. With few apartment buildings, there were fewer landlord-tenant problems but more zoning and land-use issues, greater concern with traffic congestion, youth loitering problems, and park and playground development.

General complaints were numerous, however, with over 5,000 processed in the first year of operation. Director Irving Newman, who has lived in the area 20 years, felt the NCH was a considerable convenience for the citizen, eliminating the necessity for a long trip downtown.

The prime objective of the program in this area was to help maintain neighborhood stability. Most residences are single-family homes occupied by owners, and many rental properties are under rent stabilization.

Queens Councilman Donald Manes and Assemblyman Martin Rodel used space in the NCH on Saturdays for meetings. "These were not political meetings," said Newman. "Citizens would object if this were not an equal service to all, regardless of their politics."

Newman did not see himself as coordinator of other organizations in the area, but did help to form civic groups such as the West Cunningham Civic Organization, created to insure better use of a local park; and the Hollis Hills Organization, which grew out of a zoning variance problem over a gas station.

Each member of his six-man staff functioned as a neighborhood ombudsman in a specific field, such as housing, schools, social welfare, etc., but spent most hours within the building. This staff was the first to serve both the NCH and UATF. Combining staffs for both functions seemed most logical and was followed in other areas. UATF performed as the citizen participation component of the program. Newman felt that citizen involvement was effective in Flushing-Hillcrest, and that "as much as three-fourths of the borough was involved in the program in some way."

UATF Office Performance

The performance of UATF local offices and task force chairmen and their committees is important. Douglas Yates, in an October, 1970, Rand Institute study of the task forces, indicated that the offices were understaffed (in several cases, staffed by a lone receptionist-secretary) and difficult to find (in many cases, in unmarked store fronts). They were not geared to handle a heavy volume of requests; therefore, some officials wanted to keep them secluded—somewhat counterproductive of their purpose. Task force office addresses were not listed in full in the telephone book, and there was no systematic collection of records and grievances to enhance overall evaluation and management techniques.

Their most visible activities, Yates stated, "are dispensing hydrant spray caps, Yankee baseball tickets, films, free buses (for group meetings), and plastic garbage cans." But even in this non-controversial mission, he pointed out, they made as many enemies as friends because the demand outstripped the supply. Meetings were attended by the same small group of established community leaders, and apparently others rarely found their way into task force offices. He criticized the bureaucratic attitude of many task force workers and noted the fallacy in assuming that indigenous employees will automatically provide the desired outreach into the community. "The special location of government offices may have little bearing on root problems of government responsiveness and effective service delivery," he stated.

Yates reported that because of time limitations and other responsibilities, most chairmen were unable to get involved in the day-to-day business of the task forces; a recurrent complaint was that promises made in crisis situations were not honored; fragmentation at the neighborhood level (by dozens of neighborhood groups and offices) was paralleled at City Hall by numerous offices dealing in community affairs; and there was "much loose talk" about neighborhood government which, he warned, could only lead "to disappointment at this point, if it is taken seriously."

In his conclusion on task force effectiveness, Yates was quick to stress, however, that the task forces forged stronger communication links, were very beneficial in subduing riot or near-riot situations, performed a significant function in coordination, undoubtedly improved government's understanding of neighborhood life, developed an ability to get departments to act on grievances, produced well-designed neighborhood monitoring and reporting systems in middle-income areas, and, most important, many chairmen have been able to resolve some major problems and have developed successful ties with community groups.

Indeed, the caliber of task force chairmen has been important. Chairmen have consisted of deputy mayors, administrators, department heads, and other key officials. Deputy City Administrator Philip Finkelstein performed such a creditable job in middle-class northeastern Queens that he was assigned to Rockaway (11 percent poverty) to bring some cohesion to that community. An emphasis

on the lower- and middle-class white neighborhoods was exemplified
by the appointment of Deputy Mayor Richard Aurelio (considered the
second most powerful man in the mayor's office) to head the task
force in Bay Ridge, perhaps the city's most conservative area.

Sam Azadian, deputy commissioner of public works, was UATF
chairman in South Brooklyn, a melange of middle-class and poor
whites, Puerto Ricans, and blacks. Azadian ran Lindsay's 1969 mayoral
campaign in the same area and used his UATF position to line up
people to man store front offices called "independent clubs."

The work of UATF chairmen has probably been the most notable
accomplishment of the program, but performance among chairmen
has varied greatly, some accomplishing very little and some using
the store fronts for political purposes or simply to explain why things
cannot be done. The chairman concept was excellent when used
properly, for it forced key administrators, many of whom have direct
access to the mayor, to deal with residents and view their problems
firsthand.

Citizens become members of task forces by taking an interest
in local problems. Those who attended meetings more often than
others were given assignments. It was quite flexible, and almost any
citizen could become a member.

In the beginning, there were complaints from middle-income
communities that city resources were being diverted to those where
the task forces were operating. More attention might have been given
to some areas, but apparently not more resources. It did indicate
the extent to which the task forces had succeeded in establishing contact with residents. Eventually UATFs were created in most areas
of the city and have been successful enough so that this aspect of the
program (minus local offices) will continue. However, Mayor Lindsay
says in his book, The City:

> It can be said . . . that this whole program grew out of an
> initial decision to become a visible, accessible mayor
> whose administration was at work in the neighborhoods of
> New York. It would be nice to say that this was a care-
> fully planned, "gamed-out" strategy, applied calmly and
> surely at every stage. It would be nice to say that—but
> it wasn't the case. In fact, it grew bit by bit and piece
> by piece; each finding required a new form of response,
> and each success in establishing contact between city
> and community required an extension of the idea.[1]

In addition, Lindsay says, it is still necessary to keep his personal contacts with the community.

> The task force, however, did not end my own decision to continue walking the streets. There are many reasons for this. In the first place, I think nothing is more dangerous to an executive than isolation from the people and reliance on advisers who, however competent, may tend to tell the executive what they think he wants to hear. It's not very likely that an aide will say, "Mr. Mayor, they think you're a nigger lover in my neighborhood and they hate you for it." But it is likely that in some neighborhoods that is precisely what I will hear. . . . More important, I think it necessary to get as much of the flavor of the city as possible.

DEPARTMENTAL PERFORMANCE AND HANDLING OF COMPLAINTS

Department of Sanitation and Streets

The ability of decentralized programs to improve service depends much on the performance of departments and agencies. "The UATFs have been a help in getting information to us and making us more aware," says Griswald Moeller, former commissioner of the Department of Sanitation and Streets. "However, they sometimes commit the department to too much and the resources aren't there." Even so, he says the department is able to keep up with almost all routine complaints, and has little backlog.

In response to decentralizing public works services to the borough level, Moeller states, "It is ridiculous to believe it can be done better if controlled at the borough level. It is simply a matter of resources. With adequate numbers of men and equipment, the job can be done more effectively centrally." Some borough presidents and other officials, however, feel services started to deteriorate when the responsibility was taken away from the boroughs. Moeller indicates that district superintendents have substantial authority over household pickups, street cleaning, and snow removal, which, in his opinion, constitutes a considerably decentralized system presently.

Moeller expresses caution over giving too much community control to citizens. But he feels superintendents of the fifty-eight

districts should attend "mini-cabinet" meetings and relate more
effectively to citizens and neighborhood problems. He has utilized
community service and special project officers in each district to
respond to neighborhood residents and has requested $1 million for
ninety additional officers (annual salaries $15,000) in the 1970 budget;
this had to be refused because of lack of funds. He points out that
extra refuse collection service is provided in high-density or problem
areas. Forty-two percent of the city gets five to six collections per
week and 58 percent gets three collections per week based on these
factors.

Other Departments

Most departments operate with decentralized physical facilities—
police precinct stations, hospitals and health centers, welfare offices,
firehouses, etc. Local superintendents have been given some discretion over operations, but not enough to call it functional decentralization. District police commanders are now held responsible for anything which occurs in their area, and also have more authority. Some
dramatic results have come from this change, but it is still too early
to tell long-term effects.

Lack of resources is not the only reason for poor department
performance. In fact, an unlimited supply of funds might merely
perpetuate the problem. Strong union control, restrictive work rules,
outmoded civil service system, and low employee productivity all
contribute to poor services in most departments.

Mayor's Action Center

The Mayor's Action Center was instituted to improve results
and at least make citizens feel the city cares. As the central office
of complaint and inquiry, it responded to over 300,000 complaints
and inquiries in 1969. Its staff will be reduced from twenty-five to
twelve and merged with the Volunteer Coordinating Council under the
austerity budget.

Director Kate Klein says, "Besides answering complaints, it is
a good psychological concept because citizens feel they have the
Mayor's Office directly and are getting special concern. By merely
saying 'Good morning, Mayor Lindsay's Office,' the effect is created."
She contends, however, that their requests receive about the same
departmental response as those from other sources. "We can assist

in answering individual complaints, but that doesn't solve the basic problem." She points out, for example, that little can be done about requests for housing when there are 200,000 applicants for only 15,000 vacancies.

She indicates that citizens do not get an answer in every case because there are too many inquiries and not enough staff. Use of a computer and form letters has not solved this problem.

Not all complaints are answerable. As many as one-third of the calls received in the center are "opinion" calls in which people merely "get things off their chest." These occur mostly between 6 and 8 p.m., primarily on Friday evenings, when people stop for a few drinks on their way home and conduct gripe sessions. "On Saturday night we get a lot of calls about open hydrants, for example, but don't bother to reply," she states. (See Table 10.)

TABLE 10

Mayor's Action Center Weekly Report,
New York City, May 3-9, 1970

Classification of Calls	Number
Central Complaints	452
Health Department	28
Highways Department	30
Housing Authority	186
Parks Department	20
Police Department	102
Sanitation	232
Sewers Department	38
Traffic Department	13
W.S.G.E. (Water, Sewers, Gas, Electric)	6
Welfare Department	222
Miscellaneous	2,068
Total	3,397

Source: Mayor's Action Center, New York City.

A system called IRMA (Information Referral Manual) has been developed whereby the staff can easily locate the correct agency or department for any type of complaint. It is simply a detailed directory of services and typical requests arranged in the form of a revolving file.

Kate Klein would like to see an effective computerized system developed to improve response, as well as increases in staff and departmental resources, so that all complaints could be effectively handled. However, with the austerity budget in effect, it seems more likely that the already great number of backlogged complaints is destined only to grow larger.

COMMUNITY PLANNING BOARDS

Development

The city charter authorizes community planning boards in sixty-two planning districts for the purpose of assisting in local decisions and providing some coordination of the myriad organizations and agencies. The Citizens Union (a private citizens group organized to evaluate local government) first proposed decentralized planning districts in 1947. They were later endorsed by the City Planning Commission and put into operation, at least in Manhattan, by Borough President Robert Wagner in 1951. The history of this development is significant:

> In 1947, the Citizens Union proposed the division of New York City into districts "for more orderly planning and decentralization of municipal services and community development." The report recommended grouping city services in one location in each district, and proposed that each district develop its own plan in cooperation with the City Planning Commission. In 1950, the City Planning Commission took up the idea and proposed 66 districts as "logical units for the planning of schools, housing, hospitals, libraries, playgrounds, local street systems and other public facilities as well as for consideration of land use and zoning patterns." As Borough President of Manhattan in 1951, Robert Wagner set up a Community Planning Council, consisting of 15 to 20

members, for each of the 12 Manhattan districts suggested by the City Planning Commission. In part, Wagner
did this, because the local political clubs that had been
the source of information and mediation between districts
and the city had largely ceased to function, and administrative agencies increasingly were being overwhelmed by
local groups who took their claims and grievances
directly to city heads. Through these Local Planning
Boards, Wagner sought to set up a mediating mechanism
against the anarchic onslaught of multiple organizations
in the city.[2]

The 1961 city charter authorized planning districts and boards,
and in 1968 the City Planning Commission adopted a map delineating
sixty-two districts which appeared to be related to historic boundaries,
and less relative to political and sociological identifications. The
difficulty in aligning major factors into uniform districts makes the
concept of neighborhood government more complex.

Borough presidents were given until 1968 to appoint boards.
The City Council altered the charter in 1969 to call the community
planning boards simply community boards, increase maximum membership to fifty instead of nine, and increase their scope of concern
from physical planning and capital budgeting to general matters of
welfare and orderly community development. Manhattan and Bronx
borough presidents appointed more active boards; but with little staff,
the boards have been unable to accomplish very much. City departments have not paid much attention to them. Their meetings attract
little attention, the large membership discourages attendance, and
they have mostly reacted to issues rather than initiating their own
ideas.

Until the 1961 charter changes, borough presidents had considerable authority and responsibility for the administration of their
boroughs, such as design and maintenance of streets, sewers, street
signs and traffic signals. They were comparable with mayors within
their range of control. However, charges of partisanship, provincialism, and corruption forced them to cede most of their authority
to the mayor. They are still charged with less important duties,
such as conducting public hearings; developing community planning
boards and borough improvement boards; processing citizen complaints; recommending capital improvement projects; and maintaining
a topographical bureau which concerns itself with street and map
changes, title acquisition, house numbering, establishing street guides
and street lines, and certain other engineering functions. Their

membership on the Site Selection Board and Board of Estimate are
most significant. Land cannot be acquired or disposed of, nor can
capital improvements take place, without their approval.

Composition and Function of Boards

Members of community boards are appointed by borough presidents and generally include professionals and those politically active
in the borough. Councilmen from the district are automatically
members. Queens Borough President Sidney Leviss tries to see that
at least one architect, engineer, and physician are appointed to each
board. Bronx President Robert Abrams, formerly a state assemblyman for four years, introduced an innovation by advertising for
residents who wished to be appointed to the community boards and
other borough committees. He received over 1,000 applications and
held hundreds of interviews to select a board which he felt represented
a good cross-section of the community, including young and old. In
other boroughs membership is not broadly representative.

Abrams has gone a step further and set up borough task forces
in health, education, social services, etc., to deal with local problems
and relate to comparable overall city task forces of the mayor.
"Problems may be endemic to each borough," says Abrams, "and
this is why I feel I need task forces which are advisory directly to
me." His borough faces most urban ills of today.

"The borough president has the mandate of the people, is elected
for four years, and functions in an area of natural boundaries and
identifiable interests," he says. "He has a broad overview of the
entire area which makes his office a natural vehicle to find solutions.
However, it is not being given this attention. The press is unwilling
to come to borough sessions or to give sufficient attention to problems
from a borough point of view, so it is difficult for borough presidents
to reach the people." To attract interest in local problems, under
this strong-mayor government, borough presidents must primarily
use their voting leverage on the Board of Estimate.

Plan for Borough Government

Abrams, in an October, 1970, Plan for Borough and Neighborhood
Government in New York City, cites the city's present efforts at
decentralization as halfway proposals. He recommends that each
community board have thirty-five elected members, with two-year

overlapping terms; form the basis for a single complaint office (plus mobile units for outreach) and for physical, economic, and social planning; be guaranteed a minimum budget for operating and capital outlay; and appoint an executive director responsible to it. He recommends, further, that the Board of Estimate share responsibility for taxation; that school construction be controlled at the borough level; that borough presidents select district superintendents (who would constitute district cabinets) responsible to them as well as community boards; that borough service coordinators be appointed by borough presidents to supervise district superintendents of each service; and that coterminous districts be established (based on census tracts) for all services, including councilmanic districts, which could be made coterminous with one or more community districts.

He suggests further analysis to determine which functions should be decentralized to city, borough, and district levels. According to his plan, there would be service commissioners at the city level to set standards, give technical advice, perform research and evaluation, and administer city-level aspects of programs such as garbage disposal. The City Planning Commision would be abolished, retaining only the staff to advise the mayor on integration of city and regional matters. Comptroller, purchasing, and contracting functions would remain central. In brief, boroughs would assume aspects of cities in a federal system.

The mayor's staff is not in favor of more powerful boroughs. Citizens generally see them as just another layer of government, "like downtown." Citizens changed the charter in 1961 to diminish borough powers because of provincialism and corruption. Many question the desirability of returning to a system which did not work. "Nothing seems to work," they say. Maybe neighborhood government is an answer where boards can work with viable population sizes, relating to one central government. This is the sense of the Plan for Neighborhood Government.

LINDSAY'S PLAN FOR NEIGHBORHOOD GOVERNMENT

Board and Functions

The experience of UATFs and community planning boards and districts has promoted better understanding of decentralized government. In a proposal for a Plan for Neighborhood Government, Mayor Lindsay expresses concern with the fragmentation and frustration of citizen involvement in governmental decision making: "Our city has never had an overall plan for neighborhood government. I believe it is time for the adoption of such a plan for New York to provide a single, coordinated structure in each community—one local forum for debate, one formal channel for direct communication, one city official responsible for monitoring local services." For example, policy boards exist for Head Start, day care, employment, education, community action, Model Cities, and other programs. Under the mayor's plan, one board in each neighborhood would try to coordinate some elements of these programs in addition to assuming some of their own powers.

Board membership for each district would be formed as follows:

1. Mayor, borough president, and district councilman and councilman-at-large would appoint seven members each, for a total of twenty-one

2. District community school board would appoint three

3. Community corporation boards and Model Cities advisory committees would each appoint up to three, in proportion to the total population they serve.

Thus, there would be a minimum of twenty-four members with as many as six additional in areas served by Model Cities and community corporations. Ultimately members could be elected and one "community election day" established for community school boards, community corporations, Model Cities committees, and other neighborhood boards. "The net effect would be to secure greater public awareness of and support for all locally elected bodies," the report states. Borough presidents tend to favor a community election day but would prefer election of community boards from the outset. Elections would give the boards more credence and make it easier to give them greater responsibiliites. In turn, it would make the borough presidents stronger if relatively independent boards with power were under their jurisdictions.

A step toward implementation of the plan occurred by the placement of NCHs, UATFs, Operation Better Block, and the Neighborhood Conservation Bureau under the Office of Neighborhood Government. Under this plan, the task forces, now substituting for citizen participation, would be replaced by community boards. "Only by

combining the two can we build the strongest and most broadly representative neighborhood structure," Lindsay states in his proposal.

In addition to community boards, there would be community
cabinets, chaired by community directors and composed of district
line officials, borough presidents, and councilmen (similar to the
informal "mini-cabinets" now functioning in some areas). Cabinets
would help to coordinate and elicit better performance of departments
through direct communication.

The proposal suggests a community hall for each district, with
offices for staff, councilmen, and the borough president. The mayor
would appoint a community director from a list of five names selected
by the board, with a beginning staff of two persons for each board.
However, borough presidents prefer to appoint community directors.
For example, Abrams visualizes borough presidents as chief executives who would appoint not only community directors but also certain
key district department heads.

The plan does not contemplate a budget increase, but suggests
combining functions into one budget and operation:

Mayor's UATF	$ 600,000
Neighborhood Conservation Bureau	581,000
Borough Improvement Boards	625,000
Community (Planning) Boards	250,000
	$2,056,000

With elimination of UATF offices, this budget is reduced further.

The proposal states that community boards would prepare
annual reports and capital improvement programs, gather essential
information for management purposes, hold public hearings, evaluate
services, and assume responsibilities of departments placed under
their control. The Office of Neighborhood Government would act as
liaison to community boards, supervise redistricting of boundaries,
identify agency resources, and help strengthen neighborhood government.

Need for Coterminous Boundaries

The plan sanctions the present sixty-two community planning
districts; however, none of the boundaries for councilmen, assemblymen, state senators, congressmen, policy and advisory boards,

community action corporations, Model Cities advisory committees, community school boards, city agencies, and departments are coterminous. This is a monumental problem, particularly alignment of political districts.

John Forrer, assistant director in the Bureau of the Budget, says: "Coterminous boundaries for agencies and departments are unlikely. The School Board and many other agencies are not under the mayor's control. This would make it difficult to accomplish." He adds, "Alignment of boundaries would not lead to as much of an improvement in services as more authority for local supervisors over their operations and making them more responsive." Many city officials feel time could be better spent concentrating on department efficiency rather than uniform districting. But it appears that uniformity should be accomplished where possible. Certainly new programs should be placed in logical districts, if nothing more.

Some departments are now being placed in coterminous districts: the Recreation Department, Youth Service Agency, Park Maintenance and Operation, and Mayor's Organizational Task Force for Comprehensive Health Planning. The Office of Neighborhood Government recommends the following steps:

1. Formal designation by the mayor of existing community planning district lines as the basis for neighborhood government, with provisions for modifications of these lines.

2. Mayoral mandate that all programs setting new administrative lines conform to community planning districts or to aggregations or fractions thereof.

3. Establishment of an interagency review team to develop the process by which agency administrative lines are aligned with community planning district lines.

4. Direction of agencies to submit to this interagency review team suggestions for immediate changes to conform some districts to community planning district lines. In certain peninsula areas, such as Washington Heights and the Rockaways, this could be done quickly, with a minimum redistricting for many city agencies. In other areas, certain service lines could be made conforming with a minimum shift.

5. Consolidation by the state and the federal governments of existing program lines to conform to community planning districts

and incorporation in any new legislation of provisions that require
conformity to already existing state and federal programs. If such
provisions had existed, for example, the Model Cities, community
corporations, comprehensive health planning, multiservice center,
and OEO special impact area designations would all have been required
to be related to one another, instead of the present haphazard and
unrelated set of lines that so confuse people and diffuse local efforts.

6. The state and federal governments should be called upon to
provide funding incentives and support for local government units
that take on the task of conforming their administrative boundaries
by redistricting existing municipal agency service lines.

The Plan's Future

To change the legal status, the City Council must prepare a
home rule message for the state legislature, which in turn must enact
it into law. There is considerable speculation and much doubt about
this. Lindsay states, "We must move with deliberation in this area,
taking great care to avoid raising excessive expectations, and maintaining the flexibility to alter and develop our approaches according
to the needs of each neighborhood and the lessons of experience."

A spokesman for the City Council has said, "There's now a
reasonable chance this revamped plan will go through."

Council Majority Leader Thomas J. Cuite, in a June, 1970, issue
of the New York Times stated, "I'm happy that the mayor apparently
responded to legitimate objections of many council members who
feared his little city halls' program would become a series of political
club houses. However, I will not endorse the proposals until the
mayor presents them to us in legislative form."

Queens Borough President Sidney Leviss says, "I would recommend doing away with task forces. They do the same thing as
the Community Boards and are controlled by the mayor, who is too
strong now. I feel Community Boards should be independent of the
mayor. The chairmen of the UATFs are not going to embarrass the
mayor. It takes someone independent of him to scrutinize the executive branch." Leviss believes that citizens with problems prefer to
go to borough presidents, who he says "are the true ombudsmen of
their areas."

In his 1969 annual report, former Queens Borough President
Mario J. Cariello reported that during his term of office, over

100,000 communications from residents were processed and followed up by the Queens Public Services Section in borough hall:

> Call it an ombudsman, or just plain public servant, but
> your borough president has been performing every ser-
> vice to Queens residents that could possibly be offered
> by the mayor's pet project. Queens needs no little city
> halls and it's about time the mayor abandoned this quest.
>
> They supersede the city charter, are an invasion of duly
> established responsibilities, and constitute a raid on the
> taxpayers by wasteful and unnecessary spending of public
> funds for purely political motives.
>
> What's more, they snub the more than 400 civic organi-
> zations that are active in Queens every day of the year,
> and the community planning boards that examine, debate
> and take action on every matter, large and small, affecting
> the people of their borough.

Bell and Held, in the Summer, 1969, issue of Public Interest, profess that Lindsay is building a new political base by "putting black militants on the community action payrolls, tying them in with the UATFs and using them as a battering ram against the older political machines." They say community programs are designed too much for political reasons:

> In short, what the Poverty Program and the Lindsay ad-
> ministration have tended to do is to "place their bets"
> on the militants and activists as the source of new com-
> munity leadership. What may be effective for local poli-
> tical base building is not, however, functional for institu-
> tion-building and strengthening of community ties.[3]

There is a feeling, however, that what is wrong with city government is that the old-style political clubs have been destroyed with no
replacement. As one citizen puts it, "Why deny that Lindsay wants
to create some clubhouse base? At least in the corrupt old days,
one could go down to the neighborhood ward heeler and complain
about some officious bureaucrat downtown." Some observers believe
Lindsay is trying to gain the old clubs' advantage. "What's wrong
with patronage," they ask, "as long as the city is inefficient and
corrupt anyway? And how are you going to attract qualified people
without it? There is a shortage of well-meaning types who want to
go to meetings every night for no apparent reward other than moral

satisfaction. Is that enough motivation to keep a man up late arguing
while neglecting his family?"

But there are those who argue on the other side: patronage and
favors are dispersed inequitably; are unfair to those without clout,
dull the spirit, and are corrupt in themselves. Surely government
can be run better and enough dedicated people found to serve on boards,
even if a system of compensation must be worked out.

With the neighborhood plan, Lindsay has realized that he has to
give a slice of power to other elected officials to get them to go along.
When he tried to grab it all for himself, they balked. Now he must
seek support by a number of schemes. If he gets the assistance of
Council President Sanford D. Garelik, who was his running mate in
the last election, it would assure him eight votes on the Board of
Estimate, sufficient to prevent a two-thirds majority from overriding
his vetoes. This could provide necessary leverage to work a "trade-
off" on specific programs and also could be a strong enough influence
to swing the thirty-seven members of City Council, which also needs
a two-thirds majority to override vetoes. But he cannot count on
Garelik's support.

And it is not only elected officials he must convince. There
are many powerful figures with whom compromises must be made,
such as Albert Shanker of the United Federation of Teachers (UFT);
City Comptroller Abe Beame, who has been fighting Lindsay's
spending policies lately; David Rockefeller of the Chase Manhattan
Bank; Alex Rose of the Liberal Party; and many more. He must
resolve differences among community corporations and Model Cities
committees. And the real interplay is among unions and various
entrenched bureaucracies.

The UFT, various uniformed service unions, (sanitation, fire,
and police) and the Building Trades Council are very powerful and
will have to be convinced about any local government which might
interfere with established rights. Lindsay has been unable to gain
control of day-to-day work in certain key departments, such as Personnel, Purchase, and Real Estate which run rather independently.
He has been able to shift the Bureau of the Budget to his direction,
but it is controlled internally by conservatives who drag their feet
on human resource expenditures. Neighborhood government may not
fare any better.

A December 7, 1970, report of the mayor to citizens relates
that a series of over 200 meetings with representatives of over 3,000
community groups drew the following conclusions:

1. There is strong support for neighborhood government.

2. In almost every community a remarkable "informal" system of neighborhood government already exists, consisting of civic and block associations, parish councils, fraternal organizations, advisory boards, etc.

3. People identify with and commit themselves most strongly to their own neighborhoods. They view borough government as just another "downtown."

4. Community boards need more power if they are to be a major improvement over the present system of advisory planning boards.

5. Legislation is needed to give neighborhood government legitimacy, certainty, and a precise legal framework for a more effective system of community boards.

6. While legislation is pending, a pilot program should be undertaken to test alternatives.

7. Neighborhood government, to be effective, must meet the following needs:

a. Greater accessibility of physical facilities at one neighborhood location in each community, and perhaps with one phone number.

b. Greater accessibility of key officials, to overcome the feeling that technical experts are running the lives of residents, and to offer greater accountability for deficiencies and mistakes.

c. Greater authority for local government officials to eliminate the feeling that nothing can be done because all decisions are made "downtown."

Reservations to the mayor's plan centered on the need to change certain boundaries to make all areas coterminous with city service districts; the proposed method of selecting board members; and the absence of residence requirements for board members. Suggestions were made to give boards a stronger role in selection of community directors and more power in general; enlarge staffs; increase number of local offices; and require key officials to attend community cabinet meetings. In brief, citizens want strong local participation; however, it may not come about unless borough presidents are given additional strength too.

On citizen participation and decentralization Philip Finkelstein, deputy city administrator, says, "Decentralization is not a panacea in itself. I'm interested in it to the extent that it improves the delivery of services." He adds, "Most people are alienated and frustrated, not so much because they want to make decisions themselves but because they want decisions that affect their well-being to be implemented, even if they are other people's decisions. It's not that you can't fight city hall that upsets people—you can fight city hall (and win), but nothing happens anyway." Although he is concerned about the creation of more layers of bureaucracy, he stresses that he is still in accord with the Plan for Neighborhood Government.

In community hearings to discuss the plan, additional power for boards was recommended (besides assuming responsibilities of the agencies placed under their control) if they were to function more as neighborhood governments:

1. Assignment of meter maids; housing and building inspectors; sanitation, health, and consumer affairs inspectors.

2. Issuance of summons for violations of health, environmental pollution, sanitation, and housing codes.

3. Participation in determining priorities and resources, and in allocating personnel for street sweeping, refuse collection, and trash pickup.

4. Participation in selection and evaluation of local supervisors.

5. Responsibility for determining expenditure priorities for trees, lighting, and street repairs.

HUMAN RESOURCES ADMINISTRATION

Background and Functions

One objective of UATFs is to coordinate agencies and departments which now act independently. The Human Resources Administration (HRA) was established in September, 1966, also to coordinate many disconnected projects falling under its jurisdiction, to centralize administration of the attack on poverty, to eliminate duplication, and to concentrate action where it is most needed.

Its reorganization was recommended by a study group headed
by Mitchell Sviridoff, then executive director of the community action
program in New Haven, and later appointed the first administrator
of HRA. In December, 1967, he was succeeded by Mitchell I. Ginsberg,
who was succeeded by Jule Sugarman in 1970.

The following agencies were brought under HRA's direction:
Department of Social Services, Community Development Agency (CDA),
Manpower and Career Development Agency, Youth Services Agency,
Addiction Services Agency, and Office of Education Affairs. The 1970
budget request is $1,945,200,000 of which $560,400,000 are city funds,
$828,700,000 federal funds, and $520,100,000 state funds.

The city contributes 27 percent to the total HRA program and
53 percent to the Council Against Poverty (CAP) locally determined
(versatile) program, a ratio which compares favorably with the 20
percent local contributions to versatile programs in Chicago, Los
Angeles, and Detroit. Most cities make their contributions by in-kind
services, while New York contributes in cash. In the past year HRA
expended over $1.6 billion, of which $1.52 billion was spent by the
Department of Social Services on public assistance grants and medical
assistance to persons on welfare. The remaining $155 million was
spent on other departments under HRA which work with problems of
poverty. It is estimated that about 2 million New Yorkers (one-fourth
of the city's population) fall within poverty limits.

The central staff of CDA—some 488 persons, working with a
budget of $5.6 million—formulates policies, provides administrative
supportive services, and helps integrate the operations of its agencies;
but it does not operate programs. The central staff is part of city
government, while in most cities it is independent. Ginsberg feels
this is an advantage, for it provides increased influence over programs
yet gives poverty residents greater identification with and trust in
public agencies and the city. "They have a growing sense that their
problems are being taken seriously by the 'establishment,'" he said
in a statement to a special committee of the City Council in February,
1969.

Ginsberg reinforces the concept of central administration in the
report: "I remain convinced of the absolute necessity for comprehensive planning, centralized management, decentralized delivery of
services and community participation."

CDA helps coordinate roles of community corporations and
assists CAP (the community action board). This council is composed

of fifty-one members, of whom twenty-five are chosen by residents of poverty areas, seventeen designated public officials, and nine chosen by designated citywide civic groups. City councilmen may automatically become members of community corporations within their districts. There are twenty-five community corporations serving a clientele of 200,000 persons in twenty-five poverty areas. All of HRA's programs serve a poverty group of over 760,000 persons within a much larger population area.

The community corporations held elections in 1967, 1968, and 1970 but turnouts were usually below 10 percent of registrations. Programs have been the usual recreation, job referral, and tenant organizing. New leadership developed that otherwise would not have come forth in the established bureaucratic and political environments, and much credit is given to corporations for "cool" summers. They have involved substantial numbers of poor people in the decision-making process and have developed a new middle class.

Ginsberg reports that CAP has 50 percent representation of poor, while most other cities have only 33 percent of the poor on the central policy-making board. He adds that in New York "eighty percent of local initiative programs are run by governmental, non-traditional social agencies. In Los Angeles this is 34 percent, Chicago 10 percent, and Detroit 2 percent."

The total budget for central staff, community corporations, 280 delegate agencies and other related programs is $64 million. Full-time staff of these programs is 7,061 and part-time staff is 7,415, of which 80 percent are poverty-area residents. The programs also involve some 6,500 community people in advisory roles on boards or in projects. To improve performance and management techniques, personnel are now selected through the merit service system, which has been revamped to accept persons of less traditional qualifications.

Multiservice System

HRA has been working closely with Model Cities in developing a multiservice system, to consist of a citywide network of community facilities with a large community service center at the hub of each system. Subsidiary units called multiservice centers would serve a maximum of 50,000 persons, and smaller units called multi-purpose centers would serve 25,000 people. All units would work in conjunction with each other and would link the system with similar services in other neighborhoods. The centers are being planned, generally, within walking distance of residents and near natural centers of community life. The Hunts Point multiservice center was the pilot project begun in the fall of 1967. HRA has requested a 1969-70 budget of $47 million for the system.

CDA developed the original concept of multiservice centers in New York City because no system was available whereby agencies could work together on the varied problems of individuals or families. Studies showed that teachers, probation officers, and housing project employees, for example, might all be involved in separate aspects of an individual's problem, but nowhere was concern given to the total human being or the whole family.

Physical design of multiservice centers aims at creating an informal, noninstitutional atmosphere where "discussion over a cup of coffee rather than interrogation at a desk may serve as a hallmark of the New York approach."

There are presently six centers in operation or in program development stages: Hunts Point, Brownsville, East Harlem, Central Harlem, Bushwick, and Corona-East Elmhurst. Federal grants of $3.1 million for Central Harlem and $2.9 million for East Harlem were the highest approved in the nation. Services are typical of most community action programs, including few traditional city hall functions; however, NCHs and UATFs have taken up some of this slack, particularly in handling city complaints. Services in the multiservice centers are in the following areas:

1. Central staff services
2. Family planning
3. Family care
4. Family day care
5. Parent and child center
6. Youth services
7. Assistance to ex-offenders
8. Education and school decentralization
9. Comprehensive health planning and care
10. Mental health
11. Mental retardation
12. Manpower training
13. Economic development
14. Housing sponsorship
15. Code enforcement
16. Rodent control.

Citizen Participation and Citizen Boards

The Kerner Commission Report (National Commission on Civil Disorders) of 1968 indicated that no matter how comprehensive and systematic the operations of a multiservice center may become, it may not do its job effectively. In the same vein, HRA states, "The multiservice center may never accomplish its mission, unless community residents, themselves, somehow make it more real than simply a more convenient collection of various programs." The Kerner Commission Report further states:

> Ghetto residents increasingly believe that they are excluded from the decision-making process which affects their lives and community. This feeling of exclusion, intensified by the bitter legacy of racial discrimination, has engendered a deep seated hostility toward the institutions of government. It has severely compromised the effectiveness of programs intended to provide improved services to ghetto residents.

In the New York City program, HRA Associate Director Tino Calabria, assigned as liaison to the Model Cities program, reports that residents have been extensively involved in planning and program development of the centers. He cites the Brownsville multiservice center, where the community grappled with questions of personnel and space allocations and were forced to come to grips with concrete limitations that then strengthened the community's ability to deal with more overriding questions—questions related to existing neighborhood services and setting of program priorities in light of limited space and dwindling future resources. Services and priorities in most centers were determined through a citizen process.

In Brownsville, he reports, a joint committee representing both antipoverty and Model Cities boards "succeeded in setting a standard for the kind of working cooperation necessary between two such community participation structures." The same process was followed in East Harlem and Central Harlem.

More recently, in the Model Cities program, citizens have charged that the spirit of maximum feasible participation had been violated in development of Model Cities plans, and that few citizens were allowed an opportunity to review and understand them. There were charges that everyone was given some Model Cities money except community corporations, and that CAP representatives were being bypassed. It was indicated that the multiservice center citizen participation structure tended to become separate from CAP and Model Cities boards and resulted in triplication of citizen participation and "jockeying" for recognition which has hampered comprehensive planning.

In a report on community action in Model Cities in May, 1969, Calabria stated, "Situations of this kind only underline the fact that most localities cannot long afford to be repeatedly experimented with through one 'innovation' after another—with a separate citizen participation structure for each program. Public resources and neighborhood energies become gradually depleted through endless rounds of campaigning and elections and then through conflicts between competing groups thus structured in the same community." He feels it is more advantageous to maximize funds earmarked for new urban programs by utilizing them as additional resources for strengthening and broadening existing citizen participation structures and their programs.

Policy boards for Head Start, day care, schools, and other programs have also been formed, causing further proliferation. And now the federal government has ruled that programs under Title I of the Elementary and Secondary Education Act must have local citizen advisory boards. The NCH and UATF structure has not caused serious confusion because citizen boards have been very informally organized, allowing membership from any neighborhood group. The proposed neighborhood plan, however, may complicate matters, even though it is designed to coalesce many different groups into some form of control mechanism.

An agreement in November, 1968 between HUD and OEO urged eventual consolidation of CAP and Model Cities policy boards and exchange of staff representatives in areas where they both operate. The boards have not been consolidated, but there has been a good degree of interchange of staff. Much of the blame for the proliferation of governing bodies and the confusion of control must be laid at the doorstep of the federal government. Combining boards with different levels of citizen power is difficult; therefore, a new approach such as the proposed Plan for Neighborhood Government and the concept of one community board to represent each area may be a way out of the frustration.

"You can't put an apple and an orange together," says Bernard Shiffman, former HRA deputy administrator of planning and research. "The degree of citizen participation in OEO is higher and more definitive than the advisory role in HUD's interpretation. The Council

Against Poverty can't be overridden in its allocation of funds, which is a right given to them by the mayor. Because Model Cities is a broader package which includes interlocking unions, labor relations, different educational systems, etc., responsibilities necessarily are greater." He feels, however, that Model Cities and CAP will eventually merge as a necessity. "One or the other of the departments will come out on top and merger will occur," he believes.

Ginsberg believed it more likely that the two policy boards of Model Cities and HRA would continue as separate entities but that they would meet together on key programs to reach agreement, then delegate a third agency to operate programs.

Judge Joseph Williams, administrator of Model Cities, does not see it in competition with CAP at all. He says, "We are not an operating agency. Tensions will be reduced when we allow Community Corporations and others to operate programs designated by us."

Neither are NCHs in competition with Model Cities, Williams believes. He says NCHs are complaint clearinghouses and monitoring agents for Model Cities and other programs. "NCH is sitting right down in the center of the community and not connected with others; therefore, it can evaluate more independently," he states.

Program Funding

Competing boards dramatize competition for funds. Cutbacks in OEO and higher costs have made it necessary to eliminate some programs. Model Cities was somewhat forced by logic to consider appropriating $1 million for the community action program in the three Model Cities areas because the programs were needed. This funding never took place. CDA Commissioner Major Owens attacked Model Cities for its inability to spend allocated money and blamed them for not giving his agency some of the surplus.

UATFs could also be competing for money. Shiffman points out the dangers in stimulating demands without financial resources to fill them. "How do you keep your budget down and respond to these increased demands?" he asks. "If you send out a whole bunch of people to stimulate a desire for service, you must have the system that's capable of delivering it or there will be an explosion. If you send out a task force in drug addiction and they all come back and request treatment centers the city can't deliver, they say, 'Look, commissioner, so and so doesn't respond.' Then the mayor chews him out and he gets upset and doesn't respond to the task force any-more."

Shiffman does believe the UATF program is worthwhile. "Neigh-borhood City Halls don't deliver any services. They depend on the agencies and I think that's great," he says. "The closer people are to the place where they can complain and put heat on, the more responsive the bureaucracy becomes. You get a more humane system.

"Neighborhood City Halls are excellent for communication be-cause you get a signal long before a problem becomes a crisis and you have a possibility for correction. It gives you some running room."

THE MODEL CITIES PROGRAM

Reorganization of Model Cities

The $65 million Model Cities program operates in three areas—South Bronx, Bedford-Stuyvesant, and East Harlem. The recently reorganized Model Cities Advisory Board (policy board) has rep-resentation from each program; the directors are ex-officio mem-bers. In addition, union, business, and agency representatives, as well as others, have been proposed. The final number and composition is still undetermined, and the board has not met since proposed in August, 1970. The previous board consisted of key city officials appointed by the mayor from HRA, CAP, Bureau of the Budget, the Housing and Development Administration, and the New York City Housing Authority. Residents had representation on the three neigh-borhood boards, formed by a combination of elections and appoint-ments. Since the control board was weak, residents had strong con-trol of programs and policy, although local boards were decidedly middle-class and had little electoral participation. Many members had become disgruntled with or had been rejected by community corporation boards.

There was gerrymandering of districts to form certain groups and pressure from ad hoc personnel committees to appoint particular directors. The Bar Association report indicates that the central Model Cities staff, with some assistance from neighborhood staff but no contact with citizen policy committees, wrote the original three proposals which were shown to neighborhood policy committees on one day, presented to the Board of Estimate for its approval the next day, and submitted to Washington. There was a rush to get a large piece of federal pie, and little citizen contribution.

Eventually, local boards developed considerable power, but the intent of reorganization is to centralize much of this authority. Administrator Joseph Williams does not believe Model Cities should be decentralized in the sense that local boards should have autonomous power. "I am not for local control," he says, "but I am for local participation." He wants to see a very simple centralized structure with sufficient interchange to localized boards—a system which gives local residents the advantage of more experienced persons from a representative citywide board—something he feels has been lacking to date and, as a result, has given the program a very limited point of view. Local policy committees would perform planning functions and choose programs for their own neighborhoods, passing this information on to the main policy board.

The New York Model Cities program had not been moving as rapidly as desirable and some new mechanism was needed to pull diverse groups together and "get it off dead center." Williams, with his prestige and leadership as a former judge, was expected to provide this. Former Model Cities executive secretary, Eugenia Flatow, and local directors were on a horizontal level, all reporting directly to the mayor. Now, directors report to Williams, the overall administrator. This change was intended to provide stronger control but, long accustomed to independence, local directors resist taking direction.

Some strength has been injected into Model Cities since it became a separate administration, similar to HRA and the other "superagencies." It previously was directed from the Mayor's office by a six-person policy-making committee which was to decide policy questions. But so seldom was it called upon that its members became aggravated and disinterested. "It became really almost a joke and everyone knew it was," says Michael Ainslee, formerly a private consultant to the program. "They knew they were a rubber stamp and that it was not feasible to run a program of this size without an administrator with some power. That's why the present administrator sits in the mayor's supercabinet, which enables him to get more things accomplished." However, even Director Williams' prestigious leadership is finding it difficult to make a significant difference. In the first action grant year (1969-70) only a few million dollars of the $65 million were spent. By January, 1971, about $30 million was expended. In April, 1971, the second action grant year was approved by HUD, even though progress has been slow. It has been difficult

for Model Cities to improve behavior of the complex system of
departments in New York. It has had little clout, and little assistance
from city agencies, and thus has been unable to progress very far to
date.

Citizen Participation in Model Cities

Citizen participation has been more successful. According to
the original leaders, this has been because development of effective
neighborhood groups was the prime order of business in the beginning.
Citizen boards have always had considerable strength, and the most
Flatow could do was negotiate with them. "If they could not be persuaded to go along with a program, as presented, for practical reasons, we didn't adopt that program," she says of the citizen boards.
The Bar Association report on decentralization states, "Partly as a
legacy of the community action experience, maintaining city hall
control over Model Cities funds (that the statute permitted) was in
1967 literally not conceivable."

Judge Williams, being both male and black, may command more
neighborhood discipline, but Flatow feels this may not be a successful
approach. She says, "They need to have control over planning decisions or the thing would be meaningless because decentralizing services is only a first step, but making programs more responsive to
needs as the neighborhood sees them is a necessary second step.
If you don't do both, you are not strengthening your institutions. If
the neighborhood continues to fight the institutions delivering the services, perception of service is necessarily dark and perception of
improvements poor." Williams may be actually in a weaker position
than Flatow, without any real constituency and bargaining power.

Model Cities and the UATFs

Model cities and the UATFs apparently do not conflict. Flatow
believes that during the initial development years, UATFs were
primarily crisis-oriented toward keeping peace and did not relate
closely to Model Cities. Now they do, however, because they constitute
a day-to-day operation for letting agencies know what needs to be done
in a neighborhood. "Model Cities has a planning function requiring
a longer-range view. It needs all the information the task forces
can produce, including reasons why agencies cannot respond and what
corrective steps are necessary to make them more responsive.
Model Cities can provide some of the resources and leverage necessary
to assist the task forces," she says.

PURPOSES OF DECENTRALIZATION

The UATFs, community action program, and Model Cities are all involved, in some way, in decentralizing services and in transferring varying degrees of power to local residents. What form decentralization should take and how much power neighborhoods should have are key issues.

Deputy City Administrator Finkelstein, who cautions against expecting too much from decentralization per se, says:

> We need to know the kinds of functions that are best performed at what levels and be less concerned about "power input to the neighborhood" and similar fashionable rhetoric. There is a deliberate "cop-out" from the tough questions involved. For example, in the school decentralization question, nobody at any time ever demonstrated or tried to demonstrate that more locally-oriented schools were inherently better.

> I would submit that the lady with five kids in Bedford-Stuyvesant who is living in a really rotten rat hole would rather not get involved and have a decent apartment than get involved and still not have a decent apartment. Most residents feel getting involved is not in itself all that exciting. Most people don't have time to get involved. It's usually the guy with time on his hands, or the pensioner or political activist.

The concern about local activists is also mentioned by Bell and Held:

> What unites all of Harlem is essentially an anger at "The Man," and groups compete in utilizing and exacerbating this anger. The new activists, thus, have no authority, but they do have power: the power to interfere, to raise hell, to shut things down.

> There are different groups of activists, each of whom has staked out a claim on an issue. If you want to open a business in Harlem—you go to the Harlem Chamber of Commerce, or to Roy Innis of CORE, and clear it with them. If you want to appoint a principal of a school, you go to another group. The Harlem Architects Committee

(ARCH), which led the fight against Columbia's intention
to build a gymnasium in Morningside Park, has no constituency, but it has the ability, as do many of the multi-
favor groups in Harlem, to put any outsider on the spot.[4]

Power already exists to varying degrees in most New York
communities. Model Cities boards, community action boards, the
1,200 welfare organizations and tens of thousands of nongovernmental
groups which operate in New York all have some power or influence.
The question is whether this power can be made viable by a group
that is acceptable to both the community and the establishment.
Even if neighborhood governments have power, they will still be
subordinate to city and state governments, which retain preeminent
powers of taxation and allocation of resources.

Kristol and Weaver point out the barriers to neighborhood control:

It will be the restraint of the citywide majority—which,
in New York, will for a long time remain a white, middle
and lower-income majority. No more perfect script for
perpetual civil conflict can be imagined. These people
may be willing to give the ghetto control over its own
housing, in a spirit of apartheid. But, despite any original
promises, will they be so obliging about education? Anyone who really thinks that this majority will cheerfully
pay taxes so that black nationalism (with its inevitable
racist overtones) can be taught in ghetto schools is being
unworldly, to put it mildly.

In the last analysis, then, what is really interesting about
decentralization in New York is not reform itself, but
rather that its liberal publicists and supporters embraced
it without giving it even as much thought as the average
graduate student does to the choice of a wife.[5]

Dr. Seymour Mann, director of the Department of Local Government Affairs, Hunter College, New York City, expresses serious
concern that the neighborhood boards, visualized as local policy
makers, are to be composed of representatives from the executive
as well as the legislative branches. This may mean, he fears, that
they will never be given a true transfer of legal authority for local
policy determination. Despite this possibility, Lewis Feldstein
believes the division of power might still prove acceptable to most
local groups and elected officials, and that the important thing is to

establish the boards now, if only experimentally, and hold elections later.

Strong feelings persist that absolute power should never go to local boards or back to borough presidents, for fear that the same provincialism and ineptness which forced the 1961 charter revisions may again prevail. In fact, one of the reasons for the present neighborhood government proposal is to examine the raison de'être of borough government altogether.

And there are also feelings that continuous restructuring of government ("every ten years") may not necessarily improve it, but may instead overshadow other, more important issues. Recently, Dr. David B. Hertz, vice-chairman of the Mayor's Operations Research Council, and staff member Adam Walinsky proposed abandoning the superagencies, restoring many operating departments to their pre-superagency status, and regrouping them under four deputy mayors in a way that better expresses the programmatic priorities of the city. The proposal is intended to improve coordination and allow more flexible utilization of resources, but there is skepticism over whether it would be successful. Administrative or political decentralization may be more important.

Functional decentralization of limited scope exists in New York for some services. For example, community action corporations exercise almost complete local autonomy in the operation of social welfare programs; Model Cities funds decentralized housing enforcement personnel and emergency repairmen; local school boards have a high degree of autonomy; police precincts, branch libraries, health centers, street and refuse operations, and many other city programs are physically decentralized, with varying degrees of independent district authority. The physical decentralization has generally proved to be more efficient, productive, time-saving, and apt to provide greater neighborhood responsiveness. A more difficult consideration is decentralization of authority. Whether placing greater authority in the hands of district superintendents or giving decision-making power to local citizen councils will improve services varies from situation to situation. Already many citizen planning boards exist with varying levels of power and success, some of which have already been discussed: sixty-two community planning boards; twenty-five community action corporations; thirty health advisory boards; local groups participating in housing and urban renewal activities in twenty areas (there are sixty membership organizations in the Morningside Urban Renewal Council, for example); three local Model Cities boards; seventy-six police precinct citizen councils set up to

promote recreational and social events; numerous youth service
advisory boards; thirty-two school districts with local boards; advisory
boards for day care and Head Start, and proposed boards for implementation of Title I of the Elementary and Secondary Education
Act.

Degrees of responsibility and authority vary with district superintendents, as well. In most cases, department heads are able to
delegate significant authority to their superintendents. For example,
Police Commissioner Patrick Murphy has placed responsibility for
eliminating police corruption in the hands of each precinct captain.
Street and refuse superintendents, health directors, school principals,
and other agency heads have local responsibilities now but could be
given increased authority over productivity, economy, neighborhood
appearance, citizen communication, etc. They could also be made
accountable to neighborhood councils for greater responsiveness.

The Bar Association's decentralization study ponders whether
decentralization would improve service quality, whether efficiency
would be lost, and whether performance would vary from district to
district. It concludes that either administrative (functional) or political
(territorial) decentralization would tend to improve city government.
The study suggests functional decentralization for social services
(employment, training, day care, old age, etc.); outpatient health;
trash collection and street cleaning; education through high school;
and some aspects of housing, such as development, maintenance,
relocation, and environmental control, but not land use. Some experimental police programs would be decentralized, such as controlling
gambling and prostitution, community courts, domestic relations,
drugs, rehabilitation, etc. There are also other logical areas: public
land and parks, recreation and library facilities, sidewalks, lighting,
parking regulations, and planning.

Development of work standards and some central controls would
be needed to control abuses. For both administrative and political
decentralization the report recommends thirty-five to forty-five second-
tier districts, each containing 150,000 to 200,000 persons, coterminous
with as many departments and agencies as possible. The present
sixty-two community districts would be used as a base to consolidate
into the smaller number. Boundary changes would have to be made
to achieve uniformity with the seventy-five police precincts (sixteen
divisions), fifty-eight sanitation districts (eleven borough commands),
thirty health districts, forty-four social service centers, and thirty-
two school districts.

Under political decentralization, local boards would be smaller than the present fifty-member community board in order to attract members and create more effective dialogue. Each board would have an elected or appointed chief executive. Boards would not have exclusive or autonomous powers over all aspects of the functions mentioned. Taxing powers, fiscal control, purchasing, key aspects of union negotiations, most aspects of the personnel system, and overall city planning would be retained by the higher tier of government. As a practical matter, the report recommends retention of the Board of Estimate, which would perform borough-wide fiscal and policy decision making outside the scope of multiple provincial boards.

Public comments on the report indicate that it may go too far in shifting power to local groups and may cause further splintering of an already diffused government. But some believe it would be best to concentrate power in local boards in order to consolidate and more effectively coordinate the many local organizations. Most of the Bar Association's concepts are sound, and its alternative suggestion to try a few pilot programs may be the most acceptable approach. As described earlier, the city is now experimenting in six pilot areas.

ANALYSIS AND RECOMMENDATIONS

The analysis and recommendations are made in anticipation that they will assist in the further discussion of neighborhood government for New York.

Budget Cuts and a Fresh Start

Citizens do not fully participate in government if their only involvement occurs at election time every four years. Participation must be a continual process if alienation is to be reduced, the image of government improved, and services bettered. Particularly where government performance has deteriorated, responsible citizen groups working in partnership with city officials may be invigorating. NCHs, UATFs, and the Plan for Neighborhood Government have been worthy experiments in this direction.

Although New York's fiscal crisis has caused disbanding of local task force offices, no less effort should be made to strengthen development of the six community boards under the Neighborhood Action Program. Cutbacks in the UATF program were almost a necessity, since basic services were also cut at the same time. Perhaps to

dramatize the city's financial condition to Governor Nelson Rockefeller
and the New York State Legislature, Mayor Lindsay cut one of his
favorite programs. It appears this may be a blessing, because now
the city's limited resources and the attention of its officials can be
concentrated in a few remaining areas. Unplanned neighborhood
government in fifty or sixty-two districts could be a nightmare.

Confusion, misunderstanding of purpose, and political entangle-
ment in initial decentralization attempts welcome a fresh start. Any
disenchantment from areas which do not have Neighborhood Action
Program offices can be held to a minimum if, instead of allocating
greater resources to these areas, community boards are given
decision-making authority over their fair share of citywide allocated
resources. It is commendatory that the City Council and Board of
Estimate have increased the 1971 action program decision-making
allocation by 33 percent (from $3 million to $4 million) for the existing
six boards.

An End to Political Game-Playing

With more cooperation between executive and legislative branches,
real progress may now occur, for it is important that the legislature
share in the fruits of successful decentralization; otherwise, the
concept will never get very far and the political turmoil which so
marked its history will continue, not only to the disadvantage of the
mayor but to the misfortune of New York's citizens. Where the
legislative majority is assured, as it is with Mayor Richard Daley
in Chicago, the city treasury can be used to tighten one's political
grasp, but this is unlikely in cities where political philosophies are
quite different. Building "clubhouses" in the political milieu of New
York (or Boston) can only lead to delay and limited success, at best.
New York may be able to accomplish more with its six local boards
and nonpartisan approach than with its previous comprehensive and
too political program.

"But it takes political clout and patronage to run big cities!"
The old-style political clubs that have been destroyed and not replaced
are beginning to be missed in some circles. At least in the corrupt
old days, this camp believes, one could go to the ward heeler and
complain about some officious bureaucrat downtown. For a while
Lindsay hoped to use this approach but soon realized he had to slice
his power with councilmen and borough presidents. Is there clear
evidence that it does take patronage to run a government? Chicago's
machinery runs smoothly for much more elaborate reasons than

patronage, including favorable revenues and state assistance as well
as Mayor Daley's personal abilities to achieve unity among diverse
groups. Without patronage Los Angeles runs well and corruption-
free, with services comparable with or better than Chicago's. In
place of patronage, what New York and other big cities need are
impartial neighborhood ombudsmen with authority and ability to get
the job done.

Continued Role of City Officials

Some aspects of the present program ought to be continued,
such as the fifty UATF chairmen and their local committees. They
have contributed a valuable service and can continue to do so even
without local offices. As part of the obligation of city service, key
officials should welcome taking a leading role in neighborhood life,
receiving information firsthand, assisting in developing a government
formula that works, and resolving neighborhood problems. The concept is fundamentally sound, and we have witnessed better chairmen
making progress. In the evolution of neighborhood government,
chairmen would continue as advisors to community boards.

Neighborhood Government

In the various plans for neighborhood government, a number of
similarities are evident. Mayor Lindsay, Borough President Abrams,
the Association of the Bar of the City of New York Decentralization
Study Committee, and many citizen groups favor decentralization
through strong community boards with power to appoint executive
directors and eventually some district superintendents, authority for
local planning and capital budgeting, and control over some functions.
Planning districts, or a consolidation of some, would be used as
boundaries for local government. There appears to be concurrence
in the need for minimum operating and capital budgets and eventual
election of boards. Key reservations are the role of borough government and the extent of board power.

Ideally, New York would function more effectively with a two-
tier system—general and neighborhood government. An additional
layer of borough bureaucracy is unnecessary and, from its earlier
experience of inefficiency and corruption, undesirable. Tighter controls could prevent corruption, but it would be hard to deal effectively
with a middle layer of government. As a practical matter, however,
many constituents look to borough government for responsiveness

and, most importantly, it would be difficult to devise any new organizational scheme without borough presidents' approval.

There is a very meaningful and desirable role for borough presidents. Rather than increasing their operating authority over departments, which would only tend to make government more cumbersome, they should become full-fledged ombudsmen, with these responsibilities spelled out in the City Charter. The city needs institutional change more than basic government reorganization. Already borough presidents admit to being the "true ombudsmen" of their boroughs. They have independence, tenure, high rank, and salary. Only specific subpoena and investigating powers are needed to put them on a par with their Scandinavian counterparts. Instead of running departments, although their present responsibilities would be retained, they would demand changes of the executive, creating a more favorable balance of powers. The chief executive would retain his leadership strength but would be invigorated by intense evaluation. In addition, positions of borough presidents would be strengthened and central government's diminished with restructuring of community boards and the development of neighborhood government.

Power of Community Boards

Neighborhood government may eventually call for the election of community boards. Presently, shared appointment by the mayor, borough presidents, and councilmen can get the program started; however, better balance would be achieved if at least 50 percent of the board were chosen by consensus (polling) techniques. If formal elections are eventually held and a single community election day fails to turn out a respectable number of voters or machine politics dominates the electorate, selection by consensus (independently administered) may prove preferable.

Neighborhood government should have limited powers; otherwise, central government will face the proliferation of dozens of autonomous units with as many viewpoints and bureaucracies. Streamlining government means simultaneously improving services and getting citizens meaningfully involved. Local power should be directed primarily at poorly operated services and other carefully selected areas where it could do the most good. Second, it should prevail over programs which are strictly local in nature, and only third should it have a place in projects broader in scope.

In New York, sanitation, police, social services, code enforcement, and some other services need special attention. Items of more local concern are neighborhood parks, recreational facilities, branch libraries, parking control, planning, and capital outlay budgeting. Finally, planning and capital budgeting must be correlated with city-wide efforts.

More difficult than deciding which functions to decentralize is deciding where control should be placed. To create new levels of government for systems of personnel, finance, purchasing, auditing, contract negotiation, and taxing is unsound. Basic housekeeping authority should be centrally maintained; otherwise, local boards will spend most of their time dealing in routine, unproductive matters. And because they would be held legally responsible under this arrangement, they could not cast aside these matters lightly.

Examination of community corporations and Model Cities committees will clearly verify the time-consuming nature of their functions. Better that local boards concern themselves with selecting and evaluating key district personnel, negotiating union work rules and incentive pay (but not base salaries), local program policy and evaluation, departmental investigatory responsibility, local budget and capital outlay allocations, zoning and land use, and local planning and its necessary citywide integration. Community boards should specialize in techniques for improving government and two-way communication under an existing flexible framework. Preferably, effort should be spent on things which most legislative bodies cannot find time to do or are unwilling to confront.

Because of possible conflict with one man/one vote rulings and because city government should retain the ability to comprehensively and fairly allocate resources and rule the city, decisions should be subject to review by general government. Most decisions would not reach the review stage, but when necessary, such capability should exist and be exercised by both executive and legislative branches within their existing jurisdictions. To reverse local decisions, a two-thirds legislative majority and more stringent than usual administrative procedures should be required. Special projects or portions of departmental operations could be subcontracted to local government with full operating responsibilities on a district-by-district basis.

Continued Pilot Program

To proceed at this time with the pilot Neighborhood Action Program in six areas means conducting a worthwhile experiment without requiring charter changes, but merely executive order and legislative cooperation. In fact, almost all the items described above can be done by delegation of administrative authority and cooperation of borough presidents. And with executive and legislative branches sharing board appointments, partisan political conflict is weakened. It is weakened still further if boards are allowed to select neighborhood staff. This approach to executive and legislative unity, plus the reasonable and significant involvement of the community, are important steps forward for New York.

The following is a summary of recommendations:

1. The fifty UATF chairmen and their local committee structures should be continued at this time, to assist in resolving neighborhood problems. Some local office staff should be obtained from Model Cities and community action programs, as has been done in other cities. Selection of local staff should be done by structured community boards which would eventually absorb UATFs.

2. Borough presidents should not be given increased operational authority over departments; rather, they should function as ombudsmen with subpoena and investigatory powers to create a more favorable balance of government and to improve services.

3. Government should be decentralized according to the New York Bar Association's decentralization report to thirty-five to forty consolidated districts of viable operational and roughly equal size.

4. At this time, membership of community (district) boards, including those under the Neighborhood Action Program, may be determined by shared appointment of the mayor, borough presidents, and councilmen; preferably, a method of community consensus should be used. Eventually, a combination of election and community consensus may be most appropriate.

5. The power of community boards should be directed first at poorly operated services; second, at local functions; and third, at those broader in scope. Basic systems of personnel, finance, purchasing, auditing, contract negotiation, and taxing should not be empowered locally. Boards should concern themselves primarily with selection of key district personnel; evaluation of programs; and local planning, zoning, and budgeting matters. Decisions of local boards should be subject to review by city government.

6. A newly sponsored group or an existing citizen organization should undertake a role similar to the Chicago Better Government Association, which investigates, brings suit, and uses other means

to improve government. The city itself should consider providing
funds for borough presidents or a city-sponsored agency (different
from internal investigating units which concentrate on bribes and
corruption) to investigate and bring suit against improperly functioning
civil service units, restrictive work rules, services of low productivity,
and other matters.

NOTES

1. John V. Lindsay, The City (New York: W. W. Norton & Co.,
1969), p. 111.

2. Daniel Bell and Virginia Held, "The Community Revolution,"
The Public Interest (Summer, 1969), p. 148.

3. Ibid., p. 169.

4. Ibid.

5. Irving Kristol and Paul Weaver, "Who Knows New York?—
and Other Notes on a Mixed-up City," The Public Interest (Summer,
1969), p. 53.

9

ATLANTA
MAKES USE
OF
EXISTING FACILITIES

Area: 131 square miles
Population: 487,553
Black: 187,461

THE CITY AND ITS GOVERNMENT

The City

Atlanta, the capital and largest city of Georgia, is the leading commercial, industrial, and distribution center of the southeastern United States. It is also a port of entry and cultural center. There are more than 1,000 manufacturing plants in the area, and it is a financial center and home of a Federal Reserve district bank.

A building boom has seen construction of an $18 million sports stadium and a giant civic center for conventions. The Atlanta Memorial Arts Center, opened in October, 1968, contains a museum, symphony hall, art school, and theater. The city is planning to construct a memorial to Martin Luther King, Jr., who was born in Atlanta.

Atlanta began construction in 1969 of an inner-city community to house about 900 families and to include apartment buildings, private town houses, a school, and a shopping center.

The Atlanta Constitution, one of the nation's leading newspapers, has been a strong voice for moderation in race relations in the South. The city's image as the South's most enlightened metropolis was

marred in 1966, when riots broke out in the black section of Summer-
hill. Earlier, Atlanta had been the first city in the Deep South to
experience peaceful school integration following the U.S. Supreme
Court's 1954 ruling that racial segregation in public education is
unconstitutional.

The Government

Mayor Samuel Massell (annual salary $30,000), whose term
expires in January, 1974, functions in a weak-mayor form of government with sixteen aldermen (annual salaries $7,200) running most
departments by aldermanic committees. Aldermen are very much
involved with the administration of departments. The mayor does
appoint all department heads, but only with the approval of the Board
of Aldermen. Under this system the chief administrative officer is
primarily an adviser to the mayor and coordinator of federal programs
and those functions which fall under the mayor's office.

CITY SERVICE CENTERS

History

Near the beginning of 1967, there was general agreement in
Atlanta that the gap between the citizen and government had to be
closed—that the vacuum between expectations and response of government could be the source of considerable tension. "Citizens weren't
getting any answers, period, from City Hall," says one official. "They
couldn't even find out if they were in an urban renewal area." Fortunately, Mayor Ivan Allen, Jr., also knew how unresponsive city
government had become, and was determined to do something about
it. He had based his election campaign on the need to decentralize
government and in May, 1967, with the concurrence of the Board of
Aldermen, initiated a ninety-day pilot neighborhood center program
of four single office units located within other agency facilities.

Together with his chief administrative officer, Dan Sweat, Mayor
Allen began the decentralization plan funded largely through a grant
from the Stern Family Fund, a private philanthropic organization in
New York. Four coordinators were either hired or transferred from
other city duties and attached to the mayor's office for this program.
The coordinators were placed under direct supervision of a full-time
community development coordinator in the Office of Governmental
Liaison under the Department of Human Resources Development. A

"night duty" mayor was also established to keep City Hall open to 1 a.m. daily and on weekends.

Objectives

The project was designed to determine the value of a coordinated approach in delivery of city services; establish better communication between neighborhoods and City Hall; improve the city's relationships with neighborhoods; and prevent racial disturbances as a by-product. The need to reduce factors which were cited as basic causes in almost every disturbance in American cities was an important consideration in the formation of the project.

In 1968, the mayor continued to "beef up" all city activities in disadvantaged areas, in an attempt to respond meaningfully to the recommendations of the National Advisory Committee on Civil Disorders. The little city hall project was continued for 160 days, throughout the summer. In 1969, the project received permanent status and annual funding, with four permanent coordinators. Additional office staff was supplied by HUD interns and Urban Corps volunteers. In 1970, $60,000 was allotted to the program and money for two additional centers was requested for the 1971 fiscal year.

Physical Facilities and Staff

With an eye toward obtaining maximum effectiveness out of a small staff and slim resources, Sweat and Allen recommended four low-income areas, deploying one coordinator to each. Three of the neighborhood service centers are housed in one-room offices in community action program (CAP) buildings; the fourth is in the newly constructed Model Cities complex.

Close CAP-neighborhood service center collaboration had much to do with Sweat's influence. As former deputy director of Atlanta's CAP, he felt that sharing quarters would not only save money but would also facilitate coordination and might tend to keep at least one activity going in the event that CAP funds should ever be cut off. CAP, under auspices of Economic Opportunity Atlanta (EOA), has fourteen neighborhood service centers located in high-poverty target areas throughout the city.

One reason for locating coordinators within CAP facilities was to achieve coordination among the various agencies and programs in the structure. However, city service coordinators do not coordinate these agencies, nor do they provide direction to the programs. Their prime function has been to carry resident complaints through the maze of agencies. In a number of cases CAP personnel have expressed jealousy and unresponsiveness to these coordinative efforts.

Much of this lack of responsiveness, however, has been ameliorated through the central office of the chief administrative officer, Dan Sweat. With a good deal of success, he has pulled together, in cooperative relationships, federal as well as private and other public programs. Even though most city departments are not under Sweat's direction, he has managed to keep most officials informed and to effect a reasonable degree of understanding and cooperation between them and other programs.

Selection of coordinators is largely the responsibility of John Robinson, appointed in 1969 to head the city's Department of Human Resources. Like Sweat, Robinson had prior experience with CAP, and it was he who laid much of the groundwork for the program with civic and community groups and black business leaders.

Although coordinator applicants come through regular civil service channels, their job descriptions are loose enough to leave much room for Robinson's personal judgment. He can eliminate all candidates on the civil service list until he finds an acceptable type. The jobs are sensitive ones, and he considers communications skills and personality extremely important. He also looks for people who know the city well and are committed enough to the little city hall concept to be able to defend it both inside and outside government. While present coordinators have varied backgrounds, all have had some prior experience with social service agencies. They are salaried at $7,500.

Functions

Since the city's service centers are one-room offices with one staff person, they offer only services that the coordinator can provide from his own knowledge or referral to other agencies. The center is primarily a complaint and information source and the coordinator a neighborhood ombudsman, in the sense that he is a citizen's advocate.

Problems brought to the attention of coordinators include typical but important ones of housing deterioration, rodent control, poor lighting, inadequate parks and streets, police tensions, health problems, and insufficient jobs.

A sample survey of complaints from May 26, 1969, to August 31, 1969, indicated that most citizen dissatisfaction involves the Police Department, Sanitation Department, and Building Inspection Department—although a strike of city employees occurring during the reporting period affected not only garbage pickup but also caused deployment of police for other than their regular duties.

The strike was a good example of how decentralization of communication functions can diffuse tensions even in situations where, ideologically, the government and citizens are on opposing sides. Coordinators reported that when they explained reasons for the strike to complaining citizens, most of them sided with the striking workers against the city. Nevertheless, they felt they were helping workers by cooperating with the city in disposing their own trash and following the emergency procedures which the coordinators recommended.

The volume of complaints varies from area to area and month to month. In March, 1970, for example, Nathaniel Maddox, coordinator for the Nash-Washington center corrected seventy-four complaints, while Clarence Green in the Southeast and Central City center handled only six. But Green's problems are different. In his section, which includes a Model Cities area and another known locally as "the hippie area," he finds that medical and social problems occupy a great deal of his time. Obtaining funds, through the Georgia Lions Lighthouse, for a child needing an eye operation, and getting hospital space for a terminal cancer patient are two examples of the types of assistance he provides. Green is also frequently called upon for problems dealing with drugs and firearms. He is primarily project-oriented.

The type of complaint and the personal ability of the coordinator to get cooperation from department heads are two critical factors in the success of the neighborhood ombudsman aspect of the program. As John Robinson points out, no two complaints can be handled in exactly the same way, and coordinators must know just which approach works best with which department head. At present, simple "bread and butter" problems, involving limited resources, are being well handled by the program; more difficult problems are still going unresolved. In the four-month survey period, 80 percent of complaints

involving the Sanitation Department were corrected; among those
involving the Police Department, only 30 percent could be corrected.

Problems involving large expenditures cannot be resolved by
service coordinators. This takes action from the Board of Aldermen
and a commitment of funds which normally must be previously budgeted. It is also difficult for department heads to reallocate resources
to meet new demands when they are limited even in maintaining existing services. Some lower-expenditure items of rodent control,
street lighting, street maintenance, and sewer cleaning can be implemented through the process, however. Unresolved complaints are
then used by management to set priorities for the future budget year.
This citizen feedback is an excellent management tool.

CITIZEN PARTICIPATION

In addition to dealing with department heads, coordinators spend
a great deal of their time meeting with families and "on the street"
talking with residents. In March, 1971, for example, Maddox put in
thirty-five hours of meeting time. Other coordinators reported
similar schedules.

Street work seems to have paid off, and all coordinators have
good rapport with residents in their immediate neighborhoods. Green,
who had established himself in his particular area during previous
work in housing and urban renewal, is obviously well-known and
admired by "hippies" as well as "straights"—all of whom call him
"Pops." Maddox, too, enjoys widespread popularity, some of which
is undoubtedly due to extensive participation in his area's recent
Easter project to buy shoes for disadvantaged children. Eldridge
Jackson, the only non-Atlantan among the four, feels that "people
trust us." Through Jackson's influence, Georgia Tech students,
whose campus borders his area, have rehabilitated an old building
for use as a health service center.

In 1968, following guidelines of the Kerner Commission Report,
Mayor Allen gave impetus to establishment of neighborhood task
forces in each of the six target areas which were assigned coordinators in that year. These joint government-community organizations
consist of (1) an EOA citizens neighborhood advisory council (CNAC);
(2) an EOA center staff, representing health, welfare, social service,
employment, recreation, and legal aid programs; (3) a city service
coordinator; (4) and a citywide resources task force on an "as-needed"
basis. The latter consists of representatives from the following city

departments: Atlanta Housing Authority, Atlanta Public Schools, Fulton County Health Department, EOA, Atlanta Youth Council, the Fire and Police Departments, Atlanta Public Library, and the Departments of Public Works, Building Inspection, Sanitation, Traffic Engineering, Parks and Recreation, and Planning.

A number of block organizations have also been set up. They elect members to the CNACs—one per block—and the CNACs, in turn, elect one representative for three neighborhoods to serve on the Citizens Central Advisory Council (CCAC).

Citizen groups function only in an advisory capacity, helping to pinpoint particular problems within each neighborhood. They have no real power per se, but they do provide input in determining program content. Important links in communication, particularly between black residents and City Hall, are also provided here through the four service coordinators and councils.

MODEL CITIES

Model Cities has a citizen advisory council of fourteen members, including the mayor as chairman, two aldermen, chairman of the county commission, president of the board of education, a state representative, two citizens appointed by the mayor on a citywide basis, and six citizens elected from the target areas.

John Johnson, its director, says, "Ninety-eight percent of the Model Cities board decisions have been approved by the Board of Aldermen." It funds fourteen different agencies and functions as a catalyst to stimulate other programs. "It is the biggest sleeper in years. Cities lost control of it and now must wrestle it back," Johnson says. He feels that the Model Cities program is responsible directly to the mayor and not to any of his designated assistants. Because of its relatively independent operation, some aldermen believe it may be a threat to the aldermanic committee system. Johnson believes reporting to an aldermanic committee is not an answer unless the program was placed under the Department of Human Resources, which would coordinate county, state, and federal functions as well. The state and county would have to be deeply involved in this structure, since about 80 percent of community projects and services are administered by county and state governments.

Johnson believes Model Cities should not take responsibility for

coordinating city service centers or other agency programs. "It is
too early to tell how to do it," he states. The problem of coordinating
all programs in the city has not yet been solved, but placing them
under the Department of Human Resources is viewed as a possible
answer.

Model Cities and CAP have had only minimal working relationships, and even city officials have been kept at arm's length by Johnson.
The chief administrative officer, Daniel Sweat, at times wonders to
whom Model Cities is responsible, but he is trying to mold stronger
central direction. One city service center is located in the Model
Cities headquarters, but Model Cities staff views the centers primarily
as community "pacifiers" providing few services. Most recently,
residents have expressed discontent with the slow progress of Model
Cities by staging a "sit-in" in Johnson's office, sufficiently serious
to have him called back to Atlanta from a Model Cities conference.

ECONOMIC OPPORTUNITY ATLANTA

The Economic Opportunity Atlanta (EOA) community action
program involves a multitude of counties and has a governing board
of thirty-three persons, seven appointed by the Fulton County Commissioners, seven by the mayor and Board of Aldermen, a chairman
appointed jointly by the above, two appointed by Swinnett County and
two by Rockdale County, and two by any other county coming under
the program; fourteen are elected by each CNAC representing the
fourteen areas served under the program.

Each target area has a center providing some twenty-four
services in manpower, education, child development, legal assistance,
home management, recreation, health, planned parenthood, housing,
crime prevention, senior citizen and youth projects, and many other
related areas. With this vast array of programs, it is easier to
visualize why Atlanta chose to work within the existing service center
structure rather than create new centers. However, the problems of
reaching people of all income levels, providing sufficient in-house
city services, and effecting proper coordination do become more
apparent with this approach.

In general, relationships between the CAP staff and service
coordinators have been smooth, except that there is a tendency for
each to go its own way rather than approach problems jointly. There
have been criticisms in both directions, and competition between
agencies is apparent in a number of cases.

Perhaps more characteristic is the comment of the CAP director of the East Central neighborhood center that they had "found the program to be of tremendous benefit to the center and the entire target area. The coordinator represented the decentralization of City Hall and worked closely with staff, individuals and community groups in opening direct lines of communication."

PERCEPTIONS OF SERVICE CENTERS
BY THE CITY AND CIVIC GROUPS

Indications are that city department heads consider the neighborhood service center operation praiseworthy. At the very least, to quote John Robinson, "Nobody has said anything derogatory about it." A representative of the Building Department has, in fact, stated outright that his department has received fewer irrelevant complaints since the coordinators have been at work channeling complaints to the right people. A Police Department spokesman stated, "We have better community relations in these areas." The program has relieved department heads from a "first line citizen attack," and it has been a good source of information for them.

Civic organizations, such as Georgia Lions and the National Alliance of Businessmen, have voiced strong support for the program. They seem to recognize it as an "escape valve" for citizen dissatisfaction. They look to the program as a sign of hope that Atlanta's hot spots can be cooled down.

Sharing this view are many of the city's fifteen aldermen, who exercise a great deal of policy-making and administrative power in Atlanta's weak-mayor form of government. More and more aldermen are beginning to ask that city service coordinators be located within their districts. Aldermen themselves do not get deeply involved in solicitation of neighborhood complaints.

ANALYSIS

Atlanta's city service centers have made considerable impact both in improving the city's image among the disadvantaged and alienated, and in providing much-needed services to areas that tended to be neglected in the past.

They have also helped in tying together services of nongovernmental agencies and in informing citizens of what assistance is

available in the city. In 1967 the program was the core around which
the city built its plans to expand all its efforts in disadvantaged areas.
Atlanta's previously minimal recreation program, for example, was
beefed up as part of the whole movement to get things going. The
mayor and his staff were initially effective in obtaining commitments
from many public and private agencies as well as in allocating city
department funds to the designated areas in order to make a significant
impact in filling the gap between expectancy and response. This
originally touched off the program nicely, but recently resources have
not been so readily available, particularly since other areas of the
community demand their fair share of tax monies. Without resources,
even good concepts will weaken.

Racial tension, it is felt, has eased in the city. Although the
city service center program cannot claim sole credit, it is undoubtedly
one of the contributing factors.

On the negative side, the program is too small, its resources
are too limited, and though location of coordinators in CAP buildings
helps to facilitate coordination, it also lowers visibility of the neighborhood service centers. Signs on buildings advertising their presence
would help. Also, while use of HUD interns to staff offices saves
salary expenses, it lessens efficiency. On loan to the coordinators
for their six-month training periods, the interns are retrieved by
HUD, it seems, just when they begin to make a contribution to the
office.

Robinson's biggest regret is that the administration did not hold
out for a bigger program initially. While two more centers are being
planned for next year, he feels that four more are needed—eight in
all—to be able to make decentralization effective. Robinson also
wants each center to have its own truck and crew so that it can handle
some minor, but annoying, problems itself. Picking up garbage or
dead animals, for example, could be taken care of immediately without
having to go through departments. This would create a better impression for the program.

Sweat, too, feels that more centers are needed. He envisions
each center as a full-time, computerized, multiservice facility where
citizens can go for all problems and in many cases receive answers
on the spot. One staff person working from each center, without
clerical and other staff support, does not make a multiservice center.
Sweat would like to have more manpower.

The question of how the program can best be coordinated—where it fits into the bureaucratic structure of Atlanta—cannot yet be answered. Making it into a department, as Robinson has suggested, has the advantage of firmly cementing it as an institution but has the disadvantage of subjecting it to aldermanic day-to-day administration—a point that some make in arguing to keep the service centers outside the administration, as a program reporting directly, through Robinson and Sweat, to the mayor. Currently, the program is within the mayor's budget and is not a separate division.

Although the mayor's deep interest might not ordinarily be enough to keep the program going in a city where aldermen have as much to say as they do in Atlanta, the fact that aldermen have seen its advantages is a hopeful sign for its future. It appears that the recently elected mayor, Samuel Massell, will continue the program at about the same scale. Massell's interest in improving communication and services is strong, and he is showing it through his support of existing programs as well as stimulating new ideas.

Perhaps the largest and most frustrating problem for the program is one by no means confined to Atlanta, but endemic to all municipalities in the nation—that in most substantive functions, such as education or welfare, it is really the county or state which makes the decisions and holds the purse strings. As Johnny Johnson, Atlanta's Model Cities director, puts it, "The city really can't do much in 80 percent of the problems."

Sweat, through his position, has been able to pull many agencies together and will do better when the Model Cities multiservice center is completed. It will come closest to a little city hall and will house many agencies around which the city can effect some coordination. The chief administrative officer will have closer coordination with Model Cities because the multiservice center operation will fall under Robinson and the city's Department of Human Resources.

RECOMMENDATIONS

Based upon a review of the Atlanta experience, the following suggestions are offered for improvement.

1. In order to make the existing program more effective, sufficient staff is necessary to ensure that personnel are available,

at least during regular hours, at each city service center. Citizens will tend not to come back if they continually find empty offices. The economy of a small staff may not be the most productive in the long run.

2. Central collection and management of data should be effected through the chief administrative officer, with whatever technical resources are necessary, in order to make locally collected information more useful. This system should be eventually tied into other departments and agencies.

3. Coordination of agencies and programs is now being handled on an informal basis. The mayor should take the initiative to form a cabinet of agency and service organizations to review local problems and to carry information back to their headquarters toward a concerted effort to solving city issues. Key department heads would also sit on this larger cabinet-type structure. In some cases, district "mini-cabinets" may be created.

4. Additional services should be added to present centers to make them more meaningful. These may include collections for the Finance Department, sale of licenses and permits, housing and environmental inspection, Social Security and senior citizen programs, and projects from other interested agencies not duplicative of CAP programs. This would have to be done with the cooperation of the agency operating the building. The city administration should take initiative in placing additional city services in existing or new centers.

5. Centers should be made more visible from the city's standpoint, so that city functions are not submerged within other agency structures. A renewed, vital image of City Hall would most likely come about.

Area: 426 square miles
Population: 1,213,064
Black: 281,670

THE CITY AND ITS GOVERNMENT

The City

Houston is the leading industrial metropolis of Texas and the surrounding region. It is the largest city in the South, sixth largest in the nation, and the country's largest inland port. Strategically located in an area rich in oil, gas, sulphur, salt, lime, timber, industrial soil, seawater, and fresh water, Houston ranks first in the nation as a refinery center, first in manufacture and distribution of petroleum equipment, and first in pipeline transmission.

South of Houston is the $250 million National Aeronautics and Space Administration's Manned Space Flight Center. In 1965, the $31.6 million Astrodome enclosed sports arena was built. In 1968, construction was completed on a $12 million convention and exhibit center and the $3.3 million Alley Theatre with its fan-shaped auditorium. The $110 million Intercontinental Airport was opened in June, 1969.

The Government

Mayor Louie Welch (salary $20,000), who was re-elected for a new term beginning in January, 1972, is a strong mayor in a strong mayor-council form of government and has control over all departments. Eight councilmen (salaries $3,600) are elected at-large, provided with a limited staff, and serve chiefly as legislators, with minimum involvement in servicing neighborhood complaints.

NEIGHBORHOOD CITY HALLS

History

In 1966, Mayor Welch felt a strong need for a communications link with residents, particularly minority groups, if the city was to begin to solve its urban ills. His strong hope was to be able to prevent problems and to improve existing conditions. He began personal visits to black and Mexican-American neighborhoods in "meet the mayor" sessions, in which he openly discussed problems.

Various approaches to the poor were tried. Through the mayor's office, Human Relations Division, then under the direction of Dr. Blair Justice, a social psychologist, 7,500 interviews were conducted by city teams over several years in twenty black, poverty neighborhoods. Survey results indicated that problems fell into three broad categories: environment, which included housing and police relations; employment, concerned with upgrading skills as well as new jobs; and education, primarily related to acquiring job skills.

A fourth problem soon became evident: communications between City Hall and the poor, and between the police and minority groups. This was the underlying key to the success of the other three and, therefore, was placed at the top of the mayor's priority list, summed up in the acronym CEEE for communications, environment, employment, and education.

CEEE was approached in many forms: police-community relations, job fairs for disadvantaged youth, a service center in the mayor's office in City Hall, Houston-Harris County Youth Opportunity Council (to provide recreational and cultural activities for, and communication with, ghetto youth), Jobs in the Business Sector, Project

Helping Hand (church and service groups working with minorities),
Peacekeeper Corps (designed to persuade crowds to "cool it" during
tense periods), the city plan for public emergency, Rumor Central
(to give factual information during crises), Open Door Policy, Meet
the Mayor Program, Project Person-to-Person (unscheduled walking
tours of ghetto areas by the mayor), Project Distribution (distribution
of informative service booklets by the city and civic groups), and the
neighborhood city hall (NCH) program—perhaps the most dramatic of
all.

Facilities and Locations

In December, 1966, Project Partner was started in the Bottoms
area in northeast Houston, probably the worst concentration of slums
in the city. It had received no benefit of federal poverty or urban
renewal funds and was chosen partly to demonstrate that if progress
could be made here, it could be made anywhere in Houston. In order
to establish a base of operation and motivate residents, an NCH was
opened in a renovated house in the area.

The success of Project Partner led to programs in other areas.
Following authorization by the City Council, the first mobile NCH
was established in 1968, and two more were established in 1969. The
trailers are small (thirty feet by eight feet), unaesthetic, and relatively
inexpensive units.

Staff and Budget

Staff consists of one mayor's aide assigned to each of three
trailers plus a fourth aide, a doctoral-level social worker with community organization specialization, who "floats" to the more intense
problem areas and works out of the main office. They work under
the direction of Dr. Justice of the Human Relations Division. Aides
are salaried at $8,000 to $15,000, appear to be qualified for their
positions, are nonpolitical, and in each case are acceptable to the
neighborhood. Total operating budget is $60,000. Clerical staff
assistance is provided on a part-time basis by the Neighborhood
Youth Corps program and other federally assisted projects. This
clerical arrangement is not the best, for it leaves the trailers unoccupied much of the time while aides work the neighborhoods.
However, residents are close enough to the trailers that transportation
does not seem to be a major problem if repeat calls are necessary.

Objectives

Objectives of the program are clear: to establish a mode of communication to minority neighborhoods (primarily to show that city government is aware of and concerned about resident problems); to provide new services and improve others; and to improve the physical condition of the neighborhoods.

The mayor and City Council, as well as the business community, view the program as an approach to relieving tensions and creating goodwill. Minimal services are offered, but the facilities do provide a base of operation for receiving complaints and inquiries, and for conducting neighborhood projects through leadership of a city representative acceptable to residents.

Functions

NCHs are used for distribution of pamphlets and literature on many subjects, complaint processing, police and other city employee recruitment, tax collection and payment of utility bills, special projects, and meetings held by the mayor and City Council and other groups. During special recruitment campaigns for policemen, firemen, and other city personnel, city staff are stationed at NCHs to help recruit and process applicants.

All types of complaints, regardless of their nature, are handled by the three special aides. A simple form for processing complaints was developed by one aide and is now used in all NCHs. It indicates the date of the complaint, the name and address of the complainant, the nature of complaint, to whom it is referred, and results achieved. Copies are kept by aides until satisfactory answers are received and citizens properly notified. Aides say that complaints from NCHs are given priority response and receive faster action.

Aides resemble ombudsmen in their zeal to handle complaints and act as citizen advocates. Close rapport has been established with most citizens in each area, and communication with each household is achieved through distribution of pamphlets and other literature. Aides attend numerous community meetings and work closely with as many neighborhood groups as possible. They feel that their chief responsibilities are to develop leadership within the neighborhood and to teach people how to process complaints through the maze of government and private agencies. They make it known that they will not be available forever and that the mobile units are established on

a temporary basis only. Citizens must learn to develop their own
resources and handle their own problems. This is the education
function of the program.

One trailer has already been moved three times, which has not
seemed to create adverse neighborhood reactions. Apparently, citizens
will accept removal of an NCH if the neighborhood has already received results in improved services and new facilities. In the two
areas where the mobile unit was removed, aides feel achievements
were satisfactory. All three aides, with some hesitancy, concurred
that there would not be any adverse reaction from residents if present
trailers were moved to other areas. To citizens, the trailers mean
results. Accomplishments mean the trailers will move on.

When citizens become accustomed to obtaining information,
applying for jobs, and getting other kinds of services at the neighborhood level, there is some hardship and inconvenience when they can
no longer do so. But, according to the staff, these services are "so
minor anyway, their absence does not make a great deal of difference."

A fundamental concept of the program is to physically and
socially upgrade a neighborhood. If the city does not have the finances
or the ability to make such a commitment, it does not enter a community, nor is an NCH located there unless citizens request it.
Citizens have trust in the city commitment, therefore, when a neighborhood unit is located in their community; they feel something is going
to happen.

Demography and Program Results

Bordersville Project

In the Bordersville area, presently a very depressed area composed mostly of low-income black families and part of the last area
to be annexed to the city, special treatment is being applied. It does
not have an NCH structure but operates as an extension of the mayor's
office; this, however, is somewhat similar to the NCH approach. The
area has a full-time representative, Harry G. Taylor, whose services
have been loaned to the city by the Humble Oil and Refining Company
on a public service leave of absence. He has been assigned to the
mayor's office in the Human Relations Division, but spends much of
his time in neighborhood rehabilitation efforts.

Success here has been accomplished by efforts of almost all

elements of the community: Bordersville citizens, the mayor's office, University of Houston students, civic and church groups, United Fund agencies, city departments, private industry, and many diverse groups of concerned citizens. This joint effort is a function of the Committee on Coordinated Action in Neighborhoods (CCAN), which was established to tackle difficult city problems. The idea grew out of a conference sponsored by the mayor's office and the University of Houston Graduate School of Social Work in June, 1969. A follow-up conference was held in June, 1970, to review progress and plans.

Harry Taylor believes accomplishments made so far have developed a desirable image for both city government and the community. He says, "It was one of the best examples of how coordination can be achieved with all groups, and is indicative of the success of the mayor's program of direct neighborhood involvement."

The following are results obtained in the Bordersville project, after eight months, as reported by the mayor's office:

1. A sidewalk 900 feet long was constructed to provide the children with a safe route to walk to and from elementary school. This project was accomplished almost entirely with donated materials and volunteer labor, and illustrates the meaning of coordinated action. The following participated in this project:

a. Office of the mayor
b. Architecture seniors, University of Houston
c. Jaycees
d. Houston Brick & Tile Company
e. Texas Industries, Inc.
f. Gaylord Construction Company
g. University of Houston Student Volunteer Corps
h. University of Houston faculty volunteers
i. Texas Southern University students
j. Volunteers in Service to America
k. Acme Brick, Inc.
l. Disciples United Methodist Church
m. Texas State Highway Department
n. Harris County Community Action Association
o. City of Houston Public Works Department
p. City of Houston Treasury Department.

2. Three dirt streets, badly rutted and impassable in wet weather, were graded, provided with drainage ditches, and covered with an all-weather gravel surface. These streets total 1,650 feet in length.

Following completion of road work, regular garbage collection was instituted and street signs were put in place, as were "Dead End" and "Stop" signs.

3. Delivery of city water by a tank truck was started, with residents charged the same rate as other low-volume city customers. This has resulted in a considerable reduction in the cost of water for those Bordersville residents who purchased water from a contractor in the past.

4. A mobile health unit now visits the community on a regular basis. It is equipped for immunizations, testing for diseases such as diabetes and tuberculosis, and provides health counseling and information.

5. Additional speed limit signs were erected and a speed enforcement program has improved traffic conditions.

6. The Boys Club is being rehabilitated with donated materials, volunteer labor, and labor paid by a donor.

7. A large-scale clean-up program removed several hundred cubic yards of trash. Many vacant lots and large tracts were cleared of brush and weeds, and poisoned rat bait has been placed at several hundred locations. About thirty houses were painted by University of Houston students and Jaycees using donated paint.

8. The senior architecture class at the University of Houston is developing plans for a community center. Funds for construction were obtained from church and foundation sources.

9. The Business Resource Development Department of Houston presented a series of eleven consumer information programs, each preceding a regularly scheduled Bordersville neighborhood council meeting.

10. The employment subcommittee of CCAN has met with twenty-seven employers at the new Houston Intercontinental Airport to inform them of the existence of unemployed people at Bordersville, which has resulted in increased jobs for area people.

Second Ward Neighborhood City Hall

At the request of the United Families of Second Ward (an indigenous neighborhood organization), a mobile trailer was located at Settegast Park in the Second Ward, an area of 25,000 people, almost

90 percent Mexican-American. Since April, 1969, Eddie Carral, a
Spanish-speaking Chicano (bilingual ability is a prerequisite for this
job location), has managed this area. The designation Second Ward
is a historical use of the term dating from the time the city operated
by wards. It has no significance today, except that some persons and
documents still refer to certain areas as numbered wards.

A tour of the area reveals substandard, deteriorated houses,
open ditches, few sidewalks, dirt streets, and most of the other conditions of a depressed neighborhood. However, items which the city
could deal with immediately were satisfactory, such as street lighting,
refuse collection and rodent control, and cleanup and weed cutting.
The other, more costly and time-consuming items, were in the
planning stages.

Accomplishments of what has been a joint effort by the neighborhood and city government include the following:

1. 135 ditches cleaned
2. Fifty-five streets repaired
3. Forty-five lots cut and cleaned
4. Thirty-one traffic lights installed
5. Rodent control program established
6. Settegast Park improvements: sidewalks repaired, drainage
around the streets bounding the park corrected, rest-room fixtures
installed, softball field reworked, additional park lights installed
7. Drainage around Canales Court (an extremely depressed,
privately owned housing complex) corrected
8. Survey of the lighting in this area made by the Street
Lighting Division, Public Service Department
9. Plans under way for a much-needed community building
and day-care center with financial assistance from church groups.
10. A grant to establish a school dropout, delinquency prevention
project approved by HEW.

In employment, neighborhood residents have been encouraged
to apply for positions in city government. So far, twelve area citizens
have been employed in the Fire Department.

The program has united neighborhood residents with groups
from other parts of Houston. For example, United Families of the
Second Ward has worked with Memorial Presbyterian Church for the
betterment of the Second Ward. Similarly, the office of the bishop of
the Catholic Galveston-Houston diocese has awarded a grant to assist
youths in a return-to-school project. A graduate student from the

University of Houston Graduate School of Social Work, specializing
in community organization and receiving field instruction from a
doctoral-level staff member, was primarily responsible for the making
of several voluntary service organizations and writing grant applications.

There are few English-speaking residents, but by working with
neighborhood groups, the NCH helped place some of the area's leaders
into English classes. A program is being arranged to bring tutors to
the area three times a week. In cooperation with a Houston TV channel,
NCH and the Presbyterian church arranged programming to teach
English to preschool youngsters.

A paint-up, fix-up campaign was held in cooperation with the
city, Harris Country Community Action Association, and the Jaycees.
Also, the NCH was instrumental in bringing together interested
people so that two very successful Christmas parties were held for
needy children from different parts of Second Ward.

Other areas of the city are also getting results from this NCH:
(1) Port Houston is getting some of its ditches cut and cleaned; (2)
Port Houston Park has received a $10,000 play pad, and will also get
a covered basketball court; (3) Port Houston had twelve stop signs
installed; (4) the Fifth Ward/North Side has received help with various
problems, including drainage, streets, weed cutting of four lots, and
posting of "No Dumping" signs; (5) Magnolia had at least ten ditches
cleaned and eleven lots cut; (6) Denver Harbor was surveyed by
traffic and transportation personnel and traffic control signs were
installed; (7) a radio program on Spanish-speaking station KLVL is
presented weekly by Eddie Corral to inform citizens on what is taking
place and to answer questions; (8) a Spanish newspaper is distributed
through the NCH.

The mobile unit provides space for training, through the Concentrated Employment Program "Job Opportunities for Youth," for
a young woman who does office work in the mobile trailer. Employment is also furnished during the summer for a high school youth
hired through the job fair program.

Each of the trailers has a phone, which also rings in the mayor's
office to back up a system short of staff. In emergencies, the central
office contacts aides by a one-way radio buzzer system unit, which
each aide carries with him. These units run about $300 apiece and
allow aides to remain in constant communication with the central office,
regardless of where they are.

Corral believes that the main city hall does not have the opportunity to get the feel of the citizen as he does "out here" in the community. Since he is the only special aide who speaks Spanish in a city where there are approximately 140,000 Mexican-Americans, he says, "Any one of them may call me."

Citizens in the area respond favorably to the program. Mrs. Elida Baez, a citizen involved in several neighborhood projects, stated strongly that the whole climate of the neighborhood has changed since the NCH was installed, and it would be a great loss to the neighborhood if it were removed. She says, "It is one of the best signs that the city is concerned with the Mexican-Americans living in this area. We are pleased with improvements that have already been made."

Clinton Park NCH

Clinton Park NCH, in northeast Houston, has been managed by Brenda Green since it opened in July, 1969. It serves Fidelity, Clinton Park, Clinton View, and Pleasantville, predominantly black, low-income areas. In Fidelity, the NCH, in cooperation with the Inter-Community Council (a large community organization operating in this area), has produced a number of results, which include the following:

1. Some 103 street lights installed throughout Clinton Park, Clinton View, and Fidelity, with twenty additional installations recommended

2. Twelve traffic control and street signs installed, eight more recommended

3. Reshelling of ten streets in the Fidelity Addition, one in Clinton Park, and three in the Clinton View Addition

4. Some thirty-two blocks of street repairs in Fidelity and Clinton Park Additions, with thirteen additional blocks recommended

5. Complete digging and cleaning of fifty-seven blocks of drainage ditches in Fidelity and Clinton Park Addition, thirty additional blocks recommended

6. Three vacant lots cut and cleared in Fidelity Addition, twenty-two additional lots scheduled for cutting and clearing

7. Two dilapidated houses scheduled for demolition in Fidelity Addition

8. Some twenty-seven locations baited for rodents, all four communities sprayed several times for mosquitoes

9. Grounds of Clinton Park improved: all playground equipment repaired; thirty-five acres of weeds cut and cleared; a recreation center approved by the City Council, with bids taken by the Parks and Recreation Department.

In addition to these accomplishments, the NCH has assisted these areas in several "clean-up, fix-up, and paint-up" projects. Attention is now being focused on long-range community goals.

Brenda Green likes the mobile nature of the program because neighborhoods can be treated on an as-needed basis, whereas "with a permanent store-front type structure, this cannot be done. If demands and complaints change, movement cannot take place very easily.

"Things can be done immediately with the mobile unit as a base, such as weed cutting, street lights added, street construction through special assessments and many other items. Some of these items may seem trivial to some people, but they are very important to the residents who live in the neighborhood," she says.

Sunnyside Park NCH

Ernest Carswell, the first person to manage an NCH in Houston, heads Sunnyside, opened in July, 1969. It is an area of 80,000 persons, about 95 percent black and 5 percent white. There are very few Mexican-Americans. Some 43 percent of the populace is estimated to be at poverty level.

The city reveals the following items accomplished:

1. A clean-up campaign removed 1,100 tons of trash (fifty-five truck loads). The NAACP, through Reverend C. Anderson Davis and church leaders in the area, cooperated with residents and city government in this clean-up drive

2. Some forty-five miles of drainage ditches on twelve major streets cleaned and deepened, trash removed

3. Nine streets repaired

4. "Thru Trucks Prohibited" signs installed to stop heavy truck traffic on five streets in residential areas

5. In response to residents' complaints, inspections made of private junk yards in cooperation with the Health Department. Three violations found and remedied

6. An estimated thirty-seven miles of street shoulders shelled. Two miles of street surface shelled

7. Recruits signed up for employment in the Fire Department and the Public Works Department

8. Hours being set up for recruitment of police officers.

Carswell was previously stationed in the Bottoms area, which eventually was almost completely rehabilitated. He was then transferred to the Blossom Heights area in the western part of the city, which consists of 75 percent blacks and 25 percent Mexican-Americans, mostly poor citizens surrounded by affluence. He was there from June, 1968, to May, 1969, when he was able to leave the area because he felt citizens "had sufficient independence to carry on programs themselves at this point." The office still exists in Bottoms and is manned by Carswell only when particular problems arise.

"Dealing with normal city services is not enough," Carswell believes. "Other things excite people and get them involved." He cites a street festival which he helped to arrange and which attracted over 6,000 persons.

"Moving the units isn't a problem as long as proper information is provided the citizens and they see results before you decide to leave," he says. He soon will be moved to another area, known as South Union, which has typical problems of drainage, street repairs, lighting, and police-community relations. He too receives calls and service requests from all parts of the city. Since he has been in three different areas of the city, he is in greater demand than other aides.

Meet-the-Mayor Neighborhood Programs

In addition to the NCHs, the mayor has brought City Hall to the neighborhoods by a program he calls Meet the Mayor. A desk is

moved by his staff to various NCH locations and certain other areas
to receive complaints and requests. He personally takes part in the
sessions. A sample list of complaints is shown below:

Street repairs	79
Improved water drainage	47
Requests for park improvements and weed cutting	29
Additional traffic signals	26
More adequate police patrols	16
Insufficient water for personal and public use	13
Unsanitary conditions and waste removal	7
Miscellaneous requests: bridge repairs, requests for parks, swimming pools, etc.	7
Removal of immediate safety hazards	5
Clarification of sewer and building permits	4

DEPARTMENTAL PERFORMANCE
AND COMPLAINTS

The NCH program in Houston has involved mostly city government services. Few public or private agencies are involved, and
there are few in-house services and little staff; therefore, coordination
is not a vital concern. Mayor's aides must deal directly with city
departments in getting complaints resolved, although they perform
much as neighborhood ombudsmen in pursuing complaints involving
any agency. They also attend meetings of most agencies in their areas
in order to transmit relevant information to the central staff.

The mayor has widely publicized his program and has made it
clear to department heads that priorities are to be given to NCHs.
NCHs handle complaints from any area of the city (not only an NCH
area); therefore, department heads feel it is a much broader program
and tend to respond to mayor's aides on matters related to all areas.
Departmental response is generally satisfactory but has been criticized
by some in the NCH program. Departmental commitment appears to
be stronger here than in most cities, however.

A scattered approach to resolving complaints is not only less
efficient but is also less visible to residents; therefore, Houston has
approached its neighborhoods by committing large amounts of resources
in each area so that results can be readily seen. Because reports are
accumulated comprehensively for an entire neighborhood, program
priorities and operational efficiencies are implemented more effectively.

In Bottoms, for example, almost the total area was physically transformed. Other areas have experienced extensive improvements, sufficient to hold down the day-by-day complaint level and raise the level of departmental performance.

The mayor's office receives complaints centrally on any matter through its Central Information and Referral Center, but does not have the massive volume of requests of some other large cities. Much of the work load is referral, and it has not had the kind of publicity which brings a large volume of complaints to one source.

COMMUNITY ACTION PROGRAM

The Harris County Community Action Association (HCCAA) is the policy board of the community action program, and functions with a twenty-five-member board of directors consisting of ten persons elected from among the poor in the ten target areas, seven representatives of private groups, and eight public representatives (three appointed by the Harris County judge, one from Houston Independent School District, and one each from the city governments of Baytown, Pasadena, and Houston). The executive director is Samuel Price.

In addition, there are ten area boards, both elected and appointed. Other groups within target areas include ten area councils and numerous neighborhood councils, all advisory.

The program has thirty-five HCCAA centers and thirty-five child development centers operating within the county. Child development centers will be increased to fifty with Model Cities funding. HCCAA representatives from the three areas which fall in Model Cities boundaries serve on the Model Cities board. Many HCCAA personnel have transferred to the Model Cities program for higher salary and more responsibility. There appears to be adequate joint planning with Model Cities regarding development of the proposed Model Cities multiservice center. Planning efforts have concentrated on job development, training, and child care.

HCCAA has been criticized for failure to organize and coordinate programs properly. It apparently bogged down a number of "clean-up/fix-up" programs with NCHs because workers failed to show up. "They have also gotten bogged down so much in paper work and administration that they are considered a 'paper tiger' by the community. They think city structure is bad, but they are much worse. Area councils have meetings that go on to three o'clock in the morning with personal hassles, so they never get down to solving the true community problems. They end up running themselves rather than running programs," states one NCH official.

Johney Smith, deputy director, relates that HCCAA believes the NCH program is a "good one" and that the two groups have related well, without jealousies or conflicts. The community action staff believes the mayor and his administration want to revitalize the community, and the Human Relations Division staff has strengthened this commitment.

"Citizens are in favor of Neighborhood City Halls and so are we. We believe, however, that they should be placed in permanent structures attached to each neighborhood," says Smith. This seemed to be the opinion of other HCCAA supervisory personnel as well. Apparently there has been little conflict between the two programs. NCHs do not provide in-house social services because of the large number of HCCAA centers; therefore, some jealousies and differences have been avoided.

MODEL CITIES PROGRAM

The Model Cities program in Houston, funded for $13 million and involving fifty-nine projects, is entering its action stage. The advisory board apparently has functioned well, made more representative and effective through the assistance of the NCH program, which provided Model Cities "with built-in communications and assistance in its formation."

Model Cities Director George McGonegal expressed favor for a combination multiservice center/NCH in the Model Cities area which will provide most city services as well as social services. This is presently in the planning stages.

CITIZEN PARTICIPATION

The city administration has said that NCHs would not be located in neighborhoods where residents did not want them. This apparently has held true and, as a result, NCHs have been received well wherever they have been located. Through neighborhood meetings, citizens have helped to formulate programs and suggest changes. Many communication methods described previously, plus thousands of interviews held in neighborhoods, have provided sources of considerable input from residents as to what is needed in each area. However, there are no citizen advisory councils attached to NCHs. More formal citizen advice comes from community action and Model Cities boards, on which the city seems to rely. Residents do not choose NCH staff, but they do make recommendations to the administration. Aides are closely associated with neighborhoods in which they work, attend many neighborhood meetings, and seem to have established good rapport with residents.

RELATIONSHIPS AND PERCEPTIONS

In the last City Council vote taken on funding NCHs, there were no opposing votes. The mayor and Council seem to agree on program objectives, and both accept credit for successes. Political disagreement is minimal. Initially, some councilmen felt the project would uproot political strength in their districts and argued about NCH locations. There was fear the project would merely "stir up the people" and encourage them to bring more complaints and problems to light. "When nothing can be done, this will cause further trouble," some said. But as the program progressed satisfactorily, councilmen changed their minds and now even use it as a favorable political campaign issue.

Initially, the city leased the trailers, but the temporary nature of the program was dispelled when the City Council agreed to purchase them. There is indication that the City Council may approve use of three additional trailers on a temporary basis and one on permanent status, but would not authorize a major expenditure for expansion of permanent sites at this time.

Most city department heads, human relations personnel, and the chief administrative officer view the project favorably. Many department heads feel that by having complaints handled at the neighborhood level, citizen pressure has been eased. Mayor's aides feel response from department heads and supervisors is good. The program is administered by the Human Relations Division, which appears to be the best structural arrangement. The chain of command is clear and without organizational "hang-ups."

Much of the business community and many civic groups give credit for a relatively "cool" city to the NCH project and city-related communicative achievements. These groups seem to strongly favor continuing the program and would offer considerable resistance to proposals to disband it. The possibility of discontinuing it if another mayor were elected brings this reaction: "Another mayor would have very great difficulty in eliminating this program. It would be an advantage to any mayor or City Council to continue it."

Residents' perceptions of NCHs generally are favorable, for they feel the program gets things accomplished and provides a method of communication previously lacking. Dr. Justice has pointed out that citizens have very little contact with the main city hall. "Neighborhood City Halls . . . have provided a one-station contact point for citizens who would normally have to choose among some 239 sites in the city [health centers, library branches, parks, police precincts, etc.]," he says. "Their mobility [NCHs] has allowed us to have them where they are most needed at the time. Residents are interested in the more pressing problems. Permanent neighborhood services of tax and utility collections are not foremost in the minds of citizens. Grocery stores and other businesses perform these services now." Mobility was a more important factor to him than creating permanent structures.

"The important thing about Neighborhood City Halls," says Brenda Green, "is their reliability and convenience. People have enough to worry about—paying light bills and where their next meal is coming from. They couldn't care less about attending City Council meetings and trying to get a response out of city hall! With something nearby and someone to talk to whom they know, they feel closer, and feel that maybe city hall is concerned about them."

"Some people felt Neighborhood City Halls were put out here," relates Ernest Carswell, "to keep black folk from going downtown to the big city hall. But this feeling has changed."

Attitudes of militant groups appear to have hardened in 1970, making it more difficult for the city's programs and NCHs to cope with them. In a Washington Post article of June 23, 1970, Mayor Welch stated:

Local tension levels are higher this year than last. Another year has passed without the gap between [black] expectations and realization being closed further. There's been another year of frustration, of problems of inflation, under-employment and student demonstrations and militant demands which cannot be met, all of which have raised the tension level of our city and other cities as well. It's not as bad as 1967, but already worse than 1969. . . . If the temperature level in Houston was 90 in

1967 [a year of sharp conflict between black students and
police] I would say it was 85 now, or maybe 89.

In the same article it was reported that Operation Bootstrap,
run by Pluria Marshall and Kelton Sams (Houston activists for better
economic opportunities), had boycotted several firms and succeeded
in getting better and more jobs for blacks, investments in black banks,
and scholarships for blacks. But Sams says, "Right now I don't see
any way for black people. The white radicals have heightened action,
but then they fade into the landscape, hard for the man to find. But
he can always find black folks. I see black people becoming the
common enemy of the right and left. I don't see any way for blacks
to win in America and there damn sure ain't no way out." He believes
the United States is headed for a fascist solution to its racial troubles,
at most, and toward an apartheid society, at least. This may typify
the feelings of the more extremist groups, but the overwhelming
feeling is more moderate and hopeful. Some shootings and violence
erupted during the summer of 1970, but the city has held together
fairly well and much of this can be credited to the city's attempts at
reaching the people.

ANALYSIS AND RECOMMENDATIONS

The following recommendations and comments are made in the
hope that they may stimulate thought about neighborhood programs
and be of some assistance.

The strong leadership of Mayor Louie Welch has opened many
avenues of communication for Houston's city government. One of
them is through the NCH program, whose prime objectives have been
to establish more effective and sincere communications and to
establish a base of operations toward rehabilitating neighborhoods.
It has created a feedback of complaints and requests from residents
directly to a mayor's representative in each NCH and, in turn, to the
mayor, making the citizen feel closer to city government.

Scattered trailers have given an impression that someone from
City Hall is physically there, listening and concerned, even though
the trailers themselves are not attractive and do not improve the
appearance of the neighborhood.

The total budget of $60,000 and staff of four special aides are
small, but other city resources contribute to the content of the program. It has been a program in which services are more concentrated

than decentralized. In one case, almost an entire neighborhood in Bottoms was successfully rehabilitated. In other areas, results were impressive but not as comprehensive because of limitations on resources and time.

Residents like NCHs because "things do get done." Priorities are placed in these neighborhoods and department heads are instructed to give them special attention. The city budget is programmed to provide a certain level of expenditure in these neighborhoods. Operations are not started in neighborhoods unless sufficient resources are available to make some impact, and until residents request that an NCH be brought into their area, two most significant factors in the high acceptance of the program. It is not a random placing of trailers but a finely calculated and well-prepared plan.

The trailers are too small to be able to provide all the services citizens get at the main city hall. There are very limited tax and utility collections. Employment processing has been a significant function, but performed on a part-time basis only. The main services provided are handling complaints and disseminating information—particularly beneficial to the elderly, the uninformed, those who speak little or no English, and those who need to trust someone before they will deal with him. The mayor's aides provide this touch in their role of neighborhood ombudsmen; they also educate and develop leadership skills in some residents so they can find their way through the process when no one is available to help them. Developing leadership skills is one of the key objectives of the program.

The city administration feels the mobility of the program is one of its key assets because it allows trailers to be placed wherever they are most needed at the time. Permanent stations for tax and utility collections and similar in-house services are not vital local needs of citizens, Dr. Blair Justice believes. More pressing problems have been made priorities of the program. For example, neighborhood rehabilitation and public works projects effectively utilize NCHs as a base of operation while specially treating a particular neighborhood.

Even though some officials believe the mobility of the program is not harmful, there is little evidence to feel it is helpful. The community action agency, local citizen groups, and residents have expressed a strong desire to make NCHs a permanently based operation. Once residents get used to the services, however limited, they feel their loss and neglect by the city when they are taken away. Neighborhood improvements tend to become forgotten, and a permanent, visible reminder that service is close is necessary.

Where a community expresses little concern over the removal of a trailer, it is probably not providing significant on-site services. Although the Houston program has emphasized the complaint and information processing aspects, it should now consider adding other services in order to treat multiple family problems at a one-stop center. Services may include social services work, family counseling, health, employment, housing inspection, probation and parole, drug and alcoholic programs, food distribution, day care, adult education, Social Security assistance, senior citizen projects, and many more. With permanent neighborhood sites, loaned staff from existing agencies could staff the program to keep it as economical and efficient as possible. (Baltimore's mayor's stations are a good example of this technique.)

The community action program provides some of these services in some areas; however, coordination of agencies and programs has not been effective and groups above poverty level have been eliminated.

With a rise in feelings of alienation from many quarters of the city, permanent service centers and neighborhood citizen councils should be considered in additional areas. The proposed Model Cities multiservice center and its local council are a step in this direction.

Much of the success of the Houston program depends on the capabilities of NCH aides and their performance as neighborhood ombudsmen, which appears to have been highly satisfactory. These ombudsmen types have done much to increase goodwill between citizens and city hall; however, their effectiveness would be diminished if they were to work from a central city hall office alone, which reinforces the desirability of neighborhood centers.

In most cities, neighborhood programs have been placed directly under the office of the mayor. In Houston, they have been placed primarily under the Human Relations Division, an arm of the mayor's office, because of the positive image of this division. However, success of the mayor's personal style has weighed heavily in the acceptance of the program.

In many cities, however, decentralization would not be as successful under the Division of Human Relations because the division has not been so well accepted by citizens. Each city must review its own organizational structure for best placement of neighborhood programs.

Most neighborhood center programs have not been able to do much about quelling racial tensions, primarily because they have lacked development of a comprehensive program. Centers cannot sit in a community, hoping that their mere presence will have an effect on such problems. In Houston almost every communicative device imaginable has been used in a well-rounded program, closely associated with the NCH project. The program, therefore, can be credited with considerable influence in reducing tensions.

The following are further recommendations:

1. The NCH program should be expanded to include additional city as well as public and private agency functions. Additional staff should be provided on a loan basis to make the project as economical as possible. Consideration should be given to locating centers in areas not serviced by the community action program, where need and alienation also exist. Some centers should work in conjunction with the community action program.

2. Once the initial impact of NCH neighborhood rehabilitation projects begins to wear away, more permanent multipurpose centers should be located in these areas. Mayor's aides (ombudsmen) should be continually available to neighborhood residents through the centers. The present temporary nature of this program tends to create frustration by providing only periodic services to those who need them constantly.

3. If permanent sites are selected and area boundaries established, some attempt should be made at creating coterminous service districts between city departments and other public agencies. At minimum, new programs should be aligned in similar districts in order to effect better coordination and common use of statistical data.

4. With or without coterminous districts, as permanent NCHs are located, mayor's aides should begin to conduct "mini-cabinet" sessions between district department and agency heads to improve understanding of neighborhood problems and priorities. These sessions should develop programs for a more concerted effort at dealing with a neighborhood's social, as well as physical, problems.

5. The program concept of listing proposed improvements in each neighborhood and then faithfully following them through to completion is its key success factor. This pattern should be continued; however, thought should be given to forming local citizen councils in

each NCH location to help establish priorities for neighborhood
improvements and services. More in-depth citizen involvement is
needed in all areas where the program operates. Formation of
councils and determining their powers, however, are matters which
must be pretty much tailor-made for Houston.

Area: 46 square miles
Population: 628,215
Irish: 138,207
Italian: 69,104
Black: 63,439

THE CITY AND ITS GOVERNMENT

The City

Boston, incorporated in 1822 and the capital of Massachusetts, is New England's largest city. It is the financial and trading center of New England, a leading U.S. port, and an important market for fish, seafood, and wool. The electronics industry has been a significant factor in reviving its economy since World War II.

In 1959, it embarked upon an ambitious urban renewal program which inspired development of the Prudential Center, a fifty-two-acre government center with a new $30 million city hall completed in 1969, start of a massive conversion of the waterfront and rehabilitation of the Faneuil Hall area, and substantial activity in the Washington Park, Charlestown, and North Harvard areas.

Irish-Americans and white Protestants are spread throughout the city, Italian-Americans are concentrated in various neighborhoods, blacks are concentrated in the central areas (almost half in Roxbury and the South End), and Jews are concentrated in Brighton, Back Bay, Dorchester, and Mattapan.

The Government

Boston has a strong-mayor/council form of government. Mayor Kevin H. White (annual salary $40,000), who was re-elected for a new term beginning January, 1972, formulates the budget and is accountable for all expenditures. The City Council can veto but not add to this budget, but the mayor cannot override the Council's veto. The mayor appoints almost all department heads except the police commissioner, the corporation council, building commissioner, fire commissioner, and penal institutions commissioner. He also appoints members of boards and commissions, with a few key exceptions appointed by the governor. There is no chief administrative officer who manages or coordinates all departments. The mayor tends to rely on several key staff persons for this function. A mayor-appointed Home Rule Commission recommends reorganization of city government, including an Executive Office of Administration designed to induce better direction and coordination.

The City Council's legal responsibilities are comparatively small, and even its own members agree that it has no responsibility for delivery of services. It is responsible, however, for analyzing service failures, which can be done through its budgetary and inquiry functions. The nine councillors run for reelection every two years, each has a two-man staff (special assistant and secretary), and they supervise the city clerk and city messenger. There is also a post, (presently unfilled), for a director of research for the council.

City Council elections were made at-large in a 1949 charter revision largely because reform groups felt the previous twenty-two-man, ward-based council was too vulnerable to abuses and too parochial in its concerns. Some of the parochialism has hung on. Even though elected at-large, most councillors tend to be more concerned about constituents from the areas where they reside and are somewhat apprehensive about others' handling problems in their areas. State legislators are even more sensitive about this, since they are elected by districts and do not wish to see competitors mature in their political domains.

Boston has had continuous financial difficulties for a longer time than many other major cities. It is caught in a spiral of inflation, increasing and difficult to control costs, and, like most cities, over-dependence on the property tax, which provides 69 percent of its revenue. There were suggestions in 1950 that the city go into bankruptcy and have the state run it. It has been bailed out by the state several times, and many believe that the city's problems cannot be

solved locally where home rule powers are quite limited. Mayor
White and previous mayors have repeatedly filed legislation to lessen
the property tax burden but have met defeat on Beacon Hill (state
legislature). The cities are now turning to the federal government
for some form of revenue-sharing to ease their burdens.

LITTLE CITY HALLS

History

It seems that no one person can claim all the credit for the
idea of little city halls (LCH) in Boston. City Councilman Frederick
C. Langone talked about the idea for a couple of years. Councilmen
Thomas I. Atkins and John L. Saltonstall campaigned on the concept
in 1967.

However, it did remain for Mayor White to put the program into
effect, fulfilling a 1967 campaign pledge. He promised that, if elected,
he would find some way to make it easier for residents to make their
needs known to City Hall. His goals were more effective communication and better delivery of services.

The first LCH was opened on July 25, 1968, in a stationary
trailer parked in Maverick Square, East Boston—an area of 40,000
persons, predominantly (80 percent) Italian-American—to provide a
limited number of services, information and complaint processing,
and to act as a catalyst for community improvement projects.

Facilities and Hours of Operation

By 1970, most of the present fourteen LCHs were in operation
in almost every major section of the city, designed to serve all residents, rich and poor alike. The North End and Brighton locations are
substations with two-person staffs. Four persons perform as special
liaisons to Chinatown, Uphams Corner (Dorchester), Back Bay-Beacon
Hill-Fenway, and to the scattered Spanish-speaking community. These
are not included in the total of fourteen. A twenty-four-hour Inquiry
and Information Center in City Hall is considered a fifteenth LCH.

The Mayor's Office of Public Service (OPS), a central management office, particularly for the LCHs, is located in the main city hall,
and was formed soon after Mayor White took office in January, 1968.

It developed LCH locations by market-oriented studies of where people transacted business and the most heavily used shopping and transportation areas.

Five LCHs in Allston, Dorchester, East Boston, Mattapan, and West Roxbury are located in fifty-foot trailers, which cost the city $5,000 each plus site preparation and installation costs. Seven—located in Brighton, Jamaica Plain, Charlestown, Hyde Park, Roslindale, South Boston, and the South End—are in former, virtually forgotten and unused, municipal buildings built around 1921.

For example, one of these municipal buildings, located in the South End, is a gray brick structure which housed, among other activities, public showers, a branch library, and an auditorium. The LCH operation has revitalized the building—the auditorium is now frequently used by the community, the gym is heavily used, the Youth Activities Commission has its headquarters upstairs, and a well-child clinic and a library are housed downstairs.

The North End LCH is in a well-used community building, and the Roxbury center is on the second floor of a renovated office building, in well-lighted and pleasant quarters. All units are centrally located in a population center with good visibility. There is generally no over-crowding and, except for trailers, all operations are located in used structures. (See Map 2.)

Hours of operation are generally from 8 a.m. to 6 p.m., but centers may remain open later when there are special programs—e.g., voter registration, resident parking permit distribution, etc. Most LCH managers maintain evening and weekend hours by attending neighborhood meetings and working on special projects.

Budget

The 1970 OPS budget was a little under $1.1 million for operations and a staff of 125, which mans both central OPS and the fifteen LCHs. A supplementary appropriation of $121,000 (federal share was $300,000) was approved for a summer work program, making the total budget $1.2 million. Budgets have been approved pretty much as Mayor White presented them since the inception of the program.

But things have changed. In the year 1970, particularly, several councillors criticized LCH expenditures, indicating they wanted more proof of effectiveness. Certainly, there would be no additions to the program.

MAP 2
Boston's Little City Halls

Charlestown

East Boston

○ Maverick Square

Boston Harbor

Brighton

○ Harvard Ave.
at Commonwealth

□
20 Chestnut
Hill Ave.

Boston Proper

Shawmut Ave. at
W. Brookline St.
□

□ 535 E. Broadway

South Boston

20 Roxbury St.
◇
Roxbury

North Dorchester

South St.
□

Jamaica Plain

Dorchester
Ave. at
Park St. ○

Roslindale

Cummins Hwy. at
□ Washington St.

○ Blue Hill Ave. at
Morton St.

West Roxbury

○

Mattapan

Hyde Park

□

□   Municipal building

○   Trailer

◇   Leased space

Source: Office of Public Service, Boston.

Then in January, 1971, Mayor White announced a general austerity policy to help the city's financial plight. The OPS (LCH) budget would be cut 31 percent, or $397,000, including $276,000 in payroll cuts. However, much of it would be done by transferring four employees to other city departments and by paying the salaries of nineteen (nine to Roxbury LCH and ten to OPS Planning and Development) employees with Model Cities funds under a $177,000 contract for salaries and other costs. Councillor Thomas I. Atkins calls it a "shell game" and nonsense to say payrolls have been reduced. But apparently the Model Cities-funded OPS employees will carry out planning functions for both Model Cities and the entire city. OPS will operate with about 100 employees cut from the original 125, and all fifteen LCHs will continue to function with reduced staffs.

Staff

The average staff in each center includes a manager, assistant manager, service coordinator, and secretary-receptionist. The remaining OPS staff serve as field liaisons, in the twenty-four-hour service, or have administrative and research positions. Many non-OPS employees work in the LCHs either full- or part-time. These include, in every LCH, a fire inspector, Social Security adviser, and senior (citizen) aide; and in some LCHs there are a housing inspector, policeman, and Small Business Administration workers.

The first director of OPS was Daniel J. Finn, a Boston native, graduate of Boston University Law School, former commissioner of Boston's Housing Inspection Department, and an interim director of the Model Cities program under former Mayor John Collins.

In 1969, David Davis, formerly with the Brookings Institution and then Boston's budget director, was appointed director of OPS. Davis has now been transferred to the position of director of the city's Economic Development Commission. The present director of OPS is Edward C. Dwyer.

Other assistance to the LCHs has come from the Boston Urban Corps (a federally financed work-study program for college students). It has provided over 350 college students from thirty-four colleges with summer work in seventeen city agencies and LCHs. OPS coordinates this program and supervises the high school-level Neighborhood Youth Corps program, which has added as many as 400 young people to its program to build parks, construct boccie courts, paint traffic lights and fire hydrants, and perform similar neighborhood projects.

A Division of Urban Volunteers, established in September, 1969, to enroll citizens in special projects, has provided assistance to the LCHs through clean-up/fix-up projects, parks and playground improvements, and other projects.

At the inception of the program in 1968, recruitment assistance for several of the mayor's top administrators and a definition of structure and goals for OPS was provided by a Harvard study group, under the direction of Professor Samuel P. Huntington. The high standard of OPS directors and the mayor's insistence on quality have resulted in a skilled and competent staff. Several managers, however, are political favorites of the mayor—a facet of the program several councillors do not appreciate, although some city officials as well as some outside observers are of the opinion that in certain communities, politically oriented managers have been able to do a better job because of political skills and their ability to reach citizens.

Residents may express preferences in the recruitment of managers, but selection decisions rest with the mayor and director. There are job specifications for managers, but Eric Butler, OPS personnel officer, says, "The need is for manager types of such great diversification that job specifications must be very flexible." He indicates that OPS tries to adapt the manager's ability to community needs and seeks persons who can act as catalysts for change and help formulate policy decisions. Salaries range from $11,000 to $16,000 with some of the more highly paid managers receiving base salaries from departments from which they were borrowed plus the OPS increment.

John R. Hitchcock, associate professor in the Department of Urban and Regional Planning, University of Toronto, who recently studied LCHs in Boston, lists the following as manager's responsibilities, thus providing further insight to recruitment considerations:

1. Provide information to the community
2. Educate citizens about city operations, and the legal and other constraints under which it operates
3. Give the city information about the community and act as an advocate for the community's point of view
4. Make referrals to nonmunicipal agencies for services of various kinds
5. Act as ombudsman for citizens
6. Act as catalyst or energizer in the initiation of community activities, and help provide resources for community activities
7. Act as mediator where there is community conflict
8. Participate in development of city policy and in central research and evaluation of city activities.

In almost all cases, managers are not chosen from the area where they work, to avoid their becoming potential political rivals of state legislators who are elected by districts. In a couple of cases, they have lived and worked in the same areas, but Allan Jarositis is currently the only manager whose home is in his district. Some feel this rather inflexible policy may do as much harm as good because there are times when the most effective person lives in the area.

Managers vary in background. For example, Fred Salvucci, manager of the East Boston center (salary $16,000), worked five years for the Boston Redevelopment Authority, has a degree in transportation planning from MIT, and was a Fulbright scholar. Dick McKinnon, former manager of the Mattapan center, had been a police sergeant for twenty-two years and was given a leave of absence, first to be a housing code inspector and then to be an LCH manager. He now supervises a city-sponsored civilian auxiliary police force program under the Safe Streets program. Manager Kay Morrissey has about thirty years of government experience as a career civil servant and is loaned to OPS from the accounting department. OPS supplements her basic salary.

Assistant managers also need community skills. They handle complaints and delivery of services, assist the manager at community meetings, write articles, and may have to act as substation managers.

Objectives, Functions, and Demography

"Complaint processing and information distribution is the 'bread and butter' operation of the Little City Halls," states David Davis, but adds, "this is not enough to justify our existence by playing a numbers game with complaint statistics, even though the numbers are impressive." Edward Dwyer, the new director, relates in a February, 1971, progress report that requests have increased over 60 percent from 1969, to 9,000 per week (excluding the thousands of calls which come in during a snow or flooding emergency) and that walk-ins are half of this volume. Only one-sixth of these are complaints—most are citizen contacts for service or information. Estimates indicate 55 percent of the total complaints are handled downtown by OPS. The concentration is on city services rather than those services where the city has little control. (See Appendix C.)

Davis says, "We are improving our administrative arrangements with other city departments to yield response to complaints, facilitating (or inaugurating) new programs, and advising the administration on policy decisions which are important to neighborhoods that the Little City Halls serve." He feels it is a program that looks to the future so that sustained city progress will result.

Each LCH provides notary public service; has a part-time Social Security representative, fire inspector, and one to three senior aides working with the elderly; accepts water, sewer, and real estate tax bill payments;* handles applications for common tax abatements and review of rent increases; helps citizens get marriage, birth, and death records, and to apply for public jobs and public housing; and helps register voters (13,000 in 1970). The Internal Revenue Service annually processes about 1,600 people through the centers. Over 45,000 people picked up their residential parking permits at the LCHs last year.

The centers distribute service directories, ordinances, handbooks, maps, vehicle forms, birth certificate forms, job applications, income tax forms, notices, City Council meeting and hearing announcements, recreation information and other items. An information and referral directory (containing 50,000 items) serves as a guide to all services which are available through private and public agencies in the city.

OPS directs and administers the LCH program, including personnel and training, payroll, bill payment, dissemination of information to the centers, continuous updating of the OPS directory of services, and other administrative functions. And it is a management arm of the mayor's office, frequently aiding in the preparation of neighborhood-related grant applications and research programs.

It maintains a twenty-four-hour service primarily to handle emergency complaints, such as flooding, heating, and other problems. This service was particularly useful before most areas had LCHs; but even now that they do, it receives about the same volume of calls. Such a service improves communication by increasing citizen access points into the system.

The Planning and Evaluation Section statistically analyzes complaints to highlight problems in city departments and identify specific service tie-ups. Complaint forms are coded, programmed,

———————————

*Previously, voter registration and tax bill payments were decentralized during peak times, but only for brief periods. The volume of this work has gone up substantially in decentralized locations.

and processed by computer, but there is criticism that only about three-fourths of the complaints are computerized. OPS's response is that it is too burdensome to put all complaints on forms and some are less important than others. Commissioners and department heads have criticized the increase in paper work, particularly the use of a six-part form which has since been abandoned for a three-part form.

Complaint volumes are high. In a six-month period, 10,000 Sanitation Department complaints were received, which has proved an excellent sample for statistical analysis and pinpointing weak areas, for the first time providing hard data to show where improvements should be made. "This was the kind of information OPS needed to place leverage on the totally, privately contracted refuse service," says Tom Hargadon, chief planner of OPS.

Analysis showed that from the kind of complaints the city was receiving, it had power in about 90 percent of the cases to do something about them. (See Table 11.)

Hargadon feels that city departments cannot simply go about their business answering complaints—that centralized planning must take place if fundamental changes are to be made. He feels even the best system has scheduling problems, and that a systematic review of complaints and requests can pinpoint trouble areas sufficiently so that much of the "slack in unused manpower" can be tightened.

Davis, as an ex-budget director, has used much of his budget experience as leverage with department heads to get things done. OPS works closely with the budget office to see that neighborhood priorities are incorporated in capital budgeting plans.

OPS sees itself as a tool for institutional change and as a facilitator for neighborhood change. It systematically monitors the bureaucracy citywide through its network of LCHs and is searching for the most effective way to use the information collected. It is working with commissioners of departments responsible for the bulk of complaints, to restructure departments and shift resources. It has worked closely with the Home Rule Commission to see that its views are incorporated in any legislation that may call for department restructuring.

Most importantly, OPS believes that by providing the mayor with an alternative source of information about department performance, he is better able to judge and influence departmental behavior.

TABLE 11

Summary of Citizen Requests for Service, Boston, 1968-70

Complaint	Division	Percent
No Heat, Hot Water	Housing Inspection	13.3
Open Lots—Garbage, Litter	Housing Inspection	10.1
Garbage and Refuse on Streets	Sanitary Div., P.W.D.	7.0
Catch Basin, Sewer Malfunction	Sewer Div., P.W.D.	5.3
Streets—Surfacing, Cleaning	Highway Div., P.W.D.	4.5
Defective Plumbing	Housing Inspection	4.5
Building-Garbage, Litter	Housing Inspection	4.2
Water Leaks (nonhydrant)	Water Div., P.W.D.	3.8
Sidewalks—Surfacing, Cleaning	Highway Div., P.W.D.	3.4
Cars—Abandoned, Stolen, Speeding, Illegally Parked	Police Department	3.2
Vermin, Rodents	Housing Inspection	2.8
Vacant, Abandoned Buildings	Building Department	2.7
Physical Defects in Houses	Housing Inspection	2.3
Water Pressure	Water Div., P.W.D.	2.2
Teenagers—Vandalism, Loitering	Police Department	1.6
Street Sign Requests	Traffic and Parking	1.6
Adults—Loitering, Citizen Harassment	Police Department	1.5
Broken Street Lights	Lighting Section, P.W.D.	1.4
Business Establishments	Health and Hospital Dept.	1.3
Tree Pruning	Parks and Recreation Dept.	0.9
All Others		22.4

Source: Office of Public Service, Boston (February, 1971).

Some procedural changes have taken place as a result of OPS initiative or through its assistance to other departments. Some councillors and city commissioners, however, feel that its accomplishments do not match its claims; but where questioned, OPS responds that it provided the statistical analysis without which change may never have taken place. Although dramatic changes have not occurred, the following procedural changes have come about.

1. An inspection team utilizing personnel from six city departments was begun as an experiment, and the most efficient aspects of this pilot program were retained. A recommendation for a single, unified city inspection department has been made as a result of this experience.

2. Inspectors from city departments now call daily at each LCH to pick up requests and to act directly on routine problems, thus eliminating the more involved procedures which formerly delayed responses.

3. OPS data and analysis led to a new "skim-coating" approach to patching streets, consisting of covering large areas of street surface rather than spotpatching. It allows five times more streets to be completed with the same budget.

4. OPS statistical analysis showed a disproportionate number of Parks Department complaints concerning tree maintenance. Further study indicated need for a new civil service classification, more manpower, and a change in work schedules, all of which have been accomplished.

5. Innovations have been effected in the civil service system for positions that have been difficult to fill, such as tree trimmers. In some cases, individuals are now hired without formal examination on a three-month trial basis to determine their abilities, after which oral examinations are given to those who pass the training period satisfactorily.

6. OPS did the staff work for a study leading to the redeployment to patrol functions of 265 policemen who were doing nonpolice duties.

Other changes, either in progress or recommended by OPS, are a special housing court to expedite cases; housing inspection, park maintenance foreman and supervisors of public work yards to report regularly to LCHs for work loads; redistricting of park maintenance crews and addition of a special crew for small parks; in conjunction with public works personnel, new snowplowing plans using LCHs

to establish local priorities and help coordinate the several city departments involved; special kinds of public works equipment and local
priorities for street skim-coating; and major revisions in foreclosure
and auction procedures to expedite use of available city land for housing
and community recreation use.

The fourteen LCH areas average 50,000 to 75,000 persons each;
however, they range in actual size from 17,000 (Charlestown) to over
100,000 (Dorchester). The smaller neighborhoods generally have a
district geographical-historical identity, many of them having been
independent political units before annexation by the city.

The South End has 17,000 residents, about one-third black, one-
third Puerto Rican, and the remainder a mixture of Arabic, Greek,
and other nationalities. When John Thomas was manager here in July,
1969, he called it a "United Nations community." Adequate housing is
the main problem. In its more prosperous times, the wealthy lived in
stately five-story, brownstone structures—most of them now cut up
into apartments and rooming houses.

East Boston has 40,000 residents, 80 percent of Italian origin
and most of the rest Irish. Mattapan has 68,000 persons, 75 percent
black. Once a predominantly Jewish area, now most white people are
moving out and its transitional state makes lasting changes difficult
and the citizen's council hard to keep together.

South Boston is 99 percent white, made up of 41,000 Irish, Polish,
and Italians. Twelve thousand elderly create special service problems.
There is a lunch program for the elderly and a visitation program for
shut-ins. Twenty-eight percent of the population live in five housing
projects.

The Allston-Brighton area has a higher-income population, fewer
normal day-to-day problems, and greater ability to cope with the
system. Overcoming alienation might be the biggest task here.

The fourteen areas vary in income, ethnic groups, type of problems, number of old and young, and numerous other factors. They
and the multitude of neighborhoods within them characterize special
concerns and take unique approaches and special abilities to cope
with them.

Managers have been involved in mundane as well as dramatic
issues. Fred Salvucci of the East Boston LCH has successfully fought
the expansion of Logan International Airport. Ed Kennedy of South

TABLE 12

OPS Activity, Boston, 1969 and 1970

	Total Business			Percent Business Handled Locally		
	1970	1969*	Percent Increase	1970	1969	Difference
Allston	21,677	15,700	38.1	96.9	91.4	5.5
Brighton	6,821	2,100	225.8	99.4	95.1	4.3
Charlestown	17,559	11,900	47.6	80.6	89.5	8.9
Dorchester	23,800	17,300	37.6	84.8	78.0	6.8
East Boston	23,467	13,900	68.8	95.0	83.8	11.2
Hyde Park	11,014	5,700	93.2	89.7	89.8	.1
Jamaica Plain	17,854	12,800	39.5	84.9	86.1	1.2
Mattapan	23,245	11,900	95.3	93.7	82.5	11.2
North End	7,354	5,900	24.6	90.5	90.0	.5
Roslindale	19,408	18,800	3.2	95.2	87.9	7.3
Roxbury	23,751	15,900	49.4	86.0	53.6	32.4
South Boston	17,559	13,100	34.0	90.5	80.9	9.6
South End	20,421	11,200	82.3	89.6	76.9	12.7
West Roxbury**	14,771	–	–	79.7	–	–
Total LCH	248,701	156,200	59.5	89.6	81.5	8.1
24-Hr. Service	159,020	155,300	2.4	–	–	–
Total	408,737	311,500	30.9	93.1	88.2	4.9

*1969 figures are rounded off, due to a slightly different system of record keeping.

**The West Roxbury hall opened in May, 1970.

Source: Office of Public Service, Boston (February, 1971).

TABLE 13

OPS Walk-in Business, Boston, 1969 and 1970

	1970 (percent)	1969 (percent)
Allston	57.0	37.0
Brighton	43.8	—
Charlestown	52.0	44.3
Dorchester	50.8	35.0
East Boston	71.3	70.1
Hyde Park	48.4	45.8
Jamaica Plain	51.4	39.6
Mattapan	32.3	29.4
North End	69.2	61.9
Roslindale	51.0	49.7
Roxbury	23.9	23.5
South Boston	66.2	44.5
South End	50.2	21.7
West Roxbury	65.2	—
Total LCH	52.3	40.6
24-Hr. Service	20.6	6.6
Total	39.9	22.8

Source: Office of Public Service, Boston (February, 1971).

Boston convinced two railroad corporations to remove tracks for the construction of a major street, and he has also been successful in enlisting the aid of financial institutions for new home construction and rehabilitation projects. Managers have put together school lunch programs, day-care and community centers, encouraged construction of parks, improvements in bus service, food for the elderly, half-fare transportation rates, and the development of a heating force to give aid to those without heat during the winter.

For youth, centers sponsor trips, basketball leagues, forums between adults and youth, educational programs on drugs, establish recreation and work programs, and help secure employment.

TABLE 14

Citizen Requests for Service, by Department,
OPS Activity, Boston, 1970

Department		Percent of Total
Building Department		5.3
Health and Hospitals Department		2.2
Housing Inspection Department		44.1
Parks and Recreation Department		1.6
Police Department		7.8
Public Works Department		30.3
Highway Division	9.2	
Sanitation Division	7.0	
Sewer Division	4.4	
Street Lighting	1.9	
Water Division	7.8	
Traffic and Parking Department		4.3
All Other		4.4

Source: Office of Public Service, Boston (February, 1971).

Spanish-speaking employees of several centers assist the approximately 30,000 Spanish-speaking residents in the city, and the only full-time Chinese-speaking staff of any public or private agency is provided by OPS. Conferences and assorted exhibits have been held, bilingual schools established, a welcome wagon for Spanish-speaking residents started, information for a weekly radio show provided, and an extensive translation service in the courts and police stations has been set up. The centers help distribute and provide information to two newspapers—one Spanish and one Chinese.

Managers use a variety of techniques to get the job done. When Rick McKinnon was manager of Mattapan, he was sensitive to the reluctance of many residents to go downtown for assistance. He found the elderly, in particular, have a fear of the unknown, of large structures, of poor reception, and they prefer to talk to someone they know and feel they can trust. When one resident could not get her landlord to repair an old boiler in severe weather, McKinnon went directly to the landlord's house and sat there until he agreed to correct the matter. This kind of tactic not only gets results, it teaches the citizen how to get things done. McKinnon was successful at it, and in his opinion, the LCHs averted a "near riot" in their first year of operation.

Allen Jarositis, manager of the Charlestown center, operates from an old municipal building by the Charles River, one of Boston's oldest sections, where the battle of Bunker Hill was fought. The area has been in turmoil recently, primarily because of urban renewal problems. Where the city's program was first started, residents here said they "did not want a Little City Hall or any more government interference in their daily lives." Nine months later, however, 2,000 registered voters signed petitions demanding a center.

Some managers have proved that they can get large projects accomplished by knowing how to maneuver outside the system. Managers Kay Morrissey and Frank Mollica have been around government for twenty years and know department superintendents "blindfolded." They are known for their ability to get things done.

One manager who had been unable to get things done came under severe criticism by residents and has since been relieved of his position. His own philosophy was that you could not accomplish much on a complaint-by-complaint basis—that a much broader and systematic approach was necessary. He was unable to accomplish any significant projects.

Professor Hitchcock indicates that all managers interviewed by his staff "had a genuine feeling that there were community-level values which had been neglected in the city in the past," and that some managers were more ideologically committed than others. Managers felt they were there to reduce an imbalance. Speaking of managers' divided loyalties, Hitchcock says, "This did not appear to threaten the survival of the program," explaining that the city was guilty of inaction rather than the wrong kind of action, and that actual threats to community values stemmed largely from other agencies, such as the State Highway Department, Massachusetts Port Authority, Metropolitan District Commission, Boston Housing Authority, or the Massachusetts Bay Transportation Authority. Also, since this was the mayor's program, he was prepared to listen and accept some criticisms. "It was legitimate for the managers to express community opposition and even to stir some up without being traitors," Hitchcock points out.

Managers have acted as moderators in the absence of local citizen councils and they have forced department heads to deal with

them as visible spokesmen for a newly developed constituency. And
managers have also helped departments by coordinating those unable
to coordinate themselves. They have helped to fill a vacuum, and this
creative role may be their greatest contribution.

DEPARTMENT PERFORMANCE AND TECHNIQUES
OF COORDINATION

There would be little program success if Mayor White did not
stress full cooperation from commission and department heads in their
relationships with LCH managers. Department heads tend to give preference to managers, but an overabundance of requests makes expeditious handling difficult. Boston's bureaucracy is slow and unproductive.
Union rules are restrictive, making economies less likely. All employees, except commissioners, are under civil service; and a strong
emphasis on seniority makes it difficult to promote the most efficient
workers.

OPS has annoyed some commissioners because of cumbersome
procedures; but some have praised it as a buffer between them and
citizens, conserving time because they do not have to deal directly
with residents.

Housing Inspections

About 80 percent of the 25,000 annual housing enforcement
complaints are still received through regular channels to the Housing
Inspection Office in City Hall, reports Frank Henry, director of the
Housing Inspection Department. Approximately 400-500 complaints
are received monthly from the LCHs. As in most cities, enforcement
and correction of problems is difficult because of lack of adequate
relocation housing, slow and cumbersome court proceedings, absentee
ownership, and high construction and rehabilitation costs. Yet many
severe housing problems are corrected.

Under the housing commissioner are the Housing Inspection
Board and sixty inspectors in forty-five inspection districts. Twenty-
five inspectors are stationed in Roxbury alone (an area of severe
housing deterioration) in a district unit which would continue to operate
in a decentralized fashion whether there were LCHs or not. The
department believes decentralization generates greater productivity
and neighborhood concern by its employees. Many LCHs have housing
inspectors reporting to them. Action for Boston Community Development (ABCD) and the city have combined funds to train ten additional

inspectors. The model cities agency has also funded a program to train ten housing rehabilitation inspectors. This interagency cooperation and stationing of inspectors in LCHs has created greater responsiveness to citizen complaints. In addition, the citizen now receives a copy of the violation report and results of the investigation, as well as a booklet informing him of his rights and responsibilities. Most important, the Housing Inspection Department sees the value of decentralization.

Public Works

Public works complaints have increased because complaint stations are closer to the people. Citizens believe there is a better chance to get results under the LCH program because its workers are striving for unusual results. However, basic operations have not changed. LCHs are used primarily to get complaints to the right people, reports Joseph F. Casazza, commissioner of the Department of Public Works. The two departments have cooperated well on publicity and organization for clean-up programs and other special projects. "If you weigh the pluses and minuses, Little City Halls come out on the plus side," he says. "There is no question the program should be continued, but with modifications." His chief criticisms were that paper work increased too much and the complaint process had become too complex. He says, "There are too many copies and too many people looking at them. People want results—not paper."

OPS recognized these faults and reduced their six-part complaint form to three parts and simplified the structure. But with the considerable increase in number of complaints and the new policy of answering everyone, the process necessarily became more complex.

Operations of the fifteen decentralized public works yards vary with the competence and motivation of district superintendents. And LCH managers' abilities to work with these superintendents are very important in getting complaints handled promptly and effectively. Initially, some superintendents complained that managers had too much to say about operations and were trying to develop "kingdoms of their own." Casazza feels this problem "has been licked," but there is still a question about how much authority managers should have.

Casazza suggested staff meetings as a possible solution for better communication between superintendents and managers and more effective coordination of projects. More importantly, he placed high priorities on revitalization of the Public Service Board (enlarged city action cabinet), and greater understanding and commitment by city commissioners to overall objectives. Priorities and scheduling are changed too frequently and OPS does not work closely enough with departments. Casazza felt that someone from his office ought to be assigned to the OPS staff to achieve more effective working relationships. A systems analyst from OPS has assisted in studies of manpower and equipment, snowplowing, skim-coating, and sanitation procedures, but closer liaison seems necessary.

In regard to these relationships, David Davis says, "Most city employees working with Little City Halls are cooperative and try, within the limits of their resources, to do what is necessary for citizens. Many problems with which we deal are structural—agencies working at cross purposes and bottlenecks because of disputes over jurisdiction. We try to provide the viewpoint of the consumer, and then work toward the resolution of his problems. This subtle and difficult process takes a long time and we expect daily frustration."

There seems to be consensus among city employees, elected officials, and private interests that basic changes are needed in the established mechanism of department operations, if complaints are to be handled effectively and major improvements made.

Mayor's Cabinet

To improve working relationships, Mayor White established a Public Service Board, the first in Boston's history. It started with over thirty participants, including department heads and key mayor's staff, and was designed to streamline city services and improve coordination. Developing new policies and procedures, effecting institutional changes, and improving coordination were its main goals. Originally, it was intended that the cabinet structure would oversee only LCHs, but the comprehensiveness of problems changed its course to one of overall planning and coordination. When it met, the mayor served as chairman and the director of OPS as executive director. Though the cabinet started with good intentions, it has not continued to meet regularly or function effectively.

Size, lack of an appropriate agenda, and lack of strong leadership were some of its faults. The mayor has found it more convenient to meet weekly with a smaller cabinet of only some department heads and key staff who make important policy recommendations. Formal, regular contact with all department heads does not take place, even though some officials feel this form of communication would improve relationships considerably. (Mayor Lindsay in New York, for example, finds it useful to meet regularly with a large cabinet of thirty to forty key figures, as well as with a smaller body.) Smaller cabinets seem essential for dealing with immediate matters, whereas more encompassing bodies can deal more effectively with more complex issues, such as working out agreements for coterminous districting, development of formal procedures for contacts between superintendents and local office managers, interchange of problems and solutions beneficial to other districts, setting priorities for resources, and obtaining a clearer understanding of the mayor's mandates for his team. Without cabinets, too many feel left out.

Mini-Cabinets

More recently, development of mini-cabinets in some districts is seen as an asset to problem solving. A few managers are now developing them. They normally consist of public works foremen, the housing chief, park supervisor, and similar district supervisory personnel. The feeling is that this will help improve neighborhood services because local supervisors become more knowledgeable about the totality of local problems, more sensitive about neighborhood feelings, and more experienced at finding solutions through better coordination. Under the system, district foremen are required to attend resident meetings in their areas, making them more cognizant of citizen problems and what should be done to solve them. In turn, they explain their operations and learn firsthand what citizen reaction means. Some managers feel mini-cabinets in their areas would not be useful or do not fit their operating style; therefore, the city has not made them mandatory.

To achieve more effective coordination, OPS is studying realignment of department districts so that as many boundaries as possible can be made coterminous. Presently, for example, housing inspectors work areas different from those of public works inspectors, and LCH boundaries sometimes overlap several private and public agency boundaries. Different procedures and forms are used. One section of a neighborhood may be served by several district offices of the same agency because of poorly planned boundaries. This is not peculiar to Boston but is a phenomenon of most large urbanized areas. Uniform districts help achieve coordination by reducing the number of agency heads a manager must deal with; allow development of more efficient mini-cabinets responsible to a similar area; permit more effective and understandable use of statistics and other information; allow joint use of facilities and personnel; and create stronger neighborhood identity for development of citizen councils and a sense of community.

Internal Coordination

Besides problems of external coordination, managers have insufficient authority to achieve coordination within their centers. Coordination is accomplished primarily by a manager's personal abilities and the working relationships he develops with other agency heads. It is helped by the fact that agencies are located in the same building, use a common pool of clerical assistance and common statistical data, and deal with the same neighborhood clientele. OPS plans to rotate other civil servants through LCHs as a way of further improving city personnel. Internal staff meetings and formalized agreements between the city and agencies would improve relationships.

CITIZEN PARTICIPATION

Mayor White promised he wouldn't put LCHs where residents did not want them. This was the first indication that residents were to be involved in the program.

Consequently, more citizens have become involved in city affairs, which is apparent from increases in the number of requests and visits for service. Many residents who did not complain or request service before apparently do so now because they have been encouraged and feel they may get results. In this way citizens are participating more than ever.

Citizen Councils

Local advisory councils (LAC) have been organized in five neighborhoods and are meeting regularly. In most other areas they are being organized. Joe Smith, head of LAC development and formerly a community organizer in Boston's community action program, helps in LAC formation. He indicates that more advisory councils than LCHs will be developed to adequately cover the city. Smith believes it would have been better to develop the advisory councils before LCHs were established; but OPS feels that a slower, evolutionary development of local councils is better, because no clear community "exists in any area, but rather, many voices." Some neighborhoods are over-organized already, and there is also apprehension that better articulated community demands coming through formal citizen councils might cause problems because of the inability to deliver steadily. (See Appendix F.)

One of the most effective councils is Frank Mollica's in Dorchester, where he meets several times per month with the main committee or one of about ten subcommittees. It was not formed by an elective process but merely came together by common resident interest and leadership of the manager.

Some councils have been formed by elections using regular city polling places. The only guideline is that membership must be open to anyone in the community over eighteen years of age. Schedules of meetings and membership recruitment are advertised in the press. LCH personnel will staff them and the Boston Redevelopment Authority will assign a planner to some.

Smith believes it is better to let the community decide how to set up its council. He opposes general elections as a method of council selection because there is a tendency to elect political "hacks," a predominance of activists, and those unfavorable to the client majority. Control stays in a few hands and the same hands. Smith feels a door-to-door referendum whereby citizens can be challenged, confronted with all the issues and candidates, and speak freely is a good approach. Though his views have been criticized, he believes citizen councils must get involved in the political process if they are to be effective.

Director Dwyer reports that each LAC (and, in areas without one, concerned community residents) worked with the Parks Department to review major plans for 1971, helped designate uses for drug program funds, and advised on Community Improvement Area boundaries. He says that in some areas, LACs have been granted substantial decision-making power. In East Boston, for instance, the LAC health subcommittee chose the staff for the community health center and specified what services should be provided.

Community Action Program

The parent body of the community action program (CAP) in Boston is Action for Boston Community Development (ABCD), which has fifty-one members. Fifty-one percent are elected annually from various neighborhoods and the remainder are appointed from business groups, local agencies, and three civil rights organizations. ABCD's neighborhood program operates through community corporations,

under the Area Planning Action Councils (APAC), which initially were
advisory and then were incorporated to operate their own programs.

Community corporations operate side-by-side with LCHs in
many areas. Some CAP boundaries overlap those of several LCHs;
therefore, CAP chooses the LCH with which it wishes to work. If
results are inadequate at this level, CAP can go directly to department
heads at City Hall.

Frank Mollica indicates that the CAP agency in Dorchester works
in only about one-fourth of the territory and tends to specialize in problems of poverty clientele. He believes that other groups will not use
services if they are too closely associated with the "war on poverty"
program. Therefore, he thinks it necessary to have LCHs in all areas
of the city, to insure that all types of problems and all income levels
are being served. "People choose the organization with which they
want to work," he says.

Some feel that CAP agencies should have been the organizations
under which the LCH program was developed rather than creating new
institutions. Doris Graham, director of the Dorchester APAC, believes
LCH was not organized properly. "There is too much competition and
duplication of services, and it causes confusion for residents," she
says. "They don't know which center to go to."

However, she believes it has not affected her operation very
much because the same number of people are coming in with complaints.
Also, many other organizations in the area, such as the Dorchester
Information Center and civic associations, use her council for assistance in processing all types of complaints, Mrs. Graham explains.

In many areas, community action groups work well with LCHs.
In East Boston, the CAP agency assisted in organizing the Little City
Halls operation. Many citizens elected to the APAC boards provide
considerable input into LCHs through advisory councils and programs,
and one CAP center is used partially as an LCH.

Initial opposition by the CAP, stemming from the assumption
that the city was going to "take over," has passed with realization
that the city will not interfere with CAP operations. Also, there is
favorable sentiment that higher-income neighborhoods must be serviced,
and that CAP cannot do this under its program. And, of course, APAC
operates more traditional poverty-type programs, such as manpower
training, employment, Head Start, social welfare, etc., while LCHs
emphasize City Hall programs.

MODEL CITIES AGENCY

Boston's Model Neighborhood Board operates in the two target areas of Roxbury and North Dorchester, and has eighteen citizen members elected from six subareas. The agency has a staff of 180 persons and has been approved for $7.7 million for twenty-two programs in its first operation year. The Model Cities area is 1,953 acres and consists of 63,000 residents. The area is doughnut-shaped around the Washington Park urban renewal area, making it difficult for the LCH manager to deal with Model Cities as the exclusive representative of residents of that community.

Some coordination takes place between Model Cities and LCH, however. For example, Model Cities funds provide inspectors for the Roxbury LCH, which in turn houses Model Cities. There are other programs jointly planned, but some city officials feel that there has not been enough use made of Model Cities funds for improving existing city services.

The Roxbury Family Life Center is Boston's first comprehensive health center under Model Cities. It provides one-stop health services to 10,000 people. Full multiservice centers are not planned, apparently because LCH and CAP programs are providing many of these functions.

Paul Parks, Model Cities administrator, believes a coordinated service delivery approach to Model Cities must be developed and should include health, day care, housing, police protection, street cleaning, trash removal, garbage collection, and economic development. "We hope by redefining and showing by example the redefinition of the service delivery mechanisms that we can begin to spend tax dollars far more efficiently," he says in a letter to citizens. Model Cities officials would like to see the Model Cities area become a laboratory for more efficient use of the tax dollar. And with Boston's poorly operated services and inefficient employee system, this would be an achievement.

POLITICS AND PERCEPTIONS

Elected Officials

There is a mixed reaction to LCHs from elected officials. Some city councillors openly opposed the program at first but subsequently requested LCHs in their areas. For some, the program was an accepted fact and, if there were political advantages to be gained by Mayor White, they would use it to their advantage too. Some of these officials perceived that opposition to a particular LCH might arouse voter resentment.

A few councillors and state legislators hold neighborhood meetings independent of the LCH organization. Some legislators have district offices, and are concerned that the program is diminishing their visibility in constituent districts. For some officials opposition has declined; for others it has become more serious. LCHs have been an issue since 1968, and it was an issue in the 1971 mayoral campaign. But the program probably helped White, as he won more easily than most expected.

"It ought to be called the department of injustice. It is a great disservice—the biggest hoax perpetrated on the people in the history of Boston," Councillor Joseph Timilty says flatly. He feels it has not provided better services even though it was billed as an end to citizen problems. "It is more public relations and projection than performance," he says, "and the $1.5 million expenditure is an excellent way for Mayor White to build a political machine." He feels that only five LCHs are needed and that most appointments to the centers are patronage. His higher expenditure figure is based on costs he believes OPS does not consider, such as the base salaries of some employees who are paid from other departments.

Timilty believes the most important way to improve services is to develop different and more effective ways for city departments to handle complaints. In his estimation, internal administrative and organizational changes are the most necessary elements for more effective government.

"We haven't put our own house in order and now have created another layer of government which has further alienated the public," says Timilty. He refers to certain departments which are not over-worked yet fail to produce and managers, though talented, who have failed to get things done because they could not move the system. He believes that the nine city councillors, acting as ombudsmen, are in a better position to do this. OPS counters by saying councillors do not have the machinery to handle thousands of weekly complaints, although it feels that on some difficult cases it is desirable to use councillors to break through the system they are both fighting.

Councillor John L. Saltonstall believes that the program has not come close to meeting its full potential, that citizens should become more directly involved in program operation, and that specific decision-making authority should be given to managers, so that LCHs are not simply referral agencies.

"It is the extra imagination of staff at some centers that tends to get things done," he says. "Managers have made connections and it seems you can't get things done unless it is done as a favor."

Councillors say the program was initially sold to them as an experiment, and program operators feel that more time is necessary to evaluate results fairly.

Until recently, a majority of the City Council has supported the program at budget time, but Saltonstall says, "If we don't get better proof of its effectiveness, this will not be true for long. There certainly will not be any expansion." In 1970, the council turned down a request for two additional LCHs.

In an April 9, 1970, article in the Christian Science Monitor, Gabriel F. Piemonte, City Council president, asked, "What purpose is served by the Little City Halls?" He has criticized the program, which began with an appropriation of $305,000 in 1968 and is now costing over $1 million.

"The Little City Hall manager must still call the department concerned," Piemonte says. "Why couldn't the citizen first call the department directly?" Why do citizens need a middle man to talk to their employees? Little City Halls are just a buffer between the public and the administration."

Councillor Thomas I. Atkins said, "If the Little City Hall program stops at the complaint level, with no follow-up, then it is just another layer of government."

Councillor Langone staunchly defends the concept of an LCH in each neighborhood, maintaining, "If one area gets one, every neighborhood should get one, too." "Nobody has proved them a failure," he adds.

Some councillors believe that the program simply makes the mayor stronger at their expense, in this already strong-mayor form of government, but political theory suggests that consolidation of power in the mayor's office is a positive—not negative—effect, to allow mayors to move their cities. City Councils, however, naturally believe in a more balanced approach, citing Chicago, where under a

weak-mayor system, Richard Daley is powerful because most of the
council supports him as a team, even though a political team.

Since councillors are elected at-large in Boston, name recognition
is important for reelection. They are heavily dependent on getting their
names in the news, yet the press pays little attention to the substance
of their debates. Attacking mayors (including former mayors John
Collins and John Hynes), even by councillors favoring the mayor, is
the easiest way to attract attention. Criticizing LCHs as a large
expenditure and calling for economy are favorite council attacks.
Since the city's most serious problem is perhaps its financial condition,
LCHs, being new, visible, and associated with change, are easy targets.

The nature of Boston politics was brought out by former head
of the Boston Redevelopment Authority, Hale Champion. In his resigna-
tion, after an attempt to reorganize the Authority, he commented that
politics in Boston was conducted on a new personal level, and that
personalities were immediately and thoroughly associated with programs,
resulting in petty and often vindictive attacks.

Yet criticisms go deeper than politics, and councillors are concerned about the effectiveness and expenditures of this program. Mayor
White too realized the program's faults. In an April 9, 1970, Christian
Science Monitor article he voiced three concerns: (1) failure to establish LACs to the city administration to relate how best to service
neighborhoods; (2) backlog of unserviced complaints, which totaled
8,000 at the end of 1970; and (3) failure to translate the "more sophisticated service and better talent" at the LCH level "up to the top of the
system."

Five LACs have been formed. OPS has improved paper work
and the processing of complaints, but it does not yet appear that
employee competence and dedication have rubbed off at the department
level.

Business Community

The Chamber of Commerce and business community are unsure
of the program's accomplishments. "We are not sure LCHs are much
more than mayor's listening posts and a little candy store operation."
They feel reduction of racial tensions cannot be attributed to the
program because it is not relevant to the most pressing racial issues
of school integration, housing, and police problems. "Decentralization
should come at City Hall first by allowing department heads to act

with precision and authority," they say. "Now it is no good to complain, because nothing happens."

William F. Chouinard, of the Greater Boston Chamber of Commerce Governmental Relations Division, says, "The City Council wouldn't be knocking them so hard if they were doing a good job." But there are those who attribute City Council criticism more to politics than to analysis of the program; however, criticism is difficult without specific allegations.

Chouinard believes that the general theory of LCHs to improve communications is good but is critical of going far beyond normal city operations and feels progress has been slowed because the concept preceded any formal plan of decentralization.

League of Women Voters

The League of Women Voters believes the LCH program was prompted by a sincere desire of city officials to provide citizens better service, although some political involvement was inevitable.

"The able director [Davis] of the Little City Hall program has made it a responsive and positive organization of government," says Mrs. Saul Pearlman, president of the League. "Requests for services at Little City Halls do bring response and action." She feels that a number of creative and effective governmental programs have been instituted by Mayor Collins and Mayor White, that city government has improved and is more responsive than in the past.

Municipal Research Bureau

The Boston Municipal Research Bureau (a private, not-for-profit organization funded by contributions from private citizens and corporate bodies) makes the following comments concerning the program:

The Little City Halls program is an attempt by the city administration to respond better to service needs of its citizens. As such, it represents part of a nationwide trend, and part of what might be termed an administrative and political cyclical movement. American governmental processes tend to move from forms of decentralization to forms of centralization and back, as witness the

fact that some Little City Halls have been set up in old
"municipal buildings."

However, the program has had many problems since
its inception. The Research Bureau initially felt that the
program should have been established on a pilot basis, to
let some of the bugs get ironed out before it expanded. A
pilot program can legitimately run out of a mayor's office.
A major line operation should not. In Boston's case, since
the mayor was known to be interested in the governor's
job, the fact of having this large group of noncivil service
employees working out of his office led to suspicion about
the Little City Halls program.

Academe

The advantages outweigh the disadvantages, believes Eric
Nordlinger, associate professor of politics, Brandeis University, in
a review of the LCH program. It has hastened service delivery, provided new services, and improved communications; however, he believes
it has not had anything to do with reducing racial tensions, nor has it
created institutional change, paramount to lasting improvement. Some
fundamental changes may occur by giving citizen councils decision-
making authority, he feels.

Davis wanted to create institutional change, but the mayor was
not significantly involved in the program to add the necessary strength,
Nordlinger states. The program has had an impact on the bureaucracy
only informally, for things get done mostly by asking favors. Commissioners are reluctant to break their routines, he says.

The civil service seniority system and lack of employee discipline
are two factors cited by Nordlinger that damage the system. "There
is an ethos in the whole system of 'don't cause any strain,'" he feels.
Supervisors have set performance standards below acceptable norms,
and they avoid doing anything which may displease subordinates.
Consequently, the entire system suffers from underutilization of
human and material resources, creating a pervasive sluggishness
particularly evident in service delivery. Alone, OPS and LCH managers cannot change it.

City Employees

In almost all cities originators and administrators of decentralized
programs feel they are successful, and Boston is no exception.

Commissioners and department heads generally feel the program is
designed to reach people and help deliver services more satisfactorily.
They feel effects of some changes in priorities, and as long as Mayor
White is in office, they are ready to accept the program but are unwill-
tin to relinquish any control to LCH managers or OPS.

LCH managers naturally favor the program, but some are disenchanted with progress. Gail Rotegarde, OPS planner, believes managers
have an "overlayer of protective cynicism" about LCHs but, when
pressed, are able to measure and evaluate successes and failures.
She feels they tend to overlook their own good works, the fact that
demand for good works often outweighs capacity to deliver, and the
fact that their voices are counted in decisions affecting neighborhoods
where they work. OPS and managers have had a clear impact on
important policy decisions (moratorium on highway construction,
city rent control, opposition to airport expansion) which have made
a significant difference to many people, she says, and points out that
managers' own abilities are often strengthened by citizen backing.
The manager may be a live advocate, a mediator among many factions,
or one who has to spend much of his time developing effective community organizations, she says.

Managers like to think that they will become autonomous and
will be given considerable decision-making authority. In reality, they
know, even with the mayor backing the program, the most effective
way to get better department response is through their own personalities and abilities to deal with city and agency heads. They do not see
LCHs as being significantly expanded or strengthened at this time.

Some managers have been chosen because of their close political
alliance to Mayor White. The staff gives them credit for a great deal
of competence in keeping order and resolving conflicting demands.
They feel that in many cases political backgrounds have proved a
distinct asset in dealing with people, whether voters or nonvoters.

Agency Perceptions

APAC Director Doris Graham feels LCHs have not changed
things very much, are really a "political thing" on the part of the
mayor, and get very little done. She says they were supposed to
stay open until 11 p.m. but most of them close around 5 p.m. "What
have they done?" she asks. Some community action agency officials
speak favorably of the program, crediting it with achieving better
response to neighborhood problems and demonstrating city concern.

Agencies which work within LCH facilities generally feel the program has helped them relate to the city and reach citizens more effectively by their proximity. Some feel employee performance has improved. Agencies not in the physical structures see the beginnings of improvements through mini-cabinets, better coordination, and more thorough complaint follow-up.

Resident Feelings

It appears that the bulk of residents generally feel government has become more responsive and is at least trying to solve problems. Neighborhood meetings sometimes draw as many as 1,500 people to meet with the mayor and his staff. Hyde Park, for example, had not seen a mayor in the neighborhood for nine years before this program. Public reception has been good and neighborhood sessions have been informative, worthwhile experiences.

The program has helped thousands of individuals solve problems, many of whom probably would not have made the effort because of past experiences of despair. For example, many heating and home maintenance complaints have gone unanswered in the past. Now LCH managers, acting as neighborhood ombudsmen, pursue landlords and even harass them into making corrections. When courts and regular procedures became ineffective, managers instituted innovative techniques and persistence to get results. A survey of citizens served reinforces this conclusion.

In the past, a resident who called to have a vehicle removed, for example, might have had to call several places before he found the correct department, depending on whether the car was stolen, on private or public property, abandoned, or vandalized. It takes more than the average citizen to unravel this mystery. Now he can do it with one call—a routine case for LCHs to handle.

In evaluating the program, it is difficult to determine how many persons have benefited who otherwise might not, but the weekly volume of requests received and answered since LCHs were established suggests that service has improved considerably.

Though LCHs are located in all sections of Boston, some citizens still view the program as a "give-away" for blacks. Some neighborhoods feel the money should be spent on "law and order" and have, according to one city official, exaggerated the crime rate in their areas to prove their point. And yet, if other neighborhoods have

LCHs, they want them too. Backlash from "forgotten Americans" is of considerable proportion in Boston.

Dealing with problems on a citywide basis has proved advantageous to the city by giving officials time to head off crises while focusing attention quietly. Because he has focused attention on poverty areas, on problems of racial equality and poverty, Kevin White is widely known as Mayor Black among whites (who constitute 80 percent of the population) in spite of large public works and public facilities programs located in white neighborhoods. But this does not prevent countercharges by some blacks of "city hall tokenism" and "white paternalism."

Citizen reaction on LCHs is mixed. Many say a referendum on the program would be very close. Residents less able to get through the system appreciate its advantages. The more adept need it less and tend to concentrate on the big issues facing their neighborhoods, using the managers as a catalyst to organize the community. While both groups have benefited, the key question is whether the program is worth the cost.

A survey of the Boston area based on citizen interviews conducted during the past year by the Joint Center for Urban Studies of MIT and Harvard concludes: "Being responsive and communicating concern is clearly part of winning community backing; and our data suggest that this task is even harder to do, but perhaps more important to people, than delivering services." (See Appendix 6.)

Seven out of ten gave City Hall only a fair-to-poor rating, although the services of police, schools, and trash collection got majority approval in the survey. Few were happy with parks and playgrounds in their neighborhoods. Irish residents are the most satisfied with most services, while blacks are the most critical.

The study concludes that no matter what a city administration does for people, it will face a certain amount of serious dissatisfaction. It suggests that a key problem of a mayor of a city like Boston is convincing city residents that things are actually being accomplished in their behalf. A great proportion of the population seems to think that government is always most concerned with helping someone else.

Gail Rotegarde feels the report implies need for continued attention to communication with neighborhoods. She says, "It suggests that the city administration may have been too apolitical in its efforts—that it has devoted its attention to making changes, positive efforts,

in the neighborhoods, and has not gone far enough in letting people
know what has been achieved."

RECOMMENDATIONS OF THE HOME RULE
COMMISSION

Feeling the need to move decision making closer to the people,
Mayor White appointed a Home Rule Commission in 1968 composed
of "blue ribbon" citizens to make recommendations on restructuring
of Boston's government. The key staff person, Professor Frank
Michaelman of Harvard Law School, has been paid from the mayor's
budget, and the commission has served without compensation.

The commission's report, "The Decentralization of Government
Services," has been presented to the City Council for review; but for
it to become law, it would need to be passed by the state legislature.
There is strong feeling that Boston's government needs drastic changes,
but there is also apprehension about giving too much control to neighborhoods. It appears that the commission's proposal will have "rough
sledding" from city councillors as well as state legislators.

The issue of decentralization in Boston revolves primarily
around citizen hostility, distrust of local government (the front-line
service agency), and frustration with service. The Home Rule Commission reports serious problems of communication and cooperation
have arisen between City Hall and local people: "In the South End,
concern has been voiced about urban renewal planning and building
demolition, rehabilitation, and construction; in East Boston, about
the airport; in Jamaica Plain, about management of public housing;
in West Roxbury, about high-rise construction; in Roxbury, about
neighborhood schools; in Jamaica Plain, Dorchester, and elsewhere,
about "infill" housing; throughout the city, about the Southwest Express-
way and the Inner Belt; and so forth."

The commission feels that existing programs of Model Cities,
community action, LCHs, and various citizen councils have not been
enough to close the gap. It cites five lessons from the city's recent
decentralization experience:

1. Frank recognition of authentic community groups and open
dealing with them on the basis of mutual respect are needed. Determinations of form and legitimacy must themselves have the confidence
and participation of commission members.

2. Purely voluntary and dependent committees (i.e., those without staffing or explicit budgetary or policy-making powers) are of little long-term value and can be a harmful source of cynicism when the substantial efforts invested in them yield paltry results.

3. Involvement of local people should be organized through simple, straightforward, easily comprehensible structures. (Intricate and laborious committee, subcommittee, and board relationships of Model Cities seem to have contributed to diffusion of energies and dissipation of commitment.)

4. Decentralization with regard to any citizen-based group must involve firm commitments by the city administration to clearly defined and significant functions, powers, and responsibilities for the local group. In addition, the group must have some fiscal independence, at least to the extent of being entitled to its own continuing staff and administrative service.

5. Administrative decentralization (i.e., the rationalization and organization of departmental service areas around local community territories) pursuant to firm central administrative decentralization policies, objectives, and procedures must proceed in concert with development of popularly based community bodies. Without the city administration geared, prepared, and organized to respond to local concerns and initiatives, the relationship between city government and the local community will be one of constant crisis and considerable confusion, rather than a day-to-day working relationship.

The commission's proposals are designed to establish more effective communication and cooperation between city government and neighborhoods; to construct legitimate forms of local representation; to enable city departments to design services which vary in response to differing expressions of need and services that are delivered most economically; and to foster (through smaller units) more participation in government by individuals, the sense of personal effectiveness, and the sense of community identity and pride.

It supports territorial or community decentralization by a formal decision-making body in each neighborhood which would concern itself with all matters affecting that community. It does not believe decentralization is some magic panacea, and it cautions against the plan becoming "a dogmatic imposition of an unwanted system on city government and the local community."

The commission recommendations are as follows (see Appendix F for detailed proposals):

1. Decentralization should become an integral part of the major administrative decisions of the city. Its implementation, review, and evaluation should be done by OPS and the proposed Executive Office of Administration.

2. The city administration should divide the city into fourteen logical and acceptable contiguous districts. Other agencies should be encouraged to make their district boundaries coterminous with the city's.

3. The city administration should propose some form of popular approval of the plan through LACs, conventions, or any appropriate method, which may differ from community to community.

4. An acceptable electoral system should be established to be operative within two years (end of 1972) in each community. The commission proposes a model and a staff for the citizen councils.

5. The city should encourage decentralization experiments in different areas of the city, such as Model Cities is doing. All agencies in the district would be encouraged to participate in the program.

6. Powers of the local elected body should be as follows:

a. Be entitled to articulate policies and preferences of municipal services within the district, budgets, planning process, and minimum standards of service. The councils would be brought into the executive budget-making process and into an annual evaluation of departments

b. Be entitled to full discussion and accounting from central authorities and line agencies

c. Be entitled to review and decision by the office of the mayor in case of dissatisfaction with line agencies

d. Be entitled to all budgetary and other information

e. Be entitled to its own professional staff responsible to the local council alone.

Finally, the commission views the future of decentralization as permitting local elected councils discretion over a portion of the total city budget, and eventually giving them taxing powers. It views consideration of regionalization as important as decentralization and envisions a possible future city of Boston interrelated with a federation of metropolitan Boston.

ANALYSIS AND RECOMMENDATIONS

The following comments and recommendations are made in anticipation that they may stimulate further discussion of Boston's decentralization concepts.

The Issues

Boston's LCH program is the most interesting and perhaps most controversial attempt at decentralization of city services of the twelve cities in this full study. Its objectives—improving city services and communications with citizens—show a sincere desire to create more responsive government. But the LCH program has not had enough attention from the mayor or sufficient confidence and participation of the City Council. Too many commissioners and department heads are jealous or apprehensive, and some of the program's most dedicated employees are frustrated over lack of significant change.

Moreover, restrictive unions, lackadaisical civil service, fiscal problems, petty jealousies, political battles, and the inability of any one person to pull together all the loose ends and move the system operate to further inhibit progress. These barriers to change exist in many American cities, but they seem more deeply entrenched in Boston. And in their attempt to do something about it, LCHs are getting kicked about like so many footballs.

More is needed than LCHs: fundamental structural and procedural changes; some private contracting of services; a common determination by elected officials and commissioners to tackle the main issues; an effective coalition of business, union, and civic groups to assist elected officials; and formal neighborhood councils to confront problems more established groups are unwilling to challenge.

The urgency of the problems, coupled with the inability to make rudimentary changes have forced LCHs to work around the system, much to the dissatisfaction of some councillors who would like to see the main issues confronted. Outside of political implications, the inability to make major changes and its expenditures have been the chief reasons for criticism of the LCH program.

Citywide vs. Limited Program

While a $60,000 annual operation with three or four facilities
and as many paid city personnel (as in Baltimore, Houston, and Atlanta)
might have quieted expenditure arguments, it may not have been politically feasible in Boston, and would have presented an even less potent
force for change. On the political side, concentration in the most
severe problem areas might have helped keep things "cool" and establish a reasonable sampling of problems and priorities for central
management purposes. It certainly would have been less of a threat
to established bureaucracy and would have disarmed the political
"clubhouse" argument considerably. Only in Boston and New York,
where approaches have been citywide, has the concern over politics
been so intense.

Arguments for a limited program were considered by the mayor,
but did not outweigh, in his judgment, the compelling reasons for making
LCH citywide: widespread alienation and the need for all citizens to
feel the presence of City Hall; exodus of middle- and higher-income
residents and the need to prevent further neighborhood deterioration;
issues of crime, airport expansion, neighborhood deterioration, and
delivery of services affecting almost every community; and petitions
for LCHs coming from diverse communities. Other important advantages of a citywide program included the ability to construct a base
for comprehensive and effective analysis of city priorities and the
opportunity to pursue the concept of citywide neighborhood government
and citizen councils. Besides, the mayor feared that a pilot program
would have too great a chance of fading away and realized the ethnic,
political, and social makeup of Boston would not allow concentration
of tax revenues in several areas alone. And, too, there is little
disagreement that Mayor White envisioned the LCH process as a
politically expedient way of reaching the mass of citizens to create
voter goodwill.

The program's potential attributes of communication and service
would bring favor to any mayor without the need to gear it to politics.
The operation and location of LCHs is preferably the work of both
executive and legislative branches, their credit or discredit to be
shared equally. A strong-mayor form guided by the partnership of
City Council is eminently more successful, more efficient, and less
frustrating to citizens than an individual approach to running government. Concentration of power is less important than unity of forces.

By good planning and management standards, a citywide approach
to better government is unquestionably sounder than dealing with

special districts—depending, of course, on available resources.
(Emphasis in the nation's Model Cities program is now on citywide
orientation for planning, organization, and distribution of resources,
but with resource emphasis in needy areas.)

Cities with extremely limited resources and uncertainty about
their approach to decentralization might best begin with a pilot program.
And, depending on the assessment of its social and political climate in
1968, this could have been a legitimate course for Boston. However,
Boston's service problems are too widespread, and it has had its pilot
program and initial years of experimentation. Most logically, it now
should continue citywide.

To conserve funds, staff may be cut and smaller quarters found
in less needy areas; however, it may be important to expand services
in other areas.

The citywide system is still important for the development of
communication links, coordination of agencies, development of citizen
councils, and creation of citizen awareness that City Hall cares. Even
without dramatic improvement of service, creating greater citizen
acceptance and trust in government are worthwhile achievements.
In this, Boston has made some gains, but political differences over
LCHs have hurt the program more than anything else because a
confused public does not know what to believe. Since LCHs are
designed to improve government, there should be no embarrassment
about selling them. However, to maintain enduring citizen trust,
improvements in service must continue and program faults must be
corrected.

Criticisms

One of the most intense objections to the program, regardless
of how well these appointees may do their jobs, is the appointment of
political favorites to LCH staffs. To diminish partisan political implications and gain greater acceptance by residents, appointment of local
staff ought to be shared equally by the mayor and City Council in
partnership with citizen councils. Preferably, the community should
pose a list of candidates from which the mayor and a councilmanic
committee make selections. Hopefully, this process would improve
mayoral-councilmanic relationships, at the same time legitimatizing
reasons for formation of LACs. And it should not detract from hiring
persons adept at political maneuvering, some of whom make excellent
staff members.

Besides political objections, the program has been criticized for having a cumbersome reporting system, inability to get sufficient response from district superintendents, lack of rapport with department heads, backlog of complaints, and the creation of another layer of bureaucracy.

Paperwork was reduced when OPS shortened its request form, but there will necessarily be more processing under a central complaint system. To relieve this burden, departments should be encouraged to receive more of their own complaints, use OPS follow-up procedures, and submit periodic summaries to central management. OPS should handle any complaints it receives, with particular attention to the most difficult cases. The basic complaint-answering responsibilities of departments should not be decentralized but strengthened, if departments are to be improved.

The charge that LCHs are another layer of bureaucracy would have less impact if, instead of acting as buffers between citizens and departments, the centers would concentrate on streamlining the present system by making departments respond more rapidly and take a greater concern with problems LCHs handle. The work load should eventually fall back to regular departments.

Passing complaints from departments to LCHs and back again is bureaucratic, but complaints which go directly to OPS and are channeled to LCHs where sufficient staff is available for follow-up is not unnecessarily bureaucratic as long as better results are obtained. The extra layer formed by LCH is a necessary one to the elderly, poorly informed, those in need of bilingual assistance or transportation, and citizens who previously gave up because they could not get results. To these people, the expense is worth it.

Need for Councilmanic Help

Councilmanic help in getting results where OPS has failed is a welcome part of the system. Failure to get results in every case need not discredit OPS, yet intervention of a councillor's prestige and strength in helping to move a worn-out departmental system is a credit to him. In most cities councilmen do continue to receive critical complaints—and should—for it keeps them abreast of and sensitive to problems. This should not, however, detract from a formal, well-structured, and responsive administrative approach to resolving the bulk of complaints. Without a system to absorb the flood of requests, councillors too would become impotent.

Handling Complaints

Even without LCHs, a central complaint and information office, such as Boston's twenty-four-hour service, should continue to operate (other examples are New York, Chicago, and Kansas City) so that citizens can get service by dialing one phone number. There should be complete follow-up and reply to citizens in all cases (Chicago uses automatic typewriters, each capable of 350 responses daily). Central offices prod departments into quicker responses and improve the government image.

Strengthening the Program

Reducing the backlog of complaints requires not only additional resources but increased departmental efficiency. LCHs will not substantially improve this unless the mayor and councillors attack the sources. Employee productivity and motivation must be improved, agencies and departments made more responsive, and stronger links drawn between managers. The Public Service Board and mini-cabinets could strengthen these relationships by clarifying issues, establishing priorities, developing sensitivities to local situations, coordinating territorial and policy decisions, and putting a team together to help support the mayor's programs and policies.

To strengthen the LCH program, additional services should be added, particularly in areas not adequately served by community action and Model Cities. Some communities are large enough to warrant both LCHs and CAP centers. Where social-welfare and other functions are desirable, greater use should be made of borrowed personnel from other agencies to provide a comprehensive program. Baltimore's mayor's stations, for example, are very economical and allow whole families to receive attention for myriad problems in one visit to one center.

In addition, greater effort should be made to coordinate and combine facilities and staff of the community action and LCH programs. Model Cities is now contributing to the city's program, and it is time to consider placing city representatives and programs in CAP centers and vice versa, especially in those areas where efforts are clearly being duplicated. At some point it will be necessary to sort out the multitude of neighborhood programs, and combining some resources now is a good start.

In Model Cities, where its doughnut-shaped area leaves out some citizens, additional city resources and staff could be combined in a Model Cities center to ensure service to all residents. (Atlanta placed its neighborhood city hall representatives in community action and Model Cities facilities, for example.)

Citizen Councils

Moreover, consideration should be given to combining some community action councils with city LACs. An additional citizens' council should not be added to the Model Cities area if the existing council equitably represents the area or can be made to do so.

In creating LACs, selection by community consensus closely supervised by an impartial observer is a legitimate method. LACs should be formed in all areas and given some decision-making authority, if they are to function effectively: review of the city budget, setting local capital improvement priorities, sharing responsibility for appointing managers, determining LCH programs and hours of operation, and evaluating staff and all local programs which affect their neighborhoods. (Kansas City's citizen councils remain weak because of lack of reasonably authority.) Sufficient staff should be made available to them. The true potential of LCHs may be realized only when they are backed by effectively functioning citizen councils, which refuse to accept a system where "things just don't work." The mayor and councillors should welcome this innovation.

The Importance of Managers

The most important contribution of OPS and the LCH managers has been their ability to make procedural changes and act effectively as community advocates. The managers' advocacy role in fighting airport expansion, getting railroad corporations to agree on track removal, enlisting the aid of financial institutions for home construction, improving bus service, creating special task forces to solve problems, and a host of other items, has made LCH a significant program. The potential exists, through their efforts, for even greater success and institutional change.

OPS's analytical role and central management function, as well as its ability to gain the mayor's support, is invaluable. Furthermore, the support of formal citizen councils could strengthen the manager's role, but it could also make it a little more difficult for him to balance his role between city officials and residents. This ambivalence has survived because in most cases the mayor has supported the manager;

but this may not always be the case, and he may have to choose
loyalties. However, it would be easier for his conscience to prevail
if his selection and dismissal were shared equally by the administration
and a citizen's council.

Private Help

In addition to resident councils, an impartial, privately funded
citizens group consisting of business, union, news media, government,
civic associations, and private individuals is desirable for Boston.
Not a research organization, but action-oriented, it would effect change
through the courts and news media. Since many of Boston's problems
are metropolitan in scope (e.g., water, transportation, park police,
parks, air pollution), this body could act as leverage on the whole
system. The mayor and City Council, being interested in the improvement of government, might initiate it.

Summary of Key Recommendations

1. The LCH program should be continued on a citywide basis,
but a review should take place of all facilities and staff for possible
joint operations with community action and Model Cities programs.
In some areas services could be reduced; in other areas, increased.
Social welfare and other functions could be added with little expense
by borrowing personnel from other agencies, similar to the Baltimore
experience. Mayor's complaint desks could be added to community
action and Model Cities centers.

2. To add immediate strength, LACs should be formed in all
areas where other local bodies do not equitably represent the public.
They should be given some authority and staff, as described in the
foregoing analysis. At this time and level of responsibility, citizen
councils should be chosen by some method of community consensus
acceptable to each area and with the aid of outside, impartial observers.
Their authority should extend only to problems of their immediate
neighborhoods. Too much responsibility (as placed on general government) would dissipate their efforts and destroy effective handling of
critical problems.

3. Managers should be appointed jointly by the mayor and City
Council, on the one hand, and LAC, on the other, to diminish political
implications and strengthen the manager's advocacy role.

4. Regardless of the City Council's legal authority, the mayor should give it a role in LCH policy decisions, so that it may assist the project in more effectively carrying out its goals and encourage councillors to support him in restructuring institutions. A team approach would have greater chance for success. Centralizing all power in the mayor does not help much, if potential supporters are diffused. The fundamental problem is more with institutions and the system than individual councillors or the mayor.

5. Managers and LACs should be given authority to evaluate local services and personnel and to make recommendations to the mayor and City Council. Recommendations could have the strength to cause transfer of ineffective personnel and influence salary increases, with final review always in the hands of the mayor, however. Some district personnel may be unhappy about this, but the competent ones would welcome it, and fear of causing antagonism between some supervisors and managers should be subordinated to the desire for improving services. LACs, rather than managers (who must balance their credibility between residents and the bureaucracy), should accept the brunt of responsibility and criticism. OPS should assist in designing evaluation techniques.

6. The mayor should appoint a task force to review civil service procedures or convene the Civil Service Commission to critically analyze their rules in regard to employee performance. Seniority should be deemphasized, rating systems improved, and performance made the prime requisite for promotion and retention. Incentives should be used, such as employee awards and performance bonuses. Employee groups and unions should be asked for suggestions of how to serve the public better. And the Civil Service Commission should accept employee evaluation reports from managers and LACs as standard procedure. In November, 1970, the National Civil Service Leagues adopted the Model Public Personnel Administration Law, and similar innovations should be explored for new civil service concepts.

7. The Public Service Board should be revitalized by the mayor's support, given an agenda as recommended in this analysis, and broadened to include outside agency representatives so a comprehensive review of city affairs can take place. The mayor should adopt the "responsible city" concept whereby he assumes some accountability for all issues facing his city, whether he is legally responsible or not. (The planned variation program of Model Cities stresses citywide orientation, mayor's checkoff of federal programs, and other increased city responsibilities, for example.)

8. The mini-cabinet concept should be reinforced and used in all districts (Washington, D.C., has established mini-cabinets in nine districts encompassing the entire city) and district supervisors instructed to attend all meetings and devote part of their schedules to involvement in neighborhood affairs. Some evening and weekend duties should be part of supervisory responsibility. When requested, district supervisors should be required to attend LAC meetings, and serve as part-time staff as well. Where service is particularly poor, LACs might be given greater authority over district supervisors. (New York proposes that in some districts, superintendents be selected and directed by neighborhood councils.)

9. OPS should take steps to establish coterminous districts for as many functions as possible. It particularly should place new programs in uniform districts that are logical to existing programs.

10. OPS reports of LCH performance should be reviewed by the mayor and councillors monthly to determine reasons for service breakdown and, particularly during budget deliberations, to judge department requests and employee salaries.

11. Additional city employees should be drawn through the LCH process to increase motivation, neighborhood concern, and productivity.

12. Although LCHs must align themselves with the city's chain of responsibility to expedite change, they must remain flexible, non-bureaucratic, and project-oriented if they are to continue to be innovative and grow with the needs of the community. Creative, nonbureaucratic managers are the key to its success.

13. The mayor, or some element of the general community, should initiate an action unit similar to the Chicago Better Government Association. Such an independent body may be necessary where the political system is too dependent on gathering votes, is unwilling to sacrifice for change, or is unwilling to confront issues.

Area: 78 square miles
Population: 895,222
Black: 316,451

THE CITY AND ITS GOVERNMENT

The City

Baltimore, the largest city in Maryland, is an industrial and
commercial center and major seaport. It handles the fourth largest
volume of foreign trade of any American port. It has attracted diverse
industries, including sugar and food processing, petroleum and chemicals, aircraft, guided missiles, and steel and gypsum products.
Bethlehem Steel Company's Sparrows Point complex, the largest
steel plant in the world, is located here.

In 1957, the Baltimore Urban Renewal and Housing Agency was
established to execute a long-range redevelopment program. The
Charles Center project, an integrated complex of office buildings,
two residential buildings, a hotel, theater, and shopping facilities
was begun in 1962. The following year a new civic center was completed. Currently under way is $260 million inner harbor redevelop-
ment program, which will include a municipal government center to
replace the old city hall, a thirty-two-story pentagonal trade center,
a marina, and a hotel.

The Government

Mayor Elm Shaffer (annual salary $25,000), whose term expires in December, 1975, functions in a strong-mayor/council form of government with eighteen councilmen (annual salaries $6,500). The mayor, comptroller, and president of the City Council are elected at-large. Three councilmen are elected from each of the six districts.

MAYOR'S STATIONS

History of Decentralized Services

Campaigning for mayor in 1966, former Mayor Thomas J. D'Alesandro promised neighborhood stations to improve community services. Then president of the City Council, he had extensively reviewed decentralized service systems in Cleveland and Chicago and was enamored of the concept.

Once elected, he moved to fulfill his pledge. His chief stumbling block was the outgoing administration, which, responsible for preparing the first year's budget for the new mayor, allocated no funds for the project.

Therefore, while Mayor D'Alesandro had promised mayor stations, he had no money to fulfill the promise. So he improvised— D'Alesandro released one of his assistants from other responsibilities to visit cities experimenting with the concept of decentralized city services.

Dan Zaccagnini, special assistant to the mayor, had the task of establishing the first mayor's station in Baltimore. The plan was to develop neighborhood multipurpose centers that would provide public services in a visible and accessible manner to the entire city of Baltimore.

Steps taken to organize and implement the first mayor's station were the following:

1. D'Alesandro decided on the need for decentralized services and campaigned for establishment of mayor's stations which would serve as little city halls.

2. The mayor assigned his assistant to develop a feasible program for Baltimore, after review of programs in other cities.

3. The mayor introduced the concept to cabinet members for sanction and approval.

4. City agencies met with the mayor to discuss their involvement in the mayor's station concept.

5. State and federal agencies met with the mayor to discuss possibilities and advantages of the concept in terms of their involvement.

6. A neighborhood was selected. Because of friction and opposition, the first mayor's station was located outside boundaries of the community action agency.

7. After selecting the neighborhood, the director of housing was requested to determine what city buildings were available for immediate occupancy.

8. A mayor's representative was appointed to manage the first station.

Major opposition to the mayor's station concept came from the community action agency, which saw it as a duplication of its own effort. Other opposition came from groups which felt they should have a hand in selecting the mayor's representative, and from communities outside the community action target area which did not want to be labeled "poverty areas." Support for the mayor's station came from the president of the City Council, the commissioner of housing, and the Community Council of Govans, Inc., which represents eleven different neighborhoods in the northeast area.

Essentially, the mayor's concept of neighborhood multipurpose centers was limited because of lack of funds, organizational opposition from those who felt that the stations competed with their own interests, and lack of structural alteration in the city's departmental organization and delivery system.

Objectives and Functions

Goals of the program are to create more effective communication with citizens and develop improved delivery of services. Objectives are proper and accurate information referral, more effective coordination, prompt attention to problems and complaints of the community, and more effective family and individual casework. Many people do not know where to go with problems and become very frustrated at

having to go from one department to another. Mayor's stations are
designed to eliminate much of this travel.

One function is to match problems or complaints to the most relevant agency or community resource. Service is made more thorough
by prompt coordinative and supportive assistance rendered by various
agency representative. Coordination is achieved primarily by locating agencies in the same building, thus enabling a family to receive
assistance from several agencies in a single stop. Mayor's representatives in two of the three stations hold staff meetings, are sufficiently
qualified, and demand sufficient respect that they can achieve some
coordination among the various agencies and departments operating
within their facilities.

In almost all cases, the mayor's representative initially screens
and interviews families or individuals, and directs them to one of
twelve services connected with the mayor's stations. In some cases,
general information is all that is requested. In others, individual
assistance of a supportive nature and follow-through action are provided.
In a typical month in 1970, each center averaged 700-800 visits for
the kinds of services listed in Table 15. Additionally, as many or
more telephone calls are handled monthly.

The following agencies and programs primarily compose the
mayor's station program, although not all are located in each facility:

1. Maryland State Employment
2. Department of Public Welfare
3. Baltimore City Health Dept.
4. Baltimore Police Dept.
5. Community Organizer
6. Planned Parenthood
7. Planning Dept.
8. Legal Aid Society
9. Bureau of Building Inspection
10. Dept. of Public Works
11. Community Action Agency
12. Dept. of Labor and Industry
13. Training Program (e.g., CEP, OIC, etc.)
14. Job Bank

Staff and Budget

The three mayor's representatives, chosen in cooperation with
community groups and with final approval by the mayor, are residents

TABLE 15

Service Report of Steuart Hill
Mayor's Station, Baltimore,
January, 1970

Service	Client Visits
Department of Employment Security	312
Department of Social Services	62
Department of Parole and Probation	342
Community Action Agency	18
Vocational Rehabilitation via Mayor's Representative	3
Medical Assistance	1
Health Sanitarians	9
Customer Services	3
Code Enforcement	1
Salvation Army	1
Legal Aid	1
General Information, Counseling	3
Visitors—Information: Reference to Station	4
Total	760

Activities of Mayor's Representative

City Hall Meetings	2
Community Meetings	2
Staff Meetings	1
Rotary Meetings	1
Home Visits	1
Field Trips	13

Source: Office of the Mayor, Baltimore, July 1970.

of the areas they serve. They started at a salary of $6,500 annually, which was raised to $8,400 to reflect responsibilities more closely. During the first year of operation, the centers operated from the mayor's contingency fund. Second-year program requests were for $204,000; however, this figure was reduced by the City Council to $47,000. New budget requests are for $66,000. Until this year the Pratt Street-Steuart Hill station received free quarters by operating

in the same building as the Department of Housing and Community
Development, and the Govans station received its first year's rent
from the Community Council of Govans, Inc. Now the rent of all three
stations must be paid city funds.

Staff expenditures are low because almost all personnel are on
loan from other agencies and departments.

Facilities, Demography, and
Station Services

Pratt Street-Steuart Hill Station

This station, opened March 4, 1968, is located in a large store-
front in the main business area in southwest Baltimore. In the past,
the facility was shared with the Department of Housing and Community
Development, but this department moved its local office elsewhere.
Its code enforcement program generated community hostility that
affected the image of the mayor's station, so separate operations
seemed a desirable step.

The mayor's representative occupies a desk in the main reception
area, so he can screen and initially refer all potential clients to the
proper agencies. He interviews from ten to thirty clients a day.

The Pratt station is to be expanded by some twelve offices and
twenty-eight staff persons, the bulk of which will be additional case-
workers for the social service function. Space is available in the
same building and on the same floor.

The center primarily serves an area of nine city blocks and is
situated on a street that divides a predominantly white low-middle-
income population from a black low-middle-income population. The
station has links to both communities. Statistics tend to confirm a
50 percent black and 50 percent white use of services. There are
some interesting service differentials. For instance, the employment
program shows 65 percent black use to 35 percent white, while the
social service program reverses this ratio.

Representatives of eight agencies are physically located in the
center on a full or part-time basis:

1. Welfare Services
2. Family Planning

3. Community Action
4. State Dept. of Labor
5. Employment Security
6. Building Inspection
7. Police-Community Relations
8. State Dept. of Probation and Parole

The Mayor's station has developed contacts with a number of agencies not housed in the facility. These agencies include Vocational Rehabilitation, Public Health, Legal Aid, Small Business Administration, Veterans Administration, and city departments.

Emergency funds are available and can supply a family with forty-eight hours of food needs. A family can use the fund only once a year, however.

The Rotary Club of Baltimore had adopted the Pratt Street mayor's station as their major community service project. It supplies resources for tangible aid and a variety of community improvement programs. The activities of the Rotary Club in the Pratt Street area are coordinated by the mayor's representative.

The station operates from 8:30 a.m. to 4:30 p.m., five days a week, thus excluding many working persons in the area from participation in the program.

Center Director Pearl Scheufele cites good coordination and cooperation among the various agencies in the building, and holds weekly staff meetings for this purpose. She explains that residents are hesitant to go downtown for services, especially to the main employment service office, and that the mayor's station makes a vital contribution by bringing functions closer to the people.

Govans Station

The Govans mayor's station is located in a large, accessible building on the main commercial thoroughfare in an area largely interracial and lower-middle and middle-class. Operations are set to some degree by recommendations of the Community Council of Govans, Inc., which played a major role in the center's creation and location, and is still active in funding and supporting the effort.

Center Director Robert Ayd estimates Govans handles some 1,500 contacts, including phone calls, per month. Much of the intake (about 500 cases) in every station, however, is related to compulsory services, such as parole and probation. About the same work load is in employment services.

The following services are housed in Govans on a full-time basis:

1. State Dept. of Probation and Parole
2. City Social Services
3. Housing and Community Development
4. Employment Security
5. City Health Dept., Sanitary Enforcement
6. City Planning

Part-time services include mental health, Veterans Administration, vocational rehabilitation, and Police and Fire Department community relations. Govans' mayor's representative has developed contacts with the Small Business Administration, Social Security Administration, U.S. Civil Service Office, Post Office customer relations, and such voluntary groups as women's clubs, Kiwanis, church groups, etc. It maintains an emergency loan account for persons in need of immediate cash, and lenders are obligated to pay back loans interest-free.

The station seems to lack adequate clerical resources, a fault common to all three stations, but it does provide a meeting place for local community groups, which is viewed as an important community resource. The station's service hours are 8:30 a.m. to 5 p.m., five days a week. These hours seem to severely limit use of the center by many persons in the community.

Northwest Mayor's Station

This station, opened October 3, 1969, is a tenant in a building used primarily for commercial purposes. This makes it difficult to find or identify the station, whose facilities are dispersed throughout the building. There is no adequate sign that can be seen from the street, and the location is not close to a residential area. Rather, it is integrated into a primarily light industrial complex, placed there because space was available. Knowledge of the station's whereabouts is so poor that a survey of twenty persons in the immediate vicinity, including a family walking directly in front of the building, revealed not one who could identify the mayor's station or its location. Such an out-of-the-way location also poses a transportation problem for poor persons.

However, there still seems to be a fair amount of use of the facility because community groups and other organizations know of its existence. The mayor's representative was recommended by a local community group.

Northwest mayor's station serves the broadest range of socio-economic groups of any of the centers, ranging from lower middle-class to upper middle-class. The area served is interracial, with significant increases in the nonwhite population during the last few years.

The mayor's representative provides direct supportive and counseling help to the community, but coordination of agencies and departments at this station is not as effective as at the other two. Staff meetings and other methods of coordination are not fully utilized, though there has been an attempt to survey community problems through students and to develop a comprehensive filing system for more effective management.

Full-time services offered are the following:

1. Dept. of Housing and Community Development
2. City Health Dept., Sanitary Enforcement
3. Dept. of Social Services
4. State Employment Service
5. State Dept. of Parole and Probation

Part-time services are offered for alcoholism, vocational rehabilitation, fire and police department, and community relations.

The station's hours are 8:30 a.m. to 4:30 p.m., five days a week.

Carlene (Wendy) Morgan, head of the Community Services Division, says a considerable number of residents do avail themselves of services. She estimates that she sees over 100 people per month.

Miss Morgan would like to see better coordination both with City Hall and within the facility itself. Greater program motivation, more publicity to reach residents, and addition of professional administrators to the staff are desirable, she feels. She would also like to see additional mayor's stations created.

The mayor's representative, Rebecca Bain, views her role as one of keeping in close contact with neighborhood groups rather than managing and coordinating departments and agencies.

CITIZEN PARTICIPATION

Each mayor's station has a unique history in terms of citizen involvement in the selection of neighborhood representatives, sites, and staff.

Pratt Street-Steuart Hill had the first established mayor's station. The mayor asked city officials, councilmen, and community organizations to submit names of low-income residents of the community with experience in community organization. The mayor chose the representative from three names submitted. Neighborhood residents had no hand in planning the mayor's station nor in its present operation.

Selection of the mayor's aide for the Govans mayor's station was somewhat different. The Community Council of Govans, Inc., an active citizen group, demanded that a mayor's station be established in their area. Although the city maintained it had no money to finance another station, the Govans community pledged to raise money for lease of the facility, if the mayor would provide the staff. Because of its financial involvement, the Council felt it should also be involved in selecting the mayor's representative.

Unlike Steuart Hill, Govans residents participated in planning their station; but like Steuart Hill, the Govans community organization was not given decision-making responsibilities. Consequently, their input is minimal in decisions on other staff, programs, and services. Nevertheless, their choice for representative, Robert Ayd, runs the center, and the Council's strong voice sees to it that the city provides for most of their needs.

Development of the Northwest Baltimore station, third to be established, was different from the other two centers. The mayor, by this time, had gained experience in setting up mayor's stations; therefore, he attempted to take the best from both previous stations and use it in the third. He brought most community elements, including residents, into the process of deciding who would be his representative, although the final selection rested solely in his hands. A local resident, Rebecca Bain—the only mayor's representative who is black—was chosen.

There are no present plans for formal citizen councils or increased citizen participation besides that of responding to and participating in local neighborhood organization meetings and projects.

COMMUNITY ACTION PROGRAM

The community action program in Baltimore is a public agency established by charter and is called the Economic Opportunity Commission (EOC). Its director is Lenwood Ivey. The commission has twenty-one members, ten members and the chairman appointed by the mayor and ten elected from target areas.

Three-fourths of Baltimore is in the target area, and the program operates only within boundaries of the city. There are thirty neighborhood centers and a staff of 300 people in the program, with a $20 million budget emphasizing manpower, community organization, community development, housing, and education programs. There are formally elected citizen advisory councils for each of the thirty centers.

The community organization project has successfully placed target area citizens in state elective office and on the ballot for local elective office. The community development project has placed residents in cooperative food programs, a housing development, a service station project, a credit union, and other enterprises.

A joint agreement was reached by EOC and the city not to place mayor's stations within EOC centers or EOC target areas. However, since EOC has not been able to reach many citizens of foreign ancestry, it was felt the mayor's stations should serve those areas where there were mixed ethnic groups and varied income levels.

At one time, EOC centers provided a considerable number of services. Now their emphasis is primarily on jobs, housing, and referral services. EOC apparently found its operation of in-house services unsuccessful and has dropped down to a minimum service level. Many of its clients are referred to mayor's stations for assistance, and EOC provides a staff person to one of the stations to help coordinate efforts between the two programs and expedite requests for city services.

MODEL CITIES AGENCY

The Model Cities Policy and Planning Board (called "Partnership Board" by Mayor D'Alesandro) consists of twenty-eight members, eight appointed by the mayor and twenty elected from six target areas. The $10.5 million program has a staff of fifty, and the director is William Slayer. The mayor's emphasis is on providing additional housing and greater economic development.

Model Cities funds one senior citizen center, known as a multi-purpose center but which provides services only for older persons. There are, however, two multipurpose centers in the planning stages, one to be located in Lafayette Square and the other in the Laurence Street area.

At this point there is only discussion of joint operations with mayor's stations, particularly in housing development. Some referrals are now made from the stations to the Model Cities office on housing matters.

There are plans for Model Cities to work with the community action program on a combined training and technical assistance program. They are now working together on Operation Champ, a youth program for recreation and training.

Conflicts within the Model Cities board itself over program priorities has stalled the program—delays which may be overcome after successful completion of its growing pains and leadership development.

PERCEPTIONS

Political View

The mayor sees the mayor's stations program as a success for two primary reasons: on a practical level, because decentralization results in better service, and psychologically, because they are a last resort for the "little man" in solving problems.

The mayor feels there have not been any real political problems concerning the program. Politicians are supporting the effort and are encouraging constituent groups to use its facilities and services, even though some feel it separates them a little further from their constituencies.

View from the Mayor's Office

The mayor's special assistant, Dan Zaccagnini, feels the centers provide valid services, are cheap to run and politically feasible, as well as being useful and well received by residents. Zaccagnini was closely involved in the creation of the first two centers. Another mayor's aide, Joseph Smith, assistant for neighborhood services, was in large measure overseer for development of the Northwest center.

Zaccagnini cites four ways in which the program could be improved:

1. Addition of legal aid services
2. Creation of health clinics
3. Increased staff, with perhaps some devoted to ombudsman functions
4. Addition of new centers.

He says, "The mayor's stations are one of the most effective things the mayor has done." Two additional centers are now being planned.

Joe Smith feels that mayor's representatives should have roots and ties to the community, be capable of operating formally and informally, be able to negotiate and bargain with residents as well as professional persons, be committed to program goals, and possess the ability to operate despite financial constraints.

View of City Department Heads

Generally, department heads feel the program is designed to improve the communication link between residents and City Hall and make services more convenient for citizens. Its greatest asset, they believe, is its identification with City Hall and the mayor.

Budgetary problems and lack of personnel have caused some departments to withdraw their employees from the stations. Also, some feel the emphasis is on social services rather than city functions.

Department heads most active in the program identify these deficiencies: lack of adequate budget and staff; no conceptual framework from which to work; relationships and responsibilities not spelled out; and mayor's representatives have no power or authority for innovative ideas, positive direction, or coordination.

They also feel that before more stations are established, there should be a redefinition of staff qualifications and responsibilities. According to department heads, stronger direction of each center is

needed as well as a more positive concern by the mayor for the
program.

Agency Views

Some agency personnel see the mayor's station concept as a
composite of confusion, with no clear guidelines as to purposes or
objectives. They feel the future of the program is bleak unless the
people's satisfaction and benefits are measured.

Other agency personnel, working within stations, see them
making a significant contribution, creating understanding among
agency personnel, improving coordination merely by having diverse
agencies work in the same building under some common direction,
and bringing convenience and improved service to citizens.

Views of Residents

Pratt Street-Steuart Hill Area— Conversations with Residents

1st resident: "I know where to come for help, because I live in
the area. I was here when they first moved in. I have made several
visits into the station for a job. They never have any for me because
I am seventeen years old. I feel there is no discrimination, the people
are generally 'quite'—'good'—'polite.' If they are too crowded, I go
home and come back another day." He did not understand the complex
housing arrangement within the building, nor did he understand the
relationship of the Housing and Community Development Office
located in the same building. He felt the only thing he would change
would be the services that were oriented toward the seventeen-year-
old.

2nd resident: "A friend of mine got a job here, and he told me
to come in for one; the first time I came in, I got a job bank offer, but
when I applied, they didn't hire me. The services as a whole are
good because they try to send people on the job they like. There are,
however, some bad points, such as sending people out on jobs that
they know they cannot get, and sending people out on jobs that will
not pay enough to even put food in your mouth. If I were in charge,
I would make the following changes: (1) solicit better-paying jobs;
(2) fix it so that education or lack of it would not prevent a person
from getting a job; (3) correct the situation where whites get better

jobs than blacks, such as office work for whites, dirty jobs for blacks. We would all get the same regardless of color. It seems that whites are trying to keep the black man down. All we want is an equal chance to gain employment."

3rd resident: "I heard about the station through a newspaper article. I am working now as a result of the mayor's station, at an American service station. I got my training at Job Corps. The services are generally good; the only problem is that the community people cannot wait. [Sometimes the mayor's station may have a job, sometimes it may not.] I think a strength is its location between the white and colored area. There are no bad things I can think of; however, the office space is too small and needs remodeling. Everybody needs a private office and a lunch room is needed, because there is no place you can eat if you have a three- or four-hour visit. Last, I guess I would put more people on the switchboard, because they lose a person's call who is on the outside—and even sometimes within the building."

4th resident: "A friend told me about this place last year. I am interested in a job. I think the services need some changes because they send people on 'lost causes.' We are paying out more money than we make. I hate this place. Why? Because they wouldn't allow me to use the toilet facilities, and suggested that I use the filling station across the street. The only strength I see is the fact that I don't have to go downtown. I see a number of weaknesses, such as (1) not enough services for eighteen-year-olds; (2) too many people are sent on the same job (six to eight per station); (3) there should be a phone call or some kind of message before a person is sent out for an interview (staff reports this is done); (4) attitudes are bad—no direction of any kind; (5) we can't eat or drink in the reception area, yet no other area is provided (staff indicates this is not snack time but job-hunting time); (6) the receptionist "loud-talks" people.

If I were in charge, I would make a lot of changes, such as (1) giving $1 for lunch when sending someone out on a job; (2) allow eating and coffee drinking, etc.; (3) make telephone calls before sending out interviewees (staff reports this is done); (4) get rid of one of the agencies in the building because it gives the impression that people are not being served properly.

Govans Station—Meeting with Members of the
Community Council of Govans, Inc.

It was the consensus here that the mayor's station is an asset to the community. The Community Council of Govans, Inc., has had greater impact with its mayor's station than any of the others. They informed the community about it with flyers and sound trucks for a week. The Greater Govans Committee, Inc. (business group), serves the same functions as the Rotary Club does for the Steuart Hill-Pratt Street area—working on special projects and acting as a resource group for expenses not covered by others.

Council members' concept of the mayor's station is that of a little city hall, constituting an improved communications link between the community and downtown city hall.

They generally felt the services were good, but wanted probation and parole functions taken away from their station. They wanted medical and police-community relations services added; and, because police-community relations men cannot arrest people, they wanted a policeman assigned to their station.

They felt the strengths were the following:

1. Decentralization of services
2. Relationships with other community organizations
3. Community orientation
4. Good relationship with schools and officials.

The weaknesses included the following:

1. Though the station is good for some things, other things still require a trip downtown for service
2. The staff is not sufficiently community-oriented
3. Parole and probation should not be there, because they bring "bad men" into neighborhood (staff reports 80 percent are residents)
4. Lack of coordination between downtown office and mayor's representatives
5. Powerlessness of mayor's representative
6. Lack of community power in or out of the mayor's stations
7. Administrators from different agencies employ personnel without consent of neighborhood
8. No neighborhood policy-making decisions
9. Hours are bad for working families (8:30 a.m. to 4.30 p.m.)
10. No operating budget
11. Some agencies do not fill out mayor's representative sheets with facts of intake
12. Sanitation people provide the most comprehensive service in the Govans station.

They would make the following changes:

1. Demand that center staff be committed to solving the problems of the community
2. Establish a system for coordination and planning
3. Establish a system of communication with the neighborhood
4. Create a position for legal aid representatives.

The group's general conclusions were the following:

1. The mayor is not interested in the station—he is only interested in running for governor
2. The community does not have any say as to what comes in or goes out of the station
3. The mayor's station can be used only for certain things and is not really available for community use.

Northwest Station—Conversations with Residents

1st resident: "I was sent here by the Maryland State Employment Office, because they told me they had decentralized their services. I have been here three times since Tuesday looking for the right type of job. I feel the mayor's station is helpful, and the people are nice, concerned, and really care. The only weakness is that they should be open better hours than they are, and someone should be there at lunch time to let people in so they don't have to go back home. I feel the applicant should have the listing of jobs before him, before his or her interview."

2nd resident: "I found the mayor's station through the sign on the door. I am mainly concerned with job possibilities. I first went to Maryland Employment but had no luck. The mayor's station seems to be an equal opportunity employer, and that's good. The weakness of mayor's stations is that they never have the right jobs, service is slow, no one is ever here, and college students can't even decide on which jobs they prefer. The changes I would make would be to let people explore employment files, etc."

3rd resident: "I became aware of the mayor's station through church. I am interested in the social services they offer through the Department of Public Welfare. I like the station because it offers a number of social services and the social service staff is excellent."

4th resident: "I just became aware of the station today. A friend told me. I am looking for a better job. I don't know what to

say about the services except Mrs. Bain, the mayor's representative,
received me well. The job counselor didn't want to spend time with
me, because he said Friday was a bad day for everyone, Monday is
a holiday, and said for me to come back on Tuesday. I feel, on the
whole, the services are good because they are decentralized and they
are convenient for neighborhood residents."

ANALYSIS AND RECOMMENDATIONS

These comments and recommendations are made with the intention that they may be of some assistance to the Baltimore program.

The mayor's station program was put together in Baltimore
because Mayor D'Alesandro felt it would improve the level of services
and communications with people of varied income levels, because he
was impressed with operations in other cities which he and his staff
visited, and because it could be done very economically.

There was a need to reach Italians, Greeks, and other ethnic
groups. And the agreement with the community action program to
place stations in neighborhoods which EOC was not servicing was
satisfactory because it allowed the mayor to reach some of the "forgotten Americans" and did not severely infringe upon EOC "territory"
or duplicate its service clientele.

Some groups did not favor the stations because they did not
want to be labeled "poverty areas." This was partially overcome
when the city indicated it might locate stations in all six councilmanic
areas of the city and that it was important for all citizens to receive
equal benefits.

Politics has played a minor role in the program because the
City Council has not felt the mayor was using it to build a constituency,
but rather that it was designed to provide a more convenient service
to people. The mayor did not dictate appointments of station representatives. He allowed city councilmen and community organizations
to develop a list of candidates from which he chose one for each center.
In almost all cases the representatives selected were identical to the
people's choice, and this helped to give the program a positive image.

Budgets have been extremely low. It is difficult to criticize a
program which does not cost the taxpayer significant amounts of new
money and which provides services equal to or greater than their
cost. The most pleasing and encouraging thing about this program

is that it places existing employees from city departments and other public and private agencies into a less bureaucratic, localized facility to increase effectiveness and performance. It helps to change an existing bureaucratic structure into something a little better.

Nor have the stations been permitted to evolve into structures so large as to create more bureaucracy, as has happened in similar programs in other cities. This would have defeated one of the original purposes of the program.

Expansion is taking place at a reasonable pace, in a reasonable manner. However, some city departments pulled out of the centers because of their own manpower shortages and because they felt the service emphasis was not related to them. It was a mistake to let some departments pull out too early, for it appears that insufficient time was allowed for experimentation and growth of these city services and that some of them should be relocated in the stations. In fact, additional city services should be added. Greater publicity and citizen involvement are necessary to make each city department more productive and better utilized by residents.

Greater emphasis should be placed on the mayor's role in complaint and information. Although a community action agency employee serves in this capacity in one station, greater visibility ought to be created for a mayor's desk of complaint and inquiry in each station and the persons in charge should be responsible to the mayor and City Council. The mayor should direct department heads to give priority to complaints from this source in order to create a higher level of credibility for the program. Preferably, the mayor's representative should direct this function and use loaned staff.

The center director should be chosen more for administrative skills than social service abilities and should not be required to conduct unreasonable numbers of client interviews. He should spend most of his time coordinating the various agencies within the center through regular staff meetings and day-to-day direction of agency and city department personnel. Also, he should conduct mini-cabinet meetings of district city and agency heads in order to analyze neighborhood problems and develop priorities. Some authority should be given the director in directive form in order to extend his ability to coordinate city and agency personnel within the entire district. In absence of legal authority, each entity should agree upon certain administrative procedures. A manual for this purpose should also be prepared.

The station director should help develop neighborhood projects which will bring meaningful change to the community and should perform as a neighborhood ombudsman in support of the citizen and legitimate complaints about bureaucratic "hang-ups." Institutional and procedural changes should be advocated by the director toward improving the system. Additional funds or transfers of existing persons to his direction should be made to provide a workable number of neighborhood ombudsmen.

Additionally, the mayor's aide in City Hall in charge of neighborhood services should call regular meetings of his three station representatives to convey the best of each program, exchange neighborhood facts that would be mutually advantageous, and begin to develop uniform reporting procedures toward development of a central management system.

The Customer Service Division, Bureau of Consumer Services, is the city's central office of complaint and inquiry. It handles about 1,000 calls during the week and about 500 on weekends, operates on a twenty-four-hour basis, but is primarily a referral service. Complete follow-up is needed. If a citizen can get his complaints resolved through one office, it would benefit both him and the city's image.

Department heads feel the program has a psychological impact in improving the citizen's image of City Hall, but it must do more than this or it will fail in what will have been a short-lived experiment. Improved procedure between departments and the registration of a complaint must take place. Except for a few cases, there is no strong commitment by department heads to improve these techniques or to improve coordination with the mayor's representatives.

The mayor and City Council should consider as important approval of a comprehensive package of projects which will make meaningful changes in each neighborhood. New streets, additional lights, housing rehabilitation, more policemen, effective rodent control, and a number of other projects could very well be directed from and credited to each station.

Internally, the stations provide services to individuals and families in a convenient, one-stop center. For the thousands of citizens who receive good service, obtain jobs, and get family problems resolved, the program is an excellent one. It is "one of the best things the mayor has done," and it performs satisfactorily, given staff, budget, and related resource limitations. Bearing in mind that three neighborhood people, paid modest salaries, are primarily responsible for operation of the three stations, it is commendatory how much is achieved. Only continual improvement, however, will guarantee lasting success.

An area which needs improvement is citizen participation. Several citizen organizations have expressed concern over lack of citizen input into the program, and a more formal mechanism of reaching citizens and receiving suggestions should be explored. A citizen's advisory council for each station may be an answer, and it might very well be a mixed body of representatives from several area organizations. Some concrete authority must be given them if it is to be truly meaningful.

The citizens' council may be the device to sustain an ongoing mayor's station program—one that changes with the needs and desires of neighborhood people.

The following is a summary of recommendations and additional suggestions:

1. Greater advantage should be taken of EOC centers for outreach purposes, particularly since they support so few services. Mayor's stations should be developed into true multipurpose centers to which EOC personnel could make increased referrals.

2. Station services should be increased to include programs most relevant to the particular neighborhood: environmental inspection, Social Security assistance, senior citizen programs, payment of bills and licenses, issuance of permits, public works functions, Model Cities office, and other public and private agency functions.

3. The mayor's representative should be designated director of the center, with appropriate agreements and directives from the mayor and agency heads that he will function as coordinator and director. The person in this position must be able to administer a multipurpose center and coordinate agencies.

4. A mayor's desk of complaint and inquiry, supervised directly by a mayor's appointee, should be visible in each center. Only with the mayor taking a more personal interest in this function will City Hall's image continue to improve in complaint servicing. Now only twenty to thirty complaints monthly come through this source from each station, while some cities experience thousands of complaints and inquiries monthly through similar programs. This function is not realizing its full potential.

5. The station director should fulfill the role of neighborhood ombudsman in support of local projects and resolution of citizen problems. Additional staff is needed in each center for this purpose, for they must get out into the community as well as function within the building. The ombudsman approach has the potential of changing citizen attitudes more positively toward city hall than possibly any other program.

6. The mayor's representative (director) should conduct regular internal staff meetings, monthly mini-cabinet meetings with district department and agency heads, and regular meetings with the city's head of neighborhood services. City Hall staff is of high enough caliber to direct these changes and establish necessary procedures to put them into effect. Exchange of ideas will make more effective centers. Interagency and departmental meetings at the local level will help to achieve better coordination.

7. Assignment of staff should be so arranged that the stations are open evenings and some weekend hours. Their effectiveness is now limited by daytime operation.

8. The city should increase the effectiveness of its twenty-four-hour Office of Complaint and Inquiry in City Hall by providing staff which will follow up complaints and not merely refer them.

9. The city administration should consider establishing a formal mechanism of citizen councils to work with each station. Either an existing citizens' group or new council composed of representatives from all neighborhood groups might fulfill this role. It is a logical step toward development of a permanent communications link which would provide a continual flow of neighborhood ideas and concerns. Dispensing city services alone will not establish full communications, nor will it create the sense of community which appears to be so important with city officials today.

Area: 120.8 square miles
Population: 533,418
Black: 150,296

THE CITY AND ITS GOVERNMENT

The City

Columbus, the capital of Ohio, is the state's largest city in area.
About 25 percent of its working population is employed by the federal,
state, or municipal government. Industry is also a large employer;
and among the city's products are coal-mining machinery, concrete
mixers, aircraft assemblies, auto parts, paints, shoes, glassware,
and refrigerators.

Efforts are being made to expedite urban renewal and pollution
control programs. In the 1960's private developers began restoring
German Village, a 232-acre, wedge-shaped area settled in the late
1830's by immigrants from Bavaria. The area had become increasingly dilapidated after World War 1 but is now a tourist spot.

The Government

Mayor Thomas Moody (annual salary $30,000), whose term expires
in January, 1976, functions in a mayor-council form of government
with seven councilmen elected at-large, who receive annual salaries
of $8,000. The Mayor utilizes an executive assistant who functions as
a coordinator of various city departments and programs.

THE MINI-CITY HALL

History

The mini-city hall concept was developed in September, 1967, after Mayor Sensenbrenner received the recommendation from his staff and an endorsement of the idea from business and community leaders. A building was remodeled and made ready for this purpose in 1968.

Need for additional room for the Youth Opportunity Program and the Community Relations Department was the prime reason for acquiring space. But combining this reason with a service center concept in a neighborhood where social problems are most severe was an excellent approach. City Hall did not have additional space for programs, and it seemed most appropriate to locate new projects closer to the problems.

Clifford Tyree, director of community relations, recommended that these functions be placed in the Mt. Vernon Avenue area because of problems of physical as well as social deterioration. James P. Bally, executive assistant to the mayor, chaired the Mayor's Eastside Task Force (composed of business and community leaders), which worked closely with the Mt. Vernon Avenue District Improvement Association to study the area's problems and recommend solutions, as well as to create an arm of city government more easily accessible to residents. Monthly meetings were held in churches, store fronts, and agency centers with city government and agency officials and area residents. Some grievances were corrected; however, because of the preponderance of problems, it was decided that a permanent service center was needed to effect day-by-day solutions.

The fear that civil disruption might occur in Columbus, as it had in other parts of the nation, to some degree motivated the concept, although the city had experienced no serious violence. It was not until July 21, 1969, when a white person shot a black individual that the city experienced some disruption, but never anything on the scale of a riot.

Location and Demography

The center's location in a predominantly black residential and business area was supported by city officials, members of the business

community, and some area residents; however, others opposed its
being located in a largely black area and some residents felt it was
being designed to keep them from having direct contact with the downtown city hall. Housing a representative of the Police Department in
it further complicated the matter because some citizens viewed it as
having possible elements of suppression in case of riots. The consensus
remained, however, that a center was needed and would help the
community.

Mt. Vernon Avenue, site of the mini-city hall, is the main street
of Columbus' Near East Side. The area is often referred to as the
inner belt of the city, since it is in an approximate radius of one mile
from the center of downtown. It claims a high proportion of poor
(39 percent of the families have annual incomes of less than $3,000),
three times the arrest frequency of the remainder of Franklin County,
and 17 percent of the county's deteriorated and dilapidated housing.

The facility is a store front operation (approximately 3,500 square
feet) consisting of five offices, a meeting room for thirty to forty persons, and a reception area very similar in size to the centers in Boston
and Baltimore, for example. It has been adequately remodeled to serve
its purpose.

Initially some thought was given to construction of a new facility
or one more appropriate to the multiservice concept; however, it was
decided that no construction should be done until plans were submitted
by the Model Cities Coordinating Unit Committee, since the location
was to be in the Model Cities area. Because of the importance of the
project and the possible delay of two years' time under Model Cities
planning, the city of Columbus decided to go ahead immediately by
using existing facilities.

Budget, Staff, and Functions

The budget is approximately $30,000 of city funds plus salaries
of various department staff which operate in the center. The Department of Lands and Buildings, responsible for all city property, initially
remodeled the building and continues to maintain it from its own budget
allocations. Monthly rent is $250.

The Community Relations Department provided furniture and
pays the telephone bills. Basically, each department pays its own
operating costs from its designated city budget. Personnel are not
considered to be on loan for this operation but, rather, stationed here
as part of their main offices.

Because of the low budget, some staff members solicit financial assistance from churches and other organizations in order to meet certain program needs.

Four persons of the six-member Community Relations Department compose the core city staff of the mini-city hall. They appear to be the most influential in establishing citizen links to City Hall and in receiving citizen complaints and resolving problems. They deal with problems of housing, employment, welfare, and almost any matter which arises. One acts as assistant to the director of community relations and supervises the other three staff persons. However, no one functions in the capacity of coordinator of the entire mini-city hall operation.

The following represent functions of the program and its complement of twenty-five full and part-time personnel:

1. The Community Relations Department has four persons in the center.

2. The Youth Opportunity Office serves as a clearing house for all programs involving children in Columbus. The youth coordinator, who staffs this operation, initiates youth programs and assists in overall program planning for the city. There are several part-time helpers. Funding is 80 percent federal and 20 percent city.

3. Neighborhood Youth Corps has four counselors who provide employment opportunities and counseling for school children. Some 400 youths are placed in jobs each funding period.

4. The housing section has from eight to twelve persons who handle individual complaints as well as a systematic, block-by-block inspection program. Inspectors indicate they are able to handle complaints more effectively and expeditiously by being located closer to the citizens and away from more bureaucratic city hall procedures.

5. The Police Department has one police officer who works from the mini-city hall answering individual complaints, but who functions primarily in an educational role by distributing literature and participating in community meetings and lecturing to various groups.

Two policemen have held this position: The first was a young, eager black officer who related well to the community and was considered genuinely helpful and friendly. He was replaced by a surly, hostile

white, who reportedly acted as though he did not want to be assigned
here and complained that there was not enough work for him to do.
He was soon relieved but has not been replaced. However, at various
times police officers participate in the program when the need is felt.

6. The Health Services Division does not have staff in the building
but makes available leaflets and other information for general distribution.

Tyree reports the work load for the center is about 300-350 cases
per month. Most involve youth counseling, employment, and general
complaints and requests for service. Since the program does not
emphasize adult or family counseling, there is little processing of
families through many diversified agencies.

The program is designed to handle city functions primarily.
Tyree feels welfare functions are not significant to the operation because
the State Welfare Department and community action centers operate
close by and adequately fulfill this role. He does feel that citizens
tend to trust the center staff more than people at City Hall; consequently, decentralized services are desirable.

Hours of operation are normal city working hours on a five-day
basis.

Housing enforcement complaints seem to be more expediently
and efficiently handled in the mini-city hall than at the main city hall.
City departments appear to respond well to complaints filed by the
community relations staff. Volume is low, however, which presents
a stronger focus on this function.

MODEL CITIES PROGRAM

The Columbus Model Cities program has experienced conflict
over which of two citizen bodies was to represent the city. The initial
assembly of twenty-five people apparently split into factions. The most
recent elections, held in sixteen neighborhoods of the Model Cities
area, have resolved the controversy to the satisfaction of most. Two
representatives were elected from each neighborhood, for a total of
thirty-two persons, and twenty different organizations were designated
to appoint their own representatives, for a combined total of fifty-two
persons to constitute the model neighborhood assembly.

The Model Cities area is 2.5 square miles and consists of
55,000 persons. The first action year ended May 1, 1971. The

assembly is ruled by a strong president empowered to select the
personnel and important committees. The personnel committee
recommended one person for the post of Model Cities director, whom
the city administration accepted. The latest Model Cities administrator,
John Francis, was a local attorney, appointed to his new position in
June, 1970.

Paul Shearer, assistant administrator of Model Cities, appointed
in September, 1970, indicates there are no Model Cities funds programmed for the mini-city hall project, which is located in the Model
Cities area. He has not visualized the mini-city hall program as part
of a multiservice center concept, but views it as an administrative
center to stimulate and coordinate other programs. He feels the Blackburn recreation center, also located in the Model Cities area, was
established to provide the variety of services needed by the community.
Recreation, day care, education classes, art and cultural classes,
homemaking, and other related functions are provided at Blackburn;
however, it does not provide social welfare, employment, and municipal
services.

COMMUNITY ACTION PROGRAM

The community action agency in Columbus is the Columbus
Metropolitan Area Community Action Organization (CMACAO) whose
board of trustees is composed of fifty-one members, twenty-five elected
from the poverty areas, eight appointed by the mayor and City Council,
and the remainder appointed from selected representative agencies.
Its executive director is A. Brooks Curtis.

CMACAO operates in Franklin County, whose population is 734,
300, and which is estimated to have 190,000 poor persons. Columbus
is the largest city in the county, with about 69 percent of the total
county population and 80.7 percent of the urban population.

CMACAO directs its programs in three critical areas: economic
development, housing, and education. It operates seven centers (two
in the Model Cities area) which provide typical community action
services: day care, credit union, sewing program, professional
upholstery class, concentrated employment program, adult education,
housing location, training of workers, senior citizen program, tutoring,
planned parenthood, legal aid, neighborhood Youth Corps, child development, Head Start, special impact training in the building trades and
basic literacy and computational skills, new careers, and recreation
and cultural programs.

With this vast number of services and the close proximity of community action centers to mini-city hall, it is obvious why the city's program operates so few social services and concentrates on municipal functions. Brooks has never been briefed on the purpose or functions of mini-city hall but is under the impression that it functions primarily as a referral center.

CITIZEN PARTICIPATION

There is no citizen advisory council attached to the mini-city hall nor do residents participate in staff selection, planning, or operations of the program. Individual departments select their own staffs from regular employees of the department, and operate their programs independently of citizen groups.

Tyree sees no need for a citizen's advisory council at this time. He indicates he is a member of at least twenty-five different community groups and other organizations and that his staff also has memberships on many additional community bodies. Relationships with other groups, he feels, are excellent; and he expresses the belief that another committee may merely add a bureaucratic layer. He indicates there has been no adverse reaction to the program from citizens and that the building has never been damaged. "The community knows we're here," says Tyree, "and citizens know what we are doing for the community."

PERCEPTIONS OF THE PROGRAM

Mayor and City Council

The mayor and City Council see the mini-city hall program as a worthwhile and important way to communicate with citizens. They would like to see an expansion of the program, perhaps three more mini-city halls located in the outer fringe or more transitional problem areas. There is a feeling that other income levels and ethnic groups should also be served.

Political conflicts have not been influential in the development of this program, nor has politics affected location of the center.

Mayor's Office

James Bally views the program as a desirable step to reach citizens and to more clearly determine their feelings and ways of solving some of the more critical problems. The staff feels it makes city government more accessible to Columbus residents.

Mini-City Hall Staff

Mini-city hall employees want to see adequate funding for the program, establishment of a petty cash fund, expansion to evening and weekend hours, and better coordination of departments within the facility. Some felt more coordination was desirable and some felt it was not a problem.

Staff appeared interested in their duties and willing to make improvements in the operation. An overall sense of mission and purpose, however, appeared to be lacking or not understood.

Agencies and the Business Community

Outside agency personnel generally view the operation as a referral and administrative center with few in-house services. Some visualize it as an extension of some city government offices but with most requests sent back to main city hall departments to be handled. Coordination among the various agencies and organizations in minimal.

The business community favors the program as a good way to communicate with neighborhood residents, to help keep the city calm, and to show that City Hall is sincerely concerned.

Residents

Residents who have been served satisfactorily like the program. Some, however, feel it is a waste of taxpayers' money and others feel it is in the wrong location. The general feeling is positive, tempered by the view that the program has not yet made a significant impact on the community and is not designed to effect change. When some citizens were questioned whether they would be upset if the mini-city hall were closed, the reply was "no." Those who received help with specific problems, however, felt differently, indicating that much more needs to be done and in more areas of the city.

Some residents are apparently confused about the program because the sign on the building reads "City of Columbus Special Service Center," whereas most publicity refers to the location as the "mini-city hall."

The following are randomly selected comments made by neighborhood residents:

"Mini-city hall is easily accessible. Parking could be better."

"We need more of them and people need to know where they can go to get help. They need to know who to contact when they have a problem. We need one in every area."

"Do away with it. The services are not helping people in the area. The money running mini-city hall is being wasted. I am white."

"Change locations. Most people wouldn't go over on Mt. Vernon Avenue for that kind of help. Otherwise, it's all right."

"I have so much to tell you about the run-around I got at that place. I can't write it all. May I come to see you and talk about it?"

"They helped me get back on my feet."

"I didn't know that was what that place was called."

There have been some related problems which have caused concern to the program. In January, 1970, a fifteen-year old high school student, fleeing from a school in the evening, was shot and killed by police. The next night, two young men were shot and killed breaking into a cigarette machine. In yet another incident, a police officer, using his privately owned machine gun, shot and killed a burglar. All the victims were unarmed. There have been many cries since then for a police civilian review board, and an organization known as The Committee was formed to formalize citizens' demands for such a board and for such other relief as was deemed necessary.

The initial burst of outrage, however, has had little follow-up by community action, the Model Cities agency, or East Columbus Community Organization, a nonprofit delegate agency of CMACAO.

The mini-city hall appears not to have been successful in bringing
citizens and the Police Department together in resolving these conflicts
or in making its police-community relation function operate effectively
in this matter. Impressions of area residents are that little has been
done in this regard and that little will be accomplished through the
mini-city hall structure. It appears the matter is primarily one involving the Community Relations Division.

ANALYSIS AND RECOMMENDATIONS

Recommendations in this section are made in the hope that they
may be of some benefit to the persons developing the mini-city hall
concept.

The mini-city hall in Columbus was established primarily to
provide needed space for the city's Community Relations Division and
Youth Opportunity Program. Since an expenditure for rent would have
to be made anyway, it appeared a good opportunity to create a more
comprehensive program by combining these functions with several
others and forming some semblance of a service center. It was a
reasonable approach and an efficient way to use city monies. Influence
from citizen groups was apparently minimal, except to endorse the
project.

Other city departments, such as Police, Community Relations,
and Housing Inspection, also needed to be close to residents they serve,
so the center was a chance to accomplish this. In any case, housing
inspectors most likely would be located in the neighborhood whether
there was a mini-city hall or not because of greater efficiency in being
closer to their job sites, increased effectiveness resulting from a less
bureaucratic atmosphere, and closer contact with residents and their
immediate problems and priorities.

However, development of the decentralized center, with its emphasis on providing space rather than a comprehensive attack on community
problems, reveals some shortcomings: specific goals and objectives
for community change have not been delineated, comprehensive services
for a one-stop service center have not been provided, coordination
internally or externally has not been pursued, staff direction is minimal,
the city's commitment to the solution of broad neighborhood problems
is lacking, citizen participation is weak, and positive publicity regarding
the benefits of the program and its concern for residents has been
insufficient.

Most of these concerns can be corrected. The mini-city hall
serves a large portion of the city rather than concentrating on specific
neighborhoods, which tends to dissipate its effect on an individual
community. In order to demonstrate progress, concentration of
resources is desirable.

Some citizens and private organizations have questioned locating
the facility in a predominantly black area already being served by a
number of "war on poverty," Model Cities, and other related agencies.
However, since the area needs more assistance than others in the
city, city direction and commitment of resources here is proper, unless
and until this direction can come about through the Model Cities agency.

In order to preserve the delicate balance in "transitional"
neighborhoods, however, the city needs to put effort into other areas
as well. It must show interest and concern in these areas if it is to
stabilize them, and the mini-city hall approach could be a step in
this direction.

The present facility might have been more effectively located
farther from other public and private agencies to avoid some duplication and overconcentration in one neighborhood. Since it is located
in the Model Cities area, and if Model Cities eventually develops a
multiservice center, it may best be moved to another location. However, if it substitutes for the Model Cities center, as it now is doing,
then it should try to provide all the services that would truly fulfill
the multiservice concept, and with the assistance of Model Cities
funding.

Since the mini-city hall is very near community action centers
and state welfare and employment centers, it should either join forces
with some of these operations or bring more of these functions within its own center. Placing more community action and state services
in the mini-city hall will conserve agency space and funds, and broad-
en the participation level of the city's program. Adding these services,
plus including programs most crucial to a particular neighborhood,
would establish a sound base for city involvement. These may include
drug and alcoholic rehabilitation, city collection services for bills and
taxes, advocacy city planning, city personnel recruitment, health
inspection, delinquency prevention, housing rehabilitation, and so on.

The kinds of services to be provided by each mini-city hall will
depend greatly on what is needed in the neighborhood and may include
only a few of the above or others not mentioned. Thought should be
given to providing social service and family counseling functions so

that a family can resolve its problems in one building, during one visit. These services are particularly beneficial to the elderly, the poor, and the uninformed; and the approach can considerably reduce bureaucratic "hang-up." (Baltimore is a good example of this approach.)

The mayor and City Council should establish appropriate goals for neighborhood stabilization and rehabilitation, better communication between citizens and City Hall, improved delivery of specific neighborhood services, priorities of capital outlay projects, and other short- and long-range targets. Guidelines on how the city intends to achieve its goals should be set down in detail and resources committed. As citizens view progress toward achieving these goal, realization that City Hall is really concerned about residents and the city's image should improve.

It should be made clear to department heads that priorities are to go to mini-city halls and that employees, particularly in sensitive functions such as police-community relations, should be assigned permanently to each center, in an effort to make it successful and of real value to residents.

The director of the city's Community Relations Division should be placed clearly in charge of the neighborhood services program and he, in turn, should appoint one person to be assigned to each center as director and coordinator, fully in charge of all center staff. A city directive should instruct employees from all departments within the mini-city hall operation to be responsible to the center director, who, in turn, would hold regular staff meetings with representatives from departments and agencies in the facility. As additional centers are developed, the community relations staff could be assigned to different centers rather than concentrating all of them in one location.

The center director might very well hold mini-cabinet meetings with district supervisors and heads of departments and agencies within the program area, as well as internal staff meetings. Common objectives and agreed-upon priorities should be developed and local forces directed in concerted action on the area's problems. In this manner, program duplication could be avoided and future plans developed through more effective utilization of resources.

In addition to mini-cabinet meetings, the mayor might develop and conduct city cabinet meetings of department heads and some key private and public agency heads to review and plan an overall city approach toward reaching established goals. This may diminish

overlapping of programs and develop common understanding of the
city's needs and priorities.

Additionally, a central office of complaint and inquiry should be
established by the mayor, whereby a citizen may call one phone number
for service on any problem within the city, regardless of its nature or
the agency involved. The mayor's staff should be equipped to follow
up complaints completely and respond to the citizen in every case.
A smaller version of the central office should be located in each mini-
city hall to encourage local citizen inquiries and to develop systematic
methods of handling complaints rather than the somewhat haphazard
approach now being used.

Pursuit of the above concepts, particularly development of an
effective citywide cabinet, can bring the mayor closer to the "responsible city" concept, whereby he is better able to influence agencies
and organizations which critically affect his city.

In regard to communication with residents and information feedback, the city is presently relying on the citizen councils of other
agencies, plus input from its own staff who attend meetings of public
and private organizations. For more accurate and timely information,
and for development of stronger leadership and a more positive image
in the community, the city should develop its own citizen participation
structure.

Each center should have a citizens' advisory group with some
voice in programming, staff selection, development of neighborhood
goals, and capital budget determination for its area.

Efforts were made to keep the public informed and to involve the
community in some decisions during initial stages of development
of the mini-city hall; however, this participation level appears to have
decreased. For the center to remain viable, continual input from local
residents is needed.

If there is common agreement by the city and local citizen councils on selection of directors for each center, they may be able to
perform more effectively as neighborhood ombudsmen or citizen
advocates. Directors may also act as the mayor's ombudsmen in pursuing government's concerns about performance of other agencies.
This dual role is being played effectively by neighborhood city hall
directors in a number of cities.

In short, Columbus has taken a forward step in the development
of better neighborhood services and more effective ways to communicate

with citizens through its establishment of a mini-city hall. It is now entering a second stage whereby it should strengthen the concept, improve its management techniques, add services, involve citizens, and eventually expand the number of centers.

FURTHER RECOMMENDATIONS

1. Specific goals and objectives for a citywide neighborhood services program need to be developed. They should be reinforced with a strong desire to effect change and by a commitment of sufficient city resources to make an impact on the city's problems.

2. Consideration should be given to providing additional mini-city halls in other critical problem neighborhoods and to developing some pattern for reaching most of the city. Existing staff of the Community Relations Department and some other departments should be distributed to new centers.

3. Additional services should be added to the present center to increase clientele usage, and to enable present staff to be used more efficiently. Some community action functions could be added as well as several additional city department services. There should also be joint planning with Model Cities to provide increased funding and programming.

4. One person in each center should be designated the director in charge of all employees in the facility, who will call staff meetings, coordinate all agencies operating from the center, and act as a catalyst and motivator of programs in the neighborhood.

5. The center director should be empowered to call mini-cabinet meetings of district agency heads and department superintendents in order to achieve greater coordination, avoid duplication, and develop common goals and priorities.

The mayor should consider development of a city cabinet of key persons to help establish goals and priorities on a citywide basis and to better achieve coordination and concerted action on city problems.

6. A central office of complaint and inquiry should be established in City Hall with its counterpart in each mini-city hall. The office should accept complaints on any matter, follow them up completely, and answer the citizen in every case.

Ombudsmen in the mini-city halls and mayor's office should pursue all complaints and, where necessary, attempt to effect change in departments and agencies. The mayor, most likely, is as interested in change in some agencies as the citizen clientele. This entire process would encourage the "responsible city" concept, whereby the mayor and City Council accept greater responsibility for agencies and organizations affecting their city.

7. The mayor and City Council should consider formation of a citizen advisory council attached to each mini-city hall, rather than relying on secondary sources of citizen input. The citizen council should consist of representatives from key organizations in the area, as well as residents, in order to establish a representative group. This may tend to discourage a greater proliferation of organizations.

The citizen council would advocate necessary changes in all matters, help plan the neighborhood, help select the neighborhood center director, and help improve delivery of services from all sources.

Area: 44.6 square miles
Population: 704,209
Black: 101,000
Spanish: 66,000
Chinese: 62,000
Japanese: 11,000

Although San Francisco lacks a little city hall or its equivalent, it does boast employees on the mayor's staff who function as outreach personnel in various neighborhoods. Despite campaign promises of Mayor Joseph Alioto, who spoke out strongly for governmental decentralization, the city still functions from a downtown city hall, with the mayor taking a personal lead in establishing communication with citizens.

THE CITY AND ITS GOVERNMENT

The City

San Francisco, coextensive with California's San Francisco County, is the financial center of the West and, together with the San Francisco Bay area, the largest port on the Pacific Coast. San Francisco is the home of the Pacific Coast Stock Exchange and a Federal Reserve district bank. More than sixty-five industrial parks lie within a fifty-mile radius of the city. Major industries include food processing, shipbuilding, petroleum refining, and manufacture of metal products and chemicals.

The city has completed a 3.6 mile transbay tube, first step in
the $1.3 billion Bay Area Rapid Transit (BART) project. It will be
the largest locally financed public works project in U.S. history and the
world's first fully automated rapid transit system.

The Japan Cultural and Trade Center, with hotels, restaurants,
and shops, was dedicated in 1968. There are plans to construct a
Chinese ethnic center in the near future. A projected fifty-five-story
world headquarters of Transamerica Corp. will have a 240-foot spire,
making it the tallest building west of the Mississippi.

The Government

Under the city's present weak-mayor form of government, the
mayor achieves administrative strength through his personal abilities
to deal with others. Charter revision proposals to increase his role
and decrease those of two other leading city officials (chief administrative officer and comptroller) were defeated several years ago.

The city's Board of Supervisors (City Council) consists of
eleven members elected at-large to two-year terms. San Francisco's
city charter requires that the Board involve itself in everything the
mayor does. The chief administrative officer (CAO) holds one of the
city's strongest posts—appointed by the mayor to a life term (and
thus not always the appointee of the mayor currently serving), and
removable only for malfeasance at the discretion of the Board of
Supervisors. The CAO has administrative authority over many key
city departments but in practice over the past thirty-eight years has
been fully aware of his responsibility to the mayor. He is generally
more responsive and cooperative than many of the mayor's own
commissions. The charter states: "The mayor shall be the chief
executive officer of the city and county," and in another section reads,
"The chief administrative officer shall be responsible to the mayor
and to the Board of Supervisors for the administration of all affairs
placed in his charge. . . ." Some students of government would call
this a mayor-chief administrative officer form of government rather
than weak-mayor.

San Francisco is reputed to have an honest, graft-free government, partially because of a series of checks and balances growing
out of the weak-mayor form. Indicative of this open system is the
unusual fact that city employees are not "hatched"; that is, no Hatch
Act regulations preclude their taking part in limited political activities.
They may campaign actively on issues, but not for particular candidates,
and are supposed to remain overtly nonpartisan. Even police are
allowed this freedom.

The mayor's executive assistant, John de Luca, sees Mayor Alioto as responsible for the excellent rapport established between himself, Chief Administrative Officer Thomas Mellon, the comptroller, and the city attorney. He sees his city as having strong, diverse ethnic and interest groups and feels Alioto encourages this pluralistic society, involving each point of view in government problems and processes. For example, de Luca says, when Alioto goes to Washington, D.C., to testify before a Congressional committee, he is prone to taking not one or two close aides, but a dozen or two dozen citizens closely involved in a given issue. The mayor is also usually accessible to the press, makes frequent radio appearances, conducts a weekly television show, and in general works hard to establish communication between his office and residents of the city.

City departments in San Francisco are directly beholden to commissions appointed by the mayor. These commisssions, in turn, appoint department heads and set policy. Again, they may outlast a given mayor. Since Alioto came into office in January, 1968, he has had the opportunity to appoint only six commission members out of twenty; the Board of Education has members nominated by the mayor and confirmed by voters.

Everyone under the level of department head is in civil service. Indeed, this merit system, together with labor unions, is quite strong in San Francisco. Because political patronage is thus virtually non-existent, it is even harder for the mayor to assure that his mandate is carried out. Some officials admittedly "long for some sort of spoils system, if for nothing else than to make employees more responsive."

DECENTRALIZATION

The absence of little city halls in San Francisco is due, according to John de Luca, to the compactness of the city, as well as to its highly developed, actively civic, pluralistic society.

"Labor, business, and minority groups are represented on almost all city committees," he indicates, "and it is the mayor's style to encourage this kind of participation. These factors diminish the need for little city halls."

De Luca feels that the city may be better off without them. "You can buy as many problems as you can settle with little city halls," he says, "as there are power fights in many sections of the city." And you only get frustration "when citizens realize that the resources are not there to follow through."

John H. Anderson, assistant deputy for development, and an assistant to de Luca, agrees. He feels the question of little city halls relates directly to finances; one can't promise what can't be delivered.

One "city supervisor," as they are known in San Francisco, Bob Mendelson, sees the Economic Opportunity Council (EOC, a community action board) as filling the functions of little city halls. He feels that through these kinds of programs the "have nots" are becoming increasingly sophisticated, and they are having less and less trouble reaching "the establishment" as now constituted.

He points out that an idea for a mobile unit, to fill some of the functions of a little city hall, was proposed by the San Francisco Foundation some years back, but later dropped. The unit would have cost some $12,000 and would have been used mainly to handle citizen complaints.

EOC Director John Dukes is dubious about the concept. He feels a little city hall may lead away from true citizen participation, placing residents in a subservient role. "They tend to bastardize the real problems and are therefore suspect," he says. Expressing a much more aggressive outlook, Dukes favors community corporations, under which citizens take power directly for themselves. He strongly believes, however, that a happy medium must be reached so that one does not get bogged down in too much citizen involvement.

"There is neighborhood hostility toward City Hall," says Jack Morrison, former city supervisor and unsuccessful mayoral candidate in the last election and now an EOC planning official, "and it's Alice in Wonderland stuff to think otherwise." People just don't know who to contact or how to get through to the right place, he believes.

Morrison believes some innovative technique to reach the citizens is necessary. He leans toward community action as more able to make decisions based on what people want, but feels little city halls or ombudsmen would be helpful in reaching the people. But he also believes that "Little city halls just don't get to the heart of it." It takes a deeper city commitment.

Sal Cordova, community relations director, Mission Neighborhood Health Center, says, "We don't have the traditional city hall problems, and besides we have good rapport with them. We're not that far away, and I can't see where it is really needed." He stresses a desire for community independence, that City Hall does not know how to get things done, and that there are too many political

appointments—people who do not know how to accomplish things.
City Hall is not viewed as an enemy, however. It is seen as a place
to get things on their way, if you have a plan.

San Francisco's defeated charter revision proposals contained
a section which would have created an ombudsman system for the
entire city. Although this particular section was not a point of contention, the entire charter revision was defeated two to one, and the
idea died.

Nevertheless, Bernie Orsi and John Moynihan, both working out
of the mayor's office, act as liaisons between City Hall and the people
answering complaints and working on projects. Orsi views his role
with mixed feelings. Although his job is as a mayor-citizen advocate,
he feels others, particularly minority group staffers within the Model
Cities program, can relate better to neighborhood groups. The
mayor's aides are not truly neighborhood ombudsmen, and citizens
have not participated in their selection.

Tom Miller, assistant to Chief Administrative Officer Mellon,
sees a definite need for both ombudsmen and a complaint office to
pull together the work of what he considers a fragmented government
structure. He indicates that San Francisco has fifty-five different
department heads, with over 20,000 employees, and he feels strongly
that some sort of ombudsman system would keep this vast network
sharper. He would favor one-stop service centers, particularly in
depressed areas. But he too expressed the view that there may not
be enough money to set up such a program. Dukes has another
suggestion. "The mayor should appoint ten more community aides,
in addition to the several he has, to work in the neighborhoods," he
says. "But their selection must heed the voice of the people."

ECONOMIC OPPORTUNITY COUNCIL

San Francisco's community action agency is private, nonprofit,
and was incorporated in the state of California in 1964 to function
solely in the city and county of San Francisco. Its basic purpose is
"to stimulate better focusing of all available local, state, private,
and federal resources toward enabling low-income families and
individuals, of all ages, to attain skills, knowledge, motivation and
opportunities needed to become fully self-sufficient."

The EOC has five neighborhood-based organizations, each
located in poverty pocket "target areas": central city, Chinatown-
North Beach, Hunter's Point-Bayview, Mission, and Western Addition.

Each target area office is a private, nonprofit corporation serving the particular needs of low-income residents in the area. Target area board members are democratically selected and broadly representative of the different neighborhoods and major groups within its area.

To provide support, guidance, training, and technical assistance, a central office was established with a central board whose members come from each target area, as well as public and private agencies. They are also sixteen district offices.

Relations between EOC and City Hall have not been the best. Yet the program enjoys strong support from the city's business sector. EOC Public Relations Director Frank Clark notes a strong coalition between business and the poverty program, a "coalition to keep peace," as he puts it. David A. Marcelle, Chamber of Commerce systems manager, works closely with the program, particularly in employment and minority enterprise.

EOC Director John Dukes confirms the poor relations between his program and City Hall but characterizes them as lack of communication rather than overt hostility. He also feels that EOC clients are basically fearful of City Hall.

This feeling is reinforced by citizens in the neighborhoods. San Yuen, head of the senior citizen center in the city's Chinatown (an EOC funded operation), who considers himself an ombudsman, says the Chinese fear the downtown city hall. He was moved to aid his people in a variety of official and semiofficial capacities. The mayor's aide in that area, Yuen says, is a white man with absolutely no understanding of problems confronting the Chinese. "They will not relate to him, so it is very much a waste of manpower," he states. Yuen would accept a mayor's aide working from his office if the community were involved in his selection and if the city administration expressed a sincere desire to work with the area's problems.

His neighbors rely on him to such an extent that Yuen believes many would "commit suicide" should his center close its doors. "The old are not militant. They would not riot. But they would do worse to themselves," he sadly expresses.

MODEL CITIES

San Francisco received its first Model Cities planning grant in 1968 in HUD's second round of planning grant fundings. One model

neighborhood was approved: the predominantly black, Bayview-
Hunter's Point area.

Mayor's Assistant Mike McCone has coordination of the Model
Cities program assigned as one of his duties, but overall responsibility
for the program is vested in the Model Cities Commission, a twenty-
one-member policy-making body appointed by the mayor. By ordinance,
at least fifteen members of the commission must be residents of the
model neighborhood.

Principal vehicle for citizen participation in the Model Cities
program is the Citizens Advisory Council (CAC), chosen by the commission by majority vote, and confirmed in writing by the mayor.
The Model Cities ordinance prescribes representation from the following groups: employment, labor, racial, religious, ethnic, housing,
appropriate governmental agencies, and such others as the agency
shall deem advisable. The purpose is to provide a means of widespread community participation and involvement in development of the
Model Cities program.

Thirteen task forces were set up by CAC to study and advise on
various subjects, including employment and economic satisfaction;
housing, community development, and transportation; education;
health; law and justice; leisure time activities; and citizen participation
and community communication. The task forces are coordinated by
the executive committee of CAC.

The staff, appointed by the city from within its ranks, consists
of an executive director, program coordinator, social services
coordinator, junior management assistant, three model neighborhood
assistants, and clerical and janitorial help. Some staff is loaned from
other agencies and organizations, such as city planning, social
services, and the redevelopment agency.

The flow of decision making is prescribed by ordinance. Task
forces make recommendations to CAC and its executive committee,
which in turn makes its recommendations to the commission. When
a proposal is agreed upon by the commission, it is forwarded to the
mayor; and after consultation and review within city government
and by the county supervisors, it is forwarded to HUD.

It should be noted that while there is sometimes talk of Model
Cities in San Francisco's Mission district, no such program exists
as yet. A private, nonprofit group is being organized, and reportedly
plans to seek direct funding from HUD. As of this writing, however,
no proposals have been submitted.

CITIZEN PARTICIPATION

Citizen participation in San Francisco takes several forms. There are the five councils from the five target community action organizations, which are almost autonomous and enjoy close rapport with neighborhood people. They are composed of twenty-six neighborhood people and twenty-five city officials, for a total of fifty-one each, with majority control still in the hands of the neighborhoods.

EOC Director Dukes sees this structure as a "happy medium for citizen participation." "You do not want to get too bogged down in this concept," he says, "or nothing gets done." He lauds the initial neighborhood involvement in early EOC elections but feels the groups grow less representative as time goes on. One problem Dukes sees is that representatives do not always speak for the groups they are picked to serve. More important than citizen representation, he believes, is a coalition of "money and votes" to gain greater control, break old coalitions, and foster new power bases.

Other citizen participation structures center about the Model Cities program, and include the commission, citizens' advisory council, and task forces, as described above. Citizens in the Hunter's Point Model Cities area have strong voice, including veto power over key elements of the program. Future Model Cities councils are not likely to have this control because of new federal guidelines. Sal Cordova indicates that greater citizen control is necessary, and citizens' council and staff must be independent of local government to remain effective. "As soon as you are on the payroll of City Hall, you are one of them and begin to lose the trust of the people," he emphasizes. He indicates he would not want to work for the city, for his rapport with the citizens would be lost. "Citizen councils could be funded by taxes, but the money should go directly to the citizens without any strings attached. This is true decentralization. Otherwise," he says, "control will come from City Hall."

Warns Cordova, "There is fear of government. People stay off welfare because they are afraid they may be deported and because many have too much dignity." Immigration and language problems may well account for the low level of citizen participation where twenty-six Latin American nationalities are represented in the Mission area.

There are a multitude of civic organizations, clubs, unions, business groups, ethnic societies, and other citizen units that find a way to express themselves in San Francisco. Groups seem to be more closely knit and sophisticated, and therefore know how to get things accomplished.

ANALYSIS

Initiative for neighborhood decentralization has come primarily from neighborhood groups in the way of health centers, community action centers, and Model Cities citizen councils. The state has established a series of multiservice centers throughout California, with one in San Francisco.

The city apparently has not felt the need for neighborhood city halls or their equivalent because San Francisco is compact geographically; struggle for control of these institutions might cause unnecessary conflict among existing organizations; effective citizen contact already exists through the mayor's unusual ability to communicate with citizens; and citizens already know how to get through the "system" in this highly educated and mobile society.

However, many citizens and officials believe that additional methods of reaching citizens are necessary, and new techniques should be tried. Feelings are that the preferable method is through effective citizen councils which independently run their neighborhoods and through formalized use of ombudsmen.

The city's approach to decentralization is by having several outreach aides working from the mayor's office, assigned to deal with specific problem areas. But there is strong criticism that they have been selected with greater emphasis on political considerations than on their abilities to reach specific ethnic groups. To be more effective, neighborhood leaders feel local citizens should have some say in their selection. Local people like the idea of help from City Hall, but they want a voice in personnel selection and program priorities.

Because of the city's fragmented departmental structure, it appears that a central mayor's office of complaint and inquiry (where all complaints are processed) would help the citizen immeasurably. Working in conjunction with the chief administrator's office, it would be a convenience for citizens, who would be able to obtain service at one source, and it would further develop central management techniques by processing information from all departments through the chief administrative officer.

RECOMMENDATIONS

The following recommendations may be worth pursuing in San Francisco:

1. Greater city impact could be made upon neighborhoods if city-funded ombudsmen were assigned to existing community action programs or delegate agencies, the state multiservice center, and proposed Model Cities center. Neighborhood ombudsmen should be assigned to all major areas of the city. There should be mutual agreement between the city and citizen groups as to the acceptability of these persons to achieve maximum effectiveness.

2. The mayor should consider establishing mayor's field offices of complaint and inquiry in some existing programs. One, established in the state multiservice center, for example, would give it a new dimension of concern and bring city government closer to other important operations. Other city functions, such as housing and environmental inspections, financial transactions, police-community relations, etc., could also be added. The mayor's representative could be designated coordinator of all programs operating within a specified district. He could call mini-cabinet meetings of district superintendents and, hopefully, create a greater responsiveness to neighborhood problems among government personnel. The process would tend to bring the various levels of government closer together, diminish duplication, and achieve some coordination and common effort toward solving related problems.

3. Consideration should be given to creating a central mayor's office of complaint and inquiry in City Hall and the eventual development of central management techniques that would effectively centralize information from all departments through the chief administrative officer so it could be more easily used by the mayor and Board of Supervisors.

4. The city should develop coterminous districts for all its departments and programs to improve coordination and the development of uniform statistical areas. To begin this concept, all new programs should be placed in logical alignment with existing departments and agencies.

5. Consideration should be given to the establishment of citizen councils in all parts of the city and, in some areas, physical facilities in the form of little city halls. The councils should be given reasonable powers to make them truly effective bodies and to assist in the development of a greater sense of community.

PART

III

COMMON PROBLEMS
AND TECHNIQUES—
A COMPARATIVE
ANALYSIS

PERFORMANCE: OVERALL IMPACT
OF DECENTRALIZATION

In this chapter and those that follow we will analyze the same
cities' programs comparatively from the standpoints of overall
performance, management, use of ombudsmen, politics, citizen participation, and community impact.

Neighborhood offices can solve only a portion of city problems.
To ensure success of decentralization, cross-fertilization of department, agency, and neighborhood center resources is necessary.
Centers particularly need the commitment of elected officials and
urban administrators, and they need formal links to existing systems.

The charge leveled at Chicago's large urban progress centers—
that they have become just additional layers of bureaucracy infected
with the same ills they were designed to cure—is not easy to refute.

Large centers may develop bureaucratic tendencies. To improve
them suggestions have been made for additional receiving areas sub-
dividing some functions, smaller waiting rooms, sufficient citizen
advocates to follow through on complaints and help process clients,
and lessening information and eligibility requirements. The best
solution may be further decentralization, for the chosen population
area may be too large.

In Boston, there is some criticism that little city halls have
added another layer of bureaucracy, but for the thousands of citizens
who receive satisfactory service, it is anything but an additional

331

hindrance. Councillor Joseph Timilty, for one, believes citizens can get faster response by contacting their elected representatives. This is most likely true; and little city hall managers recognize the need for councillor help on particularly difficult problems, and are glad to see citizens get it. The problem is that nine part-time councillors cannot be expected to effectively handle 15,000 to 20,000 complaints per month without an additional staff and increased administrative responsibility. Chicago processes over 800,000 inquiries annually— an impossible task for fifty aldermen whose first obligation is determining city policies.

A reliable and effective institutionalized system must be established in the normal operations of government. The neighborhood office staff is part of this system. Proper handling of some cases may take several hours or several days to follow up, and neighborhood ombudsmen are geared to spending this kind of time. It is desirable for councilmen to process a sampling of difficult cases so they know problems firsthand, but they cannot do the entire job themselves.

It has been demonstrated that many elderly or uninformed people, and those with language barriers or without adequate transportation, never make the effort to approach City Hall departments, and thus continue without service. Rapport established by the neighborhood ombudsman lessens resident fear and achieves satisfaction in most cases. However, it also increases the number of complaints, whereas most city officials would rather keep things as quiet as possible. The success of the neighborhood officer will depend very much on support of councilmen and their understanding of the necessity of outreach stations.

Educators and urban administrators have been searching for ways to improve the image of government for a long time. The "rhetoric of concern" has been adopted by many public officials, and indications are that this has had some positive effect. A 1969 study by the Harvard-MIT Joint Center for Urban Studies, based on 3,000 interviews in Boston, reveals a more positive citizen attitude toward responsive government, and concludes:

Being responsive and communicating concern is clearly part of winning community backing; and our data suggest that this task is even harder to do, but perhaps more important to people, than delivering services.

But rhetoric alone has only a temporary effect. Actual performance must follow if the image is to remain positive. In most cities that have decentralized, images have improved—through establishment of communication units, if nothing more. In Boston and New York, for example, resentment has also been created by decentralization because of inability to deliver on promises. In contrast, Houston listed commitments to residents, allocated the proper resources, and carried through on promises.

There is no doubt that any lasting improvement in the relationship between citizen and government requires improved services. If attempts to improve are to be effective, close coalition between urban administrators and neighborhood managers is necessary. Preferably the administrator should take the initiative for planning and creating local offices and incorporating them into the city's structure. Establishing decentralized facilities without department head understanding and concurrence may leave the network stranded. The mayor, too, must stress a desire for complete cooperation for the program within the city's hierarchy. Local offices must be brought into the city structure if they are to have authority. Standing alone may bring attention but little change.

Cooperation from most department and agency heads has been gained because the centers have been able to act as buffers for complaints between officials and citizens. Proper citizen contacts have diminished ill will even when complaints were not resolved, allowing department heads to continue their own operations without friction.

On the other hand, some department heads have become annoyed because of continual pressures to do things that are impossible because of lack of resources. It is essential that the center director, as well as the department head, have a clear understanding of the city's financial limitations. The director, as a neighborhood advocate, normally is more able to convince residents of the city's restraints and therefore make life more bearable for the department head in his relations with citizens.

Decentralization has made principal officials, as well as their subordinates, more cognizant of neighborhood problems and more willing to do something about them; therefore, it has also increased the level of department and agency performance.

COORDINATION

Coordination is indispensable to the delivery of services. If coordination is effective both within centers and between centers and other agencies, harmonious understanding of neighborhood problems, realistic development of priorities, less duplication, and more effective use of resources result. If it is poor, the whole delivery system may be damaged.

Internal Coordination

Coordination is more easily achieved within centers than it is among agencies, usually scattered throughout the city, county, or metropolitan area. However, many centers have failed to achieve even internal coordination.

Columbus has no director for its mini-city hall, which means services within the center operate independently with insufficient direction and coordination. In San Antonio, the engineers in charge of service centers direct only public works functions. Other functionaries report directly to City Hall. In Los Angeles, district heads are in charge of their departments only. In these operations, there is a significant administrative vacuum for tying all functions together.

In Chicago's larger centers particularly, there is an inability to coordinate all functions, even though overall directors are assigned to centers. There are too many diverse operations, and the directors have neither clear-cut guidelines nor sufficient authority for coordinative responsibilities. Some coordination is achieved through staff meetings. In Chicago's multiservice centers, coordination is more effective because of smaller size, fewer functions, and stronger administrative leadership.

Managers in Boston and Norfolk have been given clear responsibility to coordinate and direct their centers, resulting in greater harmony and singleness of purpose among agency staffs. Also, because there is a deemphasis of social services in the city's operation, there is less need to process families from one agency to another.

The mayor's aides in Baltimore have been given coordinating responsibilities, and in two of the three centers they hold staff meetings with functional heads. Because of the workable size of the centers, much coordination is done informally, its effectiveness dependent upon the skills and motivation of each director. Individuals and families are usually received by the center director, who ensures proper processing by taking the family to the right person or by bringing several service heads together to deal with the family. Families are given immediate and comprehensive attention. But coordination could be improved by employing directors with better administrative responsibility.

Other difficulties have arisen in the program. Some department heads have withdrawn employees from the centers because of lack of funds or because they felt the emphasis was too much on social services and not enough on traditional city functions. Some officials criticize lack of a broad, conceptual framework; confused relationships and responsibilities; lack of power or authority on the part of mayor's representatives to effect innovative ideas, positive direction, and coordination. Nevertheless, internal coordination of existing staff works better than in large centers, and the mayor and his staff have started to correct some of these obvious faults.

External Coordination

External coordination is as important as internal coordination, and in some cases, more so. Boston and New York, for example, focus mainly on the delivery of services from city departments, so the need to establish links to department heads is vital. Various formal and informal methods of facilitating coordination are being tried.

Mini-Cabinets

New York and Boston are the only two cities attempting to legitimize the concept of mini-cabinets, which are still highly informal arrangements. Little city hall managers call monthly meetings of direct department and agency heads in each center area to discuss problems of individual neighborhoods and to determine how the group may utilize resources from various agencies to solve them cooperatively. Bringing these officials together in a local climate has generated greater awareness and concern about needs and has demonstrated that needs are met more effectively by working together on the same priorities.

Mini-cabinet members are usually second-echelon personnel, but those who can make important decisions affecting their districts. Typical representatives have been street superintendents, refuse superintendents, police precinct captains, district health directors, welfare supervisors, employment office directors, mayor's representatives, district city councilmen, state legislators, chamber of commerce officials, and sometimes representatives from civic organizations. As yet, neither New York or Boston has formalized

the establishment of its district cabinets by decree; however, the
mayors in each case have endorsed the concept and instructed city
department officials to attend meetings regularly. It is somewhat
more difficult to get attendance from officers outside city government.
The success of each cabinet depends very much on personal abilities
of the local manager to motivate local officials, on city administrative
leadership, and on the importance of the issues.

The concept has given new responsibilities to employees who
otherwise would never have become involved, and it has developed
new and improved working relationships among agencies. In turn,
this has helped to more effectively attack neighborhood problems.

Task Forces

Task forces have been used successfully in a number of cities
to tackle specific problems, such as air pollution, mass transit,
housing, crime, youth employment, and other special concerns.
Usually department and agency heads, as well as civic representatives,
serve on them. Sometimes they take on the flavor of mini-cabinets
even within their circumscribed areas of concern and short lifespan.

In New York, along with mini-cabinets and specialized city task
forces, Mayor Lindsay utilizes fifty UATFs to perform some of the
same functions. The difference is that on UATFs, residents are the
members, with city staff and department heads only advisers. Borough
presidents, too, have appointed task forces, which tackle problems
similar to those of city task forces, but on the borough level. In
New York, the vast proliferation of governmental and nongovernmental
agencies, commissions, and study groups has made governing so
complex that a single form of neighborhood government is being
sought.

Mayor's Cabinet

Mayor's cabinets are more likely to function in larger cities.
In council-manager and chief administrative officer systems, the
urban administrator takes the leadership in convening department
head (cabinet) meetings to achieve more effective coordination and
direction. John Taylor (Kansas City) and James Kunde (Dayton) are
managers who have experienced success with this tool. New York
and Chicago have effective cabinets because of strong mayoral leadership, which, in Chicago's case, has overcome a basically weak-mayor
structure. However, in Los Angeles, also a weak-mayor system,

Mayor Samuel Yorty has not promoted the idea. The City Council has not given him that kind of authority, though recently it proposed giving him greater leeway in appointment and direction of department heads.

Mayor White formed a Public Service Board (cabinet) in Boston, but it has met infrequently and has had little influence. It consisted of a much broader range of officials than the small group of chief advisers he meets with now. Officials outside government as well as many within feel it could be a very effective force in dealing with city problems, if Mayor White would only make use of it.

Besides being effective coordinative devices, cabinets pinpoint problems and priorities, act as sources of intelligence not only for the mayor but also for those in attendance, provide opportunity for developing innovation and style, place stress on key issues, and effect the teamwork necessary to deal with complex and diversified problems.

It makes sense to expand cabinets to include representation from key state and other nonmunicipal public agencies so that a wider scope of city problems can be treated. For too long mayors and city administrators have tended to assume responsibility for only those departments under their legal jurisdiction, on the assumption that they have no business delving into other agencies' matters and have enough problems of their own; however, many officers have begun to realize that matters falling under the jurisdiction of other public agencies may be significant sources of city headaches. Recommendations of professional organizations and federal agencies support involvement of mayors and administrators in human resource programs and intergovernmental relations. It is the development of this "responsible city" concept that is giving the mayors and urban administrators greater strength and ability to coordinate, tie into regional plans, effect annexations, perform comprehensive planning, and become involved in every program that passes through their cities or metropolitan areas. As they soon learn, each program has some effect on their ability to operate municipal government.

Area-Wide Councils

Regional coordination of programs is vitally important to local government. Regional commissions can make it easier or more difficult for local government to conduct programs or make sense out of them. Some success in area-wide coordination has been achieved through regional organizations such as councils of government (COG), urban coalitions, regional task forces, and interstate groups formed by contracts.

Promotion of COGs has come about primarily because of federal requirements for comprehensive transportation planning in metropolitan areas, but the councils have expanded to include more physical and human resource functions. Success is mixed and powers limited. One success story is the Twin Cities Metropolitan Council in Minneapolis-St. Paul, which went from being a paper tiger to gaining power to conduct programs, levy taxes, and veto plans of other agencies inconsistent with regional objectives. The St. Louis metropolitan area East-West Gateway Coordinating Council is an excellent example of a COG which has developed interstate contracts and agreements for mass transportation, airports, health programs, and other concerns.

Urban coalitions (business, union, civic, neighborhood groups) have had some success in bringing business and private citizens together, particularly in helping to alleviate problems of unemployment, housing, discrimination, and other urban ills. Governmental involvement has been secondary, and a lack of permanent financing leaves the future of such coalitions in doubt.

Task forces and legal corporations established by local government bodies to operate area-wide projects (comprehensive health programs, mass transit systems, air pollution control bodies, housing development corporations, and many other functions) appear to be an important way to get specific projects started quickly and effectively. More and more, regional and local corporations are ways of getting projects immediately and maintaining them on a long-term basis.

Regional bodies are not in conflict with neighborhood government and should not be. Too many community action, Model Cities, and other local programs have operated without links to regional plans; but there are good examples where compatibility exists, such as the St. Louis metropolitan experience. Basis principles are that neighborhood government must operate what best suits it; plans of all governments must be coordinated; and higher levels must have the power of veto or correction. It is unnecessary for these philosophies to conflict.

Summary of the Five Techniques

Decentralization very much depends on the ability of agencies and governments to coordinate at higher levels. Proper direction of priorities and resources along the hierarchical ladder means less need to unscramble at the local level. This is accomplished with a

certain measure of centralized control. Centralization and decentralization are complementary, and it is desirable that both processes be
refined and extended within our society.

The five techniques discussed above are interrelated:

1. Internal coordination: Through staff meetings and effective
managerial direction, neighborhood center personnel are coordinated
and informed.

2. Mini-cabinets: Center managers and district chiefs inform
each other and establish priorities.

3. Special task forces: Specialized lay persons and technicians
evaluate and help solve wide and local problems; a task force usually
remains in existence only as long as it takes to complete the project.

4. Mayor's cabinet: Department heads and principal agency
officials create policies together; mini-cabinets and task forces feed
information to the cabinets.

5. Area-wide councils: Principal task force and cabinet officials
from various levels of government achieve faster communication
and coordination to solve local problems from a regional point of
view.

Coterminous Districts

Coordination and performance would be improved through
uniform districting of departments and agencies. Several cities have
recently established coterminous boundaries for some functions. A
few administrators feel it is not worth the time and effort to achieve
single districts when other administrative changes are easier to
effect and may make greater improvement in service. They feel time
should be expended on more effective agency heads, more productive
employees, fewer union restrictions, and citizen councils with some
authority to solve problems. But most agree that energies should be
spent on resolving all these problems.

San Antonio already has uniform districts for public works
functions. Officials in Los Angeles and New York feel they can
readily establish uniformity for sanitation, street maintenance, and
traffic functions. New York has already taken steps to move the following operations to uniform districts: Recreation Department, Youth

Service Agency, Parks Maintenance and Operation, and Mayor's
Organizational Task Force for Comprehensive Health Planning. At
least this is a beginning and sets a jurisdictional pattern for new
programs, so the problem of overlapping districts does not become
worse.

Washington, D.C., has been able to accomplish a great deal
with uniform districting because of local leadership and because most
functions fall under the authority of Congress, which approved the
concept. But it has taken a good deal of persuasion, "brow beating,"
and enticements to bring some agencies around, says Jim Alexander,
director of community services. Some agencies which saw benefits
in the plan encouraged others. For example, the park district saw
how it could benefit from recreation funds if the two departments
worked together, and the sanitation department visualized health
department inspectors assisting their inspection teams. Staff shortages
in one department were assisted by another, and two more operations
were able to make use of a single physical facility. The goal of
coterminous districts seems possible here.

The concept also involves creation of service area committees
(SACs), which consist of district agency heads who are required to
devote at least one-fifth of their time to correcting neighborhood
problems through a coordinated team approach (similar to mini-
cabinets). A service area representative is assigned as the key staff
person to the committee. Some agencies are apprehensive because
they fear the area representative may develop into an overall manager
who may diminish the authority of other chiefs. The program does
envision district heads reporting to the SAC representative for localized problems and to their own agency heads for problems of wider
scope. In order for the plan to work, agency heads must be committed to the concept and be willing to exchange some of their authority
for the benefits of the new organization. It has not required additional
appropriations for it uses staff from existing departments. It appears
to be working and worth emulating. (See appendixes I, J, and K for
service area criteria, SAC activities, and SAC obligations which
show why district uniformity was necessary.)

The structure of the state of Virginia eliminates some problems
of overlapping districts. Here, cities and counties are single entities
and almost all operational functions are under the jurisdiction of
municipal government. When Tom Maxwell was city manager in
Norfolk, he indicated that this situation lessened problems with federal
programs too. Since the community action program operates in
several contiguous cities, he felt that uniform districting with other

federal programs in just one city was not practical. Virginia is a
case where good state planning has eliminated many jurisdictional
and coordinative problems.

There are sound justifications for establishing coterminous
districts, some of which follow:

1. To facilitate coordination by limiting contacts with only one
head from each department and agency. Mini-cabinets can be more
readily formed, giving administrators and political leaders a professional group to which they can turn for problems at the local level.

2. To develop a statistical and informational base for identifying
social, economic, and physical problems in each area in order to
achieve more realistic budgets and plans.

3. To foster joint planning and operations and shared use of
facilities and staff.

4. To reduce duplication in such activities as outreach, intake,
and follow-up.

5. To make services more readily available at one-stop centers
in each area rather than a multitude of centers.

6. To develop closer ties with citizens to assure that programs
are increasingly responsive to actual needs. Neighborhood identity
and local councils responsible for a defined area can be more easily
established.

CENTRAL MANAGEMENT TECHNIQUES

Computers

There are other techniques to improve performance in decentralized operations. Feedback from neighborhood centers placed into a
central computer can provide valuable information in usable form,
if the number and variety of complaints are sufficient to warrent it.
If not, periodic hand tabulation can be just as effective. Most intelligence gathering does not readily lend itself to computer processing;
complaints change very little from month to month, and it is fairly
easy to predict the various general problems a neighborhood will
have. Key issues will come forward with little effort because they are
usually more intense and involve a large portion of the community.

The computer is hardly the answer to urban problem solving, but it can be used as a time-saver in processing bills, accounts, records, and other information. It can help in traffic regulation, crime statistics analysis, and comprehensive planning, for example, but it has yet to offer real insight into human problem solving.

Boston probably makes the best use of computer processing of complaints from decentralized offices. The staff has developed a computer model with the assistance of the MIT Urban Systems Laboratory, and is feeding many of its 9,000 weekly complaints and other information into it regularly. The process has helped to develop priorities and provide the staff with enough information to influence the policies of department heads and elected officials. However, it is likely that much of this information could have been gleaned from ordinary inspection. Boston's public works and environmental complaints lend themselves more readily to data processing than social service and family casework problems. Intricate problem analysis is possible, even to the extent of building emotions into the model, but basic human problems are still difficult to analyze under our limited utilization of machines. The proper utilization of computers can save the urban administrator time to spend on human problems.

Offices of Inquiry and Complaint

We have already illustrated how effectively cities handle complaints, but we have not discussed how they are processed. Larger cities tend to create central offices of complaint because there are just too many functions, scattered over too many areas, for the average citizen to be able to comprehend the system or know where to go.

It is truly an asset for a citizen to be able to dial one phone number or approach one office to get an answer to any problem. A look at the phone book listing of departments and services is enough to understand how a poorly informed citizen can become confused and frustrated. Some people cannot even find the listings.

Most cities handle only municipal complaints and refer other matters to appropriate agencies. However, in New York and Chicago, the mayors' offices of complaint accept all inquiries and provide information or assistance in each case. If the citizen merely asks where to receive a service, he normally is referred to the proper office; however, if he registers a complaint, it is processed.

Chicago's Office of Information and Inquiry answers 50,000 complaints by use of a seven page request form and provides information to another 300,000 callers annually. Because of the large volume of complaints to the Department of Streets and Sanitation, an additional complaint office is used, which is separate from but works in conjunction with the central office and handles an annual volume of 300,000. In the central office, automatic electric typewriters are used to answer 350 complaints per day (as opposed to 125 per day by a manual operator), and a reply is sent in each case by the ten-member staff, with an average of two-weeks' reply time. Additional staff works in the Department of Streets and Sanitation.

New York's Mayor's Action Center processes over 300,000 complaints annually with a staff of sixteen, but has accumulated a tremendous backlog because of the inability to service the complaints that the system has lost some of its effectiveness. There is less of an attempt to reply to each complainant. Citizens do not get an answer in every case because there are too many inquiries and not enough staff. Use of a computer and form letters did not solve the problem, but a system called IRMA (Information Referral Manual, a revolving file) has improved performance. Through it, the staff can easily locate the correct agency or department for any type of complaint.

There is also the "night owl mayor," a responsible executive from one of the city agencies stationed in City Hall after regular office hours to handle complaints and emergencies throughout the night.

Boston's Office of Public Service, in conjunction with its little city hall operation, responds to all complaints; but here, too, the inability to correct problems has created a significant backlog. Of the 9,000 requests it receives weekly, one-fifth are complaints and the rest referral and requests for information and service.

Kansas City's Public Information Office is staffed by two persons and handles 4,000 complaints and 8,000 requests for information annually. It easily keeps abreast of the work load, which mainly involves environmental complaints.

Baltimore's Customer Service Division operates on a twenty-four-hour, seven-days-a-week basis and receives about 1,000 requests on weekdays and 500 on weekends. This division has a separate phone number but may also be reached through the main switchboard. A form is made out on each call which is sent to the appropriate department for action.

Atlanta does not have a central complaint system but does coordinate much of this effort under its Office of Governmental Liaison. The city has a night-duty "mayor" who responds to problems till 1 a.m. weekdays and on weekends. Some aldermen feel a properly staffed central office is needed, particularly considering the number of grievance calls received by the local newspaper's Action Line." The latter's success in resolution of its complaints is high (as it is with elected officials) because it is free to exert intense pressure, but still needed is a process to effectively handle the great bulk of complaints which come through other channels.

Los Angeles believes a central complaint office is not necessary. Each department appears to be able to keep up with complaint processing, helped immeasurably by the branch city hall operation. Citizens need call only one number at a branch city hall, and an operator will connect them with the appropriate department. The councilmanic system of answering complaints in district offices also diminishes the need for a more formal central complaint office. The city clerk's office (as is usually the case in most cities) also receives requests and passes them on to the appropriate departments. None of these takes the place, however, of a fully staffed central office which follows up all complaints.

Effects of Central Complaint
Office on Neighborhood Centers

For a large number of citizens, the city's or neighborhood center's image is based simply on how well complaints are handled. Very often, the performance of a neighborhood center is dependent on the performance of the central complaint office servicing it. If it works well, the central complaint office can absorb the bulk of routine requests, allowing little city hall operations to concentrate on more critical issues. In some cases, the central offices utilize neighborhood ombudsmen from local offices to assist in personal follow-up of complaints or to reassure residents who need additional guidance. The programs complement one another.

Central offices of complaint and information also provide a single base for collecting data from all departments necessary for evaluating and comparing departmental performance and setting citywide priorities. It also opens doors for the chief administrative officer to begin systematically to review departments and can become an excellent management tool in assessing many problems. Decentralized centers are likely to provide information that may not normally come to a central office.

16

Another crucial factor affecting the performance of decentralized operations is the quality of the center director. His ability to coordinate and motivate staff and to establish close working relationships with department and agency heads are highly important. He must follow up all types of complaints through regular channels, cajolery, or any other method necessary to obtain satisfactory results for the citizen—in short, to act as a neighborhood ombudsman. But he must be equally responsive to the person who appoints him, usually the mayor or chief administrative officer. He inherits two bosses—one in the neighborhood and one in City Hall.

This dual responsibility in one way lessens the effectiveness of the neighborhood ombudsman because he cannot be fully responsive to either faction; but in another way it increases performance because he not only receives the complaint but also has access to the system— the means to get it resolved. He has been called a "pseudo ombudsman" because, in most cases, he is appointed by the executive branch, has little independence, performs informational and general services in addition to processing complaints, and usually has low salary and rank, without tenure.

Elaborating on these points, Dr. Paul Dolan, in an article entitled "Pseudo-Ombudsmen" in the July, 1969, issue of the National Civic Review, concluded that the role of ombudsmen in this country has tended more and more to become encumbered by formal procedures and elaborate mechanisms for receiving and answering complaints that completely defeat the original purpose. He states: "It appears that ombudsmen will become errand boys and "Mr. Fixits" working at the delivery end of the administration rather than correcting fundamental procedures." The complaint officers he observed were

made incapable of investigating sua sponte by poor records, lack of
independence of the executive, and inadequate budgets.

OMBUDSMEN IN EUROPE

In Sweden, England, Ireland, Denmark, and Norway, ombudsmen
review written complaints and request action from the administrative
agency involved. To gather additional facts, they may ask the police
to investigate. They may initiate hearings on their own, even if a
complaint is not filed, and they are assisted by professional staff who
are usually lawyers. They may order prosecution, issue reprimands,
and obtain compensation for damages.

Kenneth Wilson, staff director for the Los Angeles Charter
Commission when it was functioning, believes that the trend in the
United States to have ombudsmen appointed by the executive branch
with few powers is undersirable. He feels it may result in sterilization
of the pure concept. He is partially correct, except that the neighborhood ombudsman performs in the neighborhood and has a different
function. The central ombudsman concept should not be diluted because
of this innovative process on the local level designed to help multitudes
of residents with day-to-day problems, many of which will persist
even with institutional change.

AMERICAN OMBUDSMEN

Interpreted in the Scandinavian sense, we would be hard-pressed
to find any true ombudsmen in this country. However, there have been
some close approximations on both central and neighborhood levels.
The state of Hawaii, Nassau County and Buffalo (New York), and
Savannah (Georgia) have adopted central ombudsman-type systems.
Stockton, California, has created the position of "neighborhoodman,"
a person who serves as liaison between government and residents to
improve community relations. The efforts of ombudsmen in these
governmental units have helped substantially to correct administrative
errors and improve interagency communications and coordination.
The concept has been proposed at the state level in California,
Wisconsin, Maine, New York, New Mexico, and Washington. Other
states and local governments, as well as the U.S. Congress, have
considered the concept of ombudsman; but costs, existence of other
complaint machinery, and bureaucracy have held it up.

Cities with citizen advocates operating from neighborhood offices
have taken a new and effective approach to the ombudsman concept.

There, ombudsmen are usually dedicated neighborhood representatives who work long into the evenings and weekends in streets and back yards, finding problems and seeing that they are resolved. As is true with so much in this country, we have added an American twist: the citizen advocate who not only pursues complaints but also engages in projects desired by residents, often changing the character of the community. The projects may include housing construction, playground development, advocacy planning, job fairs, rent strikes, mass (town hall) meetings, community corporations, community schools, large cultural events, and a host of other items. Through mini-cabinets, agency coordination, formalized request systems, and administrative support, the neighborhood advocate may cause change in local service functions. Local center personnel assist in staffing neighborhood councils, many of which have become powerful citizen advocate organizations and have changed institutions.

The effectiveness of the citizen advocate depends greatly on his acceptance by neighborhood residents, who should play a part in his selection. In most cases, he resides in the area where he works or at least is familiar with the various ethnic and social groups and their problems. The performance of the American ombudsman is usually increased when he works from a neighborhood city hall or other local facility.

The neighborhood facility, even if only a one-room store front office, provides greater visibility and a base of operations for the ombudsman and is preferable to operating out of the main city hall. The local office gives a continuous view of government in action, showing residents that someone is always present and concerned, in contrast with central ombudsmen, who may only be encountered briefly when special problems arise. If the local facility provides in-house services, there is even a better chance to meet clients and establish neighborhood rapport.

The ombudsmen who work out of neighborhood city halls in New York, Boston, Atlanta, Houston, and the small multiservice centers in Chicago come closest to citizen advocates. In Chicago's Near North centers, advocates are appointed and removed by a neighborhood board, rather than a government body. In addition, they primarily coordinate rather than operate services, and are also responsible for evaluating services and solving citizen problems. Still, they lack sufficient authority and rank, are poorly paid, have no tenure, and depend on the city and OEO for funding.

In the other cities mentioned above, the mayor or administrative officer appoints neighborhood advocates. They have had success because these officials have been as concerned about improving services as most citizens. Mayors, administrators, and residents have usually lined up together to correct agency deficiencies. Many mayors have inherited bureaucratic jungles and welcome citizen support in their attack on the system. Urban administrators, by the leadership of the mayor or their own moral and philosophical convictions, have begun to insist that change take place and that government truly begin to solve our cities' problems.

New York

The insistence on change is particularly strong in New York, where Mayor Lindsay is battling unions and entrenched civil service systems. He has proposed neighborhood councils which would appoint their own advocates. The staffs of neighborhood city halls and urban action task forces now act in this capacity. In addition, principal city officials (deputy mayor, department heads, and other administrators) chair the fifty UATFs and act as neighborhood advocates, although some use this role as a forum to communicate why things cannot be done. Nevertheless, most of the task forces have been highly successful in resolving neighborhood problems of zoning, refuse collection, crime reduction, park development, and street repairs; and in some cases they have changed or improved basic service delivery systems.

Boston

Boston's little city hall managers (director-ombudsmen) have proved to be highly successful as advocates. In conjunction with the planning and evaluation section of the central Office of Public Service (which has programmed complaints and developed statistics to back up suspicions of poor service) neighborhood ombudsmen brought about some rudimentary changes: new tree pruning methods, team code inspections, new methods of patching streets, and innovations in civil service practices.

Many of Boston's city councillors and state legislators see themselves as ombudsmen, although they do not have the staffs to assist properly. However, they cherish their ability to solve complaints, and some look with skepticism on little city hall managers as people who are competing for the favors of their constituencies. Some managers have been politically appointed, diminishing their professional effect but not necessarily their performance, since some political types have been able to command more vocal constituent groups for change.

Los Angeles

The fifteen councilmen in Los Angeles have more attributes of ombudsmen than other elected officials in this country. They are elected, have high rank, four-year term of office, adequate compensation ($17,500 annually), responsibility for evaluating the executive branch, and staffs of eleven full-time persons each. Most of them have neighborhood offices and take their jobs seriously. However, with their heavy legislative duties, it is impossible for them to meet the demands of thousands of clients; and as politicians, it is difficult for them to retain the trust and confidence of suspicious citizens. Since they develop basic policies and approve procedures, it is also difficult for them to give an unbiased evaluation of their own work. The Charter Revision Committee in 1970 recommended the creation of an independent office of ombudsman with an eight-year term and two-thirds council vote for removal, but the City Council would have no part of this.

Besides city councilmen, city (citizen) commissions (appointed to most departments) feel they perform as ombudsmen. They hold hearings on complaints if requested to do so; however, since the clerk of the board is able to process most grievances satisfactorily, few hearings are held.

San Francisco

An ombudsman system was defeated in San Francisco in proposed charter revisions. Although the ombudsman section was not a point of contention, the entire charter failed two to one, and the idea died. Tom Miller, assistant to the chief administrative officer, states that there are fifty-five department heads and 20,000 employees, and that some sort of ombudsman approach would make "this vast network sharper." John Dukes, community action director, suggests, "The mayor should appoint ten more aides in addition to the several he has, but their selection must heed the voice of the people." There are many officials and citizens who believe that the present appointees are too political, do not relate to the people well, and because of this are a "waste of manpower."

There are over 100 outreach workers, called community representatives ("reps"), (thirty-five in the Urban Life Department of the Montrose center) operating from the urban progress centers and outposts. They go door-to-door, receiving grievances, passing out information, providing counsel and referral services, and assisting in program recruitment. They live in the area and know its people

and neighborhood life, but are of little value as neighborhood ombudsmen because they are untrained, poorly qualified, and not motivated
to act in the capacity of true advocates. This project has been an
employment and pacification program rather than service-oriented
to the tens of thousands of residents.

THE FUTURE OF OMBUDSMEN
IN THE UNITED STATES

How well will the ombudsman concept work in the United States?
First, most mayors and administrators want to do as much to change
the system as citizens do, so their appointment of ombudsmen is not
necessarily bad. Second, most problems are in the area of human
resources outside city jurisdiction, so using the mayor's strength to
help equalize the imbalance is not a bad idea. Third, more and more
community representatives are being appointed by citizen councils or
with their participation, giving the citizen advocate some independence.
And last, if the neighborhood advocate continues to develop projects
which cause change, and if he helps the evolution of strong citizen
councils, he will effect community development and improvements
regardless of the classic definition of ombudsman.

Regardless of city size, the urban administrator should consider
an ombudsman to handle problems citywide or for a particularly
disadvantaged area. In cities of 10,000 persons, there may be neighborhoods where 200 or 300 families, for example, live in depressed
conditions requiring extra help from City Hall to solve problems.
A neighborhood office and an ombudsman are ways of reaching these
citizens.

INDEPENDENT INVESTIGATION
AGENCIES AS OMBUDSMEN

Ombudsmen alone will not cure all citizen ills. Community
corporations, Model Cities programs, legal aid societies, special
task forces, multiservice centers, and independent investigating groups
may be needed.

A good example of an independent body, privately funded by business and civic groups, is the Chicago Better Government Association,
which has a staff of ten, composed mostly of lawyers and former newspaper reporters. It is a nonpartisan watchdog organization which
investigates waste, inefficiency, and corruption at all levels of

government anywhere in the state of Illinois, but concentrates on
Cook County. It should not be confused with government-appointed
internal investigating units, which primarily review employee fraud
and bribery cases. It has no more arrest or subpoena powers than
private citizens, but it does have the cooperation of the local news
media to expose findings. The rationale seems to work, since the
association has received national and international recognition for its
effectiveness, has forced many operational changes, and is credited
with saving millions of dollars of taxpayers' money.

Its investigation of the Chicago Bureau of Forestry, for example,
caused the bureau to be placed under jurisdiction of the Department
of Streets and Sanitation, resulting in greater efficiency. It has exposed
state expense account padding, illegal urban renewal activities, cigarette tax cheating, noncompliance with Illinois Personnel Code in
job placements by the Illinois Youth Commission, illegal scavenger
operations, vote frauds, abuses in the Department of Mental Health,
conflict of interest in Model Cities, and many other matters. And it
has caused procedural changes in a number of departments at various
levels of government. The formation of this type of independent
investigating agency deserves consideration in cities which feel the
impact of bureaucracy or inefficiency. It should receive moral as
well as financial support from the community.

There are various techniques for change. Today's bureaucracies
could use most of them. Congress, federal agencies, and state and
local governments should accept innovation, establish independent
offices of ombudsmen as well as neighborhood-ombudsmen, and welcome criticism that may improve the general welfare. Even in
communities which appear to be free of corruption, outmoded civil
service regulations, organized work restrictions, inequitable service
delivery, and erroneous priorities may be corrected by a courageous,
independent body. The urban administrator must assess whether he
needs this help and be unafraid to seek it.

17

Decentralized offices are instruments of mayors and administrators and, for the most part, they were designed by public officials and are run by them. Nevertheless, in various ways citizens are involved beyond the passive role of service recipients. Some citizen councils assist in selecting directors and establishing local programs, for example. And since decentralized programs are public, under influence of elected officials, a few programs have become involved in politics.

LARGE BUT APOLITICAL CITIES

Politics has not played a noticeable role in the more traditional programs of neighborhood decentralization. Emphasis in Los Angeles, San Antonio, and Kansas City has been simply to provide more convenient service. Elected officials have not tried to reach their constituents through the programs, nor have they been concerned about developing a sense of community or activating citizens by these means. Mayors and city councils in these cities fully agree that programs should be continued and, in Los Angeles and San Antonio, expanded. Perhaps, if these programs provided special functions that other neighborhoods did not receive, there would be more political and citizen interest.

The predominant government in California is the weak-mayor form. In Los Angeles, Mayor Samuel Yorty has little say over the operation of branch city halls and each branch of government closely checks the other; therefore, there is little chance of political play. It is a system full of "checks and balances," but Dave M. Wilkins, chief administrative analyst in the chief administrative officer's office, calls it "a system of all checks and no balance." Councilmen, who are elected by district, carry the weight of dealing with difficult citizen complaints.

The charter has been amended 261 times in the city's history. In 1970 the City Council approved some items which would have given the mayor greater strength, but the entire set of charter proposals was resoundingly defeated by the electorate in November, 1970, and again in April, 1971. They proposed that city commissions be advisory and the mayor be given the right to appoint all department heads with City Council approval. Other departments would be brought under the mayor's control and the chief administrative officer made primarily responsible to the mayor. Even with this, Mayor Yorty felt the proposed changes would have given him little additional power, primarily because the City Council would still approve his appointments and dismissals. The most controversial point, to make the four independent revenue departments less autonomous, was eliminated from the 1971 charter, but it was still defeated. Yet the belief is that Los Angeles' greatest failing might well be its lack of positive, pragmatic, on-the-scene leadership needed for new programs and for reforming established practices and institutions.

The city manager form of government in San Antonio and Kansas City allows little room for the mayor and councilmen to process com-plaints, or to bypass the manager in dealing with department heads. Elected officials are encouraged to go through the city manager; and since the manager is the operating head, there is less chance that political figures will interfere with administrative functions or use neighborhood facilities to their political advantage.

San Francisco's weak-mayor system does not give Mayor Alioto much administrative control. In practice, however, the system may be classified a mayor-chief administrative officer form. The mayor's chief administrative officer holds one of the strongest posts, for he is appointed for life and can only be removed for malfeasance by the Board of Supervisors. The city charter makes him responsible to the mayor and Board of Supervisors, however. And in practice, he has been more responsive than many of the mayor's commissioners, for example. In this system, the city charter requires the Board of Supervisors to become involved in everything the mayor does. In spite of these handicaps, Mayor Alioto seems to have close relation-ships with the supervisors and the chief administrative officer. Poli-tical differences or even discussion between Alioto and the Board of Supervisors is minimal over the creation of little city halls or the office of ombudsman; however, recently the city has joined forces with the community action program to explore creation of neighborhood councils.

The city manager system in Norfolk operates like those in San Antonio and Kansas City, allowing little room for the mayor or councilmen to involve themselves politically in administrative operations. And although Norfolk's multipurpose center does provide special services not found in other areas, business and labor, as well as civic groups, support the center, for they believe it will improve the general community. It is seen as making good use of an abandoned federal building located in one of the city's most depressed areas. Several more centers are planned in the other deteriorated areas. These factors have aroused support for the program without stirring political opposition.

There have been no visible disputes between mayor and City Council in Chicago. Even though this is a weak-mayor system, Mayor Daley proves to be the strongest mayor in the country because of his strong political machine and the loyalty of his followers. He has a tight rein on his Democratic colleagues, who fall in line easily; but some Republican and independent aldermen favor city programs too. Alderman Depres, for example, believes that the city's service centers are necessary to uplift depressed areas; and even though they are controlled securely from the top, they have satisfactorily served and improved the conditions of many Chicagoans. But he also feels greater efficiency and less bureaucracy are vitally necessary. There is frustration that staff is appointed politically; yet many, particularly in the case of key appointees, can get the job done. Political influence is strong in Chicago's program, but its force is used to keep the program intact; and there is no serious challenge among City Council factions.

The average citizen knows little about the effectiveness of the program or even about its objectives, but generally believes that the services would not be given if they were not needed and does not quarrel with the assumption that they help to keep the city calm. Naturally, program administrators and supervisors praise its effectiveness (much in a self-serving way), and its history is too short to be able to judge long-term effects. The consensus among most professionals is simply that it has not yet proved itself, and that politics and rivalry among staff appear to be service problems. Legal aid staff pulled out of Chicago's centers because they resent interference from center directors and city hall officials.

LOW-KEY POLITICS

Political conflicts over neighborhood city halls between mayor and City Council, or opposition to them from business, labor, and civic groups has been very low-key in Columbus, Baltimore, Atlanta, and Houston. The general citizenry believes they will improve deteriorated neighborhoods and upgrade the city as a whole. Most city councilmen would like centers in their areas of influence but are not pushing. Because the mayors in these cities have not been particularly interested in using the program to develop a political base, councilmen have been more prone to support it. And since NCHs are concentrated in poverty areas, where political favoritism might do more harm than good, citywide there is little motivation, even among councilmen, to exploit them politically. Fear of resentment from the "silent majority" has tempered any oversell, and in addition these cities are just not as political as others, such as Chicago, where rewards for political ambition are more tangible. Atlanta's weak-mayor form does not give the mayor much opportunity for independence. In the other cities, which operate with the mayor-council form, the City Council seems to have a close rapport and understanding with the mayor, thus diminishing political conflict.

Some politicians and business people in Columbus questioned locating the mini-city hall in an area with several other centers when some areas have none. Officials in Baltimore astutely spread their centers among poor white and black populations. In Atlanta, the program uses space in already established and accepted community action centers. And in Houston, although some councilmen were apprehensive that the NCHs might uproot some of their political strength and merely encourage more complaints, most officials and civic groups seemed pleased that the city was doing something about its problems before the major "blow-up" occurred. In addition, these programs are of such low cost that few politicians argue about them.

POLITICS AT HIGH PITCH

The story has been entirely different in New York and Boston, where politics has bombarded the programs. Both took the citywide approach, knowing it was political dynamite not to serve middle America as well, although in New York this lesson was not learned in time to do the most good. In both cities, the citywide approach opened communications with all income and ethnic groups and indicated that City Hall was concerned with everybody's problems, but it also

developed a hotbed of political criticism because councilmen and state
legislators felt that the mayors were creating "political clubhouses"
to benefit themselves. Mayor Lindsay did not deny this. White appointed several little city hall managers who were political favorites,
as did Lindsay to an even greater degree. Many of Lindsay's 300-mem-
ber UATF and NCH staff were politically in tune with him. But how
else can a big city mayor crack the bureaucracy and get his program
across, when the city is inefficient and corrupt? Some observers
believe that what is wrong with New York is that the old-style political
clubs have been destroyed but not replaced. "How else," they ask,
"are sixty-two neighborhood boards going to attract qualified people?"
Even with political ambitions, both Lindsay and White tried to serve
the best interests of the people by improving services and communications.

New York councilmen and borough presidents have not been
happy with the NCH program because they feel it makes the strong-
mayor system even stronger. As a result, they refused to fund it
from the beginning. In 1970 funds were approved for some aspects
of it because Lindsay sought bipartisan membership of policy boards
under a Plan for Neighborhood Government.

In October and November, 1970, more than 200 neighborhood
meetings were held with representatives from over 3,000 community
organizations to discuss Lindsay's proposal. After further community
discussion and City Council deliberation, a bill may be presented to
the New York State Legislature which would give preliminary approval
to the idea. It must pass the City Council and Board of Estimate and
be returned to the state legislature for final enactment into law. However, most observers believe this will not happen in the near future.
They believe, in fact, that such a bill might never pass because of
opposition from employees and other groups with vested interests in
preserving the status quo. It may mean that New York will have to
plod along with informal citizen councils, which will then have to be
given as much power only as existing laws permit. At least by proposed sharing of board power, various political factions now see good
reason to work together to help solve some of New York's sticky
problems. The six experimental neighborhood councils mentioned
previously are a step in this direction.

Boston's city councillors also have felt that the little city hall
program would make the mayor in this strong-mayor situation even
stronger. The Boston City Council has so little power that even a
slight decrease appears very critical. They have no responsibility
for service delivery but do have the important responsibility of

analyzing service failures, accomplished through their budgetary and
inquiry authorities. Any councillor wishing to attract the news media
must normally attack the mayor, because almost everything is in his
control. And there have been plenty of attacks since the little city
hall program was started.

Although city councillors have approved the program each year,
they have done so more and more reluctantly. Councillor Joseph F.
Timilty calls the program "the biggest hoax perpetrated on the people
in the history of Boston." He believes that in order to realistically
appraise the program, patronage underlying managerial appointments
must be recognized. Few deny the patronage appointments, but most
also believe that in some cases it has been a most effective way to
force one's way through the system by organizing pressures from a
voting constituency.

Councillor John F. Saltonstall has stated that more proof is
needed of the program's effectiveness if it is to continue to be funded.
In 1970, the City Council turned down a request for two additional
LCHs, but the biggest blow came in 1971 budget deliberations, when
Mayor White put into effect across-the-board budget cuts. Former
director Davis believes that the LCH cuts should not seriously affect
overall performance because most of it eliminated "deadwood" and
certain nonessential technical services.

There always has been criticism that the program was too big.
The new budget may satisfy some critics temporarily, but there will
be continued reviews of the program. White's reelection seems to indicate that the electorate approves of the way it is going on and that
citizens want to give him further opportunity to show what the program
can do.

MAYOR VS. CITY COUNCIL

The relationship between mayor and City Council means a great
deal to the success of most programs and certainly to the whole concept of decentralization. When a mayor begins to enhance his personal
image at the expense of the City Council, struggles ensue which
benefit no one and impair output to the citizen clientele. As top elected
officials quarrel, citizens suffer.

Strong-mayor forms may be needed to move cities, but strong
mayors should share formulation of ideas and implementation of programs with councils on a nonpartisan basis. This shared-partnership

is more likely to get budgets passed and services improved. Most mayors in the cities reviewed here have found this true. Mayor Lindsay clearly sees this as the best approach, and it seems that Mayor White is leaning in this direction.

In council-manager systems, shared responsibility is more evident, for it takes a majority of the council to hire or fire the city manager or to set policy. The manager not only caters to the mayor but also is responsible to and establishes rapport with the whole council. Here cooperation is a must if government is to succeed. But regardless of the form of government, reality demonstrates that little gets done without the cooperation of the legislative branch, and the executive may only hinder progress by taking special advantage of city programs.

CITIZEN PARTICIPATION

The impact of citizen participation in most decentralized programs has been minimal; but it is growing as city officials begin to see the importance of developing a communication system which, in the long run, will expedite programs rather than delay them.

Citizen Participation in Traditional Forms

The traditional form of decentralization has produced little citizen involvement, except in Kansas City, where it developed under different circumstances and for different reasons. Los Angeles and San Antonio have left citizen participation largely up to community action and, more recently, to Model Cities agencies.

In San Antonio there are no citizen councils operating under city direction now. Sam Granata, public works director, expresses concern with organized citizen involvement as a process which creates delays and irrelevant arguments over issues. He feels that if departments act competently and in a dedicated manner, citizen advisory councils are not needed. "I have a 650,000 [city population] man board which never adjourns," he points out. His dedication is high, but dedication alone does not help citizens understand or appreciate the processes of government.

City Manager Donald Henckel has been toying with the idea of four citizen councils, each serving one-fourth of the city. They would act as coordinating bodies and absorb some of the power of existing

citizen groups. The community action program and other social welfare programs may be placed under the wing of the city's newly created
Department of Human Resources. Nine community corporations,
started under community action programs, are in the development
stages and would eventually operate some programs of the parent
community action body. Representation on the four citizen councils
would most likely consist of appointments from the city and neighborhood groups.

Although the Model Cities agency is merely one of twenty city
departments, the board acts independently and has held up approval
of programs until the City Council changed its established policies
on hiring and other matters. Four multiservice centers will be built
to include city services.

Citizen councils and independent neighbormen (ombudsmen)
offices were recommended by the Los Angeles City Charter Commission and also by a special charter study committee of the City Council,
but the proposal was turned down by the full council. (See Appendix
A.) Cost was a factor, but primarily the City Council was unwilling
to share significant power with diverse and scattered community
groups. And they feel they already serve as ombudsmen.

Several councilmen feel strongly that there should be some
form of citizen councils, even if established only by ordinance or
simple resolution, so that citizen groups would be encouraged to come
together. Council President John Gibson says he formed citizen
councils and has been meeting with them ever since his initial election
some thirty years ago. But such purely "advisory" councils have
existed in most cities for as long and seldom have achieved meaningful
citizen participation. It does not look as though Los Angeles will
formalize citizen structures in the near future. Even the Model
Cities citizen structure is weak, as control emanates mostly from
the top. A few pilot citizen councils, adequately staffed, might be a
worthy experiment.

In Los Angeles, the issues are big ones (air pollution, unemployment, rapid transit, and housing) which do not lend themselves readily
to neighborhood councils. Services are good. There is little backlog
of complaints. The civil service system has not yet strangled the
city. And even slum housing in Watts is not as bad as it is in other
big cities. Until neighborhood problems become more critical, there
may not be a search for citizen help. But there is little sense of
community, and Mexican-Americans and blacks have already shown
signs of unrest. Some kind of community forum or communication
structure is needed, for the present system is not working.

Kansas City uses a unique kind of citizen involvement. To com-
bat a rising rate of juvenile delinquency in 1943, forty-five community
councils were formed. They have continually expanded their role to
matters of zoning, junior college location, traffic, pollution, and other
neighborhood problems. Some councils are active, print newsletters,
raise funds, and evaluate services; but most are inactive and have
found little reason to exist. Two of them became Model Cities neighborhood planning councils, however, and extended their lives and meaning.
(See Appendix B.)

The program has twelve community workers who act more as
convenors than as citizen advocates, and an operating budget of
$128,000 which was almost cut in 1970 by certain councilmen who,
because of citizen criticism, felt: "We don't have to support our
enemies." The budget funds have continued and it appears that the
City Council has greater sympathy for the program.

City Manager John Taylor and the Community Services Division
director, James Reefer, feel community councils can play a key role
in improving communications between residents and City Hall, can
help to get bond issues passed, and can improve some of the community. "We lost the $140 million December 16, 1969, bond issue because
we lost contact with the citizens," says Taylor. It looks as though
Taylor and Reefer will seek to strengthen the councils and may make
greater use of community workers as area generalists or some
variation of ombudsmen. Reefer's staff will also operate the new
Model Cities multiservice center, bringing the city closer to neighborhoods.

Citizen Participation in Multiservice Centers

Programs created to deal primarily with poverty have been
directed toward greater citizen involvement. For example, Chicago's
urban progress centers utilize advisory citizen councils appointed
by each center director, City Hall, and councilmen. Since citizens
are virtually handpicked, they have few powers. They do, however,
have a voice in center programming, which is being strengthened
by a new policy called Neighborhood Programming Project. Tyrone
Kenner, deputy director of Chicago Community on Urban Opportunity,
says the city has never forced a program on local citizens they did
not want. Programs have been turned down because of lack of resources, he states, but otherwise everything has been granted. This
may be true, but Independent Alderman Depres says programs are
conceived and controlled from the top.

Staff selection is even more centrally controlled. Citizen councils may make recommendations, and there is some superficial use
of civil service procedures at the local level; but city administrators
know who they want (particularly for key jobs), with final selection
made by City Hall or councilmen. The Chicago emphasis on "maximum
feasible participation," as required in OEO's regulations, has been
to employ residents but to involve them very little in the decision-
making process.

On the other hand, citizen councils operating with the five Near
North (Lincoln Park) multiservice centers (under the Department of
Human Resources) determine their own membership and programs.
Councils have the complete confidence of the community and are
probably the strongest citizen structures in any city studied, similar
to community corporations but dependent on the city for funding. How
long the city administration will let them exist is problematical, for
they are too critical of the machine and the system.

Model Cities has made progress for citizens in Chicago. Although
the community action boards are appointed, half of each of the four
Model Cities boards are elected and half appointed—a victory for
citizens in this tightly controlled structure. Recommendations by
the federal government and a city-appointed commission helped bring
this about. Mayor Daley felt he also wanted an element of decisiveness
in these boards which would be helped by the electoral process. Four
$2.8 million, 55,000-square-foot Model Cities multiservice centers
are being developed and will include city services of Mayor's Office
of Inquiry and Information, police and fire services, library, housing
and weights and measures inspections, as well as comprehensive
social services.

A Citizen's Advisory Council (CAC), formed in the early 1960's
to meet the requirements of the federal urban renewal workable program, functions as the citizen input in Norfolk, but is called an establishment tool. Members are appointed by the mayor and consist
mostly of civic and business types. The council has engaged mainly
in "clean-up/fix-up" projects but has also been valuable in disseminating information and gathering intelligence. Department heads sit
in on meetings held in each neighborhood to receive and answer
complaints.

When Thomas Maxwell was city manager, he believed the
council made a significant contribution and held down tensions. But
black Councilman Joseph Jordan feels it is strictly an establishment
tool which deals in trivial programs and has no authority. He says,

"The City Council won't listen to them unless it's what they want anyway." Any broadening of citizen participation will be done "begrudgingly
and negatively," he emphasizes.

Although citizens believe much more communication is necessary,
there is feeling that they are gaining on the system. As one resident
put it, "We have come a long way, but then we were so far behind.
This game of catching up is hard, but I can see the light just ahead."
And the Model Cities assemblies have opened the door a little more.
Election of fifteen of twenty-five Model Cities board members gives
citizens greater voice.

Neighborhood City Halls as Vehicles for
Citizen Involvement

Community action and Model Cities programs offer the main
opportunities for citizen involvement in Houston, Atlanta, and Columbus,
since there are no citizen councils which function with the cities'
neighborhood centers.

Mayor Louie Welch and his human relations team have made no
effort to develop neighborhood councils in Houston. However, the
Human Relations Division has tried to fill the gap through communications. The division is regarded, even by activist groups, as an institution sensitive to minority problems, establishing a high degree of
communication with residents through massive interviews, job fairs,
and neighborhood meetings. It administers the neighborhood city hall
program and coordinates the physical and human resource projects
which go with it. In most other cities, the Department of Human
Relations would not be the best agency to supervise the little city
hall program because human relations functions have traditionally
concentrated on matters of discrimination, and some have even
generated hostilities within some sectors of the community.

Although there are no formal citizen councils, the NCH program
has improved citizens' attitudes toward government. "It is one of
the best signs that the city is concerned with Mexican-Americans
living in this area. We are pleased with improvements that have
already been made," says Mrs. Eliot Baez, a citizen active in several
neighborhood projects. Citizens have an opportunity to express their
voice in the selection of aides with whom they can best communicate.
And it has been the policy of the city never to locate a neighborhood
city hall in an area where residents did not want it.

The elected fifty-six-member Model Neighborhood Residents Commission is a private, nonprofit corporation and has established a good deal of independence. It and the combination Model Cities multiservice center-neighborhood city hall will provide a closer link between residents and City Hall.

In late 1970, Atlanta's Community Relations Commission developed a sixty-member board of citizens appointed by the mayor to consider all types of problems arising anywhere in the city. It did not need aldermanic approval, but it has no formal powers. It has experienced a lack of participation from the police department but apparently is making headway in other areas. It needs power and more responsibility to be effective.

Previous to this former Mayor Ivan Allen, Jr., established task forces in each of six target areas, consisting of representatives from the community action program, Citywide Resource Task Force, and city service center coordinators. Block organizations were also established which elected representatives to the Citizens Neighborhood Advisory Council, which in turn elected members to the Citizens Central Advisory Council. This structure has not continued with any effectiveness, and appears to be a plan to be used in times of crisis only.

The Model Cities Advisory Council consists of a majority of neighborhood citizens and has obtained a good deal of power and independence. Almost all of its decisions have been approved by the Board of Aldermen.

Columbus has no neighborhood citizen councils formed by the city. The Mt. Vernon Avenue District Association, a private neighborhood organization, assisted in the planning of the mini-city-hall. Other civic groups provide input to City Hall, but there are no plans for formal citizen boards throughout the city. The Model Cities agency absorbs only part of this gap, and the community corporations are not city structures. Model Cities has an elected board. The program does not plan any multiservice centers at this time.

A unique private, nonprofit corporation founded in 1965 is the East Central Citizens Organization (ECCO), whose executive council of twenty-one is elected by general assembly and is funded privately and by OEO for about $200,000. It has youth programs in delinquency prevention, recreation, job training, education, nurseries, day care, veterinary clinic, credit union, cooperative code enforcement with the city, housing rehabilitation, small business assistance, and plans for joint ventures with the employment and health agencies, among several other social service functions. It has been successful. Milton Kotler says it has liberated the political spirit of the residents for internal government and external struggle against the city on such issues as police conduct, administration of public schools, jobs, welfare, and many other issues of public interest.

"ECCO residents are now orators and officials, and practical political wisdom is developing in a community where earlier the only expressions were frustration and escape," he says. "The mark of practical organization is not the tranformation of a poor community into a paradise overnight, if ever. It is the liberation of practical polical deliberation."*

Reliance has been on private citizen groups in Baltimore. A citizen's organization in each mayor's station area has participated in selecting station directors, formulating local programs, raising funds, and actually operating a few projects. Long-term center operations, however, are not of interest to these organizations unless permanent staff and real responsibilities are provided.

The Model Cities Policy and Planning Board (called "Partnership Board" by Mayor D'Alesandro) consists of twenty-eight members, eight appointed by the mayor and twenty elected from six target areas. A senior citizen multipurpose center is in operation and two general multipurpose centers are planned. Conflicts within the board and little assistance or encouragement from city officials have delayed the progress of this program.

Community action and Model Cities boards have undertaken the role of citizen involvement in San Francisco. In the past, city officials believed sufficient communication was generated by Mayor Alioto, and that there were too many diverse factions to make community councils workable. While the city's highly pluralistic nature is a complicating factor, it never eliminated the need for citizen involvement. Most recently the city has changed its position and has taken leadership in negotiating assistance with the community action program for a structure of citywide citizen councils.

The idea of local advisory councils (LACs) has been discussed from the very outset of the little city hall program in Boston, but only

---

*Milton Kotler, Neighborhood Government (Indianapolis: Bobbs-Merrill, 1969), pp. 44-50.

a few of the fourteen managers have experimented with the concept.
Most of them have been using existing citizen groups. Councils were
reemphasized in 1970, when Mayor White requested that they be created
in all areas. They are to be informal structures patterned according
to the will of local residents and, so far, have been given little responsibility. Programming, zoning deliberations, capital improvement
allocations, and other neighborhood matters would be some of their
responsibilities. Some officials view them as possible catalysts for
improving the efficiency of more stubborn employee groups and
bringing innovation into a strangled bureaucracy.

The staff believes community consensus and door-to-door polling
techniques are usually better than formal elections because they elicit
higher participation and are less apt to be strongly influenced by regular political parties or monetary considerations. In Boston, each
community is choosing its own method, and most councils are in the
formative stages. (See Appendix F.)

A Home Rule Commission appointed by Mayor White recommended in 1970 that citizen councils eventually be elected and given
expanded powers, including taxation. City councillors have reviewed
the proposal; however, their approval has not yet come. If approved
locally, the city must then go to the state legislature for approval
in order to change the city charter. It is all still very much in the
discussion stage. However, existing programs of Model Cities,
community action, little city halls, and various citizen council structures have not been enough to close the communication gap.

New York's Plan for Neighborhood Government calls for citizen
boards in all sixty-two of its community planning districts. A December 7, 1970, report of the mayor to citizens relates that a series of
over 200 meetings with representatives of over 3,000 community
groups drew strong support for neighborhood government. Reservations to the plan centered about the need to change certain boundaries
in order to make all areas coterminous with city service districts;
the proposed method of selecting board members; and the absence
of residence requirements for board members. Suggestions were
made to give the boards a stronger role in the selection of community
directors and more power in general; enlarge staffs; increase the
number of local offices; and require key officials to attend community
cabinet meetings. In brief, citizens want strong local participation;
however, it is not very realistic to believe that most city councilmen
and borough presidents will let them have it to the degree they want
it.

OTHER DECENTRALIZED PROGRAMS

Dayton's city manager, James F. Kunde, received City Commission approval in 1970 to create six neighborhood priority boards which are responsible for allocating small city grants in the amounts shown below.

Area	Population	1970 Grant Allocation
Southeast	88,000	$ 68,480
Northeast	13,000	10,120
North Central	41,000	31,910
Northwest	37,000	28,970
Model Cities	36,000	38,020
Southwest	42,000	32,680
	257,000	$200,180

The method of selection, composition, and number of board members are decided by each community. This arrangement is similar to that followed in Boston and recommendations made at community meetings recently held in New York. Dayton boards are very informal at this point and have very limited authority; however, if the experiment proves successful and citizen boards handle funds well, there is a good chance they will receive additional powers. The boards define neighborhood goals and try to demonstrate how grant funds may aid in their achievement. Some $500,000 requested for this program may be in next year's budget. The boards can use the funds for whatever legal purpose they wish. The only thing turned down so far has been a request for a block party.

The strongest citizen participation structure in Dayton is the Model Cities satellite corporations, which constitute the basis for the city's partnership arrangement. These are legal, nonprofit corporations licensed by the state and are composed of citizens appointed by the city and the Model Cities Planning Council (elected central policy board), the majority of whom are residents. They deal in housing, manpower, social services, health, and education. HUD has not permitted this strong a structure in any other Model Cities program. The City Commission employs a contract with the Planning Council which is morally, but not legally, binding. The arrangement has been effective and is probably the most advanced citizen mechanism employed.

The city of Hartford has operated neighborhood service centers, formerly called field team centers, since 1963. Centers provide space for local, state, federal, and voluntary personnel in the fields of welfare, employment, relocation, code enforcement, planning, special education, addiction, Social Security, etc. The largest center houses over 110 people. An assistant to the manager, Community Services, is in charge at each center, relates to neighborhood groups, and coordinates the work of the center with all municipal departments. In addition, the city operates a portable center called Info-Mobile in the summer months which serves as headquarters for a play-street program, and out of which operate special youth activities, employment personnel, health programs, etc. Complaints and information are also handled under supervision of an assistant to the city manager, Community Services, and involves the community in the program. The city budgets $100,000 per year for the operation of these programs.*

The Model Cities agency and the city administration have not been able to resolve their differences, so progress has been slow. Development of a satisfactory and workable citizen participation structure in Hartford has been difficult to accomplish and apparently will require a great deal more time and effort.

Through the experience of the Model Cities program, Seattle's Mayor Wesley Ulman is now reviewing the possibility of creating citizen structures similar to those of Model Cities throughout the city. A Community Development Department is seriously engaged in human resource planning as well as the traditional physical concerns. The Neighborhood Improvement Office is meeting in neighborhoods to develop resident councils, but it appears that councils will not be given substantial powers at this time.

Indianapolis' mayor, Richard Lugar, has not only developed uni-gov (consolidation of cities in the county into one city-county government) but has also presented the state legislature with a mini-gov proposal to create neighborhood units of government with many of the powers of general government, except powers of taxation, eminent domain, annexation, and creation of conflicting ordinances and agreements. Mini-gov would be able to hire its own staff, contract with the city and other bodies, enact ordinances, and share with the city the operation of local government. It will be interesting to follow this development. (See Appendix L.)

---

*Report on the Task Force on Sense of Community: Managing for Neighborhood Identity (Washington, D.C.: ICMA, August 8, 1970), p. 3.

The East St. Louis Model Cities Council is one of the strongest citizen components in the nation. Although a formal contract for partnership does not exist between the city and the citizen's council, it is as morally binding and effective as Dayton's plan. Almost every decision made by the citizen's group has been accepted by the City Council. Initially programs were slowed, but since the structure has matured and citizens have become involved in plans from their initial stages, Model Cities projects have met their deadlines and general government has been enlivened and improved.

The Citizens League of Minneapolis, in its report "Sub-Urbs in the City," recommends popular election of community councils in districts of 24,000 to 50,000 people, with the power to initiate plans for the development of their areas; review and comment on all zoning changes, vacancies, permits, licenses, and public improvements requested or within their boundaries; nominate persons to statutory boards and commissions in the city; and appoint representatives to citywide or area advisory boards.

> The problems that led the League to recommend community councils are familiar ones: the proliferation of neighborhood advisory boards and commissions, low levels of voter participation, inadequate methods of selecting aldermanic candidates, unrepresentative membership on citywide boards and commissions, and a growing frustration on the part of residents who lack the opportunity to influence the many public decisions that affect them. In the words of the report, "Minneapolis government is having increasing trouble winning the 'consent of the governed'. . . ."*

Opposition to this proposal may come from residents who believe the idea is too little, and too late, or from those in power who think it is too much. But some form of citizen structure will develop to give residents greater voice.

---

*Frank Beal, "Mini-Governments for Maxi-Cities," American Society of Planning Officials Newsletter, xxxvi, 8 (September, 1970), 107.

18

CONCLUSIONS
ABOUT
NEIGHBORHOOD PROGRAMS
AND
CITIZEN INVOLVEMENT

Once a community has decided on some form of neighborhood involvement, it must determine level of participation and manner of organization. Regardless of city size, some mechanism (citizen council, little city hall, ombudsman, etc.) is appropriate even for 200 or 300 families in a depressed area of the city. The guidelines and most examples presented in this work hold true for cities or counties of any size. The principal elements are discussed below.

SENSE OF COMMUNITY
AND DECENTRALIZATION

The decentralization of city operations can both strengthen the democratic process and improve government services. Better government does not only imply making services more efficient, the flow of command smoother, and technological improvements. It also means citizens assisting in the decision-making process and creating a community in which people trust their institutions and live harmoniously in a city endowed with opportunities.

LEVEL OF NEIGHBORHOOD POWER

Advisory task forces and citizen councils with little power are still desirable ways to make studies, evaluations, and recommendations on some services, particularly at the citywide level. On the other hand, power to neighborhood councils can be increased because the types of decisions encountered primarily affect the neighborhoods in which council members reside.

However, councils of any nature should not be formed unless they have specific goals and the means to reach them. When elected officials and urban administrators decide to create citizen councils, and if they are serious about their permanence and effectiveness, they must give them responsible decision-making authority in order to maintain the interest of members and create true participation. Anything less is bound to end in failure.

Some believe power should be general and absolute. Milton Kotler's neighborhood governments, for example, are really the addition of cities.* He criticizes anything less as merely an administrative mechanism for carrying out centrally devised programs—the "enduring mark of liberal reform."

Autonomous power for some functions through nonprofit corporations is legitimate and desirable to improve services and participation. There are over 1,000 corporations in the country that demonstrate this technique. But general neighborhood government should have limited powers; otherwise, central government will face the proliferation of dozens of independent units with as many viewpoints and bureaucracies. Streamlining government means simultaneously improving services and getting citizens meaningfully involved, not necessarily abdicating all authority. Local power should be directed primarily at poorly operated services and other carefully selected functions where it can do the most good. Second, it should prevail over programs which are strictly local in nature, and only third should it have a place in broader projects. But where central governments are generally incompetent, residents should have the opportunity for greater sharing in citywide decisions.

For example, neighborhood government might stress control over sanitation, police, social services, code enforcement, and other services which need special attention. Of secondary concern would be items more local in nature, such as neighborhood parks, recreational facilities, branch libraries, parking control, local planning, and neighborhood capital budgeting. Finally, local power should involve local planning and capital outlay issues and their relationship to citywide policies.

To create new levels of general government for systems of personnel, finance, purchasing, auditing, contract negotiation, and

---

*Milton Kotler, Neighborhood Government (Indianapolis: Bobbs-Merrill, 1969).

revenue raising is unsound. Basic housekeeping authority should be centrally maintained, or local boards will spend most of their time dealing in routine, unproductive matters. And because boards would be held legally responsible for all functions under their control, they could not cast aside these matters lightly.

Many corporations have full control over specific functions, however. But examination of them and Model Cities committees will clearly verify the time-consuming nature of housekeeping functions. Better that local boards concern themselves with selecting or evaluating key district personnel, negotiating union work rules and incentive pay (but not base salaries), local program policy and evaluation, and local planning and its necessary citywide integration. Community councils should specialize in techniques for improving government and two-way communication with City Hall by making the existing organizational framework more flexible and responsive to them.

Because of possible conflict with one man/one vote rulings, and because city government should retain the ability to comprehensively and fairly allocate resources and rule the city, neighborhood council decisions should be subject to review. Most decisions would not reach review stage; but, when necessary, such capability should exist. To reverse local decisions, a two-thirds legislative majority and more stringent than usual administrative procedures should be required.

METHOD OF BOARD SELECTION

The method of neighborhood board selection should be based on local characteristics. Regular procedures used to select municipal officials may be employed. Where a strong political organization dominates, money normally is used to buy the electoral process, or too few participate (as little as 2 to 5 percent in most poverty and Model Cities programs, for example), and other methods should be used.

In some neighborhoods, existing organizations may be plentiful and broadly representative, so that appointments from these groups may constitute a fair selection process. On the other hand, in some areas it may be best to use door-to-door or other types of polling techniques, conventions, or mailed ballots to determine consensus. The American Arbitration Association (with headquarters in Washington, D.C., and regional offices representing most of the nation) contracts with cities and neighborhood groups to conduct elections where local parties need help. (See Appendixes M and N.) To ensure confidentiality and widespread participation, it has successfully used the technique of mailing ballots to eligible voters utilizing a three-envelope arrangement: one for mailing to the voter, one postpaid and preaddressed envelope to mail back to election officials with a place to verify the eligible's signature, and an envelope to enclose a confidential ballot without signature.

To begin the process of selection, an organizing committee of impartial observers should be appointed by the mayor or chief administrator. This committee will oversee the city's staff or specially hired persons chosen to conduct the poll or election. Likely candidates are automatically placed on the list of eligibles, and additional candidates may be petitioned by a small number of signatures. If the city feels it may have difficulty in maintaining an impartial image, private associations may conduct elections or consensus proceedings.

LOCATION OF LITTLE CITY HALLS

Little city halls and other forms of neighborhood centers can be effectively located in poverty areas or throughout the city. In a number of cases it has been preferable to locate them in mixed income and ethnic areas in order to stem alienation from groups which feel they have been forgotten, to effect comprehensive information gathering and communication, to test reaction of programs from higher income groups, to provide a base from which the city can inform not only the poor but also those with the resources to assist them, and to help stabilize all areas of the community.

The approach need not be citywide to serve mixed income and ethnic groups. Pilot areas may be chosen. Baltimore, for example, chose mixed income and ethnic areas encompassing only part of the city.

New York chose mixed income areas but moved cautiously at first by establishing six neighborhood city halls and three mobile units as a pilot project. But in order to reach most of the city, citizen task forces were established covering 70 percent of the city.

Boston has taken the citywide approach but has received criticism on its expenditures; however, developers of the program feel this was the only course that they could have taken politically, for alienation was widespread. They also felt that a pilot approach might simply have ended being that and nothing more, for history has shown that pilot programs have been used to delay or kill projects. However, where there is no fear of losing sight of original objectives, a pilot program can serve to work out the kinks, developing a foundation for a more comprehensive system, and save money.

Most of the cities experimenting with this new concept of communication and neighborhood service chose poverty areas for their projects and received general community support, primarily because people felt that what was good here would also benefit the entire city. And federal programs emphasized the target area approach. To citizens outside these areas, general city progress and reduction of racial tensions were acceptable goals for the program. They would wait their turn for centers.

The most acceptable approach is best determined by assessment of each community's political and social climates. Either is acceptable, but for most new programs there has been less criticism when the needy areas were served first. However, if officials wish to develop a citywide network of communication and management information to improve services in all areas and reach the "forgotten" American, they must proceed citywide and be prepared to defend higher expenditures.

SIZE OF CENTER STAFFS

Where resources are available, it is advisable to develop comprehensive multiservice centers in conjunction with outreach centers (outposts). With limited funds, rented or shared office space with one staff person can constitute the beginning of an outreach program. Preferably, a minimum of two persons should staff an office, so that it is not left unoccupied for long periods of time.

Chicago uses about ten people in each of its outreach centers and from 100 to 400 persons in the comprehensive centers. Most of the outpost staff are community representatives who make referrals to agencies or help process residents through the larger centers.

In contrast, Atlanta makes use of a one-room office for each of four centers, donated by the community action and Model Cities programs. The main city expenditures are for four coordinators and their auto expenses. Although inhouse services are not provided by the city through this program, local offices make it easier for the mayor's representatives to direct and coordinate the many overlapping neighborhood projects. Houston uses a similar approach, except that small, inexpensive trailers are used as centers.

INNOVATIVE BUDGETS

Combined use of community action, Model Cities, and city monies is best for the development of multiservice centers, to achieve economy and more effective coordination. Many cities are now planning multiservice centers funded jointly by Model Cities and the city. In most cases, some functions of community action programs will be placed within these centers. Chicago finances most of its program with community action money, while Norfolk uses only Model Cities funds. To improve Boston's financial posture, its Model Cities program for the first time is assisting little city halls, to the tune of $200,000 in 1971.

One of the most novel aspects of the neighborhood multiservice concept is that comprehensive centers can be started with little city outlay by utilizing existing city and agency personnel. Through this approach, even with limited budgets almost all cities can create service centers. The best example is the city of Baltimore, which uses $66,000 of city funds to pay three center coordinators and the rent for three store fronts. In this system, public agencies and city departments transfer some headquarters staff to field offices, for the first time pulling together interrelated agencies and programs in a meaningful way and with minimum expense. Employees are in neighborhoods where they are most needed and where they appear to have greater motivation to perform more effectively. From fifteen to thirty persons representing about ten agencies operate each of Baltimore's centers. Residents and the city benefit from this program.

SIZES OF BUILDINGS

Although comprehensive, one-stop centers are desirable, they should not be designed to bureaucratic levels, where hundreds of employees create typical agency atmosphere. Some Chicago centers are guilty of this. The New York Human Resources Administration profited from lessons learned about agency bureaucracy and held its multiservice centers workable sizes. Others have done the same including: Baltimore, Norfolk, Boston, and most of Chicago's smaller centers. Citizen acceptance is apparent in the smaller multiservice centers in Chicago because neighborhood residents have become quite familiar with directors and staff and have learned to trust workers. The centers are therefore in continuous use and the people treat them as their own.

Baltimore has hit upon an ideal size (space for about ten agencies) which provides enough room for efficient service and expeditious follow-through by agencies and enough waiting space for entire families. The "right" size is a very important factor—one which can ease coordination, improve communication among staff members, and result in better and more convenient service to clients.

COMMUNITY ACTION, MODEL CITIES, AND THE CITY

Community action and Model Cities programs have taken considerably more initiative in reaching neighborhood residents than city government has. However, mayors and city councilmen can begin to share this partially developed communication channel by assigning city appointees (administrator-ombudsmen) to mayor's desks of complaint and information in the community action and Model Cities offices. In anticipation of little city halls and multiservice centers, mayors can take such immediate action and use this experience as the basis for judging the needs for a larger program. It also places the city in a more responsive and cooperative position in regard to these programs. In some cases, it has provoked planning for combining community action and Model Cities boards into one city board for each sector of the city.

Chicago has programmed Model Cities funds for a Mayor's Office of Inquiry and Information in each of four Model Cities multiservice centers under development. The city already has mayor's desks in the community action centers.

Baltimore has mayor's complaint desks in its centers. One is staffed by the community action program. Atlanta uses the community action centers for its city neighborhood offices, which function as complaint and information centers for the mayor. In Boston the community action program houses one little city hall, and Model Cities provides $200,000 to the city's program.

In most cities, Model Cities has cooperated fully with city government, primarily because there are close ties. Community action people have been more distant from city officials for fear of domination and because City Hall did not want to associate with poverty programs. Lately, there has been an improvement in the willingness to work together.

COORDINATION WITHIN
CENTERS AND DISTRICTS

Because so little positive coordination is now taking place in most service centers—and less in districts where a variety of programs operate—mayor's representatives may become center or district coordinators. In some cases, the coordinator might be the same person assigned to the mayor's desk in the neighborhood center. Because of the complexity of coordination, he must be well qualified and properly salaried. Such appointments are steps toward developing strong city initiative in assessing and evaluating programs, and in reducing duplication and proliferation. Overall effectiveness of all programs affecting the life of the city could well be increased.

"RESPONSIBLE CITY" CONCEPT

Coordination plus an overall mayor's cabinet could provide the nucleus of a "responsible city" concept. This occurs when the mayor and City Council begin to assume substantial responsibility for all programs operating or planned in their city (not just those for which they are legally responsible) by whatever means available. Mayors cannot afford to let poorly managed job and educational programs deteriorate their cities, for example.

Departments of human resources have been established in several cities to coordinate human-oriented programs of the federal, state, and local governments. Sometimes a single person, appointed by the mayor or chief administrative officer, performs human resource coordination. In Chicago and New York, departments of human resources have consolidated several departments under a single direction. San Antonio and Atlanta are headed toward a similar path, each having appointed a coordinator for federal and state programs. However, none of the cities in this review have made impressive strides toward the development of the overall mayor's cabinet concept.

MINI-CABINETS

A number of appointed local coordinators (or center directors) hold mini-cabinet meetings, consisting of district, city, department, and public agency heads. To assure meaningful performance, mini-cabinets should be provided some operating funds and staff assistance. Through such meetings, neighborhood problems are brought more definitively to the attention of district personnel, priorities are better established, concentration on key issues is effected, and greater neighborhood sensitivity and responsiveness are developed among officials.

Boston and New York utilize neighborhood city hall managers to conduct mini-cabinet meetings; they are not mandatory, but a good beginning for bringing the right people together to discuss mutual problems. In smaller cities, without numerous service districts, one overall city cabinet structure may be sufficient.

COMPUTERS AND CENTRAL OFFICES OF COMPLAINT AND INFORMATION

Municipal governments should consider some form of central office of complaint and information, even if it is a single phone number which citizens can use to receive information on any problem, regardless of the department, agency, or level of government involved. One look at most phone books will demonstrate why the average citizen is confused and frustrated.

Equally important is staff to follow complaints to conclusion, rather than passing citizens down the line from one agency or department to another.

The central complaint office should function in conjunction with field offices and, along with the city's central management staff, be responsible for compiling and analyzing data from all sources to permit a unified management and planning process. Computer systems may be developed from this information to evaluate program performance and productivity. This would provide the mayor and chief administrative officer a clearer picture of what is happening in the whole city and allow them to pass this information on to other policy makers. Boston's Office of Public Service appears to do the most effective job with computers and analysis of complaints.

Chicago, New York, Boston, and Kansas City operate effective central complaint and information offices which are more than referral services. But New York and Boston have developed a backlog of complaints because of low department productivity and lack of resources. Although the above cities respond to complaints from all agencies, none has developed a system of overall data gathering and evaluation which would result in the effective coordination of all agencies. There is still insufficient data accumulation and poor record maintenance. Computerized social data are difficult to interpret and not very meaningful. And in most cities, machine processing is unnecessary and has not significantly improved programs.

COMMON SERVICE DISTRICTS

Most cities are faced with the problem of proliferation and overlapping of city department and public and private agency service districts. There are numerous beneficial effects if agencies operate in coterminous areas: uniform development of a statistical and information base, joint use of facilities and staff, reduction of program duplication, fewer agency heads to deal with, and establishment of stronger neighborhood identity.

Washington, D.C. has created nine coterminous service districts encompassing the entire city and is beginning to realize some benefits. However, there are still agencies outside the system which will take further convincing (showing how one agency can help another under the system) before they will join.

Los Angeles feels it can easily accomplish uniform districting with its public works functions, and is proceeding to do so. San Antonio has had coterminous public works districts for many years, with an area engineer in charge of each territory. Because of favorable state laws in Virginia, Norfolk conveniently has most of the usual state and county functions under its control, thus reducing the districting problem considerably. And New York has taken several important steps in this direction by negotiating uniform districts in some parts of the city for the Recreation Department, Youth Service Agency, Parks Department, and Task Force on Health Planning.

No city has yet completely solved the problem. Many administrators feel it may not be worth the effort or time to pursue this objective, particularly if time can best be spent on improving agency performance. It appears that the concepts of mini-cabinets, overall city coordinators, one-stop service centers, and consolidation of departments will receive greater attention at this time, and that uniform districting will fall more naturally in line as each agency begins to see the advantages of working together. The effort should be made, however, to place existing city departments; and new programs should not be allowed to start without approval from the city's central coordinating body or cabinet. This will alleviate a buildup of the problem. Cities should be looking at logical and satisfactory boundary lines now, so as to eventually achieve this objective.

OMBUDSMEN

Center coordinators and community representatives are the neighborhood ombudsmen (citizen advocates) of little city hall programs. They are not like Scandinavian ombudsmen, who are independent of the executive branch, have significant authority by law, have high rank and salary, and usually are fully staffed. On the contrary, they are opposite of these characteristics, calling themselves neighborhood ombudsmen. They have the dual responsibility of supporting both City Hall and the citizen; and for the most part, their success is due to their personal ability to get through the bureaucracy. Neighborhood ombudsmen are particularly successful in dealing with other agencies because, in most cases, the city administration is just as fed up with poor public agency performance as the citizen; therefore, City Hall and the citizen become allies. In many cases, new mayors want to change the city's bureaucratic setup, as well. Neighborhood ombudsmen can assist them, increase the communication level, and improve the image of City Hall enough that mayors should not pass up the opportunity to perfect this concept.

Neighborhood ombudsmen perform best when they are acceptable to local residents (for example, chosen jointly by a neighborhood organization and the city), speak the language of the neighborhood and understand its culture, and, most important, are dedicated and competent people who understand and want to improve the system.

INDEPENDENT INVESTIGATIVE STAFF

It does not appear likely that the more formal, authoritative ombudsmen concept will develop rapidly in the United States, although some cities, school districts, and state governments are experimenting with versions of it. There are alternatives. One is the model of the Better Government Association in Chicago. Here, business and civic organizations fund an investigative staff which makes wide use of mass media, lawsuits, and other forms of pressure to achieve government reforms. Aggressive mayors and city councils in pursuit of the "responsible city" concept might take the initiative in forming such an investigative unit, or at least support the idea by council resolution and offer cooperation and assistance, if responsible private groups initiate it.

Internal governmental investigative staffs, such as exist in Chicago and New York, which investigate internal matters of corruption

should not be confused with the above concept. The independent body
evaluates all agencies and levels of government, not only in matters
of corruption but also in performance, productivity, expenditures,
and improved service. It functions with greater independence than
the Scandinavian ombudsmen but also with less authority. Candid
city officials who are vitally concerned about government effectiveness should welcome such a body or, better still, create a formal,
legal office of ombudsman. In many cities, the independent ombudsman office, like so many nonprofit law centers in other fields, could
be the single most important, immediate step toward creating equal
and effective local government services. Suits against incompetence,
lackadaisical civil service systems, restrictive work rules, patronage, abuse of tax expenditures, corruption, and illogical priorities
are all reasonable areas of concern.

MAYOR AND CITY COUNCIL

The approach to neighborhood decentralization is one best taken
by the mayor and City Council acting together. Normally, it is a
matter of initiation and leadership on the mayor's part, but for success it is almost always necessary to have a harmonious understanding
and effort by both parties. It does the citizen little good to have two
political branches in dispute while he continues to suffer. Surely the
basic philosophies of decentralization should be agreed upon and then
a city commitment of resources and method approved. It has worked
in most cities.

In only a few cities have there been extreme political differences in program and concepts. It is well understood that political differences cannot be overcome quickly, but this is one of
the reasons citizens are disenchanted with government and why
greater attention should be paid to the problem. As programs are
improved and success achieved, the political climate, hopefully, will
also mellow.

RESOURCES AND COMMITMENT

A national commitment of additional resources and the redistribution of existing resources are necessary to provide an appropriate
level of services which will be sufficient to correct the nation's most
serious problems. Functional decentralization, neighborhood government, and other structural changes cannot alone support major goals.
Revenue sharing based on need; liberalization of annexation laws to

improve the economic base; regional centralization of certain functions for greater efficiency and effectiveness; diminution of the proliferation of certain types of governmental units; creation of coordinating cabinets; and the development of coalitions between governments and other organizations are all desirable means of creating an impact on local residents which must not be overlooked in the search for the solutions to neighborhood problems.

Together with the above, little city halls, citizen councils, community corporations, and other decentralized techniques can provide the necessary links between the administration of resources and residents so that citizens truly have some control over their environment and destiny.

Additionally, the mayor and other city officials must develop a style and temperament that register sincere community concerns. It is this motivating atmosphere which may move a community and help establish a sense of community, which some feel is even more important than structural or institutional changes. It is the development of a basic trust between government officials and citizens. And it involves the proper distribution of resources to accomplish goals. It can be facilitated by the development of improved communication channels between government and citizens. It can hardly endure otherwise.

Officials, by careful scrutiny of politics and social conditions, must determine what is best for their community in order to develop sense of community and innovations to reach citizens. They must determine which combination of techniques is best or develop a new approach. But they must first be convinced of the importance of faithfully involving citizens in the process of government. This will come primarily by what they believe about the effectiveness of our democratic structure and how it relates to the improvement of services and better neighborhood life. The leadership role is best taken by the team of mayor, urban administrator, and community organizer. It will never really work without a team and its honest participation.

ANALYSIS OF INTERNATIONAL
CITY MANAGEMENT ASSOCIATION
AND CENTER FOR GOVERNMENTAL STUDIES
JOINT SURVEY ON
DECENTRALIZED GOVERNMENT SERVICES

<u>Little City Halls</u> (20)

Phoenix, Ariz.	Boston, Mass.
Los Angeles, Calif.	Kansas City, Mo.
Riverside County, Calif.	Elizabeth, N.J.
Adams County, Colo.	New York, N.Y.
Hartford, Conn.	Columbus, Ohio
Atlanta, Ga.	Toledo, Ohio*
Chicago, Ill.	Chester, Pa.
Springfield, Ill.	Houston, Texas
Baltimore, Md.	San Antonio, Texas
Prince George's County, Md.	Seattle, Wash.

<u>Planned Facility</u> (1)

Charlotte, N.C.

<u>Special Programs That Represent a Type of Decentralization</u> (4)

Fort Lauderdale, Fla.	Flint, Mich.
Louisville, Ky. (planning stage)	Memphis, Tenn.

---

*Neighborhood conservation and rehabilitation offices represent a type of little city hall whose basic interest is urban renewal. These offices function to improve and maintain the condition of their areas.

Multiservice Centers (42)

Phoenix, Ariz.   Malden, Mass.
Little Rock, Ark.   Detroit, Mich.
Fresno, Calif.   Kalamazoo, Mich.
Glendale, Calif.   Saginaw, Mich.
Ontario, Calif.   Duluth, Minn.
Riverside County, Calif.   Minneapolis, Minn.
Santa Clara County, Calif.   Elizabeth, N.J.
Solano County, Calif.   Nassau County, N.Y.
Adams County, Colo.   New York, N.Y.
Denver, Colo.   Yonkers, N.Y.
Hartford, Conn.   Charlotte, N.C.
New Castle County, Del.   Columbus, Ohio
Wilmington, Del.   Dayton, Ohio
Jacksonville, Fla.   Portland, Ore.
Champaign, Ill.   Chester, Pa.
Chicago, Ill.   Dallas, Texas
Peoria, Ill.   Houston, Texas
Springfield, Ill.   Lubbock, Texas
New Orleans, La.   Chesapeake, Va.
Montgomery County, Md.   Norfolk, Va.
Prince George's County, Md.   Portsmouth, Va.

Planned Multiservice Centers (5)

Baltimore, Md.   Fort Worth, Texas
Utica, N.Y.   King County, Wash.
Toledo, Ohio

Program Functions of Little City Halls

Program Functions	No. of Cities Reporting	Percent of Total Cities
Total, All Cities	20	100
Housing Inspection	12	60
Community Action	12	60
Health	11	55
Sanitation	11	55
Employment Services	10	50
Police Affairs	10	50
Public Housing	9	45
Recreation	9	45
Welfare	8	40

Program Functions	No. of Cities Reporting	Percent of Total Cities
Streets	8	40
Urban Renewal	6	30
Model Cities	5	25
Mental Health	5	25
Financial Services*	3	15
Other**	8	40

Program Functions of Multiservice Centers

Program Functions	No. of Cities Reporting	Percent of Total Cities
Total, All Cities	42	100
Health	29	69
Welfare	26	62
Employment Services	26	62
Community Action	25	60
Recreation	22	52
Police Affairs	19	45
Mental Health	14	33
Housing Inspection	13	31
Sanitation	12	29
Model Cities	11	26
Public Housing	10	24
Educational Services	8	19
Legal Services	8	19
Streets	7	17
Urban Renewal	7	17
Counseling Services	4	10
Library Services	3	7
Transportation	3	7
Rehabilitation	3	7

---

*Includes the issuing of licenses and certificates and payment of taxes and fees.

**Includes engineering, planning, fire inspection, youth opportunities, zoning, voter registration, neighborhood cleanup and stabilization, and drugs.

Program Functions	No. of Cities Reporting	Percent of Total Cities
Aid to the Aging	2	5
Other	13	31

NOTE: These materials appear in more detailed form in Judith E. Grollman, The Decentralization of Municipal Services, Urban Data Service, III, 3 (Washington, D.C.: International City Management Association, March, 1971).

B

RECOMMENDATIONS
AND PROPOSED LEGISLATION
ON NEIGHBORHOOD SUBUNITS
OF GOVERNMENT

A growing body of opinion points to the need for increasing
citizen involvement in the governmental activities of neighborhoods
within large cities. Some observers believe that the disappearance
of any meaningful sense of community among residents of large cities
and counties in our metropolitan areas has been one of the major causes
of the "crisis in the cities." The complaint is frequently voiced that
the gap between the neighborhood and the city hall or the county
building has lengthened continually until the distance seems astronomi-
cal rather than a few blocks or a few miles.

States should consider legislation authorizing large cities and
county governments in metropolitan areas to establish neighborhood
subunits of government with limited powers of taxation and local
self-government.* While the establishment of neighborhood centers
is by no means the complete answer to the unrest which exists in
many of our large cities, there is a definite need to stimulate individual
areas to develop programs of neighborhood improvement and self-
improvement.

The following suggested legislation authorizes city and county
governments to create neighborhood subunits of government with
elected neighborhood governing bodies. The legislation provides that
these subunits may be dissolved at will by the city or county governing
body. The legislation is not intended to fragment further local

---

*Advisory Commission on Intergovernmental Relations, Fiscal
Balance in the American Federal System (Washington, D.C., 1967).

government structure in metropolitan areas. However, it is designed to make it possible, through the neighborhood subgovernment device, for existing large units of local government to harness some of the resources and aspirations of their inner communities. The proposed legislation suggests a means through which a local government can actively involve a neighborhood in the governmental process.

Section 1 declares that the purpose of the act is to encourage citizen participation by permitting limited self-government through the establishment of neighborhood councils as legal entities of city or county governments. Section 2 defines a neighborhood service area and a neighborhood area council. Section 3 permits the establishment of neighborhood service areas, and authorizes neighborhood area councils to finance certain governmental services at a different level than the overall city or county tax rate, so that only recipients must pay for a particular service. It should be noted that a constitutional amendment may be necessary in some states in order to permit the use of this device.

Section 4 defines the procedures for establishing a neighborhood service area, and emphasizes local initiative as reflected by the submission of a petition to the city or county by the neighborhood residents. Since the area's success depends largely on neighborhood initiative and local leadership and decisions, no provision is made for a city or county governing body unilaterally to create neighborhood service areas. Section 4 provides for a public hearing and final approval by the city or county governing body of the establishment of these areas. Section 5 permits the extension of the boundaries of an existing neighborhood service area. Section 6 prescribes legislative standards for determining neighborhood service area boundaries, and Section 7 specifies the procedures for dissolution of a service area.

Section 8 provides for the election of council members and the filling of vacancies to serve unexpired terms. Sections 9 sets forth council powers and functions. A council may exercise only those powers and functions that are authorized by the city or county governing body. A power may be transferred to a neighborhood council in its entirely or may be shared with the local governing body. Neighborhood councils are authorized to initiate and carry out such self-help projects as supplemental refuse collection, beautification, street fairs and festivals, and cultural activities. Limited budget and finance authority, subject to city or county audit, may be shared or transferred to neighborhood councils for the acceptance of funds from public and private sources to meet overhead costs of administration and costs for services rendered. Neighborhood councils may also levy a uniform tax to finance certain special services.

Section 10 describes procedures for council meetings and provides that members shall receive no compensation other than that
for actual and necessary travel and other expenses incurred in the
performance of their duties. Section 11 permits the council to employ
a staff consultant, while Section 12 requires the council to make an
annual report to the city or county.

Suggested Legislation

[Title should conform to state requirements.
The following is a suggestion: "An act to
authorize cities and counties to establish
neighborhood service areas to advise, undertake, and finance certain governmental
services."]

(Be it enacted, etc.)

Section 1. Purpose. It is the purpose of this act to encourage
citizen involvement in government at the neighborhood level in urban
areas by permitting limited self-government through the establishment of neighborhood councils as legal entities of the city or county
government.

Section 2. Definitions. As used herein:

(1) "Metropolitan area" means an area designated as a "standard metropolitan statistical area" by the U.S. Bureau of
the Census*

(2) "City" means any municipality of more than [50,000] population, as determined by the latest official census, located
within a metropolitan area.

(3) "County" means any county located, in whole or in part,
within a metropolitan area.

(4) "Neighborhood service area" means an area within a city

---

*Particular states may find it necessary for constitutional
reasons, or otherwise desirable, to apply a somewhat different definition, tailored to their special circumstances.

or county, located within a metropolitan area, with limited
powers of taxation and local self-government.

(5) "Council" means a neighborhood area council created by
section 8 of this act to govern a neighborhood service area.

Section 3. Establishment of Neighborhood Service Areas. The
[governing body] of any city or county located within a metropolitan
area may establish within its borders one or more neighborhood
service areas to provide and finance those governmental services or
functions that the city or county is otherwise authorized to undertake,
notwithstanding any provision of law requiring uniform property tax
rates on real or personal property within the city or county.*

Section 4. Creation by Petition. (a) A petition signed by [ ]
percent of the [qualified voters] [residents] within any portion of a
city or county may be submitted to the city [governing body] or county
[governing body] requesting the establishment of a neighborhood
service area to provide any service or services which the city or
county is otherwise authorized by law to provide. The petition shall
describe the territorial boundaries of the proposed service area and
shall specify the services to be provided.

(b) Upon receipt of the petition and verification of the signatures
thereon, the city [governing body] or county [governing body], within
[30] days following verification, shall hold a public hearing on the
question of whether or not the requested neighborhood service area
shall be established.

(c) Within [30] days following the public hearing, the city
[governing body] or county [governing body], by resolution shall
approve or disapprove the establishment of the requested neighborhood
service area. A hearing may be adjourned from time to time, but shall
be completed within [60] days of its commencement.

(d) A resolution approving the creation of the neighborhood
service area may contain amendments or modifications of the area's
boundaries or functions as set forth in the petition.

----

*If a service is to be financed wholly or partly from property
tax revenues, some states may have to amend constitutional provisions
which require uniform tax rates within a city or county.

Section 5. Boundary Changes of a Neighborhood Service Area. The city [governing body] or county [governing body], pursuant to a request from the council, or pursuant to a petition signed by at least [ ] percent of the qualified voters living within the neighborhood service area, may enlarge, diminish, or otherwise alter the boundaries of any existing neighborhood service area following the procedures set forth in section 4(b),(c), and (d).

Section 6. Considerations in Setting Boundaries. In establishing neighborhood service area boundaries and determining those services to be undertaken by the neighborhood area council, the city [governing body] or the county [governing body] shall study and take into consideration the following:

(1) The extent to which the area constitutes a neighborhood with common concerns and a capacity for local neighborhood initiative, leadership, and decision-making with respect to city or county government;

(2) City or county departmental and agency authority and resources over functions that may be either transferred or shared with the council;

(3) Population density, distribution, and growth within a neighborhood service area to assure that its boundaries reflect the most effective territory for local participation and control;

(4) Citizen accessibility to, controllability of, and participation in neighborhood service area activities and functions; and

(5) Such other matters as might affect the establishment of boundaries and services which would provide for more meaningful citizen participation in city or county government.

Section 7. Dissolution of Neighborhood Service Area. (a) A city [governing body] or county [governing body], after public hearing, may dissolve a neighborhood service area on its own initiative or pursuant to a petition signed by at least [ ] percent of the qualified voters living within the neighborhood service area.

(b) The city [governing body] or county [governing body] shall give notice of a public hearing in [ ] newspapers of general circulation in the neighborhood service area of its intention to hold a public hearing on a proposed dissolution, the notice to be given not less than [14] days before the date at the public hearing.

Section 8. Election of Council; Vacancies.

(a) The council shall consist of [five to nine] members. The term of office of each member shall be [four] years, and members shall serve until their successors are elected and qualified.

(b) The council members shall be elected at large by the voters of the neighborhood service area at the time as provided by law for holding general elections. Members shall be residents of the neighborhood service area who are qualified to vote in elections for local government officials.

(c) A vacancy shall be filled by the [council] [city [governing body] or county [governing body]]. Members so appointed shall serve for the remainder of the unexpired term.

Section 9. Council Powers and Functions. A council may exercise any powers and perform any functions within the neighborhood service area authorized by the city [governing body] or county [governing body], which may include but not be limited to:

(1) Advisory or delegated substantive authority, or both, with respect to such programs as the community action program; urban renewal, relocation, public housing, planning and zoning actions, and other physical development programs; crime prevention and juvenile delinquency programs; health services; code inspection; recreation; education; and manpower training;

(2) Self-help projects, such as supplemental refuse collection, beautification, minor street and sidewalk repair, establishment and maintenance of neighborhood community centers, street fairs and festivals, cultural activities, recreation, and housing rehabilitation and sale;

(3) Budget and finance authority, subject to city or county audit, to accept funds from public and private sources, including public subscriptions, and to expend monies to meet overhead costs of council administration and support for self-help projects; and authority to raise revenue for special services by adoption of a uniform annual levy, not to exceed [five (5)] dollars, on each [resident] [head of household] of the neighborhood service area.

Section 10. Compensation; Meetings; By-Laws; Quorum.

(a) Members of a council shall receive no compensation but may receive reimbursement of actual and necessary travel and other expenses incurred in the performance of official duties, up to a maximum of [   ] dollars in any one calendar year.

(b) All meetings of a council shall be open to the public.

(c) A council shall adopt by-laws providing for the conduct of its business and the selection of a presiding officer and other officers.

(d) A majority of the members of a council shall constitute a quorum for the transaction of business. Each member shall have one vote.

Section 11. Staff. The council may employ staff and consult and retain experts as it deems necessary.

Section 12. Annual Report. The council shall make an annual report of its activities to the city or county.

Section 13. Separability. [Insert separability clause.]

Section 14. Effective Date. [Insert effective date.]

A neighborhood organization will be formed in the following manner. An initiative petition stating the proposed name and boundaries of the neighborhood area must be signed by not less than 5 percent of the registered voters in the defined area and filed with the city clerk. If the petition is adequate, an election is held; and if the majority vote is affirmative, with at least 30 percent of the voters participating, the neighborhood is formed. At the same election, voters would also choose a neighborhood board. Population limits of 5,000 to 30,000 are stipulated and provision is made for dissolution and boundary changes.

This type of organization would be available to all sections of the city. It would not necessarily be established in all areas, and the number that would develop would grow out of separate determinations by the residents of individual neighborhoods. Such entities will be successful only if they are formed as a product of neighborhood interest and action. The boundaries of a neighborhood should be ascertained by the residents of the area, who would make their determination within the prescribed population range. A key aspect of this proposal is its reliance on community initiation and control.

The neighborhood board will consist of at least seven elected members. Provisions for its organization and functioning are not specified in the charter in order to provide as much flexibility as possible for each neighborhood to determine its own arrangement.

The board will serve as a forum for discussions and the reaching of conclusions about neighborhood issues, problems, and goals. It will act in an advisory capacity and transmit recommendations on neighborhood matters to the appropriate public authorities, whether within the city government or in other jurisdictions. Regular meetings are required, and the board will appoint a neighborman, who will be responsible to the board.

The neighborman will be a liaison, a channel of communication, and a developer of mutual understanding between the neighborhood and the city government (and other governmental agencies as well). He will handle citizen complaints and seek their resolution with the appropriate public officials and agencies. He will maintain an office in the neighborhood, and will work with the neighborhood board and other local organizations in developing public and private programs and goals for the area. He will attend and participate in meetings of the neighborhood board and make reports to it, but he may not be a member. He will cooperate with the proposed ombudsman in the exchange of information about complaints by citizens in his area. In brief, the job of neighborman will be that of expediting and coordinating, as well as increasing the rapport between the citizens of the neighborhood and the city.

To carry out his duties completely, the neighborman will have to be knowledgeable about the organization, operations, and interrelations of governmental services. His principal concern will be with city services; but he will also be familiar with those of other local units, and the state and national governments as well.

Although not specified in the charter, it is expected that the neighborman will be a resident of the area who is familiar with its problems and needs. He will be selected by the neighborhood board, and will serve at its pleasure. To avoid the development of a neighborhood bureaucracy, the population of a neighborhood is limited and there may only be one neighborman in each neighborhood.

Neighborhood costs, as specified in the proposed charter, will be paid from the city general fund. Only basic costs will be funded in this manner, and they will consist of compensation for the neighborman and his clerical staff and the operating expenses of his office. Funding will be provided on the basis of a neighborhood budget, to be submitted in accordance with the city's budget procedure. The neighborhood board will establish the salary for the neighborman, subject to the review and approval of the mayor and Council as an item in the neighborhood budget, but the charter provides that the salary will be no less than that paid a field deputy of a city councilman. Any additional costs could be paid from other sources, but the neighborhood will not have the power to levy taxes or assessments. It could receive grant funds and private contributions for neighborhood purposes.

APPENDIX

D

STATEMENTS OF
VARIOUS ORGANIZATIONS AND CITIES
ON NEIGHBORHOOD GOVERNMENT
AS CITED BY THE LOS ANGELES
CITY CHARTER COMMISSION

1. The Advisory Commission on Intergovernmental Relations, a body made up largely of public officials, recommends enactment of state legislation authorizing large cities and county governments to establish neighborhood subunits of government with limited powers of taxation and administration over certain federal, state, and local programs.

2. The Commission for Economic Development, a prominent private organization composed of leading businessmen and educators, suggests small, popularly elected neighborhood councils and districts, the latter on the order of magnitude of about 50,000 residents each, and operations paid by city government.

3. The Kerner Commission, in its Report of the National Advisory Commission on Civil Disorders, recommended neighborhood action task forces and neighborhood city halls in areas with a high proportion of low-income minority citizens, in order to provide opportunities for meaningful citizen participation and also to serve as the eyes and ears of the mayor and council.

4. In 1969 the U.S. Department of Health, Education and Welfare formulated the concept of neighborhood service centers to help residents in referrals, clients' rights, legal and day care counseling, training and placing for employment, health, and to act as a nucleus for organizing residents in specific common problems. More than 800 neighborhood centers are now in operation in the country, most being run by indigenous community organizations.

5. Milton Kotler, Institute of Policy Studies, in a paper to the Subcommittee on Urban Affairs of the Joint Economic Committee of

the United States Congress, suggested that the vast distance between
a city administration and its citizens is the greatest defect of contemporary city government. He advocates a transfer of a portion of a
city's authority to the legally organized locality through neighborhood
corporations established by local neighborhood initiative, leadership,
and decision. He adds that the national government must provide
some initial funding. He feels that certain functions, such as day care,
recreation, libraries, schools, health, and welfare, could be better
handled by neighborhood corporations. The city would then become
a federated structure.

6. The Chicago Riot Report, studying the 1967 Chicago riots,
stated that progress will be made in the solution of ghetto problems
only if there is effective communication between ghetto residents
and city government. There should be community organizations which
can act as influential representatives of residents before local bodies.

7. The National Commission on Urban Problems in its report,
Building the American City, 1968, recommends offices in neighborhoods
for information, counseling, and referral.

8. Two California localities have launched efforts to bring
local government closer to the people.

In East Palo Alto, an unincorporated area in San Mateo County,
an advisory municipal council to develop public safety, welfare, public
works, and planning was established by resolution of the County Board
of Supervisors in July, 1969. They do not decide questions bearing
on this area before action is taken by the Municipal Council, which
consists of five members, one elected from each of five districts,
and aided by a full-time executive assistant to the county manager
and a secretary.

In Stockton, the office of neighborman has been established and
two persons appointed who work citywide, where their services are
most needed.

Little City Hall	Complaints Sent to Departments	Requests Answered Directly Complaints	Requests Answered Directly Services	Requests Answered Directly Total	Parking Stickers	Voter Registration	Total	Total Business
Allston	677 3.1%	6,815	8,942	15,757 72.7%	3,917	1,326	5,243 24.2%	21,677
Brighton	38 0.6%	1,910	2,495	4,405 64.6%	1,655	723	2,378 34.9%	6,821
Charlestown	3,408 19.4%	5,467	6,636	12,103 68.9%	1,598	450	2,048 11.7%	17,559
Dorchester	3,617 15.2%	6,732	7,135	13,867 58.3%	5,160	1,156	6,316 26.5%	23,800
East Boston	1,165 5.0%	5,394	12,063	17,457 74.4%	3,375	1,470	4,845 20.6%	23,467
Hyde Park	1,135 10.3%	1,120	7,334	8,454 76.8%	1,050	375	1,425 12.9%	11,014
Jamaica Plain	2,696 15.1%	7,014	4,485	11,499 64.4%	2,750	909	3,659 20.5%	17,854
Mattapan	1,473 6.3%	6,266	11,759	18,025 77.5%	2,270	1,477	3,741 16.1%	23,245
North End	697 9.5%	2,164	2,858	5,022 68.3%	1,280	355	1,635 22.2%	7,354
Roslindale	941 4.8%	5,320	8,502	13,822 71.2%	3,975	670	4,645 23.9%	19,408
Roxbury	3,337 14.0%	9,036	9,749	18,785 79.1%	1,175	454	1,629 6.9%	23,751

404

Little City Hall	Complaints Sent to Departments	Requests Answered Directly			Parking Stickers	Voter Registration	Total	Total Business
		Complaints	Services	Total				
South Boston	1,667 9.5%	3,347	5,367	8,714 49.6%	6,360	818	7,178 40.9%	17,559
South End	2,129 10.4%	13,606	2,325	15,931 78.0%	1,500	861	2,361 11.6%	20,421
West Roxbury	3,002 20.3%	3,127	4,181	7,308 49.5%	2,400	2,061	4,461 30.2%	14,771
Total Little City Hall	25,982 10.4%	77,318	93,831	171,149 68.8%	38,465	13,105	51,570 20.7%	248,701
24-Hour Service	2,002 1.3%	83,730	66,694	150,424 94.6%	6,594	—	6,594 4.1%	159,020
Back Bay Chinatown	230				100			330
Total	27,984 6.9%	161,278	160,525	321,803 78.9%	45,159	13,105	58,264 14.3%	408,051

Source: Boston Office of Public Service, City of Boston, January 1971.

F

**LOCAL ADVISORY
COUNCIL GUIDELINES
DRAWN UP BY A COMMITTEE
OF LITTLE CITY HALL MANAGERS,
BOSTON**

1. The LAC will be the first voice in community affairs. As
the logical extension of the LCH, the LAC will be the prime mechanism
through which the LCH will work with the community. The same
holds true for the overall city administration and city departments.
(This will begin by incorporating existing city neighborhood programs,
e.g., police-community relations program and neighborhood recreation
councils, into the LAC structure.)

2. There will be a two-way channel of information between the
LAC and the LCH. The LCH manager will be responsible for ensuring
that the LAC is kept informed of all pertinent city activity. Any difficulties in fulfilling this responsibility with particular departments
will be resolved through Joe Smith.

The LAC will be expected to direct its activities with city
departments and services through the LCH manager as the person
who keeps daily contact with city departments. If the LAC feels the
manager is not fulfilling this function, the LAC chairman will notify
Joe Smith.

3. The LAC will be an issue-oriented, community-based organization. It is assumed that comprehensive city services also fall within
this context. It will be the manager's responsibility to ensure that
the LAC is representative of all issue-interests in his LAC area and
that each subcommittee is a functioning group relevant to problems
as the community sees them.

4. The LAC will be a local planning body. In addition to the
normal "response" functioning which we can expect from LAC subcommittees, it must be made explicit to the LAC that it has the

responsibility for acting as the main planning body for that LAC area.
In order to adequately fulfill this role, adequate planning expertise
must be made available to each LAC. It will be the responsibility of
the manager of the LCH, through OPS, to secure whatever city expertise
for comprehensive community planning is available. The LAC chairman
is encouraged to seek out whatever additional professional aid is necessary.

The LAC will serve as a catalyst only to ensure adequate programming for their area. It will not execute programs on its own as
an official function of the LAC.

5. Each LAC and its subcommittees will be open and representative of the community at large. Each LAC will kick off with a "town
meeting" (preferably with the mayor present). After the "town meeting,"
the manager will be responsible for convening as soon as possible a
meeting of all individuals who expressed an interest in the LAC, plus
representatives of community organizations. This group will propose
how to structure the LAC, what committees it should have, and will
pick a chairman (temporary or acting). This proposed structure will
be submitted in writing to Joe Smith.

6. LAC must be related to present neighborhood programs and
activities. The LAC is designed to be the broadest-based issue group
in the community, encompassing existing groups working on community
issues as well as providing the openness for new inputs from individuals
and elements not already providing an input. With this end in mind,
the following are basic models preferable for the LAC executive
committee and the subcommittee structures:

a. The executive committee is composed of the chairmen
of the subcommittees

b. The LAC subcommittee is an amalgam of existing committees, plus any interested residents.

Variations on either of these models will be submitted to Joe
Smith by the LCH manager.

The goal of the LAC subcommittee is not to duplicate existing
efforts, but to rechannel those which are already working in particular
issue areas. The LAC subcommittees will be open to all parties
interested in their subject matter; the responsibility will be upon the
LCH manager to ensure maximum community input, coordination,
and cooperation, and that no limitations be placed upon the membership
in any of the sub-committees.

7. There will be a reporting system to the community at large by the LAC. Major decisions will be open to this large public meeting, which should be held periodically. No public meetings will be called in the community by the city without going through the LAC. It is understood that a public meeting will be called by vote of the LAC or by request of the LCH manager.

8. Each LAC is responsible for ensuring relevant area representation on planning issues. Respective neighborhoods must be represented if a department is going to present plans to one of the LAC subcommittees which are pertinent to a particular neighborhood or civic organization.

G

**BOSTON CITY SERVICES
AND CITY GOVERNMENT,
EXCERPTS FROM THE REPORT
BY THE JOINT CENTER FOR
URBAN STUDIES OF HARVARD-MIT**

This appendix is based on citizen interviews conducted during 1969.

There is constant debate about the quality of the city services offered in Boston; and it is, therefore, both interesting and useful to find out how people at large—and not just the vocal minority—rate city services. We chose four major service areas: (1) the education that children receive in the schools, (2) parks and playgrounds, (3) police, and (4) trash and garbage collection. For each we asked our sample of the population to rate the provision of service as "very good," "fair," or "poor." We also asked them to rate in the same manner how good a job they think the city government is doing.

For the total city population, fully 80 percent rated trash and garbage collection "very good" or "good," 57 percent gave these ratings to the police and 55 percent to the schools, while parks and playgrounds fell at the bottom with 35 percent. The differences between these ratings were substantial. Yet it is also interesting to note that over half the population gave a "good" or better rating to each of the services, with the exception of parks and playgrounds. In view of that, it may be somewhat surprising that only 30 percent of the population of Boston approves of the job that the city government is doing.

Survey data on attitudes will necessarily deal with something other than the objective quality of the city services. But citizens can and do judge services; and their degree of satisfaction becomes an important measure of the adequacy of these services. With respect to parks and playgrounds, it seems that the various groups in Boston generally agree on what constitutes good service. The major differences are among areas. While the neighborhoods in which Negroes live generally had lower ratings, none of the others were high.

At the other extreme are the evaluations of the schools. They are extreme, first, in that they appear, in many cases, to have more to do with who is doing the rating than with what is being rated. Second, there is little agreement among both Negroes and whites in Roxbury-South End and in North Dorchester that the schools are not as good as elsewhere in the city. However, there is much more difference between Negroes and whites in those same areas than among whites in different areas. Even among whites, the differences between native Bostonians and those born elsewhere in the United States are at least as great as differences among whites living in the different neighborhoods of the city.

The problem for a city government is obvious: do you try to reform a school system with which many people are very satisfied, but with which about an equal number are not satisfied? If the differences result from different standards and expectations, can there be a single school system that will be more acceptable to the city as a whole? Similar questions can be asked about other key services. It may be impossible to please all segments of a heterogeneous population.

If the difficulty of pleasing different groups with services is perplexing, an equally difficult problem for local government is raised by the consistently poor ratings that it received from different groups in the city, even from those groups that were generally positive about important services. Clearly, providing the services discussed here, even at a very satisfactory level, does not necessarily win the backing of the community.

The finding that most people think the city government is most concerned about helping someone else is perhaps central to the problems that any city government must face, regardless of its political bent. It seems reasonable to speculate that there is a general sense of taxes increasing while city problems multiply and city services do not improve markedly. In the absence of evidence that things are improving that matter to him, the average citizen may conclude that the city government must be helping someone else, or no one at all. It is interesting that those who do not hold the city government primarily responsible for city problems are most positive about the job the city government is doing. Yet there remains—even for many of those who hold the people responsible—the fact that a positive rating of a local government is tied up with the degree to which the government is seen as concerned about and responsive to people. Being responsive and communicating concern are clearly part of winning community backing; and our data suggest that this task is even harder, but perhaps more important to people, than delivering services.

APPENDIX

**RECOMMENDATIONS
ON THE DECENTRALIZATION
OF GOVERNMENT SERVICES,
HOME RULE COMMISSION,
BOSTON, JUNE, 1970**

1.   The mayor should designate a top-ranking member of his administration to press forward with the decentralization recommendations of the Commission.   Beyond this immediate responsibility, decentralization policy must become an integral part of the major administrative decisions of the city.   It therefore should be viewed as requiring the ongoing attention of the Executive Office of Administration proposed in the Commission's Report on the Reorganization of Staff Services.   We urge that the Planning, Administrative, and Budget Divisions of the Executive Office of Administration, in conjunction with OPS, be charged with periodic review and evaluation of implementation of decentralization of the city.

The Executive Office of Administration would be responsible for aligning capital and operating budgets and procedures, the long-range capital improvement program, and the organization and allocation of line agencies (1) to conform to the district boundaries established according to the standards proposed in the following subsection; (2) to budget for and accommodate the staff for district councils proposed in subsection 6 (e); and (3) to establish in the budget preparation process a time and procedure for local area input to and dialogue with line agencies with respect to the "accountability" powers outlined in subsections 6(a)-(d) below.

2.   The city administration should be charged with proposing a set of boundaries dividing the city's territory into fourteen contiguous districts.   (This number would, of course, be subject to marginal revision in light of considerations brought to light in the boundary-drawing process.)   Factors to be recognized in arriving at these boundaries should include the following:

a. Natural and man-made physical boundaries

b. Existing clusters of concentrations of people sharing recognized traits of ethnicity, socioeconomic character, and/or culture

c. "Turfs," insofar as these can be recognized, of highly visible voluntary organizations

d. Established patterns of daily interchange or transactions which seem to center around shopping areas, transit stops, parks, churches, etc.

e. Fixed locations of major capital plants, such as schools, police stations, and parks, and other technical considerations in treating the proposed district as a unit for the provision of various services

f. Existing boundaries under established and ongoing programs and projects, such as Model Cities, urban renewal, and APAC

g. Territories covered by less formalized community-engaging activities.

Despite the fantastic complexity in the abstract of an attempt to weigh all these factors "rationally" in a boundary-drawing process, we believe it will be discovered in short order that in Boston many districts will practically define themselves: Brighton-Allston, Charlestown, East Boston, and South Boston, for example, are "naturals." The Model Cities area should be incorporated as a district with the Washington Park area, which it presently surrounds, subject to some peripheral revision. In other areas there will be real problems.

Immediately upon promulgation of the proposed boundaries, all public agencies conducting programs or providing services to or through territorial subdivisions of the city would be encouraged to conform their "maps" and associated operations to the boundary proposals. Insofar as this recommendation applies to line departments of the city of Boston, it would fall to the mayor, through the Executive Office of Administration, to oversee and encourage this development. It is most important, however, to note that other agencies are involved: quasi-public corporations such as ABCD, and state agencies such as the Departments of Mental Health and Public Welfare. Recommendation of conformity in field operations to the OPS-proposed boundaries is intended to apply to all these, and strong efforts should be made to assure the cooperation of state agencies.

I

SERVICE AREA BOUNDARIES AND SERVICE AREA COMMITTEE REPRESENTATION, WASHINGTON, D.C.

In Washington, D.C., boundaries of the service areas are determined by a combination of criteria, including location of:

1. Model neighborhood
2. Manmade barriers
3. Natural boundaries
4. Areas commonly identified as neighborhoods
5. Community organizations
6. Existing agency boundaries.

The service delivery agencies represented on the SAC are the following:

1. Health service
2. Employment services and training programs
3. Maintenance of streets and highways
4. Control, counseling, and guidance of persons in custody and on parole or probation
5. Collection of trash and cleaning of streets
6. Enforcement of housing codes and regulations
7. Public assistance programs
8. Public education
9. Public housing
10. Public safety
11. Recreation for youth and adults
12. Rehabilition for the physically handicapped
13. Human relations programs
14. Library programs
15. Planning, rehabilitation, and economic development of areas
16. Others, as may be designated from time to time.

Each member is required to devote at least 20 percent of his time to his service area assignment.

Each SAC is required to develop a comprehensive service delivery report which will do the following:

1. Review the problems and the needs of the people in the service area
2. Identify the services currently available to residents of the service area
3. Indicate steps to improve coordination in the current service delivery system that will be implemented by individual members of the SAC, within their existing authority
4. Identify other desirable steps which cannot be accomplished under present legislative authority or budget availability, or which otherwise require action at higher levels.

1. Creation or strengthening of an interagency referral and follow-up system—a system to insure that any individual who needs help gets it even if one individual agency cannot provide for the totality of his and his family's needs.

2. Teamwork when necessary to solve a family's problems or to address a recurring problem of family or community, solution of which usually involves more than one agency.

3. Creation of an easy-to-update, area-level guide for interagency and community reference that will include names, positions, locations, telephone numbers, etc., of public and private services available in and to that area.

4. Use of professional and paraprofessional outreach workers to provide outreach, information, and follow-up services for more than one program or agency. For example, a public nurse or health nutrition worker or fire inspector can carry information and referral directions for all area service programs.

5. Although a unified intake form should be initiated on a citywide basis, the area-level committee can take initial steps to unify their area's intake system and can recommend further changes to the central agencies.

6. A coordinated follow-up system can be developed which will fit the unique needs and assets of each service area. For example, a follow-up system may be designed by designating different agencies' generalist and paraprofessional staff as "family workers" who divide the area on a geographic or functional basis to insure complete and effective follow-up coverage.

7. Forms, procedural requirements, and telephone and clerical duties can be examined and revamping of current operations carried out, where necessary, to maximize the efficiency and morale of personnel. For example, instead of a request for information from another agency being sent back to the central office and routed over to another central office and then down the line to the area-level operation, a procedure for direct area-level exchange of information could be worked out to shorten the process and the time involved.

8. Examine and improve client-staff relationships. Many staff problems are of a common nature despite different settings, so mutually devised and sometimes jointly held training and staff development operations can be beneficial. For example, teachers, recreation workers, and police all deal with children and youth, and some staff development activities on the psychology and special needs of youth would be useful to all these workers, despite differences in their day-to-day functions.

9. Many area-level operations are in the field (not in the office), which often means visiting of homes, stores, schools, and playgrounds for the actual delivery of service. Common functions and problems related to field visits can be examined in detail and improved jointly.

10. Some area-level facilities are overused and some underused. The committee can work out arrangements to improve use of existing facilities and public spaces, such as schools, recreation centers, public libraries, public housing facilities, playgrounds and play streets, etc.

11. The committee can recommend what kind of improved police coverage might be needed for critical areas and times, including school sites, public housing developments, parks, shopping areas, etc. Ideas for giving the police and fire stations a positive image in the community can be developed as well.

12. Workers can be scheduled for various area-level facilities when program use or costs do not make permanent satellite units feasible.

13. An interagency referral and reference guide and system, once established, can be extended from the area's public and private agencies to other service-oriented community institutions, such as church groups and tenant councils.

14. The SAC itself can provide training and staff development to various area operations, such as schools and police stations.

In-house staff meeting with SAC members could be arranged for a full discussion of the linkage of services and the problems and possibilities of integrating services for the consumer.

15. The SAC can also address and work out ways for assisting member agencies in time of crisis, such as a tense incident in an area-level school, vandalism of the local library, or sudden fund cutback for a health clinic or employment training program. For example, an employment program loses some of its funds for supportive services. Until those funds can be restored, other agencies can work out ways to fill the void so that the people undergoing training can finish.

16. When local conditions arise over which public agencies have jurisdiction, the SAC could initiate block meetings with community residents to identify ways to alleviate the situation.

17. Many service delivery-level problems are caused by traditional policy requirements or federal guidelines. Not all of these delivery-level problems are visible to central offices or to community leaders. SAC members, with their unique "inside" experience, can identify these kinds of guideline and policy-caused problems and work out recommendations for change.

18. SAC members can assess the quality of area-level public facilities and make recommendations or initiate improvements.

These are only some of the many kinds of activities a SAC can engage in for the improvement of service delivery in their community.

The Community Services Advisory Committee will perform the following functions:

1. Advise the director, OCS, in implementation of the service area system

2. Assist in review of reports, plans, and proposals from the SACs

3. Advise the director, OCS, on the consolidation of the nine service delivery reports into a comprehensive service delivery report for the city

4. Recommend service priorities between service areas

5. Recommend budgetary allocations necessary to change existing services or initiate new ones

6. Provide advice, exchange information, and assist in implementation of the Model Cities program

7. Advise the director, OCS, on procedures which will insure effective linkage between city service programs

8. Recommend policy or programs aimed at improvement of the district government's service delivery system

9. Develop, via a working subcommittee, recommended evaluation procedures for coordinated efforts among agencies to assess the effectiveness of the service area alignment process and its effect on delivery of services

10. Advise and assist in planning and establishment of community service centers integrated into the service delivery system of the various service areas.

Within their departments, agencies, or offices, CSAC representatives will be expected to assure the following:

1. Adequate department input into CSAC and service area system activities

2. Provision of items for CSAC consideration

3. Suitable communication of information concerning CSAC and the service area system

4. Systematic orientation, direction, and liaison between the office of the director, major staff sections and suboffices, and the departmental representatives on the service area committees

5. Systematic orientation and ongoing guidance to the department's SAC representatives.

Staff support to CSAC will be provided by the Office of Community Services.

SECTIONS OF A BILL
AUTHORIZING THE CREATION
AND ELECTION OF COMMUNITY COUNCILS
TO GOVERN IN LOCAL AFFAIRS,
INDIANAPOLIS

SEC. 7. Referendum on Organization. At the first primary election following the effective date of the first Plan adopted in accordance with Section 3 hereof, a referendum shall be held in each Community created by such Plan to ascertain whether the voters thereof desire to establish a Community Council for such Community and to become an Organized Community with the rights and powers conferred by this Act. The question shall be submitted to the voters in the following form: "Shall a Community Council be established in _____ Community?," the names of the respective Communities appearing in the blank provided therefor; except that in each Included Town established by the Plan as a separate community the question shall be submitted in the following form: "Shall the town of _____ become an Organized Community of the City?," the name of the Included Town to appear in the blank provided therefor. The ballots shall have printed thereon the words "Yes" and "No." The proposition shall be adopted only if fifty percent (50%) of the total number of persons voting in such primary in the Community shall vote thereon, and if a majority of the voters voting thereon shall vote "Yes." The returns of such referendum shall be certified by the Election Board of the County and shall be filed with the Council within ten (10) days after such referendum. In each Community in which the proposition shall have been adopted in accordance with this section, an election shall be held at the next General Election to select a Community Council, in accordance with the further provisions of this Article.

SEC. 8. Organization of Community Councils. In any Community which shall not become an Organized Community in accordance with Section 7 hereof, a petition may be filed at any time with the Council bearing the signatures of fifty (50) registered voters in such

Community, requesting the establishment of a Community Council for such Community. If such petition is found to be valid, a further referendum shall be held in the Community at the next primary election following the filing of such petition. Such referendum shall be conducted in accordance with Section 7 hereof.

SEC. 9. Election of Community Councils. (a) At the first General Election following the referendum establishing a Community Council there shall be elected, in accordance with the general election laws governing General Elections in a City, a Community Council consisting of one (1) councilman from each precinct in the Community, the voters of each precinct voting only for the councilman representing such precinct. In the case of a Community having fewer than three (3) precincts, there shall additionally be elected that number of councilmen at large within the Community which will result in a Community Council of three (3) members.

(b) Candidates may be nominated for the office of councilman only in the manner provided in this section. On or before September 1 of a year in which councilmen are to be elected under the provisions of this Chapter, the name of any qualified person may be presented by petition in writing, signed by the candidate and at least five (5) registered voters of the Community, which petition shall be filed with the Clerk of the Circuit Court of the County. No petition shall propose the name of more than one (1) candidate; and no person shall sign more than one (1) petition for nomination for councilman for any election. At the time required by law, the Clerk shall certify such nominations to the Election Board. Any person so nominated may withdraw his name from nomination by a written declaration filed with the Clerk prior to certification of the same. The Clerk shall not certify the name of any candidate who shall appear to be ineligible under the provisions of this Article.

(c) The names of the candidates for councilman in each precinct, and for each at-large seat on the Community Council, shall be listed on the ballot in alphabetical order. Nothing shall appear on the face of the ballot to indicate the political affiliation of any candidate; nor shall any election officer, challenger or poll book holder indicate to any elector offering to vote what he believes or understands to be the political affiliation of any candidate for councilman. The candidates shall not advertise their political affiliation, if any, in the course of the campaign, and no political party or group representing a political party shall endorse any such candidate.

(d) The councilmen shall serve without pay for terms of two (2) years. Their terms shall begin on January 1 of the year following their election, and shall terminate on December 31 of the year in which the next General Election shall be held, at which General Election their successors shall be elected. A Community Council shall be deemed elected in any Community only if a councilman shall be elected in a majority of the precincts in such Community, or if at least three (3) councilmen shall be elected in the case of any Community having fewer than five (5) precincts. In the event no Community Council is elected at the General Election following the referendum authorizing the election of a Community Council, the Community Council shall be dissolved, and no Community Council shall be elected in such Community until a new referendum is held in accordance with the provisions of Sections 7 and 8 hereof.

SEC. 10. Qualifications of Community Councilmen. Every person elected to membership on a Community Council pursuant to this Article shall have been a resident of the Community for at least six (6) months immediately preceding his election, and shall be a registered voter and resident in the precinct from which he is elected, or if he is elected at large, in the Community. No member of the Council nor officer of any political party shall be eligible to election as a Community Councilman.

SEC. 11. Vacancy. If a councilman shall die, resign, remove his residence from the Community, become incapacitated, fail to perform his duties for a period in excess of six (6) months, or be removed from office under any law of this State, his office shall become vacant. The remaining members of the Community Council shall elect a qualified person to fill such vacancy for the unexpired term.

SEC. 12. Election by Included Town. Any Included Town which may at any time be located in whole or in part within the territory of a City may, by ordinance duly adopted by its Board of Trustees, elect to surrender its status as a town and to be governed by the provisions of this Chapter. A copy of the ordinance adopted by the Board of Trustees surrendering its status and electing to accept the provisions of this Chapter, certified by the Clerk-Treasurer of the town under the seal thereof, shall be filled with the Clerk of the Circuit Court of the County and with the Council, and such Town shall thereupon be dissolved, and shall become an Organized Community in accordance with this Chapter. The incumbent members of the Board of Trustees of such Town shall continue to serve as the Community Council, as thus constituted, and shall have the power to elect additional councilmen in accordance with this Chapter, if the Community thus established is entitled to additional councilmen under the provisions of this Chapter; but no reduction in the number of councilmen shall be required prior to the next General Election.

SEC. 13. Procedures. Each Community Council created pursuant to this Chapter shall hold monthly stated meetings at a location within the Community, and may hold other meetings at such places as the Council shall determine. A majority of the duly qualified and acting councilmen from time to time shall constitute a quorum. The Community Council shall designate one (1) of its members as President, and may select such other officers as it may deem appropriate. All meetings of the Community Council shall be open to the public. The Council may by ordinance or resolution prescribe uniform procedures governing notices, meetings, and the manner in which Community Councils shall take action by ordinance, resolution or otherwise: Provided, that unless and until the Council shall otherwise provide, Community Councils shall follow the same procedures as shall be prescribed for Boards of Town Trustees by applicable law, not inconsistent with the provisions of this Chapter.

SEC. 14. General Powers of Community Councils. Except as otherwise provided in this Chapter, the Community Councils created under the provisions of this Chapter shall have the following general powers and duties:

(1) To exercise all powers conferred, and to perform all duties imposed, by the laws of this State on Boards of Town Trustees except such powers as are expressly denied to Community Councils by general ordinance adopted by the Council, provided, however, that Community Councils shall not:

(a) levy or collect any tax;

(b) issue any general obligation bonds;

(c) adopt any regulation or ordinance in conflict with, or permitting a lesser standard than, any applicable ordinance of the Council;

(d) exercise any power exclusively conferred by law on any department of the city, except as expressly authorized by, and in conformity with, an ordinance duly adopted by the Council, or except in accordance with the terms of any agreement between the Community and the department possessing such power, which agreement shall be approved by the Council before becoming effective;

(e) exercise the power of eminent domain, except as expressly authorized by, and in conformity with, any ordinance duly adopted by the Council;

(f) exercise any power outside the boundaries of the Community;

(g) enter into any agreement with, or receive funds from, any unit of government other than the City and its departments without the prior approval of the Council; or

(h) annex territory or otherwise cause its boundaries to be altered.

(2) To appropriate funds placed to the credit of the Community by ordinance of the Council;

(3) To hire its own clerk and to hire other officials permitted by ordinance of the Council upon such terms and conditions as may be established by general ordinance of the Council;

(4) To contract with the City and the various departments thereof, or with private individuals or organizations having authority to provide the services contracted for, for special services, additional police and fire protection, community improvements and park and recreational facilities;

(5) To enact ordinances for the regulation of speed, parking, and movement of vehicles and pedestrians on streets and roads within the Community, other than on a road or street designated as a thoroughfare on the metropolitan thoroughfare plan of the County, subject, however, to the power of the Transportation Board, after hearing, to invalidate any such ordinance on the ground that such ordinance is unreasonable, or that it is incompatible with the objectives of safe and convenient movement of traffic in the City;

(6) To receive notice of any proposed ordinance relating to a road or street within the Community designated as a thoroughfare on the metropolitan thoroughfare plan of the County, at least thirty (30) days prior to enactment thereof, and transmit to the Transportation Board and the Council its written report and recommendations with respect to such proposed ordinance;

(7) To enter into agreements with other Organized Communities to exercise jointly powers conferred on them by this Chapter or by ordinance of the Council;

(8) To exercise any powers, in addition to those specifically conferred by this Section, which shall be conferred on Community Councils by ordinance duly enacted by the Council.

Any ordinance enacted by a Community Council shall be enacted in accordance with the general laws governing towns in this State, and additionally shall be filed with the Council and with the Legal Division of the City for a period of thirty (30) days before becoming effective. If the Corporation Counsel of the City shall, within such thirty (30) day period, submit to the Council and to the Community Council his written opinion that any such ordinance is illegal or invalid because it exceeds the power of a Community Council under this Chapter, conflicts with applicable City, State, or Federal law, violates any state or federal constitutional requirement or limitation, was adopted without observance of procedures required by law, or for any other reason, the effective date of such ordinance shall be further postponed for an additional period of sixty (60) days following the rendering of such legal opinion. Prior to expiration of such additional sixty (60) day period the Council may by resolution veto any Community Council ordinance which the Corporation Counsel has so advised to be illegal or invalid.

Ordinances enacted by Community Councils shall be enforced by the appropriate officers of the City in the same manner as city ordinances enacted by the Council.

This Chapter shall not be construed to give any Community created under the provisions of this Chapter the status of a municipal corporation or special taxing district.

SEC. 23. Community Fund. The City Controller shall, at the time any Community becomes an Organized Community under the provisions of this Chapter, establish a special fund of the City for the use of such Community. There shall be credited to such fund:

(1) All amounts appropriated by the Council for the use of such Community in accordance with the further provisions of this Chapter; and

(2) All amounts representing such Community's share of revenues from any distribution of funds from the State of Indiana, in accordance with any general ordinance adopted by the Council providing for distributions to Organized Communities.

Such fund shall be administered by, and shall be subject to all budget and auditing procedures of, the Department of Finance of the City; and any payments of money from such fund shall be made only on warrant authorized by the Community Council in accordance with general law. Payment shall be made by the Controller or his delegate

directly to the person designated in such warrant to receive such
funds.

SEC. 24. Budgets. On or before the first day of July in any
year, the Department of Finance shall furnish to the Community Council of each Organized Community a statement setting forth:

(1) The balance in such Community's special fund as of December 31 of the year preceding, indicating the restrictions, if any, on
the uses to which any part of such fund may be put;

(2) The anticipated additions to such fund during the current
calendar year, by source; and

(3) An estimate of the additions to such fund during the next
succeeding calendar year, by source.

The Community Council shall, on the basis of the statement so
furnished, prepare a budget for the next succeeding calendar year
in accordance with the general laws of the State of Indiana applicable
to towns, which budget shall be submitted to the Department of Finance
on or before the first day of August, and which, if found by such department to conform to law, shall be included as a part of the budget
of the City for such calendar year. Such budget shall be subject to
review by the Council, but shall not be changed unless

(1) The Department of Finance or the Community Council has
overestimated the amount of the fund available for use by the Community; or

(2) The budget, or any items therein, do not conform to applicable
law. The budget shall be subject to review by State and County agencies
only as a part of the budget of the City. The Community Councils
shall be entitled to assistance by the staff of the Department of Finance
in the preparation and presentation of any budget.

SEC. 25. Council Appropriations. The Council shall have the
power to appropriate, upon petition therefor by any Community Council, from the general and special funds of the City (other than the
Special Funds of the Communities) to the extent not expressly prohibited by law, amounts specifically designated to be expended for
local improvements or services or for any other purpose for which
a town may expend monies under the laws of this State, either generally
or for specific types of improvements, such as for street maintenance
and construction, parks and recreation, and street lighting. There

shall be credited to the special fund of each Organized Community
that percentage of such designated appropriation which is equal to
the ratio of the population of such Community based on the most
recent Federal census to the population of the City based on such
census (or, in the case of an appropriation made out of funds obtained
from taxes levied on an area other than the City, the ratio of the population of such Community to the population of such area). All amounts
not credited to the special fund of any Organized Community in accordance with this Section shall be credited to the appropriate fund
of the City, and shall be expended only on local improvements of the
type for which such appropriation shall have been made, within the
areas of the City (or other area) not lying within any Organized Community. Amounts credited to the special fund of any Community shall
be expended in strict accordance with any limitations imposed by the
Council in connection with the appropriation.

SEC. 26. Designated Revenues. The Council may by ordinance
designate that all or any portion of any distribution made to the Consolidated City from the State of Indiana under the provisions of any
law, including, without limitation on the generality of the foregoing,
any inheritance tax, motor fuel tax, excise on tobacco products, excise
on alcoholic beverages of any sort, general sales tax, and income tax,
shall be specifically designated for local use; and the amounts so
designated shall be apportioned among the special funds of the Organized Communities and the appropriate fund of the City, and shall be
expended in accordance with the provisions of Section 26 hereof.

American Arbitration Association
1815 H Street, N.W., Washington, D.C.

PART I AGREEMENT

THIS AGREEMENT, entered into this _____ day of _____
1968, by and between the City of Rochester, New York, and the American Arbitration Association, a private, nonprofit corporation organized under the laws of the State of New York, of the City of New York, State of New York, herein called the Contractor.

WITNESSETH THAT:

WHEREAS, the City of Rochester proposes to enter into a contract with the United States of America for a grant for the planning and developing of a Comprehensive City Demonstration Program for a certain area, hereinafter referred to as the "Model Neighborhood Area," pursuant to Title I of the Demonstration Cities and Metropolitan Development Act of 1966; and

WHEREAS, the City of Rochester desires to engage the Contractor to render certain services in connection therewith:

NOW, THEREFORE, the parties hereto do mutually agree as follows:

1. <u>Scope of Services.</u> The Contractor shall, in a satisfactory and proper manner as determined by the City of Rochester, perform the following services:

A. Administer the election of 18 District Representatives to the Model Neighborhood Council, one from each of 18 Voting Districts as established by the City of Rochester. Specific activities to be undertaken in this regard include, but are not limited to, the following:

(1) Coordinate the entire District Election process with related public activities affecting the Model Neighborhood Program.

(2) Develop the bilingual nomination petition and instruction to nominees.

(3) Receive completed petitions, verify them, and certify eligible candidates.

(4) Secure photographs of candidates, if they desire them, prepare and print ballots for each district.

(5) Establish polling places for each Voting District.

(6) Canvass the Model Neighborhood Area to distribute information and promote the election.

(7) Conduct the election at 18 fixed polling places and on 3 mobile units.

(8) Count votes cast, certify results, and seal ballot boxes.

(9) In the event of a tie high vote in any District, conduct a run-off election, count the votes cast therein, certify results, and seal ballot boxes for delivery to the City of Rochester, Department of Public Safety, Police Property Clerk.

B. Administer the election of 18 Organization Representatives to the Model Neighborhood Council, 9 to be elected at each of two Conventions of Neighborhood Organization Delegates. Specific activities to be undertaken in this regard include, but are not limited to, the following:

(1) Coordinate the Convention Election process with related public activities affecting the Model Neighborhood Program.

(2) Invite all Neighborhood Organizations, as defined by
the City of Rochester, within or serving the Model
Neighborhood Area to transmit request for authorization
to send a Delegate to one or both of the Conventions of
Neighborhood Organizations.

(3) Receive completed authorization requests, verify them,
certify eligible organizations.

(4) Transmit delegate authorization to eligible organizations.

(5) Conduct and administer two Conventions of Neighborhood
Organizations at times and places determined by the
City of Rochester.

(6) Count votes cast, certify results, and seal ballot boxes
for delivery to the City of Rochester, Department of
Public Safety, Police Bureau Property Clerk.

2. <u>Time of Performances</u>. The services of the Contractor are
to commence as soon as practicable after execution of this Contract
and shall be undertaken and completed in such sequence as to assure
their expeditious completion in the light of the purposes of this Contract, but in any event, all of the services required hereunder shall
be completed within sixty (60) consecutive calendar days from the
date of this Contract.

3. <u>Data to be Furnished to the Contractor.</u> The City of Rochester
shall supply the Contractor with general information concerning the
Model Neighborhood Program, promotional and informational material
supporting election activities, and the vehicles to be used as mobile
voting units.

4. <u>Compensation and Method of Payment.</u>

A. Compensation. Compensation for the services to be rendered under the terms of this Contract shall be based upon
actual costs plus fifteen (15) percent. Actual costs shall be
limited to the following expenses:

(1) Staff time, at the following rates:
        Regional Manager @$10 per hour
        Election Manager @$10 per hour
        Tribunal Administrator @$5 per hour
        Secretarial @$3 per hour

Election Clerks @$2.50 per hour
Canvassers @$2.50 per hour

(2) Arbitrator fees

(3) Printing of ballots and related materials

(4) Photographing of candidates

(5) Postage and telephone

(6) Office supplies

(7) Travel, at the following rates:
Privately owned automobile @ 12 cents per mile
Common carrier @ actual cost
Highway tolls @ actual cost

(8) Subsistence not to exceed $25 per day, with overnight
lodging to be approved in advance by the Administrator
of the Department of Urban Renewal and Economic
Development.

B. Method of Payment. The City of Rochester agrees to pay
to the Contractor the amount of his actual costs incurred
plus fifteen (15) percent, which shall constitute full and
complete compensation for the Contractor's services under
this Contract. Payment will be made upon completion of all
said services upon receipt of an invoice for payment from
the Contractor specifying that the expenses were incurred
in connection with the performance of work under this Contract and that he is entitled to receive the amount invoiced.
The Contractor agrees to keep a record of his expenses
which shall be open to inspection by the City of Rochester.

C. Maximum Compensation. It is expressly understood and
agreed that in no event will the total compensation and
reimbursement to be paid hereunder exceed the maximum
sum of Twelve Thousand Dollars ($12,000) for all of the
services required.

5. Terms and Conditions. This agreement is subject to and incorporates the provisions attached hereto as Part II, Terms and Conditions (Form HUD-7003b, dated 7-67).

IN WITNESS WHEREOF, the City of Rochester and the Contractor have executed this Contract as of the date first above written.

Attest   _____

**SAMPLE ELECTION RULES,
CITIZENS GOVERNING BOARD
OF THE MODEL NEIGHBORHOOD AREA
OF DETROIT, INC.
AND THE HEALTH COUNCIL, INC.**

American Arbitration Association
1815 H Street, N.W.
Washington, D.C.

Date: June 29, 1971   Hours: 7:00 a.m. to 8:00 p.m.

All matters pertaining to the election—qualifications, nominations, regulations, election, etc.—will be based on each Sub-Division of the Sub-Area.

OFFICES TO BE FILLED:

For the Citizens Governing Board, Inc.:

> Twenty-seven (27) positions on each of four Sub-Area Boards, a total of 108 to be elected. Nine (9) from each Sub-Division of each Sub-Area (A,B,C, and D).

For the Health Council, Inc.:

> One (1) from each Sub-Division of each Sub-Area shall be elected to the Health Council, Inc. (a City of Detroit Model Neighborhood Program).

PERSONS MAY NOT RUN FOR BOTH THE CITIZENS GOVERNING BOARD AND THE HEALTH COUNCIL.

POLLING PLACES:

There shall be a minimum of one or a maximum of three per Sub-Division of each Sub-Area, selected by each Sub-Division Board.

(Sub-Division Boards must notify the Citizens Governing Board and the Model Neighborhood Agency of the locations not later than May 20, 1971. The Model Neighborhood Agency will verify locations within two weeks, after which there will be no change in polling places.)

QUALIFICATIONS TO VOTE:

Only registered voters of the Sub-Division of the Sub-Area in which they reside will be eligible to sign petitions and vote for candidates in that Sub-Division of the Sub-Area.

VOTER REGISTRATION:

Sub-Area residents who have moved or who are not currently registered should register at the City-County Building or other authorized locations by 4:30 p.m. on or before June 4, 1971.

NOMINATIONS:

To be eligible to run for the Sub-Area Board, a candidate must:

1. Be a registered voter living for one year in the Sub-Division of the Sub-Area prior to June 4, 1971.

2. File a petition with the City Election Commission, Second Floor, City-County Building, located at Two Woodward Avenue, Detroit, Michigan 48226, by 4:30 p.m. June 17, 1971, with no less than fifty (50) valid signatures of registered voters of the Sub-Division in which the candidate is running. Petitions will also be received by the Election Commission at the CGB office, 3627 Cass Avenue, on Saturday, June 12, 1971, from 9:00 a.m. to 5.00 p.m.

3. File in person the required nomination petitions signed with no less than fifty (50) valid signatures at the City Election Commissioner's Office as provided in #2 above. He must sign the register provided.

NO PERSONS RECEIVING SALARY OR WAGES FROM MODEL CITY SUPPLEMENTAL FUNDS MAY BE A MEMBER OF THE CITIZENS GOVERNING BOARD.

This restriction applies not only to the Citizens Governing Board and Model Neighborhood Agency employees but also to the employees of any project funded in whole or in part with Model Neighborhood Supplemental Funds.

BALLOTS:

The Detroit Election Commission shall be responsible for placing
the names of all candidates eligible on the voting machines.

Incumbents (current members of the Citizens Governing Board or the
Health Council, Inc.) will be so designated on the ballot.

When there is a conflict of similarity of names, a candidate may
request ballot designation by occupation.

There shall be absentee ballots under the same conditions as in the
regular elections. No request for absentee ballots will be honored
after June 5, 1971.

There shall be no eligibility for election by write-in or sticker.

No withdrawals will be allowed after June 18, 1971.

ELECTION AND TERM:

All 108 candidates elected to the Citizens Governing Board and 12
candidates elected to the Health Council, Inc. shall serve for a TWO
year term. Members are eligible to run for re-election.

The nine candidates for the Citizens Governing Board receiving the
greater number of votes in each Sub-Division shall be deemed the
elected members of their respective Sub-Division Board.

The one candidate for the Health Council, Inc. receiving the greatest
number of votes in each Sub-Division shall be deemed the elected
member of the Health Council, Inc. from that respective Sub-Division.

"Runners-up" will fill any vacancies that may arise, in the order of
the number of votes received in the election, unless a majority of the
Sub-Division determine another method of selecting the candidate for
the vacancy. In the event that a Sub-Division does not have enough
persons running for the election to fill the positions or vacancies
which may occur, the elected Sub-Division Board may fill the vacancies
on their Sub-Division Board in any manner they determine. In the
event that a Sub-Division does not have enough persons running for
the election to fill a vacancy on the Health Council, the elected Sub-
Division Board may select a person in any manner which it determines.
Any person chosen to fill a vacancy on a Sub-Division Board or the
Health Council (either as a "runner-up" or selected by a Sub-Division
Board) must meet the qualifications of original candidates for the
election.

After the Board members have been elected, the present Vice-Chairmen of the Citizens Governing Board will convene the entire elected membership on July 8, 1971. The officers of the previous Board will serve until the new Board is organized and officers elected according to the procedures outlined in the By-Laws.

The Health Council, Inc. will convene its Board whenever the Council decides.

The American Arbitration Association will arbitrate all matters, such as, but not restricted to, eligibility of voters, eligibility of candidates, determination, by lot, of winners in the event of tie votes. Challengers of candidates for infraction of "Election Rules" will be responsible to the American Arbitration Association for proper documentation and reasonable substantiation of charges.

CHALLENGES:

Each candidate may have as many challengers for election day as there are voting places in that Sub-Division, and the official challenge cards may be picked up at the Model Neighborhood Agency, after June 21, 1971.

>   -Approved by the Citizens Govern-
>   ing Board
>   February 23, 1971.

>   -Amended by the Citizens Govern-
>   ing Board
>   March 12, May 14 and May 18, 1971

GEORGE J. WASHNIS is director of municipal studies for the Center for Governmental Studies in Washington, D.C. Prior to this he was chief administrative officer for the city of East St. Louis, Illinois, for seven years; assistant city manager for Evanston, Illinois; and held two managerial positions in private industry. He received his MGA (Master of Governmental Administration) degree from the Fels Institute, Wharton School of Business Administration, University of Pennsylvania.

Mr. Washnis has had extensive experience in public administration and has been a consultant to cities and national governmental organizations. In East St. Louis he developed a partnership between residents and City Hall which has allowed that city to continue to enjoy increased funding and progress. He has served on the International City Management Association (ICMA) Task Force on Sense of Community and Neighborhood Identity and the National League of Cities/United States Conference of Mayors Finance Committee. He is presently assisting ICMA in several projects in their quest for more effective local government.

Eighth Edition

SMALL BUSINESS MANAGEMENT

An Entrepreneurial Emphasis

Justin G. Longenecker
Baylor University

Carlos W. Moore
Baylor University

COLLEGE DIVISION South-Western Publishing Co.

CINCINNATI

Publisher: Roger L. Ross
Developmental Editor: Edward A. Parker
Production Editor: Diane Longworth Myers
Production House: WordCrafters Editorial Services, Inc.
Cover and Interior Designer: Joseph M. Devine
Marketing Manager: David L. Shaut

Cover and Part-Opener Photos © Michael Wilson

GG70HA
Copyright © 1991
by South-Western Publishing Co.
Cincinnati, Ohio

Library of Congress Cataloging-in-Publication Data

Longenecker, Justin Gooderl
    Small business management : an entrepreneurial emphasis / Justin G.
Longenecker, Carlos W. Moore. — 8th ed.
        p.   cm.
    Includes bibliographical references and index.
    ISBN 0-538-80789-X
    1. Small business—Management.   I. Moore, Carlos W.   II. Title.
HD62.7.L66   1991
658.02′2—dc20   90-9842
                                                                   CIP

        2 3 4 5 6 7 8 9 RN 7 6 5 4 3 2 1

        Printed in the United States of America

PREFACE

Small Business Management, An Entrepreneurial Emphasis, Eighth Edition, presents a thoroughly contemporary treatment of the startup and management of small firms. We have included a strong emphasis on entrepreneurial opportunities and new-venture activities needed for the successful operation of small firms. Revision highlights of this Eighth Edition include the following:

1. A new section on entrepreneurial alternatives that analyzes the various types of opportunities—startup, buyout, franchising, and family business.
2. A complete chapter (Chapter 6) devoted to preparation of a new-venture business plan.
3. A new chapter (Chapter 24) on social and ethical responsibility.
4. Expanded coverage of customer orientation and customer service in small-firm strategies.
5. Increased attention to the importance of cash flow and methods of cash management.
6. Increased emphasis on international business opportunities for small businesses.
7. Amplified discussion of tax issues pertaining to small businesses.
8. Expanded coverage of computer software applications for small businesses.
9. Discussion of legal aspects of doing business is now found in two chapters—Chapter 10, Choosing a Legal Form of Ownership, and Chapter 25, Working Within the Law.

Instructional Aids in the Textbook

Small Business Management, An Entrepreneurial Emphasis, Eighth Edition, employs numerous features to facilitate student learning. The primary learning aids included are:

1. An "opener" for each chapter (Spotlight on Small Business) that features a specific small-business firm in the context of that chapter.
2. Small Business in Action reports that dramatize text material with experiences of real-world entrepreneurs.
3. Numerous new photographs, graphs, tables, and illustrations that communicate key concepts.
4. Looking Ahead and Looking Back sections for each chapter that give a preview and review of basic chapter topics.
5. Experiential Exercises at the end of each chapter.
6. Discussion Questions for each chapter, some of which review chapter content and some of which stimulate further thinking about chapter concepts.
7. Annotated References to Small-Business Practices at the end of each chapter that identify articles describing applications of chapter topics.
8. Two short incidents at the end of each chapter (You Make the Call) that permit application of chapter concepts.
9. A group of 25 cases that present many of the practical problems involved in starting and managing a small firm.
10. A glossary of terms used in the text.

Supplementary Materials

Several supplements are also available to assist in the teaching and learning process. These include:

1. *Small Business Management Using Lotus 1-2-3,* Second Edition. This workbook and its accompanying diskette, prepared by Terry S. Maness, complement the textbook by allowing students to use a personal computer in preparing a business plan and in solving problems related to other parts of the textbook.
2. *Student Learning Guide.* This supplement presents key points of each textbook chapter, brief definitions, creative exercises, programmed self-reviews, and a series of pretests.

3. A set of 100 two-color transparencies for use in the classroom discussion of chapter material.
4. To further facilitate instruction, the instructor has available a comprehensive *Instructor's Manual.*
5. A Solutions Manual for problems in *Small Business Management Using Lotus 1-2-3.*
6. A *Test Bank,* and MicroSWAT Testing Diskettes.

Acknowledgments

In preparing the Eighth Edition, the authors have been aided by colleagues, students, business owners, and others in providing case materials and in numerous other ways. For their helpful revision suggestions, we are especially grateful to the following individuals:

Richard Benedetto
Merrimack College

Jack E. Brothers
Calvin College

George R. Butler
Michigan Technological University

Gene Gomolka
University of Dayton

Frank Hoy
University of Georgia

Daniel F. Jennings
Baylor University

Robert Kemp
Drake University

James Paradiso
College of Lake County

Nick Sarantakes
Austin Community College

James K. Seeck
William Rainey Harper College

Terri Tiedeman
Southeast Community College

Donald Wilkinson
East Tennessee State University

We especially acknowledge the contributions of Terry S. Maness and Philip R. Carpenter. We also acknowledge the assistance of Kris K. Moore in supplying material for Chapter 22, the support of Mr. and Mrs. Edwin W. Streetman and our Dean, Richard C. Scott, and the typing of Doris Kelly and Sandy Tighe. We are especially indebted to H. N. Broom for the material that was shaped by his co-authorship over the first six editions. We also appreciate the understanding and support of our wives, Frances and Gwen.

Justin G. Longenecker
Carlos W. Moore
Baylor University

CONTENTS IN BRIEF

CONTENTS

PART VII—SOCIAL AND LEGAL ENVIRONMENT

CASES

NATURE OF SMALL BUSINESS

1

ENTREPRENEURS: THE ENERGIZERS OF SMALL BUSINESS

Courtesy of Stew Leonard

Stew Leonard is an entrepreneur in every sense of the word. When the state of Connecticut decided to put a highway through his dairy farm near Norwalk, he opened a dairy products store. But it was no ordinary store. His innovative approaches to retailing produced sales per square foot that are about 10 times the national average for grocery stores. According to Tom Peters and Nancy Austin, the trick is that

> He's made it a delight to shop for chicken, cheese, eggs, and other foods. He has a petting zoo for kids. Two robot dogs sing country music, and a robot cow and farmer sing nursery rhymes. The egg department features a mechanical chicken, "the world's fastest egg layer." On one wall there are about 1,000 pictures of Stew's customers displaying the store's shopping bags. He happens now to have a picture taken under water of a

customer with a bag on a deep-sea dive, another of a Leonard regular atop the Great Wall of China.

Stew Leonard's extraordinary success as an entrepreneur has made him a celebrity of sorts. He has been featured in many books, including *A Passion for Excellence,* by Tom Peters and Nancy Austin (New York: Random House, 1985). As a result, some of his time must now be devoted to television interviews and speeches to business groups.

Source: Tom Peters and Nancy Austin, "A Passion for Excellence," *Fortune,* Vol. 111 (May 13, 1985), p. 30. Copyright by Random House, Inc. Reprinted with permission.

Looking Ahead

Watch for the following important topics:
1. Examples of highly successful entrepreneurs.
2. Rewards of entrepreneurship.
3. Personal characteristics of entrepreneurs.
4. Personal readiness for entrepreneurship.
5. The various kinds of entrepreneurship.
6. New terms and concepts:

entrepreneur	precipitating events
need for achievement	founders
internal locus of control	general managers
external locus of control	franchisees
foreign refugee	marginal firms
corporate refugee	attractive small firms
parental (paternal) refugee	high-potential ventures
feminist refugee	craftsman entrepreneur
housewife refugee	opportunistic entrepreneur
society refugee	entrepreneurial team
educational refugee	

In a private enterprise system, entrepreneurs take the risks necessary in producing goods and services. In this way, they act as energizers of the business system. Each year, thousands of individuals, from teenagers to senior citizens, launch new business firms of their own. Using methods that are innovative and competitive, they provide dynamic leadership that leads to economic progress.

Although some writers restrict the term **entrepreneur** to founders of business firms, in this text we use a broadened definition that includes all active owner-managers. This definition includes second-generation members of family-owned firms and owner-managers who buy out the founders of existing firms. However, the definition excludes salaried managers of large corporations, even those who are described as "entrepreneurial" because of their flair for innovation and their willingness to assume risk.[1]

Have you ever wondered what sorts of opportunities knock on the doors of would-be entrepreneurs? How attractive can the rewards of entrepreneurship be? Are there any special characteristics or personalities that entrepreneurs must possess in order to succeed? Is there a "right" time to plunge into entrepreneurship, or must some special events take place to trigger this plunge? What kinds of entrepreneurs are there, and what kinds of businesses do they operate? This chapter will discuss each of these questions and thereby provide an introduction to the formation and management of small firms.

Stories of Successful Entrepreneurial "Energizers"

The reality of entrepreneurial opportunities can be communicated most vividly by giving examples of a few entrepreneurs who have succeeded. Reading these brief accounts of successful ventures should give you a "feel" for the potential that you can achieve if you dream of having your own business. Even though these ventures are unique in that each became a "smashing" success, they can be highly informative. They demonstrate the continued existence of opportunities and show the vast potential for at least some new ventures. And you should realize that less spectacular business ventures can still provide highly attractive career options!

Laura Caspari/SHE (Minneapolis, MN)

As a buyer for Dayton Hudson, a department store chain, Marjory Williams conceived the idea of a boutique that would cater to professional working women like herself. She took the idea to her boss, to his boss, and even to the president, but she encountered rejection at each level.

Williams, who earned a Harvard M.B.A. after a degree in literature from Wellesley College and a teaching stint in India, then began working

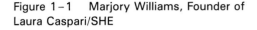

Figure 1–1   Marjory Williams, Founder of
Laura Caspari/SHE

© *Mitch Kezar*

on a business plan of her own for a boutique or possibly a whole chain of them. As she visualized it, they would create a mix of merchandise and meet the needs of busy career women and working mothers—people like herself. In March, 1979, she submitted her ten-page business plan to the First Bank of Minneapolis. A month later, she received a $90,000 loan backed by the Small Business Administration.

Williams found space in a local shopping mall for her first boutique, dubbed "SHE," and quit her job with Dayton Hudson. In her first store window, she displayed three efficient-looking suits and a copy of *The Wall Street Journal.*

The new firm prospered and was profitable in its very first month— a decidedly unusual achievement for a new business! The profits enabled Williams to open three more stores the first year. Sales grew to $500,000, and the number of employees jumped from 8 to 60. By 1989, the business had 17 stores, 140 employees, and sales of nearly $5 million!

Williams is a classic entrepreneur. She broke new ground by developing a novel idea for a new type of business. She saw its potential even though the "establishment" had no inkling of what it could become. By pursuing the idea on her own and assuming the risks associated with such an undertaking, she built the first chain of boutiques catering specifically to executive women. In doing so, she also freed herself from the constraints of corporate life and undoubtedly enriched herself financially.[2]

Federal Express (Memphis, TN)

With annual revenue in excess of $5 billion, Federal Express Corporation is no longer a small business! But Federal Express is a relatively new business, having started operations only in 1973. The company delivers parcels overnight to all major cities all over the world. Using a hub-and-spokes pattern, its planes converge on Memphis nightly with incoming freight and then fly out with shipments to their respective home bases.

Federal Express originated in the mind of Frederick W. Smith, a student at Yale.[3] In 1965, he wrote a paper for an economics course proposing a new type of air freight service. According to his thesis, later proved successful by Federal Express, a company with its own planes dedicated to freight distribution should be superior to existing freight forwarders, who were limited by the shifting schedules of passenger airlines.

Smith's professor (who surely made a name for himself in the annals of business history) pointed out the fallacy of Smith's reasoning and gave the paper a C! But entrepreneurs are not deterred by professors or others who lack their vision of the future. After his subsequent distinguished tours of military duty in Vietnam, Smith "dusted off" the idea and persuaded enough people of its potential value to obtain financial backing.

This venture has been unique in many ways. It was forced to start with a fleet of planes that could cover the entire country. The founder also came

Figure 1–2   Frederick W. Smith, Founder of Federal Express

Courtesy of Federal Express Corporation

from a wealthy family and was able, as well as willing, to risk a substantial part of the family fortune by investing several million dollars. Nevertheless, the capital requirements were great, and Smith found it necessary to obtain the major portion of the financing from the venture capital industry. Ultimately, over a dozen equity groups participated in three major rounds of financing.

Although the startup is unusual in many ways, it is especially significant in showing the ability of one person, a potential entrepreneur, to conceptualize an entirely new type of business by studying business methods and new trends. Smith's concept was implemented so successfully that it changed the very way in which business in America communicates and ships its freight.

Proctor and Gardner Advertising (Chicago, IL)

After earning an English degree at a small Alabama college, Barbara Gardner Proctor found a job as an advertising copywriter in Chicago.[4] As she gained experience in advertising, she also developed an appreciation

Figure 1–3   Barbara Gardner Proctor, Founder of Proctor and Gardner Advertising

Proctor & Gardner Advertising Inc.

for quality in advertising. One particular concept suggested for a TV commercial struck her as tasteless and offensive, and this difference of opinion led to her being fired.

Following her dismissal, Proctor applied to the Small Business Administration for a loan. She obtained $80,000 in this way and promptly opened her own agency in 1970.

Proctor and Gardner Advertising is still relatively small among advertising agencies, but it is well established and respected (having almost $15 million in billings in 1988). It specializes in advertising targeted to the black community and counts Kraft Foods and Sears among its clients. And Chicago's big Jewel Food Stores chain credits Proctor with helping make its generic foods campaign a success in 1978.

Barbara Gardner Proctor, as an entrepreneur in the area of business services, selected a strategic niche in which she could compete effectively. She also demonstrated the ability of black women to function successfully in independent business careers, once considered to be largely the province of white males.

Unlimited Entrepreneurial Opportunities

In a private enterprise system, any individual is free to enter business for himself or herself. In this chapter thus far, we have read of four different kinds of persons who took that step—a milkman in Connecticut, a department store buyer in Minneapolis, a wealthy heir in Memphis, and an advertising copywriter in Chicago. In contrast to many others who have tried and failed, these individuals achieved outstanding success.

At any time, such potentially profitable opportunities exist in the environment. But these opportunities must be recognized and grasped by individuals with abilities and desire that are strong enough to assure success. The examples cited here can help you visualize the wide variety of opportunities that awaits you. Of course, there are thousands of variations and alternatives for independent business careers. In fact, you may achieve great success in business endeavors that are far different from those described here. In these varied types of entrepreneurship, there are a number of potential rewards. We turn now to a consideration of these benefits.

Rewards and Weaknesses of Entrepreneurship

Individuals are *pulled* toward entrepreneurship by various powerful incentives, or rewards (Exhibit 1–1). These rewards may be grouped, for the

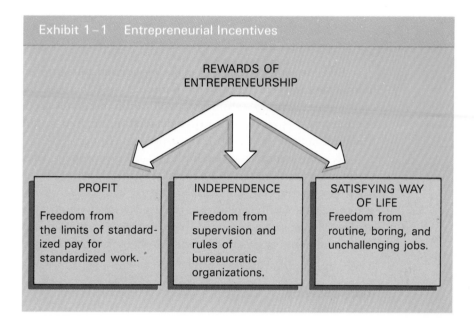

Exhibit 1–1 Entrepreneurial Incentives

REWARDS OF
ENTREPRENEURSHIP

PROFIT	INDEPENDENCE	SATISFYING WAY OF LIFE
Freedom from the limits of standardized pay for standardized work.	Freedom from supervision and rules of bureaucratic organizations.	Freedom from routine, boring, and unchallenging jobs.

sake of simplicity, into three basic categories: profit, independence, and a satisfying life-style.

Profit

The financial return of any business must compensate its owner for investing his or her personal time (a salary equivalent) and personal savings (an interest and/or dividend equivalent) in the business before any "true" profits are realized. All entrepreneurs expect a return that will not only compensate them for the time and money they invest, but also reward them *well* for the risks and initiative they take in operating their own businesses. Not surprisingly, however, the profit incentive is a more powerful motivator for some entrepreneurs than for others. For example, people like Billy J. (Red) McCombs of San Antonio, TX, have a rather simple objective of making as much money as they can. Even as a boy, Red McCombs possessed an obvious entrepreneurial instinct, as noted by one writer's account:

This single-mindedness baffled and sometimes distressed his gentle, middle-class parents. "When I was 11, I'd wash dishes in a cafe downtown from 4 p.m. until midnight and deliver newspapers at 5 a.m.," he recalls. "My mother would get tears in her eyes. 'You don't need to do this,' she'd say, and of course she was right. My father was an auto mechanic and we never wanted for anything. But I wanted to make money."[5]

Red McCombs' desire to make money led him into many entrepreneurial ventures. He has ownership interests in a chain of 100 Mr. M convenience stores, 7 radio stations, oil exploration in 2 states, a contract drilling company, real estate, a Rolls-Royce dealership, and San Antonio's NBA (National Basketball Association) franchise—the Spurs.

Red McCombs is an example of an entrepreneur who possesses an extremely strong interest in financial rewards. However, there are also those for whom profits are primarily a way of "keeping score." Such entrepreneurs may spend their profit on themselves or give it away, although most of them are not satisfied unless they make a "reasonable" profit. Indeed, some profit is necessary for survival because a firm that continues to lose money eventually becomes insolvent.

Independence

Freedom to operate independently is another basic reward of entrepreneurship. We know that the United States has long been known as a nation of rugged individualists. Many of us have a strong, even fierce, desire to make our own decisions, take risks, and reap the rewards for ourselves. Being one's own boss seems an attractive ideal.

The entrepreneurial desire for independence is evident in the experiences of entrepreneurs who sell out to large corporations and then stay on to run their firms as divisions of such corporations. Although some make the necessary adjustment, most find happiness elusive in these circumstances.

One entrepreneur who did not adjust well to the constraints of corporate life is Irwin Selinger. Selinger sold his medical supplies business to Squibb Corporation and continued on as chief executive. Following is a description of the conflict between this independent entrepreneur and the corporation:

> "No one was a more gung-ho Squibb man than I was. I mean, my wife wore Opium perfume because it was made by a Squibb subsidiary."
> Within months, the perfume didn't smell so sweet. A company officer criticized Selinger for flying coach, cautioning him that corporate executives flew first class. Then Selinger initiated an acquisition without so much as convening a committee. "I just went to the company president and said, 'Let's make a deal.'" Squibb was appalled. So was Selinger—at Squibb's reaction. "There are no bad guys in this story, just two cultures, two irreconcilable mentalities," he says.[6]

As a result of these differences, Selinger left Squibb Corporation and started a new firm with a line of medical instruments that Squibb had turned down. He was once again his own boss.

Of course, independence does not guarantee an easy life. Most entrepreneurs work very hard for long hours. But they do have the satisfaction of making their own decisions within the constraints imposed by economic and other environmental factors.

A Satisfying Way of Life

Entrepreneurs frequently speak of the personal satisfaction they experience in their own businesses. Some even refer to business as "fun." Part of this enjoyment may derive from the independence described above, but some of it also apparently comes from the peculiar nature of the business, the entrepreneur's role in the business, and the entrepreneur's opportunities to be of service.

After retiring from military service in 1981, Roger Craig and his wife

Figure 1–4   A Satisfying Way of Life Is One Reward for Entrepreneurship

Jean visited friends in Texas and helped them clear mesquite trees from their ranch.[7] After discovering that restaurants would buy this type of wood, they began cutting mesquite trees from other ranches and selling the cord wood, briquets, and chips to restaurants in the United States, Europe, Japan, and Australia. Although they now employ a number of people to cut and process the wood, both Roger and Jean are actively involved in and enjoying what they call the "leisurely-paced outdoor work," even though they work 10 hours a day, 6 days a week. They explained their enjoyment as follows:

> *Jean:* "We don't think about the time because its our own business. We both decided that we were going to do what we wanted to do."

> *Roger:* "It's something that we really get a kick out of. We wake up every morning looking forward to the next adventure in the mesquite business."

Weaknesses of Entrepreneurship

Although the rewards of entrepreneurship are enticing, there are also drawbacks and costs associated with business ownership. Starting and operating one's own business typically demand hard work, long hours, and much emotional energy. Many entrepreneurs describe their careers as exciting but very demanding. In fact, the strain of running a business is often listed as a reason for the breakup of entrepreneurial families.

The possibility of business failure is a constant threat to entrepreneurs. No one guarantees success or agrees to bail out a failing owner. As noted later in this chapter, entrepreneurs must assume a variety of risks related to failure. No one likes to be a loser, but that is always a possibility for one who starts a business.

In deciding upon an entrepreneurial career, therefore, you should look at both positive and negative aspects. The dangers noted here call for a degree of commitment and some sacrifice on your part if you expect to reap the rewards.

Characteristics of Entrepreneurs

Entrepreneurs have some qualities that distinguish them from the general population and even from professional managers. Researchers have emphasized such qualities as the need for achievement, willingness to take risks, self-confidence, and the need to seek refuge from any of various environmental factors. However, research on this topic is far from definitive, and statements that identify entrepreneurial characteristics should be taken somewhat tentatively. Furthermore, since there are exceptions to every rule, some "unlikely" prospects may turn out to be highly successful entrepreneurs.

High Need for Achievement

Psychologists recognize that people differ in the degree of their need for achievement. Individuals with a low need for achievement are those who seem to be contented with their present status. On the other hand, individuals with a high **need for achievement** like to compete with some standard of excellence and prefer to be personally responsible for their own assigned tasks.

A leader in the study of achievement motivation is David C. McClelland, a Harvard psychologist.[8] He discovered a positive correlation between the need for achievement and entrepreneurial activity. According to McClelland, those who become entrepreneurs have, on the average, a higher need for achievement than do members of the general population. Even among entrepreneurs, there are differences in achievement needs. Entrepreneurs heading faster-growing firms appear to have higher achievement needs than both nonentrepreneurs and entrepreneurs in slow-growth firms.[9]

This drive for achievement is reflected in the ambitious individuals who start new firms and then guide them in their growth. In some families, such entrepreneurial drive is evident at a very early stage. For example, sometimes a child takes a paper route, subcontracts it to a younger brother or sister, and then tries another venture. Also, some college students take over or start various types of student-related businesses or businesses that can be operated while pursuing an academic program.

Willingness to Take Risks

The risks that entrepreneurs take in starting and/or operating their own businesses are varied. Patrick R. Liles, a former Harvard professor, has identified four critical risk areas.[10] These are:

1. *Financial risk*. Entrepreneurs invest their savings and guarantee their bank loans.
2. *Career risk*. Entrepreneurs who fail may find it difficult to find employment afterward.

3. *Family risk.* The entrepreneur's spouse and children may suffer from inattention and the emotional stress of coping with a business failure.
4. *Psychic risk.* The entrepreneur may be identified so closely with a venture that he or she takes business failure as a personal failure.

David C. McClelland discovered in his studies that individuals with a high need for achievement also have moderate risk-taking propensities.[11] This means that they prefer risky situations in which they can exert some control on the outcome, in contrast to gambling situations in which the outcome depends on pure luck. This preference for moderate risk reflects self-confidence, the next entrepreneurial characteristic that will be discussed.

Self-Confidence

Individuals who possess self-confidence feel they can meet the challenges that confront them. They have a sense of mastery over the types of problems they might encounter. Studies show that successful entrepreneurs tend to be self-reliant individuals who see the problems in launching a new venture but believe in their own ability to overcome these problems.

Some studies of entrepreneurs have measured the extent to which they are confident of their own abilities. According to J. B. Rotter, a psychologist, those who believe that their success depends upon their own efforts have an **internal locus of control.** In contrast, those who feel that their lives are controlled to a greater extent by luck or chance or fate have an **external locus of control.**[12] On the basis of research to date, it appears that entrepreneurs have a higher internal locus of control than is true of the population in general but that they may not differ significantly from other managers on this point.

A Need to Seek Refuge

Although most people go into business to obtain the rewards of entrepreneurship discussed earlier, there are some who become entrepreneurs to escape from some environmental factor. Professor Russell M. Knight of the University of Western Ontario has identified a number of environmental factors that encourage or "push" people to found new firms and has labeled such entrepreneurs as "refugees."[13]

In thinking about these kinds of "refugees," we should recognize that many entrepreneurs are motivated as much or more by entrepreneurial rewards than by an "escapist" mind set. Indeed, there is often a mixture of positive and negative considerations in this regard. Nevertheless, this characterization of some entrepreneurs as "refugees" does help clarify some important considerations involved in much entrepreneurial activity.

The "Foreign Refugee"   There are many individuals who escape the political, religious, or economic constraints of their homelands by crossing national boundaries. Frequently such individuals face discrimination or handicaps in seeking salaried employment in the new country. As a result, many of them go into business for themselves. For example, Chris Nguyen came to the United States from South Vietnam at the age of 18 with no capital, no knowledge of business, and only a minimal proficiency in English.[14] After studying chemical engineering and business, he quit school in 1971 to start his own business. With a brother and sister, he founded a business to make Oriental eggrolls that he believed were far superior to those being sold in the United States. By 1984, the company was achieving sales of $4 million.

The "Corporate Refugee"   Individuals who flee the bureaucratic environment of big business (or even medium-size business) by going into business for themselves are identified by Professor Knight as **corporate refugees.** Some corporations spawn so many entrepreneurial offspring that they are described as "incubator organizations." For example, the Silicon Valley, a section south of San Francisco, CA, is populated by small electronic firms that have been "spun off" from large companies or otherwise started by corporate refugees.

Other "Refugees"   Other types of "refugees" mentioned by Professor Knight are the following:

1. The **parental (paternal) refugee** who leaves a family business to show the parent that "I can do it alone."
2. The **feminist refugee** who experiences discrimination and elects to start a firm in which she can operate independently of male chauvinists.
3. The **housewife refugee** who starts her own business after her family is grown or at some other point when she can free herself from household responsibilities.
4. The **society refugee** who senses some alienation from the prevailing culture and expresses it by indulging in entrepreneurial activity—selling paintings to tourists or operating an energy-saving business.

Figure 1–5   The Entrepreneur as ''Refugee''

By permission of Johnny Hart and Creators Syndicate

> **5.** The **educational refugee** who tires of an academic program and
> decides to go into business.

Readiness for Entrepreneurship

Many people think about getting into business for themselves but are
waiting for the right opportunity to come along. Others become so well
established in careers that they tend to get "locked into" salaried employment. No doubt many individuals look back over their careers as salaried
personnel, thinking of "what might have been" if only they had gone into
business for themselves, but recognize that it is now too late.

Age and Entrepreneurial Opportunity

Education and experience are a part of the necessary preparation for
most entrepreneurs. Although requirements vary with the nature and demands of a particular business, some type of "knowhow" is required. In
addition, prospective entrepreneurs must build their financial resources in
order to make initial investments.

Even though there are no hard and fast rules concerning the right age
for starting a business, some age deterrents exist. As Exhibit 1–2 shows,
young people are discouraged from entering entrepreneurial careers by in-
adequacies in preparation and resources. On the other hand, older people
develop family, financial, and job commitments that make entrepreneur-

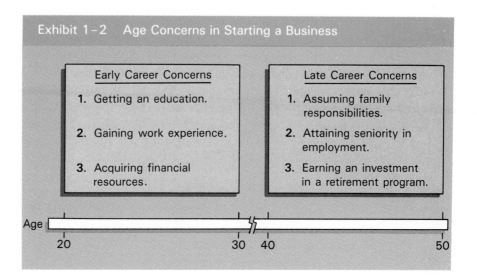

Exhibit 1-2   Age Concerns in Starting a Business

Early Career Concerns	Late Career Concerns
1. Getting an education.	1. Assuming family responsibilities.
2. Gaining work experience.	2. Attaining seniority in employment.
3. Acquiring financial resources.	3. Earning an investment in a retirement program.

Age

20   30   40   50

ship seem too risky. They acquire interests in retirement programs and achieve promotion to positions of greater responsibility and higher salaries.

The ideal time appears to lie somewhere between these two periods, perhaps from the late 20s to the early 40s, when there is a balance between preparatory experiences on the one hand and family obligations on the other. Obviously, there are exceptions to this generalization. Some teenagers start their own firms. And other persons, even at 50 or 60 years of age, walk away from successful careers in big business when they become excited by the prospects of entrepreneurship.

Precipitating Events

As suggested earlier, many potential entrepreneurs never take the fateful step of launching their own business ventures. Some of those who actually make the move are stimulated by **precipitating events** such as job termination, job dissatisfaction, or unexpected opportunities.

Charles E. Van Vorst has described how his dismissal from a large corporation caused him to start a small landscaping business.[15] After his executive job was abolished, he spent more than a year unsuccessfully seeking employment elsewhere and suffering the humiliation of standing in line for unemployment compensation. Finally, he started helping his two sons, who had a weekend landscaping route. He enjoyed the work and began to build the route into a full-time business of his own, adding customer after customer as the weeks went by. His dismissal from corporate life had triggered his entry into a personally owned business.

Getting fired is only one of many types of experiences that may serve as a catalyst to "taking the plunge" as an entrepreneur. Some individuals become so disenchanted with formal academic programs that they simply walk away from the classroom and start new lives as entrepreneurs. Others become exasperated with the rebuffs or perceived injustices at the hands of superiors in large organizations and leave in disgust to start their own businesses.

In a more positive vein, prospective entrepreneurs may unexpectedly stumble across business opportunities. A friend may offer, for example, to sponsor an individual as an Amway distributor. Or a relative may suggest that the individual leave a salaried position and take over a family business.

Many prospective entrepreneurs, of course, simply plan for and seek out independent business opportunities. There is little in the way of a precipitating event involved in their decision to become entrepreneurs. We cannot say what proportion of new entrepreneurs make their move because of some particular event. However, many who launch new firms or otherwise go into business for themselves are obviously helped along by precipitating events.[16]

Preparation for Entrepreneurial Careers

Proper preparation for entrepreneurship requires some mixture of education and experience. How much or what kind of each is necessary is notoriously difficult to specify. Different types of ventures call for different types of preparation. The background or skills needed to start a company to produce computer software are obviously different from those needed to open an automobile garage. There are also striking differences in the backgrounds of those who succeed in the same industry. For these reasons, we must be cautious in discussing qualifications, realizing there are exceptions to every rule.

Some fascinating entrepreneurial success stories feature individuals who dropped out of school to start their ventures. This should not lead one to conclude, however, that education is generally unimportant. As shown in Exhibit 1–3, the formal education of new owners is superior to that of the general adult public. This suggests that one should not expect success based on a substandard education.

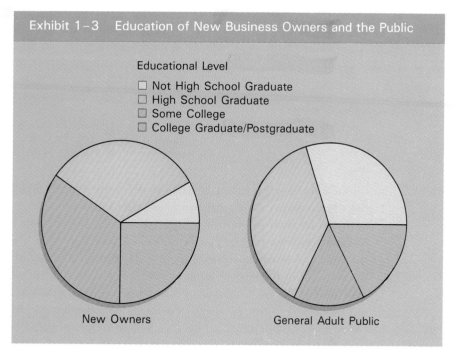

Exhibit 1-3   Education of New Business Owners and the Public

Educational Level

☐ Not High School Graduate
☐ High School Graduate
☐ Some College
☐ College Graduate/Postgraduate

New Owners   General Adult Public

Source: Data developed and provided by the NFIB Foundation and sponsored by the American Express Travel Related Services Company, Inc.

In recent years, colleges and universities have greatly expanded their offerings in entrepreneurship and small business. The Wharton School was the first to offer a degree in entrepreneurship (in 1973), and in 1988 it had 750 students taking entrepreneurship classes.[17] Karl Vesper, an authority on entrepreneurship education, has estimated that between 7,000 and 10,000 students across the country are taking how-to-start-your-own-business courses. The usefulness of such courses is debated, some holding that entrepreneurs are born and not made or that early childhood influences are more important than education. Those who offer entrepreneurship courses believe that small-business education can contribute positively even though it will not be perfectly correlated with success.

What do business owners themselves perceive to be the contributors to success in small business? A study by A. B. Ibrahim and J. R. Goodwin identified three general factors that business owners regarded as important.[18] These factors were as follows:

1. *Entrepreneurial values* (including intuition, extroversion, risk taking, creativity, flexibility, a sense of independence, and a high value of time).
2. *Managerial skills* (including a niche strategy, effective management of cash flow, a simple but efficient budgetary system, preownership experience, education, and a simple organization structure).
3. *Interpersonal skills* (including a good relationship with a credit officer or banker, good customer relations, and good employee relations).

Even though it is not possible to delineate educational and experiential requirements with great precision, we urge prospective entrepreneurs to maximize their preparation within the limits of their time and resources. At best, however, such preparation can never completely prepare one for the world of business ownership. Warren Buffett, the noted investor, has expressed it in this way: "Could you really explain to a fish what it's like to walk on land? One day on land is worth a thousand years of talking about it, and one day running a business has exactly the same kind of value."[19]

The message seems to be this: Get as much relevant education and experience as you can, but realize that you will still need a lot of on-the-job entrepreneurial training.

Kinds of Entrepreneurship

The field of small business encompasses a great variety of entrepreneurs and entrepreneurial ventures. In this section, we examine this spectrum of entrepreneurship by identifying the varied types of people and firms that exist.

Women Entrepreneurs

The number of women becoming entrepreneurs has risen dramatically during the last two decades. Newspapers and business and news magazines frequently feature women as successful entrepreneurs.[20] From 1980 to 1985, the number of women-owned proprietorships increased 47.4 percent, to a total of 3.7 million or 28.1 percent of all such businesses.[21] Women's business ownership has been expanding much more rapidly than men's business ownership, but we must remember that women are expanding from a smaller base of ownership.

Women are not only starting more businesses than previously, but they are also starting businesses in nontraditional industries and starting them with ambitious plans for growth and profit. Not too many years ago, women entrepreneurs confined themselves, for the most part, to operating beauty shops, small clothing stores, or other establishments regarded as women's work. Even though most women's business starts are still in services, women's ownership of mining, construction, and manufacturing businesses increased by 116.3 percent between 1980 and 1985.[22]

As an example of a woman entrepreneur in a nontraditional area, Nona J. Cunane runs a $6 million-a-year Delaware company that is involved in construction, environmental cleanup, and equipment leasing.[23] When she graduated from high school, she started work for DuPont and held secretarial and administrative positions there for a number of years. After the birth of her third child, however, her husband Joe, partner in a construction business, encouraged her to go into business for herself. She started by submitting a winning bid on a lawn-maintenance job for DuPont. She did the work herself and grossed $25,000 the first year. Today, her business has 120 employees (including her husband), and she is an obvious success in a male-dominated field. Having invested heavily in equipment and human resources in the early days of the business, her stated goal now is to make money—not merely to be profitable, but to be *very* profitable!

Women entrepreneurs obviously face problems common to all entrepreneurs. However, they must also contend with difficulties associated with their newness in entrepreneurial roles. Lack of access to credit has been a problem frequently cited by women who enter business. This is a troublesome area for most small-business owners, but many women entrepreneurs feel they carry an added burden of discrimination. Loan officers point out that women applicants often lack a "track record" in financial management and argue that this creates problems in approving loans. Even so, women find it irritating to be told by bankers that their husbands must countersign or that the bank does not finance hobbies such as they are proposing. Solution of this problem will require further education and experience on the part of loan officers in working with women entrepreneurs, as well as thorough preparation by women in defending financing proposals submitted to skeptical lenders. Many women have succeeded in spite of the annoyances and sex stereotyping they have faced. One winner expressed her con-

fidence this way: "Since I started the business in 1975, I have only been called 'honey' once. . . . I fired him!"[24]

Another barrier for some women is the limited opportunity they find for business relationships with others in similar positions. It takes time and effort for them to gain full acceptance and to develop informal relationships with others in local, mostly male, business and professional groups. Women are attacking this problem by increasing their participation in predominantly male organizations and also by forming networks of their own—a female equivalent of the "old boy network."

Founders and Other Entrepreneurs

Although categories tend to overlap, entrepreneurial leadership may be classified into three types: founders, general managers, and franchisees.

Founding Entrepreneurs   Generally considered to be the "pure" entrepreneurs, **founders** may be inventors who initiate businesses on the basis of new or improved products or services. They may also be craftsmen who develop skills and then start their own firms. Or they may be enterprising individuals, often with marketing backgrounds, who draw upon the ideas of others in starting new firms. Whether acting as individuals or in groups, these people bring firms into existence by surveying the market, raising funds, and arranging for the necessary facilities. After the firm is launched, the founding entrepreneur may preside over the subsequent growth of the business or sell out and move on to other ventures.

General Managers   As new firms become well established, founders become less innovators and more administrators. Thus, we recognize another class of entrepreneurs called **general managers.** General managers preside over the operation of successful ongoing business firms. They manage the week-to-week and month-to-month production, marketing, and financial functions of small firms. The distinction between founders and general managers is often hazy. In some cases, small firms grow rapidly, and their orientation is more akin to the founding than to the management process. Nevertheless, it is helpful to distinguish those entrepreneurs who found and substantially change firms (the "movers" and "shakers") from those who direct the continuing operations of established firms.

Franchisees   It is helpful to recognize a third category of entrepreneurs—that of the franchisee. **Franchisees** differ from general managers in the degree of their independence. Because of the constraints and guidance provided by contractual relationships with franchising organizations, franchisees function as limited entrepreneurs. Chapter 4 presents more information about franchisees.

High-growth and Low-growth Firms

Small-business ventures differ greatly in their potential for growth and profits. Some create millionaires, while others produce less spectacular results. To account for these differences, we may distinguish firms according to the following categories: marginal firms, attractive small companies, and high-potential ventures. In thinking about small business, one can easily fall into the trap of considering only one end of the spectrum. Some writers treat only the tiny, marginal firms whose owners barely survive, while others focus entirely on high-growth, high-technology firms. A balanced view must recognize the entire range of ventures with the varied problems and rewards presented by each point on the spectrum.

Marginal Firms   Very small dry cleaners, independent garages, beauty shops, service stations, appliance repair shops, and other small firms that provide a very modest return to their owners are the **marginal firms.** We do not call them "marginal" because they are in danger of bankruptcy. Some marginal firms, it is true, are on "thin ice" financially, but their distinguishing feature is their limited ability to generate significant profits. Entrepreneurs devote personal effort to such ventures and receive a profit return that does little more than compensate them for their time. Part-time businesses typically fall into this category of marginal firms.

Attractive Small Companies   In contrast to marginal firms, numerous **attractive small firms** offer substantial rewards to their owners. Entrepreneurial income from these ventures may easily range from $50,000 to $200,000 annually. These are the strong segment of small business—the "good" firms that can provide rewarding careers even to well-educated young people.

High-Potential Ventures   A few firms have such great prospects for growth that they may be called **high-potential ventures.** Frequently these are also high-technology ventures. At the time of the firm's founding, the owners often anticipate rapid growth, a possible merger, or "going public" within a few years. Some of the more spectacular examples within recent years include Digital Equipment Corporation, Polaroid, Amway Corporation, and Wendy's. In addition to such widely recognized successes, there are at any time thousands of less-well-known ventures being launched and experiencing rapid growth. Entrepreneurial ventures of this type appeal to many engineers, professional managers, and venture capitalists who see the potential rewards and exciting prospects.

Craftsman Entrepreneurs and Opportunistic Entrepreneurs

Perhaps because of their varied backgrounds, entrepreneurs display great variation in their styles of doing business. They analyze problems and approach decision making in drastically different ways. Norman R. Smith has suggested two basic entrepreneurial patterns: craftsman entrepreneurs and opportunistic entrepreneurs.[25]

The Craftsman Entrepreneur   According to Smith, the education of the **craftsman entrepreneur** is limited to technical training. Such entrepreneurs

---

SMALL BUSINESS IN ACTION
Handcrafted Crystal—Craftsman Entrepreneur

One type of entrepreneurship is that of the craftsman who operates a business. Handcrafted crystal is the basis for such a business operated by Jim and Kim Maxwell in Tiffin, OH. Jim had earlier worked for Tiffin Glass, cutting intricate designs in glass, but Tiffin closed its doors, a casualty of the plastics revolution.

When Jim Maxwell became unemployed, he and Kim decided to open a small glassmaking shop. They remodeled a storefront building, complete with a nursery for their youngest child. They hired one full-time employee, a veteran glassblower who had also worked for Tiffin.

Jim's orientation toward craftsmanship is evident in his remark that "I think basically I just have a tremendous attraction to craftsmanship of any kind." The business succeeded; they expected to achieve a $100,000 sales volume in 1986. They have purchased part of the old Tiffin glassworks and have plans to add skilled craftspeople as they expand this business.

Source: Gene Logsdon, "Cutting It With Glass," *In Business*, Vol. 8, No. 1 (January–February, 1986), pp. 26–28.

have technical job experience, but they lack good communication skills. Their approach to business decision making is characterized by the following features:

CRAFTMAN Entrepreneurs

1. They are paternalistic. (This means they direct their businesses much as they might direct their own families.)
2. They are reluctant to delegate authority.
3. They use few (one or two) capital sources to create their firms.
4. They define marketing strategy in terms of the traditional price, quality, and company reputation.
5. Their sales efforts are primarily personal.
6. Their time orientation is short, with little planning for future growth or change.

The mechanic who starts an independent garage and the beautician who operates a beauty shop illustrate the craftsman entrepreneur.

The Opportunistic Entrepreneur   Smith's definition of the **opportunistic entrepreneur** is one who has supplemented technical education by studying such nontechnical subjects as economics, law, or English. Opportunistic entrepreneurs avoid paternalism, delegate authority as necessary for growth, employ various marketing strategies and types of sales efforts, obtain original capitalization from more than two sources, and plan for future growth. An example of the opportunistic entrepreneur is the small building contractor and developer who uses a relatively sophisticated approach to management. Because of the complexity of the industry, successful contractors use careful record keeping, proper budgeting, precise bidding, and systematic marketing research.

In Smith's model of entrepreneurial styles, we see two extremes of managerial approach. At one end, we find a craftsman in an entrepreneurial position. At the other end, we find a well-educated and experienced manager. The former flies "by the seat of his pants," and the latter uses systematic management procedures and something resembling a scientific management approach. In practice, of course, the distribution of entrepreneurial styles is less polarized than suggested by the model, with entrepreneurs scattered along a continuum in terms of their managerial sophistication. This book is intended to help the student move toward the opportunistic end and away from the craftsman end of the continuum.

Entrepreneurial Teams

In the discussion thus far, we have assumed that entrepreneurs are individuals. And, of course, this is usually the case. However, the entrepreneurial team is another possibility that is becoming popular, particularly in ventures of substantial size. An **entrepreneurial team** is formed by bringing together two or more individuals to function in the capacity of entrepreneurs.

By forming a team, founders can secure a broader range of managerial talents than is otherwise possible. For example, a person with manufacturing experience can team up with a person who has marketing experience. The need for such diversified experience is particularly acute in creating new high-technology businesses.

One study of 890 company founders found that 39.1 percent had one or more full-time partners.[26] Even though the study underrepresented very small firms, it does suggest that founding teams are not unusual.

Looking Back

1. Entrepreneurial opportunities are unlimited, as evidenced by various dramatic success stories of successful entrepreneurs.
2. Entrepreneurial rewards include profits, independence, and a satisfying way of life.
3. Individuals who become entrepreneurs have a high need for achievement, a willingness to take moderate risks, and a high degree of self-confidence.
4. The period between a person's late 20s and early 40s is the period in which entry into entrepreneurial careers tends to be easiest. Although individuals prepare for entrepreneurship by gaining education and experience, their entry into business is often triggered by precipitating events such as losing a job.
5. Entrepreneurship includes various kinds of entrepreneurs (women entrepreneurs, founding entrepreneurs, general manager entrepreneurs, franchisees, craftsmen entrepreneurs, opportunistic entrepreneurs, and entrepreneurial teams) and various kinds of ventures (marginal firms, attractive small firms, and high-potential ventures).

DISCUSSION QUESTIONS

1. What is meant by the term entrepreneur?
2. When we read the outstanding success stories at the beginning of the chapter, we realize they are exceptions to the rule. What, then, is their significance in illustrating entrepreneurial opportunity? Are these stories misleading?
3. Some corporate executives receive annual compensation in excess of $3 million. Profits of most small businesses are much less. How, then, can profits constitute a meaningful incentive for entrepreneurs?
4. What is the most significant reason for following an independent business career by the entrepreneur whom you know best?
5. The rewards of profit, independence, and a satisfying way of life attract individuals to entrepreneurial careers. What problems might be anticipated if an entrepreneur were to become obsessed with one of these rewards, that is, have an excessive desire for profit or independence or a satisfying way of life?
6. In view of the fact that entrepreneurs must satisfy customers, employees, bankers, and others, are they really independent? Explain the nature of their independence as a reward for self-employment.
7. What is shown by the studies of David C. McClelland regarding an entrepreneur's need for achievement?
8. What types of risks are faced by entrepreneurs, and what degree of risks do they prefer?
9. Explain the internal locus of control and its significance for entrepreneurship.
10. Compare the advantages and dangers of an extremely strong internal locus of control in a heavyweight fighter such as Mike Tyson and in an entrepreneur.
11. On the basis of your own knowledge, can you identify a "foreign refugee" who is an entrepreneur?
12. What are the societal implications of the growth trend in women's entrepreneurship?
13. Why is the period from the late 20s to the early 40s in a person's life considered to be the best time for becoming an entrepreneur?
14. What is a precipitating event? Give some examples.
15. What is the difference between a marginal firm and a high-potential venture?
16. Distinguish between a craftsman entrepreneur and an opportunistic entrepreneur.
17. What is the advantage of using an entrepreneurial team?

YOU MAKE THE CALL

Situation 1

Following is a statement of an entrepreneur in which he attempts to explain and justify his orientation toward slow growth in his business:

> I limit my growth pace and make every effort to service my present customers in the manner they deserve. I have some peer pressure to do otherwise by following the advice of experts—that is, to take on partners and debt to facilitate rapid growth in sales and market share. When tempted by such thoughts, I think about what I might gain. Perhaps I could make more money, but I would also expect a lot more problems. Also, I think it might interfere somewhat with my family relationships, which are very important to me.

Questions
1. Should this venture be regarded as entrepreneurial? Is the owner a true entrepreneur?
2. Do you admire or dislike the philosophy expressed here? Is the owner really doing what is best for his family?
3. What kinds of problems is this owner avoiding?

Situation 2

After growing up in the service station business, Amy Clark would like to have a station of her own. Her father had owned several service stations where she learned to pump gas and developed some knowledge of station operation. When she graduated from high school, she entered business college and trained to be a secretary. She married soon after school, and her husband also entered the service station business. A station with three service bays and facilities for minor auto repair is available if she can persuade the oil company that she is qualified to have a franchise.

Clark has expressed her philosophy as follows: "I'm a person who likes to get things done. I like to keep excelling and do bigger and better things than I've ever done before. I guess that's why I'd like to have a station of my own."

Questions
1. Evaluate Amy Clark's qualifications for the proposed venture. Should the oil company accept her as a dealer?

2. As a woman entrepreneur, what problems may she anticipate in relationships with customers, employees, the sponsoring oil company, and her family?

EXPERIENTIAL EXERCISES

1. Analyze your own education and experience as qualifications for entrepreneurship. Identify your greatest strengths and weaknesses.

2. Explain your own interest in each entrepreneurial reward—profit, independence, satisfying way of life, or other. Point out which of these is most significant for you personally and tell why.

3. Interview one entrepreneur who has started a business, asking for information regarding that entrepreneur's background and age at the time the business was started. In the report of your interview, show whether the entrepreneur was in any sense a "refugee" and how the timing of the startup related to the "ideal" time explained in this chapter.

4. Interview a female entrepreneur and report on what problems, if any, she has encountered because she is a woman.

REFERENCES TO SMALL-BUSINESS PRACTICES

Bacas, Harry. "Leaving the Corporate Nest." *Nation's Business,* Vol. 75, No. 3 (March, 1987), pp. 14–22.
> An account of several successful businesses started by fugitives from corporate life.

Feinberg, Andrew. "Inside the Entrepreneur." *Venture,* Vol. 6, No. 5 (May, 1984), pp. 80–86.
> A psychological study of 77 individuals, all of whom ran businesses that gave them personal incomes of $90,000 or more, is reported.

Lofflin, John. "A Burst of Rural Enterprise." *The New York Times* (January 3, 1988), Section 3.
> A description of a number of farm women who are setting up small businesses to supplement sagging farm incomes.

Nelton, Sharon. "The People Who Take the Plunge." *Nation's Business,* Vol. 72, No. 6 (June, 1984), pp. 22–26.
> Characteristics of entrepreneurs are illustrated by citing examples of specific individuals. The article also includes a test that purportedly measures the qualities of the successful entrepreneur.

"What Do Women Want? A Company They Can Call Their Own." *Business Week,* No. 2978 (December 22, 1986), pp. 60–62.
> A description of several firms that have been started and are being successfully operated by women entrepreneurs.

ENDNOTES

1. For an extended discussion of the nature of entrepreneurship, see John G. Burch, *Entrepreneurship* (New York: John Wiley & Sons, 1986), Chapter 1; also see Justin G. Longenecker and John E. Schoen, "The Essence of Entrepreneurship," *Journal of Small Business Management,* Vol. 13 (July, 1975), pp. 26–32.

2. Dyan Machan, "Taking Charge," *Forbes,* Vol. 143, No. 5 (March 6, 1989), pp. 154–156.

3. The account given here is drawn from a number of different sources. One particularly helpful source is "Frederick W. Smith of Federal Express: He Didn't Get There Overnight," *Inc.,* Vol. 6, No. 4 (April, 1984), pp. 88–89.

4. This story of Barbara Gardner Proctor is reported in Jill Bettner and Christine Donahue, "Now They're Not Laughing," *Forbes,* Vol. 132, No. 12 (November 21, 1983), p. 124.

5. "Red McCombs: Making Money's Fun," *Forbes,* Vol. 126 (September 15, 1980), p. 124.

6. "Two-Timer: The Once and Future CEO," *Inc.,* Vol. 8, No. 5 (May, 1986), pp. 58–60.

7. "Mr. and Mrs. Mesquite," *Waco Tribune-Herald* (August 29, 1988), pp. 1B, 11B.

8. David C. McClelland, *The Achieving Society* (New York: The Free Press, 1961); see also David C. McClelland and David G. Winter, *Motivating Economic Achievement* (New York: The Free Press, 1969).

9. Norman R. Smith and John B. Miner, "Motivational Considerations in the Success of Technologically Innovative Entrepreneurs," in John A. Hornaday, *et al.* (eds.), *Frontiers of Entrepreneurial Research,* 1984 (Wellesley, MA: Babson College), pp. 488–495.

10. Patrick R. Liles, "Who Are the Entrepreneurs?" *MSU Business Topics,* Vol. 22 (Winter, 1974), pp. 13–14.

11. McClelland, *The Achieving Society, op. cit.,* Chapter 6. See also Robert H. Brockhaus, Sr., "Risk-Taking Propensity of Entrepreneurs," *Academy of Management Journal,* Vol. 23 (September, 1980), pp. 509–520. He questions the extent to which entrepreneurial risk-taking propensities differ from those of managers and the general population.

12. See J. B. Rotter, "Generalized Expectancies for Internal Versus External Control of Reinforcement," *Psychological Monographs,* 1966a. A recent review is given in Robert H. Brockhaus, Sr., "The Psychology of the Entrepreneur," in Calvin A. Kent, Donald L. Sexton, and Karl H. Vesper (eds.), *Encyclopedia of Entrepreneurship* (Englewood Cliffs, NJ: Prentice-Hall, Inc., 1982), pp. 39–57.

13. Russell M. Knight, "Entrepreneurship in Canada," a paper presented at the Annual Conference of the International Council for Small Business, Asilomar, CA, June 22–25, 1980.

14. Carter Henderson, "An American Dream Fulfilled with Eggrolls," *In Business,* Vol. 6, No. 4 (July–August, 1984), pp. 20–23.

15. Charles E. Van Vorst, "Behind the White Line," *In Business,* Vol. 4 (March–April, 1982), pp. 25–26.

16. For a study of job dissatisfaction as a precipitating event, see Robert H. Brockhaus, Sr., "The Effect of Job Dissatisfaction on the Decision to Start a Business," *Journal of Small Business Management,* Vol. 18 (January, 1980), pp. 37–43.

17. "The Three Rs," *Venture,* Vol. 10, No. 6 (June, 1988), pp. 55–56.

18. A. B. Ibrahim and J. R. Goodwin, "Perceived Causes of Success in Small Business," *American Journal of Small Business,* Vol. 11, No. 2 (Fall, 1986), pp. 41–50.

19. "Your Toes Know," *In Business,* Vol. 10, No. 3 (May–June, 1988), p. 6.

20. See, for example, "She Calls All the Shots," *Time* (July 4, 1988), pp. 54–57.

21. *The State of Small Business: A Report of the President* (Washington: United States Government Printing Office, 1988), pp. 40–43.

22. *Ibid.*

23. Sharon Nelton, "Making It From the Ground Up," *Nation's Business,* Vol. 76, No. 6 (June, 1988), pp. 37–38.

24. Robert D. Hisrich and Candida G. Brush, *The Woman Entrepreneur* (Lexington, MA: Lexington Books, 1986), p. 18.

25. See Rein Peterson and Norman Smith, "Opportunistic/Craftsman Entrepreneurs Reconsidered," a paper presented at the 1987 International Council for Small Business conference, Vancouver, BC, June 10–12, 1987. A similar model was earlier presented in Norman R. Smith, *The Entrepreneur and His Firm: The Relationship Between Type of Man and Type of Company,* Occasional Paper (East Lansing: Division of Research, Graduate School of Business Administration, Michigan State University, 1967).

26. Arnold C. Cooper and William C. Dunkelberg, "Influences upon Entrepreneurship—A Large-Scale Study," paper presented to Academy of Management, San Diego, CA, August 4, 1981.

2 SMALL BUSINESS: VITAL COMPONENT OF THE ECONOMY

Spotlight on Small Business

Courtesy of Snyder-General Corporation

As this chapter explains, small business operates in a highly competitive economy—one that includes big corporations, middle-size businesses, and small firms. To succeed in such an economy, small businesses must demonstrate competence, even superiority. Fortunately, many small firms are led by entrepreneurial managers who are not only competent but able to "run circles" around large corporate competitors.

As an example, consider the exploits of Richard Snyder, who at one time managed Singer Company's Climate Control Division—a low-margin, supposedly mature business. Snyder bought the division in 1982 and quickly injected new life into it. He cut inventory, speeded up collections, introduced productivity incentives, and lured capable managers from other firms by appealing to their entrepreneurial spirit. The new company, Snyder-General Corporation, repaid $14 million of its initial bank debt in only nine months. In only four years, Snyder increased his personal net worth from $750,000 to more than $300 million. Singer regarded the division as a slow-growth business, but Snyder made it a big winner!

Source: Adapted from "Cool Millions," *Forbes,* Vol. 138, No. 1 (July 14, 1986), p. 86.

Looking Ahead

Watch for the following important topics:
1. The definition of small business—that is, what types of firms may be classified as small businesses.
2. The types of industry in which small businesses operate.
3. The proportion of all business activity accounted for by small businesses.
4. Unique contributions of small businesses to our society.
5. The rate and causes of small-business failure.
6. New terms and concepts:

size criteria	distribution function
SBA standards	supply function
major industries	failure rate
economic competition	Dun & Bradstreet

It is easy to overestimate the importance of big business because of its high visibility. Small businesses seem dwarfed by such corporate giants as General Motors (811,000 employees), Citicorp ($120 billion in deposits), Prudential of America ($645 billion worth of insurance in force), and IBM (over $5 billion of annual profits). Yet small firms, even though less conspicuous, are a vital component of our economy. In this chapter, we not only examine the extent of small-business activity but also the unique contributions of small businesses that help preserve our economic well-being. But first, we need to look at the criteria used to define small business.

Definition of Small Business

Specifying any size standard to define small business is necessarily arbitrary because people adopt different standards for different purposes. Legislators, for example, may exclude small firms from certain regulations and specify ten employees as the cutoff point. Moreover, a business may be described as "small" when compared to larger firms, but "large" when compared to smaller ones. Most people, for example, would classify independently owned gasoline stations, neighborhood restaurants, and locally owned retail stores as small businesses. Similarly, most would agree that the major automobile manufacturers are big businesses. And firms of in-between sizes would be classified as large or small on the basis of individual viewpoints.

Size Criteria

Even the criteria used to measure the size of businesses vary. Some criteria are applicable to all industrial areas, while others are relevant only to certain types of business. Examples of criteria used to measure size are:

1. Number of employees.
2. Sales volume.
3. Asset size.
4. Insurance in force.
5. Volume of deposits.

Although the first criterion listed above—number of employees—is the most widely used yardstick, the best criterion in any given case depends upon the user's purpose.

SBA Standards

The Small Business Administration (SBA) establishes size standards that determine eligibility for SBA loans and for special consideration in bidding on government contracts. In 1984, the SBA issued a revised set of standards, some of which are stated in terms of number of employees and others of which are stated in terms of sales volume. Some of these standards are shown in Exhibit 2–1. Size standards for most nonmanufacturing industries are now expressed in terms of annual receipts. As you can see, $3.5 million is a common upper limit in the service and retail areas in which small business is strong. In mining and manufacturing, however, the SBA classifies firms with fewer than 500 employees as small.

Exhibit 2–1   Examples of SBA Size Standards

Type of Business	Number of Employees or Sales Dollars
Advertising Agencies	$ 3.5 million
Copper Ores Mining	500 employees
Employment Agencies	$ 3.5 million
Furniture Stores	$ 3.5 million
General Contractors—Single-family Houses	$17.0 million
Insurance Agents, Brokers, and Service	$ 3.5 million
Metal Can Manufacturing	1,000 employees
Mobile Home Dealers	$ 6.5 million
Newspaper Publishing and Printing	500 employees
Poultry Dressing Plants	500 employees
Radio and Television Repair Shops	$ 3.5 million
Radio Broadcasting	$ 3.5 million

Source: Small Business Size Standards, SBA Rules and Regulations, Part 121, published by the Small Business Administration, February 9, 1984.

Size Standards Used in This Book

To provide a clearer image of the small firm discussed in this book, we suggest the following general criteria for defining a small business:

1. Financing of the business is supplied by one individual or a small group. Only in a rare case would the business have more than 15 or 20 owners.
2. Except for its marketing function, the firm's operations are geographically localized.
3. Compared to the biggest firms in the industry, the business is small.
4. The number of employees in the business is usually fewer than 100.

Obviously, some small firms fail to meet *all* of the above standards. For example, a small executive search firm—a firm that helps corporate clients recruit managers from other organizations—may operate in many sections of the country and thereby fail to meet the second criterion. Nevertheless, the discussion of management concepts in this book is aimed primarily at the type of firm that fits the general pattern just described.

Small Business as Producer of Goods and Services

In this section, our purpose is to understand the contribution made by small business as part of our total economic system. The following questions will be answered:

1. In which industries does small business make its greatest contribution?
2. What proportion of our total economic output comes from small business?

Small Business in the Major Industries

Small firms operate in all industries, but they differ greatly in their nature and importance from industry to industry. In thinking about their economic contribution, therefore, we first need to identify the eight major industries (as classified by the U.S. Department of Commerce) and note the types of small firms that function in these industries. These eight **major industries** and examples of small firms in each are as follows:

1. *Wholesale Trade*
   Wholesale drug companies
   Petroleum bulk stations
2. *Construction*
   General building contractors
   Electrical contractors
3. *Retail Trade*
   Hardware stores
   Restaurants
4. *Services*
   Travel agencies
   Beauty shops
5. *Finance, Insurance, and Real Estate*
   Local insurance agencies
   Real estate brokerage firms

6. *Mining*
   Sand and gravel companies
   Coal mines
7. *Transportation and Public Utilities*
   Taxicab companies
   Local radio stations
8. *Manufacturing*
   Bakeries
   Machine shops

Number of Small Businesses

Widely divergent statements about the number of U.S. businesses appear in print. You may read of 4 million business units in one account and 19 million in another! Much of the confusion arises from varying definitions of what constitutes a business.

The large numbers are typically based on Internal Revenue Service data. An estimated 19 million business tax returns were filed in 1988.[1] Does this mean that 19 million businesses exist? It all depends on the definition used. Many, probably most, business tax returns report business activities of an owner who has no employees. In many such cases, furthermore, the business activities are merely part-time, seasonal, or one-time activities. A housewife, for example, may give piano lessons to two or three neighborhood children and file a business tax return to report the income.

Rather than including all businesses submitting tax returns, we have included in Exhibit 2–2 only those enterprises which the Small Business Administration has in its data base. The numbers include only businesses having one or more employees, but these businesses account for 93 percent of all private employment.

As you can see, the vast majority of the 3.8 million businesses are small. Ninety-eight percent have fewer than 100 employees. Based on the number of business units, therefore, small business is the most common form of enterprise in the U.S. economy. These figures give a distorted view of the relative importance of small business, however, because of the huge number of very small firms.

Relative Economic Importance of Small Business

The fact that numerous small firms appear in each industry does not tell us much about their relative importance. Small firms might be merely

Exhibit 2–2 Number of Enterprises by Enterprise Size and Major Industry, 1986

Industry	Total	Employment Size of Enterprise	
		Less than 100	100 or More
U.S. Total	3,805,368	3,719,337	86,031
Agriculture	104,768	103,946	822
Mining	33,852	33,029	823
Construction	527,373	522,394	4,979
Manufacturing	358,007	336,178	21,829
Transportation, Communications, Public Utilities	135,744	131,798	3,946
Wholesale Trade	420,681	415,022	5,659
Retail Trade	1,044,761	1,032,503	12,258
Finance, Insurance, Real Estate	273,574	266,484	7,090
Services	906,608	877,983	28,625

Source: The State of Small Business: A Report of the President Transmitted to the Congress 1989 (Washington: U.S. Government Printing Office, 1989), pp. 84–85.

a tiny fringe in some industries. Or they may be so numerous and productive that their collective output exceeds that of large firms. The question before us is this: What percentage of the economy's total output of goods and services comes from small business?

One simple way to measure this is to compare the number of employees who work in small firms with the number of employees who work in large firms. We can do this for each industry and for the economy as a whole. Exhibit 2–3 presents such a comparison.

As you can see, the small-business share of total U.S. employment is

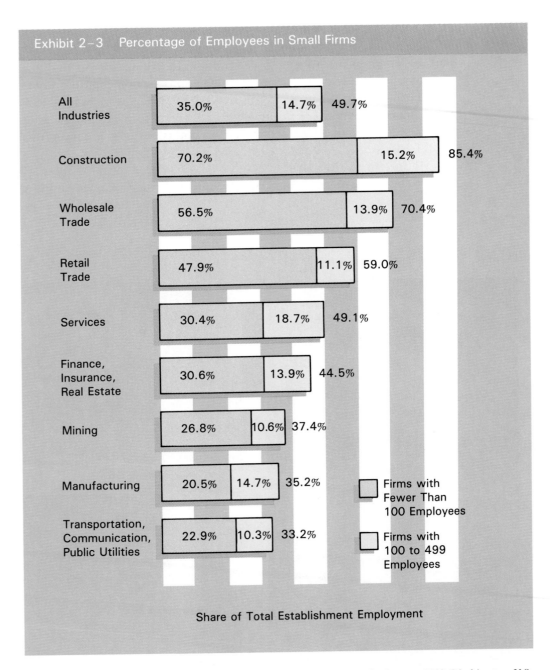

Exhibit 2–3   Percentage of Employees in Small Firms

	Firms with Fewer Than 100 Employees	Firms with 100 to 499 Employees	Total
All Industries	35.0%	14.7%	49.7%
Construction	70.2%	15.2%	85.4%
Wholesale Trade	56.5%	13.9%	70.4%
Retail Trade	47.9%	11.1%	59.0%
Services	30.4%	18.7%	49.1%
Finance, Insurance, Real Estate	30.6%	13.9%	44.5%
Mining	26.8%	10.6%	37.4%
Manufacturing	20.5%	14.7%	35.2%
Transportation, Communication, Public Utilities	22.9%	10.3%	33.2%

Share of Total Establishment Employment

Source: *The State of Small Business: A Report of the President Transmitted to the Congress 1988* (Washington: U.S. Government Printing Office, 1988), pp. 62–63.

35.0 percent, based on the 100-employee criterion, with an additional 14.7 percent added for firms with 100 to 499 employees, making a total of 49.7 percent based on the 500-employee criterion. Individual industries differ, naturally, from this overall average. In the construction industry, where small business is strongest, 85.4 percent of all employees work in firms with fewer than 500 employees. Assuming that all workers are equally productive, we can infer that 85.4 percent of that industry's output comes from small business.

In four of the industries portrayed in Exhibit 2–3, small business appears to be as important as or relatively more important than big business. These industries are construction, wholesale trade, retail trade, and services. (In services, small business is slightly less important—having 49.1 percent

Figure 2–1   Small Firms in Different Industries

Dean Foods Company

Retail

Real Estate

U.S. Department of Commerce

Construction

versus 50.9 percent for large firms.) In the other four industries, large business is clearly dominant. It is strongest in the transportation, communications, and public utilities category, with 66.8 percent of all employment.

For industry as a whole, as previously noted, firms with fewer than 500 employees account for 49.7 percent of the nation's employment and, presumably, the same percentage of the nation's output. Regardless of the exact point at which one draws the line, it is apparent that much—roughly 40 to 50 percent—of American business may be classed as small.

The most rapid growth is occurring in nonmanufacturing industries—industries such as services, retailing, insurance, and real estate.[2] Someone has called it the "new economy of services and high technology." Although both large and small firms exist in each industrial area, growth appears relatively favorable to small business—with more rapid expansion occurring in areas of traditional strength for small firms.

Special Contributions of Small Business

As part of the business community, small firms unquestionably contribute to our nation's economic welfare. They produce a substantial portion of our total goods and services. Thus, their general economic contribution is similar to that of big business. Small firms, however, possess some qualities that make them more than miniature versions of big business corporations. They make exceptional contributions as they provide new jobs, introduce innovations, stimulate competition, aid big business, and produce goods and services efficiently.

Providing New Jobs

As the population and the economy grow, small businesses must provide many of the new job opportunities. It seems clear, indeed, that small businesses must produce the "lion's share" of the new jobs.

Data released by the Office of Advocacy, Small Business Administration, show clearly the special contribution of small firms in expansion of employment. As you can see in Exhibit 2–4, small firms were the leaders in adding jobs between 1980 and 1986. Firms with fewer than 20 employees added more jobs than did firms of 500 or more employees. In fact, small and medium-size firms, those with fewer than 500 employees, accounted for almost two-thirds of all jobs added during those six years.

Of course, as newer firms grow in employment size, they become part

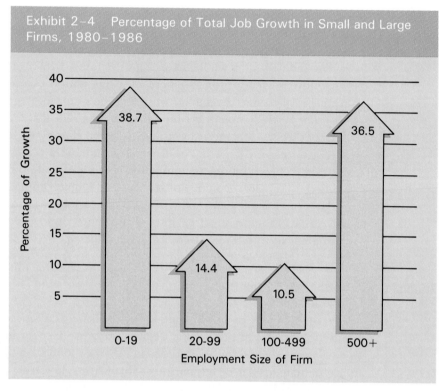

Exhibit 2–4 Percentage of Total Job Growth in Small and Large Firms, 1980–1986

Source: The State of Small Business: A Report of the President Transmitted to the Congress 1988 (Washington: U.S. Government Printing Office, 1988), p. 38.

of the big-business sector. We should also note that not all small firms grow at an even rate. David L. Birch concludes that 12 to 15 percent of all small enterprises create most of the growth.

> It is thus incorrect to speak of small enterprises as a uniformly expanding and active group. It is better to think of them as a large collection of seeds, a few of which sprout and become large plants. Their job-creating powers flow from the few, not the many.[3]

New jobs, therefore, come from the birth of new firms and their subsequent expansion. Also, some growth in employment comes from large corporations that expand and create additional jobs. The statistics reported here, however, reveal the unique, disproportionate contribution of small business to the creation of new jobs.

Introducing Innovation

New products that originate in the research laboratories of big business make a valuable contribution to our standard of living. There is a question, however, as to the relative importance of big business in achieving the truly significant innovations. The record shows that many scientific breakthroughs originated with independent inventors and small organizations.

SMALL BUSINESS IN ACTION
Cat Box Filler: A Case of Nontechnical Innovation

Not all innovation is "high tech." Small firms often introduce into ordinary products practical improvements that appeal to purchasers of those products. One example is the development of cat box filler, a product that eliminates cats' biggest drawback as house pets. Some 27 million American households own at least one cat, and many, if not most of them, have become users of this product.

Businesses are born under most unlikely circumstances. Forty years ago on a cold January day in Cassopolis, Michigan, Kay Draper's sandpile froze solid. As a result, she had to fill the cat's box with ashes, but the pet began tracking black smudges through the house. So Mrs. Draper scurried over to Ed Lowe for some sawdust. At 27, Lowe was just back from the war and struggling to keep his father's coal, ice, sawdust, and we-haul-anything business on its feet. In the trunk of his '43 Chevy coupe was some granulated dried mineral clay that he'd been trying, without much success, to sell to chicken farmers as nesting material.

"Try this," he said, pouring some of the absorbent clay in a paper bag and sending Mrs. Draper on her way. Soon she was back for more little bags. So were her friends. Lowe, tickled by the chance to make a few cents, decided to take a flier. He filled ten brown paper bags with clay, picked up a grease pencil, wrote two words on each bag, and took off down the road in his Chevy. Those words were KITTY LITTER.

Today Ed Lowe owns 13 homes (28 kitchens, and 19 fireplaces), 3,000 acres of land, an elegant yacht, a stable of quarter horses, and his own railroad. He also owns Edward Lowe Industries, the Indiana-based leader in the $350-million-a-year cat box filler industry. Sales of Lowe's Tidy Cat 3 and Kitty Litter brands were about $110 million last year. "This is a recession-proof business," he exults. "People will go without a lot of things before they'll go without their cats. And they're not going to have cats without litter."

Source: Penny Ward Moser, "Filler's the Name, Odor's the Game," *Fortune*, Vol. 117, No. 9 (April 25, 1988), p. 107.

The following is a list of some twentieth-century examples of new products created by small firms:

1. Photocopiers.	**7.** Automatic transmission.
2. Insulin.	**8.** Jet engine.
3. Vacuum tube.	**9.** Helicopter.
4. Penicillin.	**10.** Power steering.
5. Cottonpicker.	**11.** Color film.
6. Zipper.	**12.** Ball-point pen.

It is interesting to note that research departments of big businesses tend to emphasize the improvement of existing products. In fact, it is quite likely that some ideas generated by personnel in big businesses are side-tracked because they are not related to existing products or because of their unusual nature. Unfortunately, preoccupation with an existing product can sometimes blind one to the value of a *new* idea. The jet engine, for example, had difficulty winning the attention of those who were accustomed to internal combustion engines.

Studies of innovation have shown the greater effectiveness of small firms in research and development. Exhibit 2–5, based on a study by Edwards and Gordon, shows that small firms are superior innovators in both increasing-employment and decreasing-employment industries. Others believe that small companies are somewhere between 1.8 and 2.8 times as innovative per employee as large companies.[4]

Innovation contributes to productivity by providing better products and better methods of production. The millions of small firms that provide the centers of initiative and sources of innovation are thus in a position to help improve American productivity.[5]

Stimulating Economic Competition

Many economists, beginning with Adam Smith, have expounded the values inherent in **economic competition.** In a competitive business situation, individuals are driven by self-interest to act in a socially desirable manner. Competition acts as the regulator that transforms their selfishness into service.

When producers consist of only a few big businesses, however, the customer is at their mercy. They may set high prices, withhold technological developments, exclude new competitors, or otherwise abuse their position

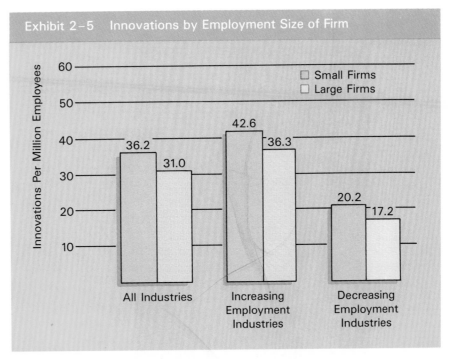

Exhibit 2–5   Innovations by Employment Size of Firm

Source: The State of Small Business: A Report of the President Transmitted to Congress 1985 (Washington: U.S. Government Printing Office, 1985), p. 128; Keith L. Edwards and Theodore J. Gordon, "Characterization of Innovations Introduced on the U.S. Market in 1982" (Glastonbury, CT: Prepared for the U.S. Small Business Administration, Office of Advocacy, Under Award No. SBA-6050-OA-82, March 1984), p. 46.

of power. If competition is to have a "cutting edge," there is need for small firms.

Even socialist economies such as that of China tolerate and encourage the formation of small businesses as a means of stimulating economic growth. As China's leaders have in recent years introduced elements of capitalism, including privately owned businesses, the country has experienced a dramatic rise in living standards.[6] Once-scarce bicycles, radios, and watches have become commonplace, and higher-income families now hope to acquire refrigerators, washing machines, and motorcycles. Chinese policy makers recognize the importance of entrepreneurial activity to a vigorous economy. "For the past three decades, the Chinese people have been deprived of their creativeness," says Jing Shuping, a former capitalist and un-

Figure 2–2   China Encourages Small Businesses

© R. Ian Lloyd/THE STOCK MARKET

official economic advisor.[7] Since the 1989 Tienanmen Square massacre, however, we are less optimistic about future prospects.

Not every competitive effort of small firms is successful, but big business may be kept on its toes by small business. Some entrepreneurs have no qualms about competing with giant corporations. For example, in Winchester, KY, a small soft-drink producer is marketing a ginger-ale-like product that outsells Coke, Pepsi, RC, and Dr Pepper in its home territory. And the younger member of the firm's family management team, Frank "Buddy" Rogers III, is quoted as saying, "My goal is to make Coca-Cola the No. 2 soft-drink company in this country."[8]

However, there is no guarantee of competition in numbers alone. Many tiny firms may be no match for one large firm or even for several firms that dominate an industry. Nevertheless, the existence of many healthy small businesses in an industry may be viewed as a desirable bulwark of the American capitalistic system.

Aiding Big Business

The fact that some functions are more expertly performed by small business enables small firms to contribute to the success of larger ones. If small businesses were suddenly removed from the contemporary scene, big businesses would find themselves saddled with a myriad of activities that they could perform only inefficiently. Two functions that small business can perform more efficiently than big business are the distribution function and the supply function.

Distribution Function   Few large manufacturers of inexpensive consumer products find it desirable to own wholesale and retail outlets. Take, for example, the successful small-business operation of Genesco retail cast-offs.[9] Genesco, Inc., a $1 billion manufacturer of footwear and clothing, sold off a number of its lackluster retail divisions to entrepreneurs who changed them into thriving businesses. One of its retail divisions—Gidding Jenny, a fashionable women's store in Cincinnati, OH—was sold in July, 1978, to Barry Miller, a former executive with Federated Department Stores. Genesco's main problem, according to Miller, was that "they couldn't adjust to stores that were atypical, that served a select trade."

Supply Function   Small businesses act as suppliers and subcontractors for large firms. General Motors, for example, purchases goods and services from more than 25,000 small businesses. Approximately three-fourths of these small firms employ fewer than 100 persons.

In addition to supplying services directly to large corporations, small firms provide services to customers of big business. For example, they service automobiles, repair appliances, and clean carpets produced by large manufacturers.

Producing Goods and Services Efficiently

In considering the contributions of small business, we are concerned with an underlying question of small-business efficiency. Common sense tells us that the efficient size of business varies with the industry. We can easily recognize, for example, that big business is better in manufacturing automobiles but that small business is better in repairing them.

The continued existence of small business in a competitive economic system is in itself evidence of efficient small-business operation. If small firms were hopelessly inefficient and making no useful contribution, they would be forced out of business quickly by stronger competitors.

SMALL BUSINESS IN ACTION
Small Business as Supplier of Granite

When AT&T needed granite for its new building, it went to a small firm in Providence, RI—an interesting example of the partnership between big business and small business.

Gerald Castellucci remembers that his hand was shaking. The architects for the new AT&T building wanted to buy as much pink granite as Castellucci & Sons Inc., in Providence, had taken out of its Connecticut quarry in a *decade*—and all for *one* building. "I thought, 'God, if we fail, it's unbelievable,'" he recalls of the meeting that sealed nine months of discussions. Castellucci went to work. He quickly expanded his work force at the Stony Creek Granite quarry from 4 to 15, then lured several master stonemasons out of retirement to train recruits in the art of shaping granite into arches, corners, and mullions. He invested $1 million in new equipment—more than the previous year's sales. And he kept his crews working overtime for three years cutting 60,000 pieces of granite, some weighing as much as 7,000 pounds. When the work finally started to subside, the prestige of the AT&T contract helped bring in dozens more. "It was the rebirth of our company," says Castellucci.

Source: Reprinted with permission, *Inc.* magazine (May, 1986). Copyright © 1986 by Goldhirsh Group, Inc., 38 Commercial Wharf, Boston, MA 02110.

Although research has identified some cost advantages for small firms over big businesses, the economic evidence related to firm size and productivity is limited. The following summary points out some of the reasons for the relative strength of small business:

New contributions to the theory of business organization and operation suggest that small firms are less encumbered by the complex, multi-echelon decision-making structures that inhibit the flexibility and productivity of many large firms. Because the owners of small firms are often also their managers, small firms are less likely to be affected adversely by the separation of owners' interests from managerial control. Empirical evidence of small firm survival and productivity suggests that, where firm size is concerned, bigger is not necessarily better.[10]

Additional economic research will undoubtedly shed more light on the most effective combination of small and large businesses. In the meantime, we believe that small business contributes in a substantial way to the economic welfare of our society.

The Small-Business Failure Record

A balanced view of small business in the economy requires us to consider also its darker side, that is, the record of business failure. While we wish to avoid pessimism, we must deal realistically with this matter.

Small-Business Failure Rate

Business failure data compiled by **Dun & Bradstreet, Inc.** have been used over the years to track the fortunes of business in general and small business in particular.[11] In general, the rate of failure has been low during periods of prosperity and high during economic recessions.

The frequent citation of failure data has tended to create an erroneous impression about the likelihood of failure.[12] In 1987, for example, 102 firms out of each 10,000 in Dun & Bradstreet's records failed. This means that only one percent failed. Viewed in this way, one can conclude that chances for success are excellent! The prospective entrepreneur should be encouraged to consider business ownership because of its bright prospects, rather than shun it because of fear of failure.

There are a number of reasons for the gap between the low Dun & Bradstreet failure rate and the much higher rates so often cited in the news media. Some of these are as follows:

1. A business may discontinue operations merely because profits are unsatisfactory. Dun & Bradstreet classifies discontinuances as failures only if there is a loss to creditors.
2. A business may close one branch office or store to consolidate operations, and this may appear to be a business failure.
3. A business may relocate, and the empty building with a "For Rent" sign may create an impression of failure.

The failure rate would vary, of course, if a different definition of failure were used. If discontinuances were considered failures, for example, the rate would be higher.

Recent research using the data base of the Small Business Administration has shown that the percentage of newly formed firms that survive is much higher than commonly believed.[13] This research indicated that 40 percent of new firms survive six or more years. Moreover, most firms that do not survive are closed voluntarily, without loss to creditors. Furthermore, survival rates more than double for firms that grow. In fact, two out of three growing firms were found to survive six or more years.

Research by David L. Birch found that about three-quarters of the firms included in his study survived from 1983 to 1987.[14] The younger companies in the group studied were only slightly less likely than older companies to make it through the four-year period.

It is desirable, of course, that we learn from the experiences of those who fail. However, apprehension of failure should not be permitted to stifle inclinations toward independent business careers. While prospective entrepreneurs should understand that failure is possible, they should also recognize that the odds are far from overwhelming.

The Costs of Business Failure

The costs of business failure involve more than financial costs. They include costs of a psychological, social, and economic nature, too.

Loss of Entrepreneur's and Creditors' Capital   The owner of a business that fails suffers a loss of invested capital, either in whole or in part. This is always a financial setback to the individual concerned. In some cases, it means the loss of a person's lifetime savings! The entrepreneur's loss of capital is augmented by the losses of business creditors. Hence, the total capital loss is greater than the sum of the entrepreneurial losses in any one year.

Injurious Psychological Effects   Individuals who fail in business suffer a real blow to their self-esteem. The businesses they started with enthusiasm and high expectations of success have "gone under." Older entrepreneurs, in many cases, lack the vitality to recover from the blow. Many unsuccessful entrepreneurs simply relapse into employee status for the balance of their lives.

However, failure need not be totally devastating to entrepreneurs. They may recover from the failure and try again. Albert Shapero has offered these encouraging comments: "Many heroes of business failed at least once. Henry Ford failed twice. Maybe trying and failing is a better business education than going to a business school that has little concern with small business and entrepreneurship."[15] The key, therefore, is the response of the one who fails and that person's ability to learn from failure.

Social and Economic Losses   Assuming that a business opportunity existed, the failure of a firm means the elimination of its goods and services that the public needs and wants. Moreover, the number of jobs available in the community is reduced. The resulting unemployment of the entrepreneur and employees, if any, causes the community to suffer from the loss of a business payroll. Finally, the business that failed was a taxpayer that contributed to the tax support of schools, police and fire protection, and other governmental services.

Causes of Business Failure

As shown in Exhibit 2–6, Dun & Bradstreet cite "economic factors" as the leading cause of business failures—57.8 percent of the total. In this category, they include such factors as "inadequate sales," "insufficient profits," and "poor growth prospects." Another important category is "finance causes," which includes such components as "heavy operating expenses" and "insufficient capital."

The most intriguing class of failures is that of "experience causes"—contributing to 12 percent of the failures. These causes are obviously related to the quality of management, including as they do "lack of business knowledge," "lack of line experience," and "lack of managerial experience."

Exhibit 2–6   Causes of Business Failure

Cause	Percentage of Failures
Neglect Causes	2.0
Disaster	0.0
Fraud	0.9
Economic Factors Causes	57.8
Experience Causes	12.0
Finance Causes	26.4
Strategy Causes	0.9

Source: Business Failure Record (New York: Dun & Bradstreet, Inc., 1989), p. 19.

Attributing the cause of failure to experience, therefore, is equivalent to saying failure results from substandard management.

Other, less-obvious causes cited by Dun & Bradstreet may also serve as masks for the underlying cause of managerial weakness. Such factors as "inadequate sales," "insufficient profits," and "heavy operating expenses" often serve as euphemisms for inferior management. Although one should not be dogmatic on the point, it seems likely that the quality of management plays a major part in the majority of small-business failures.

Looking Back

1. Definitions of small business are necessarily arbitrary and differ according to purpose. Although there are exceptions, we generally think of a business as small when it has one or a small group of investors, operates in a geographically restricted area, is small compared to the biggest firms in the industry, and has fewer than 100 employees. Size standards issued by the Small Business Administration relate to eligibility for SBA loans and to considerations in bidding for government contracts.

2. Small firms operate in all industrial areas but are particularly strong—in terms of number of employees on their payroll—in the fields of construction, wholesale trade, retail trade, and services.

3. The proportion of total business activity accounted for by small business ranges from 40 percent to 50 percent.

4. Small businesses make several unique contributions to our economy. They provide a disproportionate share of new jobs needed for a growing labor force. They are responsible for introducing many innovations and originating such scientific breakthroughs as photocopiers and insulin. Small firms act as vigorous economic competitors and perform some business functions (such as distribution and supply) more expertly than large firms in many ways. Small firms can also produce goods and services more efficiently in some areas.

5. The rate of business failure is much lower than commonly believed—amounting in 1987 to only one percent of the firms in Dun & Bradstreet's records. Although "economic factors" is cited as the most frequent reason for failure, it seems probable that management weakness is the leading underlying cause.

DISCUSSION QUESTIONS

1. In view of the numerous definitions of small business, how can you decide which definition is correct?

2. Of the businesses with which you are acquainted, which is the largest that you consider to be in the small-business category? Does it conform to the size standards used in this book?

3. On the basis of your acquaintance with small-business firms, give an example of a specific small firm in the field of transportation and other public utilities.

4. Suppose you decided to publish a tax advisory newsletter for small-business owners. How would you define your target market in terms of business size? What difference would this decision make?

5. What generalizations can you make about the relative importance of large and small business in the United States?

6. In which sectors of the economy is small business most important? What accounts for its strength in these areas?

7. As noted in this chapter, small business is stronger in some industries than in others. Would it be logical, therefore, for prospective entrepreneurs to concentrate their search for opportunities more in the strong small-business industries—for example, in wholesaling more than manufacturing?

8. What special contribution is made by small business in providing jobs?

9. How can you explain the unique contributions of small business to product innovation?

10. What changes would be necessary for Ford Motor Company to continue operation, if, for some strange reason, all firms with fewer than 500 employees were outlawed? Would the new arrangement be more or less efficient than the present one? Why?

11. In what way does small business serve as a bulwark of the capitalistic system?

12. List and describe some of the nonfinancial costs of business failure.

13. Explain the significance of the quality of management as a cause of failure.

14. What is the difference between saying that "most firms fail within five years" and that "most firms that fail do so within five years"? Which is more nearly correct? Based on the statistics on business failure, would you describe the prospects for new business starts as "bright" or "bleak"?

15. How can "economic factors," when cited as a cause of business failure, serve as a mask for other contributing causes?

YOU MAKE THE CALL

Situation 1

In the 1980s, a major food company began a push to increase its share of the nation's pickle market. To build market share, it used TV advertising and aggressive pricing. The price of its 46-ounce jar of pickles quickly dropped in one area from $1.89 to 79 cents—a price some believed was less than the cost of production. This meant strong price competition for a family business that had long dominated the pickle market in that area. This family firm, whose primary product is pickles, must now decide how to compete with a powerful national corporation whose annual sales volume amounts to billions of dollars.

Questions

1. How should the family business react to the price competition?
2. What advertising changes might be needed?
3. How can a family business survive in such a setting?

Situation 2

An entrepreneurial failure, that of Ron A. Berger, is described in the following account:

> In 1979 Berger was hot. His four-year-old brainchild, Photo Factory, was pulling in $40 million a year. He had 57 stores in eight states, and he was rolling.
>
> Then, suddenly, he was broke.
>
> His business had been leveraged with a $1 million line of credit. Interest rates skyrocketed, and the bank called in his loan. Because Berger had personally guaranteed the loan, he was forced to declare personal bankruptcy. Overnight, Berger plummeted from a net worth of about $5 million to zip. Job searches and depression followed. "I couldn't come to grips with it," Berger says today. "I felt like a total failure. I questioned my own worth and every business decision I'd ever made."
>
> **Source:** "Building on Failure," *Nation's Business*, Vol. 75, No. 4 (April, 1987), p. 50. Copyright 1987, U.S. Chamber of Commerce.

Questions

1. What was the cause of Berger's failure? Explain your answer.
2. What should he learn from this failure, and how should he deal with his feelings of failure?

EXPERIENTIAL EXERCISES

1. Visit a local firm and prepare a report showing the number of owners, geographical scope of operation, relative size in the industry, number of employees, and sales volume (if the firm will provide sales data). In your report, show the size of the firm (whether large or small) in terms of standards outlined in this chapter and the industry of which it is a part.

2. Interview a small-business owner-manager concerning the type of big business competition faced by his or her firm and that owner-manager's "secrets of success" in competing with big business. Report on the insights offered by this entrepreneur.

3. Select a recent issue of *Inc.* and report on the types of new products or services being developed by small firms.

4. Select one section of 20 businesses in the Yellow Pages of the telephone directory, label each of these businesses as large or small on the basis of that limited information, and give your rationale or assumptions for your classification of each. Then call five of these firms and ask whether the firm is a large or small business. Compare the responses to your own classification.

REFERENCES TO SMALL-BUSINESS PRACTICES

Beckner, Steven K. "The Boom That Won't Quit." *Nation's Business,* Vol. 74, No. 4 (April, 1986), pp. 26–36.

    A description of several successful small firms that have emerged in the services industry—an expanding industry that offers many opportunities for new startups.

Greco, Gail. "Nurturing the Inventor Spirit." *In Business,* Vol. 8, No. 4 (July–August, 1986), pp. 39–40.

    A description of a variety of innovative products, the inventors who produced them, and the process of making successful business ventures from them.

Kotkin, Joel. "The Great American Revival." *Inc.,* Vol. 10, No. 2 (February, 1988), pp. 52–63.

    An account of some small, flexible manufacturers who are helping restore U.S. industrial competitiveness in an industry dominated by big business.

Richman, Louis S. "Tomorrow's Jobs: Plentiful, But. . . ." *Fortune,* Vol. 117, No. 8 (April 11, 1988), pp. 42–56.

    A discussion of the job creation that is occurring in our economy and a description of some entrepreneurial ventures that are adding substantial numbers of new jobs.

"Small Railroads on a Fast Track." *In Business,* Vol. 7 (May–June, 1985), pp. 33–36.

    Transportation, particularly railroads, is generally regarded as a big-business industry. This article reports on many small firms that thrive in this area.

ENDNOTES

1. *The State of Small Business: A Report of the President Transmitted to the Congress 1989* (Washington: U.S. Government Printing Office, 1989), p. 21.

2. For an explanation of the rapid growth in services and numerous examples of new, thriving service businesses, see Dyan Machan, "How Gus Blythe Smelled Opportunity," *Forbes*, Vol. 142, No. 7 (October 3, 1988), pp. 104–113.

3. *The Contribution of Small Enterprise to Growth and Employment* (Cambridge, MA: Program on Neighborhood and Regional Change, Massachusetts Institute of Technology, undated), p. 10.

4. Tom Richman and Susan Benner, "Stanley Mason Is Growing Oil on Trees," *Inc.*, Vol. 3 (August, 1981), p. 34. Also see a National Science Foundation study (which overstated the advantage of small business), U.S. Congress, Senate, Joint Hearings before the Select Committee on Small Business and other committees, *Small Business and Innovation*, August 9–10, 1978, p. 7.

5. For an extended discussion of small-business contributions to productivity in manufacturing, including numerous examples, see Joel Kotkin, "The Great American Revival," *Inc.*, Vol. 10, No. 2 (February 1988), pp. 52–63.

6. "Capitalism in China," *Business Week*, No. 2876 (January 14, 1985), pp. 53–59.

7. *Ibid.*, p. 53.

8. "Going after Coke," *Fortune*, Vol. 101, No. 8 (April 21, 1980), p. 19.

9. "Revamping Genesco's Cast-Offs," *Venture*, Vol. 2, No. 11 (November, 1980), pp. 14–16.

10. *The State of Small Business: A Report of the President 1987* (Washington: U.S. Government Printing Office, 1987), p. 105.

11. The most comprehensive statistics pertaining to failure and changes in rate of failure are collected by Dun & Bradstreet, a business firm devoted to the analysis and rating of the credit standing of other firms. Failures, as defined by Dun & Bradstreet, include only those discontinuances that involve loss to creditors; voluntarily liquidated firms with all debts paid are excluded.

12. Professor M. Z. Massel of De Paul University argues that writers generally have become so preoccupied with the minority of firms that fail that they paint an unnecessarily pessimistic picture of chances for success in business. See Michael Z. Massel, "It's Easier to Slay a Dragon Than Kill a Myth," *Journal of Small Business Management*, Vol. 16, No. 3 (July, 1978), pp. 44–49.

13. Bruce D. Phillips and Bruce A. Kirchoff, "Formation, Growth and Survival: Small Firm Dynamics in the U.S. Economy," *Small Business Economics*, Vol. 1 (1989), pp. 65–74.

14. David L. Birch, "Live Fast, Die Young," *Inc.*, Vol. 10, No. 8 (August, 1988), p. 23.

15. Albert Shapero, "Numbers That Lie," *Inc.*, Vol. 3, No. 5 (May, 1981), p. 16.

EXPLORING ENTREPRENEURIAL ALTERNATIVES

3 STARTUP AND BUYOUT OPPORTUNITIES

Spotlight on Small Business

© Mark Perlstein

Entrepreneurs often create businesses after "escaping" from the corporate life of big business. Tuan Huynh, owner of H&A Fashions in Dallas, TX, began his apparel-manufacturing business after literally escaping from South Vietnam.

Huynh was a captain in the South Vietnamese army when the U.S. involvement ended in 1975. In 1980, the Huynh family came to Dallas after escaping on a boat that took them to an Indonesian refugee camp.

After five years, the family had saved over $50,000, and Huynh was ready to launch his own company, dubbed H&A Fashions after the family name and his wife's name. He hired a general manager, a designer, a salesperson, and a secretary, and he set up shop in a 3,000-square-foot warehouse.

H&A's initial product line was the American Shirtdress—a belted dress that has a man's-style collar. The company's first-year profits were under $50,000. Huynh says, "I am happy here because I have freedom.... I work hard so I have money. I can sleep all night here."

Source: Sally Bell, "Surviving and Thriving." Reprinted by permission, *Nation's Business,* March, 1990. Copyright 1990, U.S. Chamber of Commerce.

Looking Ahead

Watch for the following important topics:
1. The alternatives for starting a small business.
2. Types of startup ideas.
3. Sources of ideas for creating startups.
4. Reasons for buying an existing business.
5. How to determine the value of a business being considered for purchase.
6. New terms and concepts:

startup	market value approach
buyout	replacement cost approach
Type A startup ideas	liquidation value approach
Type B startup ideas	earnings approach
Type C startup ideas	capitalization of profit
serendipity	

In this chapter and the two that follow, we explore four different types of small-business ownership opportunities: startups, buyouts, franchises, and family businesses. Exhibit 3–1 depicts each of these options.

Building a business from "scratch"—a **startup**—is the route most often thought of when discussing new-venture creation. There is no question that startups represent a significant opportunity for many entrepreneurs. However, even more individuals realize their entrepreneurial dreams through other alternatives—either franchising, purchasing an existing firm (buyout), or entering a family business.

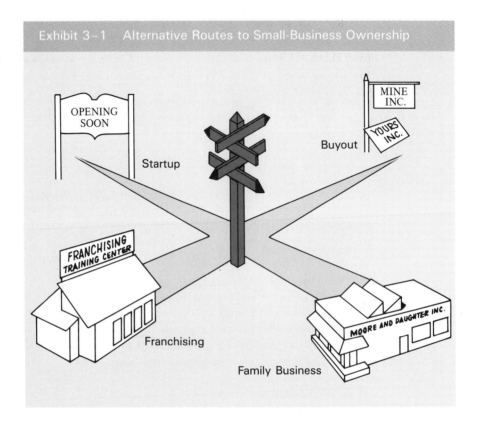

Exhibit 3-1   Alternative Routes to Small-Business Ownership

The startup and buyout options for entering small business are examined in this chapter. Franchising is discussed in Chapter 4, and the family business is analyzed in Chapter 5.

The Startup: Creating a New Business

Reasons for developing a startup, rather than pursuing the other alternatives, include the following:

1. Invention of a new product or service that necessitates a new type of business.
2. Freedom to select the ideal location, equipment, products or services, employees, suppliers, and bankers.
3. Avoidance of undesirable precedents, policies, procedures, and legal commitments of existing firms.

Q13

Regardless of the reason, the would-be entrepreneur should ask the following questions before deciding to implement a concept for a new venture: Have I found a genuine new-venture idea? What sources of new-venture ideas are available? Have I refined the idea? Do I have the necessary education and experience for this type of venture?

Importance of a Differential Advantage

Whatever type of business opportunity is involved, it must be genuine. This means that the new business must have some type of advantage that will provide a competitive edge. This special edge is necessary because the marketplace generally does not welcome a new competitor. The prospective entrepreneur must visualize some new product or service or location or "angle" that will not only "get the foot in the door" but keep it there.

Some apparent opportunities are insufficient for the long-term success of a new venture. For example, an increase in population during the construction of a large power plant or dam may provide a sizable market now, but the market may be inadequate later because of the population decline when construction is completed. Of course, in this situation, an entrepreneur could purposely go into business—for instance, a mobile food service—with plans for temporary operation, large profits, and closure or relocation when the "boom" is over.

Kinds of Startup Ideas

The startup ideas depicted in Exhibit 3–2 portray different types of new-venture ideas. Note that the lightbulbs—the types of ideas—shed light on the entrepreneur's search for a startup opportunity.

Many startups are developed from **Type A ideas**—providing customers with a product or service that does not exist in their market but already exists somewhere else. An example would be a maid-service venture in a city that previously had no service of this type.

Startups are also based on **Type B ideas**—a technically new process. One example is David Olson's startup, named STARS, based in Austin, Texas. He used satellite dish technology to form a mobile satellite transmitter and receiver business that he now uses to carry data and voice transmissions for such corporate clients as Tenneco, Inc.[1] Another example is a small Redwood City, CA, company, Advanced Polymer Systems, Inc. The company has developed a microsponge technology allowing oils to be contained inside billions of microscopic sponges. "It's a unique technology and it is applicable to a lot of different industries," states one investor.[2]

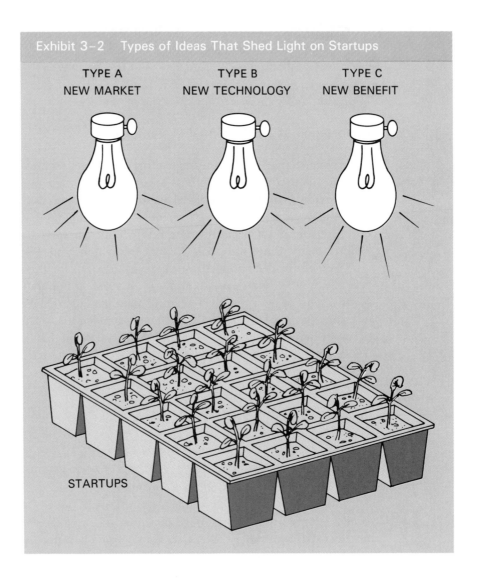

Exhibit 3–2   Types of Ideas That Shed Light on Startups

TYPE A
NEW MARKET

TYPE B
NEW TECHNOLOGY

TYPE C
NEW BENEFIT

STARTUPS

Type C startup ideas probably account for the largest number of all new-venture startups. These are concepts for performing old functions in new and improved ways. One example would be the baby stroller that Phil and Mary Baechler designed and now manufacture. It performs the function of transporting young children—nothing really new—but in an improved manner. It pushes more easily and is more difficult to overturn than previous designs. Their primary market is young parents who are joggers who want to push their babies as they run.[3]

Sources of Startup Ideas

Since startups begin with ideas, let us consider the circumstances that tend to spawn such new ideas. Several studies have addressed the question of where new product ideas for small-business startups originate. Exhibit 3–3 gives the results of a study conducted by the National Federation of Independent Business Foundation, which found that "prior work experience" accounted for 45 percent of the ideas for new businesses. The next highest source was "personal interest and hobbies," with 16 percent of the total. A "chance happening" accounted for 11 percent of the new ideas reported in the research.

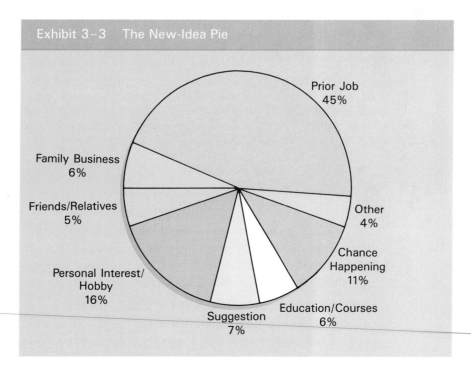

Exhibit 3–3   The New-Idea Pie

Prior Job
45%

Family Business
6%

Friends/Relatives
5%

Other
4%

Personal Interest/
Hobby
16%

Chance
Happening
11%

Suggestion
7%

Education/Courses
6%

Source: Data developed and provided by the NFIB Foundation and sponsored by the American Express Travel Related Services Company, Inc.

SMALL BUSINESS IN ACTION
Bringing an Existing Product into Focus

Max Morris, at age 57, was unable to drive or work. He had suddenly developed cataracts. Unable to read without great difficulty, he began to experiment with various reading aids. And even after surgery, which restored his sight, he continued to work with more efficient ways to read.

Eventually he developed his Kwikscan system, which emphasizes keywords in a passage in boldface print. These keywords, when linked by the reader, form their own meaningful sentences. Morris obtained a patent for the process and then formed his own business, Micro-Books, Inc. But what should he publish?

Max Morris with Kwikscan New Testament

''I knew how much of a problem reading is for many people today—and how few actually read books—yet some publications have vast audiences,'' he recalls . . . ''So we decided to publish a series of 'how-to' titles in Kwikscan that would sell for less than $2, and sell them in supermarkets and other mass-market outlets.''

Later, however, Morris had a better idea—publish the Bible with the Kwikscan system. Since the Bible is the best-selling title of all time and is unprotected by copyright, Morris decided to give it a try. Working in the den of his home with his wife and two children, he turned the Kwikscan version of the New Testament into a reality.

Source: William G. Flanagan. "In the Beginning Was the WORD," *Forbes,* April 20, 1987, pp. 100–101. ©Forbes Inc., 1987.
Photo Source: ©1988. *Photo by Acey Harper*

Let us consider in more detail the circumstances that tend to create new ideas. Since there are numerous possibilities (a new idea can come from virtually anywhere), we have developed four categories to examine: personal experience, hobbies, accidental discovery, and deliberate search.

Personal Experience   One basis for startup ideas is personal experience, which is obtained both at home and on the job. Consider "Saved By The Bell," a small business in New York City that handles a variety of chores for busy women, men, and corporations. Started by Susan Bell in 1984, the company serves over fifty clients who pay a fee to get the grocery shopping done, pick up shirts at the laundry, or a variety of other household chores.

SMALL BUSINESS IN ACTION
An Idea Fits a Need

In August, 1985, a women's shoe store by the name of Magnifete opened in downtown Cincinnati. The entrepreneur owner is Shelagh Watson, who recalls that her idea for the store started when "I couldn't find fashion shoes in my size—11½. That started me thinking about the concept of a women's shoe store that catered to the oversize range." And that's what she did. Magnifete sold 6,500 pairs of shoes in 1986 and grossed over $367,000 in sales.

Watson wants customers in her store to be able to find large sizes in stock so they can try the shoes and take them home without special ordering. The store maintains 5,000 pairs of shoes in inventory.

Lacking business experience, Watson took a course in starting a business before she opened Magnifete. She also hired a consultant to help develop a business plan. Two years later, in 1987, Watson has begun franchising her store concept.

Source: Marcia King, "Having a Football," *Nation's Business*, Vol. 76, No. 2 (February, 1988), p. 75. Reprinted by permission, *Nation's Business*, February, 1988. Copyright 1988 U.S. Chamber of Commerce.

The idea for her personal-service business came from her own experience. One day, while sitting on her apartment floor surrounded by notes on things to do, she "realized that there are a lot of other people like me—people who need a 'wife' to help them with the details of their lives."[4] Shortly after this experience, she started the business.

Also, from knowledge gleaned from their present or recent jobs, some employees see possibilities in modifying an existing product, improving a service, or duplicating a business concept in a different location. For example, a furniture salesperson may see the possibility of opening a new furniture store in a different area of the city. The new store may follow the business strategy of the existing store, or it may feature different, restricted, or expanded lines of merchandise. It may also adopt credit or delivery policies that are more appealing to customers in that area. Work experience may well be the most productive of all sources of new-venture ideas.

Hobbies   Sometimes hobbies grow beyond their stature as hobbies to become businesses. For example, a coin collector who buys and sells coins to build a personal collection may easily become a coin dealer. In 1976,

Eleanor Mills made one of her ceramic plates, adorned with hand-painted sketches, for her sister. Friends and neighbors loved it and wanted to place orders. This was the beginning of Millscraft, The Plate Place. Today, Mrs. Mills works full time in the business.[5]

Hobbies are often turned into startups by business executives who retire. For example, Bob Howard, at age 58, retired from a corporate position in Scottsdale, AZ, to pursue his tennis hobby full time. He now teaches tennis courses for senior players.[6]

Accidental Discovery   As a source of new startup ideas, accidental discovery involves something called **serendipity**—the faculty for making desirable discoveries by accident. Any person may stumble across a useful idea in the ordinary course of day-to-day living. This was true of Patty Ludwin, founder of Calamity Jeans and Jewels, in Canonsburg, PA. Her firm sells jeans riddled with bullet holes. Her inspiration came when a sharpshooter girlfriend shot up a pair of her boyfriend's jeans in a lover's spat. (He was not wearing the jeans at the time!) The man liked the "new" jeans even better than before. Currently, the bullet-hole jeans are sold through mail order.[7] Products like this are very faddish, but profits can be made while they are "hot."

Deliberate Search   A startup idea may also emerge from a prospective entrepreneur's deliberate search—a purposeful exploration to find a new idea. Entrepreneurs can survey their own capabilities and then look at the new products or services they are capable of producing, or they can first look for needs in the marketplace and then relate these to their own capabilities. The latter approach—beginning with a look at market needs—has apparently produced more successful startups, especially in the field of consumer goods and services, than the former.

Magazines and other periodicals are excellent sources of startup ideas. One way of generating startup ideas is by reading about the creativity of other entrepreneurs. For example, a 1987 edition of *Venture* described 100 such ideas.[8]

A deliberate search also helps in a general way by stimulating a readiness of mind. Prospective entrepreneurs who are thinking seriously about new-business ideas will be more receptive to new ideas from any source.

Since a truly creative person may find useful ideas in many different ways, the sources of new-venture ideas mentioned here are suggestive, not exhaustive. We encourage you to seek and reflect upon new-venture ideas in whatever circumstances you find yourself.

Refining a New-Venture Idea

A new-venture idea often requires an extended period of time for refinement and testing. This is particularly true for original inventions that require developmental work to make them operational. The need for refining a new idea is not limited to high-technology ventures, however. Almost any idea for a new business deserves careful study and typically requires modification as the aspiring entrepreneur moves toward opening day for the new business.

An example is found in the case of John Morse, who founded Fratelli's Ice Cream in Seattle. A course with Karl Vesper at the University of Washington required him to bring some practicality to his abstract ideas for this business.

> "When I first mentioned the ice cream idea to Karl, he told me I was crazy. He pointed out that we had experience bordering on weeks, no contacts, and that we'd be up against big hitters," says Morse. "The idea was 99% inspiration and 1% thought. Karl forced me to think it through." Responding to Vesper's challenges over the next two years, Morse finally signed an agreement with a local dairy to produce Fratelli's ice cream. "They had 76 years of experience—and connections," he says. Today he annually sells $1 million of ice cream in three states.[9]

The process of preparing a business plan, as discussed later in this book, helps the individual to think through an idea and consider all aspects of a proposed business. Outside experts can be used to review the business plan, and their questions and suggestions can help to improve it. One writer reported the case of the founders of a rotary-drill venture whose initial strategy was to price its products below the competition even though they had a superior product innovation in a growing market.[10] Outside experts persuaded them to price 10 percent over the competition, and this decision contributed significantly to later profits.

Buying an Existing Business

Would-be entrepreneurs can choose to buy an existing business as an alternative to buying a franchise, starting from scratch, or joining a family business. This decision should be made only after careful consideration of the advantages and disadvantages of buying an established business.

Reasons for Buying an Existing Business

All decisions in life have pros and cons. The decision to buy an existing business is no exception. An extensive listing of these pros and cons follows.[11]

Pros

1. Prior successful operation of a business increases your chances of success with the same business.
2. Prior successful operation provides the location of the business previously selected and in use.
3. If the business has been profitable or is headed toward profit, you will be profitable sooner than if you start up your own business.
4. The amount of planning that may be necessary for an ongoing business will probably be less than that for a new business.
5. You will already have established customers or clientele.
6. You will already have established suppliers and will not have to look for them.
7. You may already have inventory on hand and will not lose the time necessary for selecting, ordering, and waiting for the order to arrive before you can make your first sales.
8. Necessary equipment is probably already on hand.
9. Financing will be necessary for the single transaction of purchasing the business.
10. You may be able to buy the business at a bargain price.
11. You will acquire the benefit of the experience of the prior owner.
12. Much of the hard work of startup is avoided, including finding the location, purchasing the equipment, and so forth.
13. If employees are on board, they are probably already experienced in the business.
14. You may be able to finance all or part of the purchase price through a note to the owner.
15. Existing records of the business may help you and guide you in running the business.

Cons

1. You will inherit any bad will that exists because of the way the business has been managed.

2. The employees who are currently working for the company may not be the best or the best for you and the way you manage.
3. The image of the business is already established. If it is a poor image, it will be difficult to change.
4. Precedents have already been set by the previous owners. They may be difficult to change.
5. Modernization may be needed.
6. The purchase price may create a burden on future cash flow and profitability.
7. It is possible that you can overpay due to misrepresentation or an inaccurate appraisal of what the business is worth.
8. The business location may be a drawback.

This list of the pros and cons of buying an existing business can be condensed into three main considerations in the decision to purchase an existing business: (1) reduction of uncertainties, (2) acquisition of ongoing operations and relationships, and (3) a bargain price. We will examine each of these in more detail.

Reduction of Uncertainties   A successful going concern has demonstrated an ability to attract customers, control costs, and make a profit. Although future operations may be different, the firm's past record shows what it can do under actual market conditions. For example, the satisfactory location of a going concern eliminates one major uncertainty. Although traffic counts are useful in assessing the potential value of a location, the acid test comes when a business opens its doors at that location. And this test has already been met in the case of an existing firm, with the results available in the form of sales and profit data.

Acquisition of Ongoing Operations and Relationships   The buyer of an existing business typically acquires its personnel, inventories, physical facilities, established banking connections, and ongoing relationships with trade suppliers. Consider the time and effort otherwise required in acquiring them "from scratch." Of course, this situation is an advantage only under certain conditions. For example, the firm's skilled, experienced employees constitute a valuable asset only if they will continue to work for the new owner. The physical facilities must not be obsolete, and the relationships with banks and suppliers must be healthy.

A Bargain Price   A going business may become available at what seems to be a low price. Whether it is actually a "good buy" must be determined by

Figure 3-1   Ongoing Relationships with
Suppliers Are Acquired with the Business

the prospective new owner. The price may appear low, but several factors could make the "bargain price" anything but a bargain. For example, the business may be losing money; the location may be deteriorating; or the seller may intend to reopen another business as a competitor. However, the business may indeed be a bargain and turn out to be a wise investment.

Finding a Business to Buy

Frequently in the course of day-to-day living and business contacts, a would-be buyer comes across an opportunity to buy an existing business. For example, a sales representative for a manufacturer or a wholesaler may be offered an opportunity to buy a customer's retail business. In other cases, the would-be buyer may need to search for a business to buy.

Other sources of business leads include suppliers, distributors, trade associations, and even bankers, who may know of business firms available for purchase. Also, realtors—particularly those who specialize in the sale of business firms and business properties—can provide leads. In addition, there are specialized brokers, called "matchmakers," who handle all the arrangements in closing a buyout. "Now about 1,000 to 1,500 matchmakers are handling mergers and acquisitions of companies with sales under $75 million," reports Jerome S. Siebert, head of Siebert Associates.[12]

Investigating and Evaluating the Existing Business

Regardless of the source of business leads, each opportunity requires a background investigation and careful evaluation. As a preliminary step, the buyer needs to acquire information about the business. Some of this information can be obtained through personal observation or discussion with the seller. Also important is the need to talk with other parties such as suppliers, bankers, and possibly customers of the business. Although some of this investigation requires personal checking, the buyer can also seek the help of outside experts. The two most valuable sources of assistance in this regard are accountants and lawyers.

The seller's real reasons for selling a going business may or may not be disclosed. Robert Haas, general partner of Intercapco, a venture capital firm, expresses this concern by saying, "When somebody puts a company on the market, you wonder why they are trying to get rid of it. Either the company is not doing well, or it has a skeleton in the closet that will affect its future performance."[13]

The buyer must be wary, therefore, of taking the seller's explanations at face value. Here, for example, are some of the most common reasons why owners offer their businesses for sale:

1. Old age or illness.
2. Desire to relocate in a different section of the country.
3. Decision to accept a position with another company.
4. Unprofitability of the business.
5. Discontinuance of an exclusive sales franchise.

The buyer will also be interested in the history of the business and the direction in which it is moving. To form a clear idea of the firm's value, however, the buyer must eventually examine the financial data pertaining to its operation. Although valuation is not a science, the entrepreneur must decide how much the business is worth. A logical starting point is an independent audit of the firm offered for sale.

The Independent Audit The major purpose of an independent audit is to reveal the accuracy and completeness of the financial statements of the business. It also determines whether the seller has used acceptable accounting procedures in depreciating equipment and in valuing inventory. If financial statements are available for the past five or ten years, or even longer, the buyer can obtain some idea of trends for the business.

Adjustment of Audited Statements   Even audited statements may be misleading and require "normalizing" to obtain a realistic picture of the business. For example, business owners sometimes understate business income by failing to report some cash receipts as taxable income. Adjustment may also be required if the pricing of goods and/or services is abnormally low—lower than necessary to attract a satisfactory volume of business.

Other items that may need adjustment include personal or family expenses and wage or salary payments. For example, costs related to the family use of business vehicles frequently appear as a business expense. And in some situations, family members receive excessive compensation or none at all. "I don't touch 80% of the businesses ... even when you have the books and records, it's a fiction ... the owners hide the perks," cautions Stanley Salmore, a Beverly Hills business broker.[14] All items must be examined carefully to be sure that they relate to the business and are realistic. Exhibit 3–4 shows an income statement that has been adjusted by a prospective buyer. Notice carefully the reasons for the adjustments that have been made. Naturally, many other adjustments can be performed.

The buyer should also scrutinize the seller's balance sheet to see whether asset book values are realistic. Property often appreciates in value after it is recorded on the books.[15] In other cases, physical facilities or inventory or receivables decline in value so that their actual worth is less than their inflated book value.

Valuation of the Business   A word of caution is needed for those who see the valuation process as simple. It is not easy or exact. Officers of Corporate Investment Business Brokers describe the situation as follows:

> A lot of them [small businesses] are still run out of shoe boxes. . . . What to do? Ask to examine federal tax returns and state sales tax statements. . . . You can gain a better fix on the business by looking through invoices and receipts with both customers and suppliers, as well as bank statements.[16]

Even with accurately adjusted financial statements, the business valuation process is difficult. Each of several valuation methods focuses on different elements of value, but none is without its unique limitations. There are four common approaches to business valuation based on the following: (1) market value, (2) replacement cost, (3) liquidation value, and (4) earnings.

Exhibit 3-4   Income Statement as Adjusted by Prospective Buyer

Original Income Statement			Required Adjustments	Adjusted Income Statement	
Estimated sales	$172,000			$172,000	
Cost of goods sold	84,240			84,240	
Gross profit		$87,760			$87,760
Operating expenses:					
Rent	$20,000		Rental agreement will expire in six months; Rent is expected to increase 20 percent.	$24,000	
Salaries	19,860			19,860	
Telephone	990			990	
Advertising	11,285			11,285	
Utilities	2,580			2,580	
Insurance	1,200		Property is underinsured; Adequate coverage will double present cost	2,400	
Professional services	1,200			1,200	
Credit card expense	1,860		Amount of credit card expense appears unreasonably large; Buyer assumes that approximately $1,400 of this amount may be better classified as personal expense.	460	
Miscellaneous	1,250	60,225		1,250	$64,025
Net income		$27,535			$23,735

73

In this section we describe these approaches and provide a calculated example of how to apply the earnings approach.

The Market Value Approach   The **market value approach** relies on previous sales of similar businesses. These transactions establish the value of the one currently being appraised. Obviously, successful application of this method depends on the similarity of the businesses and the recency of the sales. If good data can be obtained, this approach is highly desirable because it is simple and reflects market values. Real estate appraisals rely extensively on this method.

The Replacement Cost Approach   The **replacement cost approach** to business valuation is one of several asset-based methods. A buyer following this approach tries to find the replacement value of property being purchased. A practical starting point is the most recent balance sheet of the business. Replacement cost would then be determined for all assets contributing to the business; some balance-sheet assets may be obsolete and of no continuing value to operations. Although this method of valuation usually ignores nontangible assets, it can increase the accuracy of asset values shown on the unadjusted balance sheet. This method is also difficult to use when a small business has been operating out of a "cigar box" and has no formal financial statements.

The Liquidation Value Approach   The **liquidation value approach** is another asset-based method of establishing value. The value of the business is equated with the salvage value of the business if operations ceased. Although liquidation is not the typical goal of the entrepreneur, this method does provide a minimum value of the business under a "worst scenario" assumption.

The Earnings Approach   The **earnings approach** centers on estimating the amount of potential income that may be produced by the business in the next year. A desired rate of return is then applied to the income estimate. The amount of investment equating these two factors is the estimated value of the business. This method is a practical approach consistent with the entrepreneur's desire to reap the operating benefits of the business.

The earnings approach can be further refined by incorporating year-by-year estimates of future income and "discounting" their value to determine current value. This refinement accounts for the greater value of a certain sum of money today compared to some time in the future. We develop the "discounting" concept much more fully in Chapter 21.

Because of the popularity and usefulness of valuation based on earnings, we wish to elaborate on this approach with a calculated example. We will use adjusted net income as our measure of earnings. According to David W. Nicholas, a vice-president of American Appraisal of New York, this method is the best valuation approach for entrepreneurs.[17] Valuation based on net income requires the use of a process known as **capitalization of profit.** Using this process, the buyer first estimates the dollars of profit that may be expected and then determines the dollar amount of investment that should logically earn the estimated dollars of profit. The dollar amount of investment constitutes the value of the business.

To illustrate, suppose that the adjusted income statement of a business shows that its annual net income is $80,000. What should a buyer be willing to pay for such a business? To answer this question, the buyer should follow four steps:

Step 1: Estimate the probable future profit for next year on the basis of past profit data. In doing this, the buyer must adjust past profit figures to eliminate nonrecurring gains or losses—for example, a loss from a fire. The buyer must ask himself or herself what operating profit the business can be expected to earn in the future.

Step 2: Allow for personal time invested in the business. In the case of a proprietorship, see whether the expenses shown on the income statement include a proper salary for the owner-manager. If no allowance has been made for the owner-manager's salary, a reasonable amount should be deducted before capitalizing the profit. Of course, this assumes that the buyer intends to devote personal time to the business—time that might otherwise be spent productively elsewhere. In the case of both proprietorships and partnerships, the "salary" for a proprietor or partner is not identified as an expense but is included as part of the firm's net profit.

Step 3: Estimate the degree of risk involved in the business. One might expect a 30 to 40 percent return on investment in businesses that entail considerable risk; in a less hazardous venture, 20 or 25 percent might be quite satisfactory.

Step 4: Determine the existence and amount of goodwill, if any. Goodwill derives from the loyalty of customers or other advantages that cause earnings to be exceptionally high in view of the physical resources involved. Goodwill tends to be less durable than other assets and thus is worth proportionately less to the buyer.

Following these four steps, let us now calculate the value of that business whose annual income we estimated to be $80,000. According to Step 1, we must decide whether the $80,000 can be expected to continue in the future. An examination of the income statement may show no unusual expense or income items. A general review of business prospects, moreover, may suggest no drastic changes in the foreseeable future. We might assume, therefore, that the $80,000 constitutes a reasonable prediction of future profit.

Following Step 2, we may find that no salary expense has been shown for the owner-manager in arriving at the $80,000 profit. If the buyer places a value of $45,000 on personal time and effort, this amount should be deducted from the $80,000, leaving $35,000 to be capitalized. This $35,000 is the profit that will compensate the buyer for the dollars invested in the business.

When estimating the degree of risk involved in the business as prescribed in Step 3, we assume that the buyer considers the business to be moderately safe and feels that a 20 percent profit would be a good return on investment (ROI) in comparison with alternative investment opportunities. We can then calculate the value of the business as follows, assuming that no goodwill exists:

Value of business × Desired rate of return = Net profit
Value of business × 20% = $35,000
Value of business = $35,000 ÷ 0.20
Value of business = $175,000

Thus, the $175,000 provides a benchmark for use in negotiating the purchase price of the business.

In following Step 4, the buyer inquires about the existence of goodwill. If the profit is unreasonably high in view of the physical resources of the business, the buyer will be purchasing goodwill along with the physical assets of the business. And if a substantial amount of the firm's profit is attributable to goodwill, the buyer should value the firm more conservatively due to the intangible and somewhat fragile nature of goodwill. Under these circumstances, the buyer needs to use a higher rate for capitalizing the profit. Assuming that the higher rate, adjusted for goodwill, is 30 percent rather than 20 percent, the value of the business can then be calculated as follows:

Value of business $\times$ Desired rate of return = Net profit
Value of business $\times$ 30% = $35,000
Value of business = $35,000 $\div$ 0.30
Value of business = $116,667

Clearly, the estimated value of the business is lower when we assume that we are paying for goodwill, which may soon disappear.

Other Factors to Evaluate A number of other factors remain to be explored when evaluating an existing business. Some of these are:

1. *Competition.* The prospective buyer should look into the extent, intensity, and location of competing businesses. In particular, the buyer should check to see whether the business in question is gaining or losing in the race with competitors.
2. *Market.* The adequacy of the market to maintain all competing business units, including the one to be purchased, should be determined. This entails market research, study of census data, and personal, on-the-spot observation at each competitor's place of business.
3. *Future community developments.* Examples of community developments planned for the future include:
   a. Changes in zoning ordinances already enacted but not yet in effect.
   b. Land condemnation suits for construction of a public building, municipally operated parking lot, or public park.
   c. Change from two-way traffic flow to one-way traffic.
   d. Discontinuance of bus routes that will eliminate public transportation for customers and employees.
4. *Legal commitments.* These may include contingent liabilities, unsettled lawsuits, delinquent tax payments, missed payrolls, overdue rent or installment payments, and mortgages of record against any of the real property acquired.
5. *Union contracts.* The prospective buyer should determine what type of labor agreement, if any, is in force, as well as the quality of the firm's employee relations.
6. *Buildings.* The quality of the buildings housing the business, particularly the fire hazard involved, should be checked. In addition, the buyer should determine whether there are restrictions on access to the building. For example, is there access to the building without crossing the property of another? If necessary, a right of way should be negotiated before the purchase contract is closed.

SMALL BUSINESS IN ACTION
Let's Make a Deal

Cash up front is sometimes the preferred method in a buyout deal because the seller-entrepreneur wants to fund another new venture. "If I were interested in stock, I'd be in the stock market," says Laurence Smith, who sold his Boston-based Associated Mobile X-Ray Services, Inc., in 1984. Smith remained with the new owners on salary.

In other buyouts, the sellers may not want all cash. Consider the situation of Jan and Al Williams when they sold their Bio Clinic Company in Southern California. When they sold their firm, they were getting a divorce and each had different objectives for the sale. "I wanted stock," says Jan; "My husband wanted as much cash as possible." The purchaser wanted to give all cash, but after a long negotiation gave cash to Al and stock to Jan.

Source: Sandra Salmans, "Cutting the Deal." Reprinted from the January, 1988, issue of *VENTURE, For Entreprenerial Business Owners & Investors,* © 1988.

7. *Future national emergencies.* The buyer should determine the potential impact of possible future national emergencies such as price and wage controls, energy shortages, human-resources shortages, raw-material shortages, and the like.
8. *Product prices.* The prospective owner should compare the prices of the seller's products with manufacturers' or wholesalers' catalogs or prices of competing products in the locality. This is necessary to assure full and fair pricing of goods whose sales are reported on the seller's financial statements.

Negotiating the Purchase Price and Terms

The purchase price of the business is determined by negotiation between buyer and seller. Although the calculated value is not the price of the business, it gives the buyer an estimated value to use in negotiating price. Typically, the buyer tries to purchase the firm for something less than the full estimated value. Likewise, the seller tries to get more than the estimated value.

An important part of this negotiation is the terms of purchase. In many cases, the buyer is unable to pay the full price in cash and must seek extended terms. The seller may also be concerned about taxes on the profit from the sale. Terms may be more attractive to the buyer and seller as the amount of the down payment is reduced and/or the length of the repayment period is extended.

Closing the Deal

As in the purchase of real estate, the purchase of a business is closed at a specific time. The closing may be handled, for example, by a title company or an attorney. Preferably the closing should occur under the direction of an independent third party. If the seller's attorney is suggested as the closing agent, the buyer should exercise caution. Regardless of the closing arrangements, the buyer should never go through a closing without extensive consultation with a qualified attorney.

A number of important documents are completed during the closing. These include a bill of sale, certifications as to taxing and other governmental authorities, and agreements pertaining to future payments and related guarantees to the seller.

Looking Back

1. There are many alternatives for starting a small business, but these options can usually be grouped into one of four categories: startups, buyouts, franchising, and joining a family business.
2. The many different types of startup ideas can generally be classified into one of three groups: existing concepts redirected to new markets, technologically derived ideas, and ideas to perform existing functions in a new and improved manner.
3. Ideas for new startups come from many different sources, including personal experiences, hobbies, accidental discovery, and deliberate search. Such ideas require study and refinement before the business is launched.
4. A number of reasons exist for buying a business. Fewer uncertainties are involved than in launching an entirely new firm. Also, the facilities, personnel, and other elements of a going business are already assembled. The business may also be available at a bargain price.

> **5.** After corrected financial statements are available, a buyer can estimate the value of the business by the market value approach, the replacement cost approach, the liquidation value approach, or the earnings approach.

DISCUSSION QUESTIONS

1. Why would an entrepreneur prefer to launch an entirely new venture rather than buy an existing firm?
2. Describe a business that grew out of the entrepreneur's hobby and one that resulted from the entrepreneur's work experience.
3. Suggest a product or a service not currently available that might lead to a new small business. How safe would it be to launch a new small business depending solely on that one new product or service? Why?
4. Classify the business of a mobile car service that changes oil and filters in parking lots according to the Exhibit 3–2 categories. Can you think of a similar but different service that might fit the other two categories? Explain.
5. Explain the concept of serendipity. What do you think is the typical reaction of an individual after experiencing serendipity?
6. Do you perceive any ethical questions when an entrepreneur bases a startup on someone else's new-venture idea? Explain.
7. Do you believe some individuals are able to think of new-venture ideas more easily than others because they are born with more creativity? Explain.
8. Which reasons for buying an existing business, in contrast to starting from scratch, appear most important to you?
9. Is uncertainty eliminated or merely minimized when an existing business is purchased? Explain.
10. What are the advantages and disadvantages of using a business broker when considering a buyout?
11. What are the advantages of purchasing an existing business with all cash up front? What are the disadvantages?
12. How should a buyer determine the estimated profit and rate of return to use in capitalizing business profits?
13. Suppose that a business firm available for purchase has shown an average net profit of $40,000 for the past five years. During these years, the amount of profit fluctuated between $20,000 and $60,000. State your

assumptions and then calculate the value that you might use in negotiating the purchase price.

14. What is the significance of a seller's real reasons for selling? How might you discover them?

15. Contrast the market value valuation approach with the earnings approach. Which is easier to apply? Which is the most appropriate?

YOU MAKE THE CALL

Situation 1

After selling his small computer business, James Stroder set out on an 18-month sailboat trip with his wife and young children. He had founded the business several years earlier, and it had become a million-dollar enterprise. Now, he was looking for a new venture.

While giving his two sons reading lessons on board the sailboat—they each had slight reading disabilities—he had an inspiration for a new company. Stroder wondered why a computer could not be programmed to drill students in special-education classes who needed repetition to recognize and pronounce new words correctly.

Source: The Wall Street Journal. [Names are fictitious.]

Questions

1. How would you classify Stroder's startup idea?

2. What source of a new idea, according to this book, would describe Stroder's circumstance?

3. Do you think Stroder might develop his idea with a startup rather than a buyout? Why?

Situation 2

Four years after starting their business, Bill and Janet Brown began to have thoughts of selling out. Their business, Bucket-To-Go, had been extremely successful, as indicated by an average 50 percent increase in revenue each of its years in existence. Their business began when Bill turned his hobby of making wooden buckets into a full-time business. The buckets were marketed nationwide in gift shops and garden centers.

Sam Kline learned of the buyout opportunity after contacting a business broker. Kline wanted to retire from corporate life and thought this business was an excellent opportunity.

Questions

1. Which valuation technique would you suggest Kline use to value the business? Why?
2. What accounting information should Kline consider? What adjustments might be required?
3. What qualitative information should Kline evaluate?

EXPERIENTIAL EXERCISES

1. Research small business periodicals in your school's library and locate five or six new startups that have been profiled by the magazine. Report to the class, describing the source of the idea.
2. Consult the Yellow Pages of your local telephone directory to locate the name of a business broker. Contact the business broker and report to the class on how that broker values businesses.
3. Select a certain startup that you are personally familiar with and then write out a description of your experiential and educational background and evaluate the exent to which it would qualify you to operate that startup.
4. Consult your local newspaper's new-business listings and then contact one of the firms to arrange a personal interview. Report to the class on how the new-business idea originated. Classify the type of new-business idea according to Exhibit 3–2.

REFERENCES TO SMALL-BUSINESS PRACTICES

Cooper, Glen. "How Much Is Your Business Worth?" *In Business,* Vol. 6, No. 5 (September–October, 1984), pp. 50–54.

    An in-depth look at business valuation is provided by the author. An actual appraisal with somewhat involved computations is included.

Galant, Debbie. "The Stuff Dreams Are Made Of." *Venture,* Vol. 10, No. 1 (January, 1988), pp. 52–56.

    This article describes several entrepreneurs who have turned their hobbies into successful businesses. The pros and cons of building a business from a hobby are examined through the entrepreneurs' experiences.

Harrell, Wilson. "Entrepreneurial Terror." *Inc.* Vol. 9, No. 2 (February, 1987), pp. 74–76.

The author of this article shares his own personal terror as he explains his entrepreneurial experiences.

Kotite, Erika. "Reinventing the Wheel Part I." *Entrepreneur,* Vol. 16, No. 7 (July, 1988), pp. 54–59.

The theme of this article is that "anything that has been done can be done better." The background of the idea to develop a cloth diaper with all the convenience of a disposable diaper is recounted. How the idea for a new bicycle seat came about is also described.

Posner, Bruce G. "Good Vibrations." *Inc.,* Vol. 10, No. 7 (July, 1988), pp. 64–68.

This article describes the anatomy of a startup—a new recording studio. Problems of marketing and financing are discussed.

ENDNOTES

1. Paulette Thomas, "The Big Idea," *The Wall Street Journal* (June 10, 1988), p. 8R.

2. Jerry E. Bishop, "Tiny Sponges Try to Capture a Big Role in Many Products," *The Wall Street Journal* (June 20, 1986), p. 19.

3. Rachell Orr, "Merrily They Roll Along," *Nation's Business,* Vol. 75, No. 11 (November, 1987), p. 65.

4. Georganne Fiumara, "Busy Woman Needs 'Wife,'" *Family Circle,* Vol. 101, No. 12 (September 1, 1988), p. 30.

5. Ellen M. Weber, "Retirees Go to Work for Themselves," *USA Today* (August 21, 1986), p. 1.

6. Earl C. Gottschalk, Jr., "More Ex-Managers Seek to Turn Hobbies into Full-Time Businesses," *The Wall Street Journal* (December 23, 1986), p. 21.

7. Laurie Kretchmar, "Taking a Pop at the Jeans Market," *Venture,* Vol. 10, No. 6 (June, 1988), p. 10.

8. "100 Ideas for New Businesses," *Venture,* Vol. 9, No. 12 (December, 1987), pp. 35–70.

9. Stephen Robinett, "What Schools Can Teach Entrepreneurs," *Venture,* Vol. 7, No. 2 (February, 1985), p. 58.

10. Jeffry A. Timmons, "A Business Plan Is More Than a Financing Device," *Harvard Business Review,* Vol. 58, No. 2 (March–April, 1980), p. 30.

11. William A. Cohen, *The Entrepreneur and Small Business Problem Solver* (New York: John Wiley & Sons, 1983), pp. 126–127.

12. "Selling Your Small Company," *Business Week,* No. 2879 (February 4, 1985), p. 101.

13. Ronald Tanner, "When It's Better to Buy," *Venture,* Vol. 6, No. 6 (June, 1984), p. 76.

14. Stanford L. Jacobs, "Asian Immigrants Build Fortune in U.S. by Buying Cash Firms," *The Wall Street Journal* (October 1, 1984), p. 29.

15. Standard accounting practice requires land, for example, to be recorded

at cost. No adjustments are subsequently made to recognize its increasing or decreasing value. When real estate values are changing substantially, therefore, the amounts shown on the books do not correspond with reality.

16. John A. Byrne, "The Business of Businesses," *Forbes,* Vol. 134, No. 4 (August 13, 1984), p. 112.

17. William Meyers, "Determining a Value," *Venture,* Vol. 7, No. 1 (January, 1985), p. 35.

4 FRANCHISING OPPORTUNITIES

Spotlight on Small Business

Courtesy of ProForma

Successful small-business ventures are not limited to startups with spectacular new products or buyouts of existing firms. Many times they are a matter of recognizing a need and providing ordinary products to willing customers through appropriate marketing strategies.

Greg Muzzillo is an entrepreneur who took existing business products and developed the successful marketing program that he franchised. His $20 million company, with 106 franchises in 1989, began when he quit his job as an accountant and invested in a $250 answering machine. Now his company, called ProForma, Inc., distributes business forms, commercial printing, office supplies, and computer supplies to businesses.

Muzzillo says, "We're looking to be a $3 billion-plus business by the year 2000." The entrepreneurial team is dedicated to supporting all its franchisees and looks long and hard at all prospective franchisees before offering a franchise. "Most importantly, we're looking for someone who's willing to invest themselves full-time in the business. We're not representing this as any type of get-rich-quick scheme," cautions Muzzillo.

Source: Adapted from "Formidable Franchise." Reprinted with permission from *Entrepreneur,* Magazine, April 1988.

Looking Ahead

Watch for the following important topics:
1. Types of franchising systems.
2. Advantages and limitations of becoming a franchisee.
3. Considerations in evaluating a franchise.
4. Advantages and disadvantages of becoming a franchisor.
5. The future of franchising.
6. New terms and concepts:

franchising	piggyback franchising
franchisee	master franchising
franchisor	subfranchising
franchise contract	System A franchising
franchise	System B franchising
product and trade name	System C franchising
franchising	disclosure document
business format franchising	

In Chapter 3 we explained the new-business alternatives of creating an entirely new venture and buying an existing business—startups and buyouts. In this chapter, we examine the third alternative—beginning a business with franchising.

Scope and Development of Franchising

Franchising offers an attractive option for starting a small business. The franchising concept helps thousands of entrepreneurs realize their

business-ownership dreams each year. Initially, let us examine the language and structure of franchising.

Franchising Terminology

The term franchising is defined in many ways. In this text, we use a broad definition to encompass its wide diversity. **Franchising** is a marketing system revolving around a two-party legal agreement whereby one party (the **franchisee**) is granted the privilege to conduct business as an individual owner but is required to operate according to methods and terms specified by the other party (the **franchisor**). The legal agreement is known as the **franchise contract,** and the privileges it contains are called the **franchise.**

The potential value of any franchising arrangement is determined by the rights contained in the franchise contract, and the extent and importance of these rights are quite varied. For example, a potential franchisee may desire the right to use a widely recognized product or name. The term commonly used to describe this relationship between supplier and dealer is **product and trade name franchising.** Gasoline service stations and soft drink bottlers are typical examples. Product and trade name franchising consistently accounts for over two-thirds of all franchise sales.

Alternatively, the potential franchisee may seek an entire marketing system and an ongoing process of assistance and guidance. This type of relationship is referred to as **business format franchising.** The volume of sales and number of franchise units owned through business format franchising have increased steadily since the early 1970s. Fast-food outlets and business services are examples of this type of franchising.

The term piggybacking has recently been used to describe a new franchising strategy. **Piggyback franchising** refers to the operation of a retail franchise within the physical facilities of a host store. Examples would be a cookie franchise doing business inside an Arby's fast-food outlet or a car-phone franchise within an automobile dealership. This form of franchising benefits both parties. The host store is able to add a new product line, and the franchise is located near the customers.

Another franchising strategy gaining widespread usage is **master franchising** or **subfranchising.** A master franchisor is an individual who has a continuing contractual relationship with a franchisor to sell its franchises.[1] This independent businessperson is a type of sales agent. Master franchisors are responsible for finding new franchisees within a specified territory.

Sometimes they will even provide support services such as training and warehousing traditionally provided by the franchisor.

Types of Franchising Systems

Three types, or levels, of franchising systems offer opportunities for entrepreneurs. Exhibit 4–1 depicts each of these systems and provides examples. In **System A,** the producer/creator (the franchisor) grants a franchise to a wholesaler (the franchisee). This system is often used in the soft-drink industry. Dr Pepper and Coca-Cola are examples of System A franchisors.

In the second level, designated as **System B,** the wholesaler is the franchisor. This system prevails among supermarkets and general merchandis-

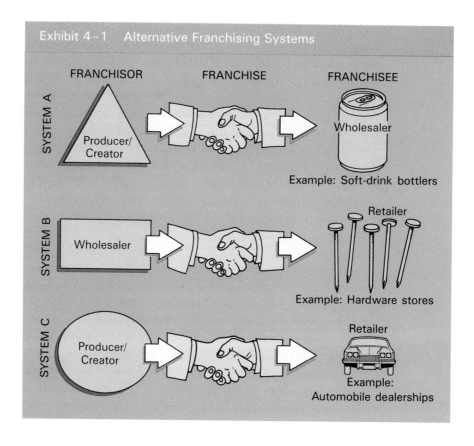

Exhibit 4–1   Alternative Franchising Systems

FRANCHISOR   FRANCHISE   FRANCHISEE

SYSTEM A

Producer/Creator

Wholesaler

Example: Soft-drink bottlers

SYSTEM B

Wholesaler

Retailer

Example: Hardware stores

SYSTEM C

Producer/Creator

Retailer

Example: Automobile dealerships

ing stores. Ben Franklin, Gamble-Skogmo, and Ace Hardware are examples of System B franchisors.

The third type, **System C,** is the most widely used. This system finds the producer/creator as franchisor and the retailer as franchisee. Automobile dealerships and gasoline service stations are prototypes of this system. In recent years, this system also has been used successfully by many fast-food outlets and printing services. Notable examples of System C franchisors are Burger King and Kwik-Kopy.

Buying a Franchise

"Look before you leap" is an old adage that should be heeded by potential franchisees. Entrepreneurial enthusiasm should not cloud the eyes to the realities, both good and bad, of franchising. We shall first look at the advantages of buying a franchise and then examine the weaknesses of this decision. Study these topics carefully, and remember them when you are evaluating a franchise.

The Pros and Cons of Franchising

The choice of franchising over alternative methods of starting your own business ultimately is based on adding up the pluses and minuses of franchising after considering the entrepreneur's personal goals and aspirations. Exhibit 4–2 depicts the major considerations for this evaluation. Franchising obviously will not be the choice for all prospective entrepreneurs, because each consideration will carry different weight for different individuals. However, in their particular circumstances, many people find the franchise form of business to be the best choice.

Advantages of Franchising

A franchise is attractive for many reasons. Three advantages in particular warrant further analysis. A franchise can offer (1) formal training, (2) financial assistance, and (3) marketing and management benefits. Naturally, all franchises may not be equally strong on all these points. But it is these advantages which motivate many persons to consider the franchise arrangement.

Formal Training The importance of formal training received from the franchisor is underlined by the managerial weakness of many small entre-

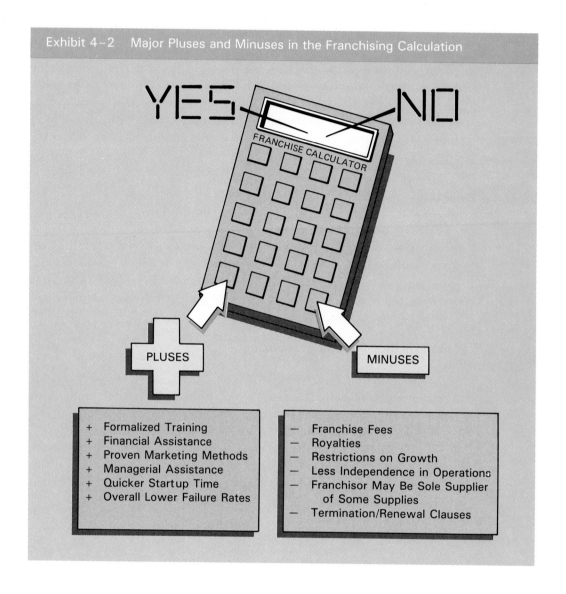

Exhibit 4–2 Major Pluses and Minuses in the Franchising Calculation

YES   NO

FRANCHISE CALCULATOR

PLUSES

MINUSES

+ Formalized Training
+ Financial Assistance
+ Proven Marketing Methods
+ Managerial Assistance
+ Quicker Startup Time
+ Overall Lower Failure Rates

− Franchise Fees
− Royalties
− Restrictions on Growth
− Less Independence in Operations
− Franchisor May Be Sole Supplier
   of Some Supplies
− Termination/Renewal Clauses

preneurs. To the extent that this weakness can be overcome, therefore, the training program offered by the franchisor constitutes a major benefit.

The value and the effectiveness of training are evident from the records of business failures, a large majority of which are caused by deficiencies in management. For example, franchisors such as McDonald's and Kentucky Fried Chicken reputedly have never experienced a failure. Some franchisors admit to purchasing a weak operating franchisee to keep it from going under, thereby maintaining its image. However, there appears to be little question that the failure rate for independent small businesses in general is much higher than for franchised businesses in particular.

Operating as a franchisee, however, in no way guarantees success. A particular franchisor may offer unsatisfactory training, or the franchisee may not apply the training correctly or may fail for some other reason.

Initial Training Training by the franchisor often begins with an initial period of a few days or a few weeks at a central training school or at another established location. For example, the Holiday Inn franchise chain operates the hotel industry's largest training center, Holiday Inn University, which was built in 1972 at a cost of $5 million. Initial training programs cover not

---

SMALL BUSINESS IN ACTION
Franchise Boot Camp

At Kwik-Kopy School new franchisees receive a crash course on how to avoid failure. "My job is to have them leave here with the attitude they can lick the world," says Nathan Winfield, the training director.

Despite the tennis courts and the swimming pool of the 23-acre campus, the three weeks' training is no picnic. Although the course teaches franchisees how to deal with paper jams and the other challenges of printing and duplicating, most of the time is devoted to managing and selling. The 64-year-old founder, Bud Hadfield, has no

KWIK-KOPY SCHOOL

pretensions about the Kwik-Kopy School. "We take someone who's been wearing a green eyeshade for 20 years and train them to run a business in three weeks. At one time it was four weeks," he says, "but we found that at the end of three weeks they want to kill you."

The end of the course is marked by hugs, photos, and exchange of addresses. At the commencement ceremony, Mr. Winfield concludes by saying, "Welcome to the Kwik-Kopy family."

Source: Thomas Petzinger, Jr. "Kwik Kopy College," *The Wall Street Journal* (June 10, 1988), p. 27R. Reprinted by permission of *The Wall Street Journal.* © Dow Jones & Company, Inc. 1988. All Rights Reserved.
Photo Source: KWIK-KOPY SCHOOL courtesy of KWIK-KOPY CORPORATION.

only the operating procedures to be used by the business, but also broader topics such as record keeping, inventory control, insurance, and human relations.

The Mister Donut franchise requires an initial training course of four weeks, including such topics as doughnut making, accounting and controls, advertising and merchandising, scheduling of labor and production, purchasing, and so on. Naturally, the nature of the product and the type of business affect the amount and type of training required in the franchised business. In most cases, training constitutes an important advantage of the franchising system and permits individuals who have had little training and education to start and succeed in businesses of their own.

Continuing Guidance   Initial training is ordinarily supplemented with subsequent training and guidance. This may involve refresher courses and/or training by a traveling representative who visits the franchisee's business from time to time. The franchisee may also receive manuals and other printed materials that provide guidance for the business. However, guidance shades into control, so that in particular cases it may be difficult to distinguish the two. The franchisor normally places a considerable emphasis upon observing strict controls. Still, much of the continued training goes far beyond the application of controls. While some franchising systems have developed excellent training programs, this is by no means universal. Some unscrupulous promoters falsely promise satisfactory training.

Exhibit 4–3 displays selected listings from the U.S. Department of Commerce Publication entitled *Franchise Opportunities Handbook*. This handbook contains a comprehensive listing of franchisors with a brief statement about the nature and requirements of each franchise. Notice the description of training provided by the four franchises listed.

Financial Assistance   The costs of starting an independent business are often high and the prospective entrepreneur's sources of capital quite limited. The entrepreneur's standing as a prospective borrower is weakest at this point. But by teaming up with a franchising organization, the aspiring franchisee may enhance the likelihood of obtaining financial assistance.

If the franchising organization considers the applicant to be a suitable prospect with a high probability of success, it frequently extends a helping hand financially. For example, the franchisee seldom is required to pay the complete cost of establishing the business. In addition, the beginning franchisee is normally given a payment schedule that can be met through successful operation. Also, the franchisor may permit delay in payments for

*PROFORMA, INC.
4705 Van Epps Road
Cleveland, Ohio 44131
John Campbell, Director of Franchise
Development

Description of Operation: Business products. Distributors of business forms, commercial printing, office supplies, computer supplies, and computers. This is not a quick print shop or retail operation.

Number of Franchisees: 33 in 17 States

In Business Since: 1978, franchising started 1985

Equity Capital Needed: $15,000–$25,000

Financial Assistance Available: Available for qualified and needy individuals.

Training Provided: Up to 2 weeks intensive training program covering industry/product knowledge and selling skills.

Managerial Assistance Available: Franchise owner does not need to hire any administrative employees because most administrative functions are performed by franchisor. Franchisor answers franchisee's telephone (toll free number), generates billings, does computer input, logs cash receipts, and generates monthly business reports. Continuous managerial advice is available from an experienced team of professionals in selling, product knowledge, manufacturer sourcing, and administration.

*THE PRO IMAGE
380 North 200 West
Suite 203
Bountiful, Utah 84010
Mark Gilleland, National Marketing Director

Description of Operation: The Pro Image carries "Everything for the Sports Fan." These unique retail stores feature gifts and clothing that is licensed and approved by the professional and collegiate teams. The stores are generally 1,000 square feet and are located in regional shopping malls.

Number of Franchisees: 100 in 25 States

In Business Since: 1985

Equity capital Needed: $60,000 to $90,000

Financial Assistance Available: None. The Pro Image assists in arranging third party financing.

Training Provided: The franchisee is trained in all phases of operations, merchandising, advertising, inventory control, management, bookkeeping, customer relations, and purchasing. Five to 10 days home office and field training.

Managerial Assistance Available: The Pro Image assists the franchisee in site selection and leasehold arrangements. The company provides complete operating manuals and accounting system. The Pro Image also allows the franchisee access to company purchasing system and its discounts. The company assists with grand opening and provides ongoing assistance for new products, promotions, and merchandising ideas.

*BEN FRANKLIN STORES, INC.
500 East North Avenue
Carol Stream, Illinois 60188

Description of Operation: Ben Franklin Stores is a general merchandise division of Fox Meyer, which provides both merchandise and retailing assistance to franchisees in 50 States. The franchisee operates a private business with the advantages of chain-store buying, merchandising and promotional expertise, with a nationwide reputation for professional service to the public.

Number of Franchisees: 1,320 in 50 States

In Business Since: 1877

Equity Capital Needed: $80,000–$120,000— may be less for existing stores.

Financial Assistance Available: Financing is arranged through local and regional commercial lending institutions.

Training Provided: The new franchisee is required to attend one week of classroom instruction in headquarters, and two weeks in-store training at one of our training stores.

Managerial Assistance Available: Assistance is available in site selection, lease negotiations, sales promotion and all phases of operation by regular visits of trained field and headquarters personnel.

(Continued)

Exhibit 4–3   *(Continued)*

*LITTLE KING RESTAURANT CORPORATION
11811 I' Street
Omaha, Nebraska 68137
Sidney B. Wertheim, President
David K. Kilby, Vice President,
Franchise Development

Description of Operation: The Little King Restaurant Corporation operates and directs a successful chain of company and franchised-owned submarine/deli-style sandwich and pizza outlets. Emphasis is on fresh-foods-fast, with the products being prepared from the freshest of ingredients directly in full-view of the customers, fresh bread baked on the premises, and a special 300 calorie or less "lite menu." Product quality, customer service, and store cleanliness are the standards of the Little King operation for over 18 years.

Number of Franchisees: 38 units in 14 States plus 26 company-owned outlets.

In Business Since: 1968—franchising began in 1978

Equity Capital Needed: $85,000–$125,000 (approximate) single restaurant. Multi-unit development program available to qualified candidates.

Financial Assistance Available: Equipment lease programs available through non-affiliated sources. Differed payment of multi-unit development program franchise fee.

Training Provided: Total 4 weeks. 2 week course in company head-quarters, Omaha, Nebraska, which includes in-store and classroom studies of operations, managerial methods, accounting procedures, marketing techniques. 2 weeks training and supervision is provided by field representatives in franchisee's restaurant prior to and during initial opening.

Managerial Assistance Available: Field representation and consultation is provided at franchisee's restaurant quarterly, in addition to weekly communications, verbal and written materials. Company provides promotional and marketing ideas and concepts to franchisees through monthly marketing report. Each facet of the operation is supported by detailed manuals.

Source: Andrew Kosteka. *Franchise Opportunities Handbook,* United States Department of Commerce (Washington: U.S. Government Printing Office, 1988).

products or supplies obtained from the parent organization, thus increasing the franchisee's working capital.

Association with a well-established franchisor may also improve the new franchisee's credit standing with a bank. The reputation of the franchising organization and the managerial and financial controls that it provides serve to recommend the new franchisee to a banker. Also, the franchisor frequently will cosign notes with a local bank, thus guaranteeing the franchisee's loan.

Exhibit 4–3 shows that, among these four franchisors, three mention a willingness to assist prospective franchisees with third-party financing and two offer to provide franchisor financing to some degree. (Notice that one of the franchisors in Exhibit 4–3 is ProForma, Inc., the franchise featured in this chapter's "Spotlight on Small Business.")

Marketing and Management Benefits   Most franchised products and services are widely known and accepted. For example, customers will readily buy McDonald's hamburgers or Baskin-Robbins ice cream because they know the reputation of these products. Or travelers who recognize a restaurant or a motel because of its name, type of roof, or some other feature may turn into a Denny's Restaurant or a Holiday Inn motel because of their previous experience and the knowledge that they can depend upon the food and service that these outlets provide. Thus, franchising offers both a proven successful line of business and product identification.

The entrepreneur who enters a franchising agreement acquires the right to use the franchisor's nationally advertised trademark or brand name. This serves to identify the local enterprise with the widely recognized product or service. Of course, the value of product identification differs with the type of product or service and the extent to which it has received widespread promotion. In any case, the franchisor maintains the value of its name by continued advertising and promotion.

In addition to offering a proven successful line of business and readily identifiable products or services, franchisors have developed and tested their methods of marketing and management. The standard operating manuals and procedures they supply have permitted other entrepreneurs to operate successfully. This is one reason why franchisors insist upon the observance of standardized methods of operation and performance. If some franchises were allowed to operate at substandard levels, they could easily destroy the customer's confidence in the entire system.

The existence of proven products and methods, however, does not guarantee that a franchised business will succeed. For example, what appeared to be a satisfactory location as a result of the franchisor's marketing research techniques may turn out to be inferior. Or the franchisee may lack ambition or perseverance. Yet the fact that a franchisor can show a record of successful operation proves that the system can work and has worked elsewhere.

Limitations of Franchising

Franchising is like a coin—it has two sides. We have examined the positive side of franchising, but we must look on the other side of the coin and examine its negative side. In particular, three shortcomings permeate the franchise form of business. These are: the cost of a franchise, the restric-

SMALL BUSINESS IN ACTION
The Other Side of the "Coin"

Franchising appears to be doing well going into the 1990s. The lure of being one's own boss and gaining financial success continues to attract aspiring entrepreneurs to franchising. But as with any story, there is always another side to the coin—the dark side of failure and disappointment. It is always wise to examine both sides before choosing franchising. The following experiences of a few franchisees represent this other side:

Louis Kallos's wife, Beata, cries as Kallos, a Hungarian immigrant, tells how he lost his $75,000 life savings. . . . Kallos and his lawyer claim . . . (the franchisor) . . . misrepresented the potential sales and profits. . . .
Agostine Maleiba of Philadelphia learned . . . the unpleasant way. In 1980 Maleiba owned 12 Arthur Treacher's Fish & Chips franchises. . . . By 1984, he had closed them all and lost $2.5 million. His troubles began when the original franchisor sold the company to Mrs. Paul's kitchens. Franchisees were told by the new owners that the only products they could use were Mrs. Paul's.
Stephen Gharakhani paid $95,000 to buy and equip a Wil Wright's Ice Cream Shop franchise—only to discover that "training" consisted of a manual and one visit from the franchisor.
Jose Ruiz of San Diego didn't take the time to see if an office cleaning franchisor was registered with California's Department of Corporations. Within eight months, he lost over $12,000.

You should never think of franchising as a sure, get-rich method of operating a business. However, by using common sense and doing your homework, you can improve your chances of success with franchising.

Source: Ellen Paris, "Franchising—Hope or Hype?" *Forbes,* December 15, 1986, pp. 42, 43. © Forbes Inc, 1986.

tions on growth that can accompany a franchise contract, and the loss of absolute independence on the part of the franchisee.

Cost of a Franchise The total franchise cost consists of several components. Only after all of these cost components have been examined can a realistic picture be drawn. The cost of a franchise begins with the franchise fee. Generally speaking, higher fees will be required by the well-known franchisors.

Other costs include royalty payments, promotion costs, inventory and supplies costs, and building and equipment costs. When these costs are considered with the franchise fee, the total investment may look surprisingly large. A McDonald's or Burger King franchise may require over $500,000 in startup costs. Other franchises, such as the Novus Windshield Repair franchise, which operates out of a car, requires under $10,000.[2] In addition to startup costs, it is often recommended that funds be available for at least six months to cover pre-opening expenses, training expenses, personal expenses, and emergencies.[3]

If entrepreneurs could earn the same income independently, they would save the amount of these fees and some of the other costs. However, this is not a valid objection if the franchisor provides the benefits previously described. In that case, franchisees are merely paying for the advantages of their relationship with the franchisor. And this may be a good investment indeed.

Restrictions on Growth   A basic way to achieve business growth is to expand the existing sales territory. However, many franchise contracts restrict the franchisee to a defined sales territory, thereby eliminating this form of growth. Usually, the franchisor agrees not to grant another franchise to operate within the same territory. The potential franchisee, therefore, should weigh territorial limitation against the advantages cited earlier.

Loss of Absolute Independence   Frequently, individuals leave salaried employment for entrepreneurship because they dislike working under the direct supervision and control of others. By entering into a franchise relationship, such individuals may simply find that a different pattern of close control over personal endeavors has taken over. The franchisee does surrender a considerable amount of independence upon signing a franchise agreement.

Even though the franchisor's regulation of business operations may be helpful in assuring success, it may be unpleasant to an entrepreneur who cherishes independence. In addition, some franchise contracts go to extremes by covering unimportant details or specifying practices that are more helpful to others in the chain than to the local operation. Thus, as an operator of a franchised business, the entrepreneur occupies the position of a semi-independent businessperson.

Evaluating Franchise Opportunities

Once an interest in becoming a franchisee emerges, much remains to be done before the dream materializes. The prospective franchisee must locate the right opportunity, investigate the franchise, and examine the franchise contract carefully.

Locating a Franchise Opportunity

With the growth of franchising over the years, the task of initially locating opportunities has become easier. Sources of franchise opportunities are promoted widely.

Often an entrepreneur's interest in franchising is sparked by franchisor advertisements in newspapers or magazines. These advertisements generally have headlines that appeal to the financial and personal rewards sought by the entrepreneur. Figure 4–1 shows a page from a popular business magazine advertising to a readership interested in small business. *The Wall Street Journal, Franchising Today, In Business,* and *Inc.* are examples of other publications that include information on franchise opportunities.

Investigate the Franchise Offer

The nature of the commitment required in franchising justifies a careful investigation inasmuch as a franchised business typically involves a substantial investment, possibly many thousands of dollars. Furthermore, the business relationship is one that may be expected to continue over a period of years.

Ordinarily, the investigation process is a two-way effort. The franchisor wishes to investigate the franchisee, and the franchisee obviously wishes to evaluate the franchisor and the type of opportunity offered. Time is required for this kind of investigation. One should be skeptical of a franchisor who pressures a franchisee to sign at once without allowing for proper investigation.

What should be the prospective entrepreneur's next step after becoming aware of a franchising opportunity? What sources of information are available? Do governmental agencies provide information on franchising? These and other questions should be considered as the entrepreneur evaluates franchising. Basically, three sources of information should be tapped: First, there are the franchisors themselves; second, there are existing and previous franchisees; third, there are several third-party sources. We will now examine the merits of each of these sources.

The Franchisor as a Source of Information   The most logical source of the greatest amount of information about a franchise is the franchisor. Obvi-

Figure 4–1   Franchise Opportunities Advertisements

FRANCHISE OPPORTUNITIES

For additional information circle desired numbers on Reader Service Card, page 64.   For advertising rates call: National 800-237-9851; Florida 800-553-8288

BE YOUR OWN BOSS!

What Comes Off the Drawing Board Can Make the Difference

Ben Franklin is the largest and oldest general merchandise franchise, established in 1927. Our program has been carefully designed—our "Blueprint for Success" clearly drafted and refined. We offer:

- Site Selection
- Financial Assistance
- Merchandising
- Group Insurance
- In-Store Guidance
- Store Planning
- Advertising
- Training
- Accounting & Payroll
- Weekly Delivery

If you have retail experience and a minimum equity investment of $100,000, let us help you put that to work for yourself. Ben Franklin makes it easy to own a store. Get the full story, (offered by prospectus only).

Ben Franklin® Stores, Inc.

Subsidiary of FoxMeyer Corporation
Write: Franchise Department G
Ben Franklin Stores, Inc.
P.O. Box 5938
Chicago, IL 60680

CIRCLE NO. 73 ON READER SERVICE CARD

OWN YOUR OWN SPORTS FRANCHISE

Be part of the 3rd fastest growing franchise in the U.S. as rated by Venture Magazine.

We offer sports fans gift stores located in high traffic malls. Investment level approx. 85K-100K.

For more information write:

EVERYTHING FOR THE SPORTS FAN

380 North 200 West, Bountiful, Utah 84010 or Call Collect (801) 292-8777

CIRCLE NO. 75 ON READER SERVICE CARD

Cashing Checks Is Big Business

We have cashed hundreds of millions of dollars worth of checks for a fee! This liquid and recession-resistant business has been in a few major cities for years. We have refined the art of cashing checks into a professional, computerized check cashing system that works. A total investment of $75K - $100K per location is required for this dynamic and financially rewarding opportunity. Single or multi-unit territories are available.

 Check Express

800-521-8211

Paint a Bright Financial Picture with a Koenig Art Emporium Franchise.

Koenig offers a proven business selling artist supplies, picture framing and framed graphics since 1933 with 110 stores now open. Minimum cash investment $50,000 with additional financing. To learn more about our successful team, call: **1-800-367-3500 or 203-877-4541**

Artist Supplies • Custom Framing
Where Creative People Shop

1777 Boston Post Road, Milford, CT 06460

FL, GA, IL, MA, MD, MI, NC, NJ, NY, OH, TN & VA.

CIRCLE NO. 74 ON READER SERVICE CARD

LITTLE KING RESTAURANT CORPORATION

TYPE OF BUSINESS: Little King operates and directs a successful chain of company and franchise-owned submarine/deli-style sandwich and pizza outlets. Emphasis is on Fresh-Foods-Fast, with the products being prepared from the freshest of ingredients directly in full view of the customer, fresh bread baked on the premises and a special 300 calorie "Lite Menu". Product quality, customer service, and store cleanliness are the standards of the Little King operation.

HISTORY: 19 years of select growth, 82 operations open and under development. Franchises available in 47 states.

CASH INVESTMENT: $50,000-$110,000 (approximately) single restaurant. Includes $19,500 franchise fee. Multi-unit (5 restaurants) $59,500. Financing assistance available.

CONTACT: David K. Kilby, Vice President, 11811 "I" Street, Omaha, NE 68137.
800-228-2148   In NE: 800-642-1629

LITTLE KING
America's Greatest Hero
Serving
FRESH FOOD FAST

CIRCLE NO. 76 ON READER SERVICE CARD

Source: Reprinted from the March, 1988, issue of *VENTURE, For Entrepreneurial Business Owners & Investors,* by special permission. © 1988 Venture Magazine, Inc., 521 Fifth Ave., New York, NY 10175-0028.

ously, information provided by a franchisor must be viewed in light of its purpose—to promote a franchise. However, there is no quicker source of information than this.

There are several ways to obtain information from a franchisor. The franchisor can be contacted directly, or information can be requested by responding to "Reader Service Cards"—a service provided by most business magazines. Notice in Figure 4-2 the references to the Reader Service Card at the bottom of four of the five advertisements. To demonstrate the Reader Service Card system, the authors responded to the Pro Image advertisement. Within a few days, we received an attractive brochure describing the Pro Image, an application form, and a cover letter from their marketing representative. These three items are the items typically received in an initial contact. Additionally, the Pro Image response included the question-and-answer document shown in Figure 4-2.

Financial data are usually provided in this information packet. However, it is important for potential franchisees to remember that many of the financial figures are only estimates. Reputable franchisors are careful not to represent that any franchisee can expect to attain certain levels of sales, gross income, or profits. After a potential franchisee has expressed further interest in a franchise by completing the application form and the franchisor has tentatively qualified the entrepreneur, a meeting is usually arranged to discuss the disclosure document. Sometimes this document is simply mailed to the individual.

The **disclosure document** is required by the Federal Trade Commission, and failure to make it available subjects the franchisor to possible fines. The document is somewhat technical, and some prospective entrepreneurs mistakenly fail either to read it or get professional assistance. For example, Gail Casano and her husband claim they were misled as to the potential of the Movieland U.S.A. franchise they eventually purchased in 1986. Now they are heavily in debt and the franchisor has folded. Casano was given a disclosure statement but admits she did not understand it because it was so technical.[4] All disclosure statements must carry a warning on the front page that advises the reader to study it and show it to an accountant or lawyer.

Existing Franchisees as a Source of Evaluation   There may be no better source of franchise facts than existing franchisees. Sometimes the location of a franchise may preclude an early visit to the business site. However, a simple telephone call can provide the viewpoint of someone in the position

Figure 4–2   Question-and-Answer Sheet

EVERYTHING FOR THE SPORTS FAN

380 No. 200 West, Suite 203 • Bountiful, UT 84010

ANSWERS TO QUESTIONS FREQUENTLY ASKED ABOUT THE PRO IMAGE® FRANCHISE PROGRAM

1
Q. **What do I need to obtain a Pro Image® franchise?**
A. Complete the Qualification Report and send it to us. If you meet our qualifications you will be invited to **our corporate office** to begin the process of owning your own The Pro Image® franchise.

2
Q. **What will a franchise cost?**
A. The first franchise is $13,000 payable at the time the franchise agreement is signed. A second franchise may be purchased for $7,500.

3
Q. **How much cash will I need beyond the franchise fee?**
A. You will need approximately $5,000 in working capital, $35,000 for inventory, and $6,000 for fixtures and equipment.

4
Q. **What about leasehold improvements?**
A. The leasehold improvements for your location within the mall can be expected to cost between $15,000-$40,000.

5
Q. **So, how much total cash do I need to secure a Pro Image® franchise?**
A. Franchise Fee $13,500
Inventory 35,000
Fixtures & Equipment 6,500
Leasehold Improvements *15,000
Working Capital 5,000
Total $75,000

6
Q. **Do you offer a finance program?**
A. No, but we can assist your banker to help you with financing. The amount you can finance depends on your qualifications and financial condition.

7
Q. **Is the price of all equipment competitively priced?**
A. Yes. Our equipment prices are specially priced because of our volume purchasing, however you are not obligated to buy it through our suppliers.

8
Q. **What is the term of the franchise?**
A. The term is for 10 years, with two five year renewal options at no additional charge.

*Leasehold improvements vary from mall to mall and ranges from $10,000 to $40,000.

Courtesy of The Pro Image, Inc.

(Continued)

Figure 4–2   *(Continued)*

9 Q. **Where will my store be located?**
A. We have a number of current locations available. If you would like your own location we will also evaluate it for you.

10 Q. **What is the charge for continuing services and royalty fee?**
A. 4% of gross sales exclusive of any sales tax.

11 Q. **Am I given territorial rights?**
A. Yes. The territory is defined as the mall in which your shop is located.

12 Q. **Do I receive training and assistance in opening my The Pro Image® store?**
A. Yes, Franchisees receive a 3-day training program conducted at The Pro Image® headquarters in Salt Lake City, Utah. Also, we help you with your initial store set-up and your opening day of business.

13 Q. **What form of continuing guidance will I receive?**
A. First of all, you will receive The Pro Image® Operations Manual covering the important facets of your retail operation. You will receive newsletters containing lower price negotiations on products, management tips and industry changes. We will also support you with advertising tips, merchandising and continuing guidance on purchasing inventory. Inventory control forms have been designed to help you efficiently run your business.

14 Q. **Do you have an inventory control system?**
A. Yes. We have a designed computer software system specifically for The Pro Image® franchise stores. It helps owners to control inventory, control employees, re-order of inventory, etc.

15 Q. **Do you have volume purchasing power?**
A. Yes. Since we are the largest franchisor of "Sports Fan Gift Stores" in the U.S., our franchisees get discounts with most vendors. We also have a warehouse facility that any franchisee can join.

16 Q. **What about advertising?**
A. Each franchisee is required to spend 1% of his gross sales on local advertising and promotion.

17 Q. **How soon can I be in operation once I have been accepted as a franchisee?**
A. Location is a determining factor. Once you have selected a location it can be completed within 90-120 days.

18 Q. **I'm ready to go! What should I do?**
A. First, fill out the Qualification Report. Upon receipt of your application, we will set up a visit with a corporate officer for final approval.

If you have any more questions, please call
or write The Pro Image, Inc., as listed below.

380 No. 200 West, Suite 203
Bountiful, UT 84010
Phone: (801) 292-8777

you are considering. If possible, also talk with franchisees who have left the business. They can offer valuable input about their decision.

Governmental and Trade Sources of Franchise Information   State and federal governments are valuable sources of franchising information. Since most states require registration of franchises, a prospective franchisee should not overlook these offices for assistance. The federal government publishes *Franchise Opportunities Handbook* and *Franchising in the Economy*. (The information in Exhibit 4–3 is taken from the first of these two publications.) Pilot Books publishes several franchising guides. The International Franchise Association is a trade association of franchisors that sponsors legal and government affairs symposiums, franchise management workshops, franchisor–franchisee relations seminars, and trade shows.

Business Magazines as Sources of Franchise Information   Many magazines include articles on specific franchisors, and several include regular features on franchising. *Entrepreneur, Inc., In Business, Nation's Business,* and *The Wall Street Journal,* to name a few, can be found in most libraries.

Continuing with our hypothetical evaluation of the Pro Image franchise, we researched business magazines and in the process located an informative article describing Pro Image and its operating strategy.[5] The article also provided useful information on Pro Image's three chief competitors. Most of the material provided in the article is not available through the franchisor's own promotions or in the governmental information.

Articles in these publications will often give an extensive profile of franchise problems and strategy changes.[6] The third-party coverage of these circumstances adds credibility to the information in the article.

Franchise Consultants   In recent years franchise consultants have appeared in the marketplace to assist individuals seeking franchise opportunities. Some of these consulting firms present seminars on choosing the right franchise. One such firm is Franchise Seminars, Inc., of Minneapolis, MN.

As in choosing any type of consultant, the prospective franchisee needs to select a reputable consultant. Since franchise consultants are not necessarily attorneys, a recognized franchise attorney should be used to evaluate all legal documents.

Examine the Franchise Contract

The basic features of the relationship between the franchisor and the franchisee are embodied in the franchise contract. However, to protect potential franchisees, the Federal Trade Commission requires that the franchisor also provide a disclosure statement to prospective franchisees that contains information in the following areas:[7]

1. Identifying Information as to Franchisor;
2. Business Experience of Franchisor's Directors and Executive Officers;
3. Business Experience of the Franchisor;
4. Litigation History;
5. Bankruptcy History;
6. Description of Franchise;
7. Initial Funds Required to Be Paid by a Franchisee;
8. Recurring Funds Required to Be Paid by a Franchisee;
9. Affiliated Persons the Franchisee Is Required or Advised to Do Business with by the Franchisor;
10. Obligations to Purchase;
11. Revenues Received by the Franchisor in Consideration of Purchases by a Franchisee;
12. Financing Arrangements;
13. Restriction of Sales;
14. Personal Participation Required of the Franchisee in the Operation of the Franchise;
15. Termination, Cancellation, and Renewal of the Franchise;
16. Statistical Information Concerning the Number of Franchises (and Company-Owned Outlets);
17. Site Selection;
18. Training Programs;
19. Public Figure Involvement in the Franchise;
20. Financial Information Concerning the Franchisor.

The contract is typically a complex document, often running to several pages. Because of its extreme importance in furnishing the legal basis for the franchised business, no franchise contract should ever be signed by the franchisee without legal counsel. As a matter of fact, many reputable franchisors insist that the franchisee have legal counsel before signing the agreement. An attorney would be useful in anticipating trouble and in noting objectionable features of the franchise contract.

In addition to consulting an attorney, as a prospective franchisee you should use as many other sources of help as possible. In particular, you should discuss the franchise proposal with a banker, going over it in as much detail as possible. You should also obtain the services of a professional accounting firm in examining the franchisor's statements of projected sales, operating expenses, and net income. The accountant can give valuable help in evaluating the quality of these estimates and in discovering projections that may be unlikely to occur.

One of the most important features of the contract is the provision relating to termination and transfer of the franchise. Some franchisors have been accused of devising agreements that permit arbitrary cancellation. Of course, it is reasonable for the franchisor to have legal protection in the event that a franchisee fails to obtain a satisfactory level of operation or to maintain satisfactory quality standards. However, the prospective franchisee should avoid contract provisions that contain overly strict cancellation policies. Similarly, the rights of the franchisee to sell the business to a third party should be clearly stipulated. Any franchisor who can restrict the sale of the business to a third party can assume ownership of the business at an unreasonable price. The right of the franchisee to renew the contract after the business has been built up to a successful operating level should also be clearly stated in the contract.

Beware of Franchising Frauds

Every industry has its share of shady operations, and franchising is no exception. Unscrupulous fast-buck artists offer a wide variety of fraudulent schemes to attract the investment of unsuspecting individuals. The franchisor in such cases is merely interested in obtaining the capital investment of the franchisee and not in a continuing relationship.

The possibility of such fraudulent schemes requires alertness on the part of prospective franchisees. Only careful investigation of the company and the product can distinguish between fraudulent operators and legitimate franchising opportunities. Mark J. Klein, a Kansas City, MO, lawyer, says, "Sometimes the best advice a lawyer can give a client is to stay away from a particular franchisor."[8]

Selling a Franchise

Franchising contains opportunities on both sides of the fence. We have already presented the franchising story from the viewpoint of the potential franchisee. Now we shall look through the eyes of the potential franchisor.

Why would a businessperson wish to become a franchisor? At least three general benefits can be identified.

1. *Reduced capital requirements.* Franchising allows you to expand without diluting your capital. The firm involved in franchising, in effect, through fee and royalty arrangements, borrows capital from the franchisee for channel development and thus has lower capital requirements than does the wholly owned chain.
2. *Increased management motivation.* Franchisees, as independent businesspeople, are probably more highly motivated than salaried employees because of profit incentives and their vested interest in the business. Since franchising is decentralized, the franchisor is less susceptible to labor-organizing efforts than are centralized organizations.
3. *Speed of expansion.* Franchising lets a business enter many more markets much more quickly than it could using only its own resources.

There are also distinct drawbacks associated with franchising from the franchisor's perspective. At least three of these can be isolated:

1. *Reduction in control.* A franchisor's right of control is greatly reduced in the franchising form of business. This is a major concern for most franchisors.
2. *Sharing of profits.* Only part of the profits from the franchise operation belongs to the franchisor.
3. *Increasing operating support.* There is generally more expense associated with nurturing the ongoing franchise relationships, providing accounting and legal services, than there is with centralized organization.

Amid the older and highly successful large franchisors, such as McDonald's, are many small businesses that are finding success as franchisors. For example, Exquisite Crafts, started by entrepreneur Marianne Montagna in 1972, will start selling franchises in New York, New Jersey, and

SMALL BUSINESS IN ACTION
I Must Have Control

A major reason for not franchising a business is the loss of control. A dedication to product or service quality is often the major factor in a decision not to franchise or to greatly reduce the number of franchises sold. Consider the attitude of Alvin A. McCall, Jr., who shut the door on franchising of Ryan's Family Steak Houses

because, says McCall, an ardent advocate of uniformity, "You can't exercise control." Not only does it take five to eight franchise units to produce the same income as one company-owned store, McCall figures, "but you have about five to eight times as many problems." . . . "There are too many people wanting to franchise just for the money who don't understand the work involved in a restaurant," explains McCall. . . . Besides, says McCall, "Our concept is too sophisticated. It's not like serving hamburgers. We cut our own beef, we're a service organization, and we're a food preparer—a combination of businesses within one. And that can't be franchised."

Alvin A. McCall, Jr. (left) and Son

Ryan started out to franchise but quickly stopped. Today there are only twelve franchise units. There are over 50 units of Ryan's Family Steak Houses in the corporate chain.

Source: Reprinted with permission, *Inc.* magazine, (July, 1986). Copyright © 1986 by Inc. Publishing Company, 38 Commercial Wharf, Boston, MA 02110.
Photo Source: © *Rhoda Baerr, 1988*

Connecticut after carefully analyzing the market and structuring the franchise package over a period of four years. Her franchise offers classes to customers on floral arranging, stenciling, needlework, and numerous other arts-and-crafts activities. During her four years of planning Montagna hired a consultant to help with the franchising plan. The initial franchise fee is $7,000, with recommended capital for other needs of over $20,000. Franchisees will pay a 3 percent royalty on gross sales for the first two years and 4 percent thereafter.[9] Montagna currently has a waiting list of potential franchisees.

Some entrepreneurs are finding that one key to building a successful franchise system is perfecting a prototype. By developing a model unit, franchisors are able to show potential franchisees how a well-planned and -managed unit can run. After only one year of franchising Entré Computers,

Steven B. Heller, 43, and James J. Edgette, 42, have sold over 200 franchises and they continue to sell at the rate of 10 per month. They say, "A prototype will enable you to do a tremendously refined job of opening a center."[10]

Franchising has undoubtedly enabled many individuals to enter business who otherwise would never have escaped the necessity of salaried employment. Thus, franchising has contributed to the development of many successful small businesses.

Future of Franchising

The growth pattern for franchised businesses historically has been steady. One of the first franchise arrangements involved a relationship between Singer Sewing Machine Company and its dealers during the nineteenth century. Post-World-War-II franchise growth was based on the expansion of the franchising principle into areas such as motels, variety shops, drugstores, and employment agencies. Then came the boom in the 1960s and 1970s, which featured franchising of fast-food outlets. Franchising growth continued into the 1980s.

Both dollar sales and number of establishments are expected to continue to increase into the 1990s. John Naisbitt, author of the best-selling *Megatrends,* predicts that "sales by business format franchisees will likely reach $1.3 trillion in the year 2010."[11] He sees the biggest increases occurring in construction and home services, recreation, nonfood retailing, business services, and fast food. Naisbitt feels that the following five major emerging trends support his predictions:[12]

- Franchising abroad [See Exhibit 4–4 for the strong international flavor of franchising already existing in 1986.]
- A rise in consumer demand for specialty items.
- Consumer preference for convenience and consistent quality.
- The transition from a manufacturing-based to a service economy.
- The increasing numbers of women and minorities in franchising.

It is not surprising to see, in Exhibit 4–4, that Canada accounts for the most foreign franchise outlets, since U.S. franchisors understandably begin international expansion in the most familiar environments. Continental Europe has the next highest number of franchising outlets. But how do U.S. franchisors enter these foreign markets?

The most popular approach to international franchising is through master franchising or subfranchising, which we described earlier in this chapter. Master franchising is a franchise sales and management system that

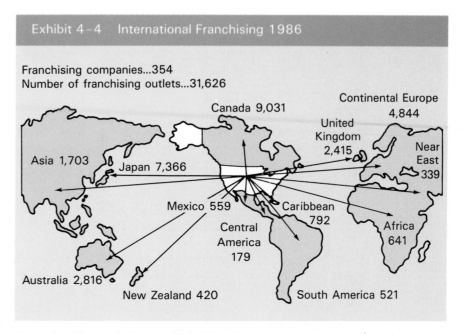

Exhibit 4-4 International Franchising 1986

Franchising companies...354
Number of franchising outlets...31,626

Canada 9,031

Continental Europe 4,844

United Kingdom 2,415

Near East 339

Asia 1,703

Japan 7,366

Mexico 559

Caribbean 792

Africa 641

Central America 179

Australia 2,816

New Zealand 420

South America 521

Source: Franchising in the Economy: 1986–1988, U.S. Department of Commerce (Washington: U.S. Government Printing Office, 1988), p. 8.

creates master franchisors who have the authority to sell and supervise individual franchises. Master franchisees, in effect, establish minifranchise companies of their own. "Subfranchising is the only method we consider when developing a new foreign market," says Dennis Steinman, director of international development for National Video, Inc. "It gives us tight control over a market, but at the same time it gives the subfranchisor enough autonomy so we don't have to look over his shoulder all the time."[13]

A franchisor must be careful to select master franchisors who understand the market, its language and political system, and other factors of the local culture. Startup costs may be higher in many foreign markets, but this is usually offset by less competition and large population bases.

Looking Back

1. Three basic types of franchising systems are System A, in which the producer is the franchisor and the wholesaler is the franchisee; System B, in which the wholesaler is the franchisor and the retailer is the franchisee; and System C, in which the producer is the franchisor and the retailer is the franchisee. The most widely used is System C.

2. Franchising provides three main advantages to the franchisee: formal training, financial assistance, and marketing and managerial expertise—all provided by the franchisor. Franchising also has its disadvantages. These include its costs, restrictions on growth, and loss of independence.

3. A franchise should be carefully evaluated before signing an agreement. Useful information can be obtained from the franchisor and nonfranchisor sources such as business magazines, other franchisees, governmental agencies, and private professionals.

4. Reduced capital requirements, increased management motivation, and speed of expansion are three reasons for becoming a franchisor. Drawbacks are reduction in control, sharing of profits, and increasing operating support.

5. The future of franchising continues to look bright at home and abroad. The biggest increases are forecasted in the areas of home services, construction, recreation, nonfood retailing, business services, and fast food.

DISCUSSION QUESTIONS

1. What makes franchising different from other forms of business? Be specific.

2. What is the difference between trade name franchising and business format franchising? Which one accounts for the majority of franchising activity?

3. Explain the three types of franchising systems. Which is most widely used?

4. Discuss the advantages and disadvantages of franchising from the viewpoints of the potential franchisee and the potential franchisor.

5. Should franchise information provided by a franchisor be discounted? Why or why not?

6. Do you believe the government-required disclosure document is useful to franchise evaluation? Defend your position.

7. Evaluate "loss of control" as a disadvantage of franchising from the franchisor's perspective.

8. What is the advantage of a franchisor's developing a prototype?

9. What are some reasons, in addition to those listed in the chapter, why an entrepreneur would consider franchising a new-business concept?

10. What are some of the trends that support a forecast of increased growth of franchising in the 1990s? Discuss.

11. Discuss how subfranchising is used in foreign franchising.

12. What types of restrictions on franchisee independents do you believe might be included in a typical franchise contract or restaurant franchise contract?

13. What problems could result when consulting previous franchisees in the process of evaluating a franchise?

14. What types of franchise information could you expect to obtain from business magazines that you would not secure from the franchisor?

15. Why are not all new businesses franchised?

YOU MAKE THE CALL

Situation 1

While still a student in college in 1989, Adrian Johnson began his first business venture. He took his idea for a laundromat to a local bank and brought back a $90,000 loan. After finding a suitable site close to his campus, he signed a 10-year lease and opened up for business. Over the first three days, the business averaged over 1,000 customers per day.

The attraction of Adrian's laundromat was its different and unique atmosphere. The business was carpeted, with oak paneling and brass fittings. There was a snack bar and a big-screen TV for patrons to enjoy while waiting for their laundry. Within a week of opening day, Adrian had an offer to sell his business at twice his investment. He rejected the offer in favor of the possibility of franchising his business concept.

Questions

1. Do you think Adrian's business concept can be franchised successfully? Why or why not?

2. Would the subfranchising concept work for this type of business?

3. If Adrian does indeed franchise his business, what types of training and support systems would you recommend he provide to franchisees?

Situation 2

Hard times in the agricultural commodities market led broker Bill Landers to leave his independent business and look for new opportunities. This time around Bill was committed to going into business with his wife Gwen and their teenage son and daughter. His goal was to keep the family close and reduce the stress in their lives. In his previous job as a broker, Bill would leave home early and return late, with little time for his wife or children.

Before leaving his job, Bill looked at several franchise opportunities. One he and Gwen were seriously considering was a custom-framing franchise that had been in existence for over 10 years and had almost 100 stores nationwide. However, the Landers were concerned about their lack of experience in this area and also about how long it would take to get the business going.

Questions

1. How important should prior experience be in the Landers's decision?
2. What other characteristics of the franchise should they investigate? What sources for this information would you recommend?
3. Can they reasonably expect a different life-style with a franchise? Explain.

EXPERIENTIAL EXERCISES

1. Interview a franchisee from the local community. Try to contact the owner-manager of a widely recognized retail franchise such as McDonald's. Ask the person to explain how he or she first obtained the franchise and the advantages of franchising over starting a business from scratch.
2. Find a franchise advertisement in a recent issue of a business magazine. Research the franchise and report back to class with your findings.
3. Consider the potential for a hypothetical new fast-food restaurant to be located next to the campus. (Be as specific about the assumed location as you can.) Divide into two groups. Ask one group to favor a franchised operation and the other to support a nonfranchised business. Plan a debate on the merits of each operation for the next class meeting.
4. Report in class on the articles cited in the References to Small-Business Practices at the end of this chapter.

REFERENCES TO SMALL-BUSINESS PRACTICES

Hartman, Curtis. "Fear of Franchising." *Inc.,* Vol. 9, No. 7 (June, 1987), pp. 104–122.
A detailed description of the rise and fall of the Pop-Ins franchise chain is provided in this article. The franchise was once called "the McDonald's" of maid services. It is now bankrupt and covered with litigation.

Hotch, Ripley. "Converting to a Franchise." *Nation's Business,* Vol. 75, No. 6 (June, 1987), pp. 28–34.
This article explores the advantages of converting an existing business into a franchise store. Several businesses that have made the change are described.

Justis, Robert. "Franchisors: Have You Hugged Your Franchisee Today?" *Nation's Business,* Vol. 73, No. 2 (February, 1985), pp. 46–49.
This article is a special report on unique efforts in cultivating ongoing franchisor-franchisee relationships. Numerous franchises are used as examples of franchise advisory councils, regional and national seminars, and other formalized ways of structuring the relationship.

Raffio, Ralph. "Double-Decker Franchising." *Venture,* Vol. 8, No. 11 (November, 1986), pp. 60–64.
Subfranchising has enabled many franchisors to grow big quickly. Several of the success stories are described.

Urbanski, Al. "The Franchise Option." *Sales and Marketing Management,* Vol. 140, No. 2 (February, 1988), pp. 28–33.
This article provides a profile of several franchisees and the franchise businesses they own and operate. Each entrepreneur in the article was previously in a corporate sales position. A change of life-style was the principal reason for going into franchising.

ENDNOTES

1. For a more complete analysis of master franchising, see Robert T. Justis and Richard Judd, "Master Franchising: A New Look," *Journal of Small Business Management,* Vol. 24, No. 3 (July, 1986), pp. 16–21.

2. John P. Hayes, "Be Your Own Boss—Sort Of," *In Business,* Vol. 10, No. 4 (July–August, 1988), p. 56.

3. For further discussion of franchise financing, see Andrew Sherman, "Financing the Franchise," *Nation's Business,* Vol. 75, No. 10 (October, 1987), pp. 41–44.

4. Jeannie Ralston, "Promises, Promises," *Venture,* Vol. 10, No. 3 (March, 1988), pp. 55–56.

5. Sheryl Jean, "Jockeying for Position," *Venture,* Vol. 10, No. 9 (September, 1988), pp. 76, 80.

6. See for example the article discussing the Naked Furniture Franchise found in Steven P. Galante, "Fine Art of Franchising Eludes Traditional Furniture Retailer," *The Wall Street Journal* (August 3, 1987), p. 15.

7. Taken from the disclosure statement of T-Shirts Plus, Inc.

8. Teri Agins, "Owning Franchises Has Pluses But Wealth Isn't Guaranteed," *The Wall Street Journal* (October 22, 1984), p. 33.

9. Nancy L. Droft and Meg Whittemore, "Finding the Right Franchise," *Nation's Business,* Vol. 76, No. 2 (February, 1988), p. 60.

10. Kevin Farrell, "Franchise Prototypes," *Venture,* Vol. 6, No. 1 (January, 1984), p. 38.

11. Meg Whittemore, "Franchising's Future," *Nation's Business,* Vol. 74, No. 2 (February, 1986), p. 47.

12. *Ibid.*

13. John F. Porsinos, "New Worlds to Franchise," *Venture,* Vol. 9, No. 11 (November, 1987), p. 50.

5 FAMILY BUSINESS OPPORTUNITIES

Spotlight on Small Business

© James Hamilton

A family business may involve several generations of a family. Such is the case with Charles Komar & Sons, a family firm in the garment-manufacturing industry. One writer states:

> In the family, they already tell stories about Herman Komar's son, young Charlie. How at two he crawled up on to his great-aunt's lap to show her the picture he had crayoned—"My factory," he announced proudly. How at five he would sit in a garment bin while his father pulled him through their New Jersey plant, down the long rows of sewing machines, past the piles of lace and trim. Day after day he would hear the tales of his grandfather, an immigrant just eight years over from Russia, starting out back in 1908 on New York's Lower East Side with a few seamstresses and $500 borrowed from the Hebrew Free Loan Association. Even before he

could read, Charlie would perch at the kitchen table with his dad, trying to decipher the day's CVO (cuts versus order)—the pulse beat of the family's lingerie-manufacturing business.

Source: Reprinted with permission, *Inc.* magazine, November, 1984. Copyright © 1984 by Inc. Publishing Company, 38 Commercial Wharf, Boston, MA 02110.

Looking Ahead

Watch for the following important topics:
1. The way family and business interests overlap.
2. Special advantages and distinctive values deriving from family involvement.
3. How its culture affects operation of a family business.
4. Special concerns of nonfamily employees.
5. Roles of Dad, Mother, sons, daughters, in-laws, and others.
6. The process of succession—how the next generation takes over.
7. New terms and concepts:

family business	cultural governance pattern
family and business overlap	cultural configuration
cultural business pattern	stages in succession
cultural family pattern	transfer of ownership

Millions of small businesses are also family businesses, and these firms provide still another type of opportunity for many young people. Rather than starting entirely new businesses, buying out existing firms, or becoming franchisees, they may elect to join Dad and Mother or some other relative in a family business.

Joining a family business is not an easy decision for most second- or third-generation family members. Family firms are different from other types of businesses, and the young person who considers such a career is immediately confronted with feelings about family loyalty, family expectations, and family rivalries as well as questions about profitability and growth potential. In this chapter, we examine some of the unique features that characterize a family business and set it apart as a special type of entrepreneurial alternative.

The Family Business: A Unique Institution

A number of features distinguish the family firm from other types of small businesses. In its decision making and culture, for example, we observe a mixture of family and business values. This section examines the family business as a unique type of institution.

What Is a Family Business?

To speak of a **family business** is to imply an involvement of the family in the life and functioning of that business. The nature and extent of that involvement varies. In some firms, family members may work full time or part time. In a small restaurant, for example, the entrepreneur may serve as host and manager, the spouse may keep the books, and the children may work in the kitchen or serve as waiters or waitresses.

The business also comes to be distinguished as a family business when it passes from one generation to another. For example, Thompson's Plumbing Supply may be headed by Bill Thompson, Jr., son of the founder, who is now deceased. His son, Bill Thompson III, has started to work on the sales floor, after serving in the stockroom during his high school years. He is the heir apparent who will some day replace his father. People in the community recognize Thompson's Plumbing Supply as a family business.

Most family businesses, and the type we are concerned with in this book, are small. However, family considerations may continue to be important even when these businesses become large corporations. Companies such as DuPont, Levi Strauss and Company, Ford Motor Company, and Bechtel Corporation are still recognized, to some extent, as family businesses.

Family and Business Overlap

The family business is composed of both a family and a business. Although these are separate institutions—each with its own members, goals, and values—they are brought into a condition of **overlap** in the family firm.

Families and businesses exist for fundamentally different reasons.[1] The family's primary function relates to the care and nurture of family members, whereas the business is concerned with the production of goods and/or services. The family's goal is the fullest possible development of each member, regardless of limitations in ability, and the provision of equal opportunities and rewards for each member. The business goal is profitability and survival. There is a possibility for either harmony or conflict in these goals, but it is obvious that they are not identical. In the short run, what is best for the family may or may not be what is best for the business.

Business Decisions and Family Decisions

Family relationships complicate the management process of the family firm. Some *business* decisions are also *family* decisions, and nonfamily managers may be surprised at the way in which family interests influence business operations. Rene Plessner, whose executive search firm specializes in finding executives for family-owned companies, explains how family decisions dominate the business:

> In a family company, you may have the title and the responsibility, and one day you walk into the office and you don't know that two cousins, a brother-in-law, sister, and the Papa had dinner over the weekend and made a decision upsetting what you expected to do. . . . Nobody was out to get you; it's simply, to be trite about it, blood is thicker than water. The family members talk among themselves. You have to be flexible enough to handle that.[2]

If the business is to survive, its interests cannot be unduly compromised to satisfy family wishes. Firms that grow must recognize the need for

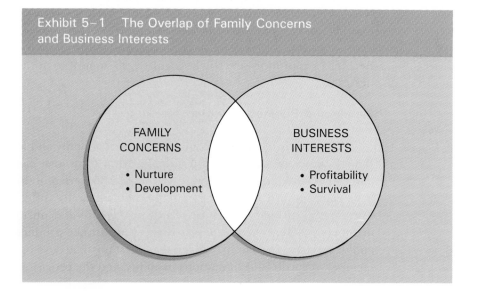

Exhibit 5–1   The Overlap of Family Concerns and Business Interests

FAMILY CONCERNS
- Nurture
- Development

BUSINESS INTERESTS
- Profitability
- Survival

professional management and the necessary limitations on family concerns. An example is found in the experience of Pierre DuPont:

> As far as Pierre was concerned, the large firm did not have the obligation to provide the family with jobs; instead, it should ensure them of large dividends. Of course, when the firm expanded, there would be increased employment opportunities for younger relatives. Family traditions were meaningful to Pierre, and he saw the family as playing a different role rather than being forgotten.[3]

The health and survival of the family business, therefore, requires a proper balancing of business and family interests. Otherwise, results will be unsatisfactory to both the business and the family.

Advantages of Family Involvement in the Business

Problems associated with family businesses can easily blind young people to the advantages deriving from family participation in the business. There *are* values associated with family involvement, and these should be recognized and used in the family firm.

One primary benefit comes from the strength of family relationships. Members of the family are drawn to the business because of family ties, and they tend to stick with the business through "thick and thin." A downturn in business fortunes might cause nonfamily managers to seek greener pastures elsewhere. A son or daughter, however, is reluctant to leave. The family

---

SMALL BUSINESS IN ACTION
Business Benefits from Family Relationships

One benefit deriving from family relationships is the willingness of family members to help out when needed. When Angus Wurtele attended Stanford Business School in 1961, he aspired to run a rapidly growing electronics firm like Hewlett-Packard or Control Data.

However, Minnesota Paints Company, an unglamorous paint manufacturer founded by a great-uncle in 1870, needed a helping hand after the death of its company president. Wurtele reluctantly agreed to help ''for a while'' after graduation. Rather than moving on quickly, however, he stayed with the company (now Valspar Corporation), acquired other paint companies, and made the firm the industry's profit leader.

Source: "Bargain Hunter," *Forbes*, Vol. 133 (June 4, 1984), pp. 177–178.

name, the family welfare, and possibly the family fortune are at stake. In addition, his or her personal reputation as a family member may be at stake. Can he or she continue the business that Dad or Grandfather built?

Family members may also sacrifice income needed in the business. Rather than draw large salaries or high dividends, they permit such resources to remain in the business for current needs. Many families have gone without a new car or new furniture long enough to let the new business get started or to get through a period of financial stress.

Family firms also possess certain features that can contribute to superior business decision making. To achieve their full potential, family businesses must develop some key advantages. According to Peter Davis, three such advantages are the following:[4]

1. *Preserving the humanity of the workplace.* A family business can easily demonstrate higher levels of concern and caring for individuals than are found in the typical corporation.
2. *Focusing on the long run.* A family business can take the long-run view more easily than corporate managers who are being judged on year-to-year results.
3. *Emphasizing quality.* Family businesses have long maintained a tradition of providing quality and value to the consumer.

The Culture of the Family Business

The imprint of its founder is often evident in the family firm. The founder may emphasize values that become part of the business and family code. Observance of such values becomes a matter of family pride. Of course, the founder cannot merely impose his or her values upon the organization. As Stein has pointed out, these basic assumptions can become part of the culture only if they work and become accepted by the group.[5]

The founder, for example, may develop the business by catering to customer needs in a special way. Customer service becomes a guiding principle for the business, and legends may be passed on to illustrate the extreme measures taken by the founder to satisfy customer needs. Any business operates according to some set of values, but the family business follows with special care those values clearly emphasized by the founding family.

In addition to regarding culture as a collection of individual values and practices, we can also look at it as the arrangement of such values and practices into cultural patterns. This means that any given family firm has a grouping of beliefs and behaviors that makes it like some other family firms but also sets it apart from others. By carefully examining the cultural pattern of a specific family business, therefore, we may be able to recognize it as a particular type of culture found in many family firms.

W. Gibb Dyer, Jr., has identified a set of cultural patterns that apply to three facets of family firms: the business itself, the family, and the governance (board of directors) of the business.[6] These patterns are outlined in Exhibit 5–2. The **business pattern, family pattern,** and **governance pattern**

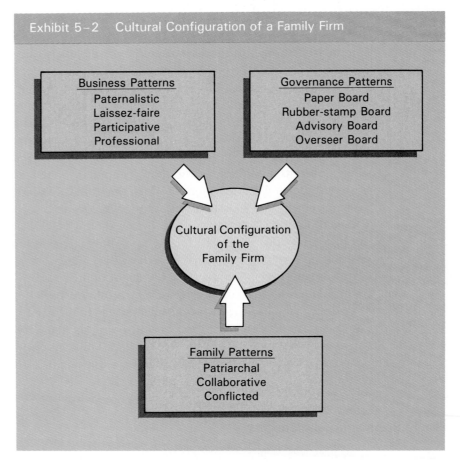

Exhibit 5–2 Cultural Configuration of a Family Firm

Business Patterns
Paternalistic
Laissez-faire
Participative
Professional

Governance Patterns
Paper Board
Rubber-stamp Board
Advisory Board
Overseer Board

Cultural Configuration
of the
Family Firm

Family Patterns
Patriarchal
Collaborative
Conflicted

Source: W. Gibb Dyer, Jr., *Cultural Change in Family Firms* (San Francisco: Jossey-Bass Publishers, 1986), p. 22.

presumably combine to form an overall **configuration** that constitutes a family firm's total culture.

In the early stages of a family business, according to Dyer, a common cultural configuration includes a paternalistic business culture, a patriarchal family culture, and a rubber-stamp board of directors. To simplify, this means that family relationships are more important than professional skill, that the founder is the undisputed head of the clan, and that the board automatically supports the founder's decisions.

Nonfamily Members in a Family Firm

Even those employees who are not family members are nevertheless affected by family considerations. In some cases their opportunities for promotion are lessened by the presence of family members who seem to have the "inside track" for promotion. What father is going to promote an outsider over a competent son who is being groomed for future leadership? The potential for advancement of nonfamily members, therefore, may be limited, and they may experience a sense of unfairness and frustration.

The extent of such limitation will depend on the number of family members active in the business and the number of managerial or professional positions in the business to which a nonfamily member might aspire. It will also depend on the extent to which the owner demands competence in management and maintains an atmosphere of fairness in supervision. To avoid a stifling atmosphere, the owner should make clear the extent of opportunity that does exist for the nonfamily member and identify the positions, if any, that are reserved for family members.

Nonfamily members may also be caught in the crossfire between family members who are competing with each other. Family feuds in family businesses make it difficult for outsiders to maintain strict neutrality. If a nonfamily employee is perceived as siding with one contender, he or she will lose the support of other family members. Some hard-working employees no doubt feel they deserve hazard pay for working in a firm plagued by an unusual amount of family conflict.

Family Roles and Relationships

As noted earlier, a family business involves the overlapping of two institutions—a family and a business. This fact makes the family firm incredibly difficult to manage. In this section we examine a few of the numerous possible family roles and relationships that contribute to the complexity of such a firm.

Mom or Dad, the Founder

A common figure in the family business is the man or woman who founds the firm and plans to pass it on to a son or a daughter. In most cases, the business and the family grow simultaneously. Some founders achieve a delicate balance between their business and family responsibilities. In other situations, parents must exert great diligence to squeeze out time for weekends and vacation time with the children. In some cases, business pressures are such that the family suffers neglect. In any event, parents generally experience tension in trying to reconcile business demands and family responsibilities.

Entrepreneurs who have sons and daughters typically think in terms of passing the business on to the next generation of the family. Parental concerns in this process include the following:

1. Does my son or daughter possess the temperament and ability necessary for business leadership?
2. How can I, the founder, motivate my son or daughter to take an interest in the business?
3. What type of education and experience will be most helpful in preparing my son or daughter for leadership?
4. What timetable should I follow in employing and promoting my son or daughter?
5. How can I avoid favoritism in managing and developing my son or daughter?
6. How can I prevent the business relationship from damaging or destroying the parent–child relationship?

ITT Corporation

Of all relationships in the family business, the parent–child relationship (especially the father–son relationship) has been most sensitive and troublesome. The problem has been recognized informally for generations. In more recent years, counseling has developed, seminars have been created, and books have been written about such relationships. In spite of extensive discussion, however, the parent–child relationship continues to perplex numerous families involved in family businesses.

Couples in Business

Some family businesses involve husband–wife teams. Their roles may vary depending on their backgrounds and expertise. In some cases, the husband serves as general manager and the wife runs the office. In other cases, the wife functions as operations manager and the husband keeps the books. Whatever the arrangement, both parties are an integral part of the business.

A potential advantage of the husband–wife team is the opportunity it provides for them to share more of their life. For some couples, however, the potential benefits tend to become eclipsed by problems related to the business. Differences of opinion about business matters may carry over into family life. And the energies of both parties may be so dissipated by their work in a struggling family firm that little zest remains for a strong family life.

One couple who have experienced both the joys and strains of working together as business partners are Adele Bihn and Murray P. Heinrich of San Jose, CA.[7] After 12 years of marriage and collaboration in their business, Data Marketing, Inc., they are described as "still blissfully happy." Adele, mother of their four children, owns 50 percent of the company and serves as president. Murray owns the other 50 percent and heads up product research. To maintain their happiness, they must deal with strains imposed by the business. They have worked together to resolve these pressures by using a variety of methods, including semi-annual visits with a marriage counselor, annual away-from-work business strategy sessions, Saturday morning breakfast dates with just the two of them, and annual separate vacations. Their experience shows that entrepreneurial couples can maintain good marriages, but it also shows that such couples may need to devote special effort to both business and family concerns.

Sons and Daughters

Should sons and daughters be groomed for the family business, or should they pursue careers of their own choosing? This is a basic question facing the entrepreneurial family. A natural tendency is to think in terms of a family business career and to push the son or daughter, either openly or subtly, in that direction. Little thought, indeed, may be given to the basic issues involved.

One question is that of talent, aptitude, and temperament. The offspring may be a "chip off the old block," but the offspring may also be an individual with different bents and aspirations. The son or daughter may prefer music or medicine to what he or she perceives to be the mundane world of business. He or she may fit the business mold very poorly. It is also possible that the abilities of the son or daughter may simply be insufficient for the leadership role. (Of course, a child's talents may be underestimated by parents simply because there has been little opportunity for development.)

A second issue is that of freedom. We live in a society that values the rights of individuals to choose their own careers and way of life. If the entrepreneur wishes to recognize this value—a value that is typically embraced by the son or daughter—that son or daughter must be granted the freedom to select a career of his or her own choosing.

The son or daughter may feel a need to go outside the family business, for a time at least, to prove that "I can make it on my own." To build self-

---

SMALL BUSINESS IN ACTION
Choosing to Enter the Family Business

Freedom to choose a career often leads family members to opt out of the family business. That almost happened to two third-generation members of the Seaman family as they graduated from the Wharton school of business. However, their fathers, who operate the highly successful retail furniture chain, Seaman's Furniture, made the family business highly attractive to the third generation without resorting to "golden handcuffs."

At first the boys were reluctant to get involved in the family business. At Wharton, Morton Seaman's son, Jeffrey, gravitated toward futures trading. Carl's son, Jordon, also at Wharton, was headed toward law. Both graduated with honors and did not have to fall back on the family business.

Yet today both Jeffrey and Jordon credit Morton and Carl's wise decision to allow for generational differences. "My father was from the old school that said you have to start at the bottom," explains Morton Seaman. "I opened crates and polished furniture. Nothing could be more boring to a kid who's going to college than starting him at that level."

Instead, the second-generation Seamans tried to make the business attractive, so that the third generation wouldn't want to work anywhere else. The strategy worked.

Source: Burr Leonard, "Heir Raising," *Forbes,* Vol. 140, No. 5 (September 7, 1987), pp. 74–80.

esteem, the young person may wish to operate independently of the family. Going back to the family business immediately may seem stifling—"continuing to feel like a little kid with Dad telling me what to do."

If the family business is profitable, it does provide opportunities. The son or daughter may well give serious consideration to accepting such a challenge. If the relationship is to be satisfactory, however, family pressure must be minimized. And both parties must recognize the choice as a business decision, as well as a family decision—a decision that may conceivably be reversed. In the case of a large family, another problem arises if the business is not large enough to support all of the children who wish to join it.

Sibling Cooperation, Sibling Rivalry

In families having a number of children, two or more of them may become involved in the family firm. This depends, of course, on the interests of the individual children. In some cases, parents feel themselves fortunate if even one child elects to stay with the family firm. Nevertheless, it is not unusual for two or more, sometimes all, of the children to take positions in the family business. Even those who do not work in the business may be more than casual observers on the sidelines because of their stake as heirs or partial owners.

At best, the children work as a smoothly functioning team, each contributing services according to his or her respective abilities. Just as some families experience excellent cooperation and unity in their family relationships, so family businesses can benefit from effective collaboration among brothers and sisters.

But just as there are squabbles within the family, so can there be sibling rivalry within the business. Business issues tend to generate competition internally (within the firm), as well as externally (in the marketplace), and this affects family as well as nonfamily members. Two sons, for example, may disagree about business policy or about their respective roles in the business.

One older son, Howard, described a power struggle that developed between him and his younger brother, Charles, over which one would run the company after their father relinquished control:

> In his mid-twenties, when I was about thirty-five, Charles let me know he planned to succeed Dad in the top spot. Years before, when he was in high school, I had assured him I envisioned him taking the company's lead.

But the passing of time and my own grasp on power made that memory very dim. Now, sitting in my office, his words bombed me:

"Howard, what are your long-range plans?"

"I don't know," I said. "One day at a time."

"We've got to think about the future," he said, "and if I'm going to stay, then I'm going to be in charge. Leadership can't work undefined."

I spat out my answer. If words could be flames, mine would have burned up that desktop.

"Well, I don't plan to leave."

Charles insisted on knowing precisely who was in command. He refused to work under a part-time brother as a boss. He demanded our company hierarchy be spelled out.[8]

After reacting furiously to his younger brother's challenge, Howard reflected more calmly on his own interests and the overall welfare of the family and the business. Eventually, he agreed that leadership should be assumed by the younger brother and, as he expressed it, "a family mess turned into a family miracle."[9]

In-Laws in and out of the Business

As sons and daughters marry, the sons-in-law and daughters-in-law become significant actors in the family business drama. Some of them may be directly involved when one, a son-in-law, for example, is employed in the family firm. If a son or daughter is also employed in the same firm, the potential for rivalry and conflict is present. How are the performance and progress of a son-in-law to be rewarded equitably as compared with the performance and progress of a son or daughter?

For a time, effective collaboration may be achieved by assigning family members to different branches or roles within the company. Eventually, the competition for top leadership will require decisions that distinguish among sons, daughters, sons-in-law, and daughters-in-law employed in the business. Being fair and retaining family loyalty become difficult as the number of family employees increases.

Sons, daughters, sons-in-law, and daughters-in-law who are on the sidelines are also participants with an important stake in the business. For example, they may be daughters-in-law whose husbands are employed, or husbands of daughters who are on the family payroll. Whatever the relationship, the view from the sideline has both a family and a business dimension. A decision by Dad affecting one member is seen from the sideline as a family *and* a business decision. Dad is giving the nod to a son or a son-in-law, and that is more than merely changing another employee in a business. Both the business and the family come to involve highly sensitive relationships.

The Entrepreneur's Spouse

One of the most critical roles in the family business drama is that of the entrepreneur's spouse. Traditionally and typically, this is the entrepreneur's wife and the mother of his children. (Note, however, that women are increasingly becoming entrepreneurs and that many husbands have also assumed the role of spouse.) As wife, she plays a supporting role to her husband's career; as mother, she monitors the socialization of their children for careers in the family business. This leads to a need for communication between spouse and entrepreneur. The spouse can contribute by being a good listener. To do so, the spouse needs to hear what's going on in the business; otherwise, the spouse feels detached and must compete for attention. The spouse can offer understanding and act as a sounding board only if there is communication on matters of such obvious importance to them both individually and as a family.

It is easy for the spouse to function as "worrier" for the family business. This is particularly true if there is insufficient communication about business matters. One spouse said:

> I've told my husband that I have an active imagination—very active. If he doesn't tell me what's going on in the business, well, then I'm going to imagine what's going on and blow it all out of proportion. When things are looking dark, I'd rather know the worst than know nothing.[10]

The spouse also serves as mediator in relationships between the entrepreneur and the children. Comments such as the following may illustrate the nature of this function:

1. "John, don't you think that Junior may have worked long enough as a stockboy in the warehouse?"
2. "Junior, your father is going to be very disappointed if you don't come back to the business after your graduation."
3. "John, do you really think it is fair to move Stanley into that new office? After all, Junior is older and has been working a year longer."
4. "Junior, what did you say to your father today that upset him?"

Ideally, the entrepreneur and spouse form a team committed to the success of both the family and the family business. They share with each other in the processes that affect the fortunes of each. Since such teamwork does not occur automatically, it requires a collaborative effort by both parties to the marriage.

The Process of Succession

The task of preparing family members for careers and turning the business over to them is difficult and sometimes frustrating. Professional and managerial requirements tend to become intertwined with family feelings and interests. In this section we look at the development and transfer process and some of the difficulties associated with it.

Available Family Talent

A stream can rise no higher than its source, and the family firm can be no more brilliant than its leader. The business is dependent, therefore, upon the quality of leadership talent provided by the family. If the available talent is deficient, the entrepreneur must provide outside leadership or supplement family talent in some way. Otherwise, the business will suffer decline under the leadership of the second- or third-generation family members.

In some family businesses, key positions are reserved for family members. They may be retained in key positions because of their family relationship, even though they are professionally weak. One family entrepreneur's attempt to correct a lack of management skill is described below:

> In one case the founder's son, who was in command, diagnosed the business' problem as a lack of specialized talent. His solution was to become the firm's all-purpose expert—lawyer, accountant, and personnel specialist all wrapped into one. And to implement his solution, he went to night school. Little did he know that hiring someone outside the family who already had the necessary knowledge would have been better. His choice had several negative consequences, including his own physical exhaustion. The lesson here is that, when the money is available or the need is critical, there is no substitute for genuine expertise.[11]

Thus, decisions that sacrifice efficiency in the interest of preserving family interests can easily destroy the vitality of the family firm's management.

The question of competency of family members presents both a critical and delicate issue. With experience, individuals can improve their abilities; so, younger people cannot be judged too harshly too early. Further-more, potential successors may be held back by the reluctance of a parent-owner to delegate realistically to them.

Perhaps the most appropriate philosophy is to recognize the right of family members to prove themselves. A period of testing may occur either in the family business or in another organization. As children show themselves to be capable, they earn the right to increased leadership responsibility. If the fairly judged leadership abilities of potential successors are inadequate, preservation of the family business and even the welfare of family members demand that they be passed over for promotion. The appointment of competent outsiders to these jobs, if necessary, increases the value of the firm to all family members who have an ownership interest in it.

Stages in the Process of Succession

Sons or daughters do not typically assume leadership of a family firm in a moment of time. Dad or Mom does not step down on Friday with the son or daughter taking over Monday morning. Instead, a long, drawn-out process of preparation and transition is customary—a process that extends over years and often decades. We may visualize this process as a series of stages as portrayed in Exhibit 5–3.[12]

Pre-Business Stage   In Stage I, the successor becomes acquainted with the business as a part of growing up. He or she accompanies the parent to the office or store or warehouse, or plays with equipment related to the business. There is no formal planning of the youngster's preparation in this early period in which he or she might be only four or five years of age. This first stage forms a boundary that precedes the more deliberate process of socialization.

Introductory Stage   Stage II includes experiences that occur before the successor is old enough to begin part-time work in the family business. It differs from Stage I in that family members deliberately introduce the child to certain people associated directly or indirectly with the firm and to other aspects of the business. The parent explains the difference between a front loader and a backhoe or introduces the child to the firm's banker.

Introductory Functional Stage   In Stage III, the son or daughter begins to function as a part-time employee. This often occurs during vacation periods or after the school day is completed. During this time, the son or daughter develops an acquaintance with some of the key individuals employed in the

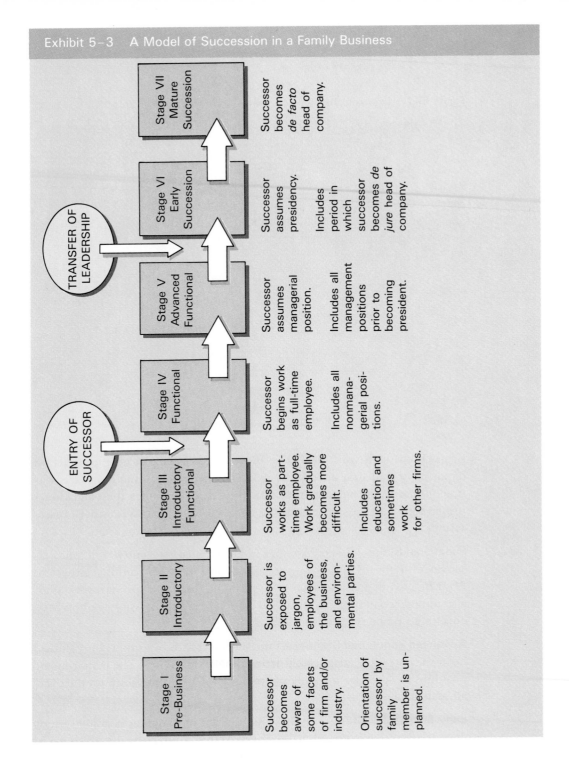

Exhibit 5-3   A Model of Succession in a Family Business

Stage I
Pre-Business

Successor becomes aware of some facets of firm and/or industry.

Orientation of successor by family member is un-planned.

Stage II
Introductory

Successor is exposed to jargon, employees of the business, and environ-mental parties.

Stage III
Introductory
Functional

Successor works as part-time employee. Work gradually becomes more difficult.

Includes education and sometimes work for other firms.

ENTRY OF SUCCESSOR

Stage IV
Functional

Successor begins work as full-time employee.

Includes all nonmana-gerial posi-tions.

Stage V
Advanced
Functional

Successor assumes managerial position.

Includes all management positions prior to becoming president.

TRANSFER OF LEADERSHIP

Stage VI
Early Succession

Successor assumes presidency.

Includes period in which successor becomes *de jure* head of company.

Stage VII
Mature Succession

Successor becomes *de facto* head of company.

Figure 5–1　Learning the Family Business from the Ground Up

firm. Often, such work begins in the warehouse or office or production department and may involve assignments in various functional areas as time goes on. The introductory functional stage includes the educational preparation and the experience the son or daughter gains in other organizations.

Functional Stage　Stage IV begins when the successor enters full-time employment, typically following the completion of an educational program. Prior to moving into a management position, the successor may work as an accountant, a salesperson, or an inventory clerk and possibly gain experience in a number of such positions.

Advanced Functional Stage　As the successor assumes supervisory duties, he or she enters the advanced functional stage, or Stage V. The management positions in this stage involve directing the work of others but not the overall management of the firm.

Early Succession Stage　In Stage VI, the son or daughter is named president or general manager of the business. At this point, he or she presumably exercises overall direction of the business, but the parent is still in the background. The leadership role of an organization does not transfer as easily or absolutely as does the leadership title. The successor has not necessarily mastered the complexities of the presidency, and the predecessor may be reluctant to give up all decision making.

Mature Succession Stage   Stage VII is reached when the transition process is complete. The successor is leader in fact as well as in name. In some cases, this does not occur until the predecessor dies. Perhaps optimistically, we assume progress on the part of the successor and regard Stage VII as beginning two years after the successor assumes the presidency of the firm.

Reluctant Fathers and Ambitious Children

Let us assume the business founder is preparing his son or daughter to take over the family firm. The founder's attachment to the business must not be underestimated. Not only is he tied to the firm financially—it is probably his primary if not his only major investment—but he is also tied to it emotionally. The business is "his baby," and he is understandably reluctant to entrust its future to one who is immature and unproven. (Unfortunately, fathers often have a way of seeing their children as immature long after their years of adolescence.)

The child may be ambitious, possibly well-educated, and insightful regarding the business. His or her tendency to push ahead—to try something new—often conflicts with the father's caution. As a result, the child may see the father as excessively conservative, stubborn, and unwilling to change.

At the root of many such difficulties is a lack of a clear understanding between father and child. They work together without a map showing where they are going. Children in the business, and also their spouses, may have expectations about progress that, in terms of the founder's thinking, are totally unrealistic. The successor tends to sense such problems much more acutely than does his or her father. But much of the problem could be avoided if a full discussion about the development process took place. The problem is highlighted in the following comments:

> Where Dad means to be open and generous, his children tend to see him as stubborn and inconsistent. As far as they can see, he refuses to move on anything even slightly important. When he does move, his decisions seem to vary day to day—and they rarely seem to be in the successor's favor.
> Where the successors are trying to do their jobs (as they see them) by pushing for changes, investment, and a little more risk, Dad sees them as spendthrift and economically naive. Where the successors' spouses only

want to make sure their own families are on the right track, Dad sees them as uncommitted and disloyal.

Each of these perceptions, real though they may seem, are seldom true. They're seldom even close. Yet everybody operates on them—their individual versions of reality.[13]

Cultural Patterns and Leadership Succession

The process of passing the leadership reins from one generation to another is complicated by, and interwoven with, changes in the family business culture. To appreciate this point, think about the paternalistic-patriarchal culture mentioned earlier in the chapter—a culture that is quite common in the early days of a family business. Changing conditions may render that culture ineffective. As a family business grows, it requires a greater measure of professional expertise. Thus, the firm is pressured to break from the paternalistic mold that gave first priority to family authority and less attention to professional abilities. Likewise, aging of the founder and maturation of the founder's children tend to weaken the patriarchal family culture with its one dominant source of authority— a father who "always knows best."

Succession may occur, therefore, against the backdrop of a changing culture. In fact, leadership change may itself play an important role in introducing or bringing about changes in the culture and making a break with traditional methods of operation. To some extent, the successor may act as a change agent as he or she assumes decision-making authority. For example, we are not surprised to see a son or daughter with a college degree eliminate musty managerial practices and substitute a more professional approach.

As W. Gibb Dyer, Jr., has pointed out, each generation faces its own set of cultural challenges.[14] In the first generation, there are centralized decision-making practices that increasingly lead to inefficiency in operation. The challenge is to retain the founder's values without losing effectiveness in operation. In the second and third generation, the founder's departure creates a vacuum that can lead to family conflicts and power struggles or to collaboration. The challenge is to work together in ways that preserve family relationships and also protect the business. In each stage of succession, the leadership goal is to preserve the best of the existing culture while eliminating its most serious defects.

SMALL BUSINESS IN ACTION
New Generation and New Culture

Management succession in a family firm can lead to changes in prevailing cultural patterns. This is illustrated by a transition from first- to second-generation management at Pittsburgh Glove Manufacturing Company. Suzanne Caplan had worked as an assistant to her father for two years prior to his death, at which time she was abruptly thrust into the leadership role. Although she lacked careful preparation for the position, she proceeded to move the company away from her father's paternalistic business culture to a more participative culture. Following is her description of that change:

"My father was a relatively autocratic manager. I gave line supervisors and others more autonomy. I really expounded the philosophy of humanistic capitalism: producing something you're proud of and doing it with people in a humane way. There's a certain sense of communalism here that hasn't hurt our bottom line."

Source: Jeffrey Lener and Tom Post, "Does Father Really Know Best?" Reprinted from the February, 1986, issue of *VENTURE, For Entrepreneurial Business Owners & Investors,* © 1986.

Transferring Ownership

A final and often complex step in the succession process is the **transfer of ownership** in the family firm.[15] Questions of inheritance affect not only the successor or potential successor in management, but also other family members with no involvement in the family business. In distributing their family estate, parents typically wish to treat all their children fairly, both those involved in the business and those on the outside.

One of the most difficult decisions is that of determining the future ownership of the business. If there are several children, for example, should they all receive equal shares? On the surface, this seems to be the fairest approach. However, such an arrangement may play havoc with the future functioning of the business. Suppose that each of five children receives a 20 percent ownership share when only one of them is active in the business.

The child active in the business—the successor—becomes a minority stockholder completely at the mercy of relatives on the outside.

Ideally, the entrepreneur is able to arrange his or her personal holdings so that he or she creates wealth outside the business as well as within it. In this way, he or she may be able to bequeath comparable shares to all heirs while allowing business control to remain with the child or children active in the business.

Tax considerations are relevant, of course, and they tend to favor gradual transfer of ownership to all heirs. As noted above, however, this arrangement may be inconsistent with future efficient operation of the business. Tax laws cannot be allowed to dominate decisions about transferring ownership without regard for these other practical considerations.

Planning and discussing the transfer of ownership is not easy, but such action is recommended. Over a period of time, the owner must reflect seriously on family talents and interests as they relate to the future of the firm. The plan for transfer of ownership can then be "firmed up" and modified as necessary when it is discussed with the children or other potential heirs.

Leon A. Danco describes an arrangement worked out by a warehouse distributor in the tire industry.[16] The distributor's son and probable successor was active in the business, but his daughter was married to a college professor at a small southern university. Believing the business to be their most valuable asset, the owner and his wife were concerned that both the daughter and the son receive a fair share. Initially, the parents decided to give the real estate to the daughter and the business itself to the son, who would then pay rent to his sister. After discussing the matter with both children, however, they developed a better plan whereby the business property and the business itself would both go to the son. The daughter would receive all *nonbusiness* assets plus an instrument of debt by the son to his sister which was intended to balance the monetary values. In this way, they devised a plan that was not only fair but also workable in terms of the operation and management of the firm.

Good Management in the Process of Succession

Good management is necessary for the success of any business, and the family firm is no exception.[17] Significant deviations for family reasons from what we might call good management practices, therefore, will only serve to weaken the firm. Such a course of action would run counter to the interests of both the firm and the family. In concluding this discussion of

Figure 5–2 Good Managers Are Important in the Process of Succession

succession, we should recall and emphasize those management concepts which are particularly relevant to the family firm.

The first concept relates to the competence of professional and managerial personnel. A family firm cannot afford to accept and support family members who are incompetent or who lack the potential for development.

Second, the extent of opportunities for nonfamily members and any limitations on those opportunities should be spelled out. They should know and not have to wonder whether they can aspire to promotion to key positions in the firm.

Third, favoritism in personnel decisions must be avoided. If possible, the evaluation of family members should involve the judgment of nonfamily members—those in supervisory positions, outside members of the board of directors, or managers of other companies in which family members work for a time.

Fourth, plans for succession, steps in professional development, and intentions regarding changes in ownership should be developed and discussed openly.[18] Founders who recognize the need for managing the process of succession can work out plans carefully rather than drift haphazardly. Lack of knowledge regarding plans and intentions of key participants creates uncertainty and possible suspicion. This planning process can begin as the founder or the presiding family member shares his or her dream for the family firm and family participation it it. John L. Ward and Laurel Sorenson have spoken of the "joy" of family meetings and described such meetings that aired family issues, reviewed company performance, or talked about the future.[19] As Ward and Sorenson point out, family conferences (for all family members, both in and out of the business) may be held at posh resorts or around a table in the dining room or cafeteria. Whatever the site, the important feature is the communication that occurs.

The family firm is a business—a competitive business. The observance of these and other fundamental precepts of management will help the business to thrive and permit the family to function as a family. Disregard of such considerations will pose a threat to the business and impose strains on family relationships.

Looking Back

1. A family business is one in which the family has a special involvement. Such a business involves an overlapping of business interests (production and profitability) and family interests (care and nurture).

2. A family business often benefits from the strong commitment of family members to the welfare of the business and the ability of management to focus on human potential, quality, and long-run decisions. Potential weaknesses include a tendency to place family interests before business interests.

3. The culture of a family business includes three segments: the business culture (e.g., paternalistic), the family culture (e.g., patriarchal), and the governance or board-of-directors culture (e.g., rubber-stamp board). Changes in culture often occur as leadership passes from one generation to another.

4. It is difficult to provide strong motivation for nonfamily employees whose promotional opportunities are limited. This problem can be minimized by open communication concerning the extent of these opportunities.

5. A primary family relationship is that between the founder and the son or daughter who may succeed the founder in the business. Sons, daughters, in-laws, and sometimes other relatives have the possibility for collaboration or conflict with the founder and among themselves in the operation of the business. The role of the founder's spouse is especially important, often as a mediator between the founder and other family members.

6. Succession is typically a long-term process starting early in the successor's life. Tension often exists between the founder and the successor as the latter gains experience and becomes qualified to make business decisions independently. Transfer of ownership involves issues of placing control in the hands of the successor, being fair to all heirs, and facing tax consequences. A carefully formulated plan is helpful in the proper resolution of these issues.

DISCUSSION QUESTIONS

1. How would you define a family business? How does the size of the business affect your definition?

2. A computer software company began operation with a three-member management team that included skills in engineering, finance, and general business. Is this a family business? What might cause it to be classified as a family business or to become a family business?

3. Suppose that an entrepreneur's son-in-law is employed in a family firm. What conflict might possibly occur between family interests and business interests in the career of this son-in-law?

4. Suppose that you, as founder of a business, have a vacancy in the position of sales manager. You realize that sales may suffer somewhat if you promote your son from sales representative to sales manager. However, you would like to see your son make some progress and earn a higher salary to support his wife and young daughter. How would you go about making this decision? Would you promote your son?

5. To what extent should business interests be compromised or sacrificed because of family considerations?

6. What benefits result from family involvement in a business?

7. Why does a first-generation family business tend to have a paternalistic business culture and a patriarchal family culture?

8. Assume that you are an ambitious, nonfamily manager in a family firm and that one of your peers is a son or daughter of the founder. What, if anything, would keep you interested in pursuing your career with this company?

9. On the basis of your own observations, describe a founder–son or founder–daughter relationship in a family business. What strengths or weaknesses do you see in that relationship?

10. Does the involvement of both husband and wife in a family business

strengthen or weaken their family relationship? Can you cite any situations you have observed to support your answer?

11. Should a son or daughter feel an obligation to carry on a family business? What is the source of such a feeling?

12. Identify and describe the stages outlined in the model of succession shown in Exhibit 5–3.

13. What steps can be taken to minimize conflict between parent and child in family business decisions?

14. As a recent graduate in business administration, you are headed back to the family business. As a result of your education, you have become aware of some outdated business practices in the family firm. In spite of them, the business is showing a good return on investment. Should you "rock the boat"? How should you proceed in correcting what you see as obsolete traditions?

15. Should estate tax laws or other factors be given greater weight than family concerns in decisions about transferring ownership of a family business from one generation to another? Why?

YOU MAKE THE CALL

Situation 1

One of Manhattan's prestige restaurants, The Quilted Giraffe, is operated by a husband-and-wife team, Barry and Susan Wine, who have been married for 20 years. They have divided the business into two areas, and each takes responsibility for one area. The organizational arrangement is described as follows:

> Susan Wine runs the restaurant—the dining room end of things. She says husband Barry, the chef, is "an irritant" when he wanders out of the kitchen. Likewise, Susan has learned to stay clear of the kitchen. "I had to respect her turf and learn that we were both good at certain things," says Barry.
>
> *Source:* Dyan Machan, "My Partner, My Spouse," *Forbes*, Vol. 140, No. 13 (December 14, 1987), pp. 240–242.

Questions

1. Are the business relationships described here the type that would strengthen or weaken a marriage relationship? What additional steps might they take to strengthen their marriage?

2. What are some types of decisions that would fall outside their respective

areas of management? How would the structure described here affect such decisions?

3. Assuming that you are properly qualified, would you like to work for this firm? Why? What more would you like to know before answering that question?

Situation 2

Harrison Stevens, second-generation president of a family heating and air conditioning business, was concerned about his 19-year-old son, Barry, who worked as a full-time employee in the firm. Although Barry had made it through high school, he had not distinguished himself as a student or shown interest in further education. He was somewhat indifferent in his attitude toward his work, although he did reasonably, or at least minimally, satisfactory work. In the view of his father, Barry was immature and more interested in riding motorcycles than in building a business.

Harrison Stevens had wanted to provide his son with an opportunity for personal development. This could begin, as he saw it, by learning to work hard. If he liked the work and showed promise, he might eventually be groomed to take over the business. His father also held a faint hope that hard work might eventually inspire Barry to get a college education.

In trying to achieve these goals, Harrison Stevens sensed two problems. First, Barry obviously lacked proper motivation. The second problem related to his supervision. Supervisors seemed reluctant to be exacting in their demands on Barry. Rather than making him toe the line, they allowed him to get by with marginal performance. It may have been their apprehension that they might antagonize the boss by being too hard on his son.

Questions

1. In view of Barry's shortcomings, should Harrison Stevens seriously consider him as a potential successor?
2. How can Barry be motivated? Can Harrison Stevens do anything more to improve the situation, or does the responsibility lie with Barry?
3. How can the quality of Barry's supervision be improved so that his work experience will be more productive?

EXPERIENTIAL EXERCISES

1. Interview a college student who has grown up in a family business concerning the way that he or she may have been trained or educated, both

formally and informally, for entry into the business. Prepare a brief report, relating your findings to the stages of succession shown in Exhibit 5-3.

2. Interview a college student who has grown up in a family business concerning parental attitudes toward his or her possible entry into the business. Submit a one-page report showing the extent of pressure to enter the business and the direct or indirect ways in which expectations were communicated.

3. Locate a family business and prepare a brief report on its history, including its founding, family involvement, and any leadership changes that have occurred.

4. Most libraries have biographies or histories pertaining to families in business or the family businesses themselves. Read and report on one such book.

REFERENCES TO SMALL-BUSINESS PRACTICES

Feinstein, Selwyn. "Almost Heaven: How One Couple Integrates Work with a Satisfying Way of Life." *The Wall Street Journal* (June 10, 1988), pp. 5R–6R.

A description is given of a couple who are struggling to build a ski center business in the Green Mountains of Vermont. Both husband and wife are heavily involved in the business.

Goldstein, Nora. "When Brothers Run the Show." *In Business,* Vol. 5 (May–June, 1983), pp. 29–31.

The nature of family relationships in a business is discussed in this report on a family firm involving four brothers and one sister, with the prospect of still more relatives to come.

Nelton, Sharon. *In Love and in Business.* (New York: John Wiley & Sons, 1986).

In this book, the author describes and analyzes the family and business lives of a number of entrepreneurial couples.

Riggs, Carol R. "Growing with the Times." *D&B Reports,* Vol. 36, No. 4 (July–August, 1988), pp. 26–28.

The Chas. C. Hart Seed Company was founded in 1892. An account is given of its adaptation to a changing environment and its continuation as a family business, now under fourth-generation management.

ENDNOTES

1. This distinction between family and business is carefully examined in Ivan Lansberg, "Managing Human Resources in Family Firms: The Problem of Institutional Overlap," *Organizational Dynamics,* Vol. 12 (Summer, 1983), pp. 39–46, and Elaine Kepner, "The Family and the Firm: A Coevolutionary Perspective," *Organizational Dynamics,* Vol. 12 (Summer, 1983), pp. 57–70.

2. Priscilla Anne Schwab, "Matchmaker Discourages Love at First Sight," *Nation's Business,* Vol. 69 (January, 1981), p. 64.

3. Pat B. Alcorn, *Success and Survival in the Family Owned Business* (New York: McGraw-Hill Book Company, 1982), p. 107.

4. Peter Davis, "Realizing the Potential of the Family Business," *Organizational Dynamics*, Vol. 12 (Summer, 1983), pp. 53–54.

5. Edgar H. Schein, "The Role of the Founder in Creating Organizational Culture," *Organizational Dynamics*, Vol. 12 (Summer, 1983), pp. 13–28.

6. W. Gibb Dyer, Jr., *Cultural Change in Family Firms* (San Francisco: Jossey-Bass Publishers, 1986), Chapter 2.

7. Marie-Jeanne Juilland, "The Good, the Bad, and the Ugly," *Venture*, Vol. 10, No. 1 (January, 1988), p. 42.

8. Howard Butt, *The Velvet Covered Brick* (New York: Harper and Row, Publishers, 1973), pp. 5–6.

9. *Ibid.*, p. 9.

10. Katy Danco, *From the Other Side of the Bed: A Woman Looks at Life in the Family Business* (Cleveland: The Center for Family Business, 1981), p. 21.

11. Elmer H. Burack and Thomas M. Calero, "Seven Perils of the Family Firm," *Nation's Business*, Vol. 69 (January, 1981), p. 63.

12. For an earlier, extended treatment of this topic, see Justin G. Longenecker and John E. Schoen, "Management Succession in the Family Business," *Journal of Small Business Management*, Vol. 16 (July, 1978), pp. 1–6.

13. Donald Jonovic, *The Second-Generation Boss* (Cleveland: The Center for Family Business, 1982), p. 85.

14. W. Gibb Dyer, Jr., *op. cit.*, pp. 57–58.

15. Transfer of ownership is discussed by a specialist in tax accounting in Irving L. Blackman, "A Financial Guide to Turning over the Helm," *Nation's Business*, Vol. 74, No. 1 (January, 1986), pp. 40–42.

16. Leon A. Danco, *Inside the Family Business* (Cleveland: The Center for Family Business, 1980), pp. 198–199.

17. For an excellent treatment of leadership transition in a family firm, see John L. Ward, *Keeping the Family Business Healthy* (San Francisco: Jossey-Bass Publishers, 1987), Chapter 8.

18. An excellent treatment of this topic appears in Richard Beckhard and W. Gibb Dyer, Jr., "Managing Continuity in the Family Owned Business," *Organizational Dynamics*, Vol. 12 (Summer, 1983), pp. 5–12.

19. John L. Ward and Laurel Sorenson, "The Joy of Family Meetings," *Nation's Business*, Vol. 76, No. 6 (June, 1988), p. 33.

6 PREPARING THE BUSINESS PLAN

© Peter Poulides

   Nonplanners who succeed in spite of lack of planning may later recognize the wisdom of planning. This is true of Julie and Bill Brice, a brother-and-sister team who used $10,000 of their own money to buy two faltering frozen yogurt stores.

   "We just winged it" in the beginning, Julie Brice recalls. "When you are in school, you think you are invincible." But winging it soon grew too complicated for the Brices as they expanded their business to four stores within the first year.

   Julie soon signed up for an entrepreneurship course at Southern Methodist University. At the end of the semester, she emerged with a business plan. Planning has continued as the business expanded into a nationwide franchise network of more than 120 I Can't Believe It's Yogurt stores.

In hindsight, Julie conceded the value of preliminary planning. "If I had to start over again, I definitely would do a business plan to take a look at all the opportunities, the positives and the negatives," she says.

Source: Roger Thompson, "Business Plans: Myths and Reality," *Nation's Business,* Vol. 76, No. 8 (August, 1988), pp. 16–23.

Looking Ahead

Watch for the following important topics:
1. The reasons for preparing a business plan and how it is used.
2. How to prepare a business plan.
3. Features of a business plan that appeal to investors.
4. The content of a business plan.
5. New terms and concepts:

business plan	management plan
executive summary	operating plan
products and services plan	financial plan
marketing plan	legal plan

An early, important step in the launching of any business is preparation of a business plan. Obviously, a plan of some type exists in the mind of any person who is thinking about a new business venture. However, this is a weak substitute for a written business plan. In this chapter, we are concerned with the transformation of those often vague ideas into a written document that lays the groundwork for the proposed venture.

Need for a Business Plan

The **business plan** describes the new-venture idea and projects the marketing, operational, and financial aspects of the proposed business for the first three to five years. Its preparation permits analysis of the proposal and helps the prospective entrepreneur avoid a downhill path that leads from wild enthusiasm to disillusionment to failure. Although we will explain the planning process and present an outline for a business plan in this chapter, we wish to make it clear that you should use the ideas presented throughout this book and particularly those in Chapters 7 through 10 when preparing such a plan.

What Is a Business Plan?

If you were to consider starting your own business, an advisor might tell you to begin by preparing a business plan. This plan would present your basic business idea and all related operating, marketing, financial, and managerial considerations. In a sense, it would represent your "game plan." It would crystallize the dreams and hopes that provide your motivation. It is sometimes called a "deal" by those who invest in new ventures. Whatever the name, it should lay out your idea, describe where you are, and point out where you want to go and how you propose to get there.

The business plan may present a proposal for launching an entirely new business. More commonly, perhaps, it may present a plan for a major expansion of a firm that has already started operation. For example, an entrepreneur may open a small local business and see the possibility of opening additional branches or extending its success in other ways. More mature businesses also prepare strategic and operational plans that contain many of the features described in this chapter. In fact, planning should be a continuing process in the management of any business. The concepts presented in this chapter are not limited, therefore, to businesses that are just beginning operation.

Benefits of Preparing a Business Plan

A moment's reflection would alert a prospective entrepreneur to the danger of jumping into a business venture with a "half-baked" idea or "wild-eyed" proposition. Any activity that is initiated without adequate preparation tends to be haphazard and unsuccessful. This is particularly true of such a complex process as initiating a new business. Although planning is a mental process, it must go beyond the realm of thought. Thinking about a proposed business becomes more rigorous as rough ideas must be crystallized and quantified on paper. The written plan is essential to assure the systematic coverage of all important features of the new business.

One benefit derived from preparing a formal written plan is the discipline provided for the prospective entrepreneur. For example, in order to prepare a written statement about marketing strategy, he or she must perform some market research. Likewise, a study of financing requirements will require a review of receipts and expenditures month by month. Even good business ideas may fail because of negative cash flow. In short, business plan preparation forces a prospective entrepreneur to exercise the discipline that good managers must possess.

Tendency to Neglect Initial Planning

Prospective entrepreneurs tend to neglect the planning stage of a new venture. They are eager to get started, and they do not always realize the importance of a written plan. They may also lack sufficient funds or necessary expertise to conduct an adequate feasibility study. Of course, sometimes they are forced to engage in a minimum of planning in order to gain a hearing from the potential investors in their business.

The neglect of initial planning is evident from a study by G. M. Naidu of business startups in Wisconsin.[1] For example, Naidu found that:

1. 63 percent of the new entrepreneurs did not evaluate the location of the business.
2. 72 percent did not conduct a trade-area analysis.
3. 52 percent did not evaluate their competition.
4. Almost 25 percent did not even estimate revenues and expenses.

Failure to prepare an initial written plan for a new venture undoubtedly contributes to the early failure of some firms.

Using the Business Plan Internally in Managing

A business plan is more than a device for raising funds. More fundamentally, it is a basis for operating a business. In it, an entrepreneur charts the course for a new firm. As we just noted, the process of formulating the plan can uncover weaknesses or alert the entrepreneur to sources of possible danger. The well-conceived plan thus offers a sound basis for operation.

The goals identified in the business plan become targets for operating control. If the new firm substantially exceeds or falls short of these goals, the entrepreneur must act. The plan itself may require modification, or other management action may be needed.

The business plan also provides a basis for communicating the business mission to insiders, the employees of the firm. Some, indeed, suggest that it can be used as a tool in recruiting key personnel. Exhibit 6-1 shows the various users of the business plan.

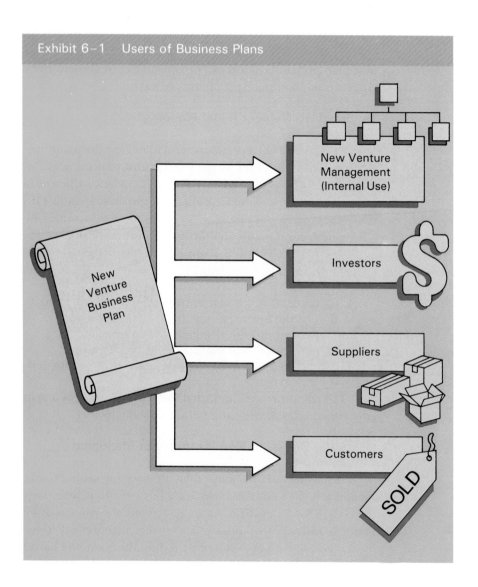

Exhibit 6–1   Users of Business Plans

The Business Plan and Outsiders

Investors and lenders are the primary, although not the only, outside users of business plans. Almost anyone starting a business faces the task of raising financial resources to supplement personal savings. Unless the entrepreneur has a "rich uncle" who will supply funds, he or she must appeal to bankers, individual investors, venture capitalists, or other sources. The business plan is the entrepreneur's "calling card."

Both lenders and investors can use the business plan to gain an idea of the business, the type of product or service, the nature of the market, and the qualifications of the entrepreneur or entrepreneurial team. A venture capital firm or other sophisticated investor would not think of investing in a new business without seeing a properly prepared business plan. The plan can also be helpful in establishing a good relationship with a commercial bank, a relationship that is important for a new firm.

Relationships with nonfinancial outside groups may also benefit from exposing those groups to the business plan. Suppliers, for example, extend trade credit, which is often an important part of the firm's financial plan. A well-prepared business plan may be helpful in gaining a supplier's trust and quickly securing favorable credit terms. Occasionally, a business plan can also improve sales prospects—for example, by convincing a potential customer that a new firm is likely to be around to service a product or to continue as a procurement source.

How to Prepare a Business Plan

Preparation of a business plan is a difficult, frustrating, and often unrewarding task, as reflected in the following quotation:

> Here's a financing riddle: What costs upwards of $5,000 to prepare, commands a few moments of an investor's time, and fails 98% of the time?
>
> Answer: The typical business plan.[2]

To gain the approval, or even the attention, of an investor, an entrepreneur must prepare and present the plan in the right way. Both style and substance are important. This section relates to the style and format of the report, and the following section discusses its content. Although business plans have varied uses, as noted earlier, the primary focus here is on their use in securing funding.

The Five-Minute Reader

Joseph R. Mancuso uses the phrase, "the five-minute reader," to picture a busy venture capitalist who spends only a few moments to glance at a business plan.[3] Very few plans are read in detail from cover to cover. Far

Figure 6–1   Venture Capitalist Scans a Business Plan

Unisys Corporation

too many proposals are received by the typical venture capital firm to permit such careful examination. George Kalan, managing general partner of Orien Ventures Inc., New Caanan, CT, has been quoted as follows: "We got 750 plans last year and made 11 deals. I look at the executive summary, and if it's clearly out of our scope, in a few minutes we send it back with a no-thank-you letter."[4]

The speed with which business plans are reviewed means that they must be designed to communicate effectively even to the speed reader. They must not sacrifice thoroughness, however, or substitute a few snappy phrases for basic factual information. After all, someone is going to read the plan carefully if it ever succeeds. To get that careful reading, however, the plan must first gain the interest of the reader, and it must be formulated with that purpose in mind. This raises the question as to what features of a plan make it appealing to investors.

Business Plans That Attract Investors

To appeal effectively to prospective investors, the plan cannot be extremely long or encyclopedic in detail. Such plans should seldom exceed 50 pages in length. Those who work with venture capitalists have reported their tendency to go for brief reports and to avoid those that take too long to read. It follows also that the general appearance of the report should be attractive and that it should be well organized, with numbered pages and a table of contents.

Venture capitalists are more market-oriented than product-oriented, and there is a reason for this orientation. They realize that most inventions, even those patented, never earn a dime for the inventors. It is desirable for budding entrepreneurs to join them in their concern about market prospects (see Exhibit 6–2).

Factors that presumably "turn on" investors are the following:[5]

- Evidence of customer acceptance of the venture's product or service.
- An appreciation of investors' needs, through recognition of their particular financial-return goals.
- Evidence of focus, through concentration on only a limited number of products or services.
- Proprietary position, as expressed in the form of patents, copyrights, and trademarks.

Prospective investors may also be "turned off" by a business plan. Some of the features that create unfavorable reactions are the following:[6]

- Infatuation with the product or service rather than familiarity with and awareness of marketplace needs.
- Financial projections at odds with accepted industry ranges.
- Growth projections out of touch with reality.
- Custom or applications engineering, which make substantial growth difficult.

Computer-Aided Business Planning

The computer is being used more and more to facilitate preparation of the business plan. Its word-processing capabilities, for example, can speed up the writing of narrative sections of the report, such as the description of the product and the review of key management personnel. By using a word-processing software package, the planner can begin with an original version of the narrative, go through a series of drafts as corrections and refinements are made, and print out a final plan as it is to be presented to investors or others. Several such software packages are described in Chapter 22.

The computer is an even more helpful tool in preparing the financial statements needed in the plan. Since the various parts of a financial plan

Based on their experience with the MIT Enterprise Forum, Stanley R. Rich and David E. Gumpert have identified the type of plan that wins funding. (The MIT Enterprise Forum sponsors sessions in which prospective entrepreneurs present business plans to panels of venture capitalists, bankers, marketing specialists, and other experts.) Following are the "winning" features:

- It must be arranged appropriately, with an executive summary, a table of contents, and its chapters in the right order.
- It must be the right length and have the right appearance—not too long and not too short, not too fancy and not too plain.
- It must give a sense of what the founders and the company expect to accomplish three to seven years into the future.
- It must explain in quantitative and qualitative terms the benefit to the user of the company's products or services.
- It must present hard evidence of the marketability of the products or services.
- It must justify financially the means chosen to sell the products or services.
- It must explain and justify the level of product development which has been achieved and describe in appropriate detail the manufacturing process and associated costs.
- It must portray the partners as a team of experienced managers with complementary business skills.
- It must suggest as high an overall "rating" as possible of the venture's product development and team sophistication.
- It must contain believable financial projections, with the key data explained and documented.
- It must show how investors can cash out in three to seven years, with appropriate capital appreciation.
- It must be presented to the most potentially receptive financiers possible to avoid wasting precious time as company funds dwindle.
- It must be easily and concisely explainable in a well-orchestrated oral presentation.

Source: "Plans That Succeed" (pp. 2–3) and dialogue on pp. 126–127 from BUSINESS PLANS THAT WIN $$$: Lessons from the MIT Enterprise Forum by Stanley R. Rich and David E. Gumpert. Reprinted by permission of Sterling Lord Literistic, Inc. Copyright © 1985 by Stanley R. Rich and David E. Gumpert.

SMALL BUSINESS IN ACTION
Plans That Are Too Long

By using a computer, a prospective entrepreneur can easily generate reams of material—sometimes too many pages. An official of a venture capital firm has complained about this tendency as noted here:

Robert J. Crowley

"There's this horrible disease going around right now," says Robert J. Crowley, vice-president of Massachusetts Technology Development Corp., a state-owned venture firm. "It's called spreadsheet-itis. It's the most common ailment in business plans today." And the venture capitalists blame word processors and spreadsheet software, especially Lotus 1–2–3, the landmark package from Lotus Development Corp. Recently, Crowley received a 98-page plan: 48 pages of spreadsheets, 30 pages of technology description, and 20 pages on management. He was horrified. Most venture capitalists say plans should run no longer than 40 pages. "Word processors allow you to just ramble on," continues Crowley, "because there's no person, no secretary, saying, "You want me to retype *what?*""

Source: Reprinted with permission, *Inc.* magazine (February, 1987). Copyright © 1987 by Goldhirsh Group, Inc., 38 Commercial Wharf, Boston, MA 02110.
Photo Source: © *1990 Stephen Sherman*

are interwoven in many ways, a change in one item—sales volume or interest rate or cost of equipment, for example—will cause ripples to run through the entire plan. If the planner wishes to check out a number of assumptions, this requires a long, tedious set of calculations.

By using a computer simulation, the planner can accomplish this task electronically. Such a program is available in Terry S. Maness, *Small-Business Management Using Lotus 1–2–3* (Cincinnati: South-Western Publishing Company, 1991). That publication, designed for use with this text, provides a program for developing a complete financial plan. By using this type of simulation, a planner can experiment with various scenarios and quickly ascertain their impact on cash flow and operating profits.

Format and Writing Suggestions

The quality of a completed business plan is obviously dependent on the quality of the underlying business concept. A defective venture idea cannot be rescued by good writing. A good venture concept may be destroyed, however, by writing that fails to communicate.

Skills of written communication are necessary to present the business concept in an accurate, comprehensible, and enthusiastic way. Space does not permit discussion of general writing principles here. Nevertheless, it may be useful to include some practical suggestions specifically related to the business plan. Following are some hints given by the public accounting firm Arthur Anderson and Company in their booklet, *An Entrepreneur's Guide to Developing a Business Plan:*

1. Provide a table of contents and tab eacn section for easy reference.
2. Use a typewritten 8½″ × 11″ format and photocopy the plan to minimize costs. Use a looseleaf binder to package the plan and to facilitate future revisions.
3. To add interest and improve comprehension—especially by prospective investors who lack the day-to-day familiarity that your management team has—use charts, graphs, diagrams, tabular summaries, and other visual aids.
4. You almost certainly will want prospective investors, as well as your management team, to treat your plan confidentially, so indicate on the cover and again on the title page of the plan that all information is proprietary and confidential. Number each copy of the plan and account for each outstanding copy by filing the recipient's memorandum of receipt.
5. Given the particularly sensitive nature of startup operations based on advanced technology, it is entirely possible that many entrepreneurs will be reluctant to divulge certain information—details of a technological design, for example, or highly sensitive specifics of marketing strategy— even to a prospective investor. In that situation, you still can put together a highly effective document to support your funding proposal by presenting appropriate extracts from your internal business plan.
6. As you complete major sections of the plan, ask carefully chosen third parties—entrepreneurs who have themselves raised capital successfully, accountants, lawyers and others—to give their perspectives on the quality, clarity, reasonableness, and thoroughness of the plan. After you pull the entire plan together, ask these independent reviewers for final comments before you reproduce and distribute the plan.[7]

Assistance in Preparing a Business Plan

The founder of a business is most notably a "doer." Such a person often lacks the breadth of experience and know-how needed in planning.

Consequently, he or she must supplement personal knowledge and personal skills by obtaining the assistance of outsiders or adding individuals with planning skills to the management team.

Securing help in plan preparation does not relieve the founder of direct involvement. The founder must be the primary planner simply because it is his or her plan. The founder's basic ideas are necessary to produce a plan that is realistic and believable. Furthermore, the plan may eventually require defense and interpretation to outsiders. An entrepreneur can be prepared for such a presentation only by having complete familiarity with it.

Granted, then, that the founder must be involved, he or she can draw upon the skills of those with greater experience in this area. Outside professionals who can provide assistance include the following:

1. *Attorneys,* who can make sure that the company has necessary patent protection, review contracts, consult on liability and environmental concerns, and advise on the best form of legal organization.
2. *Marketing specialists,* who can perform market analysis and evaluate market acceptance of a new product.
3. *Engineering and production experts,* who can perform product development, determine technical feasibility of products, and assist in plant layout and production planning.
4. *Accounting firms,* which can guide in developing the written plan, assist in making financial projections, and advise in establishing a system of financial control.
5. *Incubator organizations,* which offer space for fledgling companies and supply management counsel in structuring new businesses. (Incubators are discussed at greater length in Chapters 8 and 15.)

Content of a Business Plan

A prospective entrepreneur needs a guide to follow in preparing a business plan. Although there is no one standard format in general use, there are many similarities among the general frameworks proposed for business plans. Exhibit 6–3 presents a simple condensation of the major segments common to many of these organizing patterns. Its special value lies in the excellent bird's-eye view it gives. Before becoming immersed in the details of a plan, you can form a general idea of the various segments of a plan and how they are related to each other.

Exhibit 6-3   Overview of a Business Plan

Executive Summary: **A one- to three-page overview of the total business plan. Written after the other sections are completed, it highlights their significant points and, ideally, creates enough excitement to motivate the reader to read on.**

General Company Description: Explains the type of company and gives its history if it already exists. Tells whether it is a manufacturing, retail, service, or other type of business.

Products and Services Plan: Describes the product and/or service and points out any unique features. Explains why people will buy the product or service.

Marketing Plan: Shows who will be your customers and what type of competition you will face. Outlines your marketing strategy and specifies what will give you a competitive edge.

Management Plan: Identifies the ''key players''—the active investors, management team, and directors. Cites the experience and competence they possess.

Operating Plan: Explains the type of manufacturing or operating system you will use. Describes the facilities, labor, raw materials, and processing requirements.

Financial Plan: Specifies financial needs and contemplated sources of financing. Presents projections of revenues, costs, and profits.

Legal Plan: Shows the proposed type of legal organization—proprietorship, partnership, or corporation. Points out special, relevant legal considerations.

Major Elements of a Business Plan

The overview given in Exhibit 6–3 portrays the overall scope of a plan, but it lacks detail. In this section, we provide more specific guidelines for each of the major segments identified in Exhibit 6–3.

Note that the executive summary in Exhibit 6–3 differs from the other sections of the plan in that it presents a general picture of the business by giving highlights from the sections that follow. Because of its nature, we do not provide a set of exploratory questions relative to the executive summary.

Each of the other sections of the plan can be developed by responding to a set of questions pertaining to it. In Exhibit 6–4, for example, you will find questions related to the general company description. Similarly, in Exhibits 6–5 through 6–10, you will find questions related to the products and services plan, marketing plan, and each subsequent section of the plan.

The business plan for each new venture is unique to some extent. The guidelines and questions, therefore, will not apply identically to every business. A business plan will not merely answer these questions in the order they are given. Rather, the questions are intended to suggest areas that deserve attention. Moreover, the questions do not necessarily cover every issue with which you will be concerned. You may discover additional features that go beyond the outline given here and that must be covered in the plan for your particular business.

Turn now to Exhibits 6–4 through 6–10 to find the questions to be answered. These can be used in developing each section of the business

---

Exhibit 6–4 General Company Description

1. Is this a startup, buyout, or expansion?
2. Has this business started operation?
3. When and where was this business started?
4. What is the basic nature and activity of the business?
5. What is its primary product or service?
6. What customers are served?
7. Is this company in manufacturing, retailing, service, or another type of industry?
8. What is the current state of this industry?
9. What is the company's stage of development—"seed stage," full product line, or what?
10. What are its objectives?
11. Does the company intend to become a publicly traded company or an acquisition candidate?
12. What is the prior history of this company?
13. What achievements have been made to date?
14. What changes have been made in structure or ownership?
15. What is the firm's distinctive competence?

Exhibit 6–5 Products and Services Plan

1. What product or service is being offered?
2. What does the product look like?
3. What is the stage of product development?
4. What are the unique characteristics of the product or service?
5. What are its special advantages?
6. What additional products or services are contemplated?
7. What legal protection applies—patents, copyrights, or trademarks?
8. What government regulatory approval is needed?
9. How does the product relate to the state of the art for such products?
10. What are the dangers of obsolescence?
11. What dangers are related to style or fashion change?
12. What liabilities may be involved?
13. How has the product been tested or evaluated?
14. How does the product or service compare with products or services of competitors?
15. What makes this firm's service superior?

Exhibit 6–6 Marketing Plan

Market Analysis

1. What is your target market?
2. What is the size of your target market?
3. What market segments exist?
4. What is the profile of your target customer?
5. How will customers benefit by using your product or service?
6. What share of the market do you expect to get?
7. What are the market trends and market potential?
8. What are the reactions of prospective customers?

Competition

1. Who are your strongest competitors?
2. Is their business growing or declining?
3. How does your business compare with that of competitors?
4. On what basis will you compete?

Exhibit 6–6 *(Continued)*

Marketing Strategy

1. How will you attract customers?
2. How will you identify prospective customers?
3. What type of selling effort will you use?
4. What channels of distribution will you use?
5. In what geographic areas will you sell?
6. Will you export to other countries?
7. What type of sales force will you employ?
8. What special selling skills will be required?
9. What selling procedures will be used?
10. How will you compensate your sales force?
11. What type of sales promotion and advertising will you use?
12. What pricing policy will you follow?
13. What credit and collection policy will you follow?
14. What warranties and guarantees will you offer?
15. How do your marketing policies compare with those of competitors?

Exhibit 6–7 Management Plan

1. Who are members of the management team?
2. What are the skills, education, and experience of each?
3. What other active investors or directors are involved, and what are their qualifications?
4. What vacant positions exist, and what are the plans to fill them?
5. What consultants will be used, and what are their qualifications?
6. What is the compensation package of each key person?
7. How is the ownership distributed?
8. How will employees be selected and rewarded?
9. What style of management will be used?
10. How will personnel be motivated?
11. How will creativity be encouraged?
12. How will commitment and loyalty be developed?

Exhibit 6-8 Operating Plan

1. How will you produce your product or service?
2. What production will be accomplished by subcontracting?
3. What production or operating facilities will be used?
4. What is the capacity of these facilities?
5. How can capacity be expanded?
6. What methods of production will be used?
7. What type of plant layout will be used?
8. What production control procedures will be used?
9. What quality control system will be used?
10. How will inventory be controlled?
11. What is the environmental impact of the business?
12. What are the advantages and disadvantages of the location?
13. What production or operating advantages exist?
14. What are the labor requirements?
15. What are the major production costs?
16. What materials or components are critical to production?
17. What sources of supply exist?
18. What will be the production cost at each level of operation?

Exhibit 6-9 Financial Plan

1. What assumptions are used for financial projections?
2. What revenue level is projected by months and years?
3. What expenses are projected by months and years?
4. What profits are projected by months and years?
5. What cash flow is projected by months and years?
6. What financial position exists now, and what is anticipated at various points during the next five years?
7. When will the business break even?
8. What financial resources are required now?
9. What additional funds will be required?
10. How will these funds be used?
11. How much has been invested and loaned by the principals?
12. What additional potential sources will be explored?
13. What proportions of funding will be debt and equity?
14. What type of financial participation is being offered?

> **Exhibit 6–10   Legal Plan**
>
> 1. Will the business function as a proprietorship?
> 2. Will the business function as a general or limited partnership?
> 3. Will the business function as a regular corporation or Subchapter S corporation?
> 4. What are the legal liability implications of the form of organization chosen?
> 5. What are the tax advantages and disadvantages of this form of organization?
> 6. Where is the corporation chartered?
> 7. What was the date of incorporation?
> 8. What attorney or legal firm has been selected to represent the firm?
> 9. What type of relationship exists with this attorney or law firm?
> 10. What legal issues are presently or potentially significant?

plan. We realize, of course, that any planner will adapt the suggested pattern to the particular type of venture and emphasize the questions most relevant to that venture.

What to Highlight in Each Section

The questions in Exhibits 6–4 through 6–10 draw attention to major issues that need consideration. Let us think now about the thrust or purpose of each section in order to put those questions in perspective.

Executive Summary   This section is crucial in getting the attention of the five-minute reader. It must, therefore, convey a clear picture of the proposed venture and, at the same time, create a sense of excitement regarding its prospects. This means that it must be written and rewritten to achieve clarity and interest. Even though it comes at the beginning of the business plan, it summarizes the total plan and must be written last. A sample executive summary for an all-natural baby and children's food company is shown in Exhibit 6–11.

General Company Description   The body of the business plan begins with a brief description of the company itself. If the firm is already in existence, its prior history is included. By examining this section, the reader will know, for example, whether the company is engaged in retailing or construction or some other line of business, where the business is located, and whether

Exhibit 6–11   Executive Summary for Good Foods Incorporated

This business plan has been developed to present Good Foods Incorporated (referred to as GFI or The Company) to prospective investors and to assist in raising the $700,000 of equity capital needed to begin the sale of its initial products and finish development of its complete product line.

The Company

GFI is a startup business with three principals presently involved in its development. The principal contact is Judith Appel of Nature's Best, Inc., 24 Woodland Road, Great Neck, New York (516–555–5321).

During the past three years, GFI's principals have researched and developed a line of unique children's food products based on the holistic health concept—if the whole body is supplied with proper nutrition, it will, in many cases, remain healthy and free of disease.

Holism is the theory that living organisms should be viewed and treated as whole beings and not merely as the sum of different parts. The holistic concept, which *Health Food Consumer* determined is widely accepted among adult consumers of health foods, is new to the child-care field.

Hence, GFI plans to take advantage of the opportunities for market development and penetration that its principals are confident exist. GFI also believes that the existing baby-food industry pays only cursory attention to providing high-quality, nutritious products, and that the limited number of truly healthy and nutritious baby foods creates a market void that GFI can successfully fill.

Based on the detailed financial projections prepared by The Company's management, it is estimated that $700,000 of equity investment is required to begin The Company's operations successfully. The funds received will be used to finance initial marketing activities, complete development of The Company's product line, and provide working capital during the first two years of operation.

Market Potential

GFI's market research shows that the United States is entering a "mini baby boom" that will increase the potential market base for its products. This increase, combined with an expected future 25-percent annual growth rate of the $2.4 billion health food industry, as estimated by *Health Foods Business* in 1985, will increase the demand for GFI's products. Additionally, health food products are more frequently being sold in supermarkets, which is increasing product visibility and should help to increase popularity.

The Company will approach the marketplace primarily through health food stores and nature-food centers in major supermarket chain stores, initially in the Northeast and California. Acceptance of the GFI concept in these areas will enable The Company to expand to a national market.

The specific target markets GFI will approach through these outlets are:

Parents who are concerned about their health and their children's health and who thus demand higher quality and more nutritionally balanced foods and products.

Operators of child-care centers who provide meals to children.

164

Exhibit 6–11   *(Continued)*

Major Milestones

Approximately two-thirds of GFI's product line is ready to market. The remaining one-third is expected to be completed within one year.

Distinctive Competence

GFI is uniquely positioned to take advantage of this market opportunity due to the managerial and field expertise of its founders, and its products' distinct benefits.

Judith Appel, George Knapp, MD, and Samuel Knapp, MD all possess several years of experience in the child-care industry. Ms. Appel is a nutritionist and has served as director for the Children's Hospital for Special Services in White Plains, New York. In addition, she has nine years of business experience, first as marketing director for Healthy Harvest Foods in Yonkers, New York, then as owner/president of Nature's Best, Inc. Both of the Doctors Knapp have worked extensively with children, in hospital-based and private practices.

Together, the principals have spent the last three years developing, refining, testing, and selling GFI's products through Nature's Best, Inc., the retail outlet in Great Neck, a Long Island suburb of New York City.

GFI's product line will satisfy the market demand for a natural, nutritious children's food. The maximum amount of nutrients will be retained in the food, providing children with more nutritional benefit than most products presently on the market. The menu items chosen will reflect the tastes most preferred by children. A broad product line will also provide a diverse meal plan.

Financial Summary

Based on detailed financial projections prepared by GFI, if The Company receives the required $700,000 in funding, it will operate profitably by year three. The following is a summary of projected financial information (dollars in thousands).

	Year 1	Year 2	Year 3	Year 4	Year 5
Sales	$1,216	$1,520	$2,653	$4,021	$5,661
Gross margin	50%	50%	50%	50%	50%
Net income after tax	$(380)	$(304)	$15	$404	$633
Net income after tax/sales	—	—	0.6%	10.0%	11.2%
Return/equity	0.0%	0.0%	10.8%	73.9%	53.6%
Return/assets	0.0%	0.0%	2.6%	44.5%	36.2%

it is serving a local or international market. In many cases, issues noted in the legal plan—especially the legal form of organization—are incorporated into this section of the plan.

Products and Services Plan   As implied by the title, this section discusses the products and/or services to be offered to customers. If a new or unique physical product is involved and a working model or prototype is available, a photograph should be included. Investors will naturally show the greatest interest in products that have been developed, tested, and found to be functional. Any innovative features should be identified and patent protection, if any, explained. In many instances, of course, the product or service may be similar to that offered by competitors—for example, starting an electrical contracting firm. However, any special features should be clearly identified. Chapter 7 discusses this topic at greater length.

Marketing Plan   As stated earlier, prospective investors and lenders attach a high priority to market considerations. A product may be well engineered but unwanted by customers. The business plan, therefore, must identify user benefits and the type of market that exists. Depending upon the type of product or service, you may be able not only to identify but also to quantify the user's financial benefit—for example, by showing how quickly a user can recover the cost of a product through savings in operating cost. Of course, benefits may also take the form of convenience, time saving, greater attractiveness, better health, and so on.

The business plan should follow the establishment of user benefits by documenting the existence of customer interest, showing that a market exists and that customers are ready to buy the product or service. The market analysis must be carried to the point that a reasonable estimate of demand can be achieved. Estimates of demand must be analytically sound and based on more than assumptions if they are to be accepted as credible by prospective investors. The marketing plan must also examine the competition and present elements of the proposed marketing strategy—for example, by specifying the type of sales force and methods of promotion and advertising that will be used. Chapter 7 presents a fuller discussion of the marketing plan.

Management Plan   Prospective investors look for well-managed companies. Unfortunately, the ability to conceive an idea for a new venture is no guarantee of managerial ability. The plan, therefore, must detail the organizational arrangements and the backgrounds of those who will fill key positions in the proposed firm.

Ideally, investors desire to see a well-balanced management team, one that includes financial and marketing expertise as well as production experience and inventive talent. Managerial experience in related enterprises and in other startup situations is particularly valuable in the eyes of outsiders reading the business plan. The factors involved in preparing the management plan are discussed more fully in Chapter 8.

Operating Plan This section of the plan shows how you will produce the product or provide the service. It touches on such items as location and facilities—how much space you will need and what type of equipment you will require. The importance of the operating plan varies from venture to venture, but this plan is necessary even for firms providing services. The operating plan should explain the proposed approach to assuring production quality, controlling inventory, using subcontracting, or meeting other special problems related to raw materials. This area is treated at greater length in Chapter 8.

Financial Plan The financial analysis constitutes another crucial section of the business plan. In it, the entrepreneur presents projections of revenues and profits and reveals the basic financial structure. Revenues and profits are projected not only for the first year of operation but for five years or more. In fact, projections should be prepared monthly for the first year and quarterly for the second and third years. Projections must also consider cash flow, because a business may be profitable and still fail to produce a positive cash flow.

The intended financial structure is disclosed by showing the proposed configuration of the firm's resources—how much of the money will be devoted to equipment, inventory, and so on. It also shows the proposed sources of funds—how much will be borrowed and how much invested. Chapter 9 discusses financial decisions that are relevant to this section of the plan.

Legal Plan In the legal plan, the entrepreneur sets out the basic legal form of organization. The three major alternatives are proprietorship, partnership, and corporation. There are variations, however, that deserve consideration. A special type of corporation, for example, may serve to minimize federal taxes paid by the firm and its owners. As noted earlier, the legal plan does not necessarily stand as a totally separate section of the business plan but is often made a part of the general company description. The legal issues are important, however, and deserve careful consideration. These issues are discussed further in Chapter 10.

Sample Plans and Plan-Preparation Manuals

A prospective entrepreneur typically likes to see a sample plan and have specific guidelines available as he or she begins preparation of a business plan. Used carefully, such aids can facilitate the planning process. One should be cautious, however, about trying to follow another plan too closely by changing the numbers and adapting it for another venture. Each business is unique, and the plan should capture the essence of that specific business.

By exercising caution, however, the planner can benefit by referring to manuals that are now available. One part of a business plan, the executive summary, was shown in Exhibit 6–11. Unfortunately, we cannot reproduce the entire plan here because of space limitations.

Most, if not all, major accounting firms have compiled manuals on preparation of business plans. Private publishers and other groups have also issued books, manuals, and workbooks on this subject, and many of these publications contain sample plans. In concluding this chapter, we list a number of such sources. This list is by no means exhaustive, but merely suggestive in indicating the types of publications available.

The Arthur Young Business Plan Guide by Eric Siegel, Loren Schultz, Brian Ford, and David Carney (New York: John Wiley and Sons, 1987)

The Business Plan: A Touche Ross Guide to Writing a Successful Business Plan (Los Angeles: Touche Ross, 1986)

An Entrepreneur's Guide to Developing a Business Plan (Chicago: Arthur Anderson and Company, 1986)

The Business Plan by Michael O'Donnell (Natick, MA: Lord Publishing, Inc., 1988)

The Business Planning Guide (Dover, NH: Upstart Publishing Company, 1988)

How to Write a Successful Business Plan by Julie K. Brooks (New York: American Management Association, 1987)

How to Prepare and Present a Business Plan by Joseph R. Mancuso (Englewood Cliffs, NJ: Prentice-Hall, Inc., 1983)

Looking Back

1. Preparing a business plan forces the prospective entrepreneur to examine a business idea systematically and to deal with potential difficulties before they happen. It can be used internally as the basis for operating the business and externally as a device for raising funds or explaining the business to others.
2. A business plan should be well organized, have a table of contents, and make extensive use of charts, graphs, diagrams, tabular summaries, or other visual aids. A computer can be used in preparing the narrative sections and also, more importantly, in developing the financial section. Outside professional assistance in preparing the plan can also be obtained.
3. Investors like brief reports that are more market-oriented than product-oriented. Such reports must contain believable financial projections and portray the management team as experienced and capable of directing the venture.
4. A business plan should begin with an executive summary, which presents highlights of the overall plan for the busy reader. After the executive summary, the plan devotes sections to a general company description, products/services, marketing plan, operating plan, management plan, and financial plan.

DISCUSSION QUESTIONS

1. Sometimes an investor will put money into a new business even though it lacks a business plan. Would this be riskier in a very small (less than $1 million sales) business or in a somewhat larger (more than $25 million sales) business? Why?
2. A business plan was described in this chapter as a "game plan." What features of such a plan justify this label?
3. Why would a business plan be described as a "deal"? Does this word convey an accurate picture of a business plan?
4. Suppose a student plans to start a very small sideline business—one

that will require less than a $200 investment. Is there any point in preparing a written business plan? Why?

5. What benefits are associated with the preparation of a written new-venture plan? Who uses it?

6. Why do entrepreneurs tend to neglect initial planning? Why would you personally be most tempted to neglect it?

7. In what way could a business plan be used in recruiting key management personnel?

8. Recall the statement that the venture capitalist is a "five-minute reader." Would a really intelligent investor make decisions based on such a hasty review of business plans? Is it possible they are acting like financial wizards while throwing money away?

9. Venture capitalists were described as being more market-oriented than product-oriented. What does this mean? What is the logic behind this orientation?

10. Why shouldn't longer business plans be better than shorter ones in view of the fact that more data and supporting analysis can be included?

11. What advantages are realized by using a computer in preparing narrative sections of a business plan? In preparing the financial section?

12. Evaluate the practical planning suggestions for preparing a business plan presented on page 156. Would these suggestions apply equally well to the preparation of reports or papers for a college class?

13. In selling a new type of production tool, how might you quantify user benefit?

14. The founders of Apple Computer, Inc., eventually left or were forced out of the company's management. What implications does this have for the management section of a business plan?

15. If the income statement in a business plan shows the business will be profitable, what is the need for a cash flow forecast?

YOU MAKE THE CALL

Situation 1

New ventures are occasionally more successful than projected in their initial business plans. One example relates to Compaq Computer Corporation. Ben Rosen and L. J. Sevin invested in this company even though they had reservations about its projected sales volume. They were then astonished by the excellent results.

> In 1982, Rosen and partner L. J. Sevin, a couple of lucky guys, invested in a company then called Gateway Technology Inc. Gateway's plan said the company would make a portable computer compatible with IBM's personal computer and would sell 20,000 machines for $35 million in its first year—"Which we didn't believe for a moment," says Rosen. The sales projection for the second year was even more outrageous: $198 million. "Can you imagine seeing a business plan like this for a company going head-on against IBM, and projecting $198 million?" he asks. He and Sevin told the fledgling company to scale down its projections.
>
> Gateway later changed its name to Compaq Computer Corp. In its first year the company sold an estimated 50,000 machines, more than twice the plan's forecast, for $111 million. In the second year Compaq's sales were $329 million.
>
> *Source:* Reprinted with permission, *Inc.* magazine (February, 1987). Copyright © 1987 by Goldhirsh Group, Inc., 38 Commercial Wharf, Boston, MA 02110.

Questions

1. In view of the major error in projected sales, what benefits, if any, may have been realized through initial planning?
2. What implications for preparation of a business plan are found in the investors' skepticism concerning sales projections?
3. In view of the circumstances in this case, do you think that entrepreneurs or investors are likely to be more nearly accurate and realistic in projections in new business plans? Why?

Situation 2

A young journalist contemplated launching a new magazine that would feature wildlife, plant life, and the scenic beauty of nature throughout the world. The prospective entrepreneur intended that each issue would contain several feature articles such as the dangers and benefits of forest fires, features of Rocky Mountain National Park, wildflowers found at high altitudes, danger of acid rain, and so on. It would make extensive use of color photographs, but its articles would also contain discussions that were scientifically correct and interestingly written. Unlike *National Geographic,* the proposed publication would avoid articles dealing with the general culture and confine itself to topics closely related to nature itself. Suppose you are a venture capitalist examining a business plan prepared by this journalist.

Questions

1. What are the most urgent questions you wish to have answered in the marketing plan?

2. What details would you look for in the management plan?
3. Do you think this business plan would need to raise closer to $10,000 or $10 million in invested funds? Why?
4. At first glance, are you inclined to accept or reject the proposal? Why?

EXPERIENTIAL EXERCISES

1. Assume that you wish to start a business to produce and sell a device to hold down picnic table cloths so that they will not blow in the wind. Prepare a one-page outline of the marketing section of a business plan for this business. Be as specific and comprehensive as possible.
2. A former chef wishes to start a temporary help business to supply kitchen help (banquet chefs, sauce cooks, bakers, meat cutters, and so on) to restaurants that are short of staff during busy periods. Prepare a one-page report showing which section or sections of its business plan would be most crucial and why it or they would be most crucial.
3. Suppose you wish to start a tutoring service for students in college elementary accounting courses. Outline on one page the benefits that you would realize by preparing a written business plan.
4. Interview a person who has started a business within the past five years. Prepare a report showing the extent to which the founder engaged in preliminary planning and the founder's views about the value of business plans.

REFERENCES TO SMALL BUSINESS PRACTICES

Hand, Jason. "'They Told Us to Focus.'" *Forbes,* Vol. 142, No. 10 (October 31, 1988), pp. 134–136.
    This article describes the history of Etak, Inc., a company whose first plan was a product plan scratched on the back of an envelope. The company produces computerized navigational systems for cars, but it almost failed because of an error in the marketing plan.
Larson, Erik. "The Best-Laid Plans." *Inc.,* Vol. 9, No. 2 (February, 1987), pp. 60–64.
    In this article, the author describes the experiences of several companies in preparing and in failing to prepare adequate business plans.
Rhodes, Lucien. "Winning Is a State of Mind at Nike." *Inc.,* Vol. 3, No. 8 (August, 1981), pp. 52–57.
    This article describes the original business plan of Nike as a student paper and the subsequent growth of the firm as a major producer and marketer of athletic shoes.

Thompson, Roger. "Business Plans: Myth and Reality." *Nation's Business,* Vol. 76, No. 8 (August, 1988), pp. 16–23.

    The business plans developed by a number of small firms are reviewed in this account.

ENDNOTES

1. G. M. Naidu, "Problems and Perceptions of Emerging Businesses in Wisconsin: Some Implications," a paper presented at the International Council for Small Business Conference, Western Carolina University, Cullowhee, NC, June, 1978.

2. Warren Strugatch, "Wooing That Crucial Business Plan Reader," *Venture,* Vol. 10, No. 5 (May 1988), p. 80.

3. Joseph R. Mancuso, *How To Start, Finance, and Manage Your Own Small Business,* Revised Edition (Englewood Cliffs, NJ: Prentice-Hall, Inc., 1984), p. 56.

4. Warren Strugatch, *op. cit.,* p. 80.

5. Stanley R. Rich and David E. Gumpert, *Business Plans That Win $$$* (New York: Harper and Row, Publishers, 1985), p. 22.

6. *Ibid.,* p. 23.

7. *An Entrepreneur's Guide to Developing a Business Plan* (Chicago: Arthur Anderson and Company, 1986), p. 10.

7 THE MARKETING PLAN

Courtesy of Vencor Corporation

Good market information is often the key to the successful introduction of a new product. The experience of Culley Davis, founder of Vencor International, is a testimony to this fact. Davis relied on market research to evaluate and perfect a self-fastening, all-cloth, washable diaper and to select an appropriate target market.

Davis's product idea originated with his brother-in-law, who sold Davis the product rights for $1,000 after he became tired of working on the concept. Davis went through nine different prototypes, testing each with willing mothers until, three and one-half years later, he was ready to market the product. The primary advantages of the new product, named Didee Snug, are its Velcro fastenings and the retention of its prefolded shape even after washing.

Davis selected the final consumer market as his target market primarily because of its size—estimated according to his research to be a $3 billion industry. He estimated that supplying a baby with disposable diapers for thirty months costs some $2,000 more than cloth diapers. Research also showed that many babies were allergic to materials used in disposable diapers. These considerations prompted Davis to tap this market first, rather than other market segments such as hospitals and other medical facilities.

Davis says, "A lot of us dream about things, but putting it to work is another story." He is already analyzing market potential in other countries, where he has found that customers have a limited product selection.

Source: Erika Kotite, "Reinventing the Wheel Part I." Reprinted with permission from *Entrepreneur* Magazine, July, 1988.

Looking Ahead

Watch for the following important topics:
1. Developing a marketing orientation.
2. Benefits and techniques of collecting marketing information.
3. Three types of market segmentation strategies.
4. How to develop a sales forecast.
5. Elements of a formal marketing plan.
6. New terms and concepts:

customer-satisfaction strategy	single-segmentation strategy
small-business marketing	segmentation variables
core marketing activities	benefit variables
marketing research	demographic variables
secondary data	sales forecast
primary data	breakdown process
market niche	buildup process
strategic decision	direct forecasting
market	indirect forecasting
market segmentation	customer profile
unsegmented strategy	market tactics
multisegmentation strategy	

Entrepreneurs need formal marketing plans not only to convince potential investors of the worth of the venture, but also to guide in the initial days and months of operation. Unfortunately, many entrepreneurs will work on the cart and neglect the horse—develop the product but neglect the marketing plan that will pull the product into the market.

Consider the following conversation between a first-time female entrepreneur and a market consultant:

"Do you have a marketing plan?"

"No," she answered, "but we have a great product, and we know that once people see it they will buy it."

"How do you know that?" I asked. "Did you do some consumer research?"

"No, but all our friends told us it was a fantastic idea that would sell like hotcakes."[1]

Before we describe the formal marketing plan, we must first examine small-business marketing more generally. What should be the ultimate goal of all marketing efforts? What activities are within the scope of small-business marketing? How can marketing help the entrepreneur understand the market? Answers to these questions will help to explain the role of marketing in a new venture and the specific activities that must be conducted in the process of developing the formal marketing plan.

Developing a Consumer Orientation

Ultimately, the success of a business rests on an acceptable level of sales, and sales depend on customers. Those activities that have the most direct impact on achieving success in sales are marketing activities. It is vital, therefore, that entrepreneurs recognize the importance of marketing and understand how to develop good marketing strategies. A business cannot just rely on a good financial strategy or a sound organizational plan as a substitute for good marketing.[2]

Adopting a Marketing Philosophy

A person's philosophy will naturally influence the tactics used to achieve a particular goal. For example, a football coach who believes in "three yards and a cloud of dust" uses the running attack as the major offensive weapon. Similarly, an entrepreneur must choose between major marketing philosophies. The philosophy adopted will shape the small firm's marketing activities.

Types of Marketing Philosophies   Historically, three distinct marketing philosophies have been evident among firms. These are commonly referred to as production-oriented, sales-oriented, and consumer-oriented philosophies. From the late nineteenth century to the present, big business has shifted its marketing emphasis from production to sales to a consumer orientation. Is this same evolution necessary within a single small business? The answer is no. It need not be. Indeed, it should not be. Is one philosophy more consistent with success? The answer is yes. A small business, therefore, should adopt a consumer orientation at the time it begins operation. Nothing is better than a consumer orientation!

Factors That Influence a Marketing Philosophy   Why have many small firms failed to adopt a consumer orientation? The answer lies in three crucial factors. First, the state of competition affects a firm's orientation. If there is little or no competition and if demand exceeds supply, a firm's activities will likely emphasize production efficiency. Usually this is a temporary situation.

Second, small-business managers show a wide range of interests and abilities in gathering market-related information and interpreting consumer characteristics. For example, some small-business managers are strongest in production and weakest in sales. Naturally, production considerations receive their primary attention.

Third, some managers are merely shortsighted. A sales-oriented philosophy, for example, is a shortsighted approach to marketing. Emphasis on "moving" merchandise can often create customer dissatisfaction if high-pressure selling is used with little regard for customers' needs. On the other hand, a consumer orientation contributes to long-range survival by emphasizing customer satisfaction.

Each philosophy may occasionally permit success. However, the consumer orientation is preferable because it not only recognizes production-efficiency goals and professional selling, but also adds concern for the customer's satisfaction. In effect, a firm that adopts a consumer orientation considers the consumer as both the beginning and the end for its exchange transactions.

Customer Satisfaction—The Key Ingredient

In 1986, the Gallup Organization polled executives of 615 companies on the importance of several factors to the success of businesses. Almost one-half of the respondents picked service quality as the number one factor.[3] Another customer service survey by a private consulting firm pointed out three major causes of service dissatisfaction:

- About 20 percent of dissatisfaction is caused by the attitude or performance of employees.
- About 40 percent of dissatisfaction is caused by companies whose structure, rules, or operating procedures are not designed for customer satisfaction. . . . "The person who deals with the consumer must have the authority to help the consumer in almost any way possible, without always transferring him or her to someone else."
- . . . 40 percent of dissatisfaction is caused by customers who misuse products or don't read directions.[4]

According to Bonnie Jansen, associate director of the division of information at the U.S. Office of Consumer Affairs, consumers are "sick and tired of being battered around; they're sick of getting poor service all the time."[5]

What is the special message of these findings for small business? The answer is that small firms are *potentially* in a much better position to achieve customer satisfaction than are big businesses! Why? Re-read the three causes of customer dissatisfaction found in the private consulting firm survey. Ask yourself if the problems are not reduced by having fewer employees in a firm. For example, with fewer employees, a small firm can vest authority for dealing with complaints in each employee. On the other hand, a large business will usually charge a single individual or department with that responsibility.

Consider the following two firms' successes. L. L. Bean, a Freeport, ME, mail-order business, is famous for its goal of "100% satisfaction." Its customers can return a product at any time for a refund, replacement, or credit at the option of the customer. It has been reported that customers have received replacements for boots returned ten years later. Another company known for its emphasis on customer satisfaction is "Bugs" Burger Bug Killers (BBBK) of Miami, FL, started by Alvin L. "Bugs" Burger in 1960 and later sold to Johnson's Wax. Mr. Burger built the pest-extermination company on this service guarantee to hotel and restaurant clients:[6]

> You don't owe one penny until all pests on your premises have been eradicated.

> If you are ever dissatisfied with BBBK's service, you will receive a refund for up to 12 months of the company's services—plus fees for another exterminator of your choice for the next year.

Figure 7–1   Customer Service Is the Rule; Customer Satisfaction the Goal

If a guest spots a pest on your premises, BBBK will pay for the guest's meal or room, send a letter of apology, and pay for a future meal or stay.

If your facility is closed down due to the presence of roaches or rodents, BBBK will pay any fines, as well as all lost profits, *plus* $5,000.

Customer service can provide a competitive edge for small firms regardless of the nature of the business. A **customer-satisfaction strategy** is a marketing plan that emphasizes the goal of customer service. It applies to consumer products and services as well as industrial products. There is no reason why customer service should be the exception rather than the rule.

High levels of customer service do not come cheaply. There is definitely a cost associated with offering superior service before, during, and after a sale. However, many customers are willing to pay for good service. These costs can be reflected in a product's or service's price, and they can sometimes be scheduled separately based on the amount of service requested. Karmock Software, Inc., in Carlinville, IL, has adopted a service policy that asks customers to pay more if they want more support. Customers sign up in advance for the level of service they want—that is, various degrees of consultation on how to use computer programs they have bought.[7]

SMALL BUSINESS IN ACTION
Software Retailer Hard on Service

   Victor Alhadeff's Egghead Software stores are successful because he saw an opportunity to apply to the computer software industry a marketing strategy that he had personally observed in the clothing industry—commitment to service. While in college, Alhadeff worked at Nordstrom, a Seattle-based department store where he witnessed a "commitment to customer satisfaction and willingness to absorb the losses associated with improper merchandise returns. . . ."

   Alhadeff opened his first computer software store in 1984 with a focus on "service, convenient location, a clean store, and fair shopping." "We apply these basics with religious fervor," he says. Five years later his business, based in Issaquah, WA, is a leading retailer of software.

   Alhadeff believes his marketing strategy will work for all small businesses. "You're going to have to charge a little higher price in order to provide for service . . . ," but "service is a bigger component in why people shop than price," according to Aldaheff.

Source: Ripley Hutch, "Treat Customers with Respect," *Nation's Business,* Vol. 76, No. 11 (November, 1988), p. 30.

   Remember, customer satisfaction is not a means to achieving a certain goal; rather, it *is* the goal! A customer is anyone's customer, but a satisfied customer is *your* customer.

Scope of Marketing Activities

   Marketing was once defined as the performance of business activities that affect the flow of goods and services from producer to consumer or user. Notice that this definition emphasizes distribution. Unfortunately, many entrepreneurs continue to view marketing in this manner. Others see marketing as nothing more than selling. Actually, marketing is much more. Many marketing activities occur even before a product is produced and ready for distribution and sale! In order to portray the complete scope of marketing, we will use a broader definition. **Small-business marketing** consists of those business activities that relate directly to identifying target markets; determining target market potential; and preparing, communicating, and delivering a bundle of satisfaction to these markets.

   This definition reveals the marketing activities that are essential to

Exhibit 7–1   Core Marketing Activities for Small Business

Key Terms from Our Definition of Marketing	Core Marketing Activities	
Identifying Target Markets	1. Market Segmentation	Market Analysis
Determining Target Market Potential	2. Market Research 3. Sales Forecasting	
Preparing a Bundle of Satisfaction	4. Product Plans 5. Pricing Plans	Marketing Tactics
Communicating a Bundle of Satisfaction	6. Promotion Plans	
Delivering a Bundle of Satisfaction	7. Distribution Plans	

every small business. These activities, called **core marketing activities,** are depicted in Exhibit 7–1. Notice that the core marketing activities have been appropriately matched with the key terms in our definition of small-business marketing. The activities numbered 1 through 3 constitute the market-analysis phase of a firm's marketing. The activities numbered 4 through 7 comprise the marketing tactics phase of marketing.

It is important that market-analysis activities precede the development of the marketing tactics. Target markets must be identified even prior to the final preparation of product plans. Then, and only then, can decisions be made regarding marketing tactics.

Collecting Marketing Information

Entrepreneurs can make marketing decisions based on intuition alone, or they can base their judgment on sound marketing information. It is often a good idea to put entrepreneurial enthusiasm on "hold" until market research facts are evaluated. According to Elaine Romanelli, director of the Center for Entrepreneurial Studies at Duke University, "A lot of them think, 'I experience a need and so does everyone else.'"[8] The availability of research information in no way guarantees good marketing decisions, but it is a major ingredient.

Nature of Marketing Research for Small Business

Marketing research may be defined as the gathering, processing, reporting, and interpreting of marketing information. A small business typically conducts less marketing research than a big business.

Part of the reason for this situation is cost. Another factor is a lack of understanding of the marketing research process. Our coverage of marketing research will emphasize the more widely used practical techniques that small-business firms can use as they analyze their market and make other operating decisions.

Evaluating the cost of research against the expected benefits is another step that the small-business manager should consider. Although this is a difficult task, some basic logic will show that marketing research can be conducted within resource limits.

Neglect of Marketing Research

Many entrepreneurs avoid marketing research, not fully understanding what it can do for them. Four common misconceptions related to marketing research are described by one author as myths:[9]

- *The "survey myopia" myth.* With its random samples, questionnaires, computer printouts, and statistical analyses, marketing research is synonymous with field survey research.
- *The "big bucks" myth.* Marketing research is so expensive that it can only be used by the wealthiest organizations, and then only for their major decisions.
- *The "sophisticated researcher" myth.* Since research involves complex and advanced technology, only trained experts can and should pursue it.
- *The "most research is not read" myth.* A very high proportion of marketing research is irrelevant to managers or is simply confirming what they already know.

The entrepreneur should recognize these myths and thereby be more open to gathering marketing information.

Steps in the Marketing Research Procedure

A knowledge of good research procedures benefits the small-business manager. It helps in evaluating the validity of research done by others and in guiding the manager's own efforts. The various steps in the marketing research procedure include identifying the problem, searching for second-

SMALL BUSINESS IN ACTION
Is It Worth It?

Entrepreneurs are widely known to prefer their own "gut feel" over hard, research facts. But this appears to be changing! One reason for the trend is the number of success stories among those who have used market research. Also, there is increasing pressure from suppliers of funding to include research in an entrepreneur's business plan.

- Julius Jensen, with Copley Venture Capital in Boston, says his firm does not even bother these days with companies that have no hard market research data to support their gut feeling about a product.
- John Werner had a vision. He decided to translate an Asian nut-coating process into a gourmet peanut business in his Connecticut home state. He came up with a loose business plan but after a year was persuaded to put his vision to the test with market research. The research showed him his original plan would not work.
- Kevin Callaghan, the Director of Marketing for DioLight Technology Inc., of Pontiac, MI, did some of his own research when targeting a new market niche for its long-lasting light bulb. He visited office buildings to count the number of exit signs needing bulbs. "We learned that the industrial institutional market, rather than the consumer market, was definitely the place to go."
- Polygon Software Corp. in New York has learned the value of research the hard way. Regarding the introduction of its first software package, George Cushner, co-founder, says ". . . we made too many assumptions about the market, relying on our own views rather than going out and evaluating . . ." As a result, the software package has sold poorly. But Cushner believes his company has learned its lesson. The company is spending about $20,000 in marketing research prior to introducing its newest product.

Source: Reprinted from the October, 1985 issue of *VENTURE, For Entrepreneurial Business Owners & Investors,* © 1985.

ary data and primary data, and interpreting and reporting the information gathered.

Identify the Problem The first step in the marketing research procedure is to define precisely the informational requirements of the decision to be made. Although this may seem too obvious to mention, the fact is that needs are too often identified without sufficient probing. If the problem is not defined clearly, the information gathered will be useless.

Search for Secondary Data Information that has already been compiled is known as **secondary data.** Generally speaking, secondary data are less expensive to gather than new data. Therefore, the small business should exhaust all the available sources of secondary data before going further into the research process. Marketing decisions often can be made entirely with secondary data.

Secondary data may be internal or external. *Internal* secondary data consist of information that exists within the small business. *External* secondary data abound in numerous periodicals, trade associations, private informational services, and government publications. A helpful source of external data for the small business is the Small Business Administration. This agency publishes extensive bibliographies relating to many decision areas, including market analysis.

Unfortunately, several problems accompany the use of secondary data. One problem is that such data may be outdated and, therefore, less useful. Another problem is that the units of measure in the secondary data may not fit the current problem. For example, a firm's market might consist of individuals with incomes between $20,000 and $25,000, while the secondary data show the number of individuals with incomes between $15,000 and $25,000. Finally, the question of credibility is always present. Some sources of secondary data are less trustworthy than others. Publication of the data does not in itself make the data valid and reliable!

Search for Primary Data   If the secondary data are insufficient, a search for new information, or **primary data,** is the next step. Several techniques can be used in accumulating primary data. These techniques are often classified as observational methods and questioning methods. Observational methods avoid contact with respondents, while questioning methods involve respondents in varying degrees.

Observational Methods   Observation is probably the oldest form of research in existence. Indeed, learning by observing is quite a common occurrence. Thus, it is hardly surprising that observation can provide useful information for small businesses, too. Observational methods can be used very economically. Further, they avoid a potential bias that results from a respondent's contact with an interviewer during questioning.

Observation can be conducted by a human or a mechanical observer. The small-firm manager can easily use the less sophisticated personal observation method. The major kinds of mechanical observation devices are usually beyond the budget of most small businesses. A major disadvantage of observational methods is that they are limited to descriptive studies.

Questioning Methods   Both surveys and experimentation are questioning methods that involve contact with respondents. Surveys include contact by mail, telephone, and personal interviews. Mail surveys are often used when respondents are widely dispersed; however, these are characterized by low response rates. Telephone surveys and personal interview surveys involve verbal communication with respondents and provide higher response rates. Personal interview surveys, however, are more expensive than mail and telephone surveys. Moreover, individuals often are reluctant to grant personal interviews because they feel that a sales pitch is forthcoming.

Developing a Questionnaire   A questionnaire is the basic instrument for guiding the researcher and the respondent when surveys are being taken. The questionnaire should be developed carefully and pretested before it is used in the market. Several major considerations in designing a questionnaire are listed below:

1. Ask questions that relate to the decision under consideration. An "interesting" question may not be relevant. Assume an answer to each question, and then ask yourself how you would use that information. This provides a good test of relevance.
2. Select a form of question that is appropriate for the subject and the conditions of the survey. Open-ended and multiple-choice questions are two popular styles.
3. Carefully consider the order of the questions. The wrong sequence can cause biases in answers to later questions.
4. Ask the more sensitive questions near the end of the questionnaire. Age and income, for example, are usually sensitive subjects.
5. Carefully select the words of each question. They should be as simple and clear as possible.

Exhibit 7–2 shows a one-page questionnaire developed for a small business by one of the authors of this textbook. The firm's research problem was to assess the market potential for its new product—wooden pallets. Potential users of wooden pallets were identified and mailed the one-page questionnaire. Notice the use of both multiple-choice and open-ended questions in this questionnaire. Responses to Item 6 were particularly useful for this firm.

Interpret the Information   After the necessary data have been accumulated, they should be transformed into usable information. Large quantities

Exhibit 7-2 Questionnaire for a Mail Survey

QUESTIONNAIRE

Special Note. If you would like to receive information on our wooden pallets once production is started, please check the square below and write in your current mailing address.

I would like to receive this information ☐
Address: _____
_____
_____

1. Does your business currently use wooden pallets? (If *No,* skip to Question 7.)

   Yes _____ (1.1)
   No _____ (1.2)

2. What percentage of your wooden pallet needs require *Expendable Pallets* (pallets used only one time)?

   0–25% _____ (2.1)
   26–50% _____ (2.2)
   51–75% _____ (2.3)
   76–100% _____ (2.4)

3. For each of the following types of wooden pallets, please indicate the approximate quantity you require each year.

Type	Quantity	
Pallet Bins (All Sizes).........	_____	(5–10)
Pallet Bases (All Sizes)	_____	(15–20)
Other (Please Specify)........	_____	(25–30)
_____	_____	(35–40)
_____	_____	(45–50)

4. Please indicate which one of the following statements best describes your firm's buying patterns for wooden pallets. (Please check only one.)

   Purchase each month .... _____ (60.1)
   Purchase about twice a year.............................. _____ (61.1)
   Purchase only once a year................................ _____ (62.1)

5. Approximately how close to your business site is your major supplier of wooden pallets?

   Less than 20 miles.................................... _____ (63.1)
   20 to 50 miles....................................... _____ (63.2)
   51 to 80 miles....................................... _____ (63.3)
   81 to 120 miles...................................... _____ (63.4)
   121 to 150 miles..................................... _____ (63.5)
   Over 150 miles .... _____ (63.6)

Exhibit 7-2   *(Continued)*

6. What suggestions would you make to help us provide wooden pallets to better meet your needs?

_____

_____

_____

7. Please indicate the major products of your firm.

_____

_____

Please mail the questionnaire in the enclosed self-addressed envelope.

THANK YOU FOR YOUR COOPERATION!!!

---

of data are only facts without a home. They must be organized and molded into meaningful information. Numerous methods of summarizing and simplifying information for users include tables, charts, and other graphic methods. Descriptive statistics, such as the mean, mode, and median, are most helpful during this step in the research procedure. Inexpensive personal computer software is now available to perform statistical calculations and generate report-quality graphics. Some of these programs are listed in Chapter 22.

Determining Market Potential

A small business can be successful only if a market exists for its product or service. Therefore, one would expect every entrepreneur to be knowledgeable about his or her market. To find out if this is true, simply ask the manager of a small firm to describe that firm's market. Be prepared for vague generalities! Surprisingly enough, you will find how little thought small-business managers give to understanding their markets.

Analyzing a market is particularly important prior to starting a business. Without it, the entrepreneur enters the marketplace much like a high diver who leaves the board without checking the depth of the water. Many types of information from numerous sources are required for a market analysis.

Selecting a Market Niche

Many new ventures fail because of poor market positioning or lack of a perceived advantage by customers in their target market. To minimize this chance of failure, an entrepreneur should consider the benefits of exploiting gaps or niches in a market. A **market niche** is a target market that has not been zeroed in on by a marketing effort. The choice of a niche strategy by a small firm is suggested by, but not restricted to, the following marketing activities:[10]

- Strict concentration on a single market segment.
- Concentration on a single product.
- Reliance on close customer contact and intuitive knowledge of the market.
- Restriction to a single geographical region.
- Emphasis on substantive superiority of the product.

If a firm's strategy focuses on a unique target market, it must also use marketing tactics that match this strategy. Consider the following example of a marketing-niche strategy and related marketing tactics:

Figure 7–2   Geographical Location Is Important in the Niche Strategy

Indiana Department of Commerce

Sue and Jim Acres operate the Blue Ribbon Car Wash in an affluent part of the city. They do not market their car wash to the general public, and the general public would not typically frequent it anyway. This is because of both the cost and the nature of the service provided. Charging more than thirty dollars for a wash job and fifty for a wash and wax, Blue Ribbon caters only to owners of Audis, Cadillacs, and Lincolns. Cars are accepted by appointment only and must be left for at least four hours. The car is washed by hand using only top quality cleaners and waxes, and it is cleaned and vacuumed inside. A fabric protector is applied if desired. Wheels are scrubbed and wire wheels are carefully attended to—if necessary with a toothbrush. For an additional charge, the engine compartment can be cleaned, the trunk can be vacuumed, and the oil can be changed. Sue reports that business is brisk—six cars a day. Some owners wait as long as two weeks for an appointment.[11]

Notice how the pricing strategy of Blue Ribbon Car Wash reflects the uniqueness of the service. Also, by requiring appointments, it creates an air of exclusiveness—not just anyone can drive in and get the service.

SMALL BUSINESS IN ACTION
New Product Waits on Marketing Strategy

In 1987, Bill Sanford became the president of Steris Corporation after being hired by a venture capital firm the year before to evaluate the company for potential investment. Sanford was a marketing specialist, but he inherited a firm with a great new product and "not a whit of marketing strategy."

The product is a sterilizing system for endoscopes that reduces the sterilization time from 10 hours to 20 minutes. While the system's inventor, Ray Kralovic, worked on the system, Sanford was conducting research to determine a target market. The market niche selected was hospitals. More specifically, the system would be targeted to operating room nurses. Sanford's reasons were as follows:

"First of all, you know where they are. Second, they know all about sterilization, so you don't have to educate them. Third, they have tremendous discretionary budgets since they generate vast revenues" for their hospitals . . . or nurses . . . "wield incredible power in recommending equipment like this."

The company has used trade magazine advertising, direct mail campaigns, and booths at nurses' association meetings to promote the product. The system sells for just under $10,000.

Source: Frank Bentayou, "Fertile Ground for Sterilization." Reprinted from the October, 1988, issue of *VENTURE, For Entrepreneurial Business Owners & Investors,* © 1988.

By selecting a particular niche, an entrepreneur thereby decides upon the basic direction of the firm. Because such a choice affects the very nature of the business, we call it a **strategic decision.** A firm's overall strategy is formulated, therefore, as its leader decides how it will relate to its environment—particularly to the customers and competitors in that environment.

Selection of a very specialized market is, of course, not the only possible strategy for a small firm. Nevertheless, finding a niche that can be exploited is a popular strategy because it allows a small firm to operate in the "crack" between larger competitors. If a small firm chooses to go "head-to-head" in competition with other businesses, particularly large corporations, it must be prepared to distinguish itself in some way—for example, by attention to detail, highly personal service, or speed of service—in order to make itself a formidable competitor.[12]

Components of a Market

The term market means different things to different people. Sometimes it simply refers to a location where buying and selling take place, as when we hear, "She went to the market." On other occasions the term is used to describe selling efforts, as when business managers say, "We must market this product aggressively." Still another meaning is the one we use in this chapter. We define a **market** as a group of *customers* or potential customers who have *purchasing power* and *unsatisfied needs.*

Notice carefully the three components of our definition of a market. First, a market must have a buying unit, or customers. These units may be individuals or business entities. For example, consumer products are sold to individuals and industrial products are sold to business users. Thus, a market is more than a geographic area. It must contain potential customers.

Second, customers in a market must have purchasing power. Assessing the level of purchasing power in a potential market is very important. Customers who have unsatisfied needs but who lack money and/or credit are poor markets because they have nothing to offer in exchange for a product or service. In such a situation, no transactions can occur.

Third, a market must contain buying units with unsatisfied needs. Final consumers, for instance, will not buy unless they are motivated to do so. Motivation can occur only when an individual has unsatisfied needs. It would be difficult, for example, to sell tent dehumidifiers to desert nomads!

In light of our definition of a market, therefore, determining market potential is the process of locating and investigating buying units that have

purchasing power and needs that can be satisfied with the product or service that the entrepreneur can offer.

Understanding Market Segmentation Strategies

Even though all people are similar, they are different in many ways.
Market segmentation is built on those differences. Formally defined, **market
segmentation** is the process of analyzing one market to find out whether it
should be viewed as more than one market. A small business may view its
market in either general or specific terms. It may consider its market as all
women or as only the 24- to 35-year-old single women living in the eastern
United States. In the latter case, the firm is segmenting its market. "The
main mistake made in startup situations is heading off in all directions,"
says Grid Systems Corporation of Santa Clara, CA. "The key thing is to identify the market."[13]

The Need for Market Segmentation If a business had control of the only
known water supply in the world, its sales volume would be huge. This business would not be concerned about differences in personal preferences for
taste, color, or temperature. It would consider its customers to be *one* market. As long as the water product was "wet," it would satisfy everyone. However, if someone else discovered a second water supply, the view of the market would change. The first business might discover that sales were drying
up and turn to a modified strategy. The new approach could well emerge
from an understanding of consumer behavior.

In the real world, a number of preferences for liquid drinks exist.
What may seem to be a homogeneous market is actually heterogeneous. The
different preferences may take a number of forms. Some preferences may
relate to the way consumers react to the taste or to the container. Other
preferences may relate to the price of the liquid drink or to the availability
of "specials." Preferences might also be uncovered with respect to different
distribution strategies or to certain promotional tones and techniques. In
other words, markets may actually be composed of several submarkets.

Types of Market Segmentation Strategies The three types of market segmentation strategies discussed in this text can best be illustrated by using an
example of a hypothetical firm—the Community Writing Company. These
strategies are the unsegmented approach, the multisegmentation approach,
and the single-segmentation approach.

The Unsegmented Strategy   When a business defines the total market as its target market, it is following an **unsegmented strategy.** This strategy can be successful occasionally, but it assumes that all buying units desire the same general benefit from the product or service. This may hold true for water but probably not for shoes, which satisfy numerous needs through many styles, prices, colors, and sizes. With an unsegmented strategy, the firm would develop a single marketing mix, which means one combination of the product, price, promotion, and distribution plan. For the unsegmented strategy of Community Writing Company, see Exhibit 7–3. Community Writing Company's product is a lead pencil that is sold at the one price of 79 cents and is communicated with a single promotional and distribution plan. Notice how the marketing mix is aimed at everybody. With this strategy only one sales forecast is required.

The Multisegmentation Strategy   With a view of the market that recognizes individual segments that have different preferences, a firm is in a position to tailor-make different strategies. If a firm feels that two or more

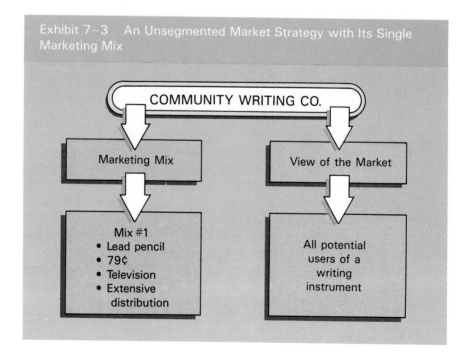

Exhibit 7–3   An Unsegmented Market Strategy with Its Single Marketing Mix

COMMUNITY WRITING CO.

Marketing Mix

View of the Market

Mix #1
- Lead pencil
- 79¢
- Television
- Extensive distribution

All potential users of a writing instrument

homogeneous market segments can be profitable, it will be following a **multi-segmentation strategy** if it develops a unique marketing mix for each segment.

Let us now assume that Community Writing Company has discovered three separate market segments: students, professors, and executives. Following the multisegmentation approach, the company develops three mixes, which might be based on differences in pricing, promotion, distribution, or the product itself, as shown in Exhibit 7–4. Mix #1 consists of selling felt-tip pens to students through vending machines at the slightly higher-than-normal price of $1.00 and supporting this effort with a promotional campaign in campus newspapers. With Mix #2, the company might market the same pen to universities for use by professors. Personal selling is the only promotion used in this mix, distribution is direct from the factory, and the product price of 49 cents is extremely low. Finally, with Mix #3, which is aimed at executives of companies of the Fortune 500 type, the product is a solid gold ink-writing instrument sold only in exclusive department stores. It is promoted in prestigious magazines and carries the extremely high price of $50. Although students might conceivably buy the solid gold pens for classroom writing, they are not viewed as members of this target market.

Notice the dramatic differences in the three marketing mixes. Small businesses, however, tend to postpone the use of multisegmentation strategies because of the risk of spreading resources too thinly among several marketing efforts.

The Single-Segmentation Strategy   When a firm recognizes that several distinct market segments exist but chooses to concentrate on reaching only one segment, it is following a **single-segmentation strategy.** The segment selected will be one that the business feels will be most profitable. One real-life example is a quick-service alteration shop called ASAP (Alter Soon As Possible). Beverly and Paul Malham opened their first store in 1984 in an Atlanta, GA, mall after deciding to concentrate on a relatively small but very profitable market. Its target market, about 60 percent of sales, are stores in the mall who prefer not to do alterations themselves.[14] The Malhams have used the single-segmentation strategy to build a reputation among the target market that they feel will spread to other markets as they expand their services.

Community Writing Company, our hypothetical example, selects the student market segment when pursuing a single-segmentation approach, as shown in Exhibit 7–5.

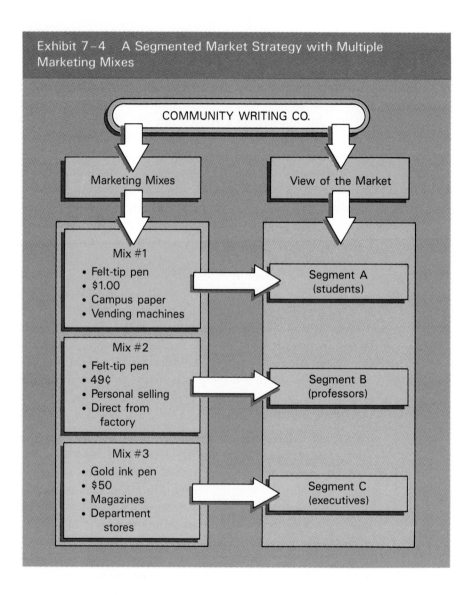

Exhibit 7–4   A Segmented Market Strategy with Multiple Marketing Mixes

COMMUNITY WRITING CO.

Marketing Mixes

View of the Market

Mix #1
- Felt-tip pen
- $1.00
- Campus paper
- Vending machines

Segment A
(students)

Mix #2
- Felt-tip pen
- 49¢
- Personal selling
- Direct from factory

Segment B
(professors)

Mix #3
- Gold ink pen
- $50
- Magazines
- Department stores

Segment C
(executives)

The single-segmentation approach is probably the best strategy for small businesses during initial marketing efforts. This approach allows them to specialize and make better use of their more limited resources. Then, when a reputation has been built, it is easier for them to enter new markets.

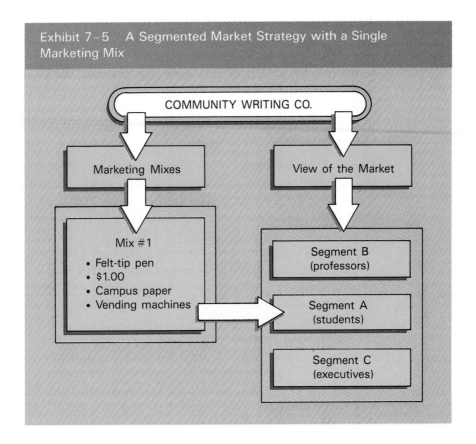

Exhibit 7–5 A Segmented Market Strategy with a Single Marketing Mix

COMMUNITY WRITING CO.

Marketing Mixes

View of the Market

Mix #1
- Felt-tip pen
- $1.00
- Campus paper
- Vending machines

Segment B (professors)

Segment A (students)

Segment C (executives)

Segmentation Variables   A firm's market could be defined very simply as "anyone who is alive"! However, this is too broad to be useful even for a firm that follows an unsegmented approach. With any type of market analysis, some degree of segmentation must be made. Notice in Exhibit 7–3, which represents an unsegmented market strategy, that the market is not everyone in the universe; rather, it includes only potential users.

In order to divide the total market into appropriate segments, a business must consider segmentation variables. Basically, **segmentation variables** are labels that identify the particular dimensions that are thought to distinguish one form of market demand from another. Two particular sets of segmentation variables that represent the major dimensions of a market are benefit variables and demographic variables.

Benefit Variables Our earlier definition of a market highlighted the unsatisfied needs of customers. **Benefit variables** are related to this dimension in that they are used to divide and identify segments of a market according to the benefits sought by customers. For example, the toothpaste market has several benefit segments. The principal benefit to parents may be cavity prevention for their young children. On the other hand, the principal benefit to a teenager might be freshness. In both cases, toothpaste is the product, but it has two different markets.

Demographic Variables Benefit variables alone are insufficient for market analysis. It is impossible to implement forecasting and marketing strategy without defining the market further. Therefore, small businesses commonly use demographics as part of market segmentation. Typical demographics are age, marital status, sex, occupation, and income. Remember again our definition of a market—customers with purchasing power and unsatisfied needs. Thus, **demographic variables** refer to certain characteristics that describe customers and their purchasing power.

The market scenario for Segment A in Exhibit 7–4 can easily be divided into additional segments with benefit variables and demographic variables. (Occupation as a demographic variable was used in Exhibit 7–4.) This possibility is illustrated in Exhibit 7–6. Notice that the Segment A market, consisting of students, can be subdivided into Segments A–1 and A–2 according to the demographic variable of marital status. In addition, Segment A–1 can be subdivided into Segments A–11 and A–12 according to the benefit variables of convenience and economy.

Based on this hypothetical case, a sales forecast for a single-segmentation approach could be structured and included in the marketing plan. The single-segmentation strategy could aim at the number of people in a geographic market who are single students looking mainly for convenience features in the writing instruments they purchase. Such precision in market delineation makes sales forecasting easier.

The Sales Forecast

Formally defined, a **sales forecast** is the prediction of how much of a product or service will be purchased by a market for a defined time period. The sales forecast can be stated in terms of dollars and/or units.

Notice that a sales forecast revolves around a specific market. This means that the market should be defined as precisely as possible. The market description forms the forecasting boundary. For example, consider the

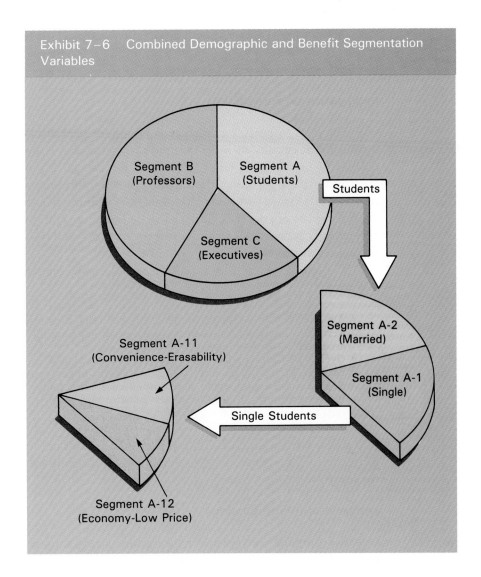

Exhibit 7–6   Combined Demographic and Benefit Segmentation Variables

sales forecast for a manual shaving device. If the market for this product is described simply as "men," the potential sales forecast would be extremely large. Alternatively, a more precise definition, such as "men between the ages of 15 and 25 who are dissatisfied with electric shavers," will result in a smaller but more useful forecast.

Also note that the sales forecast implies a defined time period. One sales forecast may cover a year or less, while another extends over several, maybe five years. Both the short-term and the long-term forecasts are needed in the entrepreneur's business plan.

Importance of Forecasting

The sales forecast is a critical component of the business plan for assessing the feasibility of a new venture. If the market is insufficient, the business is destined for failure. The sales forecast is also useful in other areas of business planning. Production schedules, inventory policies, and personnel decisions—to name a few—all start with the sales forecast. Obviously, forecasts can never be perfect. Furthermore, the entrepreneur should remember that forecasts can be in error in either of two ways—an underestimation or an overestimation of potential sales.

A recent survey of sales executives among small companies found the following:[15]

- About 40 percent of the respondents estimated that their sales forecasts were 75–89 percent accurate; 23 percent said they were 90–94 percent accurate.
- Over 90 percent stated that no consultants were used in sales forecasting.
- Secondary purposes for their sales forecast were budget preparation, setting quotas for salespeople, determining advertising and sales promotion expenditures, hiring personnel, advance purchasing of raw materials and parts, and making cash forecasts.

These statistics indicate both the importance of sales forecasting and the tendency for entrepreneurs to shoulder the entire burden of developing the forecast.

Limitations to Forecasting

For a number of practical reasons, forecasting is used more successfully by large firms than by small companies. First, the entrepreneur's forecasting circumstances are unique. Inexperience coupled with a new idea represents the most difficult forecasting situation, as depicted in Exhibit 7–7. An ongoing business that needs only an updated forecast for its existing product is in the most favorable forecasting position. Second, the typical small-business manager is unable to use or to appreciate the methods of quantitative analysis. This is not to say that all forecasting must be quantitatively oriented. Qualitative forecasting is helpful and may be sufficient.

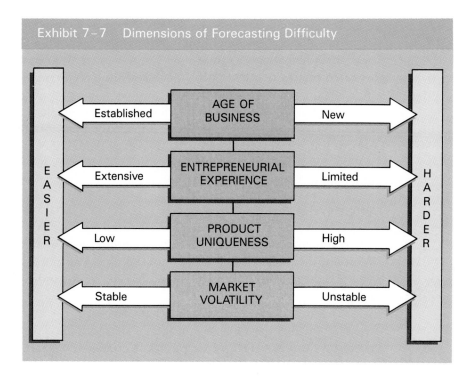

Exhibit 7-7 Dimensions of Forecasting Difficulty

Established	AGE OF BUSINESS	New
Extensive	ENTREPRENEURIAL EXPERIENCE	Limited
Low	PRODUCT UNIQUENESS	High
Stable	MARKET VOLATILITY	Unstable

EASIER ← → HARDER

However, quantitative methods have proven their value in forecasting over and over again.

Third, the small-business entrepreneur is not familiar with the forecasting process, and it is unlikely that the small firm employs a forecaster. To overcome these deficiencies, some small firms attempt to keep in touch with industry trends through contacts with their trade association. From the standpoint of its professional staff members, the trade association is frequently better qualified to engage in business forecasting. Also, small-business entrepreneurs provide themselves with current information about business trends by regularly reading trade publications and economic news-letters such as the *Kiplinger Washington Letter, Business Week,* and *The Wall Street Journal.*

Government publications, such as *Survey of Current Business, Federal Reserve Bulletin,* and *Monthly Labor Review,* are also of interest in a general way. Then there is the possibility of subscribing to professional forecasting services, which provide forecasts of general business conditions or specific forecasts for given industries.

Yet the small business should not slight the forecasting task because of its limitations. Remember how important the sales outlook is to the business plan when obtaining financing! The statement "We can sell as many as we can produce" does not satisfy the information requirements of potential investors.

One business consultant described entrepreneurs' lack of forecasting concern by saying, "They don't know if the market needs it, but they are in love with it . . . they don't know the market potential, they don't know the market size. I ask how many they need to sell to break even . . . and they don't know."[16]

Steps in the Forecasting Process

Estimating market demand with a sales forecast is a multistep process. Typically, the sales forecast is a composite of several individual forecasts. The process of sales forecasting then must merge the individual forecasts properly.

The forecasting process can be characterized by two important dimensions: (1) the point at which the process is started, and (2) the nature of the predicting variable. The starting point is usually designated by the terms breakdown process or buildup process. The nature of the predicting variable is denoted by either *direct* forecasting or *indirect* forecasting.

The Starting Point   The **breakdown process,** sometimes called a "chain-ratio" method, begins with a macro-level variable and systematically works down to the sales forecast. This method is frequently used for consumer products forecasting. The starting point might be a population figure for the targeted market. By using percentages, the appropriate link is built to generate the sales forecast. For example, consider the market segment identified by our hypothetical company, Community Writing Co., in Exhibit 7–6. The targeted market is single students seeking convenience in their writing instrument. Furthermore, assume that the initial geographic target is the state of Idaho. Exhibit 7–8 outlines the chain-ratio approach. Possible sources for each number are shown in parentheses. Obviously, the more "links" in the forecasting chain, the greater the potential for error.

The **buildup process** calls for identifying all potential buyers in a market's submarkets and then adding up the estimated demand. This method is especially helpful for industrial goods forecasting. Census of Manufacturers data are often used to estimate potential. The information can be segmented with the Standard Industrial Classification (SIC) code. This classifi-

Exhibit 7-8 Sales Forecasting with the Breakdown Approach

Linking Variable	Source Reference	Value	Market Potential
a. Idaho State Population	U.S. Census of Population		1,000,000
b. State Population in 18–24 Age Category	*Sales & Marketing Management* Survey of Buying Power	12%	120,000
c. Single, 18- to 24-year-olds in Idaho	*American Demographics*	50%	60,000
d. Single, 18- to 24-year-olds in Colleges and Universities	Idaho Department of Education	80%	48,000
e. College Students Preferring Convenience Over Price	Student Survey in Marketing Research Class	35%	16,800
f. "Convenience-Oriented" Students Likely to Purchase New Felt-tip Pen within Next Month	Personal Telephone Interview by Entrepreneur	75%	12,600
g. People Likely to Purchase Who Actually Buy	Article in *Journal of Consumer Research*	35%	4,410
h. Average Number of Pens Bought per Year	Personal Experience of Entrepreneur	4 units	17,640
SALES FORECAST FOR IDAHO			17,640 units

cation system identifies potential industrial customers by SIC code, allowing the forecaster to locate information on number of establishments, location, number of employees, and annual sales. By summing this information for several relevant SIC codes, a sales potential can be constructed.

The Predicting Variable   In **direct forecasting,** sales is used as the predicting variable. This is the simplest form of forecasting. Many times, however, sales cannot be predicted directly. In this case other variables related to sales must be forecasted. **Indirect forecasting** takes place when the other forecasts are used to project the sales forecast. For example, a firm may lack information about industry sales of baby cribs but may have data on births. The figures for births can help forecast an industry sales estimate for baby cribs.

Preparing the Formal Marketing Plan

After preliminary marketing analysis is completed—such as market research, market segmentation, and sales forecasting—the entrepreneur is ready to finalize the formal marketing plan. A general guide to various components of a marketing plan was presented in Exhibit 6–6 of Chapter 6. When questions in that outline are answered sufficiently, the entrepreneur will have the necessary information to write the final document.

It is important to remember that each business venture is different and therefore each marketing plan will be unique. An entrepreneur should not feel that he or she must develop a cloned version of someone else's plan.

In the following paragraphs we will describe the major elements of the formal marketing plan. A detailed discussion of marketing activities for both new and ongoing small businesses is provided in Part IV of this book.

Market Analysis

In this initial section of the marketing plan, the entrepreneur should discuss target market customers. The description of potential customers is commonly called a **customer profile.** Information compiled with market research—both secondary and primary data—can be used to construct this profile. A detailed discussion of the major customer benefits characterizing the new product or service should be included. Obviously, these benefits must be reasonable and consistent with statements in the "Products and Services" section of the business plan.

If an entrepreneur envisions several target markets, then each segment must have its corresponding customer profile. Likewise, several target markets necessitate an equal number of different marketing strategies.

Another major element of market analysis is the sales forecast. It is usually desirable to include more than one sales forecast—"most likely," "pessimistic," and "optimistic." This provides investors and the entrepreneur with three sales scenarios upon which to base their evaluation.

As pointed out earlier in this chapter, forecasting sales for a new venture is extremely difficult. Assumptions will be necessary but should be minimized. The forecasting method should be noted and supported by empirical data wherever feasible.

Competition

Frequently, entrepreneurs ignore the reality of competition for their new ventures. Apparently they believe that the marketplace contains no close substitutes or that their "certain success" will not attract other entrepreneurs! Stephen J. Warner, president of Merrill Lynch Venture Capital, Inc., New York, states that investors want to see a section on competition to demonstrate that an entrepreneur has considered his or her competition. He says, "I'm very pleased when I see a section on the competition that's well done ... I'm very worried when it's missing."[17]

Existing competitive firms should be studied carefully. They should be profiled, and the names of key management personnel should be included. A brief discussion of competitors' overall strengths and weaknesses should be a part of this section. Also, a list of related products currently marketed or being tested by competitors should be noted. An assessment and explanation of the likelihood that each of these firms will enter the entrepreneur's target market should be made.

Marketing Tactics

A well-prepared market analysis and a discussion of competition are important to the formal marketing plan. But this section—covering the entrepreneur's marketing tactics—is the most detailed and, in many respects, subject to the closest scrutiny by potential investors. **Marketing tactics** are the action part of the marketing plan. They plot the course of marketing action that will activate the entrepreneur's venture.

There are four areas of marketing tactics that should be addressed within the marketing plan. First, the plan includes marketing decisions that transform the basic product or service idea into a "total product." Second, the plan includes promotional decisions that will communicate the necessary information to target markets. Third, there are decisions regarding the distribution of a product to customers. Finally, there are pricing decisions that will set an acceptable value on the total product or service.

Obviously, the nature of a new venture has a direct bearing on the emphasis given to each of these areas. For example, a service business will not have the same distribution problems as a product business. Also, the promotional challenge facing a new retail store is quite different from that of a new manufacturer. Despite these differences, we can still offer a generalized format for presenting marketing tactics in a business plan.

The Total Product/Service   Within this section, the entrepreneur needs to include the product or service name and why it was selected. Any legal protection that has been initiated or currently exists should be explained. It is very important to explain the logic of the name selected. An entrepreneur's family name, for certain products or services, may make a positive contribution to sales. In other situations, a descriptive name that suggests a benefit of the product may be more desirable. Regardless of the strategy of the name, it should be defended.

Other components of the total product, such as the package, should be presented via a drawing. Sometimes it may be desirable to use professional packaging consultants to develop the package. One such consultant expresses the importance of packaging to the total product by saying, "It's not something you add on at the last moment. The consumer doesn't think of the package as a separate entity when he picks up the product but sees it as a part of the product itself."[18]

Customer service plans such as warranties and repair policies need to be discussed also. These elements of the marketing plan should be tied directly to the customer-satisfaction emphasis of the venture.

Promotional Plans   This section should cover the entrepreneur's approach to creating customer awareness of the product or service and motivating customers to buy. The entrepreneur has many options. Personal selling and advertising are two of the most popular alternatives.

If personal selling is appropriate, the plan should outline how many salespeople will be employed and how they will be compensated. Plans for training the sales force should be mentioned. If advertising is to be used, a listing of the specific media should be included and the advertising themes described.

Often it is advisable to seek the services of a small advertising agency. In this case, the name and credentials of the agency should be discussed. A brief mention of successful campaigns supervised by the agency can add to the value of this section of the marketing plan.

Distribution Plans   Quite often, new ventures will use established intermediaries to structure their channels of distribution. This strategy expedites distribution and reduces investment.

How these intermediaries will be convinced to carry the new product should be explained. If the business plans to license its product or service, this strategy should also be covered in this section.

Some new retail ventures require fixed locations; others require mobile stores. The layouts and configurations of these retail stores should be explained.

Sometimes a new business begins with exporting. When this is the strategy, the marketing plan must discuss the relevant laws and regulations governing exporting. Knowledge of exchange rates and distribution options must be reflected by the material included in this section.

Pricing Plans   At the very minimum, a price must reflect the costs of bringing a product or service to the customer. Therefore, this section of the plan must include a schedule of both production and marketing costs. It is advisable to label each of these costs as either fixed or variable so that break-even computations can be generated for alternative prices. The sales figures from the market analysis section were obviously forecasted assuming a certain sales price. Naturally, the analysis in this section should be consistent with the forecasting methods of the market analysis section.

However, setting a price for a reasonable break-even volume ignores other aspects of pricing. If the entrepreneur truly has a unique niche, she or he may be able to charge a premium price—at least for initial operating periods.

The closest competitor should be studied to learn what that firm is charging. The new product or service will most likely have to be in a reasonable range of that price. One pricing consultant gives this advice: "Being on the high end is pretty good, because you can always fall back. . . . In the long run, however, the market is going to tell you what your pricing should be."[19]

Looking Back

1. The three major marketing management philosophies are production-oriented, sales-oriented, and consumer-oriented. The consumer-oriented philosophy is the essence of the marketing concept. Entrepreneurs need to adopt a strategic position that includes an emphasis on customer service and satisfaction.
2. The first step in the marketing research procedure is to identify accurately the problem to be solved. The second step is to search

for secondary and primary data, which are two forms of marketing information. Data are collected by observational and questioning methods. Finally, the data are interpreted and prepared for use in the business plan.

3. Market segmentation is the process of analyzing a market to decide whether it should be considered as more than one market. There are three types of market segmentation strategies: the unsegmented strategy, the multisegmentation strategy, and the single-segmentation strategy.

4. Estimating market demand with a sales forecast involves a multistep process. The starting point of the sales forecast can be designated as a build-up process or a break-down process. Direct forecasting and indirect forecasting are two basic forms of forecasting sales. Forecasting techniques are usually classified in two ways: qualitative techniques and quantitative techniques.

5. A formal marketing plan is the component of the overall business plan that describes the marketing plan of action. It covers a description of the market, competition, and marketing strategy.

DISCUSSION QUESTIONS

1. Can you think of one purchase experience in which you were completely satisfied? If so, explain the circumstances surrounding that purchase. If not, what made the purchase less than satisfactory?

2. Do you believe that small businesses can achieve a higher level of customer satisfaction than big businesses? Why or why not?

3. What research methods would you use to measure the number of males with brown eyes at your school?

4. What research method would you use to determine whether or not a warranty helped product sales? Be specific.

5. Explain why the three components in our definition of a market must be viewed as having a multiplicative relationship rather than an additive relationship.

6. Explain the concept of a market niche as it might relate to an entrepreneur's desire to market a new poison-alert product. The device emits an electronic warning whenever a cabinet or drawer containing harmful materials is opened.

7. Why is it so important to understand the target market? What difference would it make if the entrepreneur simply ignored the characteristics of market customers?

8. How do the three marketing management philosophies differ? Select a consumer product and discuss your marketing tactics for each philosophy.

9. How does a multisegmentation view of the market differ from a single-segmentation approach? Be specific.

10. Assume that your instructor desired to design this course using benefit variables. What various types of benefits do you believe exist for your classmates (consumers)? How would this influence your instructor's course requirements?

11. Assume that you are planning to market a new facial tissue product. Write a detailed market profile of your target customers. Use benefit and demographic variables in your profile. Then change one or more of these variables. How would this change the marketing mix?

12. Distinguish between direct sales forecasting and indirect sales forecasting. Give examples.

13. What promotional techniques do you feel would be most effective to promote a new retail clothing store to its customers?

14. Comment on the statement "You get what you pay for" when you buy any product.

15. Select several new product names from recent issues of a magazine and discuss how conducive the names will be to marketing.

YOU MAKE THE CALL

Situation 1

James Mitchell was born and raised in the cattle country of southern Oklahoma, where he continued to ranch for almost 20 years until falling beef prices in the middle 1970s drove him out of business. After a brief try at the restaurant business, Mitchell, now age 64, decided to try a venture in the car-care service business.

His business will be an automobile inspection sticker service. There is currently no other business of this type in the city of 150,000 residents where he lives, and he has leased a good location adjacent to a major traffic artery of the city. Mitchell does not plan to do mechanical work other than minor jobs necessary to get a car up to inspection standards, such as fuse and headlight replacements. Since the state mandates that automobiles pass an inspection yearly, he feels market demand will be stable.

Questions

1. Write a brief description of what you see as Mitchell's strategic marketing position. Do you think it is a worthy strategy? Why or why not?
2. What methods of marketing research can Mitchell use to gather helpful marketing information?
3. What name might be appropriate for Mitchell's business? What forms of promotion should be in his marketing plan?
4. What type of pricing strategy would you suggest Mitchell adopt? Why?

Situation 2

Mary Wilson is a 31-year-old wife and mother who wants to start a business. She has no previous business experience but has an idea to market an animal grooming service using a pizza delivery concept. In other words, when a customer calls, she will arrive, in a van, in less than 10 minutes and provide the grooming service.

Many of her friends think the idea is unusual, and they usually smile and remark, "Oh really." However, Wilson is not discouraged; she is setting out to purchase the van and necessary grooming equipment.

Questions

1. What target market or markets can you identify for Mrs. Wilson? How could she forecast sales for her service in each market?
2. What advantage do you see in her service compared to existing grooming businesses?
3. What business name and what promotional strategy would you suggest to Mrs. Wilson?

EXPERIENTIAL EXERCISES

1. Interview a local small-business manager to determine what he or she believes is (are) the competitive advantage(s) offered by the business.
2. Select a recent issue of a business publication and report on the marketing strategy described in one of the articles.
3. Select a new product that most of the class knows about. Divide into three or more groups, and write a brief description of what you believe is the best target market for that product. Be specific in your market profile. Read the description to the class.
4. Visit a local small-business retailer and observe its marketing efforts—

such as salesperson style, store atmosphere, and warranty policies. Report to the class and make recommendations for improving these efforts for greater customer satisfaction.

REFERENCES TO SMALL-BUSINESS PRACTICES

Brown, Paul B. "Fame." *Inc.,* Vol. 10, No. 8 (August, 1988), pp. 43–48.
> The "star" status of several entrepreneurs is profiled in this article. The majority of the entrepreneurs attribute their success to a customer orientation.

Brown, Paul B. "On the Cheap." *Inc.,* Vol. 10, No. 2 (February, 1988), pp. 108–110.
> This article describes the inexpensive marketing information used by an entrepreneur opening a men's specialty store. The most valuable two sources of information were his own retailing experience and data developed and paid for by others—secondary data.

Cole, Wendy. "You're Only As Good As Your Last Meal." *Venture,* Vol. 10, No. 2 (February, 1988), pp. 55–58.
> The problems of a weak marketing plan are described by a restaurant owner. Other management problems that lead to failure are also discussed.

Kelleher, JoAnne. "Getting to Know Your Market." *Venture,* Vol. 5, No. 5 (May, 1983), pp. 70–74.
> The firsthand experiences of numerous entrepreneurs' use of marketing research is related in this article. The development of computerized data bases is emphasized as a major development in analyzing markets.

Persinos, John F. "Reaping Profit in the Heartland." *Inc.,* Vol. 5, No. 1 (January, 1983), pp. 65–66.
> A strong customer orientation is the philosophy of the small manufacturer described in this article. His approach has enabled the small farm machinery company to compete successfully in a depressed agricultural economy.

ENDNOTES

1. Wilson Harrell, "But Will It Fly?" *Inc.,* Vol. 9, No. 1 (January, 1987), p. 85.

2. A recent study supporting the importance of marketing is Alfred M. Pelham and Dennis E. Clayson, "Receptivity to Strategic Planning Tools in Small Manufacturing Firms," *Journal of Small Business Management,* Vol. 26, No. 1 (January, 1988), p. 47.

3. Bro Uttal, "Companies That Serve You Best," *Fortune,* Vol. 116, No. 13 (December 7, 1987), p. 98.

4. Scott Matulis, "The Customer Is King," *Entrepreneur,* Vol. 16, No. 9 (September, 1988), p. 69.

5. *Ibid.,* p. 65.

6. Christopher W. L. Hart, "The Power of Unconditional Service Guarantees," *Harvard Business Review,* Vol. 66, No. 4 (July–August, 1988), p. 54.

7. "It Doesn't Have to Be Free to Be Good," *Inc.,* Vol. 10, No. 12 (December, 1988), p. 139.

8. Marie-Jeanne Juilland, "A Bright Idea Isn't Enough," *Venture,* Vol. 10, No. 4 (April, 1988), p. 78.

9. Alan R. Andreasen, "Cost-Conscious Marketing Research," *Harvard Business Review,* Vol. 61, No. 4 (July–August, 1983), p. 74.

10. Ronald E. Merrill and Henry D. Sedgwick, *The New Venture Handbook* (New York: AMACOM, 1987), pp. 107–108.

11. Charles R. Stoner and Fred L. Fry, *Strategic Planning in the Small Business* (Cincinnati, OH: South-Western Publishing Co., 1987), p. 109.

12. For an excellent discussion of the success of marketing strategies in established markets, see John L. Wood and Stanley F. Stasch, "How Small Share Firms Can Uncover Winning Strategies," *The Journal of Business Strategy,* Vol. 9, No. 5 (September–October, 1988), pp. 26–31.

13. Dave Kemp, "Who Wants Your New Product?" *Inc.,* Vol. 3, No. 11 (November, 1981), p. 161.

14. Patricia Winters, "Alteration Shops Sew Up Mall Market," *Venture,* Vol. 7, No. 9 (September, 1985), p. 14.

15. Excerpted from Harry R. White, *Sales Forecasting: Timesaving and Profit-Making Strategies That Work* (Glenview, IL: Scott, Foresman and Company, 1984), Chapter 3.

16. Kevin McDermott, "Selling High Technology," *D&B Reports,* Vol. 35, No. 5 (September–October, 1987), p. 36.

17. Warren Strugatch, "Wooing That Crucial Business Plan Reader," *Venture,* Vol. 10, No. 5 (May, 1988), p. 81.

18. Warren Strugatch, "Marketing By Design," *Venture,* Vol. 10, No. 10 (October, 1988), p. 88.

19. Carol R. Riggs, "A Marketing Plan for Service Businesses," *D&B Reports,* Vol. 36, No. 5 (October, 1988), p. 25.

8 HUMAN AND PHYSICAL RESOURCE PLANS

Spotlight on Small Business

Photo courtesy of Mark Dulaney

What is the world's best location for a sailboarding business? It may be Corpus Christi, TX. Mark Dulaney's MD Surf & Skate Shop is located there, and Dulaney is working to make Corpus Christi the nation's capital for the increasingly popular sport of sailboarding. Sailboarding is basically surfboarding with a sail, and Corpus Christi, with its good wind, big waves, warm water, and warm air, provides an excellent location for this sport. The city's competitive edge rests on these factors:

1. It is more accessible than Hawaii for most sailboarders.
2. It has better wind conditions than San Diego and Florida.

211

3. It has warmer water than San Francisco, Santa Barbara, and Hood River.
4. There are no dangerous reefs.

The sport's annual U.S. Open has drawn live television coverage and brought thousands of spectators to Corpus Christi. As the sport continues to develop, MD Surf & Skate Shop should reap the benefits of its ideal location.

Source: Greg Fieg Pizano, "Dulaney Rode Right Wave: Skateboards and Sailboards Are Business," *Corpus Christi Caller-Times,* July 31, 1988, p. 20.

Looking Ahead

Watch for the following important topics:
1. Selecting the management team.
2. Considerations in choosing a location.
3. Renting versus buying a building.
4. Homes and business incubators as locations.
5. Efficient layouts for small factories and retail stores.
6. Equipment and tooling needs of small factories and retail stores.
7. New terms and concepts:

management team	free-flow pattern
business incubator	self-service layout
process layout	general-purpose equipment
product layout	special-purpose equipment
grid pattern	

Every new business requires human and physical resources. Accordingly, an entrepreneur must select employees, find a suitable location, build or rent an appropriate building, and procure equipment needed to begin operation. In this chapter, we look at the practical considerations involved in these areas of new-venture planning.

Human Resource Planning

In a very small business, a founder may personally perform most or all of the work. In most firms, however, additional personnel are needed, and choosing them becomes one of the most important initial decisions. Chapter 17 will treat the process of personnel management at some length. In this chapter, we limit discussion to the initial task of assembling a strong, properly balanced management team.

Value of a Strong Management Team

In Chapter 2, we pointed out the causal relationship between weak management and business failure. A business may be founded on a viable idea but fail because of management deficiencies. Strong management can make the best of any business idea and the resources available to make it work. Of course, even a highly competent management team cannot rescue a firm that is based on a totally weak business concept or has totally inadequate resources.

The importance of management in starting a new venture is evident in the attitudes of venture capitalists who examine business plans. A review of the management team is one of their first steps in evaluating a business plan.

Building a Management Team

Unless a firm is extremely small, the founder will not be the only individual in a leadership role. The concept of a management team, therefore, is relevant. In general, the **management team,** as we envision it here, includes both managers and other professionals or key persons who help give the new company its general direction. This team includes individuals with managerial responsibilities and also those performing other key functions for the new business. For example, the new firm may have only one person to head up its marketing effort. Eventually, this individual may become a sales manager. Even prior to that time, however, he or she may still play an important role in the firm's operations.

The type of competence needed in a management team depends upon the type of business and the nature of its operations. For example, a software development firm and a restaurant call for different types of business experience. Whatever the business, the small firm needs managers with an appropriate combination of educational background and experience. In evaluating the qualifications of those who will fill key positions, one needs to know whether an applicant is experienced in a related type of business, whether the experience has included any managerial responsibilities, and whether the individual has ever functioned as an entrepreneur.

SMALL BUSINESS IN ACTION
Blending the Skills of Partners

A successful management team requires a combination of complementary skills and personal compatibility. When Dena Robbins and Judith Cills, friends for 20 years, launched a time-management service, they knew or quickly discovered each others' strengths and weaknesses.

Because they had years of trust to build on, they were able to be honest when deciding how to divide up the responsibilities for their company, Robbins-Cills Associates Inc., Philadelphia. When each took a stab at writing a piece of literature for the business, Robbins was able to tell Cills that she thought her own writing was better. Cills agreed. So writing, in addition to other paperwork and the books, became Robbins's responsibility. Cills is the resource and quality control person. Both handle clients and employees.

The firm that they operate sells "time" by providing such services as buying groceries or gifts or taking pets to the vet.

Source: Sheryl Jean, "Divide and Conquer." Reprinted from the April, 1988, issue of *VENTURE, For Entrepreneurial Business Owners & Investors,* © 1988.

Not all members of a management team need competence in all areas. The key is balance. Is one member competent in finance? Does another possess an adequate marketing background?

In addition to identifying the key positions or individuals, the entrepreneur should work out and specify the organizational structure. Relationships among the various positions need to be understood. Although such relationships need not be worked out in great detail, it is desirable to have sufficient planning to permit orderly functioning of the enterprise and to avoid a jumble of responsibilities that invites conflict.

The management plan should be drafted in such a way as to provide for business growth. Unfilled positions should be specified. Job descriptions should spell out the duties and qualifications for such positions, and methods for selecting key employees should be explained.

The ownership share, if any, needs to be thought out carefully. Likewise, the compensation arrangements, including bonus systems or other incentive plans for key organization members, warrant scrutiny and planning.

Outside Professional Support

The managerial and professional talent of a new-venture management team can be supplemented by drawing upon outside assistance. This may take various forms. As one example, an active board of directors can provide counsel and guidance to the leadership group. Directors may be appointed on the basis of their business or technical expertise as well as on the basis of their financial investment. Selection and use of directors is discussed at greater length in Chapter 16.

Occasionally, also, a firm may "shore up" weak areas by special arrangement with consultants or individuals who have needed expertise. A few firms even offer part-time assistance in special areas of management.[1] Financial Managers Trust, Cambridge, MA, provides part-time financial management—usually several hours a week for one or two years. As another example, Richard Ward and Associates, Chicago, IL, provides part-time sales management assistance for companies with less than $3 million in annual sales.

Formal relationships with outside professional and business organizations are likewise important. Typically, these include an association with a commercial bank. Public accounting firms also provide a useful type of service to a beginning business. In addition, the new business can benefit by establishing a relationship with a legal firm and consulting with a reputable insurance agent.

Planning the company's leadership, then, should produce a team that is able to give competent direction to the new firm. It should be balanced in covering the various functional areas and in offering the right combination of education and experience. It may be comprised of both insiders and outside specialists.

Nonmanagerial Personnel

In many cases, the entrepreneur or the managerial team are the only employees when the business begins operations. However, additional personnel may be required initially or as the business grows. Human resource planning, therefore, must also consider the selection of nonmanagerial, nonprofessional personnel. The selection and training of such employees are treated in Chapter 17.

Human resources—the people involved in the business—require physical resources in the form of a place to work. We turn now to these physical resources: a location, a building, and equipment.

Selecting a Location

For most small businesses, a location decision is made only when the business is first established or purchased. Occasionally, however, a business considers relocation to reduce operating costs, get closer to its customers, or gain other advantages. Also, as a business expands, it sometimes becomes desirable to begin additional operations at other locations. The owner of a custom drapery shop, for example, may decide to open a second unit in another section of the same city or even in another city.

Importance of a Good Location

It is not the frequency but the lasting effects of location decisions that make them so important. Once the business is established, it is costly and often impractical, if not impossible, to "pull up stakes" and move. If the business depends upon a heavy flow of customer traffic, a shrewdly selected site that produces maximum sales will increase profits throughout its existence at that location. In contrast, a site with light traffic will reduce sales volume throughout the life of the business. If the choice is particularly poor, the business may never be able to "get off the ground," even with adequate financing and superior ability in purchasing and selling merchandise. This enduring effect is so clearly recognized by national chain-store organiza-

Figure 8–1　A Mall Is a Good Location for a Business That Depends on a Heavy Flow of Customer Traffic

Courtesy U.S. Shoe Corporation

tions that they spend thousands of dollars investigating sites before establishing new stores.

The choice of a location is much more vital to some businesses than to others. For example, the site chosen for a dress shop can make or break it. In contrast, the exact location of a painting contractor is of relatively minor importance. Even painting contractors, however, may suffer from certain locational disadvantages. All cities have buildings that need painting, but property is kept in better repair and painted more frequently in some communities than in others.

General Considerations in Choosing a Location

Only careful investigation will reveal the good and bad features of any particular location. Four general factors are important in this investigation. These factors are: personal preference, environmental conditions, resource availability, and customer accessibility. In a particular situation, one factor may be more important than the others, but each always has an influence. These factors and their impact on location decisions are depicted in Exhibit 8–1. Notice that the compass needle is influenced by all four factors, moving restlessly and unable to point to the best location until specific venture circumstances are provided.

Personal Preference   All too often, a prospective entrepreneur considers only the home community for locating the business. Frequently, the possibility of locating elsewhere never enters the mind. Home community preference, of course, is not the only personal factor influencing location.

Choosing one's hometown for personal reasons is not necessarily illogical. In fact, there are certain advantages. For one thing, the individual generally accepts and appreciates the atmosphere of the home community, whether it is a small town or a large city. From a practical business standpoint, the entrepreneur can more easily establish credit. The hometown banker can be dealt with more confidently, and other businesspersons may be of great service in helping evaluate a given opportunity. If customers come from the same locality, the prospective entrepreneur would probably have a better idea of their tastes and peculiarities than an outsider would have. Relatives and friends may also be one's first customers and may help to advertise one's services. The establishment of a beauty shop in the home community would illustrate a number of these advantages.

Personal preferences, however, should not be allowed to cancel out location weaknesses even though such preferences may logically be a pri-

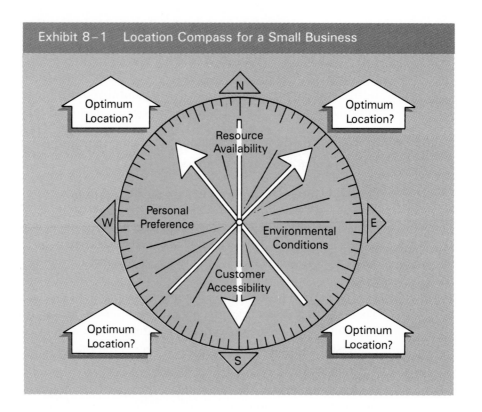

Exhibit 8-1   Location Compass for a Small Business

mary factor. Just because an individual has always lived in a given town does not automatically make it a satisfactory business location!

Environmental Conditions   A small business must operate within the environmental conditions of its location. These conditions can hinder or promote success. For example, weather is an environmental factor that has traditionally influenced location decisions. One business owner justifies his preference for a southern coastal state by saying, "You can swim in December, pick oranges virtually year-round, and go to the beach on your lunch hour."[2] Other environmental conditions, such as competition, laws, and public attitudes, to name a few, are all part of the business environment. The time to evaluate all these environmental conditions is prior to making a location decision.

Resource Availability   Resources associated with the location site are an important factor to consider when selecting a location. Land, water supply, labor supply, and waste disposal are just a few of the site-related factors that have a bearing on location costs.

Raw materials and labor supply are particularly critical considerations to the location of a manufacturing business. A wholesale business is also dependent on a convenient location to receive the goods for redistribution to its customers. The location compass in Exhibit 8–2 symbolizes the prominent role of resource availability to manufacturers and wholesalers. The

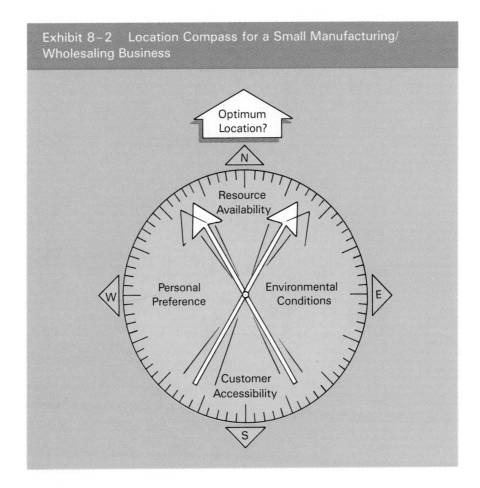

Exhibit 8–2   Location Compass for a Small Manufacturing/ Wholesaling Business

compass needle has settled considerably and now points in one general direction—a location that favors resource availability. However, personal preference or environmental conditions may exert a stronger influence on the final location decision and thus sacrifice some resource advantage.

Customer Accessibility   Sometimes the foremost consideration in selecting a location is customer accessibility. Retail outlets and service firms are typical examples of businesses that must be located conveniently to customers. Exhibit 8–3 shows the compass needle settling in the general direction of the customer-accessibility variable, reflecting its importance in locating service/retail businesses. Once again, the precise location may be influenced more strongly by the variables of personal preference or environmental conditions.

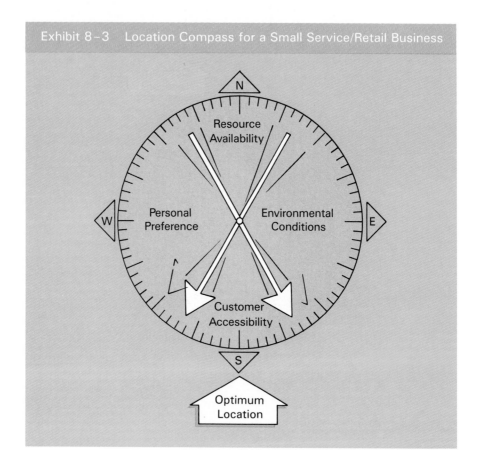

Exhibit 8–3   Location Compass for a Small Service/Retail Business

Regions, Cities, and Sites

For some businesses—a barbershop or drugstore, for example—the choice of a region is simple. These businesses can operate successfully in most areas of the country. Other types of small business, however, need to analyze the problem of geographical location with extreme care. Their location decision need not be played entirely by chance as in the Monopoly game in Figure 8–2. A logical step-by-step process in evaluating the region, city, or actual site for the business can aid the entrepreneur in making this decision.

Choice of Region Some markets for goods and services are restricted to specific regions. For example, a ski lodge is practical only in an area with slopes and snow, and a boat repair service must locate near the water. However, most new firms have the option of selecting any of several regions. Factors that affect regional choice, particularly for manufacturing businesses, are nearness to the market, availability of raw materials, and adequacy of labor supply.[3]

Figure 8–2 Selecting a Location Is Not a Game of Chance

"I'm putting two hotels on Park Place, a house on Boardwalk and a McDonald's on Marvin Gardens."

Reprinted from The Saturday Evening Post, © 1981 BFL&MS, Inc.

SMALL BUSINESS IN ACTION
Exceptions to the Rule

The personal preferences of an entrepreneur can sometimes over-shadow location considerations, such as being near your customers. The Western Fair, founded by Judge R. W. Hailey, who is now deceased, is an excellent example of how there are exceptions to every rule.

The Fair is a specialty western store located in Lott, TX, a small town of around 900 people. The store's sale of high-quality merchandise at a low price brings customers from all over the U.S. Some days Lott will see five or six times its population in the Western Fair store. The outside appearance of the store is plain and the inside is stacked with merchandise.

The owner's grandson, Bert Hailey, manages the store, which has grown from a sales volume in 1956 of $750,000 to $1.9 million in 1988. Bert concedes that their operation isn't always run by the textbook, but things have seemed to work out okay.

Source: Personal conversation with Dr. Helen Ligon, daughter of the Western Fair founder.

Nearness to the Market   Locating near the center of the market is desirable if other factors are approximately equal in importance. This is especially true of industries in which the cost of shipping the finished product is high relative to its value. For example, packaged ice and soft drinks require production facilities that are close to the consuming markets.

Availability of Raw Materials   If the raw materials required by the business are not abundantly available in all areas, the region in which these materials abound offers special locational advantages. Bulky or heavy raw materials that lose much of their bulk or weight in the manufacturing process are powerful forces that affect location. The sawmill is an example of a plant that must stay close to its raw materials in order to operate economically.

Adequacy of Labor Supply   A manufacturer's labor requirements depend upon the nature of its production process. In some cases the need for semi-skilled or unskilled labor justifies locating in a surplus labor area. Other firms find it desirable to seek a pool of highly skilled labor—the highly skilled machine trade of New England is a well-known example of such a labor supply. In addition, wage rates, labor productivity, and a history of peaceful industrial relations are particularly important considerations for labor-intensive firms.

Choice of City   For several decades many cities have tried to attract new industry. Much of this effort has been directed toward obtaining new manufacturing plants, but other types of business are welcomed also.

Growth or Decline of a City   Some cities are on the upgrade. They are growing in both population and business activity, and the income levels of their citizens are advancing. In contrast, other cities are expanding slowly or even declining in population. Economic factors, such as shifts in markets, technological changes, and transportation advantages, apparently favor some cities at the expense of others.[4]

Exhibit 8–4 lists the 10 most rapidly growing counties in the United States. As you can see, they are located in the South and West. Most are also located on the fringes of major metropolitan areas. For example, Gwinnett and Fayette counties are close to Atlanta, and Rockwall county is near Dallas.

Extent of Local Competition   Most small businesses are concerned about the nature and the amount of local competition. Manufacturers who serve

Exhibit 8–4   Rapidly Growing Counties, 1980–1987

County	Percentage of Population Growth
Average County Growth	**7.4**
Mantanuska-Susitna, AK	119.5
Hernando, FL	96.4
Flagler, FL	88.6
Gwinnett, GA	81.0
Fayette, GA	79.2
Rockwall, TX	78.3
Osceola, FL	76.5
Douglas, CO	69.3
Nye, NV	66.4
Hood, TX	66.3

Source: USA Today, October 13, 1988. Copyright 1988, USA TODAY. Excerpted with permission.

a national market are an exception to this rule, but overcrowding can occur in the majority of small-business fields. The quality of competition also affects the desirability of a location. If existing businesses are not aggressive and do not offer the type of service reasonably expected by the customer, there is likely to be room for a newcomer.

Published data can be used to shed light upon this particular problem. The average population required to support a given type of business can be determined on a national or a regional basis. By comparing the situation in the given city with these averages, it is possible to get a better picture of the intensity of local competition.

Unfortunately, objective data of this type seldom produce unequivocal answers. The population's income level and nearness to other shopping centers might account for certain discrepancies. There is no substitute for personal observation. In addition, the entrepreneur will do well to seek the opinion of those well acquainted with local business conditions. Wholesalers frequently have an excellent notion of the potential for additional retail establishments in a given line of business.

Other Factors As in the choice of region, the supply of labor may be a significant factor in the choice of city. The prevailing wage scale is particularly important for manufacturers competing with other firms that have lower wage costs.

The amount and the character of industry in a given city are likewise significant. A one-industry town is often subject to severe seasonal and cyclical business fluctuations in contrast to a city of diversified industries. In addition, the necessary customers and suppliers of essential services should be available.

Local government can help or hinder a new business. In choosing a city, the prospective entrepreneur should be assured of satisfactory police and fire protection, streets, water and other utilities, street drainage, and public transportation. Unreasonably high local taxes or severely restrictive local ordinances are to be avoided.

Finally, the city might also qualify with respect to civic, cultural, religious, and recreational affairs that make it a better place in which to live and do business.

Choice of Site After choosing a region and a city in which to locate, the next step is to select a specific site for the business. Some critical factors to consider at this stage include costs, customer accessibility, amount of customer traffic, neighborhood conditions, and the trend toward suburban development.

Costs Some firms stress the operating costs and purchasing costs associated with a specific business site. Examples of these firms are most manufacturers, wholesalers, bookkeeping services, plumbing contractors, and painting contractors. It would be foolish for these firms to locate in high-rent districts.

Customer Accessibility Earlier we recognized customer accessibility as a general consideration in selecting a location. This factor becomes even more critical when evaluating a specific site for many types of retail stores. For example, a shoe store or a drugstore may fail simply because it is on the wrong side of the street. On the other hand, a store that sells a specialty good—such as pianos—has greater freedom in selecting a site. Furthermore, some restaurants have achieved such distinction that customers drive for miles to patronize them in spite of their relatively inaccessible locations.

Unless one has a product or a service sufficiently powerful to attract the customer, however, one must locate where the customer wants to buy. In the case of motels and service stations, this means a location convenient to many motorists. For clothing stores and variety stores, it probably means a suburban shopping center location. For some drugstores and food stores, it means a location in or close to the residential areas.

Amount of Customer Traffic Customer traffic is discussed more frequently than it is measured. To count pedestrian traffic, an investigator observes the potential site and records the number of passersby. This may be done at alternate half-hour intervals during the day for enough different days to get a representative sample of the traffic. The results should be compared with the amount of traffic at other available sites and at sites known to be successful. Naturally, the traffic must also be evaluated carefully to tell whether it includes prospective customers for the particular business. A ladies' shoe store, for example, will profit little from a high flow of pedestrian traffic that is primarily male.

Of course, other factors in addition to amount of traffic must be taken into consideration. The general location must be in keeping with the prestige of the product or service. Business neighbors may likewise contribute to making a given site either desirable or undesirable. To illustrate, a high-class restaurant generally could not locate successfully in a low-income neighborhood. Neither would it locate next to a laundry.

Neighborhood Conditions   We pointed out earlier that certain cities are on the decline while others are growing more or less rapidly. What is true of cities is also true of sections within cities. City growth occurs in a given direction, and that section thrives as a result of the development. Older sections of the city become blighted. Small retail firms and, to some extent, small service businesses must consider this factor in the selection of a business site. However, since blight can be eliminated, the small retailer should also consider the impact of urban renewal programs on site values in or close to renewal areas.

Suburban Development   The trend toward suburban shopping centers has been an impressive development of recent decades. Increasing suburban population, greater use of the family car, traffic congestion, lack of parking space downtown, and other factors have contributed to the relative decline of central business district activity in many cities. Suburbanites who find it difficult or unpleasant to shop downtown turn to shopping centers located nearer the residential areas.

This shift in business has created problems in the downtown area, as well as offered opportunities in the suburbs. For the small retail business, a shopping center or other suburban location often presents a better opportunity than a downtown spot.

The Building and Its Layout

A new business ordinarily begins by occupying an existing building. For this reason, an existing structure may make a given site either suitable or unsuitable. Thus, the location decision must be coupled with an analysis of building requirements.

Rent or Buy?

Assuming that a suitable, existing building is available, the founder must decide whether to rent or buy such a facility. Although ownership confers greater freedom in modifying and using a building, the advantages of renting usually outweigh these considerations. Two reasons why most new firms should rent are the following:

1. A large cash outlay is avoided. This is extremely important for the new small firm, which typically lacks adequate financial resources.

2. Risk is reduced by avoiding substantial investment and by post-poning commitments for building space until the success of the business is assured and the nature of building requirements is better known.

In entering into a leasing agreement, the renter should check the landlord's insurance policies to be sure there is proper coverage for various types of risks. If not, the renter should seek coverage under his or her own policy. It is also important to have the terms of the rental agreement reviewed by an attorney. A renter should not be unduly exposed to liability for damages that are not caused by the renter's own gross negligence. An example has been cited of a firm that wished to rent just 300 square feet of storage space in a large complex of offices and shops.[5] On the sixth page of the landlord's standard lease was language that could have made the tenant responsible for the entire 30,000-square-foot complex if it burned down, regardless of blame!

Home-Based Businesses

Many small-business firms are based in their owners' homes. Rather than renting or buying a separate building, they house the business operation in a basement, garage, or spare bedroom.

Some home-based businesses are simply Stage I firms that will move out of the home as soon as growth makes it economically feasible. An example is Blue Chip Ice Company, Whitney, TX, which started as an ice machine in Ed Peters's garage.[6] Each time he sold the capacity of one machine, he would buy another, until his entire garage was lined with ice makers. To expand, he eventually bought an existing ice plant and built up the business to produce as much as 150 tons of ice a day.

Other home-based businesses can function indefinitely in a home setting because of their modest space demands and/or the desire to blend business activities and family care. An example of the latter is Judy's Maternity Rentals, started by Judith Schramm in Arlington, VA, when her son was born. She expressed her rationale for the location as follows: "I wanted to stay home with Michael, but I also wanted to earn money.... This lets me be with the baby, keeps the overhead down, and lowers the overall risk of a startup."[7]

To function successfully, owners of home-based businesses need to establish both spatial and nonspatial boundaries between the business and the home. Without boundaries, the home and the business can easily interfere with each other. An owner may establish boundaries, for example, by setting aside specific business space in the home and/or by scheduling definite hours for business matters. Client calls, indeed, may require the observance of regular business hours. The owner needs to protect the business from undue family or home interference and also to protect the home from unreasonable encroachment by the business. Since the owner never leaves the home to go to the office or place of business, he or she may find the business absorbing every available waking moment.

Space in a Business Incubator

In recent years, **business incubators** have sprung up in all areas of the country. Incubators are organizations that rent space to new businesses or to people wishing to start businesses. They are often located in recycled buildings such as abandoned warehouses or schools, and they serve fledgling businesses by making space available, offering administrative services, and providing management advice. An incubator tenant can be fully operational the day after moving in, without buying phones, renting a copier, or hiring office employees.

The purpose of incubators is to see new businesses "hatch," grow, and leave the incubator. Most incubators, although not all, have some type of

Figure 8–3   An Incubator: Hamilton County Business Center

Courtesy of Hamilton County Business Center

governmental or university sponsorship and are motivated by a desire to stimulate economic development.

Although the building space provided by incubators is significant, their greatest contribution lies in the business expertise and management assistance they provide. A more extensive discussion of incubators is included in Chapter 15.

Functional Requirements

When planning the initial building requirements, the entrepreneur must avoid commitments for a building space that is too large or too luxurious. At the same time, the space should not be too small or too austere for efficient operation. Buildings do not produce profits directly. They merely house the operations and personnel that produce the profits. Therefore, the ideal building is practical but not pretentious.

The general suitability of a building for a given type of business operation relates to its functional character. For example, the floor space of a restaurant should normally be on one level. Other important factors to consider are the shape, age, and condition of the building; fire hazards; heating and air conditioning; lighting and restroom facilities; and entrances and exits. Obviously, these factors carry different weights for a factory operation as compared with a wholesale or retail operation. In any case, the comfort, convenience, and safety of employees and customers of the business must not be overlooked.

General-purpose buildings are preferable to buildings that have features that limit their resale value. Although some types of business require specialized buildings, most can operate efficiently in less specialized structures. A standard prefabricated building typically is better than a custom-designed building for a new firm.

Expansion possibilities should also be considered when making the original building plan. For example, a building might provide excellent expansion opportunities by having a temporary wall on the side when there is vacant land.

Building Layout

Layout refers to the logical arrangement of physical facilities in order to provide efficiency of business operations. To provide a concise treatment of layout, we will limit our discussion to two different layout problems—

layout for manufacturers (whose primary concern is production operations) and layout for retailers (whose primary concern is customer traffic).

Factory Layout The factory layout presents a three-dimensional space problem. Overhead space may be utilized for power conduits, pipelines for exhaust systems, and the like. A proper design of storage areas and handling systems makes use of space near the ceiling. Space must be allowed also for the unobstructed movement of machine parts from one location to another.

The ideal manufacturing process would have a straight-line, forward movement of materials from receiving room to shipping room. If this ideal cannot be realized for a given process, backtracking, sidetracking, and long hauls of materials can at least be minimized. This will reduce production delays.

Two contrasting types of layout are used in industrial firms. One of these is called **process layout** and has similar machines grouped together. Drill presses, for example, are separated from lathes in a machine shop layout. The alternative to such a process layout is called a **product layout.** This is used for continuous-flow, mass production—usually conveyorized, with all machines needed for balanced production located beside the conveyor. Thus, similar machines are used at the same points on the different conveyor lines set up to process a given product.

Smaller plants that operate on a job-lot basis cannot use a product layout, because it demands too high a degree of standardization of both product and process. Thus, small machine shops are generally arranged on a process layout basis. Small firms with highly standardized products, such as dairies, bakeries, and car wash firms, however, can use a product layout.

Retail Store Layout The objectives for a retail store layout include the proper display of merchandise to maximize sales and customer convenience and service. Normally, the convenience and attractiveness of the surroundings contribute to a customer's continued patronage. An efficient layout also contributes to operating economy. A final objective is the protection of the store's equipment and merchandise. In achieving all these objectives, the flow of customer traffic must be anticipated and planned. The grid pattern and free flow pattern of store layout are the two most widely used layout designs.[8]

The **grid pattern** is the plain, block-looking layout typical of supermarkets and hardware stores. It provides more merchandise exposure and simplifies security and cleaning. The **free-flow pattern** makes less efficient use of space but has greater visual appeal and allows customers to move in any direction at their own speed. The free-flow patterns result in curving aisles and greater flexibility in merchandise presentation.

Many retailers use a **self-service layout,** which permits customers direct access to the merchandise. Not only does self-service reduce the selling expense, but it also permits shoppers to examine the goods before buying. Today practically all food merchandising follows this principle.

Some types of merchandise—for example, ladies' hosiery, cigarettes, magazines, and candy—are often purchased on an impulse basis. Impulse goods should be placed at points where customers can see them easily. Products that the customers will buy anyway and for which they come in specifically may be placed in less conspicuous spots.

Various areas of a retail store differ markedly in sales value. Customers typically turn to the right upon entering a store, and so the right front space is the most valuable. The second most valuable are the center front and right middle spaces. Department stores often place high-margin gift wares, cosmetics, and jewelry in these areas. The third most valuable are the left front and center middle spaces. And the left middle space is fourth in importance. Since the back areas are the least important so far as space value is concerned, most service facilities and the general office typically are found in the rear of a store. Certainly the best space should be given to departments or merchandise producing the greatest sales and profits. Finally, the first floor has greater space value than a second or higher floor in a multistory building. Generally the higher the floor, the lower its selling value.

Equipment and Tooling

The final step in arranging for physical facilities involves the purchase or lease of equipment and tooling. Here again, the types of equipment and tooling required obviously depend upon the nature of the business. We will limit our discussion of equipment needs to the two diverse fields of manufacturing and retailing. Of course, even within these two areas there is great variation in the required tools and equipment.

Factory Equipment

Machines in the factory may be either general-purpose or special-purpose in character. **General-purpose equipment** for metalworking includes lathes, drill presses, and milling machines. In a woodworking plant, general-purpose machines include ripsaws, planing mills, and lathes. In each case, jigs, fixtures, and other tooling items set up on the basic machine tools can be changed so that two or more shop operations can be accomplished. Bottling machines and automobile assembly-line equipment are examples of **special-purpose equipment**.

Advantages of General-Purpose Equipment   General-purpose equipment requires a minimum investment and is well adapted to a varied type of operation. Small machine shops and cabinet shops, for example, utilize this type of equipment. General-purpose equipment also contributes the necessary flexibility in industries in which the product is so new that the technology has not yet been well developed or in which there are frequent design changes in the product.

Advantages of Special-Purpose Equipment   Special-purpose equipment permits cost reduction where the technology is fully established and where a capacity operation is more or less assured by high sales volume. The large-volume production of automobiles, for example, justifies special-purpose equipment costing hundreds of thousands of dollars. Not all special-purpose equipment is that expensive, however. Even though it is used most in large-scale industry, the same principle can be applied on a more modest scale in many small manufacturing plants. A milking machine in a dairy illustrates specialized equipment used by small firms. Nevertheless, a small firm cannot ordinarily and economically use special-purpose equipment unless it makes a standardized product on a fairly large scale.

Specialized machines using special-purpose tooling result in greater output per machine-hour operated. Hence, the labor cost per unit of product is lower. However, the initial cost of such equipment and tooling is much higher, and its scrap value is little or nothing due to its highly specialized function.

Retail Store Equipment

Small retailers must have merchandise display counters, storage racks, shelving, mirrors, seats for customers, customer push carts, cash registers (see Figure 8–4), and various items necessary to facilitate selling. Such equipment may be costly but is usually less expensive than equipment for a factory operation.

If the store attempts to serve a high-income market, its fixtures typi-

Figure 8–4   Modern Check-Out Equipment
for a Retail Store

cally should display the elegance and beauty expected by such customers. Polished mahogany and bronze fittings of showcases will lend a richness of atmosphere. Indirect lighting, thick rugs on the floor, and big easy chairs will also make a contribution to the air of luxury. In contrast, a store that caters to lower-income-bracket customers would find luxurious fixtures inconsistent with an atmosphere of low prices. Therefore, such a store should concentrate on simplicity.

Automated Equipment

Automation, which takes many forms, has come into use in many small-business operations. For example, the use of computers is commonplace in such businesses as travel agencies and repair shops. Supermarkets and department stores use electronic devices to read product codes, thereby facilitating the sales and record-keeping processes.

Small manufacturing firms face greater difficulties, however, in using automated equipment. The major barrier to automation is found in short production runs. But if a small plant produces a given product in large volume, with infrequent changes in design, the owner should seriously consider the many benefits derived from automation. Among these are the following:

1. Operator errors are minimized.
2. Processing costs are lowered by speed of operation and machine efficiency.
3. Human resources are conserved while personnel skill requirements are upgraded.
4. Safety of manufacturing and handling operations is promoted.
5. Inventory requirements tend to be reduced because of faster processing.
6. Maintenance and inspection are improved by incorporating lubrication systems and devices in the automatic transfer machine.

Looking Back

1. A competent and properly balanced management team is needed to provide leadership for a new venture. Outside professional assistance is often used to supplement the efforts of employed staff members.
2. Four general considerations affect selection of a business location: personal preference, environmental conditions, resource availability, and customer accessibility. Their relative importance depends upon the nature of the business.
3. Most new firms rent rather than buy their building space. The primary reasons for renting are conservation of cash and reduction of risk.
4. Basements, garages, and spare rooms provide building space for many small businesses that are starting and for others that have limited space requirements. Business incubators also offer economical facility arrangements for many firms during their first one or two years of operation.
5. Proper layout depends upon the type of business. Manufacturing firms use layout patterns that facilitate production operations and provide for the efficient flow of materials. Retailers lay out building space in terms of customer needs and the flow of customer traffic.
6. Most small manufacturing firms use general-purpose equip-

ment, although some have sufficient volume and a standardized operation, which permit the use of special-purpose equipment. The type of equipment and tooling in retail firms should be related to the general level and type of the business.

DISCUSSION QUESTIONS

1. Why do investors tend to favor a management team for a new business in preference to a lone entrepreneur? Is this preference justified?

2. Would you rather have your grade in a course be based on your own work or on that of a team of which you are a member? Why? What does your answer say, if anything, about the use of management teams in small businesses?

3. How much competence in financial management is needed by a business founder who has an experienced finance person on the management team?

4. Since most small-company boards of directors are little more than "rubber stamp" boards, how can they make a meaningful contribution to the management team of a new business? If you were an investor, would you consider a qualified director as an asset? Why?

5. Is the hometown of the business owner likely to be a good location? Why? Is it logical for an owner to allow personal preference to influence the decision on a business location? Why?

6. For the five small businesses that you know best, would you say that their locations were based upon the evaluation of location factors, chance, or something else?

7. In the selection of a region, what types of businesses should place greatest emphasis upon (a) markets, (b) raw materials, and (c) labor? Explain.

8. In the choice of specific sites, what types of businesses must show the greatest concern with customer accessibility? Why?

9. Suppose you were considering a location within an existing shopping mall. How would you go about evaluating the pedestrian traffic at that location? Be specific.

10. Under what conditions would it be most logical for a new firm to buy rather than rent a building for the business?

11. In a home-based business, there is typically some competition, if not conflict, between the interests of the home and the interests of the business. What would determine whether the danger is greater for the home or the business?

12. What is a business incubator and what advantages does it offer as a home for a new business?

13. When should the small manufacturer utilize process layout, and when product layout? Explain.

14. Discuss the conditions under which a new small manufacturer should buy general-purpose and special-purpose equipment.

15. Describe the unique problems concerning store layout and merchandise display that confront a new small jeweler.

YOU MAKE THE CALL

Situation 1

A husband-and-wife team operated small department stores in two midwestern towns with populations of about 2,000 each. Their clientele consisted of the primarily blue-collar and rural population of those two areas. After several years of successful operation, they decided to open a third such store in a town of 5,000 people.

Most of the businesses in this larger town were located along a six-block-long strip—an area commonly referred to as "downtown." One attractive site for the store was situated in the middle of the business district, but the rental fee for that location was very high. Another available building had once been occupied by Montgomery Ward, but was vacated several years earlier. It was located at one end of the business district. Other businesses in the same block were a TV and appliance store and some service businesses. Two clothing stores were located in the next block—closer to the center of town. The rent for this latter site was much more reasonable, a three-year lease was possible, and a local bank was willing to loan sufficient funds to accomplish necessary remodeling.

Questions

1. Does the location in the middle of the business district seem to be substantially better than the second site?

2. How might this owner evaluate the relative attractiveness of these two sites?

3. To what extent would the department store benefit from having the service businesses and a TV and appliance business in the same block?

4. What other market or demographic factors, if any, should the owners consider in opening a store in this town?

Situation 2

A business incubator rents space to a number of small firms that are beginning operation or are very young. In addition to supplying space, the incubator provides a receptionist, computer, conference room, paper cutter, and copy machine. In addition, it offers management counseling and assists new businesses in getting reduced advertising rates and reduced legal fees.

Two clients of the incubator are the following:

1. A jewelry repair, cleaning, and remounting service that does such work on a contract basis for pawn shops and jewelry stores.
2. A home health care company that employs a staff of nurses to visit the homes of elderly people who need daily care but who cannot afford or are not yet ready to go to a nursing home.

Questions

1. If these businesses did not use the special services provided by the incubator, would they still find it advantageous to locate in the center? What would make it logical or illogical for them?
2. Evaluate each of the services offered by the incubator in terms of its usefulness to these two businesses. Do the benefits seem to favor this location if rental costs are similar to rental costs for space outside the incubator?

EXPERIENTIAL EXERCISES

1. Prepare a one-page résumé of your own qualifications to launch a term-paper-typing business at your college or university. Add a critique that might be prepared by an investor evaluating your strengths and weaknesses as shown on the résumé.
2. Identify and evaluate a nearby site that is now vacant after a business closure. Point out the strengths and weaknesses of that location for such a business and comment on the part the location may have played in the closure.
3. Interview a small-business owner concerning the strengths and weaknesses of that owner's business location. Prepare a brief report summarizing your findings.
4. Visit a retail store and study its layout. Prepare a report describing, explaining, and evaluating the layout.

REFERENCES TO SMALL-BUSINESS PRACTICES

Brown, Paul B. "Piggyback." *Inc.,* Vol. 10, No. 8 (August, 1988), pp. 92–93.
    A description is given of various businesses that have located within other businesses—for example, a cookie shop located inside a fast-food establishment.
Quirk, Beatrice Taylor. "Gaining a Stronghold in the Billion Dollar Video Industry." *In Business,* Vol. 4, No. 6 (November–December, 1982), pp. 39–43.
    This article describes the personal experiences of a husband-wife entrepreneurial team as lack of space forced a relocation from their home to an unused churchhouse.
Richman, Tom. "Beyond the Start-Up Team." *Inc.,* Vol. 9, No. 13 (December, 1987), pp. 53–55.
    This article reports on the effectiveness of the original management teams of several rapidly growing firms and the tendency for some companies to outgrow their original managers.
Schultz, Leslie. "A Good Garage Is Hard to Find." *Inc.,* Vol. 5, No. 4 (April, 1983), pp. 91–97.
    Picture after picture of garage-based businesses are included in this article. Each picture has a brief narrative discussing the business and the circumstances of its garage site.

ENDNOTES

1. Mary Guterson, "Officers by the Hour," *Venture,* Vol. 10, No. 8 (August, 1988), p. 72.

2. Glenn R. Singer, "An Entrepreneurial Place in the Sun," *Venture,* Vol. 4, No. 10 (October, 1982), p. 41.

3. One study showing the principal importance of these factors is described by Roger Schmenner, "How Firms Set Sights on Sites," *Nation's Business,* Vol. 69, No. 11 (November, 1981), pp. 14A–18A.

4. For an interesting discussion of how many towns are developing reputations as hospitable places for small businesses, see Margaret Coffey, "Towns Entrepreneurs Love," *Venture,* Vol. 4, No. 3 (March, 1982), pp. 34–40.

5. Marisa Manley, "Look Before You Lease," *Inc.,* Vol. 8, No. 8 (August, 1986), p. 91.

6. Karen Svendsen Werner, "Whitney-Based Blue Chip Has Ice Business Down Cold," *Waco Tribune-Herald,* June 18, 1987.

7. Nora Goldstein, "Home, Usually Sweet, Home," *In Business,* Vol. 10, No. 4 (July–August, 1988), p. 28.

8. A detailed discussion of these two layout patterns can be found in Barry Berman and Joel R. Evans, *Retail Management: A Strategic Approach* (4th ed., New York: Macmillan Publishing Co., 1989), Chapter 14.

9 INITIAL FINANCIAL PLANNING

Photo by Randy Matusow

Ellen Sherry

This is a story of how two entrepreneurs opened a boutique in Bloomingdale's department store. But wait! The real story is what happened after they conceptualized the idea and before they opened the boutique.

Ellen C. Sherry and Joan Schwager, both practicing nutritionists, began their partnership in 1980. Through their firm, Sherry-Schwager Associates, they provided one-on-one nutrition counseling. A few years later, they "began to realize there was an untapped niche in the . . . market."

> With this in mind, we thought it would be a wonderful idea to open boutiques in leading department stores to sell nutritional products in an

elegant and fashionable format, much the way fragrances are marketed. We would take vitamins out of the standard brown bottles and put them in attractive packaging.

Their idea was favorably received by a buyer for Bloomingdale's. The next step was to seek funding. A meeting with an investment banker drew the advice, "put together a comprehensive business plan—one that would make it crystal clear to investors just what we were proposing and how they would profit by risking their capital with us."

After writing a detailed plan, the entrepreneurs "hit the road," contacting prospective investors. They were not always received well, however, sometimes being treated like "goodlooking women fiddling around with some sort of hobby...." But finally, things fell into place. A commercial banker looked at their plan and said, "You're going to be millionaires." The banker directed them to a CPA who had contacts with a group of private investors. Again, with their business plan in hand, they made their proposal.

Within a few months, a financing package was in place. The business, named Vibrance, received $315,000 in seed capital in return for an equity interest in the company. The first boutique in Bloomingdale's opened in August 1987. These entrepreneurs' success in obtaining funds was due to hard work, a good idea, and a business plan.

Source: Mark Stevens, "Raising $315,000 From Scratch," *Working Woman,* Vol. 4, No. 4 (April, 1988), pp. 48–49. Reprinted with permission from WORKING WOMAN magazine, Copyright © 1988 Working Woman/McCall's Group.

Looking Ahead

Watch for the following important topics:
1. Analyzing the nature of financial requirements of a new business.
2. Estimating the dollar amounts of required funds.
3. Selecting the types of initial capital.
4. Locating the sources of funds.
5. Using pro-forma financial statements.
6. New terms and concepts:

current assets	average collection period
circulating capital	fixed-asset turnover
fixed assets	break-even analysis

owner capital	venture capitalist
creditor capital	conditional sales contract
ownership equity	asset-based lending
debt capital	factoring
angels	private placement
small-business investment companies	pro-forma financial statements

"Water, water everywhere and not a drop to drink," is a famous literary statement, which after minor adaption—"Money, money everywhere and not a cent for my new business"—describes many entrepreneurs' feelings about the financing of their new ventures. These entrepreneurs must quickly change their attitude in order to make positive and confident preparations for obtaining venture funding.

An entrepreneur's confidence may be increased if she or he recognizes that the financing process closely parallels a much more familiar activity—planning a family vacation. Let us briefly examine a few of these similarities. First, most people agree that the least fun aspect of a family vacation is paying for it. Therefore, the entrepreneur should not be surprised if the excitement of the business idea and the thrill of starting up are temporarily suppressed while financial planning is conducted! Despite this feeling, it is obviously necessary to see how the new venture will be paid for. Second, vacations of any major scope should be guided by a formal itinerary. Otherwise, family members will constantly be wondering what is happening next. Entrepreneurs also need a schedule, or financial plan, to guide their operations. This plan should include how much money is needed, when it is needed, and how it will be used. Finally, most family vacationers will admit that despite good planning they still spent more on their vacations than estimated. The proverbial truth that "everything seems to cost more than we estimate" applies to a new venture as well. After considering the parallel between planning a family vacation and preparing a financial plan, the entrepreneur should understand that financing a new venture is not a totally unfamiliar process.

Let us examine the financial planning process in more detail. Remember that in Chapter 6 we briefly examined the content of the financial plan by proposing in Exhibit 6–9 numerous questions that must be answered in writing the financial plan. In this chapter, we explain how to find the answers to these questions. We have grouped our discussion into the following four categories:

1. Determining the nature of financial requirements.
2. Estimating the amount of funds required.
3. Finding sources of funds.
4. Using pro-forma financial statements to show venture profits and funding needs.

Determining the Nature of Financial Requirements

The specific needs of a proposed business venture govern the nature of its initial financial requirements. If the firm is a food store, financial planning must provide for the store building, cash registers, shopping carts, inventory, office equipment, and other items required in this type of operation. An analysis of capital requirements for this or any other type of business must consider its needs for current-asset capital, fixed-asset capital, promotion-expense capital, and funds for personal expenses.

Current-Asset Capital

Current assets are the plus side of the working-capital equation.[1] Three current-asset items are cash, inventories, and accounts receivable. The term **circulating capital** is sometimes applied to these three items, emphasizing the constant cycle from cash to inventory to receivables to cash, and so on. Careful planning is needed to provide adequate current-asset capital for the new business.

Cash Every firm must have the cash essential for current business operations. Also, a reservoir of cash is needed because of the uneven flow of funds into the business (as income) and out of the business (as expense). The size of this reservoir is determined not only by the volume of sales, but also by the regularity of cash receipts and cash payments. Uncertainties exist because of unpredictable decisions by customers as to when they will pay their bills and because of emergencies that require substantial cash outlays. If an adequate cash balance is maintained, the firm can take such unexpected developments in stride.

Inventories Although the relative importance of inventories differs considerably from one type of business to another, they often constitute a major part of the working capital. Seasonality of sales and production affects the size of the minimum inventory. Retail stores, for example, may find it desirable to carry a larger-than-normal inventory during the Christmas season.

Accounts Receivable The firm's accounts receivable consist of payments due from its customers. If the firm expects to sell on a credit basis—and in many lines of business this is necessary—provision must be made for financing receivables. The firm cannot afford to wait until its customers pay their bills before restocking its shelves.

Fixed-Asset Capital

Fixed assets are the relatively permanent assets that are intended for use in the business rather than for sale. For example, a delivery truck used by a grocer to deliver merchandise to customers is a fixed asset. In the case of an automobile dealer, however, a delivery truck to be sold would be part of the inventory and thus a current asset.

The types of fixed assets needed in a new business may include the following:

1. Tangible fixed assets—such as buildings, machinery, equipment, and land (including mineral rights, timber, and the like).
2. Intangible fixed assets—such as patents, copyrights, and goodwill. Many new firms have no intangible fixed assets.
3. Fixed security investments—such as stock of subsidiaries, pension funds, and contingency funds. In most cases a new business has no fixed security investments.

The nature and size of the fixed-asset investment are determined by the type of business operation. A modern beauty shop, for example, might be equipped for around $80,000, whereas a motel sometimes requires 50 or more times that amount. In any given kind of business, moreover, there is a minimum quantity or assortment of facilities needed for efficient operation. It would seldom be profitable, for example, to operate a motel with only one or two rooms. It is this principle, of course, that excludes small business from automobile manufacturing and other types of heavy industry.

A firm's flexibility is inversely related to its investment in fixed assets. Investments in land, buildings, and equipment involve long-term commitments. The inflexibility inherent in fixed-asset investment underscores the importance of a realistic evaluation of fixed-asset needs.

Startup Expenses

Persons who expend time and money establishing or promoting a business expect repayment of their personal funds and payment for their services. Payment to these promoters may take the form of a cash fee or an ownership interest in the business. Of course, many new businesses come into being as proprietorships, with the entrepreneur acting as the promoter. In this case the proprietor must have sufficient funds to pay all necessary out-of-pocket promotional costs. Also, there are other startup expenses.

For example, insurance premiums may be due before the business actually opens or utility deposits may be demanded before the electricity at the business can be turned on. Each of these expenses may be small, but together they can be quite substantial.

Funds for Personal Expenses

In the very small business, financial provision must also be made for the owner's personal living expenses during an initial period of operation. Technically, this is not part of the business capitalization, but it should be considered in the business financial plan. Inadequate provision for personal expenses will inevitably lead to a diversion of business assets and a departure from the financial plan.

Estimating the Amount of Funds Required

When estimating the magnitude of capital requirements for a small business, the entrepreneur quickly feels the need for a "crystal ball." The uncertainties surrounding an entirely new venture make estimation difficult. But even for established businesses, forecasting is never exact. Nevertheless, when seeking initial capital, the entrepreneur must be ready to answer the question "How much?"

The amount of capital needed by various types of new businesses varies considerably. High-technology companies, such as computer manufacturers, designers of semiconductor chips, and gene-splicing companies, often require several million dollars in initial financing. Stephen A. Duzan, president of Immunex Corp. of Seattle, WA, estimates that it takes $60 million to bring a new biotech company from development stages to the market.[2]

Most service businesses, on the other hand, require smaller amounts

Figure 9–1   Estimating Capital Requirements Is Difficult Without a Crystal Ball

of initial capital. For example, Debora Tsakoumakis started her business, HB Bakery Connection, in Boulder, CO, with $1,000. For a fee, Tsakoumakis will arrange delivery of a personalized cake for clients who call her on the telephone. She has developed a network of 400 bakeries in almost every state that bake and deliver cakes. In her first year of operation, she filled over 350 orders.[3]

The explanations that follow will show how a prospective entrepreneur may use a "double-barreled" approach to estimating capital requirements by (1) applying industry standard ratios to estimate dollar amounts, and (2) cross-checking the dollar amounts by break-even analysis and empirical investigation. Dun & Bradstreet, Inc., banks, trade associations, and other organizations compile industry standard ratios for numerous types of businesses. If no standard data can be located, then estimating capital requirements inevitably involves educated guesswork.

Calculating Asset Needs

Having arrived at a sales estimate as objectively as possible (see Chapter 7), the entrepreneur next must compute the dollar value of all assets consistent with the particular sales volume.

Cash Requirements   Anticipated payments for labor, utilities, rent, supplies, and other expenses following the initiation of the firm must be studied in estimating cash requirements. A generous amount of cash must be set aside for those items, as well as for any unexpected expenses. For a new business, the standard amount of cash that is typical for the industry may be too small. Some additional cash may be needed for a margin of safety.

In many types of businesses, a cash balance adequate to pay one or two months' expenses is desirable. This is a good rule of thumb. But the prospective entrepreneur should realize that much subjective judgment is needed in estimating the desired cash balance for a particular business.

Inventory Requirements   Adequate levels of inventory must be maintained. Industry ratios help estimate these levels. Suppose a retailer's estimated sales is $800,000 and the standard sales-to-inventory ratio is 8. This means that the retailer would need $800,000 \div 8 = $100,000$ worth of inventory to keep up with the industry ratio of 8.

In cross-checking inventory requirements through empirical investigation, the entrepreneur must consider the specific types and quantities of items to be kept in inventory. In the case of a clothing retailer, for example, the entrepreneur must make a distribution by sizes and styles of items to be sold to customers. The costs of stocking this merchandise can then be computed by reference to prices quoted by suppliers. Likewise, a prospective manufacturer would need to identify the types and quantities of raw materials to be kept on hand, considering the rate of usage, the location of suppliers, and the time required to replenish supplies.

Accounts Receivable Requirements   Since accounts receivable, in effect, are loans to customers, these assets tie up capital. It is important to know how much capital will be involved in these assets. To estimate the amount of capital tied up in accounts receivable, we must first determine the estimated **average collection period** for the industry. (This period is the average length of time that a firm must wait before it receives cash from a credit sale.) The estimated level of accounts receivable may then be computed in two steps:

1. Divide annual credit sales by 360 to get the average daily credit sales.
2. Multiply the average daily credit sales by the average collection period for the industry.

Suppose that the average collection period for a particular type of retailing (that is, the average for the entire industry) is 36 days. Suppose, further, that a beginning retailer in this industry anticipates annual credit sales of $600,000. The level of accounts receivable that this retailer must maintain to conform to the industry standard may be calculated as follows:

Step 1. $\dfrac{\$600,000 \text{ (annual credit sales)}}{360 \text{ (days)}} = \$1,666$ (average daily credit sales)

Step 2. $1,666 (average daily credit sales)
$\underline{\times \quad\ 36}$ (average collection period)
$59,976 (daily average accounts receivable balance)

Fixed-Asset Requirements   The **fixed-asset turnover,** defined as the ratio of sales to fixed assets, can be used to calculate fixed-asset requirements. It measures the extent to which plant and equipment are being utilized productively. Suppose that the industry fixed-asset turnover is 4 in the case of the retailer with an estimated sales of $800,000. This means that the retailer would require $800,000 ÷ 4 = $200,000 in fixed assets.

Verifying Asset Needs with Break-Even Analysis

Ratio analysis is a useful approach for estimating asset requirements. However, since its estimates are closely tied to the estimate of sales, more than one sales level should be evaluated with the calculations. Also, these same sales levels should be cross-checked with break-even analysis to ascertain whether they are above, below, or at the break-even level of sales. Potential investors are always eager to determine the break-even point for sales as this has a direct bearing on their investment decision.

Break-even can be explained either with graphs, by algebraic formulas, or by simple subtraction and division. The graphic presentation is included in Chapter 12 in connection with pricing. In this chapter we explain break-even with the simplest method—subtraction and division.

Break-even analysis is a method of showing the relationship between sales revenue and costs of producing that revenue. The focal point of the analysis is the **break-even point**—the particular sales volume at which total costs will equal total revenue. At the break-even point a firm neither earns a profit nor sustains a loss.

In order to develop the application of break-even analysis to asset requirements, consider the following symbols and definitions:

P = Product unit selling price
V = Variable cost per unit (includes all costs that vary directly with the volume produced/sold)

> F = Total fixed costs (includes all costs that are constant at various levels of production/sales)
>
> CM = Contribution margin (the difference in product unit selling price and variable cost per unit, or P − V)
>
> BEP = Break-even point (the point at which total costs equal total revenue)

The break-even relationship is expressed by the following equation:

$$F \div CM = BEP$$

Let us consider an entrepreneur selling a single product in a proposed retail outlet. After estimating initial asset requirements with ratio analysis based on anticipated yearly sales of $800,000, break-even analysis can be used to discover the sales volume at which the venture will likely become profitable. Assume that total fixed costs are $400,000, variable cost is $6 per unit, and selling price is $10 per unit. The break-even point is found by substituting the following numbers into the break-even equation.

$$F \div (P - V) = BEP$$
$$\$400,000 \div (\$10 - \$6) = 100,000 \text{ units}$$

Break-even revenue computes to be 100,000 units × $10 selling price = $1,000,000. This shows that the number of units forecasted to be sold— $800,000 ÷ $10 = 80,000—is 20,000 units below the break-even point in the first year.

Break-even analysis helps evaluate the ratio-analysis estimates by relating them to the break-even point. In this hypothetical example, the break-even point will likely be reached in the second year of operation. If this appears realistic to investors, they will have more confidence in the ratio-analysis estimates. If not, further investigation is required.

Verifying Asset Needs by Empirical Investigation

Although break-even analysis is useful in cross-checking asset requirements, it should not be the only validation effort. The prospective entrepreneur should also make an independent, empirical investigation of capital needs.

For example, inventory requirements of a business should be checked with those who have experience in the same line of business. Similarly, cost estimates for land, building, and equipment may be compared with prices asked by sellers. If there are substantial discrepancies in estimates provided by the two different approaches, rechecking is necessary to decide which is more likely to be accurate.

Liquidity Considerations in Structuring Asset Needs

The need for adequate working capital deserves special emphasis. A common weakness in small-business financing is the disproportionately small investment in current assets relative to fixed assets. In such weakly financed firms, too much of the money is tied up in assets that are difficult to convert to cash. Danger arises from the fact that the business depends upon daily receipts to meet obligations coming due from day to day. If there is a slump in sales or if there are unexpected expenses, creditors may force the firm into bankruptcy.

The lack of flexibility associated with the purchase of fixed assets suggests the desirability of minimizing this type of investment. Often, for example, there is a choice between renting or buying property. For perhaps the majority of new small firms, renting provides the better alternative. A rental arrangement not only reduces the initial cash requirement but also provides the flexibility that is helpful if the business is more successful or less successful than anticipated.

Finding Sources of Funds

To this point, we have examined the nature of financial needs and ways to estimate how much funding is required. Now we turn our attention to locating the sources of these funds and establishing the necessary financial arrangements to obtain them.

The initial financing of a small business is quite often patterned after the typical personal financing plan. A prospective entrepreneur will first canvass his or her own savings and then those of family and friends. Only if these sources are inadequate will the entrepreneur turn to the more formal channels of financing such as banks and venture capitalists.

Every lender wants a feeling of confidence in the borrower and the borrower's idea. A well-prepared assessment of capital needs and sources of funds can help to win that confidence.

Types of Initial Capital

Initial capital consists of **owner capital** and **creditor capital.** Sometimes the terms **ownership equity** and **debt capital** are used, respectively. Traditionally owner capital in a new firm should be at least two-thirds of the total initial capital. This two-thirds dictum is quite conservative, and many small businesses are started with ownership equities that are smaller. Sometimes initial ownership equity is even nonexistent!

Avon, Campbell Soup, and McDonald's were each started with a 100 percent debt structure. However, many small firms fail every year due to inadequate ownership equity. The conservative approach thus provides the prospective entrepreneur with a margin of safety that the shoestring operator lacks.

The major sources of equity financing are personal savings, venture capitalists, wealthy individuals (angels), and the securities market. The major sources of debt financing are individuals, commercial banks, government-assisted programs, business suppliers, and asset-based lenders. Of course, the use of these and other sources of funds is not limited to initial financing. They can also be tapped to finance growing day-to-day operating requirements and business expansion. Exhibit 9–1 gives a visual overview of the funding sources discussed in this chapter.

Individuals as Sources of Funds

A popular avenue for funding begins close to home. The entrepreneur invests his or her own funds and often persuades parents, relatives, and other acquaintances to supply capital. These investors typically make loans (debt capital) to the entrepreneur rather than sharing ownership (owner capital).

An entrepreneur who so desires can also appeal to individual investors beyond the circle of close friends and relatives by accepting both owner and creditor capital. If the entrepreneur uses owner capital, the ownership of the new company can be shared with many individuals.

Personal Savings   A financial plan that includes the entrepreneur's personal funds helps build confidence among potential investors. It is important, therefore, that the entrepreneur have some personal assets in the business. Indeed, the ownership equity for a beginning business typically comes from personal savings.

A recent study conducted by the National Federation of Independent

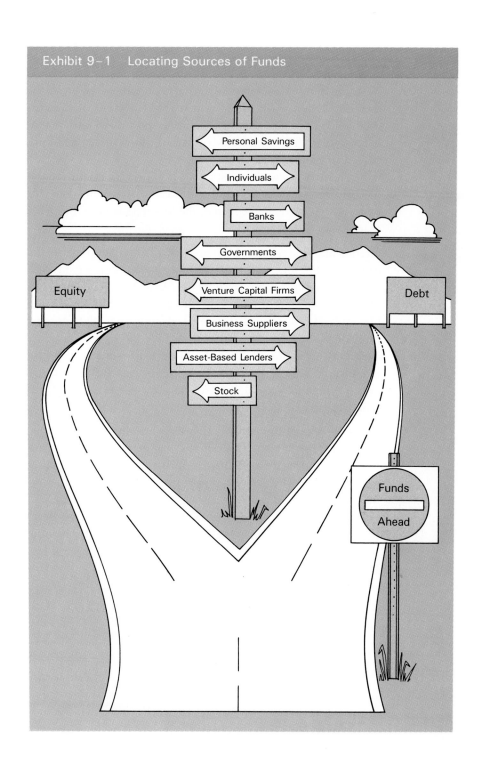

Exhibit 9–1   Locating Sources of Funds

Business found that personal savings is the most frequently used financing method.[4] Exhibit 9–2 shows that over 60 percent of the entrepreneurs in their study used personal savings when they purchased or started a business from scratch. The frequency of use of other financing sources is also displayed in Exhibit 9–2.

Personal savings invested in the business eliminate the requirement of fixed interest charges and a definite repayment date. If profits fail to materialize exactly as expected, the business is not strapped with an immediate drain on capital.

Friends and Relatives   At times, loans from friends or relatives may be the only available source of new small-business financing. Friends and relatives can often be a shortcut to financing. As a Dallas banker put it, "If Momma's got the money, get it from her. She loves you. She knows you're great, and her interest rate is low."[5] However, friends and relatives who provide business loans sometimes feel that they have the right to interfere in the management of the business. Hard business times may also strain the bonds of friendship. If relatives and friends are indeed the only available source, the entrepreneur has no alternative. However, the financial plan should provide for repayment as soon as is practical.

Other Individual Investors   Investors outside the immediate social circle of the entrepreneur—for example, lawyers, physicians, or others who wish to invest funds—are also sources of financing. But the small firm must compete with other investment opportunities for the resources of such financial backers. Local capitalists are not inclined to invest money in a risky small-business venture unless it bears the prospect of a significantly better rate of return than is available elsewhere. **Angels** is a term sometimes applied to these private investors. Consider Bob McCray, who ran his own company for 26 years until he sold out for $50 million:

> He's made four investments, each within 50 miles of his house. Like most angels, he invests anywhere from $10,000 to $100,000 in a deal, and usually brings other angels into the picture. In return, the average angel seeks 30% per annum return on any investment, fully aware that up to half the companies he backs will fold.[6]

The traditional path to locating angels is through contact with deal-makers such as business associates, accountants, and lawyers. A more recent approach involves formal angel networks or "clubs." One example is Venture Capital Network, Inc., in Durham, NH. This network receives proposals from potential investors and entrepreneurs and, for a fee, attempts to find

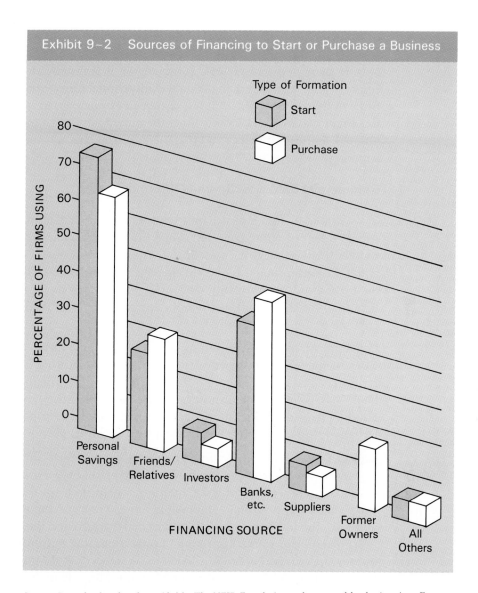

Exhibit 9–2   Sources of Financing to Start or Purchase a Business

Source: Data developed and provided by The NFIB Foundation and sponsored by the American Express Travel Related Services Company, Inc.

a match. These networks can increase the odds of finding an investor. However, "successful angels say it is best to try both formal and informal grapevines. . . ."[7]

Financing from informal, unorganized sources—informal capital financing—is the most significant source of equity funds for entrepreneurs outside their personal savings. For example, it is estimated that informal equity capital is greater than the total equity capital raised annually by small firms in the public market.[8] It has also been estimated that informal investors finance as many as "twenty times the number of firms financed by institutional venture capitalists and that the aggregate amount they must invest is perhaps twice as big."[9]

Commercial Banks as Sources of Funds

Although commercial banks tend to limit their lending to working-capital needs of going concerns, some initial capital does come from this source. If the small firm is adequately financed in terms of equity capital and if the entrepreneur is of good character, the commercial bank may lend on the basis of signature only. Of course, this is less likely for the beginning firm than for the established one. In any event, collateral and/or personal guarantees are often required.

Collateral Arrangements On some notes, the name of the co-signer provides adequate security to satisfy the bank. If the borrowing firm is a corporation, such an arrangement is often used to hold the principals personally liable. Assets such as life insurance policies, equipment, and real estate may also be pledged. Chattel mortgages and real estate mortgages are particularly useful in supporting longer term loan requests.

Line of Credit The entrepreneur should arrange for a line of credit in advance of actual need because banks extend credit only in situations about which they are well informed. Obtaining a loan on a spur-of-the-moment basis, therefore, is virtually impossible.[10] If the entrepreneur attempts this and fails, the business usually becomes bankrupt. When the line of credit is arranged prior to the beginning of operations, the entrepreneur should ask for the maximum amount likely to be needed as shown by projected business plans. And, when subsequently requesting a loan, he or she should be ready to demonstrate that the firm's current financial condition still provides an adequate basis for borrowing. In one recent survey of over 800 entrepreneurs which assessed satisfaction with commercial banks, the most satisfied group (56 percent of the respondents) had an average credit line of $30,000.[11]

Long-Term Loans Permanent working capital and fixed assets should be financed by ownership equity or long-term loans. It is often disastrous to finance a substantial portion of the fixed investment by short-term loans. This is because the debt matures before the fixed investment can be amortized from the income it yields.

Long-term borrowing actually is divided into intermediate-term and long-term. Intermediate-term loans mature in two to five years. Long-term loans mature after five years, and they are likely to be 10- to 25-year loans.

Selection of a Bank The varied services provided by banks make the choice of a bank important. For the typical small firm, the provision of checking-account facilities and the extension of short-term (and possibly long-term) loans are the two most important services of a bank. Normally loans are negotiated with the same bank in which the firm maintains its checking account. In addition, the firm may use the bank's safety deposit vault or its services in collecting notes or securing credit information. An experienced banker can also provide management advice, particularly in financial matters, to the beginning entrepreneur.

The factor of location limits the range of choices possible for the small firm. For reasons of convenience in making deposits and in conferring with the banker concerning loans and other matters, it is desirable that the bank be located in the same vicinity as the firm. Any bank is also interested in its home community and therefore tends to be sympathetic to the needs of business firms in the area. Except in very small communities, however, two or more local banks are available, thus permitting some freedom of choice.

Some banks actively seek small-business accounts. The Bank of New Haven is one example:

> Everything Bank of New Haven does is aimed at making small-business people feel that the bankers care about their business. Each account is handled by a senior officer. "No games, no gifts, no gimmicks . . . just banking," promised one newspaper ad.[12]

Lending policies of banks are not uniform. Some bankers are extremely conservative, while others are more venturesome in the risks they will accept. If a small firm's loan application is neither obviously strong nor obviously weak, its prospects for approval depend as much upon the bank as upon the borrowing firm. Such differences in willingness to lend have been clearly established by research studies, as well as by the practical experience of many business borrowers.

In addition to variations in their conservative or venturesome orientation, banks also differ in length of loans, interest rates, types of security required, and other such features. The bank's reputation for sticking with

SMALL BUSINESS IN ACTION
Strike One, Strike Two, Home Run

Putting together a financial package to purchase a business requires hard work and a commitment to keep on trying after one or two failures. Three entrepreneurs who can attest to this are Bob Phillips, Gary Edman, and Charles Stewart. They successfully purchased the Chambers Belt Company of Phoenix, AZ, where they had worked as corporate vice-presidents, but only after several refusals from bankers who they felt wanted too much or simply didn't want to take the risk. They needed between $4 and $5 million for the deal. Each of the three had no personal capital other than the equity they had in their homes. "We really didn't know what we were going to do," said Phillips. "We didn't know where to start, and we only had about two weeks to pull everything together."

As a team, they approached their first bank, which wouldn't consider the loan until the three could raise $500,000 of additional equity—beyond the value of their homes. They were also told that "it would be impossible to get a loan approved without going through several layers of committees." Strike one. . . .

At the next bank, they were also told they must have more personal equity. This bank recommended they seek another partner who could invest funds. Phillips remembers, "We found one person who wanted 51 percent of the company for investing less than $800,000." This was, of course, unacceptable. Strike two. . . .

Finally, the team located a small bank in Phoenix that was willing to talk to them. Fully expecting the same type of questions that were asked by the first two banks, they were surprised when the business loan director wanted to know their marketing plans, details about their backgrounds, and how well they got along with each other. Within a few days, the $4-million package was put together. Home run . . . !

Source: Reprinted with permission, *Inc.* Magazine, September, 1984. Copyright© 1984 by Goldhirsh Group, Inc., 38 Commercial Wharf, Boston, MA 02110.

a firm in times of adversity is also pertinent. Some banks are more flexible than others in assisting a firm that is experiencing temporary difficulty. The beginning small business certainly needs a banker who is willing to make reasonable concessions in times of stress.

Government-Sponsored Agencies as Source of Funds

There are several government programs that provide financing to small businesses. The availability of these funds varies with the economic condition of the nation and states. Sometimes entrepreneurs need to consider government-sponsored agencies because they can be a source of last resort.

Federal Government Sponsorship   The federal government has a long-standing reputation for helping new businesses get started. Some types of loans available through the Small Business Administration and Small Business Investment Companies are discussed in the next two sections.

Small Business Administration (SBA) Loans   There are two basic types of Small Business Administration business loans. Guaranty loans are made by private lenders and guaranteed up to 90 percent by the SBA. These loans are usually made through commercial banks. For loans exceeding $155,000, the guaranty percentage is 85 percent. A loan up to $500,000 can be guaranteed. To obtain a guaranty loan, the small business must submit the loan application to the lender—such as a bank—who, after initial review, will forward the loan application to the SBA. When approved, the lender closes the loan and disburses the funds.

The SBA also makes direct loans. This form of lending is available only after the small business has been unable to obtain a guaranty loan. This form of lending is much more limited and is usually for a maximum of $150,000.

Figure 9–2   SBA Logo

Courtesy Small Business Administration

The maximum maturity of SBA loans is 25 years. Interest rates are negotiated between the borrower and the lender but are subject to maximum rates set by the SBA. The SBA also requires assets to be pledged for security of the loan. Personal guaranties and liens on personal assets may also be required.

The general size standards imposed by the SBA are as follows:[13]

Manufacturing: Maximum number of employees may range from 500 to 1,500, depending on the type of product manufactured.

Wholesaling: Maximum number of employees may not exceed 100.

Services: Annual receipts may not exceed $3.5 to $14.5 million, depending on the industry.

Retailing: Annual receipts may not exceed $3.5 to $13.5 million, depending on the industry.

Construction: General construction annual receipts may not exceed $9.5 to $17 million, depending on the industry.

Special Trade Construction: Annual receipts may not exceed $7 million.

Agriculture: Annual receipts may not exceed $0.5 to $3.5 million, depending on the industry.

Small Business Investment Companies (SBICs)   In 1958, Congress passed the Small Business Investment Act, which provides for the establishment of privately owned capital banks whose purpose is to provide long-term and/ or equity capital to small businesses. SBICs are licensed and regulated by the Small Business Administration. They may obtain a substantial part of their capital from the SBA at attractive rates of interest.

Although SBICs may either lend funds or supply equity funds, the Act was intended to place a strong emphasis upon equity financing. The SBIC that provides equity financing may do so either by directly purchasing the small firm's stock or, quite commonly, by purchasing the small firm's convertible debentures (bonds), which may be converted into stock at the option of the SBIC.

Many SBICs have provided not only funds but also counsel and advice to the small firms they have served. It is not uncommon for an SBIC to have a representative on the board of directors of the borrowing firm. The SBIC does not normally wish to assume operating control of a business, but it is

SMALL BUSINESS IN ACTION
Worth the Wait

John Douglas

The wheels of government often move slowly, but the wait can be well worth it—especially when an entrepreneur needs startup capital. Such was the situation facing potential television station owner John Douglas. Way back in 1975, Douglas had completed his business plan describing his vision to start a UHF television station in San Jose, CA. But his government application for a license was delayed by the Federal Communications Commission in order to consider a competitor's application. Three years later, Douglas overcame this obstacle by buying out the competitor.

Next, Douglas turned to raising the startup capital. He put together a financing package that included equipment vendor financing, a bank loan, and a loan from the federal government's Minority Enterprise Small Businesses' Investment Companies (MESBICs). Finally, six years behind schedule, Douglas happily went on the air with KSTS-TV in May of 1981. After six years, Douglas sold his station for $17 million. Douglas's 1975 business plan had proven to be wrong in two areas: when the business would start and how much it would be worth after six years of operation. Douglas had forecast a net worth of only $15 million!

Source: Iris Lorenz-Fife, "Small Business Help from the Government." Reprinted with permission from *Entrepreneur* Magazine, November, 1988.
Photo Source: *Photo courtesy of Douglas Broadcasting*

often able to provide constructive advice, particularly of a financial nature. Some SBICs provide management counsel and advice on a fee basis, in addition to the unofficial counsel that accompanies the original investment or loan.

State and Local Government Sponsorships State and local governments are increasingly becoming involved in financing new businesses. The nature of state financing varies from state to state, but each program is geared to augment other sources of funding.

California was one of the first states to create a business and industrial development corporation to lend money to new businesses. Michigan has also been very active in establishing a state funding program. "We are trying to get private seed funds going by giving them a little government boost," according to Steve Rohde, of the Michigan Strategic Fund.[14]

Some large cities are also providing funds for new-business ventures. For example, Des Moines, IA, has established a Golden Circle Loan Guarantee Fund to guarantee bank loans to small companies. Loan amounts are available up to $250,000.[15]

Venture-Capital Firms as Sources of Funds

Technically speaking, anyone investing in a new-business venture is a venture capitalist. However, the term **venture capitalist** is usually associated with those corporations or partnerships which operate as investment groups. Each year more venture-capital groups are being organized. The investment philosophy of many venture-capital companies is shown by the following quote:

> Technology Venture Investors (TVI) is a privately held venture-capital partnership organized in 1980 to make equity investments in businesses having the potential for extraordinary increases in value over the long term. We are patient, capital-gains-oriented investors; i.e., we have the same overall objectives as the entrepreneurs in whom we invest.
>
> Our interests run the gamut from startups to secondary stock purchases in mature venture companies. Indeed, our initial TVI investments have ranged from "two guys and an idea" to profitable growth companies who are seeking their first significant outside capital as a means to obtain help and counsel in guiding further rapid growth.[16]

Some venture-capital companies provide management assistance to the young business. They also can assist in later financing needs. One such venture-capital firm is Onset, based in Palo Alto, CA. Started in 1984, it had $5 million in capital two years later. It is what is called a seed or incubator fund. Entrepreneurs have access to capital, management skills, and product-design advice, all from one source.[17]

Special resource directories are available for the entrepreneur seeking venture capital. One such book, compiled by Stanley Pratt, lists over 700 venture-capital sources plus several informative articles written by venture capitalists.[18]

Exhibit 9–3 displays part of *Venture* magazine's 1988 "Venture Capital 100." Notice the large number of business plans received by each firm and how relatively few seed startups and buyouts were actually financed. Mr. Joseph Horowitz, a general partner of U.S. Venture Partners (ranked number 21 in the Exhibit 9–3 listing) expressed the challenge of obtaining financing from his firm by saying:

Exhibit 9-3 A Profile of Venture Capitalist Firms

This Year's Rank	Last Year's Rank	Total 1987 Investments $ In Mil.	Total 1987 Investments No. of Deals	Firm Location	Paid-In Capital $ In Mil.	Seed/Startup Investments $ In Mil.	Seed/Startup Investments No. of Deals	Later-Stage Investments $ In Mil.	Later-Stage Investments No. of Deals	Follow-On Investments $ In Mil.	Follow-On Investments No. of Deals	Buyouts $ In Mil.	Buyouts No. of Deals	No. of Business Plans Received	No. of Over-the-transom Deals Funded
1	4	374.76	50	Warburg, Pincus Ventures Inc., New York	1,000.00	59.32	7	161.21	15	154.23	28	0.00	0	1,350	N.A.
2	1	290.59	57	Citicorp Venture Capital Ltd. (SBIC).* New York	323.60	2.34	3	15.65	5	62.90	36	209.70	13	2,000	0
3	3	216.40	52	First Chicago Venture Capital/First Capital Corp. of Chicago (SBIC),* Chicago	556.00	5.90	3	13.70	6	28.70	28	168.10	15	350	N.A.
4	2	140.16	57	TA Associates, Boston	523.66	17.70	6	39.60	12	43.03	35	39.83	4	6,500	1
5	7	107.89	62	Security Pacific Capital Corp./First SBIC of Calif.,* Costa Mesa, Calif.	257.00	8.72	9	25.19	14	3.36	12	70.62	27	2,000	N.A.
6	16	105.50	33	Welsh, Carson, Anderson & Stowe, New York	540.00	0.00	0	0.00	0	14.00	26	91.50	7	1,000	0
7	—	94.30	19	Morgan Capital Corp./Morgan Investment Corp. (SBIC),* New York	N.A.	0.00	0	63.60	14	0.00	0	30.70	5	200	1
8	8	94.00	46	Aeneas Venture Corp./Harvard Management Co. Inc.,[a] Boston	760.00	20.50	10	16.60	7	10.90	20	46.00	9	1,000	1
9	5	89.62	80	Hambrecht & Quist Venture Partners, San Francisco	600.00	8.19	9	13.74	8	65.10	62	2.58	1	1,000	0
10	6	79.23	49	Hillman Ventures Inc., Menlo Park, Calif.	N.A.	8.74	8	1.00	1	35.36	30	34.13	10	1,400	3
11	13	70.98	48	Chemical Venture Partners/Chemical Venture Capital Assoc. LP (SBIC),* New York	250.00	1.04	3	10.73	7	3.74	14	55.47	24	1,000	0
12	15	69.56	52	BancBoston Capital Inc./BancBoston Ventures Inc. (SBIC),* Boston	N.A.	2.23	5	0.00	0	12.81	20	54.53	27	1,550	1
13	10	64.11	250	Clinton Capital Corp. (SBIC)/Columbia Capital Corp. (MESBIC), New York	15.80	7.45	22	37.92	199	18.74	29	0.00	0	2,000	N.A.
14	21	51.33	81	New Enterprise Associates, Baltimore	386.00	24.80	26	7.03	11	19.50	44	0.00	0	1,000	2
15	9	49.57	22	Manufacturers Hanover Venture Capital Corp./M.H. Capital Investors Inc. (SBIC),* New York	138.00	0.96	1	3.05	2	0.55	2	45.01	17	300	0
16	27	46.60	12	Prudential Venture Capital Management Inc., New York	650.00	0.00	0	38.60	9	8.00	3	0.00	0	1,000	0
17	41	46.13	55	The Vista Group, New Canaan, Conn.	203.00	4.07	11	28.30	24	6.91	17	6.85	3	2,000	N.A.
18	28	42.67	215	Allied Capital Corp./Allied Investment Corp. (SBIC)/Allied Financial Corp. (MESBIC)/Allied Lending Corp. (SBLC), Washington	N.A.	20.66	162	11.95	36	7.14	14	2.91	3	5,000	40
19	37	41.28	46	Allstate Insurance Co. Venture Capital Division, Northbrook, Ill.	N.A.	11.50	12	1.11	1	19.39	30	9.27	3	1,250	1
20	40	38.82	50	Burr, Egan, Deleage & Co., Boston	195.00	3.65	4	14.34	9	16.63	34	4.20	3	1,200	4
21	19	38.10	39	U.S. Venture Partners, Menlo Park, Calif.	206.67	7.40	8	3.33	3	23.67	26	3.69	2	1,000	N.A.
22	38	36.60	30	T. Rowe Price Associates Inc., Baltimore	108.85	0.00	0	26.66	14	9.94	16	0.00	0	375	N.A.

[a] Subsidiary of Harvard University   *Bank-affiliated   N.A. Not available/not applicable

Source: "Venture Capital 100." Reprinted from the June, 1988, issue of *VENTURE, For Entrepreneurial Business Owners & Investors,* © 1988.

No idea gets far unless its promoter pursues it with obsession. If a person doesn't have a sense of urgency . . . then it's difficult to imagine it's going to get done at all. . . . You need people who understand the skills and discipline of running all facets of a business. . . . Ethics are absolutely essential. . . . [19]

Business Suppliers as Sources of Funds

Companies with which a new firm has business dealings also represent a source of funds for the firm's merchandise inventory and equipment. Thus, both wholesalers and equipment manufacturers/suppliers can be used to provide trade credit or equipment loans and leases.

Trade Credit Credit extended by suppliers is of unusual importance to the beginning entrepreneur. In fact, trade (or mercantile) credit is the small firm's most widely used source of short-term funds. Trade credit is of short duration—30 days being the customary credit period. Most commonly, this type of credit involves an unsecured, open-book account. The supplier (seller) sends merchandise to the purchasing firm. The buying firm then sets up an account payable for the amount of the purchase.

The amount of trade credit available to a new firm depends upon the type of business and the supplier's confidence in the firm. For example, shoe manufacturers provide business capital to retailers by granting extended payment dates on sales made at the start of a production season. The retailers, in turn, sell to their customers during the season and make the bulk of their payments to the manufacturers at or near the end of the season. If the retailer's rate of stock turnover is greater than the scheduled payment for the goods, cash from sales may be obtained even before paying for the shoes.

Suppliers are inclined to place greater confidence in a new firm and to extend credit more freely than bankers because of the former's interest in developing new customers. A bank might require financial statements and possibly a cash-flow budget. A supplier, on the other hand, may simply check the general credit standing of the purchaser and extend credit without requiring detailed financial statements. The supplier also tends to be less exacting than a banker or other lender in requiring strict observance of credit terms.

Equipment Loans Some small businesses—for example, restaurants—utilize equipment that may be purchased on an installment basis. A down payment of 25 to 35 percent is ordinarily required, and the contract period

SMALL BUSINESS IN ACTION
''Defogging'' the Financial Plan

The typical entrepreneur is so eager to get the business started that he or she will usually ignore funding requirements beyond initial startup needs. This lack of planning can obviously be fatal if initial sales are less than anticipated, but it can also result in delays when the successful venture begins expansion into additional product lines.

Todd Nesler

Consider the experiences of Todd G. Nesler, a successful entrepreneur operating his TN International, Inc., company in Brighton, MI. Nesler, a professional racer, invented a patented self-ventilating goggle for motocross. ''My goggles kept sweating and fogging up, and this would drive me crazy,'' he recalls. After unsuccessfully trying to sell his design to equipment manufacturers, he decided to start his own business.

After four years of effort seeking funding, he was finally able to sell a 33 percent equity deal to a retired president of a major department store. First-year sales were $200,000. Nesler's assessment of the first year was, ''We sold enough to put us on the map.''

Therefore, after only one year of operation, Nesler could see additional opportunities for expansion with other new products. But the initial financial planning had not addressed this need.

> Nesler's entrepreneurial imagination had gone into overdrive, but it became obvious that he couldn't give away a third of the company every time he wanted to launch a product. With his 1987 success under his belt, Nesler was ready to expand—and fast. He needed about $80,000 to start producing a new year-round goggle for auto and motorcycle racing, but there were, he says, ''no potential investors on the horizon.''

Eventually, Nesler turned to the tool shops that would manufacture the new products and worked out a financing arrangement with them. The toolmakers agreed to borrow the money to manufacture the tools necessary for them to produce the new products, and Nesler would pay the interest on the loan. Nesler would also pay the toolmakers a royalty per goggle sold up to a maximum limit.

Source: Debbie Galant, "Giving a Little to Get a Lot." Reprinted from the August, 1988, issue of *VENTURE, For Entrepreneurial Business Owners & Investors,* ©1988.
Photo Source: Courtesy of Todd Nesler

normally runs from three to five years. The equipment manufacturer or supplier typically extends credit on the basis of a **conditional sales contract** (or mortgage) on the equipment. During the loan period, the equipment cannot serve as collateral for a bank loan.

The small-business firm should be aware of the danger in contracting for so much equipment that it becomes impossible to meet installment payments. It is a mark of real management ability to recognize the limits in this type of borrowing.

Asset-Based Lending Companies as Sources of Funds

Asset-based lending is financing secured by working-capital assets. Usually, the assets used for security are accounts receivable or inventory. However, other assets such as equipment and real estate can be taken for loan collateral. Asset-based lending is a viable option for young, growing businesses that may be caught in a "cash-flow bind."

There are several categories of asset-based loans, the oldest of which is factoring. **Factoring** is an option that makes cash available to the business *before* accounts receivable payments are received from customers. Under this option another firm, known as a factor, purchases the accounts receivable for their full value. The factor charges a servicing fee, usually 1 percent of the value of the receivables, and an interest charge on the money advanced. The interest charge may range from 2 percent to 3 percent above the prime rate, which is the interest rate that commercial banks charge their most creditworthy customers.

Assume, for example, that the retailer sells products valued at $10,000 to a customer on 30-day credit terms. The $10,000 is listed as an account receivable on the retailer's books. Normally, the retailer would receive the $10,000 from the customer within 30 days. However, by selling the receivable to a factor, the retailer can receive $9,801 immediately. The $199 factoring cost includes the 1 percent servicing fee (1 percent of $10,000 = $100) and the interest charge (12 percent of $9,900 prorated for 30 days = $99). The 12 percent interest charge assumes a 9 percent prime rate plus a 3 percent factoring premium.

Of course, the proportion of cash sales to credit sales significantly affects the size of receivables, as do the terms of sale offered to credit customers. The size of the receivables is likewise affected by seasonality of sales and changes in business conditions, which influence promptness of payment by many customers.

SMALL BUSINESS IN ACTION
Asset-Based Lenders Keep Entrepreneur
in the Dough

Ken Rawlings

Kenneth Rawlings, founder of Otis Spunkmeyer, Inc., of San Leandro, CA, turned to an asset-based lender after banks would not give his cookie-dough-making business a needed loan. Expansion of the company's plant from an original 8,000 square feet to over 50,000 square feet had given the company a less desirable debt-to-equity ratio. "Banks use formula lending. If they look at debt-to-equity, they're not going to loan us money," remarked Rawlings, And he was correct.

So Rawlings turned to Commonwealth Financial Corporation in Oakland, CA—an asset-based lender. The president, William F. Plein, was very receptive to Rawlings' needs. "What interested me most is that they understood our position," commented Rawlings. "These people were mainly concerned about the value of our assets and the strength of our receivables."

Plein in turn liked what he saw. "Otis Spunkmeyer's sales were all invoiced to customers, making them easy to find, and most customers were paying their bills quickly . . . the inventories had a value we could dispose of quite easily in a distressed situation."

A deal was closed in less than 50 days. Spunkmeyer "would borrow $100,000 against inventories, $200,000 against equipment, and up to 80% of his receivables." Rawlings was back in the dough.

Source: Edmund L. Andrews, "The Cookie Dough Also Rises." Reprinted from the December, 1987, issue of *VENTURE, For Entrepreneurial Business Owners & Investors,* ©*1987.*
Photo Source: Otis Spunkmeyer, Inc.

Stock Sales as a Source of Funds

Another way to obtain capital is through the sale of stock to individual investors beyond the scope of one's immediate acquaintances. Periods of high interest rates turn entrepreneurs to this equity market. This is commonly called "going public."[20] Going public provides both benefits and drawbacks. These have been identified by one public accounting firm as:

Benefits
1. Future financing.
2. Merger and acquisition framework.
3. Enhanced corporate image.
4. Estate planning.

Drawbacks
1. Loss of control.
2. Sharing success potential.
3. Confidentiality.
4. Costs.
5. Periodic reporting requirements.[21]

Whether the owner is wise in declining to use outside equity financing depends upon the firm's long-range prospects. If there is an opportunity for substantial expansion on a continuing basis and if other sources are inadequate, the owner may decide logically to bring in other owners. Owning part of a larger business may be more profitable than owning all of a smaller business.

Private Placement   One way to sell capital stock is through **private placement.** This means that the firm's capital stock is sold to selected individuals, who are most likely to be the firm's employees, the owner's acquaintances, local residents, customers, and suppliers. Private sale of stock is difficult because the new firm is not known and has no ready market for its securities. However, the entrepreneur avoids many requirements of the securities laws when a stock sale is restricted to a private placement.

Public Sale   Some small firms make their stock available to the general public. These are typically the larger small-business firms. The reason often cited for a public sale is the need for additional working capital or, less frequently, for other capital needs.

In undertaking the public sale of stock, the small firm subjects itself to greater public regulation. There are state regulations pertaining to the public sale of securities, and the Securities and Exchange Commission (SEC) also exercises surveillance over such offerings.

Common stock may also be sold to underwriters, who guarantee the sale of securities. The compensation and fees paid to underwriters typically make the sale of securities in this manner expensive. The fees themselves may range from 10 percent to 30 percent, with 18 percent to 25 percent being typical. In addition, there are options and other fees that may run the actual costs higher. The reason for the high expense is, of course, the element of uncertainty and risk associated with public offerings of stock of small, relatively unknown firms.

Studies of public sale of stock by small firms reveal the fact that small companies frequently make financial arrangements that are not sound. Indeed, the lack of knowledge on the part of small-firm owners often leads to arrangements with brokers or securities dealers that are not in the best interest of the small firms.

The condition of the financial markets at any given time has a direct bearing on the prospects for the sale of capital stock. Entrepreneurs found the early years of the 1980s to be strong for new-venture stock sales. For example, consider this quote from a 1980 article: "Today's venture market is so hot that if you had a corner hot dog stand, you could take it public. There is a push to take companies public."[22] Market conditions do change, however, and therefore must be studied carefully. Consider the situation of MediVision, Inc., following the 500-point decline of the Dow in October, 1987.[23]

> The Boston-based operator of eye surgery centers was just a week away from filing a $30 million initial public offering (IPO). Rather than take a lower valuation in an IPO, MediVision rounded up ... private debt financing. ... "Debt money is no more expensive than the depletion we would have suffered had we gone public after October 19," explains Christopher Grant, Jr., chief financial officer of the four-year-old concern.

There are differences in opinion regarding initial public offerings (IPOs) for startup companies. Some market professionals say IPOs should be avoided for new businesses because they lack operating histories.[24] In any case, the new venture can rarely make a successful initial public offering. Most new startups are simply too small and unimpressive at the beginning to attract serious public interest.

Using Pro-Forma Financial Statements to Communicate Funding Needs

Once the entrepreneur has determined what capital is needed, how much is needed, and the most likely sources of these funds, she or he must structure the financial plan. A potential investor in the business wants something concrete to substantiate the entrepreneur's claims of profit and success. The financial plan section of the business plan can be used to show the capital needs and the sources for funding those needs.

Exhibit 9–4   Pro-Forma Income Statement for Maness, Inc.

	January	February	March	April	May	June	July	August	September	October	November	December
Sales	10000	15000	30000	50000	70000	75000	65000	80000	55000	40000	40000	55000
Cost of Goods Sold	7000	10500	21000	35000	49000	52500	45500	56000	38500	28000	28000	38500
Gross Margin	3000	4500	9000	15000	21000	22500	19500	24000	16500	12000	12000	16500
Operating Expenses: Selling and Adm.	20000	15000	12000	12000	12000	12000	12000	12000	12000	12000	12000	12000
Depreciation	500	500	500	500	500	500	500	500	500	500	500	500
Inventory Charge	35	53	105	175	245	263	228	280	193	140	140	193
Operating Income	-17535	-11053	-3605	2325	8255	9738	6773	11220	3808	-640	-640	3808
Interest Expense	0	0	61	218	434	647	730	638	673	510	282	219
Earnings Before Taxes	-17535	-11053	-3666	2107	7821	9090	6042	10582	3134	-1150	-922	3589
Taxes	-8768	-5526	-1833	1054	3911	4545	3021	5291	1567	-575	-461	1794
Net Income	-8768	-5526	-1833	1054	3911	4545	3021	5291	1567	-575	-461	1794

Source: Terry S. Maness, *Small-Business Management Using Lotus 1-2-3* (Cincinnati, OH: South-Western Publishing Co., 1991), Chapter 3.

Exhibit 9–5   Pro-Forma Balance Sheet for Maness, Inc.

	January	February	March	April	May	June	July	August	September	October	November	December
ASSETS:												
Cash	11733	4000	4000	4000	4000	4000	4000	4000	4000	4000	4000	4000
A/R	10000	20000	37500	65000	95000	110000	102500	112500	95000	67500	60000	75000
Inventory	10500	21000	35000	49000	52500	45500	56000	38500	28000	28000	38500	21000
Current	32233	45000	76500	118000	151500	159500	162500	155000	127000	99500	102500	100000
Fixed	20000	20000	20000	20000	20000	20000	20000	20000	20000	20000	20000	20000
(Acc. Depr.)	500	1000	1500	2000	2500	3000	3500	4000	4500	5000	5500	6000
Net fixed	19500	19000	18500	18000	17500	17000	16500	16000	15500	15000	14500	14000
Total Assets	51733	64000	95000	136000	169000	176500	179000	171000	142500	114500	117000	114000
LIABILITIES & EQUITY:												
LIABILITIES												
Trade Payables	10500	21000	35000	49000	52500	45500	56000	38500	28000	28000	38500	21000
S. T. Bank Notes	0	7294	26127	52073	77662	87617	76596	80805	61238	33813	26274	38980
Total Current	10500	28294	61127	101073	130162	133117	132596	119305	89238	61813	64774	59980
L. T. Debt	0	0	0	0	0	0	0	0	0	0	0	0
Total Liabilities	10500	28294	61127	101073	130162	133117	132596	119305	89238	61813	64774	59980
EQUITY												
Common	50000	50000	50000	50000	50000	50000	50000	50000	50000	50000	50000	50000
Retained Earnings	-8768	-14294	-16127	-15073	-11162	-6617	-3596	1695	3262	2687	2226	4020
Total Equity	41233	35706	33873	34927	38838	43383	46404	51695	53262	52687	52226	54020
Total Liab. & Equity	51733	64000	95000	136000	169000	176500	179000	171000	142500	114500	117000	114000

Source: Terry S. Maness, *Small-Business Management Using Lotus 1-2-3* (Cincinnati, OH: South-Western Publishing Co., 1991). Chapter 3.

Exhibit 9-6   Pro-Forma Cash Budget for Maness, Inc.

	January	February	March	April	May	June	July	August	September	October	November	December
Sales	10000	15000	30000	50000	70000	75000	65000	80000	55000	40000	40000	55000
Cash Receipts												
Cash Collections:												
Month of Sale	0	0	0	0	0	0	0	0	0	0	0	0
1 Month After	0	5000	7500	15000	25000	35000	37500	32500	40000	27500	20000	20000
2 Months After	0	0	5000	7500	15000	25000	35000	37500	32500	40000	27500	20000
3 Months After	0	0	0	0	0	0	0	0	0	0	0	0
Cash Receipts	0	5000	12500	22500	40000	60000	72500	70000	72500	67500	47500	40000
Cash Disbursements:												
Purchases	7000	10500	21000	35000	49000	52500	45500	56000	38500	28000	28000	38500
Selling and Adm.	20000	15000	12000	12000	12000	12000	12000	12000	12000	12000	12000	12000
Inventories	35	53	105	175	245	263	228	280	193	140	140	193
Interest Expense	0	0	61	218	434	647	730	638	673	510	282	219
Taxes	-8768	-5526	-1833	1054	3911	4545	3021	5291	1567	-575	-461	1794
Cap. Expenditure	0	0	0	0	0	0	0	0	0	0	0	0
Dividends	0	0	0	0	0	0	0	0	0	0	0	0
Cash Disbursement	18268	20026	31333	48446	65589	69955	61479	74209	52933	40075	39961	52706
Net Cash Flow	-18268	-15026	-18833	-25946	-25589	-9955	11021	-4209	19567	27425	7539	-12706
Beginning Cash Bal	30000	11733	4000	4000	4000	4000	4000	4000	4000	4000	4000	4000
Unadjusted Ending	11733	-3294	-14833	-21946	-21589	-5955	15021	-209	23567	31425	11539	-8706
Minimum Cash Bal	4000	4000	4000	4000	4000	4000	4000	4000	4000	4000	4000	4000
Borrow	0	7294	18833	25946	25589	9955	0	4209	0	0	0	12706
Repay	0	0	0	0	0	0	11021	0	19567	27425	7539	0
Ending Cash Bal	11733	4000	4000	4000	4000	4000	4000	4000	4000	4000	4000	4000

Source: Terry S. Maness, *Small-Business Management Using Lotus 1-2-3* (Cincinnati, OH: South-Western Publishing Co., 1991), Chapter 3.

you feel the greatest personal obstacles will be in obtaining funds for the new venture? Why?

YOU MAKE THE CALL

Situation 1

Tom Parum is a Yale business school graduate who has previously started several businesses—all of which have failed. These failures have left him with personal debt exceeding $80,000. However, Parum is not giving up. His latest idea is to produce and sell a high-quality tweezer.

Parum is understandably concerned about financing his new venture. He owes money to most of his family and friends, and his current cash resources are less than $1,000. Parum does have hope. His idea is to use credit cards to finance his startup. He currently owns a Visa card and feels certain he can obtain several more.

Source: Based on a story in Debbie Galant, "Don't Start Up Without It," *Venture,* Vol. 10, No. 7 (July, 1988), p. 87.

Questions

1. Do you think Mr. Parum will have much difficulty in obtaining credit with these cards? Why or why not?
2. What are the major limitations of using credit cards for financing a business? What are the advantages?
3. Does Mr. Parum have any better alternatives to obtaining funds for his new venture? If so, what are they?

Situation 2

Mary Watson has been a mother and housewife for most of her married life. She is a creative person and has always had a special interest in arts and crafts projects. For the last several years, she has created her own craft projects at home, traveling to occasional arts and crafts shows to sell her wares.

Recently, she has decided to open an arts and crafts shop to sell supplies and finished crafts. She lives in a small rural community and knows of other women who produce various craft items that could supplement her own products. Watson believes a shop could be successful if several artists would display their work. She knows of a vacant building in the local town that would be an ideal location.

Watson's husband has been supportive of her idea and has promised to help with obtaining financing. However, he does not have time or the patience to estimate the nature of the financial needs or how much is needed.

Questions

1. What do you see as the nature of Watson's financial requirements?
2. Is this venture too small to justify preparation of a financial plan? Why or why not?
3. Which sources of funds described in this chapter do you think would not be suitable for this venture? Explain your reasoning.

EXPERIENTIAL EXERCISES

1. Interview local small-business firms to determine how funds were obtained to start their businesses. Be sure you phrase questions so that they are not overly personal, and do not ask for specific dollar amounts. Report on your findings.
2. Interview a local banker to discuss the bank's lending policies for small-business loans. Ask the banker to comment on the importance of a business plan to the bank's decision to loan money to a small business. Report on your findings.
3. Review recent issues of *Entrepreneur, Inc.,* or *In Business,* and report on the financing arrangements of firms featured in these magazines.
4. Interview a stockbroker or investment analyst and discuss his or her views regarding the sale of capital stock by a small business. Report on your findings.

REFERENCES TO SMALL-BUSINESS PRACTICES

Asinof, Lynn. "Begging for Money: Young Firms Find Venture Capital Harder to Get." *The Wall Street Journal* (April 1, 1985), p. 25.

The experiences of three firms with venture capitalists are described.

Aspaklaria, Shelley. "Down But Not Out." *Venture,* Vol. 8, No. 3 (March, 1986), pp. 58–60.

Some of the financing efforts of entrepreneurs who have experienced business failures are presented in this article.

Finegan, Jay. "Are Bigger Banks Bad for Small Business?" *Inc.,* Vol. 9, No. 13 (December, 1987), pp. 161–166.

The experiences of several entrepreneurs as they sought funds from large banks are described in this article.

Juilland, Marie-Jeanne. "Alternatives to a Rich Uncle." *Venture,* Vol. 10, No. 5 (May, 1988), pp. 62–68.

> This article describes eleven alternatives for startup capital. Some of the sources mentioned provide funds directly to entrepreneurs while other sources act as intermediaries providing access to other investors.

Thompson, Roger. "How to Find Under $1 Million." *Nation's Business,* Vol. 75, No. 11 (November, 1987), pp. 14–20.

> This article discusses several ideas for cashing in on new financing opportunities. Addresses of several venture-capital organizations are included.

ENDNOTES

1. Current liabilities—debts that must be paid within the near future—represent the minus side of the working-capital equation. Accountants technically define working capital as the difference between current assets and current liabilities.

2. Sally O'Neil, "Financing 'Ivory Tower' Companies," *Venture,* Vol. 6, No. 2 (February, 1984), p. 86.

3. "100 Ideas for New Businesses," *Venture,* Vol. 10, No. 11 (November, 1988), p. 51.

4. *Small Business Primer,* a publication of the NFIB Foundation, 1988, p. 13.

5. Sanford L. Jacobs, "Aspiring Entrepreneurs Learn Intricacies of Going It Alone," *The Wall Street Journal* (March 23, 1981), p. 23.

6. William Bryant Logan, "Finding Your Angel," *Venture,* Vol. 8, No. 3 (March, 1986), p. 39.

7. Bradley Hitchings, "Finding Startups with Star Quality," *Business Week,* No. 2948 (May 26, 1986), p. 137.

8. *The State of Small Business: A Report of the President* (Washington: United States Government Printing Office, 1988), p. 156.

9. William E. Wetzel, Jr., "Informal Risk Capital Knowns and Unknowns," appearing in Donald L. Sexton and Raymond W. Smilor, Eds., *The Art and Science of Entrepreneurship,* (Cambridge, MA: Ballinger Publishing Co., 1986), p. 88.

10. An interesting discussion of creating a line of credit with a bank can be found in Jeffrey L. Seglin, "Court a Banker Now, Borrow Money Later," *Venture,* Vol. 10, No. 8 (August, 1988), pp. 65–68.

11. Nancy Madlin, "Can You Bank on Your Banker?" *Venture,* Vol. 7, No. 12 (December, 1985), p. 20.

12. Ashok Chandrasekhar, "New Haven Bank Targets Small Firms," *The Wall Street Journal* (September 21, 1984), p. 33.

13. *Business Loans from the SBA* (Washington: U.S. Small Business Administration, June, 1987).

14. Steven P. Galante, "States Cultivating Seed Funds to Spur Early Stage Ventures," *The Wall Street Journal* (January 12, 1987), p. 23.

15. Steven P. Galante, "Des Moines Has Its Own Way to Back Small-Business Loans," *The Wall Street Journal* (September 29, 1986), p. 37.

16. From a draft of a brochure for Technology Venture Investors provided by Burton J. McMurtry through personal correspondence.

17. Udayan Gupta, "California Venture Capitalists Take Earlier Role in Start-Ups," *The Wall Street Journal* (February 3, 1986), p. 14.

18. Stanley Pratt, Ed., *Guide to Venture Capital Sources,* 11th ed. (Wellesley Hills, MA: Capital Publishing Company, 1987).

19. Peter Waldman, "Taking a Flier," *The Wall Street Journal* (June 10, 1988), p. 10R.

20. An excellent discussion of going public is contained in James M. Johnson and Robert E. Miller, "Going Public: Information for Small Business," *Journal of Small Business Management,* Vol. 23, No. 4 (October, 1985), pp. 38–44.

21. A booklet entitled *Deciding to Go Public,* Ernst & Whinney, 1984.

22. Loretta Kuklinsky Huerta, "The Ups and Downs of Going Public," *Venture,* Vol. 2, No. 11 (November, 1980), p. 22.

23. Sallie Hofmeister, "Sailing on Stormy Seas," *Venture,* Vol. 10, No. 9 (September, 1988), p. 23.

24. Francine Schwadel, "Stock Market Pros Offer Some Tips on Judging Initial Public Offerings," *The Wall Street Journal* (February 21, 1986), p. 21.

10 CHOOSING A LEGAL FORM OF OWNERSHIP

Spotlight on Small Business

© 1984 Arnold Zann/BLACK STARR

The general partnership, one form of organization discussed in this chapter, has its weaknesses. One of these is illustrated by the experiences of Michael Valentine and Jim Jaeger, who once were students at the University of Cincinnati and later partners in manufacturing and selling radar detectors. Their Cincinnati Microwave company, which distributed products exclusively through the mail, was managed by Valentine, and Jaeger supervised production. Prosperity brought disagreements over strategy. Eventually, the partnership was terminated. Jaeger and Valentine parted with a great deal of money but extremely hard feelings. Says Jaeger, "I think if the company had plodded along and we were making reasonable salaries, we'd still be fast friends."

Source: Barry Stavro, "A License to Speed," *Forbes,* Vol. 134, No. 6 (September 10, 1984), pp. 94–102. Reproduced with permission.

Looking Ahead

Watch for the following important topics:
1. Forms of legal organization.
2. Characteristics of the proprietorship option.
3. Characteristics of various types of partnerships.
4. Characteristics of a regular corporation and a Subchapter S corporation.
5. Licensing requirements for a new business.
6. New terms and concepts:

proprietorship	corporation
partnership	legal entity
articles of partnership	Section 1244 stock
agency power	board of directors
limited partnership	corporation charter
general partner	S corporation
limited partners	C corporation

A number of legal and regulatory issues grow out of the initial business planning discussed in previous chapters. For example, in buying a business, reviewing a franchise contract, selecting a business location, leasing a building, or obtaining a loan, the entrepreneur needs a clear understanding of relevant laws and regulations. Therefore, consideration of business and tax laws needs to be a part of the entrepreneur's planning as she or he starts a business. In this chapter, we examine the major legal forms of business organization and the related issues of taxes and licensing.

Forms of Legal Organization

Various legal forms of organization are available to organize small businesses. Several options are, however, appropriate only for very specialized applications. We confine our attention here to the forms widely used by small business. These forms are shown in Exhibit 10–1. At one level we have the proprietorship, the partnership, and the corporation. Within the partnership form, there are two basic types—the general partnership and the limited partnership. Also, in addition to the regular corporation, there is a legal form known as a Subchapter S corporation.

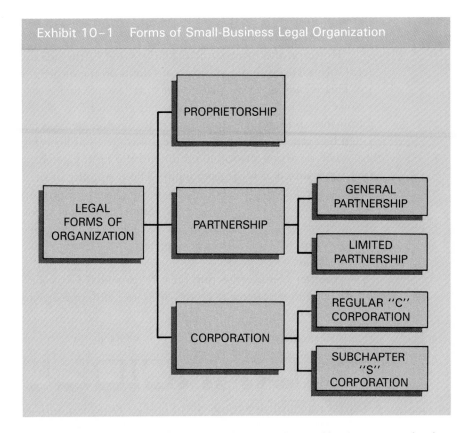

Exhibit 10-1 Forms of Small-Business Legal Organization

The proprietorship is the most popular form of business organization among small businesses. This popularity exists across all industries. There are, however, many small businesses operating as partnerships and as corporations, which suggests that there are circumstances that favor these forms. In the next several sections, we will examine each of the more popular legal forms of organization.

The Proprietorship Option

The **proprietorship** is a business owned and operated by one person. The individual proprietor has title to all business assets, subject to the claims of creditors. He or she receives all profits but must also assume all losses, bear all risks, and pay all debts of the business. The proprietorship is the simplest and cheapest way to start operation and is frequently the most appropriate form for a new business. In the proprietorship, the owner is free from interference by partners, shareholders, directors, and officers.

However, the proprietorship lacks some of the advantages of other legal forms. For example, there are no limits on the owner's personal liability. This means that the owner's personal assets outside the business can be taken by creditors if the business fails. In addition, proprietors are not employees and cannot receive some of the tax-free benefits customarily provided by corporations—for example, insurance and hospitalization plans.

The death of an owner terminates the legal existence of a business that is organized as a proprietorship. The possibility of the owner's death may cloud relationships between the business and its creditors and employees. The need for a will is suggested because the assets of the business less its liabilities belong to the heirs. In a will, the owner can give an executor the power to run the business for the heirs until they can take over or until it can be sold.

Another contingency that must be provided for is the possible incapacity of the proprietor. If he or she were badly hurt in an accident and

Figure 10-1   Cianciolo's Grocery: A Proprietorship

unconscious for an extended period, the business could be ruined. But the proprietor can guard against this by giving a legally competent person a power of attorney to carry on.

In some cases, the proprietorship option is virtually ruled out by the circumstances. For example, a high exposure to legal risks may require a legal form that provides greater protection against personal liability, as in the case of a manufacturer of potentially hazardous consumer products.

The Partnership Option

A **partnership** is a voluntary "association of two or more persons to carry on as co-owners a business for profit." Because of its voluntary nature, a partnership is quickly set up without many of the legal procedures involved in creating a corporation. A partnership pools the managerial talents and capital of those joining together as business partners.

Qualifications of Partners

Any person capable of contracting may legally become a business partner. Individuals may become partners without contributing to capital or sharing in the assets at the time of dissolution. Such persons are partners only as to management and profits.

Aside from legal aspects, however, partnership formation deserves serious study. A strong partnership requires partners who are honest, healthy, capable, and compatible.

One engineering and management consulting firm with four partners that has made a partnership work is Dynamic Systems. The founding partner in the business, David H. Bennet, expressed his views of the advantages of a partnership this way:

> You lower your own risk and required investment; you share the burden of decision-making and benefit from the strengths of each other; and you add one or more cooperative, hard-charging members to your team—members as highly motivated as yourself.
>
> A partnership is very much like a marriage. . . . As you work with each other, you will get to know each other's strengths, limitations, idiosyncrasies, goals, values, skills, and behavior patterns. How well these human characteristics complement or conflict with one another and how much they help or harm a young company are the often-hidden forces that heavily influence long-term success.[1]

Figure 10-2   Legal Firms Are Frequently Organized as Partnerships

Rights and Duties of Partners

Partners' rights and duties should be stated explicitly in the **articles of partnership.** These articles should be drawn up during the pre-operating period and should cover the following items as a minimum:

1. Date of formation of the partnership.
2. Names and addresses of all partners.
3. Statement of fact of partnership.
4. Statement of business purpose(s).
5. Duration of the business.
6. Name and location of business.
7. Amount invested by each partner.
8. Sharing ratio for profits and losses.
9. Partners' rights, if any, for withdrawals of funds for personal use.
10. Provision for accounting records and their accessibility to partners.
11. Specific duties of each partner.

12. Provision for dissolution and for sharing the net assets.
13. Restraint on partners' assumption of special obligations, such as endorsing the note of another.
14. Provision for protection of surviving partners, decedent's estate, etc.

Unless specified otherwise in the articles, a partner is generally recognized as having certain implicit rights. For example, partners share profits or losses equally if they have not agreed on a profit-and-loss sharing ratio.

In a partnership each partner has **agency power,** which means that a partner can bind all members of the firm. Good faith, together with reasonable care in the exercise of management duties, is required of all partners in a business. Since their relationship is fiduciary in character, a partner cannot compete in business and remain a partner. Nor can a partner use business information solely for personal gain.

Termination of a Partnership

Death, incapacity, or withdrawal of a partner ends a partnership and necessitates liquidation or reorganization of the business. Liquidation often results in substantial losses to all partners. It may be legally necessary, however, because a partnership is a close personal relationship of the parties that cannot be maintained against the will of any one of them.

This disadvantage may be partially overcome at the time a partnership is formed by stipulating in the articles of partnership that surviving partners can continue the business after buying the decedent's interest. This can be facilitated by having the partners carry mutual life insurance. Or the executor might act as a partner until the heirs become of age. In the latter case, the agreement should also provide for liquidation in the event of unprofitability or in the event of major disagreements with the executor as partner.

The Limited Partnership

A small business sometimes finds it desirable to use a special form of partnership called the **limited partnership.** This form consists of at least one general partner and one or more limited partners. The **general partner** remains personally liable for the debts of the business, but all **limited partners** have limited personal liability as long as they do not take an active role in the management of the partnership. In other words, limited partners risk only the capital which they invest in the business.[2] Because of this feature, an individual with substantial personal assets can invest money in a limited partnership without exposing his or her total personal estate to liability claims that might arise through activities of the business.

Historically, the limited partnership was frequently used to provide tax shelters to the limited partners. For example, the limited partnership might acquire a piece of undeveloped real estate, apartment houses, or commercial buildings. Most of the interest and other costs of the partnership were prorated to the limited partners, who reported them as tax-deductible expenditures on their personal income tax returns. (Of course, income from the property likewise had to be reported on the partners' tax returns, but the costs frequently exceeded revenue in the early going.) When the property was finally sold, it often produced a capital gain, which was taxed at a lower rate than ordinary income.

However, the Tax Reform Act of 1986 has restricted the tax advantages of investing as a limited partner. First, lower personal tax rates have effectively reduced the value of deductible losses against personal income—a feature that limited partnership ventures often provided in early operations. Second, capital gains are now taxed at the same rate as ordinary income. This reduces the incentive to use a limited partnership investment to build value in a firm for a later sale and conversion to a capital gain. Also, the Tax Reform Act has created a "passive" income category, which is defined as income that a taxpayer does not materially participate in producing. This usually includes limited partners! Passive income losses cannot be offset against regular "earned" income. Obviously, this reduces the value of limited partnership losses in offsetting other personal income.[3]

The Corporation Option

In the Dartmouth College Case of 1819, Chief Justice John Marshall of the United States Supreme Court defined a **corporation** as "an artificial being, invisible, intangible, and existing only in contemplation of the law." By these words the court recognized the corporation as a **legal entity.** This means that a corporation can sue and be sued, hold and sell property, and engage in business operations stipulated in the corporate charter.

The corporation is a creature of the state, being chartered under its laws. Its length of life is independent of its owners' (stockholders') lives. It is the corporation, and not its owners, that is liable for debts contracted by it. Its directors and officers serve as agents to bind the corporation.

Figure 10–3   A Corporate Office Scene

Photo courtesy of Xerox Corporation

Rights and Status of Stockholders

Ownership in a corporation is evidenced by stock certificates, each of which stipulates the number of shares held by the given stockholder. An ownership interest does not confer a legal right to act for the firm or to share in its management. It does evidence the right to receive dividends in proportion to stockholdings—but only when they are properly declared by the board of directors. And it typically carries the right to buy new shares, in proportion to stock already owned, before the new stock is offered for public sale.

In the initial organization of a corporation, the owner does well to consider a type of stock known as **Section 1244 stock.** By issuing stock pursuant to Section 1244 of the Internal Revenue Code, the stockholder is somewhat protected in case of failure. If the stock becomes worthless, the loss (up to $100,000 on a joint return) may be treated as an ordinary tax-deductible loss.

A stockholder casts one vote per share in stockholders' meetings. Thus, the stockholder indirectly participates in management by helping elect the directors. The **board of directors** is the governing body for corporate activity. It elects the firm's officers, who manage the enterprise with the help of management specialists. The directors also set or approve management policies, receive and consider reports on operating results from the officers, and declare dividends (if any).

The legal status of stockholders and managers is fundamental, of course, but it may be overemphasized. In the case of many small corporations, the owners may also be directors and managing officers. The person who owns most of the stock can control the business as effectively as if it were a proprietorship. In such a case, this person can name his or her spouse and an outsider as fellow directors. The directors can meet only when legally required to do so, and they can elect the principal owner as president and general manager of the firm. This is not to imply that it is good business practice to ignore a board of directors but simply to point out that direction and control may be exercised as forcefully by a majority owner in a small corporation as by an individual proprietor. The corporate form is thus applicable to individual and family-owned businesses.

Major stockholders must be concerned with their working relationships, as well as their legal relationships, with other owners, particularly with those who are active in the business. Cooperation among the entire owner-manager team of a new corporation is necessary for its survival. Legal technicalities are important, but they provide an inadequate basis for successful collaboration by those who are in reality "partners" in the enterprise.

Limited Liability of Stockholders

One of the advantages of the corporate form of organization is the limited liability of its owners. However, new small-business corporations often are in somewhat shaky financial circumstances during the early years of operation. As a result, the stockholders, few in number and active in management, frequently assume personal liability for the firm's debts by endorsing its notes.

Death or Withdrawal of Stockholders

Unlike the partnership, ownership in a corporation is readily transferable. Exchange of shares of stock is all that is required to convey an ownership interest to a different individual.

In a large corporation, stock is being exchanged constantly without noticeable effect upon the operations of the business. In a small firm, however, the change of owners, though legally just as simple, may produce numerous complications. To illustrate, suppose that two of the three equal shareholders in a business for one reason or another sold their stock to an outsider. The remaining stockholder would then be at the mercy of the outsider, who might decide to remove the former from any managerial post he or she happened to hold. In fact, a minority stockholder may be legally ousted from the board of directors and have no voice whatsoever in the management of the business.

The death of the majority stockholder could be equally unfortunate. An heir, executor, or purchaser of the stock might well insist upon direct control, with possible adverse effects for the other stockholders. To prevent problems of this nature from arising, legal arrangements should be made at the time of incorporation to provide for management continuity by surviving stockholders, as well as for fair treatment of heirs of a stockholder. As in the case of the partnership, mutual insurance may be carried to assure ability to buy out a decedent stockholder's interest. This arrangement would require an option for the corporation or surviving stockholders to: (1) purchase the decedent's stock ahead of outsiders, and (2) specify the method for determining the stock's price per share. A similar arrangement might be included to protect remaining stockholders if a given stockholder wished to retire from the business at any time.

The Corporate Charter

In most states, three or more persons are required to apply to the secretary of state for permission to incorporate. After preliminary steps, including required publicity and payment of the incorporation fee and initial franchise tax, the written application is approved by the secretary of state and becomes the corporation's charter. A **corporation charter** typically provides for the following:

1. Name of the company.
2. Formal statement of its formation.
3. Purposes and powers—that is, type of business.
4. Location of principal office in the state of incorporation.
5. Duration (perpetual existence, 50-year life and renewable charter, etc.).
6. Classes and preferences of classes of stock.

7. Number and par (or stated value) of shares of each class of stock authorized.
8. Voting privileges of each class of stock.
9. Names and addresses of incorporators and first year's directors.
10. Names and addresses of, and amounts subscribed by, each subscriber to capital stock.
11. Statement of limited liability of stockholders (required specifically by state law in many states).
12. Statement of alterations of directors' powers, if any, from the general corporation law of the state.

A corporation's charter should be brief, in accord with the law, and broad in the statement of the firm's powers. Details should be left to the bylaws. The charter application should be prepared by an attorney.

The Subchapter S Corporation

The name **S corporation** comes from Subchapter S of the Internal Revenue Code, which permits corporations to retain the limited-liability feature of regular corporations—now commonly called **"C corporations"**—while being taxed as partnerships. A corporation's desire to obtain S corporation status is motivated entirely by tax considerations. To make the election, a corporation must meet certain eligibility requirements. The major requirements are as follows:

- No more than 35 stockholders are allowed. Husband and wife count as one stockholder.
- All stockholders must be individuals or certain qualifying estates and trusts.
- There can be only one class of stock outstanding.
- It must be a domestic corporation.
- There can be no nonresident alien stockholders.
- The S corporation cannot own more than 79 percent of the stock of another corporation.

Once S status is elected by a corporation, it stops paying corporate income taxes and instead passes taxable income or loss to the stockholders. This allows stockholders to receive dividends from the corporation without double-taxation on the corporation's profit—once as corporate tax and again as personal tax.

SMALL BUSINESS IN ACTION
The Allure of the S Corporation

As personal income tax rates have fallen, the S corporation has become an even more attractive form of organization. It is attractive because the top corporate tax rate exceeds the top personal tax rate and because the S corporation can be taxed as a partnership. Following is a typical example of a small-business shift to a new form of organization:

> A construction-equipment-leasing company outside Washington, D.C., for instance, decided after 34 years as a regular corporation to switch to S status in 1987. "We couldn't afford not to make the change," says the treasurer. "Corporate rates are more stringent, and they are more likely to increase than individuals' rates."

Source: "When An S Corp May Spell Tax Relief," *Business Week*, No. 3105 (May 15, 1989), p. 160.

The 1986 Tax Reform Act has had considerable impact on the S corporation arrangement.[4] Therefore, a competent tax attorney should be consulted before making the S status election. A sample of the limitations of S corporation status under the new tax regulations are as follows:[5]

1. Except for certain exceptions, an S corporation must use the calendar year for tax reporting.
2. Only stockholder employees owning less than 5 percent of the S corporation can borrow from the corporation's pension and profit-sharing plans.
3. Medical-plan premiums paid by the corporation and other fringe benefits received by stockholder employees are taxable income.
4. An S corporation may be required to pay corporate tax if its passive income exceeds 25 percent of gross receipts.

Despite these and other limitations, it appears that S corporations will remain desirable in many cases primarily because of potential tax advantages.

The four major legal forms of organization are contrasted in Exhibit 10-2 according to the appropriate tax treatment of selected items. Notice the similarity between tax treatment for partnerships and S corporations. Also notice the contrasting treatment between regular corporations and proprietorships.

Exhibit 10–2   Comparison of Tax Treatments Among Various Forms of Doing Business

Treatment of Income and Expenses	Proprietorship	Partnership	Regular Corporation	S Corporation
Character of Income and Deductions	Tax attributes are reflected in the individual's return and, as such, maintain their character.	Conduit—no tax to partnership.	Taxed at corporate level.	Conduit—could be passive income. Potential corporate built-in or capital gains taxes.
Capital Gain	Capital gains are taxed as ordinary income.	Conduit—taxed as ordinary income at the partner level.	The 28% alternative tax rate for net capital gains is repealed for taxable years when the new corporate tax rates are fully effective.	Possible corporate capital gains or built-in gains tax; conduit—taxed as ordinary income at the shareholder level.
Capital Loss	Limited to $3,000 per year; excess is carried forward indefinitely. Losses offset ordinary income on a dollar-for-dollar basis.	Conduit—limitations apply at the partner level.	Carry back three years and carry over five years as short-term capital loss offsetting only capital gains.	Conduit—limitations apply at the shareholder level.
Section 1231 Gains and Losses	Taxed at individual level, combined with other Section 1231 gains or losses of individual; net gains are capital; net losses are ordinary.	Conduit—limitations apply at the partner level; taxed as ordinary income.	Taxable or deductible at the corporate level.	Possible corporate capital gains or built-in gains tax; conduit—limitations apply at the shareholder level; taxed as ordinary income.

Exhibit 10-2 *(Continued)*

Treatment of Income and Expenses	Proprietorship	Partnership	Regular Corporation	S Corporation
Expensing of Depreciable Business Assets	Election to expense is allowed up to $10,000 a year. Expensing allowance phases out dollar for dollar when the cost of qualified property placed in service during the taxable year is between $200,000 and $210,000.	Same	Same	Same
Organization Costs	Not amortizable.	Amortizable over 60 months. Conduit— limitations apply at the partner level.	Amortizable over 60 months. Deduction is limited to 10% of modified taxable income. Unused portion may be carried forward five years.	Amortizable over 60 months. Conduit— limitations apply at the shareholder level.
Charitable Contributions	Subject to limits for individual. Generally, gifts to public charity: cash, 50% of adjusted gross income (AGI); appreciated property, 30% of AGI. Other limitations for specific items contributed. Unused portion may be			

(Continued)

Exhibit 10–2 *(Continued)*

Treatment of Income and Expenses	Proprietorship	Partnership	Regular Corporation	S Corporation
	carried forward five years.			
Dividends Received	Treated as ordinary income; no exclusion or deduction. Treated as portfolio income.	Treated as portfolio income.	80% to 100% dividend-received deduction. Special rules on portfolio income for closely held corporations.	Treated as portfolio income.
Alternative Minimum Tax (AMT)	For individuals, the alternative minimum tax rate is 21%. The exemption amount is determined by filing status and alternative minimum taxable income.	Conduit for preference items. The alternative minimum tax is calculated at the partner level.	For corporate taxpayers, the alternative minimum tax rate is 20%. The alternative tax is imposed on alternative minimum taxable income in excess of $40,000, but only if the amount is more than the regular corporate tax. Portion of AMT tax may be applied as a credit against future regular tax.	Conduit for preference items. The alternative minimum tax is calculated at the shareholder level.
Tax Preferences	Depletion, accelerated depreciation, excess drilling costs, passive losses, net	Conduit— preference items separately stated and reflected in the calcula-	Book-tax difference, depletion, accelerated depreciation, net unrealized	Conduit— preference items separately stated and reflected in the calculation of

Exhibit 10–2 *(Continued)*

Treatment of Income and Expenses	Proprietorship	Partnership	Regular Corporation	S Corporation
	unrealized gain on certain charitable contributions, among others.	tion of AMT at the partner level. No book-tax preference.	gain on certain charitable contributions, among others.	AMT at the partner level. No book-tax preference.
Accounting Methods	Cash or accrual.	Cash or accrual; but partnership with C corporation partners with more than $5 million gross receipts and tax-shelter partnerships cannot use cash method.	Accrual, but cash available to C corporations with $5 million or less gross receipts.	Cash or accrual.

Source: Seymour Jones, M. Bruce Cohen, and Victor V. Coppola, *The Coopers & Lybrand Guide to Growing Your Business,* pp. 114–116. Copyright © 1988, John Wiley & Sons. Reprinted by permission of John Wiley & Sons, Inc.

Licenses for Startup Businesses

Most new businesses will not be required to obtain any type of federal license or permit. However, in most cases a number of local and state permits must be issued. The number and types of permits vary from state to state. Also, exact licensing requirements depend on the specific legal form of business being used. For example, see Exhibit 10–3, which summarizes the state licensing requirements of one state and indicates which form of business must comply with each requirement. Fortunately, most licensing fees are small.

Exhibit 10–3   Checklist of Texas Permit and Licensing Requirements by Type of Organization

	Proprietorship	Partnership	Corporation
State License	X	X	X
Franchise Tax Report			X
Sales Tax Permit	X	X	X
Sales Tax Bond	X	X	X
Resale Certificate	X	X	X
Exemption Certificate	X	X	X
Local Property Tax Forms	X	X	X
Subject to Oil and Gas Taxes	X	X	X
Subject to Well Service Taxes	X	X	X
Subject to Mineral Taxes	X	X	X
Unemployment Insurance Taxes	X	X	X
Assumed Name Certificate			
County Level	X	X	
State Level			X
Articles of Limited Partnership		X	
Articles of Incorporation			X
Articles of Amendment			X
Restated Articles of Incorporation			X
Articles of Dissolution			X
Certificate of Authority (for foreign corporations)			X
Antitrust Affidavit (for foreign corporations)			X

Source: Michael D. Jenkins and Donald L. Sexton, *Starting and Operating a Business in Texas* (Milpitas, CA: Oasis Press, 1987), pp. 11–18.

Looking Back

1. Various legal forms of organization are available to organize small businesses—the proprietorship, the partnership, and the corporation.
2. In a proprietorship the owner receives all profits and bears all losses. The principal limitation of this form is the owner's unlimited liability.

3. A general partnership should be established on the basis of a partnership agreement. Partners can individually commit the partnership to binding contracts. In a limited partnership, general partners are personally liable for the debts of the business, while limited partners have limited personal liability as long as they do not take an active role in managing the business.

4. Corporations are particularly attractive because of their limited-liability feature. The fact that ownership is easily transferable makes them well suited for combining the capital of numerous owners. S corporations are corporations that enjoy a special tax status that permits them to avoid corporate tax by passing taxable gains and losses to individual stockholders.

5. Compliance with local and state licensing requirements is extremely important to the small business.

DISCUSSION QUESTIONS

1. Discuss the relative merits of the three major legal forms of organization.

2. Does the concept of limited liability apply to a proprietorship? Why or why not?

3. How does the death of the owner of a proprietorship affect the legal operation of the business?

4. Suppose a partnership is set up and operated without formal articles of partnership. What problems might arise? Explain.

5. What is the purpose of the articles of partnership?

6. Explain why the agency status of business partners is of great importance.

7. How does the death of an owner in a partnership affect the legal operation of the business?

8. What is a limited partnership, and how does it differ from a general partnership?

9. How has recent tax law revision restricted the tax advantages of investing as a limited partner?

10. How does the death of an owner affect the legal operation of a corporation?

11. What is typically covered in a corporation charter?

12. What is a Subchapter S corporation, and what is its advantage?

13. What has been the impact of the 1986 Tax Reform Act on S corporation election?

14. What are some of the typical licenses required of a startup business?
15. Evaluate the three major forms of organization from the standpoint of management control by the owner and the sharing of the firm's profits.

YOU MAKE THE CALL

Situation 1

Ted Green and Mark Stroder became close friends as 16-year-old teenagers while both worked part time for Green's dad in his automotive parts store. After high school, Green went to college and Stroder joined the National Guard Reserve and devoted his efforts to supporting his weekend auto racing habit. Green continued his association with the automotive parts store by buying and managing two of his dad's stores.

In 1989, Green conceived the idea of starting a new business that would rebuild automobile starters, and he asked Stroder to be his partner in the venture. Stroder was somewhat concerned about working with Green because their personalities were so different. Green had been described as "outgoing and enthusiastic" while Stroder was "reserved and skeptical." However, Stroder was out of work at the time, and he agreed to the offer. He set up a small shop behind one of Green's automotive parts stores. Stroder did all the work; Green supplied the cash.

The "partners" realized the immediate need to decide on a legal form of organization. They had agreed to name the business "STARTOVER."

Questions

1. How relevant are the individual personalities to the success of this entrepreneurial team? Do you think Green and Stroder have a chance to survive their "partnership"? Why or why not?
2. Do you think being the same age is an advantage or disadvantage to this team?
3. Which legal form of organization would you propose for STARTOVER? Why?
4. If Stroder and Green decide to incorporate, would they qualify as an S corporation? If so, would you recommend this option? Why or why not?

Situation 2

Mark and Trey Denton were the only two brothers of a rural farm family in the southern United States. Both brothers had worked on the 500-acre family farm until they went off to college. After completing their formal education, both began teaching at a four-year university approximately 40 miles from the farm.

After two years of city life, the younger brother, Trey, moved with his wife and children to live on the farm and began commuting to his university job. A few years later, the older brother, Mark, moved back to the family farm also and likewise continued with his teaching profession.

Mark and Trey decided to take over the farm operation from their parents, who both had minor health problems.

Questions

1. What form of legal organization would you recommend to the Denton brothers? Why?
2. Should they consider S corporation status? Why or why not?
3. Will the issue of passive income be important to the legal organization decision?

EXPERIENTIAL EXERCISES

1. Interview an attorney whose practice includes small-business clients. Inquire about the legal considerations in choosing the form of organization for a new business. Report your findings to the class.
2. Interview a tax professor or lawyer. Inquire about the tax considerations in choosing the form of organization. Report your findings to the class.
3. Interview the owners of a local partnership business. Inquire about their partnership agreements. Report your findings to the class.
4. Interview the owner of a small business in your community. If possible, select one that has recently opened for business. Inquire about what licenses and permits the owner was required to obtain. Report your findings to the class.

REFERENCES TO SMALL-BUSINESS PRACTICES

Andrews, Edmund L. "I'll Take a Limited Partnership with a Twist, Please," *Venture*, Vol. 10, No. 5 (May, 1988), pp. 70–72.
  The experiences of a young business in need of additional funding are described in this article. The creative financing plan is explained along with its disadvantages.
Bahls, Steven C. and Bahls, Jane Easter. "When a Partner Retires," *In Business*, Vol. 19, No. 4 (July–August, 1988), pp. 51–53.

This article covers many of the key issues that should be included in a formal partnership agreement.

Starr, Samuel P. and Dunn, William J. "S Corporations: Knowing When to Say When," *Journal of Accountancy,* Vol. 168, No. 1 (July, 1989), pp. 46–52.

This article explains many of the advantages and limitations of S corporation status for small businesses.

Wylie, Peter and Grothe, Mardy. "Breaking Up Is Hard to Do," *Nation's Business,* Vol. 76, No. 7 (July, 1988), pp. 24–25.

The dissolution of a business partnership is compared to a married couple going through a divorce. Differences and similarities in the processes are discussed in a creative and readable format.

ENDNOTES

1. David H. Bennet, "Making a Partnership Work," *Nations' Business,* Vol. 72, No. 5 (May, 1984), p. 66.

2. Even when a deal goes bad the limited partner can take some positive actions. See, for example, Richard Greene, "All Men Are Not Created Equal," *Forbes,* Vol. 133, No. 6 (March 12, 1984), p. 158.

3. For additional discussion of the impact of the Tax Reform Act of 1986 on limited partnerships, see Lindsay K. Wyatt and Elizabeth S. Styers, *Financial Planning Under the New Rules* (Longman Financial Services Institute, Inc., 1987), Chapter 11.

4. An excellent article that discusses this impact is Kent Royalty, Robert Calhoun, Radie Bunn, and Wayne Wells, "The Impact of Tax Reform on the Choice of Small Business Legal Form," *Journal of Small Business Management,* Vol. 26, No. 1 (January, 1988), pp. 9–17.

5. Based on discussions in Ted S. Frost, "Opting for 'S' Status," *D & B Reports* (November/December, 1987), p. 6.

PART

IV

SMALL BUSINESS MARKETING

11 PRODUCTS, SERVICES, AND CUSTOMER BEHAVIOR

Spotlight on Small Business

©C. Thatcher 1988

Most new businesses are launched with a single product or service. When successful, such ventures typically attract competitors. Too often, entrepreneurs are complacent and slow to react to this competition. Others are wiser and embark on a diversification strategy before sales of the initial product begin to level off.

Such was the strategy used by Kevin Howe, president of DacSoftware, based in Dallas, TX. Its computer software, named Dac-Easy, was launched in 1985. The integrated accounting package was offered on one floppy disk and priced at an unbelievably low $50.00. It was an immediate success! But

Howe did not rest easy. He knew the importance of "not falling in love with success."

> "I had always been conscious of the perils of being a one-track pony," he says. "With the creation of Dac-Easy, the company had produced its one death-defying act. So the question was what do we do next? How do we keep the momentum going?"

The answer was diversification. His strategy was to keep current customers coming back rather than relying entirely on new customers. Howe now estimates that 40 percent of DacSoftware's revenues are from repeat customers. Dac-Easy add-ons have been introduced each year.

Howe is pleased with his early diversification strategy and points to an array of products and more than 300,000 customers and says, "I think I'll be the last vendor in my industry to be hurt in a recession."

Source: Adapted from Karen Berney, "If At First You Do Succeed," *Nation's Business*, Vol. 76, No. 6 (June, 1988), pp. 14–20. Copyright 1988, U.S. Chamber of Commerce.

Looking Ahead

Watch for the following important topics:
1. Customer service management.
2. Concepts of consumer behavior.
3. Product strategies for small business.
4. Tools for strategy management.
5. Completing the total bundle of satisfaction.
6. New terms and concepts:

needs	cognitive dissonance
perception	product
perceptual categorization	product mix
motivations	product line
attitude	product item
culture	product mix consistency
social class	product strategy
reference groups	brand
opinion leader	warranty

In Chapter 7, The Marketing Plan, we examined several marketing considerations that have a direct impact on generating sales—developing a consumer orientation, collecting marketing information, and determining market potential. We also presented an outline of the components of a marketing plan—product/service plans, pricing plans, promotional plans, and distribution plans. Part IV of this book develops each of these marketing plan components more fully.

In this chapter, we will examine product/service strategies and related issues. It is important to remember that all components of a marketing strategy are interrelated. Therefore, they should be developed concurrently.

Customer Service Management

In our earlier discussion of the marketing plan, in Chapter 7, we introduced several important points regarding customer service and customer satisfaction. Specifically, we made the following three statements:

1. Customer satisfaction is not a means to achieve a certain goal; rather, it *is* the goal.
2. Customer service can provide a competitive edge.
3. Small firms are potentially in a much better position to achieve customer satisfaction than are big businesses.

These three statements, particularly the last one, suggest that *all* small-business managers should incorporate customer service management into their firms. A small business that ignores customer service is definitely jeopardizing its chances for success!

Importance of Customer Service

The use of outstanding customer service to earn customer loyalty is not new. Stanley Marcus, of Dallas-based Neiman-Marcus, is famous for his commitment to customer service. More recently, Stew Leonard has received media attention for his motto "The customer is always right," which is chiseled in a piece of granite outside the entrance to his Norwalk, CT, dairy products store. What is new to small businesses is the wide recognition that customer service is smart business. Consider these statistics:

- Attracting a new customer costs five times as much as keeping an old one . . .
- An estimated 65 percent of the average company's business comes from its present customers . . .
- 91 percent of dissatisfied customers will never again buy from the offending company and will tell at least nine other people about their bad experiences. . . . [1]

To be effective, customer service must be genuine, ethical, and not a gimmick. The family-owned business of Jack Miller is a good example of true customer service. Miller's Chicago office supply mail-order firm is operated with a total commitment to frankness and openness with customers. Miller says, "When you're running a business, there are certain basic things

---

SMALL BUSINESS IN ACTION
Consumer Service Supports Market Niche

Small firms should be constantly searching for marketing techniques to ward off competition. Increasing customer service is one approach that usually works.

Consider the situation facing Donald L. Beaver, Jr., and his company, New Pig Corp. of Tipton, PA. Beaver was faced with the challenge of competing with companies that had copied his product—a tubular sock filled with ground-up centers of corncobs. The product, named "Pig," absorbs oil on factory floors. Beaver chose customer service as the means to fight competition. Some of his services, which are unique in his industry, include:

- Three-day delivery.
- Complete satisfaction guarantee.
- Emergency delivery system.
- Catalog ordering.

Extensive customer service such as that offered by Beaver does not come cheaply. Approximately one-third of his company's employees are involved in servicing customers. But his firm remains committed to customer service. "We discovered a neat exchange in the marketplace," Beaver says. "When you're really service-oriented, it doesn't matter how big or slick the competition is. You'll always find a niche."

Source: Rachel Meltzer, "Fending Off the Copycats." Reprinted From the February, 1989, issue of *VENTURE, For Entrepreneurial Business Owners & Investors,* © 1989.

that are true and that work. Being totally honest and open with your customers, and treating them extremely well, is one. I don't understand how
anyone could think of [ethics and customer service] separately."[2]

Evaluating Customer Service

The delivery of customer service begins with an understanding of customer attitudes. Typically, a gap is found between these attitudes and the
level of service being offered in any given industry. Most customers of auto
repair shops, restaurants, retail stores, and other businesses recognize weaknesses in the service they receive from these firms. This, indeed, presents
an opportunity to the small firm that is able to excel in its management of
customer service.[3]

The Grubb brothers, who own a construction repair firm in San Francisco, simply asked customers what they saw as the worst features of their
competitors. They found that customers did not like the old, beat-up construction trucks that were parked in customers' lots during a construction
job. Customers also complained of workers with bad manners who tracked
dirt across the clients' carpets. The brothers responded with a company that
had new trucks and workmen with jackets and ties![4]

Often, there are problems with the delivery of good service. Employees do not always share the owner's dedication to service. Therefore, employee attitudes must be changed before customers can receive maximum
service. Scott Hanson recognized this in his management of Hanson Galleries
in Sausalito, CA. He works with his salespeople—called "art consultants"—
to educate them in the difference between "selling a customer and servicing
a client." And it has worked. The best consultants make nearly $1 million
in sales each year.[5]

Problems with customer service are recognized in a number of ways.
Probably the most common is through customer complaints. Every firm
strives to eliminate customer complaints. When they occur, however, they
should be analyzed carefully to discover possible weaknesses in customer
service. Customer hotlines should be available whenever possible.

Managers can also learn about customer service problems through
personal observations and undercover techniques. A manager can evaluate
service by talking directly to customers or by playing that role anony-
mously—for example, by a telephone call to one's own business. Also, there

are professional undercover shopping services that play the customer role for business clients and make service evaluations.[6] Some restaurants and motels invite feedback on customer service by providing comment cards to customers.

Reaping the Benefits of Customer Service

The old adage "Actions speak louder than words" is nowhere truer than it is regarding customer service. Therefore, let the following real-world examples speak in support of customer service:

- Draegner's [is] a grocery store in Menlo Park, Calif. . . . with a growing base of customers willing to pay extra for top service. Draegner packs box lunches for customers on their way to events . . . it sells prepared meals that customers can pick up after work and reheat at home. A regular customer . . . can charge the cost of groceries. The store enjoyed a 57 percent growth in sales over the past three years by combining the convenience of a modern supermarket with old-fashioned service.[7]
- Norrell Temporary Services, in Atlanta, promises clients that they do not have to pay if they are disappointed with the performance of Norrell's temporary services. "Sales growth in the last five years has out-stripped the average rate of growth for the temporary-employment industry as a whole."[8]
- Mini Maid Services, with franchises in 24 states, . . . reports that every customer is contacted the day after receiving service, and all comments, whether favorable or unfavorable, are recorded. This information is fed back to the employee who performed the service.[9]
- A major problem area . . . in 800-Flowers was the lack of repeat customers. . . . excellent customer service and a toll-free order hotline is the arrangement . . . to keep customers calling back. If a customer is dissatisfied—for any reason—800-Flowers will replace the order or refund the customer's money. . . . Today, 800-Flowers is a thriving company with $10 million in revenue.[10]
- Upon purchasing a car from Sewell Village [Dallas, TX], each customer is assigned a personal service adviser whose sole job is to take the hassle out of maintaining and repairing his customers' automobiles. . . . The relationship between Sewell Village Cadillac owner and service adviser extends over the life of the car and more closely resembles the bond between patient and therapist than it does your basic car owner/mechanic arrangement. . . . "Earl [Sewell] has paid the price you have to pay to give high-quality service to the customer. And he profits by it. . . ."[11]

As you study the remainder of this chapter, remember that every marketing decision begins and ends with the customer!

Concepts of Consumer Behavior

The small-business manager needs to understand certain realities of consumer behavior. This is, however, a difficult challenge considering the complexity of the subject matter. Therefore, we offer a simplified presentation isolating only the most essential concepts for the small-business situation. The most successful small-business manager of the future may well be the best student of consumer behavior. Exhibit 11–1 contains our model of consumer behavior structured around three major topics: psychological concepts, sociological concepts, and decision-making processes.

Psychological Concepts

Psychological factors may be labeled as hypothetical because they cannot be seen or touched. By process of inference, however, several factors have been identified. The four factors that have the greatest relevance to small business are needs, perceptions, motivations, and attitudes.

Needs We define **needs** as the basic seeds of (and the starting point for) all behavior. Without needs, there would be no behavior. There are many lists of consumer needs, but the major points we wish to convey do not require an extensive listing.[12] Needs are either physiological, social, psychological, or spiritual.

Needs are never completely satisfied. This favorable characteristic of needs assures the continued existence of business. A complicating characteristic of needs is the way they function together in generating behavior. In other words, various "seeds" (remember the definition) can blossom together. This makes it more difficult to understand which need is being satisfied by a specific product or service. Nevertheless, a careful assessment of the need–behavior connection can be very helpful in developing marketing strategy. For example, many food products in supermarkets are purchased by consumers to satisfy physiological needs. But food is also selected in status restaurants to satisfy social and/or psychological needs. A need-based strategy would add a different flavor to the marketing strategy in each of these two situations.

Perception Our second psychological factor in Exhibit 11–1 is perception. **Perception** describes those individual processes which ultimately give meaning to the stimuli that confront consumers. The "meaning" is not easily

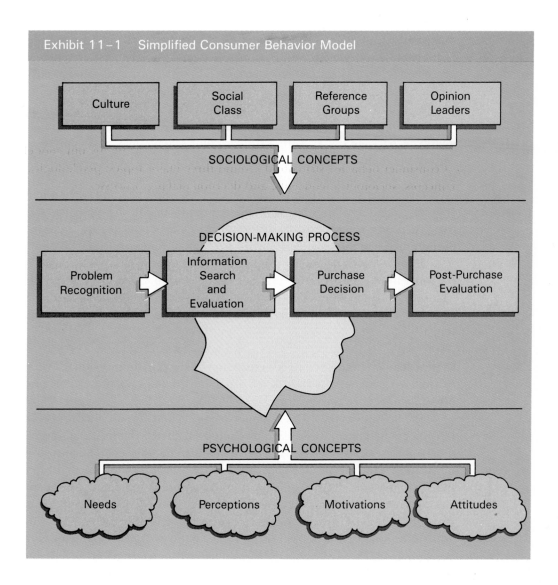

Exhibit 11–1   Simplified Consumer Behavior Model

understood, however. It may be severely distorted or entirely blocked. Perception by customers can screen a small firm's marketing effort and make it ineffective.

Perception is a two-sided coin. It depends on the characteristics of both the stimulus and the perceiver. For example, it is known that consumers attempt to manage huge quantities of incoming stimuli by a process of **perceptual categorization.** This means that things that are similar are perceived as belonging together. Therefore, if a small business wishes to position its product alongside an existing brand and have it accepted as a comparable product, its marketing mix should reflect an awareness of perceptual categorization. A similar price can be used to communicate similar quality. A package design with a similar color scheme may also be used to convey the identical meaning. These techniques will help the customer fit the new product into the desired product category.

Firms that select a family brand name for a new product rely on perceptual categorization to "presell" the new product. On the other hand, if the new product is generically different or of a different quality, a unique brand name may be selected to avoid perceptual categorization.

If an individual has strong brand loyalty to a product, it is difficult for other brands to penetrate that person's perceptual barriers. Competing brands will likely experience distorted images because of the individual's attitude. The perceptual mood presents a unique communication challenge.

Motivations Unsatisfied needs create tension within an individual. When this tension reaches a certain level, a person becomes uncomfortable and attempts to reduce the tension.

We are all familiar with "hunger pains." These are manifestations of tension created by an unsatisfied physiological need. What is it that directs a person to seek food so the "hunger pains" can be relieved? The answer is motivation. **Motivations** are goal-directed forces within humans that organize and give direction to tension caused by unsatisfied needs. Marketers cannot create needs, but they can create and offer unique motivations to consumers. If an acceptable reason for purchasing is provided, it will probably be internalized as a motivating force. The key for the marketer is to determine which motivation the consumer will perceive as an acceptable solution for the "hunger pains." The answer is found in analyzing the other consumer behavior variables.

For example, Slim-Fast, a meal replacement product, was first introduced in 1977, but it was not promoted heavily until after the Cambridge Diet received nationwide attention in 1983. Slim-Fast was offered to the diet-conscious consumer as an alternative to appetite suppressants. The product was positioned to remove the tension associated with using the suppressants while also satisfying the motivation to lose weight.[13]

Each of the other three classes of needs—social, psychological, and spiritual—is similarly connected to behavior via motivations. For example, when a person's social needs create tension due to incomplete satisfaction, a firm may show how its product can fulfill those needs by providing acceptable social motivations to that person. A campus clothing store might promote the styles that communicate that a college student has obtained group membership.

Understanding motivations is not easy. Several motives may be present in each situation. Many times the motivations are subconscious, but they must be investigated if the marketing effort is to have an improved chance for success.

Attitudes   Like the other psychological variables, attitudes cannot be observed, but all persons know that they have attitudes. Do attitudes imply knowledge? Do they imply a feeling of good/bad or favorable/unfavorable? Does an attitude have a direct impact on behavior? If you answered "yes" to all these questions, you were correct each time. An **attitude** is an enduring opinion that is based on a combination of knowledge, feeling, and behavioral tendency.

An attitude can be an obstacle or a catalyst in bringing a customer to your product. Armed with an understanding of the structure of an attitude, the marketer can approach the consumer more intelligently. One of the more popular structural views of an attitude is based on the original work of Martin Fishbein.[14] As adapted to a marketing situation, Fishbein's idea is that a person's attitude toward a brand results from the belief that the brand has certain attributes that are weighted by the importance of these attributes to that person. A more precise formulation is:

$$A_0 = \sum_{i=1}^{j} B_i I_i$$

where: A_0 = attitude toward an object (brand)
       B   = belief that the brand has a certain attribute
       I   = importance of the attribute to the individual
       i   = the particular attribute of concern
       j   = number of relevant attributes

Exhibit 11–2 shows that two hypothetical market segments for a ballpoint pen have equal attitude scores but relatively different unfavorable attitudes. The strategies to improve these individual attitudes would be totally different. To improve the attitudes of consumers in Segment A, the seller needs to persuade them that the pen is attractive because attractiveness (importance rating of 7) is important to them. Currently they do not believe the pen is attractive (belief rating of 2). They recognize that the pen is inexpensive to buy (belief rating of 7), but this is obviously not very important to them (importance rating of 1). If the seller feels that price is a distinct marketing advantage, consumers need to be persuaded to place more importance on low price.

The company has a different problem with consumers in Segment B. How well the pen writes is very important to them. They see the pen as being attractive, but this attribute is not important to them. Mathematically, you can see various possibilities for increasing their attitude score.

Sociological Concepts

We cannot ignore the people around us and their influence on our actions. Among these social influences are culture, social class, reference groups, and opinion leaders. Notice that each of the sociological concepts represents different degrees of people aggregation. Starting with culture, we see large masses of people. Then we see smaller groups—social classes and reference groups—until we find a single individual who exerts influence, the opinion leader.

Culture A group's social heritage is called its **culture.** This heritage has a tremendous impact on the purchase and use of products. Marketing managers will often overlook the cultural variable because its influences are so neatly concealed within the society. Cultural influence is somewhat like the presence of air. You really do not think about its function until you are in water over your head! Then you realize the role that air has played in your existence. On the other hand, international marketers who have experienced more than one culture can readily attest to the reality of cultural influence.

It is the prescriptive nature of culture that most concerns the marketing manager. Cultural norms create a range of product-related, acceptable behavior that influences consumers in what they buy. Culture does change, however. It adapts slowly to new situations. Therefore, what works today as a marketing strategy may not work a few years later.

An investigation of culture with a narrower definitional boundary, such as age, religious preference, ethnic orientation, or geographical location, is called **subcultural analysis.** Here, too, the unique patterns of behavior and social relationships concern the marketing manager. For example,

Exhibit 11-2   Attitude Structures of Two Market Segments

Object = Community Ballpoint Pen®

	SEGMENT A			**SEGMENT B**	

Attribute	$B_i * I_i$ *		**Attribute**	$B_i * I_i$ *	
Attractive—	$2 \times 7 =$	14	Attractive—	$6 \times 1 =$	6
High quality—	$3 \times 4 =$	12	High Quality—	$5 \times 6 =$	30
Writes well—	$5 \times 6 =$	30	Writes well—	$3 \times 7 =$	21
Inexpensive—	$7 \times 1 =$	7	Inexpensive—	$2 \times 3 =$	6
**A_0		= 63	**A_0		= 63

---

*The scale ranges from 1 to 7, with a higher value meaning greater importance of the attribute to the individual or a greater belief that the attribute is present in the product.
**The most favorable attitude score would be 196 [$(7 \times 7) \times 4$].

the needs and motivations of the youth subculture are far different from those of the senior-citizen subculture. Certain food preferences are unique to Jewish culture. Cigarettes do not sell well among Mormons. If small-business managers familiarize themselves with cultures and subcultures, they can prepare better marketing mixes.

Innovative entrepreneurs can use what they know about local and cultural preferences to start successful businesses. One example is Alvin Copeland, the president and founder of Popeye's Famous Fried Chicken and Biscuits, which began in New Orleans. He provided a menu emphasizing Cajun cuisine and super-spicy fried chicken that appealed to the taste preferences of Louisiana consumers. A tenth-grade dropout and native of New Orleans, he now drives a red Mercedes convertible with "SPICY" on his license plate.[15]

Social Class   Another sociological concept in consumer behavior is social class. **Social class** describes divisions in a society with different levels of social prestige. There are important implications for marketing in a social-class system. Different life-styles correlate with the different levels of social prestige, and products are often symbols of life-styles.

Unlike a caste system, a social-class system provides for upward mobility. The status position of parents does not permanently fix the social class of their child. Occupation is probably the single most important determinant of social class. Other determinants that are used in social-class research include possessions, source of income, and education.

For some products, such as consumer packaged goods, social-class analysis will probably not be very useful. For others, such as home furnishings, it may help to explain variations in shopping and communication patterns.

Reference Groups Although social class could, by definition, be considered to be a reference group, we are more generally concerned with small groups such as the family, the work group, a neighborhood group, or a recreational group. Not every group is a reference group. **Reference groups** are only those groups from which an individual allows influence to be exerted upon his or her behavior.

The existence of group influence is well established.[16] The challenge to the marketer is to understand why this influence occurs and how the influence can be used to promote the sale of a product. Individuals tend to accept group influence for the benefits perceived. These perceived benefits allow the influencers to use various kinds of power. Bertram Raven and John French have classified these forms of power as reward, coercive, expert, referent, and legitimate. Each of these power forms is available to the marketer.

Reward power and coercive power relate to a group's ability to give and to withhold rewards. Rewards can be material or psychological. Recognition and praise are typical psychological rewards. A Tupperware party is a good example of a marketing technique that takes advantage of reward power and coercive power. The ever-present possibility of pleasing or displeasing the hostess-friend tends to encourage the guest to buy.

Referent power and expert power involve neither rewards nor punishments. These types of power exist because an individual attaches a unique importance to being like the group or perceives the group as being in a more knowledgeable position than the individual. Referent power causes consumers to conform to the group's behavior and to choose products selected by the group's members. Young children will often be influenced by referent power. Marketers can create a desire for products by using cleverly designed advertisements such as the one shown in Figure 11–1.

Legitimate power involves the sanction of what one ought to do. We saw legitimate power at the cultural level when we talked about the prescrip-

Figure 11–1   Using Reference Group Appeal to Sell a Product

© 1990 Kraft General Foods, Inc.

tive nature of culture. This type of power can also be used at a smaller group level.

Opinion Leaders   The concept of opinion leaders is largely a communication idea. According to this concept, consumers receive a significant amount of information through individuals called opinion leaders. Thus, an **opinion leader** is a group member playing a key communications role.

Generally speaking, opinion leaders are knowledgeable, visible, and exposed to the mass media. A small-business firm can enhance its own product and image by identifying with such leaders. For example, a farm-supply dealer may promote agricultural products in a community by arranging demonstrations on the farms of outstanding farmers. These farmers are the community's opinion leaders. Also, department stores may use attractive students as models in showing campus fashions.

Consumer Decision Making

Having discussed the psychological and sociological concepts influencing consumer behavior, we turn attention to the very core of consumption—consumer decision making. One theory about human information processing holds that humans are problem solvers. According to this theory, the stages of consumer decision making are:

1. Problem recognition.
2. Information search and evaluation.
3. Purchase decision.
4. Post-purchase evaluation.

We can use this framework to examine consumer decision making. A consumer must first recognize a problem before making a purchase. This initial stage cannot be circumvented. As obvious as this seems, many small firms appear to be marketing to consumers as if they were at later stages, when, in reality, they have not yet recognized a problem!

The time required for the second stage varies with the product and the consumer. The scheduling of various communication strategies should reflect such time-dimension differences. The decision to buy a new product—the third stage—will naturally take longer than a decision involving a known product. For example, an industrial-equipment dealer may find it necessary to call on a prospective new customer over a period of months before making the first sale. Some decisions become routine and programmed; others do not.

The decision process does not terminate with a purchase. A small firm that desires repeat purchases from its customers should follow them into the post-purchase stage. A helpful concept for understanding the post-purchase process is **cognitive dissonance,** which takes the form of an uncomfortable psychological tension or a feeling of inequity. Cognitive dissonance tends to occur when a consumer has purchased one brand from among several which had attractive features. Second thoughts or doubts about the decision are bound to occur. The firm whose product was purchased should attempt to reduce the consumer's tension by communicating with that customer after the sale.

Consumers are complex creatures and will never be completely understood. However, the concepts we have presented are relevant to strategy development. Even a simple recognition of their existence, without a thorough understanding, can save a small business from serious mistakes.

However, knowledge alone is insufficient. The small-business manager must translate consumer-behavior concepts into product strategy. The process of strategy development is described in the next section.

Product Strategies for Small Business

Small-business managers are often weak in their understanding of product strategy. This creates ineffectiveness and conflict in the marketing effort. In order to provide a better understanding of product strategy in small business, we will now examine product strategy in greater detail.

Product/Service Terminology

There is confusion in marketing circles regarding the language of marketing strategy. In particular, some authors challenge the usage of the phrase "product marketing" to include services. Traditionally, marketers have used the word product as a generic term describing both goods and services. More recently, there has been a debate that goods marketing and services marketing are distinctly different.[17]

This debate is relevant to our discussion of strategy because there is a favorable future for small business in the services sector. ("Services" is used here in a more inclusive sense than in our Chapter 2 discussion of the services industry as one of eight major industries.) Consider the assessment of one researcher:

> Over half of all service-sector employment and output now originates in 5.5 million small businesses, which account for 99 percent of the sector's enterprises. In addition, the service sector is assuming an increasingly significant role in U.S. economic growth, accounting for 76 percent of the work force. . . . [18]

When we examine this debate, we find that the argument for a significant distinction between the two takes place on several dimensions. As shown in Exhibit 11–3, these dimensions are tangibility, production and consumption time separation, and standardization. For example, a pencil would fit the "pure goods" end of the scale and a haircut would fit the "pure services" end. The major implication of this debate is that services present challenges to strategy development that are different from those of goods.

Although we recognize the benefit of examining the marketing of services as a unique form of marketing, space limitations in this book require us to include the services area within the more comprehensive category of product marketing. A **product,** then, will be considered to include the total

Exhibit 11-3   Contrast of Services and Goods Marketing

Pure Services Marketing	Combination Services/Goods Marketing	Pure Goods Marketing
Intangible	TANGIBILITY	Tangible
At the Same Time	PRODUCTION/CONSUMPTION	At Different Times
Less	STANDARDIZATION	More

"bundle of satisfaction" that is offered to customers in an exchange transaction—whether it be a good or a service.

A physical product includes not only the main element of the "bundle," which is the physical product itself, but also complementary components such as packaging. Of course, the physical product is usually the most important component. But sometimes the main element of a product is perceived by customers to be like that of all other products. The complementary components can then become the most important features of the product. For example, a particular cake mix brand may be preferred by consumers, not because it is a better mix, but because of the toll-free telephone number on the package that can be called for baking hints.

A **product mix** is the collection of product lines within a firm's ownership and control. A **product line** is the sum of the individual product items that are related. The relationship is usually defined generically. Two brands of bar soap would be two product items in one product line. A **prod-**

Figure 11-2   Selecting from a Product Line

uct item is the lowest common denominator in a product mix. It is the individual item.

The more items in a product line, the more depth it has. The more product lines in a product mix, the greater the breadth of the product mix. **Product mix consistency** refers to the closeness, or similarity, of the product lines. **Product strategy** describes the manner in which the product component of the marketing mix is used to achieve the objectives of a firm.

Product Strategy Alternatives

The overall product strategy alternatives of a small business can be presented in the following eight categories:

1. Initial product/initial market.
2. Initial product/new market.
3. Modified product/initial market.
4. Modified product/new market.
5. New related product/initial market.
6. New related product/new market.

7. New unrelated product/initial market.
8. New unrelated product/new market.

Each alternative represents a different approach to product strategy. Some strategies can be pursued concurrently. Usually, however, the small firm will find that it will pursue the alternatives in basically the order listed above. Keep this premise in mind as you read about each one. Exhibit 11–4 displays each of these strategies in matrix format.

Initial Product/Initial Market   In the earliest stage of a new venture, the initial product/initial market product strategy is followed. Most entrepreneurs start with one product. Growth can be achieved under this strategy in three ways. First, current customers can be encouraged to use more of the product. Second, potential customers within the same market can be sold on the product. Third, current customers can be educated to use the existing product for additional purposes, thereby increasing demand. An example is Minnetonka's Softsoap, which was originally positioned as a replacement for bar soap. More recently, it has been promoted as a gift item and a skin-care product. As indicated in Exhibit 11–4, these same three growth strategies can be applied within each of the remaining product strategies.

Initial Product/New Market   An extension of the first alternative is the initial product/new market product strategy. With a small additional commitment in resources, a current product can often be targeted to a new market. Taking a floor-cleaning compound from the commercial market into the home market would be an example. Marketing the same product abroad after first selling it domestically would also be an example of this strategy.

Modified Product/Initial Market   Customers seemingly anticipate the emergence of "new, improved" products. With the modified product/initial market strategy, the existing product can be either replaced, gradually phased out, or left in the product mix. If the existing product is to be retained, the impact on sales of the modified product must be carefully assessed. It doesn't do much good to make an existing product obsolete unless the modified product has a larger profit margin. The product modification can involve a very minor change. For example, adding colored specks to a detergent can give the product a "new" and sales-attractive appeal. Some people, of course, would question the social value of such "improvements."

Modified Product/New Market   A modified product can also be used to reach a new market. The only difference in the modified product/new mar-

Exhibit 11-4   Product Strategy Matrix

PRODUCT DIMENSION

	Initial Product	Modified Product	New Related Product	New Unrelated Product
Initial Market Segment	**1.** Convince current customers to use more. Find new customers. Promote new uses for the product.	**3.** Convince current customers to use more. Find new customers. Promote new uses for the product.	**5.** Convince current customers to use more. Find new customers. Promote new uses for the product.	**7.** Convince current customers to use more. Find new customers. Promote new uses for the product.
New Market Segment	**2.** Convince current customers to use more. Find new customers. Promote new uses for the product.	**4.** Convince current customers to use more. Find new customers. Promote new uses for the product.	**6.** Convince current customers to use more. Find new customers. Promote new uses for the product.	**8.** Convince current customers to use more. Find new customers. Promote new uses for the product.

MARKET DIMENSION

Note: The three sub-strategies—"Convince current customers to use more," "Find more customers," and "Promote new uses for product"—are identical strategies applied within separate target markets.

ket strategy from the previous one is its appeal to a new market segment. For example, a furniture manufacturer currently selling finished furniture to customers might market unfinished furniture to the "do-it-yourself" market.

New Related Product/Initial Market   Current, satisfied customers make good markets for new additions to the product assortment of a small business. Many products can be added that are more than product modifications but are still similar to the existing products. These new products are considered to be similar when they have a generic relationship. For example, Celestial Seasonings, Inc., of Boulder, CO, has moved into a caffeine-free hot drink called Breakaway, which is a recent addition to its herb teas.[19] The new product is generically similar to the tea products. It is aimed at the same health-care market.

New Related Product/New Market   Going after a different market with a new but similar product is still another product strategy. This approach is particularly appropriate when there is concern that the new product may reduce sales of the existing product in a current market. For example, a firm producing wood-burning stoves for home use might introduce a new gas-burning furnace targeted for use in office buildings.

New Unrelated Product/Initial Market   A product strategy that includes a new product generically different from existing products can be very risky. However, the new unrelated product/initial market strategy is sometimes used by small businesses, especially when the new product fits existing distribution and sales systems. For example, a local dealer selling Italian sewing machines may add a line of microwave ovens.

New Unrelated Product/New Market   The final product strategy occurs when a new unrelated product is added to the product mix to serve a new market. This strategy has the most risk among all the alternatives since the business is attempting to market an unfamiliar product to an unfamiliar market. For example, one electrical equipment service business added a private employment agency.

With this product strategy, however, a hedge can be built against volatile shifts in market demand. If the business is selling snowshoes and suntan lotion, it hopes that demand will be high in one market at all times.

Special Tools for Strategy Management

The management of the firm's product mix is guided by many considerations. Competition, market demand, pricing flexibility—to name just a few—are important influences in this regard.

Two marketing concepts are extremely useful to the small-business manager in any efforts to control and develop the firm's product mix. These are the product development curve and the product life cycle. Both of these concepts provide concise summaries of activities or circumstances relating to the management of the product mix.

The Product Development Curve

A major responsibility of the entrepreneur is to recognize, prepare, and implement any of the product strategy alternatives discussed earlier. Many of these strategies require a structured mechanism for new-product development. In big business, committees or even entire departments are created for that purpose. In a small business this responsibility will usually rest with the entrepreneur.

The entrepreneur usually views new product development as a mountainous task. Therefore, we show the product development curve in Exhibit 11–5 in the form of a mountain. The left slope of the mountain represents the gathering of a large number of ideas. Beginning at the mountain peak, these ideas are screened as you move down the right slope until the base of the mountain—the retention of one product ready to be introduced into the marketplace—is reached. In our discussion, we emphasize product development by manufacturers rather than distributors.

The first phase of the product development curve, labeled *Idea Accumulation*, shows the need to increase the number of ideas under consideration. New products start with new-product ideas, and these ideas have varied origins. Some of the many possible sources of ideas are:

1. Sales, engineering, or other personnel within the firm.
2. Government-owned patents, which are generally available on a royalty-free basis.
3. Privately owned patents listed in the Official Gazette of the U.S. Patent Office.
4. Other small companies that may be available for acquisition or merger.

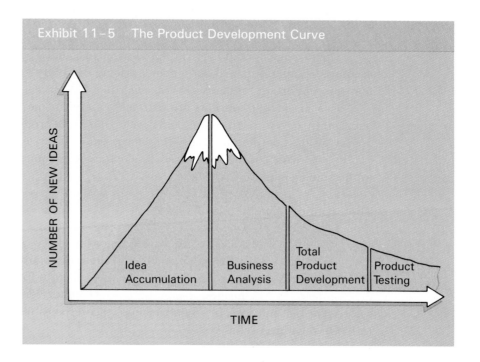

Exhibit 11–5   The Product Development Curve

NUMBER OF NEW IDEAS

Idea Accumulation   Business Analysis   Total Product Development   Product Testing

TIME

5. Competitors' products and advertising.
6. Requests and suggestions from customers.

Business Analysis is the next stage in the process. Every new-product idea must be carefully analyzed in relation to several considerations.

Relationship to Existing Product Line   Any product to be added should be consistent with, or properly related to, the existing product line. For example, a new product may be designed to fill a gap in the company's product line or in the price range of the products it currently manufactures. If the product is completely new, it should normally have at least a family relationship to existing products. Otherwise, the new products may call for drastic and costly changes in manufacturing methods, distribution channels, type of promotion, or manner of personal selling.

Cost of Development and Introduction   One problem in adding new products is the cost of development and introduction. The capital outlays may be considerable. These include expenditures for design and development, market research to establish sales potential and company volume potential, advertising and sales promotion, patents, and the equipment and tooling that must be added. It may be from one to three years before profits may be realized on the sale of the contemplated new or altered product.

Personnel and Facilities   Obviously, having adequate skilled personnel, managers, and production equipment is better than having to add personnel and buy equipment. Hence, introducing new products is typically more logical if the personnel and the required equipment are already available.

Competition and Market Acceptance   Still another factor to be considered is the character of the market and the potential competition facing the proposed product. Competition must not be too severe. Some authorities, for example, think that new products can be introduced successfully only if a 5 percent share of the total market can be secured. The ideal solution, of course, is to offer a sufficiently different product or one in a cost and price bracket that avoids direct competition.

The next stage, *Total Product Development,* entails the planning for suitable branding, packaging, and other supporting efforts such as pricing and promotion. After these components are considered, many new-product ideas may be discarded.

The last step in the product development curve is *Product Testing.* This means that the physical product should be proven to perform correctly. While the product can be evaluated in a laboratory setting, a test of market reaction to the total product should also be conducted. This test can be performed only in the marketplace.[20]

The Product Life Cycle

Another valuable concept for managing the product mix is the product life cycle. Our portrayal of the product life cycle in Exhibit 11–6 takes the shape of a roller-coaster ride. This is actually the way many entrepreneurs describe their experiences with the life cycle of their products. The initial stages are characterized by a slow and upward movement. The stay at the top is exciting but relatively brief. Then, suddenly the decline begins, and the movement down is fast.

The product life cycle gives the small-business manager a valuable

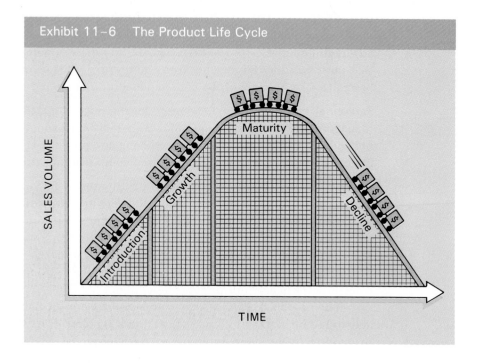

Exhibit 11-6 The Product Life Cycle

planning tool. Promotional, pricing, and distribution policies can all be adjusted to reflect a product's position on the curve.[21]

When a small business is committed to the product development concept, it can look forward to expanding its product mix successfully and to staying above the nemesis of the "roller-coaster ride" pictured in Exhibit 11-6.

Completing the Total Bundle of Satisfaction

A major responsibility of marketing is to transform a basic product into a total product. An idea for a unique new writing pen that has already been developed into a physical reality is still not ready for the marketplace. The total product, in this example, would incorporate more than the materials molded into the shape of the new pen.[22] To be marketable, the basic product must be named, have a package, perhaps have a warranty, and be

SMALL BUSINESS IN ACTION
Applying the Product Life Cycle Concept

It is extremely difficult for some entrepreneurs to focus on new product development while their existing products are selling like hotcakes! These entrepreneurs need to realize that nothing lasts forever and, therefore, preparations should be made for the time when demand slackens. The product life cycle concept is applicable to this problem. One small-business manager who has successfully applied the concept is Thomas L. Venable, chairman of Spectrum Control, in Erie, PA. Venable's assessment of the problem is expressed as follows:

It's amazing, isn't it? . . . companies get so caught up pushing products out the door . . . they're totally unprepared for the moment when demand slackens or a better mousetrap comes along.

Spectrum makes technology-based business products such as "filters" to prevent garage-door openers from activating other home electronic devices. In this industry, change is inevitable. Therefore, Spectrum, under Venable's leadership, has used the product life cycle to plan for new products.

The success of the planning tool at Spectrum Control has been reflected in its earnings. "The whole idea behind the process is to avoid crises," says Venable. "You want to be ready to go with the second product just as the first one is about to die off."

Source: Reprinted with permission, *Inc.* magazine (June, 1988). Copyright © 1988 by Goldhirsh Group, Inc., 38 Commercial Wharf, Boston, MA 02110.

supported by many other product components. We will now examine a few of these components.

Branding

An identification for a product is termed a *brand*. A brand includes both the identification which can be verbalized and that which cannot. The name Xerox is a brand, as are the "golden arches" of McDonald's. A name and a trademark are important to the image of the business and its products. Therefore, considerable attention should be given to every decision in a branding strategy.

In general, there are five rules to follow in naming a product:

1. *Select a name that is easy to pronounce.* You want customers to remember your product. Help them with a name that can be spoken easily. An entrepreneur's own name should be carefully evaluated to be sure it is acceptable. The founder of a major fast-food chain used his daughter's name for the company. Her name? Wendy. The name of the business? Wendy's.

2. *Choose a descriptive name.* A name that is suggestive of the major benefit of the product can be extremely helpful. The name Elephant for a computer memory disk correctly suggests a desirable benefit. The name Rocky Road would be a poor selection for a mattress!

3. *Use a name that can have legal protection.* Be careful that you select a name that can be defended successfully. This is sometimes difficult, but do not risk litigation by intentionally copying someone else's brand name. A new soft drink named Prof. Pepper would likely be contested by the Dr Pepper company.

4. *Consider names that have promotional possibilities.* Exceedingly long names are not, for example, compatible with good copy design on billboards, where space is at such a premium. A competitor of the McDonald's hamburger chain is called Wuv's. This name will easily fit on any billboard.

5. *Select a name that can be used on several product lines of a similar nature.* Many times customer goodwill is lost when a name doesn't fit a new line. A company producing a furniture polish called Slick-Surface could not easily use the same name for its new sidewalk surfacing compound, which purports to increase traction.

A small business also should carefully select its trademark. The mark should be unique, easy to remember, and related to the product.[23]

Trademark registration for products in interstate commerce is handled through the U.S. Patent and Trademark Office under the authority of the Lanham Trademark Act. This Act also covers the registration of service marks, certification marks, and collective marks.

Once a trademark is selected by a small business, it is important to protect its use. Two rules can help. One is to be sure the name is not carelessly used in place of the generic name. For example, the Xerox company never wants a person to say that he or she is "xeroxing" something. Second, the business should inform the public that the brand is a brand by labeling it with the symbol ™ or the symbol ®. If the trademark is unusual or written in a special form, it is easier to protect.

Packaging

Packaging is another important part of the total product. In addition to protecting the basic product, packaging is also a significant tool for increasing the value of the total product. Consider for a moment some of the products you purchase. Do you buy them primarily because of preference for the package design and/or color?

Packaging is also used for promotional purposes. It is important for some food products, for example, to be visible through the package. The manager of Dryden & Palmer Co. in Norwalk, CT, which employs 30 people and produces rock candy, talks about the package for his product this way: "Basically you've got a round product that's put in a square box. Rock candy needs to be seen. It's really quite attractive."[24]

Packaging can also open the door to new markets. Sam Gallo, president of a small Baton Rouge company, has introduced coffee bags as a new type of packaging for coffee. Coffee bags have been tried before but failed due to packaging, which allowed the coffee to become stale. Mr. Gallo guarantees a nine-month shelf life for his product and calls it "Morning Treat."[25]

Labeling

Another part of the total product is its label. Labeling is particularly important to manufacturers, who apply most labels. A label serves several purposes. It often shows the brand, particularly when branding the basic product would be undesirable. For example, a furniture brand is typically shown on a label and not on the basic product. On some products, visibility of the brand label is highly desirable. Calvin Klein jeans would probably not sell as well with the name labeled only inside the jeans.

A label is also an important informative tool for the small business. It can include information on product care. It can inform consumers how to use the product correctly. It can even include information on how to dispose of the product.

Laws on labeling requirements should be consulted carefully.[26] Be innovative in your labeling information. Include information that goes beyond the specified minimum legal requirements.

Warranties

A **warranty** is simply a promise that a product will do certain things.[27] It may be express (written) or implied. An implied warranty refers to the seller's clear title to the product and to its quality. An express warranty on a product is not always necessary. As a matter of fact, many firms operate without written warranties. They are concerned that a written warranty will only serve to confuse customers and make them suspicious. Figure 11–3 may be somewhat representative of this attitude among small businesses.

The Magnuson-Moss Warranty Act of 1974 has had an impact on warranty practices. This law covers several warranty areas, including warranty terminology. The most notable change in terminology is the use of the terms "Full" and "Limited" on an express warranty for a product that costs over $15.00. In order to give the Full Warranty designation, the warranty must state certain minimum standards such as replacement or full refund after reasonable attempts at repair. Warranties not meeting all the minimum standards must carry the Limited Warranty title.

Warranties are important for products that are innovative, relatively expensive, purchased infrequently, relatively complex to repair, and posi-

Figure 11–3   Warranties Can Be Confusing

"But we are completely satisfied with your money."

Reprinted from The Saturday Evening Post, © *1981 BFL&MS, Inc.*

tioned as high-quality goods. The major considerations that help decide the merits of a warranty policy are:

1. Costs.
2. Service capability.
3. Competitive practices.
4. Customer perceptions.
5. Legal implications.

Looking Back

1. Small firms need to incorporate customer service management into their organizations. Customer service should be genuine and ethical, and not treated as a gimmick. The delivery of customer service begins with an analysis of customer attitudes. Employees do not always share the same dedication to service as owners.
2. Psychological concepts include perception, needs, motivations, and attitudes. Sociological concepts include culture, social class, reference groups, and opinion leaders. The stages of consumer decision making include problem recognition, information search and evaluation, the decision to purchase, and post-purchase evaluation.
3. The eight product strategy alternatives are initial product/initial market, initial product/new market, modified product/initial market, modified product/new market, new related product/initial market, new related product/new market, new unrelated product/initial market, and new unrelated product/new market.
4. Two concepts useful to the management of the product mix are the product development curve and the product life cycle. The product development curve consists of four phases: idea accumulation, business analysis, total product development, and product testing. The product life cycle consists of four stages: introduction, growth, maturity, and decline.
5. When choosing a good brand name, the entrepreneur should follow five basic rules. Packaging can be used for protection, promotion, and opening new markets. Labels are informative tools for the marketer. A warranty is simply a promise that a product will do certain things.

DISCUSSION QUESTIONS

1. What is the meaning of the statement "Customer satisfaction is not a means to achieve a certain goal, but, rather, it is the goal"?

2. How can a small firm know whether it is providing sufficient customer service? Be specific.

3. Do you feel that small firms in general provide better customer service? Why or why not?

4. Select a magazine advertisement and analyze it for perceptual techniques.

5. Select a magazine advertisement and analyze it for the use of reference-group influence and cultural uniqueness.

6. Give some examples of the way in which legitimate power is used in marketing.

7. What kinds of consumer behavior occur in the post-purchase stage? Be specific.

8. What are the three ways to achieve additional growth within each of the market strategies?

9. How does the new related product/new market strategy differ from the new unrelated product/new market strategy? Give examples.

10. A manufacturer of power lawn mowers is considering the addition of a line of home barbecue equipment. What factors would be important in a decision of this type?

11. List some of the major activities in the business analysis stage of the product development curve.

12. Select two product names and evaluate each with the five rules for naming a product listed in this chapter.

13. Would a small business desire to have its name considered to be the generic name for the product area? Defend your position.

14. For what type of firm is the packaging of products most important? For what firms is it unimportant?

15. How important do you believe warranties are in selling products? Discuss.

YOU MAKE THE CALL

Situation 1

Paul McKinney is the owner and operator of a small restaurant located in the downtown area of Oklahoma City, OK. McKinney is a college graduate with a major in accounting. His ability to analyze and control costs has been a major factor in keeping his five-year-old venture out of the red.

The restaurant is located in an old but newly remodeled downtown building. His business is built on the strategy of high volume and low overhead. However, space limitations provide seating for only 25 to 30 people at one time. McKinney is concerned that customers stay too long after their meal, thereby tying up seating. He has considered using a buzzer system to remind customers that it is time to move on. He is concerned that this method is too obvious and may create customer dissatisfaction.

Questions

1. What is your opinion regarding McKinney's proposed buzzer system?
2. What other suggestions to help increase turnover can you make? Why are these ideas better?
3. What type of diversification strategy would be consistent with McKinney's restaurant business? Be specific.

Situation 2

In 1980, Chris Longfelder opened a cosmetics store with her savings of $500 and a $10,000 bank loan. The focus of her appeal was on price. One of her newspaper ads urged, "If you're tired of overpriced department store cosmetics, visit Generic Makeup." The first store was profitable, and Longfelder opened a second Generic Makeup store only four months later.

In 1986, a study of customer attitudes revealed a number of negative attitudes about her company. Some customers felt the products were leftovers and must be lower quality. Furthermore, she found that price was not the major reason customers came to her store—service, selection, and store atmosphere were all mentioned more frequently.

Longfelder has decided to change the name of her store. Two names are candidates: Kriselle and Faces.

Source: Tom Watson, "Retailer Adds Profits and 'New Faces.'" Reprinted from *In Business* magazine (Box 323, Emmaus, Pa 18049).

Questions

1. Do you believe a name change is warranted? If so, what other factors make you feel this way?
2. What factors should be evaluated in making the choice between the two names under consideration?
3. Could the perceived need to change names have been avoided? How?

EXPERIENTIAL EXERCISES

1. Obtain permission from a local mall to conduct shopper interviews. Ask customers about their major service complaints. Report your findings.
2. Over a period of two or three days, carefully note your own shopping experiences. Summarize what you consider to be the best customer service you received.
3. Visit a local retail store and observe brand names, package designs, labels, and warranties. Report your thoughts to the class.
4. Consider your most recent purchase. Relate the decision-making process you used to the four stages of decision making presented in the textbook. Report your conclusions.

REFERENCES TO SMALL-BUSINESS PRACTICES

Daescher, William F. "A Lesson in Competitiveness." *D & B Reports,* Vol. 37, No. 2 (March/April, 1988).
> A small office supply company is used as an example of how a firm can remain competitive through diversification and customer service.

Huffman, Frances. "Services." *Entrepreneur,* Vol. 16, No. 9 (September, 1988), pp. 91–98.
> Six service firms are profiled in this article. Each business has been successful in providing a special service in a unique manner.

Kahn, Joseph P. "Whipped!" *Inc.,* Vol. 7, No. 2 (February, 1985), pp. 35–44.
> A small firm battles Kraft, Inc. when Kraft contends the firm's Yogowhip trademark is in violation of its Miracle Whip brand.

Larson, Erik. "Forever Young." *Inc.,* Vol. 10, No. 7 (July, 1988), pp. 50–62.
> This article provides an intriguing account of how a new business starting as a simple ice-cream parlor has diversified while retaining its unusual commitment to the needs of its employees and community.

Mamis, Robert A. "Real Service." *Inc.,* Vol. 11, No. 5 (May, 1989), pp. 80–89.
> A mail-order company that has provided extensive customer service is profiled in this article.

ENDNOTES

1. Harry Bacas, "Make It Right for the Customer," *Nation's Business,* Vol. 75, No. 11 (November, 1987), p. 50.

2. Michael Barrier, "Brothers Act," *Nation's Business,* Vol. 77, No. 1 (January, 1989), pp. 41–42.

3. For example, see Thomas L. Powers, "Identify and Fulfill Customer Service Expectations," *Industrial Marketing Management,* Vol. 17, No. 4 (November, 1988), pp. 273–276; Laura A. Liswood, "A New System for Rating Service Quality," *The Journal of Business Strategy,* Vol. 10, No. 4 (July–August, 1989), pp. 42–45.

4. Steven P. Galante, "More Firms Quiz Customers for Clues About Competition," *The Wall Street Journal* (March 3, 1983), p. 1.

5. Tom Richman, "Come Again," *Inc.*, Vol. 11, No. 4 (April, 1989), pp. 177–178.

6. Mark Stevens, "Learn Your Firm's Inside Story," *Nation's Business,* Vol. 77, No. 8 (August, 1989), pp. 59–60.

7. Joan C. Szabo, "Service = Survival," *Nation's Business,* Vol. 77, No. 3 (March, 1989), p. 18.

8. *Ibid.*

9. *Ibid.*, p. 19.

10. Judith A. Rogala, "Turning Problems into Profits," *Business Age,* Vol. 3, No. 4 (August, 1989), p. 20.

11. Joseph P. Kahn, "Caddy Shack," *Inc.*, Vol. 9, No. 5 (May, 1987), pp. 80–81.

12. Several more complete listings can be found in Del I. Hawkins, Roger J. Best, and Kenneth A. Coney, *Consumer Behavior: Implications for Marketing Strategy,* 4th ed. (Homewood, IL: BPI/Irwin, 1989), Chapter 10.

13. "A Company That's Getting Fat Because America Wants to Be Thin," *Business Week,* No. 2869 (November 19, 1984), p. 70.

14. *Op. cit.*, Hawkins, pp. 433–436.

15. Jo Ellen Davis, "Blackened Fish, Red Beans, and a Cake to Go, Please," *Business Week,* No. 2920 (November 11, 1985), pp. 66–67.

16. For a good discussion of social group influence, see Chapter 9 in David L. Loudon and Albert J. Della Bitta, *Consumer Behavior: Concepts and Applications,* 3d ed. (New York: McGraw-Hill Book Company, 1988).

17. See for example Christopher H. Lovelock, *Services Marketing* (Englewood Cliffs, NJ: Prentice-Hall, Inc., 1984).

18. Joan C. Szabo, "Slower Growth Expected for the Service Sector," *Nation's Business,* Vol. 77, No. 1 (January, 1989), p. 12.

19. "What's Brewing at Celestial," *Business Week,* No. 2679 (March 16, 1981), p. 138.

20. For a more detailed discussion of product development, see Carlton A. Maile and Donna M. Bialik, "New Product Management: In Search of Better Ideas," *The Journal of Small Business Management,* Vol. 22, No. 3 (July, 1984), pp. 40–48.

21. A detailed discussion of these changes is beyond the scope of this book. For more details, see Charles D. Schewe and Reuben M. Smith, *Marketing: Concepts and Applications,* 2d ed. (New York: McGraw-Hill Book Company, 1983), Chapter 10.

22. An intangible service is also a basic product that requires additional product development.

23. For more extensive treatment of trademarks, see Chapter 2 of Louis W. Stern and Thomas L. Eavaldi, *Legal Aspects of Marketing Strategy: Antitrust and Consumer Protection Issues* (Englewood Cliffs, NJ: Prentice-Hall, Inc., 1984); Thomas M. S. Hemnes, "How Can You Find a Safe Trademark?" *Harvard Business Review,* Vol. 64, No. 2 (March–April, 1985), pp. 36–44.

24. Doron P. Levin, "Rock-Candy Maker Takes Its Licks: An Ailing Vestige of Simpler Times," *The Wall Street Journal* (June 17, 1981), p. 25.

25. "Morning Treat Tilts with Giants," *Sales and Marketing Management,* Vol. 122, No. 7 (May 14, 1979), p. 13.

26. Laws that affect packaging and labeling are treated in Joe L. Welch, *Marketing Law* (Tulsa, OK: The Petroleum Publishing Company, 1980), pp. 127–133.

27. An excellent discussion of the merits of service warranties is given in Christopher W. L. Hart, "The Power of Unconditional Service Guarantees," *Harvard Business Review,* Vol. 66, No. 4 (July–August, 1988), pp. 54–62.

12 PRICING AND CREDIT POLICY

Yuppie Gourmet Inc.

Credit involves a sale on the basis of trust. Therefore, a creditor must have confidence in the debtor and vice-versa. Unfortunately, a firm may sometimes use this relationship to take unfair advantage of a small business. Just such a situation was encountered by Hollis Savin, founder of Yuppie Gourmet, Inc., a Wisconsin manufacturer of upscale snacks.

Savin, who admits her own company tried to avoid extending credit to customers, experienced difficulty when a contract producer of her trade secret, Chips Au Chocolat™ (gourmet chocolate-covered potato chips), revoked credit terms. Savin contends that the manufacturer offered to buy out her company, and he cut off credit as a pressure tactic.

"He had us backed against a wall," Savin recalls. "He had our inven-

335

tory locked up in his warehouse." The inventory was needed to fill over $400,000 in orders by Yuppie Gourmet's customers.

Eventually, Savin obtained the packaging materials held hostage by the manufacturer and located another candy producer with the necessary production facilities. But this unpleasant experience left a bad taste surrounding credit that will not be soon forgotten.

Source: Jeannie Ralston, "Specialty Food with all the Trimmings." Reprinted from the February, 1989, issue of *VENTURE, For Entrepreneurial Business Owners & Investors,* © 1989.

Looking Ahead

Watch for the following important topics:
1. Cost and demand considerations in pricing.
2. Break-even analysis applied to pricing.
3. Setting the selling price and calculating markups.
4. Kinds of consumer and trade credit.
5. Managing credit activity.
6. New terms and concepts:

price	skimming-price strategy
credit	price line
total cost	consumer credit
total variable costs	trade credit
total fixed costs	open charge account
average pricing	installment account
prestige pricing	revolving charge account
elasticity of demand	trade-credit agencies
elastic demand	credit bureau
inelastic demand	aging schedule
penetration pricing	bad-debt ratio

A product or service is not ready for sale until it is priced, and, increasingly, pricing must be augmented by credit. The **price** of a product or service is the seller's measure of what he or she is willing to receive in exchange for ownership or use of that product or service. **Credit** involves an agreement that payment for a product or service will be made at some later date.

Price and credit decisions are vital to a business because they directly impact the revenue and cash flow stream of the firm. Also, initial pricing and credit decisions are important because customers dislike price increases and often react negatively to more restrictive credit policy changes. Therefore, care should be exercised when first making these decisions to reduce the likelihood of such changes. We will examine both the pricing and credit decisions of the small firm in this chapter.

Pricing Activities

Pricing is the systematic determination of the right price for a product. While setting just any price is easy, systematic pricing is complex and difficult. Before we examine the process of product pricing for the small business, let us first consider why this process is important.

Importance of Pricing

The revenue of a small business is a direct reflection of two components: sales quantity and product price. In a real sense, then, the product price is half of the revenue figure. Yet a small change in price can drastically influence total revenue. For emphasis, consider the following situations.[1]

Situation A

Quantity sold	×	Price per unit	=	Revenue
500,000	×	$10	=	$5,000,000

Situation B

Quantity sold	×	Price per unit	=	Revenue
500,000	×	$9.90	=	$4,950,000

The price per unit in Situation B is only 10 cents lower than in Situation A. However, the total reduction in revenue is $50,000! Thus, a small business can lose revenue unnecessarily if a price is set too low.

Another reason pricing is important is that price has an indirect impact on sales quantity. In the examples just given, quantity sold was assumed to be independent of price—which it may well be for a change in price from $10.00 to $9.90. However, a larger change, up or down, from $10.00 might change the quantity sold.

Pricing, therefore, has a double impact on total sales revenue. It is important *directly* as one part of the revenue equation and *indirectly* through its impact on quantity demanded.

Cost Considerations in Pricing

In a successful business, price must be sufficient to cover total cost plus some margin of profit. **Total cost** includes three elements. The first is the cost of goods (or services) offered for sale. An appliance dealer, for example, must include in the price the cost of the appliance and freight charges. The second element is the selling cost. This includes the direct cost of the salesperson's time as well as the cost of advertising and sales promotion. The third element is the general overhead cost applicable to the given product. Included in this cost are such items as office supplies, utilities, taxes, office salaries, and management salaries. Profit is the necessary payment for entrepreneurial services and the risk of doing business.

Another cost consideration concerns the way costs behave as the quantity marketed increases or decreases. **Total variable costs** are those that increase as the quantity marketed increases. Sales commission costs and material costs for production are typical variable costs. These are incurred as a product is made and sold. **Total fixed costs** are those that remain constant at different levels of quantity sold. An advertising campaign expenditure and factory equipment cost would be fixed costs.

By understanding the behavior of these different kinds of costs, a small-business manager can avoid pricing too low to cover costs. If all costs are considered, incorrectly, to behave in the same way, pricing can be inappropriate. Small businesses often disregard differences between fixed and variable costs and treat them identically for pricing. An approach called **average pricing** is an example of this disregard. Average pricing occurs when the total cost over a previous period is divided by the quantity sold in that period. The resulting average cost is then used to set the current price.

Consider the cost structure of a hypothetical firm selling 25,000 units of a product in 1990 at a sales price of $8.00 each (Exhibit 12–1). The average unit cost at the 1990 sales volume of 25,000 units is $5.00 ($125,000 ÷ 25,000). The $3.00 markup on the average cost provides a satisfactory margin at this sales volume.

However, consider the profit impact if next year's sales reach only 10,000 units and the selling price has been set at the same $3.00 markup based on 1990's average cost (Exhibit 12–2). At the lower sales volume (10,000 units), the average unit cost has increased to $9.50 ($95,000 ÷ 10,000). Such a procedure overlooks the reality of a higher aver-

Exhibit 12-1   Hypothetical Firm Cost Structure

Year 1990

Sales Revenue		$200,000
(25,000 units @ $8.00)		
Total Costs:		
Fixed Costs	$75,000	
Variable Costs ($2 per unit)	50,000	125,000
Gross Margin		$ 75,000

---

age cost at a lower sales level. This is, of course, due to a constant fixed cost spread over fewer units.

Demand Considerations in Pricing

Cost considerations provide a floor below which a price would not be set for normal pricing purposes. Cost analysis does not tell the small-business manager how far the "right" price should exceed that minimum figure. Only after considering the nature of demand can this be determined.

Demand Factors   Several factors affect the demand for a product or service. One is the appeal of the product itself. If consumers perceive the product as an important solution to their unsatisfied needs, there will be demand.

Exhibit 12-2   Hypothetical Firm Cost Structure

Year 1991

Sales Revenue		$ 80,000
(10,000 units @ $8.00)		
Total Costs:		
Fixed Costs	$75,000	
Variable Costs ($2 per unit)	20,000	95,000
Gross Margin		$(15,000)

Only in rare cases are identical products and services offered by competing firms. In many cases the products are dissimilar in some way. Even when products are similar, the accompanying services typically differ. Speed of service, credit terms, delivery arrangements, personal attention by a top executive, and willingness to stand behind the product or service are but a few of the areas that distinguish one product from another. The pricing implications depend on whether the small firm is inferior or superior in these respects to its competitors. Certainly, there is no absolute imperative for the small business to conform slavishly to the prices of others. Its unique combination of goods and services may well justify a premium price.

Another factor that has a major influence on demand is the product price itself. This factor is the basis of what is called prestige pricing. **Prestige pricing** is setting a high price to convey the image of high quality and uniqueness. The influence of prestige pricing varies from market to market and product to product. Higher-income-level markets are less sensitive to price variations than lower-income groups. Therefore, prestige pricing typically works better in these markets. Also, products sold to markets with low levels of product knowledge are candidates for prestige pricing. When cus-

---

SMALL BUSINESS IN ACTION
Prestige Pricing Lures Customers

Sometimes entrepreneurs can successfully price their products well above costs due to the uniqueness of the items. Such is the case for Tink Nathan, of McLean, VA, who sells a product to deer hunters at prices well above costs.

Nathan has been able to sell his product to hunters throughout the United States at enormous markups because they know that his buck-lure product has the scent that will attract buck deer within hunting range better than any other technique. One year he sold 700,000 1-ounce bottles of the product to distributors at $5.00 to $6.00 each. His costs at that time were only 25 cents per bottle!

Nathan's favorite reply to the question of "How's business?" is a confident "It stinks." Business has more than doubled each year for the last five years of operation.

Source: Viveca Novak, "This Business Stinks." Reprinted from the September, 1987, issue of *VENTURE, For Entrepreneurial Business Owners & Investors,* © 1987.

tomers know very little about product characteristics, they will often use price as an indicator of quality.

A company selling windshield-washer fluid found that it could use prestige pricing for its product. The product cost pennies to manufacture and, therefore, sold at an extremely low price even with a large markup. The firm recognized an opportunity and raised its price repeatedly until it was selling at a price several times greater than it had been originally. Sales made the product extremely profitable.[2]

Another small business, G.O.D., Inc., an overnight freight business, also experienced the benefits of prestige pricing. Walter Riley, the president of G.O.D., had kept prices competitive from the time the company first began operations. "We were toe to toe with them," he says, "and we still weren't getting any new business." In 1986, the company increased its prices to a 5 percent to 7 percent premium. "Raising our prices startled purchasing agents into seeing that we weren't just like our competitors. And they were willing to pay extra for overnight delivery."[3]

Elasticity of Demand   The effect that a change in price has on the quantity demanded is called **elasticity of demand.** A product is said to have **elastic demand** if an increase in its price lowers total revenue or a decrease in price raises total revenue. A product is said to have **inelastic demand** if an increase in its price raises total revenue or a decrease in price lowers total revenue.

In some industries, the demand for products is very elastic—when prices are lower, the amount purchased increases considerably, thus providing higher revenues. An example of this can be found in the personal computer industry. For other products, such as salt, the industry demand is very inelastic. Regardless of its price, the quantity purchased will not change significantly because consumers use a fixed amount of salt.

The concept of elasticity of demand is important to a small firm because it suggests an optimum situation for the firm—inelastic demand for a given firm's products. Regardless of industry demand, the small firm should seek to distinguish its product or service in such a way that small price increases will result in increasing total revenues.

Break-Even Analysis in Pricing

Break-even analysis entails a formal comparison of cost and demand for the purpose of determining the acceptability of alternative prices. There are two stages of a complete break-even analysis: cost break-even and cost-

Figure 12–1   Demand Is Elastic in Computer Software

Courtesy of The Future Now Shops

adjusted break-even. Break-even analysis can be explained via formulas or graphs. We will use the graphic presentation in this chapter.

Cost Break-Even Stage   The objective of the cost break-even stage is to determine the quantity at which the product, with an assumed price, will generate enough revenue to start earning a profit. Exhibit 12–3(a) presents a simple cost break-even chart. Total fixed costs are portrayed as a horizontal section in view of the fact that they do not change with the volume of production. The variable-cost section slants upward, however, because of the direct relationship of total variable costs to output. The area between the slanting total cost line and the horizontal base line thus represents the combination of fixed and variable costs. The area between the revenue and total cost lines reveals the profit or loss position of the company at any level of sales. The intersection of these two lines is called the break-even point because sales revenue equals total cost at this point.

Additional revenue lines at other prices can be charted on the break-even graph to evaluate new break-even points. This gives a flexible break-

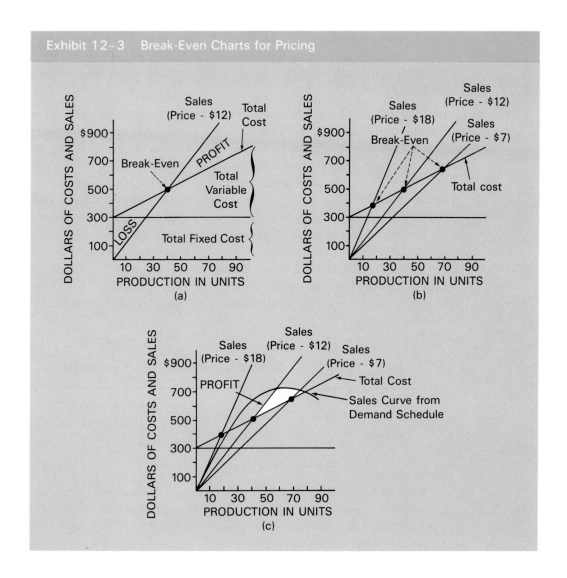

Exhibit 12-3   Break-Even Charts for Pricing

even chart as shown on Exhibit 12–3(b). The assumed higher price of $18.00 in Exhibit 12–3(b) plots a more steeply sloped revenue line, resulting in an earlier break-even point. Similarly, the lower price of $7.00 produces a "flatter" revenue line, increasing the break-even point. Additional sales revenue lines could be plotted to evaluate other proposed prices.

The cost break-even chart implies that quantity sold can increase continually (as shown by the larger and larger profit area to the right). This is misleading and can be clarified by adjusting the cost break-even analysis with demand data.

Cost-Adjusted Break-Even Stage   The indirect impact of price on quantity sold is a confounding problem for pricing decisions. Typically, less of a product is demanded as price increases. In exceptional cases, as mentioned earlier, price may influence demand in the opposite direction, resulting in more demand for a product at higher prices. The estimated demand for a product at various prices needs to be incorporated into the break-even analysis. Marketing research can be used to estimate demand at various prices.

The usefulness of break-even analysis can be greatly increased by incorporating the estimated demand. A cost-adjusted break-even chart is built by using the cost break-even data and adding a demand curve. A demand schedule showing the estimated number of units demanded and total revenue at various prices is listed below and is used to plot the demand curve in Exhibit 12–3(c).

Price	Demand (Units)	Revenue ($)
$ 7	90	$630
12	60	720
18	15	270

When this demand schedule is plotted on a flexible break-even chart, a more realistic profit area is identified, as shown in Exhibit 12–3(c). The break-even point in Exhibit 12–3(c) for an $18.00 unit price corresponds to sales quantities that cannot be reached at the assumed price. Therefore, the optimum of the three prices in Exhibit 12–3(c) is $12.00. This price shows the greatest profit potential as indicated by the shaded profit area in Exhibit 12–3(c).

Setting the Selling Price

After careful consideration of cost and demand data with break-even analysis, the small firm should have a better understanding of which prices are feasible. However, the seemingly precise nature of break-even analysis should not mislead the small-business manager. Break-even analysis is only one tool of pricing and does not in itself determine the "right" price. In other words, price should never be determined in isolation from the current marketing strategy. Several examples of these strategy considerations are discussed in the following sections.[4]

Penetration Pricing　The strategy called **penetration pricing** involves pricing products or services lower than a normal, long-range market price in order to gain more rapid market acceptance or to increase existing market share. This strategy can sometimes discourage new competitors from entering the market if they view the penetration price as a long-range price. Obviously, this strategy sacrifices some profit margins to achieve other marketing goals.

Skimming Pricing　A **skimming-price strategy** sets prices for products or services at very high levels for a limited period before reducing the price to a lower, more competitive level. This strategy assumes that certain customers will pay the higher price because they view the product or service as a prestige item. This strategy is most practical when there is little threat of short-term competition or when startup costs must be recovered rapidly.

Follow-the-Leader Pricing　The probable reaction of competitors is a critical factor in determining whether to cut prices below a prevailing level. A small business in competition with larger firms seldom is in a position to consider itself the price leader. If competitors view the small firm's pricing as relatively unimportant, they may permit a price differential. This may well be the reaction if the price-cutting firm is sufficiently small. On the other hand, established firms may view a smaller price-cutter as a direct threat and counter with reductions of their own. In such a case, the smaller price-cutter accomplishes very little.

Variable Pricing　In some lines of business, the selling firm makes price concessions to individual customers even though it advertises a uniform price. Concessions are made for various reasons, one of which is the customer's knowledge and bargaining strength. In some fields of business, therefore, pricing decisions involve two parts: a stipulated "list price" and a range of price concessions to particular buyers.

Flexible Pricing　Although many firms use total cost as a point of resistance, most of them take into consideration special market conditions and practices of competitors in arriving at their prices. The following cases illustrate this point:

1. *Contractor A* estimates the full cost of building a house, but he modifies the price to meet market conditions. Even his concept of cost reflects variable estimates of the opportunity costs of his time. His time is less valuable in the winter, when business is slack, than at other seasons; he adjusts his estimates of cost accordingly. He also shaves price on a cash sale of a house, recognizing the avoidance of a risk as compared with sales involving complicated financing. Thus, the stress on full cost does not mean inattention to demand.

2. *Printing Company B* also pays considerable attention to full-cost estimates. While the management insists that prices should be kept on a full-cost basis, actual practice is more flexible. The managers are critical of "rate cutters," who, they claim, are responsible for the low industry profits, but they themselves show some willingness to adjust to market conditions when the necessity arises.

3. *Furniture Company C* starts with a cost estimate, including an allocation of indirect labor and factory overhead. But the management modifies the target return to meet market conditions.

On certain occasions it may be logical to price at less than total cost. For example, if the facilities of a business are idle, some costs may be continuing. In any case, the price should cover all marginal or incremental costs—that is, those costs specifically incurred to get the added business. In the long run, however, all overhead costs must be covered as well.

Price Lining   A **price line** is a range of several distinct prices at which merchandise is offered for sale. For example, men's suits might be sold at $150.00, $200.00, and $250.00. The general level of the different lines would depend on the income level and buying desires of a store's customers. Price lining has the advantage of simplifying choice for the customer and reducing the necessary minimum inventory.

What the Traffic Will Bear   The policy of pricing on the basis of what the traffic will bear can be used only when the seller has little or no competition. Obviously, this policy will work only for nonstandardized products. For example, a food store might offer egg roll wrappers that the competitors do not carry. Busy consumers who want to fix egg rolls but who have neither the time nor the knowledge to prepare the wrappers will buy them at any reasonable price.

Calculating Markups

Up to this point in our discussion of pricing, we have made no distinction between pricing by manufacturers and pricing by intermediaries. Such a distinction was not necessary since the concepts apply to all small businesses, regardless of their position in the distribution channel. Now, however, we will discuss some of the pricing arithmetic that is used in the retail trade. Since retail businesses often carry many products, a system of markup pricing has emerged as a manageable framework for pricing.

With this cost-plus system of pricing, retailers are able to price hundreds of products much more quickly than they could with a system involving individual break-even analyses. In calculating the selling price for a particular item, the retailer must add a markup percentage to cover the following:

1. Operating expenses.
2. Profit.
3. Subsequent price reductions—for example, markdowns and employee discounts.

Markups may be expressed as a percentage of either the *selling price* or the *cost*. For example, if an item costs $6.00 and is selling at $10.00, the markup of $4.00 would be 40 percent of the selling price $(4.00 \div 10.00 \times 100)$ or $66\frac{2}{3}$ percent of the cost $(4.00 \div 6.00 \times 100)$. Although either method is correct, consistency demands that the same method be used in considering the components entering into the markup. If operating expenses amount to 35 percent of sales and a profit of 5 percent of sales is desired, the markup (assuming no markdown) must be 40 percent of selling price. This is clearly different from 40 percent markup based on cost. In fact, an incorrect application of the 40 percent figure to cost would produce a markup amounting to less than 29 percent of sales, which is not enough to cover operating expenses. Exhibit 12–4 presents simple formulas for markup calculations.

Additional Considerations in Pricing

In some situations local, state, and federal laws must also be considered in setting prices. For example, the federal Sherman Antitrust Act provides a general prohibition of price fixing. Most federal pricing legislation

Exhibit 12–4   Formulas for Markup Calculations

Cost + Markup = Selling price
Cost   = Selling price − Markup
Markup   = Selling price − Cost

$$\frac{Markup}{Selling\ Price} \times 100 = Markup\ expressed\ as\ a\ percentage\ of\ selling\ price$$

$$\frac{Markup}{Cost} \times 100 = Markup\ expressed\ as\ a\ percentage\ of\ cost$$

If a seller wishes to translate markup as a percentage of selling price into a percentage of cost, or vice versa, the two formulas below are useful:

$$\frac{Markup\ as\ a\ percentage\ of\ selling\ price}{100\% - Markup\ as\ a\ percentage\ of\ selling\ price} \times 100 = Markup\ as\ a\ percentage\ of\ cost$$

$$\frac{Markup\ as\ a\ percentage\ of\ cost}{100\% + Markup\ as\ a\ percentage\ of\ cost} \times 100 = Markup\ as\ a\ percentage\ of\ selling\ price$$

is intended to benefit small firms as well as consumers by keeping large businesses from conspiring to set prices that stifle competition.

Some states have passed pricing legislation. One example is the Unfair Trade Practice Laws, which require retailers to price products based on their cost, thereby limiting their pricing decisions to a formula contained in the law. A small retailer should thoroughly understand this legislation in order to avoid possible conflict.

If a small business markets a line of products—some of which may compete with each other—pricing decisions must also examine the effects of a single product price on the rest of the line. Pricing becomes extremely complex in these situations.

Constantly adjusting a price to meet changing marketing conditions can be both costly to the seller and confusing to buyers. An alternative approach is to make adjustments to the stated price—to arrive at the actual price offered to prospective buyers—by special price quotes. This is achieved with a system of discounting designed to reflect a variety of needs.

For example, a seller may offer a trade discount to a buyer (such as a wholesaler) that lowers the stated price by a certain percentage because the buyer performs a certain marketing function such as distribution. The stated price or list price is unchanged, but the seller offers a lower actual price via the discount.

A final word about pricing. Pricing mistakes are not the exclusive domain of small business. Large firms make pricing errors also. Remember that pricing is not an exact science. If the initial pricing decision appears off target, make the necessary adjustments and keep going!

Credit in Small Business

In a credit sale, the seller conveys goods or services to the buyer in return for the buyer's promise to pay. The major objective in granting credit is an expansion of sales by attracting new customers and an increase in volume and regularity of purchases by existing customers. Some retail firms—furniture stores, for example—cater to newcomers in the city, newly married couples, and others by inviting the credit business of individuals who have established credit ratings. In addition, credit records may be used for purposes of sales promotion by direct-mail appeals to credit customers. Adjustments and exchanges of goods are also facilitated through credit operations.

Benefits of Credit to Buyers and Sellers

If credit buying and selling did not benefit both parties to the transaction, its use would cease. All buyers obviously enjoy the availability of credit, and small firms, in particular, benefit from the judicious extension of credit by suppliers. Credit supplies the small firm with working capital, often permitting continuation of marginal businesses that might otherwise expire. Additional benefits of credit to buyers are:

1. It gives customers the ability to satisfy immediate needs while paying later.
2. It provides better records of purchases with credit billing statements.
3. It provides better service and ease of exchanging purchased items.
4. It offers greater convenience.
5. It builds a credit history.

Sellers extend credit to customers because they can obtain increased sales volume in this way. They expect the increased revenue to more than offset credit costs so that profits will increase. Other benefits of credit to the seller are:

1. It creates a closer association with customers because of implied trust.
2. It provides a marketing tool for easier selling through telephone and mail-order systems.
3. It tends to smooth out sales peaks and valleys since purchasing power is available throughout the month.
4. It provides a tool to stay competitive.

Kinds of Credit

There are two broad classes of credit: consumer credit and trade credit. **Consumer credit** is granted by retailers to final consumers who purchase for personal or family use. However, a small-business owner can use consumer credit to purchase certain supplies and equipment for use in the business. **Trade credit** is extended by nonfinancial firms, such as manufacturers or wholesalers, to customers who are other business firms.

Consumer credit and trade credit differ as to types of credit instruments used and sources for financing receivables. Another important distinction is the availability of credit insurance for trade credit only. Consumer and trade credit also differ markedly as to terms of sale.

Consumer Credit   The three major kinds of consumer-credit accounts are: open charge accounts, installment accounts, and revolving charge accounts. Many variations of these are also used.

Open Charge Accounts   Under the **open charge account,** the customer obtains possession of goods (or services) when purchased, with payment due when billed. Stated terms typically call for payment at the end of the month, but customary practice allows a longer period for payment than that stated. There is no charge for this kind of payment if the balance of the account is paid in full at the end of the period. Customers are not generally required to make a down payment or make a pledge of collateral. Small accounts at department stores are a good example of such use.

Installment Accounts   The **installment account** is the vehicle of long-term consumer credit. A down payment is normally required, and finance charges can be 20 percent or more of the purchase price. The most common payment periods are from 12 to 36 months, although in recent years automobile dealers have extended payment periods to 60 months. An installment account is useful for large purchases such as automobiles, washing machines, and television sets.

Revolving Charge Accounts The **revolving charge account** is another variation of the installment account. The seller may grant a line of credit, and the customer may then charge purchases at any time if purchases do not exceed this credit limit. A specified percentage of the outstanding balance must be paid monthly, which forces the customer to budget and limits the amount of debt that can be carried. Finance charges are computed on the unpaid balance at the end of the month. Credit cards use this type of credit. Because of their significance, credit cards are discussed in a separate section following trade credit.

Trade Credit Business firms may sell goods subject to specified terms of sale, such as 2/10, n/30. This means that a 2 percent discount is given by the seller if the buyer pays within 10 days of the invoice date. Failure to take this discount makes the full amount of the invoice due in 30 days. Other discount arrangements in common use are shown in Exhibit 12–5.

Sales terms in trade credit depend on the kind of product sold and the buyer's and seller's circumstances. The credit period often varies di-

Exhibit 12–5 Trade Credit Terms

Sales Term	Explanation
3/10, n/60	Three percent discount for first 10 days; net on 60th day.
E.O.M.	Billing at end of month, covering all credit purchases of that month.
C.O.D.	Amount of bill will be collected upon delivery of the goods.
2/10, n/30, R.O.G.	Two percent discount for 10 days; net on 30th day—but both discount period and 30 days start from the date of receipt of the goods.
2/10, n/30, E.O.M.	Two percent discount for 10 days; net on 30th day—but both periods start from the end of the month in which the sale was made.

rectly with the length of the buyer's turnover period, which obviously depends on the type of product sold. The larger the order and the higher the credit rating of the buyer, the better the sales terms that can be granted if individual sales terms are fixed for each customer. The greater the financial strength and the more adequate and liquid the working capital of the seller, the more generous the seller's sales terms can be. Of course, no business can afford to allow competitors to outdo it in reasonable generosity of sales terms. In many lines of business, credit terms are so firmly set by tradition that a unique policy is difficult, if not impossible.

Credit Cards   In recent years, credit cards, sometimes referred to as "plastic money," have become a major source of retail credit. As mentioned earlier, credit cards are usually based on a revolving credit system. There are basically three types of credit cards, as distinguished by their sponsor—bank credit cards, entertainment credit cards, and retailer credit cards.

Bank Credit Cards   The best known bank credit cards are MasterCard and VISA. Exhibit 12–6 shows a credit agreement for a credit card issued by a credit union through a bank. Bank credit card systems are widely used by retailers who want to offer credit but do not feel they can offer their own cards. Most small-business retailers would fit into this category. In return for paying the bank a set fee (usually 5 to 6 percent of the purchase price), the bank takes the responsibility for making collections. Recently, some banks have charged annual membership fees to cardholders. Cardholders are frequently able to receive cash up to the credit limits of their cards. In Chapter 9, we mentioned that some entrepreneurs have used this source of credit for financing their business startups—a risky type of financing.

Entertainment Credit Cards   Well-known examples of this form of credit are American Express and Diner's Club cards. These cards have traditionally charged an annual fee. Although originally used for charging services, these cards are now widely accepted for sales of merchandise. Just like bank credit cards, the collection of credit charges is the responsibility of the sponsoring agency.

Retail Credit Cards   Many companies issue their own credit cards for use in their stores or for purchasing their products in other outlets. Department stores, oil companies, and telephone companies are typical examples. Customers are usually not charged any annual fees or any finance charges if balances are paid each month.

Exhibit 12-6 Credit Card Agreement

LINE OF CREDIT (CREDIT CARD) AGREEMENT

_____ Credit Union

Address _____ , Texas
　　　　　Street　　　　　　　　　　City　　　　Zip　　　County

BORROWER(S) _____ Account Number: _____

TERMS USED IN THIS AGREEMENT: "You" and "your" mean any person who signs this Agreement or uses the card. "The card" means any credit card issued to you or those designated by you under the terms of this Agreement. "Use of the card" means any procedure used by you, or someone authorized by you, to make a purchase or obtain a cash advance whether or not the purchase or advance is evidenced by a signed written document. "Unauthorized use of the card" means the use of the card by someone other than you who does not have actual, implied, or apparent authority for such use, and from which you receive no benefit.

EXTENSIONS OF CREDIT: If your application is approved, the Credit Union may, at its discretion, establish a MasterCard and/or VISA Card account in your name and cause one or more cards to be issued to you or those designated by you. In such an event, you authorize the Credit Union to pay for your account, all items reflecting credit purchases and cash advances obtained through use of the card.

CREDIT LIMITS: You promise that payments made for your account resulting from use of the card will, at no time, cause the outstanding balance in your account to exceed your credit limit as disclosed to you at the time you receive your card or as adjusted from time to time at the discretion of the credit union.

PROMISE TO PAY: You promise to repay the Credit Union all payments made for your account resulting from use of the card plus a **FINANCE CHARGE** on the unpaid balance. At the end of each monthly billing cycle, you will be furnished with a periodic statement showing (i) the "previous balance" (the outstanding balance in the account at the beginning of the billing cycle), (ii) the amount of all cash advances, purchases and **FINANCE CHARGES** posted to your account during the billing cycle, (iii) the amount of all payments and credits posted to your account during the billing cycle, and (iv) the "new balance" which is the sum of (i) and (ii) less (iii).

You agree to pay on or before the "payment due date" shown on the periodic statment either the entire "new balance" or a minimum payment equal to _5_ % of the "new balance", or $_18.00_, whichever is greater. If the "new balance" is $_18.00_ or less, you will pay in full.

COST OF CREDIT: You will pay a **FINANCE CHARGE** for all advances made against your account at the periodic rate of _.030356_% per day, which has a corresponding **ANNUAL PERCENTAGE RATE** of _1_ %. Cash advances incur a **FINANCE CHARGE** from the date they are posted to the account. New purchases will not incur a **FINANCE CHARGE** on the date they are posted to the account if you have paid the account in full by the due date shown on your previous monthly statement or if there was no previous balance. No additional **FINANCE CHARGE** will be incurred whenever you pay the account in full by the due date. The **FINANCE CHARGE** is figured by applying the periodic rate to the Balance Subject to **FINANCE CHARGE** which is the "average daily balance" of your account, including certain current transactions. The "aver-

(Continued)

Exhibit 12-6 *(Continued)*

age daily balance" is arrived at by taking the beginning balance of your account each day and adding any new cash advances, and, unless you pay your account in full by the due date shown on your previous monthly statement or there is no previous balance, adding in new purchases, and subtracting any payments or credits and unpaid **FINANCE CHARGES.** The daily balances for the billing cycle are then added together and divided by the number of days in the billing cycle. The result is the "average daily balance." Each **FINANCE CHARGE** is determined by multiplying the "average daily balance" by the number of days in the billing cycle and applying the periodic rates to the product. You may pay any amounts outstanding at any time without penalty for early payment.

CREDIT INSURANCE: If available, credit insurance is not required for any extension of credit under this agreement. However, you may purchase any credit insurance available through the credit union and have the premium added to the outstanding balance in your account. If you elect to do so, you will be given the necessary disclosures and documents separately.

LIABILITY FOR UNAUTHORIZED USE: You may be liable for the unauthorized use of your card. You will not be liable for unauthorized use that occurs after you notify the Credit Union (for Credit Union's designee) orally or in writing, the loss, theft, or possible unauthorized use. In any case, your liability will not exceed $50.00.

The Decision to Sell on Credit

Nearly all small businesses can sell on credit if they wish, and so the entrepreneur must decide whether to sell for cash or on credit. In some cases this is reduced to the question, "Can the granting of credit to customers be avoided?" Credit selling is standard trade practice in many lines of business, and in other businesses credit-selling competitors will always outsell the cash-selling firm.

Factors That Affect the Credit Decision. Numerous factors bear on the decision concerning credit extension. The seller always hopes to increase profits by credit sales, but each firm must also consider its own particular circumstances and environment.

Type of Business Retailers of durable goods, for example, typically grant credit more freely than small grocers who sell perishables. Indeed, most consumers find it necessary to buy big-ticket items on an installment basis, and the product's life makes installment selling possible.

Credit Policy of Competitors Unless a firm offers some compensating advantage, it is expected to be as generous as its competitors in extending credit. Wholesale hardware companies and retail furniture stores are businesses that face stiff competition from credit sellers.

Income Level of Customers   The income level of customers is a significant factor in determining a retailer's credit policy. Consider, for example, a corner drugstore adjacent to a city high school. High school students are typically unsatisfactory credit customers because of their lack of maturity and income.

Availability of Adequate Working Capital   There is no denying the fact that credit sales increase the amount of working capital needed by the business. Money that the business has tied up in open-credit and installment accounts cannot be used to pay business expenses.

The Four C's of Credit   In evaluating the credit standing of applicants, the entrepreneur must answer the following questions:

1. Can the buyer pay as promised?
2. Will the buyer pay?
3. If so, when will the buyer pay?
4. If not, can the buyer be forced to pay?

Before credit is approved, the answers to questions 1, 2, and 4 must be "yes"; to question 3, "on schedule." The answers depend in part on the amount of credit requested and in part on the seller's estimate of the buyer's ability and willingness to pay. Such an estimate constitutes a judgment of the buyer's inherent credit worth.

Every credit applicant possesses credit worth in some degree, so that extended credit is not necessarily a gift to the applicant. Instead, a decision to grant credit merely recognizes the buyer's credit standing. But the seller faces a possible inability or unwillingness to pay on the buyer's part. In making credit decisions, therefore, the seller decides the degree of risk of nonpayment that must be assumed.

Willingness to pay is evaluated in terms of the four C's of credit: character, capital, capacity, and conditions.[5] *Character* refers to the fundamental integrity and honesty that should underlie all human and business relationships. In the case of a business customer, it takes shape in the business policies and ethical practices of the firm. Individual customers who apply for credit must also be known to be morally responsible persons. *Capital* consists of the cash and other assets owned by the business or individual customer. In the case of a business customer, this means capital sufficient to underwrite planned operations, including adequate owner capital. *Capacity* refers to the business customer's ability to conserve assets and faithfully and efficiently follow financial plans. The business customer with capacity utilizes the invested capital of the business firm wisely and capitalizes to the fullest extent on business opportunities. *Conditions* refer to such factors as business cycles and changes in price levels, which may be either favorable or unfavorable to the payment of debts. Other adverse factors that might limit a customer's ability to pay include fires and other natural disasters, new legislation, strong new competition, or labor problems.

Managing the Credit Activity

Unfortunately, most small businesses pay little attention to their credit management system until bad debts become a problem. Often this is too late. Credit management should begin prior to the first credit sale with a thorough screening process and continue throughout the credit cycle. The

---

SMALL BUSINESS IN ACTION
Credit Management a Must

Small businesses typically attach low priority to managing accounts receivable. This is truly unfortunate since a lack of attention to this critical component of the cash flow cycle will usually lead a business into troubled waters.

Steve Irby, founder of Stillwater Designs, Inc., in Stillwater, OK, is a case in point. Irby's business manufactures stereo speakers for automobiles. Cash flow was a minor problem when customers paid cash upon delivery; but later, due to competition, Stillwater Designs was forced to sell on credit. The company had no formal system of managing credit. As a result, 30-day credit terms quickly stretched to 55 days before collections. Then the firm realized it had a major problem.

Irby finally addressed the problem by hiring a credit manager, who quickly took charge. He established an accounts-receivable aging system—on a computer—and formalized a credit policy. The system is working, and the collection period is back down to less than 40 days.

Source: Abby Livingston, "The Squeaky Wheel Syndrome." Reprinted from the February, 1989, issue of *VENTURE, For Entrepreneurial Business Owners & Investors,* © 1989.

major issues in a comprehensive credit management program for a small business are discussed in the following sections.

Credit Investigation of Applicants   In most retail stores, the first step in credit investigation is the completion of an application form. The information obtained on this form is used as the basis for examining the applicant's financial responsibility.

Nonretailing firms should similarly investigate credit applicants. One small clothing manufacturer has every sales order reviewed by a Dun & Bradstreet-trained credit manager who maintains a complete file of D&B credit reports on thousands of customers. Recent financial statements of dealer-customers are filed also. These, together with the dealer's accounts-receivable card, are the basis for decisions on credit sales, with major emphasis on the D&B credit reports.

Credit Limits   Perhaps the most important factor in determining a customer's credit limits is the customer's ability to pay the obligation when it becomes due. This in turn requires an evaluation of the customer's financial resources, debt position, and income level.

The amount of credit required by the customer is the second factor that requires consideration. Customers of a drugstore need only small amounts of credit. On the other hand, business customers of wholesalers and manufacturers typically expect larger amounts of credit. In the special case of installment selling, the amount of credit should not exceed the repossession value of the goods sold. Automobile dealers follow this rule as a general practice.

Sources of Credit Information   One of the most important and frequently neglected sources of credit information is found in the seller's accounts-receivable records. Properly analyzed, these records show whether the customer regularly takes cash discounts and, if not, whether the customer's account is typically slow.

Manufacturers and wholesalers frequently can use the financial statements submitted by firms applying for credit as an additional source of information. Obtaining maximum value from financial statements requires a careful ratio analysis, which will reveal a firm's working-capital position, profit-making potential, and general financial health.

Pertinent data may also be obtained from outsiders. For example, arrangements may be made with other suppliers to exchange credit data. Such credit interchange reports are quite useful in learning about the sales and payment experiences of others with one's own credit customers or applicants.

Another source of credit data, on commercial accounts particularly, is the customer's banker. Some bankers are glad to supply credit information about their depositors, considering this a service in helping them obtain credit in amounts they can successfully handle. Other bankers feel that credit information is confidential and should not be disclosed in this way.

Organizations that may be consulted with reference to credit standings are trade-credit agencies and local credit bureaus. **Trade-credit agencies** are privately owned and operated organizations that collect credit information on business firms. After they analyze and evaluate the data, they make credit ratings available to client companies for a fee. These agencies are concerned with trade-credit ratings only, having nothing to do with consumer credit. Dun & Bradstreet, Inc., is a general trade-credit agency serving the nation. Manufacturers and wholesalers are especially interested in its reference book and credit reports. The reference book covers all United States businesses and shows credit rating, financial strength, and other key credit information. It is available to subscribers only.

A **credit bureau** serves its members—retailers and other firms in a given community—by summarizing their credit experience with particular individuals. A local bureau can also broaden its service by affiliation with either the National Retail Credit Association or the Associated Credit Bureaus of America. This makes possible the exchange of credit information on persons who move from one city to another. A business firm need not be a member of some bureaus in order to get a credit report. The fee charged to nonmembers, however, is considerably higher than that charged to members.

Billing Procedures   Timely notification of customers regarding the status of their accounts is one of the most effective methods of keeping credit accounts current. Most credit customers will pay their bills on time if the creditor provides them with the necessary information to verify the credit balance. Failure to send the correct number of invoices or other billing errors will only delay timely payments.[6]

Cash discounts can also be offered as an incentive for quick payment. Discounts reduce the invoice amount by a stated percentage if payment is made within a specified time period. This concept of providing a motivation to pay promptly was discussed earlier under the topic of trade credit.

Collection of Past-Due Accounts   Slow credit accounts are a problem because they tie up the seller's working capital, prevent further sales to the slow-paying customer, and lead to losses from bad debts. Even if the slow-paying customer is not lost, relations with this customer are strained for a time at least.

Inadequate records and collection procedures often fail to alert the small firm in time to permit prompt collections. Also, the personal acquaintance of seller and customer sometimes tempts the seller to be less than businesslike in extending further credit and collecting overdue accounts. Conceding the seriousness of the problem, the small firm must know what steps to take and how far to go in collecting past-due accounts. It must decide whether to undertake the job directly or to turn it over to an attorney or a collection agency.

Collection Procedure   Perhaps the most effective weapon in collecting past-due accounts is the debtors' knowledge of possible impairment of their credit standing. This impairment is certain if an account is turned over to a collection agency. Delinquent customers who foresee continued solvency will typically attempt to avoid damage to their credit standing, particularly when it would be known to the business community generally. It is this knowledge that lies behind and strengthens the various collection efforts of the business.

Many business firms have found that the most effective collection procedure consists of a series of steps, each of which is somewhat more forceful than the preceding one.[7] Although these typically begin with a gentle written reminder, they may include additional letters, telephone calls, registered letters, personal contacts, and referrals to collection agencies or attorneys. The timing of these steps may be carefully standardized so that step two automatically follows step one in a specified number of days, with subsequent steps similarly spaced.

Aging Accounts Receivable   Many small businesses can benefit from an **aging schedule**, which divides accounts receivable into age categories based on the length of time they have been outstanding. Usually, some accounts are current and others are past due. Various collection actions can be used for different-aged accounts. With successive scheduling, troublesome trends can be spotted and appropriate action taken. With experience, the probabilities of collecting accounts of various ages can be estimated and used to forecast cash conversion rates.

Exhibit 12–7 shows a hypothetical aging of accounts receivable. It shows that four customers have overdue payments totaling $200,000. Only Customer 005 is current. Customer 003 has the largest amount ($80,000) of overdue credit. In fact, the schedule shows that Customer 003 is overdue on all charges and has a past record of slow payment (a credit rating of "C"). Immediate attention to collecting from this customer is necessary. Customer

Exhibit 12–7   Hypothetical Aging of Accounts Receivable

Account Status	Customer Account Numbers					
	001	002	003	004	005	Total
120 days	—	—	$50,000	—	—	$50,000
90 days	—	$10,000	—	—	—	10,000
60 days	—	—	—	$40,000	—	40,000
30 days	—	20,000	20,000	—	—	40,000
15 days	$50,000	—	10,000	—		60,000
Total Overdue	$50,000	$30,000	$80,000	$40,000	0	$200,000
Not Due (beyond-discount period)	$30,000	$ 10,000	0	$10,000	$130,000	$180,000
Not Due (still in discount period)	$20,000	$100,000	0	$90,000	$220,000	$430,000
Credit Rating	A	B	C	A	A	

002 should be contacted also. The status of this customer is critical because, among overdue accounts, Customer 002 has the largest amount ($110,000) in the "Not Due" classifications. This customer could quickly have the largest amont overdue.

Customers 004 and 001 need a special kind of analysis. Customer 004 has $10,000 less overdue than Customer 001. However, Customer 004's overdue credit of $40,000, which is 60 days past due, may well have a serious impact on the $100,000 not yet due ($10,000 in the beyond-discount period plus $90,000 still in the discount period). On the other hand, even though Customer 001 has $50,000 of overdue credit, he or she is overdue only 15 days. Also, Customer 001 has only $50,000 not yet due ($30,000 in the beyond-discount period plus $20,000 still in the discount period) as compared to $100,000 not yet due from Customer 004. Both customers have a credit rating of "A."

In conclusion, Customer 001 is a better potential source of cash; so, collection efforts need to begin with Customer 004 rather than with Customer 001. Customer 001 may simply need a reminder that he or she has an overdue account of $50,000.

The Bad-Debt Ratio   In controlling expenses associated with credit sales, it is possible to use various expense ratios. The best known and most widely used ratio is the **bad-debt ratio**, which is computed by dividing the amount of bad debts by the total credit sales.

The bad-debt ratio reflects the efficiency of credit policies and procedures. A small firm may thus compare the effectiveness of its credit management with that of other firms. There is a relationship between the bad-debt ratio on the one hand and the type of business, profitability, and size of

---

SMALL BUSINESS IN ACTION
Bad Debt Not All Bad

Credit is a powerful sales tool. However, extending credit to maximize sales without regard to credit risk can lead to trouble. Nevertheless, zero credit risk may not be the wisest of goals either!

Consider the credit philosophy of James K. Ullery, who is credit manager for the small firm of Albany Ladder in Albany, NY. Ullery does not believe his only job responsibility is to keep bad-debt totals low. Lester J. Heath, III, president of the building supplies company, agrees. He contends that "sales and market share . . . are the key things you should look at, not bad debt. If your bad debt isn't high enough, you aren't taking enough risk." Albany Ladder's bad-debt ratio is nearly twice the industry average!

Heath began implementing his liberal credit policy when he grew tired of losing potential customers who did not have the ability to get loans to purchase building supplies from his company. "If you extend credit to a person who couldn't get it elsewhere, he'll remember that gesture forever and could be a customer for life."

Despite Albany Ladder's liberal credit policy, its collection policy is aggressive, beginning the first day that an account is overdue. "We make mistakes, no question about it," says Ullery. However, Albany Ladder is based on treating customers as human beings and recognizing that a few bad debts are only human.

Source: Paul B. Brown, "Bad Debt Can Be Good for Business." Reprinted with permission, *Inc.* magazine (March, 1988). Copyright © 1988 Goldhirsh Group, Inc., 38 Commercial Wharf, Boston, MA 02110.

firm on the other. Small profitable retailers have a much higher loss ratio than large profitable retailers. The bad-debt losses of all small-business firms, however, range from a fraction of 1 percent of net sales to percentages large enough to put them out of business!

Credit Regulation

The granting of credit is regulated by a variety of federal and state laws. Prior to the passage of legislation, credit customers were often confused by credit agreements and were sometimes victims of credit abuse. As is usually the case, legislation covering credit practices varies considerably from state to state. Therefore, our brief discussion of credit legislation is limited to federal laws.

By far the most significant piece of credit legislation is the Federal Consumer Credit Act, more often called the 1968 Truth-in-Lending Act. Its two primary purposes are to inform consumers about terms of a credit agreement and to require creditors to specify how finance charges are computed. The law requires that the finance charge be stated as an annual percentage rate (see Exhibit 12–6). The law also requires creditors to clearly specify the procedures for correcting billing mistakes.

Other legislation related to credit management includes:

1. *The Fair Credit Billing Act*—This law provides protection to credit customers for cases involving incorrect billing. A reasonable time period is allowed for corrections.
2. *The Fair Credit Reporting Act*—This act gives certain rights to credit applicants regarding credit reports prepared by credit bureaus.
3. *The Equal Credit Opportunity Act*—This act protects widowed and divorced women against credit denial because of a lack of credit history.

Looking Back

1. Cost considerations in pricing involve an understanding of the components of total variable costs and of total fixed costs. Demand considerations involve such factors as product appeal, marketing effort, and product price, all of which exert an influence on demand. An understanding of elastic demand and inelastic demand is also important.

2. Break-even analysis in pricing entails a formal comparison of cost and demand for purposes of determining the acceptability of alternative prices. Fixed and variable costs are used to construct a cost break-even chart. Demand factors can be incorporated to construct a cost-adjusted break-even chart.

3. In setting the actual price for a product or service, a firm should also consider specific marketing objectives. Penetration pricing, skimming pricing, follow-the-leader pricing, flexible pricing, price lining, and what-the-traffic-will-bear pricing all reflect different objectives. Markup calculations should be understood by all businesses—especially retailers.

4. Consumer credit is credit granted by retailers to final consumers and includes open charge accounts, installment accounts, and revolving charge accounts. Trade credit is credit extended by nonfinancial firms to customers who are other business firms. Credit cards are a major source of retail credit.

5. Credit management should begin prior to the first credit sale and continue throughout the credit cycle. Collection of past-due accounts first involves an aging of accounts receivable and then a series of collection steps.

DISCUSSION QUESTIONS

1. Explain why both pricing and credit decisions are so vital to a small business.

2. How can average-cost pricing sometimes result in a bad pricing decision?

3. Explain the importance of fixed and variable costs to the pricing decision.

4. How does the concept of elasticity of demand relate to prestige pricing? Give an example.

5. Contrast the cost-break-even stage of break-even analysis with the cost-adjusted stage. Which is better? Why?

6. What is the difference between a penetration and a skimming pricing strategy? Under what circumstances would each be used?

7. What is the psychology behind price lining?

8. If a small business has conducted its break-even analysis properly and finds break-even at a price of $10.00 to be 10,000 units, should it price its product at $10.00? Discuss.

9. What percentage markup on cost is a 70 percent markup on selling price? What percentage markup on selling price is a 40 percent markup on cost?

10. What is the difference between consumer credit and trade credit?

11. What are the major benefits of credit to buyers? What are the major benefits to sellers?

12. How does an open charge account differ from a revolving charge account?

13. What is meant by the terms 2/10, n/30? Does it pay to take discounts?

14. What is the major purpose of aging accounts receivable? At what point in credit management should this activity be performed? Why?

15. What impact has the Truth-in-Lending Act had on credit policies? What information in Exhibit 12–6 is a direct result of this legislation?

YOU MAKE THE CALL

Situation 1

Steve Jones is a 35-year-old owner of a highly competitive small business supplying temporary office help. Like most businesspeople, he is always looking for ways to increase profits. However, the nature of competition makes it very difficult to raise prices for the temps' services, and reducing their wages makes recruiting difficult. Jones has, nevertheless, found an area where improvement should increase profits—bad debts.

A friend and business consultant met with Jones to advise him on improved credit-management policies. Jones was extremely pleased to have help since bad debts were costing him about 2 percent of sales. Currently, Jones has no system of managing credit.

Questions

1. What advice would you give Jones regarding screening of new credit customers?

2. What action should Jones take to encourage current credit customers to pay their debts? Be specific.

3. Jones has considered eliminating credit sales. What are the possible consequences of this decision?

Situation 2

Mom's Monogram is a small firm manufacturing and imprinting monogramming designs for jackets, caps, T-shirts and other articles of clothing. The business has been in operation for two years. In the first year, sales reached $50,000. The next year, sales raced up to $300,000. Pricing of the firm's service has been a straight, cost-plus approach.

Success has spawned plans to double plant and equipment. The owners have never spent money advertising and figure that the expansion will double sales within the next three years. The owners plan to continue pricing their services using a cost-plus formula.

Questions

1. What problems may be encountered by the business if it continues to use cost-plus pricing?
2. How should the firm's total costs be analyzed to ascertain its pricing strategy?
3. What types of discounts might be offered customers of Mom's Monogram? Be specific.

EXPERIENTIAL EXERCISES

1. Interview a small-business owner regarding his or her pricing strategies. Try to ascertain whether the pricing policy used reflects fixed and variable costs in the business. Prepare a report of your findings.
2. Interview a small-business owner regarding his or her policies for evaluating the credit risks of credit applicants. Summarize your findings in a report.
3. Invite a credit manager from a retail store to speak to the class on the benefits and problems of credit to buyers and sellers.
4. Interview a sample of small-business owners in your community who extend credit. Ask each owner to describe what credit management policies he or she uses to collect bad debts. Report your findings to the class.

REFERENCES TO SMALL-BUSINESS PRACTICES

Barrier, Michael. "Kemmons Wilson Changes His Mind." *Nation's Business,* Vol. 77, No. 3 (March, 1989), pp. 77–78.
    An older and successful entrepreneur describes his new motel venture, including his pricing plan.

Goold, Christine. "From Crafts to Cash." *Entrepreneur,* Vol. 16, No. 7 (July, 1988), pp. 144–150.

    The pricing strategy of a female entrepreneur is described in this article.

Henry, Fran Worden. "The Price Is Right ... Or Is It?" *In Business,* Vol. 8, No. 3 (May–June, 1986), pp. 26–29.

    In this article the author has presented a case study of pricing for a small retailer which incorporates both a quantitative and qualitative analysis.

Mamis, Robert A. "The Price Is Wrong." *Inc.,* Vol. 8, No. 5 (May, 1986), pp. 159–164.

    In this article the founders of a small manufacturing firm admit to their pricing mistakes. They describe how they conducted no market analysis and did not consider what the market would bear.

Olmsted, Betty A. "Give Your Customer Relations a Charge." *Entrepreneur,* Vol. 16, No. 7 (July, 1988), pp. 26–30.

    In this article the author provides reasons why credit is an essential marketing tool. Methods to improve credit collections are also discussed.

ENDNOTES

1. Perfectly inelastic demand is assumed to emphasize the point.

2. Charles W. Kyd, "Pricing for Profit," *Inc.,* Vol. 9, No. 4 (April, 1987), p. 120.

3. "Higher Price, Higher Sales," *Inc.,* Vol. 10, No. 10 (October, 1988), p. 112.

4. An excellent discussion of pricing strategies is contained in Stephen L. Montgomery, *Profitable Pricing Strategies* (New York: McGraw-Hill Book Co., 1988).

5. Gerald Pintel and Jay Diamond, *Retailing,* 4th ed. (Englewood Cliffs, NJ: Prentice-Hall, Inc., 1987), p. 428.

6. A useful reference for examples of billing procedures and other credit collection policies is Myron J. Biggar, *Practical Credit and Collections for Small Business* (Boston: CBI Publications, 1983).

7. See, for example, Mark Stevens, "Winning Strategies for Collecting on Bad Debts," *Entrepreneur,* Vol. 16, No. 6 (June, 1988), pp. 18–20.

13 PERSONAL SELLING, ADVERTISING, AND SALES PROMOTION

Spotlight on Small Business

Courtesy of Onyx Enterprises, Inc.

How can a tiny firm promote a new product when it lacks the huge advertising resources of large corporations? One answer is to adopt promotional strategies that are creative without being too costly. Gus Blythe and his Paso Robles, CA, firm used this approach to promote "SecondWind," a product for cleaning sneakers.

Blythe first tried advertising in running magazines, but his budget was too small to be effective. He then conceived the idea of collaborating with running-shoe manufacturers. Blythe argued that his product was good and that promoting its use would also help the sneaker manufacturer.

At first, shoe manufacturers were reluctant to endorse SecondWind, feeling that clean shoes would deter repeat purchases. However, Blythe had an answer to this concern: "If you have two pairs of shoes in your closet, one clean and one dirty, which are you likely to wear?" asked Blythe. "The

367

clean ones, right? If you wear them more, they wear out faster, which means you have to buy new ones," he added.

He eventually convinced nine of the top ten sneaker manufacturers to recommend SecondWind as a cleaner for their shoes. In return, Blythe agreed to include pictures of their shoes on the product's package.

Source: Reprinted with permission, *Inc.* magazine (July, 1989). Copyright © 1989 by Goldhirsh Group, Inc., 38 Commercial Wharf, Boston, MA 02110.

Looking Ahead

Watch for the following important topics:
1. Considerations in developing a promotional mix.
2. Methods of determining promotional expenditures.
3. Preparing and making a sales presentation.
4. Advertising options for the small business.
5. Types of sales promotional tools.
6. New terms and concepts:

promotion	product advertising
promotional mix	institutional advertising
personal selling	sales promotion
prospecting	publicity
advertising	

Belief in the old adage, "Build a better mousetrap and the world will beat a path to your door," does not eliminate the entrepreneur's need for promotion. Why? Because potential customers must be informed of the new, improved "mousetrap" and how to get to the door! They may even need to be persuaded that the mousetrap is better. This process of informing and persuading is essentially communication. Therefore, we view **promotion** as communication between the small business and its target market.

Naturally, small businesses use promotion in varying degrees. Any given firm can use all or some of the many available promotional tools. The three groupings of promotional methods presented in this chapter are personal selling, advertising, and sales promotion.

Promotional Planning

Small businesses sometimes stand in awe of promotional planning. They are confused by rate schedules, reach, and frequency terminology, as well as the numerous options that are available. Promotion is admittedly a complex area, and most entrepreneurs are not "turned" in that direction. But you can begin to understand promotion by realizing the simple fact that promotion is largely communication. In fact, promotion is worthless unless it communicates. Let's briefly look at the communication process and see how promotion needs to be built on these concepts.

The Communication Process

All of us communicate each day. However, we may not have stopped to analyze our communications to realize that communication is a process with identifiable components. Exhibit 13–1 depicts the various components of communication. Part A in the figure represents a personal communication. Part B represents a small-business communication (promotion).

As you can see, the differences between Parts A and B in Exhibit 13–1 are in form, not in basic structure. Each communication involves a source, a channel, and a receiver. In Part B the receiver for the small-business communication from the XYZ Company is the customer. The receiver for Gwen Doe's personal communication is Charles Buck. She has used three different channels for her message: personal conversation, the telephone, and a special window message. The XYZ Company has used similar message channels: face-to-face communication (personal selling), the radio (advertising), and a hot-air balloon circling the city (sales promotional tool).

At this point your understanding of promotion and its roots in personal communication should be clearer. We now will turn to the particulars of molding a strong promotional plan. A good promotional plan must consider three major topics: which promotional tools to mix together, how much to spend, and how to create the messages.

The Promotional Mix

A **promotional mix** is a blend of personal selling and nonpersonal selling by marketers in an attempt to achieve promotional objectives. The mixture of the various promotional methods—personal selling, advertising, and sales promotion—is influenced by three major factors. First is the geo-

Exhibit 13–1   Analogy of Personal and Small-Business Communication

PART A: A PERSONAL COMMUNICATION

Source

(Gwen Doe)

Channel

(Conversation)

(Telephone)

I luv
you

(Window Message)

Receiver

(Charles Buck)

PART B: A SMALL-BUSINESS COMMUNICATION

Source

XYZ Co.

(Small Business)

Channel

(Personal Selling)

(Advertising)

XYZ
Co.

(Sales Promotion)

Receiver

(Customer)

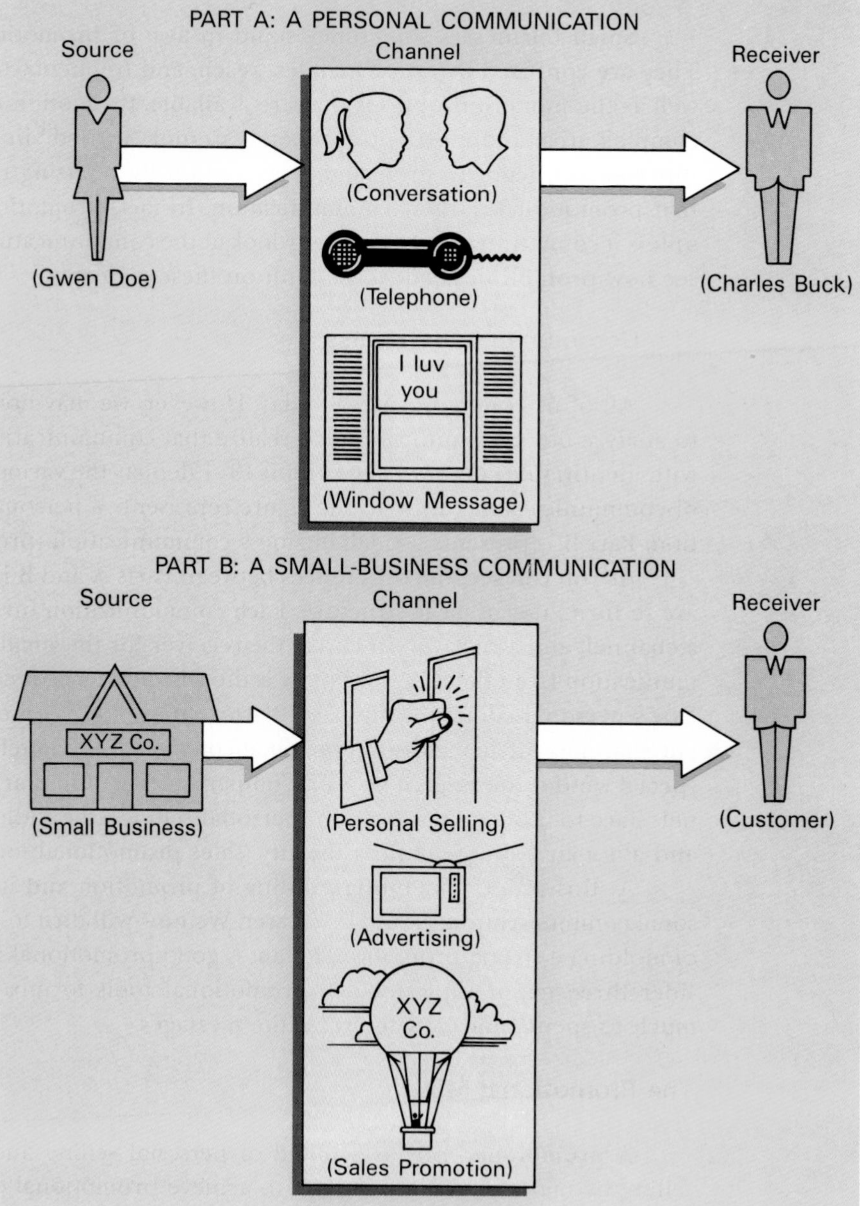

graphical nature of the market to be reached. A widely dispersed market tends to favor mass coverage by advertising, in contrast to the more costly individual contacts of personal selling. On the other hand, if the market is local with a relatively small number of customers, personal selling will be more feasible. Personal selling is more widely used for marketing to industrial customers.

Second, a small business must also understand (as discussed in Chapter 7) who its customers are. It is expensive to use shotgun promotion, which "hits" potential customers and nonpotential customers alike. This error can be minimized by knowing media audiences. The media are extremely helpful in profiling their audiences. But a small business cannot obtain a media *match* until it has specified its target market carefully.

The third factor that influences the promotional mix is the product's own characteristics. If a product is of high unit value, personal selling will be a vital ingredient in the mix. Personal selling will also be prominent for promoting highly technical products. On the other hand, sales promotion will more likely be used with an impulse good than with a shopping good.

There are, of course, other considerations that must ultimately be considered when developing the promotional mix. For example, the high cost of the optimum mix may necessitate substitution of a less expensive and less optimum alternative. But promotional planning can be used to determine the optimum mix and then make cost-saving adjustments if absolutely necessary.

Methods of Determining Promotional Expenditures

There is no formula to answer the question, "How much should a small business spend on promotion?" There are, however, some helpful approaches to solving the problem. The most common methods of earmarking funds for promotion are:

1. A percentage of sales (APS).
2. What can be spared (WCS).
3. As much as competition spends (ACS).
4. What it takes to do the job (WTDJ).

A Percentage of Sales (APS)   Earmarking promotional dollars based on a percentage of sales is a simple method for a small business to use. A company's own past experiences are evaluated to establish a promotion–sales ratio. If 2 percent of sales, for example, has historically been spent on promotion, the business would budget 2 percent of forecasted sales. Secondary data can be checked to locate industry ratio averages for comparison.

The major shortcoming of this method is its inherent tendency to spend more dollars when sales are increasing and less when they are declining. If promotion stimulates sales, the reverse would seem desirable.

What Can Be Spared (WCS)   The most widely used approach to promotional funding is to spend what is left over when all other activities have been completed. Or a budget may be nonexistent and spending determined only when a media representative sells the entrepreneur on a special deal. Such a piecemeal approach to promotional spending should be avoided.

As Much as Competition Spends (ACS)   If the small business can duplicate the promotional mix of close competitors, it will be spending approximately as much as the competition. If a competitor is a large business, this approach is not feasible. However, it can be used to react to a special short-run effort by close competitors.

What It Takes to Do the Job (WTDJ)   The preferred approach to estimating promotional expenditures is to decide what it takes to do the job. This method requires a complete analysis of the market and promotional alternatives. Assuming reasonably accurate estimates, this approach determines the amount that truly needs to be spent.

Our recommendation to a small business for estimating promotional expenditures incorporates all four approaches. This idea is represented by the flowchart in Exhibit 13–2. Start with an estimate of what it takes to do the job (WTDJ). If this estimate is equal to or smaller than any of the other three estimates, proceed to invest that amount in promotion. If the WTDJ estimate is larger than any of the others, compute the average of the four estimates [(WTDJ + APS + WCS + ACS)/4]. Then compare the WCS estimate with this average. If WCS equals or exceeds the average estimate, proceed to develop the promotion at the average estimate. On the other hand, if the WCS is less than the average, additional funds for promotion should be sought.

Sources of Promotional Expertise

Most small businesses must rely on others' expertise in creating promotional messages. There are several sources for this specialized assistance: advertising agencies, suppliers, trade associations, and the advertising media.

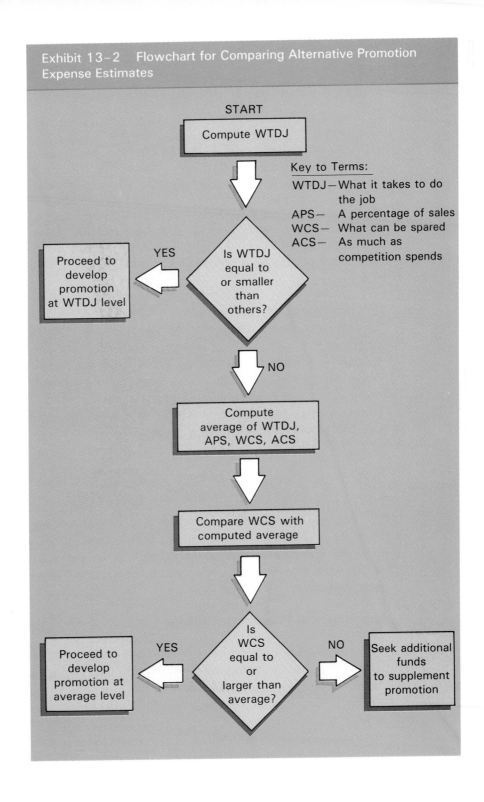

Exhibit 13–2 Flowchart for Comparing Alternative Promotion Expense Estimates

START

Compute WTDJ

Key to Terms:
WTDJ—What it takes to do the job
APS— A percentage of sales
WCS— What can be spared
ACS— As much as competition spends

Is WTDJ equal to or smaller than others?

YES → Proceed to develop promotion at WTDJ level

NO

Compute average of WTDJ, APS, WCS, ACS

Compare WCS with computed average

Is WCS equal to or larger than average?

YES → Proceed to develop promotion at average level

NO → Seek additional funds to supplement promotion

Some of the services that advertising agencies provide are:

1. Furnishing design, artwork, and copy for specific advertisements and/or commercials.
2. Evaluating and recommending the advertising media with the greatest "pulling power."
3. Evaluating the effectiveness of different advertising appeals.
4. Advising on sales promotions and merchandise displays.
5. Making market-sampling studies for evaluating product acceptance or area sales potentials and furnishing mailing lists.

Since an advertising agency may charge a fee for its services, the advertiser must make sure that the return from those services will be greater than the fees paid. Only a competent agency can be of real assistance to the advertiser.

Other outside sources may also provide assistance in formulating and carrying out promotional programs. Suppliers often furnish display aids and even complete advertising programs to their dealers. Trade associations also are active in this area. Finally, the advertising media can provide some of the same services offered by an ad agency.

Personal Selling

Many products require personal selling. **Personal selling** is promotion delivered in a one-on-one environment. It includes the activities of both the inside salespersons of retail, wholesale, and service establishments and the outside sales representatives who call on business establishments and ultimate consumers.

Importance of Product Knowledge

Effective selling must be built upon a foundation of product knowledge. If a salesperson knows the product's advantages, uses, and limitations, she or he can educate the customers and successfully meet their objections. Most customers look to the salesperson for such information—whether the product is a camera, a suit of clothes, an automobile, paint, a machine tool, or an office machine. Customers seldom are specialists in the products they buy; however, they immediately sense the salesperson's knowledge or ignorance. The significance of product knowledge is revealed by the fact that personal selling degenerates into mere order-taking when such knowledge is not possessed by the salesperson.

The Sales Presentation

The heart of personal selling is the sales presentation to the prospective customer. At this crucial point the order is either secured or lost. The first step in preparing an effective sales presentation is **prospecting,** a systematic process of continually looking for new customers. The time to look is before you need them.

Techniques of Prospecting   One of the most efficient techniques of prospecting is through *personal* referrals. Such referrals come from friends, customers, and other businesses. The initial contact with a potential customer is greatly facilitated by the ability to mention that, "You were referred to me by. . . ."

Another technique of prospecting is through *impersonal* referrals. Examples of impersonal referrals are media publications, public records, and directories. Newspapers and magazines, particularly trade magazines, also help identify prospects. These publications report on new companies entering the market, as well as on new products. Prospects can be derived from this information. For example, wedding announcements in the newspaper are impersonal referrals for a local bridal shop.

Public records of property transactions and building permits can also provide prospects. For example, a garbage pick-up service might find prospective customers from those who are planning to build houses or apartments.

Prospects can be identified without referrals through *marketer-initiated contacts.* Telephone calls or mail surveys, for example, isolate prospects. One market survey conducted for a small business by an author of this text used a mail questionnaire to identify prospects. The questionnaire, which asked technical questions about a service, concluded with the following statement: "If you would be interested in a service of this nature, please check the appropriate space below and your name will be added to the mailing list."

Finally, prospects can also be identified by recording *customer-initiated contacts.* Inquiries by a potential customer that do not conclude in a sale would classify that person as a "hot" prospect. Small furniture stores will often require their salespeople to create a card for each person visiting the retail store. These prospects are then systematically contacted over the telephone, and records of these contacts are updated periodically.

Harvey Anderson, chief executive officer of Servamatic, a company selling solar heaters, has developed an elaborate prospecting system that has helped his sales force achieve a 25 percent closing rate. They identify potential customers by visually covering the target market area. Next, they screen the potential customers by telephone. Finally, they give the "hot" prospects an in-home sales presentation.[1]

Practicing The old saying that "practice makes perfect" applies to the salesperson prior to making the sales presentations. If you are a salesperson, make the presentation to your spouse, a mirror, or a tape recorder. You may feel a little silly the first few times, but this method will improve your success rate.

The salesperson should also be aware of possible objections and should prepare to handle them. Experience is the best teacher here; how-

---

SMALL BUSINESS IN ACTION
Locating Sales Leads

The value of an effective sales prospecting system is high when selling costs are high. Consider the situation of Steve Bedowitz, who estimates that each sales call in his company costs over $100!

Bedowitz is founder of Amre, Inc., a small firm located in Irving, TX, that sells aluminum siding to homeowners. Due to the longtime poor image of the siding industry, sales are difficult. Without prospecting, closing rates are very low. Therefore, Bedowitz has developed a prospecting plan for his salespeople to help improve closing rates.

Bedowitz's prospecting plan begins with a computer analysis of a target neighborhood that develops a demographic profile of all homeowners. Next, fliers and local television advertisements are targeted to these homeowners. After that, telemarketing is used to contact homeowners who respond to the fliers and the television ads. Finally, appointments are made with these prospects, who are then contacted by company salespeople.

"The whole trick is in producing the leads," comments Amre's sales manager. "That's where Amre is head and shoulders above the rest." Bedowitz points out that "What we're looking for is not the least expensive lead," but "the least expensive sale."

Source: Mark Henricks, "A Tin Man with a Purse of Gold." Reprinted from the August, 1988, issue of *VENTURE, For Entrepreneurial Business Owners & Investors,* © 1988.

ever, there are 10 frequently used techniques that have proven helpful.[2] These are listed and briefly discussed below.

1. *Product comparison.* When the prospect is mentally comparing a product being used now or a competing product with the salesperson's product, the salesperson may make a complete comparison of the two. The salesperson lists the advantages and disadvantages of each product.

2. *Relating a case history.* Here the salesperson describes the experiences of another prospect similar to the prospect to whom he or she is talking.

3. *Demonstration.* A product demonstration gives a quite convincing answer to a product objection because the salesperson lets the product itself overcome the opposition.

4. *Giving guarantees.* Often a guarantee will remove resistance from the prospect's mind. Guarantees assure prospects that they cannot lose by purchasing. The caution, of course, is that guarantees must be meaningful and must provide for some recourse on the part of the prospect if the product does not live up to the guarantee.

5. *Asking questions.* The "why" question is of value in separating excuses from genuine objections and in probing for hidden resistance. The same question is useful in disposing of objections. Probing or exploratory questions are excellent in handling silent resistance. They can be worded and asked in a manner that appeals to the prospect's ego. In making the prospect do some thinking to convince the salesperson, questions of a probing nature get the prospect's full attention.

6. *Showing what delay costs.* A common experience of salespeople is to obtain seemingly sincere agreements to the buying decisions concerning need, product, source, and price, only to find that the prospect wants to wait some time before buying it. In such cases, the salesperson can sometimes take pencil and paper to show conclusively that delay of the purchase is expensive.

7. *Admitting and counterbalancing.* Sometimes the prospect's objection is completely valid because of some limitation in the salesperson's product. The only course of action in this case is for the salesperson to agree that the product does have the disadvantage to which the prospect is obviously objecting. Immediately after the acknowledgment, however, the salesperson should direct the prospect's attention to the advantages that overshadow the limitation of the product.

8. *Hearing the prospect out.* Some prospects object mainly for the opportunity to describe how they were once victimized. The technique recommended for this type of resistance is that of sympathetic listening.

9. *Making the objection boomerang.* Once in a while the salesperson can take a prospect's reason for not buying and convert it into a reason for buying. This takes expert handling. Suppose the prospect says, "I'm too busy to see you." The salesperson might reply, "That's why you should see me—I can save you time."

10. *The "Yes, but" technique.* The best technique for handling most resistance is the indirect answer known as the "Yes, but" method. Here are two examples of what salespeople might say when using this technique: (1) "Yes, I can understand that attitude, but there is another angle for you to consider." (2) "Yes, you have a point there, but in your particular circumstances, other points are involved, too." The "Yes, but" method avoids argument and friction. It respects the prospect's opinions, attitudes, and thinking, and operates well where the prospect's point does not apply in a particular case.

Making the Sales Presentation   Salespersons must adapt their sales approach to the customer's needs. A "canned" sales talk will not succeed with most buyers. For example, the salesperson of bookkeeping machines must demonstrate the capacity of the equipment to solve a customer's particular bookkeeping problems. Similarly, a boat salesperson must understand the special interests of particular individuals in boating and speak the customer's language. Every sales objection must be answered explicitly and adequately.

There is considerable psychology in successful selling. The salesperson, as a psychologist, must know that some degree of personal enthusiasm, friendliness, and persistence is required. Perhaps 20 percent of all salespersons secure as much as 80 percent of all sales made. This is because they are the 20 percent who persist and who bring enthusiasm and friendliness to the task of selling.

Some salespersons have special sales "gimmicks" that they use with success. One automobile salesperson, for example, offered free driving lessons to people who had never taken a driver's training course or who needed a few more lessons before they felt confident enough to take the required driving tests. When such customers were ready to take the driving tests, this salesperson accompanied them to the driver examination grounds

Figure 13–1   Sale Presentation Demonstrating Product Use

Thompson & Family Inc.

for moral support. Needless to say, these special efforts could hardly be turned down by new drivers who were in the market for cars.

Cost Control in Personal Selling

There are both economical and wasteful methods of achieving the same volume of sales. For example, routing traveling salespersons economically and making appointments prior to arrival can conserve time and transportation expense. The cost of an outside sales call on a customer may be considerable—perhaps $150 to $250. This emphasizes the need for efficient, intelligent scheduling. Moreover, the salesperson for a manufacturing firm can contribute to cost economy by stressing products that most need selling in order to give the factory a balanced run of production.

Profitability is increased to the extent that sales are made on the basis of quality and service rather than price-cutting. All products do not have the same margin of profit, however, and the salesperson can maximize profits by emphasizing high-margin lines.

SMALL BUSINESS IN ACTION
Personal Selling Through 1–800–686–2377

Telemarketing is a growing method of selling. One aspect of telemarketing is the use of special toll-free 800 numbers called *anagram numbers*—phone numbers that spell out a product or company's name. Examples are 800–IBM–PCJR and 800–NABISCO.

Many marketing experts believe that this use of anagrams is an effective promotional technique. Greg Griswold, of Madison, WI, used 1–800–BEEHIVE to help take his beekeeping supply house from sales of $480,000 to $3.2 million in two years. "If you hear the 'number' once, you remember it for life, and that can be a tremendous marketing edge," says Griswold. He is so convinced of their merit that he has asked AT&T for over 5,000 anagram numbers, which he hopes to re-sell to other businesses.

Other marketing people, such as Ernan Roman of Campaign Communications Institute of America, Inc., New York City, say that "There's absolutely no conclusive data to suggest that anagram numbers outperform easy-to-remember regular numbers."

What do you think? Can you dial the telephone number in the title of this report without looking at it again? What if you now know that the anagram for the number is 1–8–NUMBERS?

Source: Reprinted with permission, *Inc.* magazine, (July, 1983). Copyright © 1983 by Inc. Publishing Company, 38 Commercial Wharf, Boston, MA 02110.

Compensating the Salespeople

Salespeople are compensated in two ways for their efforts: financially and nonfinancially. Creating an effective compensation program must begin by recognizing that salespeople's goals may be different from the entrepreneur's goals. For example, the entrepreneur may be seeking nonfinancial goals, but the salespeople may not. A good compensation program will allow its participants to work for both forms of rewards.

Nonfinancial Rewards   Personal recognition and the satisfaction of reaching a sales quota are examples of nonfinancial rewards. A person can be motivated by these goals. Many retail small businesses will post the photograph of the top salesperson of the week on the bulletin board for all to see. Plaques are also used for a more permanent record of sales achievements.

Financial Rewards Nonfinancial compensation is important to sales-people, but it doesn't put bread on the table. Financial compensation is typically the more critical issue. There are two basic plans of financial compensation: commissions and straight salary. Each has specific advantages and limitations.

Most small businesses would prefer to use a commission plan of compensation, which is simple and directly related to productivity. Typically a certain percentage of the sales generated is the salesperson's commission. A commission plan incorporates a strong incentive into the selling activities—no sale, no income! With this type of plan, there is no drain on cash flow until there is a sale.

With the straight salary form of compensation, salespeople have more security because their level of compensation is assured regardless of personal sales made. However, this method can tend to make a salesperson lazy.

A combination of the two forms of compensation can give the small business the "best of two worlds." It is a common practice to structure the combination plans so that salary represents the larger part for new salespeople. As the salesperson gains experience, the ratio is adjusted to provide a greater share from commissions and less from salary.

Building Customer Goodwill

The salesperson must look beyond the immediate sale to build customer goodwill and to create satisfied customers who will patronize the company in the future. One way to accomplish this is to preserve a good appearance, display a pleasant personality, and demonstrate good habits in all contacts with the customer. One can also help build goodwill by understanding the customer's point of view. Courtesy, attention to details, and genuine friendliness will help to gain acceptance with the customer.

Of course, high ethical standards are of primary importance in creating customer goodwill. This rules out misrepresentation and calls for confidential treatment of a customer's plans. Certainly the salesperson who receives secret information from a firm should preserve the confidence of that customer.

Advertising

Advertising is the impersonal presentation of an idea that is identified with a business sponsor and is projected through mass media. Common

Figure 13-2   Advertising Billboard

media include television, radio, magazines, newspapers, and billboards. Advertising is a vital part of every small-business operation. As Steuart Henderson Britt has expressed it, "Doing business without advertising is like winking at a girl in the dark. You know what you are doing, but no one else does!"

Objectives of Advertising

A primary goal of advertising is to draw attention to the existence or superiority of a firm's product or service. To be successful, advertising must rest upon a foundation of product quality and efficient service. Advertising can bring no more than temporary success to an inferior product. Advertising must always be viewed as a complement to a good product and never as a replacement for a bad product. This is the attitude of Frank Perdue, a highly successful marketer of chicken. He says:

> The quality of the product is number one; our advertising is number two.... In advertising, you have to tell people why [they should buy the product]. [That means] you have to have a product that's better than most—if possible, the best in your field ... too many people take a mediocre product and fail. Eighty percent of all newly advertised products fail. The manufacturers decide the consumer is a fool. That's why it fails. They think advertising is a cure-all. But when you advertise something, you stick it in the consumer's mind that [your product] is better. They expect something a little more.[3]

The entrepreneur should not create false expectations with advertising. This can reduce customer satisfaction. Advertising may also accentuate a trend in the sale of an item or product line, but it seldom has the power to reverse such a trend. It must, consequently, be closely related to change in customer needs and preferences.

Used superficially, advertising may appear to be a waste of money. It seems expensive, while adding little utility to the product. Nevertheless, the major alternative is personal solicitation of potential customers, which is often more expensive and time-consuming.

Types of Advertising

There are two basic types of advertising—product advertising and institutional advertising. **Product advertising** is designed to make potential

Figure 13–3   Product Advertisement

Courtesy of David Shellenberger

customers aware of a particular product or service and of their need for it. **Institutional advertising**, on the other hand, conveys an idea regarding the business establishment. It is intended to keep the public conscious of the company and of its good reputation. Figures 13–3 and 13–4 illustrate the differences between product advertising and institutional advertising.

No doubt the majority of small-business advertising is of the product type. Retailers' advertisements, for example, stress products almost exclusively, whether those of a supermarket featuring weekend specials or a women's shop focusing upon sportswear. At times the same advertisement carries both product and institutional themes. Furthermore, the same firm may stress product advertising in newspapers and, at the same time, use institutional appeals in the Yellow Pages of the telephone book. Decisions

Figure 13–4   Institutional Advertisement

Courtesy of David Shellenberger

regarding the type of advertising used should be based upon the nature of the business, industry practice, media used, and objectives of the firm.

How Often to Advertise

Frequency of advertising is an important question for the small business. Advertising should be done regularly. Attempts to stimulate interest in a company's products or services should be part of a continuous advertising program. One-shot advertisements that are not part of a well-planned advertising effort lose much of their effectiveness in a short period.

Some noncontinuous advertising, of course, may be justified. This is true, for example, of advertising to prepare consumers for acceptance of a new product. Similarly, special advertising may be employed to suggest to customers new uses for established products. This is true also in advertising special sales.

Where to Advertise

Most small firms are restricted in their advertising efforts either geographically or by class of customer. Advertising media should reach—but not overreach—the present or desired market. From among the many media available, the small-business entrepreneur must choose those that will provide the greatest return for the advertising dollar.

The selection of the right combination of advertising media depends upon the type of business and its governing circumstances. A real estate sales firm, for example, may rely almost exclusively upon classified advertisements in a local newspaper, supplementing these with listings in the Yellow Pages of the telephone book. A transfer and storage firm may use a combination of radio, billboards, and telephone directory advertising to reach individuals planning to move household furniture. A small toy manufacturer may place greatest emphasis on television advertisements and participation in trade fairs. A local retail store may concentrate upon display advertisements in a local newspaper. The selection should be made not only on the basis of tradition but also upon an evaluation of the various ways to cover the particular market.

The best way to build a media mix is to talk with representatives from each medium. The small-business manager will usually find these representatives willing to recommend an assortment of media, not just the ones they represent. Before you meet with these representatives, study as much as possible about advertising so you will know both the weaknesses and the strengths of each medium. Exhibit 13–3 gives a concise summary of several important facts about media.[4] Study these pages carefully. Note particularly the advantages and disadvantages of each medium.

Sales Promotion

Sales promotion is promotion that serves as an inducement to perform a certain act while also offering value to recipients. The term sales promotion includes all promotional techniques that are neither personal selling nor advertising.

When to Use Sales Promotion

The small firm can use sales promotion to accomplish varied objectives. For example, small-business manufacturers can use sales promotion to stimulate commitments among channel intermediaries to market their product. Wholesalers can use sales promotion to induce retailers to buy inventories earlier than normally needed. Finally, with varied sales promotional tools, retailers may be able to induce final consumers to make a purchase.

Sales Promotional Tools

Sales promotion should never comprise the entire promotional effort of a small business. It should always be interlaced with advertising and personal selling. A partial list of sales promotional tools follows:

1. Specialties.
2. Publicity.
3. Exhibits.
4. Sampling.
5. Coupons.
6. Premiums.
7. Contests.
8. Point-of-purchase displays.
9. Cooperative advertising.
10. Free merchandise.

The scope of this book does not allow us to comment on each of the sales promotional tools listed. However, we will examine the first three on the list—specialties, publicity, and exhibits.

Courtesy of the Dracket Company

Specialties The most distinguishing characteristic of specialties is their enduring nature and tangible value. Specialties are referred to as the "last-

Exhibit 13-3   Media Summary

Medium	Market Coverage	Type of Audience
Daily Newspaper	Single community or entire metro area; zoned editions sometimes available.	General; tends more toward men, older age group, slightly higher income and education.
Weekly Newspaper	Single community usually; sometimes a metro area.	General; usually residents of a smaller community.
Shopper	Most households in a single community; chain shoppers can cover a metro area.	Consumer households.
Telephone Directories	Geographic area or occupational field served by the directory.	Active shoppers for goods or services.
Direct Mail	Controlled by the advertiser.	Controlled by the advertiser through use of demographic lists.
Radio	Definable market area surrounding the station's location.	Selected audiences provided by stations with distinct programming formats.
Television	Definable market area surrounding the station's location.	Varies with the time of day; tends toward younger age group, less print-oriented.
Transit	Urban or metro community served by transit system; may be limited to a few transit routes.	Transit riders, especially wage earners and shoppers; pedestrians.
Outdoor	Entire metro area or single neighborhood.	General; especially auto drivers.
Local Magazine	Entire metro area or region; zoned editions sometimes available.	General; tends toward better educated, more affluent.

(Continued)

Exhibit 13-3   *(Continued)*

Particular Suitability	Major Advantage	Major Disadvantage
All general retailers.	Wide circulation.	Nonselective audience.
Retailers who service a strictly local market.	Local identification.	Limited readership.
Neighborhood retailers and service businesses.	Consumer orientation.	A giveaway and not always read.
Services, retailers of brand-name items, highly specialized retailers.	Users are in the market for goods or services.	Limited to active shoppers.
New and expanding businesses; those using coupon returns or catalogs.	Personalized approach to an audience of good prospects.	High CPM.
Businesses catering to identifiable groups: teens, commuters, housewives.	Market selectivity, wide market coverage.	Must be bought consistently to be of value.
Sellers of products or services with wide appeal.	Dramatic impact, wide market coverage.	High cost of time and production.
Businesses along transit routes, especially those appealing to wage earners.	Repetition and length of exposure.	Limited audience.
Amusements, tourist businesses, brand-name retailers.	Dominant size, frequency of exposure.	Clutter of many signs reduces effectiveness of each one.
Restaurants, entertainments, specialty shops, mail-order businesses.	Delivery of a loyal, special-interest audience.	Limited audience.

ing medium." As functional products they are also worth something to recipients.

The most widely used specialty item is the calendar. Other examples are pens, key chains, and shirts. Actually, almost anything can be used as a specialty promotion. Every specialty item will be imprinted with the firm's name or other identifying slogan.

Specialties can be used to promote a product directly or to create company goodwill. Specialties also are excellent reminder promotions. For example, Merrymead Farm, located in Lansdale, PA, promotes its dairy products primarily with specialty advertising:

SMALL BUSINESS IN ACTION
Advertising Specialties Create Warm Relationships

There is a very special restaurant located in the small town of Barrow, AK. The restaurant's name is Pepe's North of the Border, and it specializes in Mexican–American cuisine. Its owner is Fran Tate, who started the business in 1978 in a remodeled two-bedroom house. Today, it serves about 400 customers daily.

Three facts make this restaurant special. First, it is located in the northernmost inhabited region in North America, where the average winter temperature on the Fahrenheit scale is 50° to 60° below zero. Second, it's the only restaurant in the area and does not need to use promotion. Third, Pepe's does use promotion!

Tate puts it this way, "Let's face it . . . I really don't need to advertise. Everyone who knows I'm here is *here*." Nevertheless, Tate uses specialties to create and maintain friendly communication with customers. She uses Pepe's T-shirts, caps, tote bags, thermometers, and many other items to say thank you to customers.

Tate has also used specialty items to overcome negative reactions of customers to somewhat high prices, which are necessitated by high shipping costs for some of her food items. For example, if Pepe's weekly tortilla bill is $500, the freight will be about $450.

The specialty advertising gifts are also used to smooth over the inconvenience of power failures. "The gifts are one way of showing that we really do care about them and regret any inconvenience they may experience while dining," according to Tate.

Source: Reprinted with permission from IMPRINT, copyright 1986, Advertising Specialty Institute, Langhorne, PA 19047.

Approximately 6,000 youngsters per year are led through the dairy. "We're basically a small, family-operated dairy," comments Manager Donna Quigley . . . "at the end of each visit, the participants are given reminders of their visits. We use pencils, ice cream scoops, balloons, milk mugs and erasers." Refrigerator magnets with the dairy's "smiling cow" logo, company name, address and phone number are also effective.[5]

Finally, specialties are personal. They are distributed directly to the consumer in a personal way, they are items that can be used personally, and they have a personal message. Since the small business needs to retain its personal image, entrepreneurs can use specialties to achieve this objective.

Publicity Of particular importance to retailers because of their high visibility is the type of promotion called **publicity**. Publicity can be used to promote both a product and a firm's image and is a vital part of good public relations for the small business. A good publicity program must maintain regular contacts with the news media.

SMALL BUSINESS IN ACTION
Publicity Keeps Light Glowing

Promoting a new product and gaining acceptance in a channel of distribution is always difficult. It is especially hard when there are large manufacturers in the market who have strong connections with distributors. Just ask Kevin Keating, co-inventor and founder of DioLight, of Detroit, MI.

Keating's new light bulb design reduces the power consumed and thereby extends the life of the bulb. However, design alone did not sell the product. Therefore, under the guidance of Kevin Callaghan, vice-president of marketing, a clever publicity effort began.

An article entitled "Never a Dark Moment with New Lifetime Bulb," was printed in the *Detroit Free Press*. The article caught the attention of a Cable News Network (CNN) correspondent. The network ran a video feature, which resulted in an article on Diolight in *USA Today*.

Callaghan also sent press releases to radio stations. These releases resulted in interviews with 300 radio stations. Other press stories resulted in over 100 articles in magazines and newspapers. Following every story, sales increased. According to DioLight's figures, the cost per story was about $30.

Source: Reprinted with permission, *Inc.* magazine (March, 1986). Copyright © 1986 by Goldhirsh Group, Inc., 38 Commercial Wharf, Boston, MA 02110.

This article discusses homemade commercials and how they sell even though often criticized for lack of professionalism. Several commercials of this type are described in the article.

McGlashan, Sandy and Clausen, John. "Is It Time for an Ad Agency?" *Nation's Business,* Vol. 75, No. 10 (October, 1987), pp. 74–76.

This article describes the experiences—some bad—of an entrepreneur as she learns to work with an advertising agency.

Posner, Bruce G. "A Company of Salespeople," *Inc.,* Vol. 10, No. 6 (June, 1988), pp. 123–126.

A small firm in the electronic printing business is featured in this article describing how it involves all employees in selling via a profit-sharing plan.

ENDNOTES

1. Mark K. Metzger, "Once Is Not Enough," *Inc.,* Vol. 7, No. 2 (February, 1985), p. 118.

2. Joseph Hair, Francis Notturno, and Frederick A. Russ, *Effective Selling*, 8th ed. (Cincinnati, OH: South-Western Publishing Co., 1991), pp. 254–255.

3. Robert A. Mamis, "Frank Perdue," *Inc.,* Vol. 6, No. 2 (February, 1984), pp. 21–22.

4. Reprinted with permission from Bank of America, NT&SA, "Advertising Small Business," *Small Business Reporter,* Vol. 15, No. 2, Copyright 1981.

5. Catherine M. Matecki, "Specialty Advertising Moooooves Milk . . . And Ice Cream . . . And . . . ," *Imprint,* Vol. 22, No. 2 (Summer, 1988), p. 31.

6. Leslie Bloom, "Trade Show Selling Tactics," *In Business,* Vol. 10, No. 4 (July–August, 1988), p. 43.

7. Jeffrey A. Tannenbaum, "Trade Shows Can Pay Off for New Firms," *The Wall Street Journal* (January 11, 1989), pp. B1–B2.

14 DISTRIBUTION CHANNELS AND INTERNATIONAL MARKETS

Spotlight on Small Business

© Robert Holmgren 1989

The simplest form of distribution channel involves no intermediaries. A product is sold directly by a producer to a final consumer. Entrepreneurs employing this type of distribution system typically incur high costs, but they also gain more direct control over the marketing of their products.

As an example of this simple channel, consider the distribution of fresh garlic by entrepreneur Carolyn Tognetti, of Gilroy, CA. The Tognetti family farms garlic in a community that, since 1979, has held yearly garlic festivals attracting over 100,000 people. Carolyn Tognetti started selling garlic in 1971 through a roadside stand. In March, 1986, she and her husband opened a 10,000-square-foot store costing $750,000. In 1987, Garlic World, as it is called, sold over $300,000 worth of fresh garlic! The store sells garlic-flavored food items and also Garlic World sweatshirts and napkins.

Tognetti is now developing a mail-order business—another example of direct distribution from producer to consumer. Its first catalog mailing of 6,000 copies was made in 1987. (No Scratch-n-Sniff required!) The Tognettis are also "strongly" considering starting a restaurant with, of course, a garlic-flavored menu. This would also constitute direct distribution.

Source: Adapted from Michael Barrier, "Out of This World," *Nation's Business,* Vol. 77, No. 8 (August, 1989), p. 13. Copyright 1989, U.S. Chamber of Commerce.

Looking Ahead

Watch for the following important topics:
1. Alternative channels of distribution.
2. Functions of marketing intermediaries in a channel of distribution.
3. Understanding foreign markets.
4. Sales and distribution channels for exporting.
5. Exporting assistance and trade agreements.
6. New terms and concepts:

distribution	assorting
physical distribution	agents
logistics	brokers
channel of distribution	common carriers
direct channel	contract carriers
indirect channel	private carriers
dual distribution	licensing
breaking bulk	forfaiting

At some point every product or service must be delivered to a customer. Until this exchange is consummated, the purchaser cannot derive the benefits he or she seeks. Therefore, the small business requires distribution plans to ensure that products arrive at the proper place at the correct moment for maximum customer satisfaction.

Also, given today's global marketplace, a small business may find opportunities in international marketing. Therefore, in this chapter, we examine several aspects of international distribution as well as distribution in the U.S. market.

Distribution Activities

Distribution activities are generally considered the least glamorous part of marketing. This is because distribution decisions generate less excitement than product design, packaging, name selection, and promotional decisions. Nevertheless, an effective distribution system is just as important to the small firm as a clever promotional campaign.

Prior to formalizing a distribution plan, a small-business manager should understand and appreciate certain underlying principles of distribution. These principles apply to both domestic and international distribution. In the next several sections, we will examine these principles.

Distribution Defined

The term **distribution** in marketing includes both the physical movement of products and the establishment of intermediary (middleman) relationships to guide and support the movement of the product. The physical movement activities form a special field called **physical distribution** or **logistics**. The intermediary system is called a **channel of distribution.**

Distribution is critical for both tangible and intangible goods. Since distribution activities are more visible for tangible goods, our discussion will concentrate on them. Most intangible goods (services) are delivered directly to the user. An income tax preparer, for example, serves a client directly. But even a person's labor can involve channel intermediaries as when, for example, an employment agency is used to find an employer.

Channels of Distribution

A channel of distribution can be either direct or indirect. In a **direct channel**, there are no intermediaries. The product goes directly from producer to user. If it is an **indirect channel**, one or more intermediaries may exist between the producer and the user.

Exhibit 14–1 depicts the basic ABCs of options available for structuring a channel of distribution. Channel A has no intermediaries. Door-to-door retailing and mail-order marketing are familiar forms of this channel system for consumer goods.

Channel B incorporates one intermediary. The B-type channels are used for both consumer and industrial goods. As final consumers, we are all familiar with retailers. Industrial purchasers are equally familiar with industrial distributors. Channel C shows two levels of intermediaries. This is probably the most typical channel for small businesses that have a large geographic market. The last channel in Exhibit 14–1 is labeled D. This represents the many other extensions of Channel C. For example, there may be three or more separate intermediaries in the channel. It should be noted that a small business may operate with more than one channel of distribution. This is called **dual distribution.**

Justifying Channels of Distribution   The small-business manager is often puzzled over the use of intermediaries in a channel of distribution. Are they really necessary? What kinds of small businesses really need them? The answer to the first question is "yes," and to the second, "maybe yours."

Intermediaries exist to carry out marketing functions which must be performed and which they can perform better than the producer or the user of a product. Small businesses cannot always perform these necessary

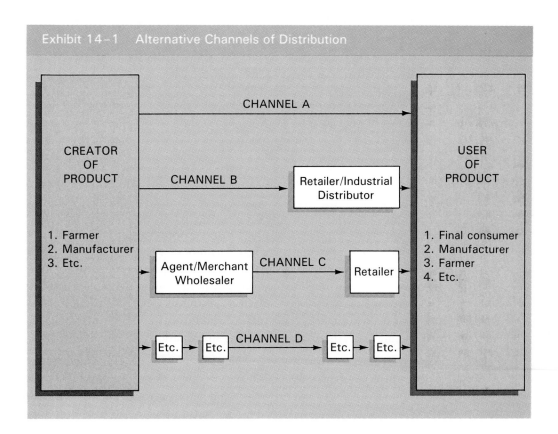

Exhibit 14–1   Alternative Channels of Distribution

SMALL BUSINESS IN ACTION
Dual Distribution Covers Market

Alternative channels of distribution in the marketplace make it possible to select the channel that best fits a given marketing strategy. But what if two channels seem feasible for the same basic product? Consider the response of Ken Dafoe to this problem.

Dafoe's company, named Dafoe & Dafoe, Inc., in Brantford, Ontario, was positioned to introduce a new disposable diaper into the U.S. market. His decision to use two distinct distribution channels came after he evaluated both alternatives and liked each one equally well. Using a distributor in Arizona, Dafoe sells the product through mail-order, specialty, and natural food stores under the name Tender Care Biodegradable. The distributor promotes the diaper by emphasizing the environmental problems associated with disposal of conventional disposables.

Dafoe's company also distributes through a Massachusetts broker, under the name Nappies, to major grocery chains. The retail price of Nappies is lower than that of Tender Care.

Some observers have asked Dafoe whether he worries about the competition between Tender Care and Nappies. His reply: "I'd rather compete against myself than someone else."

Source: Reprinted with permission, *Inc.* magazine (April, 1989). Copyright © 1989 by Goldhirsh Group, Inc., 38 Commercial Wharf, Boston, MA 02110.

---

functions as well as the intermediaries. This is why intermediaries are necessary.

As an example of the need for intermediaries, consider small producers. The small producer can perform distribution functions if the geographic market is extremely small, if customers' needs are highly specialized, and if risk levels are low. Otherwise, the producer may find intermediaries to be a more efficient means of performing distribution activities. Of course, many types of small firms also function as intermediaries—for example, retail stores. Four main functions of channel intermediaries are breaking bulk, assorting, providing information, and shifting risks.

Breaking Bulk   Very few individual customers demand quantities that are equal to the amounts produced. Therefore, there must be channel activities that will take the larger quantities produced and prepare them for individual customers. **Breaking bulk** is the distribution term used to denote these activities. Wholesalers and retailers purchase large quantities from manufacturers, store these inventories, and sell them to customers in the quantities they desire.

Assorting   Customers' needs are diverse, requiring many different products to obtain satisfaction. Intermediaries facilitate shopping for a wide assortment of goods through the assorting process. **Assorting** consists of bringing together homogeneous lines of goods into a heterogeneous assortment. For example, a small business producing a special golf club can benefit from an intermediary who carries many other golf-related products and sells to retail pro shops. It is much more convenient for a pro shop manager to buy from one supplier than from all the producers.

Providing Information   One of the major benefits of using an intermediary is information. Intermediaries can provide the producer with extremely helpful data on market size and pricing considerations.

Shifting Risks   By using intermediaries, the small-business manager can often share or totally shift business risks. This is possible by using **merchant middlemen,** who take title to the goods they distribute. Other intermediaries, such as **agents** and **brokers**, do not take title to the goods.

Choosing a Distribution System   One alternative for the small-business producer, as it decides on a distribution system, is to look at the competition. Some useful ideas about distribution are obtained from observing what others do. In all likelihood the competition will have made their decisions on the basis of practical considerations. At least a model of their distribution system can be used as a starting point.

Basically there are three main considerations in structuring a channel of distribution. We will call these the "three C's" of channel choice: costs, coverage, and control.

Costs   The small business must consider the cost of a channel carefully. A good beginning is to forget the idea that a direct channel is less expensive than an indirect channel. This is not inherently true. A small business may well be in a situation in which the less expensive channel is indirect. You should look at distribution costs as an investment. You have to spend money in order to make money. Ask yourself whether the money you would invest in intermediaries would get the job done if you used direct distribution.[1]

Coverage   Small businesses use indirect channels of distribution to increase market coverage. To illustrate this point, consider a small-business manufacturer whose sales force can make 10 contacts a week. This direct channel provides 10 contacts a week with the final users of the product.

Now consider an indirect channel involving 10 industrial distributors who (for convenience in illustration) each make 10 contacts a week with the final users of the product. With this indirect channel, and no increase in the sales force, the small-business manufacturer is now able to expose the product to how many final users a week? If you said 100, you are correct!

Gary Serdel, vice-president of Utility Chemical Company in Paterson, NJ, briefly considered hiring the company's own sales force to reach new retail customers with its swimming pool chemicals and accessories. But "we had to find a low-cost way of opening up these markets," said Serdel. He finally decided on an indirect distribution plan by which a sales representative would distribute his products.[2]

Control A third consideration in choosing a distribution channel is control. Obviously there is more control in a direct channel of distribution. With indirect channels, products may not be marketed as intended. The small business must select intermediaries which provide the desired support.

The Scope of Physical Distribution

The main component of physical distribution is transportation. Additional components are storage, materials handling, delivery terms, and inventory management. In the following sections we will briefly examine all of these topics except inventory management, which is discussed in Chapter 19.

Transportation The major decision regarding transportation concerns what mode to use. Alternative modes are traditionally classified as airplanes, trucks, railroads, pipelines, and waterways. Each mode has its unique advantages and disadvantages.[3]

Transportation intermediaries are of three types: common carriers, contract carriers, and private carriers. These are legal classifications that subject the first two types to regulations by federal and/or state agencies. **Common carriers** are available for hire to the general public, while **contract carriers** engage in individual contracts with shippers. Shippers who own their means of transport are called **private carriers**.

Storage Space is a common problem for a small business because there is never enough. When the channel system uses merchant wholesalers, for example, title to the goods is transferred, as is the storage function. On other occasions, the small business must plan for its own warehousing. If a small business is too small to own a private warehouse, it can rent space in public warehouses. If storage requirements are simple and involve little special handling equipment, a public warehouse can provide an economical storage function.

Materials Handling A product is worth little if it is in the right place at the right time but is damaged. Therefore, a physical distribution plan must consider materials-handling activities. Forklifts and special containers and packages are part of a materials-handling system. Tremendous improvements have been made through the years in materials-handling methods.

Delivery Terms A small but important part of a physical distribution plan is the terms of delivery. Delivery terms specify the following:

1. Who pays the freight costs
2. Who selects carriers
3. Who bears the risk of damage in transit
4. Who selects the modes of transport

The simplest delivery term and the one most advantageous to a small-business seller is F.O.B. (free on board) origin, freight collect. These terms shift all the responsibility for freight costs to the buyer.[4]

Figure 14–1 Physical Distribution Includes Materials Handling

Courtesy of Bergen Brunswig Corporation, Orange, CA

Having presented the basic principles of distribution, which apply to both domestic and international distribution, we will now focus on the opportunities of distribution abroad.

International Markets

International marketing for small firms is not only the wave of the future but the reality of the present! A small firm cannot afford to ignore foreign markets. Certain opportunities abroad are often more profitable than those at home.

A small firm's potential role in international marketing can be clarified by considering the following six topics: accepting the international challenge, evaluating others' experiences, researching foreign markets, sales and distribution channels, exporting assistance, and trade barriers and agreements. We will briefly examine each of these areas in the following sections.

SMALL BUSINESS IN ACTION
New Product Travels Abroad

The distribution system for a product is a vital link in an efficient marketing strategy. Increasingly, entrepreneurs recognize the need for these systems to reach beyond domestic customers into foreign markets at a very early stage in a product's life.

Consider the distribution system for Carole Chinman's product, named Smartpack. Smartpack is a set of 14 envelope-shaped garment covers that can be inserted in a suitcase to prevent wrinkles in a traveler's wardrobe. Chinman's company, Small World Travelers, began production of Smartpack in 1987. She initially distributed the product through individual stores and country clubs in the Wilmington–Philadelphia area. However, she was not content with this distribution strategy alone. Already, Chinman has contacted a trade-services company to locate a Japanese distributor. She is also working to arrange distribution in Europe.

The days of waiting until the domestic market has been saturated before looking to foreign markets for distribution may soon be gone.

Source: Adapted from Steve Golob, "Overcome Hurdles at Home: Export," *Nation's Business*, Vol. 76, No. 6 (June, 1988), pp. 48–49. Copyright 1988, U.S. Chamber of Commerce.

Accepting the International Challenge

It is a basic human characteristic that people shy away from the complex and shun the unfamiliar. Entrepreneurs and their small firms are no different. They have traditionally held this same attitude regarding foreign markets. Unfortunately, "foreign" market has meant "extraneous" market to many small businesses.

Encouragingly, this feeling appears to be changing. More and more small firms are accepting the international challenge! They are excited about international opportunities. This is, of course, good news for those most involved with U.S. trade problems. One trade representative says, "The growth in these smaller companies is where the growth in our country is."[5]

Consider the following three examples of small firms whose international involvement has reaped financial success:

> Dorr-Oliver, Inc., of Stamford, Connecticut, is a privately-owned maker of food-processing equipment which has made a long-term commitment to the China market. The company had sales of some $11.5 million in Asia in 1987.[6]

> Florod Corporation of California has about two-thirds of its $3 million annual sales coming from overseas orders.[7]

> National Graphics in St. Louis, Missouri, has about 25 percent of its total revenue of more than $15 million from exporting.[8]

A small firm can be just as successful in international markets as a large business. The idea that international markets are for big business only is extremely damaging to small firms' efforts to market abroad. Data regarding big- versus small-business involvement in international markets is at best inconclusive. However, when looking at exporting only, some writers conclude that more small firms export than do large firms.[9]

Evaluating Others' Experiences A foreign market becomes less foreign as a person learns more about it. An entrepreneur needs to study the cultural, political, and economic forces in the foreign market in order to understand why adjustments to domestic marketing strategies are required. When this is not done, costly mistakes will usually be made. Consider the following accounts of firms that did not properly research the foreign markets:

> The number "four" is a number symbolizing death in Japan. Unaware of this, a United States golfball manufacturer packaged its golfballs in sets of four for exporting to Japan.[10]

SMALL BUSINESS IN ACTION
Taking That First International Step—At Home

Many small firms are reluctant to initiate exporting because the foreign customer seems "so far away." Sometimes circumstances bring that foreign customer into a firm's own backyard. This was the experience of Plumley Cos., a small family-owned auto-parts business in Paris, TN.

In the late 1970s Mike Plumley, co-owner and CEO of the company, recognized that foreign-owned auto plants located in the United States were going to be strong competition for U.S.-owned auto plants. Therefore, he began a concerted effort to position his company as a reliable supplier to Japanese car factories being built in the southern United States. Since every auto manufacturer needs rubber hoses and ducts for its cars' heating and cooling systems, Plumley believed he could use his home-court advantage to beat out Japanese suppliers.

Plumley read extensively about Japanese culture and even took a Japanese-language course at a local college. He had his business cards and brochures printed in Japanese and, after five years of negotiation, signed his first contract with Nissan Motor Company. "Too many Americans are looking for an easy way into foreign markets," Plumley suggests. "You've got to have guts, and you've got to stick with it. But once you get one of these contracts, everyone else over there takes notice." Plumley's contracts with Nissan in the United States have now led to business with Nissan's domestic operations and other Japan-based manufacturers.

Source: Reprinted with permission, *Inc.* magazine (Fall, 1988). Copyright © 1988 by Goldhirsh Group, Inc., 38 Commercial Wharf, Boston, MA 02110.

A U.S. soft-drink firm marketed its product in Indonesia, but the drink did not sell. It was learned that the market for carbonated American soft-drinks consisted mainly of tourists and that most Indonesians preferred coconut-based drinks.[11]

An hour before an American company was to sign a contract with a Middle Eastern nation, the American executive met for tea with the responsible government official. The American propped his feet on a table with the soles facing his Arab host. The official became angry and left the room. Such an act is a grave insult in the Arab's culture. The contract was signed one year later.[12]

Sometimes a firm can transplant its product from the domestic market to a foreign market without major changes in product design. But even

---

SMALL BUSINESS IN ACTION
Have Meter, Will Travel

Frequently, a small business can make a smooth transition into a foreign market with a product it has already marketed successfully in the United States. Consider the experiences of POM, a small firm located in Russellville, AR. For years it sold parking meters exclusively in the United States. However, the 1970s' trend to large suburban shopping malls with spacious free parking, coupled with the long life of installed meters, contributed to a saturated domestic market.

Therefore, in 1981, POM made a bold move to market its meters abroad in newly industrialized countries where parking problems existed just as they had earlier in the United States. Since 1982, POM's exports have expanded by 20 percent each year. Currently, POM estimates that it has 42 percent of the world parking meter market. To maintain its competitiveness in foreign markets, POM has recently introduced the first solar-powered parking meter with a programmable timer driven by a microprocessor.

Source: Christopher Knowlton, "The New Export Entrepreneurs," *Fortune*, Vol. 117, No. 12 (June 6, 1988), pp. 94–95. © 1988 Time Inc. All rights reserved.

---

then, a change in other components of the marketing mix such as promotion and pricing may be required.

An excellent example of more extensive product changes can be seen in the experiences of entrepreneur Victor Kiam, who purchased Remington Products in 1979. At the time of this purchase, the company had incurred losses for four straight years. Kiam, the sole owner of Remington, made a bold international move which has now resulted in an estimated 45 percent share of the international shaver market. Although Remington would not be considered a small business by most definitions, its international experiences can be helpful to other entrepreneurs.

Kiam is quoted as saying that the trick in cracking foreign markets is "to keep in mind the mores, living conditions and characteristics of other lands and cultures."[13] When Kiam learned that in Britain there are few bathrooms with electric outlets, he concentrated on selling battery-powered shavers. For Japan, he redesigned the shaver to accommodate the smaller grip of the Japanese.

The concept of a market niche developed in Chapter 7 also applies to international markets. Once a market niche is defined, a small firm can develop a more precise marketing strategy. For example, when Canada adopted metric standards in 1977–78, the Bohnengel family, owners of Perfect Measuring Tape Company in Toledo, OH, saw an unfilled market niche that could take them more heavily into exporting. "We converted a machine primarily to supply our Canadian customers," says President Andrew C. Bohnengel.[14] Ten years later, the company ships 28 percent of its tapes overseas. Another small company that recognizes the power of market-niche thinking for international markets is PyMalt Corporation of Somerville, NJ. A maker of medical equipment, this privately held firm exports more blood pressure equipment to Japan than anyone else. President Paul M. Honafin says, "We have a nice little niche, and we make money on that niche."[15]

Researching a Foreign Market   Researching a foreign market should begin by exhausting as many secondary sources of information as possible. The U.S. government encourages exporting and offers an array of publications on methods of reaching foreign markets. Exhibit 14–2 lists some of these government sources.

One excellent publication prepared by the Small Business Administration is entitled *Exporter's Guide*. It, along with *A Basic Guide to Exporting*, is available from the Superintendent of Documents, U.S. Government Printing Office. Also available from the federal government is the *Exporter's Guide to Federal Resources for Small Business*, which provides names, addresses, and phone numbers of government contacts for export assistance. Elizabeth Gould, of National Graphics, who was named the 1985 Small Business Administration Exporter of the Year, credits the U.S. Commerce Department as being particularly helpful to her firm.[16]

The federal government gives strong support to small firms who desire to export. A recent example of this commitment was President Reagan's Export Now program, which was designed to increase awareness that exporting is profitable and also to publicize federal exporter-assistance programs.[17]

Banks, universities and other private organizations also provide information on exporting. The national accounting firm of Deloitte Haskins & Sells is a good example. It publishes an excellent booklet entitled *Expanding Your Business Overseas: An Entrepreneur's Guidebook*.

Talking with a native of a foreign market or someone who has visited the foreign country can be a valuable way to learn about that market. Most universities have international students who can usually be contacted through faculty members who teach in the international area.

Exhibit 14–2   Guide to Government Assistance to Exporters

	Potential Market Research	Direct Sales Leads	Agents/ Distributors	Export Regula- tions and Licences	Credit Assistance	Export and ETC Counseling	Unfair Foreign Competition	Insurance	Feasibility Studies
U.S. Department of Commerce, International Trade Administration Programs									
Office of Export Trading Company Affairs						X			
ITA Business Counseling Service	X								
Export Information Reference Room.........	X	X	X	X	X				
Exporters Licensing Service				X					
Trade Opportunitites Programs		X	X						
Agent/Distribution Service			X						
World Traders Data Reports.........			X						
Commercial News USA	X	X							
Foreign Traders Index	X	X	X						
Country Market Surveys.........	X		X						
Export Mailing Lists	X								
Overseas Business Reports............	X								
Foreign Economic Trends............	X								
National Oceanic and Atmospheric Administration............	X	X		X		X		X	
U.S. Department of Agriculture									
Product Advertising Abroad									
Commodity Credit Corporation				X	X	X			
Export-Import Bank of the U.S.									
Briefing Programs............									
Small Business Advisory Service						X			
"New to Export" Short-Term Insurance Policy						X			X
Small Business Credit Program............					X				
Working Capital Loan Guarantee Program............									
Medium-Term Credit Program					X		X		
Overseas Private Investment Corporation									
Feasibility Studies/Counseling Insurance..						X		X	X
Small Business Administration									
Export Revolving Line of Credit					X				
Counseling through SCORE or ACE.........						X			
Small Business Investment Corporations..					X				
Office of the U.S. Trade Representative							X		
U.S. Trade and Development Program								X	
USAID, Bureau for Private Enterprise (PAE).									X

Source: U.S. Department of Commerce, *The Export Trading Company Guidebook* (Washington: U.S. Government Printing Office, 1987), p. 23.

Sales and Distribution Channels

Exporting is not the only way to be involved in international markets. In fact, licensing is the simplest strategy for conducting international business. With a small investment, a firm can penetrate a foreign market. **Licensing** is an arrangement allowing a foreign manufacturer to use the designs, patents, or trademarks of the licenser. The practice of licensing is helpful in overcoming trade barriers surrounding exporting, because the product is produced in the foreign country. Superflight, Inc., of Palo Alto, CA, has used licensing to avoid tariffs in the European Community. Its frisbee-type disk, named Aerobie, has three licensees who have exclusive rights to manufacture and sell in foreign markets.[18]

A small firm can also participate in foreign-market sales via joint ventures and wholly owned subsidiaries in foreign markets. There are many tax considerations when selecting these alternatives which are beyond the scope of our discussion in this chapter.

Channel options for foreign distribution are numerous. The channels can be direct or can involve intermediaries who work for commissions or who take title and assume all risks. Exhibit 14–3 shows the channels to foreign mar-

Figure 14–2   Penetrating the Foreign Market: McDonald's in Moscow

Courtesy of McDonald's Restaurants of Canada Limited

Exhibit 14-3 Foreign Market Channels of Distribution

Sales Representatives or Agents—A sales representative is the equivalent of a manufacturer's representative here in the United States. Product literature and samples are used to present the product to the potential buyer. He usually works on a commission basis, assumes no risk or responsibility, and is under contract for a definite period of time (renewable by mutual agreement). This contract defines territory, terms of sale, method of compensation, and other details. The sales representative may operate on either an exclusive or nonexclusive basis.

Distributor—The foreign distributor is a merchant who purchases merchandise from a U.S. manufacturer at the greatest possible discount and resells it for his profit. This would be the preferred arrangement if the product being sold requires periodic servicing. The prospective distributor should be willing to carry a sufficient supply of spare parts and maintain adequate facilities and personnel to perform all normal servicing operations. Since the distributor buys in his name, it is easier for the U.S. manufacturer to establish a credit pattern so that more flexible or convenient payment terms can be offered. As with a sales representative, the length of association is established by contract, which is renewable if the arrangement proves satisfactory.

Foreign Retailer—Generally limited to the consumer line, this method relies mainly on direct contact by traveling sales representatives but, depending on the product, can also be accomplished by the mailing of catalogs, brochures, or other literature. However, even though it would eliminate commissions and traveling expenses, the U.S. manufacturer who uses the direct mail approach could suffer because his proposal may not receive proper consideration.

Selling Direct to the End-User—This is quite limited and again depends on the product. Opportunities often arise from advertisements in magazines receiving overseas distribution. Many times this can create difficulties because casual inquirers may not be fully cognizant of their country's foreign trade regulations. For several reasons they may not be able to receive the merchandise upon arrival, thus causing it to be impounded and possibly sold at public auction, or returned on a freight-collect basis that could prove costly.

State Controlled Trading Companies—This term applies to countries that have state trading monopolies, where business is conducted by a few government-sanctioned and controlled trading entities. Because of worldwide changes in foreign policy and their effect on trade between countries, these areas can become important future markets. For the time being, however, most opportunities will be limited to such items as raw materials, agricultural machinery, manufacturing equipment, and technical instruments, rather than consumer or household goods. This is due to the shortage of foreign exchange and the emphasis on self-sufficiency.

New Product Information Service (NPIS)—This special service, offered by the Department of Commerce, can facilitate your direct selling effort to potential overseas customers. It enables U.S. companies interested in selling a new product overseas to submit appropriate data through Commerce Department District Offices for placement

(Continued)

Exhibit 14-3 *(Continued)*

in the Department's publication, *Commercial News USA,* which is distributed exclusively abroad through 240 U.S. Foreign Service posts. The new product data are extracted and reprinted in individual post newsletters that are tailored to local markets. Selected product information also is broadcast abroad by the International Communication Agency's (formerly the U.S. Information Agency) Voice of America.

Commission Agents—Commission or buying agents are "finders" for foreign firms wanting to purchase U.S. products. These purchasing agents obtain the desired equipment at the lowest possible price. A commission is paid to them by their foreign clients.

Country Controlled Buying Agents—These are foreign government agencies or quasi-governmental firms empowered to locate and purchase desired goods.

Export Management Companies—EMCs, as they are called, act as the export department for several manufacturers of noncompetitive products. They solicit and transact business in the name of the manufacturers they represent for a commission, salary, or retainer plus commission. Many EMCs also will carry the financing for export sales, assuring immediate payment for the manufacturer's products.

This can be an exceptionally fine arrangment for small firms that do not have the time, personnel, or money to develop foreign markets, but wish to establish a corporate and product identity internationally.

Export Merchants—The export merchant purchases products direct from the manufacturer and has them packed and marked to his specifications. He then sells overseas through his contacts, in his own name, and assumes all risks for his account.

Export Agents—The export agent operates in the same manner as a manufacturer's representative, but the risk of loss remains with the manufacturer.

In transactions with export merchants and export agents the seller is faced with the possible disadvantage of giving up control over the marketing and promotion of the product, which could have an adverse effect on future success.

Source: Adapted from U.S. Department of Commerce, *A Basic Guide to Exporting* (Washington: U.S. Government Printing Office, 1981).

kets that are available to the small business. The export management companies (EMCs) described in Exhibit 14–3 have been popular among entrepreneurs. According to Richard J. Singer, vice-president of marketing for Singer Products Company of Westbury, NY, "There is an EMC available for virtually any entrepreneur. The advantage for the entrepreneur is that we've built the goodwill necessary to do business in foreign countries."[19]

Exporting Assistance

Difficulty in getting trade information is often mentioned as the biggest barrier to small-business exporting. In reality, there are a number of direct and indirect sources of information, including financing, that help the small firm view foreign markets more favorably. We will call attention to a few of these.

Private Banks   Commercial banks typically have a loan officer responsible for handling foreign transactions, and in large banks there may be a separate international department. Banks also participate in a system called forfaiting. **Forfaiting** is used when a U.S. exporter makes a sale abroad and receives promissory notes. A bank will then purchase the notes from the exporter at a discount. Collection of a note becomes the responsibility of the bank.[20] Banks are also used by exporters to issue commercial letters of credit and perform other financial activities associated with exporting.

Factoring Houses   A factoring house buys clients' accounts receivable and advances money to the clients. The factor assumes the risk of collection of the accounts. The Factors Chain International is an association representing factors from over 25 countries.[21] Its efforts have helped make factoring available on an international basis.

State Programs   More and more states each year are developing and implementing their own programs to help small companies finance exports. For example, California guarantees 85 percent repayment on loans used to finance receivables related to exports. Since 1985, when California began its programs, it has guaranteed over $3.7 million.[22] C. M. Magnetics, of Santa Fe Springs, CA, was a beneficiary of state assistance when the company needed capital to fill an order for its videotapes from China. "Without their help . . . we probably wouldn't be in business today," says President J. Carlos Maciel.[23]

Export-Trading Companies   In 1982, President Reagan signed into law the Export Trading Company Act for the stated purpose of increasing U.S. exports of goods and services.[24] The two areas covered by the Act relate to restrictions on trade financing and uncertainty about U.S. antitrust laws. Under the Act, an Export Trading Company (ETC) can be organized to facilitate the exporting of goods and services produced in the United States. Through a small firm's affiliation with the ETC, it could employ the resources of an ongoing organization that has exporting expertise. As of October 1989, there had been only 112 certificates issued for ETCs. Their value to small firms is still in doubt. One recent study asking users of export trading companies to evaluate the performance of ETCs concluded that there is "a lack of congruence between what services small businesses desire from exporting intermediaries and the services ETCs perform well."[25]

The Export-Import Bank   To encourage businesses to sell overseas the federal government created, as an independent agency, the Export–Import Bank (Eximbank). Although historically of greatest use to large firms, Eximbank in recent years has undertaken to overhaul its programs to benefit small firms. The following programs are particularly helpful to small-business exporters:

- Export Credit Insurance.
- New-to-Export Insurance Policy.
- Umbrella Policy.
- Working Capital Guarantee.
- Eximbank/SBA Working Capital Co-Guarantee Program.
- Direct and Intermediary Loans.

Trade Agreements

International trade is made difficult by the differences in trading systems and import requirements of each country. To appreciate the problems these differences create, consider the situation of Mentor O & O, Inc., a small manufacturer in Norwell, MA. This company produces diagnostic and surgical equipment used in eye care. Mentor markets internationally and is regularly modifying its products to meet rigid design specifications that vary from country to country. For example, an alarm bell on Mentor's testing device has an on/off switch that must be removed before it is acceptable in Germany.[26] This is typical of trade barriers throughout the world.

However, we appear to be in a period of positive change regarding trade barriers. For example, the 12 nations of the European Community have embarked on a path of deregulation with the goal of building a single market by the end of 1992. Small U.S. firms will certainly benefit from this historical movement. A recent Canada–U.S. Free Trade agreement is another example of export barrier reduction. This agreement promises to eliminate all tariffs between the two countries.

Looking Back

1. A channel of distribution can be either direct—involving no intermediaries—or indirect—incorporating one or more intermediaries. Dual distribution exists when the same product is distributed through two different channels at the same time.

2. Intermediaries in a channel of distribution exist to carry out marketing functions. Small firms cannot always perform these functions or carry them out as efficiently as the intermediary. Channels of distribution perform four main functions: breaking bulk, assorting, providing information, and shifting risks.

3. An entrepreneur must study the cultural, political, and economic forces in foreign markets in order to develop appropriate marketing strategies. Sometimes a firm can transfer its product to a foreign market without major product-design changes. On other occasions, extensive product changes may be in order. The concept of a market niche also applies to international markets.

4. A tremendous amount of exporting information and assistance is available from states and the federal government. Private banks, factoring houses, export-trading companies, and Exim-bank also provide exporting assistance to small firms. Trade agreements among nations are helping to reduce trade barriers.

DISCUSSION QUESTIONS

1. How does physical distribution differ from channels of distribution?

2. Why do small firms need to consider indirect channels of distribution for their products? Why involve intermediaries in distribution at all?

3. Discuss the major considerations in structuring a channel of distribution.

4. What are the major components of a physical distribution system?

5. Comment on the statement, "Channel intermediaries are not necessary and only increase the final price of products."

6. Discuss the importance of a careful cultural analysis before entering an international market.

7. What changes in a firm's marketing plan, if any, may be required when selling to foreign markets? Be specific.

8. Does the concept of a market niche apply to international markets? Explain with examples.

9. What is the position of the U.S. federal government regarding the potential for exporting among small U.S. firms? Do you agree or disagree? Why?

10. What are alternatives to exporting that provide small-business involvement with international markets? Which one(s) do you find most consistent with a small firm's situation? Why?

11. What is forfaiting? How does it work?

12. Explain how state governments are involved in assisting small firms with exporting.

13. What is an export-trading company? How did they come about? What success have they had?

14. Explain the exporting assistance programs of Eximbank.

15. How have trade agreements helped reduce trade barriers? Do you believe these efforts will continue?

YOU MAKE THE CALL

Situation 1

Berney and Pat Anderson own and operate a manufacturing operation named the Great Out-of-Doors Company, in Coleman, CO. Their principal product is a rifle sling.

Berney conceived the product idea in 1986, and one year later he and his wife took in two investors and began manufacturing. Currently, the plant has six employees producing the rifle sling and a few minor complementary products. Pat takes care of the accounting, and Berney supervises the plant operations.

Their rifle sling product is patented and has been received well by those who have tried it. The nylon sling is produced in 1-inch and $1\frac{1}{2}$-inch straps and is available in 25 different colors.

The firm has manufactured the sling for other brand-name sporting goods manufacturers and has sold it under its own name—Sports Sling—in sporting goods stores.

Questions

1. What do you see as the strong and weak points of the distribution channels the company is currently using?

2. What additional channels would you recommend for consideration?

3. Do you think exporting is a feasible alternative for the Andersons at this time? Why or why not?

Situation 2

John Adams is a veterinarian specializing in small-animal care in Jackson, FL. For several years he has supplemented his professional income by exporting products he has invented and patented. His best seller is a dog leash that he originally sold to other veterinarians in the United States. However, after placing a product release in a Department of Commerce publication, he received inquiries from foreign importers who wanted the product, and his exporting began.

Based on his personal experiences with exporting, Adams is currently contemplating leaving his veterinary practice and becoming a full-time exporting distributor. He believes there is a growing number of American businesses that do not want to get involved with the problems of the export business but would like the revenue from the overseas markets. His services as a distributor should be attractive to these firms.

Questions

1. Would you recommend that Adams leave his successful veterinary practice to pursue a business as an export distributor? Why or why not?
2. What would you anticipate Adams's biggest problems to be if he makes the move he is considering?
3. What private sources of assistance might he use?

EXPERIENTIAL EXERCISES

1. Contact a local banker to discuss his or her firm's involvement with international marketing. Report your findings.
2. Interview two different types of local retail merchants to determine how the merchandise in their stores was distributed to them. Contrast the channels of distribution and report your findings.
3. Review recent issues of *Entrepreneur, Inc.*, or *Nation's Business*, and report on articles discussing international marketing.
4. Interview a local distributor concerning how it stores and handles the merchandise it distributes. Report your findings.

REFERENCES TO SMALL-BUSINESS PRACTICES

"Burger Madness." *Entrepreneur*, Vol. 17, No. 4 (April, 1989), pp. 12–13.
    This article describes an unusual approach to gaining supermarket distribution for a new product. The entrepreneur called "Mad Mike" used flashy attire to draw attention to his hamburger spread.
DeYoung, H. Garrett. "Learning the Ropes." *Inc.*, Vol. 10, No. 8 (August, 1988), pp. 103–106.
    The experiences of an American firm that successfully took its product abroad

are discussed in this article. Several lessons learned from its efforts in Japan are shared with the reader.

Rondel, Stephen A. "On the Front Lines in the Trade War." *Nation's Business*, Vol. 77, No. 6 (June, 1989), p. 10.

This article describes how an entrepreneur, who began manufacturing in a horse stall in his barn, has entered exporting. His financial difficulties resulting from direct competition with foreign manufacturers are developed.

Sato, Gayle. "Bringing Your Product to Life Part V: Attaining Shelf Space—The Ultimate Goal," *Entrepreneur*, Vol. 16, No. 7 (July, 1988), pp. 49–52.

Getting a new product into stores is a difficult job. Several experiences of entrepreneurs are described.

Thompson, Roger. "A Fresh Start After 40." *Nation's Business*, Vol. 77, No. 4 (April, 1989), pp. 62–64.

The entrepreneur featured in this article started a repair- and maintenance-parts company to supply businesses with repair parts for their equipment. His creative distribution idea has made his company one of the largest independent companies in this market.

ENDNOTES

1. The reduction in product price given an intermediary is the investment cost to which we refer.

2. Carol Rose Carey, "A Low-Cost Way to Find Top Salespeople," *Inc.*, Vol. 4, No. 3 (March, 1982), p. 119.

3. A good discussion of modes of transportation is found in Chapter 12 of William M. Pride and O. C. Ferrell, *Marketing Concepts and Strategies* (Boston: Houghton Mifflin Company, 1989).

4. For a more detailed discussion of various delivery terms, see Lynn Edward Gill, "Delivery Terms—Important Element of Physical Distribution," *Journal of Business Logistics*, Vol. 1, No. 2 (Spring, 1979), pp. 60–82.

5. William J. Holstein and Brian Bremmer, "The Little Guys Are Making It Big Overseas," *Business Week* (February 27, 1989), p. 94.

6. William J. Hampton, et al., "The Long Arm of Small Business," *Business Week* (February 29, 1988), p. 65.

7. David E. Gumpert, "Turnabout Is Fair Play," *Inc.*, Vol. 9, No. 10 (September, 1987), p. 120.

8. Kevin McDermott, "What It Takes to Make It Overseas," *D & B Reports*, Vol. 37, No. 2 (March–April, 1988), p. 36.

9. David L. Birch, "Trading Places," *Inc.*, Vol. 10, No. 4 (April, 1988), p. 42.

10. Jacques Koppel, "The Quirks of Exporting," *In Business*, Vol. 5, No. 2 (March–April, 1983), p. 27.

11. Charles F. Valentine, "Blunders Abroad," *Nation's Business*, Vol. 44, No. 3 (March, 1989), p. 54.

12. *Ibid.*, p. 56.

13. Christopher Elias, "A New Razor-Sharp Approach to Old-Fashioned Capitalism," *Insight*, Vol. 3, No. 2 (January 12, 1987), p. 42.

14. *Op cit*. Hampton.

15. *Ibid*.

16. Steven Golob, "Export Expertise," *Nation's Business*, Vol. 76, No. 1 (January, 1988), p. 26.

17. Albert G. Holzinger, "A Big Boost for Small Exporters," *Nation's Business*, Vol. 76, No. 5 (May, 1988), p. 12.

18. Ted Harwood, "How to Build $1 Million Sales . . . Without Advertising," *In Business*, Vol. 8, No. 4 (July–August 1986), p. 21.

19. Kevin Farrell, "Exports," *Venture*, Vol. 5, No. 3 (March, 1983), p. 63.

20. For more discussion of forfaiting, see R. Michael Rice, "Four Ways to Finance Your Exports," *The Journal of Business Strategy* (July–August, 1988), pp. 30–31.

21. *Ibid*., p. 31.

22. Steven P. Galante, "States Launch Efforts to Make Small Firms Better Exporters," *The Wall Street Journal* (February 2, 1987), p. 17.

23. *Ibid*.

24. For a complete description of the Act, see *The Export Trading Company Guidebook*, 1987, provided by the U.S. Department of Commerce.

25. Alex F. DeNoble, Richard M. Castaldi and Donald M. Moliver, "Export Intermediaries: Small Business Perceptions of Services and Performance," *Journal of Small Business Management*, Vol. 27, No. 2 (April, 1989), pp. 33–41.

26. Roger Thompson, "EC92," *Nation's Business*, Vol. 77, No. 6 (June, 1989), p. 18.

PART

V

MANAGING SMALL BUSINESS OPERATIONS

1136 Suite 110
INNER SPACE DESIGN

PROFESSIONAL MANAGEMENT IN THE GROWING FIRM

Spotlight on Small Business

© Gregory Edwards

A tension between entrepreneurial and professional management often occurs as small firms grow. An entrepreneur's free-wheeling management style must give way to a more systematic, professional approach.

An example of the dilemma is found in the experience of the Marine Pollution Control Company of Detroit. Under the leadership of its founder, David Usher, it had grown to more than $10 million in revenues. Rapid growth and participation in a gigantic cleanup project—the *Exxon Valdez* oil tanker disaster in Alaska—created managerial tensions between the founder and the next generation, including son Charlie.

The sons contend they are hamstrung by an arbitrary-seeming, "Dave-centered" management structure in which virtually every decision must be cleared with Dave. Big jobs like the *Valdez* one stretch this kind of structure to its limits and underline its weaknesses. Charlie and the others want Dave to delegate more authority so the company has the depth of management needed for the future.

Dave, for his part, says he recognizes the need to delegate. He believes, however, in the loosely organized system that brought the company success, and he worries about losing touch with day-to-day operations. The same entrepreneurial personality that drove him to build the company won't allow him to let go of any part of it.

Source: Robert Charm, "Masters of Disasters," *Family Business,* premier issue, 1989, pp. 18–25.

Looking Ahead

Watch for the following important topics:
1. Weaknesses in small-firm management.
2. Constraints faced by managers in small firms.
3. How management is affected by the growth cycle of a small business.
4. Effective use of managerial time.
5. Sources of management assistance.
6. New terms and concepts:

professional managers	Small Business Development
Small Business Institute (SBI)	Centers (SBDCs)
Service Corps of Retired Executives (SCORE)	networking

To some extent, the management processes of large and small businesses are similar. Both require managerial direction and coordination of work activities. There are differences, however, in the sophistication of management methods and in the nature of challenges facing small-business managers. This chapter will focus on unique aspects of managing the smaller enterprise. It will also examine the growing firm's transition from simple management practices to a more professional kind of management that emphasizes formal systems of planning and control.

Distinctive Features of Small-Firm Management

Even though managers in both large and small companies perform similar management functions, their jobs as managers are somewhat different. This is readily recognized by a manager who moves from a large corporation to a small firm. He or she encounters an entirely different business atmosphere. Furthermore, the small firm experiences constant change in its organizational and managerial needs as it moves from point zero, its launching, to the point where it can employ a full staff of **professional managers**. In this section we shall examine a number of these special features that serve to challenge managers of small firms.

Prevalent Weaknesses in Small Firms

Although some large corporations experience poor management, small business seems particularly vulnerable to this weakness. Managerial inefficiency exists in tens, or even hundreds, of thousands of small firms. Many small firms are marginal or unprofitable businesses, struggling to survive from day to day and month to month. At best, they earn only a pittance for their owners. The reason for their condition is at once apparent to one who examines their operations. They "run," but it is an exaggeration to say that they are "managed."

Weak management shows up in the service received by customers. For example, consider the following comments made about hotel service:

> My guess, simply as one traveling man, is that the secret is primarily a secret of management. Capital may have something to do with it, of course; architecture, interior decoration, location, the nature of the clientele—all these doubtless figure into the equation. At bottom, I suspect, the difference between a poor hotel/motel and a good one lies in the experience, the attitude, and the personal attention of the man or woman who runs the place. If a manager does a good job of training the maids, and pays them tolerable wages, and treats them with dignity, and praises them for doing well, that manager's rooms will be comfortable rooms—for the maids will have checked the light bulbs and tried the TV before they leave. If a manager insists upon friendly courtesy on the part of his desk clerks, he can get it—or he can get some new desk clerks.[1]

Even though management weakness exists in small business, it is not universal. More important, poor management is by no means inevitable just because a firm is small.

Constraints on Management in Small Firms

Managers of small firms, particularly new and growing companies, are constrained by conditions that do not trouble the average corporate executive. Small firms have neither enough money nor enough talented people. They must face the grim reality of small bank accounts and limited managerial staff. These limitations are readily apparent to large-firm managers who move into management positions in small firms. As one writer expresses it,

> You cannot realize how lavish big business is until you try making the transition to small business. For example, a marketing man moving from a big company to a small one usually discovers, to his horror, that his new employer has no market surveys, and the sum of his research is a two-year-old article clipped from a trade magazine. Making bad matters worse, the little company desperately needs a four-color brochure for the salesmen. You can't sell without sales literature, now can you?
>
> In big business there is no question about it; you get these tools, and a major skill the new employee brings with him is knowledge of how to use the tools. In small business the new employee will likely be told by the company president, "We can't afford research. We can't afford surveys and probably don't need them anyway. As far as that brochure is concerned, if we really need one, there is always Jiffy Printing across the street. They can whip something out for $600. Nothing fancy, mind you. And ask 'em not to bill us 'til September."[2]

Thomas P. Murphy has cited the conflict between an entrepreneur and a Harvard Business School-trained senior executive whom the entrepreneur had hired.[3] The new executive had concluded that a $100,000 stainless-steel mold for making plastic extrusions was a far better investment than a $10,000 aluminum mold that wouldn't last as long. The analysis was correct, but the business did not have $100,000. The entrepreneur explained that he was more concerned about staying alive in the short run than having the best long-run solution, but this was difficult for the new executive to understand.

In a small firm, the entrepreneur also typically lacks adequate specialized staff. Most managers are generalists, and they lack the support of experienced staff in market research, financial analysis, advertising, human resources management, and other areas. The entrepreneur must make decisions involving these areas without the advice and guidance that is available in a larger business. Later in this chapter, we see that this limitation may be partially overcome by use of outside management consultants.

SMALL BUSINESS IN ACTION
A Cadillac Dealer Runs Short of Cash

During the oil crisis of the 1970s, a young Cadillac dealer in Illinois, Rob Mancuso, learned the hard way about controlling costs. After the business started losing money and checks began to bounce, Mancuso began managing in a way that reflected these financial realities.

"In all the years I'd been at my father's store, I'd never heard the word 'overdraft,'" Mancuso admits. "I quickly learned how to turn frozen assets into liquid assets. We bailed out of used cars, sent new cars back to the factory, and cut back on parts to the point where, if a guy came in for a tune-up, we'd have to run down to K mart for spark plugs."

These were desperate measures, but the business survived and went on to prosper under Mancuso's imaginative leadership.

Source: Reprinted with permission, *Inc.* magazine (June, 1984), Copyright © 1984 by Goldhirsh Group, Inc., 38 Commercial Wharf, Boston, MA 02110.

Nevertheless, the shortage of immediately available talent is a part of the reality of the entrepreneurial firm.

Stages of Growth and Implications for Management

As a newly formed business becomes established and grows, its organization and pattern of management change. To some extent, management must adapt to growth and change in any organization. However, the changes involved as business moves through periods of "childhood" and "adolescence" are much more extensive than those that occur with the growth of a relatively mature business.

As shown in Exhibit 15–1, a new firm passes through four stages of growth. Subordinates are employed and layers of management are added as it moves from Stage 1 to Stage 4.

In Stage 1, the firm is simply a one-person operation. Of course, not all firms begin at this level, but this situation is by no means rare. In Stage 2, the entrepreneur becomes a player-coach, which implies extensive participation in the operations of the business. In addition to performing the basic work—whether it be production, sales, writing checks, or record keeping—the entrepreneur must also coordinate the efforts of others.

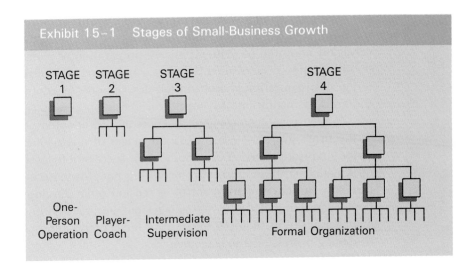

Exhibit 15-1   Stages of Small-Business Growth

STAGE 1 — One-Person Operation

STAGE 2 — Player-Coach

STAGE 3 — Intermediate Supervision

STAGE 4 — Formal Organization

In Stage 3, a major milestone is reached when an intermediate level of supervision is added. In many ways this is a difficult, dangerous point for the small firm, because the entrepreneur must rise above direct, hands-on management and work through an intermediate level of management.

Figure 15-1   A Small Hardware Store in the Early Stage

Owens Illinois, Inc.

Stage 4, the stage of formal organization, involves more than increased size and multilayered organization. The formalization of management involves the adoption of written policies, preparation of plans and budgets, standardization of personnel practices, computerization of records, preparation of organization charts and job descriptions, scheduling of training conferences, institution of control procedures, and so on.

Some formal management practices may be adopted prior to Stage 4 of the firm's growth. Nevertheless, the stages of management growth describe a typical pattern of development for successful firms. Flexibility and informality may be helpful at the beginning, but growth necessitates greater formality in planning and control. A tension often develops as the traditional easy-going patterns of management become dysfunctional. Great managerial skill is required to preserve the "family" atmosphere while introducing professional management.

Changing Skill Requirements

As a firm moves from Stage 1 to Stage 4, the pattern of entrepreneurial activities changes. The entrepreneur becomes less of a doer and more of a manager, as shown in Exhibit 15–2.

Firms that are overly hesitant to move through these organizational stages and to provide the necessary management limit their rate of growth. On the other hand, a small business may attempt to become a big business too quickly. The entrepreneur's primary strength may lie in product development or selling, for example, and a quick push into Stage 4 may saddle the entrepreneur with managerial duties and rob the organization of those valuable entrepreneurial talents.

Thomas P. Murphy has pointed out the significant nonmanagerial role played by many entrepreneurs:

> Having already set management science back to the dark ages, let me add a final heresy—the role of the boss is not to become the serene orchestra conductor while others tootle the instruments. Fine for larger companies. But small businesses are generally founded on an individual's special strength—the boss is a gifted engineer or an excellent salesman. Relegate him or her too early to the orchestra-leader role and you remove the basic strength of the business and replace it with a frustrated administrator.[4]

Murphy described a small company whose venture capitalists wanted to make it into a "real" company quickly.[5] To do so, they pulled the chief executive officer, who was also making half of the company's sales, back

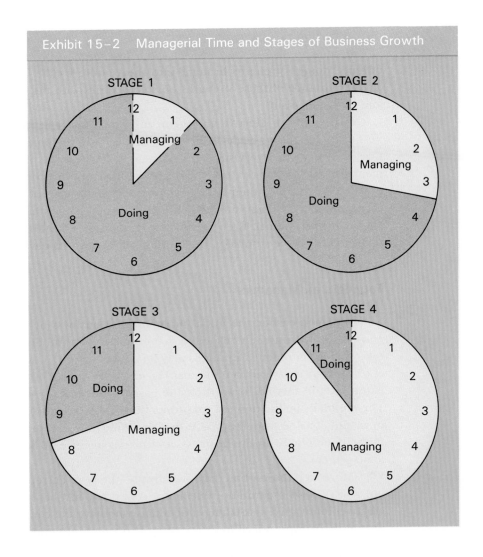

Exhibit 15–2 Managerial Time and Stages of Business Growth

into the office and hired three new salespeople. However, the new sales-people failed to sell, the new financing was lost, and the venture capitalists walked away in disgust, leaving the company to sink. But it did not sink! The chief executive fired the salespeople who didn't sell, went back to sell-ing—which he did very well—and watched the firm evolve into the "real" company the venture capitalists had tried to develop prematurely.

A tension exists, therefore, between the "doing" and "managing" roles of the entrepreneur. Care must be taken to capitalize on the special or unique "doing" strengths brought into the venture by the entrepreneur. The importance of these strengths obviously varies with the entrepreneur and the enterprise.

The need for effective management becomes more acute as the business expands, and its neglect can retard the firm's development. We recognize, of course, that very small firms often survive in spite of weakness in management. To some extent, the quality of their products or services may offset deficiencies in their management. In the early days of business life, therefore, the firm may survive and grow even though its management is less than professional. Even in very small businesses, however, defects in management place strains on the business and retard its development.

Founders as Managers

As noted earlier, the initial direction of a business by the founding entrepreneur is uniquely related to that entrepreneur and his or her interests. The entrepreneur's strengths may lie in production (in some cases the entrepreneur is basically a tradesman) or in sales. The new business is often launched and carried forward on the basis of these functional strengths. The founder's inclination toward production or sales is typically influential in shaping business operations. At the beginning, the entrepreneur may be the only employee in the business, and management may be largely self-management.

Moreover, those who create new firms—the pure entrepreneurs—are not always good organization members. As we saw in Chapter 1, they are creative, innovative, risk-taking individuals who have the courage to strike out on their own. Indeed, they are often propelled into entrepreneurship by precipitating events, some of which involve a difficulty in fitting into conventional organizational roles. As a consequence, management and organizational precepts and practices are often secondary concerns of entrepreneurs who are caught up in the excitement of creating a new business.

Founders differ from professional managers in terms of their ownership and intense commitment to the businesses they found. In many subtle ways, the orientation of founders differs from that of professional managers. Edgar H. Schein has identified many of these differences, as outlined in Exhibit 15–3. These variations show the founder as being more self-

Exhibit 15–3   How Do Founder/Owners Differ from "Professional Managers"?

Entrepreneurs/founders/owners are	Professional managers are

Motivation and Emotional Orientation

Oriented toward creating, building.	Oriented toward consolidating, surviving, growing.
Achievement-oriented.	Power- and influence-oriented.
Self-oriented, worried about own image; need for "glory" high.	Organization-oriented, worried about company image.
Jealous of own prerogatives, need for autonomy high.	Interested in developing the organization and subordinates.
Loyal to own company, "local."	Loyal to profession of management, "cosmopolitan."
Willing and able to take moderate risks on own authority.	Able to take risks, but more cautious and in need of support.

Analytical Orientation

Primarily intuitive, trusting of own intuitions.	Primarily analytical, more cautious about intuitions.
Long-range time horizon.	Short-range time horizon.
Holistic; able to see total picture, patterns.	Specific; able to see details and their consequences.

Interpersonal Orientation

"Particularistic," in the sense of seeing individuals as individuals.	"Universalistic," in the sense of seeing individuals as members of categories such as employees, customers, suppliers, and so on.
Personal, political, involved.	Impersonal, rational, uninvolved.
Centralist, autocratic.	Participative, delegation-oriented.
Family ties count.	Family ties are irrelevant.
Emotional, impatient, easily bored.	Unemotional, patient, persistent.

Structural/Positional Differences

Have the privileges and risks of ownership.	Have minimal ownership, hence fewer privileges and risks.
Have secure position by virtue of ownership.	Have less secure position, must constantly prove themselves.
Are generally highly visible and get close attention.	Are often invisible and do not get much attention.

(Continued)

Exhibit 15–3 *(Continued)*

Entrepreneurs/founders/owners are	Professional managers are
Structural/Positional Differences	
Have the support of family members in the business.	Function alone or with the support of nonfamily members.
Have the obligation of dealing with family members and deciding on the priorities family issues should have relative to company issues.	Do not have to worry about family issues at all, which are by definition irrelevant.
Have weak bosses, boards that are under their own control.	Have strong bosses, boards that are not under their own control.

Source: Reprinted, by permission of the publisher, from ORGANIZATIONAL DYNAMICS, Summer, 1983, © 1983 American Management Associations, New York. All rights reserved.

oriented and willing to take risks, in contrast to the professional manager's greater organizational concern.

As a business grows, the founder sometimes finds himself or herself in conflict with those who recognize the importance of increasing the emphasis on professional management. If the business experiences special "growing pains," the pressure grows, sometimes to the point of squeezing the founder out of the business he or she has founded. One of many such examples is found in the experience of Jon Birck, founder of Northwest Instrument Systems.[6] Birck founded the business in 1979 and went through several rounds of financing by venture capitalists. Professional managers were brought in, at the suggestion of the venture capitalists, and in 1984 they suggested that Birck should resign.

Avoidance of such extreme conflict in managerial philosophy calls for the founder to add sufficient professional management to enable the organization to grow and remain adaptive to its environment. If the founder can do this while retaining the most important elements of his or her own values, he or she can provide a strong foundation for a growing business.

The Cultural Background of Organizational Change

The culture of a small firm tends to complicate its change from a simple entrepreneurial type of management to a more professional style. Conflict among personnel can easily occur as new approaches clash with prevailing patterns of belief and behavior. New ideas bring into question the values that had previously been accepted as "the right way to do things." Traditions die hard. As a result, the process of change is more complex and difficult than it might appear to be at first glance.

To illustrate, imagine a firm that has been founded by a strong, autocratic entrepreneur. Those associated with such a leader may admire that person's brilliance and feel comfortable in accepting his or her control of each part of the firm's operation. As the firm grows, however, one-person management may become ineffective. It may be difficult for "old timers" to shift out of patterns of dependence, however, and to accept the greater personal responsibility needed to speed up the decision-making process.

W. Gibb Dyer has studied the ways that cultural change affects family firms.[7] In one example cited by Dyer, the family firm (Bennett Paint and Glass) began losing money in the late 1970s. To deal with that problem, the family brought in a consultant and later hired him as a manager. The consultant "cut out the dead wood" and succeeded in changing the culture. In this case, drastic action was taken to deal with weaknesses in the prevailing culture. Fortunately, cultural change does not always require dismissals. Nevertheless, change typically involves some degree of strain and conflict.

Managers and Decision Making

A manager constantly faces the necessity of making decisions. Proper guidance of the enterprise requires decisions on business objectives, scale of operation, marketing policies, products and product cost, product quality, work assignments, pay rates, and employee grievances, among many others. Virtually every managerial activity involves a choice among alternatives, thereby requiring a decision by the manager.

In making decisions, the business manager is often tempted to rely upon intuition. Indeed, one may be forced to do so because of the intangibles involved or the absence of necessary information. The intuitive decision may be criticized, however, if it disregards factual information that is already available or that is easy to obtain. Another basis for decisions is past experience, which has both strength and weakness. There is an important element of practicality that comes from experience; but at the same time, past experience is no sure guide to the future. In making decisions, therefore, the manager should have a healthy respect for factual data and should utilize them as extensively as possible.

Time Management

Much of an owner-manager's time during the working day is spent on the firing line—meeting customers, solving problems, listening to employee complaints, talking with suppliers, and the like. The manager of a small firm tackles management problems with the assistance of only a small staff. All of this means that the manager's energies and activities are diffused more than those of managers in large firms. It also means that time is often the manager's scarcest resource.

Problem of Time Pressure

Many entrepreneurs and key managers in small firms work from 60 to 80 hours per week. The hours worked by most new business owners are particularly long, as shown in Exhibit 15–4. A frequent and unfortunate result of such a schedule is the inefficient performance of their work. They are too busy to see sales representatives who can supply market information on new products and processes. They are too busy to read technical or trade literature in order to discover what others are doing and what improvements might be adapted to their own use. They are too busy to listen carefully to employees' opinions and grievances. They are too busy to give instructions properly and to teach employees how to do their jobs correctly.

Time-Savers for Busy Managers

One important solution to the problem of lack of time is good organization of work. This means delegating duties to subordinates, who are then permitted to discharge those duties without close supervision. Of course, this requires proper selection and training of individuals to assume responsibility for the delegated functions.

Perhaps the greatest time-saver of all is the effective use of time. If an individual flits from one task to another and back again, it is likely that little will be accomplished. The first step in planning one's use of time should be a survey of time normally spent on various activities. Relying on general impressions is unscientific and is likely to involve considerable error. For a period of several days, or preferably several weeks, the manager should record the time spent on various types of activities during the day. An analysis of these figures will reveal the pattern of activities, those projects and tasks involving the greatest time expenditure, and factors responsible for waste

Figure 15–2   On the Firing Line

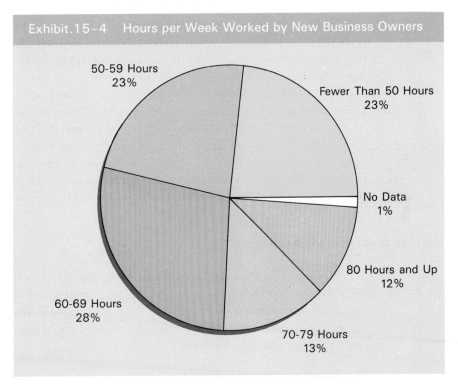

Exhibit.15–4   Hours per Week Worked by New Business Owners

50-59 Hours
23%

Fewer Than 50 Hours
23%

No Data
1%

80 Hours and Up
12%

70-79 Hours
13%

60-69 Hours
28%

Source: Data developed and provided by The NFIB Foundation and sponsored by the American Express Travel Related Services Company, Inc.

of time. It will also reveal chronic waste of time caused by excessive socializing, work on trivial matters, coffee breaks, and so on.

After eliminating practices that waste time, a manager can plan carefully the use of available time. A planned approach to a day's work or week's work is much more effective than a haphazard do-whatever-comes-up-first approach. This is true even for those small-firm managers whose schedules are often interrupted in unanticipated ways.

Many specialists in time management recommend the use of a daily written plan of work activities. This may simply be an informal listing of activities on a note pad, but it should include an establishment of priorities. By classifying duties as first-, second-, and third-level of priority, the manager can identify the most crucial tasks. That manager's attention should then be focused primarily on tasks carrying the highest priority.

Effective time management requires self-discipline. It is easy to begin with good intentions and later lapse into habitual practices of devoting time to whatever one finds to do at the moment. Procrastination is a frequent thief of time. Most of us delay unpleasant and difficult tasks. We often retreat to trivial or less threatening activities by rationalizing that we are getting those items out of the way in order to concentrate later on the important tasks.

Some managers devote much time to meetings with subordinates. Often these meetings just happen and drag on without any serious attempt to control them. The manager should prepare an agenda for such meetings, set starting and ending times, limit the conferences to the subjects to be discussed, and assign the necessary follow-through to specific subordinates. In this way the effectiveness of business conferences may be maximized and the manager's own time conserved, along with that of other staff members.

Outside Management Assistance

In view of the managerial deficiencies discussed earlier in this chapter, the entrepreneur should give careful consideration to the use of outside management assistance. Such outside assistance can supplement the busy owner-manager's personal knowledge and the expertise of the few staff specialists on the company's payroll.

The Need for Outside Assistance

The typical entrepreneur is not only deficient in managerial skills, but also lacks the opportunity to share ideas with managerial colleagues.

Although entrepreneurs can confide, to some extent, in subordinates, many of them experience loneliness. A survey of 210 owners revealed that 52 percent of them "frequently felt a sense of loneliness."[8] Moreover, this same group reported a much higher incidence of stress symptoms than those who said they did not feel lonely.

By using consultants, entrepreneurs can overcome some of the management deficiencies and reduce the sense of isolation they experience. Furthermore, an "insider" directly involved in a business problem often "cannot see the forest for the trees." To offset this limitation, the consultant brings an objective point of view and new ideas, supported by a broad knowledge of proven, successful, cost-saving methods. The consultant also can help the manager improve decision making through better organization of fact gathering and the introduction of scientific techniques of analysis. Ideally the consultant should have an "on call" relationship with the small business so that improved methods may be put into use as the need arises.

Sources of Management Assistance

The sources of management assistance given here are by no means exhaustive. No doubt there are numerous, less obvious sources of management knowledge and approaches to seeking needed help. For example, owner-managers may increase their own skills by consulting public and university libraries, attending evening college, or considering suggestions of friends and customers.

New-Business Incubators As discussed in Chapter 8, a new-business incubator is an organization and facility that offers both space and management services to new businesses. In Chapter 8, we referred to business incubators as one building-and-facilities option for startup businesses. In this chapter, we direct attention to the more important aspect of incubator operation— the management counsel and administrative services they provide.

Although some new-business incubators existed prior to 1980, their rapid growth began in the 1980s. There are now several hundred incubators in the United States, and the number is growing rapidly. Most of them involve the participation of governmental and/or university agencies, although some have been launched as purely private endeavors. The primary motivation in establishing them has been a desire to encourage entrepreneurship and thereby contribute to economic development. The logic behind their formation is evident in these words:

The primary driver of new business ventures is neither the availability of funds nor the rate of technological advance; it is the entrepreneur. New business incubators seek to maximize the potential of entrepreneurial talent within a community by providing entrepreneurs with services and support that complement their natural talents and enable them to expand their potential.[9]

Incubators provide a supportive atmosphere for a business during the early months of its existence when it is most fragile and vulnerable to external dangers and internal errors. If the incubator system works as it should, the fledgling business gains strength quickly and, within a year or so, graduates from the incubator setting.

Incubators offer new entrepreneurs on-site business expertise.[10] Very often, individuals who wish to start businesses are deficient in business knowledge and lacking in business experience. In many cases, they need practical guidance in marketing, record keeping, management, and preparation of business plans. These and other services, as portrayed in Exhibit 15–5, are available in a business incubator.

Small Business Institute (SBI) Programs   In 1972, the Small Business Administration implemented the **Small Business Institute (SBI)** program to make the consulting resources of universities available to small-business firms. SBI teams of upper-division and graduate students, under the direction of a faculty member, work with owners of small firms in analyzing their business problems and devising solutions. The primary users of such SBI consulting assistance are applicants for SBA loans, although the services are not restricted to such firms.

The program has been one of mutual benefit in providing students with a practical view of business management and in finding answers to the problems of small firms. Students from small-business, business-policy, or similar courses are typically combined in teams that provide a diversity of academic backgrounds. Individual teams, for example, may have different members specializing in management, marketing, accounting, and finance. There has been an evident enthusiasm on the part of those participating in the program, and many feel it has been one of the most successful consulting programs for small business.

Service Corps of Retired Executives (SCORE)   Small-business managers can obtain free management advice from a group called the **Service Corps of Retired Executives (SCORE)** by appealing to any Small Business Administration field office. SCORE is an organization of retired business executives who will consult on current problems with small-business managers.

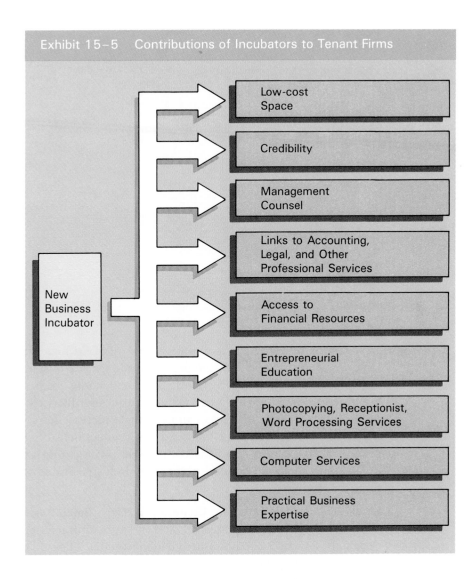

Exhibit 15-5   Contributions of Incubators to Tenant Firms

Functioning under the sponsorship of the Small Business Administration, this group provides an opportunity for retired executives to be useful to society, and it helps small-business managers solve their problems. Hence, the relationship is mutually beneficial. It may also encourage entrepreneurs to utilize paid consultants as their firms grow by demonstrating the worth of consulting service.

Figure 15–3   SCORE Counselor Gives Advice

Photo by Dave Beers, Krueger

There are numerous stories of successful SCORE assistance to small firms. A race car driver, for example, went into the tire business but experienced problems with poor records and inadequate credit control. The SCORE counselor, a retired tire manufacturer and district sales manager, provided suggestions that led to an immediate increase in profits. Another firm, a small manufacturer, established a cost reduction/profit improvement program with the aid of a SCORE counselor. The enthusiastic owner reported increased sales volume, higher-than-industry profits, and improved financial standing.

Small Business Development Centers (SBDCs)   **Small Business Development Centers**, which are patterned after the Agricultural Extension Service, were started in 1977 and now operate in most states. They are affiliated with colleges or universities as a part of the U.S. Small Business Administration's overall program of assistance to small business.

Small Business Development Centers provide direct consultation to small firms, continuing education, small business research, export services, and minority support. Their staff typically includes faculty members, SCORE counselors, professional staff, and graduate student assistants. A number of studies have concluded that the SBDC program has a positive, cost-effective impact on small business and that it is regarded as useful by most clients.[11]

Certified Public Accounting (CPA) Firms   CPA firms, both large and small, provide a range of financial and management services to small businesses. Deloitte & Touche, one of the major CPA firms, offers the services listed in Exhibit 15–6.

Management Consultants   General management consultants serve small-business firms as well as large corporations. The entrepreneur should regard the service of a competent management consultant as an investment in cost reduction. Many small firms could save as much as 10 to 20 percent

---

Exhibit 15–6   Financial and Management Services Offered to Small Businesses

Accounting and Reporting Systems

1. Developing basic accounting systems and forms, and establishing related office procedures.
2. Designing and installing cost accounting systems.
3. Designing and installing systems for the control of production and inventories.
4. Designing financial reports.
5. Planning and coordinating the use of outside computer services.
6. Assisting in recruiting, training, and evaluating accounting and clerical personnel.

Audit Services

1. Conducting a general audit of the financial statements.
2. Evaluating systems and procedures for internal control.
3. Assisting in various filings with the Securities and Exchange Commission and other regulatory agencies.

Budgets and Forecasts

1. Preparing monthly and annual operating budgets.
2. Developing long-range operating plans.
3. Installing cash-flow and other specialized forecasting systems.
4. Computing material, labor, and overhead rates for use in bidding and pricing.

Consulting

Consulting with management on the various aspects of:
1. Capital needs and alternative methods of financing business growth.

(Continued)

> ### Exhibit 15-6 *(Continued)*
>
> 2. Credit and collection policies, dividend policies, compensation plans, and insurance.
> 3. Changes in products, methods, facilities, markets, and product pricing.
> 4. Accounting for pension and profit-sharing plans, stock-option plans, and other contracts.
> 5. Applying for loans and credit.
> 6. Preparing government reports.
> 7. Preparing contract bids and proposals.
>
> #### Financial Statements
>
> 1. Assisting in the preparation of unaudited interim and year-end financial statements.
> 2. Assisting management in the interpretation of interim and year-end financial statements.
>
> #### Taxes
>
> 1. Preparing annual income tax returns.
> 2. Advising on tax planning for the organization, the individual, and the individual's estate.
> 3. Training personnel to prepare payroll, sales and use, and similar tax returns due throughout the year.

Source: Services to Small and Growing Businesses (Deloitte Haskins and Sells, 1978), pp. 7–9.

of annual operating costs. The inherent advantage in the use of able consultants is suggested by the existence of thousands of consulting firms. They range from large, long-established firms to small one- or two-person operations. Two broad areas of service rendered by management consultants are:

1. To help a client get out of trouble.
2. To help prevent trouble by anticipating and eliminating its causes.

Business firms have traditionally used consultants to help solve problems they could not handle alone.[12] But an even greater service that management consultants provide is their daily observation and analysis, which keep problems from becoming big. This view of the role of consultants greatly enlarges their service potential. Exhibit 15–7 shows a diagnostic checklist to determine whether or not the small business has a need for consultants.

Exhibit 15–7   Diagnostic Checklist to Determine Need for Consultants

The questions below may be used by owners to determine the need for management assistance and by students and other consultants who wish to "size up" a particular firm as an initial step in providing management assistance.

Management

_____   1. Does the firm have specific objectives?
_____   2. Are its objectives written?
_____   3. Does it have written long-range and short-range plans?
_____   4. Are there clear position descriptions for all key jobs?
_____   5. Are relationships among positions and departments well defined?
_____   6. Does it have an organization chart?
_____   7. Are its controls adequate for decision making?

Marketing

_____   1. What has been the sales trend for the past five years?
_____   2. Does the firm have a seasonal sales pattern?
_____   3. Has the potential market been analyzed?
_____   4. Is the nature of the firm's customers changing?
_____   5. What share of the market does it hold?
_____   6. Is its market share growing or declining?
_____   7. Have its product lines been defined?
_____   8. Does it explore new lines and delete less effective ones?
_____   9. Does it prepare sales forecasts?
_____ 10. Does it compare sales results to sales quotas or forecasts?
_____ 11. Has the firm analyzed the effectiveness of its advertising?
_____ 12. Are its personal selling practices satisfactory?
_____ 13. Does it use appropriate sales-promotion methods?
_____ 14. Does it measure customer satisfaction?
_____ 15. Does it price its products competitively?
_____ 16. Are credit accounts offered to its customers in line with industry practices?

(Continued)

Exhibit 15-7 *(Continued)*

Product/Operations

_____ 1. Is the firm's product design suitable for efficient production?

_____ 2. Is its production equipment technologically adequate and in good condition?

_____ 3. Does its physical layout contribute to operating efficiency?

_____ 4. If it is a marketing firm, does its physical layout encourage sales?

_____ 5. Is there extensive idle time for either machines or personnel?

_____ 6. Can the handling and storage of raw materials, work in process, or finishing goods be significantly improved?

_____ 7. Does it control quality adequately?

_____ 8. At what points does it check for quality?

_____ 9. Are its production operations scheduled carefully?

_____ 10. Is its plant housekeeping adequate?

Purchasing and Inventory Control

_____ 1. Does the firm buy the desired quality at the best price?

_____ 2. Does it use the best sources of supply?

_____ 3. Does it have a minimum of dead stock?

_____ 4. Is its inventory truly current and usable?

_____ 5. Does it use an effective inventory-control system?

_____ 6. Does it experience frequent stock-outs?

_____ 7. Is its inventory turnover rate adequate?

_____ 8. How does it determine its reorder point?

_____ 9. How does it determine its minimum ordering quantities?

Personnel

_____ 1. What sources does the firm use for recruiting personnel?

_____ 2. Are its selection methods adequate to assure properly qualified personnel?

_____ 3. Does it provide sufficient training for its personnel?

_____ 4. What types of training does it use?

_____ 5. Are its compensation levels and fringe benefits competitive?

_____ 6. How does its personnel turnover rate compare with that of the industry?

_____ 7. Has it prepared written personnel policies?

Exhibit 15–7 *(Continued)*

Finance

_____ 1. What is the firm's rate of return on equity?
_____ 2. What is its debt–equity ratio?
_____ 3. What is its current ratio?
_____ 4. What is its acid-test ratio?
_____ 5. Are its cash balances and working capital adequate for its sales volume?
_____ 6. Are its financial statements prepared regularly? By whom?
_____ 7. Does its accounting system provide current information on accounts payable and accounts receivable?
_____ 8. Does it use an operating budget?
_____ 9. Are its operating results compared with budgeted amounts?
_____ 10. Does it use a cash budget?
_____ 11. Does it take all available cash discounts in purchasing?
_____ 12. Does it pay its current obligations promptly?
_____ 13. Does it use the services of an outside CPA?
_____ 14. Are its operating expenses in line for its type of firm?
_____ 15. Are its credit applicants properly investigated before they are granted credit?
_____ 16. Are its bad-debt losses in line with those of the industry?
_____ 17. Are its accounts receivable aged as a part of credit control?
_____ 18. Has it made an analysis to determine which expenses are fixed and which are variable?
_____ 19. Has it prepared a break-even chart?

Risk Management

_____ 1. Have the major risks facing the firm been identified and analyzed?
_____ 2. What are its major risks?
_____ 3. Does its insurance program adequately cover the major insurable risks?
_____ 4. Are its insured amounts in line with present values?
_____ 5. Can it possibly reduce major risks in any significant way?

Other Business and Professional Services Various other business and professional groups also provide management assistance. Among these are bankers, attorneys, suppliers, trade associations, other business people, and Chambers of Commerce. One study of small-business firms found that accountants or CPAs, lawyers, and bankers were the most extensively used sources of outside management assistance.[13] In many cases, the extension of management assistance is incidental to a primary business function, for example, the provision of management assistance by a banker as a supplement to banking services.

Networks of Entrepreneurs

Entrepreneurs also gain informal management assistance through **networking**—the process of developing and engaging in mutually beneficial relationships with peers. As business owners meet other business owners, they discover a commonality of interests that leads to an exchange of ideas and experiences. The setting for such relationships may be a trade association, civic club, fraternal organization, or some other situation that brings the parties into contact with one another. Of course, the personal network of an entrepreneur is not limited to other entrepreneurs, but those individuals are typically a significant part of that network.

An example of entrepreneurial networking is found in this report:

> Alan, for example, finds his involvement with the Smaller Business Association of New England very satisfying: "Anytime you go to an SBANE meeting, you'll find people talking—not about their skiing or flying, but about business. Everybody just loves to have the chance to talk to somebody else who's not a threat. There's no concern about confidentiality or anything like that. I do a lot of talking and it helps."[14]

Networks of entrepreneurs involve a variety of ties—instrumental, affective, and moral. An instrumental tie means that the parties find the relationship mutually rewarding—for example, exchanging useful ideas about certain business problems. An affective tie relates to emotional sentiments—for example, the sharing of a joint vision about the role of small business in doing battle with giant competitors or with the government. A moral tie involves some type of obligation—for example, a mutual commitment to the principle of private enterprise or the importance of integrity in business transactions.

In personal networks of entrepreneurs, affective and moral commitments are believed to dominate those which are instrumental.[15] This suggests that a sense of identity and self-respect may be a significant product of the entrepreneur's network.

Networking has been particularly helpful to some women entrepreneurs. In the New York area, a group of ten women business owners meet monthly to help one another with business problems. They own and operate companies with annual sales of between $1 million and $10 million. One participant was quoted as saying, "The roundtable gives me the opportunity to hear what someone else has to say. They are much more capable of analyzing a problem sometimes because I am too close to it."[16]

Cost of Consulting Services

Management consultants may be hired on a fixed-fee basis (such as $100 per hour) or on a retainer basis (such as $500 per month). Retained consultants are "on call" to the small firms that have contracted for their services, thus assuring their clients of regular assistance.

The direct cost of consulting service often appears high. While the cost savings may not be immediately measurable, a benefit should be realized if competent counsel is obtained. Moreover, the small-business manager may propose a fee contingent upon demonstrable results (in the form of lower costs and higher profits, for example). This involves a hazard, however, in that a consultant might cut costs in the short run but damage the company in the long run.

Selection of a Consultant

Management consultants may be located by talking with business friends, accountants, attorneys, bankers, and trade associations. Firms that have used a particular consultant may share their opinions and provide recommendations or warnings. By talking with these firms, it is possible to evaluate this consultant's work. To check a consultant's reputation, furthermore, the prospective user can request a list of firms for whom similar projects have been completed by this consultant.

The small business may well be wary of firms that use "high-pressure" approaches. An ethical consulting firm will not engage in offensive self-promotion any more than it will haggle over fees. It is also a good idea to learn some things about the consultant such as length of time engaged in business, training and experience, and financial status. Fees to be paid and time stipulated for the accomplishment of results should be specified con-

SMALL BUSINESS IN ACTION
A Good Small Business Consultant

A small-business owner has reported the following positive experience with a management consultant:

The consultant I remember best was the first one I ever used. The company I worked for had a problem handling incoming orders—sorting, processing, recording statistics, etc. My experience was mainly in editing. But because we had so few managers, I took over the job of directing subscription processing. I had enough trouble organizing the flow of papers on my desk, so I clearly needed some help organizing a system that covered mail opening through billing. That's when Jerry Hoffman came along.

Jerry had the qualities needed in an outstanding consultant—a good teacher, a careful listener and quick analyst, a hands-on practitioner, and, perhaps most of all, the confidence to develop simple, understandable solutions for not-so-complex needs.

I worked with Jerry for about 10 years, starting with a design for sorting racks, a billing system that involved perforated cards, and eventually the more sophisticated transition from a manual to a computerized in-house system. The dollars we spent on Jerry were returned many times over to the company, and each of us who worked with him became more efficient managers.

Over the years, I've since worked with a number of other consultants. Some have approached Jerry's performance, but many exhibited the worst of the breed—a put-down attitude to persons whom they advise, a determination to force-fit a ''model'' approach, and a greater determination to establish a beachhead to become long-term residents.

These experiences overall have made me cautious about consultants—and even more so, doubly appreciative of the ones who remind me of Jerry Hoffman.

Source: Nora Goldstein, "How to Find the Right Consultant," *In Business*, Vol. 5, No. 1 (January–February, 1983), p. 35. Reproduced with permission.

tractually. And both consultant and client should require a clear definition of the consultant's task.

Cooperation between client and consultant is important. The small-business manager can contribute to the improvement of the consultant's service by throwing open the establishment and its business records. Data requested should be furnished promptly and accurately—with no pertinent facts withheld. Problems noted by either client or consultant should be promptly called to the other's attention and full exploration made so that a solution may be found quickly. Promptness in taking remedial action reduces the scope and impact of many problems.

Common Criticisms of Consultants

One frequent criticism of management consultants is that even among the reputable ones there are charlatans who claim a background of skill and experience they don't possess. While this criticism may be valid occasionally, it does not warrant suspicion of able, ethical consulting firms. Instead, it calls for care in the selection of a consultant.

Another criticism is that management consultants, unlike doctors and public accountants, need not be licensed by the state to practice and are not subject to ejection from the profession in the event of unethical practice. There are, however, several associations whose members subscribe to a code of professional practice and ethics.

A third charge against management consultants is that they may insert themselves unduly into management and take over its responsibilities. Fulfillment of responsibilities is up to the managers themselves. They cannot be forced to turn responsibilities over to a consultant. Hence, if responsibilities shift from manager to consultant, it is the manager's own fault.

A fourth common criticism concerns lack of ability. Information on percentage of satisfied clients, like that on frequency of repeat engagements, is difficult to obtain. The growth of consulting services, however, makes it obvious that consultants have many satisfied customers.

Looking Back

1. A large proportion of small-business firms is characterized by weak management. In part, this results from the lack of managerial expertise by entrepreneurs whose primary focus is creating a new business rather than managing.
2. Managers of small firms typically face two major constraints. A shortage of financial resources limits their options in decision making, and an absence of an adequate professional staff denies them the expertise that is available to large-firm managers.
3. Founders typically differ in a number of ways from professional managers, and difficulties are experienced as a firm grows. As a firm grows, its founder becomes more a manager and less a doer and moves in the direction of becoming a professional manager or bringing in professional management. The existing culture often complicates the change toward greater professionalism.

4. Small-business managers who have difficulty finding time to perform managerial tasks efficiently should learn to delegate some duties to subordinates and to organize their use of time by careful planning.

5. Outside management assistance is provided by many types of consultants, including new business incubators, SBI student consultants, SCORE (retired executives), Small Business Development Centers, CPA firms, general management consultants, and various others, as well as by networking. The use of management consultants may be thought of as an investment in cost reduction.

DISCUSSION QUESTIONS

1. Is it likely that the quality of management is relatively uniform throughout the many types of small businesses? What might account for differences?

2. What are the four stages of small-business growth outlined in this chapter? How do managerial requirements change as the firm moves through these stages?

3. Evaluate founders as managers. Why is there a tendency toward managerial weakness in those who create new firms?

4. As noted in Exhibit 15–3, entrepreneurs are thought to be primarily intuitive, whereas professional managers are thought to be primarily analytical. If this is true, how will collegiate education for business affect the development of entrepreneurs?

5. How can the prevailing cultural patterns of a firm interfere with the firm's movement toward more professional management?

6. What practices can a small-business manager utilize to conserve time?

7. Is it reasonable to believe that an outsider coming into a business could propose procedures or policies superior to those of the manager who is intimately acquainted with operations? Why?

8. What would be the advantages and drawbacks of a business-incubator location for a startup retail firm?

9. Does the rapid growth of new-business incubators in the 1980s suggest that they may be a fad? If the concept is sound, why didn't incubators emerge much earlier?

10. Explain the nature of the SBI student consulting program. Is this program of primary benefit to the client firm or to the students?

11. What might account for the fact that accountants and CPAs are among the most widely used sources of outside management assistance?

12. What is networking, and how can an entrepreneur use it to improve management within a small firm?

13. Suppose that in three years you will be operating your own retail specialty foods store and that you have heard of the value of networking. How would you find or arrange a network for yourself?

14. Would you personally be most inclined to participate in networking because of an instrumental tie, an affective tie, or a moral tie?

15. Suppose that you, as owner of a small firm, realize that you need management help and that you are approached by a management consultant who offers his or her services. How would you go about "checking out" this consultant to determine whether you would get high-quality assistance that would make it worth your money?

YOU MAKE THE CALL

Situation 1

In 1988, *Venture* published a review of time-management practices in small business. According to this study, David Alan Foster, founder and chief operating officer of Mindsight Corporation, Newbury Park, CA, works from 75 to 85 hours per week. He attributed his exceptionally long work week to the newness of the business, which had started only a few months earlier—a "startup mode" that caused them to "run on the ragged edge."

Foster's concerns about the long hours and his hope for improvement are explained in these words:

> Though Foster, 35, would also prefer more vacation time to spend with his wife and two boys, he would also enjoy shifting responsibilities in his company to allow him to be more creative. "I'd like to give up some of my hat," confesses Foster. He wishes he could cut his hours by using more administrative support and secretarial services. "I'd like more time to make contacts and work on policy—things that would help us grow faster."
>
> *Source:* Webster E. Williams, "Time is Money, So How Do You Spend It?" Reprinted from the August, 1988, issue of *VENTURE, For Entrepreneurial Business Owners & Investors,* © 1988.

Questions

1. How is time pressure related to the newness of a firm? In view of the long hours generally worked in small business, do you think Foster's reference to newness may be a rationalization?

2. How does Foster intend to change his usage of time? Is there any reason he could not make such changes immediately?
3. What other inexpensive ways to reduce time pressure can you recommend to this business founder?

Situation 2

A few years after successfully launching a new business, an entrepreneur found himself spending 16-hour days running from one appointment to another, negotiating with customers, drumming up new business, signing checks, and checking up as much as possible on his six employees. The founder realized that his own strength was in selling, but general management responsibilities were very time consuming and interfered with his selling efforts. He even slept in the office two nights a week.

No matter how hard he worked, however, he knew that his people weren't organized and that many problems existed. There was no time to set personnel policies or to draw up job descriptions for his six employees. One employee even took advantage of the laxity and sometimes skipped work. Invoices were sent to customers late, and delivery schedules were sometimes missed. Fortunately, the business was profitable in spite of the numerous problems.

Questions
1. Is this founder's problem one of time management or general management? Would it be logical to engage a management consultant to help solve the firm's problems?
2. If this founder asked you to recommend some type of outside management assistance, would you recommend a SCORE counselor, an SBI team, a CPA firm, a management consultant, or some other kind? Why?
3. If you were asked to improve this firm's management system, what would be your first steps and your initial goal?

EXPERIENTIAL EXERCISES

1. Interview a management consultant, SCORE member, SBI project director, or representative of a CPA firm to discuss small-business management weaknesses and the small firm's willingness or reluctance to use consultants. Prepare a report on your findings.
2. Select an unstructured block of one to four hours in your schedule—

that is, hours that are not regularly devoted to class attendance, sleeping, and so on. Carefully record your use of that time period for several days. Prepare a report showing your use of the time and a plan for its more effective use.

3. Interview a business owner regarding that firm's use of outside management assistance of any type and the owner's attitudes toward such assistance. Prepare a report summarizing your findings.

4. Interview a partner in a public accounting firm to discover the types of services the firm provides to small businesses. In particular, inquire about services that go beyond financial reporting and auditing, such as help in creating an organization structure, establishing controls, or employee recruitment.

REFERENCES TO SMALL-BUSINESS PRACTICES

Black, Pam. "A Little Help from Her Friends." *Venture*, Vol. 8, No. 7 (July, 1986), pp. 52–58.
> A description of the formation and operation of several female entrepreneurial networks is given in this article.

Kerwin, Kathleen. "Carry-Out Consultants." *Nation's Business*, Vol. 76, No. 6 (June, 1988), pp. 50R–51R.
> This article describes a number of small firms and the types of outside management assistance they have used.

"Publishing Magnate Pat McGovern." *Inc.*, Vol. 10, No. 8 (August, 1988), pp. 27–33.
> This article records an interview with an entrepreneur who started from scratch and built a big business. He describes how he changed from being a doer into being a manager.

Richman, Tom. "Beyond the Billable Hour." *Inc.*, Vol. 8, No. 8 (August, 1986), pp. 56–59.
> The efforts of a small public relations firm to move into professional management and to escape the limits imposed by the time constraints of the founder are described.

ENDNOTES

1. James J. Kilpatrick, "Making Life More Bearable for the Traveler," *Nation's Business*, Vol. 65, No. 12 (December, 1977), p. 12.

2. Thomas P. Murphy, "From Eagles to Turkeys," *Forbes*, Vol. 134, No. 4 (August 13, 1984), p. 136.

3. *Ibid.*

4. Thomas P. Murphy, "The Role of the Boss," *Forbes*, Vol. 130, No. 12 (December 6, 1982), p. 246.

5. *Ibid.*

6. "Dear Jon," *Inc.*, Vol. 7, No. 2 (February, 1985), pp. 79–86.

7. W. Gibb Dyer, Jr., *Cultural Change in Family Firms* (San Francisco: Jossey-Bass Publishers, 1986).

8. David E. Gumpert and David P. Boyd, "The Loneliness of the Small Business Owner," *Harvard Business Review*, Vol. 62, No. 6 (November–December, 1984), p. 19.

9. Raymond W. Smilor and Michael D. Gill, Jr., *The New Business Incubator* (Lexington, MA: Lexington Books, 1986), p. 11.

10. Studies of the effectiveness of incubators include the following: James R. Lumpkin and R. Duane Ireland, "Screening Practices of New Business Incubators," *American Journal of Small Business*, Vol. 12, No. 4 (Spring, 1988), pp. 59–81; Fred L. Fry, "The Role of Incubators in Small Business Planning," *American Journal of Small Business*, Vol. 12, No. 1 (Summer, 1987), pp. 51–61.

11. See, for example Afsaneh Naharandi and Susan Chesteen, "The Impact of Consulting on Small Business: A Further Examination," *Entrepreneurship Theory and Practice*, Vol. 13, No. 1 (Fall, 1988), pp. 29–40; James J. Chrisman, R. Ryan Nelson, Frank Hoy, and Richard B. Robinson, Jr., "The Impact of SBDC Consulting Activities," *Journal of Small Business Management*, Vol. 23, No. 3 (July, 1985), pp. 1–11; Alfred M. Pelham, "Should the SBDC Program Be Dismantled?" *American Journal of Small Business*, Vol. 10, No. 2 (Fall, 1985), pp. 41–51.

12. Professor Herbert E. Kierulff of Seattle Pacific University has described a three-phase "turnaround" process successfully used by a consulting firm in helping more than 200 smaller companies. See Herbert E. Kierulff, "Turnaround vs. Bankruptcies," *In Business*, Vol. 3, No. 3 (May–June, 1981), pp. 37–38. This shows how consultants help small firms get out of trouble.

13. Robert A. Peterson, "Small Business Management Assistance," *American Journal of Small Business*, Vol. 9, No. 2 (Fall, 1984), pp. 35–45.

14. David E. Gumpert and David P. Boyd, "The Loneliness of the Small Business Owner," *op. cit.*, p. 24.

15. Bengt Johannisson and Rein Peterson, "The Personal Networks of Entrepreneurs," paper appearing in conference proceedings, Third Canadian Conference, International Council for Small Business—Canada, Toronto, Canada, May 23–25, 1984.

16. "Women Chief Executives Help Each Other with Frank Advice," *The Wall Street Journal* (July 2, 1984), p. 19.

16

THE NATURE OF MANAGERIAL WORK

Spotlight on Small Business

Courtesy of Buddy Eanes

Effective managerial leadership in today's small business requires more than a carrot-and-stick approach. E. R. "Buddy" Eanes and his son Richard have used imaginative, nontraditional methods to motivate the 120 drivers and other employees of Warren Trucking Company in Martinsville, VA. Their first step was to set an example—to the point of going into the warehouse and helping load trucks. They also arranged schedules of long-distance drivers so they could be home several nights each week, and they provided stress-management seminars for employees and their families. To involve employees in the management process, they started weekly meetings with 10 key employees to solve problems and cut costs. This progressive approach to management enabled the firm to more than double sales in two years.

Source: Dennis T. Jaffe and Cynthia D. Scott, "Bridging Your Workers' 'Motivation Gap,'" *Nation's Business*, Vol. 77, No. 3 (March, 1989), pp. 30–32. Copyright 1989, U.S. Chamber of Commerce.

Looking Ahead

Watch for the following important topics:
1. Planning in small firms.
2. Building effective human relationships.
3. Organizing activities and people.
4. Using a board of directors.
5. New terms and concepts:

long-range plans	chain of command
short-range plans	line-and-staff organization
strategic plans	line activities
budget	staff activities
business policies	unity of command
procedures	delegation of authority
standard operating procedures	span of control
line organization	advisory council

In the previous chapter, we treated the management process in a general way. We emphasized the need for good management, the evolution of management methods as a firm grows, and sources of outside management assistance. In this chapter, we look more closely at what small-firm managers do—how they plan, how they provide leadership, how they organize, and how they use boards of directors.

Operational Planning

Someone has said, "If you don't know where you're going, any path will get you there." That statement suggests a need for objectives in operating a business. A business plan, as discussed in Chapter 6, sets out such long-range objectives for a beginning business. A long-established firm also benefits by thinking out and formulating a comprehensive plan that gives it direction.

Planning does not end, however, with the creation of a mission statement or formulation of an overall plan. To be effective, planning must become an ongoing process. Our focus in this section is the continuing process of planning that gives substance to the firm's broad objective and that enables it to carry out production, marketing, and other activities most effectively.

Need For Formal Planning

Most small-business owners and managers plan to some degree. However, the amount of planning is typically much less than the ideal. Also, what little planning there is tends to be spotty and unsystematic—dealing with how much inventory to purchase, whether to buy a new piece of equipment, and other questions of this type. Specific circumstances affect the degree to which formal planning is needed, but most businesses could function more profitably by increasing their planning and making it more systematic.

SMALL BUSINESS IN ACTION
A Plan That Actually Guides Business Operations

In 1987, Western Windshields, Inc., a distributor of automobile replacement glass, needed to retrench, having lost money on one venture and having neglected its core business. Western's president, Neil Smith, with the help of management consultant Raymond Leon and Western's own management team, put together a comprehensive plan designed to turn strategies into action.

The plan was distinctive in that it was constructed for use as a management tool—to be followed during the year rather than being placed on a shelf and forgotten. Each department had a one-page summary of the plan that laid out its activities by calendar periods.

For instance, by last July Smith was to have hired a credit manager. And in the first two weeks of September he was to have analyzed the status of collection of receivables. "That's the beauty of this thing," says Smith. "At any given point we know exactly where we are on the plan."

Smith and other managers hold monthly meetings to monitor progress, and they update the plan annually. Western's plan was credited with helping the business to more than double its 1984 sales in the plan's first two years of use.

Source: Jeffrey Lener, "A Business Plan That Grows with You." Reprinted from the December, 1988, issue of *VENTURE, For Entrepreneurial Business Owners & Investors* © 1988.

If the firm is very small, the manager may do most of the planning in his or her head with very little paperwork. Such informal planning may work satisfactorily if there is little complexity in the business. A low-technology firm with a simple product or process may be able to get by and even prosper with minimal formal planning.

Other variables affecting the need for formal planning are the degree of competition and the level of uncertainty. A small firm facing stiff competition needs to plan and monitor its operations closely. Although all companies experience some surprises and unpredictability in their operations, they differ in the degree of uncertainty that they face. If there is much uncertainty, planning can help the entrepreneur to grasp the nature of the challenges facing the firm.

Still another factor affecting the need for formal planning is the entrepreneur's experience and background. Those who are highly capable, who understand the various aspects of the business, and who are willing to involve themselves in the details of the business can do more of the planning in their heads and reduce the paperwork of formal planning. It should be obvious that such highly personalized management eventually acts as a constraint to growth by centering its planning around one or two individuals.

Making Time for Planning

Small-business managers may easily succumb to the "tyranny of the urgent." Because they are so busy "putting out fires," they may never get around to planning. Planning is easy to postpone, and that makes it easy for managers to ignore it while concentrating on more urgent issues of production and sales. And, like quarterbacks blindsided by blitzing linebackers, such entrepreneurs may be bowled over by unsuspected competitors.

Some discipline is necessary, therefore, to find time for planning and to gain its benefits. Time must be set aside and a degree of seclusion provided if significant progress is to be made. Planning is primarily a mental process, and it is seldom done effectively in an atmosphere of ringing telephones, rush orders, and urgent demands for decision.

It is a mistake, however, to think that planning calls for skills that exceed the abilities of a business owner. Planning can be practical, as John Ward has pointed out: "It's not a fancy process. It is not a high-powered, sophisticated, computer-driven or MBA-driven effort. It's basically sitting down and saying, 'O.K., how do I think about my business?'"[1]

Employee Participation in Planning

The small-business owner is directly and personally responsible for planning. Typically, he or she does not have, and cannot have, a full-time planning staff such as many large firms have. Neither the money nor the personnel are available for such a staff. Consequently, the owner must do the planning, and a great proportion of the owner's time will be spent in it. Nevertheless, this responsibility may be delegated to some extent, because some planning is required of all the members of the enterprise. If the organization is of any size at all, the owner can hardly specify in detail the program for each department. Furthermore, there is a need for some factual information that can be supplied only by other members of the organization.

The concept that the boss does the thinking and the employee does the work is rather misleading. Progressive managers have discovered that employees' ideas are often helpful in developing solutions to company problems. The salesperson, for example, is closer to the customer and usually better able to evaluate the customer's reactions. It is not enough for employees to call attention to problems—they must also turn up recommendations and solutions.

Figure 16–1   A Planning Meeting Among
Employees of a Retail Clothing Store

The practical use of participation in planning is apparently quite limited. A survey by *Venture* magazine revealed that 51 percent of their 1,090 respondents sought planning input solely from top management.[2] And only 24 percent disseminated their plans below the department-head level.

The value of such contributions by subordinates is clearly dependent on their ability. If subordinate managers and other key people lack ability and experience, they can contribute little to the firm's planning. Not all employees possess the capacity or the motivation for planning.

Kinds of Plans

Business plans may be classified in several ways. When classified according to the time period for which they are established, they are called **long-range plans** or **short-range plans**. When classified according to their frequency of use, they are known as standing plans (such as policies and procedures) or single-use plans (such as special projects and budgets). More detailed functional plans are also developed in production, marketing, finance, and other areas.

Long-Range and Short-Range Plans Long-range plans are also referred to as **strategic plans**. They include choices that will affect a firm several years in the future. As we pointed out in Chapter 7, a firm may select a special niche by choosing to concentrate on a particular segment of the market. This constitutes a long-range, strategic decision.

Even though a firm's basic direction is established when it begins, it needs to be reviewed periodically as part of the continuing planning process. Without some contemplation of the distant future on a regular basis, a firm might find itself on a "dead-end street."

The more extensive planning activities, however, involve the preparation of short-range action plans—the yearly and/or quarterly plans for production, marketing, and other functional areas that are needed to implement action toward general goals. An important part of a firm's (or department's) short-range action plans is the budget. A **budget** is a device for expressing future plans in monetary terms. It is usually prepared for one year in advance, with a breakdown by quarters or months. As a plan of action, the budget provides a set of yardsticks by which operations can be controlled. To be effective, the budget must be based on a realistic estimate of sales volume, with appropriate expense levels determined accordingly. The budget is discussed in greater detail in Chapter 20.

Policies   **Business policies** are defined as fundamental statements that serve as guides to management practice. Some policies are general in that they affect the whole business, while other policies affect only particular departments or portions of the operation. In a small manufacturing firm there are product policies, sales policies, manufacturing policies, financial policies, expansion policies, personnel policies, and credit policies, among others. For example, any small firm establishes a personnel policy when it determines the amount of vacation to which its employees are entitled. Similarly, sales policy is established when a firm determines the geographical scope of its market and the type of customer it will seek.

An already-decided policy permits a prompt decision on a specific problem. This does not mean that the policy dictates the decision—a policy should allow a certain latitude for judgment in individual cases. Nevertheless, an established policy makes it unnecessary for the manager to analyze a specific problem each time it arises. For example, an employer need not decide each year the amount of vacation each employee should receive. The general statement of vacation policy is simply applied to individual cases.

Saving time is only one of the advantages in the use of definite policies in a small firm. Policies are established on the basis of a careful consideration of all pertinent factors and are thus arrived at logically. Without policy in particular areas, the manager is forced to make decisions under pressure and without the opportunity to think through the implications of those decisions. Finally, policies also provide consistency of action from one time to another. This is a matter of value to both customers and employees of the firm.

Procedures   A **procedure** is similar to a policy in that it is a standing or continuing plan. However, a procedure is concerned primarily with methodology—how something is to be done. Once a method of work or a procedure is worked out, it may be standardized and referred to as a **standard operating procedure**. For example, the steps involved in taking a credit application, investigating the applicant, approving or disapproving the request, and subsequent authorizations of particular purchases by approved customers may be completely standardized.

Human Relationships in the Small Firm

As with any endeavor involving people, a small firm needs an atmosphere of cooperation and teamwork among all participants. Fortunately, effective collaboration among employees in small firms is entirely possible. In fact, the potential for good teamwork is enhanced in some ways by the smallness of the enterprise.

Personal Contact Between Employees and Entrepreneur

In most small firms, employees get to know the owner-manager personally within a short period of time. This person is not a faceless "unknown" but an individual whom employees see and relate to in the course of their normal work schedules. This situation is entirely different from that of large corporations, in which most employees have never even seen the chief executive. If the employer–employee relationship is good, employees in small firms naturally develop strong feelings of personal loyalty to the employer.

In very small firms—those of 20 or fewer employees—extensive interaction is typical. As a firm grows, the amount of personal contact naturally declines. Nevertheless, a significant personal relationship is characteristic of most small businesses.

Figure 16–2   Personal Contact Between Entrepreneur and Employees

Courtesy of Honeywell Inc.

There is a potential weakness in the close relationship, however, if the entrepreneur is not oriented toward people or appreciative of employee contributions. In such a case, the small firm may fail to achieve the level of employee commitment that is possible. Another danger exists if the employer is reluctant to exercise proper discipline. As an example, a supermarket owner employed a long-time acquaintance who desperately needed a job. The employee's main duty was to serve as cashier, but she was extremely choosy about her duties and neglected opportunities to stock shelves or perform other menial duties when not busy at the cash register. The long-suffering employer permitted the situation to exist because of sympathy for a friend and an unwillingness to incur her ill will.

The Entrepreneur's Pervasive Influence

In a large corporation, the philosophy and values of top management must be filtered through many layers of management before they come to those who produce and sell the products. As a result, the influence of those at the top may be diluted by the very process of going through channels.

In sharp contrast, personnel in a small firm are in a position to receive the leader's messages directly. This face-to-face contact facilitates their understanding of the leader's stand on integrity or customer service or other important issues.

This pervasive, personal influence of the owner-manager can contribute to strong relationships between management and employees. In day-to-day operations, however, a firm faces a diversity of pressing production, sales, and financial issues as well as people issues. These nonpeople issues can easily absorb management's attention and become disruptive to good employer–employee relationships. It is easy for an entrepreneur to become enmeshed in problems related to his or her personal background and neglect employee relationships and motivation.

The Quality of Leadership

Leadership that maximizes the contributions of personnel in a small firm will enable the firm to compete more effectively in the marketplace. Although larger competitors may have an advantage because of the economic resources at their disposal, they should not be permitted an advantage in their methods of leadership. By creating an environment that inspires enthusiasm, the leader of a small firm can get the best from present company personnel and also offer a strong inducement to prospective employees. For example, most professional personnel prefer an organizational setting that minimizes "politics" as a factor in getting ahead. By creating a friendly atmosphere that avoids the intrigue common in some organizations, an entrepreneur can build an environment that is much more attractive to most employees.

An example of business progress through leadership change is found in the experience of Amot Controls Corporation, an industrial controls manufacturing company in Richmond, CA, founded by Elton B. Fox in 1947.[3] The business expanded sales, showed good profits, and achieved a strong market niche. Nevertheless, Steven K. Fox, who took over management from his father in the early 1980s, felt that the company was becoming sluggish and bureaucratic and sensed mistrust and hostility between employees and management.

The younger Fox took a number of steps to change the company's culture to create a more people-oriented business. He began to hold meetings with office staff and shop-floor employees, letting them know what was going on and giving them a chance to ask questions. Interestingly, a couple of workers were wary of the change and would not have anything to do with the first meeting! Nevertheless, Fox persisted. He hired a manager of manufacturing, who broke up the one long assembly line and its repetitive, boring tasks. In its place, he organized the machines into clusters, with employees at each cluster making, as much as possible, complete parts. In making the change, he sought ideas from employees rather than calling in consultants. The changes made at Amot Controls Corporation reduced animosity between employees and management. Morale improved, and the company experienced growth and a new vitality.

Leadership that emphasizes positive, noncoercive approaches is increasingly replacing the more autocratic methods of earlier years. Positive leadership rests upon a respect for individual members of the organization and a basic fairness in decisions affecting them. Such leadership makes extensive use of communication as noted in the next section.

Effective Communication

The key to healthy interpersonal relationships lies in effective communication. To be sure, much communication flows in the form of orders and instructions to employees. But communication is a two-way process, and it is difficult for employees to be either intelligent or enthusiastic teamwork-

SMALL BUSINESS IN ACTION
Effective Two-Way Communication

Hope's Windows, Inc., is a custom manufacturer of steel and aluminum windows located in Jamestown, NY. In 1977, the company experienced a drop in orders in one of its key markets, forcing the layoff of 23 of 35 employees. The problem was caused by the bidding process, which produced bids that were consistently too high.

To solve the problem, Hope's management appealed to employees who made the windows. The company created a bidding committee made up of managers and production workers which proved successful in winning most of their subsequent bids. Dale Mansfield, a ten-year veteran at Hope's, commented as follows:

> In a lot of companies the managers act like they're too good to be speaking to a "nobody." Here they listen to people like me. No manager can do every job or understand every job. So how can he always know what needs to be done? I don't think managers are relinquishing anything by asking us what we think. We're just providing the information; management still has to make the decisions. But, with their ideas and our ideas, maybe we can come up with something that will really help the company.

Source: Reprinted with permission, *Inc.* magazine (April, 1981). Copyright © 1981 by *Inc.* Publishing Company, 38 Commercial Wharf, Boston, MA 02110.

ers if they do not know the reasons for such orders and instructions. Furthermore, the opportunity to contribute ideas and opinions *before* the manager decides an issue adds dignity to the job in the eyes of most employees.

Other aspects leading to effective communication include telling employees where they stand, how the business is doing, and what plans are for the future. Negative feedback to employees may be necessary at times, but positive feedback is the primary tool for establishing good human relations. Perhaps the most fundamental concept to keep in mind is that employees are people. They quickly detect insincerity, but they respond to honest efforts to treat them as mature, responsible individuals.

To go beyond good intentions in communicating, a small-firm manager may adopt some practical techniques of stimulating two-way communication. A few examples, by no means exhaustive, are the following:

1. Periodic performance review sessions as a time for discussing the employee's ideas, questions, complaints, and job expectations.

2. Bulletin boards to keep employees informed about developments affecting them and/or the company.
3. Suggestion boxes as a means of soliciting employee ideas.
4. Staff meetings for the discussion of problems and matters of general concern.

These methods can be used to supplement the most basic of all channels for communication—the day-to-day interaction between each employee and his or her supervisor.

Defining Organizational Relationships

While an entrepreneur may give direction through personal leadership, he or she must also define the relationships among the firm's activities and among the individuals on the company payroll. Without some kind of organization structure, the situation eventually becomes chaotic, and morale suffers.

The Unplanned Structure

In small companies, the organization structure tends to evolve with little conscious planning. Certain employees begin performing particular functions when the firm is new and retain those functions as the company matures. Other functions remain diffused in a number of positions, even though they have gained importance as a result of company growth.

This natural evolution is not all bad. Generally, a strong element of practicality exists in organizational arrangements that evolve in this way. The structure is forged in the process of working and growing, not derived from a textbook. Unplanned structures are seldom perfect, however, and growth typically creates a need for organizational change. Periodically, therefore, the entrepreneur should examine structural relationships and make adjustments as needed for effective teamwork.

Assuming that the business is more than a one-person operation, the entrepreneur must decide whether a line organization is appropriate or whether a more complex form of organization is desirable.

Establishing a Chain of Command

In a **line organization** each person has one supervisor to whom he or she reports and looks for instructions. Thus, a single, specific chain of command exists. All employees are engaged directly in getting out the work—producing, selling, or arranging financial resources. Most very small firms—for example, those with fewer than ten employees—use this form of organization. A line organization is illustrated in Exhibit 16–1.

The term **chain of command** implies a superior–subordinate relationship with a downward flow of orders, but it involves much more. The chain of command is also a channel for two-way communication, although this does not mean that communication among employees at the same level is forbidden. Informal discussion among employees is inevitable. However, the chain is the official, vertical channel of communication. Even so, not all communication between superior and subordinate is official, and not all of the superior's statements are orders. There is normal social interaction, as well as order giving, between superior and subordinate. When orders are given, the subordinate's line of responsibility or obligation to the superior to carry out the orders becomes evident.

An organizational problem occurs when managers or employees ignore organization lines. In small firms, the climate of informality and flexibility makes it easy to short-circuit the formal chain. The president and founder of the business, for example, may get in a hurry and give instructions to salespersons or plant employees instead of going through the sales manager or the production manager. Similarly, an employee who has been

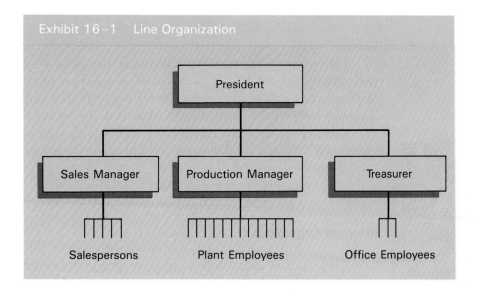

Exhibit 16–1   Line Organization

President

Sales Manager   Production Manager   Treasurer

Salespersons   Plant Employees   Office Employees

with the entrepreneur from the beginning tends to maintain that direct person-to-person relationship rather than observe newly instituted channels of communication.

As a practical matter, adherence to the chain of command can never be complete. An organization in which the chain of command is rigid would be bureaucratic and inefficient. Nevertheless, frequent and flagrant disregard of the chain of command quickly undermines the position of the bypassed manager. This is a particular danger for the small firm, and only the entrepreneur can make sure that the integrity of the structure is maintained. Occasionally, for example, the entrepreneur may need to say, "Why don't you talk with your supervisor about that first?"

As a small business expands and hires additional employees, it outgrows the simple line organization. The need for specialized management assistance leads to the type of organization described in the next section.

Adding Specialists to the Organization

The **line-and-staff organization** is similar to a line organization in that each person reports to a single supervisor. However, in a line-and-staff structure there are also staff specialists who perform specialized services or act as management advisers in special areas. Examples of staff specialists include a human resources manager, a production control technician, a quality control specialist, or an assistant to the president. Small firms ordinarily grow quickly to a size requiring some staff specialists. Consequently, this is a widely used type of organization in small business. Exhibit 16–2 shows a line-and-staff organization.

Line activities are those that contribute directly to the primary objectives of the small firm. Typically, these are production and sales activities. **Staff activities**, on the other hand, are the supporting or helping activities. Although both types of activities are important, the focus must be kept on line activities—those which earn the customer's dollar. The owner-manager must insist that staff specialists function primarily as helpers and facilitators. Otherwise, the firm will experience confusion as employees receive directions from a variety of supervisors and staff specialists. **Unity of command**—that is, receiving direction from only one boss—would be destroyed.

Informal Organization

The types of organization structure previously discussed are concerned with formal relationships among members of an organization. In

Campbell Soup Company

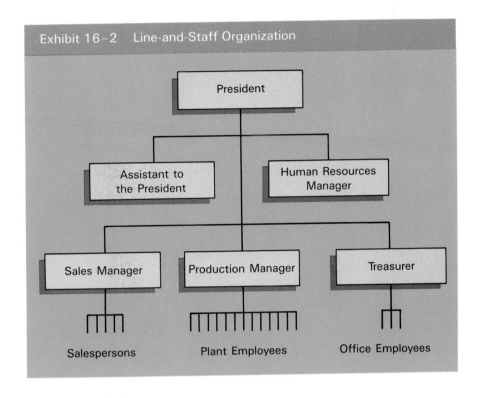

Exhibit 16-2   Line-and-Staff Organization

President

Assistant to the President

Human Resources Manager

Sales Manager

Production Manager

Treasurer

Salespersons

Plant Employees

Office Employees

any organization, however, there are also informal groups that have something in common such as jobs, hobbies, carpools, age, or affiliations with civic associations. The dotted areas in Exhibit 16–3 represent informal groups in an organization.

Although informal groups are not a structural part of the formal organization, the manager should observe them and evaluate their effect on the functioning of the total organization. Ordinarily, no serious conflict arises between informal groups and the formal organization. It is probable that an informal leader or leaders will emerge who will influence employee behavior. The wise manager understands the potentially positive contribution of informal groups and the inevitability of informal leadership. Of course, if a leader were to persist in influencing other employees to behave contrary to the wishes of management, it might become necessary to discharge such an individual.

Informal interaction among subordinates and managers can facilitate work performance and also can make life in the workplace more enjoyable

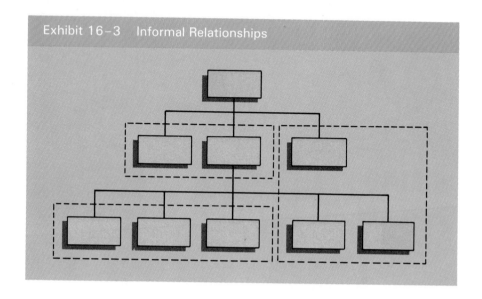

Exhibit 16-3   Informal Relationships

for everyone. The value of compatible work groups to the individual became painfully clear to one college student who worked on a summer job:

> I was employed as a forklift driver for one long, frustrating summer. Soon after being introduced to my work group, I knew I was in trouble. A clique had formed and, for some reason, resented college students. During lunch breaks and work breaks, I spent the whole time by myself. Each morning I dreaded going to work. The job paid well, but I was miserable.

Delegating Authority

Given a proper concept of **delegation of authority**, a superior will grant to subordinates, on the basis of competence, the right to act or to decide. By delegating authority, the superior can perform the more important tasks after turning over the less important functions to subordinates.

Failure to delegate may well be the weakest point in small-business organizations generally. Although the problem is found in all organizations, it is a special problem for the independent entrepreneur, whose background usually contributes to this situation. Frequently, the entrepreneur has organized the business and knows more about it than any other person in the firm. Thus, to protect the business, the owner is inclined to keep a firm hold on the reins of leadership.

Inability or unwillingness to delegate authority is manifested in numerous ways. For example, employees may find it necessary to "clear it with the boss" before making even a minor decision. A line of subordinates may be constantly trying to get the attention of the owner to resolve some issue that the subordinates lack authority to settle. This keeps the owner exceptionally busy, rushing from assisting a salesperson to helping iron out a production bottleneck to setting up a new filing system.

Delegation of authority is important for the satisfactory operation of a small firm and is an absolute prerequisite for growth. This factor alone is the reason why many firms can never grow beyond the small size that can be directly supervised in detail by the owner. One owner of a small restaurant operated it with excellent profits. As a result of this success, the owner acquired a lease on another restaurant in the same area and proceeded to operate it for one year. During this time, the owner experienced constant "headaches" with the second restaurant. Working long hours and trying to supervise both restaurants finally led the owner to give up the job. This person had never learned to delegate authority.

By allowing others to participate in decision making, an entrepreneur develops employees' abilities and thereby builds an organization. However, a manager must delegate carefully, or subordinates may simply bring their problems back to the boss. One entrepreneur suggests the following way to analyze one's practices in delegating:

> Try analyzing your time and separating your work into two general categories: problems your employees "delegated" to you and your own activities. You will quickly learn how much control you have over your own problems versus how much control your employees have.[4]

If employees have too much control, the manager must encourage them to act independently and avoid doing all their work for them. Only by real delegation can the entrepreneur build an organization rather than merely run a business.

Deciding How Many to Supervise

The optimum **span of control** is the number of subordinates who can be effectively supervised by a manager. Although some authorities have stated that six to eight people are all that one individual can supervise effectively, the proper span of control actually is a variable depending upon a number of factors. Among these are the nature of the work and the superior's knowledge, energy, personality, and abilities. In addition, if the abilities of subordinates are greater than average, the span of control may be enlarged accordingly.

In a business organization there is a limit to the number of operative employees who can be effectively supervised. Of course, the span of control is greater in the case of personnel performing routine assignments than in the case of technical, professional, or administrative personnel.

As a very small firm grows and adds employees, the entrepreneur's span of control is extended. There is a tendency to stretch the span too far—to supervise not only the first 5 or 6 employees but later all 10 or 12 as they are needed. Eventually a point is reached at which the attempted span exceeds the entrepreneur's reach—the time and ability he or she can devote to the business. It is at this point that the entrepreneur must establish intermediate levels of supervision, devoting more time to management and moving beyond the role of player-coach.

The Board of Directors in Small Corporations

All too often, the majority stockholder (the entrepreneur) in a small corporation appoints a board of directors merely to fulfill a legal requirement. Such owners make little or no use of directors in managing their companies. In fact, an entrepreneur may actively resent efforts of managerial assistance from directors. When appointing directors, the entrepreneur tends to select personal friends, relatives, or other managers who are too busy to analyze situations and are not inclined to argue. In directors' meetings, the entrepreneur and other directors may simply engage in long-winded, innocuous discussions of broad general policies, leaving no time for serious, constructive questions. Some entrepreneurs, however, have found an active board to be both practical and beneficial.[5]

Contribution of Directors

A properly assembled board of directors can bring supplementary knowledge and broad experience to corporate management. The board should meet regularly to provide maximum assistance to the chief executive. Such board meetings should be conferences in which ideas are debated, strategies determined, and the pros and cons of policies explored. In this way, the chief executive is assisted by the experience of all the board members. Their combined knowledge makes possible more intelligent decisions on major issues.

Utilizing the experience of a board of directors does not mean that the chief executive of a small corporation is abdicating active control of its operations. Instead, it means merely that the chief executive is consulting with, and seeking the advice of, the board's members in order to draw upon a larger pool of business knowledge.

An active board of directors serves management in several important ways. The first of these, of course, is the board's review of major policy decisions. But there is also the matter of advice on external business conditions and on proper reaction to the business cycle. Moreover, some directors are willing to provide individual advice informally, from time to time, on specific problems that arise.

Entrepreneurs responding to a survey by *Venture* magazine rated objectivity as the most valuable contribution of outside directors.[6] These respondents also valued their financial knowledge, ideas, management expertise, and connections.

Outside directors may also serve the small firm by scrutinizing and questioning its ethical standards. S. Kumar Jain notes that "operating executives, without outside directors to question them, may rationalize unethical or illegal behavior as being in the best interest of the company."[7] With a

---

SMALL BUSINESS IN ACTION
Directors' Valuable Counsel

Directors of small firms are supposed to offer valuable counsel to management. Here is the story of a small business owner who received just that kind of assistance from a newly formed board of directors:

> When we were planning to start a new company, our business plan called for $4 million in assets. By having our board probe alternative strategies—and make me rethink my approach to the idea—we found that we needed only $2 million. The vice-president of manufacturing who was working on the plan then came up with an even better strategy, and the new company was launched.

This owner calls the board an "inside sparring partner who tests your perceived strengths and weaknesses before you get to the main arena—the marketplace."

Source: Clayton L. Mathile, "A Business Owner's Perspective on Outside Boards," *Family Business Review*, Vol. 1, No. 3 (Fall, 1988), pp. 231-237. San Francisco: Jossey-Bass, Inc.

strong board, the small firm gains greater credibility with the public as well as with the business and financial community.

Selection of Board Members

Many sources are available to the owner attempting to assemble a cooperative, experienced, able group of directors. The firm's attorney, banker, accountant, other business executives, and local management consultants might all be considered as potential directors. However, such individuals lack the independence needed for critical review of an entrepreneur's plans. For this reason, the owner needs to consider the value of an outside board—one with members whose income does not depend on the corporation.

The importance of selecting a truly independent group of board members is expressed in these comments:

> Probably the strongest argument for adding outsiders to the family business board is to make qualified and objective confidants available to the chief executive. Too many family business directors seek to tell the CEO what he wants to hear. That is understandable if the directors are other family members, employees, or outsiders who depend on the family for income.[8]

The nature of the business and the needs of the firm will help determine the types of director qualifications needed. For example, a firm that faces a marketing problem or recognizes its marketing weakness may benefit greatly from the counsel of a board member with a marketing background. Business prominence in the community is not essential, although it may help give the company credibility and enable it to attract other well-qualified directors.

After deciding upon the qualifications needed, a business owner must seek suitable candidates. Suggestions may be obtained from the firm's accountants, attorney, banker, or other friends in the business community. Owners or managers of other, noncompeting small companies as well as second- and third-level executives in large companies are often willing to accept such positions. Some discreet checking of candidates is appropriate before offering them positions on the board.

Compensation of Directors

The amount of compensation paid to board members varies greatly, and some small firms pay no fees whatever. One survey of firms using outside boards reported the following compensation levels for individual directors:[9]

	Average Annual Compensation
Small Firms (fewer than 100 employees)	$2,465
Medium Firms (100–499 employees)	2,872
Large Firms (500 or more employees)	8,400

The "typical board" represented in the survey met quarterly for about four hours each time and usually had one other unscheduled meeting a year.

The relatively modest compensation for the service of well-qualified directors suggests that financial compensation is not the only, or perhaps even the primary, motivation in attracting them. Some reasonable compensation appears appropriate, however, if directors are making an important contribution.

An Alternative: An Advisory Council

In recent years, increased attention has been directed to the legal responsibilities of directors. Under the law, outside directors may be held responsible for illegal company action even though they are not directly involved in wrongdoing. As a result of such legal pressures, some individuals are now reluctant to accept directorships.

One alternative that is used by some small companies is an **advisory council**. Rather than being elected as directors, qualified outsiders are asked to serve as advisers to the company. The group of outsiders then functions in much the same way as a board of directors does, except that its actions are advisory only.

The following account illustrates the potential value of an advisory council:

> In another case, a seven-year-old diversified manufacturing company incurred its first deficit, which the owner-manager deemed an exception that further growth would rectify. Council members noted, however that many distant operations were out of control and apparently unprofitable. They persuaded the owner to shrink his business by more than one-half. Almost immediately, the business began generating profits. From its reduced scale, growth resumed—this time soundly planned, financed, and controlled.[10]

The legal liability of members of an advisory council is not completely clear.[11] However, a clear separation of the council from the board of directors is thought to lighten if not eliminate the personal liability of its members. Since it is advisory in nature, it may, consequently, pose less of a threat to the owner and possibly work more cooperatively than a conventional board.

Looking Back

1. Planning is easy to postpone, and small-firm managers need to set aside time for planning. Although informal planning may be done "in the entrepreneur's head," some amount of formal planning is useful for most firms. This planning should include both long-range and short-range projections and may use the contributions of managerial and other personnel.

2. Effective teamwork in small firms can be realized through the almost inevitably close employer–employee relationships and the entrepreneur's pervasive influence on all aspects of the business. Achievement of a cooperative atmosphere requires an entrepreneur who realizes the importance of people and who exercises a positive type of leadership.

3. An unplanned structure evolves if no thought is given to organizational relationships. Some conscious planning is desirable, however, to avoid weaknesses that creep into such naturally evolving structures. The line organization of a very small organization quickly becomes a line-and-staff organization as the firm grows and adds specialists. Some of the most important organizational decisions are those relating to delegating authority and determining the number of subordinates to be supervised by a given manager.

4. Boards of directors can contribute to small corporations by offering counsel and assistance to their chief executives. To be most effective, members of the board must be properly qualified and be independent outsiders.

DISCUSSION QUESTIONS

1. Some professional football coaches hold written game plans in their hands that they consult from time to time during games. If coaches

need formal plans for this kind of competition, does it follow that small business firms need them for their type of competition? Why?

2. What type of firm, if any, might operate successfully without engaging in formal planning?

3. Suggest some ways in which a very busy small-business manager might find time to create a conducive atmosphere for planning.

4. What major blunders might result from a lack of long-range planning on the part of a small manufacturing firm?

5. What determines whether the close personal contact between entrepreneurs and employees in small firms is a source of strength or weakness for the business?

6. Do you believe that most employees of small firms would welcome or resist a leadership approach that sought their ideas and involved them in meetings to let them know what was going on? Why might some resist such an approach?

7. According to one saying, "What you do speaks so loudly I can't hear what you say." What does this mean, and how does it apply to communication in small firms?

8. What advantages and difficulties do you see in an entrepreneur's use of performance review sessions as a time for discussing an employee's status, ideas, and expectations?

9. How large must a firm be before it encounters problems of organization? As it grows, do its problems become more difficult to solve? Explain.

10. What type of small firm might properly use the line type of organization? When would its structure require change? To what type? Why?

11. When one employee becomes the recognized leader of an informal organization and has goals that are at variance with those of management, what should the manager do to correct the situation?

12. What are the two most likely causes of failure to delegate authority properly? Is delegation important? Why?

13. How might a board of directors be of real value to management in a small corporation? What are the qualifications essential for a director? Is stock ownership in the firm a prerequisite?

14. What may account for the failure of most small corporations to use boards of directors as more than legal entities or rubber-stamp boards?

15. How do advisory councils differ from boards of directors? Which would you recommend to a small-company owner? Why?

YOU MAKE THE CALL

Situation 1

In one small firm, the owner-manager and his management team use various methods to push decision making onto employees at the operating level. New employees are trained thoroughly when they begin, but no supervisor monitors their work closely once they have learned their duties. Of course, help is available as needed, but no one is there on an hour-to-hour basis to make sure they are producing as needed and that they are avoiding mistakes.

Occasionally, all managers and supervisors leave for a day-long meeting and allow the operating employees to run the business by themselves. Job assignments are defined rather loosely. Management expects employees to assume responsibility and to take necessary action whenever they see that something needs to be done. When employees ask for direction, they are sometimes simply told to solve the problem in whatever way they think best.

Questions:

1. Is such a loosely organized firm likely to be as effective as a firm that defines jobs more precisely and monitors performance more closely? What are the limitations of the management style described above?
2. What do you think would be the morale effects of such management methods?
3. Would you like to work for this company? Why or why not?

Situation 2

For years, a small distributor of welding materials followed the practice of most small firms in treating the board of directors as a legal necessity. The board was composed of two co-owners and a retired steel company executive, but it was not a working board. The company was profitable and had been run with informal, traditional management methods.

The majority owner, after attending a seminar, decided that a board might be useful for more than legal or cosmetic purposes. Based on this thinking, he invited two outsiders—both division heads of larger corporations—to join the board. This brought the membership of the board to five and, in the thinking of the majority owner, should open up the business to new ideas.

Questions:
1. Can two outside board members in a group of five make any real difference in the way it operates?
2. Evaluate the owner's choices for board members.
3. What will determine the usefulness or effectiveness of this board? Do you predict that it will be useful? Why?

EXPERIENTIAL EXERCISES

1. Interview a small-business owner or manager concerning the type of planning, if any, used by the firm. Find out whether any plans are prepared in written form, whether the business uses a budget, and so on. Prepare a one-page summary of your findings.
2. Select a small-business firm and diagram the organizational relationships in that firm. In your report, note any organizational problems that are apparent to you or that are recognized by the manager or others in the firm.
3. Most students have also been employees, for temporary periods at least, at some time or other. Prepare a report on your personal experience as an employee in responding to the leadership and delegation of authority by your supervisor. Include reference to the type of leadership exercised and to the adequacy of delegation, its clarity, and problems involved.
4. Discuss with a corporate director, attorney, banker, or business owner the contributions of directors to small firms. Prepare a brief report of your findings. If you discover a particularly well-informed individual, suggest that person to your instructor as a possible speaker.

REFERENCES TO SMALL-BUSINESS PRACTICES

Andrews, Edmund L. "Keeping Directors Aboard." *Venture,* Vol. 8, No. 6 (June, 1986), pp. 36–42.
> This article describes the experiences of several small companies in attracting qualified directors and the difficulties associated with the potential liability of directors.

Posner, Bruce C. "A Board Even an Entrepreneur Could Love." *Inc.,* Vol. 5, No. 4 (April, 1983), pp. 73–87.
> Amtrol, Inc., a privately owned manufacturing company in West Warwick, RI, listens carefully to the advice of four outside directors and uses many of their ideas. The contributions of those directors have enabled the company to remain profitable and financially strong.

Rhodes, Lucien. "At the Crossroads." *Inc.*, Vol. 10, No. 2 (February, 1988), pp. 66–76.

Growth often brings management problems—especially in delegation of authority. This article describes the need experienced by one successful owner to give up extensive personal control of every decision in the firm.

Rhodes, Lucien. "The Turnaround." *Inc.*, Vol. 8, No. 8 (August, 1986), pp. 42–48.

A dying division of International Harvester was purchased by 13 employees and turned into a dynamic, profitable business. The participative leadership approach used in this turnaround is described.

ENDNOTES

1. Roger Thompson, "Winning Your Own Game," *Nation's Business*, Vol. 75, No. 7 (July, 1987), p. 21.

2. "The Venture Survey: Sticking to Business Plans," *Venture*, Vol. 7, No. 4 (April, 1985), p. 25.

3. Sharon Nelton, "Cultural Changes in a Family Firm," *Nation's Business*, Vol. 77, No. 1 (January, 1989), pp. 62–65.

4. Glenn H. Matthews, "Growing Concerns: Run Your Business or Build an Organization?" *Harvard Business Review*, Vol. 62, No. 2 (March–April, 1984), p. 35.

5. For a number of excellent articles on boards of directors for small firms, see the special issue of *Family Business Review*, Vol. 1, No. 3 (Fall, 1988).

6. "The Venture Survey: Who Sits on Your Board?" *Venture*, Vol. 6, No. 4 (April, 1984), p. 32.

7. S. Kumar Jain, "Look to Outsiders to Strengthen Small Business Boards," *Harvard Business Review*, Vol. 58, No. 4 (July–August, 1980), p. 166.

8. Gardner W. Heidrick, "Selecting Outside Directors," *Family Business Review*, Vol. 1, No. 3 (Fall, 1988), p. 271.

9. John L. Ward and James L. Handy, "A Survey of Board Practices," *Family Business Review*, Vol. 1, No. 3 (Fall, 1988), p. 294.

10. Harold W. Fox, "Growing Concerns: Quasi-boards—Useful Small Business Confidants," *Harvard Business Review*, Vol. 60, No. 1 (January–February, 1982), p. 164.

11. Fred A. Tillman, "Commentary on Legal Liability: Organizing the Advisory Council," *Family Business Review*, Vol. 1, No. 3 (Fall, 1988), pp. 287–288.

17 MANAGING PERSONNEL

© 1987 Erin Garvey

While small firms often find it difficult to pay competitive salaries, some have offered special financial incentives that enable them to attract talented personnel. Peter L. Sheeran, president of Sheeran Cleveland Architects, needed such a plan to reduce turnover among architects and designers.

"We wanted," Sheeran says, "to find a way to reward people, so that they knew the harder they worked, the more money they made. A profit-sharing plan seemed to fit the bill." That first year, Sheeran Cleveland's profit-sharing plan doled out a generous 50 percent of the firm's earnings to employees. In no time at all, productivity jumped. "People started working nights and coming in early," Sheeran recalls, "and they started taking on more responsibilities without the partners having to delegate it to them."

What's more, Sheeran Cleveland's turnover rate slowed down dramatically—almost to the vanishing point. And the firm found itself in the enviable position of being able to recruit architects and designers from competing firms. "Usually," Sheeran says, "partners want the profits for themselves. Our profit-sharing plan set us apart from those other firms."

Source: Reprinted with permission, *Inc.* magazine (November, 1984). Copyright © 1984 by Goldhirsh Group, Inc., 38 Commercial Wharf, Boston, MA 02110.

Looking Ahead

Watch for the following important topics:
1. Recruiting and selecting personnel.
2. Steps in evaluating job applicants.
3. Training and development.
4. Compensation and incentives.
5. Formal personnel systems.
6. New terms and concepts:

leasing employees	Age Discrimination in Employment Act of 1967
Job Instruction Training (JIT)	
daywork	Occupational Safety and Health Act (OSHA)
employee stock ownership plans (ESOPs)	
	National Labor Relations Act
Civil Rights Act of 1964	Immigration Reform Act

Smallness creates a unique situation in the management of human resources. For example, the owner of a small retail store cannot adopt the human resources program of Sears, Roebuck and Company, which has 500,000 employees, by merely scaling it down. The atmosphere of a small firm also creates distinctive opportunities to develop strong relationships among its members. In view of the special employment characteristics associated with smallness, the entrepreneur needs to develop a human resources program that is directly applicable to a small firm.

Recruiting and Selecting Personnel

The initial step in a sound human resources program is the recruitment of capable employees. In recruiting, the small firm competes with both large and small businesses. It cannot afford to let competitors take the cream of the crop. Aggressive recruitment requires the employer to take the initiative in locating applicants and to search until enough applicants are available to permit a good choice.

Importance of People

Employing the right people and getting their enthusiastic performance are keys to business success. Financial resources and physical resources will eventually be insufficient if adequate human resources are lacking. In many small businesses, sales are directly related to the attitudes of employees and their ability to serve customer needs. The effective use of people is also crucial because payroll expense is one of the largest expense categories for most small firms.

Since people are important, the entrepreneur must give high priority to recruiting and selecting employees. This beginning step establishes the foundation for a firm's ongoing human relationships. If talented, ambitious recruits can be obtained, the business will be able to build a strong human organization through effective management.

Attracting Applicants to Small Firms

There is competition in recruiting well-qualified business talent, just as there is in recruiting athletic talent. Small firms, therefore, must identify their distinctive advantages in making an appeal to outstanding prospects for managerial and professional positions. Fortunately, small-firm recruiters can advance some good arguments in favor of small-business careers.

The opportunity for general management experience at a decision-making level is attractive to many prospects. Rather than toiling in obscure, low-level, specialized positions during their early years, capable newcomers can quickly move into positions of responsibility in small businesses. In such positions, they can see that their work makes a difference in the success of the company.

Many such opportunities offer professional and managerial personnel greater freedom than they would have in big business. Marshall Fitzgerald, the president of a small electronics company in California, has emphasized this advantage of the small firm as follows:

> Fitzgerald says he has managed to win in the Silicon Valley bidding wars not by offering more money than his better-financed rivals, but by better understanding what motivates and attracts the different kinds of employees his company needs.
>
> "We start by identifying an expert in a key area where we need superior talent," explains Fitzgerald. "We lure him into the company by offering him more freedom than he'll probably ever get in a large bureaucracy. And then we use him as a magnet to attract a supporting staff of people who want an opportunity to work with a superstar."
>
> "Good people are motivated as much by creative challenges, by a chance to learn and grow, as they are by paychecks," Fitzgerald adds. "Here's where a small company actually has an advantage over a large organization. We can give a person a job and let him run with it."[1]

Individual contributions can be recognized rather than hidden under the numerous layers of a bureaucratic organization. It is also possible for compensation arrangements to be structured so that they provide a power-

---

SMALL BUSINESS IN ACTION
Small Business as a Great Place to Work

Although the small-business setting is sometimes chaotic, it provides exciting career possibilities for many people. Walter Weller, Jr., grew up hearing the stories of frustration related by his father, who eventually took early retirement from a giant pharmaceutical firm. Walter, Jr., went into a smaller company and became, at 34, the number two man for Crest Products, Inc., a producer of tiny metal washers for industrial use.

A boring business? Not for Weller. In the last few years Weller has restructured the firm's debt package (he learned how to do it on the job), became involved in engineering, worked on the firm's expansion to a new Lexington, Ky. plant—in short, done everything but clean the latrines. "Activity and challenge—that's what charges my batteries," says Weller.

Weller believed that he could develop his skills more effectively in a small company. As he put it, "Faster growth is here—if you're willing to take the risks."

Source: Richard Greene, "Can You Handle Chaos?" *Forbes*, Vol. 137, No. 13 (June 16, 1986), pp. 156–158.

ful incentive. The firm featured in this chapter's Spotlight on Small Business, Sheeran Cleveland Architects, developed just such an incentive plan.

The value of these features as recruiting advantages depends to some degree on the circumstances of the particular firm. Ideally, the firm should be growing and profitable. It should also have a degree of professionalism in its management that can be readily recognized by prospective employees.

Sources of Employees

To recruit effectively, one must know where and how to obtain qualified applicants. The sources are numerous, and one cannot generalize about the best source in view of the variations in personnel requirements and quality of sources from one locality to another. Some major sources of employees are discussed in the following paragraphs.

Walk-Ins A firm may receive unsolicited applications from individuals who walk into the place of business to seek employment. It is an inexpensive source for lower-skilled jobs, but the quality of applicants may be mixed. If qualified applicants cannot be hired immediately, their applications should be kept on file for future reference. In the interest of good public relations, all applicants should be treated courteously whether or not they are offered jobs.

Schools Secondary schools, trade schools, colleges, and universities are desirable sources for certain classes of employees, particularly those who need no specific work experience. Secondary and trade schools provide applicants with a limited but useful educational background. Colleges and universities can supply candidates for positions in management and in various technical and scientific fields. In addition, many colleges are excellent sources of part-time employees.

Public Employment Offices State employment offices, which are affiliated with the United States Employment Service, offer, without cost, a supply of applicants who are actively seeking employment. These offices, located in all major cities, are for the most part a source for clerical workers, unskilled laborers, production workers, and technicians.

Private Employment Agencies Numerous private agencies offer their services as employment offices. In some cases an employer receives their services without cost because the applicant pays a fee to the agency. However, most firms pay the fee if the applicant is highly qualified. Such agencies

tend to specialize in people with specific skills such as accountants, computer operators, or managers.

Employee Referrals   If current employees are good employees, their recommendations may provide excellent prospects. Ordinarily, current employees will hesitate to recommend applicants thought to be inferior in ability. Many small-business owners say that this source provides more of their employees than any other source.

Help-Wanted Advertising   The "Help Wanted" sign in the window of a business establishment is one form of recruiting used by small firms. More aggressive recruitment takes the form of advertisements in the classified pages of local newspapers. Although the effectiveness of this source has been questioned by some, the fact remains that many well-managed organizations recruit in this way.

One small firm, North American Tool and Die, Inc., exercises great care in preparing such advertisements, avoiding standard cliches and focusing attention on the company and its achievements.[2] They have pointed out, for example, that their rejects from Silicon Valley customers have averaged only 0.1 percent over the past four years—a very high quality level—and that NATD is a "fun place" to work. Their purpose is to attract people who care about the company they work for and who are looking for such opportunities.

Temporary Help Agencies   The temporary help industry, which is growing rapidly, supplies temporary employees (or "temps") such as word processors, clerks, accountants, engineers, nurses, draftsmen, and sales clerks for short periods of time. By using agencies such as Kelly Services or Manpower, small firms can deal with seasonal fluctuations and absences caused by vacation or illness. It is a less useful source when extensive training is required or continuity is important.

Selection Guidelines

The small-business manager should analyze the activities or work to be performed and determine the number and kinds of jobs to be filled. Knowing the job requirements and the capacities and characteristics of the individual applicants permits a more intelligent selection of persons for specific jobs. In particular, the small business should attempt to obtain individuals whose capacities and skills complement those of the owner-manager.

Certainly the owner-manager should not select personnel simply to fit a rigid specification of education, experience, or personal background. Rather, the employer must concentrate upon the ability of an individual to fill a particular position in the business.

Recruiting Managerial and Professional Personnel

Personnel filling managerial and professional positions are obviously important in any business, especially in one that is small. Their recruitment, therefore, deserves special attention and also involves some special considerations.

Technical competence is necessary, as it is in a large business, but versatility may be an even more important virtue in the small-firm setting. "The day will come when the engineer has to go out and make sales calls. He had better be the sort that can do it. By the same token, the marketing people should be able to get a handle on a wrench. So you need versatility and flexibility."[3]

Finding capable, experienced key employees is often difficult. For this reason, some small firms, especially high-tech firms, turn to executive search firms (headhunters) to locate qualified candidates. Armos Corporation, a new scientifically oriented firm in San Francisco, is an example of a firm using this approach in filling top management positions.[4] Although the fee is equal to one-third of each person's annual salary, the founders of this firm feel it is worth the payment because of their own lack of time to engage in such a search.

Evaluating Applicants

Many techniques for evaluating applicants are available to the small business. An uninformed, blind gamble on new employees may be avoided by following the series of steps described in the following paragraphs.

Step 1—Use of Application Forms   The value of having an applicant complete an application form lies in its systematic collection of background data that might otherwise be overlooked. The information recorded on application forms is useful in sizing up an applicant and serves as a guide in making a more detailed investigation of the applicant's experience and character.

An application form need not be elaborate or lengthy. In fact, it need not even be a printed sheet. A simple application form is illustrated in Exhibit 17–1. In drawing up such a form, the employer should remember that questions concerning race or religion are prohibited by the Civil Rights Act of 1964. Even questions about education must be demonstrably job-related.

Step 2—Interviewing the Applicant   An employment interview permits the employer to get some idea of the applicant's appearance, job knowledge, intelligence, and personality. Any of these factors may be significant in the job to be filled. Although the interview is an important step in the process of selection, it should not be the only step. Some individuals have the mistaken idea that they are infallible judges of human nature on the basis of interviews alone.

The value of the interview depends upon the interviewer's skill and methods. Any interviewer can improve the quality of interviewing by following these generally accepted principles:

1. Determine the questions you want to ask before beginning the interview.
2. Conduct the interview in a quiet atmosphere.
3. Give your entire attention to the applicant.
4. Put the applicant at ease.
5. Never argue.
6. Keep the conversation at a level suited to the applicant.
7. Listen attentively.
8. Observe closely the applicant's speech, mannerisms, and attire if these characteristics are important to the job.
9. Try to avoid being unduly influenced by the applicant's trivial mannerisms or superficial resemblance to other people you know.

To avoid the possibility of running into legal problems with the Equal Employment Opportunity Commission (EEOC), the interviewer should refrain from:

1. Direct or indirect inquiries that will reveal the applicant's national, ethnic, or racial origin.
2. Questions to female applicants on marital status, number and age of children, pregnancy, or future child-bearing plans.
3. Inquiries about arrest or conviction records, unless such information is demonstrably job-related.

Step 3—Checking References and Further Investigation   When contacted, most references listed on application forms give a rose-colored pic-

Exhibit 17–1 Simplified Application Form

APPLICATION FORM

1. PERSONAL DATA

Name _____ Social Security No. _____

Address _____ Tel. No. _____

2. WORK EXPERIENCE

Present or last job:

Name and address of employer _____

Dates of employment _____

Title of your job _____

What kind of work did you perform? _____

_____

Why did you leave? _____

Next-to-last job:

Name and address of employer _____

Dates of employment _____

Title of your job _____

What kind of work did you perform? _____

_____

Why did you leave? _____

3. EDUCATION

High School:

Name and address of school _____

Did you graduate? _____ When? _____

College or Specialized School:

Name and address of school _____

Did you graduate? _____ When? _____

Nature of course _____

4. REFERENCES (List three references not mentioned above)

NAME	ADDRESS	OCCUPATION

ture of the applicant's character and ability. Nevertheless, careful checking with former employers, school authorities, and other references can be most constructive. A written letter of inquiry to these references is probably the weakest form of checking because people hesitate to put damaging statements in writing. However, individuals who provide little useful information in response to a written request often speak more frankly when approached by telephone or in person.

For a fee, an applicant's history (financial, criminal, employment, and so on) may be supplied by personal investigation agencies or local credit bureaus. If an employer needs an investigative consumer report to establish the applicant's eligibility for employment, the Fair Credit Reporting Act requires that the applicant be notified in writing prior to the request for such a report.

Step 4—Testing the Applicant　Many kinds of jobs lend themselves to performance testing. For example, a typist may be given some material to type to verify the typing speed and accuracy reported by the applicant. With a little ingenuity, employers may improvise practical tests pertinent to most of the positions in their business.

Psychological examinations may also be used by small-business firms, but the results can easily be misleading because of difficulty in interpretation or in adapting the tests to a particular business. In addition, the United States Supreme Court has approved the EEOC's requirement that *any* test used in making employment decisions must be job-related.

Step 5—Physical Examinations　Although they are frequently neglected, physical examinations of applicants are of practical value to the small business. Few small firms have staff physicians, but arrangements can be made with a local doctor to administer the examinations. The employer, of course, should pay for the cost of the physical examination. In a few occupations, physical examinations are required by law; but even when they are not legally required, it is wise to discover physical limitations and possible contagious diseases of all new employees.

Leasing Employees

Leasing equipment or property has long been an accepted alternative to buying it. Leasing employees, as surprising as it may seem, is also an alternative to hiring one's own employees!

An estimated 300 leasing companies have emerged in recent years to

SMALL BUSINESS IN ACTION
An Example of Employee Leasing

Al Wittick's Diamond Tires Company in Elizabeth, NJ, has only five employees, but they are leased from Employee Leasing of America, a firm that specializes in employee leasing. Wittick explains the advantages of leasing as follows:

First, I don't have to deal with the Internal Revenue Service on payroll taxes; I'm insulated from their incompetence. Second, the leasing company can provide employee benefits that were very expensive for me to buy—corporate-type benefits such as hospitalization, medical and life insurance, and things which I as a small-business owner could never afford, like education expenses and eyeglasses and dental care.

Wittick even "leases himself" from the service because he wants the same benefits for himself.

Source: "Fire Them All?" *Nation's Business*, Vol. 76, No. 2 (February, 1988), pp. 62R–63R. Copyright 1988, U.S. Chamber of Commerce.

lease personnel to thousands of small businesses. For a fee of from 5 to 10 percent of payroll, the leasing company writes paychecks, pays the taxes, and files necessary reports with government agencies. Although small firms using this service escape certain paperwork, they do not usually escape the tasks of recruitment and selection. Typically, the employees of a small firm are simply shifted to the leasing company's payroll at some specified date. In most cases, the small firm still determines who works, who gets promoted, and who gets time off.

Many employees also like the leasing arrangement. Since leasing companies typically employ several hundred people, they can afford to offer benefits that are superior to those possible in most small firms.

Training and Development

Once an employee has been recruited and added to the payroll, the process of training and development must begin. The new recruit is the "raw material," and the well-trained technician, salesperson, manager, or other employee is the "finished product."

Purposes of Training and Development

One obvious purpose of training is to prepare the new recruit to perform the duties for which he or she has been employed. There are very few positions in industry for which no training is required. It would be a rare individual who had an adequate background when applying for employment. If the employer fails to provide training, the new employee must proceed by trial and error, frequently with a waste of time, materials, and money.

Training to improve skills and knowledge is not limited to newcomers. The performance of current employees may often be improved through additional training. In view of the constant change in products, technology, policies, and procedures in the world of business—even in a small business—training is necessary to update knowledge and skills. Only in this way can personnel become capable of meeting the changing demands placed upon them.

Both employers and employees have a stake in the advancement of personnel to higher-level positions. Preparation for advancement usually involves developmental efforts—possibly of a different type than those needed to sharpen skills for current duties.

In view of the fact that personal development and advancement are prime concerns of able employees, the small business can profit from careful attention to this phase of the personnel program. If the opportunity to grow and move up in an organization exists, it not only improves the morale of current employees, but also offers an inducement for outsiders to accept employment.

Orientation for New Personnel

The developmental process begins with the employee's first two or three days on the job. It is at this point that a new person tends to feel "lost." Much is confusing—a new physical layout, different job title, unknown fellow employees, different type of supervision, changed hours or work schedule, and a unique set of personnel policies and procedures. Any surprises that conflict with the newcomer's expectations are interpreted in the light of his or her previous work experience, and these interpretations can foster a strong commitment to the new employer or lead to feelings of alienation.

At this point of great sensitivity of the new employee, the employer can contribute to a positive outcome by proper orientation. Initial steps can be taken to help the newcomer adjust and to minimize feelings of uneasiness in the new setting.

In addition to explaining specific job duties, supervisors can outline the firm's policies and procedures in as much detail as possible. The new employee should be encouraged to ask questions, and time should be taken to provide careful answers. The employer may facilitate the orientation process by giving the recruit a written list of company procedures. These may include information about work hours, paydays, breaks, lunch hours, absences, holidays, names of supervisors, employee benefits, and so on.

Training Nonmanagerial Employees

Job descriptions or job specifications, if they exist, may identify abilities or skills needed for particular jobs. To a large extent, such requirements regulate the type of training that is appropriate.

For all classes of employees, more training is accomplished on the job than through any other method. The weakness of on-the-job training results from depending on haphazard learning in contrast to establishing planned, controlled training programs. A system designed to make on-the-job training more effective is known as **Job Instruction Training (JIT)**. The steps of this program, listed below, are intended to help the manager who is not a professional educator "get through" to the nonmanagerial employee.

1. *Prepare the employee.* Put the employee at ease. Find out what he or she already knows about the job. Get the employee interested in learning the job. Place the employee in an appropriate job.
2. *Present the operations.* Tell, show, illustrate, and question carefully and patiently. Stress key points. Instruct clearly and completely, taking up one point at a time—but no more than the employee can master.
3. *Try out performance.* Test the employee by having him or her perform the job. Have the employee tell, show, and explain key points. Ask questions and correct errors. Continue until the employee knows that he or she knows how to do the job.
4. *Follow up.* Check frequently. Designate the person to whom the employee should go for help. Encourage questions. Get the employee to look for the key points as he or she progresses. Taper off extra coaching and close follow-up.

Figure 17–1 On-the-Job Training

Holiday Inn Inc.

Developing Managerial and Professional Employees

The small business faces a particularly serious need for developing managerial and professional employees. Depending on the size of the firm, there may be few or many key positions. Regardless of the number, individuals must be developed in or for these key positions if the business is to function most effectively. Incumbents should be developed to the point that they can adequately carry out the responsibilities assigned to them. Ideally, potential replacements should also be available for key individuals who retire or leave for other reasons. The entrepreneur often postpones grooming a personal replacement, but this step is likewise important in assuring a smooth transition in the management of a small firm.

In accomplishing management training, the manager should give serious consideration to the following factors:

1. *Determine the need for training.* What vacancies are expected? Who needs to be trained? What type of training and how much training are needed to meet the demands of the job description?
2. *Develop the plan for training.* How can the individuals be trained?

Do they currently have enough responsibility to permit them to learn? Can they be assigned additional duties? Should they be given temporary assignments in other areas—for example, should they be shifted from production to sales? Would additional schooling be of benefit?

3. *Establish a timetable.* When should training be started? How much can be accomplished in the next six months or one year?

4. *Counsel with employees.* Do the individuals understand their need for training? Are they aware of the prospects for them in the firm? Has an understanding been reached as to the nature of training? Have the employees been consulted regularly about progress in their work and problems confronting them? Have they been given the benefit of the owner's experience and insights without having decisions made for them?

Compensation and Incentives for Small-Business Employees

Compensation and financial incentives are important to all employees, and the small firm must acknowledge the central role of the paycheck and any "extras" in attracting and motivating personnel. In addition, small firms can also offer several nonfinancial incentives that appeal to both managerial and nonmanagerial employees.

Wage or Salary Levels

In general, small firms find that they must be roughly competitive in wage or salary levels in order to attract well-qualified personnel. Wages or salaries paid to employees either are based on increments of time—such as an hour, a day, a month—or vary directly with their output. Compensation based on increments of time is commonly referred to as **daywork**. The daywork system is most appropriate for types of work in which performance is not easily measurable. It is the most common compensation system and is easy to understand and administer.

Financial Incentives

In order to motivate nonmanagerial employees to increase their productivity, incentive systems have been devised. Incentive wages may constitute an employee's entire earnings or may supplement regular daywork wages. The commission plan often used to compensate salespeople is one type of incentive plan. In manufacturing, employees are sometimes paid according to the number of units they produce.

More general bonus or profit-sharing systems are especially important for managerial or other key personnel, although such plans may also include lower-level personnel. These are plans that give personnel a "piece of the action." They may or may not involve giving them shares of stock. A given plan may simply entail a distribution of a specified share of the profits or a share of profits that exceed a target amount.

Profit sharing provides a more direct work incentive in small companies than in large companies, because the connection between individual performance and company success can be more easily understood. Any such plans should be devised with care, however, usually with the aid of a consulting and/or public accounting firm.

The potential power of a profit-sharing plan is evident in the experience of Au Bon Pain Company, a Boston-based fast-food chain specializing in fancy coffees and croissants.[5] After extensive investigation, this company's management devised a profit-sharing plan that increased company sales and profits and that enabled store managers to double or triple their compensation by hard work and creative management. The owners found, moreover, that the plan relieved them of many management headaches by turning store managers into self-starters.

Fringe Benefits

Fringe benefits (which include such items as vacations, holidays, group insurance, pensions, and severance pay) are expensive for small firms. According to the U.S. Bureau of Labor Statistics, benefits expenditures amounted to 36 percent of payroll in 1983 and were expected to exceed 40 percent of payroll in 1987.[6] The cost of such benefits, therefore, adds substantially to direct wage costs. For some small firms, the total wage costs, including fringes, account for more than 50 percent of their total operating expense.

Even though fringes are expensive, a small firm cannot ignore them if it is to compete effectively for good employees. Some small firms now use flexible benefits programs (or "cafeteria plans") that allow employees to choose the type of benefits they wish to receive.[7] All employees may receive a core level of coverage such as basic health insurance and then be allowed to choose among additional options. For example, employees might decide how some amount specified by the employer is to be divided between child care reimbursement, pension fund contributions, or additional insurance.

SMALL BUSINESS IN ACTION
Lavish Fringe Benefits

Throughout our business history, a few employers have provided lavish fringe benefits as part of their employee relations programs. Some were part of well-conceived compensation plans, some were fads, some represented crude attempts to buy employee loyalty, and some were highly paternalistic. One 69-year-old family firm that has prospered while successfully offering elaborate benefits is Fel-Pro, a highly profitable producer of gaskets and sealants for engines.

It is also renowned for some other things, such as the converted horse farm where employees can garden on weekends, or send their children to summer camp, or get married. Then there is the company-subsidized day-care center, not to mention the gym. At Fel-Pro, no holiday goes by without a gift for each worker: a box of chocolates on Valentine's Day, a canned ham on Easter, a tin of pistachio nuts on Thanksgiving, a turkey on Christmas. There are monetary gifts, too, for practically every event in the human life cycle: $100 for a birth, $500 for an adoption, and up to $5,000 for a child's college tuition. And, lest the spirit need elevating as well, the company has a half-time sculptor on the payroll, whose sole job is to create gasket art.

Source: Reprinted with permission, *Inc.* magazine (January, 1986). Copyright © 1986 by Inc. Publishing Company, 38 Commercial Wharf, Boston, MA 02110.

Employee Stock Ownership Plans

Some small firms have created **employee stock ownership plans (ESOPs)**, by which they give employees a share of ownership in the business.[8] These may be structured in a variety of ways. For example, a share of annual profits may be designated for the benefit of employees and used to buy company stock, which is then placed in a trust for the employees.

ESOPs also provide a way for owners to "cash out" and withdraw from a business without selling the firm to outsiders. The owner might sell ownership to the firm's employees, and they can borrow funds at attractive rates for this purpose. In fact, there are many tax advantages to both owners and employees that make ESOPs an increasingly popular ownership plan.

Special Issues in Personnel Management

Thus far in the chapter, we have dealt with recruitment, selection, training, and compensation of employees. In addition to managing these primary activities, the entrepreneur, as personnel manager, must treat a number of other general issues. These issues—legal constraints, union relationships, formalizing personnel management, and using a personnel manager—are the focus of this concluding section.

The Law and Management of Personnel

Employer–employee relationships, even in small firms, are affected by a variety of both federal and state laws.[9] Although some laws limit their application to employers having a minimum of 15 to 20 employees, others are more broadly applicable. The legislation, therefore, is applicable to most small-business concerns. Because of its complexity, it is important to have competent legal counsel in dealing with specific issues. Some of the more significant types of regulation are identified here.

Equal Employment Opportunity Legislation   The **Civil Rights Act of 1964** and related amendments and executive orders prohibit discrimination on the basis of race, color, religion, sex, or national origin. This legislation and many state laws apply to all employment practices, including hiring, firing, promotion, compensation, and other conditions of employment. A separate act (**Age Discrimination in Employment Act of 1967** and related amendments) requires employers to treat applicants and employees equally, regardless of age. Sexual harassment in the workplace has also become a highly sensitive issue in recent years, requiring employers to maintain a proper work environment.

Protection of People with Disabilities   In 1990, Congress was considering and seemed certain to pass a disability rights act. Under terms of the proposed law, employers with more than 15 employees could not refuse to hire a qualified, disabled applicant if the individual could do work with "reasonable accommodations." Such accommodations might include making the workplace accessible, changing schedules, and, in some cases, providing helpers.

Wage and Hour Laws   Federal legislation requires employers to pay a specified minimum hourly wage and, usually, time-and-a-half for hours exceeding 40 per week. Employers must also comply with child labor regulations.

Safety Regulations   According to the **Occupational Safety and Health Act (OSHA)**, employers must provide a workplace that is free from hazards that are likely to cause death or serious physical harm. They must also comply with various safety and health standards promulgated in accordance with the Act. Small-firm owners and managers have also been charged in some

Figure 17–2   Nondiscrimination in the
Workplace

© *Stacy Pick 1985/STOCK, BOSTON*

states with criminal liability for allowing workplace hazards that resulted in the death of employees.[10]

Plant-Closing Law   The federal plant-closing law, enacted in 1988, requires employers to give employees 60 days' advance notice of plant closings or mass layoffs. The effect on small firms will be minimal, because the law applies only to employers with 100 or more employees and to reductions affecting 50 or more full-time jobs.

Employee Unions Legislation   The **National Labor Relations Act** requires employers to avoid discrimination based on union affiliation and to bargain with a union if desired by a majority of employees in the bargaining unit.

Immigration Reform   The **Immigration Reform Act**, which became effective in 1987, requires employers to check job applicants' papers to be sure they are either U.S. citizens or aliens authorized to work in the United States.

Wrongful Discharge Litigation   At one time, employment was assumed to involve an "at-will" contract, and the employer's right to fire was virtually unchallenged. Courts are increasingly coming to hold, however, that such contracts contain implied promises to deal fairly and in good faith. This means that employers must act carefully and avoid unfairness in discharge actions if they are to avoid lawsuits. By establishing a standard disciplinary procedure that contains protection against capricious firings, an employer can help to assure fairness and avoid legal conflict.

Labor Unions and Small Business

Most entrepreneurs prefer to operate independently and to avoid unionization. Indeed, most small businesses are not unionized. To some extent, this results from the predominance of small business in such areas as services, where unionization is less common than in manufacturing. Also, unions typically concentrate their primary attention on large companies.

This does not mean, of course, that labor unions are unknown in small firms. Many types of firms—building and electrical contractors, for example—negotiate labor contracts and employ unionized personnel. The need to work with a union formalizes and, to some extent, complicates the relationship between the small firm and its employees.

If employees wish to bargain collectively, the law requires the employer to participate in such bargaining. The demand for labor union representation may arise from labor dissatisfaction with the work environment and employment relationships. By following enlightened personnel policies, the small firm can minimize the likelihood of labor organization and/ or contribute to healthy management–union relationships.[11]

Formalizing Employer–Employee Relationships

As explained earlier in the chapter, the management system of small firms is typically less formal than that of larger companies. A degree of informality can, in fact, constitute a virtue in small organizations. As personnel are added, however, the benefits of informality decline, and its costs increase. The situation has been portrayed in terms of family relationships as follows: "House rules are hardly necessary where only two people are living. But add several children, and before long Mom starts sounding like a government regulatory agency."[12] Large numbers of employees cannot be managed effectively without some system for regulating personnel relationships.

Growth, then, produces pressures toward formalizing personnel policies and procedures. The primary question is how much formality and how soon—a question that involves judgment. Probably some matters should be formalized from the very beginning. On the other hand, excessive regulation becomes paralyzing.

One way to increase the formality is to prepare a personnel policy manual or employee handbook. Although such an act may seem a bit dictatorial, it can meet a communication need by letting employees know the basic ground rules of the firm. It can also provide a basis for fairness and consistency in decisions affecting employees.

The content of a policy manual may be as broad or narrow as desired. It may include an expression of company philosophy—what the company considers important, such as standards of excellence or quality considerations. More specifically, personnel policies usually cover such topics as recruitment, selection, training, compensation, vacations, grievances, and discipline. Policies should be written carefully, however, to avoid misunderstandings. In some states, an employee handbook is considered part of the employment contract.

Procedures relating to management of personnel may also be standardized. For example, a performance review system may be established and a timetable set up for reviews, such as an initial review after six months and subsequent reviews on an annual basis.

Use of a Personnel Manager

A firm with only a few employees cannot afford a full-time specialist to deal with personnel problems. Some of the more involved personnel tools and techniques that are required in large businesses may be unnecessarily complicated for the small business. As it grows in size, however, its personnel problems will increase in both number and complexity.

The point at which it becomes logical to hire a personnel manager cannot be specified precisely. Each entrepreneur must decide whether the type and size of the business would make it profitable to employ a personnel specialist. Hiring a part-time personnel manager might be a logical first step in some instances.

Some conditions that encourage the appointment of a personnel manager in a small business are:

1. When there is a substantial number of employees. (What is "substantial" varies with the business, but 100 employees is suggested as a guide.)
2. When employees are represented by a union.
3. When the labor turnover rate is high.
4. When the need for skilled or professional personnel creates problems in recruitment or selection.
5. When supervisors or operative employees require considerable training.
6. When employee morale is unsatisfactory.
7. When competition for personnel is keen.

Until the time when a personnel manager is employed, however, the owner-manager typically functions in that capacity. His or her decisions regarding selection, compensation, and other personnel issues will have a direct impact on the operating success of the firm.

Looking Back

1. To obtain capable employees, the small firm must take the initiative in seeking applicants. Sources include walk-ins, schools, public and private employment agencies, friends and acquaintances of current employees, advertising, and temporary-help agencies. The selection process must conform to legislation applying to the hiring of minorities and other special employment groups. Leasing employees is an alternative to hiring that is used by some firms.
2. Steps in the evaluation of applicants include the use of an application form, applicant interviewing, checking references and background investigation, testing, and physical examinations.
3. Both managerial and nonmanagerial employees of small firms require training to develop skill and knowledge in their jobs and to prepare them for promotion. The need for developing personnel at the managerial and professional levels is particularly acute.
4. Small firms must be competitive in wage and salary levels and fringe benefits. They can use various types of incentive, profit-

sharing, and stock-ownership systems to provide motivation for personnel, especially for those in key positions.

5. As a firm grows, the need for formal methods of personnel management increases. This includes adoption of personnel policies, establishment of personnel procedures, and, at some point, employment of a personnel manager.

DISCUSSION QUESTIONS

1. As a customer of small-business firms, you can appreciate the importance of employees to their success. On the basis of your experience, cite one case in which the employee's contribution was positive and one in which it was negative.

2. What factor or factors would make you personally most cautious about going to work for a small business? Could these reasons for hesitation be overcome by a really good small firm? How?

3. Suppose you were trying to recruit a well-qualified graduate of your school to work in a firm of fewer than 100 employees. What arguments would you use to persuade the student to join your firm? (You may state your assumptions as you develop these arguments.)

4. Under what conditions might walk-ins be most useful as a source of employees?

5. Assuming you have worked for a small firm for five years, what would be your attitude toward recommending an acquaintance for employment? What are the implications of your attitude for employee referrals as a source of employees?

6. How might the manager of a small business be aggressive in recruiting new employees? Explain.

7. Based on your own experience as an interviewee, what do you think is the most serious weakness in interviewing? How could this be remedied?

8. How does employee leasing differ from use of a temporary-help agency? What are the greatest values to be realized by employee leasing?

9. What steps and/or topics would you recommend for the orientation program of a printing firm with 65 employees?

10. Consider the small business with which you are best acquainted. Have adequate provisions been made to replace key management personnel? Is the firm using any form of executive development?

11. What problems are involved in using incentive wage systems in a small firm? How would the nature of the work affect management's decision concerning use or nonuse of wage incentives?

12. Is the use of a profit-sharing system desirable in a small business? What major difficulties might be associated with its effectiveness in providing greater employee motivation?

13. Which type of legislation cited in the chapter seems potentially most troublesome for small firms? Why?

14. It has been said that labor unions have been more successful in organizing small manufacturing firms than in organizing small merchandising firms. Why might this be true?

15. List the factors in small-business operation that encourage the appointment of a personnel manager. Should a personnel manager always be hired on a full-time basis? Why or why not?

YOU MAKE THE CALL

Situation 1

Following is an account of an employee's introduction to a new job:

> It was my first job out of high school. They gave me a physical exam and a pamphlet on benefits, and they told me how dangerous a steel mill could be. But it was from the old-timers on the floor that I learned what was really expected of me.
>
> The company management never told me about the corporate culture or the unspoken rules. The old-timers let me know where to sleep on what shift and which foreman to avoid. They told me how much work I was supposed to do and which shop steward I was to speak with if I had a problem.
>
> *Source:* Gene Geromel, "A Good Start for New Hires," *Nation's Business,* Vol. 77, No. 1 (January, 1989), p. 21. Copyright 1989, U.S. Chamber of Commerce.

Questions

1. To what extent should a small firm use old-timers to help introduce new employees to the workplace? Is it inevitable that newcomers will always look to old-timers to find out how things really work?

2. How would you rate this firm's orientation efforts? What are its strengths and weaknesses?

3. Assuming that this firm has fewer than 75 employees and no personnel manager, can it possibly provide any more extensive orientation than

that described here? How? What low-cost improvements, if any, can you recommend?

Situation 2

Technical Products, Inc., distributes 15 percent of its profits quarterly to its eight employees. This money is invested for their benefit in a retirement plan and is fully vested after five years. An employee, therefore, has a claim to the retirement fund even if he or she leaves the company after five years service.

The employees range in age from 25 to 59 and have worked for the company from 3 to 27 years. They seem to have recognized the value of the program. However, younger members sometimes express a stronger preference for cash than for retirement benefits. Also, the 1986 Tax Reform Act reduced taxes on individual income, and this may affect employee attitudes toward the plan.

Questions

1. What are the most important reasons for structuring the profit-sharing plan as a retirement program?
2. What is the probable motivational impact of this compensation system?
3. How will age affect the appeal of this plan? What other factors are likely to strengthen or lessen its motivational value? Should it be changed in any way?

EXPERIENTIAL EXERCISES

1. Interview the director of the placement office for your college or university to discover the extent to which small firms use its services and to obtain the director's recommendations for improving college recruiting by small firms. Prepare a one-page summary of your findings.
2. Examine and evaluate the "help wanted" classified section of a local newspaper. Summarize your findings and formulate some generalizations about small-business advertising for personnel.
3. Join with another student to form an interviewer–interviewee team. Take turns interviewing each other as job applicants for a selected type of job vacancy. Critique each performance by using the interviewing principles outlined in this chapter.

4. Join with another student, taking turns role playing job instruction training as outlined in this chapter. Each student-trainer should select a simple task and teach it to the other student-trainee. Jointly critique the teaching performance after each episode.

REFERENCES TO SMALL-BUSINESS PRACTICES

Bacas, Harry. "Mandated Leave: Small Firms' Nightmare." *Nation's Business*, Vol. 75, No. 8 (August, 1987), pp. 32–33.
> This article describes the problems faced by a number of small firms as Congress considers requiring firms to grant leave for child care or disability.

Case, John. "ESOPs: Dead or Alive." *Inc.*, Vol. 10, No. 6 (June, 1988), pp. 94–100.
> The experiences of a number of small companies having employee stock ownership plans are described in this article.

Doescher, William F. "Replacing Irreplaceable You." *D&B Reports*, Vol. 36, No. 5 (September–October, 1988), pp. 10–11ff.
> This article describes the type of planning being done in several small firms to replace their owner-managers. In some cases, the preparation of a successor is simply being postponed.

Halcrow, Allen. "Temporary Services Warm to the Business Climate." *Personnel Journal*, Vol. 67, No. 10 (October, 1988), pp. 84–89.
> Of the firms surveyed in this study, 91 percent use temporary-services firms. Their use of "temps" is described.

Melohn, Thomas. "Screening for the Best Employees." *Inc.*, Vol. 9, No. 1 (January, 1987), pp. 104–106.
> The president of a company having 86 employees describes his own involvement in the processes of hiring personnel. He also describes the firm's use of application forms, interviewing, references, and trial periods for new hires.

ENDNOTES

1. James Fawcette, "Money Alone Can't Buy Top Talent," *Inc.*, Vol. 3, No. 3 (March, 1981), p. 92.

2. Thomas Melohn, "Screening for the Best Employees," *Inc.*, Vol. 9, No. 1 (January, 1987), pp. 104–106.

3. Thomas P. Murphy, "Peopling a Business," *Forbes*, Vol. 130, No. 11 (November 22, 1982), p. 270.

4. Dave Lindorff, "Assembling Your Team," *Venture*, Vol. 3, No. 5 (May, 1981), p. 44.

5. Bruce G. Posner, "May the Force Be with You," *Inc.*, Vol. 9, No. 8 (July, 1987), pp. 70–75.

6. "The Boom in Benefits," *Personnel Journal*, Vol. 67, No. 11 (November, 1988), p. 52.

7. "One Size Doesn't (Bene)fit All," *Nation's Business*, Vol. 76, No. 12 (December, 1988), pp. 35–36.

8. For an explanation of employee stock ownership plans, see George T. Milkovich and John W. Boudreau, *Personnel/Human Resource Management*, 5th ed. (Plano, TX: Business Publications, 1988), pp. 809–810.

9. For a summary of federal employment rules and regulations applicable to small business, see "Personnel Guidelines," *Small Business Reporter*, 1985, published by the Bank of America, San Francisco, CA.

10. Joseph P. Kahn, "When Bad Management Becomes Criminal," *Inc.*, Vol. 9, No. 3 (March, 1987), pp. 46–50.

11. For a further discussion of this topic, see Linda A. Roxe, *Personnel Management for the Smaller Company* (New York: AMACOM, 1979), Chapter 10.

12. "Do You Need an Employee Policy Manual?" *In Business*, Vol. 10, No. 4 (July–August, 1988), p. 48.

18 OPERATIONS MANAGEMENT

Spotlight on Small Business

Courtesy of Unison Industries

Operations management, the subject of this chapter, involves day-to-day activities that crucially affect a firm's productivity. In many small firms, unfortunately, managers find it difficult to maximize productivity. Even when they know what needs to be done, they often lack the necessary resources to do it.

Unison Industries, Inc., a tiny manufacturer of industrial motors in Rockford, IL, is such a firm. It uses aging equipment strewn haphazardly across a 135,000-square-foot factory floor. Even on a new production line, all but 2 of 30 steps required to assemble motors are still performed by hand. Frederick B. Sontag, who purchased the plant in 1980, is struggling to improve its productivity. Although Sontag has excellent qualifications (including an M.B.A. degree from Harvard), he is limited in time and money. His frustrations are commonplace in small firms. "When you only have $400,000 to spend, you can't just order up a batch of $100,000 robots," he says.

Similarly, he has no industrial relations staff to set up quality circles or to lead discussions about work improvement. In spite of such limitations, this small firm improved productivity 9 percent in just two years. And it is continuing to make those changes which it can afford. By recognizing its need for improvement and by making "affordable" improvements, it is staying competitive and profitable.

Source: Reprinted by permission of *The Wall Street Journal,* © Dow Jones & Company, Inc., 1984. All Rights Reserved.

Looking Ahead

Watch for the following important topics:
1. Differences in manufacturing and service operations and in their management.
2. Role and types of maintenance.
3. Creating and controlling quality in products and services.
4. Methods of work improvement and measurement.
5. Quantitative tools for operations management.
6. New terms and concepts:

production process	productivity
operations process	work study
operations management	laws of motion economy
intermittent operations	motion study
continuous operations	time study
corrective maintenance	micromotion study
preventive maintenance	work sampling
quality circle	statistical inference
inspection	mathematical programming
inspection standards	linear programming
statistical quality control	applied probability models
attributes sampling plan	queuing theory
variables sampling plan	simulation
work improvement	forecasting

In this chapter, we turn our attention to the operations process of the enterprise. Sometimes called production, it includes the core activities necessary to transform a firm's inputs into outputs. To a great extent, a firm's productivity and profitability depend upon the way it manages its basic operations.

Managing the Operations Process

The **production** or **operations process** consists of those activities necessary for "getting the job done," that is, for performing the work the firm was created to perform.

Nature of the Operations Process

An operations process is required whether a firm produces a tangible product such as clothing or bread or an intangible service such as dry cleaning or entertainment. It includes the production process in clothing manufacturing, the baking process in a bakery, the cleaning process in dry cleaning, and the performance process in entertainment. Production systems obviously differ for products and services, and they also differ from one type of product or service to another.

Despite their differences, operations processes are alike in that they all change inputs into outputs. These outputs are the products and/or services that a business provides to its customers. Thus, the operations process may be described as a conversion or transformation process. As Exhibit 18–1 shows, the operations process converts inputs of various kinds into products such as hot tubs and services such as window cleaning.

Inputs include raw materials, labor, equipment, information, and energy—all of which are combined in varying proportions depending on the nature of the finished product or service. Printing plants and toy manufacturers, for example, use inputs such as paper, ink, wood products, the work of employees, printing presses, lathes, product designs, and electric power to produce printed material and toys. Car-wash facilities and motor freight firms, which are service businesses, also use operating systems to transform inputs into car-cleaning and freight-transporting services.

Operations management involves the planning and control of the conversion process. It involves the acquisition of inputs and overseeing their transformation into the tangible products and intangible services desired by customers.

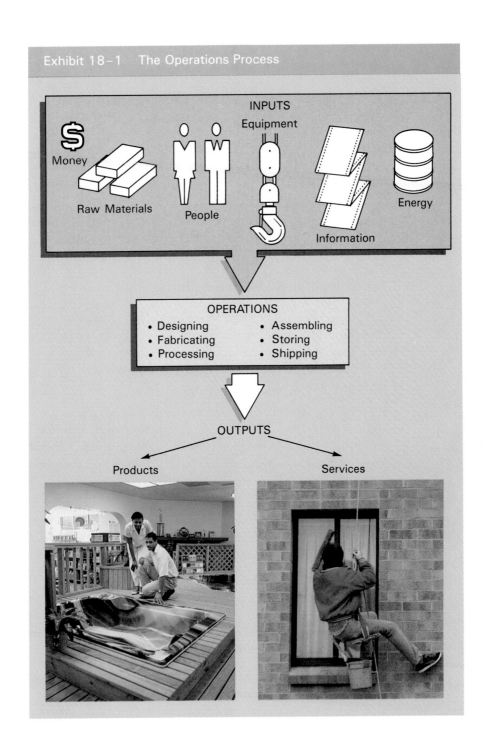

Exhibit 18–1   The Operations Process

INPUTS

$ Money

Raw Materials

People

Equipment

Information

Energy

OPERATIONS
• Designing   • Assembling
• Fabricating   • Storing
• Processing   • Shipping

OUTPUTS

Products   Services

Manufacturing and Service Operations

Manufacturing results in a tangible physical product. In contrast, a service operation produces an intangible output. Service operations usually involve more customer contact than do manufacturing operations. In addition, service operations typically use more labor and less equipment than are needed in manufacturing.

The greater customer contact involved in service firms tends to complicate their operations management. For example, consider the functioning of an automobile repair shop and a beauty shop. In both cases, the customer is involved, though in different degrees. In the beauty shop, the customer is a participant in the process as well as a user of the service.

Intermittent and Continuous Operations

Operations may be differentiated on a continuum according to the degree of repetitiveness and the quantity of goods or services produced at one time. Although some operations are performed only one time (such as building a company's plant), we can classify most operations as intermittent or continuous.

Intermittent Operations   Often described as job-order production, **intermittent operations** involve short production runs with only one or a few products or services being produced before shifting to a different production setup. General-purpose machines are used for this type of operations. Examples of businesses that use intermittent operations include print shops, machine shops, and automobile repair shops.

Continuous Operations   Firms that produce a standardized product or a relatively few standardized products use **continuous operations** that involve long production runs. Highly specialized equipment can be used. A soft-drink bottling plant is an example of a continuous operations process.

Exhibit 18–2 shows the layout of a small factory that produces a single, final product called ABC. This product is made from three machine parts: Part A, which is fabricated by the factory in three shop operations, and Parts B and C, which are purchased. The raw materials for Part A, as well as the purchased parts, flow to the plant from suppliers by rail and by truck. They are received, inspected and then sent to the storeroom for subsequent issue.

To start a production run, the raw materials for Part A move lot by lot to the storage table and then to the machines for Shop Operation #1 through Shop Operation #3. Meanwhile, Parts B and C move by conveyor

Exhibit 18-2   A Manufacturing Layout and Process

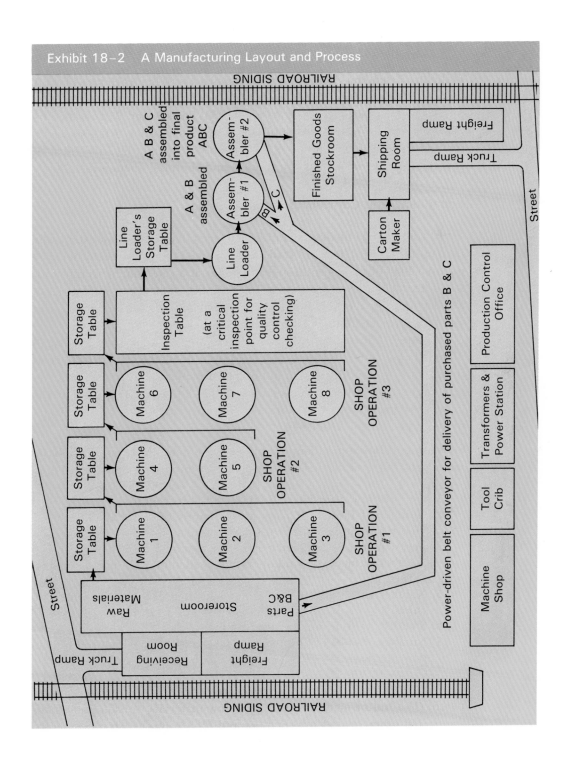

to the two assemblers near the end of the process. When each lot of Part A has passed inspection, it goes to the line loader, who places one part at a time on the conveyor going to Assembler #1. Parts A and B are joined by Assembler #1 to form subassembly AB. Then subassembly AB goes to Assembler #2, who joins Part C to subassembly AB to produce the finished product, ABC. Final inspection, storage, and shipping operations follow.

Scheduling and Controlling Manufacturing

Production control procedures have been developed most extensively in manufacturing. They consist of steps designed to achieve the orderly sequential flow of products through the plant at a rate commensurate with scheduled deliveries to customers. To attain this objective, it is essential to avoid work stoppages, to eliminate production bottlenecks when they occur, and to utilize machines and personnel efficiently.

Simple, informal control procedures are frequently used in small plants. If a procedure is simple and the output small, the manager can keep things moving smoothly with a minimum of paperwork. Personal observation might even suffice. However, there comes a time in the growth of any manufacturing organization when formal procedures must be established to attain production efficiency.

Planning and Routing   Planning involves the determination of the basic manufacturing data needed. Among the most important data needed are:

1. Kinds of raw materials and fabricated parts required.
2. Number of fabricated parts and amounts of material of each kind required per unit of finished product.
3. Best sequence of processing operations for making each product.
4. Number of machines and operators needed on each processing operation.
5. Number and kinds of tooling items needed to set up each machine.
6. Standard output rate of each machine.
7. Number of units of finished product that the plant can produce daily or yearly.

Once the manufacturing data are determined, two forms can be prepared: (1) a bill of materials listing the raw materials, consumption standards, and other related information, and (2) a route list showing the sequence of processing operations and who will perform them.

In intermittent operations, machines are shut down rather frequently and retooled to produce a different product. Therefore, the basic manufacturing data are needed well in advance of the start of production. This allows management sufficient time to make any necessary changes in plant layout, to buy new tooling items required, and to train workers.

In continuous operations, most or all of the machines run without stopping for long periods of time. Advance planning is even more essential, for once the machinery is set up and operations have begun, changes are both difficult and costly.

Scheduling and Dispatching   After a given process is planned and set up, timetables for each department and work center are established to control the flow of work. In continuous operations, which involve large-scale production and which are found in very few small factories, flow control is fairly simple and involves little paperwork. This is the case because continuous operations assure a steady flow of finished products off the final assembly line. The dispatcher must keep all lines (subassembly and final assembly) operating all the time. If delays occur, rescheduling or other adjustment is required.

In intermittent operations, which involve small- to medium-volume production where lots are produced one at a time, there are different flow-control techniques. Where a lot is in process for several days, or is slow-moving, it is possible to use visual control boards to reflect both work assignments and the progress of work toward completion. For fast-moving processes where a lot clears each machine quickly, the block control technique clears the oldest blocks first on each processing operation.

Supervising and Performance Follow-Up   Keeping the work moving on schedule is the major responsibility of the shop supervisor. Performance reports and necessary follow-up routines are established. After an order is completed, the schedules are terminated, and the work records are filed for future use.

Scheduling and Controlling Service Operations

Since service firms are tied closely to their customers, they are limited in their ability to produce services and hold them in inventory for customers. An automobile repair shop must wait until the auto arrives, and a beauty shop cannot function until a customer is available. A retail store can perform some of its services, such as transportation and storage, but it must wait until the customer arrives to perform other services.

A number of scheduling strategies are available to service firms. Appointment systems are used by many automobile repair shops and beauty shops, for example. Other service firms, such as dry cleaners and plumbers, take requests for service and delay delivery until the work can be scheduled. Still other firms, such as movie theaters, maintain a fixed schedule of services and tolerate some idle capacity. Some businesses attempt to spread out demand by offering incentives for using services at off-peak hours—an "early-bird" special at a restaurant, for example.

Plant Maintenance

According to Murphy's Law, if anything can go wrong, it will! In operating systems that make extensive use of tools and equipment, there is indeed much that can go wrong. The maintenance function is intended to correct malfunctions of equipment and, as far as possible, to prevent such breakdowns from occurring.

Role of Maintenance in Small Firms

The nature of maintenance work obviously depends upon the type of operations and the nature of the equipment being used. In an office, for example, the machines that require maintenance may simply include typewriters, office copiers, computers, and related office machines. Maintenance services are usually obtained on a contract basis—either by calling for repair personnel when a breakdown occurs or by contracting for periodic servicing and other maintenance when needed.

In manufacturing firms that use more complex and specialized equipment, the maintenance function is much more important. For all types of firms, maintenance includes plant housekeeping as well as equipment repair. Plant housekeeping contributes to effective performance, moreover, even in those operations that use simple facilities.

It is easy to underestimate the importance of maintenance. Managers often think of it as janitorial-type work and postpone it as much as possible in order to concentrate upon the production process. The increased use of expensive, complex equipment, however, has made the maintenance role a much greater factor in the firm's overall effectiveness. A major breakdown in production equipment, for example, can interfere with scheduled deliveries and cause labor costs to skyrocket as personnel are idled. Figure 18–1

Figure 18–1   Maintaining Equipment in a Printing Plant

Courtesy of The Nielson Lithographing Co.

pictures the type of equipment requiring maintenance in a production plant.

In small plants, maintenance work often is performed by regular production employees. As a firm expands its facilities, it may add specialized maintenance personnel and eventually create a maintenance department.

Types of Maintenance

Plant maintenance activities fall into two categories. One is **corrective maintenance,** which includes both the major and minor repairs necessary to restore a facility to good condition. The other is **preventive maintenance,** which includes inspections and other activities intended to prevent machine breakdowns and damage to people and buildings.

Corrective Maintenance   Major repairs are unpredictable as to time of occurrence, repair time required, loss of output, and cost of downtime. Because of these characteristics, some small manufacturers find it desirable to contract with other service firms for major repair work. In contrast, the regular occurrence of minor breakdowns makes the volume of minor repair work reasonably predictable. Minor repairs are completed easily, quickly, and economically. Therefore, many small plants use one or two of their own employees to perform such work.

Preventive Maintenance   A small plant can ill afford to neglect preventive maintenance. If a machine is highly critical to the overall operation, it should be inspected and serviced regularly to preclude costly breakdowns. Also, the frequent checking of equipment reduces industrial accidents, and the installation of smoke alarms and/or automatic sprinkler systems minimizes the danger of fire damage.

Preventive maintenance of equipment need not involve elaborate controls. Some cleaning and lubricating is usually done as a matter of routine. But for preventive maintenance to work well, more systematic procedures are needed. A record card showing cost, acquisition date, periods of use and storage, and frequency of preventive maintenance inspections should be kept on each major piece of equipment. On any given day, the machinist is handed the set of cards covering that day's required inspections. The machinist inspects each piece of equipment, makes necessary notations on the cards, and replaces worn parts.

Good Housekeeping and Plant Safety

Good housekeeping facilitates production control, saves time in looking for tools, and keeps floor areas safe and free for production work. Disregard for good housekeeping practices is reflected in a plant's production record, for good workmanship and high output are hard to achieve in an ill-kept plant.

As noted in Chapter 17, the Occupational Safety and Health Act of 1970 (OSHA) requires employers to provide a place of employment free from hazards that are likely to cause death or serious physical harm. This means that the building and equipment must be maintained in a way that minimizes safety and health hazards. Although very small firms have been relieved of some of OSHA's record-keeping requirements, they are still subject to the requirements of the law.

As far as safety of the premises is concerned, not all small manufacturers require a sophisticated security system. However, all should be aware of the security problems and of available security devices. Such devices include fences to deter intruders, security guards, burglar-alarm systems, and gates or doors equipped with access controls that are activated only by identification cards or keys given to authorized personnel.

Quality Control

Most consumers view quality subjectively as a single variable ranging from very bad to very good. The manufacturer knows, however, that there is a set of objectively measurable physical variables—such as length or diameter—which *together* determine how good or bad a product is. To approach perfection on even one variable is very costly. To make a product inferior to that of competitors, however, means that they will get the business. Thus, a product must be good enough so that it will be competitive, yet it must not be prohibitively expensive.

Building Quality into the Product

One company advertises, "The quality goes in before the label goes on." This slogan implies that quality does not originate with the inspection

---

SMALL BUSINESS IN ACTION
Maintaining Quality Through Careful Management

Quality cannot be "inspected" into a product. It must be built in, and this requires careful workmanship. Careful workmanship, in turn, depends on proper training and supervision of the operations process. Increasing production volume brings with it a threat to high quality standards. Chalif Mustard, a small Pennsylvania business operated by Nick and Liz Thomas, faced such a threat as mustard sales grew rapidly. The superior quality of their product was the key to their success, and they could tolerate no compromise with quality. Therefore, the owners trained employees thoroughly and kept a tight rein on production methods as they expanded output.

To ease that process, the Thomases developed a step-by-step checklist so that ingredients are added in the right order and in the right quantity. "In addition, we always have at least two people making the products so there is someone checking while the other is adding and mixing," she says. Nothing is ever done by eye or taste. "Every ingredient is measured to the hundredth of a pound by using a very sensitive scale," adds Thomas.

Through painstaking management, Nick and Liz Thomas succeeded in preserving the high quality of their product even in this stressful situation.

Source: Nora Goldstein, "Quest for Quality," *In Business,* Vol. 8, No. 4 (July–August, 1986), pp. 50–51.

process that checks the finished product, but with the earlier production process. Quality of a product begins, in fact, with its design and the design of the manufacturing process.

Another factor that contributes to product quality is the quality of the raw materials used. Generally the finished product is better if a superior grade of raw material is used. A contractor who uses lumber of inferior grade produces a low-quality house.

In many types of businesses, an even more critical variable is found in the performance of employees. Employees who are careful in their work produce products of a better quality than those produced by careless employees. You have probably heard the admonition, "Never buy a car that was produced on Friday or Monday!" The central role of personnel in producing a high-quality product suggests the importance of human resources management—properly selecting, training, and motivating production personnel.

Quality Circles

Quality circles, a Japanese innovation, are used in small business as well as big business. A **quality circle** consists of a group of employees, usually a dozen or fewer, performing similar or related work. They meet periodically, typically about once a week, to identify, analyze, and solve production problems, particularly those involving product or service quality. Supervisors often serve as circle leaders, but others may also be given this role.

The contribution of quality circles to quality improvement has been demonstrated by the performance of Globe Metallurgical, Inc., a small business located in Beverly, OH. This firm was one of three U.S. companies selected to receive the Malcolm Baldrige National Quality Award in 1988. Globe's use of employee participation in achieving this distinction is explained as follows:

> Communication is a key. Every level of the company has a quality committee. Workers hash out issues in their own weekly "quality circles." Finally, in each of the company's two plants, still another committee, made up of the plant manager and department heads, assembles each morning to review the previous day's performance.[1]

For quality circles to function effectively, participating employees must be given appropriate training. Also, top management must give consistent support on a long-term basis. With such support, quality circles have the potential for tapping the often unused potential for enthusiastic contributions by employees.

Inspection: The Traditional Technique

Inspection consists of scrutinizing a part or a product to determine whether it is good or bad. An inspector typically uses gauges to evaluate the important quality variables. For effective quality control, the inspector must be honest, objective, and capable of resisting pressure from shop personnel to pass borderline cases.

Inspection Standards   In manufacturing, inspection standards consist of design tolerances that are set for every important quality variable. These tolerances show the limits of variation allowable above and below the desired dimension of the given quality variable. Tolerances must satisfy the requirements that customers will look for in finished products.

Points of Inspection   Traditionally, inspection occurs in the receiving room to check the condition and quantity of materials received from suppliers. Inspection is also customary at critical processing points—for example, *before* any operation that would conceal existing defects, or *after* any operation that produces an excessive amount of defective products or components. Of course, the final inspection of finished products is of utmost importance.

Reduction of Inspection Costs   To reduce costs, the manufacturer must be alert to possibilities for mechanization or automation of inspection. Automated inspection requires only first-piece inspection and periodic rechecks. So long as the setups remain satisfactory, the production run continues without other inspection.

100 Percent Inspection   When each item in every lot processed is inspected, this is called 100 percent inspection. Supposedly it assures the elimination of all bad materials in process and all defective products prior to shipment to customers. Such goals are seldom reached, however. This method of inspection is not only time-consuming, but also costly. Furthermore, inspectors often make honest errors in judgment. A reinspection of lots that have been 100 percent inspected, for example, will show that inspectors err by placing good items in the scrap barrel and bad items or rework items in the good-item barrel. Also, some types of inspection—for example, opening a can of vegetables—destroy the product, making 100 percent inspection impractical.

Statistical Quality Control

To avoid the cost and time of 100 percent inspection, small firms can use statistical methods to devise sampling procedures of quality control. In this way, the small firm can inspect a small number of items in a group and make an inductive decision about the quality level of the entire group.

Attributes Sampling Plans Some products are judged to be either acceptable or unacceptable, good or bad. For example, a light bulb either lights up or it doesn't. Likewise, a manufactured part either falls within the tolerance size limits or it doesn't. In these cases, control of quality involves a measurement of attributes.

Suppose a small firm receives a shipment of 1,000 parts from a supplier. Rather than evaluating all 1,000 parts, the purchaser can check the acceptability of a small sample of parts and decide about the acceptability of the entire order. The size of the sample—for instance, a sample of 25 of the 1,000 parts—affects the discriminating power of an attributes sampling plan. The smaller the sample, the greater the danger of either accepting a defective lot or rejecting a good lot due to sampling error. A larger sample reduces this danger but increases the inspection cost. An **attributes sampling plan** must strike a balance between these two forces, avoiding excessive inspection costs and simultaneously avoiding an unreasonable risk of accepting a bad lot or rejecting a good lot.

Variables Sampling Plans A **variables sampling plan** measures many characteristics of an item, rather than simply judging the item as acceptable or unacceptable. If the characteristic being inspected is measured on a continuous basis, a variables sampling plan may be used. For example, the weight of a box of candy—which is being manufactured continuously throughout the day and week—may be measured in pounds and ounces. The process can be monitored to be sure it stays "in control." Periodic random samples are taken and plotted on a chart to discover whether the process is out of control, thus requiring corrective action.

The variables control chart used for this purpose has lines denoting the upper and lower control limits. For example, a shop might produce wooden pieces averaging 42 inches in length. The upper control limit might be 43 inches and the lower control limit 41 inches. A signal of a lack of control would be given by a measurement falling outside either control limit, by a trend run of points upward or downward, or by various other indicators.

To establish a specific variables or attributes sampling plan, the small-business manager may consult more specialized publications in production/operations management or statistical quality control. Or, more likely, the manager may consult a specialist in quantitative methods for assistance in devising a sound sampling plan. The savings made possible by using an efficient quality control method can easily justify the consulting fees required in devising a sound quality control plan.

Quality Control in Service Businesses

The discussion of quality control typically centers on a manufacturing process involving a tangible product that can be inspected or measured in some way. The need for quality control, however, is not limited to producers of physical products. Service businesses, such as motels, dry cleaners, accounting service firms, and automobile repair shops, also need to maintain an adequate control of quality. In fact, many firms offer a combination of a tangible product and intangible services and, ideally, wish to control quality in both areas.

Measurement problems are greater in assessing the quality of a service, however. One can measure the length of a piece of wood more easily than the quality level of motel accommodations. Nevertheless, methods can be devised for measuring the quality of services. Customers of an automobile repair shop, for example, may be sampled to determine their view of the service they received. And a motel can maintain a record of the number of "foul-ups" in travelers' reservations, complaints about cleanliness of rooms, and so on.

For some types of service firms, control of quality constitutes the single most important managerial responsibility. All that such firms sell is service, and the future of their businesses rests upon the quality of their service as perceived by customers.

Work Improvement and Measurement

Work improvement means finding work methods that demand the least physical effort and the shortest execution time at the lowest possible cost. Most large manufacturing plants employ industrial engineers who specialize in work improvement methods. In the small plant, however, the man-

Figure 18-2 Efficient Production of Milk Cartons Improves Productivity

USDA Photo

ager may have to initiate and carry out a work improvement program with the help of shop supervisors.

Improving Productivity

The standard of living of any society depends, to some extent, upon its **productivity**—the efficiency with which inputs are transformed into outputs. In recent years, productivity growth in the United States has lagged behind that of Japan, Great Britain, and France.[2] For individual firms, improving productivity provides a key to competing more vigorously and increasing profits.

We may visualize a business firm's productivity as follows:

$$\text{productivity} = \frac{\text{outputs}}{\text{inputs}} = \frac{\text{goods and/or services}}{\text{labor} + \text{energy} + \text{capital} + \text{tools} + \text{materials}}$$

A firm improves its productivity by doing more with less. This can be accomplished in many different ways. As one writer has pointed out, Mom's apple pie baking may be improved by sending Mom to cooking school, buying better apples, getting a better oven, or redesigning the kitchen.[3]

At one time, productivity and quality were viewed as competitive, if not conflicting. However, production at a high quality level reduces scrap and rework. Therefore, quality improvement, automation, and better methods are all routes to better productivity.

Improving productivity in the service sector has been especially difficult. Since it is a labor-intensive area, managers have less opportunity for improvement by using automation.

Nature of Work Study

When conducted for the entire operation of a plant, **work study** involves an analysis of equipment and tooling, plant layout, working conditions, and individual jobs. It means finding the answers to such questions as:

1. Is the right machine being used?
2. Can one employee operate two or more machines?
3. Can automatic feeders or ejectors be utilized?
4. Can power tools replace hand tools?
5. Can the jigs and fixtures be improved?
6. Is the workplace properly arranged?
7. Is the operator's motion sequence effective?

To be successful, work improvement and measurement require the collaboration of employees and management. The assistance of employees is important both in the search for more efficient methods and in the adoption of improved work procedures.

The competitive pressures on today's small-business firms provide the incentive for work improvement. Small firms can improve their productivity and stay competitive. To the extent that methods can actually be improved, there will be increasd output from the same effort (or even reduced effort) on the part of production employees.

Laws of Motion Economy

Underlying any work improvement program—whether it be for the overall operations of a plant or for a single task—are the **laws of motion**

economy. These laws concern work arrangement, the use of the human hands and body, and the design and use of tools. Some of these laws are:

1. If both hands start and stop their motion at the same time and are never idle during a work cycle, maximum performance is approached.
2. If motions are made simultaneously in opposite directions over similar paths, automaticity and rhythm develop naturally, and less fatigue is experienced.
3. The method requiring the fewest motions generally is the best for performance of a given task.
4. When motions are confined to the lowest practical classification, maximum performance and minimum fatigue are approached. Lowest classification means motions involving the fingers, hands, forearms, and trunk.

A knowledge of the laws of motion economy will suggest various ways to improve work. For example, materials and tools should be so placed as to minimize movement of the trunk and the extended arms.

Methods of Work Measurement

There are several ways to measure work in the interest of establishing a performance standard. **Motion study** consists of a detailed observation of all the actual motions that the observed worker makes to complete a job under a given set of physical conditions. From this study the skilled observer should be able to detect any wasted movements that can be corrected or eliminated. **Time study**, which normally follows motion study, involves timing and recording each elemental motion of a job on an observation sheet. **Micromotion study** is a refinement of the time study in that a motion-picture camera, rather than a stopwatch, is used to record the elemental motions, as well as the times.

As you can readily see, the methods of work measurement mentioned above require trained observers or analysts. Most small plants would find it impractical to utilize the costly methods of time study and micromotion study. A more practical method of work measurement, which provides little operating detail but estimates the ratio of actual working time and downtime, is **work sampling.** This method was originated in England by L.H.C. Tippett in 1934. Work sampling involves random observations in which the observer simply determines whether the observed worker is working or idle.

The numbers of observations are tallied in "working" and "idle" classifications; the percentages of the tallies are estimates of the actual percentage of time that the worker was working and idle.

Quantitative Tools in Operations Management

In both large and small businesses, quantitative tools may be utilized to improve decision making. Most owners of independent businesses associate these quantitative tools with big business, considering them inapplicable to small firms. However, the potential usefulness of quantitative tools to the small firm should not be overlooked.

Value of Quantitative Methods

Many decisions in small firms can be improved by adopting quantitative decision-making techniques. Unfortunately, most small-business owners lack an awareness of the power of such techniques. Much of their decision making reflects personal experience—what they have learned through trial and error—and they fail to realize that such decisions can be made more rational. Reliance on intuitive approaches can be reduced by the analytical processes that are a part of management science.

As a practical matter, few managers of small firms have sufficient knowledge of advanced mathematics and statistics to apply these tools personally. A consideration of these tools is pertinent, however, for at least two reasons. First, the small-business owner should know that such tools exist and that assistance can be obtained from individuals qualified in the use of quantitative methods. Second, the growing use of these techniques points up the need for increased training in quantitative methods on the part of small-business managers. Even though an individual lacks the necessary technical knowledge for using the tools, it is desirable that he or she appreciate their possibilities, advantages, and limitations.

The variety and complexity of quantitative methods make it impossible to provide an extensive review of them in this book. Because of space limitations, only a few such approaches can be explained.

Statistical Inference

By means of statistical analysis, one can use quantitative data to arrive at conclusions that are useful in managing a small business. Suppose, for example, that you wish to judge the quality of a large production run without inspecting each item or that you wish to understand your market without surveying each individual customer. You may accomplish these objectives by sampling the population and then applying **statistical inference,** that is, inferring something about a large group on the basis of facts known about a smaller group.

Although sampling is not the only tool that uses statistical inference, it illustrates its practical application in small business. In sampling, the manager wishes to obtain a sample that is truly representative of the underlying population. A sample is representative when it is like the population in all important respects. To assure this condition, the researcher will often use a random sample in which every item in the population has a known chance of being included. The sample should also be adequate, that is, large enough to yield a dependable answer.

Sampling is essential for the simple reason that the entire population of data can seldom be investigated. Cost and time pressures make this prohibitive.

Mathematical Programming

Several types of mathematical programming are available, such as integer programming, quadratic programming, goal programming, dynamic programming, and linear programming. They can be applied to the solution of such varied problems as resource allocation, inventory management, production planning, advertising media selection, and capital budgeting.

Linear programming, the most widely used variety of mathematical programming, involves the use of mathematical algorithms for evaluating the results from several alternative courses of action, each of which contains a number of variables. This tool is used to discover the exact solution that will minimize costs or maximize gains. It is beyond the scope of this text to illustrate advanced mathematical theories in solving problems by linear programming. Suffice it to say that this tool can be used to analyze manufacturing problems that involve the production of several products for which basic, but scarce, raw materials are used. Linear programming could determine the following information for such a problem:

1. The amount of each raw material needed for each product.
2. The profit per unit for each product.
3. Which product or combination of products to produce in order to maximize profits.

4. How much of each product should be produced.

5. How much of a low-profit product to produce in order to "take care" of certain loyal customers.

Applied Probability Models

A number of applied probability models, including queuing models, Markov chain models, and inventory models are applicable to various types of business problems. We shall limit the present discussion to queuing models.

Queuing theory is waiting-line theory. It consists of the use of calculated probabilities for determining the number of persons who will stand in a line. Examples of problems that may be solved by applying this theory might include the number of depositors who will stand in line for service at a bank teller's window, customers who will stand in line at checkout counters in a supermarket, or car owners who will wait in line at car wash establishments.

Take the case of a barber facing retirement at age 65 in order to draw a Social Security pension. The alternatives considered were: (1) to sell out, (2) to trade the two-chair shop for a one-chair shop to be operated on weekends only, and (3) to keep the two-chair shop open on Fridays and Saturdays only. Using the queuing theory for Alternative No. 2 showed that the barber would work continuously, without rest breaks or meals, from 8:00 A.M. to 10:00 P.M. if all arriving customers waited until served—even though the shop was locked for an hour at noon and after 5:00 P.M. Because this was untenable, the possibilities of Alternative No. 3 were simulated. This alternative proved to be workable, except that the barber would still make too much money to be legally entitled to the Social Security checks. Hence, the waiting-line simulations suggested a different solution: The barber sold out and contracted to work for another barber on Fridays and Saturdays only, taking full pay of services up to the limiting monthly amount and letting the shop owner take everything over that figure. This case exemplifies the application of waiting-line theory for the guidance of a small-business owner's decision to sell out.

Simulation Technique

Experience can be a good teacher, but experience is costly and time-consuming. This is true of managerial decision making as it is elsewhere. **Simulation** permits the decision maker to gain experience in something resembling the actual business situation without taking the risk existing in that situation. The basic idea in simulation is the creation of a model that acts like the system it represents. Manufacturers, for example, test products in laboratories that simulate the environment in which those products are used. A model must contain the parameters that exist in the real-life situation if it is to produce results comparable to those that would emerge in real life.

Even in a small business, the manager can occasionally create a model of a problem that requires a solution. The model will typically express the problem in mathematical terms and be structured for solution by use of a computer. By having a mathematical, computerized model available, the decision maker can easily and quickly experiment with alternative actions in reaching a sound decision. When a particular decision is fed into the computer, the computer calculates its effects. Thus, the manager can immediately determine the consequences of that decision and also alternative decisions.

Simulation can be used for such problems as determining the number of loading docks to build and the number of people to hire for a warehouse where the amount of time between truck arrivals is random. In a different context, simulation can help in deciding how many products to order for a special sale in which leftover products must be sold at a loss. There are also other types of problems in which simulation can be used, but these examples should demonstrate its possible application to practical problems in the small firm.

Forecasting

Forecasts are necessary for many types of business decisions. Managers of small firms must decide how much to buy, how many employees to hire, how many products to produce, and how much money to borrow by predicting the demand for their products. In Chapters 6 and 7, we stressed the importance of a credible forecast when preparing a business plan.

Some forecasts are merely "guesstimates," or products of entrepreneurial intuition. However, management science offers quantitative tools to assist in preparing reliable forecasts. They vary in degree of sophistication and in their usefulness in particular situations. They include such methods as moving averages, exponential smoothing, and multiple regression models, among others.

Limitations of Quantitative Tools

Quantitative tools do not preclude the exercise of managerial judgment, which is definitely required because of the human factor in any problem situation. The tools are a means to an end, not the end itself. The manager's judgment remains the decisive factor in planning.

Neither does the use of quantitative tools preclude the requirement of feedback. Any information about operating results must be fed back to the planner so that plans, programs, and instructions may be modified when necessary. For example, when feedback reports describe deviations from an existing budget, the budget may have to be modified as a means of corrective action.

It must be emphasized that quantitative tools are just that—they are tools, and no more. When used properly, they tend to improve managerial decision making. These decision-making tools do not eliminate business risk totally. Risk is inherent in the use of present resources and production facilities for the creation of new goods. It is inherent also in the purchase of merchandise for resale. Decision-making tools are designed merely to minimize risk by providing a rational approach to the solution of business problems.

Looking Back

1. Both manufacturing and service organizations use an operations process that converts inputs into products or services. Two basic types of processes are intermittent and continuous. Proper scheduling and controlling of work flow is needed in both manufacturing and service organizations.
2. The maintenance function is critical for firms that use complex and highly specialized equipment. Plant maintenance includes corrective maintenance to restore a facility to good condition and preventive maintenance to minimize breakdowns. Plant housekeeping and safety management are also part of the maintenance function.
3. Quality is built into a product during the production process, not at the inspection stage. The quality of a product is influenced by its design, the quality of raw materials used, and the

performance of employees. Quality circles draw upon the thinking of employees by bringing them together periodically to identify and solve quality and other operating problems. Inspection is the method traditionally used to maintain control of quality. Modern quality control involves the use of two statistical techniques: attributes sampling and variables sampling plans. Quality control is important in service businesses as well as in manufacturing.

4. Improving productivity requires attention both to quality of product or service and to work methods. Work study and measurement are accomplished by the use of motion study, time study, work sampling, and other tools of industrial engineering.

5. Quantitative tools useful for the improvement of decision making include methods of statistical inference such as sampling; mathematical programming; and applied probability models including queuing theory, simulation, and forecasting. The limitations of quantitative tools should be known to the entrepreneur. As tools, they assist in reaching a decision, but they do not obviate the use of personal judgment.

DISCUSSION QUESTIONS

1. Describe the operations process for the following types of service firms: (a) management consultant, (b) barber shop, (c) advertising agency.

2. What is the difference between intermittent manufacturing and continuous manufacturing?

3. Why might a small manufacturing or service firm prefer a versatile work force in its operations even though such employees might be paid more than less-versatile employees?

4. How do operations processes differ for manufacturing firms and service firms?

5. Customer demand for services is not uniform during the day, week, or other time period. What approaches or strategies can be used by service firms to relate customer demand for services to the firm's capacity to perform services?

6. Explain the difference between preventive and corrective maintenance. Explain the relative importance of each of these types of maintenance when (a) one or more major breakdowns have occurred in a small plant, and (b) shop operations are running smoothly and maintenance does not face any major repair jobs.

7. The breakdown of machines during their use is a result of failure to exercise preventive maintenance. Why should these breakdowns always be investigated promptly? What should be the outcome of such investigations? Are cost considerations or lost production of paramount importance in such situations? Why?

8. How could improved housekeeping help raise productivity?

9. What is meant by the saying, "You can't inspect quality into a product"?

10. It is said that the major problems of manufacturing inspection are where to inspect, how much to inspect, and the cost of inspection. Explain each of these inspection problems concisely.

11. A small manufacturer does not believe that using statistical quality control charts and sampling plans would be useful. Can traditional methods suffice? Can 100 percent inspection by final inspectors eliminate all defectives? Why?

12. How can a service business, such as a dry cleaner, use the concept of quality control?

13. Doing something rapidly and doing it well are often incompatible. How could quality improvement possibly contribute to productivity improvement?

14. What is meant by the "laws of motion economy"?

15. To what extent are sophisticated, quantitative decision-making tools actually applicable to small-business management?

YOU MAKE THE CALL

Situation 1

Broom making is a centuries-old craft. In the early 1980's Thurman Scheumack started a small broom-making business in the Ozark foothills. Although the workshop has only seven employees, including Scheumack and his wife, Rhonda, its output has grown to 20,000 brooms per year. Seventy-five percent of production is in standard kitchen models, and the rest have hand-carved faces in their handles. Some brooms are sold through art galleries, and some are sold at tourist attractions such as Disneyland and Colonial Williamsburg for prices up to $50 each.

The brooms are fashioned from broomcorn, a plant imported from Mexico. Most of the production equipment, initially built by Scheumack, is far from high tech. Developed in the 1700s, the machinery runs on a system of hand- and foot-operated weights and levers. One concession to technology is a single electric motor that operates a pulley for a broom-winding machine.

Source: Adapted from "Ozark Enterprise Handcrafts Brooms," *In Business,* Vol. 11, No. 1 (January–February, 1989), p. 16.

Questions

1. In view of its antiquated technology, should this firm attempt to modernize its equipment and update its manufacturing methods? Would motion study be relevant and useful?
2. How would quality be defined for this type of product? How could quality be measured?

Situation 2

A college professor opened a furniture shop in Maine and saw it grow to $5 million in annual sales volume and 85 employees. The firm produces high-quality chairs, tables, and other items for the contract furniture market. Each piece is sanded and polished, sealed with linseed oil, and finished with paste wax. No stain, color, or varnish is added, and the furniture never needs refinishing.

As the firm grew larger, it began the equivalent of mass production. Many of the original craftspeople dropped out and were replaced with production workers. The founder is seeking to maintain quality through employee participation at all levels. He believes that quality can be maintained indefinitely if the company doesn't "get too greedy." He has expressed his philosophy as follows:

> We're still not driven by profit but by meaningful relationships between employees and between the producer and the user. It's a way of life. We throw out a lot of good stuff. If we had to produce something just to make a buck, I'd go back to teaching school.

Source: Christopher Hyde, "The Evolution of Thomas Moser," *In Business,* Vol. 10, No. 4 (July–August, 1988), pp. 34–37.

Questions

1. How does this firm's growth make quality control easier or more difficult?
2. The founder recognizes that people and people relationships have a bearing on quality. What can he do to persuade or enable production employees to have the right attitude toward quality?

3. The founder's comment suggests that profits and quality may be incompatible. When does "making a buck" lead to lower quality? Can or should this type of firm use financial incentives?

EXPERIENTIAL EXERCISES

1. Visit a small manufacturing plant or service organization. Ask the manager to describe the production/operations process, the way operations are controlled, and the nature of maintenance operations. Prepare a brief report on your findings.
2. Outline the operations process involved in your present educational program, identifying inputs, operations, and outputs.
3. Assume that you are responsible for quality control in the publication of this textbook. Prepare a report outlining the quality standards you would use and the points of inspection you would recommend.
4. Outline, in as much detail as possible, your customary practices in studying for a specific course. Evaluate the methods you use and specify changes that should improve your productivity.

REFERENCES TO SMALL-BUSINESS PRACTICES

Fenn, Donna. "The Lord of Discipline." *Inc.,* Vol. 7, No. 11 (November, 1985), pp. 82–95.
  Oberg Industries is a small tool and die shop located in western Pennsylvania. Its tough management, exceptional maintenance, superior workmanship, and high standards are described.
Goldstein, Nora. "Production Strategies When Business Booms." *In Business,* Vol. 10, No. 2 (March–April, 1988), pp. 32–34.
  This article describes the steps taken by a small manufacturing firm to expand output—changes in production processes, modifications of equipment, and new methods to maintain control of quality.
Kyd, Charles W. "Quality Nightmares." *Inc.,* Vol. 9, No. 11 (October, 1987), pp. 155–158.
  The author describes the cash-flow nightmare that came to one firm as a consequence of lapses in quality control.
Logsdon, Gene. "Partners in Pasta." *In Business,* Vol. 9, No. 3 (May–June, l987), pp. 28–31.
  This article describes the production methods used by a small business in Marietta, OH, to produce pasta of exceptional quality.

ENDNOTES

1. Donald C. Bacon, "How the Baldrige Winners Did It," *Nation's Business,* Vol. 77, No. 1 (January, 1989), p. 32.

2. "The Productivity Paradox," *Business Week,* No. 3055 (June 6, 1988), p. 101.

3. Michael LeBoeuf, *The Productivity Challenge: How to Make It Work for America and You* (New York: McGraw-Hill Book Company, 1982), p. 9.

19 PURCHASING AND MANAGING INVENTORY

Spotlight on Small Business

Courtesy of Barry & Dan Schacht

Barry Schacht and his brother, Dan, own and operate Schacht's Spindle Company in Boulder, CO, a manufacturer of looms for hand weaving. They have found that astute buying of components can save thousands of dollars and that there is wide variation in prices quoted by vendors. Their ability to save money by shopping around is evidenced in Barry Schacht's description of his search for a spherical bearing:

> The first place I called had spherical bearings that cost $20 apiece, real bad news for us. But that company made bearings for rockets. All we needed was one for a tool that had been state of the art five centuries ago. The next place had spherical bearings that cost $10, for airplanes. Hmmm. After about $100 in phone calls I found a little company that made all kinds of spherical bearings, and had exactly what we needed. He asked, "How many do you want?" I said 500. He sighed. "Well if you only want a few, they are kind of expensive—54¢ each."

A self-described "former hippie," Barry Schacht started in business when he lost a university lawn-mowing job. He mowed a big peace symbol in a lawn, and campus authorities thought it was less clever than he did!

Source: Gene Logsdon, "Factory Crafting," *In Business,* Vol. 10, No. 2, (March–April, 1988), pp. 35–37.

Looking Ahead

Watch for the following important topics:
1. The purchasing cycle.
2. Purchasing policies.
3. Factors to consider in selecting suppliers.
4. Objectives of inventory control.
5. Control of inventory costs.
6. Methods of accounting for inventory.
7. New terms and concepts:

purchasing	two-bin method
purchase requisition	Kanban system
purchase order	economic order quantity
reciprocal buying	physical inventory system
make-or-buy decisions	perpetual inventory system
ABC method	retail inventory valuation
reorder point	method
safety stock	

In many small businesses, more money is spent for materials or merchandise than for any other purpose. Many firms must also carry sizable inventories that are crucial for their operation. In this chapter, we explain how small firms should deal with these important areas of purchasing and inventory management.

Purchasing

The objective of purchasing activities is to obtain materials, merchandise, equipment, and services needed to meet production and/or marketing goals. Through effective purchasing, a firm secures all production factors except labor in the required quantity and quality, at the best price, and at the time needed for its operations.

Importance of Effective Purchasing

There is a direct correlation between the quality of finished products and the quality of the raw materials placed in process. For example, if tight tolerances are imposed on a manufacturer's product by design requirements, this in turn requires the acquisition of high-quality materials and component parts. Then, given an excellent process, excellent products will be produced. Similarly, the acquisition of high-quality merchandise makes a retailer's sales to customers easier and reduces the number of markdowns required.

Delivery of goods should be timed to meet the exact needs of the buyer. In a small factory, failure to receive materials, parts, or equipment on schedule is likely to cause costly interruptions in production operations. Machines and personnel are idled until the items on order are finally received. And in a retail business, failure to receive merchandise on schedule may mean the loss of one or more sales and, possibly, the permanent loss of the customers who were disappointed.

Effective purchasing can also affect the "bottom line" directly by securing the best price for a given product or raw material. Recall this chapter's Spotlight on Small Business, which describes a small firm's success in its diligent search for a low-cost supplier.

Changing economic conditions also make purchasing and inventory management important. Such factors as shortages of materials, inflation, and high interest rates make it logical for the small business to emphasize purchasing and inventory activities.

The Purchasing Cycle

Purchasing is a process involving a number of steps as described in the following paragraphs. It is essential that all steps be followed in the proper sequence.

Receipt of a Purchase Request   A **purchase requisition** originates within the firm. It is a formal, documented request from an employee or department for something to be bought for the business. In a small business, a purchase request is not always documented. However, financial control is improved by purchasing only on the basis of purchase requests.

Location of a Source of Supply Suitable suppliers can be located through sales representatives, advertisements, trade associations, word of mouth, and company records of past supplier performance. Price quotations are obtained, and, for major purchases, bids may be solicited from a number of potential sources. The importance of good relationships with suppliers is discussed later in this chapter.

Issuance of the Purchase Order The next step in purchasing is the issuance of a **purchase order**. A standard form, such as that shown in Exhibit 19–1, should be used in all buying operations. When the signed order is accepted by a vendor (supplier), it becomes a binding contract. In the event

Exhibit 19–1 A Purchase Order

	PURCHASE ORDER THE RED WING COMPANY, INC. Fredonia, NY 14063-4925	No. 05282 SHOW THIS NUMBER ON INVOICE

June 27, 19
DATE OF ORDER

Byron Jackson & Company
4998 Michigan Avenue
Chicago, IL 60615-2218

SHIPPING INSTRUCTIONS:

Mark purchase order number
on each piece in shipment

DELIVERY REQUIRED July 24	F.O.B. Chicago	ROUTING via NYC-Buffalo	TERMS 2/10 net 30

ITEM	QUANTITY & UNIT	DESCRIPTION	PRICE & UNIT
622	35 each	Spring assembly	14.35 ea
230	200 each	Bearings	3.35 ea
272	70 each	Heavy duty relay 50V	7.50 ea
478	490 each	Screw set	.03 ea

ORIGINAL BILL OF LADING MUST ACCOMPANY ALL INVOICES FOR GOODS SHIPPED BY FREIGHT.
2% DISCOUNT FOR PAYMENT IN 10 DAYS WILL BE DEDUCTED FROM FACE OF INVOICE UNLESS OTHERWISE SPECIFIED.

INVOICE IN DUPLICATE

BY _J. Jromboski_
Purchasing Agent

of a serious violation, the written purchase order serves as the basis for adjustment.

Maintenance of Buying and Warehousing Records   Record keeping is a necessary part of the purchasing function. As an example, stores cards are maintained to show the supply of each kind of raw material, purchased part, and supply item carried in the storeroom. Other records include price quotations, outstanding orders, and vendor quality ratings.

Follow-Up of Purchase Order   The follow-up of purchase orders is necessary to assure delivery on schedule. Troublesome orders may take repeated checking to be sure materials or merchandise will be available when needed.

Receipt of Goods   The receiving clerks take physical custody of incoming materials and merchandise, check their general condition, and sign the carrier's release. Inspection follows to assure an accurate count and the proper quality and kind of items. Exhibit 19–2 shows a weekly or quarterly summary analysis of the quality of a given material.

Purchasing Policies

Purchasing policies can significantly affect the cost of purchasing, but they may be even more important for the preservation of good relationships with suppliers. Whenever possible, purchasing policies should be writ-

Figure 19–1   Verifying Receipt of Goods

Exhibit 19–2 Materials Yield Summary

Materials Yield Summary

The Iowa Manufacturing Company

Stores Item _____ Week Ending _____

Stores Item Number _____ Quarter Ending _____

Supplier	Units of Product Put in Process	Allowance per Unit of Finished Product	Total Units Allowed	Actual Units Used	Usage as % of Units Allowed
1	2	3	4=3·2	5	6=⁵⁄₄ (100) (Quotient) = %

ten. This will assure that the policies are understood and will eliminate the need for repetitive decisions.

Reciprocal Buying   Some firms try to sell to others from whom they also purchase. This policy of **reciprocal buying** is based on the premise that one company can secure additional orders by using its own purchasing requests as a bargaining weapon. Although the typical order of most small companies is not large enough to make this a potent weapon, there is a tendency for purchasers to grant some recognition to this factor. Of course, this policy would be damaging if it were allowed to obscure quality and price variations. Otherwise, there is probably little to be lost or gained from this policy.

 Making or Buying   Many firms face **make-or-buy decisions.** This choice is especially important for small manufacturing firms that have the option of making or buying component parts for the products they make. A less conspicuous make-or-buy choice occurs with respect to certain services—for example, purchasing janitorial or auto rental services instead of providing for those needs internally. Some reasons for *making* component parts, rather than buying them, are as follows:

1. Uses otherwise idle capacity, thus permitting more economical production.
2. Gives the buyer greater assurance of supply with fewer delays and interruptions caused by difficulties with suppliers.
3. Protects a secret design.
4. Reduces expenses by saving an amount equivalent to transportation costs and the supplier's selling expense and profit.
5. Permits closer coordination and control of total production operations, thus facilitating operations scheduling and control.
6. Provides higher quality products than may be available from suppliers.

Some counter arguments for *buying* are as follows:

1. May be cheaper, due to the supplier's concentration on production of the given part, which makes possible specialized facilities, added know-how, and greater efficiency.
2. Obviates possible shortage of necessary space, equipment, personnel skills, and working capital.
3. Requires less diversified managerial experience and skills.
4. Offers greater flexibility; for example, seasonal production of a given item makes its manufacture risky.
5. Frees "in-plant" operations for concentration on the firm's specialty—finished products and services.
6. Reduces the risk of equipment obsolescence by transferring this risk to outsiders.

The decision to make or buy may be expensive to reverse. It should certainly be based on long-run cost and profit optimization. The underlying cost differences need to be analyzed very carefully, since small savings in buying or making may greatly affect profit margins.

Substituting Materials or Merchandise New types of materials and merchandise are constantly being developed. Some of them may be both cheaper and better than older products. Nevertheless, the purchasing decision by a manufacturer must take into consideration not only the impact on the product and its cost but also the effect upon the process. A change in materials may alter the sequence of operations or may even cause the deletion or addition of one or more operations.

Purchasing policy should be sufficiently flexible to permit ready consideration of new or different materials or merchandise. Of course, a change must be based upon the possibility of producing or selling a better, cheaper product.

Taking Purchase Discounts One argument in favor of taking purchase discounts available is that this evidences financial strength to suppliers and tends to promote good relationships with them. Even more important is the fact that discounts provide a source of savings. If the discount is taken on terms of 2/10, n/30, the savings are equivalent to interest at the rate of 36 percent per year (under the banker's rule for interest calculation). This is such a good rate that it pays to borrow if necessary in order to take the discount.

Diversifying Sources of Supply In the purchase of a particular item, there is a question of whether it is desirable to use more than one supplier. Division of orders among several suppliers can be a form of insurance against difficulties with a sole supplier. For example, a strike or a fire might eliminate the supply for a time. Another danger is the fact that failure to "shop" may result in a loss of the lower prices, better quality, and superior service offered by other suppliers. Also, knowing that competitors are getting some of the business may cause a supplier to be more alert to providing good prices and service.

Nevertheless, the arguments on this problem do not all favor diversification of sources of supply. With centralized buying from one firm, the purchaser may acquire the right to special quantity discounts and other favorable terms of purchase. Special service, such as prompt treatment of rush orders, is more readily granted to established customers. Moreover, the single source of supply may provide financial aid to the regular customer who encounters financial stress. It will also provide management advice and market information. For some products, the total order may be too small to make it worthwhile to divide it.

Some firms follow a compromise policy by which they concentrate enough purchases to justify special treatment. At the same time, they diversify purchases sufficiently to provide alternative sources of supply.

Speculative Buying   Buying substantially in excess of quantities needed to meet actual use requirements is called speculative buying. This is done in the expectation that prices are going up. Price appreciation produces inventory profits. The great danger is that speculative buying entails gambling on the continued rise of prices. Broad price declines subsequent to heavy speculative buying could bankrupt the speculator. Unless one is very stable financially and very wise, speculative buying should be avoided. It is typically used when the business cycle is on the way up; its use during a depression would be suicidal.

Scheduled Budget Buying   Buying to meet anticipated requirements is planned buying, or scheduled budget buying. This policy involves the adjustment of purchase quantities to estimated production or sales needs. Budget buying in suitable quantities will assure the maintenance of planned inventories and the meeting of product schedule requirements without delays in production due to delayed deliveries. It strikes the middle ground between hand-to-mouth buying—with its planned understocking of materials and its occasional delays due to late deliveries—and speculative buying, with its deliberate overstocking, which entails risk as it seeks speculative profits. It represents the best type of buying for the conservative small firm.

Selection of and Relations with Suppliers

Before making a choice of suppliers, the purchaser must know the materials or merchandise to be purchased, including details of construction, quality and grade, intended use, maintenance or care required, and the importance of style features. The purchaser must also know how different grades and qualities of raw materials affect various manufacturing processes.

Selection of Suppliers   A number of considerations are relevant in deciding which suppliers to use on a continuing basis. Perhaps the most obvious of these are price and quality. Price differences are clearly significant if not offset by quality or other factors.

Quality differences are sometimes difficult to detect. For some types of materials, statistical controls can be used to evaluate shipments from specific vendors. In this way, the purchaser obtains an overall quality rating for various suppliers. In some cases, the purchaser can work with a supplier to upgrade quality. If satisfactory quality cannot be achieved, the purchaser then has a rational basis for dropping the supplier.

Location becomes an especially important factor as a firm tries to reduce inventory levels and to make possible speedy delivery of purchased items. A supplier's general reliability in supplying goods and services is also significant. For example, can the purchaser depend upon the supplier to meet delivery schedules or to respond promptly to emergency situations?

Services provided by the supplier must also be considered. The extension of credit by suppliers provides a major portion of the working-capital requirements of many small firms. Some suppliers provide merchandising aids, plan sales promotions, and furnish management advice. In times of recession, some small retailers have even received direct financial assistance from major suppliers of long standing. Another useful service for some types of products is the provision of repair work by the supplier. A small industrial firm, for example, may select a vendor for a truck or diesel engine on the basis of the vendor's service department.

Importance of Good Relations with Suppliers   Good relations with suppliers are essential for firms of any size, but they are particularly important to small businesses. Perhaps the cornerstone of good supplier relationships is the buyer's realization that the supplier is usually more important to the buyer than the buyer (as a customer) is to the supplier. The buyer is only one among dozens, hundreds, or perhaps thousands buying from that supplier. Moreover, the buyer's volume of purchases over a year and the size of the individual orders are often so small that the business could be eliminated without great loss to the supplier.

To implement the policy of fair play and to cultivate good relations, the small buying firm should try to observe the following practices:

1. Pay all bills promptly.
2. See all sales representatives promptly, according them a full, courteous hearing.
3. Do not summarily cancel orders merely to gain a temporary advantage.
4. Do not argue over prices, attempting to browbeat the supplier into special concessions and unusual discounts.

5. Cooperate with the supplier by making suggestions for product improvement and/or cost reduction whenever possible.

6. Give courteous, reasonable explanations when rejecting bids, and make fair adjustments in case of disputes.

Small buyers must remember that it takes a long time to build good relationships with a supplier but that good relations can be destroyed by one ill-timed, tactless act.

Inventory Control

Inventory control is not glamorous, but it can make the difference between success and failure. The larger the inventory investment, the more vital is its proper use and control. The importance of inventory control, particularly in small retail or wholesale firms, is attested to by the fact that inventory typically represents these firms' major dollar investments.

Objectives of Inventory Control

Both purchasing and inventory control have the same general objective: to have the right goods in the right quantities at the right time and place. This general objective requires other, more specific subgoals of inventory control.

Assured Continuous Operations Efficient manufacturing requires work-in-process to be moved on schedule. A delay caused by lack of materials or parts can cause the shutdown of a production line, a department, or even the whole plant. Such interruptions of scheduled operations is both serious and costly. Costs jump when skilled workers and machines stand idle. Given a long delay, the fulfillment of delivery promises to customers may become impossible.

Maximum Sales Assuming adequate demand, sales are greater if goods are always available for display and/or delivery to the customer. Most customers want to choose from an assortment of merchandise. Customers who are forced by a narrow range of choice and/or stockouts to look elsewhere may be lost permanently. On the other hand, the small store might unwisely go to the other extreme and carry too large an inventory. Management must walk the chalk line, so to speak, between overstocking and understocking in order to retain customers and maximize sales.

Protection of Assets   One of the essential functions of inventory control is to protect inventories against theft, shrinkage, or deterioration. The efficiency or wastefulness of storekeeping, manufacturing, and handling processes affects the quantity and quality of usable inventory. For example, the more often an article is picked up and handled, the more chance there is for physical damage. Inventory items that need special treatment can also spoil or deteriorate if improperly stored.

Minimum Inventory Investment   Effective inventory control permits inventories to be smaller without causing disservice to customers or to processing. This means that the inventory investment is less. It also means lower costs for storage space, taxes, and insurance. And inventory deterioration or obsolescence is less extensive as well.

Administrative Uses of Inventory Records   The inventory records provide data useful for various administrative uses. For example, the records provide information for determining proper purchase quantities and ordering dates. They also provide information useful for evaluating managerial performance. The inventory turnover ratio, which is explained in Chapter 20, is an important tool in such an evaluation. It is a measure of how quickly inventory is sold or placed in production. Too high a turnover as well as too low a turnover can be inefficient.

Controlling Inventory Costs

It is easy to understand how effective control of inventory contributes to the "bottom line," that is, to the profitability of a firm. It is more difficult, however, to understand how to make effective inventory decisions that will minimize costs.

Types of Inventory-Related Costs   Minimizing inventory costs requires attention to many different types of costs. Order costs include the preparation of a purchase order, follow-up, and related bookkeeping expenses. Quantity discounts must also be included in such calculations. Inventory-carrying costs include interest costs on money tied up in inventory, insurance, storage, obsolescence, and pilferage costs. These are costs of carrying items in inventory. There is also a cost of not having items in inventory, or stockouts, because of lost sales or disrupted production resulting from the stockouts. Although stockout costs cannot be calculated as easily as other inventory costs, they are nonetheless real.

ABC Inventory Analysis   Some inventory items are more valuable than others, and, therefore, more crucial in their effect on costs and profits. For this reason, managers should give most careful attention to those items entailing the largest investment.

One widely used approach, the **ABC method,** classifies inventory items into three categories—A, B, and C. The few high-value items in the A category account for the largest percentage of total dollars and deserve very close control. Category B items are less costly but deserve a moderate amount of attention because they make up a larger share of the total inventory. Items in category C contain low-cost items such as paper clips in an office or nuts and bolts in a repair shop. Their carrying costs are not large enough to justify close control.

The purpose of the ABC method is to focus managerial attention where it will do the most good. There is nothing sacred, of course, about the three classes. Four classes could be created if that seemed more appropriate.

Reorder Point and Safety Stock   In maintaining inventory levels, a manager must decide the point at which additional quantities will be ordered. Calculating the **reorder point** requires consideration of the time necessary to obtain a new supply, which, in turn, depends on location of suppliers, transportation schedules, and so on.

Because of difficulty in getting new inventory at the exact time it is desired and because of irregularities in withdrawals from inventory, firms also typically maintain a **safety stock**. The safety stock provides a measure of protection against stockouts caused by emergencies of one type or another.

The **two-bin method** is a simple technique for implementing these concepts. Inventories are divided into two portions or two bins. When the first bin is exhausted, an order is placed to replenish the supply. The remaining portion should cover needs until a new supply arrives, and it includes a safety stock as well.

Kanban Inventory   Reducing inventory levels has been a goal of operations managers around the world. A Japanese concept, known as the **Kanban system**, or "just-in-time" inventory, enables them to minimize inventory carrying costs by cutting inventory to the bare minimum. New inventory is received, presumably, just as the last item from the existing inventory is placed into service. This, in turn, contributes to the lower costs in production of autos and other products in Japan. Many U.S. firms have adopted some form of the Kanban system, and small business can likewise benefit from its use.

SMALL BUSINESS IN ACTION
The Impact of Kanban on Small Distributors

As large manufacturing firms have adopted just-in-time production and inventory systems, they have forced changes on the more than 300,000 distributors in the United States. Most distributors are small businesses with less than $5 million in sales and fewer than 30 employees. Under the just-in-time or Kanban system, distributors must work closely with manufacturers to help them meet their inventory needs.

As an example, Continental Glass and Plastic, Inc., is a Chicago distributor supplying containers to Walgreen Laboratories to package health and beauty aids for the drugstore chain. When Walgreen decided to reduce inventory levels by one-third, it gave suppliers a choice of participating in a modified just-in-time delivery program or discontinuing the relationship. Continental chose to stay and now works closely with Walgreen, projecting container needs six months in advance and locking in delivery dates four weeks prior to delivery. In this case, the manufacturer has reduced its inventory by shifting a part of it to the small distributor.

Source: Steven P. Galante, "Distributors Bow to Demands of 'Just-in-Time' Delivery," *The Wall Street Journal* (June 30, 1986), p. 23. Reprinted by permission of *The Wall Street Journal,* © Dow Jones & Company, Inc. 1986. All Rights Reserved Worldwide.

By keeping inventory at such low levels, a firm minimizes inventory costs. Careful coordination of operations is required, however, to avoid costly stockouts—for example, a mistake leading to the shutdown of a production line. If the inventory is held too low, the firm will suffer in loss of sales or production.

Economic Order Quantity If a firm could order inventory with no expense other than the cost of the merchandise or material, it would be less concerned about the amount to order at one time. However, high carrying costs associated with large orders tend to offset the lower order costs.

The goal is to purchase that quantity which minimizes the total costs of ordering and carrying the inventory. Exhibit 19–3 portrays the behavior of these costs. The total-costs curve is simply the sum of the carrying and order costs at the various quantity levels.

The **economic order quantity** is the quantity to be purchased that minimizes total costs, and it is the point labeled "EOQ" in Exhibit 19–3. Notice that it is the lowest point on the total-costs curve and that it coincides with

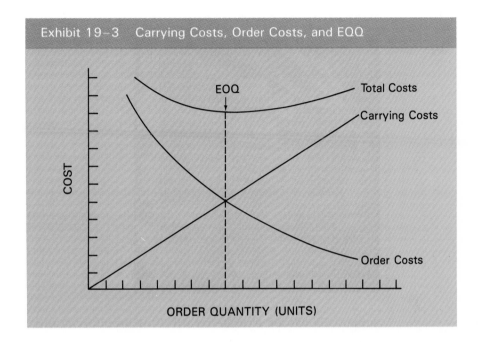

Exhibit 19-3   Carrying Costs, Order Costs, and EOQ

the intersection of the carrying-costs and order-costs curves. In rare cases, where sufficient information on costs is available, this point can be calculated with some precision.[1] In all cases, even when the economic order quantity cannot be calculated with precision, the goal is still to avoid both high ordering costs and high carrying costs.

Inventory Accounting Systems

A small business needs a system for keeping tabs on its inventory. The larger the business, the greater is the need. Also, since manufacturers are concerned with three broad categories of inventory (raw materials and supplies, work-in-process, and finished goods), their accounting for inventory is more complex than that for wholesalers and retailers.

Although some record keeping is unavoidable, small firms should emphasize simplicity of control methods. Too much control is as wasteful as it is unnecessary.

Physical Inventory Method   A **physical inventory system** involves an actual count of inventory items. Counting is done in natural physical units such as pieces, gallons, boxes, and so on. By using this method, the firm

Figure 19–2 Taking a Physical Inventory

Courtesy of Bergen Brunswig Corp., Orange, CA

supposedly has an accurate record of its inventory at one point in time. Some businesses have an annual shutdown to count everything—a complete physical inventory.

In some businesses, the process of taking a physical inventory has been simplified by using computers and bar-code systems. Bar codes are the printed patterns of lines, spaces, and numerals that appear on packaged products. The codes can be read with a hand-held wand that transmits data to a computer.

An example of its use for inventory purposes is found in the experience of a metal fabricating firm. Before bar coding was instituted at Tate Andale, a Baltimore-based metal-fabricating firm, recording inventory each year "required 24 people working two days," says Milt Thacker, the company's data-processing manager. "Then it would take 30 to 40 hours in the office to key in the data. With hand-held bar-code scanners, it takes four people eight hours in the warehouse, and manual data entry is eliminated. Not only do we save a tremendous amount of time, but the accuracy of our data is way up."[2]

Perpetual Inventory Method A **perpetual inventory system** provides a current record of inventory items. It does not require a physical count of inventory. Periodically, a physical count can be made to assure the accuracy of the perpetual system and to make adjustments for such factors as theft. The stores card illustrated in Exhibit 19–4 is the basic control tool in a perpetual inventory system covering raw materials and supplies.

With a separate perpetual inventory card for each raw material or supply item, the firm will always know the number of units on hand. If each receipt and issue is costed, the dollar value of these units is also known.

Use of a perpetual inventory system may be justified in the small factory or the wholesale warehouse. In particular, this is desirable for expensive and critical items—for example, those which could cause significant losses through theft or serious production delays.

Perpetual inventory control can also be used for finished goods, but

---

Exhibit 19–4   A Stores Card

STORES CARD

SHAFER SHOE COMPANY

Item: Metal Eyelets

		Maximum No. of Pairs	60,000
		Reorder Point No. of Pairs	24,000
		Minimum No. of Pairs	12,000

	Receipts			Issue			Balance on Hand		
Date	Pairs	Price per Pair	Cost	Pairs	Price per Pair	Cost	Pairs	Price per Pair	Cost*
Jan. 1							14,000	$.00400	$ 56.00
2				2,500	$.00400	$10.00	11,500	.00400	46.00
3	48,000	$.00420	$201.60				59,500	.004 16	247.60
3				2,000	.004 16	8.32	57,500	.004 16	239.28
4				2,100	.004 16	8.74	55,400	.004 16	230.54
7				2,000	.004 16	8.32	53,400	.004 16	222.22

*Minor discrepancies in this column are due to 5-place rounding in the preceding column. The stores card is used by routing and planning clerks to assure an adequate supply of materials and parts to complete any given factory order.

Exhibit 19–5 April Data

Sales	$75,000
Added markups	.6,000
Markdowns	.2,500
Markdown cancellations	.1,800
Purchases.	45,000 at cost ($81,000 at retail)
Freight in	.500
Starting inventory	.1,000 at cost ($1,800 at retail)

the cards used in this case are known as stock cards rather than stores cards. Techniques for the use of stock cards are the same as for stores cards.

Retail Inventory Valuation

Retailers can value their inventories at cost or at retail. The **retail inventory valuation method** requires that starting inventory and purchases be recorded at both cost and retail; sales, net markdowns, and net added markups are to be entered at retail only.[3]

Retail Inventory Valuation Procedure The procedure may be illustrated with the data shown in Exhibit 19–5 from a small department store recorded for the month of April.

To find the retail value of ending inventory for this department store,

Exhibit 19–6 Retail Value

	Cost		Retail
Starting inventory	$ 1,000		$ 1,800
Purchases.	45,000		81,000
Freight in	500		
Net added markups			6,000
Goods available for sale	$46,500		$88,800
Sales		$75,000	
Net markdowns		700	75,700
Ending inventory (retail value). . . .			$13,100

first tabulate the data so that starting inventory, purchases, freight in, and net added markups can be totaled to provide cost and retail values of goods available for sale during April. Then deduct the total of sales and net markdowns, which are separately recorded at retail, from the total retail value of starting inventory, purchases, and net added markups.

The resulting tabulation is shown in Exhibit 19–6 with $13,100 as the retail value of ending inventory.

For balance-sheet purposes, the cost value of ending inventory is needed. This unknown amount in dollars, symbolized by X, can be calculated algebraically as follows:

$$\frac{\text{Ending Inventory (Cost)}}{\text{Ending Inventory (Retail)}} = \frac{\text{Goods Available for Sale (Cost)}}{\text{Goods Available for Sale (Retail)}}$$

$$\frac{X}{\$13,100} = \frac{\$46,500}{\$88,800}$$

$$\$88,800X = \$609,150,000$$

$$X = \frac{\$609,150,000}{\$88,800} = \$6,859.80$$

The balance sheet of this department store would show the merchandise inventory at $6,860 (rounded to the closest dollar), which is its value stated in cost dollars.

Primary Use of the Retail Inventory Valuation Method   The retail inventory valuation method was developed primarily for department stores as a basis for dollar control of merchandise stocks involving a wide variety of items in a number of departments. Such inventory conditions, together with a high volume of sales, preclude the use of perpetual inventory cards for each item and also make the use of physical inventory methods arduous and unsatisfactory for control. But the retail inventory valuation method does not contribute to unit control.

Advantages of the Retail Valuation Method   The retail inventory valuation method is approved for income tax reporting. It facilitates the preparation of monthly financial statements, which would be too expensive if physical inventories were required as their basis. Moreover, this method gives a more conservative balance-sheet evaluation than historical cost data would provide because it relates the inventory values to current sales prices.

Hence, the retail inventory valuation method gives valuations equivalent to the lower of cost or market value.

Weaknesses of the Retail Inventory Valuation Method   The retail inventory valuation method has the following weaknesses:

1. Being based on averages and applied on a department-wide or class-of-merchandise basis, this method tends to overvalue certain merchandise items and undervalue others. That is, the inventory value on the balance sheet shows a cost value for total inventory that assumes that all inventory items have the same relation between cost and sales price. This is frequently untrue.

   The retailer ordinarily finds it desirable or necessary to sell merchandise with different gross margins. To the extent that sales are not proportional among the merchandise groups carrying different gross margins, the inventory value computed by the retail inventory valuation method may be distorted. That is, separate inventories, using this method, are required for each "gross margin" class for accuracy.

2. Given very frequent markups and markdowns, the record keeping for the retail inventory valuation method becomes arduous and costly. This is particularly true if separate "gross margin class" inventories are maintained individually under this method.

3. The system also ignores stock shortages and employee discounts and suffers disadvantages in the proper handling of trade-ins and customer discounts. Of course, physical inventory, used along with this method, helps reveal the "ignored" stock shortages.

The retail inventory valuation method may be an effective system, and it is certainly a unified, integrated system of inventory control in a retail store. Nevertheless, its disadvantages may sometimes outweigh its advantages. Hence, the small retailer should consider carefully both its strengths and its limitations before reaching a decision on its use.

Looking Back

1. The purchasing cycle includes the receipt and evaluation of a purchase request, location of a source of supply, issuance of the

purchase order, maintenance of buying and warehousing records, follow-up of purchases, and receipt and inspection of purchased items.

2. Policies related to purchasing include reciprocal buying, making or buying parts, substituting materials or merchandise, taking purchase discounts, diversifying sources of supply, speculative buying, and scheduled budget buying.

3. Choice of a supplier entails considerations of the supplier's price, quality rating, ability to meet delivery schedules, quality of service, and general reputation. Good relations with suppliers are particularly valuable to small firms.

4. The objectives of inventory control include assured continuous operations, maximum sales, protection of assets, minimum inventory investment, and administrative uses of inventory records.

5. Maintaining inventory involves a variety of costs, including order costs, carrying costs, and stockout costs. The minimum amount that can be carried depends on the time required to replenish the supply and on the necessary safety stock. Carrying costs are minimized by holding inventory to a minimum, the objective of the Kanban system. Total costs are minimized by calculating the economic order quantity, the purchase amount that most economically balances large-order costs and small-order costs.

6. A physical inventory system consists of taking an actual count of items on hand and recording the information. A perpetual inventory system does not require an actual count but provides a current record by recording additions and withdrawals on inventory cards. In retail businesses, the value of inventories may be calculated by using data on beginning inventory, purchases, sales, markups, markdowns, and the ratio of cost to retail prices.

DISCUSSION QUESTIONS

1. Suppose that you, as purchasing agent for a small firm, have read the story about Barry Schacht's purchasing experience in this chapter's Spotlight on Small Business and that you have vowed to find similar savings for your business. Would you shop for the best price on all purchases? How would you decide which ones to shop for most aggressively? Explain.

2. What conditions make purchasing a particularly vital function in any given business? If it is important, can the owner–manager of a small firm safely delegate the authority to buy to a subordinate? Explain.

3. Of what value are purchasing records to a small firm?

4. Under what conditions should the small manufacturer make component parts or buy them from others?

5. Compare the arguments for and against concentrating purchases with only one or two suppliers.

6. Compare the potential rewards and dangers of speculative buying. Is it more dangerous for a small firm or a large firm? Why?

7. State the factors governing a small manufacturer's selection of a supplier of a vitally important raw material.

8. In what ways is location a significant factor in the choice of suppliers? Is the closest supplier normally the best choice?

9. Does the maximization of inventory turnover also result in the maximization of sales? Explain.

10. Suppose that a small firm has excess warehouse space. What types of inventory-carrying costs would apply to an inventory decision? How would such costs differ for a firm that does not have excessive storage space?

11. Explain and justify the use of the ABC method of inventory analysis. How would it work in an automobile repair shop?

12. What is Kanban, or just-in-time, inventory? What are the advantages and dangers of using it in a small firm?

13. Inventory systems are sometimes described as "push" systems or "pull" systems. In which category does Kanban belong? Explain.

14. Explain the basic idea involved in calculating the economic order quantity.

15. Explain the retail inventory valuation method as it would be applied in a small department store.

YOU MAKE THE CALL

Situation 1

In a very general sense, a temporary-help employment agency maintains an inventory of service in the form of personnel awaiting assignment. Excel, a temporary-help agency, found that its inventory tended to disappear early each day. If assignments were not readily available, its "temps" would accept offers from other temporary-help agencies.

Excel wanted to have personnel available the moment they were requested by an employer. Much of the time, calls came early the same day that help was desired. The firm faced a dilemma in trying to match this unpredictable demand with its own inventory of temps. If an employer's request came at 10:00 A.M., for example, Excel often found that its best "temps" had already accepted assignments through other agencies. If Excel were to guarantee work, on the other hand, there was a probability that costs would be incurred for unused personnel on days when demand failed to materialize.

Questions

1. How does Excel's present system compare with a Kanban system?
2. Can the firm solve its problem by smoothing out demand in some way? How?
3. Should temps be guaranteed work? How could this be arranged?
4. If you were a consultant for this firm, how would you recommend they solve this problem?

Situation 2

The owner of a small food products company was confronted with an inventory control dilemma involving differences of opinion among his subordinates. His accountant, with the concurrence of his general manager, had decided to "put some teeth" into the inventory control system by deducting inventory shortages from the pay of route drivers who distributed the products to stores in their respective territories. Each driver was considered responsible for the inventory on his or her truck.

When the first "short" paychecks arrived, drivers were angry. Sharing their concern, their regional manager went first to the general manager and, getting no satisfaction there, appealed to the owner. The regional manager—immediate supervisor of the drivers—argued that (a) there was no question that the drivers were honest; (b) he had personally created the inventory control system that was being used; (c) the system was admittedly time-consuming, difficult, and susceptible to clerical mistakes by the driver and also by the office; (d) the system had never been studied by the general manager or the accountant; and (e) it was ethically wrong to make deductions from the small salaries of honest drivers for simple record-keeping errors.

Questions

1. What is wrong, if anything, with the general manager's approach to making sure that drivers do not steal or act carelessly? Is some method of enforcement necessary to be sure the system is followed carefully?

2. Is it wrong to deduct shortages from drivers' paychecks when the records actually show the shortages?

3. How should the owner resolve this dispute?

EXPERIENTIAL EXERCISES

1. Interview an owner-manager regarding purchasing procedures used in his or her business. In your report, compare these procedures with the steps in the purchasing cycle outlined in this chapter.

2. Outline carefully the steps involved in an important purchase you have made personally—a purchase of more than $100, if possible. Compare those steps with the steps identified in this chapter as part of the purchasing cycle, and explain any differences.

3. Using the ABC inventory system, classify you own personal possessions into these categories. Include at least two items in each category.

4. Interview the manager of your college book store (or some other book store) regarding the type of inventory control system being used. In your report, include an explanation of methods used to avoid buildup of excessive inventory and any use made of inventory turnover ratios.

REFERENCES TO SMALL-BUSINESS PRACTICES

Bodenstab, Charles J. "Surprise! Surprise!" *Inc.*, Vol. 10, No. 9 (September, 1988), p. 135.

> The chief executive officer of Battery and Tire Warehouse, St. Paul, MN, describes the "glitches" in the firm's inventory-control system and efforts over a four-year period to make the system more effective.

"President and Chief Operating Officer." *Inc.*, Vol. 10, No. 12 (December, 1988), pp. 120–121.

> When Frederick E. Zucker became president and chief operating officer of Adept, San Jose, CA, he found that inventory had gotten out of hand and that inventory turnover was much lower than the turnover rate in other companies. His efforts to bring inventory under control are described.

Slutsker, Gary. "When Quick Success Is a Mixed Blessing." *Venture*, Vol. 2, No. 10 (October, 1980), pp. 67–69.

> The importance of an inventory control system is demonstrated by the experi-

ences of a small photographic service. The system keeps track of rolls of film while they are being processed by different labs.

Strugatch, Warren. "Counting Your Chickens." *Venture*, Vol. 10, No. 7 (July, 1988), p. 88.

This article explains the inventory-control problems of a small but growing clothing manufacturer and includes recommendations of consultants for solving the problems.

Waters, Craig R. "Profit and Loss." *Inc.*, Vol. 7, No. 4 (April, 1985), pp. 103–112.

A Virginia company, Xaloy, Inc., made substantial savings by shifting to a "just-in-time" inventory system. Problems in operations management were experienced as some personnel found it difficult to adapt to the new system.

ENDNOTES

1. See an operations management text for formulas and calculations related to the economic order quantity. One example is James B. Dilworth, *Production and Operations Management* (New York: Random House, 1989), Chapter 6.

2. Leila Davis, "Wider Uses for Bar Codes," *Nation's Business*, Vol. 77, No. 3 (March, 1989), p. 34.

3. Initial markup is the excess of initial sales prices over the purchase cost of the goods and the pertinent transportation cost. Added markups are increases in selling price above initially marked prices. These may later be canceled, in part, in which case the difference is the net added markup. Markdowns are reductions below original sales prices. These may be subsequently canceled, in part, in which case the difference is the net markdown.

FINANCIAL AND ADMINISTRATIVE CONTROLS

20 ACCOUNTING SYSTEMS AND TAX ISSUES

Spotlight on Small Business

© Bob Mahoney 1989

Accounting requirements can place a tremendous burden on a small firm. The load is particularly heavy when the small business is inadequately staffed for the accounting function. Frequently, small firms find relief by using outside accounting services.

Thomas Golisano has developed a service to assist these small firms with one specific function—payroll accounting. His company, Paychex, Inc., based in Rochester, NY, has been extremely successful and was ranked 69th on *Forbes* magazine's recent 200 Best Small Companies in America list. When Golisano started Paychex in 1971, he "just wanted to get 300 payrolls in Rochester and live happily ever after." Currently, Paychex has over 100,000 clients!

Paychex has received strong competition in the accounting service market, but Golisano believes there will continue to be strong demand. He estimates that 80 percent of small businesses still prepare their own payrolls.

Source: Fleming Meeks, "Tom Golisano and the Red Tape Factory." Adapted by permission of *Forbes* magazine, May 15, 1989. © Forbes Inc., 1989.

Looking Ahead

Watch for the following important topics:
1. Considerations in establishing an accounting system.
2. Alternative accounting methods and typical accounting statements.
3. Ratio analysis of accounting statements.
4. Budgeting in small firms.
5. Tax issues in small business.
6. New terms and concepts:

cash method of accounting	profit margin on sales
accrual method of accounting	return on total assets (asset earning power)
single-entry system	
double-entry system	return on net worth (return on equity)
FIFO	
LIFO	debt-to-total-assets ratio
income statement	times-interest-earned ratio
balance sheet	operating budget
statement of cash flow	actual expenses
current ratio	imputed expenses
acid-test (quick) ratio	fixed expenses
inventory turnover ratio	variable expenses
average collection period	functional expenses
fixed-asset turnover	tax credit

A well-designed accounting system provides valuable information for planning, controlling, and evaluating the performance of a small business. Outwardly, a business may appear sound, but actually it may be in poor health. Accounting information is the firm's X-ray; it allows the entrepreneur to monitor the "medical condition" of the business. Accounting statements, financial ratios, and budgets are important aspects of a complete accounting system.We will examine each of these in this chapter.

Tax laws are technical and complex, but they directly affect the operation and profitability of small firms. Therefore, we will also examine selected tax issues in this chapter.

Accounting Activities in Small Firms

Very few small-business managers can expect to be expert accountants. But every entrepreneur should know enough about the accounting process, including the financial statements, to recognize which of the optional accounting methods will work to the advantage of the business.

Basic Requirements for Accounting Systems

An accounting system structures the flow of financial information from the initial transaction to the points necessary to develop a financial picture of business activity. Exactly where these points are depends on the firm and its financial reporting goals. Some very small firms may not even require formal financial statements. Others may need financial statements monthly and want them to be computer-generated.

Fulfillment of Objectives of Accounting Systems Regardless of the level of sophistication, any accounting system should accomplish the following objectives for a small business:

1. The system should yield an accurate, thorough picture of operating results.
2. The records should permit a quick comparison of current data with prior years' operating results and with budgetary goals.
3. The records should provide financial statements for use by management, bankers, and prospective creditors.
4. The system should facilitate prompt filing of reports and tax returns to regulatory and tax-collecting agencies of the government.
5. The system should reveal employee fraud, theft, waste, and record-keeping errors.

Consistency with Accepted Principles of Accounting   An accounting system must be consistent with accepted principles of accounting theory and practice. This means that a business must be consistent in its treatment of given data and given transactions. Since an accounting system is seldom designed well by the amateur, the services of a certified public accountant ordinarily are required for this purpose.[1]

Larger accounting firms are now paying closer attention to the accounting needs of small businesses. The fees charged by these national accounting firms are usually higher than the accountant down the street, but discounts are available. Obviously, fees are an important consideration in selecting an accountant, but there are other major factors in this decision.

Availability and Quality of Accounting Records   An accounting system provides the framework for managerial control of the firm. The effectiveness of the system rests basically on a well-designed and managed record-keeping system. The major types of accounting records and the financial decisions to which they are related are briefly described in the following list:

1. *Accounts-receivable records.* Records of receivables are vital not only to decisions on credit extension but also to accurate billing and to maintenance of good customer relations. An analysis of these records reveals the degree of effectiveness of the firm's credit and collection policies.
2. *Accounts-payable records.* Records of liabilities show what the firm owes, facilitate the taking of cash discounts, and allow payments to be made when due.
3. *Inventory records.* Adequate records are essential to the control and security of inventory items. In addition, they supply information for use in purchasing, maintenance of adequate stock levels, and computation of turnover ratios.
4. *Payroll records.* The payroll records show the total payments to employees and provide the base for computing and paying the various payroll taxes.
5. *Cash records.* Carefully maintained records showing all receipts and disbursements are necessary to safeguard cash. They yield a knowledge of cash flow and balances on hand.
6. *Other records.* Among other accounting records that are vital to the efficient operation of the small business are the insurance register, which shows all policies in force; records of leaseholds;

and records covering the firm's investments outside of its business.

To safeguard business assets and prevent errors, the accounting records should be accurately maintained, transaction by transaction. No one employee should completely control any given business transaction. For example, cashiering and account collections should be divorced from bookkeeping, and the bookkeeper should never be allowed to authorize purchases.

In addition, data analyses and reports should ordinarily depend upon the efforts of at least two persons. Of course, in a small business using cash registers, the cash register tape provides a double check on cash received by the cashier. Such procedures tend to prevent fraud and errors.

Computer software packages are now available that can be used on the small firm's own personal computer. Most of the simpler software routines fall into one of three categories:

1. Those that function as a computerized checkbook, automatically calculating the balance and printing checks.
2. Those that provide a budget and compare actual expenditures with budget expenditures.
3. Those that prepare income statements and balance sheets.[2]

Additionally, there are numerous software packages for specialized accounting needs such as graphs, cash-flow analysis, and tax preparation.

As an alternative to account keeping by an employee or a member of the owner's family, a firm may have its financial records kept by a certified public accountant or by a bookkeeping or computer service agency that caters to small businesses. Very small businesses often find it convenient to have the same firm keep the books and prepare the financial statements and tax returns. Numerous small accounting firms offer a complete accounting service to small businesses.

Mobile bookkeepers are a new type of accounting service firm that serves small firms in some areas. They bring a mobile office, including computer equipment, to the premises of the small firm, where they obtain the necessary data and prepare the financial statements. Mobile bookkeeping thereby provides some firms with a fast, cheap, and convenient approach to obtaining certain accounting services. "We go after the small companies because they usually can't afford in-house accountants," says Jack Dunn, chairman of Kansas City-based Debit One, one such firm.[3]

When a small firm's accounting system is designed by an outside consultant, it is important that certain issues be considered. Exhibit 20–1 depicts these issues in a tree-diagram format. The branches of the tree lead to appropriate design options. Notice that the four design issues are (1) the amount of time the client's firm has available to devote to accounting, (2) the client's accounting knowledge, (3) the client's form of business organization, and (4) the size of the client's firm.

Retention of Accounting Records   The life of an accounting record is not necessarily long. Nevertheless, some firms habitually keep all records without considering the future need for them. If a business is quite small and the records can be housed in just a few filing cabinets, the problem is not serious. For most firms, however, there are two weaknesses in such a policy. First, the excess storage equipment and the unnecessary handling of records are wasteful. Second, loading the files with unnecessary material makes it difficult and time-consuming to locate important information when it is needed.

Essential records, including those legally required for possible government audit, must be maintained as long as the actual need exists. The records may have to be kept for three, five, or ten years—or even longer. Nevertheless, every firm should study its needs and retain essential records only for the requisite time periods.

Once retention needs have been determined, the additional problem of reducing the cost of maintaining records should be resolved. The increased usage of personal computers for small-business accounting has helped with the problem of record retention. The floppy disks used by these computers file large amounts of data in a small physical space. These floppy disks are easy to handle and easy to store. Copies of data disks should always be retained, preferably in another location, for backup purposes. Chapter 22 of this textbook discusses these small computer systems.

Alternative Accounting Options

Accounting records can be kept in just about any form as long as they provide users with the data needed and are legally proper. This implies that the small business has certain options in selecting accounting systems and accounting methods. And this is usually the case. Most entrepreneurs want to minimize the time and effort devoted to developing and managing their firms' accounting systems. However, they should take the necessary time

Exhibit 20-1 Accounting System Design Decision Model

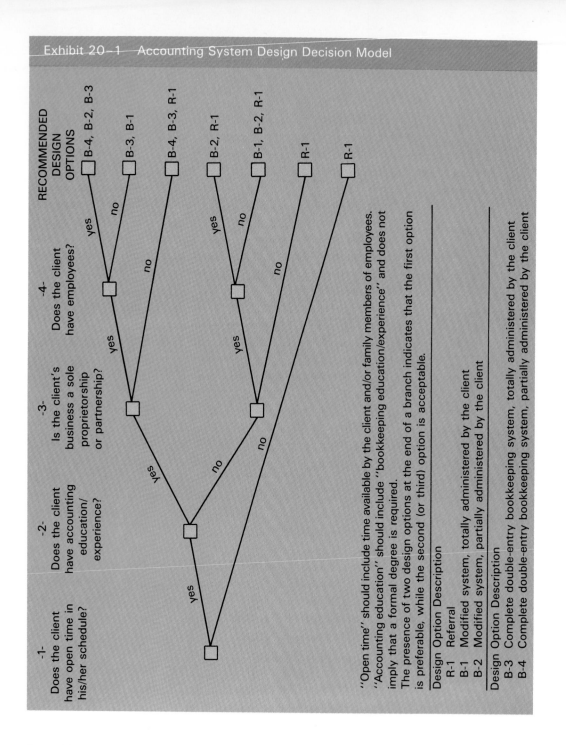

"Open time" should include time available by the client and/or family members of employees. "Accounting education" should include "bookkeeping education/experience" and does not imply that a formal degree is required.

The presence of two design options at the end of a branch indicates that the first option is preferable, while the second (or third) option is acceptable.

Design Option Description
R-1   Referral
B-1   Modified system, totally administered by the client
B-2   Modified system, partially administered by the client

Design Option Description
B-3   Complete double-entry bookkeeping system, totally administered by the client
B-4   Complete double-entry bookkeeping system, partially administered by the client

Source: Olen L. Greer, "A Decision-Tree Approach to the Design and Implementation of Accounting and Information Systems for Small Business," *Journal of Small Business Management,* Vol. 27, No. 1 (January, 1989), p. 11.

to become aware of current accounting issues and alternative accounting practices.

Three accounting options—cash versus accrual accounting, single-entry versus double-entry systems, and LIFO versus FIFO inventory valuation—are examined in the following sections. These three represent only a few of several alternative accounting methods available to the small business.

It is important to note that the accounting options chosen for financial reporting are not always required to be the same as those used for tax accounting. This fact is emphasized by the Small Business in Action entitled "Two Sets of Books?"

SMALL BUSINESS IN ACTION
Two Sets of Books?

Small-business owners logically use accounting practices that are legal and that minimize tax liabilities. However, good tax strategy is not automatically good business strategy.

David A. Towneson, a small-business accounting specialist in Wakefield, MA, feels that many of his clients want to deduct too many expenses against revenue when sometimes capitalization is a wiser alternative. "Small startup companies would be wiser to capitalize such costs . . . this boosts reported income, [but] it boosts their asset base, permitting them to borrow more and sell their concern for more."

Towneson recounts the circumstances of one client company that exemplifies his point. This company

> . . . lost a chance for $1 million contract because it had used accelerated depreciation for its equipment. Using straight-line depreciation, the equipment would have been valued on the books at $525,000, or enough to collateralize a $420,000 loan from a bank. But after accelerated depreciation, the books only showed the equipment at $300,000, so the bank would supply only a $240,000 loan. The company needed $400,000 to gear up for the new order. It lost the sale.

Small-business owners should remember that it is acceptable to use different accounting methods for financial reporting and tax reporting. Regarding keeping two sets of books, Mr. Towneson says, "It's well worth it."

Source: Lee Berton, "Dos and Don'ts," *The Wall Street Journal,* (June10, 1988), p. 41R. Reprinted by permission of *The Wall Street Journal,* © Dow Jones & Company, Inc. 1988. All Rights Reserved Worldwide.

Cash vs. Accrual Accounting   The major distinction between cash and accrual accounting is the point at which a firm "recognizes" revenue and expenses. The **cash method of accounting** is easier to use and reports revenue and expenses only when cash is received or payment is made. Under the **accrual method of accounting**, revenue and expenses are reported when they are incurred regardless of when the cash is received or payment is made.

The cash method of accounting is generally selected by the very small business, as well as those businesses whose receivables move slowly and who want to help their cash flow by avoiding the payment of taxes on income not yet received. However, the cash method does not provide an accurate matching of revenue and expenses.

On the other hand, the accrual method of accounting matches revenues when they are earned against the expenses associated with those revenues. The accrual method involves more record keeping but also provides a more realistic measure of profitability within an accounting period.

Single-Entry vs. Double-Entry Systems   The system of accounts that records financial transactions does not have to be identical in every business. The informational needs of the users will ultimately determine the number and complexity of the accounts in the system. In the very small business, a single-entry record-keeping system is still found. It is not, however, a system to be recommended to businesses that are striving to grow and become efficient in financial planning.

A single-entry system neither incorporates a balance sheet nor directly generates an income statement. A **single-entry system** is basically a checkbook system of receipts and disbursements supported by sales tickets and disbursement receipts. The sales and disbursements may be summarized daily and monthly in separate reports, but the checkbook is the focal point of the single entry of a transaction.

A **double-entry system** of accounting incorporates journals and ledgers and requires that each transaction be recorded twice in the accounts—hence the name double-entry. There are two major advantages of the double-entry system. First, it has a built-in, self-balancing characteristic. If no math errors have been made, the debits recorded will always equal the credits recorded. Second, transactions are recorded in such a way as to provide a natural flow into finished financial statements.

Introductory accounting textbooks provide considerable information on setting up a double-entry system.[4] Office supply retail stores can provide most of the actual recordkeeping journals and ledgers needed. A number of special-purpose forms are available that facilitate manual record keeping. For example, there is a One-Write System, which uses preprinted forms so that, when a payroll check is written, the entry is simultaneously entered on the payroll ledger.

FIFO vs. LIFO Inventory Valuation   Another accounting option concerns the selection of LIFO (Last-in-First-Out) or FIFO (First-in-First-Out) inventory valuation. Both FIFO and LIFO are alternatives for reporting the product cost associated with the actual product sold. **FIFO** assumes that the first product in inventory is the first product out of inventory. **LIFO** allows the most recent cost of a product placed in inventory to be charged against revenue regardless of whether that most recent unit was actually sold and delivered to a customer.

During periods of inflation, LIFO appears to be the clear choice. LIFO usually results in reporting higher costs of goods sold and therefore lower operating income. This, of course, results in lower taxes.[5]

Typical Financial Statements

The preparation of financial statements is made possible by the existence of accurate and thorough accounting records. The three major financial statements are the income statement, balance sheet, and statement of cash flow.

Two major financial statements of the LM Manufacturing Company, a hypothetical small corporation, are illustrated in this section. These statements—the income statement and the balance sheet—will be referred to in the discussion of financial ratios later in the chapter.

Income Statement   The **income statement** shows the results of a firm's operations over a period of time, usually one year. Exhibit 20–2 shows the income statement of the LM Manufacturing Company. A minor variation would be involved in preparing an income statement for a retailing or wholesaling firm rather than a manufacturing firm. Specifically, the "Cost of goods sold" section in Exhibit 20–2 would make reference to purchases rather than to manufacturing costs.

Balance Sheet   The **balance sheet** is a statement that shows a firm's financial position at a specific date. Exhibit 20–3 shows the balance sheet of the LM Manufacturing Company as of December 31, 1990. If this firm were a proprietorship or a partnership, the term "Stockholders' Equity" would

Exhibit 20–2   Income Statement

The LM Manufacturing Company
Income Statement
For Year Ended Dec. 31, 1990

Sales.			$830,200
Cost of goods sold:			
Finished goods inventory, Jan. 1, 1990		$ 77,000	
Cost of goods manufactured		589,350	
Total cost of finished goods available for sale		$666,350	
Less finished goods inventory, Dec. 31, 1990		102,000	
Cost of goods sold			564,350
Gross profit on sales.			$265,850
Operating expenses:			
Selling expenses:			
Sales salaries and commissions.	$ 57,150		
Advertising expense	38,600		
Miscellaneous selling expense	5,000		
Total selling expenses		$100,750	
General expenses:			
Officers' salaries	$ 46,120		
Office salaries.	16,600		
Depreciation—office equipment.	3,600		
Bad-debts expense	4,100		
Miscellaneous office expense.	5,580		
Total general expenses		76,000	
Total operating expenses.			176,750
Operating income			$ 89,100
Other expense:			
Interest expense.			$ 10,000
Net profit before income tax			$ 79,100
Income tax			17,390
Net profit after income tax			$ 61,710

Exhibit 20-3   Balance Sheet

The LM Manufacturing Company
Balance Sheet
Dec. 31, 1990
ASSETS

Current Assets:

Cash			$ 44,480
Accounts receivable	$ 83,000		
Less allowance for			
uncollectible accounts	5,000	78,000	
Inventories (at lower of cost or market):			
Finished goods	$102,000		
Work in process	52,000		
Raw materials	57,450	211,450	
Factory supplies		8,000	
Prepaid insurance		5,800	
Total current assets			$347,730

	Cost	Accumulated Depreciation	Book Value	
Plant Assets:				
Office equipment	$ 36,000	$ 16,200	$ 19,800	
Factory equipment	552,000	327,000	225,000	
Buildings	250,000	40,000	210,000	
Land	70,000	—	70,000	
Total plant assets	$908,000	$383,200		524,800

Intangible assets:		
Patents		55,000
TOTAL ASSETS		$927,530

LIABILITIES AND STOCKHOLDERS' EQUITY

Current liabilities:			
Accounts payable	$ 77,200		
Estimated income tax payable	17,390		
Salaries and wages payable	3,930		
Interest payable	2,500		
Total current liabilities		$101,020	
Long-term liabilities:			
First mortgage 10% notes payable			
(due 1995)		200,000	
Total liabilities			$301,020
Common stock, no-par (30,000 shares			
authorized and issued)		$300,000	
Retained earnings		326,510	
Total stockholders' equity			626,510
TOTAL LIABILITIES AND			
STOCKHOLDERS' EQUITY			$927,530

read "Capital." And the items listed in this section would show individual ownership investments.

Statement of Cash Flow   A third financial statement—the **statement of cash flow**—is now required by the Financial Accounting Standards Board, the rule-making body of the accounting profession. This financial statement shows all cash receipts and cash payments involved in operating the business and managing its financial activities. Chapter 21 discusses the importance of cash flow analysis.

Analysis of Financial Statements

A single item from a financial statement has only limited meaning until it is related to some other item. For example, current assets of $10,000 mean one thing when current liabilities are $5,000 and another when they are $50,000. For this reason, ratios have been developed to relate different income-statement items to each other, different balance-sheet items to each other, and income-statement items to balance-sheet items.

Although numerous financial-statement ratios can be computed, only those that are the most practical and widely used for small businesses will be explained here. These ratios will be grouped into four classifications, using the financial statements of the LM Manufacturing Company for illustrative purposes. It must be emphasized that a careful interpretation of ratios is required to make them useful to a particular firm. A ratio may indicate potential trouble, but it cannot explain either the causes or the seriousness of the situation. Most small firms find it helpful to compare their ratios with their own past experience and with industry standard ratios.

Ratios Related to Working-Capital Position   Adequacy and liquidity of working capital are measured by two ratios: the current ratio and the acid-test (or quick) ratio.

Current Ratio   To compute the **current ratio**, divide current assets by current liabilities. The "banker's rule" for this ratio is "at least two to one" for working capital to be judged adequate. Actually the proper size of this ratio depends upon the type of industry, the season of the year, and other factors. The current ratio of the LM Manufacturing Company is:

$$\frac{\text{Current assets}}{\text{Current liabilities}} = \frac{\$347,730}{\$101,020} = 3.44 \text{ times}$$

From this it appears that the LM Manufacturing Company has sufficient cash and other assets that will be quickly converted into cash to pay all maturing obligations.

Acid-Test Ratio   A more severe test of adequacy of working capital is provided by the **acid-test** (or **quick**) **ratio**. To compute this ratio, divide current assets less inventories by current liabilities. The exclusion of inventories from current assets is necessary because inventories are in part a fixed-capital investment and are less liquid than other current assets. The LM Manufacturing Company's acid-test ratio is:

$$\frac{\text{Current assets less inventories}}{\text{Current liabilities}} = \frac{\$347,730 - \$211,450}{\$101,020} = 1.35 \text{ times}$$

The traditional rule of thumb is a minimum of 1 to 1 acid-test ratio. At 1:35 to 1, it appears the LM Manufacturing Company's working-capital position is sound.

Ratios Related to the Sales Position   Comparisons between the level of sales and the investment in various asset accounts involve the use of three

Figure 20–1   Preparing Financial Statements

ratios: inventory turnover, average collection period, and fixed-asset turnover. These ratios indicate the need for a proper balance between sales and various asset accounts.

Inventory Turnover   The **inventory turnover ratio** shows whether or not a company is holding excessive stocks of inventory. When this ratio is computed for a going concern, two questions arise: (1) Since sales are at market prices and inventories are usually carried at cost, which is more appropriate to use as the numerator in the ratio: sales or cost of goods sold? and (2) Which inventory figure should be used: an average inventory or an inventory at one point in time?

Logic dictates that the inventory turnover should be computed by comparing cost of goods sold to inventory. As a rule, however, it is better to use the ratio of sales to inventories carried at cost because established compilers of financial ratios, such as Dun & Bradstreet, do this. Thus, the firm can compute a ratio that can be compared to the standard ratio developed by Dun & Bradstreet. It is also better to use an average inventory figure (computed by adding the year's beginning and ending inventories and dividing by 2) if there has been a marked upward or downward trend of sales during the year. The LM Manufacturing Company's inventory turnover rate is:

$$\frac{\text{Sales}}{\text{Average inventory}} = \frac{\$830,200}{\$89,500} = 9.28 \text{ times}$$

If the industry average is 9, for example, it is obvious that the LM Manufacturing Company is not carrying excessive stocks of inventory. Excessive inventories are unnecessary and reduce business profits.

Average Collection Period   The **average collection period** is a measure of accounts-receivable turnover. A two-step procedure for finding the average collection period for the LM Manufacturing Company, using 360 as the number of days in a year, is:

$$\text{Step 1:} \frac{\text{Sales}}{360} = \frac{\$830,200}{360} = \$2,306 \text{ average daily sales}$$

$$\text{Step 2:} \frac{\text{Receivables}}{\text{Average daily sales}} = \frac{\$78,000}{\$2,306} = 33.8 \text{ days}$$

If the industry average collection period is 20 days, then it would appear that the LM Manufacturing Company is experiencing serious collection problems.

Fixed-Asset Turnover   The **fixed-asset turnover** measures the extent to which plant and equipment are being utilized. For the LM Manufacturing Company, the fixed-asset turnover is:

$$\frac{\text{Sales}}{\text{Fixed assets}} = \frac{\$830,200}{\$524,800} = 1.58 \text{ times}$$

If the industry average is 4 times, this means that LM's plant and equipment are not being used effectively. This should be borne in mind when considering requests for additional production equipment.

Ratios Related to Profitability   Profitability is the net result of a firm's management policies and decisions. The ratios that may be used to measure how effectively the firm is being managed are: profit margin on sales, return on total assets, and return on net worth (or equity).

Profit Margin on Sales   The **profit margin on sales** gives the profit per dollar of sales. To compute this ratio, divide net profit by sales. For the LM Manufacturing Company, the profit margin on sales is:

$$\frac{\text{Net profit}}{\text{Sales}} = \frac{\$61,710}{\$830,200} = .0743 \text{ or } 7.43 \text{ percent}$$

If the industry average is 7 percent, LM's slightly higher profit margin indicates effective management of sales and operations.

Return on Total Assets   The **return on total assets,** or **asset earning power,** measures the return on total investment in the business. To compute this ratio, divide net profit by total assets. The LM Manufacturing Company's return on total assets is:

$$\frac{\text{Net profit}}{\text{Total assets}} = \frac{\$61,710}{\$927,530} = .0665 \text{ or } 6.65 \text{ percent}$$

If the industry average is 8 percent, LM's low rate may indicate an excessive investment in fixed assets even though its profit margin on sales is slightly better than the industry's average.

Return on Net Worth The **return on net worth,** or **return on equity,** measures the rate of return on stockholders' investments in the business. To compute this ratio, divide net profit by net worth. For LM's stockholders the return on net worth is:

$$\frac{\text{Net profit}}{\text{Net worth}} = \frac{\$61,710}{\$626,510} = .0985 \text{ or } 9.85 \text{ percent}$$

If the industry average is 12 percent, it would appear that LM's return is unsatisfactorily low. It is possible that LM's return on net worth may be improved by using more leverage, or debt.

Ratios Related to Debt Position One of the most critical aspects of the financial structure of a firm is the relationship between borrowed funds and invested capital. If debt is unreasonably large when compared with equity funds, the firm may be skating on thin ice. According to the conservative rule of thumb, two-thirds of the total capital in a business should be owner-supplied. In most lines of business, however, the industry standard is somewhat lower.

The ratios that may be used to measure the debt position of a firm are debt to total assets and times interest earned.

Debt to Total Assets The **debt-to-total-assets ratio** is a ratio that measures the percentage of total funds that have been provided by a firm's creditors. To compute this ratio, divide the total debts (current liabilities and long-term liabilities) by total assets. The LM Manufacturing Company's debt ratio is:

$$\frac{\text{Total debts}}{\text{Total assets}} = \frac{\$301,020}{\$927,530} = .3245 \text{ or } 32.45 \text{ percent}$$

It is evident that LM's debt ratio conforms to the conservative rule of thumb. This means that LM should be able, if desired, to borrow additional funds without first raising more equity funds.

Times Interest Earned The **times-interest-earned ratio** measures the extent to which a firm's earnings can decline without impairing its ability to meet annual interest costs. To compute this ratio, divide operating income by interest charges. The LM's times-interest-earned ratio is:

$$\frac{\text{Operating income}}{\text{Interest charges}} = \frac{\$89,100}{\$10,000} = 8.9 \text{ times}$$

If the industry average is 8 times, it is obvious that LM's position is strong and that it can cover its interest charges even with a substantial decline in its earnings. This reinforces the previous conclusion that LM should have little difficulty if it tries to borrow additional funds.

Observance of Accounting Principles and Conventions   In seeking to analyze and interpret financial statements, a manager must remember that certain principles and accounting conventions govern the preparation of accounting statements. For example, conservatism is a principle that guides accountants, and the most conservative method available is the one an accountant will typically choose. Another principle governing the preparation of statements is consistency. This means that a given item on a statement will be handled in the same way every month and every year so that comparability of the data will be assured. Also, the principle of full disclosure compels the accountant to insist that all liabilities be shown and all material facts be presented. This is intended to prevent misleading any investor who might read the firm's statements.

Certain accounting conventions also regulate, in part, the preparation of financial statements. One of these concerns the accrual accounting system mentioned earlier in this chapter. Receivables are valued at their cash value less an allowance for possible bad debts, while fixed assets other than land are valued at their depreciated value based on original cost. Each of these methods results in balance-sheet and income-statement values that may vary from one method to the next and thereby change ratio analysis numbers somewhat.

Budgeting in Small Firms

If your family has ever used a household budget, you are already acquainted with the basic concept of budgeting. Remember how Mom and Dad agonized over the household budget at the beginning of the month and again sometimes at the end of the month? At the start of the month, they were estimating income in the form of salaries and wages and outgo in the form of payments for groceries, utilities, rent or mortgage, and braces for Johnny. At the end of the month, they were trying to understand, after looking at the budget and actual income and expenditures, what went wrong!

In a small business the budgeting goals are much the same as in a household—to determine what the sources of income are and how it will be distributed. But the budgeting process in a small business is much more complex. The budget of a small firm is the principal short-range financial plan of the business. It allows the entrepreneur to allocate the firm's scarce funds and to forecast when additional financing may be required.

There are three key budgets used by small businesses—the operating budget, the pro-forma (or forecasted) balance sheet budget, and the cash budget. The operating budget and the pro-forma balance sheet budget will be examined in the following sections of this chapter, while the cash budget is presented in Chapter 21, in association with working-capital management.

The Operating Budget   The **operating budget** is a composite plan for each phase of the operation of the business. The operating budget is derived from several other forecasts—the sales forecast, production forecast, purchase forecast, selling and administrative expense forecast, and so forth. These individual "budgets" must be worked up in order to develop the finished operating budget—usually prepared by months. The operating budget is typically formatted as a budgeted income statement.

Exhibit 20–4 shows a monthly operating budget for a hypothetical retail firm. This particular pro-forma income statement was prepared with a personal computer using the software contained in *Small Business Management Using Lotus 1–2–3*, a workbook supplement to this textbook. Many non-computer worksheets are also available that provide various formats as guides.[6]

Notice in Exhibit 20–4 how the first line (Sales) reflects a sales forecast of $50,000 for January, fluctuating up and down throughout the year with a $120,000 projection for December. Line number two (Cost of Goods Sold) reflects a 70 percent cost on Selling Price. For example, in May, sales are forecasted at $60,000; therefore, 70 percent of this amount, or $42,000, is expected to be cost of goods sold. Various other forecasting assumptions are used to generate the budgeted income figures. As you can see from this operating budget, November is expected to be the first "profitable" month of the year ($1,669 in net income).

Pro-Forma Balance Sheet   As stated earlier in the chapter, a balance sheet is a statement of a firm's financial position at a specific date. A pro-forma balance sheet is a forecast of that financial position. It is a budget in the sense that it is a guide to what the firm's future financial position should look like. Exhibit 20–5 shows monthly pro-forma balance sheets generated by the same software used for Exhibit 20–4.

Notice that this picture of the firm's overall financial condition shows

Exhibit 20–4   Operating Budget

	Jan	Feb	Mar	Apr	May	Jun	Jul	Aug	Sep	Oct	Nov	Dec
Sales	50000	70000	100000	75000	60000	50000	50000	50000	70000	90000	100000	120000
Cost of Goods Sold	35000	49000	70000	52500	42000	35000	35000	35000	49000	63000	70000	84000
Gross Margin	15000	21000	30000	22500	18000	15000	15000	15000	21000	27000	30000	36000
Operating Expenses												
Selling and Adm.	15000	20000	35000	21000	18000	15000	15000	15000	25000	35000	25000	30000
Depreciation	500	500	500	500	500	500	500	500	500	500	500	500
Inventory Charge	175	245	350	263	210	175	175	175	245	315	350	420
Operating Income	−675	255	−5850	738	−710	−675	−675	−675	−4745	−8815	4150	5080
Interest Expense	325	346	488	843	756	529	384	343	343	526	811	960
Earnings Before Tx	−1000	−91	−6338	−106	−1466	−1204	−1059	−1018	−5088	−9341	3339	4120
Taxes											1669	2060
Net Income											1669	2060

583

Exhibit 20-5   Pro-Forma Balance Sheets

Balance Sheet	Jan	Feb	Mar	Apr	May	Jun	Jul	Aug	Sep	Oct	Nov	Dec
ASSETS												
Cash	4000	4000	4000	4000	4000	4000	4000	4000	4000	4000	4000	4000
A/R	77500	95000	135000	125000	97500	80000	75000	75000	95000	125000	145000	170000
Inventory	49000	70000	52500	42000	35000	35000	35000	49000	63000	70000	84000	56000
Current	130500	169000	191500	171000	136500	119000	114000	128000	162000	199000	233000	230000
Fixed	20000	20000	20000	20000	20000	20000	20000	20000	20000	20000	20000	20000
(Acc. Depr)	6500	7000	7500	8000	8500	9000	9500	10000	10500	11000	11500	12000
Net Fixed	13500	13000	12500	12000	11500	11000	10500	10000	9500	9000	8500	8000
Total Assets	144000	182000	204000	183000	148000	130000	124500	138000	171500	208000	241500	238000
LIABILITIES & EQUITY												
LIABILITIES:												
Trade Payables	49000	70000	52500	42000	35000	35000	35000	49000	63000	70000	84000	56000
S.T. Bank Notes	41480	58525	101194	90747	63480	46082	41112	41120	63164	97335	115165	137605
Total current	90480	128525	153694	132747	98480	81082	76112	90120	126164	167335	199165	193605
L.T. Debt	0	0	0	0	0	0	0	0	0	0	0	0
Total Liabilities	90480	128525	153694	132747	98480	81082	76112	90120	126164	167335	199165	193605
EQUITY:												
Common	50000	50000	50000	50000	50000	50000	50000	50000	50000	50000	50000	50000
Retained Earnings	3520	3475	306	253	-480	-1082	-1612	-2120	-4664	-9335	-7665	-5605
Total Equity	53520	53475	50306	50253	49520	48918	48388	47880	45336	40665	42335	44395
Total Liab. & Equity	144000	182000	204000	183000	148000	130000	124500	138000	171500	208000	241500	238000

negative retained earnings at the end of May! It also shows a buildup in the Accounts Receivable (AR) balance from $77,500 in January to $170,000 at the end of December! Both of these projections are a function of the operating budgets and the management policy of collecting receivables.

These two budgets alone do not provide the entrepreneur with sufficient planning tools. Attention must also be given to the cash flow in the business. Unanticipated cash requirements may actually cripple the business prior to reaching the "profitable" month of November! To facilitate the understanding of the interrelationship between the operating budget and the cash budget, the cash budget developed in the next chapter is based on the same hypothetical retail business used to develop the operating budget in Exhibit 20–4.

We now turn our attention to special considerations in establishing and using all kinds of budgets in a small business. Budgets are not only a valuable planning device, but also a useful guide to operations.

Budget Revisions   After the budgeted operating statement and balance sheet are prepared, they should be evaluated by the use of key financial ratios such as those that were discussed in the early part of this chapter and others found in financial management textbooks. If the ratio analysis indicates that the budgeted operations will produce unsatisfactory results, the master budget and all supporting schedules must be revised at once.

Business operation is always full of uncertainties. Thus, actual operations seldom correspond exactly, and sometimes not even closely, to the budgeted operating level. A need for budget revision during the budget year consequently arises. For example, a manufacturer budgets a given product mixture and volume for sales. If actual sales do not conform in total amount and in product mixture, the budgeted sales and the corresponding expense budgets must be revised.

In the retail or wholesale establishment, changes in advertising and sales promotion emphasis, changes in style trends, changes in customer clientele, and other changes lead to a similar need for budget revision.

Using the Budget to Control and Reduce Expenses   The budget, when properly used, is perhaps the most effective tool for controlling expenses. By providing a set of standards for expenses of each kind, the budget points up overspending or underspending. To examine the possibilities for controlling expenses, we must first understand the different classifications of expenses discussed below.

Actual vs. Imputed Expenses   Those expenses that in fact accrue and require cash outlays are called **actual expenses. Imputed expenses** are those that do not exist in the sense that they can be entered on the books of account and appear on the income statement. Consider, as an example, the interest on the owner's investment in a business. If the owner had invested the money in the stocks or bonds of other corporations or in government bonds, he or she would have received an income in the form of dividends or interest. The theory of imputing the interest expense on the owner's investment lies in the fact that an income that could have been received from another source is lost if the money is tied up in one's own assets. The lost income is the imputed interest expense. The economist refers to imputed expenses as opportunity costs. Certainly such imputed expenses cannot properly be included in the income statement. Considerations must be given to them, however, in many business decisions.

Fixed vs. Variable Expenses   Those expenses that do not vary in total amount for the accounting period are called **fixed expenses**. For example, a rental charge of $500 per month or a property tax of $1,000 per year are fixed expenses. **Variable expenses** are fixed on a per-unit basis but vary in total amount for month and year with the volume of goods manufactured or sold. As an example of a variable expense, consider machine operators in a factory who work on piece rates and receive a specified amount in dollars and cents per unit of product processed by them. If they process 100,000 units at 5 cents per unit, they receive $5,000. If they process 10,000 units at 5 cents per unit, they receive $500. Thus, the amount of the variable expense—in this case, direct labor—depends upon the number of units made.

This distinction is also important in business decisions. For example, an order might be accepted under some circumstances at a price that would cover variable costs but fail to cover all fixed costs. As a practical matter, many expenses are neither completely fixed nor completely variable in nature.

Functional Expenses   Those expenses that relate to specific selling and administrative activities of a business are called **functional expenses.** If the amounts recorded by kinds of expense in the books of account can be equitably distributed to the functional-expenses categories, then expense control can be achieved. Consider, for example, the expense of "payroll preparation," which is charged to the functional category of "control." This expense does not include the production payroll itself; rather, it involves costs of payroll preparation, distribution of paychecks, and audit. (The payroll cost itself would be distributed to the various pertinent categories.)

Controllable vs. Noncontrollable Expenses It is important that managers of small firms stress controllable expenses almost to the exclusion of noncontrollable expenses. Consider a lease with a flat rental. Once a lease has been signed, rental expense is not controllable during the life of the lease. Hence, attention should then be directed to expenses that *are* controllable.

For example, delivery expenses are controllable to some extent. The truck driver's salary, truck depreciation, and operating cost can be more effectively used and better controlled if the truck is provided with a two-way radio. In contrast, a retailer subscribing to a delivery service at a fixed amount per month is committed to noncontrollable expense. Accordingly, there is little need for attention to it until time to renegotiate the delivery service contract.

Common Budgetary Control Deficiencies in Small Businesses Even though budgets are designed to facilitate effective management, they sometimes fail to do so, particularly in the small business. Here are several reasons why small businesses suffer from unsatisfactory budgetary control:

1. *Inaccurate determination of budget standards.* When inaccurate budget standards are set, comparisons of actual results with budgeted amounts are misleading. Management may be lulled into the belief that all is well when, as a matter of fact, costs are uncontrolled and performance is inefficient.
2. *Failure to include all key business activities in the budget.* If desired overall results are to be attained, all business activities of the firm must be incorporated in the budget.
3. *Lack of full support for the budget.* When preparing the budget, managers should consult their subordinates so that the latter will feel that the budget is theirs, too. And when the budget is completed, top management must back it up and convince all employees of the value of the budget as a control system. Subordinates can show their full support by promptly submitting control reports, especially when the budget needs to be revised. Of course, any budget revisions should also be communicated promptly to the subordinates.
4. *Inability to interpret control reports.* Sometimes the manager and the employees find control reports difficult to interpret. Thus, they may fail to detect and act on controllable expenses that vary significantly between actual and budgeted amounts.

Tax Issues in Small Business

Entrepreneurs are encouraged to use outside professional assistance in many areas of small-business management. Tax planning is certainly no exception. In fact, small-business managers should seek tax advice even before they start their businesses!

Tax laws traditionally have been complex and difficult to interpret. And a major milestone in tax history, the Tax Reform Act of 1986, has continued the tradition. One accountant specializing in small-firm clients says, "This tax bill makes small business owners the forgotten people in the United States . . . . Congress has once again failed in its responsibilities to them."[7]

Many issues have arisen subsequent to passage of the Tax Reform Act, and strong opinions prevail regarding the impact of the law. Ultimately, time and experience will shed their clarifying light on these issues. For example, Section 89, enacted as part of the Tax Reform Act, created a set of rules that imposed tax penalties for employer-paid health and life insurance and other nonpension employee benefits that were judged to favor higher-paid workers. The enormous complexity of Section 89 drew sharp criticism. By late 1989, Section 89 was repealed. In spite of the confusion, however, small businesses must develop tax strategies and move on with operations. One CPA says, "Other companies may be hoping that if they ignore the rules, they'll just go away . . . . the law may impose some hardships, but it's here to stay. The only viable option is to learn the rules and to comply with them."[8]

A complete presentation of tax issues involving small firms would certainly fill a separate book.[9] Therefore, we have selected issues that not only have a direct impact on small firms but also, to some extent, are controversial. Our selection includes capital gains, tax credits, business expenses, inventory costing, tax shelters, estate freezes, and taxpayer rights.

Capital Gains

Prior to the Tax Reform Act of 1986, gains from sales of certain types of property were treated as capital gains and received preferential tax treatment. The tax status of capital gains encouraged investment in small firms because investors could avoid the higher tax obligations associated with other ways of increasing their wealth. Under the new law, capital gains are

SMALL BUSINESS IN ACTION
An Opinion on Capital Gains Reform

Prior to passage of the Tax Reform Act of 1986, certain capital gains were taxed at a rate lower than the rates for ordinary income. Now capital gains are taxed at the same rates. What impact has this change had on small businesses? One opinion comes from entrepreneur Darrell Wilburn.

Wilburn started his electronics company, Step Engineering, in Sunnyvale, CA, in 1977. From that time to the passage of the Tax Reform Act, Congress had been gradually lowering capital-gains tax rates. Wilburn remarks, "If Congress had not lowered the tax rate on capital gains, there would be no company." Because of the more lenient taxation of capital gains, Wilburn was willing to sacrifice—for example, to go for more than a year without pay—in order to keep his business strong. If Wilburn sells now, his returns for these sacrifices will be "eaten up" by the large capital-gains tax. He believes the new capital-gains treatment will discourage entrepreneurs from starting businesses.

Source: Adapted from Joan C. Szabo, "The Push to Trim Capital-Gains Tax," *Nation's Business,* Vol. 77, No. 7 (July, 1989), p. 56. Copyright 1989, U.S. Chamber of Commerce.

treated as ordinary income and subject to ordinary tax rates. Consequently, many tax-saving strategies in small firms have evaporated.

This provision of the new tax law had been criticized severely. "The U.S. now stands nearly alone in the industrialized world with its high rates of capital-gains taxation," says one tax attorney.[10] Several senators and representatives are critical of the capital-gains change. One senator has stated, "Without a capital-gains differential, investors aren't going to take a chance on small, riskier companies with a lot of growth potential. . . ."[11]

Some of the current proposals to modify capital-gains treatment would impose a rate on gains from property held for more than one year that is lower than the rate on ordinary income. Still other proposals would totally eliminate a capital-gains tax for taxpayers below a certain level of income.

Tax Credits

A **tax credit** is a direct reduction of a taxpayer's tax liability. This makes a tax credit more valuable dollar for dollar than a tax deduction.

Under old tax law, an investment tax credit (ITC) on depreciable property was available in addition to allowable depreciation deductions. These credits were actually "icing on the cake," promoting capital investment. Up to 10 percent of the cost of new equipment, under the old laws, could be written off against taxes. Therefore, it is certainly noteworthy to capital-intensive firms to learn that investment tax credits were repealed by the Tax Reform Act of 1986.

Some tax credits existing under the old laws remain intact. These include such things as a foreign tax credit and a targeted-jobs credit.

However, the Tax Reform Act did implement a change in another area that may *partially* offset the elimination of the ITC. This change relates to a one-year write-off (deduction) of certain otherwise depreciable property. Under the new tax laws, a business can treat as expense $10,000 worth of business property in any one year. This rule allows the small firm some flexibility to increase expenses under cash accounting procedures.

Business Expenses

The legitimacy of business expenses in small-business tax reporting has sparked controversy for many years. One study has even suggested that small-firm employees may view "padding of expense accounts" with greater tolerance than larger-firm employees.[12] Therefore, it comes as little surprise that the Tax Reform Act of 1986 created new provisions to cover business deductions.

Travel, meal, and entertainment deductions were scrutinized carefully during the tax reform process. Since 1987, only 80 percent of business meals can be deducted. Furthermore, travel expenses must be "ordinary and necessary." Certain travel expenses, if deemed lavish or extravagant, will be disallowed.

Even employees of small businesses are affected by the new tax provisions. For example, unreimbursed employee business expenses are now entered as a miscellaneous itemized deduction on their personal tax returns. With the 2 percent of adjusted gross income limitation on miscellaneous itemized deductions, this means employees will not be able to deduct 100 percent of unreimbursed business expenses.

There are several other restrictions on business expense deductions that are too technical to describe in this book. Small-business owners can improve the likelihood of getting business expense deductions when they follow the required documentation rules.[13]

Inventory Costing

The new law requires certain types of expenditures to be capitalized in inventory values rather than being treated as expenses. The net effect of this rule is more current tax liability! The rule applies to all inventories except those of retailers and wholesalers with gross receipts of less than $10 million.[14] Under old tax regulations, wholesalers and retailers were not required to capitalize so-called indirect costs, such as purchasing, processing, handling, and administrative expenses. Now they are required to do so.

Another change from the old tax laws is that some package design costs must also be included in inventory, rather than being deducted as an expense. However, businesses have been allowed to use a five-year straight-line depreciation option for all new products since March 5, 1989.[15] The inventory costing rule is simply another hidden tax increase that burdens small business.

Tax Shelters

In the past, individuals could put money into certain types of investments and, if losses occurred, use those losses to offset or shelter income earned from other sources. The original intent of the tax law was to provide relief to entrepreneurs who suffered losses. It was believed that this would serve to stimulate business development. Abuse occurred in this area, however, as suggested by the term *shelter*. The Tax Reform Act of 1986 placed strict limitations on this tax strategy.

Three types of income have been defined by the new law: active, passive, and portfolio. Under the tax rules, passive losses may be used to offset *only* passive income! There are, however, some exceptions to this rule—for example, real estate investments.[16]

Any small-business owner with anticipated losses from other businesses in which he or she participates either marginally or not at all, should do some careful tax planning. For example, limited partnerships would provide "passive income" or a "passive loss" to its limited partners. A passive loss could not be used to offset profits earned by a business owner in his or her primary business.

Estate Freezes

A challenging tax problem facing a family-run company is determining the best strategy to pass the business to the next generation while minimizing taxes. An estate freeze is one popular method used for this purpose. In an estate freeze, junior family members are transferred partial ownership in the business while a corporate recapitalization caps the value of a parent's ownership for estate purposes. Any future appreciation in the value of the business goes to the children. Tax legislation passed in 1987 and 1988 has severely restricted the estate-freeze strategy. Now, if an owner retains control and substantial interest in the firm, the future appreciation in the value of the business is included in his or her estate for tax purposes. Section 2036(c) of the tax law deals with these concerns.[17]

Additional highlights of recent tax reform are shown in Exhibit 20–6.

Taxpayer Rights

Most people do not enjoy preparing tax forms and paying taxes. Owners and managers of small firms are no exception. Horror stories about Internal Revenue Service audits have probably contributed to this feeling. A few taxpayers may even consider tax-planning activities as tax evasion.

Exhibit 20–6   Additional Highlights of Tax Reform

Accounting Period:
- A partnership is now required to conform its tax year to the tax year of either its majority partners, its principal partners, or a calendar year, in that order, unless it can establish a business purpose for using a different year.
- An S corporation must now use as its tax year a year that ends on December 31 (the calendar year), unless the corporation establishes a business purpose for using a different tax year.

Accounting Methods:
- The cash method may not be used by corporations (other than S corporations), partnerships having a corporation (other than an S corporation) as a partner, and by tax shelters. An exception allows businesses with gross receipts of $5 million or less to continue using the cash method. This exception does not include tax shelters.
- If the small business uses an accrual method for purchases and sales, it may use the cash method for figuring all other items of income and expense.

Going into Business Costs:
- Costs such as conducting market surveys, travel, and fees to have a lawyer organize a business or an accountant set up your recordkeeping system cannot be deducted as business expenses but rather become capital expenditures.

Exhibit 20-6   *(Continued)*

- If a business wishes to amortize startup expenditure, it must make an election to do so. Generally, these costs are deducted in equal amounts over a period of 60 months or more.

Depreciation:
- The maximum section 179 deduction for a trade or business property has increased from $5,000 to $10,000.
- A new depreciation method applies to tangible property placed in service after 1986. This system, which is referred to as the modified accelerated cost recovery system (MACRS), has eight classes of property.

Business Expenses:
- A small business may deduct advertising expenses if they are reasonable and related to the business activities. A business cannot deduct the cost of advertising if its purpose is to influence legislation. Expenses for public service advertising, such as encouraging people to contribute to the Red Cross, are deductible.
- If a business is located in the taxpayer's home, expenses associated with the part of the home used exclusively and regularly as the principal place of business can be deducted.
- Amounts paid to buy a franchise, trademark, or trade name where the transferor does not retain any significant power, right, or continuing interest (non-contingent payments) must be capitalized. Payments which are based on the productivity and use of the franchise, trademark, or trade name (contingent payments) are deductible as expenses.

Tax Rates:
- For corporations with tax years beginning after June 30, 1987, a three-bracket system shown below applies:

Taxable Income	Tax Rate
Not over $50,000	15%
Over $50,000 but not over $75,000	25%
Over $75,000	34%

An additional 5% tax, up to $11,750, is imposed on corporate taxable income over $100,000. Corporations with taxable income of at least $335,000 pay a 34% flat rate.
- For tax years beginning after 1986, corporations are subject to an alternative minimum tax. The alternative minimum tax provides a formula for computing tax that, in effect, ignores certain preferential tax treatments that are allowed in figuring the regular tax.

Source: Excerpted from *Tax Guide for Small Business,* Publication 334, 1987, Internal Revenue Service, Washington, DC.

These negative attitudes are unfortunate, and they create unnecessary tensions in small businesses. A small-business owner should take a positive approach to taxes: learn the rules, file the returns correctly and in a timely manner, and then direct attention back to operations.

Taxpayers have recently received some positive reinforcement for an improved attitude with the passage of the Technical and Miscellaneous Revenue Act of 1988. Provisions of this act include what is being called the Taxpayer Bill of Rights. The intent of the legislation is to define clearly the responsibilities of the Internal Revenue Service, taxpayer, and tax return preparer in their dealings with one another. The areas covered are the examination process, tax collection process, proceedings by taxpayers, Internal Revenue Service administration, and tax court jurisdiction.[18]

Concluding Note

It would be inappropriate to end the discussion of federal taxes by giving the impression that the Tax Reform Act of 1986 has been all bad. This is not the case. For example, the new tax law contains many positive features for family and in-home businesses. Many benefits of S-corporation status (which was discussed in Chapter 10) remain intact. Also, the cash method of tax accounting is still permitted in many situations. And, of course, recent tax reform continues a downward trend in personal tax rates.

Looking Back

1. A well-conceived accounting system may require the expertise of an accountant. It should be consistent with generally accepted accounting principles and include as a minimum certain accounting records. The entrepreneur should evaluate the accounting options of cash versus accrual accounting, single-entry versus double-entry systems, and LIFO versus FIFO inventory evaluation.
2. Three accounting statements most typically prepared by a small business are the income statement, the balance sheet, and the statement of cash flow. The income statement shows the results of a firm's operations over a period of time, usually one year. The balance sheet shows a firm's financial position at a specific date. The statement of cash flow accounts for changes in a firm's cash position.

3. Financial statements serve as the basis for computing financial ratios. These ratios can be grouped into those relating to working-capital position, sales position, profitability, and debt position.
4. The three key budgets for a small firm are the operating budget, the pro-forma balance sheet budget, and the cash budget. These budgets are valuable planning and management tools.
5. Key tax issues resulting from the passage of the Tax Reform Act of 1986 are capital gains taxation, investment credit repeal, business expenses, inventory cost, tax shelters, and estate freezes.

DISCUSSION QUESTIONS

1. Explain the accounting convention that income is realized when earned whether or not it has been received in cash.
2. Should entrepreneurs have someone else set up an accounting system for their proposed small firms or do it themselves? Why?
3. What are the major types of accounting records required in a sound accounting system?
4. What is the relationship between the income statement and the balance sheet?
5. What are the major advantages of a double-entry accounting system over a single-entry system?
6. Explain the tax advantage of using LIFO inventory valuation rather than FIFO. Would this always be an advantage? Explain.
7. Explain the purpose of each of the three major financial statements. Which one is the newest to be required in financial reporting? Why?
8. What is the disadvantage of having too low an inventory turnover?
9. Explain the danger in having too high a debt-to-total-assets ratio in a small firm.
10. What are the purposes of pro-forma balance sheet budgets? Be specific.
11. Can "fixed" expenses be controlled? Are they really always "fixed"? Cite some examples for the answers to both questions.
12. What is the nature of an expense classification by function? Of what value is it to the manager?
13. What did the Tax Reform Act of 1986 change regarding taxation of capital gains? Do you believe the change has had a negative impact on small firms? Why or why not?
14. Explain the concept of "passive income" as it relates to tax shelters.

15. In what way has recent tax reform affected employee benefits in small firms?

YOU MAKE THE CALL

Situation 1

Mary and Matt Townsel are in their early retirement years after having worked for several different businesses over the last 30 years. Now, to supplement their Social Security income, Matt operates a newspaper delivery service. He has more than 600 customers in the retirement/vacation village where they live. Mary's major contribution to the business partnership, in addition to rolling papers early in the mornings, is bookkeeping.

Mary has recently purchased a computer to assist her with the accounting function. She has no software and is therefore looking for someone to write her programs.

Questions

1. What types of accounting records do you believe Mary should maintain? Why?

2. Does it appear that a computer will benefit Mary's record-keeping task? How?

3. With what tax considerations should a very small business such as this one be concerned?

Situation 2

Sue and Ted Brown own and operate a successful, incorporated ranch that has appreciated in value to almost $10 million. Their three sons have worked on the ranch except while they were in college. At age 73, Ted is concerned with the tax problems of passing the ranch on to his sons.

Several years ago, a friend advised Ted that he could recapitalize the ranch business and allocate much of the current value to preferred stock, which he would own. The remaining value would be allocated to common stock, which he and his wife would sell to his children. Ted's understanding was that this would greatly reduce taxes on his estate at his death. He could not, however, remember all the details.

Questions
1. What approach to tax planning was the friend talking about?
2. Do you believe Mr. Brown should consult a tax accountant?
3. What area(s) of the tax law would deal with Mr. Brown's concern?

EXPERIENTIAL EXERCISES

1. Interview a local CPA who consults with small firms and determine his or her experiences with small-business accounting systems. Report to the class on what levels of accounting knowledge the CPA's clients appear to possess.
2. Contact several very small businesses and explain your interest in their accounting systems. Report to the class on their level of sophistication—such things as whether they use a single-entry system, a computer, or an outside professional.
3. Conduct a telephone survey of small-firm owners to measure their awareness of the tax issues discussed in the chapter. Determine what other tax issues they are particularly concerned about. Report your findings.
4. Interview a tax professional in your area and determine the current status of each tax issue presented in the chapter. Provide an update to the class.

REFERENCES TO SMALL-BUSINESS PRACTICES

Bahls, Steven and Bahls, Jane Easter. "The Tax Advantage." *In Business,* Vol. 10, No. 2 (March–April, 1988), pp. 50–51.
> In this article, the advantages and disadvantages to incorporating are examined within the context of the Tax Reform Act of 1986. The S-Corporation election is discussed within the analysis.

Ellentuck, Albert B. "Save Money by Getting a Jump on New Year's Tax Season." *Entrepreneur,* Vol. 17, No. 12 (December, 1988), pp. 102–106.
> This article provides suggestions on how a taxpayer can remain creative in tax planning. A number of "tips" are discussed.

Foster, Mike. "A Battle of Words with the IRS." *Nation's Business,* Vol. 77, No. 3 (March, 1989), pp. 42–44.
> This article provides an interesting and informative account of Tax Code and Tax Court rulings faced by an entrepreneur who was fighting to save certain tax deductions. The article concludes with some recommendations for taxpayers facing an audit.

Pearlstein, Steven. "Accounting Critic Robert Kaplan." *Inc.*, Vol. 10, No. 4 (April, 1988), pp. 55–67.

Harvard Business School professor Robert Kaplan is interviewed by the editor of this business magazine. Several accounting issues of interest to business, including small firms, are discussed in the course of the interview.

Szabo, Joan C. "Welcome to Tax Reform." *Nation's Business,* Vol. 74, No. 11 (November, 1986), pp. 20–28.

This article contains several comments from small-business owners regarding the Tax Reform Act of 1986. Several of the major provisions are briefly discussed.

ENDNOTES

1. An excellent article on this subject is Mark W. Dirsmith and Walter K. Kunitake, "How to Choose CPA Services for the Growing Company," *Business* (October–December, 1988), pp. 13–21.

2. Linda M. Watkins, "Users Find Personal-Accounting Software Doesn't Easily Solve All Financial Woes," *The Wall Street Journal* (March 4, 1986), p. 29.

3. Frank Mixson, "Accountants on the Move," *Entrepreneur,* Vol. 17, No. 4 (April, 1989), p. 88.

4. An even simpler example of using journals and ledgers can be found in John A. Welsh and Jerry F. White, *The Entrepreneur's Master Planning Guide* (Englewood Cliffs, NJ: Prentice-Hall, Inc., 1983), pp. 265–269.

5. There are several possible disadvantages to LIFO, and these are discussed in a booklet entitled *LIFO: An Implementation Guide* (New York: Arthur Young, 1980).

6. See for example the Operating Budget in *Financial Records for Small Business* (San Francisco: Bank of America, 1984), p. 14.

7. Joan C. Szabo, "Welcome to Tax Reform," *Nation's Business*, Vol. 74, No. 11 (November, 1986), p. 21.

8. Mark Stevens, "A Nightmare for Small Business," *D & B Reports,* Vol. 35, No. 6 (November–December, 1987), p. 42.

9. See for example, *Tax Tips for Small Business 1988–89* (Milpitas, CA: The Oasis Press, 1988).

10. Joan C. Szabo, "The Push to Trim Capital-Gains Tax," *Nation's Business,* Vol. 77, No. 7 (July, 1989), p. 57.

11. *Ibid.*

12. Justin G. Longenecker, Joseph A. McKinney, and Carlos W. Moore, "Ethics in Small Business," *Journal of Small Business Management*, Vol. 27, No. 1 (January, 1989), pp. 27–31.

13. A listing of the required documentation is included in Ted S. Frost, "Embattled Travel and Entertainment Deductions," *D & B Reports*, Vol. 36, No. 5 (September–October, 1988), p. 58.

14. *The Business Advisor,* Peat Marwick (October, 1987), p. 1.

15. For a more detailed discussion of this tax change, see Gerald W. Padwe, "A Tax Jolt by Design," *Nation's Business,* Vol. 77, No. 6 (June, 1989), p. 82.

16. An extensive discussion of this area is contained in Hans-Dieter Sprohge, "Impact of the Antitax Shelter Rules on Entrepreneurs," *Business* (October–December, 1988), pp. 47–57.

17. An excellent article providing a more detailed analysis of estate freeze changes is Lawrence Brady and David R. Currie, "Estate Freezes Limited: An Overview and Planning Opportunities," *Journal of Financial Planning,* Vol. 2, No. 2 (April, 1989), pp. 68–74.

18. An excellent discussion of this legislation is contained in R. Wayne Saubert and Cherie J. O'Neil, "The New Taxpayer Bill of Rights," *Taxes—The Tax Magazine,* Vol. 67, No. 4 (April, 1989), pp. 211–222.

21 Working-Capital Management and Capital Budgeting

Courtesy of Donald Weck, LOVE AT FIRST BITE

Rapid growth can create enormous financial problems for small businesses. Donald Weck's company, Love At First Bite, Inc., is a classic example of a firm that expanded too swiftly without careful working-capital management. Weck and a partner launched the San Mateo, CA, company in 1981 to make patés and quiches. When sales grew, the partners borrowed money to finance the expansion.

"We spent way too much money on things we had no business spending money on," says Weck. "We took out a $15,000 loan for a computer that we didn't need. We hired a controller for $30,000 when we were only grossing $400,000 a year. We were acting like a much bigger company."

Failure to manage its finances properly led this business to the brink of bankruptcy. Fortunately, Weck, after buying out his partner, was able to slash expenses, restructure loans, and pay off debt, thereby salvaging a profitable business.

Source: Jeannie Ralston, "Specialty Food with All the Trimmings." Reprinted from the February, 1989, issue of *VENTURE, For Entrepreneurial Business Owners & Investors,* © 1989.

Looking Ahead

Watch for the following important topics:
1. The cash-flow system in a small business.
2. Managing accounts receivable, inventory, and accounts payable.
3. Capital-budgeting methods in the small business.
4. Considerations in evaluating expansion opportunities.
5. New terms and concepts:

working capital	payback-period method
working-capital management	return-on-investment method
cash flow	net-present-value method
cash budgets	internal-rate-of-return method
factoring	search activity
capital budgeting	retained earnings

A small firm must plan and control the use of its financial resources properly if it is to earn a satisfactory return on its investment and meet its obligations in a timely manner. In the short run, it must carefully manage its working capital—especially its cash flow. On a longer-term basis, it must correctly evaluate the attractiveness of various investment opportunities. In this chapter, we present a practical orientation to both types of financial decision making—working-capital management and capital budgeting.

Working-Capital Management

Strange as it may sound, a profitable business may simply run out of money! This unfortunate event may result from mistakes in managing its working capital. Financial management in a small firm, therefore, requires attention to the firm's working capital. **Working capital** may be defined as a firm's current assets. **Working-capital management** begins with management of cash, but extends to other areas—accounts receivable, inventory, and accounts payable, in particular—that directly affect its cash flow.

Managing Cash Flow

At the core of working-capital management is the monitoring of **cash flow.** Cash is constantly pumping through a healthy business. It flows in, for example, as customers pay for products or services, and it flows out as payments are made to suppliers. The typically uneven nature of inward and outward flows makes it imperative that they be properly understood and regulated.

The Nature of Cash Flow   Cash flow may best be understood by focusing upon a firm's bank account. Let us assume that all cash received in the course of business operations is deposited in the firm's bank account and that all payments are made by checks drawn on that account. The firm's cash flow may then be analyzed by examining its bank account. Cash deposits during a month less checks written during the same period equal its net cash flow. If deposits for a month add up to $100,000 and checks total $80,000, the firm has a net positive cash flow of $20,000. The cash balance at the end of the month is $20,000 higher than it was at the beginning of the month. Exhibit 21–1 portrays the flow of cash through a business.

In making such calculations, it is necessary to distinguish between revenues and cash receipts. They are seldom the same. Revenues are recorded at the time a sale is made, but they do not affect cash at that time unless the sale is a cash sale. Cash receipts, on the other hand, are recorded when the money actually flows into the firm, often a month or two after the sale. Similarly, we must distinguish between expenses and disbursements. Expenses occur when the material, labor, or other item is used; payments (disbursements) for these expense items may be made later, at the time that checks are issued.

Net Cash Flow and Profit Are Different   In view of the differences just noted, it should come as no surprise that net cash flow and net profit are also different. Net cash flow is the difference between cash inflows and outflows. Net profit, in contrast, is the difference between revenues and expenses. Failure to understand this distinction can play havoc with a small firm's financial well-being.

One reason for the difference is the uneven timing of cash disbursements and the expensing of those disbursements. As an example, think

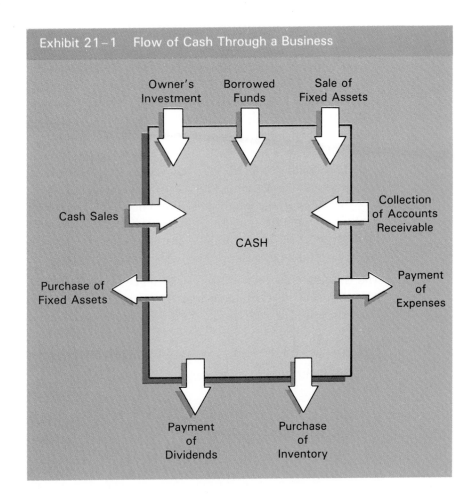

Exhibit 21-1 Flow of Cash Through a Business

about the merchandise purchased by a retail store. It may be paid for (a cash disbursement) before it is sold (when it becomes an expense). On the other hand, labor may be used (an expense) before the paycheck is written (a cash disbursement). In the case of a major cash outlay for a building or equipment, the disbursement will show up immediately as a cash outflow, but it will be recognized as an expense only as the building or equipment is depreciated over a period of years.

Likewise, there is uneven timing of sales revenue and cash receipts because of the extension of credit. A sale is made, at which time the transaction is recorded as revenue, and the cash receipt is recorded when payment for the account receivable is received 30 or 60 days later.

Some cash receipts, furthermore, are not revenue and never become revenue. When a firm borrows money from a bank, for example, it receives cash without receiving revenue. When the principal is repaid to the bank some months later, a cash disbursement occurs. However, no expense is recorded, because the firm is merely returning the money that was borrowed. (Any interest on the loan that was paid to the bank would, of course, constitute both an expense and a cash disbursement.)

Because of the important differences between net cash flow and profit, it is imperative that small firms manage cash flow as carefully as they manage revenues, expenses, and profits. Otherwise, they may find themselves insolvent while showing handsome paper profits.

The Growth Trap   Some firms experience rapid growth of sales volume. The firm's income statement may simultaneously reflect growing profits. However, rapid growth in sales and even profits may be hazardous to the

---

SMALL BUSINESS IN ACTION
Profits But No Cash

A manager needs to monitor both profits and cash flow. Otherwise, the company's checking account may "run dry" at the same time that its income statement shows profits.

The president of a small Midwestern manufacturing company made the mistake of concentrating exclusively on the firm's monthly profit-and-loss statements—statements that showed profits of $5,000 on sales of $100,000. He assumed that cash balances would not be a problem. However, one day the president received a call from an irate creditor who had not been paid. When the president looked into the situation, he found that his company had, indeed, held up payment on a number of bills because of a cash shortage. Concentration on the income statement alone had led to neglect of cash-flow analysis and to the embarrassing surprise that the company's sales dollars had not made it to the bank in time to pay the bills.

Source: Ron D. Richardson, "Managing Your Company's Cash," *Nation's Business,* Vol. 74, No. 11 (November, 1986), pp. 52–54. Copyright 1986, U.S. Chamber of Commerce.

firm's cash. This happens because growth tends to soak up additional cash more rapidly than such cash can be generated in the form of additional profits.

Inventory, for example, must be expanded as sales volume increases. This means that additional dollars must be expended for merchandise or raw materials to accommodate the higher level of sales. Similarly, accounts receivable must be expanded proportionally to the increased sales volume. It should be evident, then, that a growing, profitable business could quickly find itself in a financial bind. As Welsh and White have pointed out, "It is perfectly normal to find that a business is growing profitably while going broke down at the bank."[1]

The distinctive characteristics of small firms make the growth problem particularly acute for them:

> Larger businesses usually grow at slower rates than smaller businesses. It is possible to double sales in one year if what is being doubled is small. It is nearly impossible to double sales in one year if annual sales are already a billion dollars. Because of this, smaller businesses are more likely to have a continuous and urgent need for proportionally more money to overcome negative cash flow than their larger counterparts.[2]

In view of the small firm's characteristic difficulty in obtaining funds externally, it is apparent that the growth trap can be lethal for small businesses unless cash is managed carefully.

The Process of Cash Budgeting   **Cash budgets** are tools for managing cash flow. They differ in a number of ways from income statements. Income statements take items into consideration before they affect cash—for example, expenses that are incurred but not yet paid and income earned but not yet received. Cash budgets, in contrast, are concerned specifically with dollars as they are received and paid out.

By using a cash budget, the entrepreneur can predict and plan the cash flow of a business. An example of a cash budget for a small retail store is shown in Exhibit 21–2. The business portrayed in this example has projected an uneven monthly sales volume, ranging from $50,000 in January and June to $100,000 in March.

The forecast of monthly sales is the first step in estimating the inflow of cash. These sales figures can be taken from the operating budget which, as discussed in Chapter 20, will typically be developed first. Sales figures and cash receipts are not identical, however, because sales are made on a credit basis. In this cash budget, it is assumed that none of the payments

Exhibit 21-2   Cash Budget for a Small Business

	January	February	March	April	May	June
Sales	$ 50,000	$ 70,000	$100,000	$75,000	$60,000	$50,000
Cash receipts:						
1 month after sale	$ 27,500	$ 25,000	$ 35,000	$50,000	$37,500	$30,000
2 months after sale	20,000	27,500	25,000	35,000	50,000	37,500
Total cash receipts	$ 47,500	$ 52,500	$ 60,000	$85,000	$87,500	$67,500
Cash disbursements:						
Purchases	$ 35,000	$ 49,000	$ 70,000	$52,500	$42,000	$35,000
Selling and administrative expense	15,000	20,000	35,000	21,000	18,000	15,000
Inventory carrying cost	175	245	350	263	210	175
Interest expense	325	350	492	847	788	567
Taxes	0	0	0	0	0	0
Capital expenditures	0	0	0	0	0	0
Dividends	0	0	0	0	0	0
Total cash disbursements	$ 50,500	$ 69,595	$105,842	$74,610	$60,998	$50,742
Net cash flow	$ -3,000	$ -17,095	$ -45,842	$10,390	$26,502	$16,758
Beginning cash balance	4,000	4,000	4,000	4,000	4,000	4,000
Unadjusted ending balance	1,000	-13,095	-41,842	14,390	30,502	20,758
Borrow	3,000	17,095	45,842	0	0	0
Repay	0	0	0	10,390	26,502	16,758
Ending cash balance	4,000	4,000	4,000	4,000	4,000	4,000

will be received in the month of the sale, that one-half will be received in the month following the sale, and that the remaining one-half will be received in the second month following the sale. Since this business has been in operation for some time, the January receipts are based on sales that were made in the previous November and December.

Cash disbursements involve expenditures for a variety of purposes. In this example, we assume that the store has a gross margin of 30 percent. This means that March sales of $100,000 will cost $70,000. The order is placed in February, and the entire amount is paid in the month following the purchase. Therefore, goods sold in March must be paid for in March. Expenditures for selling and administrative activities are self-explanatory. The inventory-carrying cost includes expenditures, such as insurance payments, that vary with the investment level.

Interest expense represents interest payments on bank loans. As of January 1, this business owed $38,980 to the bank at an interest rate of 10 percent. Additional money is borrowed in months in which there is a negative cash flow, and loans are repaid in months showing a positive cash flow. The company plans to keep a minimum cash balance of $4,000 at all times.

Since the company does not anticipate a net profit during the first six months, there are no projected payments for taxes. Also, there is no plan for purchase of fixed assets or payment of dividends during this time.

As you can see, the company does not achieve a positive cash flow until April. Additional borrowing must be arranged, therefore, in each of the first three months. By preparing a cash budget, the owner of this business can anticipate these needs and avoid the nasty surprises that might otherwise occur.

On those occasions when a small business has idle funds, the cash should be invested. The cash forecast is a basis for anticipating these occasions. If unexpected excess funds are generated, they can be invested also. Many short-term investment opportunities are available. Certificates of deposit and money market certificates are just two of the many vehicles for putting excess cash to work for the firm.

Managing Accounts Receivable

In Chapter 12, we discussed the extension of credit by small firms and their practices in managing and collecting accounts receivable. In this section, we consider the impact of credit decisions on working capital and particularly on cash flow.

Figure 21-1   A Credit Sale Begins Receivables Life Cycle

Courtesy of IBM Corporation

How Accounts Receivable Affect Cash   Granting credit to customers is a marketing decision that directly affects a firm's cash account. By selling on credit, the selling firm delays the inflow of cash by allowing customers to delay payment, thereby tying up money in accounts receivable.

The total of customer credit balances is carried on the balance sheet as accounts receivable—one of the current assets of the business. Of all noncash assets, accounts receivable is closest to becoming cash. Sometimes called "near cash," accounts receivable are typically paid and become cash within 30 to 60 days.

The Life Cycle of Receivables   The receivables cycle begins with a credit sale. In many businesses, an invoice is then prepared and mailed to the purchaser. When the invoice is received, the purchaser processes it, prepares a check, and mails the check in payment to the seller.

Under ideal circumstances, each of these steps is taken in a timely manner. It is obvious, however, that delays can occur at any stage of this process. Some, indeed, may result from inefficiencies within the selling firm. One small-business owner found that the shipping clerk was "batching" invoices before sending them to the office for processing. This naturally delayed the preparation and mailing of invoices to customers. And, of course, this practice also postponed the day on which the customer's money was received and deposited in the bank so that it could be used to pay bills.

Credit management policies, practices, and procedures, as explained in Chapter 12, affect the life cycle of receivables and the flow of cash from them. It is important that, in establishing credit policies, small-business owners consider cash-flow requirements as well as the need to stimulate sales. Following are some examples of credit-management practices that can have a positive impact on a company's cash flow:

1. Minimizing the time between shipping, invoicing, and sending notices on billings.
2. Reviewing credit experience to determine impediments to cash flow, such as continued extension of credit to slow-paying or delinquent customers.
3. Providing incentives for prompt payment by granting cash discounts or charging interest on delinquent accounts.
4. Aging accounts receivable on a monthly or even weekly basis to identify quickly any delinquent account.
5. Using the most effective methods for collecting overdue accounts.

Accounts-Receivable Financing Some small businesses can speed up the cash flow from receivables by borrowing against them. By financing receivables, they can often secure the use of their money 30 to 60 days earlier than would be possible otherwise. Although at one time this practice was concentrated largely in the apparel trades, it has expanded to many other types of small business such as manufacturers, food processors, distributors, home building suppliers, and temporary employment agencies. Financing of this type is provided by commercial finance companies and by some banks.

Two types of financing are possible. In one, a firm's accounts receivable are pledged as collateral for a loan. When payments are received from customers, the payments are forwarded to the lending institution to pay off the loan. In the second type of financing, a business sells its accounts receivable to a finance company, a practice known as **factoring.** The finance company assumes the bad-debt risk associated with receivables it buys.

The obvious advantage of accounts-receivable financing is the immediate cash flow it provides for firms that have limited working capital. As a secondary benefit, the volume of borrowing can quickly be expanded proportionally to a firm's growth in sales and accounts receivable.

An obvious drawback to this practice is the high finance cost. Interest rates typically run several points above the prime interest rate, and factors also charge a fee that compensates them for their credit-investigation activities and for the risk they take that customers may default in payment. However, a borrower may escape the expense of conducting a credit investigation of customers by turning this function over to the factor. Another weakness is that pledging accounts receivable may limit a firm's ability to borrow from a bank by removing a prime asset from its available collateral.

Managing Inventory

Inventory is a "necessary evil" to the financial management system. It is necessary because supply and demand cannot be manipulated to coincide precisely in day-to-day operations. It is an evil because inventory ties up funds that are not actively productive.

Freeing Cash by Reducing Inventory   Inventory is a bigger problem to some small businesses than to others. The inventory of many service firms, for example, consists of only a few supplies. A manufacturer, on the other hand, has several inventories—raw materials, finished goods, and supplies. Also, retailers and wholesalers, especially those with high inventory turnover rates (such as those in grocery distribution), are continually involved in inventory-management problems.

In Chapter 19, we discussed several ideas related to purchasing and inventory management that were designed to minimize inventory-carrying costs and processing costs. At this point, we wish to emphasize practices that will minimize average inventory levels, thereby releasing funds for other applications. A correct minimum of inventory is the level needed to maintain desired production schedules or a required level of customer service. A concerted effort to manage inventory can trim inventory fat and pay handsome dividends. For example, the Boston-based Superior Pet Products Company tightened its inventory policies and freed up about $400,000 in capital. This released capital also meant a savings of $80,000 in interest expense, which was being paid to finance the inventory.[3]

Staying on Top of Inventory   One of the first tactics of managing inventory to reduce capital investment is to discover what is in inventory and how long it has been there. Too often, items are purchased, warehoused, and essentially lost! A yearly inventory for accounting purposes is inadequate for good inventory control. Items that are slow-movers may sit in a retailer's inventory beyond the time when markdowns should have been applied.

Computers can provide assistance in inventory identification and control. The use of physical inventories may still be required, but only as a supplement to the computer system.

Holding the Reins on Stockpiling Some small-business managers tend to overbuy inventory. There are several possible reasons for this behavior. First, the entrepreneur's enthusiasm may forecast greater demand than is realistic. Second, the personalization of the business–customer relationship may motivate the manager to stock everything customers want. Third, the price-conscious entrepreneur may overly subscribe to vendor appeal—"buy now, prices are going up."

Stockpiling is not bad per se. Improperly managed and uncontrolled stockpiling may, however, greatly increase inventory-carrying costs and place a heavy drain on the funds of a small business. Restraint must be exercised with stockpiling efforts.

Managing Accounts Payable

Cash-flow management and accounts-payable management are intertwined. As long as a payable is outstanding, the buying firm can keep cash equal to that amount in its own checking account. When payment is made, however, the company's cash account is reduced accordingly.

Even though payables are legal obligations, they can be paid at various times or even renegotiated in some cases. Therefore, financial management of accounts payable hinges on negotiation and timing.

Negotiation Any business is subject to emergencies, which may lead to a request for the postponement of its payable obligations. If a firm finds itself in this situation, it should so inform its creditors. Usually creditors will cooperate in working out a solution because they are interested in the firm and want it to succeed.

Timing It would not be surprising to find the motto "Buy Now, Pay Later, Later, Later . . ." over all enterpreneurs' desks. By buying on credit, a small business is using creditors' funds to supply short-term cash needs. The

Exhibit 21-3   An Accounts-Payable Timetable

Timetable (Days after invoice date)	Account Settlement Costs for a $100,000 Purchase (Terms: 3/10, net 30)
Day 1 through Day 10	$97,000
Day 11 through Day 30	$100,000
Day 31 and thereafter	$100,000 + possible late penalty + deterioration in credit standing

longer the creditors' funds can be "borrowed," the better. Payment, therefore, should seemingly be made as late as the agreement specifies.

Typically, trade credit will include payment terms that contain a cash discount. For example, terms of 3/10, net 30 would offer a 3 percent potential discount. With trade-discount terms, the entrepreneur's motto of "Buy Now, Pay Later" may be inappropriate. For example, Exhibit 21-3 shows the possible settlement cost over the credit period of 30 days. For a $100,000 purchase, a settlement of only $97,000 is required if payment is made within the first 10 days ($100,000 minus the 3 percent discount of $3,000). During the interim between day 11 and day 31, a settlement of $100,000 is required. After 30 days, the settlement cost may even exceed the original amount, as the exhibit indicates.

The timing question is as follows: Should the account be paid on day 10 or day 30? There is little reason for paying $97,000 on day 1 through day 9, when the same amount will settle the account on day 10. Likewise, if payment is to be made after day 10, why not wait until day 30 to pay $100,000?

By paying on the last day of the discount period, the buyer saves the amount of the discount that is offered. The other alternative, payment on day 30, allows the buyer to use the seller's money for an additional 20 days by foregoing the discount. In the example shown in Exhibit 21-3, the buyer can use the seller's $97,000 for 20 days at a cost of $3,000. The annualized interest rate that is involved can be calculated as follows:

$$\text{Annualized rate} = \frac{\text{Days in year}}{\text{Net period} - \text{Cash disc. period}} \times \frac{\text{Cash discount \%}}{100\% - \text{Cash disc. \%}}$$

$$= \frac{365}{30 - 10} \times \frac{.03}{1.00 - .03}$$

$$= 18.25 \times .030928$$

$$= 56.4\%$$

By failing to take a discount, a business typically pays a high rate for use of a supplier's money—56.4 percent in this case. Payment appears entirely logical. Recall, however, that the payment also affects cash flow. If funds are extremely short, the small firm may simply have to pay on the last possible day in order to avoid an overdraft at the bank.

Capital Budgeting in Small Business

The manager of a going concern must find time to search for alternative prospective investments if the business is to grow. After assessing the availability of expansion capital, the manager must determine the most profitable use of such funds by appraising the alternative investment opportunities open to the small firm.

Figure 21–2   New Building Construction Is One Item in Capital Budgeting

Capital budgeting assumes that the firm's supply of capital is limited and that it should be rationed in such a way as to provide funds for the best investment proposals. In its broadest sense, capital budgeting includes investments of both a long-range and short-range nature. In this chapter, however, our concern is with long-range financial commitments; the discussion that follows deals exclusively with long-range movements of funds.

What are some typical investment proposals entailing an outlay of funds that a small manufacturer might be contemplating at one time? Some examples include the following:

1. Development and introduction of a new product that shows promise but requires additional study and improvement.
2. Replacement of the company's delivery trucks with newer models.
3. Expansion of sales activity into a new territory.
4. Construction of a new building.
5. Employment of several additional salespersons for more intensive selling in the existing market.

Because capital is insufficient to finance all five investment proposals, the owner-manager must decide which of them must be postponed or rejected and which should be accepted. Both the cost of capital and the absolute limit on the volume of available funds require the rejection not only of proposals that would be unprofitable, but also of those that would be least profitable. A ranking of the alternative investment proposals according to their profitability can be made after each proposal has been evaluated.

Traditional Methods of Investment Valuation

Two rule-of-thumb methods of evaluating investment proposals are the payback-period method and the return-on-investment method. In using either of these methods, only net additions to costs or profits are considered. For example, if a partially depreciated machine is to be replaced, the book value of the old machine is ignored except for the purpose of calculating the tax impact of resale at a price differing from book value. Of course, any salvage or trade-in value of the old machine would be considered in computing the investment cost.

The greatest value of these traditional methods lies in their simplicity. They provide a rough check for evaluating an investment. Although they have definite limitations when compared with the more sophisticated valuation tools described later in this chapter, they are widely used and often provide satisfactory answers.

Payback-Period Method The **payback-period method** shows the number of years it takes to recover the original cost of an investment from annual net cash flows. Suppose that a firm is considering Project A and Project B, each of which requires an investment of $100,000. The estimated annual cash flows (profit plus depreciation) from the two projects are as shown in Exhibit 21–4.

The payback period for Project A is three years; for Project B, four years. If the firm ordinarily sets three years as its standard payback period, then Project A will be accepted and Project B rejected.

Return-on-Investment Method The simple **return-on-investment method** evaluates proposals by relating the expected annual profit from an investment to the amount invested. This method is expressed in the following equation:

$$\text{Rate of return} = \frac{\text{Annual profit}}{\text{Investment}}$$

If the expected return on an investment of $100,000 is $20,000, the rate of return will be 20 percent. Such an investment is justified if more lucrative investments are not available and if a return of 20 percent is reasonable in view of the risk involved.

Exhibit 21–4 Annual Cash Flows, Project A and Project B

Economic Life (Year)	Cash Flow Project A	Cash Flow Project B
1	$50,000	$10,000
2	40,000	20,000
3	10,000	30,000
4	10,000	40,000
5		50,000
6		60,000
	$110,000	$210,000

Weaknesses of Traditional Methods   The payback-period method and the return-on-investment method are subject to two major weaknesses. First, they fail to recognize the time value of money. For example, suppose Projects C and D, each of which costs $10,000, had net cash flows listed in Exhibit 21–5. Both projects have a three-year payback, which makes them equally attractive when judged by this criterion. But we know that a dollar today is worth more than a dollar a year from today because the dollar can earn interest during the year. Therefore, Project C, with its faster cash flow, is more desirable.

The second weakness of the traditional methods is their neglect of the economic life of a project. Going back to the annual cash flows from Projects A and B given in Exhibit 21–4, we note that the payback period of Project B is a year longer than that of Project A. But Project B's longer economic life of six years provides $100,000 more in total cash flow than Project A. In a similar manner, a simple rate-of-return method gives no indication of the length of time during which that rate of return may be expected to continue.

Theoretically Correct Methods of Investment Valuation

Two valuation methods designed to eliminate the defects of traditional methods are the net-present-value method and the internal-rate-of-return method.

Net-Present-Value Method   Present value means the value today of a stream of expected net cash flows, discounted at an appropriate rate of

Exhibit 21–5   Net Cash Flows, Project C and Project D

Year	Cash Flow Project C	Cash Flow Project D
1	$ 5,000	$ 1,000
2	4,000	4,000
3	1,000	5,000
	$10,000	$10,000

interest. The **net-present-value method** is calculated by means of the following formula:

$$V = \left[\frac{CF_1}{(1 + r)} + \frac{CF_2}{(1 + r)^2} + \cdots + \frac{CF_n}{(1 + r)^n} + \frac{S}{(1 + r)^n} \right] - C$$

Where V = excess present value over cost
CF_t = post-tax cash flow in year t (where t is 1, 2, 3, ... n)
S = terminal salvage value
r = selected rate of interest
C = cost of asset/project
n = useful life of asset/project

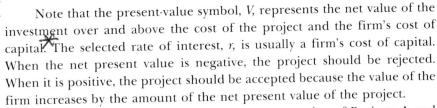

Note that the present-value symbol, V, represents the net value of the investment over and above the cost of the project and the firm's cost of capital. The selected rate of interest, r, is usually a firm's cost of capital. When the net present value is negative, the project should be rejected. When it is positive, the project should be accepted because the value of the firm increases by the amount of the net present value of the project.

To illustrate, let us calculate the net present value of Projects A and B, previously cited, assuming a 10 percent cost of capital. Also assume that neither project has any salvage value. By using the formula just given, the net present value of Project A is calculated as follows:

$$V = \left[\frac{CF_1}{(1 + r)} + \frac{CF_2}{(1 + r)^2} + \frac{CF_3}{(1 + r)^3} + \frac{CF_4}{(1 + r)^4} \right] - C$$

Where CF_1 = cash flow in year 1 = \$50,000
CF_2 = cash flow in year 2 = \$40,000
CF_3 = cash flow in year 3 = \$10,000
CF_4 = cash flow in year 4 = \$10,000
r = 10%
C = \$100,000
n = 4 years

$$V = \left[\frac{50,000}{1.1} + \frac{40,000}{1.21} + \frac{10,000}{1.33} + \frac{10,000}{1.46} \right] - 100,000$$

$$V = [45,455 + 33,058 + 7,519 + 6,849] - 100,000$$
$$V = -7,119$$

With a *negative* present value of \$7,119, Project A should be rejected.[4]

Calculating the net present value of Project B, the formula would be applied as follows:

$$V = \left[\frac{10{,}000}{1.1} + \frac{20{,}000}{1.21} + \frac{30{,}000}{1.33} + \frac{40{,}000}{1.46} + \frac{50{,}000}{1.61} + \frac{60{,}000}{1.77} \right] - 100{,}000$$

$$V = [9{,}091 + 16{,}529 + 22{,}556 + 27{,}397 + 31{,}056 + 33{,}898] - 100{,}000$$
$$V = 40{,}527$$

Since Project B yields a *positive* net present value of $40,527, this project should be accepted.[5]

Internal-Rate-of-Return Method In using the **internal-rate-of-return method,** one first finds that rate of return which equates the cost of the investment project with the present value of its expected net cash flows. The formula to be applied is the following, which is basically the same as that of the net-present-value method.

$$C = \frac{CF_1}{(1 + r)} + \frac{CF_2}{(1 + r)^2} + \ldots + \frac{CF_n + S}{(1 + r)^n}$$

Where CF_t = post-tax cash flow in year t (where t is 1, 2, 3, . . . n)
C = cost of asset/project
n = useful life of asset/project
r = unknown rate of return
S = terminal salvage value

The internal rate of return on the project may be found by trial and error, starting with any arbitrarily selected rate of interest. Then compute the present value of the cash flows and compare it with the cost of the project. If the present value is higher than the cost of the project, try a higher interest rate and go through the procedure again. Conversely, if the present value obtained is lower than the cost of the project, try a lower rate of interest and repeat the process. Continue this procedure until the present value obtained is approximately equal to the cost of the project. The interest rate that brings about this equality is the internal rate of return of that particular project.

To calculate the internal rate of return for Project A, again assuming that there is no salvage value, we can start with the firm's cost of capital, which has already been given as 10 percent. By substituting 10 percent for r, we find that the present value of the net cash flows of Project A is less than its initial cost of $100,000.

$$V = \frac{50{,}000}{1.1} + \frac{40{,}000}{1.21} + \frac{10{,}000}{1.33} + \frac{10{,}000}{1.46}$$

$$V = 45{,}455 + 33{,}058 + 7{,}519 + 6{,}849$$
$$V = 92{,}881$$

By repeating the procedure with lower interest rates, we find that the interest rate that will equate the present value of the net cash flows with the initial cost of the project is somewhere between 5 percent and 6 percent.

Once the internal rate of return of a particular project is calculated, it can be compared with the firm's current cost of capital (or cost of debt). If the internal rate of return of the particular project is calculated to be the same as the firm's cost of capital, the firm would simply be breaking even if it went ahead with the project. If the calculated internal rate of return exceeds the firm's cost of capital, the project would be profitable. But if the calculated internal rate of return is less than the firm's cost of capital, as is the case for Project A, the result would be a loss.

Criticisms of Theoretically Correct Methods Even though these methods are theoretically superior to the traditional ones, they are not widely used in small businesses. The typical small-business manager is unaware of the existence of these methods and would not readily understand the underlying reasoning and analysis involved. In addition, the solution of problems through these methods is often time-consuming and may require the use of a computer.

Perhaps the greatest deterrent to the use of theoretically correct valuation methods is the extreme uncertainty that surrounds many investment decisions. If great uncertainty about future demands or costs exists, the use of sophisticated methods may provide little practical guidance. Instead, the small-business entrepreneur may prefer to base decisions on short-run prospects—for example, approving an investment that seems likely to return the invested capital in one or two years.

Other Considerations in Evaluating Expansion Opportunities

Having focused on capital-budgeting methods for evaluating investment opportunities, let us now turn to other considerations that enter into expansion decisions. These considerations involve a firm's growth philosophy, constraints on expansion, search activity, and approach to financing the expansion.

Growth Philosophy

There are many entrepreneurs who prefer smallness. Some of them begin business with the expectation that their firms will remain small, while others come to this conclusion after experimenting with growth. As an example of the latter, Skip Kelley converted his remodeling business into a franchise of Mr. Build International and grew quickly.[6] Sales climbed from $320,000 to $1.2 million in just three years, but Kelley found himself with a company he couldn't control. Problems eventually led to liquidation of the business. "This whole thing cost me a business. It cost me a sports car. It cost me a wife," he says now. "It cost me a lot of things."[7] After Kelley closed the business, he began operating a small building-inspection company out of his house in Byfield, MA. He values his less-hectic lifestyle and recognizes he was not "the right guy to run a multimillion-dollar company."

Many other small-business owners carry growth ambitions from the very early days of starting their businesses. Growth is a continuing goal for these entrepreneurs. For example, Carl Karcher, who founded Carl's Jr. Hamburgers in California in 1941, expresses his growth philosophy by saying, "If your company decides not to grow, that's the beginning of the end."[8]

But growth is not without its problems. Expansion can strain a firm's capital position and damage current operations. It can also spread managerial skills too thin.

Constraints on Expansion

How rapidly can a small business grow? There is obviously no simple answer to such a question. Even so, a small firm must often decide how rapidly it can grow as it is faced with opportunities for expansion. Such opportunities carry the incentive of increased profits, but they can also stretch a firm's resources to their limit and sometimes beyond. The depth and quality of a company's resources, therefore, impose limits on the rate of expansion.

Some constraints are financial in nature. Long-term investments in buildings, equipment, new products, or new territories, for example, require infusions of capital that may or may not be available. Also, as noted earlier, growth of sales volume requires a corresponding increase in working capital.

There are also nonfinancial constraints that limit the scope and rapidity of expansion. As explained in Chapter 15, more sophisticated management methods are needed as small firms become big businesses. Time is needed to develop or expand a management team to the point that it can successfully manage a much larger business. Unless a small firm's leadership is truly outstanding, its expansion can sometimes outrun the growth of its management team.

SMALL BUSINESS IN ACTION
Dangers in Rapid Expansion

Spectacular success and rapid growth are sometimes matched by an equally spectacular demise. James Bildner opened his first upscale grocery store (J. Bildner & Sons, Inc.) in 1984. The store was an instant hit, and it was featured, within a month, in a *Newsweek* story on Yuppies. By 1987, the company had grown to 21 stores with 2,000 employees and $49 million in sales.

By 1988, however, the company had filed for protection under Chapter 11 of the federal Bankruptcy Code.

J. Bildner was a textbook example of the dangers of overexpansion. It grew too fast, too haphazardly. Its market research was flawed, its management ill-equipped to handle rapid growth. And it strayed from its original concept.

This failure revealed a management group that lacked extensive experience. Only one of its 10 officers, for example, was older than 35.

Source: Buck Brown, "James Bildner's Spectacular Rise and Fall," *The Wall Street Journal* (October 24, 1988), p. B1. Reprinted by permission of *The Wall Street Journal,* © Dow Jones & Company, Inc. 1988. All Rights Reserved Worldwide.

Search Activity

All growth opportunities must be scrutinized carefully. For too long, small business has been saddled with the reputation of making growth decisions without extensive **search activity.** Small-business managers have often considered growth opportunities on a one-at-a-time basis. They have been less concerned with ranking a number of growth possibilities than with trying to determine the merit of one particular proposal. Moreover, in the analysis of a single proposal, they have often jumped to a conclusion on the basis of sketchy information.

The apparent deficiencies in small-business search activity provide an opportunity for improvement in the quality of small-business investment decisions. By breaking out of the pattern of routine activity or by delegating such work to others, the small-business entrepreneur can make more time for the search activity that leads to more profitable expansion.

Friends and acquaintances who are in management positions with other firms are valuable sources of information about expansion opportunities. Many other professionals, such as lawyers and bankers, are also reliable sources of this type of information. Trade journals and publications, such as *The Wall Street Journal,* can also contain notifications of purchase opportunities that represent potential growth developments.

Methods of Financing Expansion

The financing of expansion is usually a major consideration in growth plans. Financing can be internal or external. Many of the sources of initial financing discussed in Chapter 9 also provide expansion funds. An entrepreneur's past success with a new venture will usually make the financing of expansion easier than startup financing.

Realized profits that are plowed back into the business, or **retained earnings,** constitute a major source of funds for financing small-business expansion. Such internally generated funds may be invested in physical facilities or used to expand the firm's working capital. It is likely that the majority of small firms experience an annual growth in net worth as a result of retained earnings.

In using retained earnings, the rate of expansion is limited by the amount of profits generated by the business. In the case of a rapidly expanding small firm, these funds are often insufficient to meet the heavy capital needs.

Financing through retained earnings provides a conservative approach to expansion. The dangers of overexpansion or expansion that is too rapid are largely avoided. Because the additional funds are equity, the firm has no creditors threatening foreclosure and no due dates by which repayment must be made.

The lack of an interest charge on funds secured in this way may create the impression that there is no cost involved in their use. Even though there is no out-of-pocket cost, there is a definite opportunity cost involved. This opportunity cost is the dividend foregone by stockholders. Presumably the stockholders could have reinvested their dividends in other income-generating opportunities.

Looking Back

1. The cash-flow system consists of cash flowing into a business (through sales revenue, borrowing, and so on) and cash flowing out of the business (through purchases, operating expenses, loan repayments, and so on). These inflows and outflows are reconciled in the cash budget, which involves forecasts of receipts and expenditures on a month-to-month basis. If projections indicate a negative cash flow from operations, arrangements must be made to secure additional funds through borrowing or investment.

2. Managment of working capital requires attention not only to cash flow but also to accounts receivable, inventory, and accounts payable. A firm can improve its cash flow by speeding up collections from customers, minimizing inventories, and using the maximum allowable time in paying suppliers.

3. Capital budgeting is the process of planning expenditures on which returns are expected to extend well into the future. The most popular capital-budgeting techniques among small businesses are the payback-period and return-on-investment methods. The net-present-value method and the internal-rate-of-return method are additional techniques that are considered to be theoretically correct.

4. Small-business owners have various expansion philosophies. Success in expansion is facilitated by proper search activity and an adequate base of financial and managerial resources. Most sources of initial financing can also be used for expansion. Retained earnings provide a conservative, relatively safe approach to financing expansion.

DISCUSSION QUESTIONS

1. What are some examples of cash receipts that are not sales revenue?
2. Explain how expenses and cash disbursements during a month may be different.
3. Explain how a firm may be unable to pay its bills when its income statement shows a profit.
4. Assume that a small firm is growing rapidly. What kind of pressures or problems does this create in its working-capital management?
5. If a small business has a reasonably accurate projected income statement, does it need a cash budget? Why?
6. In a typical small business, what is the source of most cash receipts shown in the cash budget?

7. Suppose you are a banker and are considering loan requests from two small firms. One of them has a cash budget. How does this fact affect your evaluation of the two requests? Explain.

8. How may a seller speed up the collection of receivables? Give examples that may apply to various stages in the life cycle of receivables.

9. Explain the difference between borrowing by pledging accounts receivable and factoring. What are the principal drawbacks to accounts-receivable financing?

10. Suppose that a small firm could successfully shift to a just-in-time inventory system. How would this affect its working-capital management?

11. Do you think a business has an obligation to pay its accounts payable before the net due date if it has the funds? Why or why not?

12. What appear to be the principal weaknesses of traditional capital-budgeting methods used by small-business firms?

13. What are the principal advantages of the internal-rate-of-return method and the net-present-value method as compared with the traditional methods of capital budgeting?

14. What is meant by "search activity," and how is it related to investment by small-business firms?

15. Explain the danger in considering investment expansion proposals one at a time (as is done by so many small-business owner-managers) instead of ranking a number of them.

YOU MAKE THE CALL

Situation 1

A small firm specializing in the sale and installation of swimming pools was profitable but devoted very little attention to management of working capital. It had, for example, never prepared or used a cash budget.

To be sure that money was available for payments as needed, the firm kept a minimum of $25,000 in a checking account. At times, this account grew larger, and it totaled $43,000 at one time. The owner felt that this practice of cash management worked well for a small company because it eliminated all of the paperwork associated with cash budgeting. Moreover, it had enabled the firm to pay its bills in a timely manner.

Questions

1. What are the advantages and weaknesses of the minimum-cash-balance practice?
2. There is a saying, "If it's not broke, don't fix it." In view of the firm's present success in paying bills promptly, should it be encouraged to use a cash budget? Defend your answer.

Situation 2

Ruston Manufacturing Company is a small firm selling entirely on a credit basis. It has experienced successful operation and earned modest profits.

Sales are made on the basis of net payment in 30 days. Collections from customers run approximately 70 percent in 30 days, 20 percent in 60 days, 7 percent in 90 days, and approximately 3 percent bad debts.

The owner has considered the possibility of offering a cash discount for early payment. However, the practice seems costly and possibly unnecessary. As the owner has put it, "Why should I bribe customers to pay what they legally owe?"

Questions

1. Is a cash discount the equivalent of a bribe?
2. How would a cash discount policy relate to bad debts?
3. What cash discount policy, if any, would you recommend?
4. What other approaches might be used to improve cash flow from receivables?

EXPERIENTIAL EXERCISES

1. Prepare a cash budget projecting your personal cash receipts and cash expenditures month by month for the next three months. Include an explanation of any unusual features.
2. Interview a small-business owner or credit manager regarding the extension of credit and/or the collection of receivables in that firm. Summarize your findings in a report.
3. Interview a small-business owner concerning some specific long-term investment that has been made by his or her business within the past five years. Find out how the investment decision was made, whether alterna-

tive investment opportunities were considered at the time, and whether the entrepreneur made any use of traditional evaluation methods or is aware of the net-present-value or internal-rate-of-return methods. Summarize your findings in a report.

4. Assume that you are starting a small business. Prepare a one-page statement outlining your personal philosophy of business growth. Include an explanation of the values and reasons that underlie this philosophy.

REFERENCES TO SMALL-BUSINESS PRACTICES

Gupta, Udayan. "Locating Those Costly Cash Leaks." *Venture*, Vol. 7, No. 12 (December, 1985), pp. 118–120.

This article describes the steps taken by several small companies to improve their management of cash flow.

Kyd, Charles W. "Formula for Disaster?" *Inc.*, Vol. 8, No. 11 (November, 1986), pp. 123–126.

Management of accounts receivable can become confusing if defective analytical tools are used. One firm's problems of this type are described.

Mamis, Robert A. "Factors to Consider." *Inc.*, Vol. 8, No. 10 (October, 1986), pp. 131–136.

The practices of several specific financial institutions in financing accounts receivable of small firms are described.

McKeown, Kate. "Go with the Cash Flow." *D&B Reports*, Vol. 36, No. 5 (September–October, 1988), pp. 30–35.

This article describes the frustrations of a small-business owner in trying to exercise financial control without adequate information on cash flow. The improvement achieved through better analysis of cash aspects of the business is explained.

Persinos, John F. "The Once and Future King." *Inc.*, Vol. 6, No. 3 (March, 1984), pp. 54–58.

This article explains the major financial problems encountered in an ill-advised major expansion by a well-established small company. The company eventually returned to its original size.

ENDNOTES

1. John A. Welsh and Jerry F. White, *Administering the Closely Held Company* (Englewood Cliffs, NJ: Prentice-Hall, Inc., 1980), p. 50.

2. *Ibid.*, p. 51.

3. "How to Unlock Your Company's Hidden Cash," *Inc.*, Vol. 2, No. 7 (July, 1980), p. 64.

4. The use of interest factors found in present-value tables would facilitate the solution of these problems.

5. Rounding off the denominators in the equation or rounding off interest factors in present-value tables would give slightly different answers.

6. "Big Dreams," *Inc.*, Vol. 9, No. 11 (November, 1987), p. 14.

7. *Ibid.*

8. Doris A. Byron, "Carl's Jr.: 306-Unit Restaurant Chain Began as a Hot Dog Cart," *Los Angeles Times* (May 26, 1981), p. 1.

22 COMPUTER APPLICATIONS

Spotlight on Small Business

© 1985 Bill Ballenberg

Predefined spreadsheets or templates provide simple worksheets that eliminate the need to start each computer project from scratch. A template can be purchased and used as is, or it can be modified by the user—even by a relatively inexperienced programmer.

Anderia Luz, a secretary at the Master Engineers and Designers consulting firm in Lynchburg, VA, is an inexperienced computer operator who has effectively used templates for spreadsheets. "When I first started doing this, I didn't even know what a spreadsheet was," recalls Luz.

Luz has created a customized spreadsheet to track the firm's 18 employees, capturing information on regular time, overtime, sick time, and "business development" time. This tracking is used to determine "chargeable" time to clients. "About all I have to do is enter the numbers and watch it recalculate," she says.

Source: Reprinted with permission from *Personal Computing*, September, 1985, pp. 55–59. Copyright 1986, Hayden Publishing Company. © 1985 Bill Ballenberg. All rights reserved.

Looking Ahead

Watch for the following important topics:
1. Components and types of computer systems.
2. Computer hardware and software.
3. Computer applications in small firms.
4. How to computerize a small firm.
5. The future of computers.
6. New terms and concepts:

computer	floppy disks
computer system	user friendly
mainframe	hard disks
minicomputers	software
microcomputers	system software
personal computers (PCs)	application software
network	word processing
hardware	mail merge
dot-matrix printers	spell check
letter-quality printers	modem
laser printers	electronic spreadsheets
magnetic disk drives	

In years past, computers were used primarily by large governmental agencies and big business. This is no longer the case. Computers are now a vital educational tool in our schools. We even use computers in our homes for leisure and recreational activities and household management. Therefore, it is to be expected that small firms can also reap the benefits of using a computer.

Probably the four factors contributing most to this remarkable development are lower computer prices, a greater understanding of what computers can do, advances in computer programs to do the work, and advances in techniques for "communicating" with computers. In this chapter, you will see the influence of these four factors as we emphasize the components of a computer system, small-business applications, and special considerations in the decision to computerize.

The Nature of Computer Systems

A **computer,** in concept, is a relatively simple device—a machine designed to follow instructions. In reality, it is a complex data-processing machine, vastly outperforming human beings in the tasks of recording, classifying, calculating, storing, and communicating information. Every **computer system** consists of four components, each of which performs a unique function—processing, storage, input, or output. Exhibit 22–1 depicts the basic relationship between these components and shows examples of typical units performing the functions. The computer (the processing unit) receives data from input and storage units and sends data to the output and storage components. Computer calculations occur within the processing unit and consist of both arithmetic computations and logic comparisons.

Types of Computer Systems

There are no clear definitions that distinguish all types of computers. However, computer systems are commonly grouped into three basic categories according to size: mainframes, minicomputers, and microcomputers. A **mainframe** computer is a very large machine capable of processing large amounts of information in a very short time. Mainframe systems are extremely expensive and provide capabilities beyond the needs of most small firms. **Minicomputers** represent the next level of computing power. Basically, minicomputers are scaled-down mainframe systems designed for a segment of the business market that has large computer needs but cannot afford a mainframe system. Many midsize businesses use minicomputer systems. Today's minicomputers are as powerful as many mainframe systems of the 1970s. Microcomputers are the third class of computer systems. A simple definition of **microcomputers** is that they are small computer systems that "you can pick up and carry."[1] Microcomputers, more commonly called **personal computers** or **PCs,** are compactly designed and intended for use by one person at a time (see Figure 22–1). However, personal computers can be linked, in so-called **network** systems, to meet the growing needs of small firms.

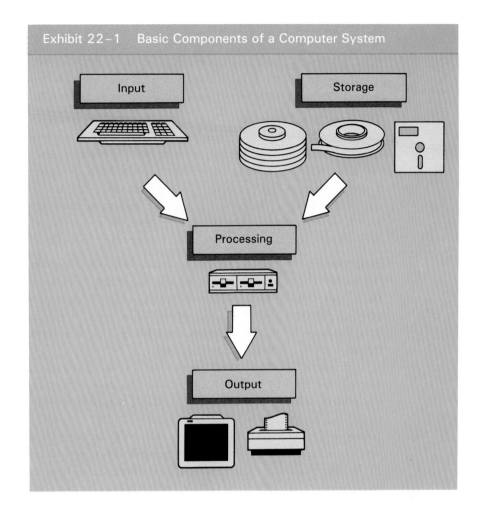

Exhibit 22–1   Basic Components of a Computer System

Input

Storage

Processing

Output

Personal computers are also distinguished from mainframes and mini-computers by the configuration of their components. Refer once again to Exhibit 22–1. Both mainframe and minicomputer systems have large separate units of hardware performing each of the four functions. A personal computer, however, performs several—and sometimes all—functions within one unit. In other words, personal computers typically have the keyboard, monitor, disk reader, and processing unit combined. Falling prices, coupled with faster processing speeds, will most likely make personal computers as common in small businesses as pocket calculators are in our homes!

Hardware

Hardware is the term that describes the computer processor and all items of physical equipment used for data input, output, and storage.[2] We will examine several types of computer hardware in the following sections.

The Computer Processor   This is the heart of the computer hardware. It consists of a central processing unit (CPU) and memory unit (MU). The electronic circuitry, or microprocessor, that processes data and instructions is contained in the CPU. The reduction in size of microprocessors has been a major impetus to the development of personal computers. A control unit within the CPU controls the operations, and an arithmetic logic unit performs the calculations. The memory unit of the processor provides temporary storage for data, programs, and intermittent calculations.

Peripherals   Input units are examples of computer peripherals. They supply data to the central processing unit. Today, the predominant method of data input is by means of a terminal consisting of a keyboard and video screen. The data and processing instructions are entered on the keyboard and displayed on the video screen for editing. The terminal is also used for displaying output from the computer.

Printers, another class of peripherals, are used as a means of obtaining "hard copy" of a computer's output. The less expensive printers are called **dot-matrix printers.** They produce readable copy of lower quality than that produced by the more expensive "letter-quality" printers. **Letter-quality printers** work more like typewriters, with a key striking an inked ribbon.

Laser printers incorporate the newest technology in printers, providing excellent-quality copy. These printers produce output at the rate of 10 to 12 pages per minute by fusing dry ink to the paper with pressure and heat. Laser printers are not only fast but quiet.

Magnetic disk drives and their respective storage media also are peripheral equipment. They are used primarily for permanent storage of information. When information such as a customer's charge account after a purchase is to be updated, information is entered from a storage disk or tape into the computer's central processing unit. The calculation, or updating of the file, is performed internally, and then the current information is returned to the external tape or disk for storage. It is important for the small-business manager to keep backup tapes or disks of all information stored on the computer.

The most popular form of external data storage for personal computers is the diskette. Commonly called **floppy disks** because of their phys-ical flexibility, diskettes are entered into disk drive units to receive data and programs or to load existing data programs into the computer. Some small-business computer systems use **hard disks,** which are capable of storing larger amounts of information. The reading and writing of data with a hard disk is much faster than is possible with a floppy disk, but the cost is much higher.

Figure 22–1 shows a grouping of computer hardware, with the user reading the "hard copy" produced by the system printer. To the right of the printer is a keyboard terminal used for data input and program control commands. The screen for viewing input and output operations is stationed atop the disk drive unit. A floppy disk is used for input and for external storage of data and programs.

Software

The programs for a computer system are called **software**. These are the instructions that operate the hardware. Software is typically divided into

Figure 22–1   A Personal Computer System

Courtesy of Hewlett-Packard Company

two types: system programs and application programs. **System software** includes programs that control the overall operations of the computer including input and output processing. These programs are the link between the hardware devices and the application programs. System software is usually provided by the computer manufacturer. **Application software** consists of programs written for particular business needs. It has been stated that "application software is the most important ingredient of any small computer system." Application programs can be created by the user or purchased as preprogrammed packages. Most small-business users will find the "canned" programs to be the best option.

Before over-the-counter software packages are purchased, it is advisable to evaluate them carefully. A helpful software evaluation checklist is shown in Exhibit 22–2.

The phrase **user friendly** applies to the ability of software to communicate simple and easily understood commands to users of personal computers. Great strides have been made in designing more user-friendly software for small-business users. One example is the "menu" feature, which allows a program user to initiate a certain operation by selecting from an assortment displayed by a menu on the computer screen.

Computer Applications for Small Business

The benefits of a personal computer to a small business are many and varied. One study, reported by the National Federation of Independent Business, found six major benefits, which are listed here in the order of their importance:[3]

1. Improves the quality of business information.
2. Improves productivity.
3. Improves work quality.
4. Makes work easier.
5. Improves the organization of the business.
6. Reduces labor costs.

Computer systems can also improve customer service and thereby pave the way for increased revenues.

For new ventures and young firms with no previous experience with computer usage, it is generally recommended that the areas of primary computer applications be covered before more advanced applications are at-

Exhibit 22-2 Software Evaluation Checklist

1. Do the basic functions of the package meet your requirements for information processing and data management? (What are you seeking to accomplish? Does the package help you reach that goal?)
2. Will this package run on your computer system? What are its requirements for:
   a. main memory
   b. disk drives
   c. printers
   d. input channels
   e. optional hardware
   f. off-line equipment
3. If any extra equipment or features are required, what are the costs and availability of these items?
4. What are the operating-system or language requirements?
5. How well do the detailed capabilities of the package match your requirements?
   a. Do the format and information content of the output meet your needs?
   b. If not, can they be changed with modest cost and limited effort?
   c. Does it contain control procedures and audit trails?
   d. What about file protection and data security?
6. How flexible is the package? Can it be changed, expanded, or modified easily?
7. Is the package easy to install and use?
   a. Do you need vendor assistance?
   b. How much user training is needed?
   c. Is there an extra charge for this training? (Even if there is no direct charge, what is the time cost for the employees involved?)
   d. Is the operating manual well documented, written in nontechnical, user-friendly language, and complete?
   e. Does the operating manual have sufficient examples of screen formats and printed reports?
8. Is there continuing support the vendor or developer will provide?
   a. What are the cost and availability of additional program assistance if it is needed?
   b. Does your agreement or contract with the vendor consider this issue?
   c. Does the vendor agree to correct any "bugs" found in the program?
9. What is the testimony of other users? (This is the best evidence you can have. Demand user names and talk with them.)

(Continued)

Exhibit 22-2   *(Continued)*

10. What is the total cost of installing and using the program?
    a. Direct cost—selling price of the package
    b. Indirect costs:
       (1) personal training
       (2) modification, adaptation, and change costs
       (3) additional equipment necessary
       (4) installation costs
       (5) annual maintenance and warranty costs
       (6) legal fees for contract and warranty review
       (7) increased audit review and participation
       (8) user personnel removed from normal operations
11. Is the cost worth the expected benefit?
12. What financing options are available?
    a. sale
    b. lease
    c. lease/purchase
    d. Is there a discount for prompt payment?
    e. Is there a discount for multiple installations in the same bank or banking organization?
    f. What is the cost of extra manuals, forms, or other support materials?
    g. If you wish to do so, can you sell the services you produce from use of the package?
13. Summary Report

	Poor	Fair	Good	Excellent
Performance	____	____	____	____
Documentation	____	____	____	____
Ease of Use	____	____	____	____
Error Handling	____	____	____	____

Source: This appeared in the February, 1984, newsletter, *Micro Digest,* published by the Center for Banking and Financial Institutions of Baylor University.

tempted. We will consider each of these two levels of computer usage in the following sections.

Primary Applications

Primary applications of computers involve highly repetitive procedures such as those required for word processing, payrolls, ordering and billing, accounts receivable, accounts payable, general-ledger systems, and inventory control.

Word Processing   Word processing is invariably the first function to be computerized in a small firm. The term **word processing** refers to any process that involves textual information and uses such equipment as typesetters, copiers, and automatic typewriters. Small businesses are overwhelmed by the need to generate many printed pages such as purchase orders, invoices, business letters, and tax information forms. Computer-based word processors have decreased the cost of this paperwork tremendously.

Computerized word processing can be thought of as typing with a computer. Words go into the computer's memory rather than onto paper, so corrections and adjustment of text material can be made easily. Word processing can also be used to insert unique data into form letters and to produce mailing labels for envelopes.

Word-processing capabilities are extremely beneficial to small direct-marketing businesses, which require large quantities of mailings each month. Word processors store addresses of customers in the computer memory and apply the addresses to form letters by a procedure called **mail merge.** This technique is also useful for billing or advertising.

A unique feature of word processing is a procedure called **spell check.** This procedure checks the text of written material for words that are spelled incorrectly and flags them. Spell-check programs include dictionaries on their floppy diskettes ranging in size from 20,000 to 80,000 or more words.

Most of the capabilities of word processing needed by the small-business person can be purchased for less than $100 per package. The more expensive packages add desktop-publishing capabilities. For example, a document can be printed with different types of print determined by special symbols placed in the text material. Even more sophisticated word-processing packages allow the user to produce documents that used to require servicing by expensive graphics and printing departments.

Some of the top word-processing packages are WordPerfect, MicroSoft Word, XyWrite III, Nota Bene, Q&A Write, Ashton-Tate's MultiMate Advantage II, and MicroPro's Wordstar. MicroSoft Word, WordPerfect, Wordstar, and XyWrite III have desktop-publishing capabilities.[4]

Payroll   Another business operation to be computerized early is payroll. (See Spotlight on Small Business for Chapter 20.) For payroll preparations, the computer input requires employee time records, wage rates, and information such as sales volume that may be necessary to calculate commission or other incentive payments. Computer output includes wage or salary amounts, incentive payments, tax deductions, FICA amounts, and other fringe benefits.

Employee records are updated to record the current pay period. The output of payroll software includes the checks for each employee, check stubs, and a summary of payroll transactions. Since computations required for payroll are repetitive, computers have been very satisfactory in performing this function.

Ordering and Billing Ordering and billing are other business functions that are quickly converted to computerized systems. A vendor may receive orders through a salesperson, by mail, by telephone, or by telegram. The computer can prepare the shipping order with customer codes, names, descriptions of items ordered, and prices rapidly and accurately. When it is time for billing, the document input to the computer is a copy of the shipping order. The output document is the invoice prepared for mailing.

Accounts Receivable The accounts-receivable system in a small business keeps records on amounts owed by each customer and the length of time the accounts have been outstanding. When a customer purchases goods or services, the information is entered and the system updates the customer's account. An invoice with the customer's charges is mailed periodically to the customer. When payments are received, the information is entered into the computer and the account becomes current again. In addition to printing all customer statements, current software can produce aging reports that show which customers are delinquent in their payments.

The importance of accuracy is obvious. Errors cause loss of revenues and annoyance to customers. Computers reduce errors in this function and present more professional-appearing statements to customers. Detailed listings of customers' charges, payments, and account balances are available in an instant after a request by a user.

Accounts Payable Accounts-payable systems keep track of the purchases of a business by using invoices from creditor companies as input to the accounts payable system. The system then generates a check and updates the balance. Most software has options to allow the user to hold, select, and release vouchers for payment according to schedules that give the user the advantage of discounts for early payment.

General Ledger The central core of the financial transactions of a business is the general ledger. In the past, accountants manually posted debits and credits for each account in a general ledger; thus, the name has carried on with computer software. The original documents—checks, vendor invoices, cash register totals, journal entries, customer invoices, and bank deposits—became the source documents for software processing. Other software systems for payroll, accounts receivable, and accounts payable can feed information to the general-ledger system.

Exhibit 22–3 shows the various components of an accounting system for which software has been developed by one successful software business. The software enables the user to determine the ending balance for every account and all information necessary for automatic generation of the balance sheet and income statement. For just a few hundred dollars, a small business can computerize its accounting system with a general-ledger program.

Current issues of computer magazines are excellent sources of information evaluating and comparing computer software. Some popular packages are DacEasy, Accpac BPI, RealWorld, and Solomon III.[5] For example, a recent issue of *PC World* evaluated the RealWorld series as a slightly unorthodox audit system that is very rigorous, one that has well-organized menus, allows for 10 million accounts, has the best printer-generated financial statements, and has excellent procedures for calculation of sales taxes and commissions. On the negative side, the magazine pointed out that RealWorld's documentation suffers because of jargon-laden descriptions, data-entry procedures that are weak, and financial reports that are difficult to design.[6]

Inventory Control   The management of inventory is important to the success of any product-based small business. The goal of inventory control is to reduce inventory investment and eliminate costly stockouts. These goals are to some degree contradictory, since a reduction of inventory investment increases the probability of stockouts. Nevertheless, computerized inventory systems can increase the effectiveness of inventory management and aid in realizing both goals.

The key to inventory management is to establish an effective method for keeping track of inventory. Bar-code technology, pioneered by the food industry in the 1970s, has aided this process. We have all shopped at supermarkets that use the Universal Product Code system, which uses an optical scanner that reads labels by distinguishing between light and dark bars on the bar code. The scanner reads each four-bar pattern, determines the number, and relays the information to the central computer. The scanning device eliminates the need for manual keystroking at the point of sale or for

Exhibit 22-3   Software and the Accounting System

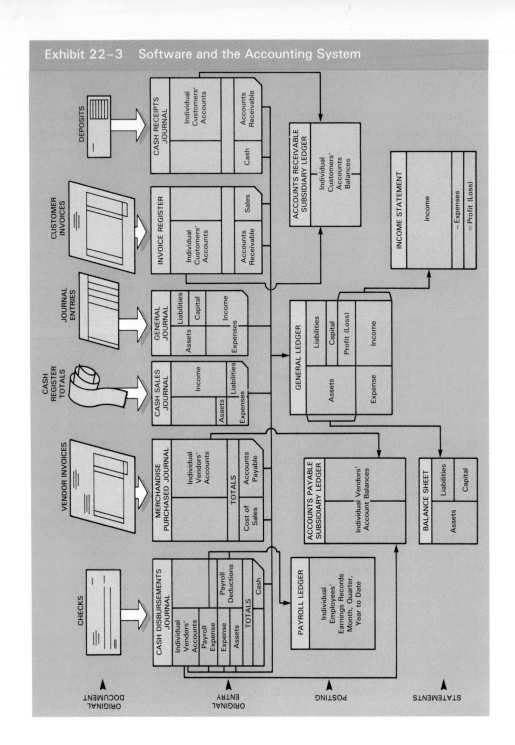

Figure 22–2   Keeping Track of Inventory
with a Bar Code Reader

*Photograph provided by Norand Corporation,
Cedar Rapids, Iowa*

inventory checks. It has taken more than a decade for bar-code technology
to penetrate all levels of business, including small firms.[7]

Secondary Applications

Secondary applications involve more advanced uses of computers and
usually follow several years of successful primary applications. Some secondary applications involve financial planning, management of information, and market research. These applications would not be recommended
for the first-time computer user.

Financial Planning   Financial management involves the management of
money. While accounting functions also involve the control of money, a
major difference exists between computerized financial-planning systems
and computerized accounting systems. The accounting system has many users; therefore, procedures for this system must be clearly defined in order
to maintain proper control. On the other hand, financial operations are
managed by fewer people—usually high-level personnel. Consequently, the
computerized financial-planning system can be flexible and quite varied

SMALL BUSINESS IN ACTION
Building an Inventory as Easy as 1–2–3

Voy Flynn and Barbara Des Prez of Norcross, GA, own a new store called "Swan Alley." They sell gifts and items for entertaining and decorating. Many of the inventory items have a high value, and the owners needed a reliable inventory system. Trying to decide when to order inventory to avoid both stockouts and excess inventory was an overwhelming task.

They hired a consultant to develop a Lotus 1–2–3 template for their inventory system. A template is a model of a particular application of a spreadsheet. The template can process different data in a specified manner. They selected this approach because with their 640K capacity machine and no add-ins, the spreadsheet could handle 3,000 inventory items and 1,500 transactions with no storage problems. This met their present demand and would be large enough for the foreseeable future. Also, Flynn and Des Prez both knew Lotus 1–2–3 and expected to learn to use the template with little additional training.

The initial startup time required approximately one month because of the data entry required to bring the system up to date. After the spreadsheet was set up, the day-to-day operation required no more time than they spent before the system, but the Lotus 1–2–3 template produced information that entrepreneurs Flynn and Des Prez needed to better manage their business.

Source: Thomas Padgett, "Building an Inventory System in Lotus 1-2-3," *Business Software,* Vol. 6, No. 8 (August, 1988), pp. 28–36.

from one small business to another. Computerized financial-planning systems, though not widely developed, are being used by small businesses.

Like the sophisticated calculator, a computer can be used to calculate cash flow, interest rates, present values, and rates of return for capital budgeting. More important, through financial-planning computer software, the computer can aid in the following financial functions:

1. Forecasting of revenues and expenses of the business operation over future years.
2. Analysis of capital expenditures by computing the costs and benefits for different plans of action.
3. Cash planning by keeping current records of cash flows, helping to avoid cash shortages, and properly investing any surplus cash.

4. Credit analysis, which is used primarily by banks and loan agencies to determine the creditworthiness of potential borrowers.

Software packages called **electronic spreadsheets** are essential to the financial-planning activity. Numbers are entered at certain column and row intersects called cells, which are then used in a particular calculation. The spreadsheet allows the manager to play a "what-if" game by entering key figures in the appropriate cells, pressing a key, and then seeing the effect of these figures on the total financial structure of the company.

Exhibit 22–4 shows four examples of spreadsheets generated by Lotus 1-2-3. The first spreadsheet is for cash-flow management. The source and use of cash application gives details of the inflow and outflow of cash in a business for nonoperating items such as notes payable, installment debt, mortgage debt, and paid-in capital. A second spreadsheet provides automatic calculation of financial ratios such as gross profit margin, net profit margin, operating profit margin, return on investment, and return on the owner's equity.

The third spreadsheet is the pro-forma financial statement, which shows the expected results of alternative decisions involving the income of the business. The cost–volume–profit analysis is the last spreadsheet shown in Exhibit 22–4. It estimates the impact of sales volume on profits. Each time alternative sales figures are entered, for example, the computer will quickly calculate new figures for the financial planner. In addition to Lotus 1-2-3, Quattro and MicroSoft Excel have been rated highly for small-business needs.[8]

Management of Information   Managers need to make decisions based on current, accurate information. They also want information quickly and in a summarized form. Computers can supply information quickly and in any form managers desire. Computers can also ease the burden of increased paperwork required by government legislation over recent years.

The management of information can be used for both long-range planning and operational planning. Long-range planning involves the future financial status of the business. Operational planning usually involves optimization and data analysis to organize daily activities such as the preparation of delivery schedules, truck routes, and purchase orders.

A successful management information system has several characteristics:

1. It converts data into information for the business decision makers.

Exhibit 22–4   Examples of Electronic Worksheets

SOURCE & USES OF CASH (INPUT TABLE)

	A	B 1985	C 1986	D 1987
	Cash Flow (Drain) from Operations	24,333	1,564	70,229
	Owner's Withdraws (Dividends)	2,500	4,000	5,000
	Notes Payable	18,975	21,110	38,000
	Installment Debt	12,853	25,668	9,678
	Mortgage Debt	110,000	106,000	102,000
	Paid-In Capital	38,000	30,000	30,000
	Total Fixed Assets	211,000	213,000	217,500

READY

FINANCIAL RATIOS (OUTPUT TABLE)

	A	B 1985	C 1986	D 1987
	Profitability Measures:			
	Gross Profit Margin	49.8%	42.8%	42.6%
	Operating Profit Margin	17.6%	16.2%	16.2%
	Net Profit Margin	10.0%	6.1%	6.1%
	Return on Investment	18.7%	16.5%	16.5%
	Return on Owner's Equity	22.6%	14.5%	14.5%

READY

PRO FORMA INCOME STATEMENT (OUTPUT TABLE)

	A	B	C
	Projected Sales		$765,433
	Cost of Goods Sold/Cost of Sales		437,828
	Gross Profit		$327,605
	Operating Expenses		
	Wages		$78,074
	Rent		11,481
	Telephone and Utilities		28,321
	Insurance		11,481
	Advertising		45,161
	Gas and Oil		10,716
	Depreciation		4,593
	Other Expenses		9,375
	Total Operating Expenses		$199,702

READY

COST-VOLUME-PROFIT STATEMENT (INPUT TABLE)

	A	B	C Amount
	Net Sales		340,000
	Fixed Costs:		
	Salaries Including Employment Taxes and Cost of Fringes		24,500
	Fixed Wages Costs Including Employment Taxes and Cost of Fringes		16,200
	Rent and Lease Payments		3,600
	Depreciation		2,000
	Insurance		12,700
	Fixed Selling Expenses		25,000
	Fixed Insurance		6,500
	Fixed Utility Costs		5,093
	Fixed Vehicle Costs		19,916

READY

2. It supports a variety of functional areas.

3. It is flexible and can adapt to changing information needs.

4. It provides system security that prevents access by unauthorized users.

Marketing   Computers can aid in the performance of marketing activities in a number of ways. For example, software is available to help make sales. Mark O'Neill, of WNEW Radio in New York, uses a software package called Saleseye to personalize sales letters and remind him of advertising customers he needs to contact. The package is also designed to prompt salespeople who communicate with prospects on the phone. Marketing software is also available to reduce the time and effort associated with conducting and tabulating market surveys.[9] These sophisticated procedures to assist marketing efforts are likely to become commonplace among progressive small-business managers.

Computerizing the Small Firm

If a small business is considering the use of a computer, it should analyze the potential benefits, estimate the costs, and work out an appropriate plan. There are no quick and easy procedures to follow in this decision process. Each business will have a unique set of problems.

The Feasibility Study

As a first step, the small business should make a feasibility study. This study should determine whether the firm has a sufficient work load or need for efficiency to justify the expense of a computer. The cost/benefit analysis is difficult to make, but it is the most important step in the decision-making process. This analysis can be performed by the business owner-manager or by an outside computer consultant.

The feasibility study may indicate that the business should not computerize. If the study shows that the business should computerize, the second step is to decide whether to use a service bureau, to opt for time-sharing, to lease a computer, or to buy a computer. If the firm decides to buy a computer, then it should select the best system for the business.

Service Bureaus

Service bureaus are computer firms that receive data from business customers, perform the data processing, then return the processed information to the customers. The service bureaus charge a fixed fee for the use of their computers. For a small firm desiring a single application and lacking computer experience, the service bureau represents a logical first choice.

Using a service bureau has several advantages. The user avoids an investment in equipment that will soon become obsolete. The user also avoids the need for specialized computer personnel. Some service bureaus even provide guidance to make it easy for the user to start and expand computer usage. The disadvantages of a service bureau include slow turnaround time in receiving processed information from the service bureau, divulgence of confidential information to outside parties, and difficulty in working with a group unfamiliar with the client company's procedures.

In the past, there have been numerous small service bureaus. However, today the small service bureaus are having difficulty competing with bigger bureaus that have larger minicomputer systems. The competition among service bureaus will no doubt become even greater in the future.

Time-Sharing

Time-sharing allows a business to have the capabilities of a computer without buying or leasing it. The business pays a variable fee for the privilege of using a computer system. As indicated earlier in this chapter, the user of time-sharing must have at least one terminal in order to input data. The terminal is connected to the time-sharing computer via a telephone line with a device known as a **modem.**

Early time-sharing systems provided computer time for professionals who knew how to operate and to program a computer. With the advancement of software, time-sharing is used more to process data and information for a company by using existing programs. The time-sharing approach is often a good first or second step for small firms that decide to computerize.

The advantages of time-sharing include control of company records, more sophisticated applications of programs, and lower cost of installing a working system. The disadvantages include variable costs, waiting time when other customers are using the system, and the need for the user to have some computer ability.

SMALL BUSINESS IN ACTION
Poor Service at Service Bureau

As owner and manager of Jones Fine Furniture, Joe Jones has 15 employees and approximately 2,000 credit customers. Although Jones was at first hesitant to use a computer, he eventually decided to automate some of the day-to-day transactions.

Before automating, Jones was using a ledger card system to keep track of accounts payable and accounts receivable. Copying-machine copies of the bills were made, and the calculation of interest charges was time-consuming. With the encouragement of his son, Jones decided to use a local service bureau that also serviced about five other customers. However, after three years with the service bureau, minor communication problems and occasional delays in mailouts finally convinced him to install his own computer system.

Jones and his son decided on a microcomputer because it was the least expensive, required little room to house, and seemed capable of meeting the firm's computing needs. Although the accountant learned the system in a week, she disliked it and left after six months. Jones hired an inexperienced replacement at a much lower salary, and he was delighted when she mastered the computer system in less than a week. The individual operating the computer system had been a furniture duster the previous year.

Mr. Jones is much happier with the microcomputer system than he was with the service bureau. "With the service bureau, you were at the mercy of the people who knew how to run their computer system, and delays often occurred. Now I can go in and get a printout anytime I want one," he says. "My system has an audit program that allows me to answer any customer's question about his or her account in a matter of seconds," he boasts.

Source: Personal conversation with the owner's son. Names have been changed.

Leasing a Computer

For most businesses, leasing a computer means possessing and using a computer without buying it. The most common leasing arrangement is the full payback lease. Usually the lease periods are fairly long term (i.e., for around eight years). A shorter lease period may be more expensive, but it reduces the possibility of having to use outdated equipment. With the current rapid advances in computer technology, some computer users claim that computer equipment becomes outdated every two years!

Two advantages of leasing are the use of a complete computer system without a large initial investment and the availability of consulting help through the leasing company's computer specialists. The disadvantages relate to the length of the lease period and the possibility of having to use outdated equipment. In addition, leasing a computer requires the lessee to have skilled computer personnel.

Buying a Computer

The advantages of buying a computer are obvious. The owner has total control and ownership of the computer. Also, depreciation expense reduces the business owner's taxable income. The disadvantages are the large expense of the computer system, the need for trained computer personnel to operate the programs and maintain the hardware, and the possible obsolescence of the equipment.

For small firms choosing to purchase a computer, the key to creating a successful computer system is a carefully planned approach. It is important for the first-time computer user to look first at the programs, not at the hardware. The following ten steps set forth an orderly approach to computerization.

Step 1. Learn about Computers   Visit other firms that are already using computers for similar applications. Ask for a vendor demonstration. Be aware that the changeover will require much time and thought. If possible, hire a data-processing manager with experience, or at least place someone in charge of the changeover. In summary, the computer is not an easy way out. If the business is in basic trouble, the computer system will not save it. The computer can help a successful business become more successful.

Step 2. Analyze the Present Manual System   Examine the transactions that involve routine actions. Restudy the routine manual actions to find a more efficient procedure if possible. Having established an efficient procedure, you are then ready to think about introducing a computer.

The detailed study of the business and the areas that might be computerized help to clarify computer needs. This is information that computer vendors need in order to propose ways to computerize a company efficiently.

Figure 22–3   Define Your Expectations of
the Computer System

THE WALL STREET JOURNAL

The Wall Street Journal, September 9, 1981, p. 25.
Permission—Cartoon Features Syndicate

ENGLEMAN.

"I don't want to talk to a middleman . . . put
me straight through to the computer!"

Step 3. Clearly Define Your Expectations of the Computer System   Having reviewed your manual system, decide what you need in a computer system. Be specific in the functions you want the computer to perform. For example, you may decide to computerize mailing lists, payroll, inventory control, or sales analysis. These needs should be outlined for five years in the future. If you are unable to determine your exact needs, you may want to seek help. Possible sources are other small businesses, computer consultants, or an employee with computer experience.

Step 4. Compare Costs and Benefits   It is easy to estimate the costs of current manual systems, but it is difficult to estimate the cost of computerization. Estimates should be obtained from several vendors to help determine the cost of changeover. Also, there are hidden costs incurred. For example, the patience and endurance of employees are tested during the conversion.

Step 5. Establish a Timetable for Installing the System   A five-year schedule should be made to install the computer system. It is best to automate the simplest manual operations first. Each computerized operation should be working before going to the next. Be aware that transactions are slow. If possible, run the manual system in parallel with the automated system until the rough spots are smoothed out. Be willing to adjust the timetable from time to time as unexpected problems occur.

Step 6. Write a Tight Contract   Both the purchaser and the vendor should be willing to sign a formal agreement on the function the computer is expected to perform. The specifications should contain details rather than general summaries of expected performance. Obligations for servicing the equipment should also be clearly specified. The contract should specify what the vendor must do before each step in the payment schedule.

Also, is it usually unwise to agree to field-test new equipment. It is best to obtain established equipment and programs that have been working in other small businesses.

Step 7. Obtain Programs First, Then Obtain the Computer   There are several options for obtaining computer programs:

1. Obtain programs that are already working at other, similar small businesses.
2. Hire a programmer to write programs.
3. Hire a consultant who has programs that can serve most business functions.

The manager must make the decision about which alternative is best for the particular business. Once the needed programs are identified, the most economical hardware to run the programs can be obtained.

Step 8. Prepare Your Employees for Conversion   It is commonplace for employees to resist the move to computers. They may feel the computer is a threat to their jobs. Assure employees that the change will be beneficial to the business and consequently beneficial to them. People who are unwilling to become involved should be moved to other departments. A good attitude, with interest in the computerization, must prevail for a successful transition from manual power to computer power.

Step 9. Make the Conversion First, assign the responsibilities carefully for the conversion process. The conversion period will require extra work because daily work must continue. Second, remember to convert operations one at a time. Again, if possible, keep the parallel manual system functioning as long as possible. Third, be patient, remembering that pitfalls will occur. Do not plan on using the system until it begins functioning.

Step 10. Reap the Benefits The goal of the transition is to obtain the following benefits:

1. Earlier, more nearly accurate, and more extensive information.
2. Better organization of information because of the discipline the computer requires.
3. Current information on costs and sales.
4. Current information on inventory levels.
5. Better cash control.

The Future of Computers

Currently fewer than 25 percent of small businesses use computers, but this percentage will surely increase.[10] By the 21st century, a small business without a computer will be like a farmer without a tractor, a car without gasoline, or a house without electricity. Even now, try to persuade the office secretary to return to a manual typewriter once he or she has experienced word processing, or convince your local grocery store clerk to manually check out groceries once optical scanners have been used. Small businesses with computers soon reach the point of no return.

The greatest improvements in computers will probably occur in communications. Visual and verbal information will likely be shared across the country as easily as a telephone call is made today. Also, robotics will be used more in small-business manufacturing, and information networks will allow a businessperson to order and sell electronically. Customers will possibly do their shopping electronically, reducing time-consuming activities and providing more leisure time.

Electronic funds transfer by financial institutions may replace much of the paper involved in banking transactions. Computer-based navigation systems may be standard equipment on transportation vehicles. As an alternative to hard-copy publishing, newspapers, books, and mail may all be transmitted and read electronically. Artificial intelligence systems (expansion of the capability of a computer to "think") may aid in medical diagnosis, business decision making, military strategy, and any operation requiring a knowledge-based system to which standard rules of logic are applied to solve a particular problem.

There is no reason to believe the improvements in computer technology will bypass small firms. Therefore, the office of George Moody may well be typical of small businesses of the future:

> After arriving at his downtown Los Angeles office on a given morning, George Moody, president of Security Pacific Corporation, decides that he would like to review the profitability of his 1,000 retail branches and check the status of Third-World loans. Instead of turning to a pile of reports and printouts or ordering studies that get bucked down the chain of command, he turns to his desktop computer, clears his throat, and—using simple oral commands—calls up the data he wants in the depth and quantity he requires.[11]

To maintain a competitive edge in the future, small-business managers must be computer literate and have the ability to determine what computer technology will help their businesses in a cost-effective way.

Looking Back

1. The components of a business computer system are input, processing, output, and storage. The three basic types of computers, based on size, are mainframes, minicomputers, and microcomputers (or personal computers). Microcomputers are the most cost effective and appropriate for small businesses.
2. Hardware is the computer processor and all items of physical equipment associated with data input, data output, and storage. Software is the programs—systems and application—for the computer.
3. First-time users of a computer system should acquire some years of experience in primary applications before proceeding to secondary applications. Primary applications involve repetitive, work-intensive functions such as word processing, payroll, accounts receivable, accounts payable, general ledger, and inventory control. Secondary applications involve more sophisticated uses of computers for financial planning, management of information, and marketing research.
4. The small-business manager who decides that a computer is feasible for business operations has several options: using a service bureau, time-sharing, leasing a computer, or buying a computer.

5. To maintain a competitive advantage, the small-business manager of the future needs to be computer literate. Computers and information will affect every aspect of an individual's life.

DISCUSSION QUESTIONS

1. List and define the four components of a business computer system.
2. What types of input units and output units are available in computer systems?
3. What are the three categories of computers?
4. Distinguish between computer hardware and computer software.
5. What is meant by the terms "floppy disk," and "user friendly?"
6. Why have computers become more commonly used in small business?
7. Identify some of the major benefits that small firms derive from personal computers.
8. What two activities in small firms are usually the initial areas of application for computers to perform? Why?
9. Explain the function of general-ledger software.
10. What are electronic spreadsheets? What areas in small business use this type of software?
11. What inventory management needs can a computer fulfill?
12. What marketing activities are aided by computer software?
13. Discuss the advantages and disadvantages of (a) service bureaus, (b) time-sharing systems, (c) leasing computers, and (d) buying computers.
14. List and discuss the 10 steps a business should take when obtaining a computer system for the first time.
15. Discuss the future of computers.

YOU MAKE THE CALL

Situation 1

Phil and Doris Kelly started their business in 1985 after a trip to Hawaii, where they made arrangements to be a distributor of macadamia nuts. The store they opened in Norman, OK, sells nuts, jams, and jellies to corporate clients and mail-order customers, as well as those in their store. In fact, only

25 percent of sales are from the store. Approximately 1,000 different items are sold by the Kellys, with gross sales at around one-half million dollars.

The store uses an IBM computer system that cost several thousand dollars in 1985. They use a software package called "In-Store." The Kellys are currently considering a plan to open additional small stores that would be stocked out of one location.

Source: Christine Adamec, "Retailers Streamline as Operation Grows," *In Business,* April, 1987, p. 44. Names have been changed.

Questions

1. What applications do you believe the Kellys should be integrating into the computer system?
2. What special computer problems does the mail-order distribution bring to the Kellys' computer system?
3. If expansion does occur, what will this do to the existing system? Be specific.

Situation 2

Brent Burton runs a retail store selling unfinished furniture. Several years ago he decided he should computerize his inventory. Therefore, he visited a local computer store and purchased an inventory software package which would run on his own IBM personal computer. The program was not very user friendly and did not do the job he needed.

Burton's daughter, Sissy, has recently finished her undergraduate computer degree in a nearby college. Therefore, Burton turned to her for advice.

Source: Kevin McDermott, "Things That Go Beep in the Night," *D&B Reports,* Vol. 36, No. 3 (June, 1988), p. 37. Names have been changed.

Questions

1. What did Mr. Burton do incorrectly when he first computerized his inventory?
2. What options do you believe his daughter will pursue? Why?
3. What type of capability should good inventory software contain?

EXPERIENTIAL EXERCISES

1. Conduct a personal interview with a local small-business manager who uses a computer system in his or her firm. Determine the types of hardware the manager purchased and why. Report your findings.

2. Locate a local small firm that does not yet use a computer. Interview the owner to determine whether he or she has ever considered computerizing the firm. Determine what reservations there are to purchasing a computer. Report your findings to the class.

3. Talk with a local computer store owner, or a salesperson representing a computer manufacturer, and ask him or her to demonstrate the hardware and software that small businesses might use. Obtain copies of literature from this individual and bring them to class.

4. Interview the manager of a local small firm to determine whether its computer applications are primary, secondary, or both. Summarize your findings.

REFERENCES TO SMALL-BUSINESS PRACTICES

Field, Roger. "Switching On for Success." *Entrepreneur*, Vol. 17, No. 5 (May, 1989), pp. 86–93.
> Two small businesses are profiled in this article to demonstrate the success that can come from automating office equipment. One firm is a manufacturing and design firm, the other a tile-importing company.

Kall, Janice. "Small Consulting Firm Solves Its Big Problem." *Business Software*, Vol. 2, No. 1 (April, 1984), pp. 46–51.
> This article describes the trial-and-error experiences of a small firm trying to find the best data base management system for use in the development and implementation of sales incentive programs for its corporate clients.

Mamis, Robert A. "Taking Control." *Inc.*, Vol. 9, No. 2 (February, 1987), pp. 82–88.
> An account of how a musical instrument store is computerized is provided in this article. The benefits of the computer system in providing management information are described.

Mandell, Mel. "Take Charge of Your Phones." *Nation's Business*, Vol. 77, No. 1 (January, 1989), pp. 25–26.
> This article describes the latest technology in telephone management systems that compile data on a small firm's telephone calls. A small firm that installed this system shares its experiences.

ENDNOTES

1. For a more detailed discussion of the three types of computer systems, see Larry Long, *Introduction to Computers and Information Processing* (Englewood Cliffs, NJ: Prentice-Hall, Inc., 1988), Chapter 3.

2. An excellent article describing the more popular personal computers, including printers, is Jon Pepper, "There's a Computer in Your Future," *Nation's Business*, Vol. 77, No. 9 (September, 1989), pp. 56–59.

3. See *Small Business Primer* (Washington, DC: National Federation of Independent Business Foundation, 1988), p. 27.

4. "Word Processing," *PC World*, Vol. 6, No. 7 (July, 1988), pp. 120–140.

5. See "The Software That Makes your Computer Useful," *Nation's Business,* Vol. 77, No. 2 (February, 1989), p. 34; and Ralph Soucie, "Accounting Software: Good for Business," *PC World,* Vol. 6, No. 9 (September, 1988), pp. 122–129.

6. *Ibid.* Soucie, p. 122.

7. Leila Davis, "Wider Uses for Bar Codes," *Nation's Business,* Vol. 77, No. 3 (March, 1989), pp. 34–36.

8. "The Software That Makes Your Computer Useful," *Nation's Business,* Vol. 77, No. 2 (February, 1989), p. 34.

9. Christine Adamec, "Computer Power," *In Business,* Vol. 8, No. 3 (May–June, 1986), pp. 42–45.

10. "Special Kit Helps Small Businesses Manage Finances," *Lotus Quarterly,* Vol. I, No. 3 (Fall, 1988), pp. 6–8.

11. Stephen Quickel, "Management Joins the Computer Age," *Business Month,* Vol. 133, No. 5 (May, 1989), pp. 42–46.

23 RISK MANAGEMENT

Spotlight on Small Business

©Bruce Zake

    A small business can never be completely sheltered from liability risks. Harry Featherstone, president of the Will-Burt Company in Orrville, OH, can attest to that! One day, in 1980, Featherstone was notified that he was being sued. An accident had occurred at a construction site in Florida, killing one worker and severely injuring another. The scaffolding—the cause of the accident—was produced by another company but included parts manufactured by Will-Burt. The scaffolding company went bankrupt and Will-Burt was sued "under the theory that all companies involved in the production and sale of a defective product are jointly liable. . . ."

    Eventually, Will-Burt's insurance company settled out of court even though Featherstone argues that his parts were never defective. He further contends that the suit might never have been filed if there had been a federal product-liability law to clarify the legal questions surrounding conflict-

657

ing state laws. According to Featherstone, "A plaintiff can win a suit in one state, lose in another and be prohibited even from filing in a third."

Faced with the settlement payment and loss of liability coverage, Will-Burt laid off employees and discontinued some of its product lines. Although it was down, it was not knocked out. In spite of adversity, this small business is still in business.

Source: Adapted from Roger Thompson, "Deciding Who's to Blame," *Nation's Business*, Vol. 76, No. 5 (May, 1988), pp. 26–27. Copyright 1988 U.S. Chamber of Commerce.

Looking Ahead

Watch for the following important topics:
1. The concepts of risk and risk management.
2. Classifications of business risks.
3. Methods of coping with business risks.
4. Basic principles of insurance.
5. Types of insurance coverage.
6. New terms and concepts:

risk	credit insurance
risk management	general liability insurance
self-insurance	employer's liability insurance
business interruption insurance	workers' compensation insurance
dishonesty insurance	key-person insurance
coinsurance clause	risk-retention group
surety bonds	purchasing group

It is said that "nothing is certain except death and taxes." Entrepreneurs would probably extend this adage to read, "Nothing is certain except death, taxes, and small-business risk." In Chapter 1, we noted the moderate risk-taking propensities of entrepreneurs and their preference for risky situations in which they can exert some control over the outcome. As a consequence, they seek to minimize business risk as much as possible. The first step toward reducing business risk tension is to understand the different types of business risks and alternatives for managing them.

Simply stated, **risk** is "a condition in which there is a possibility of an adverse deviation from a desired outcome that is expected or hoped for."[1] Applied to the small-business situation, "risk" translates into losses associated with company assets and earning potential of the business. As used here, the term "asset" includes not only inventory and equipment but also such "assets" as the firm's employees and its reputation. **Risk management** consists of all efforts designed to preserve these assets and the earning power of the business.

Risk management has grown out of insurance management. Therefore, the two terms are often used interchangeably. Actually, risk management has a much broader meaning, covering both those risks that are insurable and those that are not.

Risk management in the small firm differs from risk management in the large firm. The manager of a small business is usually the risk manager. In contrast, a large firm may assign the responsibilities of risk management to a specialized staff manager. In practicing risk management, the small-business manager should be able to identify the different types of business risks and be able to cope with them. In the next section, we shall discuss the specific nature of the more common types of small-business risks.

Common Small-Business Risks

Business risks can be classified in several ways. One simple approach is to list the causes of potential losses. Fire, personal injury, theft, and fraud would be items on such a list. Another system portrays business risks by grouping accidental losses into those that are generally insurable and those that are largely uninsurable. A fire loss would typify the first category; product obsolescence the second category.

A third system, one that we will use in this chapter, emphasizes the asset-centered focus of the definition of risk management by grouping business risks into four categories: market-centered risks, property-centered risks, personnel-centered risks, and customer-centered risks. Exhibit 23-1 portrays these four risk categories including examples of each. This classification system encompasses four key asset groups for the small business. A substantial loss in any one category could mean devastation for the small business. We will examine the forms of risk associated with each category and identify the possible alternatives for coping with them.

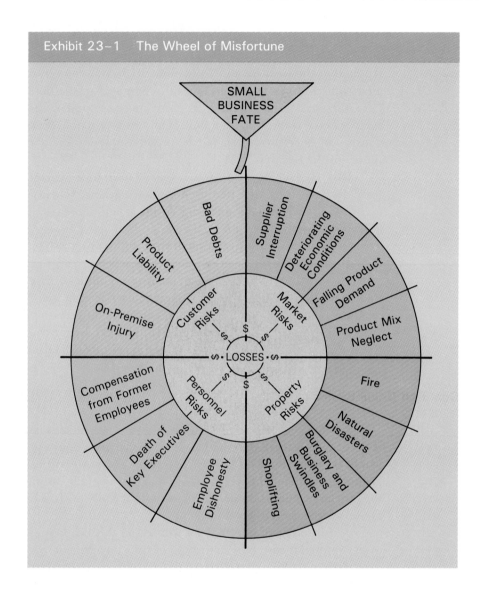

Exhibit 23–1   The Wheel of Misfortune

Market-Centered Risks

Some of the most crippling forms of business risks are found in the negative changes occurring within a firm's target market and marketing efforts. Many of these factors directly affect the firm's competitive position

Figure 23–1   Breakdown of Telephone
Service: A Market-Centered Risk

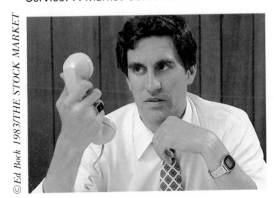

© *Ed Bock 1983/THE STOCK MARKET*

and potential for long-term survival. Characteristically, market-related risks develop slowly from day to day until, finally, they become destructive—unlike a fire that ignites and destroys a building overnight. Four examples of market-centered risks are supplier interruptions, deteriorating economic conditions, falling product demand, and product mix neglect. These market-centered risks are generally uninsurable through standard insurance policies. Firms can, of course, always practice self-insurance, which we will explain later. Let us examine each of the four examples we have named.

Supplier Interruptions   A small firm is often highly dependent on suppliers to keep its business running smoothly. When major suppliers experience an interruption of their business operations, fall-out from their hard times disrupts the operations of their customers. For example, on Mother's Day in 1988, a telephone service company experienced a major switching breakdown in one of its substations. The problem took a month and a half to solve. Local businesses who depended on the company for telephone and data-processing services were severely handicapped for the duration of the malfunction.

Deteriorating Economic Conditions   Periods of high inflation, rising interest rates, declining discretionary income, and recessions are all symptoms of a deteriorating economy and are uncontrollable variables to the small-business manager. Nevertheless, they have a major impact on the small firm's level of risk. Rapidly rising prices for materials and labor, for example, may catch the small firm in a vulnerable position, particularly if it is locked into a fixed price with customers. The increased cost of a bank loan might also be the straw that pushes a marginally profitable venture into bankruptcy.

Management of this form of risk is difficult. Entrepreneurs are extremely vulnerable to this type of risk because much discipline is required to save profits in times of prosperity to guard against a weak working-capital position.

Falling Demand for a Product   As we discussed in Chapter 11, all products go through a life cycle. Often, however, the downturn in sales occurs suddenly and with little warning. Consider the situation surrounding the demand for ceiling fans in the early 1980s. After experiencing rapid growth in the late 1970s, the demand leveled off in 1981. Fred G. Wall, the president of Robbins and Myers, a Dayton, OH, manufacturer, saw the reality of this form of risk when the roof caved in on ceiling fan growth, leaving his firm with excessive inventories. He spoke of the situation as being very painful. "We were on a long roll, and then everything happened."[2] The company had just previously halted production of other products at another plant converting to ceiling fan production!

A small firm should make every possible effort to escape this kind of situation. Keeping abreast of the market can help reduce the impact of this type of risk.

Product Mix Neglect   Product innovation is a key factor for the small business that stays competitive. The risk of trying to sell an obsolete product is increased when product innovation is lacking. A firm must adapt its product mix to survive! An excellent example of successful product mix adaptation by a firm is the Bonne Bell company, which started in 1927 when its founder Jesse Grover Bell began manufacturing cosmetic products in his basement. In 1936 Mr. Bell purchased the formula for a medicated skin wash and named it Ten-O-Six. This product became Bonne Bell's flagship product. However, the company continued to introduce new products to meet the needs of a changing market. Today, it has estimated sales of $50 million and is one of the few remaining family businesses in the cosmetics industry.[3]

The best way to avoid the risk of product mix neglect is to keep up with the pulse of the market in order to turn perceived threats into opportunities. The entrepreneur must maintain the entrepreneurial spirit and not neglect the product mix of his or her firm.

Property-Centered Risks

In contrast to market-centered risks, property-centered risks involve tangible and highly visible assets. When these physical assets are lost, they are quickly missed. Most property-centered risks are insurable. Four examples of property-centered risks are fire, natural disasters, burglary and business swindles, and shoplifting.

Fire Hazards   The possibility of fire is always present. Building, equipment, and inventory items can be totally or partially destroyed by fire. Of course, the degree of risk and the loss potential differ with the type of business. For example, industrial processes that are complex and hazardous or that involve explosives, combustibles, or other flammable materials enlarge this risk.

Fire not only causes a direct property loss, but also may interrupt business operations, resulting in a loss of profit to the firm. During the period when business operations are interrupted, such fixed expenses as rent, supervisory salaries, and insurance charges continue. To avoid losses arising from business interruptions, a business might, for example, have alternative sources of electric power, such as its own generators, for use in times of emergency.

Natural Disasters   Floods, hurricanes, tornadoes, and hail are often described as "acts of God" because of human limitations in foreseeing and controlling them. As in the case of fire, natural disasters may also interrupt business operations. Although a business may take certain preventive measures—for example, locating in areas not subject to flood damage—there is not much one can do to avoid natural disasters. Major reliance is placed upon insurance in coping with natural-disaster losses.

Burglary and Business Swindles   The forcible breaking and entering of premises closed for business with the subsequent removal of cash or merchandise is called burglary. Although insurance should be carried against losses from burglary, it may prove helpful for a business to install burglar alarm systems and arrange for private security services.

Business swindles can amount to thousands of dollars a year. Small firms in particular are susceptible to swindles. Examples of these are bogus office-machine repairers, phony charity appeals, billing for listing in nonexistent directories, sale of advertising space in publications whose nature is misrepresented, and advanced-fee deals. Risks of this kind are avoidable only through the alertness of the business manager.

Shoplifting   The theft of merchandise during store hours costs retail merchants alone upwards of $22 billion a year, and small business is not immune to this danger.[4] Various precautionary measures may be taken by the small business to minimize shoplifting. These include:

1. Limiting access to certain areas of the business premises.
2. Screening employees carefully.
3. Laying out the facilities to provide good visual coverage.
4. Keeping high-unit-value items in special-security locations.
5. Monitoring shoplifting with special equipment such as closed-circuit television.
6. Educating potential offenders to understand that they will be prosecuted.

Personnel-Centered Risks

Personnel-centered losses occur indirectly due to personal circumstances or directly through actions against the business. For example, a physically sick or injured employee causes an indirect loss. Employee spying, on the other hand, is a direct action against the business and constitutes a major concern for many small businesses. Most employee-centered risks are insurable. Three examples of personnel-centered risks are dishonesty of current employees, former-employee competition, and death of key executives.

Employee Dishonesty   One of the more visible forms of employee dishonesty is theft. Estimates of the magnitude of employee theft are difficult to make and tend to vary considerably from source to source. A recent article in one business publication used a figure of $40 billion annually.[5] This estimate would include all businesses, both large and small. Despite how much may be big business's share of the estimate, there is a strong feeling that small businesses are particularly vulnerable because their anti-theft controls are characteristically lax.

Thefts by employees may include not only cash but also inventory items, tools, metal scrap, stamps, and the like. Then there is always the possibility of forgery, raising of checks, or other fraudulent practices. The trusted bookkeeper may enter into collusion with an outsider to have bogus invoices or invoices double or triple the correct amount presented for payment. The bookkeeper may approve such invoices for payment, write a check, and secure the manager's signature. In addition to bonding employees, the firm's major protection against employee fraud is a system of internal checks or control.[6] Consider the following incidents:

> The head bookkeeper in a Florida office equipment firm starts forging company checks to finance improvements to his home, buy new clothes and take a trip to Europe. His thefts, $45,000 over six months, are not discovered until he is on the European trip and the office manager spots her own signature—forged on a returned check.

> A contract janitor at a surgical-glove factory in Alabama steals a company chain saw. His supervisor finds out and gets him to return the saw. The janitor leaves for another company, where he steals another chain saw.

> The owner of a lumber company in Indiana discovers through inventory shortages that a salesman has used false invoices to steal $20,000 worth of lumber. He brings charges and gets most of the money back. Before the case is settled, the company cashier is found to have embezzled more than $15,000 in cash. Again the owner brings charges, but this time there is no restitution.[7]

According to Mick Moritz, who is director of security for United Telephone Systems in Carlisle, PA, there are four contributing factors to employee theft: desire, a rationalization of the action, opportunity, and the perception that apprehension is unlikely.[8] It is mainly the last two factors that small businesses can eliminate.

Death of Key Executives   Every successful small business has one or more key executives. These employees could be lost to the firm by death or through attraction to other employment. If key personnel cannot be successfully replaced, the small firm suffers appreciably and loses profits as the result of the loss of their services.

In addition to valuable experience and skill, there is also the possibility that the executive may have certain specialized knowledge that is vital to the successful operation of the firm. For example, a certain manufacturer was killed in an auto accident at the age of 53. His processing operations involved the use of a secret chemical formula that he had devised originally and divulged to no one because of the fear of losing the formula to competitors. He neither reduced it to writing nor placed it in a safety-deposit box. Not even his family knew the formula. As a result of his sudden death, the firm went out of business within six months. The expensive special-purpose equipment had to be sold as junk. All that his widow salvaged was about $60,000 worth of bonds and the Florida residence that had been the couple's winter home.

Two solutions, at least, are available to the small firm faced with this contingency. The first of these is life insurance, which is discussed later in the chapter. The second involves the development of replacement personnel. A potential replacement may be groomed for every key position, including the position of the owner-manager.

Competition from Former Employees Good employees are always hard to get; they are even harder to keep. When a business has employee turnover—and it always will—it must be concerned with the risks associated with former employees. This risk is particularly acute with turnover of key executives. They are the more likely candidates to start a competing business or to leave with trade secrets.

Companies are very sensitive to former employee activities. Consider the following risk situation:

> Michael was employed by a company that manufactured equipment and supplies used in hot stamp decorating ... Michael met and became friendly with Robert, who owned a company that sold marking tools to Michael's employer.... Michael began ordering patterns and models from a second company, which was also owned by Robert.... Then Michael and Robert formed a corporation of their own.... Michael quit his job ... and began producing and selling material used for hot stamp decorating—in competition with his former employer.... The former employer sued Michael and Robert for misappropriating the manufacturing procedures manual ... and other alleged trade secrets.... The judge awarded nearly $200,000 in damages to the former employer.[9]

One common practice to help avoid this kind of employee-centered risk is to require employees to sign employment contracts clearly setting forth the employee's promise not to disclose certain information or use it in competition with the employer. But this practice is not always possible.

Customer-Centered Risks

Customers are the source of profit for small business, but they are also the center of an ever-increasing amount of business risk. Much of this risk is attributable to on-premise injury, product liability, and bad debts. Most customer-centered risks are insurable. The three types of customer-centered risks we will examine are on-premise injury to customers, product liability, and bad debts.

On-Premise Injury to Customers The small business should be aware of the risks associated with customers' claims against the business originating with an on-premise injury. Because of high store traffic, the risk is particularly acute for the small-business retailer, but it must be managed by all small businesses. Personal injury liability of this type may occur, for example, when a customer breaks an arm by slipping on icy steps while entering or leaving the business. An employer is, of course, at risk with employees who suffer similar fates; but customers, by their sheer numbers, make this risk larger.

Juries have traditionally favored customers in these types of liability. Consider the following judgments:

> An Indiana jury returned a verdict of $2,500,000 for a 6-year-old boy who suffered severe brain injury when a gasoline tank exploded. A construction company had dug up the tank while preparing a site for a new shopping center. The tank, containing gas fumes, was left unattended.

> In a Kansas supermarket, a 61-year-old woman was reaching for a bottle of Pepsi when a carton of the bottles fell to the floor and shattered. Flying glass struck the shopper's foot. She sued the market and the bottler. . . . The jury awarded her $86,000.[10]

Good management of this kind of customer-centered risk demands that a regular check of the premises for hazards be conducted. The concept of preventive maintenance applies to management of this risk factor.

Product Liability   Recent product liability decisions have broadened the scope of this form of risk. No reputable small business would intentionally produce a product that would potentially harm a customer, but good intentions are weak defenses in liability suits.

A product liability suit may be filed when a customer becomes ill or sustains property damage in using a product made or sold by a company. Class-action suits, together with individual suits, are now widely used by consumers in product liability cases. Some types of businesses operate in higher-risk markets than others. For example, the insulation business has recently been targeted with numerous product claims because of the asbestos scare.

Richard S. Betterley, a consultant, suggests the following steps to help a small company reduce product liability losses:

1. Include thorough and explicit directions for the product's use with each product. Warn customers of potential hazards and keep an eye on promotional material to make sure advertising doesn't undo the company's precautions.
2. Develop procedures for handling consumers' complaints through distributors and at the home office. Prepare a plan to handle the worst possible kind of disaster.

3. Determine whether any of the company's products are too risky to sell, given the consequences of a suit.
4. Test products internally for possible safety problems. Then obtain a "second opinion" from others in the field and consult the company's insurer.
5. Acquaint all employees with the company's concern with product safety.
6. Stay current with legislation and litigation within the appropriate industries.[11]

Bad Debts Bad debts are an unavoidable risk associated with credit selling. Most customers will pay their obligations with no more than a friendly reminder. A few customers will intentionally try to avoid payment. These accounts should be quickly turned over to a lawyer for litigation or be written off.

Customers who fall between the two groups of "quick pay" and "no pay" are the ones who cause the most trouble. These customers may be good customers but, for various reasons, may temporarily experience difficulty and become slow payers. Every effort should be made in an aggressive but courteous manner to offer these customers options that will encourage payment.

SMALL BUSINESS IN ACTION
Lawsuits Bug an Industry

All small businesses should manage product liability risks, but none are any more affected by this kind of risk than exterminators. This is an industry characterized by very small businesses—firms with two or three employees. Rising insurance premiums are placing entrepreneurs of this industry in positions similar to other industries. Richard Lipsey, vice-president of research at Kemco Chemical and Manufacturing Corporation in Jacksonville, FL, says, "I think we are starting into the same position doctors moved into 10 years ago with malpractice problems."

In one year's time, liability insurance costs for the typical "bug doctor" have gone from $1,000 a year to over $4,000. Most suits allege that customers have become ill due to pesticides used by the exterminators.

Source: Reprinted by permission of *The Wall Street Journal,* © Dow Jones & Company, Inc., 1985. All Rights Reserved.

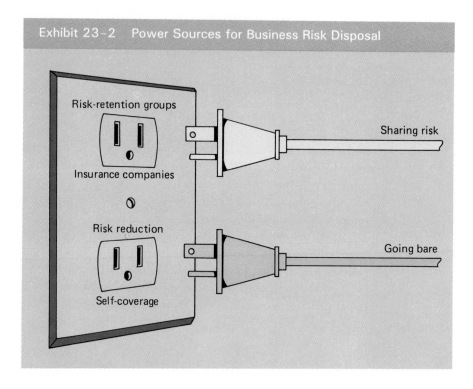

Exhibit 23–2   Power Sources for Business Risk Disposal

Risk-retention groups

Insurance companies

Risk reduction

Self-coverage

Sharing risk

Going bare

Coping with Small-Business Risks

Once a manager is fully aware of the sources of risk in his or her business, programs of risk management can be developed. Three basic alternatives of coping with risks can be pursued individually or in combination. These options are: (1) reduce the risk, (2) save funds to recover from risk losses, or (3) share the risks. Exhibit 23–2 depicts those risk-coping alternatives. Most small businesses rely heavily on sharing business risks via insurance when they should be using the three options in combination.

Reducing Business Risks

Small-business risks of all kinds can be reduced with sound, common-sense management. Preventive maintenance applied to risk management means eliminating the circumstances and situations that create risk. For example, the small firm needs to take every possible precaution to prevent fires. Some possible precautions include the following:

✝ **1.** *Use of safe construction.* The building should be made of fire-resistant materials, and electrical wiring should be adequate to carry the maximum load of electrical energy that will be imposed. Fire doors and insulation should be used where necessary.

2. *Provision of a completely automatic sprinkler system.* With an automatic sprinkler system available, fire insurance rates will be lower—and the fire hazard itself is definitely reduced.

3. *Provision of an adequate water supply.* Ordinarily this involves location in a city with water sources and water mains, together with a pumping system that will assure the delivery of any amount of water needed to fight fires. Of course, a company may hedge a bit by providing company-owned water storage tanks or private wells.

4. *Institution and operation of a fire-prevention program involving all employees.* Such a program must have top-management support, and the emphasis must always be on keeping employees fire-safety conscious. Regular fire drills for all employees, including both building-evacuation and actual fire-fighting efforts, may be undertaken.

Saving to Recover from Risk Losses

Intelligent, personal financial planning usually follows the practice of "saving for a rainy day." This concept should also be incorporated into small-business risk management. It is a difficult practice to follow in a business, but one that will pay dividends. This is a form of risk management frequently called **self-insurance.**

Self-insurance can take a general or specific form. In its general form, a part of the firm's earnings is earmarked as a contingency fund for possible future losses regardless of the source. In its specific form, a self-insurance program designates funds to individual loss categories such as property, medical, or workers' compensation. Some firms have moved quite heavily into self-insurance. Consider also Growth Enterprises Inc., a restaurant development company in Basking Ridge, NJ, which saved over $29,000 in its first year of operating a self-insurance program. Suzanne Green, Growth Enterprises's administrative manager, says, "We plan to go back out to the market and compare again. I don't think you can go along blindly with this kind of thing (self-insurance), put it in and say, 'Gee, this is going to work forever.' Self-insurance is not a panacea."[12]

SMALL BUSINESS IN ACTION
I'll Take My Chances

Going without insurance is a "risky" option for managing a small firm's product liability risks. Nevertheless, escalating policy premiums are encouraging some firms to take the chance. One such business is Sure-Grip International Corporation, a manufacturer of roller skates and skateboards in South Gate, CA. Recently, the firm was confronted with a statement for $40,000 in annual product liability premiums. Its president, Harry Ball, despite fully knowing that one major successful lawsuit could spell doomsday for his firm, takes the position, "I refuse to pay that kind of money for insurance. We'll keep the rest of our insurance, like fire, because it has remained reasonable."

Harry Ball

   Ball is stepping up quality control as a means to reduce the risk of a product liability claim. He also hopes that plaintiffs will not be as eager to sue if they realize that Sure-Grip has no insurance.

Source: Reprinted with permission, *Inc.* magazine, October, 1985. Copyright © 1985 by Goldhirsh Group, Inc., 38 Commercial Wharf, Boston, MA 02110.
Photo Source: *Courtesy of Harry Ball*

Sharing Risks

The rapid increase in insurance premiums in the 1980s—particularly for general liability coverage—has resulted in an inability of many small businesses to obtain affordable insurance.[13] Small-business owners hope this trend will be reversed. Nevertheless, insurance still provides one of the most important means of sharing business risks. A sound insurance program is imperative for the proper protection of a business.

Regardless of the nature of the business, risk insurance is serious business. Too often in the past, the small firm has paid insufficient attention to insurance matters and has failed to acquire skill in analyzing risk problems. Today such a situation is unthinkable. The small-business manager *must* take an active role in structuring an insurance package.

Insurance for the Small Business

It is often apparent that small firms fail to carry sufficient insurance protection. The entrepreneur often comes to such a realization only after a major loss. Careful risk management dictates a study of adequate insurance policies *in advance of a loss* rather than after the occurrence of the event.

Basic Principles of an Insurance Program

What kinds of risks can be covered by insurance? What kinds of coverage should be purchased? How much coverage is adequate? Unfortunately, there are no clear-cut answers to these questions. Probably the best advice to a small-business manager is to seek advice from a professional insurance agent. A reputable insurance agent can provide valuable assistance to small firms in evaluating risks and designing proper protection plans. However, the entrepreneur should enter this consultation as knowledgeable about insurance as possible. Some of the basic principles of insurance are discussed in the next paragraphs.

Identify the Business Risks to Be Covered Although the common insurable risks were pointed out earlier, other, less obvious, risks may be revealed only by a careful investigation. The small firm must first obtain coverages required by law or contract, such as workers' compensation insurance and automobile liability insurance. As part of this risk-identification process, the plant and equipment should be reappraised periodically by competent appraisers in order to maintain an adequate insurance coverage.

Obtain Coverage Only for Major Potential Losses The small firm must determine the magnitude of loss that it could bear without serious financial difficulty. If the firm is sufficiently strong, it may cover only those losses exceeding a specified minimum amount to avoid unnecessary coverage. It is important, of course, to guard against the tendency to underestimate the severity of potential losses.

Relate Cost of Premiums to Probability of Loss Because the insurance company must collect enough premiums to pay the actual losses of insured parties, the cost of insurance must be proportional to probability of occurrence of the insured event. As the chance of loss becomes more and more certain, a firm finds that the premium cost becomes so high that insurance is simply not worth the cost. Thus, insurance is most applicable and practical for improbable losses.

Requirements for Obtaining Insurance

Before an insurance company is willing to underwrite possible losses, certain requirements about the risk or the insured must be met.

The Risk Must Be Calculable The total overall loss arising from a large number of insured risks can be calculated by means of actuarial tables. For example, the number of buildings that will burn each year can be predicted with some accuracy. Only if the risks can be calculated will it be possible for the insurance company to determine fair insurance premiums to be charged.

The Risk Must Exist in Large Numbers The particular risk must occur in sufficiently large numbers to permit the law of averages to work and be spread over a wide geographical area. A fire insurance company, for example, cannot afford to insure only one building or even all the buildings in one town. It would have to insure buildings in many other towns and cities to get an adequate, safe distribution of risk.

The Insured Property Must Have Commercial Value An item that possesses only sentimental value cannot be insured. For example, an old family picture that is of no value to the public may not be included among other tangible items whose value can be measured in monetary terms.

The Policyholder Must Have an Insurable Interest in the Property or Person Insured The purpose of insurance is reimbursement of actual loss and not creation of profit for the insured. For example, a firm could not insure a building for $500,000 if its true worth is actually only $70,000. Likewise, it could not obtain life insurance on its customers or suppliers.

Types of Insurance

There are several classifications of insurance and a variety of coverages available from different insurance companies.[14] Each insurance purchaser should seek a balance between coverage, deductions, and premiums. Since the trend is toward higher and higher premiums for small businesses, the balancing act becomes even more critical.[15]

Commercial Property Coverage This class of insurance provides protection from losses associated with damage to or loss of property. Examples of property losses that can be covered are fire, explosion, vandalism, broken glass, business interruption, and employee dishonesty.

Figure 23–2   Commercial Property Coverage Can Keep This Firm in Business

Aetna Life & Casualty Co.

Most entrepreneurs will see the need for fire coverage and maybe a few other more traditional losses, but not enough small businesses realize the value of business interruption insurance. **Business interruption insurance** protects companies during the period necessary to restore property damaged by an insured peril. Coverage pays for lost income and other expenses of recovery. John Donahue, vice-president of the commercial insurance division for The Hartford Insurance Company, says that the "biggest mistake" small companies make

> is in not having sufficient . . . coverage that protects them against some catastrophe, such as a flood or fire, which would close down their business; while standard property insurance will pay to replace a building and its contents, it will not cover the payroll and other expenses that must be paid during the three or four months the factory is being rebuilt.[16]

Proving the extent of lost profits can be difficult. According to one writer, the process is difficult "because you are trying to reconstruct what never was."[17]

Dishonesty insurance covers such traditional areas as fidelity bonds and crime insurance. Employees occupying positions of trust in handling company funds are customarily bonded as a protection against their dishonesty. The informality and highly personal basis of employment in small firms make it difficult to realize the value of such insurance. On the other hand, the possible loss of money or other property through the dishonesty of persons other than employees is easy to accept. Crime insurance can cover such dangers as theft, robbery, and forgery.

Many commercial property policies contain a **coinsurance clause.** Under this clause, the insured agrees to maintain insurance equal to some specified percentage of the property value.[18] (A percentage of 80 percent is quite typical.) In return for this promise, the insured is given a reduced rate. If the insured fails to maintain the 80 percent coverage, only part of the loss will be reimbursed. To see how a coinsurance clause determines the amount paid by the insurer, assume that the physical property of a business is valued at $50,000. If the business insures it for $40,000 (or 80 percent of the property value) and incurs a fire loss of $20,000, the insurance company will pay the full amount of $20,000. However, if the business insures the property for only $30,000 (which is 75 percent of the specified minimum), the insurance company will pay only 75 percent of the loss, or $15,000.

Surety Bonds   These bonds protect against one kind of market-centered risk. **Surety bonds** insure against the failure of another firm or individual to fulfill a contractual obligation. Surety bonds are frequently used in connection with construction contracts.

Credit Insurance   Some small firms are financially able to insure themselves against certain losses. **Credit insurance** protects businesses from abnormal bad-debt losses. Abnormally high losses are those that result from a customer's insolvency due to tornado or flood losses, depressed industry conditions, business recession, or other factors. Credit insurance does not cover normal bad-debt losses that are predictable on the basis of past business experience. Insurance companies compute the normal rate on the basis of industry experience and the loss record of the particular firm being insured.

Credit insurance is available only to manufacturers and wholesalers. It is not available to a retailer. Thus, only trade credit may be insured. There are two reasons for this. The more important reason is found in the relative difficulty of analyzing business risks as compared with analyzing ultimate consumer risks. The other reason is that retailers have a much greater number of accounts receivable, which are smaller and provide greater risk diversification, so that credit insurance is less acutely required.

The collection service of the insurance company makes available legal talent and experience that may otherwise be unavailable to a small firm. Furthermore, collection efforts of insurance companies are generally conceded to be superior to those of regular collection agencies.

In addition, the credit standing of many small firms that might use credit insurance is enhanced. The small firm can show the banker that steps have been taken to avoid unnecessary risks, and thus it might obtain more favorable consideration in securing bank credit.

Credit insurance policies typically provide for a collection service on bad accounts. Although collection provisions vary, a common provision requires the insured to notify the insurance company within 90 days of the past-due status of the account and to turn it in for collection after 90 days.

Although the vast majority of policies provide general coverage, policies may be secured to cover individual accounts. A 10 percent, or higher, coinsurance requirement is included to limit the coverage to approximately the replacement value of the merchandise. Higher percentages of coinsurance are required for inferior accounts in order to discourage reckless credit extension by insured firms. Accounts are classified according to ratings by Dun & Bradstreet or ratings by other recognized agencies. Premiums vary with account ratings.[19]

Commercial Liability Insurance   There are two general classes of this form of insurance—general liability and employers' liability/workers' compensation. **General liability insurance** covers business liability to customers who might be injured on the premises or off-premises or who might be injured from the product sold to them. General liability insurance does not cover injury to a firm's own employees. However, employees using products such as machinery purchased from another manufacturer can bring suit under product liability laws against the equipment manufacturer. For example, a New Jersey court ruled that a machine manufacturer was liable for a worker's injury in a plastics plant when the worker caught his fingers in its machine. A protective guard had been removed, but the court felt that the manufacturer should have foreseen that.[20]

Employer's liability and **workers' compensation insurance** are required by all states to insure employees. As the titles imply, employer's liability coverage provides protection against suits brought by employees who suffer injury. Workers' compensation coverage obligates the insurer to pay eligible employees of the insured as required by workers' compensation law of the state.

Key-Person Insurance   By carrying life insurance, protection for the small business can be provided against the death of key personnel of the firm. This insurance is purchased by the company with the company as sole beneficiary. It may be written on an individual or group basis.

Most small-business advisers suggest term insurance for key-person insurance policies primarily because of lower premiums. How much to buy is more difficult to decide. Stan Meadow, who is a small-business specialist with McDermott, Will & Emery, a Chicago firm, recommends that the best way to determine a key executive's worth is to "calculate what it would cost to bring in someone of equal skill."[21]

Insurance Cooperatives

Another option by which a small business can share its risk via insurance is to join with other, similar, firms in a cooperative effort. This option

---

SMALL BUSINESS IN ACTION
Key-Person Insurance

Key-person insurance refers to special life-insurance coverage for top executives. It is most useful, according to Phil Dunne, chief financial officer of Sikes Corporation, for "companies that are highly leveraged or dominated by one person." The Sikes Corporation collected $6.9 million from a key-man policy on Jimmy Sikes, the chief executive officer of the Lakeland, FL, ceramic-tile manufacturer. Sikes had died suddenly at the age of 52 from a heart attack.

The key-man policy had been taken out by the firm in 1976 with yearly premiums of $200,000. Dunne viewed this cost as "just another cost of doing business." Dunne expects to purchase two more key-man policies for the company. One is on the new chief executive officer and another is for Jimmy Sikes's brother, who is chairman of the board. Dunne feels this type of coverage is still needed. "We don't have somebody who could step right into either one of those jobs, and if—God forbid—something should happen . . . then we'd need all the help we could get."

Source: "When the Man Is the Company," *Forbes*, Vol. 131, No. 7 (March 28, 1983), pp. 100, 102.

was made possible with the passage of the Federal Product Liability Risk Retention Act in 1981. This legislation allowed organizations to form special risk-retention groups or join together into a purchasing group.[22]

A **risk-retention group** is an insurance company started by a homogeneous group of entrepreneurs or professionals. The group provides liability insurance for its members. A **purchasing group** is any unincorporated group of persons that has the purpose of purchasing liability insurance for the group. It is subject to less regulation than a risk-retention group. Prior to passage of the 1981 Act, it was almost impossible for these cooperatives to function under state regulations of a nonlicensing state.

The Risk Retention Amendments of 1986 broadened the scope of risk retention and purchasing groups. The new law permits a group to provide any commercial liability coverage to its members who all face a common risk. A cooperative effort to share risks with other small businesses is not necessarily a viable option for all small firms. It does, however, offer another alternative for coping with business risk.

Looking Back

1. Risk management is an approach to management concerned with the preservation of the assets and earning power of a business against risks of accidental loss. The three ways to manage business risks are: reduce the risk, save to cover possible future losses, and transfer the risk to someone else by carrying insurance. The best solution often is to combine all three approaches.

2. Business risks can be classified by the causes of accidental loss, by insurability, or by type of assets that are preserved with risk management. In using the last system, risks are classified as market-centered, property-centered, personnel-centered, and customer-centered.

3. The small firm should carry enough insurance to protect against major losses. Beyond this, the decision on coverage requires judgment that balances such factors as magnitude of possible loss, ability to minimize such losses, cost of the insurance, and financial strength of the firm.

4. To obtain insurance, several requirements must be met. The risk must be calculable in probabilistic terms, the risk must exist in large numbers, the insured property must have commercial

value, and the policyholder must have an insurable interest in the property or person insured.

5. The basic types of insurance coverage that the small business might require are commercial property coverage, surety bonds, commercial liability, credit, and key-person insurance. Risk-retention and purchasing groups provide a mechanism for obtaining insurance coverage through nontraditional channels.

DISCUSSION QUESTIONS

1. Which of the different classifications of business risks is the most difficult for the small firm to control? Why? Which is the least difficult to control? Why?

2. Do you feel the product liability suit brought against the Will-Burt Company (Spotlight on Small Business) was fair? Why or why not?

3. If you were shopping in a small retail store and somehow sustained an injury such as a broken arm, under what circumstances would you sue the firm? Explain.

4. Review the Small Business in Action report entitled "Here Today, Gone Tomorrow." Would you feel the same way that Judy George does if you had been in her shoes? Why or why not?

5. What are the basic ways to cope with risk in a small business?

6. Can a small firm safely assume that business risks will never turn into losses sufficient to bankrupt it and therefore avoid buying insurance and taking other protective measures? Why?

7. How can a small business deal with the risk entailed in business recessions?

8. Could a small firm safely deal with such hazards as property loss from fire by precautionary measures in lieu of insurance?

9. When is it logical for a small business to utilize self-insurance?

10. Enumerate a number of approaches for combating the danger of theft or fraud by employees and also by outsiders.

11. Under what conditions would life insurance on a business executive constitute little protection to the business? And when is such life insurance helpful?

12. Are any kinds of business risks basically human risks? Are the people involved always employees?

13. Is the increase in liability claims and court awards of special concern to small manufacturers? Why?

14. What types of insurance are required by law for most business firms?

15. Explain how risk-retention groups are an alternative way for small firms to cope with risk. Do you believe these groups will become popular? Why or why not?

YOU MAKE THE CALL

Situation 1

The Amigo Company manufactures motorized wheelchairs in its Bridgeport, MI, plant under the supervision of Alden Thieme. Alden is the brother of the firm's founder, Allen Thieme. The company has around 100 employees and does $10 million in sales a year.

Like many other firms, Amigo is faced with increased liability insurance costs. It is contemplating dropping all coverage. However, it realizes that the users of its product are individuals who have already suffered pain and trouble. Therefore, if an accident were to occur and there was a liability suit, there might be a strong temptation for juries to favor the plaintiffs. In fact, the company has already experienced litigation. A woman in their wheelchair was killed by a car on the street. The driver of the car had no insurance, so Amigo was sued.

Source: Based on the information in Harry Bacas, "Liability Trying Times," *Nation's Business,* Vol. 74, No. 2, (February, 1986), p. 23. Copyright 1986 U.S. Chamber of Commerce.

Questions

1. Do you agree that the type of customer to whom the Amigo Company sells should influence its decision regarding insurance?

2. In what way, if any, should the outcome of the firm's current litigation impact Amigo's decision to renew its insurance coverage?

3. What options for going "bare" does Amigo have? What is your recommendation?

Situation 2

Pansy Ellen Essman is a 42-year-old grandmother who is chairman of a company based in Atlanta, GA, that does $5 million in sales each year. Her company, Pansy Ellen Products, Inc., grew out of a product idea Essman had as she bathed her squealing, squirming granddaughter in the bathroom tub. Her idea was to produce a sponge pillow to cradle a child in, thus freeing the mother's hands so she could easily clean her baby.

Since production of this initial product, the company has expanded its product line to include nursery lamps, baby food organizers, strollers, and hook-on baby seats. Essman has seemingly managed her product mix risk well. However, she is concerned that other sources of business risk may have been ignored or slighted.

Source: Based on the account of the firm's startup found in "It Scared the Bejeebers Out of Me," *Forbes,* Vol. 131, No. 3 (January 31, 1983), p. 48.

Questions

1. What particular other types of business risk do you think Essman might be considering? Be specific.
2. Would a risk-retention group be a good possibility for this company? Why or why not?
3. What different types of insurance coverage should a company like this carry?

EXPERIENTIAL EXERCISES

1. Locate a recent issue of a business magazine wherein you can read about new small-business startups. Select one new firm that is marketing a product and another that is selling a service. Compare their situations relative to business risks. Report to the class on your analysis.
2. Contact a local small-business owner and obtain his or her permission to conduct a risk analysis of the business. Note the business's situation in regard to risk and what preventive or protective actions you suggest. Report your findings to the class.
3. Contact a local insurance company and arrange to conduct an interview. Determine in the interview the various types of coverage the company offers for small businesses. Write a report on your findings.
4. Assume that upon graduation you enter your family business or obtain employment with an independent business back in your home town. Further assume that after five years of employment you leave the business to start your own competing business. Make a list of the considerations you perceive you would face regarding leaving the business with trade secrets after just five years of experience.

REFERENCES TO SMALL-BUSINESS PRACTICES

Brody, Michael. "When Products Turn into Liabilities." *Fortune,* Vol. 113, No. 5 (March 3, 1986), pp. 20–24.
> Some of the responses companies have taken to the increase in lawsuits are discussed in this article. Several lawsuits over product liability are described.

Crowley, Michael. "Recovering from the Ashes." *Venture,* Vol. 6, No. 3 (March, 1984), pp. 108–110.
> This article provides a vivid account of a manager's eyewitnessing of a fire and the recovery strategy after fire completely destroyed a manufacturing plant. Due to careful insurance planning, the company didn't lose a penny.

Joseph, Eileen Z. "Managing Your Risks." *Nation's Business,* Vol. 74, No. 4 (April, 1986), pp. 66–68.
> A step-by-step approach for controlling risks and lowering insurance costs is included in this article. The need for risk-management plans is emphasized by the author.

Mangan, Doreen. "None of Your Secrets Are Safe." *Venture,* Vol. 10, No. 2 (February, 1988), pp. 61–67.
> The author examines several incidents of corporate intelligence/espionage.

Waters, Craig R. "The Private War of James Sullivan." *Inc.,* Vol. 4, No. 7 (July, 1982), pp. 41–46.
> The chairman of the board of an insulation business describes the trials and tribulations surrounding more than 1,800 product liability lawsuits directed at his business.

ENDNOTES

1. Emmett J. Vaughan, *Fundamentals of Risk and Insurance,* 4th ed. (New York: John Wiley & Sons, 1986), p. 4.

2. Damon Darlin, "Sales Plateau in Ceiling Fans Hurts Concern," *The Wall Street Journal* (November 8, 1982), p. 2.

3. Gayle Olinekova, "Bringing Up Bonne," *Entrepreneur,* Vol. 17, No. 10 (October, 1989), pp. 44–51.

4. Holly Klokis, "Confessions of an Ex-shoplifter," *Chain Store Age Executive,* Vol. 61, No. 2 (February, 1985), p. 15.

5. "Employee Theft," *Inc.,* Vol. 10, No. 2 (February, 1988), p. 98.

6. Neil H. Snyder and Karen E. Blair, "Dealing with Employee Theft," *Business Horizons,* Vol. 32, No. 3 (May–June, 1989), pp. 27–34.

7. Harry Bacas, "To Stop a Thief," *Nation's Business,* Vol. 75, No. 6 (June, 1987), p. 16.

8. Joanne Kelleher, "A Thief in the Fold," *Inc.,* Vol. 4, No. 6 (June, 1982), p. 96.

9. Fred S. Steingold, "Competing with Your Former Employer," *Inc.,* Vol. 5, No. 1 (January, 1983), p. 91.

10. Fred S. Steingold, "Do Your Business Premises Present a Public Hazard?" *Inc.*, Vol. 5, No. 11 (November, 1983), pp. 189, 191.

11. "Proper Precautions Trim Product Liability Risks," *Inc.*, Vol. 2, No. 5 (May, 1980), p. 131.

12. Donna Sammons, "Risky Business," *Inc.*, Vol. 6, No. 1 (January, 1984), p. 115.

13. See for example the discussion in Archer W. Huneycutt and Elizabeth A. Wibker, "Liability Crisis: Small Businesses at Risk," *Journal of Small Business Management,* Vol. 26, No. 1 (January, 1988), pp. 25–30.

14. Much of the terminology used here to describe the different types of insurance is consistent with that used in the new Portfolio Program, suggested by the Insurance Services Office, which is a national rating bureau that publishes rates for property and liability insurance. This program introduced simplified policy terminology effective January 1, 1986.

15. A current assessment of what is happening with insurance can be found in Jill Andresky, "A World Without Insurance?" *Forbes*, Vol. 136, No. 2 (July 15, 1985), pp. 40–43; and David B. Hilder, "Small Firms Face Sharp Cost Hikes for Insurance— If They Can Get It," *The Wall Street Journal* (August 5, 1985), p. 23.

16. Nancy McConnell, "Business Insurance Good News and Bad News," *Venture,* Vol. 10, No. 9 (September, 1988), p. 64.

17. Sanford L. Jacobs, "Business-Disruption Coverage Is Inadequate at Many Firms," *The Wall Street Journal* (October 3, 1983), p. 27.

18. It should be remembered that this is value at time of the actual loss.

19. For additional discussion of credit insurance, see Emmett J. Vaughan, *op. cit.,* pp. 602–605.

20. William Steele, "The Product Liability Trap," *Inc.*, Vol. 4, No. 7 (July, 1982), p. 93.

21. Kathleen Mirin, "Key-Man Insurance," *Venture,* Vol. 5, No. 6 (June, 1983), p. 29.

22. For an excellent discussion of the Act, see Jon Harkavy, "The Risk Retention Act of 1986: The Options Increase," *Risk Management,* Vol. 34, No. 3 (March, 1987), pp. 22–34.

24 SOCIAL AND ETHICAL ISSUES

Stephen Lefkovits/USA TODAY 1990

The Body Shop, a firm started by Anita Roddick in England in 1976, gives social responsibilities a high priority in its operation. Its principal business is the sale of skin and hair care products. From its beginning as one tiny shop, this firm has made customer and community service a major objective.

One example is The Body Shop's efforts to protect the environment by offering discounts to customers who return plastic bottles, using products that are biodegradable, recycling waste, using recycled paper, and providing biodegradable carrier bags. To serve its customers well, The Body Shop places greater emphasis on health and well-being than on beauty, avoids high-pressure selling, seeks to provide adequate product information, keeps packaging at a minimum so that customers pay only for the product, and uses a range of container sizes so that customers can buy only

what they need. The Body Shop's philosophy of management is expressed
in these words:

> The company operates within the world, the environment, the com-
> munity. That is where our responsibilities lie: we want to give something
> back to society.

Source: What Is The Body Shop?, a brochure distributed in The Body Shop stores.

Looking Ahead

Watch for the following important topics:
1. Social responsibilities of small firms.
2. Types of ethical problems in small business.
3. How small firms can attain high ethical standards.
4. How small firms are regulated by federal, state, and local government.
5. The burdensome nature of small-business regulation.
6. New terms and concepts:

social responsibilities   bait advertising
environmentalism   unfair-trade practice laws
consumerism   blue-sky laws
code of ethics

Business owners obviously intend to earn a profit, and our society
agrees with that right by granting freedom to operate as part of a private
enterprise system. In addition, society expects business firms—including
small ones—to operate in a responsible manner and to contribute positively to the welfare of the community and nation.

Some social expectations are incorporated in the law—for example, a
prohibition against misleading advertising. The law, however, is not so detailed or explicit that it spells out answers to all of the social and ethical
issues confronting small and growing firms. Therefore, small-business owners need a general understanding of the social context of business operations.

Social Responsibilities of Small Business

In recent years, public attention has been focused on the social obligations of business organizations. These feelings of concern are rooted in a new awareness of the role of business in modern society. In a sense, the public regards managers as trustees and expects them to act accordingly to protect the interests of suppliers, employees, customers, and the general public, along with making a profit.

How Small Firms View Their Social Obligations

Conservation, fair hiring practices, consumerism, environmental protection, and the public welfare are popular themes in the news media. One might wonder whether entrepreneurs are aware of such issues and the extent to which they are responsive to them. Is their attention focused so closely on the bottom line that they ignore the broader social issues that affect their businesses?

One might expect to find varying degrees of social sensitivity among business owners, and this is, indeed, the case. One study asked small-business owners and managers, "How do you see your responsibilities to society?"[1] In response to this question, 88 percent mentioned at least one type of social obligation, whereas only 12 percent felt they had no specific responsibilities or did not know what to make of the term.

The majority who recognized **social responsibilities** cited obligations to customers, to employees, and to the community, as well as a general responsibility to act ethically. On the basis of these responses, we can see that most small-business owners are aware that their firms function within the context of the broader society. We recognize, of course, that actual business decisions may fall short of business ideology, but the general awareness shown by those in small firms is strongly positive.

Social Obligations and Profit Making

Small firms, as well as large corporations, must reconcile their social responsibilities with their need to earn profits. It is easy to think that only the large corporation can afford to be civic-minded. A corporate leader, George Weissman, argues otherwise, however:

You don't have to be a giant company to participate. Even the tiniest firm can return a portion of what it takes *from* the community *back* to the

Figure 24–1   Serving the Community. In Cincinnati, small-business owner Ed Hubert, of Hubert Distributing Co., has established a foundation to help finance grants and loans to non-profit organizations such as the North Fairmount Community Center, which sponsors housing renovation and makes homes available for purchase by low-income families.

Courtesy of Brock Schmidtz & Associates and the North Fairmount Community Center, Cincinnati, Ohio

community. Social responsibility has got to be a shared function of all business men and women, regardless of the size of their enterprises, if enterprise is to survive.[2]

Managers of small businesses recognize the same responsibility clearly, if not always as eloquently, as those who speak for big business. In fact, many independent entrepreneurs speak of their satisfaction in serving the community as one of the major rewards from their businesses. Of course, this does not mean that all firms share this philosophy; some fail to sense or refuse to recognize any obligation beyond the minimum necessary to produce a profit.

A sense of social responsibility may be perfectly consistent with the firm's long-run profit objective. Urban problems, for example, sometimes require small firms to take part in community projects more as a means of survival than altruism. In the 1970s, a group of local business owners on

Cleveland's southeast side headed by John Young, owner of a pest exterminating business, formed an organization to deal with the urban deterioration surrounding their businesses.[3] This organization, Old Brooklyn Community Development Corporation, financed by dues and donations, has planted trees and flowers, thrown parties for the neighborhood kids, created a residents' forum, started a garden club, opened a community theater, and organized an auxiliary police unit.

The firm that consistently fulfills certain obligations makes itself a desirable member of the community and may attract patronage. Conversely, the firm that scorns social responsibilities may find itself the object of restrictive legislation and may discover its employees to be lacking in loyalty. It seems likely, however, that the typical independent entrepreneur contributes to the community and other groups because it is a duty and a privilege to do so, and not merely because the profit potential in each such move has been cunningly calculated.

Recognition of a social responsibility does not change a profit-seeking business into a charitable organization. Earning a profit is absolutely essential. Without profits, the firm is in no position to recognize social responsibilities toward anyone. The point is that profits, although essential, are not the only factor of importance.

The Special Challenge of Environmentalism

In recent decades the deterioration of the environment has become a matter of widespread concern. One source of pollution has been business firms that discharge waste into streams, contaminants into the air, and noise into areas surrounding their operations. Efforts to preserve and redeem the environment thus directly affect business organizations, including small-business firms.

The interests of small-business owners and environmentalists are not necessarily or uniformly in conflict. Some business leaders, including those in small business, have worked and acted for the cause of conservation. For example, many small firms have taken steps to remove eyesores and to landscape and otherwise improve plant facilities. Others have modernized their equipment and changed their procedures to reduce air and water pollution. In a few cases, small business has been in a position to benefit from the emphasis on ecology. Those companies whose products are harmless to the environment gain an edge over competitive products that pollute. Also, small firms are involved in servicing pollution-control equipment. The auto

SMALL BUSINESS IN ACTION
Environmental Concerns—Recycling Paper

Environmental needs—such as the need to conserve forests and the need to reduce landfill waste—can create opportunities for small business. Allen Davis responded to this type of need by founding Conservatree Paper Company, in San Francisco, to sell fine recycled papers. As product quality has improved, this firm has been able to compete in quality and price with other types of paper. As of 1988, Conservatree's business saved well over $1 million a year in pulp processing, kept tons of recyclable paper out of landfills, and saved roughly 75,000 trees. Conservatree is an example of the small firm that solves, rather than creates, environmental problems.

Source: "Recycling Hits the Big Time," *In Business,* Vol. 10, No. 6 (November–December, 1988), p. 25.

repair shop, for example, services pollution-control devices on automobile engines.

Some small firms are adversely affected by efforts to protect the environment. Livestock feeding lots, cement plants, pet-food processors, and iron foundries are representative of industries that are especially vulnerable to extensive regulation. The cost impact on businesses of this type is often severe. Indeed, the required improvements can force the closure of some businesses.

The ability to pass higher costs on to customers is dependent upon the market situation and is ordinarily quite difficult for the small firm. Resulting economic hardships on small business must, therefore, be recognized as a cost of pollution control and evaluated accordingly. In some instances the controls are hardest on the small, marginal firm with obsolete equipment. Environmental regulation may merely hasten the inevitable closing of the firm.

The level of government regulation poses another potential problem for small business. Legislation, whether state or local, may prove discriminatory by forcing higher costs on a local firm than on competitive firms outside the regulated territory. The immediate self-interest of a small firm, therefore, is served by regulations that operate at the highest or most general level. A federal regulation, for example, applies to all U.S. firms and thereby avoids giving competitive advantages to low-cost polluters in other states.

The Special Challenge of Consumerism

At one time the accepted philosophy of business was expressed as "let the buyer beware." In contrast, today's philosophy says "let the seller beware." Today's sophisticated buyers feel that they should be able to purchase products that are safe, reliable, durable, and honestly advertised. This theme has influenced various types of consumer legislation. The Magnuson-Moss Warranty Act, for example, imposes special restrictions on sellers such as requiring warranties to be available for inspection rather than be hidden inside a package.

Small firms are directly involved in the **consumerism** movement. To some extent, they stand to gain from it. Attention to customer needs and flexibility in meeting these needs have traditionally been strong assets of small firms. Their managers have been close to customers and thus able to know and respond easily to their needs. To the extent that these potential

---

SMALL BUSINESS IN ACTION
Herman Miller's Reputation for Integrity

One of the nation's best-known family businesses is Herman Miller, Inc., Zeeland, MI, manufacturer of fine office furniture. Founded in 1923 by D. J. DePree, the firm is now headed by his son, Max DePree. Its reputation as a well-managed company rests not only on its superb products—acclaimed by some as the highest-quality office furniture made anywhere—but also by its integrity in relationships with employees, customers, and others. Following is an outsider's assessment of the company and its present leader:

> Herman Miller is a place with integrity. Max defines integrity as "a fine sense of one's obligations." That integrity exhibits itself in the company's dedication to superior design, to quality, to making a contribution to society—and in its manifest respect for its customers, investors, suppliers and employees.

Source: The statement is that of James O'Toole, University of Southern California, and appears in the foreword to Max DePree, *Leadership Is An Art* (East Lansing: Michigan State University Press, 1987), pp. xvii–xviii.

features have been realized in practice, the position of small business has been strengthened. And to the extent that small firms can continue to capitalize upon customer desires for excellent service, they can reap rewards from the consumerism movement.

Consumerism also carries threats to small business. It is hard to build a completely safe product and to avoid all errors in service. Moreover, the growing complexity of products makes their servicing more difficult. The mechanic or repairer must know a great deal more to render satisfactory service today than was needed two or three decades ago. Rising consumer expectations, therefore, provide a measure of danger as well as opportunity for small firms. The quality of management will determine the extent to which opportunities are realized and dangers avoided.

Ethical Responsibilities of Small Business

Stories in the news media concerning insider trading, fraud, and bribery have usually involved large corporations. Does that mean that ethical problems are confined to big business? Clearly not. In the less-publicized, day-to-day life of small business, decision makers also face ethical dilemmas and temptations to compromise principles for the sake of business or personal advantage. The topics of environmentalism and consumerism discussed earlier have an ethical dimension, but we move on in this section to more individual ethical issues.

Kinds of Ethical Issues in Small Firms

Only the naive would argue that small business is pure in terms of ethical conduct. In fact, there is widespread recognition of unethical and even illegal activity. There is no way of measuring the extent of unethical conduct, of course, but there is an obvious need for improvement in small, as well as big, businesses.

One glaring example of poor ethics practiced by many small businesses is fraudulent reporting of income and expenses for income-tax purposes. This conduct includes "skimming" of income (that is, keeping some income off the record) as well as improperly claiming certain business expenses. The following account illustrates the nature of these practices:

> To countless small businesses, cheating Uncle Sam is as routine as making the payroll and marketing the product.

For a Georgia cafeteria owner, it involved skimming at least $100 a day from the cash register before recording his receipts on the ledger. On the docks in Massachusetts, seafood buyers carry briefcases full of cash so their suppliers don't have to account for checks. A fashion designer refurbished his suburban Philadelphia mansion as a tax-deductible corporate expense.

The government pressed charges in these cases, but most income-tax chiseling by small business goes undetected by overworked tax agents and accountants unable to probe deep enough to find it.[4]

The reference to income-tax cheating by small business does not imply that all or even most small firms engage in such practices. It simply tells us that tax evasion does occur within small firms and that the practice is sufficiently widespread as to be recognized as a general problem.

Cheating on taxes represents only one type of unethical business practice. Questions of right and wrong permeate all areas of business decision making, as they do all areas of life itself. It may be helpful to identify some common types of ethical issues confronting small-business managers in order to better understand the dimensions of this problem.

In *marketing decisions,* the entrepreneur is confronted with a variety of ethical questions. For example, the entrepreneur must devise advertising content that sells but also tells "the truth, the whole truth, and nothing but the truth." Salespeople must walk a fine line between persuasion and deception. In some types of small business, the seller can obtain sales contracts more successfully by offering improper inducements to buyers or by joining with competitors in rigging bids.

In *management decisions,* the entrepreneur affects the personal and family lives of employees. Issues of fairness, honesty, and impartiality easily surface in decisions and practices regarding hiring, promotion, salary increases, dismissals, layoffs, and work assignments. In communication with employees, the entrepreneur may be truthful, vague, misleading, or totally dishonest.

In *financial and accounting decisions,* the entrepreneur must decide the extent to which he or she will be honest and candid in reporting financial condition and results. Even with a small firm, outsiders such as bankers and suppliers depend upon its financial reports to be accurate. Some firms reportedly keep two sets of books—a fictitious set for the government and another in which the real facts appear.

These examples are not meant to be exhaustive in outlining ethical issues in small business. Instead, they are intended to illustrate the existence of such issues in the various areas of small-business operation.

Vulnerability of Small Firms

Walking the "straight and narrow" may be more difficult and costly on Main Street than it is on Wall Street.[5] In other words, small firms—the Main Street type—may face greater temptations and pressures to act unethically because of their smallness.

As an example, a lack of resources may make it difficult for a small firm to resist extortion by public officials.

> Prof. William Baxter of the Stanford Law School notes that for such owners, delayed building permits or failed sanitation inspections can be "life-threatening events" that make them cave in to bribe demands. By contrast, he adds, "the local manager of Burger King is in a much better position" to tell these people to get lost.[6]

The small firm may also feel itself at a disadvantage in competing with larger competitors that have superior resources. As a result, the small firm owner may be tempted to rationalize bribery as a way of offsetting what seems to be a competitive disadvantage and securing an even playing field.

While these pressures do not justify unethical behavior, they help explain the context for decisions involving ethical issues. Ethical decision making often calls for difficult choices by the entrepreneur.

The temptation for entrepreneurs to compromise ethical standards as they strive to earn a profit is evident in the results of a study of entrepreneurial ethics.[7] In this study, entrepreneurs were compared with other business managers and professionals in their views about various ethical issues. Respondents were presented with 16 vignettes, each involving a business decision having ethical overtones. They were asked to indicate the degree to which they found each action compatible with their own ethical views by checking a seven-point scale ranging from 1 (never acceptable) to 7 (always acceptable). Following is an example of one vignette:

> An owner of a small firm obtained a free copy of a copyrighted computer software program from a business friend rather than spending $500 to obtain his own program from the software dealer.

On 5 of the 16 cases, entrepreneurs appeared significantly less moral (more approving of questionable conduct) than other respondents.[8] Each of these cases involved an opportunity to gain financially by taking a profit from someone else's pocket. For example, entrepreneurs were more willing to condone collusive bidding and the duplicating of copyrighted computer software without payment to the manufacturer for its use.

These choices reveal the special temptation for entrepreneurs who are strongly driven to earn profits. However, this issue must be kept in perspective. Even though entrepreneurs appeared less moral than other business respondents in their reaction to these five issues, the majority of entrepreneurs were significantly *more* moral in their responses to two other issues in which there was no immediate profit impact.[9] The evidence shows, then, that most entrepreneurs display a general ethical sensitivity but that some of them show vulnerability in issues that directly affect profits.

Ethical Leadership in Small Firms

Entrepreneurs who care about ethical performance in their firms can do something about it! They can use their powerful positions of leadership and ownership to insist that their firms display honesty and integrity in all of their operations. Ethical values are established by leaders in all organizations, and those at lower levels take their cues regarding proper behavior from the pronouncements and conduct of their leaders.

In a small organization, the ethical influence of a leader is more pronounced than it is in a large corporation. In a giant corporation, leadership becomes diffused, and the chief executive must exercise great care to make sure that his or her precepts are shared by those in the various divisions and subsidiaries. Some corporate CEOs have professed great shock to discover behavior at lower levels that conflicted sharply with their own espoused principles. The position of an entrepreneur is much simpler. In effect, the founder or head of a small business can say, "This is my personal integrity on the line, and I want you to do it this way!" Such statements are easily understood. And such a leader becomes even more eloquent as he or she backs up such statements with appropriate behavior.

We can see, then, the potential for high ethical standards in small firms. An entrepreneur who believes strongly in honesty and truthfulness can insist that those principles be followed throughout the organization. Earlier in this chapter, we cited Herman Miller, Inc., the furniture manufacturer, as a family firm exhibiting high standards of integrity. This ethical stance reflects the values of the DePree family. The ethical values of the founder and his son, the present CEO, have obviously permeated and continue to characterize this firm's operation.

In summary, the personal integrity of the founder or owner—the top management of the small firm—is a key to ethical performance. It is obviously important in any organization, but the dominant role of this one per-

son in a small firm gives him or her a powerful voice in the ethical performance of that firm.

Developing a Code of Ethics

As a small firm grows, the personal influence of the entrepreneur inevitably declines. Personal interaction with the leader occurs less and less.
The result is that the powerful, personal enunciation of ethical values is no
longer quite as effective as it was earlier. The entrepreneur's basic principles simply cannot be expressed or reinforced as frequently or consistently
as the business grows larger.

At some point, therefore, the firm should formulate a **code of ethics,**
as most large corporations have done. Such a code should express the principles to be followed by members of the firm and give examples of these
principles in action. A code might, for example, prohibit acceptance of gifts
or favors from suppliers and then point out the standard business courte-
sies, such as a free lunch, that might be accepted without violating the policy. (Sample codes can be obtained from Ethics Resource Center, Inc., 1025
Connecticut Avenue, N.W., Washington, DC 20036.)

If a code of ethics is to be effective, employees must be aware of its
nature and convinced of its importance. As a minimum, they should read
and sign it. As time goes on and employees know less about the firm's commitments, however, training is necessary to be sure the code is well understood and taken seriously. It is also imperative, of course, that management
operate in a manner that is consistent with its own principles and deal deci-
sively with any infractions.

Better Business Bureaus

In any sizable community, all shades of ethical and unethical business
practices can be found. A few businesses are little more than rip-offs. Others
use highly questionable practices—for example, **bait advertising,** which is
an insincere offer to sell in order to lure customers and switch them to the
purchase of more expensive products. Other firms are totally dishonest in
the services they provide—for example, replacing auto parts that are perfectly good.

Unethical operations reflect adversely on the honest members of the
business community. As a result, privately owned business firms in many
cities have banded together to form Better Business Bureaus. The purpose

of such organizations is to promote ethical conduct on the part of all business firms in the community.

Specifically, a Better Business Bureau's function is twofold: (1) it provides free buying guidelines and information about a company that the consumer should know *prior* to completing a business transaction, and (2) it attempts to solve questions or disputes concerning purchases. As a result, business swindles often decline in a community served by a Better Business Bureau. Exhibit 24–1 presents a small section from a code of advertising ethics developed by the Better Business Bureaus.

Governmental Regulation

Observance of social responsibilities and ethical standards is not left entirely to the discretion of small-business firms. Federal laws, as well as state laws and local ordinances, regulate business activity in the public interest. In this section, we consider some examples of regulation and the regulatory burden resting on small firms.

Types of Government Regulation

The varieties of regulation are endless. They affect the ways in which small firms pay their employees, advertise, bid on contracts, dispose of waste, promote safety, and care for the public welfare. Of necessity, the discussion here will be limited to a few key areas of regulation.

Maintenance of Free Competition   A fully competitive economic system presumably benefits customers who can buy products and services from those firms which best satisfy their needs. Of the various laws intended to maintain a competitive economy, perhaps the best known are the federal antitrust laws, especially the Sherman Antitrust Act of 1890 and the Clayton Act of 1914. Both acts were designed to promote competition by eliminating artificial restraints on trade.

Although the purpose of federal and state antitrust laws is noble, the results leave much to be desired. One would be naive to think that small business need no longer fear the power of oligopolists. These laws prevent some mergers and eliminate some unfair practices, but giant business firms continue to dominate many industries.

To some extent, at least, the antitrust laws offer protection to small firms. For example, a local distributor of petroleum products sued a major

Exhibit 24–1   Better Business Bureau Code of Advertising

Bait Advertising and Selling

A "bait" offer is an alluring but insincere offer to sell a product or service which the advertiser does not intend to sell. Its purpose is to switch consumers from buying the advertised merchandise or service in order to sell something else, usually at a higher price or on a basis more advantageous to the advertiser.

a. No advertisement should be published unless it is a bona fide offer to sell the advertised merchandise or service.

b. The advertising should not create a false impression about the product or service being offered in order to lay the foundation for a later "switch" to other, more expensive products or services, or products of a lesser quality at the same price.

c. Subsequent full disclosure by the advertiser of all other facts about the advertised article does not preclude the existence of a bait scheme.

d. An advertiser should not use nor permit the use of the following scheme practices:
  - refusing to show or demonstrate the advertised merchandise or service;
  - disparaging the advertised merchandise or service, its warranty, availability, services and parts, credit terms, etc.;
  - selling the advertised merchandise or service and thereafter "unselling" the customer to make a switch to other merchandise or service;
  - refusing to take orders for the advertised merchandise or service or to deliver it within a reasonable time;
  - demonstrating or showing a defective sample of the advertised merchandise; or
  - having a sales compensation plan designed to penalize salespersons who sell the advertised merchandise or service.

e. An advertiser should have on hand a sufficient quantity of advertised merchandise to meet reasonably anticipated demands, unless the advertisement discloses the number of items available. If items are available only at certain branches, their specific locations should be disclosed. The use of "rainchecks" is no justification for inadequate estimates of reasonably anticipated demand.

f. Actual sales of the advertised merchandise or service may not preclude the existence of a bait scheme since this may be merely an attempt to create an aura of legitimacy. A key factor in determining the existence of "bait" is the number of times the merchandise or service was advertised compared to the number of actual sales of the merchandise or service.

Source: Council of Better Business Bureaus, Inc., *Code of Advertising (1985),* pp. 8–9. Reproduced with permission.

oil company and another dealer for $6 million, charging violation of anti-trust laws. The suit alleged that the plaintiff was overcharged for gasoline, given unreasonably low allocations of petroleum products, and forced to make one station a nonbrand station. In another case, a small processor of waste material from slaughterhouses, stores, and restaurants sought treble damages of $300,000 and the prohibition of unfair practices by a larger competitor. The plaintiff claimed that the competitor had begun offering unreasonably high prices for waste products in the plaintiff's territory, far above the prices offered in the defendant's established territory. The suit alleged that the defendant's purpose was to establish a monopoly.

As an amendment to the Clayton Act, the Robinson-Patman Act of 1936 prohibited price discrimination by manufacturers and wholesalers in dealing with other business firms. In particular, the law is designed to protect independent retailers and wholesalers in their fight against large chains. Quantity discounts may still be offered to large buyers, but the amount of the discounts must be justified economically by the seller on the basis of actual costs. Vendors are also forbidden to grant disproportionate advertising allowances to large retailers. The objective is to prevent unreasonable discounts and other concessions to large purchasers merely because of superior size and bargaining power.

The effectiveness of the Robinson-Patman Act and its benefits to small business have been debated. Some have argued that it discourages both large and small firms from cutting prices and makes it harder to expand into new markets and to pass on to customers the cost savings on large orders.[10]

The majority of states have **unfair-trade practice laws,** also known as unfair-trade practices acts, unfair-sales acts, and unfair-practices acts. These laws specify that sellers may not sell goods at less than their cost, and they also specify certain percentage markups. Some of the state unfair-trade laws even cover personal services.

While unfair-trade practice laws ostensibly aim to eliminate unfair price competition, there is a question as to whether they accomplish this objective. The danger in such laws is their tendency to handicap those firms that are able to reduce prices because of their efficiency. Thus, in the guise of preservation of free competition, these laws may actually hold a price umbrella over inefficient, marginal firms, denying freedom of enterprise to efficient firms and penalizing the public accordingly.

Protection of Consumers   Insofar as freedom of competition is provided by the laws discussed above, consumers will benefit indirectly. In addition, consumers are given various forms of more direct protection by federal, state, and local legislation.

The Wheeler-Lea Act of 1938 gave the Federal Trade Commission a broad mandate to attack unfair or deceptive acts or practices in commerce. The FTC's original focus on antitrust practices has been expanded through the years to cover a wide range of business activities: labeling, safety, packaging, and advertising of products; truth-in-lending; fair credit reporting; equal credit opportunity; and many others. States have also enacted laws and created consumer protection agencies to deal with unfair or deceptive practices. A few examples of the types of trade practices scrutinized by the Federal Trade Commission are: labeling goods as "free" or "handmade"; advertising that offers unreal "bargains" by pretended reduction of unused "regular" prices; and bait advertising.

As still another measure to protect the public against unreasonable risk of injury associated with toys and other consumer products, the federal government enacted the Consumer Product Safety Act of 1972. This act created the Consumer Product Safety Commission to enforce its established

---

SMALL BUSINESS IN ACTION
Consumer Protection and the Small Firm

Efforts by the Consumer Product Safety Commission (CPSC) to protect the consumer created a major problem for Sprouts, a new small business. Ann Buscho, founder of Sprouts, discovered that her infant daughter's skin rash was caused by an allergy to formaldehyde, a product used in fabrics that are blends and in polyesters. All children's sleepwear contains formaldehyde because pure natural fibers do not lend themselves to flame retardant chemical treatments.

Buscho found that all-cotton clothing solved the rash problem and created a firm to make such clothing for children. Although the clothing was not called "sleepwear," some of it could be used for that purpose. However, the Flammable Fabrics Act requires that all children's sleepwear through size 14 be made from flame-resistant material. Consequently, the CPSC began an investigation of the new firm because of possible violation of the Flammable Fabrics Act. Trying to protect children against a skin rash involved another danger, that of fire. CPSC obviously placed greater emphasis on protection from fire than protection from formaldehyde.

Source: Nora Goldstein, "Do Babies Have Cotton Rights?" *In Business*, Vol. 5, No. 5 (September–October, 1983), pp. 42–44. Reproduced with permission.

goal. The Commission is authorized to set safety standards for consumer products and to ban those goods which are exceptionally hazardous.

Protection of Investors   To protect the investing public against fraudulent devices and swindles in the sale of stocks and bonds, both federal and state laws regulate the issuance and public sale of securities. The federal laws involved are the Securities Act of 1933 and the Securities Exchange Act of 1934. The latter Act established the powerful Securities and Exchange Commission to enforce the regulations provided by both Acts.

Because of the small amounts involved and the private nature of much of their financing, most small businesses are excluded from extensive regulation under federal law. However, they are subject to state **blue-sky laws.** In general, these laws cover registration of new securities; licensing of dealers, brokers, and salespersons; and prosecution of individuals charged with fraud in connection with the sale of stocks and bonds.

Promotion of Public Welfare   Other laws are designed to benefit the public welfare in various ways. Local ordinances, for example, establish minimum standards of sanitation for restaurants to protect the health of patrons. Zoning ordinances protect the community from the waste of unplanned development.

Environmental protection legislation—at the federal, state, and local levels—constitutes another example. The major laws of this type deal with air pollution, water pollution, solid-waste disposal, and toxic substances. As explained earlier in the chapter, antipollution laws adversely affect some small firms, although they occasionally provide opportunities for others.

State governments restrict entry into numerous professions and types of businesses by establishing licensing procedures. For example, physicians, barbers, pharmacists, accountants, lawyers, and real estate salespersons are licensed. Insurance companies, banks, and public utilities must seek entry permits from state officials. Although licensing protects the public interest, it also tends to restrict the number of professionals and firms in such a way as to reduce competition and increase prices paid by consumers.

There is a difference between licensing that involves a routine application and that which prescribes rigid entry standards and screening procedures. The fact that the impetus for much licensing comes from within the industry suggests the need for careful scrutiny of licensing proposals. Otherwise, we may be merely protecting a private interest and minimizing freedom to enter a field of business. In fact, a case of sorts can be made for the regulation of almost any business. However, failure to limit such regulation

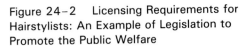

Figure 24–2   Licensing Requirements for
Hairstylists: An Example of Legislation to
Promote the Public Welfare

to the most essential cases erodes the freedom of opportunity to enter business and thereby provide an economic service to the community.

Political Power of Small Business

Although small business is the object of legislation that regulates its
activities, it is also a political force that affects the legislative process. Legislators are attuned to the needs of their constituencies, and they recognize
small business as a group having votes and political influence. Its political
influence is not surprising in view of the large numbers of small businesses
and the community leadership roles filled by small-business owners. They
are members of the Chamber of Commerce, officers in the Rotary Club,
chairpersons of committees to raise funds for hospitals, and leaders in other
civic endeavors. Legislators are not inclined to ignore their views.

The sensitivity of political leaders to small-business concerns is indicated by these comments:

> In part, small-business groups are effective because they're seeking
> special-interest legislation that often doesn't arouse passionate opposition.
> "Most legislators will follow the line of least resistance," says Iowa State

Rep. Darrell Hanson. "The only people paying attention to how the legislator votes are those who asked for the law," he adds. "The only way to lose is to vote against it."

State Sen. Brian Rude of Coon Valley, WI, adds another reason. "We tend to listen because [small-business people] are our bread and butter," he says. "Joe Smith the car dealer will be talking to 250 of my constituents in the next month, so I want to help him."[11]

These comments suggest that legislators are likely to listen carefully to the opinions of small-business leaders.

Occasionally, the political activities of small firms reflect special interests that conflict with those of the general public:

Local plumbers and electricians have been successful in stirring doubts about polyvinyl chloride (PVC) pipe and conduit. The plastic pipe is easier and cheaper to use than its metal counterparts, thus enabling homeowners to install it themselves. But plumbing and electrical associations, which help write local housing codes, have succeeded in getting PVC pipe banned as dangerous in many locales.[12]

However, we should not assume that all small-business political concern is narrowly self-serving. Many interests and causes of small-business owners are entirely consistent with the public interest.

The special needs of small business have been highlighted by White House conferences on small business in 1980 and 1986. These national conferences followed state meetings of small-business owners in which they formulated concerns that were discussed later in the White House conferences. These conferences have placed small business in the spotlight and given it a growing political identity. Those in small business exercise their influence not only individually but also collectively through trade associations and more general associations such as the National Federation for Independent Business.

The Burden of Regulation

The growth of governmental regulation has reached the point that it imposes a real hardship on small firms. To some extent, the problems arise from seemingly inevitable "red tape" and bureaucratic procedures of governments.

Even apart from the arbitrariness of regulation, its sheer weight is burdensome to small firms. The contents of the 330-page volume on the Occupational Safety and Health Act (OSHA) alone place unreasonable demands on the funds and productive energies of small companies.

SMALL BUSINESS IN ACTION
The Burden of Environmental Regulation

Some regulation of business is necessary, but it imposes an especially heavy burden on small firms. Lacking a legal staff, the entrepreneur must try to keep up with requirements of the law. Ray Morgan, owner of Morgan Sanitation, a waste collection company in Algona, IA, has described his predicament:

Morgan, who only has nine people on his payroll including himself and his wife, says he spends "four or five hours a week doing paper work and trying to keep up on regulations that come out from the Environmental Protection Agency." But it is a losing battle, he says.

He says that, on numerous occasions, he has picked up materials that neither he nor the business he was collecting them from knew had been listed as hazardous. "It's just so time-consuming to try to keep up with all the regs on what materials are dangerous," he notes. "I don't have the time, and the small companies that I deal with don't either. What I hauled a year ago, I may not be able to haul today. But who can afford to subscribe to the *Federal Register* and then spend the time to go through it?"

Source: Mary-Margaret Wantuck, "Moving the Mountain of Paper Work," *Nation's Business,* Vol. 73, No. 11 (November, 1985), pp. 64–65. Copyright 1985, U.S. Chamber of Commerce.

Recognition of the burdensome nature of small-business regulation has led to legislative attempts to reduce the problem. The Regulatory Flexibility Act of 1980, for example, requires federal agencies to assess the impact of proposed regulations on small business. They are required to reduce paperwork requirements and to exempt small firms or simplify rules when at all possible. The general purpose of the Act is to avoid unnecessary burdensome regulation of small firms. Its usefulness will depend upon the vigor and consistency of its application.

Another law recognizing the regulatory plight of small firms is the Equal Access to Justice Act of 1980. A strengthened version of the 1980 Act was passed in 1985. This law requires the federal government to reimburse court costs for small firms that win cases against regulatory agencies. Incorporated and unincorporated businesses, partnerships, and organizations having a net worth of less than $7 million are eligible for recovery of attorneys' fees.

The Need for Flexibility in Regulation

Some have argued that special consideration in the regulation of small firms is in itself unfair. According to this logic, all competitive firms should "play by the same rules." However, we should note that the marketplace is not perfectly competitive and that the hand of regulation rests more heavily upon small competitors. The Chief Counsel for Advocacy in the Small Business Administration has cited a research study on small-business regulatory costs:

> The research indicated that average regulatory costs per employee for the median small firm are three times greater than for the median large firm and two times greater than for the median mid-sized firm. When costs of complying with a regulation do not increase proportionately with firm size, small firms bear a disproportionately large share of total regulatory costs and suffer a competitive disadvantage.[13]

Rather than providing a special advantage to small business, therefore, flexibility in regulation serves to minimize a government-imposed handicap.

Looking Back

1. Society gives business firms the freedom to operate as part of a private enterprise system. In return, society expects these privately owned firms to contribute positively not only by providing goods and services but also by protecting the environment, treating customers fairly, and promoting the public welfare in various ways.
2. Small firms encounter a wide variety of opportunities to act unethically. These include temptations such as cheating on income-tax returns, deceiving customers, treating employees unfairly, and lying to employees and outsiders. The smallness of firms makes them especially vulnerable to pressures to act unethically.
3. Entrepreneurs, by virtue of their positions, can exert a powerful influence for moral virtue in small firms. As a business grows, their personal leadership can be supplemented by the adoption of codes of ethics and by support of local Better Business Bureaus.
4. Government regulation is intended to protect customers, com-

petitors, employees, and others from injurious acts of business firms. Today's regulations affecting small business deal with freedom and fairness of competition, consumer protection, and investor protection, as well as other areas of the public welfare.

5. Governmental regulation has become burdensome to small business because of its bureaucratic nature, the excessive paperwork required, and the small firm's lack of time and expertise in responding to regulation. Some legislative attempts have been made to reduce this burden by encouraging greater flexibility in regulation.

DISCUSSION QUESTIONS

1. Is it necessary for an entrepreneur to be a philanthropist to some degree in order to recognize and fulfill the firm's social responsibilities?

2. A small-business owner is asked to place an advertisement in the local high school yearbook. Is this part of a firm's social responsibility? What would be the effect on profits?

3. To what extent do small-business owners recognize that they have a social responsibility? How, if at all, could you defend the position of those who say they have no social responsibility?

4. Should all firms use biodegradable packaging? What is your answer if you know its use adds 25 percent to the price of the product?

5. What are some examples of small businesses that profit from the increased efforts to clean up and protect the environment? How do they profit?

6. What is "skimming"? How do you think owners of small firms might attempt to rationalize such a practice?

7. What are some examples of ethical issues in small-business marketing? In small-business management?

8. Give an example of an unethical business practice that you have personally encountered.

9. An auto salesman is willing to allow as much as $4,200 as a trade-in allowance. However, he tries to get the customer to settle for less by saying, "Four thousand dollars is as much as I can give." On a scale of 1 (extremely ethical) to 9 (extremely unethical), how would you rate the tactics of this salesman? Why?

10. Based on your experience as an employee, customer, or other observer

of some particular small business, how would you rate its ethical performance? Upon what evidence or clues do you base your opinion?

11. One business owner contends that competition protects the customer and that governmental regulation is simply unnecessary except for special situations such as insider trading on Wall Street. How would you argue for or against this point of view?

12. Do any of the regulatory requirements of government conflict with the interests of small business?

13. What evidence is there that indicates that small business has political power?

14. Why is governmental regulation burdensome to small firms?

15. Is it inherently unfair to accord special attention to small firms in formulating governmental regulations?

YOU MAKE THE CALL

Situation 1

When Ben Cohen, founding partner of Ben & Jerry's Homemade, Inc. (purveyor of gourmet ice cream), considered selling his share of the business, he decided instead to keep the business and run it in a socially responsible way. This was different in his mind from operating as a traditional business, and it apparently gave him a greater sense of purpose as an entrepreneur.

Following is a description of action he took based on this motivation:

> Because he felt strongly that "the community should prosper right along with the company," Cohen engineered an equity offering pitched first to Vermonters and, a year later, to fellow ice cream fanatics nationwide; $500,000 from the $5.1-million offering helped start a nonprofit foundation that, bolstered by 15% of Ben & Jerry's pretax profits, supports local causes. Internally, Cohen also instituted a five-to-one salary-ratio cap, whereby the lowliest line employee cannot make any less than 20% of what top management makes (currently $50,000).

Source: Reprinted with permission, *Inc.* magazine (May, 1986). Copyright © 1986 by Goldhirsh Group, Inc., 38 Commercial Wharf, Boston MA 02110.

Questions

1. Is selling equity to Vermonters more socially responsible than selling out in other ways?

2. In what way is the salary cap a socially responsible policy?

3. Is a business that sells double fudge ice cream to overweight customers acting in a socially responsible way?

Situation 2

A small construction company received a bid from a subcontractor. It was a very low bid—20 percent too low, according to the guess of the construction company owner. He believed the subcontractor had made an error in preparing the bid. Accepting the subcontractor's bid would greatly improve the firm's chance of winning a contract for a big project. On the other hand, an error of this size, approximately $30,000, would be most damaging to the subcontractor and could conceivably result in his failure.

The various subcontractors have delivered their bids only a few hours before the construction company owner must submit his bid, so time for reflection is short. To be fair to all of the subcontractors, the construction company cannot divulge the bid of one subcontractor to another in order to allow that subcontractor to rebid.

Questions
1. Would acceptance of the low bid be illegal? Unethical? Why?
2. What should the construction company owner do about the low bid?

EXPERIENTIAL EXERCISES

1. Visit or telephone the nearest Better Business Bureau office to discover the types of unethical business practices existing in your community and the ways in which the Better Business Bureau is attempting to raise ethical performance. Report briefly on your findings.
2. Employees sometimes take sick leave when they are merely tired, and students sometimes miss class when they are merely tired. Divide into groups of four or five and prepare a brief statement showing the nature of the ethical issue (if any) in both of these practices.
3. Examine a recent issue of *The Wall Street Journal* or another business periodical and report briefly on the nature of some ethical problem in the news. Could this type of ethical problem occur in a small business? Explain.
4. Prepare to debate the following topic: "Resolved, that the scope of small-business regulation should be reduced." Choose either the affirmative or negative side, unless you are specifically assigned to one or the other.

REFERENCES TO SMALL-BUSINESS PRACTICES

Berney, Karen. "Finding the Ethical Edge." *Nation's Business,* Vol. 75, No. 8 (August, 1987), pp. 18–26.

    The ethical problems faced by a number of small firms are described in this article.

Grossmann, John. "Milk Fight." *Inc.,* Vol. 9, No. 10 (September, 1987), pp. 37–44.

    This story describes the fight of a family dairy firm to enter the New York City market against the wishes of the New York state government.

Kahn, Sharon. "Water Fit to Drink." *Venture,* Vol. 8, No. 6 (June, 1986), pp. 76–82.

    This article reports on several small firms that are seizing business opportunities to clean up the environment and profit thereby.

Schifrin, Matthew. "Uncle Sam's Foot in the Door." *Forbes,* Vol. 133, No. 14 (June 18, 1984), p. 118.

    This article reports on the honesty of door-to-door marketers and on efforts by the Internal Revenue Service to make sure that all income is reported for tax purposes.

"Small-Business Conference Opens Today in Washington." *The Wall Street Journal* (August 18, 1986), p. 21.

    Small-business representatives met in Washington to discuss their problems and present them to those in government.

ENDNOTES

1. Erika Wilson, "Social Responsibility of Business: What Are the Small Business Perspectives?" *Journal of Small Business Management,* Vol. 18, No. 3 (July, 1980), pp. 17–24.

2. George Weissman, "The Art of Responsibility: Corporations, Arts, and Economic Development," Address to Citizens for Business and Industry in North Carolina, March 14, 1984.

3. Tom Richman, "Not Everyone Can Move to Southern California, You Know," *Inc.,* Vol. 5, No. 5 (May, 1983), pp. 115–118.

4. Sanford L. Jacobs, "Hide and Sneak," *The Wall Street Journal* (May 20, 1985), p. 13c.

5. This possibility is advanced by Michael Allen in "Small-Business Jungle," *The Wall Street Journal* (June 10, 1988), p. 19R.

6. *Ibid.*

7. Justin G. Longenecker, Joseph A. McKinney, and Carlos W. Moore, "Egoism and Independence: Entrepreneurial Ethics," *Organizational Dynamics,* Vol. 16, No. 3 (Winter, 1988), pp. 64–72.

8. These differences were significant at the .05 level.

9. These differences were also significant at the .05 level.

10. "The Antitrust Revolution," *Fortune,* Vol. 108, No. 1 (July 11, 1983), pp. 29–32.

11. Damon Darlin, "Small Business, Big Influence," *The Wall Street Journal* (May 20, 1985), p. 71C.

12. *Ibid.*

13. *Annual Report of the Chief Counsel for Advocacy on Implementation of the Regulatory Flexibility Act* (Washington: U.S. Small Business Administration, 1985), p. 1.

25 WORKING WITHIN THE LAW

Spotlight on Small Business

Courtesy of Trent & Company

Large companies sometimes add products that resemble those of small firms. If the new product resembles the original too closely, the producer may be found guilty of infringing on the trademark or trade dress of the small business. Susan Polis Schutz and Stephen Schutz, creators of Blue Mountain cards, believed that Hallmark Cards Inc. had copied the Blue Mountain line of highly emotional nonoccasion cards.

Though Hallmark, with $1.5 billion in revenues, controls 40 percent of the greeting card market, company officials were concerned enough about Blue Mountain's success to consult with the Schutzes in March 1985 about working for Hallmark or selling their company. The offer was declined. A year later, Susan Polis Schutz was browsing in a California card shop and turned over a card that appeared to be one of their own. She discovered it bore a Hallmark label.

Blue Mountain sued Hallmark for $50 million and won the first round in court. Hallmark maintained that it is not illegal to copy an item and that no artist can monopolize a special style. Nevertheless, the judge ordered Hallmark to stop selling 43 copycat card designs pending resolution of the suit.

Source: Jane Easter Bahls, "Creator Vs. Imitator: Who's Winning?" *In Business,* Vol. 10, No. 3 (May–June, 1988), pp. 25–28.

Looking Ahead

Watch for the following important topics:
1. Legal considerations in agreements and relationships with outsiders.
2. Methods of trademark, patent, and copyright protection.
3. The concept of trade dress protection.
4. Regulation of private stock placements.
5. Considerations in choosing an attorney.
6. New terms and concepts:

contracts	libel
statute of frauds	trademark
mechanic's lien	patent
statutes of limitations	utility patent
bulk sales laws	design patent
agency	plant patent
negotiable instruments	copyright
holder in due course	trade dress

Obviously, not all entrepreneurs can be lawyers. Nevertheless, they must have sufficient knowledge of the law to avoid poor business decisions. They should appreciate how the legal system can be used to safeguard their new ventures and provide opportunities for wise management decisions. We will highlight a few of the legal and regulatory issues related to operations and also investigate the choice of an attorney for the small firm. Our discussions should alert entrepreneurs to the complexity of the legal environment and emphasize the importance of professional legal counsel.

Agreements and Relationships with Outsiders

An entrepreneur should be extremely careful in making agreements with individuals and businesses outside his or her firm. Today's society seems to encourage lawsuits and legal action toward others. Therefore, it is more important than ever that entrepreneurs understand such basic elements of law as contracts, agency relationships, negotiable instruments, and libelous acts, just to name a few. (See Exhibit 25–1.)

Contracts

Managers of small firms frequently make agreements with employees, customers, suppliers, and others. In some of these agreements, called **contracts,** the parties intend to create mutual legal obligations. For a valid contract to exist, the following requirements must be met:

1. *Voluntary agreement.* A genuine offer must be accepted unconditionally by the buyer.
2. *Competent contracting parties.* Contracts with parties who are under legal age, insane, seriously intoxicated, or otherwise unable to understand the nature of the transaction are typically unenforceable.
3. *Legal act.* The subject of the agreement must not be in conflict with public policy, such as a contract to sell an illegal product.
4.. *Consideration.* Something of value, or consideration, must be received by the seller.
5. *Form of contract.* Contracts may be written or oral. Some contracts must be in written form to be enforceable. Under the **statute of frauds,** sales transactions of $500 or more, sales of real estate, and contracts extending for more than one year must be in writing. The existence of an oral contract must be demonstrated in some way; otherwise it may prove difficult to establish.

If one party to a contract fails to perform in accordance with the contract, the injured party may have recourse to certain remedies. Occasionally, a court will require specific performance of a contract when money damages are not adequate. However, courts are generally reluctant to rule in

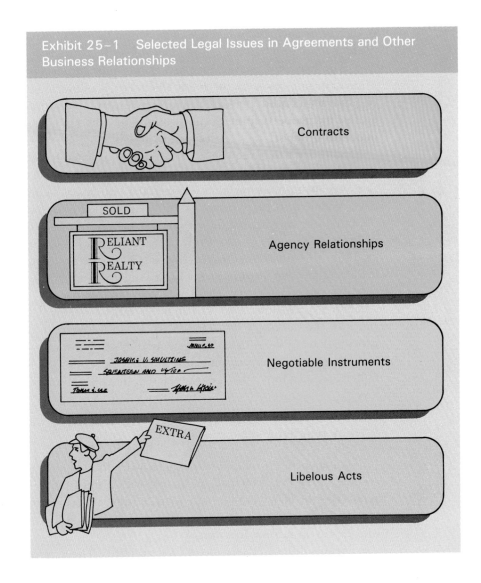

Exhibit 25–1   Selected Legal Issues in Agreements and Other Business Relationships

Contracts

Agency Relationships

Negotiable Instruments

Libelous Acts

this manner. In other cases, the injured party has the right to rescind, or cancel, the contract. The most frequently used remedy takes the form of money damages, which are intended to put the injured party in the same condition that he or she would have been in had the contract been performed. In many cases, a creditor-seller arranges for certain security devices so that he or she need not rely exclusively on the credit standing or ability of the debtor to pay.

Another claim against property that is quite important to some types of small businesses is the **mechanic's lien.** For example, materials suppliers or contractors who perform repair or construction would have a lien against the property if the property owner defaulted in payments for either materials or labor.

State laws that require creditors to be reasonably prompt in filing their claims are known as **statutes of limitations.** These laws are intended to protect debtors from claims in which the evidence is so old that the facts have become difficult to establish. Although time periods under the statute of limitations vary depending on the type of contract, an action for breach of contract on a sale of goods must be started within a few years. For small creditors, this means that legal action should not be postponed indefinitely if there is any expectation of forcing payment.

Various states have enacted **bulk sales laws,** which effectively preclude a debtor from making a secret sale of an entire business before a creditor can take the necessary legal action to collect. In general, bulk sales laws provide that any debtor's sale of a business inventory down to the bare walls must be preceded by written notification to the creditors of the business. Otherwise, such bulk sales are fraudulent and void with respect to the creditors.

Agency Relationships

An **agency** is a relationship whereby one party, the agent, represents another party, the principal, in dealing with a third person. Examples of agents are: the manager of a branch office who acts as the agent of the firm, a partner who acts as an agent for the partnership, and real estate agents who represent buyers or sellers.

Agents differ in the scope of their authority. The manager of a branch office is a general agent, whereas a real estate agent is a special agent with authority to act only in a particular transaction.

The principal is liable to a third party for the performance of contracts made by the agent acting within the scope of the agent's authority. A principal is also liable for fraudulent, negligent, and other wrongful acts of an agent that are executed within the scope of the agency relationship.

An agent has certain obligations to the principal. In general, the agent must accept the orders and instructions of the principal, act in good faith,

Figure 25-1   An Agency Relationship:
Realtor Representing the Seller

© *Michael Grecco/STOCK, BOSTON*

and use prudence and care in the discharge of agency duties. Moreover, the agent is liable if he or she exceeds stipulated authority and causes damage to the third party as a result—unless the principal ratifies the act, whereupon the principal becomes liable.

It is apparent that the powers of agents can make the agency relationship a potentially dangerous one for small firms. For this reason, small firms should exercise care in selecting agents and clearly stipulate their authority and responsibility.

Negotiable Instruments

Credit instruments that can be transferred from one party to another in place of money are known as **negotiable instruments.** Examples of negotiable instruments are promissory notes, drafts, trade acceptances, and ordinary checks. When a negotiable instrument is in the possession of an individual known as a **holder in due course,** it is not subject to many of the defenses possible in the case of ordinary contracts. For this reason, the small-business firm should secure instruments that are prepared in such a way as to make them negotiable. In general, the requirements for negotiable instruments are:

1. There must be a written, signed, unconditional promise or order to pay.
2. The amount to be paid must be specified.
3. The instrument must provide for payment on demand, at a definite time, or at a determinable time.
4. The instrument must be payable to the bearer or to the order of some person.

Libelous Acts

Libel may be defined as printed defamation of one's reputation. Unless proper precautions are taken, there is a danger of including materials in credit correspondence that may be held by the court to be libelous. Even ordinary collection letters to a debtor have in some cases been held to be libelous by virtue of being dictated by a creditor to a stenographer. This was held to constitute "publication" of the statement.

Under the Fair Debt Collection Act of 1977, it is a federal offense for debt collectors to do the following, among other things:

1. Threaten consumers with violence.
2. Use obscene language.
3. Publish "shame" lists.

Violators are liable for any actual damages, as well as additional civil damages, determined by the court up to $1,000.

Protection of Intangible Assets

In Chapter 18, we referred to the importance of safeguarding a firm's assets. In addition to managing and protecting the physical assets, a new business must protect its intangible assets. We will briefly examine the regulatory issues surrounding four of those intangible assets. Exhibit 25–2 depicts these four intangible assets.

Trademark Protection

A **trademark** is a word, figure, or other symbol used to distinguish a product sold by one manufacturer or merchant. Small manufacturers, in particular, often find it desirable to adopt a particular trademark and to feature it in advertising.

Exhibit 25–2   Trademarks, Patents, Copyrights, and Trade Dress

Trademarks

Patents

Copyrights

Trade Dress

Before a name is adopted it should be researched carefully. Joseph W. Alsop, president of Data Language Corporation of Billerica, MA, thought its name for a computer software program, Progress, was cleared for use. A trademark application was initially rejected because another company was using the name to sell educational materials. An agreement was worked out allowing both firms to use the name. But later a Houston, TX, software company, not uncovered in the trademark search, was found to be using the Progress name. However, Data Language was able to work out still another agreement with the Houston firm.[1]

Common law recognizes a property right in the ownership of trademark. In addition, registration of trademarks is permitted under the federal Lanham Trademark Act—a step that generally makes protection easier if infringement is attempted.[2] Since November 16, 1989, trademark rights have arisen from just a bona fide intention to use a mark, along with the filing of an application. Before that, a firm must have already used the mark on goods shipped or sold. A trademark registration lasts for 10 years and may be renewed for additional 10-year periods. Application for registration should be made to the U.S. Patent and Trademark Office. The different states also have trademark registration laws, although it is still the common law that provides the basic protection for the owner of the trademark. Full registration is recommended because the growth of a business firm may eventually make its trademark an extremely valuable asset. Even with proper registration, the trademark owner may be considered to have abandoned the trademark if extensive disregard of it is allowed. Ten benefits of registration are shown in Exhibit 25-3.

Proper use of a trademark in the marketing efforts of the small business serves to protect the trademark. Two rules can help. One is to be sure the name is not carelessly used in place of the generic name. For example, the Xerox company never wants a person to say that he or she is "xeroxing" something. Second, the business should inform the public that the trademark is a trademark by labeling it with the symbol ™ or the phrase "Registered in U.S. Patent and Trademark Office."

Patent Protection

A **patent** is the registered right of an inventor to make, use, and sell an invention. The two primary types of patents are utility patents and design patents. A **utility patent** covers a new process and protects the function of a product. A **design patent** covers the appearance of a product and covers

Exhibit 25-3 Benefits of Trademark Registration

1 The filing date of the application is a constructive date of first use of the mark in commerce (this gives registrant nationwide priority as of that date, except as to certain prior users or prior applicants).

2 The right to sue in Federal court for trademark infringement.

3 Recovery of profits, damages and costs in a Federal court infringement action and the possibility of treble damages and attorney's fees.

4 Constructive notice of claim of ownership (which eliminates a good faith defense for a party adopting the trademark subsequent to the registrant's date of registration).

5 The right to deposit the registration with Customs in order to stop the importation of goods bearing an infringing mark.

6 Prima facie evidence of the validity of the registration, registrant's ownership of the mark, and of registrant's exclusive right to use the mark in commerce in connection with the goods or services specified in the certificate.

7 The possibility of incontestability, in which case the registration constitutes conclusive evidence of the registrant's exclusive right, with certain limited exceptions, to use the registered mark in commerce.

8 Limited grounds for attacking a registration once it is five years old.

9 Availability of criminal penalties and treble damages in an action for counterfeiting a registered trademark.

10 A basis for filing trademark applications in foreign countries.

Source: Basic Facts About Trademarks, U.S. Department of Commerce, 1989, p. 1.

everything that is an inseparable part of the product. Utility patents are granted for a period of 17 years, while design patents are given a 14-year protection. Patent law also provides for plant patents. A **plant patent** covers any distinct and new variety of plants.

Items that may be patented include machines and products, improvements on machines and products, and new and original designs. Some small manufacturers have patented items that constitute the major part of their product line. Indeed, some businesses such as Polaroid and IBM can trace their origins to a patented invention.

The process of obtaining a patent is both complicated and expensive. The standard filing fee is $370. The issue fee for utility patents is $620. A maintenance fee is also due $3\frac{1}{2}$, $9\frac{1}{2}$, and $11\frac{1}{2}$ years after the original grant.

SMALL BUSINESS IN ACTION
Only Time Will Tell

The patent process is perplexing and sometimes treacherous. And even patent protection is never an absolute guarantee that competitors will not challenge the patent. Consider the following entrepreneurial experience:

Jack E. Caveney founded Panduit [Corporation] in his basement. In 1961, he began a research effort to create a one-piece plastic device to bind cables together. Nine years . . . later, he began selling the device, which qualified for three patents between 1970 and 1976. . . . Meanwhile, Dennison Manufacturing . . . was trying to develop its own one-piece cable tie. After eight years of trying, Dennison gave up and, according to a lawsuit later filed by Panduit, copied Panduit's tie. . . . Six years later, a court found Panduit's patents invalid.

The court's contention was that the innovation was an "obvious" design and not worthy of patent protection. By 1985, however, the newly established Federal Circuit Court of Appeal ruled that Panduit's patents were valid! In response to this decision, Dennison appealed to the Supreme Court, which later upheld the patents' validity. In 1988, Panduit agreed with Dennison to license the future production of the cable ties and also to receive from Dennison a one-time lump sum settlement. So finally the patent was clearly the property of Panduit—maybe.

Source: Clint Willis, "It Pays to Patent. Reprinted from the October, 1988, issue of *VENTURE, For Entrepreneurial Business Owners & Investors.* © *1988.*

However, small firms are required to pay only one-half of these amounts. Nevertheless, a patent attorney is often retained to act for a small-business applicant in preparing an application. One source estimates that having a patent attorney file a patent application will cost between $1,000 and $5,000.[3]

Suits for patent infringements may be brought, but they are costly and should be avoided if possible.[4] Finding the money and legal talent with which to enforce one's legal rights is one of the major problems of patent protection in small business. Monetary damages and injunctions are available, however, if an infringement can be proved.

For many years patent infringement decisions were appealed to 11 circuit courts. Each court often had its own interpretation of patent law, which resulted in much confusion about what was and was not legal. However, in 1982, the U.S. Court of Appeals for the Federal Circuit was formed, and all patent appeals are now directed to this one court. This system is helping to make patent law more understandable.

Copyright Protection

A **copyright** is the registered right of a creator (author, composer, designer, or artist) to reproduce, publish, and sell the work that is the product of the intelligence and skill of that person. According to the Copyright Act of 1976, the creator of an original work that has been copyrighted receives protection for the duration of the creator's life plus 50 years. Copyrights are registered in the Copyright Office of the Library of Congress.

Authors, to avoid loss of protection, must give notice of a copyright on all distributed materials. The notice consists of three elements (see the page following the title page of this textbook):

1. The symbol ©.
2. The year when the work was published.
3. The copyright owner's name.

The law provides that copyrighted creative work cannot be reproduced by another person or persons without authorization. Even photocopying of such work is prohibited, although an individual may copy a limited amount of material for research purposes. A copyright holder can sue a copyright violator for damages.

Figure 25-2 Authors Have the Right to Copyright Protection

Courtesy of Apple Computers

Trade Dress Protection

A small business may also possess a valuable intangible asset called **trade dress,** which describes those elements of a firm's distinctive operating image not specifically covered as a trademark, patent, and so on. It is the "look" that a firm creates to provide its marketing advantage.

Although there are currently no statutory laws covering trade dress, the courts are beginning to recognize a value to this asset. Consider the situation of Daniel and Monika Crotta, owners of NYPD (New York Pizza Department), based in San Diego. In 1983, they began their unique pizza franchise, which delivers pizza in cars that look like police cars. Their employees wear actual police uniforms. In 1987, the Crottas learned there was an Iowa company delivering pizza in police cars using the name LAPD (Los Angeles Pizza Delivery). The Crottas sued LAPD's parent company, using the argument that NYPD's trade dress should be protected. In July of 1988, an out-of-court settlement was reached whereby LAPD agreed to change its name and refrain from using a police theme.[5]

Regulation of Private Stock Placements

The sale of stock to finance business operations is not an attractive alternative for most startups. However, a small, rapidly growing business may turn to this form of financing. If so, the entrepreneur should be prepared to face the regulatory issues involved in "going public."

A private placement is one alternative to a full-scale public offering of stock. Private offerings are exempt from registration requirements of the Securities and Exchange Commission (SEC). Private placements raise capital for the business while avoiding the public disclosure requirements of public offerings. This feature allows a small firm to remain private—a desirable feature for most entrepreneurs—while also reducing the cost of raising the capital. There are several rules within Regulation D of the Securities Act of 1933 that cover qualified private placements. The following list identifies these rules and gives a brief description of what each covers:

1. Rule 501 contains common terms and definitions used in the regulation;
2. Rule 502 outlines general conditions that must be met to be exempt from registration;
3. Rule 503 describes a uniform notice of sales form (Form D) that must be used;
4. Rule 504 covers offerings not over $500,000;
5. Rule 505 refers to those involving $5 million or less; and
6. Rule 506 covers offerings greater than $5 million.[6]

Rule 504 is of primary importance to most small businesses in their early stages of operation because it covers the smaller placements. To comply with this rule the business must be a nonpublic company, file the required form, and avoid advertising for investors. Regulation D is a federal regulation and does not negate state regulations governing "going public." State regulations obviously must be researched prior to making a private placement.

Choosing an Attorney

A review of legal organizational forms and areas of business law makes evident the need for proper legal counsel. Unless an entrepreneur is trained in law, he or she cannot be expected to know the law sufficiently well to avoid the use of professionals. Nor should the small business wait until an emergency arises to establish a working relationship with a competent attorney. The small firm's team of professional counselors should include an attorney, a CPA, a banker, and other specialists.

The small firm needs an attorney experienced in legal practice related to small business. Lawyers might be selected by using the Yellow Pages, reading an advertisement, or consulting a law directory, but an informed choice requires a recommendation based on some acquaintanceship with the legal profession. Suggestions of possible attorneys may be obtained from the firm's banker, CPA, or even from other business owners. Lawyers who practice in other areas of law or law school professors, for example, may also be in a position to make recommendations.

Following is some advice to consider when searching for a good lawyer:

1. Begin by talking to other people in your community who own or operate a small business. Ask them about lawyers whom they've used. Word of mouth is an excellent way to size up a lawyer.
2. Friends, relatives, and business associates can also provide names of lawyers.
3. Shop around. It's certainly acceptable to look before you leap. You would spend time shopping for a new car, so why not for a lawyer with whom you will be spending just as much, if not more, time?
4. Check on the lawyer's experience. Lawyers specialize, and your needs may be very specific also.
5. Be sure you are comfortable with the lawyer. Evaluate his or her personality to be sure that the relationship has a chance to work.
6. Evaluate the accessibility of the lawyer. Determine whether he or she is interested in you and your business.
7. Try to select a lawyer who is a doer! Excessive delays in taking action can be extremely costly to your business.
8. Talk about fees. Have a clear understanding of what services are included. Don't be afraid to negotiate the rates.[7]

The firm's relationship with its attorney is most effective when courtroom battles are unnecessary. Much of an attorney's contribution is made by providing information when specific questions arise, when contracts or other documents are reviewed, and when counseling is needed. The relationship should preferably be a continuing one. Once an attorney–client relationship is established, the client should utilize the attorney's services promptly whenever the need arises.

One legal service emphasizes this need to stay in contact even if it's only a regular phone call to discuss a planned decision. The president of this service says, "If people took the time to check with their attorneys, the huge sum of monies spent on legal fees could be drastically reduced, and 80 percent of the matters that wind up in court would not."[8]

Looking Back

1. Contracts are binding agreements for legal acts made by competent contracting parties, and they involve something of value for both parties. A small firm should exercise care in selecting its agents and clearly stipulate their authority and responsibility. Negotiable instruments permit the transfer of credit from one party to another. Small firms may seek protection of their names and original work by registering their trademarks and applying for patents or copyrights. Libel refers to the printed defamation of one's reputation, so precautions should be taken to avoid libelous statements about others.

2. Registration of trademarks is permitted under the federal Lanham Trademark Act. The two kinds of patents are a utility patent and a design patent. A copyright is the registered right of a creator to reproduce, publish, and sell the work that is the product of the intelligence and skill of that person.

3. Trade dress describes those elements of a firm's distinctive operating image not specifically covered by a trademark or patent.

4. Private stock placements raise capital while avoiding public disclosures required in public offerings.

DISCUSSION QUESTIONS

1. Give the legal requirements that must be fulfilled to make a contract valid and binding.
2. Define the following: (a) statute of frauds, (b) mechanic's lien, and (c) statute of limitations.
3. What is meant by "agency" relationships?
4. What are the requirements of negotiable instruments?

5. Discuss the legal protection afforded by trademarks. Does registration guarantee ownership?
6. List the various types of patents. What kinds of fees should a small firm expect to pay for a patent?
7. What is a copyright? How can copyright materials be protected?
8. What is trade dress? What is the legal status of trade dress?
9. Why were the situations of NYPD and Blue Mountain cards not covered by trademark or patent law? Be specific.
10. What is a private stock placement? What advantage does it have over public stock sales?
11. Why would a small business consider a private stock placement rather than a public offering?
12. What are some of the rules within Regulation D that cover qualified private placements?
13. What are the limitations on a private stock placement under Regulation D?
14. What advice should a small firm consider when selecting a good attorney?
15. What reasons exist for establishing a continuing relationship with an attorney rather than using an attorney as needed for specific projects?

YOU MAKE THE CALL

Situation 1

A manufacturer refused to buy back a dealer's unsold inventory, citing a written contract with the dealer. One clause of the contract did indeed make repurchase by the manufacturer optional. The dealer, however, argued that he had a prior oral agreement that the manufacturer would repurchase unsold inventory.

As a further complication, the manufacturer had neither signed nor dated the contract when the dealer signed it. Also, the dealer's minimum inventory requirements were left blank, and the contract failed to mention other details.

Questions
1. Does the dealer appear to have a strong legal case to force the manufacturer to repurchase the inventory?
2. How would an attorney be useful in this case?

Situation 2

Ann Landers is president of her own company, Nationwide Drinks, Inc., which she founded in 1980 to produce and market a natural soda that she formulated in her kitchen. The company had grown and prospered over its first 10 years of operation, but a major problem emerged when Ms. Landers saw a television commercial promoting a new natural soda that an industry giant was introducing at 20 cents below her soda's price.

Ms. Landers was obviously concerned that there was a competing brand to battle, but she was also distressed that the bottle design was almost identical to Nationwide's. Ms. Landers was a fighter; therefore, she sued the competitor, charging infringement of her design—even though she had no formal ownership of a copyright or trademark. A federal judge granted Nationwide Drinks a preliminary injunction.

Questions

1. What arguments should Nationwide Drinks present to the court?
2. Do you predict that the large competitor will eventually win by forcing Nationwide Drinks to face huge legal costs? Why or why not?
3. In your opinion, what course of action should Nationwide Drinks have taken to avoid this situation? Can a small firm afford to pursue your recommendation?

EXPERIENTIAL EXERCISES

1. Interview a local patent or trademark attorney regarding small-business clients. Report what problems this lawyer has faced in this work.
2. Interview a local business owner—a manufacturer, if possible—and ask about his or her strategy to protect the intangible assets of the business.
3. Interview a local lawyer and determine what areas of law he or she considers most vital to small-firm managers. Report your findings to the class.
4. Contact a local investment banker or stockholder and ask for information on private stock placements. Summarize the information in a brief report.

REFERENCES TO SMALL-BUSINESS PRACTICES

Andrews, Edmund L. "Tell It to the Judge." *Venture*, Vol. 10, No. 4 (April, 1988), pp. 24–25.

This article describes an investor's experience with the U.S. Department of Commerce's Patent and Trademark Office and his attempt to recover legal fees under the Equal Access to Justice Act.

Coleman, Henry D. and Vandenberg, John D. "How to Follow the Leader." *Inc.,* Vol. 10, No. 7 (July, 1988), pp. 125–126.

This is a "how-to" article for researching whether or not a competitor's product is patented. If the product is indeed covered by a patent, the article proposes ways to proceed with a similar but legal product.

Krasnow, Erwin G. and Conrad, Robin S. "Managing Your Lawyer." *Nation's Business,* Vol. 77, No. 4 (April, 1989), pp. 70–72.

This article suggests a step-by-step procedure for selecting the right lawyer. There is also discussion of determining fees.

Marsa, Linda. "An Ounce of Prevention." *Venture,* Vol. 10, No. 6 (June, 1988), pp. 86–88.

This article argues that entrepreneurs are typically poor "paperwork" people and therefore should rely on the expertise of lawyers to advise them in legal matters.

ENDNOTES

1. Christine Quarembo, "Trademarking Your Name," *Venture,* Vol. 7, No. 6 (June, 1985), p. 34

2. An easy-to-understand presentation of the requirements for registration can be found in Ira N. Bachrach, "How to Choose and Use a Trademark," *Nation's Business,* Vol. 71, No. 3 (March, 1983), pp. 70–72.

3. J. A. Dunnigan, "Bringing Your Product to Life Part I: Patenting Your Product," *Entrepreneur,* Vol. 17, No. 3 (March, 1988), p. 62.

4. An excellent discussion of patent laws can be found in Louis W. Stern and Thomas L. Eovaldi, *Legal Aspects of Marketing Strategy, Antitrust and Consumer Protection Issues* (Englewood Cliffs, NJ: Prentice-Hall, Inc., 1984), Chapter 2.

5. Sheryl Jean, "Beware of Copycats," *Venture,* Vol. 10 No. 10 (October, 1988), p. 24.

6. Lon W. Taylor, "Raising Capital Through Private Placements," *The Journal of Business Strategy* (July–August, 1988), p. 62.

7. Based on the material in Fred S. Steingold, *Legal Master Guide for Small Business* (Englewood Cliffs, NJ: Prentice-Hall, Inc., 1983), Chapter 29.

8. Sid Kane, "When A Lawyer Is Unnecessary," *Venture,* Vol. 6, No. 6 (June, 1984), p. 43.

CASES

CASE 1

Robert Mulder, Sole Proprietor
Entrepreneurial motivations and attitudes

In the following account, small-business owner Robert Mulder reflects on the nature of his landscaping business in Raleigh, NC. This firm is extremely small. Mulder's testimonial is noteworthy, however, because of its vivid portrayal of issues involved in small-business ownership. These issues, which exist in most independently owned businesses, include entrepreneurial motivations, customer relations, expansion decisions, attitudes toward risk, growth orientation, family concerns, social responsibility, and personal values.

I own a small landscaping business that operates out of my house in Raleigh, N.C. The business, Amsterdam Landscaping, grosses less than $50,000 annually. I have three part-time employees, a 1976 Ford pickup truck with 102,000 miles on it, a plant nursery in my backyard, and nine regular customers who contract for my services. If you divide my income by the hours I spend doing everything I do—laying brickwork, trimming hedges, filing entries in my maintenance log—I probably earn only slightly more than minimum wage. My "salary" last year—the money I took out of the business for food, rent, and other family expenses—came to

Source: This material is reprinted with permission, *Inc.* magazine, November, 1986. Copyright © 1986 by Goldhirsh Group, Inc., 38 Commercial Wharf, Boston, MA 02110.

just under $16,000. Cash out all my assets, and I doubt you'd find me worth more than $10,000, total.

As a very small-business man, I've had to face many of the same questions confronting owners of INC.-type, fast-growth companies, yet the answers I've come up with don't always fit the conventional profile of corporate success.

I started my business seven years ago for two principal reasons: because I like working with plants and shrubs and because I don't particularly like working for other people. At various times since college—I'm 35 years old and graduated from North Carolina State University in 1975 with a degree in horticulture—I have done yard work for a Catholic diocese, run a small printing operation, been employed by a property-management firm, and driven a beer truck. Nothing has been as satisfying to me as running my own business. I'm doing what I like to do every day, looking after my accounts personally, and making sure my customers get the kind of service they've come to expect. I figure I turned away as much business as I took in last year.

Most of my accounts are residential ones, the kind of jobs where personal contact is high and the profit opportunities relatively low. Last year, however, I had the opportunity to expand my business substantially by picking up a major commercial account. By borrowing $30,000 or so in working capital (and coming up with $7,500 myself), I would have been in a position to get an exclusive landscaping contract with a Raleigh builder who was constructing houses in the $150,000-to-$200,000 range. More such contracts could have followed, and soon I would have been managing a fast-growing business.

Many friends and customers urged me to go this route. They said I'd make more money—and be that much more satisfied, I guess—if I started managing landscaping projects instead of doing them myself.

I couldn't live with that decision, though. Never having borrowed money to finance the business—I have a $1,500 line of credit on my checking account at Wachovia Bank & Trust Co. and good credit at the local plant nursery, but that's it—I suddenly found myself waking up in the middle of the night thinking, $30,000! How do I make payments if business starts drying up? Who'll I be working for, myself or the bank? After that, sleep was hopeless. I couldn't function at all.

One mentor—Bill Kopke, a client of mine who owns a very successful fruit-importing business in the New York City area—recognized this right away. Bill and I had dinner during the time I was thinking about expanding my business, and Bill told me in no uncertain terms that he thought it would be a mistake. I was tremendously relieved when he said this, because I knew in my gut he was right. In fact, as it turned out, not as many houses have been built in the project as had been anticipated. So if I'd become involved in the project, I'd probably be in Chapter 7 by now. Trusting my own instincts in this situation may well have saved my business.

Beyond keeping my own enterprise afloat, I also feel there's a subtle tendency in our society to belittle the very small-business person, to champion growth at the expense of other issues. In my view, there are people for whom growing bigger is a disaster, a promotion to incompetence, if you will. Plus there's the issue of losing touch with what I consider the fundamentals. I remember visiting my uncle in Ontario—he's a very successful car dealer up there, with a house on 70 to 80 acres—and asking him how a certain piece of equipment on one of his cars worked. He said he didn't know, that he managed the business and that wasn't his department, so he hadn't bothered to find out. That kind of attitude doesn't sit well with me. I like knowing what I'm working with, just as I like showing my employees how to do the job right the first time. I'd hate to have to go back and have them redo a project to my standards because I hadn't been around in the first place.

So I made a conscious decision to stay

small. Not because I couldn't get the business, but because it would have changed me in ways I didn't really want to change. For one thing, I would have had to drop at least some of my residential customers, the ones who helped me get started in this business. Most landscapers are all too eager to go into commercial work—that's where the big money is—and abandon the residential stuff. I feel just the opposite: I've always said I'll continue to work for these people until they either die or buy a town house and don't need me anymore.

More importantly, if I had grown my business the way the "experts" say, I would have lost the time to do the little things that make work so enjoyable to me. Having lunch with my client, a retired army lieutenant colonel who tells me about his battle campaigns in World War II. Fixing somebody's leaky faucet as a favor or listening to a personal problem because I'm an "outsider" who can. There would be less time too for things like taking my wife and two children off to the mountains for long weekends. Or for projects like The Land Stewardship Council of North Carolina, a broadly ecumenical, Judeo-Christian group I work with that tries to promote intelligent land use, alternatives to chemical pesticides, and other environmental concerns.

Since 99% of my friends and customers had urged me to expand, a lot of them took my decision to mean that I simply wasn't ambitious as a businessman. That really griped me at first. I do have ambitions, and I do consider myself a successful businessman. My ambitions just don't lie in the area of making more money. Instead of mortgaging myself to the hilt and not having time for my family, I'd rather grow along with them and have a little less now, a little more later. We all hear about chief executives who wish they'd spent more time with their families and less with their businesses. I don't want to look back in 10 years and make the same complaint.

This isn't to say that I haven't already made my share of mistakes. Years ago I had no idea how to charge for my services. I underbid on a lot of jobs simply through lack of a sophisticated cost analysis. If a job that I figured would take 80 hours actually took 100—well, there went my profit. It's tough doing business with friends, which most of my clients have become. But I can't stay in business by undercharging them. Now I provide them with a complete cost analysis of all my work and a detailed letter of explanation whenever I feel it necessary to raise my rates. And they have stayed as loyal to me as I am to them.

Being an independent sole proprietor, I probably measure the business universe differently from, say, the average INC. 500 company manager. My idea of a small company, for instance, is one with two or three employees and revenues of less than $100,000 a year. A midsize company would have maybe three or four full-time workers, an equal number of part-time workers, and no more than $500,000 in sales. Large companies? To me, that would be 20 to 25 employees and around $2 million in revenues.

Also, unlike many successful company builders, I don't consider myself to be a risk-taker. I'm actually fairly conservative by nature, although not always politically (and certainly not environmentally).

As a businessman, I like to buy good equipment, but if I can't afford what I want, I'll do without it. Individually, given the opportunity to save money, I can probably save it better than anyone I know.

My 1985 federal tax return shows I paid $3,935 in wages last year, spent $8,383 on landscaping supplies, $2,676 on insurance, $2,512 on truck expenses, $53 on office supplies, and $0 on travel and entertainment (no three-martini lunches for me). My total tax liability, state and federal, came to about $5,000. I took nothing in oil-depreciation allowances and the only stock in my investment portfolio, a fast-food restaurant chain out of Atlanta, went from $3.50 a share to Chapter 11.

I did win $1,329 in a local radio station cash-call contest. The money was nice, but I forgot to set some of it aside and that screwed up my tax situation. Right now I'm paying off the Internal Revenue Service $1,800 that I owe from last year. That's really the key to good business management, I feel. Setting aside money when you have it for the times when you really need it. Ideally, I'd have $10,000 in the bank at all times to cover emergencies. That's ideally, however. The closest I have gotten so far is $5,000, and my operating cushion is usually a lot less than that.

I know that businesses like my own aren't the sexiest part of the U.S. econ-omy. We don't hire a lot of people or rent out five floors in an office building. We don't get recruited with tax incentives by governors who want to rebuild their local economies. I have often paged through the INC. 500 issue, and I have wondered if there would be a way to measure my side of the equation. How do I fit in with the Bill McGowans (MCI Communications Corp.) and the Alvin McCall Jrs. (Ryan's Family Steak Houses Inc.) of the business world?

The effect of companies like mine is cumulative. Last year I pumped $22,910 into the local economy. Multiply that times the thousands of very small businesses in the Raleigh area, and it spells big bucks. We provide a stable and healthy local economy, one on which the McGowans and McCalls depend for growing their own companies. We can't afford to do without these people: men and women who see a small niche, a window of economic opportunity, and are determined to fill it.

If I were to measure success by the personal satisfaction I get in owning my own business, then I would consider myself as successful as the McGowans of the world. I may never make the INC. 500, but I am making my fortune every day—when I nurture my young nursery plants or have tea and gingerbread with a 90-year-old customer. These are the things that make me fortunate.

Questions

1. Is Mulder, the owner of this business, an entrepreneur? If so, is he a craftsman entrepreneur or an opportunistic entrepreneur?
2. To what extent can you support the no-growth or low-growth philosophy of Mulder?

3. Is Mulder correct in associating smallness with customer satisfaction? Would customer service inevitably deteriorate if he expanded?

4. What rewards is Mulder seeking and finding in this business? Would greater emphasis on profit interfere with attainment of the other rewards?

5. Is Mulder's attitude toward risk typical of the independent business owner? Is it commendable or deplorable? Why?

6. How can you explain Mulder's environmental concerns? Are they consistent with his role as a business owner?

CASE 2

Marty's Landscaping, Inc.
Danger of business failure

George J. Davis, a management consultant, received an urgent call from Wendell Martin, owner of Marty's Landscaping, Inc. This business was located on a county road a few miles from Atlanta. It had fallen on hard times, and the owner was seeking help that would enable it to survive and eventually prosper.

When Davis attempted to make his first visit, he experienced difficulty in finding the place of business. He passed it four times and made two inquiries before he was able to recognize it! Eventually, he saw a portable sign with the name of the business sitting back about 100 feet from the highway. It was also hard to see because a bulldozer and two pickup trucks were parked in front of the office building, making the business look more like a construction company than a landscaping company.

Upon entering the office building, Davis found a spacious outer office with several pieces of office furniture and equipment, all of which were dusty and ill-kept. There was no one in the reception area. Finally, a man (who later proved to be the landscape architect) appeared from an office at one side of the reception area. Upon asking to see the president of the company, Davis was escorted to an office at the opposite side of the reception area and introduced to Wendell Martin.

In the discussion that followed, Martin explained that the company's major

problem arose from loss of two contracts. The company had been doing landscaping for two major builders of apartment complexes in the Atlanta area, and both had stopped construction because of overbuilding in the area. Martin further explained that the company was continuing to do maintenance work at the various apartment complexes. The firm used 10 employees for this purpose in addition to the landscape architect and office personnel.

Martin believed they were losing money because of heavy payments on leased equipment they were no longer using. He felt that turning the leased equipment back might tend to destroy the company's credit. Also, the vehicles could be purchased at an attractive price at the end of the lease. Martin also mentioned that they were considering going into the nursery business as a move to turn the business around.

Davis received a copy of the balance sheet and income statement for the latest eight months. (See Exhibits C2–1 and C2–2.) In the letter accompanying the report, the CPA noted that management had failed to make all of the disclosures required by generally accepted accounting principles.

After reviewing the statement, Davis asked about the nature of two accounts receivable items, "Green Valley Ranch" and "Green Valley Youth Retreat." It was explained to him that these receivables related to a 75-acre piece of land about one-half mile from the landscaping business.

Source: This case was prepared by George J. Davis.

Exhibit C2-1   Balance Sheet

Marty's Landscaping, Inc.
Balance Sheet
August 31

ASSETS

Current assets:

Cash.	$ 195	
Accounts receivable	46,188	
Accounts receivable, Green Valley Ranch.	52,424	
Accounts receivable, Green Valley Youth Retreat	25,586	
Inventory	11,622	
Prepaid expenses	27,373	
Total current assets.		$163,388

Fixed assets:

Transportation equipment	$ 89,024	
Machinery and equipment	20,108	
Other equipment and furniture	14,986	
	$124,118	
Less accumulated depreciation.	97,922	
Total fixed assets.		26,196
TOTAL ASSETS		**$189,584**

LIABILITIES AND EQUITY

Current liabilities:

Short-term debt	$282,437	
Current portion of long-term debt	13,606	
Accounts payable.	23,779	
Accrued expenses	9,508	
Total current liabilities.		$329,330
Long-term liabilities		23,841
Total liabilities		$353,171

Stockholder's equity:

Common stock	$ 100	
Retained earnings (deficit)	(163,687)	(163,587)
TOTAL LIABILITIES AND EQUITY		**$189,584**

Exhibit C2–2 Income Statement

Marty's Landscaping, Inc.
Income Statement
Eight Months Ending August 31

	Current Month	Eight Months
Sales	$33,841	$341,517
Direct labor	$ 8,634	$ 68,929
Plants, grass, materials	13,897	121,419
Contract labor	783	88,264
Depreciation expense	1,722	13,777
Other expense	5,314	43,972
Cost of sales	$30,350	$336,361
Gross profit	$ 3,491	$ 5,156
General and administrative expense (See schedule below)	12,243	90,440
Net income (loss)	$ (8,752)	$ (85,284)

Schedule of General and Administrative Expenses

	Current Month	Eight Months
Executive salaries	$ 3,151	$ 24,384
Office salaries	1,427	12,790
Interest	4,399	24,452
Legal and accounting	350	7,233
Other	2,916	21,581
TOTAL	$12,243	$ 90,440

Martin had purchased the property for $7,500 some time earlier with the intention of developing it into a retreat site. The property was estimated to have a current value of $75,000—the approximate amount of the mortgage on that property. However, the ranch and youth retreat were maintained as a venture completely separate from Marty's Landscaping.

Martin gave Davis a tour of the Green Valley Ranch. He explained his own religious interests and his intention to build the center as a site primarily, though not exclusively, for religious gatherings. The area appeared ideal for a retreat site, but little development had been done. There was no work currently in progress. A tractor stood in a field of high grass. There was one partially completed barracks building, some stacks of lumber, one graded sports field, and a small lake. Davis quickly estimated that some $200,000 to $300,000 would be needed to complete the project even if equipment were available to clear and grade the area where buildings were to be built.

Even though business had turned sour, Martin wanted to take the steps necessary to rescue his firm and make it a winner. Additional funds were needed, but the firm had no additional collateral to pledge for a loan. "What can I do," he asked Davis, "to avoid bankruptcy and become profitable again?"

Questions

1. Evaluate the present condition of this business and its prospects for the future.
2. Evaluate Martin's idea of opening a nursery as a means of strengthening the business.
3. What steps can you, as a consultant, recommend to improve the business?
4. What appear to be the primary causes of the present dilemma? Were they avoidable?

CASE 3

Stitch Craft
Buying a small business

Helen and Martha, recent graduates from the School of Fabric Design at Webster University, are interested in going into business in some field that will utilize their education. They both have been steady customers of Stitch Craft, a nationally franchised business, since it opened a year ago, and they both know Peggy and Susan, the owners. Helen and Martha have learned from Peggy that the store is doing quite well for having been in business only a year. Just the other day, while Martha was shopping in Stitch Craft, she was approached by Susan, who told her that she and Peggy were considering selling the business. Susan said the reason they wished to sell was that they had overextended themselves in terms of time availability and were having difficulties maintaining their homes, children, outside interests, and the business simultaneously. Since Helen and Martha had expressed an interest in the business and had experience in fabric design, Peggy and Susan thought they should be given first chance to buy the business.

Helen and Martha were quite excited about this prospect and made an appointment to meet with Peggy and Susan. At this meeting they were shown the whole business from inventory procedures to ringing out the cash register at night.

Source: This case was prepared by Professor Carl Schweser of the University of Iowa.

They were quite impressed and eager to proceed with the takeover. When they discussed finances with Peggy and Susan, they were told that since the business was only one year old they were only asking Helen and Martha to assume the existing balance of the SBA loan and pay the invoice price of the inventory and $20,000 for the fixtures, leasehold improvements, and franchise fee. Helen and Martha don't know anything about finances, so they have come to you with a copy of last year's income statement and this month's income and balance sheets for you to review (Exhibits C3–1, C3–2, and C3–3).

Other points that have come up in your discussion with Helen and Martha are that thay have contacted the Stitch Craft Corp., which granted Peggy and Susan the franchise, and were informed that they could indeed take over the remaining nine years of the franchise agreement. Peggy also explained that the Stitch Craft brand is nationally known for quality and style, which accounts for its rapid acceptance in the Webster City market. Helen and Martha have given a great deal of thought to the store's current location, which is in a strip mall on the south end of town. The south end is the "lower-rent" district, and the store's customers are mainly from the higher-income northwest section of town. Helen and Martha feel the store should be moved to a location that is closer to the market. If they buy the

Exhibit C3–1 Income Statement

Stitch Craft
Income Statement
1989

		Industry Figures % of Sales
Sales		
Fabric	$144,376	82.0%
Patterns/books	16,871	10.0%
Sewing classes	6,932	7.0%
Other.	1,621	1.0%
Total sales	$169,800	100.0%
Cost of goods sold	$ 79,300	51.0%
Gross profit.	$ 90,500	49.0%
Expenses		
Wages	$ 30,600	14.0%
Supplies	2,575	1.0%
Rent	15,000	7.5%
Utilities.	2,880	1.5%
Advertising	9,572	5.5%
Displays	2,220	1.0%
Travel	375	1.0%
Phone	1,550	.5%
Services	1,875	.5%
Royalty fee (4.5% of sales)	7,436	4.5%
Depreciation and amortization	4,128	2.0%
Interest.	7,185	1.0%
Other.	5,654	5.0%
Total Expenses	$ 91,050	45.0%
Income before taxes & owner's draw	$ (550)	4.0%

business, they plan to move the store at the end of the current lease, which expires in two years. However, they have options to extend the lease for six years after the current lease expires should they decide not to move. They have talked to the landlord, and she will convert Peggy and Susan's lease to Helen and Martha as is.

Exhibit C3-2 Balance Sheet

Stitch Craft
Balance Sheet
Jan. 31, 1990

Current Assets:
Cash on hand	$ 400	
Cash in the bank	(1,245)	
Accounts receivable	0	
Inventory		
Fabrics	20,372	
Notions	3,900	
Patterns/books	2,190	
Sewing machines	1,345	
Prepaid rent:	1,250	
Total current assets		$28,212

Fixed Assets:
Fixtures	$12,000	
Less: Accumulated depreciation	(1,300)	
	$10,700	
Leasehold improvements	11,760	
Less: Accumulated depreciation	(1,820)	
	$ 9,940	
Franchise	12,500	
Less: Amortization	(1,352)	
	$11,148	
Total fixed assets		31,788
TOTAL ASSETS		$60,000

Current Liabilities:
Accounts payable–Trade	$21,873	
Withholdings payable	550	
Sales tax payable	202	
Total current liabilities		$22,625

Long-Term Liabilities:
SBA Loan—Balance due		
($50,000 over 7 yrs @ 15%)		46,025

Exhibit C3–2 *(Continued)*

Equity:
Capital—Peggy Ralson . . . . (275)
  Add: Current income/loss . . . . (1,550)

  Training expense draw. . . . . (2,500)
Plus other withdrawals. 0
  New Balance . . . . (4,325)

Capital—Susan Keightly . . . . (275)
  Add: Current income/loss . . . . (1,550)

  Training expense draw. . . . . (2,500)
Plus other withdrawals. 0
  New Balance . . . . (4,325)

  Total equity. . . . . (8,650)

TOTAL LIABILITIES AND EQUITY. $60,000

Exhibit C3–3 Income Statement

Stitch Craft
Income Statement
Jan. 31, 1990

Sales	$ 6,750
Cost of goods.	3,649
Gross margin	$3,101
Operating expense. . . .	6,001
Net income	($3,100)

Note: January/February sales are lowest in year.
October/November sales are highest.

Question

1. Your job is to review the current financial statements and all the data
presented to you and make a recommendation on whether or not Helen
and Martha should buy Stitch Craft. What counteroffer would you recommend they make if you feel the current asking price is not attractive?

CASE 4

The Medicine Shoppe
Selecting a franchise

Kara has recently graduated from pharmacy school and registered as a pharmacist in her state. She recognizes the need for professional business guidance to allow her to successfully operate her own pharmacy. She realizes that her consumers would rely upon her professional skills and seek her help because she works in the health-care profession. She wants to be her own boss, to own her own store, and not be part of a large chain.

Kara's dream has always been to open her own pharmacy, yet in today's fast economy it is difficult for anyone to start a business and make it profitable. For her, it is even more difficult to buy an existing pharmacy because of the high sale price and the low return on investment. One of her best options is to become a franchise of Medicine Shoppe International, Inc.

The Medicine Shoppe franchise offers her a way of maintaining a sound balance between professionalism and profit. It would help her find a prime location with approximately 800 to 1,000 square feet in a high-traffic area. In addition, she would receive help with interior decor, external signs, and internal fixtures, in an attempt to maximize the image exposure and efficiency of the location.

The Medicine Shoppe program enables the franchisee to purchase in volume

Source: Robert Justis and Richard Judd, *Franchising* (Cincinnati, OH: South-Western Publishing, Co., 1989), p. 268.

and develop specific inventory-control guidelines. The parent company is involved in daily marketing needs, pharmacy supplies, generic and other ethical drugs, promotional materials, fixtures and equipment, store insurance, and promotional articles. The Medicine Shoppe also has its own private label, with over 100 items currently available.

An intensive one-week training seminar at the Medicine Shoppe's corporate headquarters helps train the franchisee in all aspects of business. Additionally, a six-week grand-opening program generates tremendous exposure of the business to consumers in the marketing area. Substantial assistance is given in site selection, lease negotiation, store layout, personnel selection and training, opening procedures, purchasing, inventory control, record keeping, budgeting, and management.

The initial capital required is approximately $60,000, which includes the original franchising fee of $16,000 plus fixtures, supplies and inventory, and opening promotions. In addition, a 5 percent royalty fee on all gross receipts is to be paid to the company.

Kara has little, if any, managerial background. She is very well aware that many pharmacists have failed because of poor managerial ability, and she knows that most businesses in general fail because the owners lack management experience and expertise. Because of her lack of knowledge in management, Kara is gravely concerned about opening a Medicine Shoppe franchise.

Questions

1. Do you think Kara's professional background will be adequate to help her achieve success in the business, or does she need the assistance she has indicated?
2. What recommendations for evaluating the franchise would you give Kara?
3. What ongoing training should Kara seek from the franchisor?
4. What other alternatives does Kara have for starting her business?

CASE 5

Construction Equipment Dealership
Weighing a career with IBM against running the family business

As Professor Alan Stone talked on the telephone, he watched his graduate assistant, Jerry Westin, shifting nervously in his chair. When Stone had completed his call, the following conversation with Jerry took place.

Professor: Sorry we were interrupted, Jerry! You said you have a problem. How can I help you?

Jerry: Dr. Stone, I'll be finishing my M.B.A. next month, and I still haven't been able to decide which job offer to accept. Two of the companies want answers next week, so I simply have to make some decisions.

Professor: Well, Jerry, you will have to make the final determination yourself, but we can certainly discuss the various alternatives. As a matter of curiosity, did any of the consulting work we did for IBM ever result in a job offer?

Jerry: Yes, sir! IBM has offered me a really intriguing project-planning job in their National Marketing Division in Atlanta at $32,800. I would have a lot of responsibility from the start, and I would be coordinating the efforts of personnel from several functional departments. If all went well, they have indicated I'd probably have a good chance to be the head of product development for the entire division. Of course, they would pay all moving expenses, and they really have a package of fringe benefits.

Source: This case was prepared by John E. Schoen.

Professor: That sounds awfully good! What else do you have?

Jerry: Samsonite, Shell Development, and Boise Cascade. If my wife has her way, we'll go to San Francisco with Boise Cascade. My only question is, can two people live in San Francisco on $29,000 a year, particularly if one of them is my wife?

Professor: Say, what about the family business? Have you given up the idea of being the biggest construction equipment dealer in Billings, Montana?

Jerry: No, sir, not really! As a matter of fact, that's one of the complicating factors. I've been getting some pressure to go back to Billings.

Professor: How do you mean, Jerry?

Jerry: Well, I never really noticed how subtle Dad has been until I started thinking about it. As far as I can recall, he has never specifically said that he thought I should come into the business. But he always said that the opportunity was there if I wanted to take it. His classic statement is how good the business and Billings have been to the family, and I think it is fair to say he influenced me to go to Iowa State, his alma mater, and even to major in accounting. My uncle, who is the accountant in our company, is retiring this year, and I see now that I was probably being prepared all along for that position.

Professor: Does your mother voice an opinion?

Jerry: Yes, sir! She voices more than an opinion! To give you an idea, the last time I talked to her about some of the job offers, she burst into tears and said that it would break my father's heart if I didn't join the business. She said they built the business for me and that they hadn't worked all those years to turn it over to some stranger. Since my uncle has to retire because of his health, she accused me of turning my back on Dad just when he needs me the most. By the time she finished, she had me feeling confused, miserable, and mad!

Professor: Mad?

Jerry: Yeah! Mom made some statements about Carol, my wife. Mom thinks Carol is trying to persuade me not to go back to Billings because it's too small and I'd be too close to the family. I suppose I wouldn't have been so angry if it hadn't been partially the truth!

Professor: You mean your wife doesn't want to go to Billings?

Jerry: Oh, I'm sure she'll go if that's what I decide to do, but I think she'd greatly prefer San Francisco. She is from Seattle and likes all the bright lights and activity in big cities. In addition, she has a degree in interior design and the opportunities for employment and learning would be greater in San Francisco than any of the other places, particularly Billings. She has worked to help put me through school for the last two years, so I may owe this to her. She also believes it would be better for me to stand on my own two feet and asks why I went for an M.B.A. if all I was going to do was join the family business. She made me mad, too, last week when she said the worst thing she can imagine is being barefoot and pregnant and eating at my folks' house three times a week.

Professor: What about the Shell and the Samsonite offers?

Jerry: Oh, they're really just offers I've had. It is basically San Francisco, IBM, or home!

Professor: Well, Jerry, you do seem to have a problem. Can you compare the nature of the work in each job?

Jerry: Yes, sir! The IBM job looks very interesting, and the possibilities for advancement are good. Boise Cascade, on the other hand, has a typical cost accounting position. I suppose it would be all right for a couple of years while Carol does her thing and we see if we like San Francisco, but something else would have to come along eventually!

Professor: What about your work in the family business?

Jerry: That's the funny part of it! Everything about the IBM offer—the salary, fringes, authority, prestige, promotion possibilities, and so forth—appeals to me, but I like the family business, too. I mean I've grown up in the business; I know and like the employees, customers, and suppliers; and I really like Billings. Of course, I'd be working as an accountant for a while; but I would eventually succeed my father, and I've always thought I'd like to run the business someday.

Professor: What about salary in the family business?

Jerry: That's a part I've forgotten to tell you! Last week, my uncle was in town, and even he was dropping broad hints about the family looking forward to our return to Billings and how he will give me a short orientation and then "get the heck outa Dodge." His parting comment was that he was certain Dad would match anything the big companies could do on starting salary.

Professor: Even $32,800?

Jerry: Apparently! Well, there it is, Dr. Stone! What do you think? I've got to let IBM know by the end of the month.

Professor: I don't know, Jerry. Could you go with IBM or Boise Cascade for a couple of years and then go back to the family business?

Jerry: I thought of that possibility, but I think that if I'm going to go with the family business, this is the right time. Uncle Phil is retiring, so there is a position; and I know Dad was a little hesitant about the M.B.A. versus getting experience in the family business. Dad is approaching 60, and the business is hitting all-time highs, so I believe he will try to sell it if I go somewhere else. No, I think it's now or never!

Professor: Well, you were right about one thing, Jerry. You do have a dilemma! This reminds me of the cases in management textbooks—no easy solution! Good luck, and let me know your decision.

Jerry: Thanks, Prof!

Questions

1. Does Jerry Weston have an obligation to the family to provide leadership for the family business?

2. What obligation does Jerry have to his wife in view of her background, education, and career interests?

3. Should Jerry simply do what he wants to do? Does he know what he wants to do?

4. In view of the conflict between Jerry's own interests and those of his wife, what should his career choice be?

CASE 6

Robinson Associates, Inc.
Business plan for a new venture

This case presents a business plan for a proposed management-consulting firm. This plan was prepared by a graduate student in business as the basis for his own livelihood both during and after his period of graduate study. A few details, such as name and location, have been changed, but the situation is real.

BUSINESS PLAN
for
David R. Robinson
Minneapolis, Minnesota

SCOPE OF THE BUSINESS

Personal

I plan to start a business consulting service in conjunction with USA Consultants (a nationwide business-consulting firm).

History of USA Consultants

USA is over 30 years old. It originated in Boston and Atlanta. It started out as P. Miller Management Consultants. Paul Miller III is the current president of USA.

The name changed to USA in 1972.

They have over 160 consultants in more than 50 cities.

SPECIFIC AREAS OF ASSISTANCE

Company (brochure available on request)

Analysis Phase
Implementation Phase (selected examples)

Marketing programs
Organization planning

Personnel training programs
Cost reduction programs
Loan package preparation
Inventory control systems
Financial control and reporting
Mergers and acquisitions
Strategic business planning
Business evaluation

Personal

With my accounting background (CPA—inactive) and current experience consulting with small businesses, I would concentrate on:

1. Analysis phase
2. Implementation phase—especially on
   Organization planning
   Loan package preparation
   Strategic business planning
   Financial control and reporting systems
3. USA continuing education programs in various areas in which I could update my skills.

GOALS

Personal

1. I plan to begin the business July 1 and operate it part time for three months. I will cut back my hours to 32 per week. I will still be eligible for full-time benefits including health insurance and tuition remission. I will go into the business full time starting October 1.
2. I plan to continue pursuing a Ph.D. in business administration. This is entirely compatible with the consulting business. (See attached projected cash flow statements.)

Financial

I plan to reach the following cumulative gross billing goals:

Six months . . . . $ 22,500
Twelve months . . . . $ 86,500

Eighteen months $137,000
Twenty-four months. $191,000

MANAGEMENT CAPABILITY

See attached résumé.

Strong Points

1. Four years' consulting experience with Small Business Development Centers.
2. Admitted to Ph.D. program at the university in business administration. Major: management; minor: international business,
   with current G.P.A. of 4.0 out of possible 4.0.
3. Accepted by USA. USA advertised in *The Wall Street Journal, Inc.*,
   USA Today. To date, they have received over 3,000 applications
   but selected only 158.
4. Education will be continued through schooling and USA continuing education program.

MARKETING

Competition

External
1. Review of the Minneapolis-St.Paul *Webb's Directory* on management consultants shows no direct competition.
2. Typically consultants specialize in one to three areas. No firm
   can offer the wide range of services that USA can.

Internal
There are two other USA consultants in the Minneapolis-St.
Paul area. One started his business in December of last year,
and the second is just starting. Both are on the Minneapolis side
of the river. There appears to be plenty of room for a third USA
consultant.

Customer Analysis

USA billing rates are $125/hour to $300/hour. These rates will preclude
very small businesses from using our services in most cases. The firms that

appear to be best suited for a USA consultant would be firms with 30 to 400 employees.

These firms can be identified through the use of *Webb's Directory* and various other publications.

Reaching the Customer

There are three primary methods to reach customers:

1. Salesperson. USA will assist consultant in hiring and training.
2. MAS services to small accounting firms. USA works with accounting firms that do not have an MAS department to provide them with consulting services.
3. Personal contacts. Extensive contacts have been developed on both sides of the river and will be used to assist in identifying potential customers.

Exhibit C6–1   Projected Billable Hours for First Year

	Hours	Billings	Compensation (@ 50%)
July	10	$ 1,250	$ 625
August	15	$ 1,875	$ 938
September	25	$ 3,125	$ 1,563
October	40	$ 5,000	$ 2,500
November	50	$ 6,250	$ 3,125
December	40	$ 5,000	$ 2,500
January*	55	$ 8,250	$ 4,125
February	55	$ 8,250	$ 4,125
March	70	$10,500	$ 5,250
April	85	$12,750	$ 6,375
May	85	$12,750	$ 6,375
June	75	$11,250	$ 5,625
Totals		$86,250	$43,125

*Pay review is conducted every six months—expect increase to $150/hour.
After $50,000 in gross billings, consultant receives back $7,500 deposit. This should occur about the end of March.

Exhibit C6-2   Cash Flow Projections for David R. Robinson Family

Item	July	Aug.	Sept.	Oct.	Nov.	Dec.
Husband	$1,396	$1,396	$1,396	$ 0	$ 0	$ 0
Wife	$ 783	$ 783	$ 783	$ 783	$ 783	$ 783
USA	$ 0	$ 625	$ 935	$1,560	$2,500	$3,125
Subtotal	$2,179	$2,804	$3,497	$2,726	$3,666	$4,163
Expenses	$3,300	$3,300	$3,400	$3,500	$3,600	$3,700
Overage (Shortage)	($1,121)	($ 496)	$ 97	($ 744)	$ 66	$ 463

	Jan.	Feb.	Mar.	Apr.	May	June
Husband	$ 0	$ 0	$ 0	$ 0	$ 0	$ 0
Wife	$ 783	$ 783	$ 783	$ 0	$ 0	$ 0
USA	$2,500	$4,125	$4,125	$ 5,250	$6,375	$6,375
Other	$ 0	$ 0	$ 0	$ 7,500	$ 0	$ 0
Subtotal	$3,283	$4,908	$4,908	$12,750	$6,375	$6,375
Expenses	$5,500	$3,800	$3,900	$ 4,000	$3,800	$3,900
Subtotal	($2,217)	$1,108	$1,008	$ 8,750	$2,575	$2,475

Summary of Overages (Shortages):

July	($1,121)
Aug.	($ 496)
Sept.	$ 97
Oct.	($ 774)
Nov.	$ 66
Dec.	$ 463
Jan.	($2,217)
Additional cash needed	($3,982)

Market Trends

Many businesses today are downsizing. Typically the person businesses are outplacing is in middle management. Businesses still have the same problems as before. Businesses will then turn to a consultant to assist in solving these problems.

CAREER OBJECTIVE

To make optimal use of my organizational analysis and human relations abilities to become a skilled consultant to clients and/or management.

This will result in:
More coordinated organizations
Increased job satisfaction/productivity

QUALIFIED BY

Training and over 10 years' experience encompassing:
Organizational skills
Human relations
Leadership skills
Financial analysis
Reporting

ACHIEVEMENTS

Organizational Skills

Effectively worked with the Small Business Development Center (SBDC) director to present a highly rated conference on SBDCs for state and federal government personnel.

Supervised and coordinated other staff accountants in the preparation of audited financial statements.

Coordinated with volunteer personnel to achieve a very successful fund drive.

Developed and coordinated with other area procurement specialists to present two highly rated seminars.

Human Relations

Quickly developed an atmosphere of trust with established clients through careful consideration of their accounting and tax needs.

Successfully assisted two business partners in planning, starting, and operating their own small business.

Provided clear direction to several small businesses, which enabled them to successfully bid on government contracts.

Leadership Skills

Effectively taught a government procurement seminar in a concise and clear manner to small-business persons.

Successfully started and developed a Procurement Assistance Center in assisting local businesses obtain over $1,000,000 in government contracts in just over two years.

Financial Analysis

Developed and successfully implemented annual budgets for the SBDC and Procurement Assistance Center for over two years.

Thoroughly completed audits and prepared financial statements for corporations with assets up to $2,000,000.

Developed an accounting system for the Chaplain Fund that provided more complete documentation and permitted audits to be completed in half the expected time.

Reporting

Coordinated development of successful funding proposals for the local Small Business Development Center and Procurement Assistance Center.

Thoroughly prepared two nominations for awards, one national and one state, which resulted in the nominees' receiving the rewards.

Gathered information regarding a specific question by the Chaplain Fund council, then translated this information into a short, understandable format that permitted an immediate, well-informed decision.

EXPERIENCE

State University, Minnesota (June 1989–Present)
Procurement Specialist/small business counselor/graduate assistant

Bellhaven Hospital (November 1987–May 1989)
Advanced staff auditor

Moore, Snyder CPA, Inc. (December 1986–June 1987)
Staff accountant

Harry C. Reynolds & Co. (January 1985–November 1986)
Staff accountant

U.S. Army (1980–1984)
Fund custodian, Chaplain Fund, Illinois
Chapel activities specialist, Korea
Funds clerk, Chaplain Fund, Texas

EDUCATION

B.S. in Accounting, State University, Ohio

M.A. in industrial/organizational psychology, State University, Minnesota (Thesis title: Comparative Psychological Characteristics of Entrepreneurs vs. Small-Business Owners)

OTHER

Licensed as a CPA (inactive) in Minnesota.

FINANCIAL

Amount Needed

$ 7,500   Initial deposit*
$ 1,000   Supplies**
$ 4,000   Working capital***

$12,500   Bank financing
$ 9,500   Personal collateral (certificate of deposit)

$22,000

*To be refunded when $50,000 in gross billings have been achieved.
**Supplies include *Webb's Directory*, file cabinet, office supplies, shelving, business subscriptions, business phone.
***See attached cash flow statement for details.

Questions

1. As a potential investor, which part of this business plan would impress you most favorably?
2. As a potential investor, what are the most serious concerns or questions you would have after reading this plan?
3. What additional information should be added to strengthen the plan?
4. What changes should be made in the format or wording of the plan to enhance its communication effectiveness?
5. As a banker, would you make a working-capital loan to this business? Why?

CASE 7

HOT Magazine
Researching market potential

Kate Johnson, director of public information for a social-service organization in Waco, TX, was scanning the newspaper at lunch with her friend Susan Baldwin, an advertising account representative for the *Waco Tribune-Herald*.

"Did you see this story about the city magazine the Waco Chamber of Commerce may start?" asked Kate.

"Yeah, sounds interesting. They'd probably have to hire an editor. Would you be interested? You've had a lot of experience with publications."

"I just don't know, Sue. I think Waco is ripe for a city magazine, but I just can't get excited about a Chamber of Commerce publication. They're all so boring."

"You're right about that. But what do you expect? The editors don't have much freedom, having to answer to the business establishment," Susan added.

"I really think Waco needs a city magazine. We've got a lot going on here, and we're virtually ignored by *Texas Monthly* and the special-interest magazines. They've all written us off as a small town," Kate said. "What we really need is a high-quality, independent city magazine like *D, the Magazine of Dallas* or *Philadelphia*."

"Do you really think a magazine like that would go in Waco?"

"I know it would, and I think we're the ones who could pull it off, Sue," Kate replied.

Source: This case was prepared by Minette E. Drumwright.

"There would be quite a risk involved, and we'd have to quit our jobs," Susan commented.

"Well, I don't want to be an employee and a public servant all my life. I'm ready for something new and challenging, something on my own," said Kate.

"A city magazine would certainly be a challenge, Kate."

Background of the Would-Be Entrepreneurs

Kate, who was 35 years old, had worked in public affairs positions for local, regional, and state organizations during the past 13 years, editing a variety of organizational newsletters, magazines, and brochures. In addition, she had been editor of both a small-town newspaper and a special-interest publication about music. Kate's longest tenure in any of the jobs was less than three years. As soon as she mastered a job, she would begin looking around for a new challenge. Kate had lived in Waco a total of 11 years, including the time she spent studying journalism at Baylor University.

Although the Waco Chamber of Commerce eventually abandoned the idea of sponsoring a city magazine, Kate held tenaciously to her aspirations for an independent city magazine. She persuaded her 30-year-old sister, Debra Lunsford, and Susan Baldwin, who was 23 years old, to join her in the venture. Although Susan had been out of college for only two years, she had worked for the newspaper in her hometown since she was 16 years old. Debra was the vice-president and business manager of a shipping company in Houston. The three women would form the full-time staff of the publication with Kate serving as editor. Susan would be the advertising sales director, and Debra would be the business manager. All the stories, photography, and graphics would be contracted on a free-lance basis, providing local artists a showcase for their work.

The HOT Idea

Kate proposed to call the publication *HOT,* which was a commonly used abbreviation for "Heart of Texas." *HOT* would include an entertainment guide; features on local personalities; and a variety of stories focusing on social, economic, and political trends of the locality. The target audience would be central Texans between the ages of 25 and 55 years with annual incomes ranging from $18,000 to $50,000.

The percentage of advertising in each issue is a key variable for any publication, representing the primary source of revenue. Susan projected that the initial advertising-to-editorial-contents ratio would be 60:40 and that eventually a 70:30 ratio would be attained.

Debra determined that an initial investment of $400,000 would need to be contributed by local investors to launch the magazine. The $400,000 would be used to sustain the magazine through the initial periods of loss, providing for salaries, free-lance work, promotion, and production.

Together, the three entrepreneurs interested James Jenkins, a 32-year-old ac-

countant, in the magazine idea. James, who was from an established Waco family, was president of Downtown Waco, Inc., a group of retail merchants with a vested interest in reviving the downtown area. His family owned and operated one of the city's highly successful specialty retail businesses.

Before approaching potential investors about the city magazine, James insisted that the entrepreneurs substantiate their feelings that the magazine would be a success. In an effort to get the necessary information, Kate called a professor specializing in marketing research at Baylor University's Hankamer School of Business. The professor referred the entrepreneurs to two graduate students in his seminar in marketing research.

The Research

The graduate students set out to develop a profile of independent city magazines to determine the feasibility of initiating a successful venture in Waco. Using a structured, undisguised questionnaire, they surveyed city-magazine publishers throughout the nation. The sample included the publishers of all the city magazines with complete listings in Standard Rate and Data Service. Participants were asked to enclose a recent issue of their magazine along with the completed questionnaires. A $2 incentive was enclosed to defray the cost of the magazine and the mailing expense. Among the survey questions were those shown in Exhibit C7–1.

Analysis of the Questionnaire

The response rate to the survey was 63 percent. As the questionnaires were re-

---

Exhibit C7–1   Survey Questions

General Information

1. How many employees do you have?
   In editorial   _____
   In advertising   _____
   Other   _____

2. On the average, what percentage of the stories are written by free-lance writers? _____

3. What is your production cost per issue?
   _____ less than $25,000   _____ $40,001–$50,000
   _____ $25,000–$30,000   _____ more than $50,000
   _____ $30,001–$40,000

Advertising

4. What was the approximate ratio of advertising to editorial contents

	Advertising		Editorial
in the first issue?	_____	to	_____
after a year of issues?	_____	to	_____
currently?	_____	to	_____

5. What was the advertising revenue during the magazine's first year?
   _____ less than $100,000   _____ $500,001–$1,000,000
   _____ $100,000–$500,000   _____ more than $1,000,000

6. What was the advertising revenue last year? (Please omit this question if last year was your first year of publication.)
   _____ less than $100,000   _____ $500,001–$1,000,000
   _____ $100,000–$500,000   _____ more than $1,000,000

7. What businesses are your major advertisers in?
   _____
   _____

Subscriptions

8. At the time of the first issue, what was the total circulation of the magazine?
   _____ less than 5,000 _____ 10,001–15,000   _____ 25,001–40,000
   _____ 5,000–10,000 _____ 15,001–25,000   _____ more than 40,000

9. When the first issue was published, how many paid subscriptions did the magazine have?
   _____ less than 5,000 _____ 10,001–15,000   _____ 25,001–40,000
   _____ 5,000–10,000 _____ 15,001–25,000   _____ more than 40,000

(Continued)

Exhibit C7–1 *(Continued)*

10. What is the average income bracket of your readership?

_____ less than $15,000 _____ $30,001–$50,000 _____ more than $75,000

_____ $15,000–$30,000 _____ $50,001–$75,000 _____ don't know

11. What is the average age of your readership?

_____ less than 25 years _____ 36–45 years _____ 56–65 years

_____ 25–35 years _____ 46–55 years _____ more than 65 years

12. Please rank in priority order the subject matter your readers prefer. Let a "1" represent the most preferred topic and a "5" represent the least preferred topic.

_____ local politics _____ local news analysis _____ business news

_____ entertainment _____ local personalities

13. What adjectives would you use to describe your readership?

_____

14. What advice would you give to someone interested in starting a city magazine?

_____

_____

_____

Exhibit C7–2 Survey Tabulations

Percentage of stories written by free-lance writers	59.4%	Promotion expenditure before publication	$29,000
Percentage of advertising in the first issue	40.3%	Promotion expenditure during the first year	$39,958
Percentage of advertising after one year of issues	45.5%	SMSA population*	671,924
		Circulation**	59,178
Percentage of advertising currently	49.5%	Newsstand price***	$1.80

*The population of the Standard Metropolitan Statistical Areas (SMSA) in which the magazines were located were taken from the *1980 Census of Population and Housing: United States Summary.*

**The circulations were listed in consumer magazines and farm publications published by Standard Rate and Data Service, Inc.

***The issue prices were taken from the covers of the sample issues submitted by participants.

turned, the data were analyzed with a computer using a variety of procedures. The means for some of the quantitative variables are listed in Exhibit C7–2.

Readership Profile Ninety percent of the participants responded to the open-ended questions asking them to describe their readerships with the word "affluent." Ninety-six percent of the readership had an annual income greater than $30,000, and more than 80 percent ranged from 36 to 45 years of age. Participants ranked the subjects their readers preferred in the following order: (1) feature stories on local personalities, (2) entertainment, (3) local news analysis, (4) local politics, and (5) business news.

Major Sources of Advertising Participants were asked to list the businesses of their major advertisers to permit an analysis of the primary sources of advertising in city magazines. Eighty-eight percent of the respondents listed retail businesses, while 38 percent included restaurants and banks in their lists. Nineteen percent mentioned real estate companies.

National advertising appeared in the lists of only two respondents, and one of the two specified that the national ads were "occasional." The respondent who indicated that national advertising was a frequent source of revenue was the publisher of a magazine in an SMSA with a population exceeding 3,000,000.

Exhibit C7–3 Profile of Waco SMSA (McLennan County)[1]

Population	172,800
Population ranking in the United States	194
Number of households	63,000
Total effective buying income (in thousands of dollars)	$1,189,402
Retail sales	$840,358,000
Retail sales per household	$13,381
Age groups:	
18–24	24,000
25–34	23,000
35–49	27,000
50–64	28,000
65 or older	23,000
Undetermined	1,000
Median age	44
Income Distribution of Adult Population:	
Under $10,000	37,000
$10,000–$19,999	38,000
$20,000 or more	51,000
Median income	$16,800

[1]This abbreviated profile was obtained from federal government Census publications.

Questions

1. Do you see any flaws in the sample selection that would create a bias toward larger, metropolitan areas?
2. What other questions should have been included in the questionnaire?

3. Do the survey data support the entrepreneur's plans for the advertising-to-editorial ratio?

4. What additional information about the Waco market is needed by the entrepreneurs?

5. Given the research findings, do you recommend that a city-magazine venture be initiated in Waco? Why or why not?

CASE 8

Downtown Grocery

Problems of a downtown location

Following is the account of a business owner who purchased a grocery business in Colorado Springs describing changes necessitated by trends in the downtown business environment.

Conventional wisdom can be the graveyard of the entrepreneur. My husband and I ran into this truth many times in the course of saving our Colorado Springs grocery business and commercial property.

We had bought a downtown grocery in early 1984, and that year our business began falling off for a number of reasons: People were moving away from downtown as homes were replaced by office buildings, and supermarkets in the suburbs were attracting customers. On top of all that, Colorado's energy-based economy was going into a decline that brought the highest rate of bank and savings-and-loan failures since the Depression.

Within three years, we were at a turning point. Our customers were using us only for convenience shopping, so we had more space than we needed. We were about to yield to the conventional wisdom: Sell the business for the value of the land.

But we had an asset: a 14,000-square-foot building with 43,000 square feet of parking space in an office-building area with very little parking. The building's

major merit was spaciousness. I knew that there had to be a formula to save the business and to give the community convenience shopping. It would be a true test of our abilities.

I took on the project of selling the building or leasing all or part of it. Our first step was to scale the grocery down to a convenience store. We also leased one part of the building. Business still didn't pick up, and I wasn't having much luck finding other businesses to lease space.

One afternoon I passed the shuttered Trailways bus depot. Greyhound had bought Trailways, and I decided to call the Greyhound office to see if they might want to move their combined operations to our location. It was not entirely a shot in the dark, because their location looked cramped.

Conventional wisdom says you don't get anywhere with a blind call, but my experience proves otherwise. I remember that call very well. I merely asked the person who answered the phone if Greyhound had ever thought of moving to another location. "Of course we're looking," he said, and told me he would have the manager call me at once.

The next day the manager was driving around our parking lot. For the next couple of months there was a steady flow of Greyhound people looking at the site.

Source: This case is taken from Kathy Conners, "How to Save a Small Business." Reprinted by permission, *Nation's Business,* November 1988. Copyright 1988, U.S. Chamber of Commerce.

The catch was that they wanted only about 5,000 square feet of the building but all of the south end of the parking lot.

They were sold on the location, but it took months to negotiate the lease. In setting up the lease, we developed a way of using the building as a shared space. Greyhound would take a portion, but its lobby would be open to the rest of the building. We would operate our convenience store, add a fast-food bar and maintain all rights to concessions as long as we kept the same business hours as Greyhound.

With this plan, the idea of the service center I had been trying to push at first seemed feasible. I started calling all over again: check-cashing facilities, credit unions, small novelty retailers, T-shirt companies, video rental stores, shoe-repair stores, welcome services and florist services.

By day I did my telephoning. By night I would plan the next day's contacts and make lists of interested parties so that my husband could do the follow-ups.

We came up with nine businesses to occupy the building along with Greyhound. Seven of the nine new occupants were small-business people planning extensions of their already successful companies.

As these businesses fell into place, we needed financing for a building face-lift. It was a nightmare, even though we had a solid basis for applying for a loan. We had a long-term lease with Greyhound, written commitments for space from successful business people in the community and an appreciating property. But most bankers were unwilling to consider the project because they were facing hard times themselves from the regional economic slump.

Eventually, we found our banker in Colorado Springs, and we also got a small, low-interest construction loan from the city.

Our commercial mortgage company told us that they had never seen anyone convert a declining downtown business into a profitable enterprise by sharing the building space. But to me it appeared to be the only way to save our life's investment and everything we had worked for.

After all the exhausting and agonizing physical and mental labor, we dedicated our building and opened this past August. And we had done it contrary to the conventional wisdom that says you must have lawyers, interior designers, architects and real-estate people to bring off such a deal.

Now we can watch Greyhound expand its operation, and after all the skepticism, we can enjoy the compliments on our success—including the ultimate compliment of imitation: An East Coast investor, impressed with what we have accomplished, hopes to copy it in an old Safeway building.

So much for conventional wisdom.

Questions

1. Was the 1984 purchase of the grocery business at this location a logical decision at the time it was made?

2. What were the keys to developing a successful use plan for this facility and location?
3. Suppose Greyhound had declined to relocate. What were the owners' practical alternatives in that case?
4. Would you consider this location if you wished to start a high-fashion women's wear boutique?

CASE 9

Walker Machine Works
Financing arrangements for a new venture

Jim Walker was a management consultant on a continuing but indefinite assignment with a medium-sized plastics company. He was also an M.B.A. candidate at a nearby university. He had thought that the consultant's position would be challenging and would add a dimension of practical experience to his academic background. But after several months Jim had become very disenchanted with his job. Although he seemed to have much freedom in his duties, he began to discover that his reports and suggestions could not be translated into meaningful results and solutions. He realized that the management was interested only in maintaining the status quo and that he was hired as a more or less token consultant. His efforts to help the company were largely ignored and overlooked. It seemed as if his job was quickly becoming nothing more than an exercise in futility.

Jim discussed the situation with a few friends, most of whom urged him to seek a more fulfilling position with another company. But he had another idea: Why not start a small company of his own? He had toyed with this idea for the past couple of years, and there was no better time than the present to give it a try. At least it would be a real test of his management abilities.

Source: This case was prepared by Richard L. Garman.

After a few days and considerable thought, Jim had several potential ventures in mind. The most promising idea involved the establishment of a machine shop. Before entering college, he had worked two years as a general machinist and acquired diversified experience operating a variety of lathes, milling machines, presses, drills, grinders, and more. And he really enjoyed this sort of work. He guessed that making things on machines satisfied some sort of creative urge he felt.

After a very comprehensive and systematic research of the local market, it appeared that there was a definite need for a high-quality machine-shop operation. Thus, Jim's mind was made up. He was sure that he had an adequate knowledge of machining processes (and enough ambition to find out what he didn't know), and his general business education was also a valuable asset. The problem was money. The necessary machinery for a small shop would cost about $12,000, yet he had only about $3,000 in savings. Surely he could borrow the money or find someone willing to invest in his venture.

A visit to one of the local banks was something less than productive. The vice-president in charge of business investments was quite clear. "You don't have a proven track record. It would be a big risk for us to lend so much money to someone with so little actual experience," the vice-president said. Jim was greatly disappointed but unwilling to give up yet. After all, there were six other banks in town, and one of them might be willing to lend him the money.

Financing Proposal #1

One possibility lay in a suggestion the banker had given Jim. He was told to contact Russ Williams, the president of a local hydraulics company. The banker felt that Russ might be interested in investing a little money in Jim's venture. It was certainly worth a try, so Jim called Russ and made an appointment to see him.

Russ had been involved in manufacturing for over 40 years. As a young man, he had begun his career as Jim had—in the machine shop. After several years of experience as a journeyman machinist, Russ was promoted to shop supervisor. Rising steadily through the ranks, Russ, now in his early sixties, had been promoted to president of the hydraulics company only two years ago.

Jim had never met Russ before and knew little about the man or his background. Nevertheless, Jim soon found Russ to be pleasant in nature and very easy to talk to. Jim spent about an hour presenting his business plan to Russ, who seemed impressed with the idea. Although Russ's time and energies were currently committed to an expansion project for the hydraulics company, he indicated that he might be interested in contributing both money and management. As Jim rose to leave, Russ proposed a 50–50 deal and asked Jim to think it over for a few days.

Financing Proposal #2

A few days later, Stan Thomas came by to see Jim. They had been good friends for about a year and had even roomed together as undergraduates. Stan had talked with his father about Jim's idea and perhaps had even glorified the possibilities a little. Stan's father was intrigued with the plan and offered to meet with Jim to discuss the possibility of a partnership.

Phil Thomas, Stan's father, was a real estate investor who owned his own agency. Although he had been in business only a few years, he was very successful and was constantly looking for new investment prospects. He drove the 250 miles from his home to meet with Jim one Saturday. After looking over the business plan and some pro-forma financial statements that Jim had prepared, he agreed that it might be a worthwhile venture. "I'll contribute all of the capital you need and give you a fair amount of freedom in running the business. I know that most investors would start out by giving you only 10 or 15 percent of the equity and then gradually increase your share, but I'll make you a better deal. I'll give you 40 percent right off the bat, and we'll let this be a sort of permanent arrangement," he said. Jim was a little unsure about that, so he said he'd think it over for a few days and then let him know.

Jim didn't know quite what to do. He had several options to choose from, and he wasn't sure which would be best. The sensible thing would be to talk to someone who could offer some good advice. So, he went to the business school to talk to a professor he knew fairly well.

Financing Proposal #3

Jim found Professor Wesley Davis in his office and described the situation to him. The professor was an associate dean and a marketing specialist. Although he had no actual manufacturing experience, he had edited some semitechnical publications for the Society of Manufacturing Engineers. Thus, he had at least a general knowledge of the machining processes involved in Jim's proposed business.

The professor had been aware of Jim's interest in starting a business and frequently inquired about the progress Jim was making. At the end of this discussion, Jim was surprised to hear the professor offer to help by investing some of his own money. "It sounds like you have an excellent idea, and I'd like to see you give it a try. Besides, a little 'real-world' experience might be good for an old academic type like me," said the professor. "And I would suggest bringing in Joe Winsett from the accounting department. I know neither one of us relishes keeping the books. Besides, Joe is a C.P.A. who could provide some valuable assistance. I'll talk to him if you like." The professor suggested that the equity be split into equal thirds, giving Jim the first option to increase his share of the equity.

Questions

1. Evaluate the backgrounds of the possible "partners" in terms of the business and management needs of the proposed firm.
2. Evaluate the three financing proposals from the standpoint of Jim Walker's control of the firm and the support or interference he may experience.
3. Compare Jim's equity position under each of the three proposals.
4. What are some important characteristics to look for in a prospective business partner?
5. Which option should Jim choose? What reasons can you give to defend your answer?

CASE 10

VMG Products
Formation of a limited partnership

As a salesman of industrial adhesives, Timothy Wagner discovered a business opportunity in the disposable diaper marketplace. Although two companies (Procter and Gamble and Kimberly-Clark) dominated the market, Wagner believed that a low-cost producer located in the Pacific Northwest should be able to compete effectively in that area. He and two associates prepared a 60-page business plan and took it to William N. Prater, Jr., head of Weatherly Private Capital, an investment firm in Seattle. Prater helped them to establish a limited partnership.

The three founders would be one of two general partners in the venture. Weatherly would be the other—acting in an administrative role, just to assuage investors who might be nervous about the founders' youth and lack of experience, Prater had explained. Neither one

Source: Reprinted with permission, *Inc.* magazine, April, 1987. Copyright © 1987 by Goldhirsh Group, Inc., 38 Commercial Wharf, Boston, MA 02110.

would put any significant cash into the deal; that would come from the limited partners. In return, the limiteds would be first in line for a payback, getting nearly all the net income from the diaper line until they had recovered their original investment. Then their share would decline, stepwise, until they had earned seven times their capital. At that point the founders would get 60% of the partnership's income, the limiteds 30%, and Weatherly 10%.

Right there, Prater had said, was the beauty of the partnership structure. If he had set up a corporation right away, the founders would have had to give up most of the equity just to attract capital. This way they could work themselves up from 1% to what amounted to 60% ownership.

The partnership agreement provided that the two general partners were supposed to agree before they took significant action. The limited partners had no day-to-day authority, but they had the power, if it came to that, to kick out either or both general partners.

Questions

1. What makes such an ownership arrangement attractive to limited partners?
2. What are the advantages for Wagner and his two associates?
3. What are the disadvantages for Wagner and his two associates?

CASE 11

The Expectant Parent Center
Linking consumer behavior with a new service business

In February, 1988, Mrs. Ramona Caliban started a profit-oriented childbirth education center in Scranton, PA. On the basis of eight years' hospital experience as a registered nurse in obstetrics, Ramona made the decision to establish herself as an entrepreneur in the fast-growing service area of childbirth education.

Location and Facilities

Ramona conducted her first prenatal classes in the fellowship hall of her church, charging $20 per couple. She stated:

> At first my only clients were three ladies in the married's Sunday school class at church, so space and facilities were no problem. However, the popularity of my instruction and techniques soon grew to the point that I needed additional room and more professional facilities.

Ramona then rented a small office in a mini shopping center in May, 1988, and began operating as The Expectant Parent Center (EPC). She subsequently moved into a slightly larger facility in the same shopping center.

Nature and Growth of Services

The Expectant Parent Center provided childbirth preparation and instruction to expectant parents through four separate classes, as follows:

Source: This case was prepared by Steve R. Hardy and Professor Philip M. Van Auken of Baylor University.

1. Childbirth preparation at $45 per couple (six instructional sessions).
2. Prenatal hygienics and orientation at $20 per couple (two sessions).
3. C-section at $50 per couple (five sessions).
4. Prenatal and postpartum exercises at $25 per couple (five sessions).

Ramona shared instructional duties with two other registered nurses (RNs), who were compensated on the basis of number of teaching contact hours and class size.

The Center had experienced steady growth in enrollments despite lack of advertising. Ramona commented, "We doubled enrollment from May, 1988, to January, 1989. Between January and August of 1989, we doubled once again, peaking at 35 couples per month. Enrollment figures for the last quarter of 1989 averaged 33 couples per month."

Potential Demand

Ramona felt that the Center had only scratched the surface of demand for childbirth education in the Scranton area. She said:

> For a city with more than 100,000 people, I know we could be doing a great deal more business than we are. I have been so busy over the last year with teaching and managerial duties that I really haven't had much time for growth planning. However, I feel that we offer a service very much in demand by enlightened couples. There's no reason

why we can't continue to grow at a healthy pace. We'll need larger facilities and more teachers, but that will all come in time.

Marketing Issues

Ramona characterized her marketing strategy as a "bewildering bundle of unanswered questions and unstated assumptions." In particular, she was confused about pricing and advertising. She claimed:

> I just don't know what the market will bear in paying for prenatal education. I'm not even sure what the market is here in Scranton—to whom I should target my services.
>
> Only two hospitals in town offer alternative childbirth education, and they do it for $25 for two sessions. However, their classes are typically overcrowded, poorly taught, and offered only sporadically. There is no doubt that most expectant couples are willing to pay for better instruction, but I just don't know how high they are willing to go. Right now I'm pricing pretty much at breakeven, at least from the looks of my latest profit-and-loss statement. Now that the business has established itself locally, I want to start turning a decent profit. Prices will definitely have to go up, but I just don't know how far.
>
> Neither am I sure how to best market my services. Obviously our clients are fairly well educated and somewhat affluent, or they wouldn't be interested in paying for first-class prenatal care. Beyond this reference point, however, my customer profile is fuzzy. If I had a better feel for which people are most interested in The Expectant Parent Center, I would know how to promote and diversify my services better.

Product Line

In addition to its four areas of childbirth instruction, the Center sold a limited line of child-care books, equipment, and educational toys. Included in the products inventory was a back massager invented by Ramona to aid mothers during labor. She explained:

> The massager helps the mother to relax during labor and minimizes muscle spasms in and around the back. The thing has a simple design consisting of a handle with two attached wooden doorknobs. When rolled up and down the back, the wooden wheels greatly counteract muscle tension.
>
> I subcontract out the manufacturing at a cost of $2.40 a unit. I sell them at the Center for $7.00, and they go like hotcakes. I'm currently in the process of getting a manufacturer's rep to circulate them at medical trade shows. He thinks they have national potential if properly marketed.

Competitive Strength

Ramona summed up her perceived competitive edge as follows:

> The Expectant Parent Center offers the very finest in childbirth education, presented with tender loving care. We have good facilities, top-notch instructors, auxiliary products, and an affordable price. Given the right marketing, the Center's growth should really explode. To use a bad pun, we're really in a growth business!

Questions

1. Evaluate Ramona Caliban's pricing concerns and her firm's name in the light of consumers' perceptions of marketing stimuli. Recommend an appropriate pricing strategy.

2. What social and cultural influences may impact the demand for Ramona's services?

3. What types of social power can Ramona use if she begins to promote her services more actively? Be specific. Give an example.

4. How important do you think opinion leadership would be in "selling" Ramona's services? Why?

5. Would you recommend that Ramona continue to pursue the marketing of auxiliary products through the Center? Why or why not?

CASE 12

The Jordan Construction Account
Extending credit and collecting receivables

Bob McFarland was the president and principal stockholder of Iowa Tractor Supply Company, a farm and construction equipment distributor located in Marshalltown, IA. The firm employed 27 persons, and in 1988 sales and net profit after taxes reached all-time highs of $3.4 million and $81,500, respectively. The ending net worth for 1988 was slightly in excess of $478,000.

Bob was highly gratified by these figures as 1988 was the first full year since he had appointed Barry Stockton as general manager. Although the company had been in operation since 1957, it had prospered only from the time Bob had purchased it in 1969. Having been a territorial sales manager for the John Deere Company, he was able to obtain that account for Iowa Tractor, and it typically contributed two-thirds or more of the annual sales volume. After struggling successfully for 10 years to build Iowa Tractor into a profitable firm, he decided that it was time to take things a little easier. Accordingly, he promoted Barry and delegated many of his day-to-day duties to him. Fortunately, Barry seemed to do an outstanding job, and during the summer of 1989, Bob felt secure enough to spend six weeks in Europe with his wife.

One day shortly after Bob returned to work, he looked up from his desk and saw

Source: This case was prepared by John E. Schoen, Waco, TX.

his accountant, Marvin Richter, approaching with several ledger cards in his hand. Marvin entered the office, carefully closed the door, and began to speak earnestly. Marvin said:

> Mr. McFarland, I think you should look at these accounts receivable, particularly Jordan Construction. I've been telling Barry to watch out for Jordan for two months, but he just says they're good for it eventually. I got the latest Dun & Bradstreet monthly report today, which didn't look very good, so I've called Standifer Equipment in Ames and the Caterpillar branch at Cedar Rapids. Jordan seems to have run up some pretty good bills with both of them, and Carter at Standifer said some of the contractors in Des Moines think that the two jobs Jordan got on Interstate 80 are just too big for them to handle. If Jordan can't finish those jobs, we are going to be in trouble! Carter says they're probably going to put them on C.O.D. and call in the rental equipment.

Bob examined the data for a few minutes, asked Marvin several questions before dismissing him, and then summoned Barry to his office. The following dialogue took place between Bob and Barry:

Bob: Barry, I've just been looking over the sheets on Jordan and the amount really scares me. Apparently they are over 90 days on nearly $21,000, between 30 and 90 days on another $17,000, and the total due is more than $45,000. Payments on their account have been dropping off since April, and last month they barely covered the interest on the amount outstanding.

Barry: I know, Bob, I've been over to talk to old man Jordan twice in the last three weeks. He admits they are having some trouble with those jobs on the Interstate, but he claims it is only temporary. I hate to push him too hard because he has bought a lot of equipment from us over the years.

Bob: That's right, Barry, but we're talking about $45,000! At this rate, we'll soon have more money in Jordan's business than he does! I'm not so sure we shouldn't put Jordan on C.O.D. until he makes some substantial payments on their account.

Barry: I don't think so, Bob! Old man Jordan has a real mean streak, and the first time I went over there he really cussed me out for even questioning his account. He reminded me that he had been a good customer for more than 10 years, and he threatened to cut us off if we put any pressure on him.

Bob: Yes, but you've heard that before, Barry. Here we are contributing capital to his business involuntarily; we never get a share of his profits if he succeeds, but we sure get a share of the losses if he goes "belly-up." Barry, I don't want any $45,000 losses!

Barry: Well, I won't say that Jordan doesn't have some problems, but Harry thinks they'll be all right. It's just that if we put them on C.O.D. or pick up the rental equipment and they make it, I'm sure they'll never spend another dollar in here.

Bob: Harry thinks they'll be O.K.?

Barry: Yes, sir.

Bob: Get Harry in here!

In a few minutes Barry returned with Harry Reiser, the sales manager for Iowa Tractor. The following dialogue took place between Bob and Harry:

Harry: Barry says you wanted to talk to me?

Bob: That's right, Harry. We've just been discussing Jordan Construction, and I'd like to get any information you have on them.

Harry: Well, they're pretty good customers, of course. I rented them two tractor-backhoes last month. There are some rumors about their Interstate jobs, but I don't think there is much to it because Jordan was talking about buying a couple of crawler tractors last Friday. I think we have a good chance to get those crawlers if that joker over at Ames doesn't sell his below cost.

Bob: Just a minute. You rented them some backhoes last month?

Harry: Yes, sir, two model 310-A's.

Bob: How much are we getting for those units?

Harry: $1,400 a month each, and I think we have a good chance to convert them to a sale if Jordan gets six months' rent into them.

Bob: Did you check with anybody before you put those units out with Jordan?

Harry: Well, I think I asked Barry. No, I think he was busy that day. I'm really not certain, but Jordan Construction is one of our best accounts, isn't it?

Bob: That's what we are trying to determine, Harry. Did you know that their accounts receivable is over $45,000?

Harry: No! That's great! I knew we'd really been selling them. I'm sure those rumors. . . .

Bob: And did you know that $38,000 of the $45,000 is past due and that $21,000 is over 90 days?

Harry: Oh!

Then Bob turned to Barry and said:

Barry, I think we've established what Harry knows about Jordan. Why don't we get Marvin in here and see what information he has. Then I think the four of us need to decide the best approach to getting as much of our money back as soon as possible.

Questions

1. Evaluate the quality of the information provided Bob McFarland by each of his subordinates.
2. Evaluate the alternatives in solving the Jordan situation.
3. What action should Bob take regarding the Jordan account?
4. How could Bob improve the credit and collections procedure of Iowa Tractor to minimize problems of this nature?
5. Evaluate the performance of Marvin Richter, Barry Stockton, and Harry Reiser in handling the Jordan account. Do the circumstances warrant any type of disciplinary action?

CASE 13

Mitchell Interiors
Developing a promotional strategy

Joyce Mitchell, age 38 and married for 20 years, was a native Texan with two children. Her husband Joe, age 40, had recently taken a 20-year retirement from his firefighter's job in Dallas, TX. Together, Joyce and Joe operated an interior decorating business located on North Main Street in Corsicana, TX, a town of approximately 25,000 people.

Joyce's Background

During her early years of marriage, Joyce tried several jobs but was mainly a housewife. She was not content at being a housewife because, as she said, "I have a tendency to get everything done. I'm usually a pretty good organizer, and I just didn't feel fulfilled." When her children were older, she went back to school to pursue a home economics degree. During this time, she accepted a kindergarten teaching job at a private school.

Joyce soon found out she was not cut out to be a teacher. In her words, "I cannot train people. You know how some people play piano by ear—well, I'm that way. I feel I know how to do something, so why shouldn't you? So, teaching was frustrating to me." About this time, Joe and Joyce decided to move south of Dallas into the country. Joyce happily gave up her teaching.

Joe and Joyce decided to personally build their house on the land they purchased in Navarro County about 12 miles west of Corsicana. Therefore, the first year after Joyce had left teaching, she was busy helping with the construction project. "If I wasn't busy with a hammer and nails, wallpaper, or helping the plumber, I was running back and forth to Corsicana picking out interior decorations."

Working for a Large Chain

Joyce began helping her friends with their decorating. A large chain store in Corsicana was a place Joyce would go for her decorating purchases. The store manager was always impressed by the well-organized clippings and folders that she would bring into the store. One day the manager offered Joyce an opportunity to work with the store in a newly created interior decorating job. This chain was just getting into this type of business activity. Joyce was not interested at that time because she had enrolled for 18 credit hours at a local college. The manager persisted, "I've been watching you for four months, and I know you are what I need." Finally, Joyce consented to work on Saturdays beginning in December after the semester concluded. The manager agreed, and Joyce continued for two months under this arrangement. Then, in February, she began working full time and set up the interior design department. During the next five years, she was highly successful and reached the point where she was earning more than $1,500 a month from salary and commissions. For the Corsicana area, this was a high income and an excellent supplement to Joe's salary.

One day Joyce realized she was "working around the clock for another company." She would get up at 5 A.M. to figure bids, report to the store at 8 A.M., oversee installations, and then come home to figure more bids at night. "I really had too many clients," she recalled. She was overloaded and uncomfortable with carrying heavy carpet samples and wallpaper samples in and out of clients' houses. The weight of these samples was also wearing on her personal car. Finally, she requested a company van to carry these samples. The request was received favorably, but the company never did buy the van.

Joyce was also being asked to train interior decorators from other stores in the chain organization. "I was also getting behind in my other work. It was a nice compliment from the store, but I got to looking at it and decided they would have to compensate me or get me some help. I decided to resign." Later, Joyce was told the company was about to promote her to regional supervisor. This would have meant she would be teaching even more, something she didn't enjoy. Joyce decided, "I like decorating because that's my talent. That's the talent God gave me, so I'm going to stay with it."

Beginning Her Own Business

Since the lack of a van to transport decorating samples to clients' homes was a key issue in Joyce's departure from the chain store, Joe and Joyce decided to begin their own business with a used Dodge Motor Home—thus, Mitchell Interiors was born. The business began smoothly. All of Joyce's suppliers were eager to help because they had observed her success with the large chain store. She had no trouble opening accounts with them because they knew she could sell.

After nine months, the van became crowded. Joyce told Joe, "If we are going to do this, let's do it big." So they bought a 28-foot Winnebago and Joyce personally designed a plush interior. Joe built the interior, and they had a decorating studio on wheels. "The type of clients I want need to see what you can do the minute they step into your place," Joyce commented. "I want them to think, 'If she can do this to a van, she can do my home to please me.'"

Opening the Mitchell Interiors Store

The Mitchell Interiors store was located in Corsicana and occupied 2,000 square feet of store and warehouse space. The store allowed for increased display of many items that were also for sale to walk-in customers. The location was leased and had three neighbor tenants: Prestige Realty, Clint's Jewelers, and Pat Walker's (a reducing salon). All four businesses catered to the same type of clientele.

Joyce still used the Winnebago for travel to clients' homes. Business had been good. In fact, Joyce said, "I am so busy, I cannot take everything that comes in off the street. The first question I ask is: Have you been recommended? I cannot physically get to all the potential business. Therefore, I consider only those jobs I know I can get. I am really wasting time going out to bid on a job if they don't know whether they want me to do it or not."

Joyce was a strong believer in bringing the personal touch to a business. She always tried to bring this to her clients. Even Joe, who installed all drapes and supervised carpet installation, believed in the personal touch. Joyce said, "I hope our business never gets so big that we cannot personally oversee all our jobs."

The Product/Service Mix

Contract sales provided about 75 percent of the total business volume of Mitchell Interiors. Contract sales were those made to interior decorating clients—individual homeowners or business owners. Joyce occasionally contracted with builders for the decorating of new houses. Recently, however, because of high interest rates, there was little speculative building in the area. The main products that sold in contract jobs were carpet, vinyl floor covering, draperies, and wallpaper. Drapery sales constituted 60 percent of the contract sales, and Joyce was happy with this situation because of the higher markup associated with draperies. Since competition was much greater in carpeting and vinyls, these products produced a much lower markup. The remaining 25 percent of the business volume came from in-store sales of tables, lamps, ceiling fans, and other decorative accessories.

Joyce saw her customers as upper-middle class and upper class, 35 to 50 years old, both in Corsicana and in surrounding towns.

Promotional Practices

Most of Joyce's promotion had been accomplished through the recommendations of satisfied customers. Customers who had known Joyce when she worked for the chain store recommended her to their friends. When Mitchell Interiors was initially "garaged" at Joe and Joyce's home, few people who had a cursory interest would call because of the long-distance telephone charges. Joyce would advertise such things as a drapery sale in the newspaper or on some other special occasion such as Mother's Day. Joyce also used radio advertising on the local FM country-western radio station. Joyce had done all the design work for the firm's stationery and for print advertising.

Joyce used direct mail advertising, too. She felt very strongly that this was an effective medium for her business. These mail-outs were primarily a reminder that her store was there and that she was available. The mailing lists came mainly from an internal file of satisfied customers. This file was updated to remove customers who had not visited the store after about three mail-outs. Additional names were solicited from employees, the Corsicana telephone directory, new residents in the more elite parts of town, and listings of doctors and lawyers.

Yearly promotional expenditures were planned by Joyce at the beginning of the year when the master budget was finalized. Joyce forecasted the expenses and the sales needed to meet these expenses. Break-even sales were around $20,000 per month. In the master budget Joyce included an advertising budget because she believed that advertising was important. Last year, she allowed approximately $300 of the total budget per month for promotion on newspaper advertising, radio, direct mail, business gifts, and specialty advertising. Most of her promotion emphasized accessory items. Joyce reasoned, "I want people to come in and buy accessories. I want people to get used to having a store like this in Corsicana."

The Store Employees

The business had only one full-time employee and four part-time helpers. According to Joyce, "Joe is the only person besides me who gets outside the business and works with clients." Joyce wanted to remain as the designer-buyer for the store but was willing to take on another designer. She was also looking for someone to manage the accessories area at the store. She wanted the manager to pre-interview other employees, but she wished to make the final hiring decisions.

Questions

1. What other types of promotion would "fit" Joyce Mitchell's customers?
2. Evaluate the promotional practices of Mitchell Interiors.
3. Should Joyce continue to advertise when she already has more business than she can handle? Why or why not?
4. How can Mitchell Interiors grow and also retain the personal touch that is so important to Joyce?

CASE 14

Litter Ridder
Finding the best distribution channel for a new product

It is often said that necessity is the mother of invention. Sometimes unpleasant household chores can be that necessity. Such was the case with Don and Marsha Hostetler. Don and Marsha liked cats, but they hated cleaning the cat litter box.

Don decided there must be a better way. In 1986, he developed "Litter Ridder," a disposable cat litter box. The cat owner need never see or smell cat litter again. He or she could merely throw out the old box and install a new one each week. The box was made of two cardboard pieces. The bottom piece held the cat litter, and the top piece popped up to form a covering over the litter. The cat could then easily go in and out of the enclosed litter box.

Don's architectural drafting background helped him not only to design the product but also to design and build a small assembly line to produce Litter Ridder. Marsha proved to be a hard-nosed negotiator with suppliers, and this helped to minimize materials costs.

Don and Marsha needed assistance in two primary areas: finance and marketing. They found three local investors to provide the initial financial support. One was an attorney. The other two (father and son) were owners of a professional

services firm. Don said the investors were picked because they made the first offer to finance the business. None of the investors had marketing expertise. The financial support gave Don and Marsha the resources they needed to set up production facilities, begin production, and develop a marketing strategy.

Four major grocery chains operated in the St. Louis area: Schnucks, Dierbergs, National, and Shop 'N Save. Schnucks and Dierbergs stores were upscale stores patronized by affluent customers. Shop 'N Save was a discount grocer drawing lower-income customers. National was positioned in the middle in terms of customer appeal.

Litter Ridder was sold in the upscale Schnucks and Dierbergs stores throughout the greater St. Louis area. In order to get Litter Ridder into the stores, Don approached the respective buyers and showed them a sample of Litter Ridder. Both the Schnucks and Dierbergs buyers readily agreed to put Litter Ridder on their shelves. There were no wholesalers or food brokers involved in the process. For Schnucks, Don delivered Litter Ridder to a central warehouse, while for Dierbergs, he delivered to each store.

Marketing was not a high priority. A total of eight ads were placed with local newspapers. One was placed with the *St. Louis Post-Dispatch*, four with *The Riverfront Times* (a free weekly paper distributed throughout the metropolitan St. Louis area), and three were placed with the

Source: This case was prepared by Philip R. Carpenter. He gratefully acknowledges the support of the St. Louis University Small Business Development Center and Don Kirchgessner of the St. Louis County Enterprise Center.

Ladue News. (Ladue is the wealthiest suburb in the St. Louis area.) The company was also featured in 13 public relations articles appearing in the *Post-Dispatch* and suburban newspapers.

Don, Marsha, and the other investors intended to advertise on television, but funds ran low before the television advertising could be developed. Radio advertising had not been developed. They believed that Litter Ridder was a product that could be advertised best by using visual media.

The retail price of Litter Ridder was $3.85 per box. Competition included national and generic brands of cat litter such as the following:

Brand	Bag Size	Price
Tidy Cat 3	25 pounds	$3.50
Fresh Step	16 pounds	$4.59
Generic	25 pounds	$1.79–2.29

A 25-pound bag would typically last three or four weeks (changing the litter once a week), while Litter Ridder would last one week. Customers who bought Litter Ridder were not minimizing their costs. Rather, they were buying convenience in changing litter and avoiding the unpleasant sights and odors related to ordinary litter.

In early 1989, in-store demonstrations were held. The stores decided which personnel would demonstrate the product; Don and Marsha had no say in this. However, they did send an instruction sheet on how to present Litter Ridder. The results from demonstrations were discouraging. Several customers made negative remarks regarding the product. Discount coupons were offered, but the response was low. As if these problems weren't enough, one of the product demonstrators was quite negative toward Litter Ridder during the demonstration.

Sales were increasing slowly. See Exhibit C14–1. (No sales were recorded in May because the stores made large purchases in April in anticipation of increased sales after the in-store demonstrations.) Sales volume was still well below the break-even point. Don thought the price might be too high. He spent time redesigning the box and was able to reduce the cost of production significantly.

After current inventory was used up, Don planned to begin production of the new box. He would pass on the cost savings to the supermarkets. There was a positive response from the supermarket buyers. They said they would in turn pass on the savings by reducing Litter Ridder's price. Don started the lower pricing in June.

Don thought that by expanding their market they could increase sales. Visiting a large regional grocer in Indianapolis, he found himself unprepared for the detailed questions concerning pricing, delivery, food brokers, discounting, and couponing asked by the grocer's buyers.

By June 1989, the investors were becoming restless. While the father and son were willing to be patient and stick it out, the lawyer was not. He wanted out, and he persuaded the other two to join him. The investors had been supporting the business on a modified pay-as-you-go plan. They each made an equal initial investment. When this sum was gone, they paid the monthly expenses of the business. They stopped paying the monthly expenses at the end of June. Their total in-

Exhibit C14-1 Litter Ridder Sales History

Sales	December 88 Dollars	Units	January 89 Dollars	Units	February 89 Dollars	Units	March 89 Dollars	Units	April 89 Dollars	Units	May 89 Dollars	Units	June 89 Dollars	Units
A. Schnucks	$423	144	$846	288	$1058	360	$1058	360	$2328	792	$0	0	$1332	720
B. Dierbergs	$133	43	$151	49	$231	75	$408	131	$478	73	$0	0	$204	105
Total	$556	187	$998	337	$1287	435	$1466	491	$2807	829	$0	0	$1536	825

vestment in the corporation was $52,000, which was split evenly among them. Don and Marsha had invested no cash in the business. The agreement was that their share would be 25 percent in event the business was sold.

Don and Marsha believed there was potential for a new investor. Don had been reviewing patent applications for products similar to Litter Ridder. One day he came across one in the local St. Louis area. He called the person, who expressed an interest in providing financial and marketing assistance for Litter Ridder. The discussion had remained at a preliminary stage.

Don and Marsha stopped production in June and planned to sell their three-month backlog. During this time, they planned to make some difficult decisions regarding Litter Ridder's future.

Questions

1. How might this firm's distribution channels be related to its failure to attain a larger sales volume?
2. What distribution channels would be most appropriate for this product?
3. What types of marketing research are needed by this firm? What questions need to be answered?
4. Evaluate their sales and promotional efforts. Suggest types of advertising and advertising media that might be most appropriate.
5. What should the Hostetlers do next?

CASE 15

Burton Walls Electric
Management issues in business growth

"How big should we grow?" That was the question posed by Burton Walls of Burton Walls Electric, a small electrical contracting firm in Seattle. Walls had started the firm with one associate working out of the basement in his home. After 14 years, he had built the business to the $1 million annual revenue level, with 13 employees, projects throughout the metropolitan area and as far as 100 miles away, and $50,000 in profit (not including his own salary).

Since growth to this point had been successful, Walls naturally thought about further expansion. Should he try to make it a bigger small business by shooting for $3 million in revenue and 35 employees? "There's a 'no man's land' between 15 and 25 employees," he explained. "Adding four or five employees would stretch our present staff too far but still not give us enough volume to justify additional management personnel. If we want to grow, we should plan for somewhere between 25 and 50 employees."

Walls had completed a bachelor's degree in business administration before starting the business. However, both he and his associate performed the electrical work in the beginning stages. As the work expanded, Walls devoted more of his time to estimating and eventually devoted all of his time to management of the business. Because of this background, he understood the nature of the work and the concerns of electricians who worked for him. He operated on a non-union ba-

sis and felt that he had developed a very loyal group of employees.

The company's electrical work was varied—60 percent on commercial buildings and 40 percent on residential dwellings. More than half of the residential work was obtained through property management companies rather than through individual homeowners. Typical projects were bid through a general contractor and ranged from a few thousand dollars to $100,000. Usually, these covered the electrical portion of remodeling or tenant upgrade projects. Recently, for example, they had rewired a building to be used as a radio station. The firm also provided repair and maintenance service as needed by individual and commercial customers.

The firm's most recent income statement and balance sheet are shown in Exhibits C15–1 and C15–2. Even though the business is currently successful, profits have fluctuated considerably. The financial results in some recent years have, in fact, been disappointing. This has raised questions about the effectiveness of the managerial control system. As one example, Walls and the firm's CPA discovered a weakness in the accounting for labor cost on specific projects—a weakness that had worked to hold down profits. By following some suggestions of the CPA, the firm was able to remedy that problem and thereby help improve profitability.

Growth should bring increased profits as well as an increase in salary for

Exhibit C15-1   Income Statement

Burton Walls Electric
Annual Income Statement

Revenues		$954,801
Direct costs of revenues:		
Materials	$304,557	
Wages and salaries	220,857	
Other direct costs	108,857	634,271
Indirect costs of revenues		91,554
Gross Profit		$228,976
General and administrative expenses		178,400
NET INCOME		$ 50,576

the owner. With $3 million in revenue, profits should hit the industry average of $90,000 to $110,000. It seemed possible, in fact, that he might do better than the industry average. Throughout the firm's entire existence, Walls had tried to provide excellent service to customers—for example, meeting the needs of contractors to have electricians available at just the time needed to facilitate overall progress on construction. As a result of such reliability, the firm had established a good reputation with general contractors and occasionally obtained contracts on a negotiated bid basis.

Prospects for profitable growth, however, were not without difficulties and dangers. A substantial additional investment would be required. Although the firm used a small computer for accounting and job costing, a much larger computer system and more sophisticated software would be necessary. Also, additional working capital would be needed, because there is typically a 30- to 60-day lag in payment for work that is completed. The following investment requirements were estimated:

Computer system	$ 65,000
Additional trucks	22,000
Additional tools	10,000
Additional working capital	250,000

Overhead salary costs would increase with the addition of two supervisors (approximately $35,000 each), three estimators (approximately $45,000 each), and two clerical positions (approximately $20,000 each). Direct labor cost could be controlled in the event of a business downturn by laying off electricians. It

Exhibit C15–2   Balance Sheet

Burton Walls Electric
Balance Sheet

ASSETS

Current Assets:		
Cash	$ 33,629	
Receivables	190,954	
Inventory	20,000	
Job progress—unbilled	33,459	
Other current assets	3,844	$281,886
Fixed Assets:		
Total fixed assets	$169,809	
Less accumulated depreciation	116,743	53,066
TOTAL ASSETS		$334,952

LIABILITIES AND EQUITY

Current Liabilities:		
Trade accounts payable	$ 23,265	
Deferred income tax	34,450	
Other payables	17,737	$ 75,452
Long-term liabilities		21,752
Total liabilities		$ 97,204
Stockholder's equity		237,748
TOTAL LIABILITIES AND STOCKHOLDER'S EQUITY		$334,952

would be difficult to cut overhead costs quickly, however, in the event of a downturn. Additional borrowing would also be required, and this would increase interest expense substantially. Even so, the expansion should generate additional profits if the firm could operate as well as the average firm in the industry.

Profit margins would be threatened somewhat as the firm started bidding on projects in the $100,000 to $300,000 range. Large contracts of this type attract more bidders and more aggressive competition. Furthermore, Burton Walls Electric would need to price very competitively since it had no "track record" on projects of this size. In the past, the firm had been most successful and earned the best profit margins on contracts between $2,000 and $10,000 and on maintenance work.

Effective control of work operations would also become more difficult. The firm had been reasonably successful in effectively supervising the work of nine electricians. In addition to Walls, who served as general manager, the firm employed one supervisor and one estimator who could also give some supervision of jobs in case of emergency. With a larger scale of operation, control would necessarily become less personal. To some extent, formal systems of control and computer printouts would be needed to replace some of the personal, face-to-face direction that was possible with a smaller group of employees. The question was whether the same efficiency could be realized with more supervisors and a larger administrative structure. Production efficiency required skill in shifting electricians from one project to another and back again according to the demands of each job.

An expanded scope of operation would entail increased risk. In the past, Walls had depended upon his personal investment in commercial rental property to provide stability in the electrical business. The rental property produced a steady income flow and enabled the business to function without difficulty even when the electrical business slackened, as happened occasionally. For example, his outside income enabled him to forego taking his own salary when money was tight and taking it when conditions improved. In all of its years of operation, Burton Walls Electric had never failed to meet a payroll on schedule.

Walls was also concerned with the im-plications of expansion for key employees, who over the years had become a closely-knit group. The present congenial relationships would undoubtedly be altered as personnel were added and additional levels of supervision created. In general, Walls practiced a somewhat participative style of management that invited the input of key personnel. Once a month, for example, he held a breakfast meeting with all employees for open discussion of concerns and business conditions. He realized that these people had a stake in the business that deserved consideration and that their commitment to expansion would be necessary if it was to succeed.

A number of more personal questions were also involved in such a decision. Entrepreneurial motivations are complex, and Walls thought about the extent to which expansion might be merely an "ego trip" in which he sought community respect and recognition by his peers. An expansion would add emotional stress and perhaps take time away from highly valued family activities with his wife and two school-aged children.

Expansion offered opportunities but also entailed costs and risks—the ingredients of any entrepreneurial decision. As Walls pondered the future of Burton Walls Electric, he wanted to make an intelligent decision concerning the best size for the long-run best interests of the business, the employees, and his own family.

Questions

1. How would expansion impact the management process of this firm?
2. Do the firm's present managerial system and resources appear adequate

as a foundation for changes necessitated by expansion? How difficult will it be to adapt the management system to an expanded level of operation?

3. Is Walls's concern for the welfare of employees consistent with the best interests of the business?

4. How should the owner treat the possibility of increased stress and disruption of family time in reaching a decision on expansion?

5. Can or should such an expansion be financed by borrowing? What advantages or risks would this entail?

6. Should this firm expand to the $3 million revenue level?

CASE 16

Central Engineering
How the entrepreneur's managerial practices hampered decision making

Henry and Jami Wolfram, a husband-and-wife team, owned and operated Central Engineering, a heating and air-conditioning firm located in Huntsville, AL. The business prospered during the six years they owned it, and it served both residential and commercial accounts.

Organizational Structure

Henry served as general operations manager. (Exhibit C16–1 shows the simple organization structure of the firm.) As the business grew, more and more responsibility fell on Henry's shoulders. Although Jami assumed some of the burden by act-ing as treasurer and supervising the office work, Henry was personally involved in most of the key decisions. Henry's son, Jeff Wolfram, had started work on an installation crew. Later he moved into the position of estimator-salesman and acted as manager on those occasions when his father was away.

The Bottleneck

An unfortunate consequence of Henry's growing work load was the creation of a bottleneck at the very top of the business. Since he was a key person, his judgment seemed indispensable in many

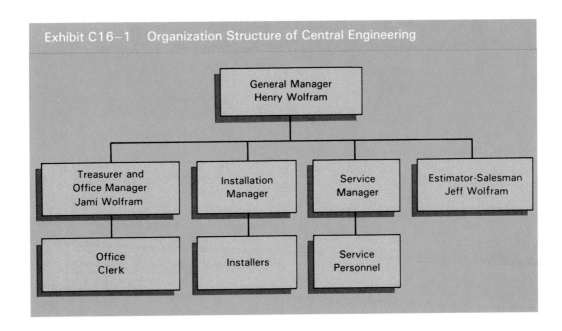

Exhibit C16–1   Organization Structure of Central Engineering

- General Manager
  Henry Wolfram
  - Treasurer and Office Manager
    Jami Wolfram
    - Office Clerk
  - Installation Manager
    - Installers
  - Service Manager
    - Service Personnel
  - Estimator-Salesman
    Jeff Wolfram

actions. As a result, decisions were sometimes delayed while waiting for his attention. Others in the organization sometimes found themselves waiting in line to get a chance to talk with him. And Henry found himself rushed, with insufficient time to think carefully about some aspects of the business. In addition, he would have liked to devote a little more time to family, church, and personal interests.

Review of Customer Billing

One task that required Henry's attention was his personal review of bills before they were sent to customers. When a management consultant asked why this was necessary, the following dialogue took place:

Henry: I really need to take a last look before bills are sent out. For example, on construction jobs there may be additions or extras that were included after we had made the original bid.

Consultant: On regular service calls, is there a similar chance of an error?

Henry: That's right. For instance, maybe the worker has left something off the work order. The worker may say he has done this and this and this, but over here on the material list he has some items that don't match up or that are missing from what he said he's done.

Consultant: Can you tell me how many hours in a day or week are required for this?

Henry: Well, it cuts into a lot of time. This is part of another problem. The office is too open, with Jeff and his customers in the same office with me. I just don't have any place where I can concentrate on this

type of work. I think that, when we get that physical arrangement changed, it will help some.

Consultant: So, how many hours a week does this take?

Henry: Sometimes we stay here at night or come in Saturday to do this. But I suppose it might run 8 or 10 hours a week.

Consultant: Is there anybody else who could do this?

Henry: Well, on service calls Jami can usually spot such discrepancies. She is getting enough experience that she can recognize them.

Consultant: What is Jeff's role? Could he do this?

Henry: He's an estimator and does sales work. He doesn't quite have the experience yet. Well, he might be close to being capable. But he's pretty busy. Also, I have a service manager who could catch a lot of this when the orders are turned in. But he does not manage that carefully. I have a more aggressive manager in installation who is better at catching things like this.

The general theme in Henry's discussion with the management consultant was the difficulty of resolving the time-management problem. Henry recognized the burden this placed on him personally and on the business, but there seemed to be no obvious answer at this stage in the life of the firm.

Review of Accounts Payable

Henry also tried to look over all payments being made on trade accounts payable. His discussion with the management consultant regarding this function ran as follows:

Henry: These payments need to be checked over because we may be charged too much on some bills.

Consultant: How does this happen?

Henry: On particular jobs we may get special pricing. Say I'm working on a bid. I may pick up a phone and say to the supplier, "We need some special pricing. Here's what we're up against, and we need the special pricing to get this job." And if they give us the special pricing, we should pay accordingly.

Consultant: And you can't depend on them to bill you at that special price?

Henry: I don't think it is anything intentional. But they give it to their clerks to bill, and they may overlook the special pricing that was promised. So, if we don't catch it, we would lose it.

Henry's Dilemma

The responsibilities relative to accounts receivable and accounts payable were typical of the overall situation. In many aspects of the business, Henry felt compelled to give his personal attention to the issues and the decisions that needed to be made. In a sense he felt trapped by the very success and work that accompanied the operation of the business. He enjoyed the work, every minute of it, but occasionally he wondered why there was no obvious solution to his dilemma.

Questions

1. Is Henry Wolfram's personal involvement in the various specific aspects of the business necessary, or is it a matter of habit or of simply enjoying doing business that way?
2. What changes would be necessary to extricate Henry from the checking of customer bills before they are mailed?
3. If you were the consultant, what changes would you recommend?

CASE 17

Gibson Mortuary

Personnel problems in a small family business

Gibson Mortuary was founded in 1929 and grew to become one of the best known funeral homes in Tacoma, WA. One of its most persistent problems over the years had been the recruitment and retention of qualified personnel.

Background of the Business

Gibson Mortuary was a family business headed by Ethel Gibson, who owned 51 percent of the stock. As an active executive in the business, Ethel had become recognized as a community leader. She had served in various civic endeavors, had been elected to the city council, and had served one term as mayor.

The mortuary had built a reputation as one of the finest funeral homes in the state. The quality of its service over the years had been such that it continued to serve families over several generations. While large corporations had bought up many mortuaries in recent years, Gibson Mortuary continued to remain competitive as an independent family firm—a "family serving families." Funeral homes in general had become the target of public criticism, and books such as *The American Way of Death* had reflected adversely on this type of business. Nevertheless, Gibson Mortuary had withstood this threat by its determined, consistent effort to provide the best possible customer service. In its most recent year it had conducted 375 funerals, which placed it in the top 9 percent of all funeral homes in the nation when measured in terms of volume of business.

Ethel's son, Max Gibson, had entered the business after completing military service and had become general manager of the firm. He was a licensed funeral director and embalmer. Both mother and son were active in the day-to-day management of the firm.

Recruitment and Retention Problem

Perhaps the most difficult problem facing Gibson Mortuary was the recruitment and retention of qualified personnel. The image of the industry made it difficult to attract the right caliber of young people as employees. Many individuals were repelled by the idea of working for an organization in which they daily and personally faced the fact of death. In addition, the challenges raised by social critics reflected poorly on the industry and conveyed to many youth the impression that funeral homes were profiteering on the misery of those who suffered bereavement.

One source of employees was walk-in applicants. Also, Gibson Mortuary worked through sales representatives who sold throughout that geographical area. They often knew of people who might be considering a change in their career.

As a small business, Gibson Mortuary also presented fewer total opportunities than a larger company or even a funeral home chain. The fact that it was a family business also suggested to prospective employees that top management would remain in the family. It was apparent to all that the two top management spots were family positions. However, Ethel and Max were the only family members employed, so there was some hope for the future for nonfamily employees. Max was 49 years old.

Training Problem

Gibson Mortuary used two licensed embalmers—Max and another individual. The pressure of other managerial work made it difficult for Max to devote sufficient time to this type of work. To become a licensed embalmer, one had to attend mortuary college and serve a two-year apprenticeship. (Mortuary science programs were part of some community-college programs.) The apprenticeship could be served either prior to or after the college training. Gibson Mortuary advised most individuals to take the apprenticeship prior to the college training so that they could evaluate their own aptitude for this type of career.

Gibson Mortuary preferred its personnel to be competent in all phases of the business. The work involved not only embalming, but also making funeral arrangements with families and conducting funerals and burials. However, some part-time employees assisted only in conducting funerals and did not perform preparatory work.

Personal Qualifications for Employment

All employees who met the public and had any part in the funeral service needed the ability to interact with others in a friendly and relaxed but dignified manner. The personalities of some individuals were much better suited to this than those of others. Ethel described one of the problem personalities she had encountered at Gibson Mortuary as follows:

> In the first place, he didn't really look the part for our community here. He was short and stocky, too heavy for his height. His vest was too short, and he wore a big cowboy buckle! Can't you see that going over big in a mortuary! He wanted to stand at the door and greet people as they came. We do furnish suits, so we tried to polish off some of the rough edges.
>
> But he was still too aggressive. He became upset with me because I wouldn't get him any business cards immediately. One day I had to send him to the printers, and he came back and said, "While I was there, I just told them to make some cards for me. I'll pay for them myself." I said to him, "Willis, you go right back there and cancel that order! When you are eligible for cards, I'll have them printed for you." We couldn't have him at that point scattering his cards with our name all over town.

Ethel also discussed a young applicant who made an impressive appearance but lacked polish. His grammar was so poor that he lacked the minimal skills necessary for any significant contact with the public.

Two characteristics of employment that discouraged some applicants were the irregular hours and the constant interruptions that were part of the life of a funeral director. A funeral director might start to do one thing and then find it necessary to switch over to another, more urgent matter. Then there was the requirement for some night and weekend duty in the work schedule.

Solving the Personnel Problems

Although Gibson Mortuary had not completely solved its need for qualified personnel, the business was working at it. While waiting for the right person to come along, Gibson Mortuary had started another apprentice prior to any college training. In addition, it was following up on a former apprentice who was attending mortuary college and working during summer vacations. The business also employed a part-time minister as an extra driver. In these ways Gibson Mortuary was getting along, but it was still seeking to do a better job in personnel staffing.

Questions

1. Evaluate the personnel problems facing this firm. Which of these appears most serious?
2. How can Gibson Mortuary be more aggressive in recruitment? How can it make such a career attractive to applicants?
3. Does the fact that Gibson Mortuary is a family firm create a significant problem in recruitment? How can the firm overcome any problems that may exist in this area?
4. Assuming you are the proper age to consider such employment, what is the biggest question or problem you would have in considering employment with Gibson Mortuary? What, if anything, might the Gibsons do to deal with that type of question or problem?

CASE 18

Delco Machines, Limited (A)
Providing adequate production facilities

Introduction

Delco Machines, Limited, incorporated in 1972 for the purpose of designing and manufacturing special machinery, tools, and gauges for a variety of automotive and automotive-related customers. Located in Centerport, NY, the firm's facility includes 6,700 square feet of manufacturing and 600 square feet of engineering and office space.

Delco's first seven years of business had brought it many solid repeat customers including Ford, Chevrolet, and Carborundum (see Exhibit C18–1). Stan Crow, manager for Delco, commented that "breaking into the tough automotive tool market was very difficult and that this accomplishment should demonstrate the skill and abilities of the Delco team."

According to Mr. Crow, problems began when the company's landlord announced that it would not renew Delco's lease. Delco Machines shared a building facility with another manufacturer, which was also the owner of the building. Apparently the landlord's business was also expanding, and it made the decision not to renew the lease in order to allow its own expansion. This gave Delco approximately six months to find a new location.

Source: This case was prepared by Professor Roger H. Ford of James Madison University.

Providing Suitable Manufacturing Space

Planning efforts for Delco determined that its new building should include an expansion to a total of 12,500 square feet, 1,875 square feet of which would be for office and engineering and the rest for manufacturing. It was felt that this increase of 70 percent would allow the company to grow for several years. Mr. Crow stated that the present plant was operating at nearly full capacity. Also included within this space would be a 20-foot clear height crane bay to house a new hoist to be purchased for $150,000.

Delco estimated the total cost of the new facility, including land, building, all mechanicals, the $150,000 hoist, and miscellaneous, would be $400,000. After an unsuccessful attempt to secure a government loan, Mr. Crow approached the Mercantile Bank and Trust to help Delco sell $400,000 worth of bonds. Crow and his staff put a great deal of effort into preparing a prospectus and other documents. Unfortunately, the bank advised Delco that selling bonds for such a relatively new and small firm would be next to impossible and impracticable.

[It must be assumed that, since a long-term bank loan was never discussed by Crow, the alternative was either not possible (perhaps due to Delco's poor financial condition) or not attractive to Delco due

795

Exhibit C18-1   Delco Machines, Limited, Customer List

A.A.I. Corp (Aircraft Armaments Inc.) Baltimore, MD	Harrison Radiator Division, GMC Lockport, NY
ACCO Chain (American Chain & Cable) Detroit, MI	J&A Keller Machine Co., Inc. Buffalo, NY
Bayex, Inc. Albion, NY	Loud Wendel Division of Skil Saw Middleport, NY
Carborundum Co. Coated Abrasives Division Niagara Falls, NY	Moore Business Forms Niagara Falls and Grand Island, NY
Chevrolet—Tonawanda Motor Division, GMC Tonawanda, NY	S.B. Whistler Products Specifications Division Batavia, NY
Chevrolet—Buffalo Buffalo Plant Buffalo, NY	Pulsafeeder Corporation Rochester, NY
E & M Division Borden Foods Middleport, NY	Rando Machine Macedon, NY
FMC Corporation Middleport, NY	Raymond Corporation Greene, NY
Ferranti-Packard Ltd. St. Catharines, Ontario and Dunkirk, NY	Guterl Steel (Simonds Steel) Lockport, NY
Ford Motor Stamping Buffalo, NY	UCC—Linde Division Tonawanda, NY
GMC of Canada Limited St. Catharines, Ontario	Garlock Corporation Palmyra, NY

to interest rates and other terms available.]

With only five months remaining on the lease, Mr. Crow contacted his C.P.A. firm, Peters and Company, for any suggestions the partners might have. After care-

ful consideration, a C.P.A. on the Delco account indicated that another client, Hudson Builders, Inc., might be interested in assisting Delco with a development project.

Hudson Builders, Inc., established in

1947, is a general contractor and real estate development firm that engages primarily in erecting prefabricated steel
buildings. Hudson buildings, generally
owned by Hudson and leased to others,
are scattered throughout a several-
hundred-mile area in the Northeastern
United States. Tenants of Hudson buildings include a wide variety of commercial,
industrial, and institutional businesses
and organizations.

Delco's Contact
with Hudson Builders

In September, 1979, Stan Crow contacted Hudson Builders and asked James
Hudson, vice-president of Hudson, to prepare a lease proposal for Delco Machines.
He provided Hudson with Delco's specifications for the new facility. Crow wanted a
per-month cost for a 15-year net lease, with
one 5-year renewal option and first right of
refusal for a second option. Hudson was to
provide a turnkey construction operation,
furnishing all financing, including the purchase of a lot selected by Delco. Delco required that the entire project be completed in mid-January, 1980, to give Delco
ample time to move without disturbing operations.

The Decision

Hudson's analysis of the total project
costs resulted in a proposed rental fee of
$6,238.69 per month. Hudson was then
faced with the question of whether or not
to rely on Delco's ability to meet such a substantial monthly rental obligation. Exhibit
C18–2 shows Delco's comparative balance
sheets for 1977 and 1978. One change from
1977 to 1978 was a decrease in stockholders' equity by 22 percent. Total liabilities

also increased 27 percent, while total assets
decreased over 7 percent.

Exhibit C18–3 shows income statements for Delco for the same years. Although a profit was shown in 1977, net in-
come/sales was under 2 percent. Return on
equity was 5.5 percent. 1978 showed an operating loss corresponding with the 1978
decrease in stockholders' equity.

In spite of the evidence accumulating
against the union with Delco, as procedure requires, Hudson prepared a modified cash flow analysis for Delco based on
pro-forma profit and loss information
provided by Mr. Crow. Exhibit C18–4
shows a cash projection for Delco Machines' first year of operation in the new
facility. According to these calculations, it
did not appear that Delco would be able
to meet this large rental obligation. Hudson discussed his analysis with the Peters
and Company accountant on the case,
who concurred that his client was not financially strong enough for a $6,238.69
commitment.

James Hudson informed Stan Crow
that first, the rental required to pay for
such a project would be $6,238.69, and
second, considering Delco's financial position, Hudson Builders, Inc. would not
be willing to enter into a lease agreement.
Hudson went on to explain that the combination of (a) high rental arising from total costs and high interest rates and (b) the
high tax and insurance expense associated with such a plant (and relative tax
rates of the area) made the project impossible to undertake.

Counterproposal

Disappointed and nearing despera-
tion, Mr. Crow insisted that the project be

Exhibit C18–2 Balance Sheet, Delco Machines, Limited

ASSETS

Current assets:	**1978**	**1977**
Cash	$ 5,985	$ 28,974
Accounts receivable	29,135	12,943
Inventories		
Material	2,547	2,237
Work in process.	8,355	13,130
Prepaid expenses	1,495	3,040
Total current assets	47,517	60,324
Plant and equipment:		
Machinery and equipment	108,724	95,701
Furniture and fixtures	2,050	2,050
Vehicles	800	800
	$111,574	$98,551
Less accumulated depreciation	55,643	47,355
Net plant and equipment	55,931	51,196
Other assets:		
Organization expenses.	95	95
Less accumulated amortization	95	84
	0	11
TOTAL ASSETS.	$103,448	$111,531

LIABILITIES AND STOCKHOLDERS' EQUITY

Current liabilities:	**1978**	**1977**
Notes payable, bank.	$ 31,300	$ 17,968
Accounts payable	8,671	7,047
Accrued expenses.	3,169	3,629
Income taxes payable	250	432
Total current liabilities	43,390	29,076
Long-term debt:		
Notes payable officers.	0	5,000
Total long-term liabilities	0	5,000
Total liabilities.	43,390	34,076
Stockholders' equity:		
Common stock	40,000	40,000
Retained earnings	20,058	37,455
Total stockholders' equity	60,058	77,455
TOTAL LIABILITIES AND		
STOCKHOLDERS' EQUITY	$103,448	$111,531

Exhibit C18-3 Statement of Income

Revenue:	1978	1977
Product sales	$264,308	$224,100
Cost of goods sold	$235,194	$183,561
Gross margin	29,114	40,539
Expenses:		
Selling, general and administrative	41,687	29,505
Interest.	4,337	4,728
Depreciation and amortization	237	245
Total expense.	46,261	34,478
Operating income	(17,147)	6,061
Other income	0	14
Income before taxes on income.	(17,147)	6,075
Provision for taxes on income	250	1,812
NET INCOME	($17,397)	$ 4,263

Note to Statement of Income

SCHEDULE OF COST OF GOODS SOLD

	1978	1977
Beginning Inventory	$ 15,367	$ 9,500
Materials and supplies	51,942	45,211
Subcontract.	14,041	7,506
Salary, wages, and benefits	124,319	102,425
Repairs and maintenance.	8,250	4,587
Freight and trucking	4,073	3,205
Rent	7,638	6,834
Utilities	5,800	4,645
Insurance	3,412	3,412
Rework	3,192	3,464
Depreciation	8,062	8,139
Goods available for sale	246,096	198,928
Less: Ending inventory	10,902	15,367
COST OF GOODS SOLD	$235,194	$183,561

given another shot. He felt confident that the citizens and officials in Centerport did not want to see Delco liquidate. With this in mind, he suggested that Delco apply for tax exemption for commercial business or industrial real property. Crow also believed he could come up with better insurance rates.

Exhibit C18-4 Cash Flow Projection

Quarter Ending	Feb. 1980	May 1980	Aug. 1980	Nov. 1980
Beginning cash . . .	$16,100.00	($5,477.38)	($21,293.45)	($36,509.52)
Net income from operations	4,000.00	6,100.00	6,800.00	6,800.00
Depreciation	2,500.00	2,600.00	2,500.00	3,500.00
Cash flow available for building expense . .	$22,600.00	$3,222.62	($11,993.45)	($26,209.52)
Rent	$12,477.38	$18,716.07	$ 18,716.07	$ 18,716.07
*Building expenses	15,600.00	5,800.00	5,800.00	1,900.00
ENDING CASH . . .	($5,477.38)	($21,293.45)	($36,509.52)	($46,825.59)

*Includes all taxes and insurance

In keeping with the spirit of austerity, several other sacrifices were agreed upon: elimination of the crane hoist and, therefore, the 20-foot crane bay; reduction of the office area from 1,875 square feet to 1,000 square feet; a modest reduction in the manufacturing area; elimination of final landscaping; and reduction of overall ceiling heights by 18 inches. This resulted in a substantial reduction in the total project costs. The new rental figure that Delco would need to pay was $3,596.94 per month.

The Outcome

Exhibit C18–5 shows an adjusted cash flow projection for the first year in the new facility, using the new rental and ad-justed for anticipated reductions in taxes and insurance. In spite of all the belt-tightening efforts, the cash flow analysis demonstrated that Delco Machines, Limited, would not be moving into a Hudson Builders' building at this time. The Hudson firm had been thriving in the building and leasing business for years, and attributed their success to staying away from long-term leases with firms whose ability to meet their financial obligations was questionable.

James Hudson realized the seriousness of Delco's position as he prepared to contact Stan Crow with Hudson's decision. He wondered what Crow's next move would be, and whether Delco Machines, Limited, would even be in business in a few years.

Questions

1. Do you agree with Hudson's analysis of Delco's financial position? Why or why not?

Exhibit C18-5 Revised Cash Flow Projection

Quarter Ending	Feb. 1980	May 1980	Aug. 1980	Nov. 1980
Beginning cash	$16,100.00	$ 4,486.12	($1,664.70)	($7,215.52)
Net income from operations	4,000.00	6,100.00	6,800.00	6,800.00
Depreciation	2,500.00	2,600.00	2,500.00	3,500.00
Cash flow available for building expense . . .	$22,600.00	$13,186.12	$ 7,635.30	$ 3,084.48
Rent	$ 7,193.88	$10,790.82	$10,790.82	$10,790.82
*Building expenses . . .	10,920.00	4,060.00	4,060.00	1,330.00
ENDING CASH	$ 4,486.12	($1,664.70)	($7,215.52)	($9,036.34)

*Exhibit C18-4 figures reduced by 30%

Exhibit C18-6 Trends In U.S. Auto Sales, Foreign vs. Domestic

(Units in Thousands)	Domestic	Imports	% of Total
1965	8763	569	6.1
1970	7119	1285	15.3
1972	9327	1623	14.8
1973	9676	1763	15.4
1974	7454	1413	15.9
1975	7053	1587	18.4
1976	8611	1498	14.8
1977	9109	2076	18.6
1978	9312	2000	17.7
1979	8328	2330	21.9

2. Given its financial condition, do you think Delco's most pressing problem is procuring plant space? If not, what do you think is its major problem?

3. What should Stan Crow do now?

CASE 19

Mather's Heating and Air Conditioning
Selecting and dealing with suppliers

Fred Mather operated a small heating and air-conditioning firm that sold and serviced heating and air-conditioning systems. Over the years the firm had changed from primary reliance on one manufacturer—Western Engineering—as the major supplier to a more balanced arrangement involving three suppliers. In the following discussion with a consultant, Fred described some points of friction in dealing with Western Engineering.

Fred: Western Engineering is so big that it can't be customer-oriented. Why, with my firm they've probably lost $600,000 or $700,000 worth of business just because of their inflexibility!

Consultant: They can't bend to take care of your needs?

Fred: Right. They're not flexible. And part of it, of course, is due to the sales reps they have. They just blew the Mather account. We sold Western equipment mostly until we just got disgusted with them.

Consultant: Did the situation just deteriorate over time?

Fred: True. Finally, after a good period of time, I started getting on them. I'm kind of temperamental. I finally just made up my mind—although I didn't tell them—that in the future our policy will be to sell other equipment also. In essence, what we've done since then is sell more Marshall Corporation and Solex equipment than we have Western.

Consultant: What bothered you about Western Engineering?

Fred: It is really a combination of things. The sales rep, for example. Instead of creating a feeling that he was going to try to take care of you and work with you and be for you, he was always on the opposite side of the fence. It was really strange. Western had certain items that were special quotes to help us be competitive. Well, he was always wanting to take different items off the special quote list every time there was a price change. But we needed every item we could get. This is a very competitive area.

Consultant: What other kinds of problems did he create?

Fred: On paperwork, he would not get it done. Let me give you an example about this sign in front of the business. We bought that sign when we bought the business, and we paid Western for it. About a year later, he came back and said, "Western has a new policy. The sign can no longer belong to the owner, so we will return the money you paid for the sign." I said, "Now that you have operated on my money for a year, the sign doesn't belong to me?" I went along with it, but it was the idea of the thing. They tell you one thing and then do something else.

Consultant: Were there other special incidents that occurred?

Fred: One time we got a job involving $30,000 or $40,000 worth of equipment. I told the rep it *appeared* that we had the job. We had a verbal contract, but that wasn't final. The next thing I knew, the equipment was sitting in Central Truck Lines out here. I hadn't ordered the equipment or anything. Fortunately, we did get the contract. But we weren't ready for the equipment for two more months and had no place to put it. And I ended up paying interest. It irritated me to no end.

Consultant: Was that what made you lean toward the other suppliers?

Fred: The final straw was the Park Lake project—a four-story renovation. I had designed the heating and air-conditioning system myself. I called the rep, intending to use Western equipment, and requested a price. So he called back and gave me a lump sum. There were lots of different items, and they were broken down into groups. I asked him to price the items by groups to provide various options to the purchaser. He replied, "We can't break it out." I said, "What do you mean, you can't break it out?" He said something about company policy. I really came unglued, but he never knew.

Consultant: What did you do about it?

Fred: As soon as I quit talking with him, I picked up the phone and called the Marshall Corporation rep. In just a few hours, we had prices that were broken down as I wanted them. The total price turned out to be $2,500 more, but I bought it! That was the end of Western Engineering as sole supplier.

Questions

1. What services did Fred Mather expect from the supplier? Were these unreasonable expectations?

2. Evaluate Fred's reaction when the Western Engineering rep declined to give him a breakdown on the price. Was Fred's decision to pay $2,500 more for the other equipment a rational decision?

3. Was Western Engineering at fault in shipping the large $30,000 or $40,000 order on the basis of an oral commitment and in the absence of an order? What should Fred have done about it?

4. Are the deficiencies that bother Fred caused by weaknesses of Western Engineering or merely the sales rep who sells for them?

5. Should Fred continue to use three separate suppliers or concentrate more purchases with one of them?

CASE 20

Style Shop
A "tough guy" uses financial and accounting information for decisions

A friend of mine recently said that 1975 is going to be the year of the tough guys, and that's right. It's for guys and gals who care enough to put everything they've got into what they're doing, and do their best. It's not the year for sitting around and letting everyone else do it for them. It's a good year for challenge and productivity because there is still money there, and there are still people who are ready to spend it. It's up to the tough guys, to the ones who merit being the ones with whom that money is spent!

Dorothy Barton, sitting at her desk in the small office just off the Style Shop sales floor, pondered this quotation which happened to catch her eye as she leafed through the latest edition of the *Dallas Fashion Retailer*.

In the women's ready-to-wear business, as in many other businesses, 1974 had been a rough year. It was particularly rough, however, for the attractive, energetic Style Shop owner. Wife and the mother of four teenage daughters, Mrs. Barton saw her sales fall 12.5 percent from 1973 to 1974; but, more significantly, her net profit plunged 62.5 percent over the same time period. She spent untold hours on the sales floor catering to her customers' eye for quality and fashion; in the office appealing to manufacturers to ship the next season's orders

Source: This case was prepared by Janelle C. Ashley, Dean, School of Business, Stephen F. Austin State University.

even though the current ones were yet to be paid; and at the Dallas Apparel Mart buying just the fashions she hoped would fit the needs and desires of her customers. At the same time, she was spending many hours each week in an effort to help her husband get his infant construction business off the ground.

She remembered hearing one "expert" say, "This is not a time for pessimism, nor a time for optimism. This is a time for realism." And an economic prognosticator had indicated that he saw a good future in the industry, despite the economic slowdown. Buyers, he noted, are working a little more cautiously right now. They are still buying, just looking at things a little more carefully.

"But what is 'realism' for me?" she asked herself. "Am I one of the tough guys who can stick it out and 'merit being the one with whom the money is spent!'?"

Style Shop Location and Background

The Style Shop opened its doors on February 12, 1954, in Lufkin, TX, and in 1969 it moved to its location in the Angelina Mall. The mall contains a major discount chain store, two full-line department stores, and a number of specialty shops. Located nearby are a twin cinema, motel, and junior college. The mall serves as the hub of a trade area extending over a radius of more than 100 miles. The only centers comparable to the Angelina Mall at the time were as distant as Houston, 120 miles to the southwest, and Dallas, 166 miles to the northwest.

Dorothy Barton began with the Style Shop as a part-time accountant in March, 1962. She became a 50–50 partner when the new shop opened in 1969 and purchased the 50 percent belonging to the other partner in January, 1974. She operates the business as a sole proprietorship.

The Style Shop up to 1974

Personnel The Style Shop employed four full-time clerks, one alteration lady, and a maid. A former employee and the teenage daughter of Mrs. Barton were frequently called in for part-time work during peak seasons.

Mrs. Flo Gates had been with the shop for 10 years. She worked as a clerk and floor manager and accompanied Mrs. Barton to market. The other three clerks had been with the Style Shop from one to three years each. Personnel turnover and apathy had been problems in the past, but Mrs. Barton was quite pleased with her present work force.

Policies The Style Shop operated with no formal, written policies. Personnel were paid wages and benefits comparable to other workers in similar capacities in the city. They enjoyed a great deal of freedom in their work, flexibility in hours of work, and a 20 percent discount on all merchandise purchased in the shop.

Competition Lufkin had an average number of retail outlets carrying ladies' ready-to-wear for cities of its size. Several department stores and other specialty shops carried some of the same lines as did the Style Shop, but they were all comparable in price. The Style Shop did handle several exclusive lines in Lufkin, however, and enjoyed the reputation of being the most prestigious women's shop in town. Its major competition was a similar, but larger, specialty shop complete with a fashion shoe department in neighboring Nacogdoches, 19 miles away.

Inventory Control The Style Shop used the services of Santoro Management Consultants, Inc., of Dallas, TX, for inventory control. IBM inventory management reports were received each month, broken down into 23 departmental groupings. These reports showed beginning inventory, sales and purchases for the month and year to date, markdowns, ending inventory, and various other information. Cost for the services was $110 per month.

Financial Position It is often quite difficult and sometimes next to impossible to evaluate the "true" financial position of a single proprietorship or a partnership due to the peculiarities that are either allowed or tolerated in accounting practices for these forms of ownership. This is evident in looking at the Style Shop's five-year Comparative Statement of Income (Exhibit C20-1), the Comparative Statement of Financial Condition (Exhibit C20-2), plus the 1974 Statement of Income (Exhibit C20-3) and 1974 Statement of Financial Condition (Exhibit C20-4). Key business ratios (median) for women's ready-to-wear stores are also given for comparative purposes in Exhibit C20-5.

Exhibit C20-1 Comparative Statement of Income

Item	1970	1971	1972	1973	1974
Sales	$200,845.43	$213,368.15	$216,927.31	$217,969.59	$190,821.85
Cost of sales	132,838.30	133,527.91	131,900.84	138,427.14	121,689.74
Gross profit	$ 68,007.13	$ 79,840.24	$ 85,026.47	$ 79,542.45	$ 69,132.11
Expenses	60,727.46	70,051.29	67,151.58	69,696.93	65,438.20
Net	$ 7,279.67	$ 9,788.95	$ 17,874.89	$ 9,845.52	$ 3,693.91

Exhibit C20-2 Comparative Statement of Financial Condition

Item	1970	1971	1972	1973	1974
Current assets*	$38,524.93	$ 70,015.11	$ 66,749.78	$ 58,530.44	$ 68,458.34
Inventory	23,039.00	37,971.00	33,803.00	36,923.00	35,228.00
Fixed assets	7,314.58	86,504.94	83,924.45	80,534.06	63,943.67
Total assets	$45,839.51	$156,520.05	$150,674.23	$139,064.50	$132,402.01
Current liabilities . . .	35,892.81	$ 19,586.45	$ 20,161.93	$ 31,587.57	$ 55,552.70
Long-term liabilities . .	0	39,042.90	33,680.07	26,841.76	20,003.45
Total liabilities	$35,892.81	$ 58,629.35	$ 53,842.00	$ 58,429.33	$ 75,556.15
Net worth	9,946.70	97,890.70	96,832.23	80,635.17	56,845.86
Total	$45,839.51	$156,520.05	$150,674.23	$139,064.50	$132,402.01

*Current-asset values include the amounts shown for inventory.

Exhibit C20-3 Statement of Income

Style Shop
Statement of Income
For Year Ended Dec. 31, 1974

Sales		$190,821.85
Cost of sales:		
Beginning inventory.	$ 36,923.00	
Purchases	119,994.74	
	$156,917.74	
Ending inventory	35,228.00	121,689.74
Gross profit		$ 69,132.11
Expenses:		
Advertising.	$ 3,034.63	
Auto expense	1,509.63	
Bad debts	(439.83)	
Depreciation	1,580.49	
Freight, express, delivery	2,545.90	
Heat, light, power, and water	1,847.96	
Insurance	1,431.80	
Interest	4,064.25	
Legal and accounting	2,034.74	
Rent.	11,220.40	
Repairs	528.98	
Salary	26,227.69	
Supplies	5,138.11	
Tax—Payroll	1,656.18	
Tax—Other.	604.62	
Telephone	784.67	
Dues and subscriptions	601.89	
Market and travel.	1,066.09	65,438.20
Net profit		$ 3,693.91

Two explanatory footnotes should be added to these statements. The jump in fixed assets between 1970 and 1971 (see Exhibit C20–2) and the subsequent changes were due in large part to the inclusion of personal real estate on the partnership books. The long-term liability initiated in 1971 was an SBA loan. Caught in a period of declining sales (due in part to the controversy over skirt length and women's pantsuits) and rapidly rising expenses in the new mall location, the Style

Exhibit C20–4 Statement of Financial Condition

Style Shop
Statement of Financial Condition
Dec. 31, 1974

ASSETS

Current assets:

Cash on hand and in banks	$ 4,923.92
Accounts receivable	21,306.42
Inventory	35,228.00
Cash value—Life insurance	7,000.00
Total current assets	68,458.34

Fixed assets:

Furniture and fixtures and leasehold improvements	$27,749.94	
Less: Allowance for depreciation	9,806.27	$ 17,943.67
Auto and truck.		9,500.00
Real estate		20,000.00
Furniture		10,000.00
Boat and motor		2,000.00
Office equipment.		2,500.00
Jewelry		2,000.00
Total fixed assets		$ 63,943.67
TOTAL ASSETS		$132,402.01

LIABILITIES AND CAPITAL

Current liabilities:

Accounts payable	$ 30,413.12
Accrued payroll tax	825.64
Accrued sales tax	1,193.94
Note payable—Due in one year	9,420.00
Note payable—Lot	10,700.00
Note payable—Auto	3,000.00
Total current liabilities	$ 55,552.70
Note payable—Due after one year	20,003.45
Total liabilities	$ 75,556.15
Net worth	56,845.86
TOTAL LIABILITIES AND CAPITAL	$132,402.01

Exhibit C20-5 Key Business Ratios for Women's Ready-to-Wear Stores

Ratio	1974	1973	1972	1971	1970
Current assets Current liabilities . . .	2.65	2.81	2.51	2.38	2.50
Net profit Net sales	2.05	2.30	1.81	1.86	2.18
Net profit Net worth.	8.92	8.53	6.68	7.14	8.73
Net profit Net working capital . .	11.43	10.96	8.64	9.98	10.92
Net sales Net worth.	3.82	3.96	3.95	3.76	3.78
Net sales Net working capital . .	4.61	4.92	4.73	4.90	4.49
Net sales Inventory	6.7	6.7	6.6	6.7	6.1
Fixed assets Net worth.	18.3	18.2	18.6	17.5	14.7
Current liabilities Net worth.	49.4	49.2	51.0	54.5	56.5
Total liabilities Net worth.	98.5	100.1	104.0	124.1	125.8
Inventory Net working capital . .	73.0	72.3	76.7	71.1	78.3
Current liabilities Inventory	84.6	87.2	87.0	93.9	86.6
Long-term liabilities Net working capital . .	30.1	33.2	29.8	34.0	30.8

Note: Collection period not computed. Necessary information as to the division between cash sales and credit sales was available in too few cases to obtain an average collection period usable as a broad guide.

Source: Dun's Review (September issues, 1970–1974).

Shop owners found themselves in that proverbial "financial bind" in late 1969 and 1970. They needed additional funds both for working capital and fixed investments. Since a big jump in sales was anticipated in the new location, additional working capital was necessary to purchase the required inventory. The new tenants also desired fixed-asset money to purchase display fixtures for their new store. They obtained this money through a local bank in the form of an SBA-insured loan.

The Style Shop, 1975

"Certainly there is no longer an arbiter of the length of a skirt or the acceptance of pantsuits," Mrs. Barton mused.

"The economic picture is looking brighter. The experts tell us there will be more disposable personal income and a lower rate in inflation. Yet this is a time for 'realism.' Am I a 'tough guy'?"

Questions

1. Evaluate the overall performance of the Style Shop. How good a business was it at the end of 1974?
2. Compute the current ratio for the shop and compare it with the industry ratio. What are the implications?
3. Evaluate the shop's ratios showing the relationships of net profit to net sales, to net worth, and to net working capital.
4. How did the shop's net-sales-to-inventory ratio compare with that of the industry? Explain.
5. Should Mrs. Barton have kept the business or sold it? What are the primary factors to be considered in reaching such a decision?

Case endnote

1. "Merchandisers Must Provide Leadership," *Dallas Fashion Retailer* (June, 1975), p. 17.

CASE 21

Barton Sales and Service
Managing the firm's working capital

Barton Sales and Service was located in Little Rock, AR. Its owners were John and Joyce Barton. John served as general manager, and Joyce as office manager. The firm sold General Electric, Carrier, and York air-conditioning and heating systems and serviced these and other types of systems as well. It served both commercial and residential customers. Although the business had operated successfully since the Bartons purchased it five years earlier, it continued to experience working-capital problems.

Barton's Financial Structure

The firm had been profitable since the Bartons purchased it. Profits for 1989 were the highest for any year to date. Exhibit C21–1 shows the income statement for that year.

The balance sheet as of December 31, 1989, for Barton Sales and Service is shown in Exhibit C21–2. Note that the firm's equity was somewhat less than its total debt. However, $51,231 of the firm's liabilities was a long-term note carrying a modest rate of interest. This note was issued at the time the Bartons purchased the business, and the payments were made to the former owner.

Barton's Cash Balance

A minimum cash balance is necessary in any business because of the uneven nature of cash inflows and outflows. John explained that they needed a substantial amount in order to "feel comfortable." He felt that it might be possible to reduce the present balance by $5,000 to $10,000,

Exhibit C21–1 Barton Sales and Service Income Statement for the Year Ended December 31, 1989

Sales	$727,679
Less: Cost of sales	466,562
Gross profit	$261,177
Less: Selling, general & administrative expenses	
(including officers' salaries)	189,031
Net income before income taxes	$ 72,086
Provision for income taxes	17,546
Net income	$ 54,540

Exhibit C21–2 Barton Sales and Service Balance Sheet as of December 31, 1989

ASSETS

Current assets:

Cash	$ 28,789
Trade accounts receivable	56,753
Inventory	89,562
Prepaid expenses	4,415
Total current assets	$179,519
Loans to stockholders	41,832
Autos, trucks, and equipment, at cost,	
less accumulated depreciation of $36,841.	24,985
Other assets—Goodwill.	16,500
TOTAL ASSETS	$235,836

LIABILITIES AND STOCKHOLDERS' EQUITY

Current liabilities:

Current maturities of long-term debt (see Note 1).	$ 26,403
Trade accounts payable	38,585
Accrued payroll taxes	2,173
Accrued income taxes	13,818
Other accrued expenses	4,001
Total current liabilities	$ 84,980
Long-term debt (see Note 1)	51,231
Stockholders' equity	99,625
TOTAL LIABILITIES AND STOCKHOLDERS' EQUITY	$235,836

Note 1: Short-Term Debt and Long-Term Debt

		Long-Term	Current	Total
(1)	10% note payable, secured by pickup, due in monthly installments of $161 including interest	$ 1,367	$ 1,827	$ 3,194
(2)	10% note payable, secured by equipment, due in monthly installments of $180 including interest	0	584	584
(3)	6% note payable, secured by inventory and equipment, due in monthly installments of $678 including interest . .	39,127	6,392	45,519
(4)	9% notes payable to stockholders	10,737	0	10,737
(5)	20% note payable to bank in 30 days . .	0	17,600	17,600
		$51,231	$26,403	$77,634

but he stated that it gave them some "breathing room."

Barton's Accounts Receivable

The trade accounts receivable at the end of 1989 were $56,753, but at some times during the year the accounts receivable were twice this amount. These accounts were not aged, so the firm had no specific knowledge of the number of overdue accounts. However, the firm had never experienced any significant loss from bad debts. The accounts receivable were thought, therefore, to be good accounts of a relatively recent nature.

Customers were given 30 days from the date of the invoice to pay the net amount. No cash discounts were offered. If payment was not received during the first 30 days, a second statement was mailed to the customer and monthly carrying charges of one tenth of 1 percent were added. The state usury law prohibited higher carrying charges.

On small residential jobs, the firm tried to collect from customers when work was completed. When a service representative finished repairing an airconditioning system, for example, the rep presented a bill to the owner and attempted to obtain payment at that time. However, this was not always possible. On major items such as unit changeouts—which often ran as high as $2,500—billing was practically always necessary.

On new construction projects, the firm sometimes received partial payments prior to completion of a project. This helped to minimize the amount tied up in receivables.

Barton's Inventory

Inventory accounted for a substantial portion of the firm's working capital. It consisted of the various heating and airconditioning units, parts, and supplies used in the business.

The Bartons had no guidelines or industry standards to use in evaluating their overall inventory levels. They felt that there *might* be some excessive inventory, but, in the absence of a standard, this was basically an opinion. When pressed to estimate the amount that might be eliminated by careful control, John pegged it at 15 percent.

The firm used an annual physical inventory that coincided with the end of its fiscal year. Since the inventory level was known for only one time in the year, the income statement could be prepared only on an annual basis. There was no way of knowing how much of the inventory was expended at other points and thus no way to calculate profits. As a result, the Bartons lacked quarterly or monthly income statements to assist them in managing the business.

Barton Sales and Service was considering changing from a physical inventory to a perpetual inventory system. This would enable John to know the inventory levels of all items at all times. An inventory total could easily be computed for use in preparing statements. Shifting to a perpetual inventory system would require the purchase of proper file equipment, but that cost was not large enough to constitute a major barrier. A greater expense would be involved in the maintenance of the system—entering all incoming materials and all withdrawals. The Bartons estimated that this task would necessitate the work of one person on a half-time or three-fourths time basis.

Barton's Note Payable to the Bank

Bank borrowing was the most costly form of credit. Barton Sales and Service paid the going rate, slightly above prime, and owed $17,600. The note was a 90-day renewable note. Normally some was paid on the principal when the note was renewed. The total borrowing could probably be increased if necessary. There was no obvious pressure from the bank to reduce borrowing to zero. The amount borrowed during the year typically ranged from $10,000 to $25,000.

The Bartons had never explored the limits the bank might impose on borrowing, and there was no clearly specified line of credit. When additional funds were required, Joyce simply dropped by the bank, spoke with a bank officer, and signed a note for the appropriate amount.

Barton's Trade Accounts Payable

A significant amount of Barton's working capital came from its trade accounts payable. Although accounts payable at the end of 1989 were $38,585, the total payable varied over time and might be double this amount at another point in the year. Barton obtained from various dealers such supplies as expansion valves, copper tubing, sheet metal, electrical wire, electrical conduit, and so on. Some suppliers offered a discount for cash (2/10, n/30), but Joyce felt the credit was more important than the few dollars that

could be saved by taking a cash discount. By giving up the cash discount, the firm obtained the use of the money for 30 days. Although the Bartons might wait a few days beyond the 30 days before paying, their suppliers quickly applied pressure. The Bartons could stretch the payment dates to 45 or even 60 days before being "put on C.O.D." However, they found it unpleasant to delay payment more than 45 days because suppliers would begin calling and applying pressure for payment.

The major manufacturers (Carrier, General Electric, and York) used different terms of payment. Some major products could be obtained from Carrier on an arrangement known as "floor planning." This meant that the manufacturer (Carrier) shipped the products without requiring immediate payment. The Bartons made payment only when the product was sold. If still unsold after 90 days, the product had to be returned or paid for. (It was shipped back on a company truck, so there was no expense in returning unsold items.) On items that were not floor-planned but were purchased from Carrier, Barton paid the net amount by the 10th of the month or was charged 18 percent interest on late payments.

Shipments from General Electric required payment at the bank soon after receipt of the products. If cash was not available at the time, this necessitated further borrowing from the bank.

Purchases from York required net payment without discount within 30 days. However, if payment was not made within 30 days, interest at 18 percent per annum was added.

Can Good Profits Become Better?

Although Barton Sales and Service had earned a *good* profit in 1989, the Bartons wondered whether they were realizing the *most possible* profit. The pressure of inflation and slowness in construction caused by high interest rates were slowing their business somewhat. They wanted to be sure they were meeting the challenging times as prudently as possible.

Questions

1. Evaluate the overall performance and financial structure of Barton Sales and Service.
2. What are the strengths and weaknesses in this firm's management of accounts receivable and inventory?
3. Should the firm reduce or expand its bank borrowing?
4. Evaluate the Bartons' management of trade accounts payable.
5. How can Barton Sales and Service improve its working-capital situation?

CASE 22

The Fair Store
Contemplating a computerized inventory-control system

The Fair Store of Lott, TX (a small town of less than 1,000 population), has built a reputation as the state's leading retailer of high-quality western wear at moderate prices. Its owner is R. W. Hailey. In the store the atmosphere of the Old West is developed by narrow aisles, crowded racks of merchandise, inexpensive fixtures, and informality in operating procedures. Many customers drive hundreds of miles to this store and, at certain times of the year, stand in line on the sidewalk in order to be admitted.

Fair Store's Sales Personnel

All of the salesclerks at The Fair Store are local people. Many of them are housewives whose husbands are farmers in the surrounding areas. For the most part, the sales personnel are not well educated and are quite provincial. However, they have always been accustomed to hard work and are pleasant to customers.

Fair Store's Merchandising Practices

In western wear, just as in other types of merchandise, style consciousness affects customer demand. Quite a variety of merchandise is sold. Many brands of boots with different price ranges are sold, but The Fair Store's two principal suppliers of handmade boots are Tony Lama and Justin Company.

Source: This case was prepared by Professor Kris K. Moore of Baylor University.

Breaking the merchandise into groups, Hailey estimates the store's merchandise assortment as follows:

Hats	8%
Jeans, pants, suits, and shirts	20%
Children's boots and cheaper adult boots	15%
Tony Lama and Justin Red Wing Boots	50%
Miscellaneous	7%

The buying of boots has to be done months ahead, usually about six months, because they are handmade. Such a time lag means that purchasing for the Thanksgiving and Christmas markets must come no later than the previous April or May. Boots, therefore, entail a large inventory investment during the period from June to November. A recent amount purchased from the Justin Company for this market period was $57,507.

Western hats (which are often custom-steamed to the customer's favorite crease) follow the seasonal demand—with straw hats for spring and summer, and felt hats for fall and winter. Hats must be purchased six months in advance. Jeans, pants, suits, and shirts must also be purchased several months in advance.

Fair Store's Inventory Practices

At present the store has no direct methods of inventory control. The sales representatives from Tony Lama and Justin Company bring samples of different styles to Hailey. Hailey then chooses styles that he believes will sell and, with the sales representatives, determines the price and the quantity to be shipped. When the merchandise is received at the store, Hailey helps unpack the goods and mark prices. There is no verification that merchandise received matches the purchase orders. No further record keeping is maintained. Merchandise is shelved, and the amount of a sale is rung up on the cash register when a customer has concluded his or her shopping.

Periodically, Hailey walks through the store and makes a visual check of merchandise, noting low levels of styles and sizes. He then places new orders on the basis of such notes. At year's end, an inventory check is made to determine the information needed for tax returns. The yearly inventory check is time-consuming and costly.

Hailey's Thoughts on Computerizing

After the store grossed over $1 million in a recent fiscal year, Hailey began wondering how he could use a computer for better control of the business. He was especially interested in two areas: (1) controlling the average daily inventory, which had grown from $94,000 to $207,000 in 1 year; and (2) having available in quantity for customers the most frequently demanded sizes of handmade boots. Although sales had increased satisfactorily, the rate of increase was lower than the growth in inventory. Hailey felt that his business would continue to grow at a rapid rate and wondered whether a computer would help him with inventory management.

Questions

1. In what areas of inventory management does R. W. Hailey seem to have the greatest problems? What cost savings might be realized by better inventory control?
2. What buying, receiving, pricing, and check-out changes would be necessary to accommodate a computerized inventory-control system? Be specific.

CASE 23

Dale's Lawn Service

Determining insurance needs of a small service business

As Donnie Conner organized his new business, Dale's Lawn Service, he thought about insurance needs and contacted an insurance agent to talk it over. The insurance agent asked Donnie to explain the nature of the business prior to discussing insurance coverage.

Nature of the Business

Donnie explained that he had worked for another lawn-care firm for three years but had decided to begin his own business. In preparation for getting into business, he had acquired three riding lawnmowers ($800 each), five push lawnmowers ($300 each), two hedge clippers ($265 each), two edgers ($225 each), a small used pick-up truck ($3,500), a trailer ($1,000), and miscellaneous other equipment.

Donnie planned to provide lawn care for apartments, commercial buildings, and residential properties. In fact, he had been servicing a number of properties on his own time while working for the other employer. The most important part of his business would be performed on the basis of 12-month maintenance contracts. These called for the care of lawns, shrubs, and trees. On some contracts, the rate for three winter months was somewhat lower than the normal monthly rate. However, since some work (such as trimming trees, pruning shrubs, and raking leaves) was necessary in the winter, a few contracts specified a uniform monthly fee throughout the year.

At the beginning, Donnie would be the only person in the business, but he expected to hire other employees when he was able to expand. While he wanted to protect himself against the most important risks that would be involved in the business, he also wished to avoid excessive insurance coverage and to minimize expenses during the early days in the business.

Donnie's Automobile Insurance Coverage

Since Donnie already owned the truck, he had included it with his car on a personal automobile insurance policy. The policy provided for collision coverage ($200 deductible), single-limit liability covering bodily injury and property damage ($50,000), and comprehensive coverage. The agent assured Donnie that his automobile insurance coverage was adequate for business purposes since he used the truck for both personal and business use.

Proposed General Liability Coverage

The agent suggested a $50,000 general liability policy at a premium of $153 per year. Donnie was a little unsure of the wisdom of buying this insurance because he needed to keep all costs to a bare minimum until he became established. On the other hand, he recalled that a mower operated by his former employer once threw a rock that struck a small girl in the face and cut the skin. There was always the outside chance that some such accident could occur because his work was always performed on the property of others.

Proposed Major Medical Insurance

The agent also recommended a major medical policy (with a small deductible) that would cover hospital, surgery, and other medical costs. On major medical expenses, the insurance company would pay 80 percent of the total that exceeded the deductible. Family coverage (for Donnie, his wife Stephany, and his one-year-old son Caleb) would cost $102 per month, plus a $15 monthly processing fee for the business. (This $15 fee would remain at this level even after Donnie placed other employees under the policy.) When Donnie decided to hire employees, he could add each of them to the policy for approximately $45 per month. The employees would have the option to pay for coverage of their families.

Proposed Six-Month Disability Coverage

If Donnie desired, he could also add a six-month disability clause. The premium on this insurance would run $17 per month. In the event he became disabled through injury or illness, this would pay two-thirds of his weekly salary for 180 days. For example, if Donnie planned to pay himself a $300 weekly salary, he would receive a compensation payment, if disabled, of $200 per week. Donnie was only 30 years old, had good health, and had no prior disabilities. However, most of his financial resources were invested in the business.

Proposed Long-Term Disability Insurance

For disability beyond six months, Donnie could secure a long-term policy which would begin after six months and run as long as he was disabled or until age 65. For the same $200-per-week coverage, the premium would run $42.50 per month. It would take a major accident or very serious illness, of course, to disable him for more than six months. He wondered whether the premium was too much for such an unlikely possibility.

After new employees were hired, they would be covered by the state's workers' compensation plan. Donnie could also elect to be included in that plan. However, the plan protected against only work-related accidents or illnesses, and the total reimbursement for lost wages would be much less than the amount provided by the disability policy. (The law specified a maximum compensation of less than $100 per week and a maximum time period for benefits, the length varying with the type of disability.)

Proposed Theft Insurance

Another hazard faced by the business was the possible theft of equipment. The principal danger, as Donnie saw it, existed while he was using equipment on the job. While he was using one piece of equipment on another part of the property, other items might be stolen from the truck or trailer. A friend of his had lost two lawnmowers in this way. The only available theft insurance had a $200 deductible on each piece of equipment and involved a premium of $40 per month. Donnie wondered whether there was any other way to protect the equipment so that he could avoid this expense.

**Donnie's Reactions
to the Insurance Proposals**

Having reviewed the various policies, the agent asked Donnie which coverages he wanted. Rather than respond immediately, Donnie asked for a few days to think it over.

Questions

1. What general liability insurance, if any, should Donnie Conner buy?
2. Should Donnie take the hospitalization insurance?
3. Should he acquire the short-term disability coverage? The long-term disability coverage?
4. Should he obtain theft insurance for the equipment used in the firm?
5. What other insurance, if any, would be desirable?

CASE 24

Walter Stanton: Employee Responsibility and the Use of Time
Ethical issues in small firms

Walter Stanton, in discussing the responsibility of an employee to his or her employer with a group of MBA students at a southwestern business school, was surprised at the number of questions he received and the diversity of opinion he found among his students regarding the use of time on and off the job. To give some focus to the discussion, he asked each student to describe a specific incident in the student's own experience in which this question had arisen. The following are a few of the incidents reported by the students.

Allen Chan

After I finished my undergraduate work in mathematics and computer science, my wife persuaded me to take a job for a couple of years so that we could pay off some of our bills and get ahead a little before I started on my MBA. She was also concerned that I wasn't spending enough time with my two young sons. Between the demands of my course work and a part-time job, I usually left early in the morning and often was not home until after they had been put to bed.

One of my undergraduate professors was instrumental in getting me a job with Nelson Data Processing. I understood before I started that they were a hard-driving firm with a reputation for high-quality

Source: This case was prepared by Professor Clinton L. Oaks, of Brigham Young University.

work. Once aboard, I found that the company had a large backlog and that management was encouraging everyone to put in overtime, for which they paid a generous hourly rate on top of the employee's salary.

We needed the money and the work was interesting. Before long, I found myself working late almost every night. Barbara, my wife, didn't say much at first, but I could tell she wasn't happy with the way things were working out. Finally one day she said, "Allen, you were spending more time at home when you were in school than you are now." I mumbled something about "trying to cut it down a little" and dropped the subject.

The next day at noon, when another employee and I were on our way out to grab a sandwich, I mentioned that my wife was unhappy about all the time I was spending away from home. He said, "Look, Allen, you don't have to punch a time clock on those extra hours. A lot of the guys just take their work home with them. Keep track of your time and turn it in just like you do now. I'm not sure what the company policy is, but I have been doing this every so often for several months now, and nobody has ever said anything about it."

The more I thought about the idea of doing my overtime at home, the better I liked it. I could spend the early evening with the family and then, after the boys were in bed, I could really get some work done. As I had expected, Barbara was elated when I explained to her what I was going to do.

The first few nights I found it hard to get up to speed again after letting down for dinner and roughhousing with the kids. As I got into the swing of it, however, I found that since there were no distractions, as there often were at the office, I could do a lot more at home in an hour than I was doing at work. Whenever I needed someone to help with the checking or sorting, Barbara was always available and seemed to enjoy working with me. I found that there were some things she could do faster and more accurately than I could. One night after we had finished a particularly long and involved task in about half the time it would ordinarily have taken me, I said, "Barbara, there ought to be some way to put you on the payroll." She laughed and said, "Why don't you just increase the number of hours put in for yourself to cover it?"

Questions

1. Should Allen Chan report his wife's working time as part of his own working time and thereby receive compensation for it?
2. Does the arrangement whereby work is performed at home present any particular ethical problems?

Lupe Diaz

I had been working for Patterson Engineering for nearly a year when I decided to come back and get my MBA. About three weeks before school was to start, I gave my supervisor, Jim, who was really a great boss, my two-week notice. Since he and I had talked a number of times about my going on to school as a preparation for a move into management, he was not at all surprised. He asked me to come in his office for a few minutes later that morning to make plans for my departure. I thought he might be concerned about several things I was working on that would be hard to turn over to anyone until I completed my present segment. I wasn't too concerned, however, because I had worked out a careful schedule and I figured I would just have time to do it all in those last two weeks.

When I entered my supervisor's office, he said, "Lupe, you have done a great job for us, and when you finish your education, we want you to keep us in mind. You said that school started right after the first of next month?" I nodded, and he went on to say, "I imagine that you have a lot of work to do to get packed and moved, don't you?" I replied, "Boy, I'll say! Moving is always such a hassle. We want to get out of our apartment by the fifteenth so that we can get our deposit back. I would like to have allowed myself a few more days, but when we figured out what we would need for school this year, we found that the money from these last two weeks was really crucial."

My supervisor smiled and leaned back in his chair. "Yes," he said, "I remember how it was. I think, though, that I can help you out. According to my records, you have accumulated about twelve days' sick leave. Is that right?" "Yes," I answered. "Well, as you know, the firm doesn't pay any sick leave unless you are actually sick. In your case, though, you are going to be sick—sick of moving. I want you to spend this afternoon acquainting Tom with where you are on each one of your projects. Then each morning for the next two weeks I want you to call in sick. If there is any question about it, I'll cover for you."

That night I thought a lot about what Jim had said—but I just didn't feel good about it. Tom was a good man, but it would take someone else at least twice as long to finish the things I was working on as it would take me. One of the projects was the kind that someone new would almost have to start over. The executives at Patterson had really been good to me in terms of the kinds of assignments they had given me—and I had been given a pay raise every six months instead of every year, as was typical with new employees.

I went in early the next morning and was right in the middle of my most important project when Jim came by. He frowned when he saw me at my desk. "I thought I told you to take these two weeks off. I don't want to see you in here after today!"

Question

1. Should Lupe Diaz accept her supervisor's offer and take sick leave during the time she is moving?

Lorraine Adams

When I was an undergraduate, I worked summers on an electronic composer for Brown Publishing. This is a typewriter with a memory that enables it to type course material in columns and justified (flush right) margins. Because it is difficult to determine how long it takes to type material into memory and play it back, I often went for four hours without taking the 15-minute break we were supposed to have both morning and afternoon. Some of the other women who had the same problem kept track of the breaks they didn't take and then used them as justification for leaving a half hour early or arriving a half hour late, recording their time as if they had left or arrived at the normal time. One woman even saved hers for two weeks and then took an afternoon off to do some shopping. I am sure that this was contrary to company policy, but our supervisor was a very relaxed and friendly woman who never seemed to notice when someone was gone.

Another problem I had with breaks is, what can constitute a break? If a friend, who wasn't an employee of the company, dropped in for a few minutes, I always thought of that as a break. But what if some other employee who is tired, bored, or worried comes by and spends a few minutes talking about her work, her plans for the weekend, her current boyfriend, or some personal problem? Should you count that as a break? One morning our supervisor talked to me for 20 minutes about job opportunities for women with MBAs. Was that a break?

Accounting for my time has always been a problem for me. Last summer, I worked as a department manager in a branch of a large department store in Los Angeles. A number of the department managers would arrive at 8:00, as we were supposed to do, and then take off across the mall to a coffee shop "to make plans for the day." They usually got back just before the store opened at 9:30. I went with them a couple of times and found that if they discussed anything related to their work in the store, it was only an incidental part of their conversation. A couple of these guys would also regularly take up to an hour and a half for lunch and then check out right after five. Since we didn't have to check in and out for breaks or for lunch, their time card would show an eight-hour day. When I said something to one of them about it one day, he answered, "Listen, Lorraine, summer is a slack time around here. You ought to be here during the Christmas rush. We work a lot of hours then that we don't get paid for. The store owes us a chance to relax a little when the heat is off."

Questions

1. What constitutes a legitimate break? Is it ethical to save up breaks and use them at other times?
2. Are the department managers acting ethically in taking extended coffee breaks and lunch hours?

Robert Jeffries

Before I came back to school, I worked for two years for a branch of Jefferson Sporting Goods. Jefferson had five large stores located in different metropolitan areas in the state and did a large volume in men's and women's sports clothes. Our branch wasn't the largest in the chain but would have been second or third.

The store manager, Rand Walker, had been manager since the store was opened. He had previously had soft-goods experience with several other stores and really knew that part of the business.

We got along really well. Not long after I came to work, Rand put me in charge of the shoe department. Later he made me manager of the men's clothing department, and, a year later, he made me assistant manager. He always saw that I got a substantial raise after each six-month review. He seemed to have a lot of trust in me. I noticed, for example, that even before I had been there for a year, he shared a lot of confidential figures with me that he didn't show to any of the other managers.

One day Rand called me into his office. He had me shut the door so that no one else would hear our conversation. "Bob," he said, "I've got a chance to buy the Blue Hills Pant Depot and I want to know what you think about it." Blue Hills was in a suburb about 10 miles north of our store. Rand proceeded to tell me the details of the offer. "It looks like a good deal as far as I can tell," I said, "but would it be as profitable for you as Jefferson's has been?" I was assuming he would quit when he bought the store. "Oh," he said, "I'm not going to quit unless Elliot Jefferson, the owner, tells me to." I was surprised because it looked like a clear case of conflict of interest. I knew that Rand had been looking at some outside investments since he had done well at Jefferson's, but I hadn't thought he would consider buying another clothing store.

I didn't say much after that, trying not to get too involved with what was happening. Many times Rand would come to me to ask my opinion on certain clothing lines. He asked me to give him a list of the top five pant vendors and their salespersons' names and addresses, which I did.

Several weeks later, I asked Rand if he had made a decision on the store. He said he had gone ahead and bought it. He said he put it under his wife's name, and she was going to run it; that way he felt he could justify continuing his work at Jefferson's.

After that, I noticed that Rand spent a lot more time in his office and less time out on the floor. Occasionally, I would drop into his office to see him and find him paying invoices and doing book work for his pant store. I never asked anything about it and, in fact, tried to keep our conversations on problems that needed attention at Jefferson's.

This situation remained unchanged for several months. I concentrated my attention on doing my job and kept my thoughts to myself. Many of the other employees kept asking me about the Pant De-pot. They wanted to know, for example, who really owned it, Rand or his wife. I would just tell them I didn't know.

In October, Rand came to me again and said that he was planning on acquiring a second pant store in another suburb about fifteen miles south of our store. A clothing store in that town was going out of business, and he had a chance to rent the building. This really surprised me. I kiddingly asked if he was planning to open a whole chain. He replied that he would like to open several stores similar to the one he had already and that all he needed was to find good locations where he could rent store space cheaply.

On November 1, Rand opened his second store. It immediately became a success, almost equalling the volume of the first.

After that, I seldom saw Rand on the floor. He was either in his office or gone. I found myself trying to cover for him when we would get calls from the home office. This situation made me very uncomfortable. When he did come in, he seemed a lot more absent-minded about things in our store.

I wondered how much Elliot Jefferson knew (or suspected) about Rand's involvement in these other stores. I wondered, too, whether I should tell the home office why our reports were slow and why our sales had stopped increasing as rapidly as they had when Rand spent full time managing the store.

Questions

1. Did Rand Walker experience a sufficient conflict of interest to constitute an ethical problem?
2. Does Robert Jeffries have an obligation to report Walker's outside business involvement to the top management of Jefferson Sporting Goods?

CASE 25

"No Strain" Testers

An inventor seeks to obtain a patent on his own

Harvey Strain was an employee of a highly successful lithographic printing equipment manufacturer in Dallas, TX. He had worked more than 15 years as a "trouble-shooter" for the company, solving customers' problems with purchased printing presses. Harvey had always been interested in mechanical devices. During his teenage days, he was constantly working in the family garage modifying automobiles for drag racing. His creative skills had remained active. For example, at age 44, he finished building a custom-designed car from new and used parts.

The Invention

Recently Harvey turned his creative talents and mechanical skills toward an idea that had the potential to be a marketable product. His invention would be used with lithographic printing presses such as those produced by his employer. His invention was an automatic testing reservoir used in connection with dampening systems on those presses. Figure C25–1 shows promotional material designed by Harvey for his invention. The device maintained a constant alcohol solution level, continuously sampling the circulating solution to give an accurate specific-gravity reading. The product overcame the existing problems, time, and expense involved in maintaining the proper alcohol percentage with existing battery-type testers.

Harvey realized the potential value of a patent but was uncertain whether he could handle the patenting process himself, or should turn it over to a lawyer. In a recent article of a trade magazine, *Machine Design,* he read some hints on how to market an invention. The article encouraged Harvey to "try it on his own." The article stated further that a patent could be obtained at a cost in the neighborhood of $1,000.

The Patenting Process

On December 22, 1985, Harvey wrote a privately owned Washington-based patent search company. Its response was cordial, requesting that he fill out the enclosed patent protection forms "giving us as detailed a sketch of your invention as possible . . ." and offering to conduct a patentability search for $100. "In the meantime," the letter continued, ". . . no attempt should be made to sell your invention since under our present laws you have nothing to sell (no legal property) until an application for patent has actually been filed in the Patent Office and you have *PATENT PENDING*."

On January 19, 1986, Harvey authorized the patent search, enclosing the completed Record of Disclosure and the $100 fee. On February 4, 1986, A. Mercedes, Managing Director for the Washington Patent Office Search Bureau, wrote Harvey saying, "We are pleased to report that your invention appears to be patentable." A. Mercedes urged Harvey to proceed with the preparation and filing

Figure C25-1   Promotional Material for Alcohol Testers

of a patent application. He also offered his company's services in helping Harvey prepare the specifications, claims, and the Official United States Patent Office Drawing.

Harvey decided to continue on his own. He prepared his own drawings and specifications. On February 16, 1986, he filed his Petition for Patent and other required documents. His letter of transmittal is shown in Exhibit C25-1.

Six months later, Harvey received a letter from the Commissioner of Patents and Trademarks. Harvey quickly opened

the letter. His application had been rejected. Although this was bad news, Harvey did not want to give up.

The rejection decision was based on three reasons, two of which were minor and one serious. One minor problem concerned the oath (or declaration) provided by Harvey in his letter of February 16, 1986. The form required to correct this problem was enclosed in the letter from the Commissioner of Patents and Trademarks. The other minor problem involved errors in the drawings, which could be corrected by the Patent Office.

Exhibit C25–1   A Letter of Transmittal

P.O. Box 3185
Irving, TX 75061
February 16, 1986

Commissioner of Patents
United States Patent Office
Washington, DC 20231

To the Commissioner of Patents

Enclosed are my Petition for Patent, Oath to Accompany my Petition, Abstract, Specifications, Claim, and a check in the amount of $50, which I understand is the initial filing fee.

The preliminary patentability search was completed by the Washington Patent Office Search Bureau, P.O. Box 7167, Washington, DC 20044, who reported that my invention appeared to be patentable.

I am unable to utilize their additional services or the services of a patent attorney and will appreciate your indulgence in considering the attached drawings and specifications which I have prepared.

Yours sincerely

(Sgd.) Harvey A. Strain

The serious problem was that the Patent Office claimed that Harvey's idea fell under the requirements that "A patent may not be obtained . . . if the differences between the subject matter sought to be patented and the prior art are such that the subject matter as a whole would have been obvious at the time the invention was made to a person having ordinary skill in the art to which said subject matter pertains." This pronouncement sounded very final.

Questions

1. Would you have believed the magazine article about a patent for less than $1,000, or would you have gone to a lawyer? What difficulties are involved in being one's own attorney?
2. What do you think Harvey Strain should have done to get his patent? Be specific.
3. Do you believe Harvey should have forgotten the patent and marketed his product without patent protection? Why or why not?

GLOSSARY

100 percent inspection   inspection of each item in every lot processed

ABC method   a method of classifying inventory into categories of high-value, less costly, and low-cost items

accrual method of accounting   accounting method by which revenue and expenses are recognized when they are incurred, regardless of when the cash is received or payment is made

acid-test (or quick) ratio   ratio of current assets less inventories to current liabilities

actual expenses   expenses that in fact accrue and require cash outlays

advertising   the impersonal presentation of an idea that is identified with a business sponsor and is projected through mass media

advisory council   a group that serves in an advisory role to management but does not have legal liability like a board of directors

affective tie   a tie among entrepreneurs that relates to emotional sentiments in their working relationships

Age Discrimination in Employment Act of 1967   federal legislation that requires employers to treat applicants and employees equally regardless of age

agency   a relationship whereby one party, the agent, represents another party, the principal, in dealing with a third person

agency power   a right of a partner to bind all members of the firm

agents   distribution intermediaries who do not take title to the goods

aging schedule   a grouping of accounts receivable into age categories based on the length of time they have been outstanding

angels   private investors who supply financing for new, risky, small ventures

application software computer programs written for particular business needs and which can be created by the user or purchased as preprogrammed packages

applied probability models quantitative models such as queuing models, Markov chain models, and inventory models that are applicable to various types of business problems

articles of partnership a written document that states explicitly the rights and duties of partners in a partnership

asset-based lending financing secured by working-capital assets

assorting the process of bringing together homogeneous lines of goods into a heterogeneous assortment

attitude a feeling toward an object organized around knowledge that regulates behavioral tendencies

attributes sampling plan a statistical method of quality control that measures the attributes of a product and checks the acceptability of a small sample of parts to decide about the acceptability of the entire lot

average collection period a measure of accounts-receivable turnover

average cost a number obtained by dividing the total cost over a previous period by the quantity sold or produced during that period

average pricing a pricing approach using average cost as a basis to set price

bad-debt ratio an expense ratio that is computed by dividing the amount of bad debts by the total credit sales

bait advertising advertising in which a low price for an article is offered merely to lure a prospect into the place of business, whereupon the prospect is talked into purchasing a more expensive product

balance sheet a financial statement that shows a firm's financial position (regarding its assets, liabilities, and net worth) at a specific date

benefit variables segmentation variables that are used to divide and identify segments of a market according to the benefits sought by customers

Better Business Bureau association of business firms that promotes ethical conduct by all business firms in a community

bill of materials a form listing the raw materials, consumption standards, and other related information

block control   a flow-control technique that clears the oldest blocks first on each processing operation

blue-sky laws   state laws that cover the registration of new securities; licensing of dealers, brokers, and salespersons; and prosecution of individuals charged with fraud in connection with the sale of securities

board of directors   the governing body elected by the stockholders of a corporation

brand   the identification for a product which can be verbalized or expressed in other symbolic terms

breakdown process   a forecasting process that begins with a macro-level variable and systematically works down to the sales forecast. Also called a chain-ratio method.

break-even analysis   a comparison of cost and demand to determine the point at which total sales revenue equals total costs. Determines the acceptability of alternative prices or evaluates prospects for capital investments.

breaking bulk   channel activities that take the larger quantities produced and prepare them for individual customers

brokers   distribution intermediaries who do not take title to the goods

budget   a device for expressing future plans in monetary terms

buildup process   a forecasting process that calls for identifying all potential buyers in a market's submarkets and then adding up the estimated demand

bulk sales laws   state laws that effectively preclude a debtor from making a secret sale of an entire business before a creditor can take the necessary legal action to collect

burglary   the forcible breaking and entering of premises closed for business with the subsequent removal of cash or merchandise

business format franchising   relationship in which the franchisee obtains an entire marketing system and an ongoing process of assistance and guidance from the franchisor

business incubator   facility that provides shared space, services, and management assistance to several new businesses

business interruption insurance   insurance that protects companies during the period necessary to restore property damaged by an insurance peril

business plan written description of a new-venture idea that projects marketing, operational, and financial aspects of the proposed business

business policies fundamental statements that serve as guides to management practice

buyout purchasing a business

C corporation a type of company that has a limited-liability feature

capital budgeting the process of planning major investments whose returns are expected to extend well into the future

capitalization of profit a process used in the valuation of a business whereby the buyer first estimates the dollars of profit that may be expected and then determines the dollar amount of investment that should logically earn the estimated dollars of profit

cash budgets budgets concerned specifically with dollars as they are received and paid out

cash method of accounting accounting method by which revenue and expenses are recognized when cash is received or payment is made

cash flow the constant flow of funds into the business as receipts and out of the business as expenditures

chain of command the superior-subordinate relationship that serves as a channel for two-way communication

channel of distribution a system of distribution that typically includes intermediaries such as retailers and wholesalers

circulating capital the current-asset items consisting of cash, inventories, and accounts receivable

Civil Rights Act of 1964 federal legislation that prohibits discrimination on the basis of race, color, religion, sex, or national origin

code of ethics official statement that specifies standards of behavior for employees

coercive power a group's ability to withhold material or psychological rewards

cognitive dissonance an uncomfortable psychological tension or a feeling of inequity

coinsurance clause a clause in an insurance policy under which the insured agrees to maintain insurance equal to some specified percentage of the property value or otherwise to assume a portion of any loss

commercial finance companies   institutions that make loans based on securities such as inventories, accounts receivable, equipment, or other items

commission agents (in foreign market distribution)   "finders" for foreign firms wanting to purchase domestic products

common carriers   transportation intermediaries that are available for hire to the general public

computer   a complex data processing machine, outperforming humans in some tasks of recording, classifying, calculating, storing, and communicating information

computer system   a system consisting of a computer and its related interactive components

conditional sales contract   a contract providing for the purchase of equipment on an installment basis

consumer credit   the type of credit granted by retailers to final consumers who purchase for personal or family use

consumerism   emphasis on providing to customers products and services that are safe, reliable, and honestly advertised

continuous operations   production operations that involve long production runs and are used by firms that provide a standardized product

contract carriers   transportation intermediaries that engage in individual contracts with shippers

contracts   legal agreements in which the parties create mutual legal obligations

copyright   the registered right of an author, composer, designer, or artist to reproduce, publish, and sell the work which is the product of the intelligence and skill of that person

corporate refugees   individuals who flee the bureaucratic environment of big business (or even medium-sized business) by going into business for themselves

corporation   a legal form of business that is an artificial being, intangible and existing only in contemplation of the law

corporation charter   the written application for permission to incorporate that is approved by a state official

corrective maintenance   plant maintenance activities that include both the major and minor repairs necessary to restore a facility to good condition

country-controlled buying agents   foreign government agencies or quasi-governmental firms empowered to locate and purchase desired goods

craftsman entrepreneurs   tradesmen who operate businesses on a personal, paternalistic basis with a short time orientation and little planning

credit   an agreement that payment for a product or service will be made at some later date

credit bureau   an organization of retailers and other firms in a given community that serves its members by summarizing their credit experience with particular individuals

credit insurance   insurance that protects nonretailing businesses from abnormal bad-debt losses

creditor capital   initial capital in a business obtained from creditors such as individuals, banks, and government programs. Also known as debt capital.

cultural business pattern   a grouping of beliefs and practices in the business facet of a family firm. The types of patterns are paternalistic, laissez-faire, participative, or professional.

cultural configuration   the total culture of the family firm that is made up of the firm's business pattern, family pattern, and governance pattern

cultural family pattern   a set of beliefs and behaviors held by the family facet of a family firm. The types of patterns are patriarchal, collaborative, or conflicted.

cultural governance pattern   a set of beliefs and behaviors in the governance facet of a family firm. The types of patterns are paper board, rubber-stamp board, advisory board, or overseer board.

culture   mankind's social heritage, which includes customary forms of belief and behavior

current assets   cash, accounts receivable, and inventories

current liabilities   obligations that must be paid within one year

current ratio   ratio of current assets to current liabilities

customer profile   a description of potential customers

daywork   compensation based on increments of time

debt capital   financing of a new business by a creditor. Also known as creditor capital.

debt-to-total-assets ratio   ratio of total debts to total assets

delegation of authority   a superior's act of granting to subordinates, on the basis of competence, the right to act or to decide

deliberate search   a purposeful exploration to find a new-venture idea

demographic variables   segmentation variables that refer to certain characteristics that describe customers and their purchasing power

design patent   a type of patent that covers the appearance of a product and everything that is an inseparable part of the product

direct channel   a channel of distribution in which there are no intermediaries

direct forecasting   a form of forecasting that uses sales as the prediction value

direct SBA loans   Small Business Administration (SBA) loans made for a maximum amount of $150,000

disclosure document   document containing technical financial data required by the Federal Trade Commission to be made available to all prospective investors

dishonesty insurance   a form of insurance including such areas as fidelity bonds and crime insurance to protect against employee dishonesty

distribution   the physical movement of products and the establishment of intermediary relationships to guide and support the product

distribution function   the distribution of products and the establishment of intermediary relationships to guide and support the movement of products

distributor (in foreign market distribution)   a merchant who purchases merchandise from a domestic manufacturer and resells it abroad

double-entry system   accounting system that incorporates journals and ledgers and requires that each transaction be recorded twice in the accounts

dual distribution   distribution that involves more than one channel

Dun & Bradstreet   a company that furnishes buyers and sellers pertinent information for use in making business decisions involving credit, insurance, marketing, and other activities. Such information is provided in the Dun & Bradstreet Business Information Report.

earnings approach   a business-valuation approach that centers on estimating the amount of total income that may be produced by the business in the future

economic competition   a situation in which businesses vie for the greatest amount of sales

economic order quantity (EOQ)   the quantity to be purchased that minimizes total costs

educational refugee   a person who tires of an academic program and decides to go into business

elastic demand   the characteristic of demand for a product in which a change in its price produces a significant change in the quantity demanded

elasticity of demand   the effect that a change in price has on the quantity demanded

electronic spreadsheets   see spreadsheets

employee leasing   an arrangement whereby a small firm's employees are leased from a firm that writes paychecks, pays employee taxes, and files necessary reports with the government

employee stock ownership plans (ESOPs)   agreements by which the employees gain a share of ownership in the business

employer's liability insurance   business coverage to provide protection against suits brought by employees who suffer injury

entrepreneurial team   a group of two or more individuals brought together to function in the capacity of entrepreneurs

entrepreneurs   people who provide the spark for our economic system by taking risks in starting and/or operating businesses

environmentalism   social concern with protection of the environment against damage by business firms as well as others

equal employment opportunity   the absence of employment discrimination based on race, color, religion, sex, or national origin

equipment leasing   leasing of equipment, which provides an alternative to equipment purchasing

ethical issues   practices and policies that raise questions of right and wrong

executive summary   one section of a business plan that gives an overview of the entire proposal

expert power   a group's ability to be perceived as being in a more knowledgeable position than the individual

export agents   agents who operate in international business in the same manner as a manufacturer's representative, but with the risk of loss remaining with the manufacturer

export management companies (EMCs)   companies that act as the export department for several manufacturers of noncompetitive products

export merchants   those who purchase their products directly from the manufacturer, have the products packed and marked to their specifications, sell the products overseas through their contacts and in their own names, and assume all risks for their accounts

external locus of control   a psychological characteristic of people who feel that their lives are controlled to a greater extent by luck or chance or fate than by their own efforts

factoring   obtaining cash before payments are received from customers by selling the accounts receivable to a factor

failure rate   the rate at which businesses fail

family and business overlap   intersection of family concerns and business interests in a family business

family business   a firm in which family relationships of the owner affect the functioning of the business

family business culture   configuration of business patterns, family patterns, and governance patterns in a family business

feminist refugee   a woman who experiences discrimination and elects to start a firm in which she can operate independently of male chauvinists

FIFO (First-In-First-Out)   inventory valuation system that assumes that the first product in inventory is the first product out of inventory

financial plan   a section of the business plan that specifies financial needs and contemplated sources of financing while presenting projections of revenues, costs, and profits

five-minute reader   venture capitalist who quickly scans a business plan to evaluate its potential

fixed-asset turnover   the ratio of sales to fixed assets

fixed assets   the relatively permanent assets that are intended for use in a business rather than for sale

fixed costs   those costs that remain constant in total amount at different levels of quantity produced or sold

fixed expenses   expenses that do not vary in total amount for the accounting period

floppy disk   a form of external data storage that is entered into disk drive units to receive data and programs or load existing data programs into the computer

follow-up routine   a pattern of making sure that a shop's machines are operating efficiently and smoothly

forecasting   projections of future sales, income, or other variables

foreign refugees   individuals who leave their native countries and later go into business as entrepreneurs

foreign retailer   a retailer located outside the United States to whom selling is accomplished through traveling sales representatives or by direct mailing of catalogs, brochures, or other literature

forfaiting   a system whereby a U.S. exporter makes a sale abroad and receives promissory notes, which are then purchased by a bank at a discount

founders   individuals who are generally considered to be the "pure" entrepreneurs because they initiate businesses on the basis of new or improved products or services

four C's of credit   character, capital, capacity, and conditions

franchise   the privileges contained in a franchise contract

franchise contract   the legal agreement between a franchisor and a franchisee

franchisee   the party in a franchise contract who is granted the privilege to conduct business as an individual owner but is required to operate according to methods and terms specified by the other party

franchising   a marketing system revolving around a two-party legal agreement whereby one party is granted the privilege to conduct business as an individual owner but is required to operate according to methods and terms specified by the other party

franchisor the party in a franchise contract who specifies the methods and terms to be followed by the other party

free-flow pattern a type of retail store with a curving-aisles layout that makes less efficient use of space than the grid pattern but has greater visual appeal and allows customers to move in any direction at their own speed

fringe benefits items such as vacations, group insurance, and pensions that supplement direct compensation of employees

functional expenses expenses that relate to specific selling and administrative activities of a business

general liability insurance insurance covering business liability to customers who might be injured on or off premises or from the product sold to them

general managers a class of entrepreneurs who are less innovators and more administrators, presiding over the week-to-week and month-to-month operation of their successful business firms

general partner any partner in a general partnership or a partner in a limited partnership who remains personally liable for the debts of the business

general-purpose equipment machines that can be used for various production functions

grid pattern a type of retail store with a block-like layout that provides more merchandise exposure and simplifies security and cleaning

growth trap a cash shortage resulting from rapid growth that soaks up more cash than is generated in the short run

guaranty loans loans granted by the Small Business Administration in cooperation with private banks in which the degree of participation by the SBA ranges up to 90%

hard disks data storage devices that are capable of storing larger amounts of information and that read and write data much faster than floppy disks

hardware a term that refers primarily to the computer processor unit and items of peripheral equipment used for data input, data output, and data storage

holder in due course the individual or business who has possession of a negotiable instrument and is not subject to many of the defenses possible in the case of ordinary contracts

home-based business   a firm that operates out of the owner's home

housewife refugee   a woman who starts her own business after her family is grown or at some point at which she can free herself from household duties

implied warranty   refers to the seller's clear title to the product and to its quality

Immigration Reform Act   federal legislation requiring employers to check job applicants' papers to be sure they are either U.S. citizens or aliens authorized to work in the U.S.

imputed expenses   expenses that do not appear on the income statement

income statement   a financial statement that shows the results of a firm's operations over a period of time, usually one year

incubator   see business incubator

indirect channel   a channel of distribution in which there are one or more intermediaries

inelastic demand   the characteristic of demand for a product whereby a change in its price does not bring about a significant difference in the quantity demanded

informal organization   unplanned relationships that develop spontaneously in the operation of a business

inspection   scrutinizing a product or service to determine whether or not it meets quality standards

inspection standards   design tolerances that are set for every important quality variable

installment account   a form of consumer credit that normally requires a down payment of the purchase price, with the balance of payments made over a period of months or years

institutional advertising   type of advertising that conveys an image regarding the business establishment

instrumental tie   a tie among entrepreneurs who find their networking relationship mutually rewarding in a practical way

intermittent operations   production operations that involve short production runs with only one or few products being produced before shifting to a different production setup. Also known as job-order production.

internal locus of control   a psychological characteristic of entrepreneurs who believe that their success depends upon their own efforts

internal-rate-of-return method   investment evaluation whereby a stream of expected net cash flows is discounted at the rate that results in a zero net present value (NPV)

inventory-carrying costs   costs that include interest costs on money tied up in inventory, insurance, storage, obsolescence, and pilferage costs

inventory turnover ratio   ratio of sales or cost of sales to inventories

Job Instruction Training (JIT)   a system designed to make on-the-job training more effective

Kanban system   a system of reducing inventory levels to minimize inventory-carrying costs. Also known as just-in-time inventory.

key-person insurance   a form of coverage that protects a small business in the event of the death of key personnel of the firm

laws of motion economy   principles concerning work arrangement, the use of the human hands and body, and the design and use of tools that are intended to increase efficiency

leasing employees   see employee leasing

legal entity   a form of organization that can sue and be sued, hold and sell property, and engage in business operations stipulated in its charter

legal plan   a section of the business plan that shows the proposed type of legal organization—proprietorship, partnership, or corporation—and points out special, relevant legal considerations

legitimate power   the sanction of what one ought to do

liability insurance   insurance that covers business liability to customers or others who might be injured from the product sold to them

libel   printed defamation of one's reputation

licensing   an arrangement allowing a foreign manufacturer to use the designs, patents, or trademarks of the licenser

LIFO (Last-In-First-Out)   an inventory valuation method that assumes that the most recent cost of a product placed in inventory is charged against revenue regardless of whether that most recent unit was actually sold and delivered to a customer

limited partners partners who have limited personal liability as long as they do not take an active role in the management of the limited partnership

limited partnership a partnership that consists of at least one general partner and one or more partners having limited liability

line activities those activities that contribute directly to the primary objectives of a firm

line organization an organization structure in which each person has one supervisor to whom he or she reports and looks for instructions

line-and-staff organization an organization structure in which staff specialists perform specialized services or act as management advisors in special areas

linear programming a quantitative tool that involves the use of mathematical algorithms for evaluating the results from several alternative courses of action, each of which contains a number of variables

liquidation value approach an asset-based approach in the valuation of a business that equates the value of the business with its salvage value if operations ceased

logistics see physical distribution

long-range plan see strategic plan

magnetic disk drive a piece of peripheral equipment that is used primarily for permanent storage of information

mail merge a procedure by which a word processor stores addresses of customers in the computer memory and applies the addresses to form letters

mainframe a large computer that is capable of processing large amounts of information in a very short time and has a large internal memory

major industries as classified by the U.S. Department of Commerce, the eight largest groups of businesses

make-or-buy decision a choice for a small manufacturing firm that has the option of making or buying component parts for the products they make

management   all the activities undertaken to secure the accomplishment of work through the efforts of other people

management plan   a section of the business plan that identifies the "key players"—the active investors, management team, and directors—and cites the experience and competence they have

management team   the group of managers and other professionals who give leadership and direction to a business firm

marginal firm   any small firm that provides insignificant profits to its owner(s)

market   a group of customers or potential customers who have purchasing power and unsatisfied needs

market niche   a target market that is not adequately served by competitors

market segmentation   the process of analyzing a market to find out whether or not it should be viewed as more than one market

market value approach   an approach used in the valuation of a business that relies on previous sales of similar businesses

marketing   those business activities which relate directly to determining target markets and preparing, communicating, and delivering a bundle of satisfaction to those markets

marketing concept   a consumer-oriented marketing management philosophy

marketing-information systems   an organized way of gathering market-related information on a regular basis

marketing plan   a section of the business plan that shows who will be the customers and what type of competition will be faced. It also outlines the marketing strategy to be used and specifies what will give a company a competitive edge.

marketing research   the gathering, processing, reporting, and interpreting of marketing information

marketing tactics   the action part of a marketing plan; the course of action that will activate the entrepreneur's venture

master franchising   an arrangement whereby a master franchisor has a continuing contractual relationship with a franchisor to sell its franchises. Also known as subfranchising.

mechanic's lien a claim by contractors, laborers, or suppliers against the property if the property owner or tenant defaults in payments for either materials or labor

merchant middlemen distribution intermediaries who take title to the goods

microcomputer a personal computer that can be operated without extensive training and technical expertise and can be upgraded to provide the memory capacity needed to handle many day-to-day activities of a small business

micromotion study a refinement of time study that uses a motion-picture camera, rather than a stopwatch, to record the elemental motions as well as the times

minicomputer a scaled-down mainframe computer system designed for a segment of the business market

modem a device that connects one computer to another computer via a telephone line

moral tie a tie among entrepreneurs that involves some type of mutual obligation or commitment in their networking relationships

motion study a detailed observation of all the actual motions that the observed worker makes to complete a job under a given set of physical conditions

motivations goal-directed forces within humans that organize and give direction to tension caused by unsatisfied needs

multisegmentation strategy the marketing strategy used by a business when it recognizes individual market segments that have different preferences and develops a unique marketing mix for each segment

National Labor Relations Act federal legislation requiring employers to avoid discrimination based on union affiliation and to bargain with a union if desired by a majority of employees in the bargaining unit

need for achievement internal desire or ambition for personal accomplishment

needs the basic seeds of (and the starting point for) all behavior

negotiable instruments credit instruments that can be transferred from one party to another in place of money

net-present-value method investment evaluation to determine the net present value (NPV) of a stream of expected net cash flows at a specified rate of return

network   a system linking personal computers

networking   the process of developing and engaging in mutually beneficial relationships with peers

new-business incubator   see business incubator

Occupational Safety and Health Act (OSHA)   federal legislation that mandates that employers provide a workplace that is free from hazards likely to cause death or serious physical harm

open charge account   the customer obtains possession of goods (or services) when purchased, with payment due when billed

operating budget   a composite plan, expressed in monetary terms, for each phase of the operation of a business

operating plan   a section of the business plan that explains the type of manufacturing or operating system that will be used and includes a description of the facilities, labor, raw materials, and processing requirements

operating process   see production process

operations management   the planning and control of the conversion process; the acquisition of inputs and overseeing their transformation into the tangible products and intangible services desired by customers

opinion leader   a group member playing a key communications role

opportunistic entrepreneurs   well-educated business owners who use sophisticated management methods

opportunity costs   the value of a lost opportunity such as the amount that could be earned on money elsewhere

order costs   costs that include the preparation of a purchase order, follow-up, and related bookkeeping expenses

ordinary charge account   a form of consumer credit whereby the customer obtains possession of goods or services when purchased, with payment due when billed

organizing   assignment of tasks and duties to departmental components and to individual employees and specification of relationships among departments and individuals

orientation   initial training of new employees that gives them general information about the company and its policies

owner capital   ownership equity in a business

ownership equity   the new business is financed by the owner

parental (paternal) refugee   a person who leaves a family business to show the parent that he or she is not dependent upon the parent to succeed

partnership   a voluntary association of two or more persons to carry on a business for profit as co-owners

patent   the registered right of an inventor to make, use, and sell an invention

payback-period method   a method of valuation that shows the number of years it takes to recover the original cost of an investment from annual net cash flows

penetration pricing   the strategy that involves pricing products or services lower than a normal, long-range price in order to gain more rapid market acceptance or to increase existing market share

perception   the individual processes that ultimately give meaning to the stimuli that confront consumers

perceptual categorization   the process whereby consumers attempt to manage huge quantities of incoming stimuli and perceive as belonging together those things which are similar

performance reports   a record of the efficiency of a work schedule

perpetual inventory system   a system that provides a current record of inventory items and does not require a physical count

personal computers (PCs)   computers compactly designed and intended for use by one person at a time

personal selling   promotion delivered in a personal, one-on-one manner

physical distribution   the physical movement activities in distribution

physical inventory system   an inventory control system that entails periodic actual counts of inventory items

piggyback franchising   the operation of a retail franchise within the physical facilities of a host store

planning the management function that requires decisions about a future course of action and involves goal setting

plant patent a patent that covers any distinct and new variety of plants

precipitating events occurrences, such as losing a job, that serve as catalysts in causing individuals to become entrepreneurs

present value the value today of a stream of expected net cash flows, discounted at an appropriate rate of interest

prestige pricing setting a high price to convey the image of high quality and uniqueness

preventive maintenance plant maintenance activities which include inspections and other activities intended to prevent machine breakdowns and damage to people and buildings

price the seller's measure of what he or she is willing to receive in exchange for ownership or use of a product or service

price line a range of several distinct prices at which merchandise is offered for sale

pricing the systematic determination of the "right" price for a product

primary data new information for which a search is made through various methods

prime rate the interest rate that commercial banks charge their most creditworthy customers

private carriers shippers who own their means of transport

private placement selling of a firm's capital stock to selected individuals

procedures plans that specify the methods or steps to be followed in business activities

process layout a type of factory layout in which similar machines are grouped together

product the total "bundle of satisfaction" that is offered to customers in an exchange transaction

product advertising type of advertising designed to make potential customers aware of a particular product or service and of their need for it

product item the lowest common denominator in a product mix—the individual item

product layout   a type of factory layout in which machines are arranged according to the need for them in the production process

product life cycle   the stages of introduction, growth, maturity, and decline in the life of a product

product line   the sum of the individual product items that are related

product mix   the collection of product lines within a firm's ownership and control

product mix consistency   the logical relationship of the product lines to each other

product strategy   the manner in which the product component of the marketing mix is used to achieve the objectives of a firm

product and trade name franchising   the relationship between a franchisor and franchisee granting the right to use a widely recognized product or name

production control   procedures that have been developed most extensively in manufacturing that consist of steps designed to achieve the orderly, sequential flow of products through the plant at a rate commensurate with scheduled deliveries to customers

production process   those activities necessary for performing the work the firm was created to perform. Also referred to as the operations process.

productivity   the efficiency with which inputs are transformed into outputs

products and services plan   a section of the business plan that describes the product and/or service provided and points out any unique features. It also explains why people will buy the product or service.

professional manager   a person who is hired to manage a business and receives payment for this service

profit margin on sales   ratio of net profit to sales

pro-forma financial statements   tools consisting of an income statement, a balance sheet, and a cash flow budget to help communicate financial plans

promotion   communication between the business and its target market

promotional mix   the mixture of various promotional methods—personal selling, advertising, and sales promotion

proprietorship   a business owned and operated by one person

prospecting   a systematic process of continually looking for new customers

publicity   disseminating information or promotional materials to gain the public's interest. A type of promotion that can be used to promote both a product and a firm's image.

purchase order   an order to buy which, when accepted by a vendor, becomes a binding contract

purchase requisition   a formal, documented request from an employee or a manager for something to be bought for the business

purchasing   a process involving receipt of a purchase request, locating a source of supply, issuing a purchase order, maintaining the buying and warehousing records, following up on the purchase order, and receiving the goods

purchasing group   any unincorporated group of persons that has the purpose of purchasing liability insurance for the group

quality circle   a group of employees, usually a dozen or fewer, performing similar or related work, who meet periodically to identify, analyze, and solve production problems, particularly those involving product or service quality

quantity discount   a reduction in cost that occurs when goods are bought in bulk or a large amount

queuing theory   a quantitative tool that consists of the use of calculated probabilities for determining the number of persons who will stand in a line. Also known as waiting-line theory.

reciprocal buying   a policy based on the premise that one company can secure additional orders by using its own purchasing requests as a bargaining weapon

reference groups   those groups from which an individual allows influence to be exerted upon his or her behavior

referent power   a group's ability to cause consumers to conform to its behavior and to choose products selected by its members

reorder point   the point at which additional quantities of materials or merchandise should be reordered

replacement cost approach   an asset-based approach used in the valuation of a business that relies on finding the replacement value of the property being purchased

retail inventory valuation method   an inventory control system used by retailers to determine the retail value of ending inventory

retained earnings   realized profits that are plowed back into a business

return-on-investment-method   a method of evaluating proposals by relating the expected annual profit from an investment to the amount invested but disregarding the time value of money

return on net worth (return on equity)   ratio of net profit to net worth

return on total assets (asset earning power)   ratio of net profit to total assets

revolving charge account   a variation of the installment account whereby the seller grants a line of credit up to a certain amount and the customer may charge purchases at any time if purchases do not exceed this credit limit

reward power   a group's ability to give material or psychological rewards

risk   a condition in which there is a possibility of an adverse deviation from an outcome that is expected or hoped for

risk management   all efforts designed to preserve assets and earning power by managing risk factors

risk-retention group   an insurance company started by a homogeneous group of entrepreneurs or professionals to provide liability insurance for its members

route list   a form showing the sequence of processing operations and who will perform them

S corporation   a name derived from Subchapter S of the Internal Revenue Code, which permits a corporation to retain the limited-liability feature of a regular corporation while being taxed as a partnership, thereby avoiding the corporate income tax. Also known as a Subchapter S Corporation.

safety stock   the level of stock maintained to provide a measure of protection against stockouts

sales forecast   the prediction of how much of a product or service will be purchased by a market during a defined time period

sales promotion   activities or techniques that provide inducements to potential purchasers of products or services

sales representatives or agents (in foreign market distribution)   the foreign counterparts of U.S. manufacturers' representatives

scheduled budget buying a policy of buying to meet anticipated requirements

secondary data information that has already been compiled

Section 1244 stock a type of stock that can be issued in the initial organization of a corporation and, pursuant to Section 1244 of the Internal Revenue Code, provides certain tax advantages to the stockholder if the stock becomes worthless

segmentation variables labels that identify the particular dimensions that are thought to distinguish one form of market demand from another

self-insurance a form of risk management whereby a part of the firm's earnings is earmarked as a contingency fund for possible future losses, specifically for individual loss categories such as property, medical, or workers' compensation

self-service layout a type of retail store layout that permits customers direct access to the merchandise

serendipity the faculty for making desirable discoveries by accident

Service Corps of Retired Executives (SCORE) an organization of retired business executives who will consult on current problems with small-business managers

short-range plans yearly and/or quarterly action plans for functional areas needed to implement action toward general goals

simulation a technique that permits the decision maker to gain experience in something resembling the actual situation without taking the risk existing in that situation

single-entry system a checkbook system of receipts and disbursement supported by sales tickets and disbursement receipts

single-segmentation strategy the marketing strategy used by a business when it recognizes that several distinct market segments exist but chooses to concentrate on reaching only one segment

single-use plan a classification used to characterize a plan such as a special project or a budget

skimming underreporting of income in order to avoid payment of taxes

skimming-price strategy the practice of setting prices for products or services at very high levels for a limited period before reducing them to a lower, more competitive level

Small Business Development Centers (SBDCs)   Small-Business-Administration-sponsored centers affiliated with colleges and universities that provide direct consultation to small firms, continuing education, small-business research, export services, and minority support

Small Business Institute (SBI)   a program implemented by the Small Business Administration to make the consulting resources of universities available to small-business firms

Small Business Investment Companies (SBICs)   privately owned capital banks that supply equity funds and loan funds to small businesses

small-business marketing   those business activities that relate directly to identifying target markets; determining target market potential; and preparing, communicating, and delivering a bundle of satisfaction to these markets

social class   a sociological concept related to the divisions in a society with different levels of social prestige

social responsibility   the obligation of business firms to meet the expectations and legal requirements of society

society refugee   a person who senses some alienation from the prevailing culture and expresses it by indulging in entrepreneurial activity—operating an energy-saving business, for example

software   the programs for a computer system that contain instructions to operate the hardware

span of control   the number of subordinates who are supervised by one manager

special-purpose equipment   machines that are designed for a specialized function in the production process

speculative buying   buying more than needed in the expectation that prices will go up

spell check   a word-processing feature that automatically checks text material for misspellings and flags them

spreadsheets   computer programs that provide rows and columns for entry of numbers, which are entered at "cells" and used to analyze actual data and to aid managers in financial decision making through "what if" exercises

staff activities   those activities which support or help line activities

standard operating procedure   a method of work or a procedure that has been worked out

startup   building a business from "scratch"

state-controlled trading companies   entities in countries that have state trading monopolies

statement of cash flow   a financial statement showing cash receipts and cash payments

statistical inference   inferring something about a large group on the basis of facts known about a smaller group

statistical quality control   quality control and assurance systems that use statistical procedures

statute of frauds   a law under which sales transactions of $500 or more, sales of real estate, and contracts extending for more than one year must be in writing

statutes of limitations   state laws that require creditors to be reasonably prompt in filing their claims

stock card   the basic control tool in a perpetual inventory system for finished goods

stockouts   not having items in inventory, which may result in lost sales or disrupted production

stores card   the basic control tool in a perpetual inventory system covering raw materials and supplies

strategic decision   a decision as to how a business firm will relate to its customers, competitors, and the external environment in general

strategic plan   a business plan characterized by choices that will affect a firm several years in the future. Also known as a long-range plan.

Subchapter S corporation   see S corporation.

subfranchising   see master franchising

supply function   when a small business acts as a supplier and subcontractor for a larger firm

surety bonds   bonds that insure against the failure of another firm or individual to fulfill a contractual obligation

System A franchising   the producer/creater (franchisor) grants a franchise to the wholesaler (franchisee)

System B franchising   the wholesaler is the franchisor

System C franchising   the producer/creator is the franchisor and the retailer is the franchisee

system software   programs that control the overall operations of the computer, including input and output processing, and are the link between hardware devices and application programs

tax credit   a direct reduction of a taxpayer's tax liability

tax shelter   a type of investment, severely restricted by law, that shelters income from taxation

temporary help agency   a business firm that supplies temporary employees ("temps") for short-term staffing needs

time study   the timing and recording of each elemental motion of a job on an observation sheet

time-sharing system   the sharing of one computer by several users. Terminals to collect data are located at the office of each user, and the computer runs the programs for all users in sequence.

times-interest-earned ratio   ratio of operating income to interest charges

total cost   includes the cost of goods or services offered for sale, the selling cost, and the general overhead cost applicable to the given product or service

total fixed costs   those costs that remain constant at different levels of quantity sold

total variable costs   those costs that vary as the quantity marketed varies

trade credit   the type of credit extended by nonfinancial firms to customers that are also business firms

trade dress   elements of a firm's distinctive operating image (the "look") that are protected by patent or copyright

trade-credit agencies   privately owned and operated organizations that collect credit information on business firms

trademark   a word, figure, or other symbol used to distinguish a product sold by one manufacturer or merchant

two-bin method   a simple technique for maintaining safety stock that divides inventory into two portions: When the first bin is exhausted, an order is placed to replenish the supply, while the portion in the second bin should cover needs until a new supply arrives.

Type A startup idea   a new business based on the idea that now there is something improved in a product already being sold

Type B startup idea   a new business based on a completely new product

Type C startup idea   a new business based on performing an old function in a new and improved way

unfair trade practice laws   laws that specify that sellers may not sell goods at less than their cost

unity of command   direction emanates from the owner-manager, while staff specialists function primarily as helpers and facilitators

unsegmented strategy   the marketing strategy used by a business when it defines the total market as its target market

utility patent   a type of patent that covers a new process and protects the function of a product

variable expenses   expenses that are fixed on a per-unit basis but vary in total amount for month and year with the volume of goods manufactured or sold

variables sampling plan   a statistical method of quality control that measures many characteristics of an item, rather than simply judging the item as acceptable or unacceptable, by taking periodic random samples that are plotted on a chart to discover whether or not the process is out of control

venture capitalist   an investor or investment group that invests in new-business ventures

visual control board   a flow-control technique used to reflect both work assignments and the progress of work toward completion

walk-ins   unsolicited applicants seeking employment

warranty   an express or implied promise that a product will do certain things

word processing   any process that involves textual information and uses such equipment as typesetters, copiers, and automatic typewriters

work improvement   finding work methods that demand the least physical effort and the shortest execution time at the lowest possible cost

work sampling a method of work measurement that provides little operating detail but estimates the ratio of actual working time and downtime

work study an analysis of equipment and tooling, plant layout, working conditions, and individual jobs to improve production efficiency

workers' compensation insurance coverage that obligates the insurer to pay eligible employees of the insured as required by the workers' compensation law of the state

working capital a firm's current assets

working-capital management the management of current assets and current liabilities

INDEX

Entries including a "G" reference can be found in the Glossary.